D1371030

introduction to Sociology 5e

Project Development Manager: Brae Buhnerkemper

Project Development Assistant: Della Brackett

Managing Editor: Joyce Bianchini

Photo Researcher: Michelle Hipkins

Design and Illustrations: Rachel Weathersbee

Typesetter: Esther Scannell

Text and Cover Printing: Quad/Graphics

Sales Manager: Robert Rappeport

Marketing Manager: Richard Schofield

Permissions Coordinator: Suzanne Schmidt

Art Director: Brandi Cornwell

ISBN: 978-1-60229-777-7

The publisher of affordable textbooks

introduction to Sociology 5e

Laurence A. Basirico
Elon University

Barbara G. Cashion
Shippensburg University of Pennsylvania

J. Ross Eshleman
Wayne State University

BVT
PUBLISHING

Brief Table of Contents

Table of Contents

CHAPTER 6

CHAPTER 7

CHAPTER 8

CHAPTER 9

CHAPTER 10

CHAPTER 11

CHAPTER 12

CHAPTER 13

CHAPTER 16

CHAPTER 17

CHAPTER 20

The Changing Community 608

CHAPTER 21

The Nature of Social Change 640

Preface

Our purpose in writing this text is to convey both the excitement of sociology and its relevance to our lives. The excitement of sociology comes from what it studies: social life and social organization. Sociology encompasses all aspects of society: family life, community change, individual development, group differences, and gender inequality, to name a few. It involves a unique way of looking at the world in which we live, forcing us to question the obvious and understand how society and behavior are patterned and organized. People are discovering that sociology provides them with unique skills and abilities in research methods, in applying social theory in the working world, and in using their understanding of social processes, organization, and change.

New to this Edition

As with each new edition, we have retained the characteristics of our introduction to sociology text that make it stand out and have incorporated updates and revisions to insure accuracy and currency. This edition continues to include an emphasis on the relevance of sociology with sections in each chapter on how students can apply specific sociological theories and/or concepts to their professional and personal lives. This edition contains over 136 new references and/or citations. There are nearly seventy revised or new tables and figures containing the most current statistics available at the time of writing, including data that incorporates the most recent decennial U.S. Census (2010) or annual updates. Twelve of the twenty-one opening vignettes have been significantly updated or revised (and the others have been updated to reflect the most up to date trends and statistics). Five are new to this edition, including vignettes on preventable disasters (Chapter 5), women in America (Chapter 10), school bullying (Chapter 14), influence peddling (Chapter 15), and health as a social fact (Chapter 20). This new edition now includes Pop Quizzes at the end of each chapter to further enhance student learning. We believe that our book offers a traditional, solid introduction to sociology that encourages students to see its relevance in their lives and the world around them.

Supplements

Supplements for Instructors

- **Study Guide** A thorough and practical student study guide includes learning objectives, chapter outlines, questions, and ideas that help the student review the material presented in this text. Also included are student activities and projects designed to enhance the practical application of sociological concepts.

- **Instructor's Manual** A comprehensive manual provides a wealth of teaching suggestions, objectives and resources, outside activities stressing the importance of sociology to personal lives, suggested readings from short stories and novels, a guide to films, and much more.

- **Test Bank** An extensive test bank of approximately 2,100 questions is available to instructors in both hard copy and electronic forms. Each chapter consists of a variety of multiple choice, short answer and essay questions. Each question is referenced to the appropriate text page to make verification quick and easy.

- **Distance Learning Solutions** BVT Publishing is committed to providing the ability to administer tests and quizzes over the Internet. We have a strong relationship with Respondus, whose Course Management Software allows for the creation of randomly-generated tests and quizzes that can be downloaded directly into a wide variety of course management environments, such as Blackboard, Web CT, Desire 2 Learn, Angel, E Learning and others.

BVT Publishing also offers direct-to-consumer availability of our textbooks and study guides in an eBook format, for added convenience and affordability.

- **Power Points** A set of PowerPoint slides is available to instructors who adopt this book. The set includes charts, tables, and graphs from the text and additional charts and graphs from other sources.

- **Customize This Book** If you have additional material that you would like to add (handouts, lecture notes, syllabus, etc) or simply rearrange and delete content, BVT Publishing's custom publishing division can help you modify this book's content, to produce a book that satisfies your specific instructional needs. BVT Publishing has the only custom publishing division that puts your material exactly where you want it to go, easily and seamlessly. Please visit **www.bvtpublishing.com** or call us at **1-800-646-7782** for more information on BVT Publishing's Custom Publishing Program.

New to this Edition!

BVT*Lab*

BVT*Lab* —a simple, robust, online lab for college instructors and their students—provides essential teaching, assessment, and communication tools. It is an affordable option for students, with student lab fees costing only $19.99 for a full-semester course. Even if you do not use the lab as your online classroom, your students can still take advantage of the many free student resources.

Course Setup

BVT*Lab* has an easy-to-use, intuitive interface that allows instructors to quickly set up their courses and grade books, and replicate them from section to section and semester to semester. Multiple choice and true/false questions can be delivered online as practice questions, homework assignments, quizzes, and tests—each of which draws from a separate bank of questions. Homework, quizzes, and tests have assigned start and end times; and tests can be proctored in the computer lab or self-proctored for distance learners. Homework and quizzes offer optional hints and instructor tips. In addition, practice questions can be linked to fully worked solutions and multimedia tutorials. Instructors can preview and manually select questions assigned to students, or they can use the "quick-pick" feature in BVTLab to generate sets of questions.

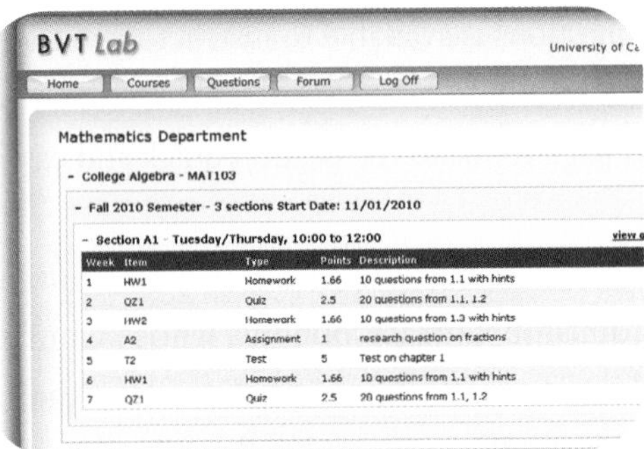

Grade Book

Using an assigned passcode, students register themselves into the grade book. All homework, quizzes, and tests are automatically graded and recorded in the grade book. In addition, instructors can manually enter or modify scores, with provisions for extra credit, attendance, and participation grades. Grade books can be replicated from section to section, semester to semester, and can be easily edited or modified if required.

Communications Tools

Instructors can post discussion threads to a class forum and then monitor and moderate student replies. Important notifications can also be sent directly to each student via email.

www.BVTLab.com

Supplements For Students

BVT*Lab* is a comprehensive online learning environment designed to help students succeed. It provides a complete online classroom, as well as the practice questions, learning aids, and communication tools that students need for success. Even if your instructor does not use the lab as a classroom, you are always welcome to visit as a guest and take advantage of the many free resources.

Practice Questions Students work through hundreds of practice questions online. Questions are multiple choice or true/false and are graded instantly for immediate feedback.

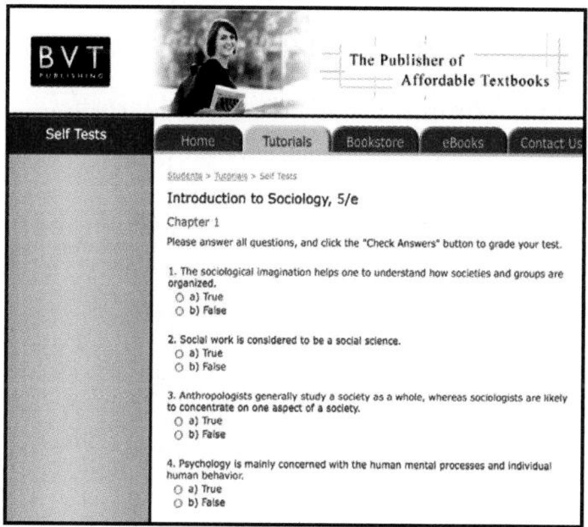

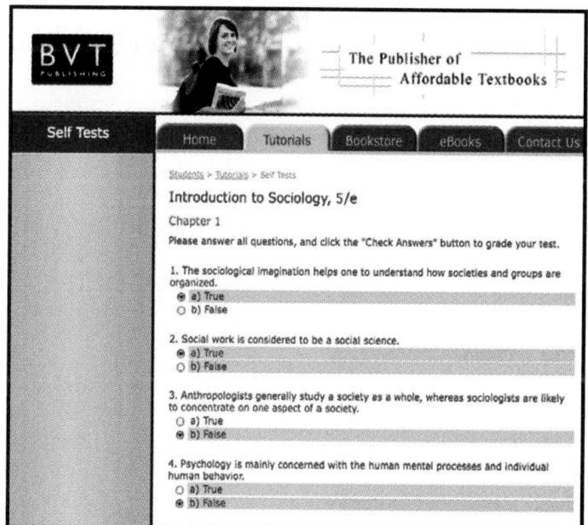

Flashcards **BVT*Lab*** includes sets of flashcards for each chapter that reinforce the key terms and concepts from the textbook.

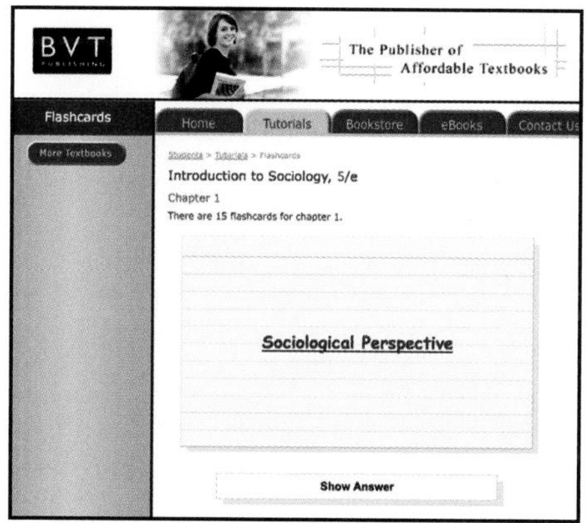

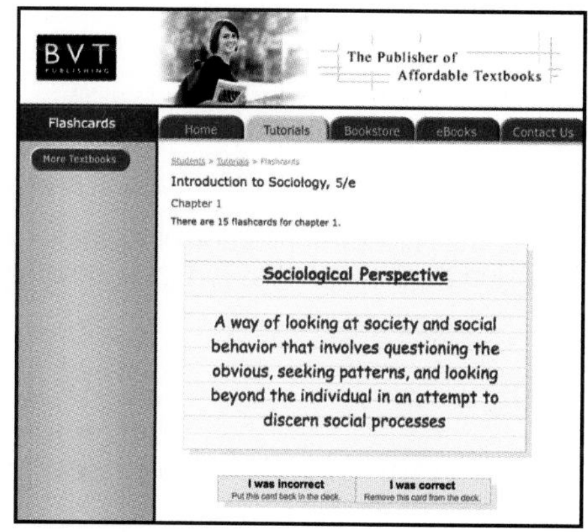

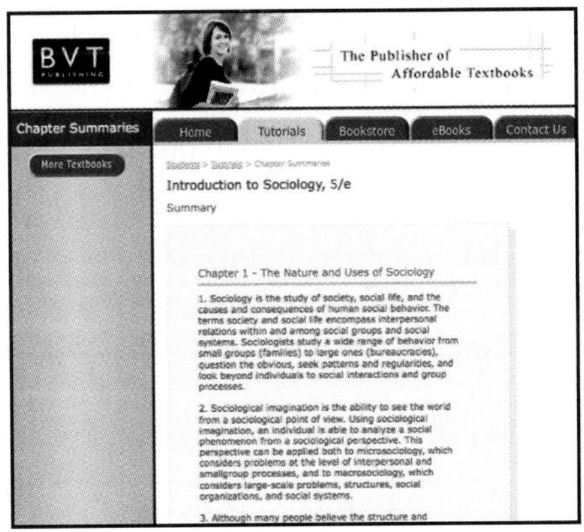

Chapter Summaries A convenient and concise chapter summary is available as a study aid for each chapter.

Discussion Forum An online discussion forum allows students to interact with each other and the instructor to explore challenging concepts and share other resources, while providing an online community for distance learning.

Review For classes taught within the lab, students can view their grades for all completed work and also review prior homework and quizzes to identify areas that require additional study.

Shop Online

1. **Textbook** For the student's convienience and pocketbook, students have the added option of purchasing this textbook in the following three formats at **www. bvtstudents.com**:

- **Hard Copy textbook**
- **Loose-Leaf Black & White**
- **eBook Subscription (6 months)**

2. **Study Guide** A thorough and practical student study guide that includes learning objectives, chapter outlines, questions, and ideas that help the student review the material presented in this text. Also included are student activities and projects designed to enhance the practical application of sociological concepts.

About the Author

Laurence ("Larry") Basirico earned his BA in sociology from Hofstra University (1972) and his MA (1974) and PhD (1983) at Stony Brook University. He is professor of sociology at Elon University where he has been since 1983. He was chair of the Department of Sociology and Anthropology from 1994 to 2004 and resumed his role of department chair in 2009. Dr. Basirico's research primarily has been in the areas of social interaction, identity, socialization, the family and culture—as applied specifically to rock groups, arts and craft communities, family reunions, and marital relationships. His major teaching areas are introduction to sociology, self and society, and the family. Dr. Basirico was also dean of international programs at Elon for five years (2004 to 2009), spearheading one of the most successful study abroad programs in the United States and overseeing efforts to internationalize the campus. While he was dean, Elon won the prestigious Paul Simon Internationalization of the Campus Award, the highest award given by NAFSA: Association of International Educators.

In 1988, he joined forces with J.Ross Eshleman and Barbara G. Cashion to write Sociology: An Introduction (Scott Foresman, Little Brown and then with HarperCollins Publisher), the precursor for this textbook. That book was one of the first sociology textbooks that focused on how students could apply sociology in their lives. He has now assumed primary responsibility for the 5th edition of Introduction to Sociology with Best Value Textbooks.

Dr. Basirico is married with three children and lives in Burlington, North Carolina. He is a lifelong music lover and learner dedicated primarily to guitar these days, but with a background in piano. He regularly walks around golf courses chasing a little white ball into never before seen natural habitats.

J. Ross Eshleman, PhD received his doctorate from Ohio State University and is currently Professor Emeritus at Wayne State University. His past teaching experience includes serving as Department Chair of Sociology at Wayne State University and Appalachian State University, two Fulbright grants to the Philippines at the University of Santo Tomas and De La Salle College, a year with the National Science Foundation, and two university teaching awards.

Dr. Eshleman has directed five institutes for teachers of high school sociology with grants through the National Science Foundation. His publications include numerous editions (ten of his own and two co- authored) of a sociology of the family text.

Dr. Cashion received her PhD from the University of Maryland and taught at a variety of universities, including Georgetown University in Washington, D.C., and Shippensburg University of PA. She has special interest in the sociology of medicine and has worked in group health insurance settings, at the National Institute of Mental Health (NIMH), and in the pharmaceutical field.

Dr. Cashion has published on related topics in a variety of journals. She is currently retired from teaching and is living in Hagerstown, MD. There she continues to develop her interests in music and fine arts, especially in the sociology of American art. Dr. Cashion has two daughters and four grandchildren.

Acknowlegments

As in the previous editions of this text, we wish to acknowledge the input and contributions of many people. How do we express an intellectual debt to the scholars, researchers, teachers, and students who provided the ideas, data, and findings used here? For the three of us, this includes many people. Special thanks to our spouses and children who have taught us as much as we have taught them. We also thank our teachers, those people who have sparked our interest in sociology and helped us develop our ability to think through the issues of the discipline. We extend our thanks to our professional colleagues at Elon University, Shippensburg University, and Wayne State University who have supported us in our daily activities.

We want to thank the many instructors who used previous editions of our text and provided us with valuable feedback. We are especially grateful for the comments and suggestions offered during preparation of this edition. We also thank the editors and contributors to this edition of the work and for their dedication to maintaining currency and relevance.

Finally, we would like to acknowledge the following scholars who, from the outset, have provided review of our manuscript, from which successive editions (including this one) have come:

David A. Gay	University of Central Florida
Lee F. Hamilton	Montana State University
Gary D. Hartley	Simpson College
Harlowe Hatle	University of South Dakota
A. C. Higgins	SUNY Albany
Tim Johnson	Central College
Tye Craig Johnson	University of South Carolina
Cheryl A. Joseph	College of Notre Dame
Barbara Karcher	Kennesaw State College
James H. Leiding	East Stroudsburg University
Martin L. Levin	Emory University
Jerry Lewis	Kent State University
Margarite Martin	Gonzago University
Barbara McCoy	Northeast Mississippi Community College
Richard B. Miller	Missouri Southern State College
Man J. Molseed	University of Michigan, Flint
Kay Mueller	Baylor University
Donna Phillips	San Bernardino Valley College
William G. Roy	University of California, Los Angeles
William A. Schwab	University of Arkansas
Dwayne M. Smith	Tulane University
Thomas Sparhawk	Georgia Southern College
James Sutton	Chattanooga State Technical Community College
Nancy Terjesen	Kent State University
Kathleen A. Tiemann	University of North Dakota
Steven Vassar	Mankato State University
Richard Veach	Whatian Community College
Robert Wooley	Mansfield University

An Open Invitation to Our Readers:

We feel it is imperative to make sure that our textbook is as current, relevant, and engaging as possible, as well as providing the greatest utility benefit to instructors and students alike. If you have any comments and/or suggestions from which future editions of this book may benefit, please let us know. We welcome your emails and will give due consideration to each and every one. Please send your communications to: contactus@bvtpublishing.com.

PART ONE

Sociology: Perspectives and Methods

People who like to avoid shocking discoveries, who prefer to believe that society is just what they were taught in Sunday school, who like the safety of the rules … should stay away from sociology.

PETER BERGER

CHAPTER 1

The Nature and Uses of Sociology

興禮門

THE SOCIOLOGY OF RAMPAGE SHOOTING

On April 16, 2007, the worst school shooting in the history of the United States took place in Blacksburg, Virginia. On that day, twenty–seven college students and five instructors were shot and killed during two separate incidents that spanned over two and a half hours. Seung-Hui Cho, who was a twenty-three-year-old English major at Virginia Polytechnic University and State School (Virginia Tech), engaged in what seems to have been a pre-meditated and methodical attack on students and faculty. Accounts of the incident suggest that his attack consisted of a ruthless, merciless series of murders that took place over a period of a few hours.

On January 18, 2011, Jared Lee Loughner opened fire at an informal political gathering outside a supermarket in Tucson, Arizona, killing six people and wounding thirteen others. One of those severely wounded was Gabrielle Giffords, a Democratic congresswoman. Those killed included one of her staff members, a federal judge, three retired people, and a nine-year-old girl. This attack, like the one at Virginia Tech, also had the markings of a methodical, pre-meditated event.

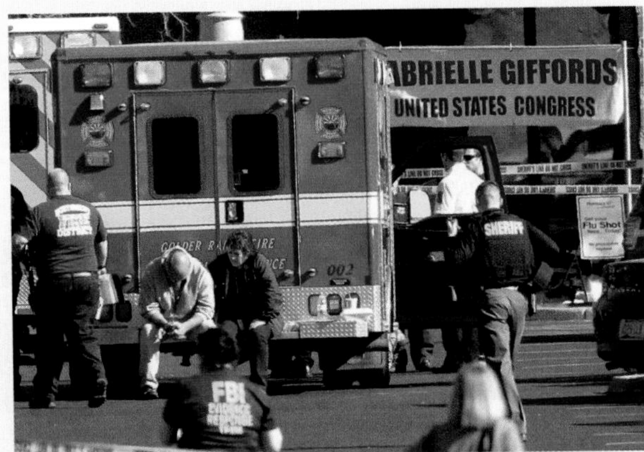

Jared Lee Loughner opened fire at an informal political gathering in Tucson, Arizona on January 18, 2011, killing six people and wounding thirteen others. (AP Photo)

During the weeks and months following both of these events, newspaper articles abounded with speculations about the possible motives for the shootings and especially about how, in retrospect, the killers had manifested problematic psychological characteristics well before the deadly incidents had taken place. Seung-Hui Cho had a record of psychological problems and psychiatric treatment throughout his childhood, moodiness, being distant, and having exhibited troublesome and sometimes bizarre behaviors with other students and teachers while in school. Jared Lee Loughner also had exhibited signs of paranoid schizophrenia (although never involuntarily institutionalized in a psychiatric hospital) and had a history of rejection: by the military, by a community college, by a girlfriend, and also by some family members. While the Virginia Tech massacre and the shootings in Arizona that surrounded Gabrielle Giffords were tragedies almost beyond belief, there have been many shooting rampages within the past fifty years, dating back to 1966 when twenty-five-year-old Charles Whitman barricaded himself in the top of the clock tower at the University of Texas in Austin. Whitman then shot and killed fourteen people and injured thirty-one others before being killed by police.

Much like yourself, the shooting victims probably thought college and informal meetings with a politician in a shopping center were very safe places to be, places where crime is limited to petty theft and other non-violent offenses. However, in recent years the media have bombarded us with images of school violence. We hear commentary from multiple news agencies and television personalities suggesting that schools, once thought to be safe havens for children, have become killing fields. How much of this is truth and how much is myth? Are young people becoming increasingly violent? Should we arm our students with bulletproof vests before sending them off to school? Are students safer if they attend schools in rural areas rather than in inner cities? After incidents as horrific as these, and others like them, it is easy to focus exclusively on the characteristics of the killers and/or to blame society for a decline in morality. Some have even suggested that such rampages are the result of severely differing values (political or otherwise) or the availability of guns. These explanations tend to be quick reactions to tragedies that may or may not be accurate or worthwhile explanations.

As sociologists, we feel that to answer these questions about why incidents such as these take place, we should first consider what Peter Berger suggests in Invitation to Sociology. Berger (1963) suggests that **"the first wisdom of sociology is this—things are not what they seem."** As a sociology student, you will be asked to examine issues based on a critical analysis, rather than simply rely on the media or your own personal experiences to answer questions related to social phenomena. Instead, it is best to examine issues from various points of view, particularly those directly affected by the phenomenon.

For example, Peter Stearns (2008) conducted an extensive social history of public violence, critically analyzing and comparing the massacre at the University of Texas with Virginia Tech. How did the media handle public reactions? How did the police handle the incidents? What types of communication were in place to help warn the public? What types of policy changes took place? What was the impact on society? Cybelle Fox and David J. Harding

(2005) investigated school shootings from the point of view of organizational deviance rather than focusing so much on the characteristics of the killers. "From a sociological perspective, what is perhaps most surprising is that, with few exceptions, school officials were unaware that the shooters in these incidents were experiencing severe emotional, social, and/or behavioral problems or that they had such rage against the institution" (Fox and Harding 2005, 69). Their approach looks not so much at the killers but at what organizations do or do not do. "Organizational deviance occurs when events that are created by or in organizations do not conform to an organization's goals or expectations and produce unanticipated and harmful outcomes (Vaughan 1999, 273). It is often an unintended consequence of the normal activities of actors within an organization" (Fox and Harding 2005, 70).

... the first wisdom of sociology is this— things are not what they seem.

Peter Berger

Our point here is not that we are shifting the blame from the individual to society. Our point is to reaffirm Berger's contention that "things are not what they seem" and that sociology offers us perspectives, theories, and methods to analyze events in such a way that we go well beyond our immediate reactions and what might seem to be common sense. Then, we can gain a more accurate and helpful understanding of the causes and consequences of events. This does not mean that sociology always finds answers that are different than our initial assumptions (although sometimes the conclusions are very different than what we initially assume). Rather, sociology employs a critical analysis that enables us to feel more confident in explanations and, hopefully, to have explanations that are more useful in helping stem disasters such as rampage shootings.

Our lives are governed by the society in which we live. Social rules and conventions influence every aspect of our daily lives. We begin to learn which rules are socially acceptable and which ones are not before we can talk; and they are reinforced, altered, or contradicted every time we enter a social situation, whether new or familiar. For example, technology has provided parents with the opportunity to find out the sex of their baby before the child is born. With this information parents can begin to plan for the arrival of their little one by purchasing clothes, room decor, and toys. It is quite likely that if parents find out they are having a boy, their first purchases will primarily be in the color blue. On the other hand, if they are told their baby is a girl, they will purchase items that are pink. The reason it is easy to predict the actions of the parents is because we have been taught that blue is a socially acceptable color for boys and pink is for girls. There are times, however, when parents may choose to decorate in gender-neutral colors such as green and yellow. Nonetheless, by the time we are young children (some evidence suggest that by the time we are thirty-months-old), traditional gender stereotypes—such as what types of toys and activities are appropriate for boys and for girls—have been ingrained in us (Miller, et. al., 2009). This, however, does not diminish their importance or pervasiveness.

The answers to many of the questions about which we wonder have at least some social components. Why, for example, do roommate situations with three people almost always have more problems than those with two? Do sororities or fraternities serve any real purpose? Why do they choose to admit some people but not others? Have you had an argument with anyone lately? If you have, the chances are that it arose at least in part from having different perceptions about how people should behave—perceptions influenced by social surroundings. The people employed in the housing offices of most schools are aware of this important sociological fact and try to place people from similar backgrounds as roommates. For example, sociologists have studied how roommate assignments can lead to interracial friendships and how a university can directly influence interracial friendships on campus (Tyson, 2004; Buchman, et. al., 2009). Why do most of us feel uncomfortable with a group of people we do not know? Part of the reason is that we do not know how to behave—our social behavior is determined by a constant exchange of social cues; and these cues may differ from group to group. Indeed, why are you attending college,

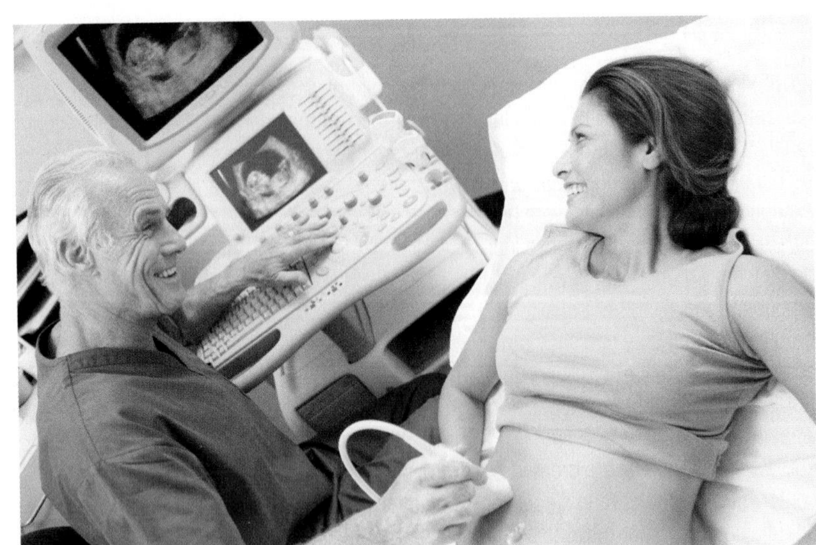

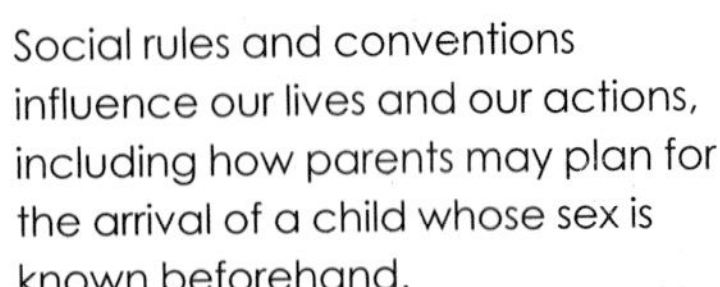

Social rules and conventions influence our lives and our actions, including how parents may plan for the arrival of a child whose sex is known beforehand.

taking this course, and reading this book right now? (Rates of college attendance differ dramatically from one social group to another.) These are not simply matters of interests for sociology but also for society at large. Concerns and efforts to achieve diversity, for example, are increasingly a part of many workplaces.

The list could be extended indefinitely, but our point should be clear: Whether or not we like it or are even aware of it, the social fabric that surrounds us dictates many aspects of how we live. One of the pleasures of studying sociology is that it not only has scientific applications, but also personal and occupational applications. Sociology attempts to explain not only the factors that draw group members together, but also why we may feel uncomfortable talking to most athletes and yet feel very comfortable talking to most members of the drama club (or vice versa). Although we may not recognize them, there are reasons for our social behavior; and having knowledge of these reasons is useful in our personal lives, in our occupations, and in understanding trends in the world around us. At its best, an understanding of sociology can bring to light an entire new dimension of social forces that influence us constantly.

WHAT IS SOCIOLOGY?

What is **sociology**? Sociology is the scientific study of human behavior, social groups, and society. The term itself, often credited to Auguste Comte (1798–1857), the founder of sociology, is derived from two root words: *socius*, which means "companion" or "associate," and *logos*, which means "word." At its most basic, then, it means "words about human associations or society."

Another way to find out what sociology is would be to observe some sociologists at work. Some might spend most of their time poring over volumes from the census bureau or traveling to northern Alaska every year to talk to Eskimos about their hunting practices. Some might use a survey to investigate sexual behavior or might study kinship systems (i.e., family relationship patterns) among natives of the South Pacific. Others might look into how college students perceive their professors or how television has influenced family life in the United States.

If you pursued all these approaches, you would probably find yourself with a bewildering variety of ideas about what sociology is. What do they have in common? They all suggest that sociology is concerned with every aspect of the self in relationships with others and every aspect of the social world that affects a person's thoughts or actions. As stated by the American Sociological Association in a booklet titled *21st Century Careers with an Undergraduate Degree in Sociology* (2009), sociology is the study of social life and the social causes and consequences of human behavior. The term *social life* encompasses all interpersonal relationships, all groups or collections of persons, and all types of social organizations. The "causes and consequences of human behavior" encompass how these relationships, groups, and organizations are interrelated; how they influence personal and interpersonal behavior; how they affect and are affected by the larger society; how they change or why they remain static; and what the consequences are of these factors. This definition reflects the belief that people can be understood only in the context of their contacts, associations, and communications with other people. The very heart of sociology then—its concern with the complexities and subtleties of human social life—makes it a discipline that is highly relevant not only to professional sociologists, but also to people in virtually every line of work and at every level.

Thus, sociology may consider a wide range of general questions such as the following:

1. How do groups influence individual human behavior?
2. What are the causes and consequences of a particular system of social order?
3. What social factors contribute to a particular social change?
4. What purpose is served by a particular social organization?
5. What are the causes and consequences of a particular social system?

Sociologists then use these general questions to help in identifying and responding to more specific questions. In the case of question five, for example, a sociologist might further inquire about a particular social system by asking questions: How do the patterns of social interaction in a small village differ from those in a large city? How do city planners help ensure social tranquility in rural areas undergoing rapid economic growth and development?

Other areas investigated by sociologists include racial and ethnic relationships, prejudice and discrimination, power and politics, jobs and income, families and family life, school systems and the educational process, social control, organizations, bureaucracies, groups and group dynamics, leisure, health-care systems, military systems, women's movements, and labor movements. The stratification of people by wealth, education, power, and such differences as gender or age may also be examined. As you can see, sociology is an extremely broad field. It provides knowledge that directly applies to occupations that involve evaluation, planning, research, analysis, counseling, and problem solving. In its most comprehensive sense, sociology can be regarded as including every aspect of social life—its causes, its forms and structures, its effects, and its changes and transformations.

The Sociological Imagination

Throughout this course you will likely be asked to step outside your "box" and to view social issues as an outsider. The purpose of this request is to help you develop a **sociological imagination**—a quality of mind that allows us to understand the influence of history and biography on our interactive processes (Mills 1959). Although published in 1959, Mills' description of what sociological thinking entails is equally as accurate today. In other words, our experiences guide our perceptions. Like the blind men who described the elephant differently, depending on whether they felt its trunk, tail, ear, body, or leg, everyone regards the world from his or her own point of view. A school building may be seen as a place of work by a teacher, as a place of study by a student, as a tax liability by a homeowner, as a fire hazard by a firefighter, and as a particular structural design by a builder. In the same way, sociologists consider the social world from their own unique perspective.

As a student, you develop not only a sociological imagination, but also a sociological perspective. Sociology is a perspective, a way of looking at society and social behavior. What is the **sociological perspective**? It is a conscious effort to question the obvious and to remove us from familiar experiences and examine them critically and objectively. This sort of *empirical* (based on observa-

nine
ate.
ions
rces
e on
s to
ion,
rnal

d in-
pret
life.

An awareness of interaction patterns and group processes can help us to understand the relationship between our personal experiences and the society in which we live.

Human behavior is, to a large extent, shaped by the groups to which people belong, by social interactions, and by the surrounding social and cultural context. Apart from the social and cultural context, for example, it may be extremely difficult to understand the spontaneous, simultaneous, and collective shout that occurs when a person with a wooden stick hits a round object over the head of a person wearing a thick leather glove on one hand but not on the other. It may be difficult to understand the anger of people in a neighborhood when children are bused to a school in a different neighborhood. It may be difficult to understand why people often become overtly vehement in their disagreements about policies concerning taxes, health care, gun control, abortion, public prayer, same sex marriages, and other persistent controversial issues. Behaviors such as these reflect the group, the institution, and the society in which they occur. Because individual behavior can be understood only in its social and cultural context, the sociological perspective considers the individual as part of the larger society. It notes how the society is reflected in individuals and attempts to discover patterns in behaviors and regularity in events.

The sociological perspective operates at two levels, termed ***macrosociology*** and ***microsociology***. The difference relates to the size of the unit of analysis. Macro level analysis deals with large-scale structures and processes: broad social categories, institutions, and social systems, such as war, unemployment, and divorce. Solutions to these problems are sought at the structural or organizational level.

One example of macrosociological analysis is the study of how societies transition from an agricultural economic system to an industrial one. Micro level analysis, on the other hand, is concerned with how individuals behave in social situations. The social problems of a veteran, an unemployed worker, or a divorcée would be subjects for microsociological research. Solutions would be sought at the personal or interpersonal level. One example of microsociological analysis is the study of university classroom conformity, where the researcher observes the day-to-day patterns of behavior and socialization occurring among those enrolled in the class. The sociological perspective involves investigations of problems on both scales.

Sociology and Popular Wisdom

It is widely assumed, sometimes accurately so, that research findings tend to support what we already know. We all have some idea as to why people act the way they do and how society works. As social beings, most of us were raised in families and communities. Everyone has learned to obey traffic signals and danger signs. We have all heard the debate and rhetoric of presidential and local political campaigns. We have all read newspapers

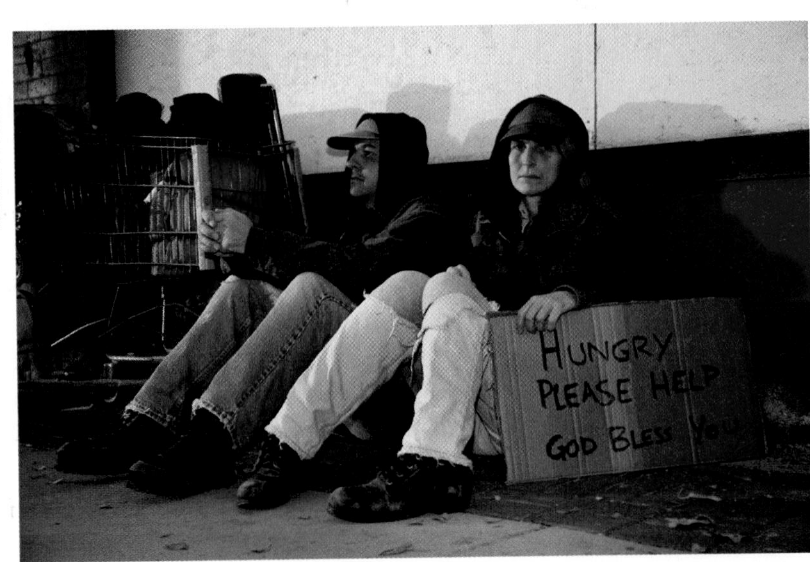

Macro level analysis is concerned with large-scale structures and processes such as war, unemployment, and divorce. Micro level analysis is concerned with how individuals, such as the unemployed, behave in social situations.

and heard television reports that remind us continually of crime, racial conflicts, poverty, inflation, pollution, AIDS, and teenage pregnancies. We all understand social life—our own experiences make us experts in human behavior and in the nature of society. Let us examine a few examples to prove our point. Aren't the following statements obviously true?

Thinking Sociologically

1. It was suggested that human behavior is, to a large extent, shaped through our social interactions and cultural contexts. Discuss ways in which members of our communities influence our everyday choices. More personally, to what extent are you solely responsible for your own condition or destiny?

2. In regard to school shootings, how does the sociological imagination help us to understand the events at Virginia Tech University?

1. People who commit rampage shootings are obviously mentally ill and suddenly snapped before the incident.
2. Because poor racial and ethnic minorities are more likely to live in larger cities, poverty is more an urban problem than a rural one.
3. Because capital punishment leads people to give serious thought to the consequences before committing crimes, crime rates are much lower in states that have capital punishment than in those that do not.
4. Because males are more prone to violence than females, suicide rates are lower for girls than for boys.
5. Because we all know that death is approaching, as we grow older, a fear of dying increases with age.

Many other examples could be given, but these common-sense ideas should illustrate our point. Although you may agree with all of them, research findings indicate that all of these statements are false. Key findings from a 2002 Safe School Initiative study conducted by the U.S. Department of Education and the U.S. Secret Service found that most perpetrators of school shootings had not previously been evaluated for psychological disorders, nor had they sought assistance from a behavioral agency. Many of the offenders had kept journals detailing their anger and rage prior to their shooting spree. For example, Charles Whitman kept a journal and asked that his body by studied after he was dead so police would know why he had homicidal tendencies. It was discovered during autopsy that Whitman had a brain tumor. The study also found that school shooters rarely "snap" but, rather, display behavior that concerns others prior to the incident. Seung Hui Cho, the Virginia Tech shooter, had several teachers note his suicidal and homicidal ideation while he was in the eighth grade. Further, several female students at Virginia Tech complained to resident advisors or to campus police that Cho was sending them unwanted messages. In 2005, an English professor was concerned about Cho's behavior and complained to the department chair that Cho was taking pictures of other students from underneath his desk and writing material that appeared to be overtly violent. Prior to the 2011 Arizona shooting of Gabrielle Giffords and bystanders, Jared Lee Loughner had placed a disturbing video on Myspace that included a handgun on top of a U.S. history textbook and had exhibited behavior that was odd enough to lead to his suspension from community college. Even though the administrators would not allow Loughner to return unless he received a mental health evaluation, he never did receive an evaluation and dropped out. There is no record of him ever having made explicit threats prior to the shooting. (Lipton, et. al, 2011)

The second statement in our list of popular wisdom suggests poverty is an urban problem not a rural one. This belief is most likely perpetuated by the media whose images of poverty often involve unwed, minority mothers and their children living in public housing within large urban areas. However, the truth is that poverty is more prevalent in rural areas than in urban communities. According to Jenson (2006), approximately 7.3 million persons living in rural communities are poor. In 2005, 15.1 percent of the rural population was living in poverty, compared to 12.5 percent of persons living in urban communities. Additionally, the Annie E. Casey Foundation (2004), reports that of the top fifty counties in the United States with the highest rates of child poverty,

The belief that poverty is an urban problem is most likely perpetuated by the media whose images portray unwed minority mothers and their children living in public housing within large urban areas.

forty–eight are located in rural America. One in five children, or 18.9 percent, living in rural communities are poor, a number higher than urban children from all minority groups. Lack of job opportunities is one reason for higher poverty in rural communities.

The third statement suggests crime rates are lower in states practicing capital punishment than in states without the death penalty. The evidence, however, suggests there is very little relationship between the rate of murder and other crimes and the use of capital punishment. The murder rates in states with the death penalty are not consistently lower than the rates in states without it. In general, the death penalty is not a deterrent to murder or other crimes. Even imprisonment does not seem to be a major deterrent, as is evident from the *recidivism* (relapse into repeating criminal behavior) rate of people who have been in prison. Rather than changing people's attitudes, punishment may make them more cautious and promote extra efforts to avoid apprehension.

The fourth statement suggests that males are more prone to commit suicide due to their violent nature. While suicide rates (Table 1-1) are higher for males than for females in most countries, including the United States, there are some countries where the rates between males and females are strikingly different, some where they are similar, and at least one (China) where they are higher for females (World Health Organization 2009). However, what the suicide data present us with is that understanding suicide is much more complex than one might initially think. For example, according to World Health Organization data, Eastern European countries have the highest rates of suicide for both males and females. The Eastern Mediterranean region and Central Asia have the lowest suicide rates. Globally, fifty-five percent of suicides are among people ages fifteen to forty-four, and forty-five percent are among those age forty-five and older. Youth suicide is increasing at the greatest rate. Sociology prompts us to to ask why the above trends are taking place. What social and cultural factors have an effect on suicide rates among different groups?

The fifth statement suggests a fear of dying increases with age as the likelihood of death approaches. A *Los Angeles Times* poll (2000) found that only seven percent of people over sixty-five think about and fear death while twenty percent of eighteen to twenty-nine year-olds are afraid of dying.

These examples illustrate that although some popular observations may be true, many others are not supported by empirical data. Without social research,

TABLE 1-1 SUICIDE RATES PER 100,000 BY COUNTRY, YEAR AND SEX (TABLE) MOST RECENT YEAR AVAILABLE; AS OF 2009

Country	Year	Males	Females
ALBANIA	03	4.7	3.3
ANTIGUA AND BARBUDA	95	0.0	0.0
ARGENTINA	05	12.7	3.4
ARMENIA	06	3.9	1.0
AUSTRALIA	04	16.7	4.4
AUSTRIA	07	23.8	7.4
AZERBAIJAN	07	1.0	0.3
BAHAMAS	02	1.9	0.0
BAHRAIN	88	4.9	0.5
BARBADOS	01	1.4	0.0
BELARUS	03	63.3	10.3
BELGIUM	99	27.2	9.5
BELIZE	01	13.4	1.6
BOSNIA AND HERZEGOVINA	91	20.3	3.3
BRAZIL	05	7.3	1.9
BULGARIA	04	19.7	6.7
CANADA	04	17.3	5.4
CHILE	05	17.4	3.4
CHINA (Selected rural & urban areas)	99	13.0	14.8
CHINA (Hong Kong SAR)	06	19.3	11.5
COLOMBIA	05	7.8	2.1
COSTA RICA	06	13.2	2.5
CROATIA	06	26.9	9.7
CUBA	06	19.6	4.9
CYPRUS	06	3.2	1.8
CZECH REPUBLIC	07	22.7	4.3
DENMARK	06	17.5	6.4
DOMINICAN REPUBLIC	04	2.6	0.6
ECUADOR	06	9.1	4.5
EGYPT	87	0.1	0.0
EL SALVADOR	06	10.2	3.7
ESTONIA	05	35.5	7.3
FINLAND	07	28.9	9.0
FRANCE	06	25.5	9.0
GEORGIA	01	3.4	1.1
GERMANY	06	17.9	6.0
GREECE	06	5.9	1.2
GRENADA	05	9.8	9.8
GUATEMALA	06	3.6	1.1
GUYANA	05	33.8	11.6
HAITI	03	0.0	0.0
HONDURAS	78	0.0	0.0
HUNGARY	05	42.3	11.2
ICELAND	07	18.9	4.6
INDIA	98	12.2	9.1
IRAN	91	0.3	0.1
IRELAND	07	17.4	3.8
ISRAEL	05	8.7	3.3
ITALY	06	9.9	2.8
JAMAICA	90	0.3	0.0
JAPAN	07	35.8	13.7
JORDAN	79	0.0	0.0
KAZAKHSTAN	07	46.2	9.0
KUWAIT	02	2.5	1.4
KYRGYZSTAN	06	14.4	3.7
LATVIA	07	34.1	7.7
LITHUANIA	07	53.9	9.8
LUXEMBOURG	05	17.7	4.3
MALDIVES	05	0.7	0.0
MALTA	07	12.3	0.5
MAURITIUS	07	16.0	4.8
MEXICO	06	6.8	1.3
NETHERLANDS	07	11.6	5.0
NEW ZEALAND	05	18.9	6.3
NICARAGUA	05	11.1	3.3
NORWAY	06	16.8	6.0

(continued)

TABLE 1-1 SUICIDE RATES PER 100,000 BY COUNTRY, YEAR AND SEX (TABLE) MOST RECENT YEAR AVAILABLE; AS OF 2009

Country	Year	Males	Females
PANAMA	06	10.4	0.8
PARAGUAY	04	5.5	2.7
PERU	00	1.1	0.6
PHILIPPINES	93	2.5	1.7
POLAND	06	26.8	4.4
PORTUGAL	04	17.9	5.5
PUERTO RICO	05	13.2	2.0
REPUBLIC OF KOREA	06	29.6	14.1
REPUBLIC OF MOLDOVA	07	28.0	4.3
ROMANIA	07	18.9	4.0
RUSSIAN FEDERATION	06	53.9	9.5
SAINT KITTS AND NEVIS	95	0.0	0.0
SAINT LUCIA	02	10.4	5.0
SAINT VINCENT AND THE GRENADINES	04	7.3	0.0
SAO TOME AND PRINCIPE	87	0.0	1.8
SERBIA	06	28.4	11.1
SEYCHELLES	87	9.1	0.0
SINGAPORE	06	12.9	7.7
SLOVAKIA	05	22.3	3.4

Country	Year	Males	Females
SLOVENIA	07	33.7	9.7
SPAIN	05	12.0	3.8
SRI LANKA	91	44.6	16.8
SURINAME	05	23.9	4.8
SWEDEN	06	18.1	8.3
SWITZERLAND	06	23.5	11.7
SYRIAN ARAB REPUBLIC	85	0.2	0.0
TAJIKISTAN	01	2.9	2.3
THAILAND	02	12.0	3.8
TFYR MACEDONIA	03	9.5	4.0
TRINIDAD AND TOBAGO	02	20.4	4.0
TURKMENISTAN	98	13.8	3.5
UKRAINE	05	40.9	7.0
UNITED KINGDOM	07	10.1	2.8
UNITED STATES OF AMERICA	05	17.7	4.5
URUGUAY	04	26.0	6.3
UZBEKISTAN	05	7.0	2.3
VENEZUELA	05	6.1	1.4
ZIMBABWE	90	10.6	5.2

Source: http://www.who.int/mental_health/prevention/suicide_rates/en/index.html

it is extremely difficult to distinguish what is actually true from what our common sense tells us should be true. Many people have suffered enormous losses in personal relationships and business deals because they acted on the basis of what they considered "common sense" about what they believed was "the truth." We believe the knowledge you gain from sociology will help to improve the quality of your personal and professional life. Even if this is the only sociology course you ever take, we hope after completing it you will have a far greater understanding of yourself, of your society, and of human behavior, as well as an increased ability to question many of the popular observations widely accepted as truth by the press and by our fellow citizens. In addition, part of what is needed to develop your sociological perspective and to comprehend "the truth" is realizing that we live in a global world and we are but one part of the big picture. Media stereotypes often lead to misconceptions about other cultures or social issues within and outside our society.

Sociology and the Other Social Sciences

All branches of science attempt to discover general truths, propositions, or laws through methods based on observa-

FIGURE 1-1 CHANGES IN THE AGE DISTRIBUTION OF CASES OF SUICIDE BETWEEN 1950 AND 2000

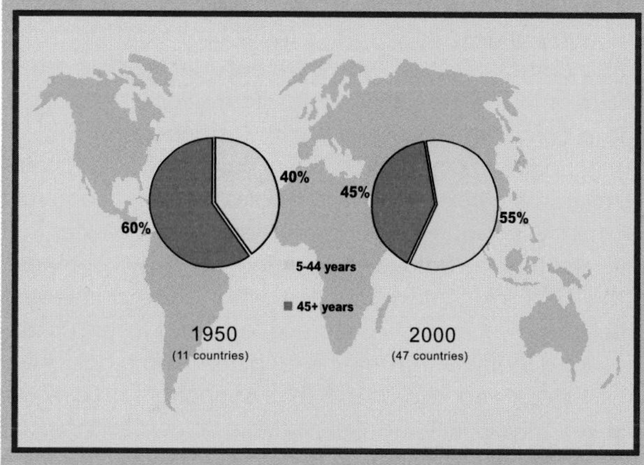

Source:
http://www.who.int/mental_health/prevention/suicide/changes/en/index.html

FIGURE 1-3 EVOLUTION OF GLOBAL SUICIDE RATES 1950-2000, PER 100,000

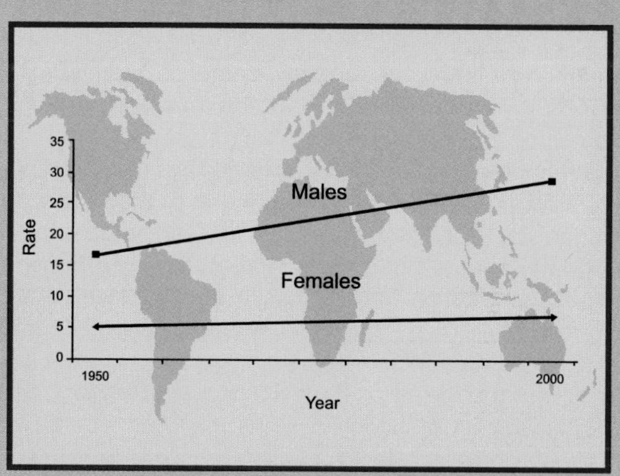

Source:
http://www.who.int/mental_health/prevention/suicide/evolution/en/index.html

FIGURE 1-2 DISTRIBUTION OF SUICIDE RATES PER 100,000 BY GENDER AND AGE, 2000

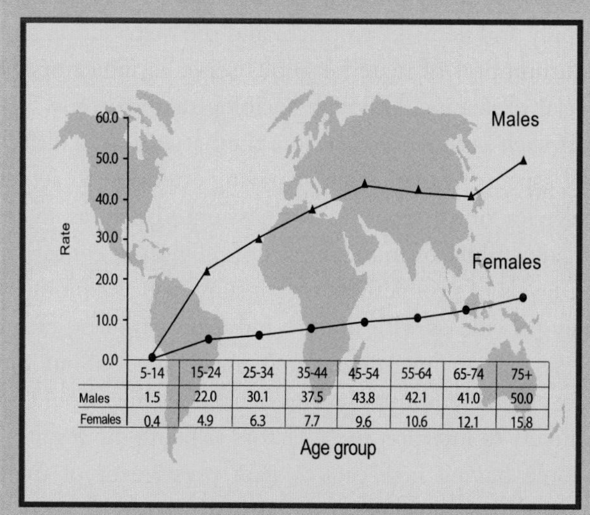

	5-14	15-24	25-34	35-44	45-54	55-64	65-74	75+
Males	1.5	22.0	30.1	37.5	43.8	42.1	41.0	50.0
Females	0.4	4.9	6.3	7.7	9.6	10.6	12.1	15.8

Source:
http://www.who.int/mental_health/prevention/suicide/suicide_rates_chart/en/index.html

tion and experimentation. Science is often divided into two categories: the social sciences and what are often referred to as the natural sciences. The natural sciences include (a) the *biological sciences*—biology, eugenics, botany, bacteriology, and so forth, which deal with living organisms, both human and nonhuman; and (b) the *physical sciences*—physics, chemistry, astronomy, geology, and so on, which deal with the nonliving physical world. The word natural must be applied to these sciences with caution, however. The **social sciences** are just as natural as those that the natural sciences embrace. Sociology, like other social sciences, applies the scientific method to studying human behavior. For example, the organization of cities, the collective action of a football team, and the patterns of interaction in a family system are just as natural as electricity, magnetism, and the behavior of insects and can be studied using a scientific approach.

Sociology is a social science, but it is important to realize that a complete understanding of a society or of social relationships would be impossible without an understanding of the physical world in which societies exist and an understanding of the biological factors that affect humans. Like the other social

HOW TO READ A TABLE

Sociologists make frequent use of tables to present the findings of their own research, to provide numerical evidence to support or reject statements they make, or to show comparisons among social groups, categories, events, or across different points in time. Numerous tables are presented throughout this text, not so much to present our own research findings as to lend numerical support to substantive content and to show comparisons among groups or periods of time. You will be able to understand the contents of a table more easily if you follow a systematic procedure. The previous table in this text is used as a model (Table 1-1) in leading you through the steps to follow in reading a table.

1. *Examine the title* At the top of a good table is a title that tells precisely what the table contains. The title in Table 1-1 informs us that this table includes information about suicide numbers and rates per one hundred thousand from selected countries.

2. *Check the source* The source of the information presented usually appears at the bottom of the table. Unless the table presents original data, it probably includes a source note listing the research journal or other publication that contains the original information. The source note tells where the data comes from and where we can go to locate the data; it helps us judge how reliable the information is. In Table 1-1, the data come from the World Health Organization.

3. *Look for any headnotes or footnotes* Headnotes generally appear below the title; footnotes are likely to appear below the table but above the source note. Headnotes or footnotes may tell how the data were collected, how a question was asked, why some information is lacking, which statistical measure was used, or why the data were presented as they were. Table 1-1 includes a footnote that lets the reader know the data is from the most recent year available, 2009. It is important to know what the figures actually indicate, or if there are any exceptions to the rest of the data in the table. Readers interested in getting further data

sciences—psychology, anthropology, economics, and political science—sociology deals with human relationships, social systems, and societies. Although the boundaries among the various social sciences are sometimes hazy, each tends to focus on a particular aspect of the world and tries to understand it. A brief description of the other social sciences and sociology's relationship to them may be helpful in providing and understanding the nature of social science, in general, and of sociology, in particular.

Sociology applies the scientific method to studying human behavior, such as the collective action of a football team.

Economics is the study of how goods, services, and wealth are produced, consumed, and distributed within societies. Figures about the gross national product, balance of payments deficits, or per-capita income may seem to belong more to the realm of statistics or mathematics than to social science, but these statistics reflect individual behavior, the relationships among groups, and the functioning of society. The effects of supply and demand on prices and the distribution and consumption of material goods serve as indicators of social exchange. Although sociologists also study factors such as these, they devote their attention to different aspects of them such as paying attention to actual behavior or attitudes, to business enterprises as social organizations, or to the impact of religion or education on levels of productivity or consumption. Economists may provide us with import and export figures, ratios of savings to investment, and information about the rate at which money changes hands, but they would be unlikely to interpret these factors as being the result of people buying new cars to gain prestige or of their starting new businesses because they are frustrated with their jobs or their bosses.

Political science studies power, governments, and political processes. Political scientists study different kinds of governments, as well as interpersonal

about suicide or in checking rates in future years can access data from the World Health Organization.

4. *Read the column and row headings* Tables contain two important types of headings. The column headings appear at the top and tell what appears below them. The row headings appear on the left and describe the information to the right of them across the table. Referring again to Table 1-1, you will see a couple of levels of headings. The top heading tells you the data found within each column: the country, year, number, and rate of suicide is found within each one. The second level of heading further divides the information into gender and total suicides for each previous heading. The first column (Countries) explains what are in the row headings below. Keep both the column and the row headings in mind as you look at the table to make comparisons.

5. *Make comparisons* Now that we know what the figures mean (numbers and rates), what the column headings refer to (gender and totals), and what the row indicates (countries), we are ready to read the table and to make comparisons. Looking back at Table 1-1, by looking at the vertical column we see the number of suicides—numbers and rates for specific countries. Looking at the horizontal row, we can compare the numbers and rates of suicides for males and females and get total number or percentage of suicides for a specific country. Comparing columns and rows, we can note similarities, differences, or trends. By doing this, we are ready for the final and highly important step: drawing conclusions.

6. *Draw conclusions* What can we conclude from the material presented? How are suicide rates different from a global perspective? What are the differences in rates between males and females in various countries? How can we explain the differences in suicide rates among developed countries? Do these data support the popular wisdom mentioned in the text that suicide is typically a male problem?

Tables will vary considerably in format and complexity, but following these six steps should assist you in understanding and grasping the information presented in any table you encounter. You will not only read tables when studying sociology, but you will also often use the ability to read and interpret tables in your personal and professional life.

processes and means through which power is exercised, focusing on both abstract theory and the actual operation of government. During elections, it is political scientists who provide us with information about voting patterns, changes from previous elections, and the characteristics of voters. Traditionally, political scientists have been interested primarily in political theory and government administration. More recently, however, they have begun to devote more attention to matters of interest to the sociologist, such as the acquisition of political beliefs, the social backgrounds of political activists, and the role of women and of ethnic, racial, and other minorities in political outcomes.

Anthropology, like sociology, is a broad and varied discipline. It includes physical anthropology, archaeology, cultural history, social linguistics, and social and cultural anthropology. *Physical anthropologists* attempt to understand both traditional indigenous and modern cultures by studying physical traits such as the shape and size of skulls, artifacts such as pottery and weapons, and genetic mutations of both human and nonhuman forms of life. The work of *cultural* or *social anthropologists*, on the other hand, is very similar to that of sociologists. Like sociologists, they are concerned with social institutions, patterns of organization, and other aspects of society. There are differences in the two fields, however. Anthropologists generally study a society as a whole, whereas sociologists are likely to concentrate on one aspect of a society. Also, anthropologists often live in the culture or community they are studying so that they can observe behavior directly. Sociologists are more likely to rely on statistics, questionnaires, or secondary data; they are frequently interested in comparing information about the social processes and structures across different cultures, whereas anthropologists often study cultures or communities individually.

Psychology is concerned primarily with human mental processes and individual human behavior. Frequent areas of study include learning, human development, behavior disorders, perception, emotion, motivation, creativity, personality, and a wide range of other mental and behavioral processes. In addition to being studied by psychologists, some of these areas are also studied by sociologists and by members of a field known as **social psychology**. These three branches of social science have different emphases, however. *Psychology* is concerned with individuals. *Social psychology* is the study of how an individual influences his or her social interactions with other individuals or with groups and of how social behavior influences the individual. *Sociology* deals primarily with groups and social systems. Much of the material covered in sociology textbooks technically is considered to be social psychology.

History is considered either a social science or one of the humanities and provides a chronological record of past events. Sociology is an analytical discipline that tries to derive general truths about society. History, on the other hand, is basically descriptive; historians traditionally consider every event to be unique, assuming that attempts at classification or generalization may impair their ability to understand exactly what happened. For example, a sociologist studying the Bolshevik revolution might therefore try to determine whether revolutions evolve through a standard series of stages or whether particular social situations are common to most prerevolutionary societies. A historian studying the same revolution would be more interested in discovering the exact sequence of the events that actually occurred, particularly as described in documents written by persons who experienced those events.

Increasingly, however, many historians are becoming more sociological in their orientation. Instead of concentrating exclusively on events—names, dates, successions of kings, and details of battles—they are analyzing broad social movements and general social patterns. Many are turning to sociological methods of analysis to determine what social forces influenced specific historical events.

Geography, often considered a natural science, is concerned with the physical environment and the distribution of plants and animals, including humans. Geographers may study such things as why a particular trade route evolved or how the formation of nations is influenced by the physical landscape. The *physical geographer* investigates climate, agriculture, the distribution of plant species, and oceanography. *Social* and *cultural geographers*, like sociologists, may be interested in how the distribution of people in a particular area influences social relationships. Sometimes, urban geographers and urban sociologists work together on such problems as how various types of housing affect family life and how a given transportation system affects employment and productivity. Although physical geography usually is not considered a social science, social geography clearly shares many areas of interest with the other social sciences.

Is **social work** a social science? Technically, it is not. Social work is the field in which the principles of the social sciences, especially sociology, are applied to actual social problems in the same way that the principles of physiology are applied in medicine and the principles of economics are applied in business. The **applied sciences**—those that directly use these principles—are often considered distinct from the **pure sciences**—those that seek knowledge for its own sake; but the two actually can be considered to occupy different points on the same continuum. At one end of the continuum would be the disciplines that use knowledge to solve actual problems. A social worker might, for example, use information obtained from family research to try to place children in foster homes or to establish centers for abused spouses. At the other end of the continuum would be the disciplines involved in research—not to solve a specific problem, but simply to increase our understanding of the world. A researcher of this sort might study child rearing or spouse abuse as a function of income or education levels. Nevertheless, few social scientists do only pure research, and few social workers do only applied science. Social workers, for example, devise their own research and techniques to help people solve personal and group problems, and the resulting applications contribute to our existing body of knowledge. For their part, sociologists have always been involved in both applied and pure research. Thus, sociologists and social workers do share some common tasks, but it is a mistake (albeit a common one) to regard sociology as equivalent to social work or social welfare. Likewise, it is a common mistake to assume that social work is the only way to apply sociology

Thinking Sociologically

1. The role of women in society is different in many parts of the world. Choose one or two of the social sciences described in this chapter and discuss how it or they would address the various roles of women throughout the world.

2. Are sociologists social workers? Are social workers sociologists? Explain your answers.

CHAPTER REVIEW

Wrapping it up

Summary

1. Sociology is the study of society, social life, and the causes and consequences of human social behavior. The terms society and social life encompass interpersonal relations within and among social groups and social systems. Sociologists study a wide range of behavior from small groups (families) to large ones (bureaucracies), question the obvious, seek patterns and regularities, and look beyond individuals to social interactions and group processes.
2. Sociological imagination is the ability to see the world from a sociological point of view. Using sociological imagination, an individual is able to analyze a social phenomenon from a sociological perspective. This perspective can be applied both to microsociology, which considers problems at the level of interpersonal and small-group processes, and to macrosociology, which considers large-scale problems, structures, social organizations, and social systems.
3. Although many people believe the structure and workings of society are a matter of common knowledge, countless sociological findings disprove popular conceptions and provide surprising insights.
4. Sociology is one of the social sciences, which are disciplines that try to systematically and objectively understand social life and predict how various influences will affect it. Each social science attempts to accumulate a body of knowledge about a particular aspect of society and the social world. Other social sciences include economics, political science, anthropology, psychology, history, and geography.

Key Terms

anthropology The study of the physical, biological, social, and cultural development of humans, often on a comparative basis

economics The study of how goods, services, and wealth are produced, consumed, and distributed

geography The study of the physical environment and the distribution of plants and animals, including humans

history The study of the past; social history is concerned with past human social events

macrosociology A level of sociological analysis concerned with large-scale units such as institutions, social categories, and social systems

microsociology The level of sociological analysis concerned with small-scale units such as individuals in small group interactions

organizational deviance Occurs when events that are created by or existwithin organizations that do not conform to an organization's goals orexpectations and produce unanticipated and harmful outcomes

political science The study of power, government, and the political process

psychology The study of human mental processes and individual human behavior

pure science The area of science in which knowledge is sought for its own sake with little emphasis on how the knowledge might be applied

social psychology The study of how individuals interact with other individuals or groups and how groups influence the individual

social science A science that has as its subject matter human behavior, social organizations, or society

social work The field in which the principles of the social sciences are applied to actual social problems

sociological imagination The ability to see how history and biography together influence our lives

sociological perspective A way of looking at society and social behavior that involves questioning the obvious, seeking patterns, and looking beyond the individual in an attempt to discern social processes

sociology The study of human society and social life and the social causes and consequences of human behavior

traditional indigenous Refers to ethnic groups who are native to a land or region, usually before the arrival of a foreign and possibly dominating culture.

Discussion Questions

1. Explain sociological perspective and discuss how it changes the way we look at societies different from our own.
2. What is the difference between macrosociology and microsociology? How would each examine police corruption?
3. Explain why common sense knowledge is not the best source of information. With this in mind, discuss why women who are victims of domestic violence stay in abusive relationships.
4. Discuss what the social sciences have in common. How is each unique or different from the others?

Pop Quiz

1. Sociology

   a. is the study of social life
   b. studies common sense and popular wisdom
   c. is a form of socialism
   d. studies the autonomy of the individual

2. The term "sociology" was coined by

   a. Comte
   b. Mills
   c. Marx
   d. Durkheim

3. Which of the following would a sociologist probably study?

   a. how groups influence individual human behavior
   b. the causes and consequences of a particular system of social order
   c. the purpose served by a particular social organization
   d. all of the above

4. At the micro level of analysis, sociology might focus on

   a. husbands and wives in interaction
   b. how divorce rates vary cross-culturally
   c. unemployment rates
   d.how social change influences the divorce rate in a particular society

5. ________ focuses on large-scale structure and process without reference to the relationships of the persons involved.

   a. Microsociology
   b. Macrosociology
   c. Political science
   d. Geography

6. The social sciences are more likely to have as a goal

   a. the direct utilization of knowledge gained through research
   b. the acquisition of knowledge
   c. the study of both human and nonhuman life
   d. defining "what should be" in a society

7. _______ is the study of how goods, services, and wealth are produced.

   a. Anthropology
   b. Political Science
   c. Sociology
   d. Economics

8. A social science that studies physical traits, artifacts, and the shape and size of skulls is

   a. cultural anthropology
   b. geography
   c. physical anthropology
   d. biology

9. Which of the following is more likely to be covered in sociology textbooks?

   a. psychology
   b. clinical social work
   c. social psychology
   d. applied research

10. In the insert, "How to Read a Table," the source of the information presented usually apears ______.

    a. at the bottom of the table
    b. right below the title
    c. in the footnote area
    d. in the column headings

11. Unlike the other social sciences, sociology does not study social institutions. T/F

12. The very heart of sociology is concerned with the complexities and subtleties of human social life. T/F

13. In its most comprehensive sense, sociology includes every aspect of social life. T/F

14. The sociological perspective entails efforts to see primarily the individual and her/his actions and thoughts. T/F

15. Macrosociology deals with how individuals behave in social situations. T/F

1. A	6. B	11. F
2. A	7. D	12. T
3. D	8. C	13. T
4. A	9. C	14. F
5. B	10. A	15. F

CHAPTER 2

The Development of Sociology

HOW THEORY AFFECTS SOCIAL POLICIES AND SOLUTIONS TO SOCIAL PROBLEMS

How did human life originate? Creationism holds that human beings came into existence according to the literal biblical account of creation as told in the Book of Genesis. That is, God created the world in six days, the sixth day being the day on which human life began. Evolutionism—the theory presented by Charles Darwin in *The Origin of the Species*—holds that humans evolved from lower forms of life over a period of tens of millions of years through a process of natural selection and organic evolution. The publication of Darwin's book in 1859 fueled a controversy between those who believed in the divine creation of life (creationists) and those who believed in a natural origin of life (evolutionists). National attention focused on this controversy in the summer of 1925, when John Scopes, a high school biology teacher in Dayton, Tennessee, was put on trial for breaking a state law that prohibited the teaching of evolution. Although John Scopes was being tried for violating a state law, the "Scopes trial"—or "monkey trial" as it is often called—became a battle about the right to hold and profess particular ideas.

William Jennings Bryan—the prosecuting attorney in the case and a Democratic nominee for president in 1896, 1904, and 1908—tried to make his case against Scopes by appealing to the religious convictions of the jury and by promoting the sanctity of the Bible. Clarence Darrow—one of Scopes's defense lawyers and an attorney of great national prominence at the time—argued that Scopes' academic freedom and his constitutional rights (specifically, freedom of speech and the guarantee of separation between church and state) had been violated. Nevertheless, Scopes had broken a state law and was therefore convicted. In order to defuse the controversy somewhat, the trial judge fined Scopes only $100 and gave no prison sentence. Later, the conviction was appealed and overturned on a technicality. The significance of the Scopes' trial is not so much in its outcome as in the intensity of passions that it aroused in the adherents of creationist and evolutionist views on life. It clearly demonstrated that the theories that people hold about matters of great import—such as the origin of life or the nature of social reality—often dictate their views on practical matters.

Even though most theologians have reconciled the evolutionist views with their religious views, the evolutionist–creationist controversy still exists, especially when matters of policy are concerned. Both of these theories have implications for the ways in which social policies are enacted. Creationism suggests that because God created humans, specific values and morals are also provided by God and are absolute. On the other hand, evolutionism implies that because human life evolved over millions of years, specific values and morals have also evolved, to serve the best interests of humankind.

Thus, these two different views require very different approaches to policy decisions. For example, policies that support a woman's right to have an abortion would be seen by creationists as unacceptable under any circumstances because of the view that God alone is responsible for decisions regarding life. Creationists would see policies that benefit homosexuals as unacceptable because sexual mores prohibiting homosexuality are contained within the Bible. Policies that give rights to unmarried heterosexual couples or unwed mothers would be seen by creationists as unacceptable because of biblical constraints against sex outside of marriage. Evolutionists might or might not find such policies—or any policies related to moral views expressed in the Bible—unacceptable, depending on their interpretations of natural or social scientific ideas. Evolutionists would make their determinations based on what they see as the positive or negative value of such policies for individuals and society, not based on what they believe that God has determined.

The sociological significance of the creationism versus evolutionism controversy goes far beyond specific issues and policy discussions. The controversy is important because it illustrates the influence of theories in determining people's perspectives on social issues and solutions to social problems. It is interesting to note that this controversy is as much alive today as it was in 1925. Further, it demonstrates the central sociological idea that social reality is subjective and open to interpretation. Nevertheless, once social reality is interpreted in a particular way—that is, once a theoretical viewpoint is accepted—it is acted on as if that interpretation is the reality. This chapter introduces you to some of the most widely used theoretical perspectives in sociology today. It is important not only to understand these theories, but also to understand that many different interpretations of social life exist and that each interpretation carries with it implicit assumptions for dealing with social issues, problems, and policies.

THE DEVELOPMENT OF SOCIOLOGY

The study of sociology is a recent development in social history. Philosophers such as Aristotle and Plato had much to say about society and human relationships, but until the late nineteenth century, no writer we know of could appropriately be considered a sociologist. In fact, the label *sociologist* was not applied to the early practitioners of the field in their own time; they have been identified as such only in retrospect.

Most early writers were interdisciplinary in orientation, drawing their ideas from philosophy and from the physical and biological sciences. Actually, as a result of developments in the natural sciences, much of the early writing in sociology was based on the assumption that laws of human behavior could be discovered in the same way that laws of nature had been discovered by astronomers, physicists, and other natural scientists. These early writers also had great faith in the power of reason, assuming that it could be used to formulate laws that could be applied to improve social life and to eliminate or diminish social problems.

These assumptions were rapidly put to a test as the Industrial Revolution presented new challenges and social problems in Europe. People began to migrate to towns and cities for factory jobs. With many of these jobs came low wages, long working hours, harsh child labor practices, housing and sanitation problems, social alienation, social conflict, encounters with crime, and a variety of other social problems that provided an abundance of conditions for concern, study, and solution. The Industrial Revolution that began in England, the social revolution in France under Napoleon, and the political upheavals throughout Europe—all provide the backdrop for the emergence of the discipline known today as sociology.

Sociology originally developed as a practical discipline intended to address social problems and social reform. Turner and Turner say:

> ... By 1880 ... the label "sociology" embraced such activities as philanthropic and reform efforts to help the "dependent classes," public edification on the need for social reform, attempts at making the church more effective in the social arena, arguments bolstering the intellectual authority of the cooperative movement, and programs for collecting statistics on the laboring classes. Each of these associations was embodied in some form of work, ranging from reformist activity and government research to college teaching and literary writings. (1990, p. 12)

We can begin to understand this discipline, now less than two hundred years old, by briefly examining a few of the early writers who were influential in its development. All knowledge, all societies, all institutions have a social history. We can examine selected aspects of this historical development by focusing on five European

The discipline of sociology as we know it today emerged from the changes brought on by the Industrial Revolution in the nineteenth century. With the Industrial Revolution, people began migrating to towns and cities for factory jobs, which brought about such social problems as harsh child labor practices.

theorists: Comte, Spencer, Marx, Durkheim, and Weber. These sociologists all lived in the nineteenth century, and their ideas stemmed from their personal circumstances and social settings. Certainly, these are not the only important European thinkers who helped shape sociology; however, their work was seminal in shaping the foundations of the discipline.

Auguste Comte

Auguste Comte (1798–1857) was born in southern France, the son of a minor government official. He was educated in Paris where his studies were concentrated in mathematics and the natural sciences. Before completing his schooling, he was expelled for participating in a student insurrection against the school's administration. He then became secretary to Henri Saint-Simon, an influential political leader and advocate of a pre-Marxist version of socialism—a system in which the people own the means of production (e.g., industry). Comte was greatly influenced by Saint-Simon; but their relationship ended when Comte was accused of plagiarism, a charge he denied. He held another job in Paris for approximately twelve years but was again dismissed. He had made too many enemies and too few friends.

Comte is usually credited with being the "father of sociology" because he coined the term *sociology*. He first called this new social science "social physics" because he believed that society must be studied in the same scientific manner as the world of the natural sciences. Like the natural sciences, Comte said, sociology would use empirical methods to discover basic laws of society, which would benefit humankind by playing a major part in the improvement of the human condition.

Comte is best known for his **law of human progress** (or law of the three stages), which basically states that society has gone through three stages: (1) the theological, or fictitious; (2) the metaphysical, or abstract; and (3) the scientific, or positivist. In addition, a specific type of social organization and political dominance accompanies each mental age of humankind. In the first stage, the theological, everything is explained and understood through the supernatural. The family is the prototypical social unit (the model or standard to which others conform), and priests and military personnel hold political dominance. In the second stage, the metaphysical, abstract forces are assumed to be the source of explanation and understanding. The state replaces the family as the prototypical social unit; and, as in the Middle Ages and the Renaissance, the political dominance is held by the clergy and lawyers. In the third and highest stage, the scientific laws of the universe are studied through observation, experimentation, and comparison. The whole human race replaces the state as the operative social unit, and industrial administrators and scientific moral guides hold the political dominance. It was Comte's assertion that the scientific stage of human knowledge and intellectual development was just beginning in his day. According to Comte, sociology, like the natural sciences, could henceforth draw on the methods of science to explain and understand the laws of progress and the social order.

A related concept originated by Comte was the view that society was a type of "organism." Like plants and animals, society had a structure consisting of many interrelated parts, and it evolved from simpler to more complex forms. Using this organic model as a base, he reasoned that sociology should focus on **social statics**, the structure of the organism, and on **social dynamics**, the organism's processes and forms of change. Comte believed that sociology was the means by which a more just and rational social order could be achieved.

APPLYING COMTE

Auguste Comte was primarily interested in applying scientific principles of social life to affect social situations. That social actions are governed by laws and principles—just as physical actions are—is a significant fact that is useful to others besides academic social scientists. Whether in our personal lives or in our occupations, if we believe that individual personalities alone or fate alone can explain why problems occur, we might look in the wrong places for solutions or become powerless to solve them. In a discussion about Comte's ideas, social theorist Lewis Coser states (1977, 4), "As long as (people) believed that social actions followed no law and were, in fact, arbitrary and fortuitous, they could take no concerted action to ameliorate them."

Although Comte wrote primarily for intellectual social leaders of his day, his ideas were useful to many people. His belief that society should be studied scientifically is the basis for all sociological research—academic and applied (hence his title, "father of sociology"). Sociologists do not merely speculate, philosophize, or use opinions to formulate theories about social behavior; rather, they rely heavily on the scientific principles emphasized by Comte: observation, experimentation, and comparison. To explain the rate and/or causes of school shootings in the United States, for example, a sociologist might first formulate hypotheses to test. Perhaps the researcher believes the cause of school shootings is directly related to the learning behaviors of the shooter, learning violent behavior from an abnormal or dysfunctional home life. The sociologist might then collect data that would enable him or her to compare the characteristics of school shooters: familial history, childhood behavioral problems, discipline style used by parents, etc.

You can use Comte's prescription for scientific analysis in many ways in your professional and personal lives. Instead of quickly making decisions based on gut feelings, you may be better off systematically collecting as much information as possible on the situation before you act. Think, for a moment, how you will go about deciding on a career and looking for a job. Very often, college graduates and others looking for jobs do what they think is the right thing—such as look at the classified ads and pray. If you are a little more scientific in your approach, however, you can significantly increase your chances of getting a satisfying and highly rewarding job—possibly even the one that you want.

For example, suppose that you are interested in computer programming and you want to work for Microsoft. You could collect data regarding Microsoft personnel:

How do they expect people to dress?
What types of personalities are they looking for?
Do they expect people to relocate?
What are their long-term goals?
From what geographical areas are they most likely to recruit people?
Where do they currently advertise their job openings?
How do they expect you to act during interviews?
What do they look for on a résumé?
Most important of all, what is the precise nature of the job for which you are applying?

If you take this more scientific approach to finding a job, you will have a better chance of getting the one you want sooner than if you leave it up to chance alone. This type of analytical thinking is useful not only for finding a job but in all areas of your life. Think, for example, how people's political views might be shaped if they relied more on a scientific approach to analyzing issues and policies rather than relying on their gut feelings.

Herbert Spencer

Herbert Spencer (1820–1903) was born in England, the son of a schoolteacher. Like Comte, he received considerable training in mathematics and the natural sciences, but little in history and none in English. Feeling unfit for a university career, he worked as a railway engineer, a draftsperson, and finally as a journalist and writer.

One of Spencer's major concerns was with the evolutionary nature of changes in social structure and social institutions. He believed that human societies pass through an evolutionary process similar to the process Darwin explained in his theory of natural selection. It was Spencer who coined the phrase "survival of the fittest"—and he was the first to believe that human societies evolved according to the principles of natural laws. Just as natural selection favors particular organisms and permits them to survive and multiply, societies that have adapted to their surroundings and can compete will survive. Those that have not adapted and cannot compete will encounter difficulties and eventually die.

Spencer's theory paralleled Darwin's theory of biological evolution in other ways. He believed that societies evolved from relative homogeneity and simplicity to heterogeneity and complexity. As simple societies progress, they become increasingly complex and differentiated. Spencer viewed societies not simply as collections of individuals but as organisms with a life and vitality of their own.

In sharp contrast to Comte, the idea of survival of the fittest led Spencer to argue for a policy of noninterference in human affairs and society. He opposed legislation designed to solve social problems, believing it would interfere with the natural selection process. He also opposed free public education, assuming that those who really wanted to learn would find the means. Just as societies that could not adapt would die out, Spencer contended, individuals who could not fit in did not deserve to flourish.

As you can imagine, Spencer's ideas had the support of people of wealth and power. His theories strengthened the position of those who wanted to keep the majority of the population impoverished and minimally educated. His ideas also tended to support a discriminatory policy: Was it not a natural evolutionary law that kept people unequal? Spencer thought that conflict and change were necessary parts of the evolutionary process (like Marx, discussed in the next section). Unlike Marx, however, he believed that planned change would disrupt the orderly evolution of society, which he thought would eventually improve the social order. (His goals are a radical departure from those of Marx in other respects, too, of course.)

Spencer was one of the earlier writers to be concerned with the special problems of objectivity in the social sciences. Comte never seemed concerned with potential conflicts among his personal views, his religious mission, and his analysis of society. Marx denied that objective social science was possible, believing that theory was inseparable from socialist practice. Spencer, however, devoted attention specifically to the problem of bias and other difficulties that sociologists face in their work.

Those familiar with contemporary politics in the United States will recognize a resurgence of ideas similar to those espoused by Spencer, but today few sociologists accept his ultraconservative theory of noninterference in social change. There is, however, widespread acceptance of the idea that societies grow progressively more complex as they evolve and an increasing recognition that evolutionary processes seem to operate in areas such as population changes or the selection by the stratification system of the "socially most fit" for particular types of education and positions.

APPLYING SPENCER

Although few contemporary sociologists accept Spencer's policy of noninterference in social problems, knowledge of his ideas is useful in helping us understand some present-day politics. By analyzing Spencer's theory of noninterference, for example, how could a politician, a political science major, or a citizen gain insight for interpreting some policies implemented under some conservative political administrations? For example, Ronald Reagan, who became president of the United States in 1980 and who died in 2004, will be remembered largely for the dictum of "getting government off the backs of the people." This dictum was manifested in policies that led to lower taxes, less government regulation of environmental pollution, cutbacks in federal aid for college loans and to colleges in general, reduction in aid for social service programs, and deregulation of many industries. Americans were told that the rationale for such noninterference was to give people more freedom; this would, theoretically, stimulate the economy. This policy was reinforced again under the administration of George W. Bush and became a central value among many conservative politics, especially that of the Tea Party. 2011 was the centennial of Ronald Reagan's birth, and many of the ceremonies that honored his life also paid homage to his views on government non-interference. As an aside, it is interesting to note that unemployment rates in the mid-1980s (when Reagan gained support for his views about "non-government interference") peaked at 10.8 percent and then declined to around 3.8 percent by 2000 (U.S. Misery Index, 2010). At the end of 2009,

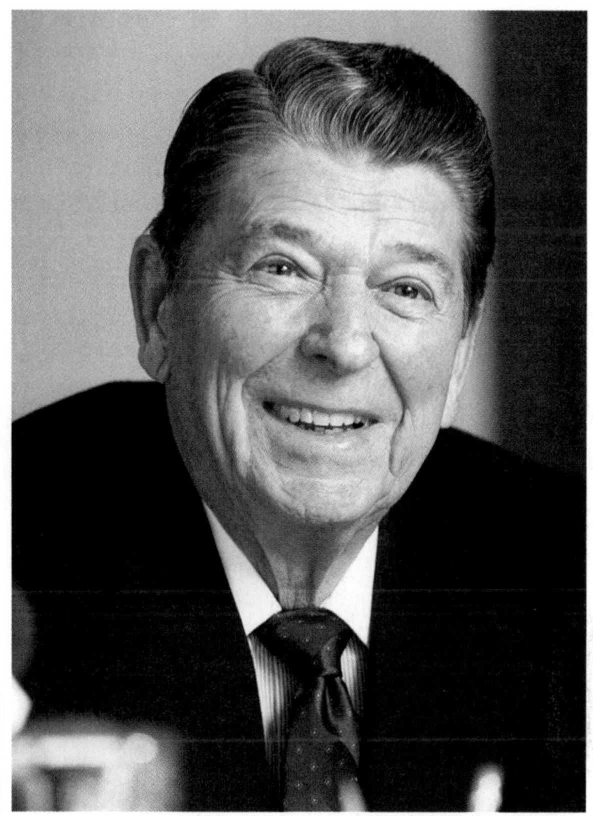

Knowledge of Spencer's ideas about noninterference is helpful in understanding past and present-day political policies, such as those of President Reagan, whose policies led to less government regulation.

the unemployment rates had again climbed to 10.1 percent. This is around the time that the Tea Party began to gain strength. Is this coincidental, or does this suggest that there is a connection between social theory, political views, and economic conditions? If so, why do you think a Spencerian philosophy of non-government interference becomes more popular during periods of high-unemployment?

If you analyze Spencer's ideas concerning noninterference and see who really benefits from them, you may begin to understand the implications of such a policy for Americans today. You may come to see that it does not necessarily lead to increased freedom and benefits for the majority but rather for those who are already wealthy and powerful.

To further illustrate this idea, suppose that your teacher placed one hundred $5-bills on the floor at the front of the classroom. The money is available for everyone to take. All you need to do is to get to it before someone else does. The teacher will not interfere in any way whatsoever. If you are sitting in the front of the classroom, how do you feel about the teacher's policy of noninterference? Being in a position of advantage, you would probably praise the teacher for such an enlightened idea that gives you so much freedom. However, suppose now that you were sitting anywhere from the middle to the back of the classroom. How, then, would you see the policy of noninterference? Would you be as "free" to get the money as the people in the front? Does the teacher's policy of noninterference give you more freedom or less? Would some sort of regulation or intervention about how much money the people in the front could take actually increase the freedom of those in the middle and back of the room?

It is important for all of us to understand that some political viewpoints give the appearance of improved social conditions for everyone; but as we look a little deeper, we see that they may really benefit only a select few. We are told, for example, that a decrease in taxes that go toward social services will provide us with more individual money. However, who really benefits from a decrease in taxes—the wealthy or the middle class—if that decrease also leads to cutbacks in services that the middle class needs, such as the availability of federal loans to college students?

Karl Marx

Karl Marx (1818–1883) was born in Germany. His father, a lawyer, and his mother were both descended from long lines of rabbis. Marx attended college, planning to practice law; but after becoming involved with a radical anti-religious group, he decided to devote his life to philosophy. Unable to get a university position, he became a writer for a radical publication and wrote a series of articles on various inhumane social conditions. His articles attracted the attention of government officials, who opposed his views; and he lost his job. Shortly thereafter, he moved to Paris and met the leading intellectuals of

the radical movements of Europe, solidifying his conversion to socialism. He began his lifelong friendship with Friedrich Engels, with whom he wrote the now-famous *Communist Manifesto* (1847). Having joined the Communist League in Brussels, he returned to Germany. He was again pressured to leave the country because of his activities. He moved to London where—with his friend Engels—he continued to promote his views until his death in 1883.

The theme common to all the writings of Marx and Engels was a profound sense of moral outrage at the misery produced in the lower classes by the new industrial social order. Marx concluded that political revolution was a vital necessity in the evolutionary process of society and that it was the only means by which the improvement of social conditions could be achieved.

Marx was a major social theorist and contributor to economic and philosophical thought. He believed that capitalism was dominant in the shaping of society. He argued that **social conflict**—struggle and strife—was at the core of society, the source of all social change. He asserted that all history was marked by

economic determinism—the idea that all change, social conditions, and even society itself are based on economic factors—and that economic inequality results in class struggles. Marx believed society was comprised largely of two social classes: **bourgeoisie** (the owners and rulers) and the **proletariat** (the industrial workers). These conflicts between the rich and the poor, the owners and the workers (also referred to as the haves and have-nots) lead to feelings of *alienation*, a feeling of frustration and disconnection from work and life among the workers. The recognition among workers that society is stratified and that they share the same plight is known as **class-consciousness**, which according to Marx, leads ultimately to revolution. It was Marx's belief that conflict, revolution, and the overthrow of capitalism were inevitable.

Today, regardless of whether they agree or disagree with Marx's ideas, few sociologists deny the importance of the contributions he made. Sociologists are still trying to understand the influence of economic determinism, social conflict, social structure, social class, and social change on society.

APPLYING MARX

Karl Marx's ideas are used in practically every area of sociology. To simplify one of Marx's tenets used by academic sociologists, there is a fundamental inequality in social relationships between those who have *assets* (land, money, jobs, equipment, prestige, etc.) that provide them with power and those who do not. This inequality allows those who have power to dominate and exploit those who do not. Thus, all social relationships contain the elements of conflict between "haves" and "have-nots."

Many academic sociologists use this idea as a premise for interpreting a variety of social relationships regarding gender and race relations, marriage, economics, politics, employment, education, religion, justice, and other matters. In developing a theory about school shootings, for example, a Marxian analyst may focus on the conflict between students who feel powerless and those who seem to be in control (teachers, principals, and other, more popular students). In trying to explain education, the focus might be on the inherent conflict between faculty (the ones who control the grades) and students, or administration (the ones who control jobs and salaries) and faculty.

It may surprise you that some clinical sociologists use Marx's ideas, also. Marx-oriented therapists, for example, can be of immediate use to their clients who have capital-related problems such as depression over failure to achieve quick financial success, frustration over being powerless at work, overwhelming fear of not being able to pay one's bills, and other problems related to money. Much suffering can be relieved by helping the clients realize that their problems are not isolated, individual ones but rather a societal matter that appears in many forms in different social classes and groups. For example, if a client experiences problems in her marriage because she's anxious and frustrated by the way she's treated by the supervisors at her job, a Marxist therapist can help her realize that her anger is rooted in the structure of capitalism and help her to defuse it. When some clients understand how economic systems create psychological stress and that other people are affected with similar problems, the pain of alienation often subsides.

Smith-Nonini (2002) is a journalist turned anthropologist who has used insights developed from Marxian theory to help call attention to and eradicate the plight of Latino migrant farm workers and workers in meat-packing plants in North Carolina. Contrary to popular ideas, the immigrant population in many areas of the United States stimulates the economy, rather than takes away from it. The Bryan School of Business and Economics for the Center for New North Carolinians, highlights how entrepreneurial activity picks up in areas with large immigrant populations and the vast majority of immigrants do not take away jobs from native-born Americans (Hummel 2004). Through her efforts (highlighted in this chapter's "Sociology at Work" box), Smith-Nonini has helped create awareness of injustices toward this group of people.

Many non-sociologists also benefit from Marx's ideas. Armed with the knowledge of how the powerful (say, factory owners) may exploit the

SOCIOLOGY AT WORK

Helping Migrant Farm Workers

Sandy Smith-Nonini is a former journalist, turned anthropologist. She earned her Ph.D. in anthropology from the University of North Carolina at Chapel Hill. Smith-Nonini's work is an example of how Marx's theories can be used to explain the origins of inequities in the workplace.

Smith-Nonini has been studying migrant farmworkers and meat packers in North Carolina and working with advocacy groups defending their labor rights. These workplaces, which now depend heavily on immigrants, have unusually high rates of injuries and even deaths. Yet many citizens have little knowledge of new immigrants, much less the working conditions of companies that stock the counters of our grocery stores. For this reason, Smith-Nonini has worked with a Unitarian-Universalist committee on a documentary project on farmworker conditions. The goal of her research and documentary is to raise awareness of the general public and of the farmworkers themselves, many of whom are not aware they have rights to fair labor conditions.

In 2004, when President Bush proposed a new legal status for immigrant workers, Smith-Nonini noted that many hoped for an end to the administration's "close the border" mentality. However, when she looked closer at the new proposals, Smith-Nonini became concerned. Under the plan, Mexican workers would be granted temporary visas to work in a specific job for an employer who participates in a "guest worker" program. The visas would be for three-year periods and could be renewed with the same employer. Having studied the existing federal guest worker program, known as H2A, Smith-Nonini realized the new proposal was likely to replicate some of the worst abuses now affecting H2A workers. In a news article criticizing the Bush plan, she noted the problems "derive from the fact that the employer is also the de facto immigration officer, with the power to deport those who grumble about work conditions or pay." From a Marxian perspective, the employers are clearly the owners of the means of production able to create working conditions the farmworkers have no choice but to accept.

"For example," Smith-Nonini states, "farmworkers employed by the North Carolina Growers Association (NCGA), the largest H2A farm labor brokerage in the country, routinely complain that workers who leave their assigned farm or who anger their farmer employer end up on a blacklist maintained by the NCGA." These workers, then, are not rehired. Smith-Nonini continues, "Abuses such as the blacklist, long contract period, and the inability of workers to change employers are possible only in a dual-labor market of the kind that is created by guest worker programs, where a class of workers lacks full citizenship and labor rights. If employers had to compete in the general market for workers, they would be forced to improve conditions to attract workers."

Migrant workers play a role in strengthening the economy in many areas of the United States. One study, at North Carolina State University, estimated that each farmworker's labor contributed $12,000 to the state's agricultural profits. Smith-Nonini's research and advocacy raise the question of whether it's fair for the larger community to benefit so handsomely from this cheap labor while the workers themselves are not reaping a fair share of the rewards and are often suffering grave injustices in the process.

powerless (the workers), labor leaders could convey to union members how they are being taken advantage of. This may help to promote "class consciousness" and solidarity among the members, and thus increase the union's bargaining power.

Finally, Marx's ideas are useful for you personally. Your knowledge that the powerful members of society seek to maintain their power may help you think more critically about issues when it comes time for you to vote in elections. When new tax laws are proposed that supposedly are designed to benefit the whole population, for example, you may find cause to question whether the wealthy and powerful will benefit more than the middle and lower classes. You may use Marxian ideas to understand your intimate relationships better. A spouse who has chosen not to be employed may realize that he or she lacks equal say in important marital decisions (such as what car to buy, where to go on vacation, or where to live) because the working partner has more resources (namely, control of the money). Realizing this, the unemployed spouse may seek employment to create more equality in the relationship.

Emile Durkheim

Emile Durkheim (1858–1917) can be considered the first French academic sociologist. Before Durkheim, sociology was not a part of the French education system although such related fields as education, social philosophy, and psychology were studied. In 1892, the University of Paris granted him its first doctor's degree in sociology. Six years later he was appointed chair of the first Department of Social Sciences at the University of Bordeaux and later was named chair of the Department of Education and Sociology, thus providing sociology the opportunity to be recognized as a science. In addition to teaching, Durkheim wrote critical reviews and published important papers and books. His best known books include *The Division of Labor in Society, The Rules of Sociological Method, Suicide,* and *The Elementary Forms of Religious Life.*

Durkheim is responsible for several important ideas. For one, he refused to explain social events by assuming that they operated according to the same rules as biology or psychology. To Durkheim, social phenomena are **social facts** that have distinctive social characteristics and determinants. He defined social facts as "every way of acting, fixed or not, capable of exercising on the individual an external constraint" (1933, 13). Since these facts are external to the individual, they outlive individuals and endure over time. They include such things as customs, laws, and the general rules of behavior that people accept without question. Stopping at traffic lights, wearing shirts, and combing one's hair are behaviors most people perform without dissent. In short, individuals are more the products of society than the creators of it.

Although an individual can come to know and be a part of society, society itself is external to the individual. For this reason, Durkheim concentrated on examining characteristics of groups and structures rather than individual attributes. Instead of looking at the personal traits of religious believers, for example, he focused on the cohesion or lack of cohesion of specific religious groups. He was not so concerned with the religious experience of individuals, but rather with the communal activity and the communal bonds that develop from religious participation (Coser 1977).

Such communal interaction gives rise to what Durkheim called a **collective conscience**—a common psyche (spirit) that results from the blending together of many individual mentalities yet exists over and above any individual. Although the collective conscience is socially created, it is a powerful reality that comes to control us and cannot be denied. From this perspective, for example, whether God exists as a supernatural being is secondary to the fact that God exists as a result of people sharing and demonstrating their belief in God. To those sharing that belief, God is unquestionably and undeniably real, and thus an inescapable force. It is no longer a matter of a personal belief, but is now a belief in something outside of any one of us.

Durkheim's work *Suicide* deserves special attention for several reasons. It established a unique model for social research; and it clearly demonstrated that human behavior, although it may seem very individual, could be understood only by investigating the social context in which the behavior takes place. After looking at numerous statistics on different countries and different groups of people, Durkheim concluded that suicide was a *social* phenomenon, related to the individual's involvement in group life and the extent to which he or she was part of some cohesive social unit. Durkheim's central thesis was that the more a person is integrated into intimate social groups, the less likely he or she is to commit suicide. Thus, people who have a low level of social integration and group involvement, such as the unmarried and those without strong religious convictions, would be expected to have higher suicide rates.

He believed that social integration was achieved through people's mutual dependence and acceptance of a system of common beliefs. An important element in the system of beliefs was religion, the ceremonies of which become common experiences—symbols shared by the association of a group of people—and thus a significant part of the collective conscience.

Durkheim played a key role in the founding of sociology. Although Comte, Spencer, and Marx introduced new ideas about society and helped convince the public that sociology and the other social sciences deserved a hearing, it was Durkheim who made sociology a legitimate academic enterprise.

APPLYING DURKHEIM

Like Comte's emphasis on the scientific method, Durkheim's concept of social facts is central to every form of sociological investigation. Many theories and concepts developed by academic sociologists are rooted in the idea that forces external to the individual affect human social behavior. Sociologists do not, for example, explain divorce in terms of individual psychological makeup. Rather, they look to social factors external to the individual, such as the economy, income, education, religion, age, or occupation. Is divorce more likely to occur when the economy is doing well or in trouble? Do people in lower or upper income groups have higher divorce rates? Are highly educated people more likely to divorce than people with less education? When the answers to these and other questions are found, sociologists can begin to analyze how certain types of social conditions (the state of the economy, degree of education, level of income, etc.) account for divorce instead of just looking at individuals.

Durkheim's ideas about social facts and the collective conscience have important applications that are indispensable in clinical settings. It is important to keep in mind that although sociologists often work in clinical settings, Durkheim's ideas benefit anyone intervening in social problems.

Emile Durkheim believed religion to be an important element in the system of beliefs through which social integration was achieved. The ceremonies and symbols associated with religion became common and shared experiences and thus were a part of the collective conscience.

To help people deal with a particular problem—whether it involves helping parents to deal with a child's poor performance in school, counseling a suicidal person, or counseling a politician on strategies for getting elected —the clinician cannot adequately understand the situation solely on the basis of individual personalities or psychological characteristics. Rather, the social world of these people—the relevant social facts and collective conscience—must be analyzed. People usually do not explore the social processes that underlie situations or their decisions and tend to look exclusively at psychological processes.

Suppose, for example, that a high school guidance counselor notices that a student getting ready to apply for college suffers a sharp decline in grade point average (GPA) two semesters in a row. Rather than assume that the student is lazy or anxious about being rejected by colleges, how could knowledge of the student's social environment—say, that her parents are getting divorced—help the counselor deal with this student's situation? Knowing that social facts and a collective conscience exist, we can better look behind the scenes to help others and ourselves and deal with most situations.

Max Weber

Max Weber (1864–1920; pronounced *Vay-ber*) was born in Germany, the son of a wealthy German politician. He was trained in law and economics, receiving his doctorate from the University of Heidelberg at the age of twenty-five. For the next several years, he taught economics, but he soon succumbed to a severe mental illness that kept him an invalid and recluse for much of his life. Despite this condition, Weber was a prolific writer. His best-known works in sociology include *The Protestant Ethic and the Spirit of Capitalism*, *The Sociology of Hinduism and Buddhism*, *Theory of Social and Economic Organization*, and *Methodology of the Social Sciences*.

Weber's mixed feelings toward authority, whether familial or political, are reflected in his writings on the topic of power and authority. Weber discussed why men claim authority and expect their wishes to be obeyed. (Typically for his period, women were not considered.) His approach to sociology, however, has probably been as influential as his ideas. His predecessors considered societies in terms of their large social structures, social divisions, and social movements. Spencer based his studies on the belief that societies evolved like organisms; Marx considered society in terms of class conflicts; and Durkheim was concerned with the institutional arrangements that maintain the cohesion of social structures. These theorists assumed that society, although composed of individuals, existed apart from them.

Weber was concerned with value-free sociology. He did not believe that society could be studied value-free because sociologists would always interject their own values and beliefs when studying society or even when choosing what to study. Weber believed that sociologists must study not just social facts and social structures but also *social actions*—external objective behaviors as well as the internalized values, motives, and subjective meanings that individuals attach to their own behavior and to the behavior of others. The goal, Weber believed, was to achieve a "sympathetic understanding" of the minds of others. He called this approach **verstehen** (pronounced "ver-shtay-en"): understanding human action by examining the subjective meanings that people attach to their own behavior and to the behavior of others. Once values, motives, and intentions were identified, Weber contended, sociologists could treat them objectively and scientifically.

This approach is evident in Weber's interpretation of social class. Whereas Marx saw class as rooted in economic determinism, particularly as related to property ownership, Weber argued that social class involves subjective perceptions of power, wealth, ownership, and social prestige, as well as the objective aspects of these factors.

APPLYING WEBER

Weber's concept of "verstehen" is a vital tool for academic and applied social researchers. As mentioned, Weber explained social class not just in terms of how much power, wealth, and prestige people have but, rather, in terms of how they see and feel about their power, wealth, and prestige. So, for example, in conducting research on inequality between upper class and middle-class groups, academic researchers need to find out not only what differences exist due to power and wealth, but also how people in each group feel about their own self-worth and the worth of others.

Verstehen is helpful to clinical sociologists working with clients. Consider a situation in which a counselor is called in to help with an interpersonal conflict among employees: An owner of an auto dealership is having a problem with conflict among the salespeople. It appears that in their struggle to acquire sales, the work environment has become the equivalent of a battlefield. Remember that for Weber, subjective meanings guide people's behavior; therefore, the clinician must try to identify with the people and their motives and try to see their actions from the involved persons' perspectives. How do the salespeople perceive their jobs? By trying to identify with them, the clinician may find out that (a) the salespeople feel threatened by one another; (b) they are uncomfortable with the close supervision of the manager; (c) they are convinced that if they do not sell enough, they will be fired; and (d) they think that aggressively competing with the others is smiled upon by management. In helping the client (in this case, the manager) deal with the problem, the techniques of verstehen can be taught to help each come to an understanding of the situation from one another's perspectives.

This technique is not only essential for clinical sociologists, it also can be used in almost any situation—personal or occupational. Certainly, a professor could teach more effectively if she were to put herself in the minds of her students. To help students understand all perspectives, a professor should examine all opinions, even the unpopular ones. Also, the students would fare better if they would try to understand where the teacher was coming from in her lectures or assignments. A salesman would also benefit from applying verstehen; he would gain more if he looked at his sales approach from the customer's perspective rather than trying to direct hard sell.

While a number of scholars established the foundation of European sociology, we cannot leave this discussion without introducing you to the "first female of sociology."

Harriet Martineau

Harriet Martineau (1802–1876) was a significant contributor to the early development of sociology. Almost completely deaf by adulthood, Martineau immersed herself in reading and self-education. She studied social life in Great Britain and, in 1834, traveled to the United States to examine American social life for two years. She published her findings in

"Society in America" in 1837 and in "Retrospect of Western Travel" in 1838. Due to her gender, much of her original research was ignored by the male dominated discipline. However, she was acknowledged for translating Comte's work, *Positive Philosophy*, into English in 1851, condensing his six-volume work into two volumes. Today, Martineau is recognized for her contributions to sociology and is considered to be one of the earliest founders of sociological thought and research.

Besides the scholars just discussed, other European thinkers—including Georg Simmel, Henri de Saint-Simon, Vilfredo Pareto, Ferdinand Toennies, and Karl Mannheim—contributed to the development of sociology. With rare exceptions, they viewed society as a social unit that transcended the individual or was greater than the sum of individuals. It was for this reason, in part, that they did not investigate the means by which individual humans come to accept and reflect the fundamental conditions and structures of their societies—a question that was an important concern of some early American sociologists.

Thinking Sociologically

1. Consider a social problem (ex. domestic violence, poverty, violent crime) and apply the ideas of early contributors Comte, Spencer, Marx, Durkheim, and Weber to the issue. Explain how each might approach the problem.
2. Looking back to your high school history classes, explain how culture in the 1800s may have contributed to the works of Harriet Martineau and other early female thinkers that were largely being ignored by the scientific community.

THE DEVELOPMENT OF SOCIOLOGY IN AMERICA

The earliest sociologists were Europeans, but much of the development of sociology took place in the United States. The first department of sociology was established in 1893 at the University of Chicago, and many important early figures of the discipline were associated with that institution. At the time sociology was arriving, rapid social change was occurring within America. Industrialization, urbanization, and immigration were three factors contributing to this change as the economy was shifting from an agricultural to an industrial society. As people began to migrate to the cities, the increase in population created tremendous social problems, including overcrowding, pollution, crime, as well as many others. In addition, massive waves of immigrants were arriving in the United States which only intensified the problems, as their culture often clashed with that of other immigrants and Americans. By the beginning of the twentieth century, communities were looking toward universities to find the answers to problems within the cities. Much like their European forerunners, American sociologists were concerned with social problems and social reform, in part because of the rapid social changes taking place in this country. These early scholars focused on urbanization and urban problems—ghettos, prostitution, drug addiction, juvenile delinquency, immigration, and race relations.

The Chicago School

From the turn of the century until the mid- to late-1940s, the University of Chicago was the leading sociological training and research center in America. The first sociology graduate program was established there in the 1890s, and many prominent American sociologists were taught at the school. Indeed, seven of the first twenty–seven presidents of the American Sociological Association (ASA) taught or were educated at that institution.

One leading figure in this group was Robert E. Park (1864–1944), who studied in Germany with a sociologist named Georg Simmel. Before beginning his work at the University of Chicago in 1914, Park worked as a journalist; and then he was invited by Booker T. Washington to work at the Tuskegee Institute on race issues in the southern United States. At the University of Chicago, Park was concerned with urban sociology and the effects that industrialization had on the lives of urban dwellers. He argued that industrialization was linked to many of the problems seen within the city and believed that scientific qualitative methods of observation should be used to study man in his natural habitat. He was the author of several important books. With Ernest W. Burgess, he wrote an early textbook in sociology (1921) and, with Burgess and R. D. McKenzie, a book titled *The City* (1925), which suggested that urban communities are areas of both cooperation and competition, much like ecological habitats that occur in nature. The multidisciplinary approach he established became known as "social ecology." Park taught at the university until his retirement in 1936.

After World War I, a group of scholars at the University of Chicago developed an approach to social psychology known today simply as the **Chicago School**. To these early scholars, Chicago was an ideal "social laboratory" because it was experiencing all the problems associated with urban life. Previously, human behavior had been explained primarily in terms of instincts, drives, unconscious processes, and other innate characteristics. The Chicago School believed a shift was needed from a philosophical paradigm to a scientific one. Besides Park, there were several earlier notable scholars at the University of Chicago. The department's first chair, Albion Small, was founder of the American Sociological Society (now known as the American Sociological Association) and first editor of the *American Journal of Sociology*. W. I. Thomas arrived on campus in 1893 and made significant contributions when he co-authored *The Polish Peasant* in Europe and America in 1918, and his formulation of the "Thomas Theorem" in 1928. Ernest W. Burgess became an assistant professor in 1916 and remained at the university until his retirement. Burgess created the Concentric Zone Model, the first explanation of the distribution of social groups within urban areas. His zones became the standard in urban demography. Other notable scholars from the University of Chicago that we will discuss in later chapters include George Herbert Mead, and Herbert Blumer.

During the 1930s, American sociology experienced a period of rapid change, and the Chicago School began to decline in popularity. During this time, the field developed its service relationship to national public policy, its theoretical focus on macro-level systems, and its methods of large-scale quantification. In the words of Lengermann (1979, 196), "The societal crisis of the thirties raised new empirical and theoretical questions for sociologists, brought new demands from public and state to bear on the professional community, opened up new sources of employment and research support, created career anxiety for many sociologists and helped produce the regional associations." Lengermann argues, however, the Great Depression of the 1930s was not the cause of changes in sociology during this decade because the methodological, theoretical, and professional transformation was in process prior to 1929. Rather, the changes were brought about by factors such as the growth and differentiation of the profession, by emerging elitist coalitions, and by the loss of momentum of the Chicago scholars.

Jane Addams

Jane Addams (1860–1935) was not a sociologist, but her work would have qualified her as an applied sociologist during her time. Addams was born to a wealthy father and a devoted mother, and she was extremely close to her father who taught her the spirit of philanthropy. However, while her father allowed Jane a modicum of feminine freedom, ultimately he expected her to get married and to devote herself to family, church, children, cooking, and cleaning. Jane didn't share his views about womanhood; and after her father's death, she and some friends went on a tour of Europe. While there she was drawn to the work being done at Toynbee Hall, a settlement house in London's poor community. Upon her return to America, Jane and one of her traveling companions, Ellen Starr, were committed to opening a settlement house in Chicago. In 1889 they opened Hull House—America's first settlement house and a place to serve Chicago's immigrant population. Addams would often invite scholars from the Chicago School to visit Hull House, and she worked closely with some, including George Herbert Mead. In 1931 Addams was awarded the Nobel Peace Prize for her work and, to date, remains the only sociologist to have received this distinguished award.

W. E. B. DuBois

W. E. B. DuBois (1868–1963), in 1896, became the first African American to receive a PhD from Harvard University in any area of study. His dissertation, *The Suppression of the African Slave Trade in America* is the first volume in Harvard's historical series and remains a respected contribution to the study of slavery in America. He accepted his first teaching job at Wilberforce in Ohio, earning $800 a year. Later he moved to Philadelphia, accepting a position teaching sociology at the University of Pennsylvania. There he began studying the black community living in the slums, afterwards publishing *The Philadelphia Negro* in 1896. DuBois was devoted to bringing attention to the divisiveness between whites and blacks and the overall plight of blacks in America. He was one of the founders of the National Association for the Advancement of Colored People (NAACP) where he worked to empower African Americans to fight for social rights. Eventually, he became a follower of Marx and Engels, increasingly becoming disillusioned by the lack of changes occurring in the U.S. Ultimately, he left America and moved to Ghana. Upon becoming a citizen there, he denounced his American citizenship. Ironically, DuBois died on the eve of Martin Luther King Jr.'s "I Have a Dream Speech" in Washington in 1963.

The Shift of Influence to the East

In the 1940s, the center of sociological research shifted from Chicago to other schools such as Harvard and Columbia. Talcott Parsons (1902–1979), who was affiliated with Harvard, rapidly became the leading social theorist in America, if not the world. Drawing heavily on the work of European thinkers such as Weber and Durkheim, he developed a very broad "general theory of action" (Parsons and Shils 1951).

Robert K. Merton (1910–2003), a student of Parsons', began his teaching career at Harvard but moved in 1941 to Columbia University. Although his general orientation was similar to Parsons', Merton was much less abstract and much more concerned with linking general theory to empirical testing. This approach came to be known as the **middle-range theory**. His contributions to our understanding of such concepts as social structures, self-fulfilling prophecies, deviance, and bureaucracies place him among the leading American social theorists.

C. Wright Mills, Peter Blau, Erving Goffman, Herbert Blumer, Ralf Dahrendorf, Randall Collins, and Jessie Bernard were other scholars who greatly contributed to sociology's development in reaching its present state. Most colleges and universities have departments of sociology, and sociologists are increasingly found in nonacademic settings. Outstanding theorists, researchers, and practitioners can be found from California, New York, and Texas to

Michigan, North Carolina, and Florida. The number of professional sociologists in the United States alone is estimated to approach fifteen thousand. Research on traditional subjects such as the family, urban sociology, race relations, and criminology continues to be funded and studied; much new work on the elderly, gender roles, popular culture, globalization, and peace studies is being undertaken. In addition, the methodological tools and procedures and the range of theories to explain social phenomena are more diverse today than ever before.

THE MAJOR THEORETICAL PERSPECTIVES IN SOCIOLOGY

Theories are explanations offered to account for a set of phenomena. *Social theories* are explanations of social phenomena, such as why people choose to marry as they do or why people behave differently in different social situations. We all develop theories (to use the term in its broadest sense) to help us explain and predict a wide variety of events. For example, if asked why juvenile violence occurs, you will likely have an opinion on the cause or causes of such crimes. A scientist will use a **theory**, a set of interrelated statements or propositions to attempt to answer the question about juvenile crime or any other social phenomenon. Theories are based on a set of assumptions and self-evident truths; they include definitions and describe the conditions in which the phenomenon exists.

While sociological theories exist to explain everything from childrearing to automobile sales, a small number of basic theories are predominate in the field. We will examine these theories and how each can be applied in work settings and in your personal life. They are also described in more detail and applied to specific settings throughout this book.

Structural Functional Theory

Structural functionalism has its roots in the work of the early sociologists, especially Durkheim and Weber. Among contemporary scholars, it is most closely associated with the work of Parsons and Merton. Structural functionalists use a macro-level analysis to explain society and social structures. *Macrosociological orientations* interpret society in terms of its large structures—organizations, institutions, social classes, communities, and nations. Others may use *microsociological orientations* and study individuals in society and their definitions of situations, meanings, roles, interaction patterns, and the like. Although theories overlap considerably, they operate from different assumptions and premises.

Structural functionalism is sometimes referred to as "social systems theory," "equilibrium theory," or simply "functionalism." The terms *structure* and *function* refer to two separate, but closely related, concepts. *Structures* can be compared to the organs or parts of the body of an animal, and *functions* can be compared with the purposes of these structures. The stomach is a structure; digestion is its function. In the same way, health care organizations and the military are social structures (or **social systems**), and caring for the sick and defending governmental interests are their functions. Like a biological structure, a social system is composed of many interrelated and interdependent parts or structures.

If you were to visit any society in the world, from the largest to the smallest, you will find that most societies, if not all, are comprised of five major structures: family, religion, education, economy, and government. According to structural functionalist, the overall function of a society is dependent on each structure performing its required duties. Those advocating this theory believe that each structure is interrelated and interdependent of the other. When working properly, a social system performs specific functions that make it possible for society and the people who comprise that society to exist. Therefore, each structure serves a function that leads to the maintenance or stability of the larger society. The educational system is intended to provide literary and technical skills; the religious system is intended to provide emotional support and to answer questions about the unknown; families are intended to socialize infants and children, and so on. The functionalist perspective assumes these social systems have an underlying tendency to be in equilibrium or balance; any system failing to fulfill its functions will result in an imbalance or disequilibrium. In extreme cases, the entire system can break down when a change or failure in any one part of the system affects its interrelated parts.

A social system can be regarded as having two types of functions: (1) the immediate purpose of what the system does and (2) the broader, less immediate consequences resulting from a particular type of structure or organization. For example, in a biological system, the immediate function of the eye is to obtain information about the environment. This function more broadly enables the viewer to seek food and shelter and to avoid danger. In a social system, one function of government might be to maintain order. An advantage of this function is people can carry on their affairs—running businesses, raising families—without having their lives disrupted.

According to Merton, a social system can have both **manifest functions** and **latent functions**. *Manifest functions* are intended and recognized; *latent functions* are neither intended nor recognized. One manifest function of education systems is to teach literary and technical skills. They also perform the latent functions of providing supervision for children while parents work and of providing contacts for dating and even for marriage. Correctional institutions have the manifest functions of punishment and removing criminals from social interaction within the larger society. They may also perform the latent functions of providing criminals with advanced training in other criminal behaviors.

Merton recognized not all consequences of systems are functional—that is, they do not all lead to the maintenance of the system. Some lead to instability or the breakdown of a system. He termed these consequences **dysfunctions**. Families have a manifest function of rearing children. The intensity of family interactions, however, can lead to the dysfunction, or negative consequence, of domestic violence and child abuse. Dysfunctions such as these may lead to the disruption of relationships within the family system or even to the total breakdown of the system.

Sociologists who adhere to the functionalist perspective examine the parts of a given system and try to determine how they are related to one another and to the whole. They observe the results of a given cluster or arrangement of parts, attempting to discover both the intended (manifest) and the unintended (latent) functions of these parts. In addition, they analyze which of these consequences contribute to the maintenance of a given system and which lead to the breakdown of the system. However, what may be functional in one system may be dysfunctional in another. For example, a function that is good for corporate profits may not be good for family solidarity, or one good for religious unity may not be good for ethnic integration.

According to the functionalist perspective, social systems exist because they fulfill some function for the society. Functionalists focus on order and stability, which has led some critics to argue it supports the status quo. With the emphasis on equilibrium and the maintenance of the system, the process of change, critics say, receives little attention.

APPLYING STRUCTURAL FUNCTIONAL THEORY

Even though it has its critics, structural functional theory is one of the most generally applicable perspectives in social science. It is used by academic sociologists to study and analyze every form of social system, including families, prisons, governments, communities, schools, sports teams, and many others.

Just as structural functionalism is broadly applicable to problems of interest to academic sociologists, so is it a useful tool for almost every type of applied sociological problem. It can be particularly useful as a means of identifying and analyzing the components and goals of a system and of ensuring that those goals are met. When we try to solve problems in any type of social system—whether it is a society, a corporation, a family, a sorority, or a sports team—we must answer some central questions. What are the parts of the system? What functions do the parts actually serve? What functions are they intended to serve? How do the parts influence each other?

A structural functionalist exploring the phenomenon of school violence may look toward the family structure for explanation. During the past forty to fifty years, the structure of the family has changed considerably. Many women, once expected to stay home and raise children, have entered the paid workforce instead of becoming stay at home wives and mothers. Even when a woman wants to stay home, the cost of raising a family today generally requires both parents provide a paycheck to make ends meet. In addition, divorce is more common today than when your parents were children, thus increasing the number of single parent families in society. From a functionalist perspective, these issues could create dysfunction in the family. Children left home alone may spend time involved in deviant behavior, such as vandalism, shoplifting, drug or alcohol use, etc. One of the intended (manifest) functions of the family is for parents to supervise the behavior and activities of their children and to socialize them about respecting the law. A latent function of families can be social isolation due to the increasing amount of independence given to children. Continuous separation from family and friends, unsupervised activities on the computer, and the belief in personal space without parental interference, may create socialization problems for a child struggling to fit in somewhere. If he or she feels like an outsider at school, other children may respond with ridicule, teasing, and bullying. In a rare situation, the child may respond with violence toward those he or she believes are responsible for the problems experienced school.

Robert Merton's theory of **functional alternatives** provides one way to avoid dysfunctions such as school violence. *Functional alternatives* are other ways to achieve the intended goal. Perhaps the family could provide an alternative for the child left alone, such as staying with a relative, attending an after school or sports program, or being involved in a community organization. It is imperative that parents recognize the problems experienced by their children and, instead of dismissing them, find a solution that works for everyone. This functional alternative would, hopefully, meet the needs of the child and lessen the chance of there being an episode of school violence.

The functional perspective can also be applied to tensions among the various parts of a system. The expectations or actions of the different parts of a system may fail to mesh. A building-supply store selling a variety of construction materials, for example, may have some employees who receive commissions from in-store sales and others who receive commissions from outside sales. Suppose that you are hired as an outside sales representative and you develop a large clientele of building contractors through contacts made while on the road. However, when one of those customers decides to purchase material directly from the store, an inside salesperson takes credit for the sale. Who should get the commission for the sale? The conflict arises not because of poor performance on the part of the salespeople but because of a systemic dysfunction. This lack of clarity and confusion over the store's specific goals and the goals of each of its parts can cause serious personnel conflicts that could undermine the business. In this situation, some type of explicit goal-setting or value-clarification process would be appropriate. These examples demonstrate how, by focusing on the functions of the parts of a system, we might be able to discover solutions to a problem.

Conflict Theory

Conflict theory also had its origins in early sociology, especially in the work of Karl Marx; among its more recent proponents are C. Wright Mills, Lewis Coser, Ralf Dahrendorf, and others. These sociologists share the view that society is best-understood and analyzed in terms of conflict and power. Like structural functionalism, conflict theory is a macro theory of analysis.

Karl Marx began with a very simple assumption: society is constructed around its economic organization, particularly the ownership of property. Marx argued that society basically consists of two classes: those who own the means of production (bourgeoisie) and those who provide the labor (proletariats). These two groups are in opposition of one another and, as a result, experience ongoing class conflict. While the proletariats provide the labor that creates the wealth for the bourgeoisie, they (the proletariats) are never paid what they are worth. The profits made from their labor remains primarily in the hands of those who own the means of production. According to Marx, in any economic system that supports inequality, the exploited classes eventually recognize their submissive and inferior status and revolt against the dominant class of property owners and employers. The story of history, then, is the story of class struggle between the owners and the workers, the dominators and the dominated, the powerful and the powerless. Ultimately, conflict theory is about the exploitation of one class of people by another class.

Contemporary conflict theorists assume that conflict is a permanent feature of social life and that, as a result, societies are in a state of constant change. Unlike Marx, however, these theorists rarely assume conflict is always based on class or that it always reflects economic organization and ownership. Conflicts are assumed to involve a broad range of groups or interests: young against old, male against female, or one racial group against another, as well as workers against employers. These conflicts occur because such things as power, wealth, and prestige are not available to everyone; they are limited commodities, and the demand exceeds the supply. Conflict theory also assumes those who have or control desirable goods, services, and other resources will defend and protect their own interests at the expense of others.

In this view, *conflict* does not mean the sort of event that makes headlines, such as war, violence, or open hostility. It is, instead, regarded as the struggle occurring day after day as people try to maintain and improve their positions in life. Neither should conflict be regarded as a destructive process leading to disorder and the breakdown of society. Theorists such as Dahrendorf and Coser have focused on the integrative nature of conflict, its value as a force contributes to order and stability. How can conflict be a constructive force? Basically, the answer is people with common interests join together to seek gains that will benefit all of those sharing these common interests. By the same token, conflict among groups focuses attention on inequalities and social problems that might never be resolved without conflict. Racial conflicts, for example, may serve to bind people with common interests together and may also lead to constructive social change, actually lessening the current conflict among groups.

There is an obvious contrast between the views of the functionalists, who regard society as balanced and in a state of equilibrium, and the views of conflict theorists, who assume that society is an arena of constant competition and change. Functionalists believe the social process is a continual effort to maintain harmony; conflict theorists believe it is a continual struggle to "get ahead." Functionalists view society as basically consensual, integrated, and static; conflict theorists believe it is characterized by constraint, conflict, and change. Whereas functionalists have been criticized for focusing on stability and the status quo, conflict theorists have been criticized for overlooking the less controversial and more orderly aspects of society.

APPLYING CONFLICT THEORY

Like structural functionalism, sociologists use conflict theory to explain the relationship between the parts of a social system and the inequalities that exist among these parts. By recognizing conflict is a permanent feature of the life of any social system, conflict theory can be used to discover and explain the sources of the conflict. In addition to discovering and explaining the sources of conflict, conflict theory may be used to help create techniques to deal with conflict or to use it constructively in the workplace and in your personal life. Sociologists working as therapists or counselors in juvenile detention centers recognize that if conflict in relationships are not resolved, problems will likely manifest and ultimately lead to a worse impact on the child, family, and community.

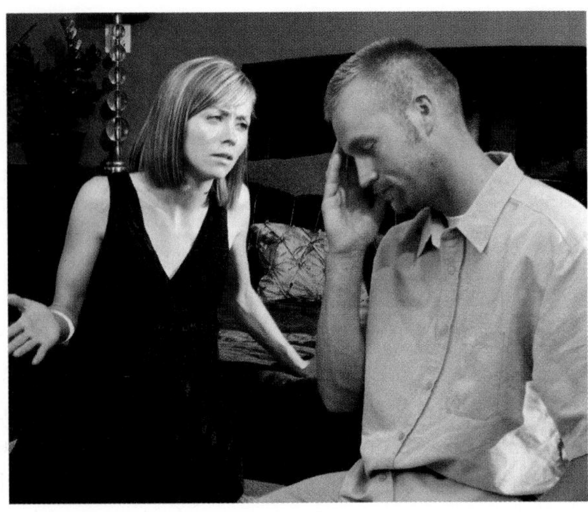

Conflict in a relationship is not always explicit and individuals do not always express it. However, certain clues can indicate inequalities in positions between such relationship members as husbands and wives.

In dealing with any situation, whether it is running a business, coaching a basketball team, teaching a class, presiding over a group, maintaining a family, or organizing a labor union, conflict theory tells us to look for the hidden strains and frustrations, particularly between those in power who make the decisions (bosses, managers, owners, administrators, teachers) and those who carry out these decisions (workers, players, students). Even when those involved do not express dissatisfaction, there may still be conflict. Conflict in relationships is not always explicit, nor do individuals always express it. Nonetheless, some clues might help you to recognize conflict.

When sociologists or counselors are looking for clues to conflict, they often look to clues that indicate inequalities in positions between schools and students, husbands and wives, or between managers and workers. Some of these clues, or expressions of power differentials, may include covert signs of anger (e.g., overeating, boredom, depression, illness, gossip), *passive aggression* (sarcasm, nitpicking, chronic criticism), *sabotage* (spoiling or undermining an activity another person has planned), *displacement* (directing anger at people or things another person cherishes), devitalization of the relationship (a relationship that has become lifeless, equivalent to "emotional divorce"), or violence (resulting from unreleased pressures and tensions) (Lamanna and Riedmann 2009). These same consequences are likely to occur in families or in any other relationship in which conflict is denied. Realizing this, a sociologist, or anyone working with a group, might try to build into the group's activities some ways of airing conflicts among members in a way that is approved and expected. Perhaps a basketball coach would initiate weekly "gripe sessions" where each member of the team is expected to discuss things that bother him or her about other players or about the coaches.

Another sign that there may be an unexpressed conflict is low morale. Imagine that you are the manager of an insurance company with a large pool of clerical workers whom the company has always promoted exclusively on the basis of seniority. To improve efficiency, you decide to change the policy and promote on the basis of merit, not number of years employed. This might cause some discontent among the clerks, especially those who have been with the company for a number of years. Suddenly, you notice a change in the secretaries' behaviors: reduced work effectiveness, poor attitudes, higher rates of absence due to "illness," and a general lack of camaraderie. Understanding conflict theory, you might realize that the abnormal behavior is probably a result of some form of conflict among the employees rather than a sudden unexplained incompetence. The employees might not openly express their discontent because they may feel powerless to change the situation. In fact, many sociologists and social psychologists have suggested that people fail to express dissatisfaction, not because conflict does not exist, but because they feel powerless to change things, may not be aware that things could be better than they are, or are resigned to the situation (Johnson 1986).

Conflict theory helps us realize that because conflict is normal and usually inevitable, it is okay to express it. In fact, some clinicians go so far as to recommend to their clients—whether they are married couples, university settings, occupational groups, or sports teams—that they periodically engage in conflict to release tensions and initiate emotional interactions. For example, faculty members within university settings are represented by a president, nominated and voted on by the body of the faculty at the university. The faculty president presides over the faculty senate comprised of members from each department within the university. The student body at the university has a similar structure when they elect a student body president and senate. To resolve conflict between the university and the students, the president of the student body will attend faculty senate meetings and express concerns of the students. The faculty senate will listen to the concerns and vote on issues brought forth by the student body president. For example, a student body president is approached by a disabled student who is concerned over smoking areas close to the entrances to classroom buildings. She is confined to a wheelchair and at the level where a cigarette being tossed or "flicked" by a smoker can possibley injure her. The student body president listens to her concern and takes it to the student body senate; they vote to ban smoking on university property. However, they have to take this vote to the faculty senate, and the faculty senate, too, must vote to pass the smoking ban. If it passes, the bill would be sent to the president of the university for review and final approval. These organizations within the university and other settings are not meant to prescribe all-out war within groups but, rather, to encourage people with conflicts to develop explicit procedures to deal with differences in a rational and constructive way, instead of pretending they don't exist or will disappear on their own.

Thinking Sociologically

1. How would structural functional theory address the issue of gender discrimination within the workplace?
2. To what extent is conflict inherent in the university settings? Is conflict primarily between student and university, student and faculty, or between student and student? Explain your answer.

Symbolic Interaction Theory

Symbolic interaction theory, although influenced somewhat by early European sociologists, was developed largely through the efforts of George Herbert Mead, W.I. Thomas, and Charles Horton Cooley, who belonged to the Chicago School. The key difference between this perspective and those discussed earlier is the size of the units used in investigation and analysis. The previous two theories use a macro-level analysis to study societies; symbolic interaction theory, on the other hand, uses a micro-level approach. This theory studies individuals within societies, particularly their definitions and meanings attached to situations, rather than focusing on the large-scale structures.

The question of how individuals influence society and how society influences individuals is central to sociology. As you recall, early sociologists (Spencer, Durkheim, and Marx, for example) regarded society as an entity existing apart from the individual. Symbolic interactionists, however, assume society exists within every socialized individual; and its external forms and structures arise through the social interactions taking place among individuals at the symbolic level.

What does "symbolic level" mean? It can be explained this way. Suppose you are driving down the road in your car, and you see a brick wall closing off the entire road. You stop, of course, because you have learned you cannot pass through a physical object. If, however, you are riding down the same road and you come to a stoplight, once again, you stop—but why? No physical object prevents you from progressing. Your reason for stopping is because you have learned the red light is a *symbol* that means, "stop." The world around us can be said to consist of these two elements: physical objects and abstract symbols. Language is a system of symbols. It represents physical objects or concepts used to communicate.

According to George Herbert Mead, who played an important role in the development of symbolic interactionism, it is the ability of humans to use symbols that sets us apart from animals and that allows us to create social institutions, societies, and cultures. People in a society share an understanding of particular symbols (the stoplight, for example). Social learning takes place

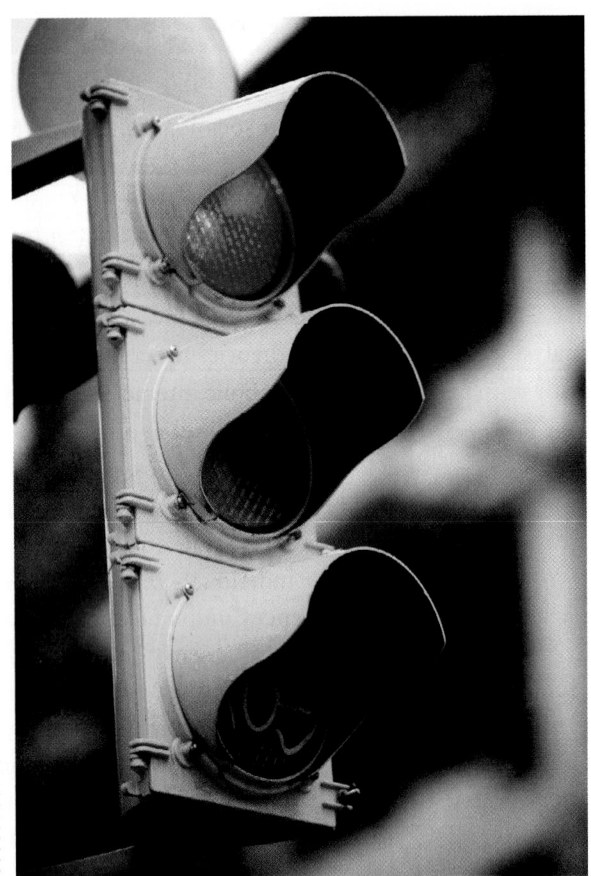

The world around us can be said to consist of two elements: physical objects and abstract symbols. A red stoplight is a symbol that we have learned to mean "stop."

at both symbolic and non-symbolic levels. By interacting with others, we internalize social expectations, a specific language, and social values. In addition, we learn to share meanings and to communicate symbolically through words and gestures. As humans, we can interact at both a physical (e.g., a slap) and a symbolic (e.g., showing a fist or making a verbal threat) level. Since we can relate symbolically, we can carry on conversations with ourselves. We can also imagine the effects of different courses of action. We can imagine what would happen if we were to throw a rotten tomato in the face of a police officer. By thinking through alternative courses of action, we can choose those we believe to be the most appropriate for a given situation. The fact that others share similar expectations makes life patterned and relatively predictable. Those who fail to recognize that a red traffic light means stop will have trouble getting any place safely in their cars.

The interactionist perspective examines patterns and processes of everyday life that are generally ignored by many other perspectives. It raises questions about the self, the self in relationships with others, and the self and others in the wider social context. Why do some of us have negative feelings about ourselves? Why is it we can relate more easily with some persons than with others? Why do we feel more comfortable around friends than among strangers? How is it possible to interact with complete strangers or to know what to do in new situations? How are decisions made in families? Symbolic interactionists try to answer such questions by examining the individual in a social context. The starting point of this examination is the social setting in which an individual is born and the interactions he or she has with parents, siblings, teachers, neighbors, or others. From these interactions, we learn what is proper or improper, whether we are "good" or "bad," who is important, and so forth. A more complete explanation of this perspective is given in other sections throughout the book.

APPLYING SYMBOLIC INTERACTION THEORY

The symbolic interactionist perspective emphasizes that people act on the basis of their interpretation of the language and symbols in a situation and not the situation in and of itself. This perspective is useful, in that it points to the necessity of having people achieve at least a minimal agreement about the definition or meaning of a situation. One potential problem to develop in any relationship—whether on the job or in the home—is the lack of consensus in people's definitions of a situation. The lack of consensus may be the result of a disagreement or a misunderstanding. The confusion may be about the roles individuals develop for themselves, the goals they think should be pursued collectively, or the ways in which resources (such as money or power) should be distributed. This could lead to a breakdown of a relationship altogether or, at the very least, to confusion, tension, strife, and general unhappiness within the relationship or social system. Some examples may show how the definition of a situation can be at the core of some interpersonal problems and how symbolic interaction theory can be used.

Imagine that you are the manager of a retail jewelry store, and you hire two salespeople. The salespeople are told their salaries will be partly straight pay and partly commission generated by their sales. Person A defines the situation as one in which potential customers should be divided equally between the two employees because they both work in the same place. Person B sees the situation as one of competition among the employees for sales. Both interpretations are possible and quite feasible. As a result, Person A sees Person B as aggressive, money-hungry, and cutthroat. Person B sees Person A as uncompetitive, complacent, and not sales oriented. The tension mounts, and each salesperson believes the other has a personality problem. The problem, though, may not be due to personalities but due to a lack of clarity about how each person defines what he or she has been employed to do. As the manager, how could your knowledge of symbolic interaction theory help you to resolve this problem? Symbolic interaction theory alerts us to the importance of effective communication among people so they can understand each other's perspectives. If this occurs, they may be able to coordinate their actions better. According to Johnson (1986), "the ultimate outcome is not only reinforcement of appropriate role performance but also the creation of a more supportive and satisfying atmosphere" (p. 60).

It is also important to understand that various individuals' definitions of a situation are related to their definitions of what constitutes a problem. Another person may not see what one person considers a problem as a problem. A male boss who continuously flirts with his female secretary through physical contact (arm touching, back rubbing, and so on) or sexually suggestive comments may think he is creating a friendly, supportive work atmosphere. He may be unaware that the secretary sees his actions as sexual overtures and feels harassed and exploited by his "friendliness."

Addressing the issue of school violence, a student who feels like an outsider, both at home and at school, may internalize the perceptions of others as hate or being unwanted. As a result he turns the perceptions of others inward and begins to see himself in the same way. Others in this individual's life may not have this perception at all but simply be focused on their own problems, completely unaware that troubled youth perceives feelings of hate and being unwanted.

In each of these examples, open communication is needed so the definition of the situation can be clarified. Often, a mediator, perhaps a sociologist but not necessarily, is needed to help explain each side to the other, in the hope of helping the parties to achieve at least a minimal agreement about the definition of the situation.

Thinking Sociologically

Discuss how a symbolic theorist would explain "classroom conformity". Why do students, when asked questions by the professor, not respond even when they know the answers?

While the previous three theories are often cited as the major perspectives within the field of sociology, you should be familiar with some others that have made tremendous contributions to the study of society, social groups, and human behavior.

Exchange Theory

Although symbolic interaction theory is the most widely used and recognized interaction perspective, exchange theory also falls within this general orientation. **Exchange theory** has a diverse intellectual heritage from sources in economics, anthropology, and psychology, as well as sociology. This perspective is based on the belief that life is a series of exchanges involving rewards and costs. In economic exchanges,

Table 2-1 Major Perspectives in Sociology

Theory	Level of Analysis	View of Society	Major Concepts	Pros and Cons of Theory
Functionalism	Macro	Society consists of interdependent parts, each fulfilling certain functions.	Structure, function, manifest and latent function, dysfunctions	**Pros:** examines structures within society; examines the "big picture"; emphasizes the impact that structures in relation to consequences for society **Cons:** does not emphasize the interactions between individuals
Conflict	Macro	Conflict between diverse groups within society competing for valuable resources.	Means of production, proletariat, bourgeoisie, social class, scarce resources	**Pros:** examines stratification and inequality and the reasons that they exist; examines who benefits from existing social relationships **Cons:** does not explore competition within society as potentially beneficial
Interactionism	Micro	Interaction between people in society is negotiated using symbols, gestures, and communication, including non-verbal.	Symbols, social construction, definition of the situation	**Pros:** examines day-to-day interactions between people; examines relationship between identity and social interaction **Cons:** does not emphasize the ways in which large-scale structures affect interaction
Exchange	Micro	Actions are determined by weighing rewards and costs.	Exchanges, rewards, costs, benefits, negotiation	**Pros:** examines day-to-day interactions between people; examines relationship between identity and social interaction **Cons:** does not emphasize the ways in which large-scale structures affect interaction
Evolutionary	Macro	Social systems evolve naturally from simple to complex.	Organism, social arrangements social systems, simple, complex, survival of the fittest	**Pros:** looks at society as evolving naturally over time; brings in the possibility of social evolution as conected with biological evolution **Cons:** does not emphasize the potential negativity of "survival of the fittest" concept

people exchange money, goods, and services, hoping to profit or at least break even in the exchange. In anthropological, psychological, and sociological exchanges, the items of exchange include social and psychic factors. Consider the following: In return for your companionship, I'll invite you to my house; in return for your positive teacher evaluation, I'll work extra hard to be a good instructor. Work, gifts, money, affection, and ideas—all are offered in the hope of getting something in return.

Social exchange theory seeks to explain why behavioral outcomes such as marriage, employment, and religious involvement occur, given a set of structural conditions (age, race, gender, class) and interaction possibilities. Women, for example, marry men of a higher social status more frequently than men marry women of a higher social status. Exchange theorists would attempt to explain this finding by examining the desirable qualities men and women have to exchange. In the United States, for men to have money or a good job is viewed as desirable; for women to be physically attractive is viewed as desirable. Thus, we might expect very attractive lower-status women could exchange their beauty for men of a higher economic and occupational status, which seems to be what happens.

Exchange theory assumes that people seek rewarding statuses, relationships, and experiences, and they try to avoid costs, pain, and punishments. Given a set of alternatives, individuals choose those from which they expect the most profit, rewards, or satisfaction; and they avoid those not profitable, rewarding, or satisfying. When the costs exceed the rewards, people are likely to feel angry and dissatisfied. When the rewards exceed the costs, they are likely to feel they got a good deal (unless they got it through exploitation or dishonesty, in which case, they may feel guilty and choose to avoid further interactions). Both parties are more likely to be satisfied with the interaction if there is perceived equity in the exchange, a feeling on the part of both that the rewards were worth the costs.

Although people may work selflessly for others with no thought of reward, it is quite unusual. The social exchange perspective assumes that voluntary social interactions are contingent on rewarding reactions from others. When rewarding reactions cease, either the actions end or dissatisfaction results.

There are two different schools of thought in the exchange theory perspective. George Homans, the theorist responsible for originating exchange theory, represents a perspective consistent with that of behavioral psychologists, who believe that behavior can be explained in terms of rewards and punishments. Behaviorists focus their attention on actual behavior, not on processes that are inferred from behavior but cannot be observed. In exchange theory, the rewards and punishments are the behavior of other people, and those involved in exchanges assume their rewards will be proportional to their costs.

Peter Blau is the advocate of a different school of exchange theory, one that is consistent with symbolic interactionism. Blau does not attempt to explain all exchanges in terms of observable behavior. He argues the exchange is more subjective and interpretive and exchanges occur on a symbolic level. As a result, money may be a just reward only if the receiver defines it as such; and psychic rewards of satisfaction with doing a good job or of pleasing someone may be as important as money, gifts, or outward responses of praise.

Both Homans and Blau agree that what is important is each party in the exchange must receive something perceived as equivalent to that which is given (to Homans, "distributive justice"; to Blau, "fair exchange"). All exchange involves a mutually held expectation that reciprocation will occur. If resources or exchange criteria are unequal, one person is at a distinct disadvantage; and the other has power over and controls the relationship. As a result, in marriage, unequal exchanges between husband and wife are likely to result in dominance of one over the other or may even end the relationship. In employment, if employee and employer do not recognize a fair exchange of rewards and costs, dissatisfaction may result. The employee may quit, or the employer may dismiss the employee.

In exchange theory, then, social life is viewed as a process of bargaining or negotiation, and social relationships are based on trust and mutual interests. In recent years, some sociologists have criticized exchange theory as overly adhering to economic and mathematical models that do not put enough emphasis on the human elements or content of a situation (Zafirovski 2003).

APPLYING EXCHANGE THEORY

Although most of us probably do not like the idea that we rationally calculate relationships in terms of rewards and costs, exchange theory is supported by much research concerning family relationships, dating, and the workplace (see, for example, Rubin, 1973; Blau, 1964; and Homans, 1974). An exemplary application of exchange theory is found in Blau's (1964) study of relationships between supervisors and workers in complex organizations such as hospitals, factories, and corporations. Blau found that supervisors often reward workers with special favors in exchange for positive evaluations. Such favors include services (such as being paid on time and taking coffee breaks), non-enforcement of some of management's rules, or the development of comradeship with the workers. In exchange for these favors, the workers express their loyalty.

For this reason the demand for fair exchange seems to be a fact of most social relationships. We might use this knowledge to ensure that cost–reward outcomes are fair and, more importantly, are perceived as fair by the people involved. Dissatisfaction in marriage and occupations, for example, often results from the belief that there is an imbalanced give-and-take in the relationship. What sometimes needs to be done in such troubled situations is to help the individuals or parties involved evaluate, rationally, the costs and rewards of the relationship. What may be perceived as an imbalanced exchange may actually not be as unfair as it seems. If this is the case, helping each party understand that there is a balanced exchange could salvage the relationship. However, if there is indeed an imbalance of rewards and costs to one or all of the parties, then there must be some form of negotiation to restore the necessary balance of exchange.

It is very possible that rampage shooters somehow feel cheated in their relationships with others within and even outside the setting in which the shooting occurred. What would lead an adult to open fire on a college or elementary school, or an informal political meet-and-greet gather, killing a number of innocent people? The aftermath of many of these horrific rampage shootings unveiled the assailants' anger with society and a history of rejection of one sort or another. From an exchange perspective, the assailants may have felt betrayed and that their contributions to society (their cost, so to speak)—be they acts of what the assailants perceived as kindness or good will or good citizenship—were not met with an appropriate reward, such as acceptance.

Exchange theory can also be used for other than troubled relationships. Rewards can be used to induce people to give more of themselves (a cost). These rewards are not necessarily material and may

People view the flower tributes in front of Dunblane Primary School in Scotland on March 16, 1996. The flowers pay tribute to the students and teacher killed at the school.

also be psychological. Think of how you could use this knowledge to enhance your interpersonal skills in your job. Imagine you are a bank manager in a large branch. You need a way to induce the head teller to come in early every day for two weeks to train some new tellers who have been hired. Instead of merely giving her the assignment, you might also mention to her that besides paying her overtime, you are going to make a note in her personnel file about her dedication to the bank. You might also express your praise openly to her so the president of the bank happens to overhear it. In this case, recognition is being exchanged for time spent. Similarly, an automobile dealership may buy newspaper space each month to give credit to the top salesperson for that period as an inducement for the salespeople to do extra work for the company.

Thinking Sociologically

1. Select a group or organization in which you are involved and explore it in terms of structural functionalism, conflict theory, symbolic interactionism, and exchange theory. What types of things would each perspective be interested in finding out? What types of answers might each perspective reach?
2. Select a contemporary social problem and examine it using the Exchange Theory.

Evolutionary Theory

The evolutionary approach is associated with biological concepts and concerned with long-term change. **Evolutionary theory** suggests that societies, like biological organisms, progress through stages of increasing complexity. Like ecologists, evolutionists suggest that societies, also like organisms, are interdependent with their environments.

Most of the early sociologists and some recent ones adhere to an evolutionary view. Early sociologists often equated evolution with progress and improvement, believing natural selection would eliminate weak societies and those that could not adapt. The strong societies, they believed, deserved to survive because they were better. It was for this reason that early theorists, such as Spencer, opposed any sort of interference protecting the weak and interfering with natural evolutionary processes.

Contemporary evolutionists, on the other hand, rarely oppose all types of intervention. They tend to view evolution as a process resulting in change, but they do not assume changes are necessarily for the better. Almost all would agree that society is becoming more complex, for example; but they might argue that complexity brings about bad things as well as good. The telephone is a good illustration of a technological improvement making our lives more complex. Surely it is an improvement—it permits us to be in contact with the whole world without stirring from our homes—but a contemporary evolutionist might point out a phone can also be an annoyance, as students trying to study and harried office workers can attest. Early evolutionists, on the other hand, would have been more likely to regard the telephone as a sign of progress and, hence, an unmixed blessing.

Evolutionary theory provides us with a historical and cross-cultural perspective from which to judge a wide range of social influences. If its basic premises of directional change and increasing complexity are valid, it should provide better comprehension of current trends and even help us to predict the future.

APPLYING EVOLUTIONARY THEORY

Although evolutionary theory is concerned mostly with long-term macro change, it applies to short-term sociological phenomena as well. For example, to a professional sociologist, city planning is not merely a matter of creating space to accommodate more people but also entails the organization of buildings and space so the evolving needs of the population will be met as society grows more complex. Sociologists in the workplace can use evolutionary theory, then, to make sure there is a balance between the relative complexity of the parts of a system and the complexity of the system itself. The city planner, for example, must make sure the number, size, and arrangement of buildings, schools, parks, and malls are in line with the needs of the entire city. It would not make sense to plan for the construction of new housing developments without also planning for the construction of additional educational facilities to accommodate the increased number of children.

For helping a small business, how could sociologists apply the basic premises of evolutionary theory so that (a) over time, social systems become more complex in their diversity, specialization, and interdependence of parts; and (b) the fittest survive? Consider the emergence of many craft businesses entered into by babyboomers (such as pottery, stained glass, and jewelry-making) that became popular during the 1970s and early 1980s. Many of these small businesses were started by craftspeople that shared an intense interest in making a living by producing a particular craft.

One of the authors of this textbook (Basirico 1983, 1986) studied the arts and craft movement that took place in the United States during the late 1970s and found that the careers of stained-glass artisans followed a typical pattern. A group of like-minded craftspeople would get together for the purpose of producing and selling stained-glass creations. Often, this took place in out-of-the-way, low-rent locations with little overhead. The common interest and activities and the simple lifestyle associated with the craft were often the basis for starting the business. In time, however, some businesses could not compete and failed, while other artisans' business affairs often became more complex with new locations, larger workplaces, higher rent and overhead, advertising costs, tax bills, different types of clientele with varied needs, and diversification of the business into areas such as selling supplies and giving lessons. As they grew more complex, many of these small businesses also began to experience difficulties; most closed down after a few years.

Had the artisans used an evolutionary perspective, some of their businesses may have been saved. Remember that evolutionary theory states that systems and the parts of systems become more complex over time. If we look at some of these craft businesses, we see some significant growth in their complexity. However, the roles of the craftspeople themselves did not change that much. In other words, there was no balance between the level of complexity of the business (the system) and the level of complexity of the artisans' roles (the parts of the system). They kept to their simple, undifferentiated, independent tasks, whereas the business—in order to survive—evolved into a system that demanded a specialization of tasks and interdependence among the artisans.

Knowledge of evolutionary theory might also be a useful perspective in your personal life. How, for example, would the theory that social systems move from simple to complex influence your decision about buying or building a house for your family? Often homeowners discover that the home they bought simply for its attractiveness and decor no longer fits the needs of their family. You might save money and headaches if you realize that families are social systems that evolve and become more complicated over time. Successful architects who design homes (and office buildings) consider more than just their clients' present needs; they also consider the evolving nature of the group for which they are designing.

Although each of the theoretical perspectives has been discussed separately with regard to how they can be applied, it is important to note that in most cases, more than one can be used; and some may even be used in conjunction with each other. It should also be noted that even though some of the applications discussed might not be exactly what the people who originally devised the theories had in mind, this does not lessen the validity of these applications. On the contrary, using scientific theories in ways that extend beyond their original purpose demonstrates the significance of the theories. A number of additional theoretical orientations are discussed briefly to conclude this section.

Additional Theoretical Perspectives and the Future of Sociological Theory

The reader should not be led to think that structural functional, conflict, symbolic interaction, exchange, and evolutionary theories compose all of the theories or theoretical perspectives in sociology. From the 1950s through the 1970s, sociology could have been more easily described in terms of these five theories with structural functionalism reigning supreme in the 1950s and conflict theory taking a strong foothold in the 1960s. However, by the mid-1980s, sociology began to become described as a "hyperdifferentiation of theories," suggesting a growing proliferation of competing perspectives (Turner 2006). However, Turner (2006) notes one distinguishing characteristic of sociology today is that there is less competition between adherents of the different sociological theories and more co-existence; however, still there is a proliferation of new theoretical perspectives. Others, such as Ritzer (1999), sees this as a time of theoretical synthesis: an integration of micro and macro ideas, an integration of Marx's ideas into structural functionalism, a joining of exchange and structural theories into a new network theory, and so forth. Ritzer's argument is that many sociological theories are borrowing heavily from one another with the result that traditionally clear, theoretical boundaries are growing increasingly blurred and porous. Ritzer's and Turner's views are not at odds with each other but reinforce the idea that sociological theories are continuing to develop and expand.

Perhaps an example of an older, interdisciplinary, theoretical linkage can be seen in *sociobiological* orientations. You may have noted that Spencer's ideas of the survival of the fittest, described earlier in this chapter, had a biological base. Today, sociobiological theories link social behavior (crime, drinking, aggression, and so forth) to genetic or biological factors. For example, a sociobiologist would probably explain male sexual dominance or female nurturance by the differing genetic makeup of the sexes. If male–female differences are biologically determined, it could be expected that social influences would not greatly modify behavior. It could also lead to justifying sexual and racial inequalities because "that's the way things are," and little can be done to change them. Yet sociologists note, in spite of biological predispositions toward a particular behavior pattern, wide variations exist in sexual domination, nurturance, and other behaviors generally assigned to one sex or the other. Beliefs that human behaviors can be changed led to other theoretical linkages, such as the two examples that follow: humanistic and feminist theories.

Humanistic theories, consistent with ideas expressed by Marx, reject the positivist position that social science can or should be value free. This perspective is based on the following beliefs and practices: Sociologists or other social scientists should be actively involved in social change; efforts should be made toward achieving social justice and equity for everyone irrespective of gender or race; the mind has "free will"; and humans are in charge of controlling their own destiny. As Chapter 13 makes clear, secular humanism (the solving of problems by humans through their own efforts) disputes the religious focus on a god or on supernatural powers. Sociologists often take a humanistic perspective with a goal of using the knowledge, skills, and tools of sociology to improve social conditions and the lives of those less fortunate.

Thinking Sociologically

Discuss the humanists' idea that sociologists should use their knowledge and skills to improve social conditions and the feminists' idea that gender is basic to all social organization and interaction.

Feminist theories and perspectives hold the belief that gender is basic to all social structure and organization. The impetus for contemporary feminist theory involves a simple question: How do women interpret and experience the world differently from men? Answers to this question are based on beliefs that gender should not be the basis of social inequality, nor should men be more valued in the political arena (as more effective leaders of the country), in the home (as heads of the house), or in the workplace (where they sometimes make more money than women). Early waves of the feminist movement focused on equal rights. Contemporary feminist perspectives include multicultural, liberal, and socialist perspectives, and examine the interlocking systems of racism, sexism, and class. This "third wave" movement is marked by a desire for personal empowerment.

Other perspectives, such as utilitarian theory, network theory, existentialism, and phenomenology, are generally closely linked to one or more of the perspectives discussed in this chapter. Numerous variations of the major theories are presented throughout the text. Regardless of the development of new theories in sociology, it is essential that you understand the five theories discussed more fully in this chapter since they are the seeds of many of the new theories.

CHAPTER REVIEW

Wrapping it up

Summary

Check out our website www.bvtstudents.com for free chapter-by-chapter flashcards, summaries, and self-quizzes.

1. Compared with the other sciences, sociology is of recent origin. Not until the 1880s was a scientific methodology applied to social phenomena. The Industrial Revolution and political upheavals in Europe encouraged various scholars to try to explain social change and the social order. Five theorists who had an especially important influence on the development of sociology are Comte, Spencer, Marx, Durkheim, and Weber.

2. In the early 1900s, the development of sociology in America grew rapidly, drawing heavily from earlier European scholars. The Chicago School of thought focused on micro level approaches with important contributions made by sociologists—such as Cooley, Mead, and Thomas—which stressed the importance of social interaction and the influence of society on human thought and action.

3. Not until the 1930s did sociology shift from the University of Chicago to other major educational institutions. In the eastern United States, Parsons, Merton, Mills, Coser, Homans, and Blau were influential in the development of social theory.

4. A social theory is a systematically interrelated proposition that seeks to explain a process or phenomena. Five major theories—three at the macro level and two at the micro level—have had an important influence on contemporary sociology: structural functional theory, conflict theory, symbolic interactional theory, exchange theory, and evolutionary–ecological theory.

5. Structural functional theory focuses on the parts of a system, the relationships among these parts, and the functions or consequences of social structures. These functions can be either manifest (intended and recognized) or latent (unintended and unrecognized). Some consequences are dysfunctional, in that they lead to the instability and breakdown of the system. Structural functional theories assume that systems have a tendency toward equilibrium and balance.

6. Conflict theory assumes that conflict is a permanent feature of social life and a key source of change. The Marxist orientation toward conflict assumes that it is rooted in a class struggle between the employers and the workers or between the powerful and the powerless. Many conflict theorists assume that conflict serves an integrative function and acts as a source of constructive change.

7. Symbolic interactionism, a micro-level theory, emphasizes relationships among individuals and between individuals and society. According to this theory, society is based on shared meanings, language, social interaction, and symbolic processes. It is the mind that differentiates humans from

nonhumans and permits people to develop a social self, to assume the roles of others, and to imaginatively consider alternative courses of action.

8. Exchange theory assumes that social life involves a series of reciprocal exchanges consisting of rewards and costs. Exchange theories endeavor to explain why particular behavioral outcomes result from a given set of structural conditions and interaction possibilities.

9. Evolutionary theory suggests that societies, like biological organisms, go through transitions or stages and are interdependent with the environment or world about them.

10. Other theoretical perspectives or orientations include sociobiology, humanism, and feminism. The latter two both reject a positivist notion of total objectivity and noninvolvement and stress instead the need for active involvement in social change.

Key Terms

bourgeoisie The class of people who own the means of production

Chicago School An approach developed by Cooley, Mead, Thomas, and others in the 1920s that emphasized the importance of social interactions in the development of human thought and action

class-consciousness Awareness among members of a society that the society is stratified

collective conscience A collective psyche that results from the blending of many individual mentalities, but exists above any one individual

conflict theory A social theory that views conflict as inevitable and natural and as a significant cause of social change

dysfunction In structural functional theory, factors that lead to the disruption or breakdown of the social system

economic determinism The idea that economic factors are responsible for most social change and for the nature of social conditions, activities, and institutions

evolutionary theory A theory of social development that suggests that societies, like biological organisms, progress through stages of increasing complexity

exchange theory A theory of interaction that attempts to explain social behavior in terms of reciprocity of costs and rewards

functional alternatives Alternate ways to achieve an intended goal in order to avoid dysfunctions

latent functions The unintended consequences of a social system

law of human progress Comte's notion that all knowledge passes through three successive theoretical conditions: the theological, the metaphysical, and the scientific

manifest functions The intended consequences of a social system

middle-range theory A set of propositions designed to link abstract propositions with empirical testing

proletariat The group in capitalist societies that does not own the means of production and has only labor to sell

social conflict A view of Karl Marx that social conflict—class struggle due to economic inequality—is at the core of society and the key source of social change

social dynamics Comte's term for social processes and forms of change

social facts Reliable and valid items of information about society

social statics Comte's term for the stable structure of a society

social system A set of interrelated social statuses and the expectations that accompany them

structural functionalism The theory that societies contain certain interdependent structures, each of which performs certain functions for the maintenance of society

symbolic interaction theory The social theory stressing interactions between people and the social processes that occur within the individual that are made possible by language and internalized meanings

theory A set of logically and systematically interrelated propositions that explain a particular process or phenomenon

verstehen Understanding human action by examining the subjective meanings that people attach to their own behavior and the behavior of others

Discussion Questions

1. What influenced the development of sociology both in Europe and in America?
2. The contributions of women and minorities in early sociology were largely overlooked. Explain what factors contributed to their lack of recognition by the field?
3. Why did early sociologists use natural science terms and methods to describe society? Discuss some shortcomings in following this approach.
4. Spencer's idea of "survival of the fittest" led to his belief in noninterference in human affairs. Explain how Spencer's beliefs would influence today's welfare system in the United States.
5. How might conflict theory apply to male and female workers in a field dominated primarily by men, such as construction work?
6. From a symbolic interactionist perspective explain why burning the American flag creates anger among most U.S. citizens. In your discussion, consider the significance of symbols and their meanings.
7. Apply social exchange theory to the interaction between you and your parents or your best friend. What are the cost and rewards of these relationships? What happens when the social exchanges are not defined as equitable?

Pop Quiz

1. The study and discipline of sociology originated approximately _________.

   a. three hundred years ago
   b. two hundred years ago
   c. one hundred years ago
   d. approximately seventy-five years ago after World War I erupted

2. According to Comte's law of human progress, the stage of human thought associated with the political dominance held by the clergy and lawyers is _________.

   a. the theological stage
   b. the metaphysical stage
   c. the positive stage
   d. the scientific stage

3. According to Marx, the recognition among workers that they share the same plight is known as _________.

   a. revolution
   b. social dynamics
   c. class consciousness
   d. economic determinism

4. When students try to see where their teacher is coming from in her/his lectures or assignments, the students are most likely applying the concepts of _________.

   a. Herbert Spencer
   b. Emile Durkheim
   c. Karl Marx
   d. Max Weber

5. Structural functional theory is sometimes referred to as _________.

   a. social systems theory
   b. equilibrium theory
   c. simply functionalism
   d. all of the above

6. Symbolic interactionists believe that __________.

   a. in interaction we internalize values and social expectations
   b. only humans are able to communicate
   c. people learn primarily through rewards and punishments
   d. all of the above

7. The ________ theory rejects the positivist position that sociology should be value-free.

   a. conflict
   b. exchange
   c. humanistic
   d. functionalist

8. Functions that are intended and recognized in a social system are called __________.

   a. latent
   b. observable
   c. manifest
   d. symbols

9. The first major center of sociological thought in the United States was __________.

   a. Harvard University
   b. Columbia University
   c. University of Michigan
   d. University of Chicago

10. The theorist who believed that all social change is rooted in social conflict was __________.

    a. Mead
    b. Weber
    c. Comte
    d. none of the above

11. Charles Darwin coined the term "survival of the fittest." T/F

12. Unmarried people have a lower rate of suicide than married people. T/F

13. The evolutionary perspective tends to be concerned with long-term change. T/F

14. Functionalists focus on order and stability, with an emphasis on equilibrium. T/F

15. Feminist theorists stress that gender is basic to all social structure. T/F

1. B	6. A	11. F
2. B	7. C	12. F
3. C	8. C	13. T
4. D	9. D	14. T
5. D	10. D	15. T

CHAPTER 3

Methods of Studying Society

中华人民共和国万岁
世界人民大团

ARE TATTOOS A SIGN OF DEVIANCE OR CULTURAL FAD?

Do you know anyone with a tattoo? Most college students either know someone with a tattoo or they have a tattoo. In fact, tattoos and body piercing are the most common forms of body modifications practiced by college students today. However, what does it mean to have a tattoo? Are those with tattoos rebellious and deviant? Does having a tattoo provide us with any information about the character of a person?

Suppose you were told that college men and women with tattoos are more sexually promiscuous than college students without tattoos. Would you believe it? If you were thinking about getting a tattoo, would it cause you to question whether or not to get one? Would you be less likely to socialize, date, or even marry someone with a tattoo if you believed tattoos were a sign of sexual prowess? What if your doctor believed that persons (particularly adolescents) with tattoos and body piercings were more likely to engage in other at-risk behaviors?

Due to the of the rise in popularity of body modification, researchers are looking to determine if those receiving tattoos, piercings, and other forms of modifications are engaging in a deviant act and, thus, more likely to engage in other deviant or rebellious behavior or if tattoos are simply a cultural fad. Following are three studies that focus on the behaviors of young people with tattoos:

- In June 2002, *Pediatrics*, the official journal of the American Academy of Pediatrics, published research titled: "Tattooing and Body Piercing as Indicators of Adolescents Risk-Taking Behavior." The researchers, Sean T. Carroll, MD, Robert H. Riffenburgh, PhD, Timothy A. Roberts, MD and Elizabeth B. Myhre, CPNP, MSN, sought to determine if there existed a relationship between body modification and deviant behavior among adolescents.
- According to "College Students, Tattoos and Sexual Activity", a research study conducted by Jerome Koch, Alden Roberts, Myrna Armstrong and Donna Owen from Texas Tech University's Departments of Sociology and School of Nursing, tattooed college students are more likely to engage in premarital sex than non-tattooed college students. In addition, tattooed college males are more likely to have engaged in premarital sex at a much earlier age than non-tattooed college males.
- Gary Foster and Richard Hummel presented a paper titled "The Commodification of Body Modification: Tattoos and Piercings from Counterculture to Campus" at the Midwest Sociological Association Conference. Their research suggests that tattooing and body piercing has become more commercialized and, simply, a popular practice among young people, rather than a sign of deviance and rebellion.

Before deciding into which research to put our trust, we need to understand the research process. To do this, we must ask four questions about the research study: What is the purpose of the study? What methods did the researchers use to collect the data? What were the results of their study? What did they conclude from their study?

Let's apply these questions to one of the previous studies.

Study: *Tattooing and Body Piercing as Indicators of Adolescents Risk-Taking Behavior*

What is the purpose of the study? The study assessed whether tattoos and body piercings serve as markers of risk-taking behaviors in adolescents.

What methods did the researchers use to collect the data? The researchers used a 58-question survey from the 1997 Centers for Disease Control and Prevention Youth Risk Behavior Survey. The survey was offered to all adolescent that came to the Adolescent Clinic. The survey contained standard Youth Risk Behavior Survey questions that inquire about eating behavior, violence, drug abuse, sexual behavior, and suicide. However, for the purpose of their study, the researchers added questions about tattoos and body piercing. A total of 484 adolescents between the ages of twelve to twenty-two years were surveyed.

What were the results of their study? The researchers found that adolescents with tattoos and/or body piercings were more likely to have engaged in risk-taking behaviors and at greater degrees of involvement than those without either. At-risk behaviors included disordered eating behavior, gateway drug use, hard drug use, sexual activity, and suicide. With regard to

Research has found that adolescents with tattoos and/or body piercings were more likely to have engaged in risk-taking behaviors.

violence, the study found an association with males having tattoos and with females having body piercings. Gateway drug use was associated with younger age of both tattooing and body piercing. Hard drug use was associated with number of body piercings. The researchers found that suicide was associated with females having tattoos and younger age of both tattooing and body piercing. Both tattoos and body piercings were found to be more common in females than males.

What do the researchers conclude from their study? Patients that come into the office with tattoos and/or body piercings may be involved in other risk-taking behaviors and should alert the practitioner to offering preventive measures, including counseling. In addition, tattoo and body piercing discovery should be an important part of the health maintenance of adolescent medical care.

Based on the information provided from the study, can we assume that tattoos are equivalent to deviance? If you read this study, what would be your thoughts about its reliability?

While the previous four questions give us some information about the researcher's purpose and findings, they do not provide us with any guidelines to evaluate the research. One problem that is apparent from the information provided in the study is the researchers did not use a control group to make comparisons with the experimental group. In other words, the researchers studied only adolescents with tattoos coming to their medical offices and, from those findings, concluded that adolescents with tattoos and piercings are more likely to engage in risk taking behavior. Tattoos have historically been viewed as a stigma associated with marginalized groups within society (sailors, prostitutes, bikers, gangs). It is possible that the researchers were biased about adolescents with tattoos and piercings prior to their initiating the study, which could influence the outcome. By using a control group, the researchers have a standard of comparison and can address any bias in their research findings.

Research Implications: Research findings are sometimes used to make policy or other changes within organizations, settings, or groups. In the above study, the researchers conclude that "When doctors see a teenager who has a piercing [or tattoo], they should ask whether they smoke, ask about their friends, and maybe spend a little more time asking about their sexual behavior. Seeing a pierced or tattooed body part should help a doctor decide how to spend his or her time with a patient."

Carroll, Sean T. MD, Robert H. Riffenburgh, PhD, Timothy A. Roberts, MD, and Elizabeth B. Myhre, CPNP, MSN. "Tattooing and Body Piercing as Indicators of Adolescents Risk-Taking Behavior," *Pediatrics* 109 No. 6 (June 2002) 1021–1027.

Foster, Gary S., and Richard L. Hummel, *"The Commodification of Body Modification: Tattoos and Piercings from Counterculture to Campus."* Paper presented at the Midwest Sociological Association. April 21, 2000.

Koch, Jerome R., Alden E. Roberts, Myrna L. Armstrong, Donna C. Owen, "College Students, Tattoos, and Sexual Activity," *Psychological Reports* 97 (2005.): 887–890.

In this chapter, we consider the use of scientific methods in sociology. We also examine standards of scientific inquiry, types of sociological research, research methods, and the process of research. In addition, we examine ethical issues within the field and how students can use sociology in their personal and occupational lives.

For a few reasons, many students are apprehensive about studying research methods. First, they often equate research methods with advanced mathematics and statistics. In reality, much advanced sociological analysis does employ statistics, but most sociological research and analysis is accomplished with only an elementary knowledge of statistics; some use no statistics at all. Second, students believe research methods are relevant only to sociologists. This is simply not true. All persons in society are affected by their knowledge (or lack of it) of basic principles of research methods. To know nothing about the scientific method is to be a victim of false claims about products and ideas when being exposed to advertising in newspapers, on TV, or from any source. It is also important to know where and how to gain access to legitimate research results when making personal decisions and choices.

We hope that after reading this chapter, you will see the relevance of research methods in all areas of your life, and you will at least begin to sense some of the exciting discoveries and insights that sociological research has to offer.

WHOSE KNOWLEDGE IS OF MOST WORTH?

How do we know something to be true? For example, how do you know a cup of coffee is hot? We can tell by touch, right? How did you come to learn the concept of hot? Can we teach someone the meaning of "hot" without their experiencing it for themselves? The parents of a toddler beginning to pull himself up to a standing position with the help of the coffee table must begin teaching the child about objects he will encounter at that level. If the child reaches for a cup of coffee on the table, the parent could caution, "No, no, the coffee is hot … it will burn the baby." Will the child know or understand the concept of hot if they have never experienced it? This is not to say the parents will have to let the child experience the pain of a coffee burn to understand the meaning of hot; rather they must teach him through some other form of experience. People arrive at their knowledge and beliefs through a number of different routes, and their notions about reality vary greatly. Some people believe politicians are crooked; others think they are dedicated public servants. Some believe hard work will lead to success; others think it is a waste of time, and for them failure is inevitable. We get ideas such as these from a number of different sources, including authority, experience, cultural tradition, faith, media, and science.

Types of Knowledge

AUTHORITY Some people are assumed to be knowledgeable simply because of their experience or position. We may consider the Pope, the President of the United States, our doctor, our professor, or our parents to be authority figures. We seldom bother to investigate or to question their information because we feel we can trust them to provide us with truths. Like ideas derived from common sense, however, the opinions of authorities may differ. The conclusions of one physician are not always identical to those of another. Even our parents sometimes disagree with each other, and they often disagree with other parents.

EXPERIENCE Our past experiences and personal observations convince us certain things are true. We see blondes having a good time and are convinced that blondes have more fun. We talk to women who want children and assume that a desire for children is instinctive in women. Experience is often confused with common sense when we assume something is the way it is just because it seems reasonable. However, others may have another conclusion, based on their own experiences, different from yours.

CULTURAL TRADITION The wisdom of previous generations is passed on and accepted as accurate. We rarely question tradition because that's the way it's always been done. We may plant corn by the phase of the moon and take a sip of brandy to cure a chest cold. Consider this: why do women wear white on their wedding day? If you ask your grandparents, they would likely say it is a symbol of purity for a woman on her wedding day. By wearing white, she is acknowledging to others that she is still a virgin.

An authoritative figure is assumed to be knowledgeable.

Symbolisms can be expressions of wisdom that are passed down from previous generations.

What about today? Is wearing white still a symbol of purity? We see previously married women wearing white dresses, as well as others, such as women in cohabitation with their husband-to-be. The constructed meaning of the white wedding dress has changed over time; the tradition of wearing it on your wedding day has not.

FAITH Faith is a belief in the unknown, an unquestionable truth. It includes revelations from divine experiences, prayer, or magic. Knowledge acquired through revelation is often considered sacred and absolute, so it is not subject to question. Some people, for example, believe wives should submit to their husbands' authority because the Bible says that they should do so.

MEDIA Today, the media has become a significant source of knowledge for many people. We often believe what we read or hear from media sources, including the Internet, television, radio, and print. The constant deluge of information can be overwhelming at times, particularly when sources of news contradict each other.

Information from the media is believed to be true.

SCIENCE Sociologists do not reject authority, experience, cultural tradition, faith, or the media as sources of knowledge; but most rely heavily on methods considered empirical or scientific. *Empirical methods* focus on observable phenomena, meaning that others should be able to observe the same phenomena and check our observations for accuracy. Unlike the common-sense observations made as part of our daily experience, researchers using empirical methods strive to be objective.

Thinking Sociologically

Of the five sources from which we gain our ideas, which would you say were most influential in what you know about (a) human sexuality, (b) life after death, and (c) communism? Why are the sources likely to be different? Which are likely to be the most correct?

THE RESEARCH PROCESS

Comte, Spencer, and other early sociologists regarded their new discipline as a science. The natural sciences had successfully formulated laws, principles, and theories about the physical world through the use of the **scientific method**, a procedure that involved systematically formulating problems, collecting data through observation and experiment, and devising and testing hypotheses. Early social theorists believed that the same method could be used to develop laws, principles, and theories about the social world. There was also a practical reason for adopting science as the model of inquiry. The Western world, particularly the United States, has regarded science as almost sacred. Sociologists seeking legitimacy for their new discipline wished to convey to a skeptical world that they too could be objective, systematic, precise, and predictive in their field of study. They also hoped to develop a social technology that could be used to direct change and resolve social problems.

Is Sociology a Science?

Not everyone regards sociology as a science (Turner 2006). Some contend that, when strictly defined, science does not include the descriptions, hunches, opinions, and statistical tendencies of sociology. It has also been argued that human behavior is too complex and unpredictable to be studied scientifically and that sociology is too young a discipline to have developed a body of laws and principles like those found in the natural sciences. An additional criticism is that sociologists are part of the societies they observe, which makes it extremely difficult for them to prevent bias from affecting their perceptions.

Defenders of sociology as a science assert that any subject may seem complex to an untrained observer but that people have been engaging in the study and practice of sociology on an informal basis for thousands of years (Fuchs 2006). In response to the criticism that sociologists must be biased because of their closeness to their subject matter, sociologists state that they can be objective researchers by separating themselves from the subject, repeating studies using multiple observers, and by making cross-cultural and historical comparisons. Thus, although one can argue correctly that many sociologists are biased, naive, limited in cultural perspective, and bound by the present, this type of argument tells us little about whether sociology can be considered a science.

How then does one proceed? To determine whether sociology is a science, we have to rephrase the question by asking, what distinguishes the scientific mode of inquiry from nonscientific modes of inquiry? Can sociology and the other social sciences follow the scientific mode? To answer this question, we consider the steps in the research process used by many sociologists to study society.

STEPS IN THE RESEARCH PROCESS

When a sociologist decides to conduct research, it is usually after he or she has become curious about some phenomenon. Sociologists may spend their entire careers seeking answers to a specific problem such as adolescent deviance. As they explore the problem, they identify a number of questions that need to be answered; these usually lead to more questions. In an attempt to find answers, they will conduct scientific research. While, there may be some variations among researchers, typically there are eight steps in the research process. Following is a discussion of each of the steps.

State and Define the Problem

Research will always begin with some questions about a social phenomenon. The first step of the research process is to discuss the purpose of the study. This is where the researcher clearly articulates the problem under investigation and defines the concept(s) being studied. A **concept** is an abstract system of meaning that enables us to perceive a phenomenon in a particular way. Concepts are simply tools that

TABLE 3-1 STEPS IN THE RESEARCH PROCESS

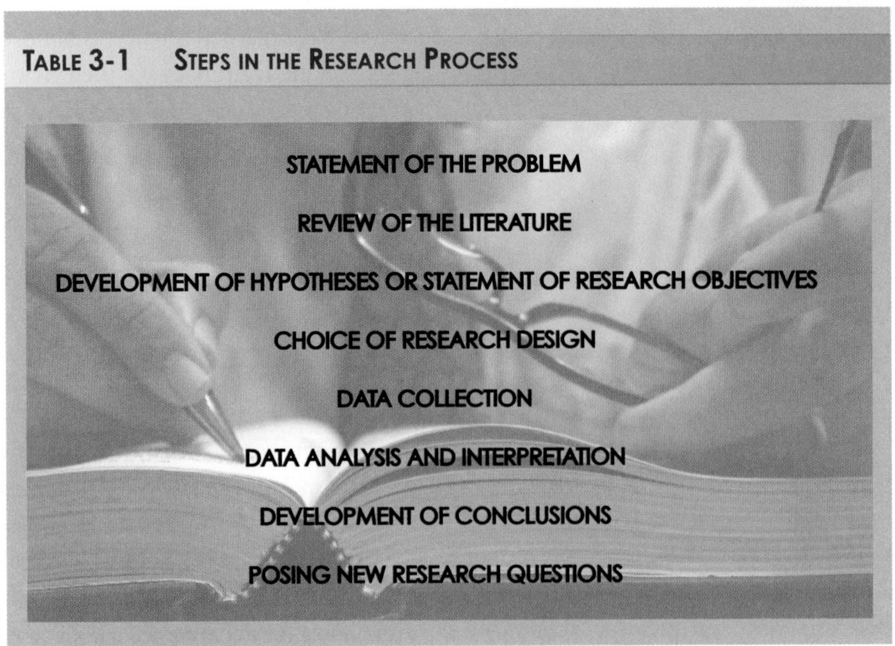

STATEMENT OF THE PROBLEM
REVIEW OF THE LITERATURE
DEVELOPMENT OF HYPOTHESES OR STATEMENT OF RESEARCH OBJECTIVES
CHOICE OF RESEARCH DESIGN
DATA COLLECTION
DATA ANALYSIS AND INTERPRETATION
DEVELOPMENT OF CONCLUSIONS
POSING NEW RESEARCH QUESTIONS

permit us to share meanings. Most of the terms in the glossary are sociological concepts: norm, status, stratification, group, mob, folkway, and so on. The concept of "stratification," for example, represents a particular type of inequality that exists in society; developing the concept made it possible for people to think and communicate about the social differentiation of people by wealth, gender, age, social position, and other characteristics.

Concepts can mean different things to different people at different times. Take the concept of deviance, for example. It varies from one culture to another and from one time period to another. Consider the act of adolescent drinking in the United States and in Germany. Until recently the legal age for drinking beer and wine in Germany was sixteen-years-old (it has been increased to eighteen), compared to twenty–one in the U.S. Germany is more permissive and tolerant of drinking by young persons while the United States is ambivalent, which is likely to result in problem drinking (Link 2008). A sociologist studying the cross cultural phenomenon of adolescent drinking may conduct research to enhance their understanding of the issue. Necessary to the study would be clarifying the components of the research problem, including concepts.

When concepts have two or more degrees or values, they are referred to as **variables**. For example, *husband* is a concept, and *years married* is a variable. *Dollar* is a concept; *level of income* is a variable. *Years of marriage* and *level of income* can both vary, but the meanings of the words *husband* and *dollar* remain constant.

Some concepts or variables are much easier to measure than others. We may all agree on how to measure the number of males and females in a room because we know how to measure quantities of people and how to determine gender. How would we, however, proceed with a study of the relationship between gender and happiness? *Happiness* is an abstract term that means different things to different people, and opinions would vary on how to measure it. In general, the more abstract a variable is and the further it is removed from direct observation, the more difficult it is to reach a consensus on how it should be measured. This is not to say that the variable *happiness* cannot be measured—it can.

The process of arriving at a means of measuring a concept or variable is referred to as *operationalization*. In this procedure, the sociologist selects indicators of an abstract concept, determining what will be observed and how it will be measured. In the preceding example, this would involve determining some criteria for assessing happiness. We might decide that happiness is whatever the individuals themselves think it is and simply ask them whether they are happy or not, or ask them to rate their own happiness on a five-point scale. On the other hand, we might decide that factors such as absence of depression, high levels of self-esteem, or

The concept of deviance varies from one culture to another. For example, the legal age for drinking beer and wine in Germany is lower than in the United States.

the ability to function successfully are indicators of happiness and attempt to measure those. Although opinions may differ on whether the criteria selected actually reflect happiness, the operationalization of the definition ensures that we understand the term *happiness* and, thus, know what it is that we are measuring. An **operational definition**, then, is a definition of a concept or variable such that it can be measured during research. Therefore, operationalization makes an abstract variable measurable and observable.

Conduct a Literature Review

The second step in the research process is to demonstrate that you have a significant understanding of the problem being examined. To accomplish this, you must conduct a literature review. In this step, the researcher attempts to find out as much information as possible about their topic of study. One of the best ways to do this is to examine the works of others. By understanding what has already been done, the researcher avoids the possibility of duplicating someone else's work; instead, they use other works to build onto their own existing knowledge base.

Resources used by the researcher in the literature review can be divided into two main categories: primary and secondary sources. Primary sources are original work and firsthand documentation of what was done by the individual(s). An example of a primary source would be a research study conducted and published in a professional journal, such as the *American Journal of Sociology*. Secondary sources are the result of an original work that has been interpreted by another and that work becomes the researcher's source. An example of a secondary source is this textbook because it provides information on numerous works by others. Both primary and secondary sources are important to researchers; however, primary sources are particularly important to a researcher's understanding of what has previously been studied about the topic.

Also found in the literature review is a theory about that which is being studied. As noted in Chapter 1, a **theory** is a set of interrelated statements or propositions used to answer questions about some social phenomenon. By using a theory, researchers attempt to find patterns and consistencies in what they are studying. Good theories are a key source of ideas for researchers to test; the information they discover through testing may be used in turn to modify and refine the theory. A good theory should be stated in abstract terms and should allow predictions to be made.

We want to emphasize the importance of conducting a thorough literature review as one of the first steps in conducting research. Consider this metaphor. Have you ever been involved in a deep, ongoing conversation with someone or with a group of friends, and someone enters the conversation late without any prior knowlege about what has been discussed so far? When that happens, have you ever noticed that the person entering the conversation late may bring up topics irrelevant to the conversation or things that have already been discussed, and as a result, the conversation gets a bit de-railed? If that has ever happened to you, have you felt like saying to the newcomer, "You need to get up to speed about what we are talking about first before spouting out irrelevant ideas or things we spoke about a while ago"? If that sounds familiar, think of research as a conversation among scientists or other academicians, a conversation that has been taking place long before you began your research. In order for your research (or your contribution to the "conversation") to be relevant, worthwhile, and valued, it is essential that you have a good foundation about what has already taken place within that "conversation" or the topic or you are investigating.

Development of Research Questions or Hypotheses

Once a thorough review of the literature has taken place, the researcher will pose either research questions or hypotheses, usually depending on the type of method he or she intends to use in the research. Sociological research involves two types of methods: qualitative and quantitative. The qualitative method will typically utilize research questions and quantitative will utilize hypotheses.

In qualitative studies, research questions (or objectives) are formulated with the purpose of answering them, using specific methods in the research process.

For example, "Do tattoos increase the likelihood of deviance among teens?" "Are college students with tattoos more likely to engage in promiscuous sexual behavior?" Research questions are specific to what is being studied and often involve more than one question in an attempt to find answers to the phenomenon.

Quantitative methods generally use propositions rather than questions. A **proposition** is a statement about the nature of some phenomenon. It generally consists of a statement about the relationship between two or more variables. The statement "Social activity is related to student grades" would be a proposition. If this proposition is formulated so that it can be tested, it is considered a **hypothesis**. A testable hypothesis would be "Students who attend more than one social activity per week have higher grade point averages than those who do not." Thus, hypotheses are propositional statements that indicate how the stated relations can be tested. In this example the hypothesis states that if social activity goes up, grade point averages will go up. In scientific studies, the variable that is presumed to cause a change or an effect is known as the **independent variable.** The variable that is presumed to be affected by the independent variable is the **dependent variable**. Thus, in the above example, grade point average is the dependent variable, the effect; the cause of the change in GPA—social activity—would be the independent variable.

This hypothesis is known as a **direct relationship** because it states that if one variable changes in some regular fashion, a predictable change will occur. **Inverse relationships** are also possible—for example, "As social activity goes up, grade point averages go down." Hypotheses that involve direct or inverse relationships are *directional hypotheses. Null hypotheses,* which state that there is no relationship between the variables of interest, can also be formulated: "There is no relationship between social activity and grade point averages."

One of the goals of scientific research is to establish a cause and effect relationship between variables. To establish a cause–effect relationship, researchers must establish an association between two variables. Variables that are not associated cannot be causally related. The age of one's grandparents is not related to one's driving ability—obviously, neither one causes the other. Even when two variables can be associated, however, it is not safe to assume that one causes the other. Hours of daylight begin to increase at the same time that the rate of drowning begins to increase, but it would be absurd to argue that one causes the other. Thus, we can see that there must also be a logical rationale for relating two variables before they can be considered to have a cause–effect relationship.

Determine the Research Design

This step in the research process outlines the methods used by the researcher to test their hypotheses or answer the research questions. **Methodology** refers to the rules and guidelines followed in sociological research. As previously mentioned, there are two means from which to choose—qualitative or quantitative research designs—each with a variety of methods to use in order to collect information or gather facts.

Qualitative methods are used to determine the essential characteristics, properties, or processes of something or someone. Rather than desiring to count how many, how much, or how often, qualitative researchers may attempt to study conditions or processes such as how police make a decision to arrest someone, the reactions or responses of a spouse or parent to the loss of a loved one, or the processes used in obtaining illegal drugs.

In a qualitative study, the researcher can use various methods to collect data, including observational methods. In **observational research**, the researcher or research team watches what is happening and makes no attempt to control, modify, or influence the ongoing activity.

Participant observation occurs when the researcher is an active participant in the event being studied. Anthropologists frequently use this method to study a particular community or subculture. Sociologists have been participant observers in studies of nudist camps, bars, prisons, the drug trade, and homosexual behavior. As a full participant observer, the researchers become directly involved in the group or community activities. Laud Humphreys (1975) took on the role of the "lookout" in his Tearoom Trade research of homosexual behavior in roadside public restrooms. As participants, researchers may learn about some of the subtleties involved in personal interactions. The researcher may, therefore, acquire a deeper understanding of the emotions and beliefs that bind the group together than would be possible if a person not participating in the group made observations. That kind of information is essential to many sociologists attempting to develop theories about particular types of groups or relationships. Other researchers may want to engage in only limited participation, where their interaction is not as involved as Humphreys, or in non- participation, where they only observe but don't participate or interact with those being studied.

Most participant observation research takes the form of a case study, in which a detailed study of an individual person, group, community, or activity is undertaken. The use of participant observation for case studies offers numerous advantages and positive outcomes. Often, such studies are sources that generate new research questions or hypotheses. Sometimes, one or two carefully selected case studies provide information that cannot be seen or could not be determined through quantitative analysis.

Suppose a researcher wants to study an entire culture or subculture of people—he or she can conduct **ethnographic research**. Ethnography has always been the primary form of investigation in anthropological research, and it has been a valued method of research for sociologists as well. Ethnography is a method of studying the social and cultural dimensions of human interaction. It is a form of research focusing on the sociology of meaning through close observation of sociocultural phenomena. Its goal is to understand communities and cultures from an insider's perspective and, then, translate that understanding to outsiders. Indeed, Max Weber's notion of *verstehen*, sympathetic understanding (discussed in Chapter 2) is testimony to the value that sociologists have placed on ethnographic research since the earliest days of the discipline. Ethnography is a method of studying the social and cultural dimensions of human interaction. Ethnographic researchers will use a variety of techniques to gather information, including participation, observation, and interviewing. This methodology is grounded in the same principles behind experiential learning—that we can learn and interpret the world as much by doing as by rational analysis.

Quantitative methods are designed to obtain numbers or amounts of something—the median age at marriage, the range of incomes or crime rates, for example. To quantify is to count, to determine frequencies, to measure amounts, or to state something in mathematical or statistical terms. This type of research design often involves methods such as surveys, experiments, or secondary analysis.

The procedure used most frequently to obtain information about the social world is **survey research**. This quantitative technique involves systematically asking people about their attitudes, feelings, ideas, opinions, behaviors, or anything else. Usually, the researcher uses a questionnaire to guide the questioning. You may have participated in a survey at some point, either an informal survey in a magazine—"Should college athletes be subject to drug tests?"—or a formal survey of your attitudes toward birth control or some other issue.

Surveys have a number of advantages over many other data-gathering procedures. They are usually easy to administer and often permit researchers to gather data on identical variables from many people simultaneously. Unlike most participant observation studies, which may take months or years, surveys provide a lot of information within periods ranging from a few minutes to several weeks.

There are problems with surveys, too, of course. First, if questions concern personal information about age, income, sex life, or criminal activities, for example, the respondents may not answer honestly. Second, if the questions or responses are highly structured, the results of the survey may not reflect the actual beliefs of the people being questioned, but

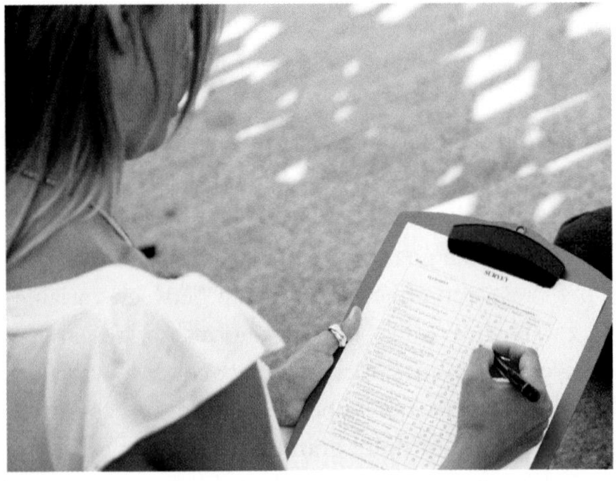

Survey research involves systematically asking people about such things as their attitudes, feelings, ideas, and opinions.

rather the researcher's conceptions of how the questions should be asked and what people's answers are likely to be. To give an exaggerated example, a survey question about attitudes toward abortion would not yield valid information if it listed as the only possible answers either "I think abortion should not be allowed under any circumstances" or "I think abortion is permissible in situations involving rape or danger to mother's health." Third, do surveys assess only the most superficial aspects of social life or cover only a limited part of the respondents' thoughts on a subject? Surveys may fail to assess areas that are difficult to examine, and people's beliefs may be far more complex than a survey indicates. Despite these problems, survey research is widely used by social scientists.

Another method used in quantitative research is **secondary analysis**—the use of existing information that was gathered by others or that exists independently of your research. Secondary materials may include *personal documents*, such as letters, diaries, e-mail, internet blogs and forums, autobiographies, and speeches; *public records*, such as health, school, police, marriage, death, and divorce; news sources, such as radio, TV, newspapers, magazines, books, professional journals, and reference materials available in most libraries; and *actual research data* gathered from other studies and available in existing data banks, such as at the National Opinion Research Center (NORC) in Chicago or the Roper Public Opinion Research Center in Massachusetts. One of the most widely used secondary data sources is the United States Census. For example, a researcher may want to examine possible patterns created by the changes in the collection methods used in the 2010 Census where persons were allowed to choose "all that apply" with regard to their race. While less than three percent of persons chose to identify themselves as biracial or multiracial, who were they? Why did some take advantage of the option, while the majority continued to use a monoracial identity?

The classic procedure used in scientific research is the **experimental design**, used to determine cause–effect relationships in carefully controlled situations. In an ideal experiment, it is possible to control all relevant factors and to manipulate, statistically or in the society itself, one variable to determine its effect.

To carry out an experiment, two matched groups of subjects are selected. In the **experimental group**, an independent variable is introduced, and it is the effect of this variable that is tested. The **control group** is identical to the experimental group in every respect, except that the variable is not introduced to this group. If we were studying the effects of dim lighting on social interaction, for example, we might randomly choose two groups of students. The experimental group would be placed in a dimly lit room, whereas the control group would be in a normally lit room. All other aspects of these settings would be identical (e.g., furnishings, size, time of day). The researcher would note differences in the behavior of the two groups: frequency of interaction, level of noise, the number of subgroups formed, and other behaviors considered germane. Differences in the social behavior of the two groups would presumably be due to the influence of the independent variable, dim lighting; however, we should be cautious at concluding the association because another unidentified variable may have influenced the outcome.

When experiments are done in a laboratory setting, it is easier to control conditions than it is in a natural or field (non-laboratory) setting, thereby making it easier to establish causation. It has been argued, however, that laboratory settings are artificial and yield distorted results.

Like other methods, there are problems with experimental techniques, particularly when studying human behavior. How is it possible to conduct experiments with humans in either a laboratory or non-laboratory setting? We cannot lock people in rooms withhold food, punish them, or remove them from friends and family? Doing this would by highly unethical and most likely unlawful. We can study circumstances that already exist in the social world: prisoners, populations of starving people, families who abuse their children, nursing homes that isolate people from their loved ones, and incarcerated juveniles placed in solitary confinement. The social world also contains populations of well-fed people, families that do not abuse their children, and so forth. It is often possible to find existing experimental and control groups that have all the characteristics in common, except the independent variable chosen for observation.

Another problem that can occur with sociological experiments is called the "Hawthorne Effect", where people's behavior changes because they realize they are

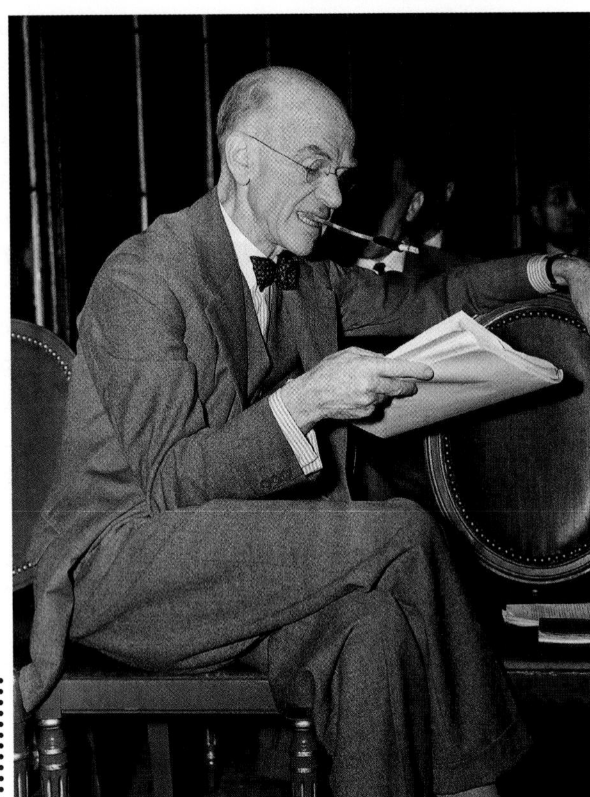

Industrial research professor Elton Mayo conducted a work-productivity study in 1939 that resulted in the "Hawthorne Effect."

being studied. Many years ago, one of the best-known experiments in sociology resulted in the "Hawthorne Effect" occurring. Before World War II, at the Hawthorne plant of Western Electric, Elton Mayo separated a group of women (the experimental group) from the other workers and systematically varied their lighting, coffee breaks, lunch hours, and other environmental factors (Roethlisberger and Dickson 1939). In the control group, work conditions went on as usual. Much to the amazement of the researchers, the productivity of the experimental group (the dependent variable) increased regardless of the variables that were introduced, including returning the workers to their original conditions. Obviously, the desired result, increased productivity, was not being caused by a specific independent variable. On the one hand, the experiment seemed to be a success—the experimental group differed from the control group when independent variables such as lighting and coffee breaks were introduced. On the other hand, the experiment appeared to be a failure, in that one independent variable seemed to have as much influence as another. The researchers concluded that the women were trying to please the researchers and enjoyed the attention they were getting. The very presence of the researchers contaminated the experiment to the point that they became a significant independent variable and caused a change in the dependent variable—work productivity.

Triangulation Studies

Today, both qualitative and quantitative research are widely used, with both recognized within the discipline as legitimate methods of social research. Throughout the research process, careful consideration must be given to the range of alternative methods or procedures that might meet one's objectives, and a variety of suitable procedures and methods do exist. In fact, many researchers choose to employ both quantitative and qualitative methods in their study. Triangulation is a method of data collection where multiple methods, usually three, are used to gather data. For example if a researcher wants to study violent juvenile behavior, she could use secondary analysis (such as crime statistics), interviews with incarcerated juveniles, and non-participant observation of the social interaction with one another during certain times of the day. Thus, the researcher has used both quantitative and qualitative methods to collect data.

In addition to choosing the method of data collection, the researcher must also outline the steps involved in measuring data. The scientific standard of precision of measurement asserts that the phenomenon being studied should be measured in precise, reliable, and valid ways. The more accurate our measurements, the better we are able to test our ideas about the social world. An ability to test or study anything, whether it is height, a religious practice, or a theory, is in large part dependent on the ability to measure it accurately. Part of the research process, then, is to establish both reliability and validity in your study.

Reliability is the extent to which repeated observations of the same phenomenon yield similar results. The scientific standard of replication asserts that research should be conducted and reported in such a way that someone else can duplicate it. The use of similar subjects and measuring procedures under similar conditions should produce results virtually identical to those of the original study. In the physical sciences, replication of studies under identical conditions is often easier than it is in the social sciences; but even in the physical sciences, it is sometimes impossible to recreate identical conditions. A California earthquake or a space shuttle explosion cannot be duplicated.

In the social sciences, the problems of replication are compounded by human factors. Some studies may be impossible to duplicate because of the nature of the problems studied. It would not be possible, for example, to duplicate studies of the reactions of East and West Germans on the day the Berlin Wall was opened and came down, or to duplicate studies of the residents of a particular town destroyed by flood or fire. It is possible, however, to perform studies on the residents of other communities or on other citizens who are granted freedom from a particular type of governmental or social repression and to note patterns of psychological adjustment, points of greatest stress, changes in kin and child relationships, or other conditions. The principle of replication of studies is based on the conviction that similar conditions and circumstances should produce highly similar results.

Studies of the reaction of Germans to the opening of the Berlin Wall are impossible to duplicate.

Validity is the extent to which observations actually yield measures of what they are supposed to measure. For example, if a bathroom scale registers different weights each time you step on it, it is not reliable. If it gives the same weight each time but it is not an accurate measure, the bathroom scale may be *reliable* (same results each time) but not *valid* (inaccurate weight). A common problem with research validity is that critics question whether the measurement instrument actually measures what it is supposed to measure. For example, on the bathroom scale, if the scale reliably and accurately determined your height, it would not be valid as a measurement of your weight. For a measure of your weight to be considered a fact, the scales must be both reliable (consistent) and valid (accurate measure of the factor or characteristic).

Data Collection

After determining our research design, we begin the data–collecting step where we identify the group of people to be studied. The group might be doctors, students, the taxpayers, voters in a given election, or any selected group that can provide the information needed to prove or disprove the hypotheses. This group is usually called the "population." Since we can rarely study all doctors, students, or taxpayers due to such factors as cost and time, we must pick an appropriate sample. A **sample** is a group of people chosen from the population who are thought to represent that population. The sample is questioned, and their answers are expected to reflect the beliefs of the population as a whole.

Samples are chosen by a variety of methods. A **random sample** is chosen by chance, so that every member of a group has an equal chance of being selected. Because it is usually impossible to place all names in a hat, sociologists often assign a number to each name and use a table of random numbers to select which persons should be included. They may also use a method known as **systematic sampling**, in which a specific pattern of selection is followed, such as selecting every twentieth name. A third method is **stratified sampling**, in which the population is divided into groups and then chosen at random from within those groups. If our population were students, we might stratify them by class rank, sex, or race and then randomly select from each of these groups. Regardless of how the sample is chosen, if every person has an equal chance of being chosen, it should be representative—it should reflect the attitudes of the total population.

Analyze the Data

After we have performed all the steps to collect the data, analyzing it requires us to consider, again, the type of research method used. Using qualitative data collection techniques requires the researcher to look for patterns, themes, or trends during the analysis of the data. While this process relies a great deal on the subjectivity of the data, it requires a great deal of objectivity from the researcher. The scientific standard of objectivity asserts that in the study of any phenomenon—social or nonsocial—the personal biases and values of the people doing the research must never influence the data reported or the interpretation of results. The political, religious, racial, or other beliefs of the investigators should in no way determine the findings of a study. Two independent researchers who study the same phenomenon should produce identical results regardless of their differences in status, belief, or personal behavior.

Quantitative data analysis involves converting the data to numbers in order to run statistical tests. The researcher might want to include some descriptive data about each of the variables. For example, if a researcher wants to provide the average age of students enrolled in their Introduction to Sociology course, he can provide measures of central tendency. This statistical technique provides averages using three possible ways. For the purpose of our example, let's say there are eleven students enrolled in the course with the following ages: forty-five, forty, twenty-seven, twenty-five, twenty, twenty, nineteen, nineteen, nineteen, eighteen, eighteen. If we want to know the most frequent response to our age question, the **mode** will provide us with the answer. However, if we want to know the midpoint, above which are one-half the students and below which are one-half, we would use the **median**. We could also determine the average, the **mean** sum of all the ages of students in our class, by dividing the total combined age of all the students by the number of people involved. Therefore, looking back on the ages of students enrolled in the class, the most frequent age of student in the class would be nineteen years of age; therefore, this is our mode. The age at which half the students are below and half are above is twenty years, and it represents the median age. Finally, the average mean age is 24.5 years—the sum (270) divided by eleven. As you can see, each one gave us a different answer; therefore, we must use caution when choosing which average to use. The mean is a great way for students to figure what grade they have in a class if the instructor uses a standard point system. By adding the total number of points you've earned and dividing that by the total number of points possible, you will determine your average. For example, if you have a total of 270 points out of a possible 300—you would be at a ninety percent.

Another frequently chosen statistical analysis is correlation, the degree to which the variables being measured can be associated to each other. A correlation exists if, when one variable increases, another variable either decreases or increases in a somewhat predictable fashion. For example, if our variables are income and education, we could determine the degree of association between the two. Suppose we find a strong correlation—as education increases so does income. We could suggest that level of education is related (correlated) to level of income. We have to be careful with our interpretations of correlations by not assuming a relationship means one variable causes another to occur. Suppose we examined the relationship between smoking and pregnancy. We conduct a survey about smoking before and during pregnancy, and our sample consists of pregnant women at a low-income clinic. Upon analyzing our data we find a correlation between smoking and pregnancy; the more women who smoked, the more who became pregnant. Can we conclude that smoking causes pregnancy? What looks like a correlation is actually misleading or spurious when no meaningful relationship exists between the variables. While there is the appearance of causality, it would be foolish to think smoking causes pregnancy. However, there may be a true correlation between smoking and income.

Interpreting a correlation between two variables—such as smoking and pregnancy—must be done carefully as other factors may contribute to the relationship.

These are just a couple examples of simple statistical techniques; there are many more complex ones used by researchers. However, even statistics can be manipulated in a way that presents bias in the study. Benjamin Disraeli, a nineteenth century British politician, once said, "There are three kinds of lies: lies, damned lies, and statistics". Data analysis can be objective as long as researchers are aware of the possibility of bias and take measures to minimize the level of subjectivity. The use of computers to analyze quantitative data has lessened the chances of human calculation errors; and as long as we don't misinterpret or falsely report the findings, then we can be confident in our research.

While specific techniques were discussed under qualitative and quantitative methods, that doesn't mean they are exclusive to one or the other. There are some data which can be analyzed using either quantitative or qualitative methods. Take for example **content analysis** and focus groups—these two data gathering techniques could be analyzed using either method. Content analysis refers to the procedure of systematically extracting data from a wide range of communications—including newspapers, journals, books, television and so on. In analyzing the data, the researcher may look at quantifying it, such as how many times aggressive behavior occurs in children's cartoons, or qualitatively assessing whether the cartoons represent violence significant to a specific time period—say Bugs Bunny versus Power Rangers. Along these same lines focus group data can be analyzed using quantitative or qualitative methods. Focus groups usually involve no more than ten persons who are led by a moderator in a discussion concerning the participant's attitudes about some event, product, etc. For example, suppose we want to examine the attitudes of college students toward co-ed dormitories. Using a quantitative approach, we could simply measure the negative and positive comments made by the group, or separate their statements into themes, such as safety, personal space, etc., for a qualitative analysis. The type of method chosen by the researcher is guided by their research objectives.

Implications and Conclusions

After the data has been collected and analyzed, the next step is to determine what it all means. Simply reporting the findings is not enough; the researcher must also discuss what the findings imply. If you are using qualitative research methods, you will want to discuss patterns, themes, characteristics, or trends. If using quantitative methods, statistical findings will be discussed and generalizations proposed. Generalization refers to the extent we can apply our findings beyond the sample group. For example, in our co-ed dormitory study, we may be able to generalize our findings to the sample, the entire population of students at the university we sampled, or perhaps go even broader—such as all college students. Generalization is a necessary part of the conclusion to our research.

The discussion and conclusion section is also where the researchers will tie their findings back to the theory proposed in the literature review and discuss how their findings contribute to the overall theoretical base. In addition, this section will explain any limitations or problems the researchers may have encountered while conducting the study.

Publish and Pose Future Research Questions

All good research should be shared with others, particularly the scientific community. Research studies are found in professional journals, monographs, or discussed in books. In addition, research is cyclical, meaning it offers new questions for future researchers. Tying the findings back to the theory is part of the research because theories serve as important sources of new research. There are many theories to explain crime, for example. Early explanations were based on biological theories, and propositions were established that attempted to relate crime to the shape of the head, the size of the body, or chromosomal abnormalities. Some psychological theories of crime led to propositions linking criminal activity to emotional immaturity, a particular personality type, or a mental defect or illness. Sociologists have developed theories of crime based on social and cultural factors. These theories have led to propositions and testable hypotheses linking crime with social inequality, socialization or learning experiences, disorganization in the social order, and lack of effective societal controls. All these theories are sets of interrelated propositions that attempt to explain crime or some criminal activity. However, they also provide direction for new research.

Thinking Sociologically

1. Formulate a quantitative research study. Follow the research process described, and provide an outline for each step.

2. Formulate a qualitative research study. Can these same steps be followed? Why or why not? Discuss.

TYPES OF SOCIOLOGICAL RESEARCH

Now that you understand the steps in the research process, a further distinction between scientific and unscientific sociology can be clarified by examining the four most common types of research designs used in sociological studies. The four basic types—exploratory, descriptive, explanatory, and evaluative—will be discussed.

Exploratory Research

Exploratory research is typically used to explore some new social phenomenon, possibly allowing the researcher to examine a new program, group, process, activity, situation, etc., and to determine how those involved in the interaction process get along. Exploratory research usually answers the question "what" and provides information on future research.

Since very little is known about a new social issue or topic, exploratory studies can be challenging with frequently changing goals and arbitrary guidelines. When conducting a literature review, a researcher may find few empirical studies related to their study. Therefore, theory development is often a goal of exploratory research, as well as methods and procedures.

Exploratory studies are common in many areas of study. For example, a criminal justice student may be interested in exploring the rising number of crimes identified as cyberstalking. Remember that exploratory studies answer the question "what"; therefore, the researcher is likely to learn that as the number of young people using the Internet continues to increase, so does the need to prevent them from becoming the target of an online stalkers. In addition, the researcher will seek to define the concept of cyberstalking. According to the United States Department of Justice, cyberstalking occurs when someone uses the Internet, email, or other electronic devices to stalk someone. The stalker is likely to make harassing, threatening, or violent comments using the computer. A cyberstalker may send repeated, threatening, or harassing messages by simply pushing a button. They may use programs to send messages at regular or random intervals without being physically present at the computer terminal. In addition, they can get other internet users involved by pretending to be the victim and posting controversial or hateful information on internet boards or chat rooms. Suppose the researcher wants to also find out what problems cyberstalking causes for police departments. The difficulty facing law enforcement is that a cyberstalker can be someone across the street or in another state from the victim, making it difficult for law enforcement to identify, locate, and arrest the offender.

Descriptive Research

Descriptive research describes social reality or provides facts about the social world. A descriptive study would be undertaken to determine whether people who have served time in prison have more trouble finding jobs than people who have not been in prison, or to determine what percentage of college students use various forms of drugs and how frequently.

All descriptive studies share the goal of providing data on *social facts,* which are reliable and valid items of information about society. A *fact* could be a *behavior* (John scored three touchdowns), an *attitude* (women want equal pay for equal work), a *law* (the speed limit is fifty-five mph), or even a *statistic* (the median married couple income in 2001 was $30,116).

There are many different types of descriptive studies, which cover many different topics and are used in many different ways. However, all of them answer questions regarding who, what, where, when, how often, and how many. Whom do particular types of wrongdoing victimize? What are the needs of a particular community for a new park? Where do people prefer to shop? When are people most likely to watch TV? How often do people buy a new car? How many people favor a particular presidential candidate? What is the level of morale of employees in an organization? To clarify these potential applications, we take an example of a descriptive study and look at how it can be used.

One study was done to determine how often and how seriously airline flight attendants are physically or verbally assaulted on routine air travel (Salinger et al., 1985). The researchers found not only that the problem is widespread but also that it occurs most during weekends in December. How is this particular research useful? First, academic sociologists might use it to develop theories and explanations about social behavior in general. What does the information found in this study tell sociologists about crowd behavior? How does time of year affect social behavior? What is the impact of fear (such as fear of flying) on human behavior? How does being in a confined area (an airplane) affect relationships? One study alone cannot lead to such generalities, but it could be used to support other theories or as a starting point for new ones.

Second, professional sociologists employed by a specific airline (say, "Friendly Sky Airways") might use the findings of that study to help plan administrative policies that would improve efficiency or would minimize assault, or they might conduct similar studies to find out how much assault occurs in "Friendly Sky Airways." Are there other forms of victimization in "Friendly Sky Airways" that management should know about? When, for example, is passenger luggage most likely to be reported lost? Are there times when passengers themselves might be at greater risk of crime (for example, victims of pickpocketing) in the airport terminal? Sociologists could use this and other information to make recommendations that would

Descriptive research describes social reality, such as whether people who have served time in prison have more trouble finding jobs than people who have not served time.

A descriptive study on air travel may be used by nonsociologists, such as airport security, to determine the amount of police

help airlines improve their services in the highly competitive air travel industry.

Third, the study could be used by many nonsociologists working in air travel. Travel agents could use it to minimize discomfort for their clients (and thus increase their business) by booking flights during more peaceful hours. Airport security could use it to determine the amount of police protection needed at various times. Flight attendants could use it to be aware of the periods when passengers are more irritable and to be more sensitive to them during those times. Finally, in making your own travel plans, knowing when these kinds of assaults or other types of annoying situations (lost luggage, etc.) are likely to occur could be useful to you personally.

Explanatory Research

Explanatory research attempts to explain why things do or do not happen. Why do people with prison records have trouble finding jobs? What factors are related to students using drugs? Questions such as these are concerned with the problem of causation. What factors make a designated phenomenon happen or change? What is the cause of a given effect?

Explanatory (or analytical) studies and descriptive studies are similar, in that they both provide useful information about social reality. The primary difference between them is that explanatory studies are also concerned with answering the question "Why?" Explanatory research answers the question "Why?" by discovering the independent variable (the cause or event that precedes the behavior in question). It may be true that assault against airline attendants is higher on weekends in December, but what are the conditions that precede or lead to this kind of behavior (that is, what are the independent variables associated with assault)? Is it because flights are overbooked more often during those times? Is it because younger people are more likely to travel then? Are the people that drink alcohol during the flight more likely to commit assault or less likely? Does assault occur more often on longer or on shorter flights? Does it occur more often in first class or in coach? In other words, what causes the behavior—in this case, the assault?

Like descriptive studies, explanatory studies are the essential material out of which academic sociologists construct their theories. Suppose that explanatory research was conducted to find out the socioeconomic position of people who supported a particular presidential candidate. This information could help academic sociologists to construct general theories and explanations about the relationship between social class and voting behavior in general. However, this information is also useful for those involved in planning political campaigns. Does this mean that applied social research (research studies conducted by professional sociologists in the workplace) and academic (basic) research are exactly the same? At times, yes; the same studies could be used in different ways. However, a major difference between academic (basic) research and applied research is that sociologists doing research in the workplace are focusing on variables that are of specific interest to specific clients. The primary goal of professional sociologists in the workplace is to help a particular client find out what leads to or what is the result of particular actions or situations.

Knowing what precedes (or causes) a particular type of behavior is important for two major reasons: It helps us to predict behavior, and it helps us to control behavior. Think of the power that kind of knowledge can give you! As a manager, you may be able to control the rate of personnel turnover by finding out what causes employee dissatisfaction. By discovering what leads to higher worker morale you might be able to stimulate greater employee production of goods and services. By knowing what attracts people to a product, you might be able to create better marketing devices. Advertising and marketing rely heavily on these kinds of studies. Most TV commercials provide very little product information, if any. Rather, they appeal to particular types of people who will use specific types of products under given types of circumstances. For example, think about the preponderance of "Bud Light" commercials on television. Do these commercials tell us anything at all about the product? Or do they focus, rather, on the type of people buying the product by appealing to the characteristics (sexy, care-free, contemporary, etc.) with which their prospective buyers want to identify?

There are many types of descriptive and explanatory studies. Although it is not very likely that most of you will become sociologists, it is very likely that most of you will do or use descriptive and explanatory research as part of your job or in your personal life. As a sales representative for a beverage distributor, you will need to know where to find the highest rates of soft-drink consumption. As a display manager in a department store, you will need to find out what stimulates customers to remain in a store. As a physician opening up a new practice, you will have to find the locations that have the highest rates of illness in your specialty, and to discover what makes people feel at ease in a medical office.

A third kind of sociological research that has come to be known more for its applications in the workplace than for its use in academic sociology is evaluation research.

Evaluation Research

Evaluation research measures how well a program or project works in relation to its goals. It determines the extent to which the intended goals are being met and provides a basis for deciding to continue, alter, or eliminate a program. Does the mandatory seat-belt law actually save lives? Does the law that requires a minimum legal drinking age of twenty-one years reduce drunk driving? Does a mandatory class-attendance policy lead to better grades? Do social programs such as the Personal Responsibility and Work Opportunity Reconciliation Act, formally Aid to Families with Dependent Children (AFDC) actually help poor people improve their situation, or do such programs create a cycle of dependency, keeping people down? Conversely, evaluation studies may precede the implementation of a program, project, or policy to help determine whether it will produce the intended results. Some researchers feel that evaluation research "is the bread and butter of applied social science" (Finsterbusch and Mars 1980, 119). It is one of the most widely used types of research in the workplace.

You may have noticed that assessment research has become an increasingly important activity in many professions including, but certainly not limited to, education. It is important to point out that assessment and evaluation are often used synonymously, but they are not the same thing. Assessment typically involves collecting data to determine where an organization "is at"

Evaluation research measures how well a program, such as the mandatory seatbelt law, works in relation to its goals.

in terms of what it wants to achieve and its long-term goals. For example, many colleges and universities have diversity as a long-term goal. This may mean diversity in what the curriculum offers, the student body, the faculty, and the staff. In attempting to achieve this goal, a first step is to determine to what extent diversity already exists and what may be needed to reach a desired goal. So, assessment is taking stock of where the organization currently is; and based upon that information, they begin identifying goals and resources and making plans. Evaluation, on the other hand, looks backward after a period of time to measure if the goals have been accomplished. It is a subtle difference but important, nevertheless, to note. The remainder of our discussion will consider evaluation research only.

Evaluation research is one of many ways in which politicians, journalists, concerned citizens, and others often try to evaluate the worth of a program informally and subjectively. *Evaluation research* uses the same methodological techniques of descriptive and explanatory research and often utilizes the findings of descriptive and explanatory studies to make its recommendations. If the results of descriptive research tell you that the number of drunk drivers is greater now than before the new minimum age law went into effect, for example, what does that tell you about the effectiveness of the law itself?

There are four steps involved in systematic evaluation research: specification, measurement, analysis, and recommendation (Gones 1984). Specification is the first and most important step. It means defining or identifying the goals to be met by the program, policy, or project. The goal of sex-education programs, for example, may be to reduce teen pregnancies. If that is the goal of sex education, then the basis for evaluating these programs must be the degree to which the programs reduce the rate of teen pregnancies. The program should *not* be judged on the basis of whether teens continue to engage in premarital sex. Clearly, it is imperative that the goal of the program being evaluated be fully understood before going any further in the research.

The *measurement* is the way in which the researchers collect the information needed to evaluate the specified goal. This can be done through surveys, interviews, observation, secondary analysis, or experimentation. To measure the rates of teen pregnancies, a researcher might compare city hospital records on this subject for the years before and after a citywide sex-education program went into effect. Perhaps a survey of teens that asks them whether they regularly use birth control could be done in order to compare high schools with sex-education programs and those without them.

Analysis, the third step in evaluation research, is the use of the information collected in the measurement stage to draw conclusions. Methods of analysis range from very complex to very simple. That is, sometimes, analysis may involve sophisticated statistical analysis of the data collected, and at other times, it may involve a simple interpretation of descriptive findings, depending on the specific research involved. Suppose that, in our evaluation of sex-education programs, we found that teen pregnancies in some participating schools increased, and in some schools, they decreased. A simple interpretation of the data here would not work. It would probably be necessary to determine whether there were other variables that account for the teen pregnancy rate, such as age of students in the school, socioeconomic status, or religion. However, if it turned out that the number of teen pregnancies declined in every school that had a sex-education program and went up in every school that did not have such a program, without doing any complex statistical analysis, it would be fairly safe to assume that the program works.

Recommendation is the final stage of evaluation research. This refers to the advice that is given, based on the analysis, regarding what should be done. Should the program continue as is, are there particular changes that should be made, or should the program be eliminated altogether? An analysis of the sex-education program might find that teen pregnancies are reduced most when birth control devices are actually brought into class and students are instructed in how to use them, but that in programs where such devices are merely discussed or described, there is no change in the number of pregnancies. In this case, the researcher might recommend that all sex-education courses include exposure to actual birth control devices and specific instructions on how to use them.

Evaluation research can be used to determine the effectiveness of any purposeful activity. Practically all of the human and public service fields regularly use evaluation research. Professional sociologists and other social scientists for social service organizations, government agencies, politicians, city planning departments, schools, hospitals, and other such organizations primarily do it. However, the results of the research are used also by many nonsociologists—such as college administrators, politicians, social workers, hospital administrators, and teachers.

Another use of evaluation research is in the commercial world. An advertising company needs to know whether its campaigns are attracting the clientele they are after. Grocery stores may need to know whether their policy to stay open twenty–four hours a day is increasing profits. More customers may be shopping there, but perhaps not enough to cover the increased costs of remaining open.

Although primarily professional sociologists and other social scientists do evaluation research, it is likely that at some point you will conduct some evaluation research of your own in your occupation. As a teacher, you may need to evaluate whether your innovative techniques are actually attracting students to your courses and holding students' attention more or whether these techniques are frightening students away and distracting them in class. As a dentist, you might want to determine whether your informal attire in the office makes your younger patients more comfortable, or whether it is perceived as a lack of professionalism and a lack of caring. As an automobile sales representative, you may need to find out whether your friendly, personal approach with customers puts them at ease or makes them distrust you. Very often, finding out the answers to these questions before you actually implement your plan can save you much time, trouble, and money.

Evaluation research might also benefit you in your personal life. Although this would not be as formal or as methodologically sophisticated as that done by professional sociologists or by someone as part of his or her job, you will still probably need to do it at some point. You may do it to evaluate your educational plans, career plans, investment strategies, or even the way you are raising your children. Will getting your MBA or PhD actually improve your chances of getting a better job and a higher salary? Upon carefully evaluating the situation, you might find that further education could actually hurt your chances of getting an entry-level position. Will the jobs that require these degrees be available when you complete your education? Does the particular employer you would like to work for really want someone with an MBA, or will this degree over qualify you for the job you want? Would you be better off starting work right after college? Will the money lost due to time not working and the cost of tuition be balanced out by any income that you might make after you receive your degree? How long will it take you to make up the difference?

You might ask similar questions regarding your personal investments. It may seem, for example, that putting money in the bank every month increases your savings. However, are you spending more on interest in credit card payments than the interest you are getting in the bank? In childrearing, will your strict rules regarding what your children can and cannot do lead them to become mature, independent people, or will they make them dependent, rebellious, and uncreative? Clearly, there are many ways that you will use evaluation research in your personal life. You may have thought of many others already.

Thinking Sociologically

1. Should the social sciences be held to the same standards of scientific inquiry as the biological and physical sciences? Why or why not?

2. Select a topic for study, such as cohabitation, female employment, or busing. What types of questions could be answered with exploratory descriptive, explanatory, and evaluation research?

SOCIOLOGY AND SCIENCE

Now that we have discussed the steps in the research process, along with some of the methods and attributes of scientific inquiry, we can return to our original question. Should sociology be considered a science? Like many questions, this one cannot be answered with a simple yes or no. The issue is not so much whether sociology is a science, but rather to what extent it is pursued with scientific modes of inquiry. According to the criteria we have discussed, some sociological studies would certainly be regarded as scientific. A sociologist

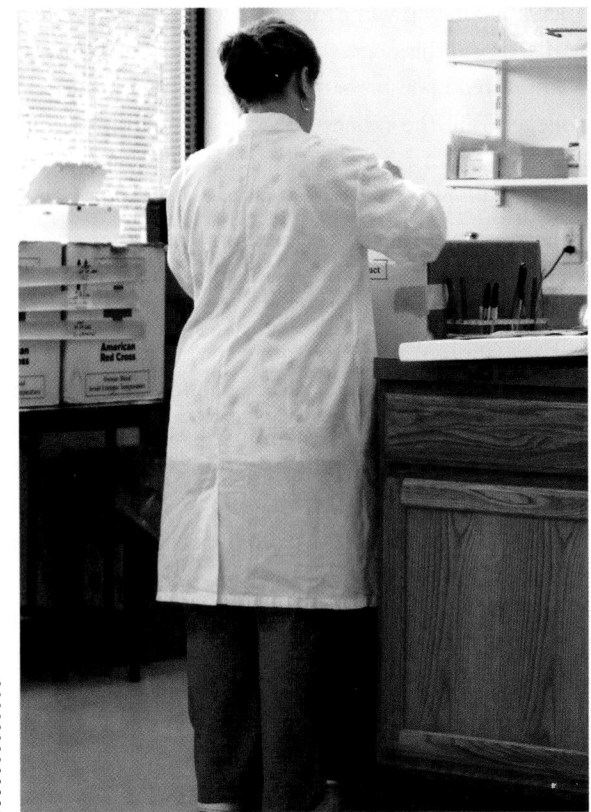

The answer to the question of whether sociology should be considered a science is not a simple yes or no.

studying the correlation between age at marriage and divorce rates would develop operational definitions and precise measurements to objectively examine the marriage and divorce phenomena in a replicable study. Studying a problem such as the relationship between gender and happiness might have to use methods that, strictly speaking, would not be considered scientific. In short, the techniques used by sociologists range from those that meet the strictest standards of scientific inquiry to those that, although still useful, fall short of that standard.

ETHICAL ISSUES IN SOCIOLOGICAL RESEARCH

When conducting research a number of ethical issues should be considered. Ethics requires persons to follow the guidelines or rules regarding the standards of conduct for their specific profession or group. In the field of sociology, there are both general ethical guidelines and specific guidelines to follow, particularly when conducting research.

There is a general understanding among social scientists: 1) Participation is voluntary, 2) there will be no harm to the participants, and 3) participants are informed of all risks associated with the study. Basically what this means is that anyone who participates in research should do so voluntarily, and the researcher will make certain the participants are not harmed in any way. Finally, there is informed consent, whereby the researchers have explained all the possible risks involved and the participants consent to participate in the study. However, while most research abides by the general guidelines, there is controversy within the field regarding the plausibility of absolute adherence to the rules. Are there studies that make it difficult to obtain voluntary participation?

One of the most controversial research studies within the field of sociology involved the dissertation of a graduate student. Laud Humphreys was attending Washington University in St. Louis when he became interested in sexual relations occurring between men in public restrooms. Humphreys began researching what he referred to as "tea room trade" or the act of sexual behaviors between two anonymous men in public restrooms. He wanted to understand why it occurred and who were the men that met in these public places. Humphreys knew that if asked to voluntarily participate in the study, the men would say no and he would not be able to move forward with his work. Therefore, Humphreys was determined to learn as much as possible about the practice and decided to become an insider so that he could study their behaviors. Focusing primarily on the restrooms in public parks, Humphreys made himself a regular when the men were engaged in sexual activities; and he offered to be a lookout and warn the participants when others were entering the restroom. Wanting to track the men he encountered, Humphreys followed the men from the restroom and jotted their license plate number down. He then went to the police department and filed a false police report on each vehicle, which allowed him to get the personal information of each man. He persuaded the investigators of another study on men's health to include his participants in their study and to allow him to be the interviewer.

TABLE 3-2 FOUR RESEARCH METHODS: A SUMMARY COMPARISON

Method	Application	Advantages	Disadvantages
Observation studies • Laboratory observation • Natural field observation • Participant observation	• Case studies • Group behaviors • Community activities • Other cultures • Explanatory, descriptive, and evaluative	• Generates qualitative data • Generates new insights and hypotheses • Can take place in natural setting	• Observer (researcher) may influence outcome • Roles of participant and researcher may be difficult to separate • May be very time consuming
Survey research • Questionnaires • Interview schedules	• Study of the nonobservable (opinions, attitudes, values) • Public opinion polls • Market research • Census taking • Cross-national studies • Explanatory, descriptive, and evaluative	• Generates easily quantifiable data • Can be used on large populations • Permits standardized questioning • Easily administered • Requires only a short time frame for gathering data	• Sampling difficulties • Exclusion of nonrespondents • Honesty of responses too personal/sensitive questions not known • Difficulty of question construction: clear, unambiguous, unloaded • Omission of relevant questions
Experimental designs • Experimental and control groups • Laboratory or field setting	• Comparison of two groups of workers, students, or children • Explanatory, descriptive, and evaluative	• Controls the specific conditions • Often permits replication of experiment • Specifies cause-effect relationships	• Artificiality of laboratory, "unnatural" setting • Cannot always control all variables • Hawthorne effect
Secondary analysis • Historical records • Official data • Public records • Mass media • Data banks	• Historical study • Permits the analysis of the content of communications • Allows observation of trends and changes • Explanatory, descriptive, and evaluative	• Data already gathered or available • Inexpensive • Sources from past or otherwise not available • Generalization difficult	• Desired variables or materials missing or omitted • Out-of-date or incomplete data • Nonsystematic, inaccurate records • No control over possible bias in data

Humphreys donned a different disguise and went to the men's houses to interview them about their health, including their sexual behavior. In all Humphreys observed 134 men in the public restroom and interviewed one hundred of them, either at the restroom or through the health study. Through his research, Humphreys discovered that over fifty percent of the men he encountered in the restroom did not see themselves as homosexual; they were happily married men with children, and worked in respectable jobs. They wanted to have quick sexual encounters without commitment or conversation, but considered themselves heterosexual. In addition, the men he met were more likely to hold conservative thoughts both politically and socially which acted as a veil of protection against suspicion.

At the time of his study, Humphreys only needed to have the approval of his dissertation committee to be awarded the PhD Without any significant dissatisfaction with his work, Humphreys was awarded his doctorate in 1970 and then went to work for a university teaching sociology. After several faculty members from the Sociology Department at Washington University heard about his actions, they petitioned the school to rescind Humphreys', PhD, believing he acted unethically in his collection of data.

Critics argued that Humphreys observed and interviewed participants without fully disclosing his intent to conduct research. He also manipulated information by writing down the vehicle tag numbers to obtain home addresses and used these, later, to interview participants again. The potential for harm was great for the participants who could have been "outed" if their identities were discovered during the research process.

One of the main problems that existed during the time of Humphreys' "Tearoom Trade" study was the absence of **Institutional Review Boards (IRB)** in higher education. Institutional Review Boards are ethical review committees whose main duties are to approve, monitor, and review research studies involving human subjects. Members of the committees are typically colleagues of the researcher or even members of the community. The role of the IRB is to be the overseer of research and to protect the rights and welfare of individual research subjects. Any agency that receives federal funding and conducts research using human subjects is required to have IRB committees to oversee the process. The goals of IRB committees are to assure the following:

1. Subjects are selected fairly.
2. Risks to subjects are minimal and reasonable.
3. Risks of participation are fully disclosed to participants.
4. Vulnerable subjects (easily coerced or influenced) are protected.
5. Informed consent is reasonably obtained by subject or his/her legal guardian.
6. Informed consent is appropriately documented.
7. Safeguards are in place to protect the privacy and confidentiality of the subjects.
8. Protection of data is outlined and monitored.

Data collected from research studies are usually kept for three years in a secured and locked location to protect research subjects. Before researchers can undertake a study involving human subjects, the IRB has to give approval—and only after the above requirements are met. In addition, research studies are reviewed on an annual basis to make certain the rules continue to be followed.

Thinking Sociologically

1. Discuss the pros and cons of the "Tearoom Trade" research. Consider how the data could have been gathered differently than the methods used by Humphreys.

2. What is the purpose of Institutional Review Boards in university settings? How can IRB committees protect participants from becoming victims of poor research practices?

The American Sociological Association (ASA) has established ethical guidelines outlining professional standards of responsibilities and conduct for sociologists. These guidelines not only address the responsibilities of researchers but also sociologists practicing in fields both inside and outside academia. The following excerpts represent the five broad principles specifically addressed by the ASA:

- **Principle A**: Professional Competence—Sociologists will strive to maintain the highest level of competence
- **Principle B**: Integrity—Sociologists should maintain the highest level of integrity by being fair, honest, and respectful
- **Principle C**: Professional and Scientific Responsibility—Sociologists should adhere to the highest level of scientific and professional standards ....
- **Principle D**: Respect for People's Rights, Dignity, and Diversity—Sociologists should respect all people and strive to be unbiased
- **Principle E**: Social Responsibility—Sociologists have a duty to share with their communities and society their knowledge

Now that you have learned in these first three chapters about the birth of sociology, as well as some of the theories and methods used within the field, how can a student benefit by taking courses in sociology? The next section provides you with some of the uses of sociology in both your personal and professional lives.

OCCUPATIONAL AND PERSONAL USES OF SOCIOLOGY

Sociology is not only for sociologists. Although sociology is used professionally in academic ("basic" or "pure" sociology) and nonacademic ("applied" or "practical" sociology) careers and occupations, sociological skills and knowledge are used in many jobs, by many different types of people, and also in our personal lives. One of the fascinating and exciting things about sociology is its diversity of applications.

Beginning students of sociology often ask a number of related questions. Some of the more common ones are the following: (a) "Why should I take sociology? If I'm not interested in a sociological career, what use will it be to me?" (b) "What is the value of sociology to society? Why should this field be supported?" (c) "What do sociologists do? If I decided to become one, what career options would be open to me?" These are important questions that we continue to address throughout this book. One of our goals for this book is to demonstrate how the subject matter in each chapter can be used in occupations and in daily personal life. For now, though, we look briefly at four applications of sociology: (1) academic sociologists, (2) professional sociologists in the workplace (nonacademic), (3) nonsociologists in the workplace, and (4) nonsociologists in society and other social environments.

Academic Sociologists

More sociologists are employed as teachers than in any other capacity. There are more than fifteen thousand sociologists in the United States today, and at least

Sociological skills and knowledge are used in many jobs and by many different types of people, as well as in our personal lives.

Of the more than 15,000 sociologists in the United States today, at least two-thirds of them consider teaching to be their primary responsibility.

two-thirds of them consider teaching to be their primary responsibility. Most teaching sociologists also serve other-functions—researcher, administrator, or social critic, for example. Most teaching positions are found in liberal arts colleges or colleges of arts and sciences, in departments devoted to sociology exclusively, or to some combination of sociology, anthropology, and social work. Increasingly, sociologists are being hired in the professional schools of such fields as medicine, nursing, law, social work, business administration, theology, and education.

In addition to teaching, most academic sociologists do research. The research function is often regarded as contributing to the society at large by providing new knowledge about society. Most researchers engage in basic or pure research—the acquisition of knowledge for its own sake, with little thought about how the results will be used. For example, the basic researcher may seek information about the causes of crime, its prevalence, and its distribution by age, gender, or geography, but not be overly concerned with how this knowledge will be used.

Professional Sociologists in the Workplace

Peter H. Rossi and William Foote Whyte (1983), two prominent applied sociologists, suggest that sociology can be applied to the workplace in three major ways: applied social research, social engineering, and clinical sociology. Collectively, this type of work is referred to as applied sociology, practical sociology, or sociological practice. As suggested in the opening vignette to this chapter, public sociologies are the concern of many sociologists.

APPLIED SOCIAL RESEARCH Many companies, government agencies, and other groups employ professional sociologists to collect and interpret research data on a variety of social issues or problems that the group may face. Applied social research is the use of sociological knowledge and research skills to obtain information for groups and organizations—such as banks, insurance companies, public utilities, retail stores, government agencies, schools, community service organizations, child-care centers, hospitals, and mental health centers, among others. An insurance company, for example, might employ sociologists to find out who the company's prospective customers are, as well as the types of insurance the prospective customers will need, their income levels and lifestyles, their values and beliefs, and the ways in which they determine which types of insurance they need.

A state government might request the services of a sociologist to evaluate the impact of a proposed law before it actually goes into effect. Will the new law have the desired consequences? How will the law be enforced? What will be the increased cost to taxpayers to ensure that the law is enforced? Will people comply with the law? Will failure to comply overburden the courts and impede the system of justice?

The questions that organizations need to have answered by sociologists are endless. There are many types of applied social research, and it would not be practical to try to discuss all of them here. There are, however, three broad categories that encompass most of the specific types: (1) descriptive studies, (2) analytical or explanatory studies, and (3) evaluative studies. These are described briefly here and are discussed in more detail when we turn to research methodology later on.

Descriptive studies are used primarily to obtain information about a particular social problem, event, or population. For example, a college administrator may need to know how many freshmen fail out of American colleges each year, as well as these freshmen's ages, genders, and races, and the types of extracurricular activities in which they were involved. Although this type of research is often a first step in arriving at cause–effect relationships and explanations, its main goal is to describe what is occurring rather than to explain why it occurs.

Analytical (or explanatory) studies are used in various careers and occupations to help explain what causes (or what is related to) some specific events or problems. Is there a relationship between a state's legal minimum drinking age and the dropout rate of students attending college in that state? Do colleges that allow freshmen to pledge to fraternities and sororities have a higher dropout rate than colleges that do not allow freshmen to pledge? Descriptive studies, on the other hand, are used mainly to obtain information about what is occurring, analytical studies focus on why events take place. Like descriptive studies, analytical studies are needed in most occupations. Sociologists doing this kind of research tend to look for social factors that precede or result from the event or problem in question.

Evaluative studies are among the most widespread forms of applied sociological research. They are used to estimate the effects of specific social programs or policies. Will a policy that prohibits freshmen from pledging to fraternities and sororities lower the dropout rate, or will it lead freshmen to engage in behavior that would increase their rate of failure? What will be the impact on a college's enrollment if sororities and fraternities are prohibited? Simply put, evaluative studies find out how well a program, policy, or project works or is likely to work.

CLINICAL SOCIOLOGY Clinical sociology is the use of sociological perspectives, theories, concepts, research, and methods for consulting and providing technical assistance to individuals, groups, or organizations. The Sociological Practice Association (which changed its name from the Clinical Sociology Association) defines clinical sociology as sociological intervention—using sociology to help in specific situations.

Clinical sociology is similar to another area of sociology, social engineering, which is attempting to change the way a society, organization, institution, or group is arranged so that a particular goal may be achieved. Both have to do with social intervention, and it is sometimes difficult to see the difference between them. Social engineering is concerned with large-scale social planning, whereas clinical sociology is concerned more with advising on specific social settings and situations. Social engineering is likely to be involved with designing policies, laws, programs, and projects, whereas clinical sociology involves consultation, counseling, therapy, and conflict mediation. It is social engineering, for example, to develop a statewide basic education program to improve the quality of education that students receive; it is clinical sociology to counsel teachers in a particular high school about how to communicate better with students in the classroom. It is social engineering to create a nationwide project that would encourage corporations to offer on-site child care for working parents; it is clinical sociology to offer group therapy to working parents to help them overcome their conflicting loyalties, anxieties, and everyday problems.

Like many other areas of applied and basic sociology, clinical sociology and social engineering often overlap. According to Rossi and Whyte (1983), "The clinician will often encounter structural factors that must be changed before the clinical treatment can produce the hoped-for results. Similarly, the social engineer must recognize that the implementation of a major structural change in an organization may be effectively facilitated by a skillful clinician" (p. 12).

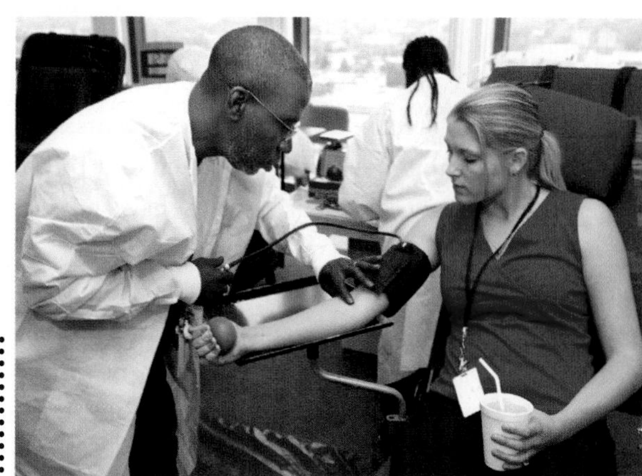

Clinical sociologists are engaged in such careers as community health care.

SOCIOLOGY AT WORK

Research Analyst

Jean Brittain Leslie is a research analyst at the Center for Creative Leadership in Greensboro, North Carolina. Prior to her current position, she was a research project manager at the *Greensboro News and Record,* a major daily newspaper in North Carolina. She received her B.A. in sociology from Elon University and her M.A. in sociology at the University of North Carolina at Greensboro.

Jean Leslie is one of those people who happened to stumble into sociology and fall in love with it. "I would like to say that I aspired to become a 'sociologist,' but that is not the case. I, like many students, did not know what I wanted to do when I 'grew up' so I took many introductory courses. Sociology was one of them. Needless to say, I enjoyed it so much that I decided to major in it. In retrospect, sociology as compared to other majors most closely fits my personal orientation toward the world. A sociology degree . . . offers an intellectually stimulating framework to address the world." She says that sociology encourages her to objectively approach her work "or at least be aware of how my own values infiltrate my perspectives. Sociology has taught me to question what appears to be reality and to not take for granted shared meanings." Besides obviously benefiting from an understanding of symbolic interactionism and knowledge about how different cultures operate, Jean feels that the macro-level perspective that sociology offers is invaluable to her when studying organizations.

Jean credits her degree in sociology to helping her obtain her current position at the Center for Creative Leadership. "I am a researcher by occupation. My employer was looking for someone with skills similar to the ones I acquired through studying sociology." She says that courses such as research methods, statistics, sociological theory, and cultural anthropology provided her with a basic understanding of human behavior that is pertinent to her job. "I am working for an organization that studies managers and leaders from diverse organizations and cultural regions. Every time I go into a new project, I must read literature from other academic disciplines (for example, business, psychology, counseling)." Jean notes that she often finds sociological perspectives in works from other disciplines. "It is not uncommon to find popular sociologists cited in non-sociological journals or presentations at Academy of Management meetings. Having attended both business and sociological professional conferences, I can tell you that both disciplines are facing similar quality research issues.

When thinking about a career, Jean thinks that there are some skills that all employers would prefer their employees have, which you can gain from sociology courses. "Writing abilities are a premium, the ability to communicate with others is another plus, and above all one must learn how to survive in a world where norms are often implicit. These things can be exercised through sociology if the student believes them to be important." Additionally, she feels that the perspective that sociology teaches is not duplicated in other academic disciplines. "Sociology offers a unique analytical approach to the world that can be applied in any career and organizational setting .... The most obvious difference between sociology and other academic disciplines is the macro orientation. The unit of measurement for most of my coworkers is the individual. Due to my sociological orientation, I am able to bring a much more global perspective to our work. I do quite a bit of cross-cultural research in which sociology (as opposed to other disciplines) has the opportunity to shine."

Clinical sociologists are engaged in careers such as legislative consultation, law and criminal justice, corporate marketing, social work, psychiatric health care, community health care, child guidance, student counseling, and family therapy. Governments, businesses, and communities often seek them out to offer suggestions or advice. Their services have been requested in court decisions on busing, in neighborhood programs for crime prevention, in the development of personnel policies for insurance companies, in discrimination cases involving automotive companies, and in the creation of community mental health centers. Sociologists seldom work as full-time consultants, however. They are used in specific situations, such as offering methodological advice to groups doing evaluation studies, assisting in data analysis, or explaining the probable consequences of a set of alternative courses of action.

Thinking Sociologically

1. Select a social phenomenon about which you are curious—such as a specific group, organization, or activity—and use as much information in this chapter as possible to discuss how you might investigate it from a sociological perspective. What would you focus on? What types of questions would you want to answer? What types of explanations would you expect to discover? How could the results of your study be useful professionally and personally?

Non-Sociologists in the Workplace

Although it is usually necessary to have a graduate degree (MA or PhD) to be employed as a professional sociologist, sociology offers knowledge and skills that can be used by non-sociologists in a multitude of careers and occupations. Even if you are not interested in a career in sociology, the study of sociology offers valuable preparation for other types of careers. You do not even have to major in sociology to take advantage of its applications within most occupations. For example, if your interests lie in business, law, education, medicine, architecture, politics, or any profession dealing with people, social life, or social organization, sociology can be useful because it provides a wealth of knowledge that can be applied to any of these fields. Besides the specific theories, concepts, and perspectives that can be useful in and of themselves in occupational settings, sociology students develop research skills, critical-thinking and problem-solving skills, interpersonal skills, and communication skills. In recent years, several studies have found that these skills are necessary for success in many careers and occupations.

RESEARCH SKILLS Research skills involve basic investigative capabilities. Essentially, they include quantitative (numerical) and qualitative (non-numerical) data-collection methods. The sociology student may develop skills in survey techniques (in-depth interviews and questionnaire construction), empirical observation, participant observation, experimentation, and library research. Lawyers, physicians, advertisers, market analysts, clerks, administrative assistants, publishers, and many others use these skills.

In business, information must often be gathered quickly. A newly employed investment banker must be able to find out very quickly who may be potential clients in a particular region. The manager of a retail store either could go with a hunch that a costly investment will pay off or could conduct a consumer survey to reduce the probability of making a financial blunder. Since research is basic to sociology, even a brief introduction to the field will acquaint you with a range of research techniques and methods you can use. Whether we use simple observation, formal structured interviews, content analysis, experimental designs, or elaborate statistical computations, an understanding of the variety of research techniques should be useful in many occupational settings and situations.

CRITICAL-THINKING AND PROBLEM-SOLVING SKILLS Research skills and knowledge of sociological theories and concepts can add to your critical-thinking and problem-solving skills. To possess critical-thinking skills means to have the ability both to analyze a situation or information and to arrive at careful, precise judgments. With theory and research, you can investigate and carefully arrive at some solutions to problems faced in many occupations. For example, a physician who is having personnel problems with office staff might attribute the conflict to clashes in personalities. A knowledge of small-group processes, along with the ability to find and analyze models of successful organizational or personnel relationships, would be more useful than continually hiring and firing staff members. A lawyer must be able to critically evaluate the terms of a settlement and to find solutions to problematic areas in that settlement to ensure the protection of the client's interests. Two young chiropractors may need to figure out how to establish their practice and develop clientele in a city where they have no existing personal connections or other patient referrals.

The ways in which sociology must be learned, which determine the nature of most sociology textbooks, facilitates the development of critical-thinking and problem-solving skills. The key to understanding sociological theories and concepts is not memorization, but rather involves carefully analyzing the meanings and implications of these abstractions and trying to come up with concrete examples. Most sociology textbooks, particularly at the advanced levels, do not merely present theories; they usually evaluate the merit of those theories as compared to other ones. This type of learning forces the student to think critically. The assignment of term papers in which sociological theories and concepts must be applied to particular situations or events helps students to sharpen their problem-solving skills. Sociology students also learn other analytical skills, such as constructing and testing hypotheses, discovering explanatory factors, and reading tables. It would be hard to think of an occupation in which the ability to think critically and solve problems is not needed.

INTERPERSONAL SKILLS Interpersonal skills are techniques that help you to efficiently manage yourself and others within an organization or in other interaction settings. These skills include management, leadership, interaction, diplomatic skills, and the ability to facilitate and coordinate group activities. Competence in setting goals, the ability to plan projects, and knowledge of how organizations work are also important interpersonal skills. Unclear objectives or poorly designed work programs could result in poor teamwork performance. For example, the business manager who is unable to coordinate the goals of the product-development staff (which stresses innovation at any cost) with the goals of the accounting department (which values cutting expenses wherever possible) is bound to have problems.

Interpersonal skills can be developed through an understanding of sociological theories and concepts that focus on interpersonal and group relationships. Some of these theories and concepts concern culture, race and ethnic relations, gender relations, social stratification, socialization, social interaction, and social organization. For example, suppose that you are an elementary school teacher who wishes to increase the involvement of your Hispanic students' parents in your school. You might choose to do this by organizing a special club for Hispanic students' parents. The knowledge that child rearing is traditionally the primary responsibility of mothers in Hispanic cultures might help give you some ideas for bringing such a group together. Health professionals might find it useful to know that people from different cultures respond to pain and symptoms in very different ways and, thus, might develop different ways of dealing with them. Both the factory managers and the workers' union managers would be interested in knowing which aspects of the work environment different types of factory workers consider to be most important. The list goes on and on. For almost every job, knowledge of sociology would be a valuable tool that could be used to enhance interpersonal skills.

COMMUNICATION SKILLS Perhaps the most important skill you need to have is the ability to communicate well. Without this ability, your other skills may not be apparent. As a student of sociology, you will have to develop both oral and written skills. Most assignments in sociology, written or oral, are concerned not only with giving correct answers, but also with developing and presenting the argument in order to get your point across. It is necessary not only to think clearly, but also to express yourself clearly so that your argument can be understood. The perpetual interplay of ideas between students and professor—via class discussions and critical analyses—provides practical experience with thinking "on your feet" and with communicating your thoughts and ideas to others. Again, this is a skill that must be developed to be a success in any career.

Sociological insight plays an important role in effective communication. Sociology tells us, for example, that people from different cultures and social groups interpret language and other symbols in different ways and that language influences a person's perception of a given situation. With this in mind, middle-aged professors would find it useful to know the jargon of the various student groups at a college (jocks, punks, preppies, honors students, etc.) to reach each of them emotionally and intellectually. Advertisers and salespeople would benefit if they could quickly find out the needs and wants of their clients through the subtle messages found in their conversations. The transplanted New Yorker who is recruited to be the director of a child-care center in North Carolina needs to understand why Southern parents might not trust "fast-talkin' Yankees." There are hundreds of other examples of how sociology can help us in our day-to-day communication problems. By now, you have probably thought of some examples of your own.

Non-Sociologists in Society and Other Social Environments

Since it is concerned with every aspect of social life, sociology should interest every social being. Just as we should have an understanding of sickness without having to be physicians and an understanding of money without having to be economists, an understanding of sociological principles can be useful in our daily lives because they are concerned with an enormous range of events. Sociologists may study topics as diverse as the intimacy between husband and wife and the dynamics of mob violence. Violent crime may be the subject of one study, the communion of persons in a religious institution the subject of another. One investigator may be concerned with the inequities of race, age, and gender, while another may investigate the shared beliefs of common culture. Sociology is interested in both the typical or normal, and the unusual or bizarre.

Sociology can teach us to consider perspectives other than our own and to look beyond the individual in our efforts to understand individual behavior. It encourages us to look not merely at how people and events are unique and different, but also at how people share perceptions and how events occur in patterns. It familiarizes us with a range of theoretical explanations of how people think and act, of how societies' structures change, and of how society operates.

Perhaps most important, though, is that sociology can help us to understand ourselves. Humans are social animals, and people can understand themselves only in the context of the society in which they live. Knowledge of the social constraints that bind us can be frustrating—we may feel trapped, angry about our inability to control our lives, and disappointed at the social inequities that surround us. Only through understanding our society, however, can we truly understand ourselves.

C. Wright Mills (1959) wrote that the "sociological imagination" enables us to distinguish between "personal troubles" and "public issues." By understanding how societies and groups are organized, we may well come to realize that problems that we thought we had caused ourselves might in fact be problems that result from social forces. Think of all the times you came down hard on yourself—or someone else—because of a problem you faced. If you knew how social forces generated the problem, you might be better able to deal with it. This one sociological idea alone—and there are hundreds of others—has implications for many of your social relationships. Consider, for example, how parents might handle a problem with their child if they could understand the cultural, structural, institutional, and group forces acting on the child instead of focusing solely on the child's problematic behavior.

Sociology is useful for more than just helping us with our problems. It also can help us with most of our important personal decisions, such as whether to get married, how many children to have, whether to buy a home, how much education to get, what kind of career to pursue, and when to retire.

Although "personal uses of sociology" have been discussed last, this is perhaps the most important section of the chapter for many of you. The author of *College: The Undergraduate Experience in America*, a report issued by the Carnegie Foundation for the Advancement of Teaching, states, "We found on most campuses a disturbing gap between the college and the larger world .... We feel compelled to ask: How can the undergraduate college help students gain perspective and prepare them to meet their civic and social obligations in the neighborhood, the nation, and the world?" (Boyer 1986, 16). This report is as relevant in 2012 as it was in 1986.

Sociology has always been one of the disciplines best able to help meet such a challenge. In light of the Carnegie Foundation's recent findings, sociology is now more relevant to a college education than ever before. This book introduces you not just to sociology as a science, but also to sociology as a tool for improving the quality of your life and the lives of those around you.

CHAPTER REVIEW

Wrapping it up

Summary

1. Although we also learn about society from everyday experiences, authority, faith, and tradition, sociology depends heavily on empirical research that uses the scientific method.

2. Is sociology a science? Some argue that it is, some that it is not. It may be more constructive to note what distinguishes scientific modes of inquiry from nonscientific modes of inquiry and then to consider whether sociology can follow a scientific mode. Following the steps involved with scientific research increases the chances the research is reliable and valid.

3. There are certain standards of inquiry basic to science. Objectivity involves excluding personal values, beliefs, and biases from the research process, findings, and interpretations. The standard of replication requires that research be undertaken and reported such that someone else can replicate it. The standard regarding precision in measurement requires that whatever is studied be measurable and that measurements be precise, reliable, and valid.

4. Sociological research is of four basic types: exploratory, descriptive, explanatory, and evaluative. *Exploratory research* is typically used to study a new phenomenon. *Descriptive research* provides reliable, valid data on social facts. *Explanatory research* goes beyond description to determine why a particular social situation occurs and to discover cause–effect relationships.

5. Sociological methods are often categorized into two types: qualitative and quantitative. *Qualitative methods* are used to determine the essential characteristics, properties, or processes of something or someone. These methods often include case studies, laboratory observations, field observations, and participatory observations.

6. *Quantitative methods* are designed to determine the amounts or numbers of something: how many, how often, how statistically significant, and so forth. Experimental research and surveys are generally quantitative methods.

7. *Surveys*, the most frequently used method of sociological research, involve systematically asking people about their attitudes or behaviors, which is usually accomplished with the use of questionnaires. Choosing an appropriate sample and wording questions carefully are crucial parts of the survey method.

8. The *experimental method* involves the use of two or more similar groups. An independent variable is

introduced into the experimental group but withheld from the control group.

9. Valuable data are often found in public records and secondary sources. Content analysis is one procedure used to critically examine this material.

10. Research generally involves a sequence of tasks, including the following: formulating the problem, reviewing the literature, developing hypotheses for testing, choosing a research design, collecting data, analyzing the findings, drawing conclusions, and disseminating the results.

11. There are often many different ways to categorize the data, to formulate tables, and to use statistical measures such as the mode, median, mean, range, and variance. When the data analysis is finished, conclusions are drawn and the results are made available to the public.

12. Ethics in sociology are meant to guide researchers in meeting the needs of human subjects involved in their studies. Among other things, maintaining integrity and protecting the confidentiality of subjects are paramount to sociological research.

13. Research methods are not only important and useful for sociologists, but also an integral part of many occupations and used often in our daily lives.

Key Terms

concept An abstract system of meaning that enables us to perceive a phenomenon in a certain way

content analysis The procedure of systematically extracting thematic data from a wide range of communications

control group In an experiment, the group not exposed to the independent variable that is introduced to the experimental group

dependent variable A variable that is changed or influenced by another variable

descriptive research Research that describes social reality or provides facts about the social world

direct relationship A relationship between two variables in which an increase in one variable is accompanied by an increase in the other; compare with inverse relationship

ethnographic research A form of descriptive research focusing on the sociology of meaning through close observation of sociocultural phenomena

evaluation research Research that measures how well a program or project works in relation to its goals

experimental design A scientific procedure in which at least two matched groups, differing only in the variable being studied, are used to collect and compare data

experimental group In an experiment, the group to which an independent variable is introduced; this variable is not introduced in the control group

explanatory research Research that attempts to explain why things do or do not happen by examining the relationship between social variables

exploratory research Research that attempts to answer the question "what" by explaining a new social phenomenon

hypothesis A statement about the relationship between variables that can be put to an empirical test

independent variable A variable that causes a change or variation in a dependent variable

Institutional Review Boards (IRBs) Committees on college/university campuses and in research organizations that provide oversight of research that is conducted on human subjects

inverse relationship A relationship between two variables such that an increase in one variable is accompanied by a decrease in the other; compare with direct relationship

mean A measure of central tendency computed by adding the figures and dividing by the number of figures; also known as the average

median A measure of central tendency in which half the figures fall above and half the figures fall below; also known as the midpoint

methodology The rules and guidelines outlined and followed in social research

mode The most frequent response in a body of data

observational research Research in which the researcher watches what is happening and makes no attempt to control or modify the activity being observed

operational definition A definition of a concept or variable such that it can be measured

proposition A statement of the relationship between two or more concepts or variables

qualitative methods The gathering and reporting of non-numerical data used to determine the essential characteristics, properties, or processes of something or someone

quantitative methods The gathering and reporting of data based on numbers or amounts of something

random sample A sample selected in such a way that every member of a population has an equal chance of being chosen

range The span between the largest and smallest amount of a variable

reliability The extent to which repeated observations of the same phenomena yield similar results

sample A number of individuals or cases drawn from a larger population

scientific method A procedure that involves systematically formulating problems, collecting data through observation and experiment, and devising and testing hypotheses

secondary analysis The use of existing information that was gathered or exists independently of one's own research

stratified sampling Sampling in which a population is divided into groups and then subjects are chosen at random from within those groups

survey research A quantitative research technique that involves asking people questions about the subject being surveyed

systematic sampling Obtaining a sample from a population by following a specific pattern of selection, such as choosing every tenth person

theory A set of logically and systematically interrelated propositions that explain a particular process or phenomenon

validity The extent to which observations actually measure what they are supposed to measure

variable A characteristic such as age, class, or income that can vary from one person to another; a concept that can have two or more values

variance A descriptive statistic that tells how the data are spread over the range

Discussion Questions

1. Are music and art sciences? Are physics and biology sciences? Is any social science discipline (including sociology) a science? Why or why not?

2. Formulate two general propositions. Can you operationalize them—that is, reformulate them in terms of testable hypotheses?

3. Why are reliability and validity important in social research? Give examples to illustrate each.

4. Compare and contrast the advantages and disadvantages of qualitative and quantitative research. Give examples of where each type could be used and where one type could be more appropriate than the other.

5. What do you think of the idea that quantitative research represents masculine characteristics and qualitative research represents feminine characteristics?

6. List examples where observation research would be appropriate. What are its strengths and weaknesses?

7. Can sociologists conduct experimental designs? Give examples.

8. After reading about the Hawthorne effect, illustrate how researchers themselves might influence or contaminate the results.

9. Suppose that you want to study police brutality. What methods could you use? What are some ethical and political issues that you should consider? Should unpopular or undesirable results or findings not be made public?

10. An instructor says that she is going to grade on a curve. She returns your exam results with a score of fifty. What types of additional data do you need to know to assess whether fifty is a good or a poor grade?

Pop Quiz

1. Most sociologists rely heavily on _______ as the sources of ideas and knowledge.

   a. common sense and everyday experiences
   b. tradition and rituals
   c. observation and empirical methods
   d. revelation and intuition

2. A _______ is an attempt to find patterns and consistencies in seemingly idiosyncratic and inconsistent events.

   a. concept
   b. theory
   c. variable
   d. measurement

3. When concepts have two or more degrees or values, they are referred to as _______.

   a. hypotheses
   b. variables
   c. propositions
   d. theories

4. If a proposition is formulated so that it can be tested, it is considered to be a _______.

   a. theory
   b. concept
   c. hypothesis
   d. fact

5. _______ hypotheses states that there is no relationship between the variables of interest.

   a. Null
   b. Directional
   c. Inverse
   d. Conceptual

6. The extent to which repeated observation of the same phenomenon yield similar results indicates _______.

   a. validity
   b. causation
   c. reliability
   d. correlation

7. Research that attempts to explain why things do or do not happen is _______.

   a. descriptive
   b. explanatory
   c. evaluation
   d. qualitative

8. In a medical study, lung cancer could be the _______ variable, while smoking would be the _______ variable.

   a. dependent, independent
   b. independent, dependent
   c. valid, reliable
   d. reliable, valid

9. The research procedure used most frequently to obtain information about the social world is _______.

   a. observation
   b. content analysis
   c. experiment
   d. survey

10. Contamination of experimental outcomes due to the influence of the researcher's presence is known as the __________.

    a. Hawthorne Effect
    b. Chicago School
    c. Qualitative Factor
    d. Sociological Imagination

11. The process of defining precise measurement of a concept or variable is known as the principle of replication. T/F

12. In research, the same variable may be independent in one context and dependent in another. T/F

13. In a stratified sample, every member of the population has an equal chance of being selected. T/F

14. The mean is one measure of central tendency. T/F

15. The mean is also known as the "average." T/F

1. C	6. C	11. F
2. B	7. B	12. T
3. B	8. A	13. F
4. C	9. D	14. T
5. A	10. A	15. T

PART TWO

Individuals Within Society

Then I began to think, that it is very true which is commonly said, that the one-half of the world knoweth not how the other half liveth.

François Rabelais

CHAPTER 4

Culture and Society

MARK ALL THAT APPLY

On January 1, 1892, seventeen-year-old Annie Moore from County Cork, Ireland became the first person processed through Ellis Island in New York. Over the next fifty–two years, more than twelve million people passed through Ellis Island to start their new lives in America. Today, an estimated forty percent of U.S. citizens can trace their ancestry to one of those early immigrants (U.S. Census Bureau 2008). Other Americans can trace their ancestors even further back to the colonial era when immigrants were arriving from England or as slaves on ships. Some recognize their ancestors as the first true Native Americans, living here before the arrival of all the others. After the Revolutionary War, money was needed to pay for the cost of the war, among other things, and the government needed to determine how to levy taxes. Familiar with population counts that had been required by the Crown, the new government devised a plan to count people who could then be required to pay taxes.

In 1790 the United States conducted its very first census, counting the number of people living within the thirteen colonies. Approximately 650 U.S. marshals rode on horseback, using only pencil and paper to count the heads of households and other persons living in their homes. It took the marshals eighteen months to count the 3.9 million people living in America at that time. The first census was relatively easy with only six questions. They included the name of the head of household and the number of people living in the household—free white men over sixteen years, free white men under sixteen years, free white women, other free people, and slaves. At that time slaves were counted as only three-fifths of a person, and Indians were not counted at all because they were not required to pay taxes.

Since that first census over two hundred years ago, one has been conducted every ten years with alterations to the questions occurring nearly as frequently. For example, racial categories have changed almost regularly, with some groups expanding while others were excluded altogether. As noted, Indians were excluded from the first census, and blacks were not considered as a complete person. During the 1850 census, racial categories included the rising number of racially mixed people. Racial classification included White, Black, and Mulatto (mixed race)—with Blacks and Mulattos further categorized as either free or slave. It wasn't until later that censuses included persons other than Whites and Blacks. For example, the 1870 Census reflected the end of slavery, but added Chinese and Indian to the racial categories. The Tenth Census in 1890 further quantified mixed race persons by adding Quadroon (one-quarter black) and Octoroon (any degree up to one-eighth black) to the Mulatto (one-half black) category. While quantifying Black racial categories may appear to have benefited persons with mixed race heritage, the distinction was designed, in fact, to limit their access to resources. Not long after slavery ended, the United States entered a period of Jim Crow segregation where persons with any degree of Black blood were considered Black, regardless of their skin color. These categories stayed in place until the 1930s; but new categories of race were also added, such as "Mexican", which was removed at the next census in 1940. Today, Mexican's are not classified as a race at all, but rather are ethnicity lumped together with other groups under the "Hispanic" category.

The biggest change to racial classifications occurred in 2000, when persons were allowed for the first time in history to mark more than one race. The 2000 Census questionnaire contained fifteen race options, including an option for "Some other race." On a questionnaire item separate from race identification, individuals were asked to indicate whether their ethnicity is "Hispanic or Latino" or "Not Hispanic or Latino."

According to the U.S. Census, this new change reflects the growing number of interracial children and the increasing diversity throughout the country. After the data was tabulated, 2.4 percent of the population had identified themselves as belonging to two or more races. Of those, 4 percent were children under the age of eighteen years. Among the population of persons who marked two or more races, 93 percent identified themselves as only two races. The largest group of two races was "White" and "Other" with over 32 percent, followed by "White" and "Native American" with 15.86 percent, and "White" and "Asian" with 12.72 percent. The percentage of persons who chose "White" and "Black" as their race was 11.5 percent. Hawaii was the state with the largest population of persons who identified themselves as multiracial (24.1 percent).

How we define race changes over time. The way race was defined in 2000 will likely change in twenty or thirty years. In addition, other cultures may see race differently than we do in the United States. For example, in the former South African system of racial separation, there were four legally defined racial categories—White, Black, Colored, and Indian. Established in 1950, those racial categories defined how people were treated, including what schools they went to, whom they could marry, whether they could vote, and much more. However, a person's racial classification could also change with their status; moving up or down the racial ladder was based on one's accomplishments. In 1991, South Africa officially abolished their system of racial separation.

The arbitrary categories of race found on the censuses throughout the history of the United States suggest that race is socially constructed, rather than biologically. Race is defined and redefined to reflect the beliefs of our society at any given time. How will adding the "mark all that apply" instruction to the census change our definition of race in the future?

DEFINING CULTURE

The term culture means different things to different people. Many people use the words culture and society interchangeably; however, they are different in their meanings. To a sociologist a **culture** is a system of ideas, values, beliefs, knowledge, norms, customs, and technology shared by almost everyone in a particular society. In other words, culture is a society's entire way of life. A **society** is a group of interacting persons who live in a specific geographical area, who are organized in a cooperative manner, and who share a common culture. Culture and society cannot exist without the other; there can be no society without a culture, and likewise, no culture without a society. A culture is a society's system of common heritage. Each of us has a culture because we were all raised in a society. We express our culture continuously in our dress, food, work, language, recreation, and other activities. We learn our culture from those within our society. Our families, friends, schools, and others teach us, and then we pass it on to future generations.

A comprehension of the elements of culture is vitally important to all interpersonal relationships, from personal life to occupation. Indeed a time honored anthropological axiom is that "in order to work with a people it is essential to understand their culture" (Foster 1952). In most discussions of culture, it is assumed that the various groups of people within a society share some expectations about how it works and how its members should behave. In America, people live in houses or apartments. We buy food in a supermarket or grow it ourselves, we have jobs, and we generally expect our spouses to be sexually faithful to us. In traditional Eskimo culture, by contrast, people lived for part of the year in houses made of snow. They hunted for food because no one had "jobs" in our sense of the word. In some circumstances, sexual infidelity was not merely tolerated but was even encouraged through a practice of "wife lending." Since behaviors of these types vary from one group or society to another, they are viewed as products of culture rather than as basic aspects of human nature. In other words, these behaviors are not programmed genetically, as in most animal life—they are determined by the culture. Humans are not born knowing which beliefs and behaviors are appropriate. These must be learned. By the time we are adults, most of what we come to recognize as culture is so embedded into our everyday lives that we often take it for granted. From the foods we eat to the religions we practice, our belief is that we are "normal" and everyone different from us are not.

Culture is one of the most complex sociological and anthropological concepts, and one of the most central concepts to understanding human behavior. Every society is made up of both material and nonmaterial culture. Material culture includes all tangible things within our society. Houses, architecture, art, clothes, toys and tools, are all examples of our material culture. All objects created within a particular society are a part of that society's material culture. Nonmaterial culture is comprised of mostly non-tangible items within a culture. Laws, language norms, values, beliefs, ideas, and customs are all components of nonmaterial culture.

Culture manifests itself in everything humans do—from birth to dying we experience culture. The clothes we place on our newborns, the way we wear our hair, our dating rituals, and our funeral and burial practices—all are parts of our culture. Culture is learned and shared with others within our society. Most people spend their entire lives in the culture in which they were born and often take for granted the way things are done. This is reinforced when visiting another country where it is not

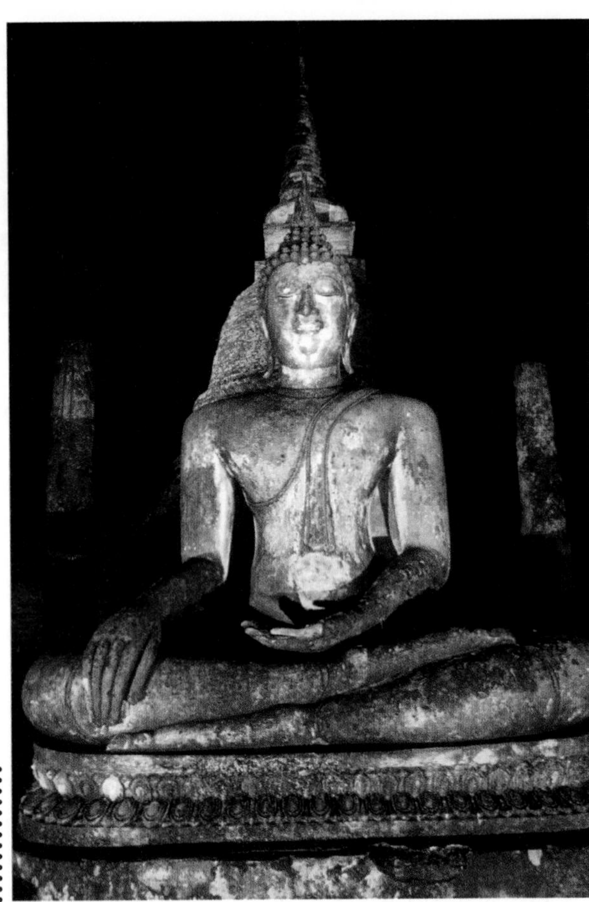

Material culture includes all objects created within a particular society, such as this statue of the Buddha.

uncommon for people to experience culture shock—a feeling of confusion, disbelief, or outrage by something found "normal" in another culture completely at odds with what is practiced in one's own culture. For example, street kids are a familiar sight in Rio de Janeiro, Brazil. These children are often abandoned by their families due to poverty and a government that has no formal social service agencies with which to deal with them. Left to survive on their own, the children often turn to begging or stealing to eat. Most street children living in alleys throughout the city were familiar with "child death squads." Merchants knew that tourists were likely to experience culture shock when they saw children begging for money or food in public. Therefore, in order to protect their businesses, merchants would sometimes turn to death squads to rid the alleys of street children. Members of death squads were mostly off duty police officers hired by a group of shop owners to rid the area of begging street children. Death squads would wait until nightfall and then move in to kill the children living in alleys around the shops. By sunrise the bodies of the children would be discovered, often with their hands tied behind their back and their tongues cut out. While the practice of targeting street children has declined, death squads continue to be an issue in Brazil, particularly among its poorest citizens. Culture shock can also occur within one's own society. While we don't expect to see homelessness and poverty in the United States to the degree found in Brazil, some would be shocked to learn that hundreds of people roam the streets of America each night in search of a place to sleep and eat. When proper shelter cannot be found, these homeless may sleep in subways, public restrooms, automobiles, and under bridges. When we look at cultural practices that are very different from our own, it is easy to become judgmental.

The attitude that our own culture is superior to others, that our own beliefs, values, and behaviors are more correct than others, and that other people and cultures do things wrong compared to our own culture is known as **ethnocentrism**. Ethnocentrism was defined by Sumner (1906, 13) as "that view of things in which one's own group is the center of everything and all others are scaled and rated with reference to it."

Most groups in any society tend to be ethnocentric. Religious groups believe that they know the "truth" and are more moral than others. Some will send missionaries to convert people, whom they consider to be backward and lost, from other religions. Scientists are equally likely to believe their methods are the best way to approach problems. Most Americans believe that monogamy is more "proper" than polygamy and that capitalism is far superior to communism. Most of us shudder when we read a headline such as "Restaurant in China Serves Rat 30 Ways" (*Wall Street Journal*, May 31, 1991). Many of us are likely to consider people who scar their bodies to be masochists. We are likely to believe that people who refuse to drink milk are ignorant and that people who walk around half-naked are shameless. However, we think it quite natural that American women paint their lips and hang jewelry from their ears, that men tie a strip of cloth around their necks, and that people eat corn, which is considered chicken food in many cultures.

The opposite of ethnocentrism is xenocentrism, the belief that what is foreign is best—that our own lifestyle, products, or ideas are inferior to those of others. The strange, distant, and exotic are regarded as having special value: cars made in Japan, watches made in Switzerland, beer brewed in Germany, fashions created in France, silks imported from India and Thailand, and gymnasts from eastern European countries are believed to be superior to our own. In some instances, feelings of xenocentrism are so strong that people reject their own group. Thus we find anti-American Americans, anti-Semitic Jews, priests who revolt against the church, blacks who reject a black identity, and family members who scorn their kin network. Xenocentrism may focus on a product, an idea, or a lifestyle. Regardless of the focus, it is assumed that native techniques and concepts are inferior.

Another form of cultural bias is temporocentrism, the belief that our own time is more important than the past or future. Accordingly, historical events are judged not in their own context but on the basis of contemporary standards. Our tendency toward temporocentrism leads us to assume that current crises are more crucial than those of other periods; therefore problems need to be solved now before it is too late. An associated belief is that actions taken now will have an enormous impact on life in the future. This belief could conceivably be warranted, as in the case of nuclear warfare that could end world civilization; but in most cases, what we do in our time will later be viewed as only a minor ripple on the stream of history.

Just as ethnocentrism is strongest among people with little education or exposure to other nations, temporocentrism is most prevalent among people who lack historical perspective. Even people with extensive educational training and a strong grasp of history tend to focus on the present, however. Politicians and social scientists view today as the critical time. Sermons, newspapers, and teachers stress that we are living in perilous times, that this is the age of transition.

Social scientists who study other cultures tend to be highly temporocentric, but most make special efforts to avoid ethnocentrism and xenocentrism. They attempt to view all behaviors, lifestyles, and ideas in their own context. The practice of examining cultures on their own terms and in relationship to their institutions and environment rather than by the standards of another culture is **cultural relativism**.

According to the cultural relativistic perspective, an act, idea, form of dress, or other cultural manifestation is not inherently right or wrong, correct or incorrect. These things should be examined only in the context in which they occur; what is appropriate in one culture or context may be inappropriate in another. Nudity in the shower or at a nudist colony is appropriate, but nudity in the classroom is inappropriate. In some hunting societies, being fat may have survival value and may serve as a source of admiration. In America, however, fatness is regarded as unhealthy and rarely serves as a source of admiration. The practice of abandoning unwanted infants would be viewed as intolerable by most contemporary cultures; however, many cultures used to follow this practice, and some still do. The point is that any aspect of a culture must be considered within its larger cultural context. Each aspect may be regarded as good if it is acceptable to the members and helps attain desired goals, and bad if it is unacceptable or fails to achieve these goals.

Cultural relativity does *not* mean that a behavior appropriate in one place is appropriate everywhere, nor does it mean that all behaviors are condoned simply because they make sense in a cultural context. It is not a license to do as one would wish. Even though having multiple wives makes sense for many Saudi Arabian men, killing female infants makes sense in a Brazilian tribe, and wearing loincloths makes sense to African Bushmen, these behaviors are not acceptable to most Americans. They make sense in some societies because they are part of a larger belief and value system and are consistent with other norms appropriate to that cultural setting. Examining other societies on the basis of cultural relativism makes us less likely to ridicule or scorn the beliefs and habits of people from other cultures; but, more importantly, we won't make mistakes similar to those of the past by acting on ethnocentric beliefs.

Ethnocentrism can encourage racism, discourage integration efforts, increase hostility and conflicts among groups, and prevent changes that could be beneficial to all. Ethnocentrism can increase resistance to change and can encourage the exclusion of outsiders who may have something good to contribute. Carried to an extreme, ethnocentrism is destructive, as evidenced by the Nazis in Germany that believed in the absolute superiority of the "white Aryan" race and culture. The result was the death of millions of people who did not fit into this category. While ethnocentric cultures have confidence in their own traditions, they discourage outsiders and thus protect themselves against change. Cultures that consider themselves superior tend to maintain the status quo—if our culture is already best, why change it?

Thinking Sociologically

1. Provide a behavior seen as "normal" in the United States but likely seen as a culture shock for people from another country.

2. Explain a time when you have experienced culture shock within your own society.

APPLYING CULTURAL RELATIVISM

The worth of cultural relativism goes beyond analyzing or judging other societies. That aspect is important for social scientists, but the cultural relativistic perspective is also important for anyone who comes into contact with people from different cultures. Consider, for example, teachers in the United States who are faced with the growing number of students from minority cultures and the prospect of teaching within bilingual education programs. Many teachers have been taught to judge students by the norms of white, middle-class children (See and Strauss 1985).

However, **norms** are different from culture to culture. For example, a Native American student might pause two or three seconds before answering a question as a courtesy to the questioner. A Hawaiian student might interrupt a questioner because such behavior displays interest. Hispanic and Asian children might not maintain eye contact with the teacher because they were raised in cultures in which it is disrespectful to maintain eye contact with someone of higher status. In these situations, it is possible that the teachers might interpret such children's actions as signs of being unprepared, inattentive, or disrespectful—treating them accordingly. This ethnocentrism on the part of the teachers could decrease their effectiveness. Ronald Tharp, a professor at the University of California who studies culture and education among ethnic groups, notes, "Every little classroom is turning into a United Nations ...with all the hazards and complexities that involves. It's as if every teacher has to be a former U.N. Secretary General Javier Perez] de Cuellar" (Marklein 1991, 9D).

Cultural relativism is important in any type of situation that involves people with different cultural backgrounds. As sociologists See and Strauss (1985, 69) note, "Utilizing the cultural [relativistic] approach in the practice of counseling, education, public administration, and the health-care and service professions means that special attention is placed on how the individual one is dealing with analyzes situations given their particular cultural backgrounds, social characteristics, and group affiliations."

The approach also makes good business sense. The would-be entrepreneur from New York who visits the South and notices the lack of Jewish delicatessens might think she has stumbled upon a "gold mine." Assuming that a commodity that is highly valued in one cultural region will be just as "hot" in another region might lead to a financial disaster.

ELEMENTS OF CULTURE

Understanding culture can sometimes be difficult; however, it can be easier if one knows the components of culture. As previously mentioned, nonmaterial culture is comprised of symbols, language, values, beliefs, and norms. In addition, material culture is highly influenced by technology or the innovations and inventions occurring frequently in our society. The following is a more comprehensive look at each of these elements of culture.

Symbols

The existence of culture depends on people's ability to create and understand symbols. A **symbol** is something

FIGURE 4-1 THE ELEMENTS OF CULTURE

Non-Material	
Symbols	An object or event that represents another object or event only because people agree as to its meaning
Values	Subjective reactions to experiences expressed in terms of good or bad, moral or immoral, the ideals that people look up to but do not necessarily achieve or pursue.
Beliefs	The ideas people hold about what is true and/or real are considered their beliefs
Norms	Shared rules that define how people are supposed to behave under particular circumstances
Emotions	Inner reactions to experiences. Societies enculturate (teach) its members to associate certain emotions with specific situations and to experience these emotional states at various intensities depending on the context
Attitudes	Likes and dislikes, and general preference for certain experiences over others
Laws	Norms defined by political authorities as principles that members of a society must follow
Perceptions	Interpretations of cultural phenomenon which may vary from person to person due to his or her unique experience as a member of society
Aspirations	Ambitions and goals that are valued and desired within a culture
Technological Knowledge	Human knowledge of the techniques and methods for subsistence (how one makes a living, acquires the calories for survival) and/or control and adaptation to the cultural and natural environment
Material	
Artifacts	The material products of culture, past and present
Technology	The tools and products used for subsistence and/or control and adaptation to the cultural and natural environment

Source: The Elements of Culture (Basirico and Bolin, in Arcaro and Haskell, 2010, p. 39.

that is used to represent something else. Words, numbers, flags, crosses, and kisses are symbols. During World War II, raising the middle and index fingers of one hand was the symbol "V" for victory. During the 1960s, the same gesture came to symbolize "peace." Raising the middle finger, or putting thumbs up or thumbs down, or spreading one's thumb and little finger ("hang loose" in Hawaii)—all convey particular meanings. In the same way, a stop sign is a symbol meaning "halt" and a cross is a symbol of Christianity.

Symbols are arbitrary designations. There is no necessary connection between a symbol and what it represents. There is nothing inherent in the act of holding one's thumb up that indicates we approve of something. Neither is there anything inherent in an "A-Okay" gesture, signaled by forming a circle with the thumb and forefinger and holding up the other three fingers. Many people in the United States use it to signify that "all is fine." However, to use that same symbol in France and Belgium would convey a message that a person is of

A symbol, such as a flag, is an integral part of a culture—a culture's existence depends on the ability of that cultures members to understand it. Symbols are arbitrary designations in that a connection between a symbol and what it represents may not necessarily exist.

little or no worth. In Greece and Turkey, it would suggest an insulting sexual invitation. In parts of Italy, it would be an offensive reference to one part of the female anatomy. It's no wonder that interpersonal relationships among people from different cultures are influenced by an awareness of the meanings attached to symbols.

It is important to realize that symbols are collective creations. They are not only products of group experiences and needs, but they also shape a group's experiences and future needs. Astute entrepreneurs—restaurateurs, physicians, retail store managers, and so forth—often use their insights about the clientele they are trying to attract and display symbols that are meaningful to their target groups (for example, yuppies, born-again Christians, Italians, or liberals). A dentist in a college town who is trying to build a clientele of students might be better off having the office radio tuned to rock music rather than to Mozart, having copies of *Rolling Stone* magazine available rather than *U.S. News and World Report*, and dressing casually rather than wearing a pin-striped suit. Many advertising agencies realize the importance of cultural symbols and distinguish between *general marketing*, aimed at the total population, and *segmented marketing*, aimed at specific ethnic, racial, or other groups. Segmented marketing uses symbols such as speech patterns (accents, slang), music, clothing, objects, hand signals, and other symbolic elements that are thought to be characteristic of the group the advertisers are trying to attract.

Only humans can assign symbols to represent the objects around them; this is one of the things that makes humans different from animals and enables us to create cultures. The difference is not one of degree. It is not that humans have better reasoning ability than animals. Rather, it is a fundamental difference in kind. Most sociologists assume that the ability to use symbols is uniquely human and that animals do not communicate symbolically or deal with abstractions. Unlike animals, human beings can use symbols to understand reality, to transmit messages, to store complex information, and to deal with an abstract symbolic world. Our success or failure in many relationships, from personal to professional, often depends on our ability to communicate symbolically.

Language

The most important set of symbols is **language**. Language, among humans, is the systematized usage of speech and hearing to convey or express feelings and ideas. It is through language that our ideas, values, beliefs, and knowledge are transmitted, expressed, and shared. Other media—such as music, art, and dance—are also important means of communication, but language is uniquely flexible and precise. It permits us to share our experiences from the past and present, to convey our hopes for the future, and to describe dreams and fantasies that may bear little resemblance to reality. Some scientists have questioned whether thought is even possible

Language is used to convey feelings and ideas; it is the most important set of symbols in a culture. Although not all societies are able to read and write their language, all societies possess a spoken language.

without language. Although language can be used imprecisely and can seem hard to understand, it is the chief factor in our ability to transmit culture.

All human societies have languages. Although there are thousands of different languages in the world, linguistic behavior, as such, is universal. Some societies cannot read or write their language, but they all have a spoken language. Like symbols, language is uniquely human, which is one of the basic distinctions between human beings and other forms of life. Like the use of symbols, the difference between humans and animals is a difference in *kind*, not merely in *degree*.

Note, for example, the difference between a human being and a chimpanzee, believed to be one of the most intelligent animals. Numerous experiments (Hayes 1951; Kellogg and Kellogg 1933) over the past sixty years by psychologists who reared both infants and chimpanzees lead most sociologists to conclude that language is the key to understanding differences between the two forms of life. Chimpanzees lack the neural equipment to either generate speech or comprehend language. Although chimps emit sounds and respond to commands, their sounds do not constitute a system of symbols and their responses do not involve a system of shared definitions and meanings. Chimpanzees also lack the type of pharynx found in humans, a pharynx with size, shape, and mobility crucial to the production of speech. Epstein (2000) sees the inability of chimpanzees to develop language as a critique of the Animal Rights movement's attempt to grant rights to prevent the capture and exploitation of chimpanzees and bonobos. One important question that this raises is whether or not language as we know it (that is, verbal communication) is the only form of language.

Language is so basic to culture and essential for human interaction and social organization that it is often taken for granted but we can only speculate as to its origins. Did it begin with the imitation of sounds of nature, such as running water or wind in the trees? Did it start with the utterance of grunts, sighs, coughs, and groans? Did it originate in calls and sounds that came to be shared by group members and later expanded to include new experiences and objects? We do not know. There do seem to be attributes shared by many of the world's languages, however. Regularities of words over time and place, and the widespread use of certain words, indicate that language is an integral and universal part of culture. Linguistic symbols are learned and shared just like other cultural elements.

Cultures develop not only a verbal and written language, but also a nonverbal language of gestures, expressions, mannerisms, and even the use of space. Latin American and North American (Canada and the United States) cultures, for example, use space between people differently during conversation. For Spanish speakers, standing close conveys cordiality and sincerity, whereas for English speakers it conveys pushiness. The distance that English speakers see as proper for conversations, Spanish speakers see as cold. Knowledge of another culture's nonverbal or "silent" language is invaluable for any type of interaction that involves people from different cultures, such as international businesspeople, lawyers, politicians, or diplomats. Business deals and international agreements often rely heavily on the private interaction of a few high-powered individuals. A deal might easily be soured if one party interprets the other's normal speaking distance as pushy or standoffish.

Suppose that you are a lawyer hired by an American electronics company that relies on Japanese parts. Part of your job entails securing a long-term contract to ensure that the company can continue to import the parts it needs for its products. It might help you in your negotiations with the lawyers that represent the Japanese firm to learn about the nonverbal language used by Japanese people in their conversations and to learn how they interpret some of our nonverbal language. What do they consider to be polite standing or sitting distance between people? Are there any American gestures that we tend to use in our communication with others that might be offensive to Japanese people? What are some Japanese gestures that convey warmth, trust, and honesty?

Language influences people's thoughts and experiences to a greater degree than generally recognized. In 1929, Edward Sapir argued that people see and interpret the world through the grammatical forms, labels, and categories provided by their language. He contended that societies with different languages actually perceive the world differently—that is, they do not just use a different set of labels to describe the same things.

This idea is known as the **Sapir-Whorf hypothesis**. While working for an insurance company, Benjamin Whorf, a student of Sapir, noted that workman handling barrels of gasoline were very careful about matches and cigarettes when the barrels were full, but they became careless and caused many accidents once the label *empty* had been applied to a barrel. In other words, the application of the word *empty* to a barrel influenced the workers' perception and consequent behavior (Whorf 1941). Intrigued by this finding, he began to study different cultures to see whether the language they used influenced people's behavior. He found that language does influence the way we perceive things and how we behave.

As examples, note how words such as *snow* or *banana* create a certain mental image. What do you see when you hear those words? Would you see something different if a precise word or symbol existed for snow, depending on whether it was falling, drifting, frozen, fresh, compacted, in a cone, and so on? Would you behave differently (drive your car, go skiing, eat it, build a snowman), depending on your perception? Is a banana just a banana? Or as to most Filipinos, do bananas differ in their size, colors, and uses and require precise words or symbols to convey the banana desired? Interpreters of languages such as Hebrew, Russian, or German often find that no parallel word exists in English for the word they are trying to translate. Thus, they can only try to convey in English the "reality" of the word they are translating. The Sapir-Whorf hypothesis appears to be valid: Our perceptions of reality are greatly influenced by our language. Languages are learned, shared, and transmitted from one generation to another; they are a central element of culture.

There has been great debate in recent years about whether or not our native language actually constrains our ability to understand a concept, such as time or space. Current research suggests that one's language does not prevent one from being able to understand something that language does shape how often and how deeply we think about certain things, and perhaps even our attitudes or feelings towards something (Deutscher 2010). For example, one thing that differentiates English from languages such as French, Italian, or German is that nouns in English are not gender specific. If an object is gendered because of language (for example, la or el in Spanish), it may be possible that affects our perceptions, our attitudes, or even the way we use an object.

Regardless of how and why the connection between perception and language exists, the Sapir-Whorf hypothesis helps us to realize the necessity of studying foreign languages. Learning a foreign language is important not only because it allows us to speak to non-English-speaking people but also because it allows us to see their view of reality and what they deem as important. For those whose work involves interaction with people from different countries—foreign diplomats, ambassadors, politicians, international businesspeople and lawyers, social workers, or others—being able to speak directly, rather than through an interpreter, is essential for complete understanding.

Thinking Sociologically

1. Is language a distinctively human activity? Explain why or why not.

2. Relate the Sapir-Whorf hypothesis to your personal life or academic field of study. Show how the language or the specific terminology in your discipline influences your perceptions of reality and your experiences.

Values

Values are ideas shared by the people in a society regarding what is important and worthwhile. Our values are the basis of our judgments about what is desirable, beautiful, correct, and good—as well as what is undesirable, ugly, incorrect, and bad. Most values have both positive and negative counterparts, which are reciprocally related. If you place a high positive value on fighting for your country, for example, you probably place a high negative value on those who refuse to fight. If you value marital sexual exclusiveness, you probably disapprove of those who engage in extramarital sexual relationships. Values are often emotionally charged because they stand for things we believe to be worth defending.

Most of our basic values are learned early in life from family, friends, the mass media, and other sources within society. The value of saving money, for example, may be conveyed directly by parents or others but may, also, be reinforced in more subtle ways as through proverbs. Most of us are familiar with common sayings such as, "A penny saved is a penny earned" or "Waste not, want not" (values that convey frugality or the value of saving money). By whatever manner they are conveyed or learned, the values are generally shared and reinforced by those with whom we interact. Placing a high value on religious faith, honesty, cleanliness, freedom, money, children, education, or work serves as a general guide for our behavior and the formation of specific attitudes. Since values indicate what is proper or improper, they tend to justify particular types of behavior and to forbid others.

When basic values are in conflict, we usually place them in a hierarchy of importance and behave in ways consistent with the most important. During a war, for example, the value of patriotism may overcome the value that human life is precious, or vice versa. When it is impossible to place our values in a hierarchy to resolve a conflict, we may feel guilty or suffer mental stress.

To give another example of value conflict, consider the case of a parent who enjoys spending time with the family. If job demands take this parent away from the family for extended periods, the parent is likely to feel stress. To avoid stress, the parent could quit his or her job, take the family along on job trips, justify the job demands as being in the best interests of the family, compromise on both family and job demands, or leave the family. Some of these choices may be impossible, however. Quitting the job or taking the family along may not be realistic alternatives, and divorce may conflict with social and religious values. Mental stress is likely to result when choices are impossible. The alternative courses of action, as well as the choice selected, will generally be consistent with the values of the society and with those most important to the individual.

Sometimes, our stated values and our behavior are inconsistent. We may place a high value on freedom of

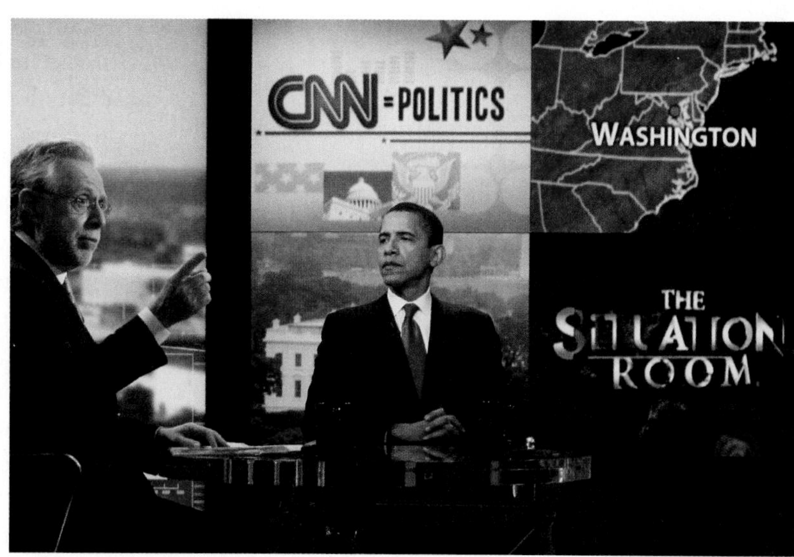

Values are the basis for our moral judgments and are shared by the members of a society. Shaped in part by television and other mass media outlets, values have reciprocally related positive and negative counterparts.

the press but want to censor communist writings. We may place a high value on individualism but want to punish people whose behavior is inconsistent with our definition of appropriate behavior. Our true values are often reflected more by what we do than by what we say. If we say we value education but have no interest in attending classes or paying for public schools, or if we say that we value simplicity but spend money conspicuously to display our wealth, our actions expose our real values.

Since values are learned cultural products, they differ from one society to another. Americans, for example, tend to be individualistic, using personal characteristics and achievements to define themselves, while societies such as Japan and the Israeli kibbutzim focus more on group harmony, unity, and loyalty. North Americans tend to see themselves as dominant over nature, while societies such as the Chinese or subcultures such as the Navajo see themselves as living in harmony with nature. Residents of Canada and the United States are more conscious of being "on time" than those in Asia and the Middle East.

Most cultures, despite diversity in their populations, tend to share certain value patterns. In American society, Sociologist Robin M. Williams (1970) described fifteen value orientations important in United States American life and are still are at the core of U.S. American culture today:

1. **Achievement and Success** We stress personal achievement, especially secular occupational achievement.
2. **Activity and Work** Every able–bodied person should work and not expect handouts.
3. **Moral Orientation** People should know the difference between right and wrong.
4. **Humanitarian Motives** We should help others who are in a crisis.
5. **Efficiency and Practicality** We should strive to be as efficient and thrifty as possible.
6. **Process and Progress** Our society favors technology and innovations.
7. **Material Comfort** Through hard work, we can use our money to buy a house, cars, and other material possessions.
8. **Equality** Everyone has an equal opportunity to succeed.
9. **Freedom** We believe in freedom to pursue our goals.
10. **External Conformity** Everyone should adhere to similarity and uniformity in speech, manners, housing, dress, recreation, politically expressed ideas, and group patterns.
11. **Science and Rationality** We know that science can solve problems, and we have faith in those who strive to make life better for us.
12. **Nationalism** We believe in the American system—it's institutions, government, and education.
13. **Democracy** Our system advocates majority rule.
14. **Individualism** We believe in personal responsibilities.
15. **Racism and Group Superiority** We evaluate people based on group performance and placement within society.

The extent to which such traditional U.S. American value orientations have changed has become a topic of study in recent years, especially in light of the effects of globalization and increased diversity in American society (Brunner 2003; Coon and Kemmelmeier 2001; Kester 2001).

It must be kept in mind that these are general themes in American values, which change constantly. They are often in conflict, and they are not all exhibited in a single person's behavior. Sometimes, they even appear to be inconsistent. How can we value both independence and conformity, or equality and racial differentiation? Some of the explanations for these inconsistencies lie in whether the value is applied generally or specifically. A person might say, for example, "Our society believes strongly in freedom of the press, but I don't want my town library to carry novels with explicit sex in them." Other explanations may reflect the beliefs of different regions of the country.

William's states that most conflicts between value systems in the United States occur between those centering on individual personalities and those organized around categorical themes or conceptions. Group discrimination and racism, as categorical themes, are contrary to other central values of the society. Each of these values has a historical base and a complexity far greater than is evident in this brief discussion. Evidence does suggest, however, a decline in racist beliefs over several

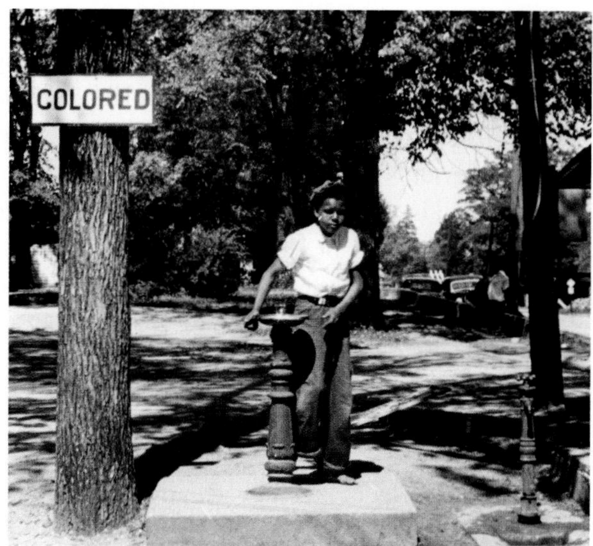

As this photo shows, racial segregation was still in existence in the twentieth century.

decades. Legislation has forced movements away from enforced segregation and public discrimination; and Congress has passed Civil Rights Acts and a series of laws that forbid discrimination because of race, sex, religion, nationality, place of birth, or place of residence. Thus, while a central value may continue to exist, which grants privilege based on group or racial affiliation, some evidence suggests that this particular theme may be fading.

An understanding of value systems can be useful for many people in their work. In a discussion of how to manage organizational conflict, for example, Hampton, Summer, and Webber (1982) emphasize the importance of being able to recognize that competing value systems are often the source of the conflict. They state the following:

> Instances of inadequate sharing of values and of competing goals are numerous. Individual self-actualization versus collective will is one value conflict that has been and will be fought on many battlefields. At a business level, salespeople value company responsiveness to the customer, while production personnel value equilibrium and predictability; engineers value ingenuity and quality, while finance values the profit margin; marketing emphasizes gross income, while the credit department values minimum credit loss, and so on. (p. 635)

A way to deal with these competing value systems is to try to create common values. Some experts on how to manage corporations suggest that successful organizations do this by developing stories, slogans, myths, and legends about the corporation (e.g., Kanter 1983; Peters and Waterman 1982). These help to decrease conflict and create a greater sense of mutuality. The "human relations school of management" relies heavily on the notion that sharing values is important for members of large corporations.

Thinking Sociologically

1. Critique the values suggested by Williams. What differences do you believe exists between the ones he suggested more than forty years ago and the ones we have today? Discuss why you think values have changed or have stayed the same.

2. To what extent do people have the right (or obligation) to impose their values on others (parents on children, a religious group on those of other religions, a culture on a subculture, etc.)? Illustrate with specific examples.

Norms

Norms are elements of non-material culture and are rules of conduct or social expectations for behavior. These rules and social expectations specify how people should and should not behave in various social situations. They are both *prescriptive* (they tell people what they should do) and *proscriptive* (they tell people what they should not do).

Whereas values are abstract conceptions of what is important and worthwhile, social *norms* are standards, rules, guides, and expectations for actual behavior. Norms and values are likely to be conceptually consistent, but values are less situation-bound and are more general and abstract. Norms link values with actual events. *Honesty* is a general value; the expectation that students will not cheat on tests is a norm. Most norms permit a range of behaviors—that is, some kinds or degrees of overconformity and underconformity are expected and tolerated, particularly in some settings or situations. We would not criticize a starving man for lying to get food, for example.

An early U.S. American sociologist, William G. Sumner (1840–1910), identified two types of norms, which he labeled "folkways" and "mores." They are distinguished not by their content but by the degree to which group members are compelled to conform to them, by their degree of importance, by the severity of punishment if they are violated, or by the intensity of feeling associated with adherence to them. **Folkways** are customs or conventions. They are norms, in that they provide rules for conduct; but violations of folkways bring only mild censure. In the United States, most adults are expected to eat vegetables with a fork rather than a spoon or knife or chopsticks, and most students attend classes in pants or skirts rather than gowns or bathing suits. If you eat vegetables with a spoon or attend class in a gown or bathing suit, the chances are you will not be arrested or beaten; however, you may receive some smiles, glances, or occasional comments from others. Why? It may be easier to use a spoon for eating vegetables, and on hot days, a bathing suit may be more comfortable attire. The reason that people would express mild disapproval is that these behaviors violate folkways that exist in the United States.

Like other norms, folkways are learned in interaction with others and are passed down from generation to generation. Folkways change as culture changes or when we enter different situations. Our tendency is to accept the folkways as appropriate without question. Why do suburbanites fertilize lawns and keep them trimmed? Why do people avoid facing one another in elevators? Why are people expected to chew food quietly and with their mouths closed? No written rules are being violated in these situations, and no one is being physically harmed. These are simply the folkways of our culture, the set of norms that specify the way things are usually done; and people who violate these norms are punished only mildly if at all.

Mores are considered more important than folkways, and reactions to their violation are more serious. They are more likely than folkways to involve clear-cut distinctions between right and wrong, and they are more closely associated with the moral values a society considers important. Violations of mores inspire intense reactions, and some type of punishment inevitably follows. The punishment may involve expulsion from the group, harsh ridicule, imprisonment, or—in some cases—even death. Why don't people have sex in public? Why don't physicians end the life of elderly people who have terminal illnesses? Why don't people betray their country's well-being for money? Actions such as these violate cultural mores. Mores that prohibit something, that state, "thou shalt not," are **taboos**. To love and care for one's children is a *mos* (the Latin singular of *mores*); to commit incest (marry or have intercourse) with them or neglect them is a taboo. In the United States, people who murder, commit treason, or engage in incest are widely regarded as sinful and wicked. They violate the mores of society by engaging in taboo behaviors.

Since folkways and mores differ only in degree, it is sometimes difficult to tell them apart. Furthermore, because folkways and mores are elements of culture, they vary from one society or subculture to another. The physical punishment of children may be a folkway in some cultures and a taboo in others. Killing may be rewarded in war but condemned in one's local community. Marriage between same sex couples may be acceptable in a few states and a strong taboo in many other states. To function effectively in a culture, one must learn the culture's appropriate folkways and mores.

Certain norms about which a society feels strongly may become laws, which are formal, standardized expressions of norms enacted by legislative bodies to regulate particular types of behaviors. **Laws** do not merely state what behaviors are not permitted; they also state the punishment for violating the law. Ideally, the punishment should reflect the seriousness of the crime or civil offense and should be carried out by a judicial system. This system legitimizes physical coercion and is above the control of any individual member of a society. Within the boundaries of their duties, members of a judicial system can use physical force, imprison, or even kill without retaliation. Laws, therefore, are formalized legislated norms that are enforced by a group designated for that purpose. In contrast, folkways and mores (unless they are made into laws) are enforced only by the members of society themselves, not by a separate group designated as enforcers.

When a law does not reflect folkways and mores, its enforcement is likely to be ignored or given low priority. Although certain actions may be formally defined as illegal in certain communities (shopping on Sundays, smoking marijuana, having sex outside of marriage), enforcement is ignored because of changing folkways or mores that grant a degree of social approval to the behavior. This suggests that conformity to the norms of society does not come from formal law-enforcement officials but, rather, from the informal interaction of members of society. Members of society follow most norms, but adherence is not rigid. Adaptations to changing conditions are possible, and a certain degree of deviation from existing norms is both possible and beneficial for the effective functioning of society.

Indeed, it is important to realize that cultural norms (folkways and mores) are not always beneficial for a society, group, or individual. Some norms may actually be harmful, what Erich Fromm (1965) calls the "**pathology of normalcy.**" Thus, we can follow cultural norms when they do not harm us, but we do not always have to follow them. You might be able to improve the quality of your life if you analyze the costs and benefits of the norms you are expected to follow by society or by your peer group. As one clinical sociologist notes,

> Is it part of your peer subculture to take the easy way through school rather than to read, research, study, learn basic skills, and treat teachers and others with respect even while you disagree with them? The benefit of following peer-group norms of little work might be a degree with "no sweat," but the costs may be educationally empty school years, boredom, a bad conscience, a lack of pride in oneself, few solid accomplishments, and lifelong deficits in skills such as reading, writing, and critical thinking. Researching and analyzing the student subculture may show a pathology of normalcy. (Cohen 1985, 46)

In this case, you might decide to deviate from the norms in order to maximize your gains. The process of violating norms beyond the range of group acceptability is called "deviance," and the process of applying sanctions to obtain social conformity is known as "social control."

Technology and Material Culture

In addition to the nonmaterial aspects of culture— symbols, language, values, norms, and laws— there are certain material techniques and products used by societies to maintain their standards of living and their lifestyles. The practical production and application of these techniques and products is a culture's **technology**. Technology applies the knowledge gained by science in ways that influence all aspects of culture. It includes social customs and practical techniques for converting raw materials to finished products. The production and use of food, shelter, and clothing, as well as commodities and physical structures, are also aspects of a society's technology.

An Ethiopian woman makes dough from banana stems. Such production and use of food is part of her material culture, which helps maintain her society's standard of living and lifestyle. It also reflects her society's technology—the knowledge gained and applied by its members.

SOCIOLOGY AT WORK

Teen Girls Help FBI Nab Cyber Stalkers

In 2008 there were an estimated 220 million Internet users in the United States, representing over 72 percent of the population. According to Nielsen Online Data (2008), the average person spends over thirty-seven hours per month on the Internet and views an average of 1,489 web pages during that time. While adults access the Internet regularly, the number of children online continues to grow. Children use personal computers for numerous reasons, including school assignments, often requiring them to access information from several online sources. In addition to school work, young persons are using the Internet to play games and to socialize. Over 90 percent of young people between twelve and seventeen years of age access the Internet regularly. In 2007, an estimated 55 percent of them had a profile on a social networking site such as Facebook or MySpace, and 47 percent admitted to uploading personal pictures onto their profile for others to view (Pew Internet and American Life Project, 2007).

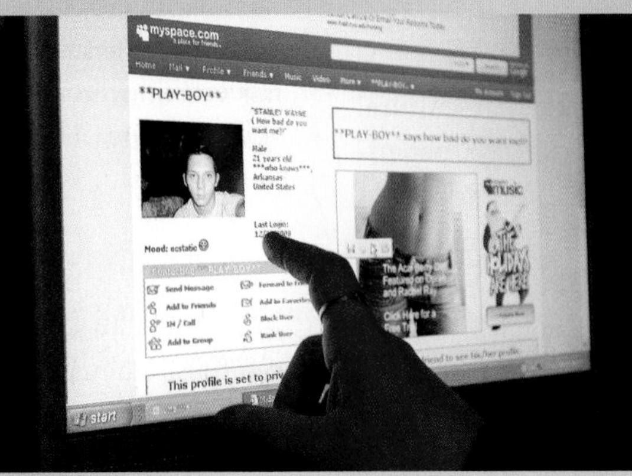

The fear of children becoming the victims of online predators continues to grow in conjunction with the number of young people accessing the Internet. Parents, law enforcement, and advocacy groups search for new ways to lessen the possibility that children will fall victim to pedophiles skilled in the behaviors of young people online. The FBI estimates that at any given time twenty thousand sexual predators are lurking online to persuade children to provide personal information about themselves or, even worse, to meet them outside their homes.

According to the Center for Missing and Exploited Children, the number of incidents of predators communicating with children is intensifying. The Federal Bureau of Investigation (FBI) began trying to learn as much about the behavior of young people online to combat the possibility they would be convinced to meet a predator offline. However, the agents were not familiar with the sites or language used by young Internet users, and pedophiles caught on quickly, lessening the chances they would be caught.

The FBI decided to enlist the help of young people to train agents in the online culture of children. An agent sought the help of his daughter and some of her friends who regularly used the Internet and were familiar with the behaviors of other young people. When the girls first arrived, they administered a multiple choice and true/false test to measure the agents' knowledge of teen culture. Every agent failed the test. According to fourteen-year-old Mary, one of the trainers, "They, like, don't know anything." Her friend Karen, another fourteen-year-old, rolled her eyes and added, "They're, like, do you like Michael Jackson?"—obviously indicating how outdated the agents were on their understanding of young people.

By 2005, the girls had trained over five hundred FBI agents from around the country on music, movies, and computer language, particularly the abbreviations used by young Internet users. As a result, within the first few years, the FBI arrested over 2,600 online sexual predators. The agents continue to receive regular training; however, Mary and Karen are no longer the trainers because, at age sixteen, they are too old. To stay on top, the FBI makes certain their training comes from young persons knowledgeable in the culture of teenagers who regularly use the Internet.

These physical products are **artifacts**. A society's artifacts can be very diverse: beer cans, religious objects, pottery, art, pictures, typewriters, computer terminals, buildings and building materials, clothes, books, and even contraceptive devices. Material artifacts reflect the nonmaterial culture—symbols, beliefs, values, norms, and behaviors—shared by the members of a society.

Artifacts provide clues to a society's level of technological development. Americans, especially those of European descent, take great pride in their level of technology. The ability to perform heart transplants, to split atoms, and to produce sophisticated patriotic missiles, supersonic jets, computers, and environmentally controlled living and working conditions leads us to perceive our type of culture as superior, advanced, and progressive. This perception is often accompanied by a belief that cultures with a low level of technological development are inferior and not progressive.

These are subjective perceptions, however, not scientific criteria for evaluating cultures. A more objective evaluation of what some call "less-developed" cultures indicates that they possess an amazing degree of skill and ingenuity in dealing with the environment. Many, apparently crude techniques are based on fundamental principles of engineering. Today, people marvel at the rice terraces built several thousand years ago on mountainsides in Asia, which included water distribution systems that seem difficult to improve on today. These rice fields produced food for generations of families and communities without the aid of diesel tractors, complex machinery, or hybrid rice plants; many are still in use. Anthropologists know of countless instances of the survival of people under conditions that few members of "highly developed" cultures could endure. The adobe huts of Native Americans, the igloos of the Eskimos, or the bamboo houses of rural southeast Asia—none of which have indoor plumbing, heating, or air conditioning—would be inadequate homes for most members of more technologically advanced cultures. Yet these people's technology is suited to and perfectly adequate for their particular lifestyles. It could be argued that in more developed nations, the technology is developed by a handful of specialists, and so the general population is less technologically proficient than members of so-called primitive groups.

The goals and consequences of technology and the production of material goods are being seriously questioned today. Does a high level of technology increase happiness and improve family life? Do complex technologies bring us clean air and pure water or help us conserve natural resources? All cultures possess a technology so that they can apply knowledge to master the environment and to interact effectively with nature. It is a mistake to dismiss a culture's technological system because it appears less developed or complex than our own.

THE WEB OF CULTURE

Where does culture come from? This is a question that sociologists and anthropologists (especially) have been examining since the birth of these disciplines. One answer is that cultures arise from agreements of people within a social system (be it among people within a geographic region, such as a country, or an organization) about things that are essential to their survival (Babbie 1977, 1980) and in response to environmental factors. Social systems develop mechanisms and sets of rules to meet basic survival needs such as how reproduction practices are regulated, how we insure that children are cared for, how we regulate power, how we insure that basic material needs are met, how knowledge is disseminated, how we provide for spiritual nourishment, and more. Some of the things that are necessary for a social system to survive are universal, and some are distinct to particular organizations. Sociologists refer to these sets of rules as "institutions" (Basirico and Bolin 2010, 42). Some of the universal institutions found throughout the world include family, economics, politics, religion, health care, and education. These certainly are not the only institutions that exist. You will learn more about these institutions in Part 4 of this book. Culture, then, refers to all of those ways of life (practices and what we think) that both stem from and shape social institutions. It is important to understand the relationship between culture and institutions because without that understanding, it is easy to become judgmental of other cultures.

Basirico and Bolin refer to a "web of culture" and emphasize that it is difficult to understand the elements of culture (Figure 4.1) without understanding the relationship between the elements of culture and institutions. They use the analogy of a rubber band ball to illustrate the relationship between the elements of culture and institutions to a rubber band ball:

"Think of the separate rubber bands as elements of culture—values, beliefs, norms, symbols, technology, and so on. Now, think not just of one value, one belief, one symbol, and so on but think of the hundreds of examples of values, beliefs, norms, symbols, and so forth in a particular place. Imagine that each rubber band represents one value, belief, symbol, norm, etc. Further, imagine that other rubber bands represent social institutions—the family, the economy, politics, religion, education, health care, and so forth. Think of how intertwined the strands of a rubber-band ball are and how they create something solid, real, and tangible that is much more than the individual strands. The relationship between the elements of culture and institutions is a little like that ball in that they create a whole culture that is greater than the individual parts" (2010, 43).

In order to help understand the relationship between the elements of culture and institutions within any

FIGURE 4-2 WEB OF CULTURE

	Non-Material Culture						Material Culture	
Structures/ Institutions	Symbols	Values	Beliefs	Norms	Emotions	Laws	Artifacts	Technology
Family Kinships								
Educational Systems								
Economic Systems								
Government/ Political systems								
Religious/Magical Systems								
Sex & Gender Systems								
Healthcare Systems								
Military Systems								
Arts and Leisure Systems								
Non-kinship Assoc./ Interest Groups								

Source: The Web of culture (Basirico and Bolin, in Arcaro and Haskell, eds., 2010, p.45.)

particular culture, Basirico and Bolin suggest using a matrix to analyze your observations of that culture (See Figure 4.2) They provide an instructive example of how you might analyze a wedding ceremony in the United States. First, think of what you might observe at such a ceremony. For example, you might notice who is performing the ceremony (priest, minister, rabbi, justice of the peace), what the bride is wearing, rings, invoking the use of the word "God," a limousine, a father "giving away" the bride, and many other things. Next, try to place each of these observations in the "web of culture "matrix. Notice that you might be able to place some of your observations in more than one box. Now think a little more conceptually about the relationship between each of the elements of culture that you observed and the institutions and how they may reinforce each other.

Imagine taking this analytical approach to examine entire cultures in detail. Imagine again using this method to examine a culture that is very different than yours, perhaps even one that may seem deviant, and how it would help you to understand that culture in a non-judgmental way. The web of culture approach is one way that you can understand cultures in a culturally relativistic manner.

CULTURAL DIVERSITY

A culture is not simply an accumulation of isolated symbols, languages, values, norms, behaviors, and technology. It is a complex and diverse system of many interdependent factors influenced by physical circumstances—climate, geography, population, and plant and animal life. Eskimos traditionally eat meat almost exclusively, live in igloos or huts made of skins, and dress in furs. Many societies in tropical rain forests have diets composed primarily of fruits and vegetables, live in shelters made of leaves and branches, and wear few clothes. Physical circumstances, however, may have less influence on a culture's functioning than such social factors as contact with other cultures, the stage of technological development, or the prevailing ideologies (the assertions and theories characteristic of the group). The complexity and diversity of a culture can be better understood by examining various units of a culture, such as subcultures, countercultures, idiocultures, the ideal and real cultures, and social institutions.

SUBCULTURES

It is rare to find a society that has a single culture shared equally by all its members. This could happen only in small, isolated, nonindustrial societies. Most societies include groups who share some of the cultural elements of the larger society yet also have their own distinctive set of norms, values, symbols, and lifestyles. These units of culture are **subcultures**. Subcultures exist within the confines of a larger culture. There are thousands of subcultures within a society, and all of us belong to several at any given time. For example, in college you may be a member of a sorority or fraternity, young Democrats or Republicans, men or women's athletic team, chemistry or social work club, or some others. More often subcultures reflect racial or ethnic differences, such as those found among Black, Polish, or Chinese Americans. Other subcultures develop around occupations: corporate, military, medical, or factory work. The Mormons, Amish, Muslims, and other groups form religious subcultures. Some are based on geography, such as those found in the South and New England; others are based on wealth and age. There are also drinking, drug, reggae, and homosexual subcultures. Every society that has diverse groups of people has subcultures. All subcultures participate in the larger, dominant culture but possess their own set of cultural elements.

At times, the dominant culture and the subculture may conflict to such a degree that tremendous stresses occur, and a crisis results. Members of the subculture may be required by the dominant culture to register for the military even though they value pacifism. The subculture may value the use of particular drugs but be forbidden by the dominant culture to obtain them. Also, note how subcultural differences are at the heart of the policy issue selected for this chapter: bilingualism. Can or should Spanish, Japanese, or Arab immigrants to the United States be able to retain their native language in their places of work? Can or should children in the public schools be given reading materials and exams in their native language when that language is not English? Subcultural differences and the rights of specific religious, ethnic, or other minority groups are central to many legal and policy debates. An understanding of subcultures makes us realize the importance of differences not merely among cultures but also in the diversity of thinking and behaving of different people within a culture as well.

Thinking Sociologically

Richard Bernstein (1990, 48) wrote the following about bilingual education:

> What's at stake ... is nothing less than the cultural identity of the country. Those who argue that bilingual education is a right, make up a kind of informal coalition with those who are pressing for changes in the way the United States is perceived—no longer as a primarily European entity to which all others have to adapt, but as a diverse collection of ethnic groups, each of which deserves more or less equal status and respect ....

Those on the other side insist that diversity is all well and good; but they argue that bilingual education could lead to an erosion of the national unity, a fragmentation of the nation into mutually hostile groups.

Use the knowledge about culture presented in this chapter to discuss why and how the policy debate over bilingual education is much more than a debate about language usage in schools.

POLICY DEBATE

Bilingual Education vs. English Immersion

One of the most controversial policy debates in the United States concerns bilingual education—education that involves two languages. In the United States, these languages are English and a minority language. This debate has had a long, stormy history in the United States. In the mid-1800s, various states with large immigrant communities passed laws that allowed education in languages other than English—for example, German in Wisconsin and Pennsylvania—but then repealed those laws after World War I, largely due to nationalistic sentiments (Romaine 1989). The debate was revived when the federal government passed the Bilingual Education Act of 1968. The legislation recognized that "the use of a child's mother tongue can have a beneficial effect upon his [sic] education" (Haugen 1987, 4) and that there are "special education needs of a great many students whose mother tongue is other than English" (Stoller 1976, 50). This spurred many sociologists, educators, and linguists to implement bilingual education programs in communities with large numbers of people with limited English proficiency (LEP). As of 2009, more than five million public school students had LEP; and the number is increasing (CQ Researcher, 2009). The hope was that bilingual education would reduce the LEP students' sense of alienation in an all-English world (Haugen 1987). Although some bilingual education programs are designed to maintain the native language and culture of the child ("maintenance programs"), most are aimed at providing a transition to English and to mainstream American culture ("transitional programs") (Hakuta 1986). Today, the minority language predominantly at issue is Spanish. This is becoming increasingly true as the U.S. continues a rapidly increasing shift in the racial make-up of the youth (under age eighteen) population and involves important issues of identity, learning and assimilation (Saulny 2011). Whites are now a minority of the youth in ten states. Not surprisingly, some of these states have the highest tensions over immigration and bilingual education. Whereas the controversy in the 1960s and 70s focused on the pros and cons of bilingual education, a backlash from opponents of bilingual education in the 1980s and 90s who decried its ineffectiveness has sharpened the debate to bilingual education vs. "English immersion" (CQ Researcher 2009). While the debate is still highly politically charged, it has shifted somewhat to include arguments about the pedagogical effectiveness of the respective programs.

Advocates of bilingual education claim that because federal policy has been responsible for the presence of a large part of the LEP population in the United States—for example, through the acquisition of territory (such as Puerto Rico) and through wars (such as Vietnam and the Mexican-American Wars)—there should be continued federal policy for bilingual education (Hakuta 1986). Proponents also claim that a "white, Anglo" education is demeaning and psychologically harmful to minority groups (Bernstein 1990). The crux of their argument is that teaching students in their native languages builds a stronger foundation for success in English and academics (Crawford 2009). They contend that this is because when students receive lessons in their native language, the teachers can teach at the same level that they teach English-speaking students, rather than having to simplify it in English to make it understandable to LEPs. Thus, the more the students develop their cognitive and literary skills overall, the more likely they are to acquire English-speaking skills. Proponents of bilingual education say that it is the best chance for LEP students to partake fully in the opportunities of American life (Bernstein 1990, 48).

High Culture, Folk Culture, and Popular Culture

Herbert Gans (1975) identified three "taste cultures" within the larger culture, including high culture, folk culture, and popular culture. **High culture** or elite culture reflects the tastes of the wealthy, affluent, or upper classes. Individuals of high culture may distinguish themselves from those considered "beneath them" through language, education, housing, etc. They will often see themselves as more "cultured" than ordinary people. Members of high culture will attend the finest restaurants, operas, ballets, and socialize with others who belong to their inner circles. Folk culture is distinctively different from high culture. **Folk culture** reflects the tastes of the working class or ethnic groups. Craft fairs, bluegrass or jazz festivals, NASCAR—all are examples of folk culture. **Popular culture** tends to reflect the tastes of the masses within a society. Music, art, dance, radio, linguistic trends, and literature produced and consumed by members of society are part of popular culture. For example, Santa Claus, the Easter Bunny, Halloween, Monday Night Football, soap operas, and baseball games are part of popular culture in the United States. In this case, culture is constructed by, and shared among, common persons such as you and me.

The National Association for Bilingual Education (NABE), for example, has argued that bilingual education programs have led to "improved academic achievement test scores, reduced rates of school dropout and student absenteeism, increased community involvement in education, and enhanced student self-esteem" for LEP students. NABE suggests that this overall improvement in the effectiveness of education benefits not only minority group members but also the future economic productivity of the United States as a whole. Additionally, it lays the foundation for improving the linguistic competencies of all Americans and enhances their understanding, tolerance, and appreciation for other cultures (Hakuta 1986)

On the other side, one of the strongest arguments presented against bilingual education and in support of English immersion contends that bilingual education delays students mastery of English (Jost 2009) and the research to support the effectiveness of bilingual education is inconsistent. Opponents of bilingual education feel that research on English immersion shows better academic gains for students. Further, however, and perhaps at the center of their argument, is their emphasis on assimilation into U.S. culture and that English is necessary for economic success in the United States (Hakuta 1986). Supporters of English immersion, additionally, feel that teaching students in their native language through bilingual programming could lead parents to the conclusion that English may not be necessary, after all, in order to succeed. The problem is compounded by the segregation of bilingual students from English-speaking students, which decreases the chances for full assimilation into American culture (Hakuta 1986). Interestingly, some opponents of bilingual education are immigrants who had to learn English and assimilate quickly upon coming to the United States at a young age. They insist that a bilingual education would have impeded their integration into American society (Romaine 1989, Porter 2009). Many opponents feel that the United States is becoming too ethnically diverse at a time when there is strong need to pull the various parts together; and the opponents argue that too much cultural diversity leads to a lack of common ground (Bernstein 1990). They maintain that bilingual education leads to cultural pluralism, rather than assimilation, and thus has negative consequences for members of minority groups and for the nation as a whole.

Clearly, the debate over bilingual education is more than a debate about language. It is a debate about cultural pluralism versus cultural assimilation and the values of each, as well as about the most effective ways of learning how to speak English.

Countercultures

A **counterculture** is a subculture that adheres to a set of beliefs and values that "rejects and opposes significant elements of the dominant culture of which it is a part" (Johnson 2000, 65). Because they accept such beliefs and values, members of a counterculture may behave in such radically nonconformist ways that they may drop out of society. Dropping out may mean either physically leaving or ideologically and behaviorally leaving, by rejecting the dominant values and working to change them.

Delinquent gangs, the Hare Krishna religious sect, hippies of the 60's, and some extreme right-wing religious groups of the 1980s can all be classified as countercultures. The norms and values of each of these groups were sharply in contrast with those held by conventional middle-class groups. Often, these values are not merely different from those of the dominant culture, but in opposition to them. Delinquent gangs may grant prestige and social approval for lawbreaking, violence, theft, or the use of drugs to achieve their goals of dominance and material success. The stated goal of the Hare Krishna religious sect is the salvation of the world through its conversion to Krishna Consciousness. The Krishna counterculture entails considerable ritualism, ceremony, shaved heads, chant-ins, proselytizing in airports, and other activities often viewed as countercultural. The youth movement of the 1960s, which included political activists, dropouts, and hippies, actively challenged the dominant cultural norms of hard work, financial success, conformity of dress, sexual restrictiveness, military superiority, and white supremacy. Perhaps the pendulum has swung away from countercultural trends among youth to countercultural trends among extreme right-wing adults. Some right-wing religious groups in the 1980s and 1990s have been behind the bombing of abortion clinics, while less extreme groups have made efforts to legalize corporal punishment, mandate prayer in the public schools, and demand the inclusion of creationism in the school curriculum. With the bombing of the Alfred P. Murrah Building in Oklahoma, and the destruction of the World Trade Center in New York, a greater awareness of terrorist countercultures exists within the United States. The individuals behind these deadly attacks, both domestic and foreign terrorists, disagreed with governmental policies and chose to take revenge on the citizens of our society.

Ideal and Real Culture

In most cultures, differences exist between what people are supposed to do and what they actually do. The **ideal culture** consists of the norms and values people profess to follow; the **real culture** is the culture they actually do follow. If you were asked to tell a foreign visitor about the norms and values of Americans, for example, you would probably describe the ideal culture, mentioning such topics as freedom, democracy, equal rights, monogamy, marital fidelity, and educational opportunity for all. The actual culture differs considerably from the ideal, however. The very poor are less likely to get a good education, marital infidelity is common, and many people have several spouses during their lives.

Some anthropologists express this distinction between real and ideal culture in terms of "explicit" culture and "implicit" culture. These terms may be more accurate than "real" and "ideal"—both types of culture are real in the sense that they actually exist. The point is that stated cultural norms and values are not always practiced. Students should be sensitive to distinctions of this sort. The speed limit may be fifty-five, but many people drive at speeds of sixty-five or higher. Honesty in the classroom may be the norm, but cheating can be widespread. Clashes between ideal and actual practices may be avoided through rationalizations or flexibility in social control. A student might defend cheating on a test by arguing, "everyone does it." Police rarely arrest all who exceed the speed limit, concentrating instead on extreme violations.

Auto racing is an example of folk culture, which reflects the tastes of the working class or ethnic groups.

Although cultures vary in their symbols, language, and behavior, and in their subcultures, countercultures, real and ideal cultures, all share some basic concerns known as **cultural universals**. People in all cultures must have food, shelter, and protection. All people face illness and death, and every society has a kinship system with taboos on incest. Like American suburbanites, African Bushmen and Mongolian nomads socialize and train their members in the ways of the culture, provide for work and leisure activities, and establish leaders and rulers.

Multicultural

As mentioned in the introduction, throughout the history of the United States the emphasis has been on monoracial categories rather than multiracial ones. In addition, the belief has been that America is a "melting pot" where all people, regardless of nationality or skin color, have assimilated into one culture. The problem with this assumption is not everyone was welcomed into the pot. Historically, only persons of white European decent were invited, with the idea they would come together and form a common culture, including language, values, norms, etc. Other groups have traditionally been excluded, including African Americans, Native Americans, Hispanics, and Asians. Multicultural refers to a move to recognize the contributions of all cultures within America. Instead of promoting assimilation, there is a need to recognize a pluralistic society where diverse groups live together and each is recognized not for their ability to lose their ancestral heritage, but for the contributions they make to the United States.

Idiocultures

Gary Fine (1979) has argued that every group forms its own culture to a certain extent and called these created cultures **idiocultures**. An *idioculture* is a system of knowledge, beliefs, behaviors, and customs created through group interactions. Members of a group share particular experiences and recognize that other members will understand references to a shared experience. Members of one group, for example, might roar with laughter whenever the word *cashew* is mentioned because it triggers a memory of a shared humorous experience. All small groups have a culture that is unique to themselves but that is, nevertheless, part of a larger cultural pattern. The group itself forms the group's idioculture; thus idiocultures do not exist when a group is first formed. They are created from the opening moments of group interaction when people begin to learn names and other information about one another. With time, rules are established, opinions expressed, information exchanged, and events experienced together.

Suppose, for example, that a newspaper has just been established and that the editors, reporters, typesetters, and other employees have come together for the first time. Initially, they will have shared no experiences, but as they work together, they will develop unique ways of interacting. At first, the reporters may go out for coffee individually, but eventually they might decide to delegate one person to get coffee for everyone. "Gathering background information" might become a euphemism for wasting time. When the Johnson Warehouse is destroyed in the biggest fire that ever happened in the town, they might come to refer to any big story as a "Johnson." Similarly, stories dealing with improper behavior by politicians might come to be called "Watergates" and the task of writing the relatively uninteresting daily reports about weddings, funerals, and meetings might come to be called the "trivia." After a few unpleasant arguments, the reporters might agree never to comment on one another's stories. After working together for an extended period, the group would develop its own jargon and set of customs that would not be understood by an outsider.

CHAPTER REVIEW

Wrapping it up

Summary

1. A *culture* is a society's social heritage, the system of ideas, values, beliefs, knowledge, norms, customs, and technology that everyone in a society shares.

2. A *society* is a group of people who share a common culture. Some of the most significant elements of a culture are symbols, language, values, norms, and technology.

3. Societies consist of material and nonmaterial culture. *Material culture* includes all things tangible within society while *nonmaterial* culture involves all intangible aspects of society, such as norms and values.

4. When we encounter a culture different from our own, we may experience culture shock. This is often the result of our own ethnocentric behavior where we judge another culture based on our own.

5. The idea of *cultural relativism* suggests that cultures must be judged on their own terms, not by the standards of another culture. Acts, ideas, and products are not inherently good or bad; they must be judged in the cultural context in which they happen.

6. *Symbols* are arbitrary representations of something. The use of symbols is a human capability that allows us to make sense of reality, transmit messages, store complex information, and deal with an abstract world.

7. Our most important set of symbols is language, which enables us to transmit and store our social heritage. The importance of language to humans is illustrated in studies comparing the development of children and of animals such as chimpanzees.

8. It has been demonstrated that language influences how we perceive and experience the world. The Sapir-Whorf hypothesis suggests that the use of different languages by different societies causes them to perceive the world very differently. Rather than simply seeing the same world with different labels, they actually perceive different realities.

9. *Values* are conceptions about what is important and of worth. They are learned and shared cultural products that justify particular types of behavior. People in the United States tend to value achievement, success, work, a moral orientation, and humanitarian concerns, among other things.

10. Values indicate what is important, whereas norms are rules of conduct, the standards and expectations of behavior. Norms are of two types: *folkways*, which are customs or conventions that provoke only mild censure if violated; and *mores*, which are far more important and provoke severe punishment if violated. Laws are the formalized and standardized expressions of norms.

11. In addition to the nonmaterial aspects of culture such as these, there are material and technological aspects as well.

12. *Subcultures* are groups within a society that share the common culture but have their own distinctive set of cultural complexes. A *counterculture* is a type of subculture adhering to a set of norms and values that sharply contradict the dominant norms and values of the society of which the group is a part. To a certain extent, all groups possess localized cultures of their own, which are known as *idiocultures*.

13. The culture a society professes to follow (its ideal culture) differs from the culture it actually does follow (its real culture).

14. Multiculturalism is beginning to replace the belief that only those belonging to the dominant group (European) make relevant contributions to our culture.

15. Understanding the various elements of culture is useful in a variety of occupational settings, including health professions, service organizations, politics, public administration, education, business, and others, as well as in your personal life. Sociologists have come to be used as cultural translators who help to lessen misperceptions and increase understandings among people from diverse cultural settings.

Key Terms

artifacts Physical products or objects created through human actions

counterculture A subculture that adheres to a set of norms and values that sharply contradict the dominant norms and values of the society of which that group is a part

cultural relativism The belief that cultures must be judged on their own terms rather than by the standards of another culture

cultural universals Aspects of culture that are shared by all people, such as symbols, shelter, food, and a belief system

culture The systems of ideas, values, beliefs, knowledge, norms, customs, and technology shared by almost everyone in a particular society

ethnocentrism The view that one's own culture is superior to others and should be used as the standard against which other cultures are judged

Folk culture The culture of the working class or ethnic groups

folkways Norms of conduct of everyday life that bring only mild censure or punishment if they are violated

high culture The materials and ideas of wealthy, affluent, or upper classes (in contrast to popular culture)

ideal culture The norms and values that people profess to follow

idioculture The system of knowledge, beliefs, behaviors, and customs that is unique to a given group

institution A stable cluster of values, norms, statuses, and roles that develops around a basic social goal

language The systematized use of speech and hearing to communicate feelings and ideas

laws Formal, standardized expressions of norms enacted by legislative bodies to regulate certain types of behaviors

mores Norms of conduct associated with strong feelings of right or wrong, violations of which bring intense reaction and some type of punishment

norms Formal and informal rules of conduct and social expectations for behavior

pathology of normalcy The concept that cultural norms are not always beneficial for a society, group, or individual

popular culture Trends, social activities, and shared experiences of everyday people (in contrast to elite culture)

real culture The norms and values that people actually follow and practice, which, may or may not be the same as the ideal culture and which represents the norms and values people profess to follow

Sapir-Whorf hypothesis The hypothesis that societies with different languages perceive the world differently because their members interpret the world through the grammatical forms, labels, and categories their language provides

society A group of interacting people who live in a specific geographical area, who are organized in a cooperative manner, and who share a common culture

subcultures Groups of persons who share in the main culture of a society but also have their own distinctive values, norms, and lifestyles

symbol Something that is used to represent something else, such as a word, gesture, or object used to represent some aspect of the world

taboos Mores that prohibit something

technology The application of nonmaterial and material knowledge by a society to maintain its standard of living and lifestyle

values Ideas and beliefs shared by the people in a society about what is important and worthwhile

Discussion Questions

1. Make a list of leisure activities that might be considered high culture. Do the same for folk and popular culture. How might you explain why you participate in some of these activities and not in others?
2. How many examples can you give of symbols using only your hand and fingers? Can you think of any that mean different things in different contexts or to people of different cultures? Have any of these changed over time?
3. Discuss the significance or accuracy of the statement, "Societies with different languages actually see or perceive the world differently."
4. How would an understanding of the Sapir-Whorf hypothesis help politicians to evaluate whether the United States should promote bilingual education programs?
5. Describe what is meant by value conflict. Give examples. How are such conflicts resolved?
6. Joe listens to his radio (quietly, with earphones, of course), and Mary reads her New York Times in their sociology class. Is this illegal, forbidden, or harmful behavior? Why is the professor likely to disapprove of such behavior?
7. Discuss ways in which existing student norms may not be beneficial or may even be harmful to students.
8. Using the concepts of ethnocentrism and cultural relativism, discuss the impact that a bilingual education might have on understanding other cultures.
9. How might multiculturalism affect people's attitudes toward bilingual education programs?
10. Think about the subcultures, countercultures, or idiocultures of which you are a member. Differentiate these, and explain the differences.
11. Differentiate between real and ideal cultures. Why are they seldom one and the same?

Pop Quiz

1. Something that is used to represent something else is a/an __________.

   a. ideal culture
   b. folkway
   c. more
   d. symbol

2. What does the Sapir-Whorf hypothesis suggest?

   a. Our language shapes both ours perceptions of reality and our behavior
   b. Language simply reflects one's perception of reality and behavior
   c. Some form of language has been found to be used by chimpanzees
   d. In some remote areas, verbal language is forbidden

3. Social norms are ________.

   a. either prescriptive or proscriptive
   b. consisting of several types

c. rules of conduct or social expectations for behavior
d. all of the above

4. Wearing a swimsuit to class most likely violates a ______.

a. folkway
b. American value
c. taboo
d. more

5. Mores that prohibit something are called _____.

a. laws
b. social censure
c. taboos
d. folkways

6. Social control is essentially the ______.

a. process of applying social sanctions
b. formal expressions of norms
c. method of prohibiting something
d. same as a taboo

7. The material techniques and products a society uses to maintain its standard of living are the society's ______.

a. culture
b. values
c. mores
d. technology

8. When does cultural lag occur?

a. Changes in material culture occur more rapidly than changes in nonmaterial culture
b. Artifacts and norms are too advanced for a culture's technology
c. Folkways and mores are inconsistent
d. Symbols in a society are misunderstood

9. Among whom is Temporocentrism most prevalent?

a. people who lack historical perspective
b. Americans from upper income families
c. people who fear foreigners
d. people who only prefer foreign goods

10. A unit of culture that rejects the society's dominant culture and prescribes an alternative one is best described as a(n) ______.

a. subculture
b. counterculture
c. idioculture
d. multiculture

11. All symbols involve words or written language. T/F

12. Only humans can assign symbols to represent the objects around them. T/F

13. Subcultures have their own norms and values, but also exist within the confines of a larger culture. T/F

14. All societies have institutions to meet their broad goals. T/F

15. For most people, values seldom conflict. T/F

1. D	6. A	11. F
2. A	7. D	12. F
3. D	8. A	13. T
4. A	9. A	14. T
5. C	10. B	15. F

CHAPTER 5

Social Structure, Social Groups, and Social Organizations

LAKERS

PREVENTABLE DISASTERS

On April 20, 2010, there was an explosion on a rig owned by the British Petroleum Oil Company (BP) one mile below the surface of the Gulf of Mexico. This led to the largest accidental oil spill in history. Nearly five million barrels (later estimated by independent researchers to be approximately 185 million gallons) of oil spewed into the Gulf of Mexico before the Macondo well was finally capped successfully, eighty-six days after the explosion. The oil spill caused catastrophic amounts of environmental damage and financial losses to tourism and fishing industries in Louisiana, Mississippi, Alabama and Florida. Many of the areas affected were small, sleepy coastal communities that have relied on the income provided by the natural resources that the Gulf of Mexico offers.

An explosion on a rig owned by the British Petroleum Oil Company (BP) one mile below the surface of the Gulf of Mexico was the largest accidental oil spill in history.

In the months following the disaster, a presidential panel studied the accident. The panel's conclusion was that the accident was preventable and was the result of BP, Haliburton, Transocean, and several other contractors having taken hazardous time-saving steps without adequate consideration for the potential risks. Surveys of workers on the Deepwater Horizon, the oil rig that exploded, revealed that many of them had concerns about safety practices prior to the explosion; but they feared reprisals if they had said anything. Many key components in the oil rig had not been inspected since 2000, even though requirements call for inspections every three to five years. Investigators also revealed concerns about the quality of cement that was used in the construction of the oil well and discovered that Halliburton and BP knew weeks before the explosion that the cement mixture they had planned to use to seal the bottom of the well was unstable (Brody 2010). In December 2010, the United States Department of Justice filed a lawsuit against BP and eight other companies that were involved with the construction of the oil well. (Retrieved from http://www.nytimes.com, 2011).

The repercussions of the oil spill were disastrous enough, but matters were made even worse by the fact that it occurred as the United States was in the midst of one of its worst economic crises since the 1930s Great Depression. The housing market, the unemployment rate, the bank closings, and other indicators signified one of the bleakest economic periods in United States history. Particularly hard hit by the economic downturn, and the least likely to bounce back quickly, were the very people who depended upon the resources from the Gulf of Mexico to sustain a livelihood. How could such a preventable disaster occur? How could decisions have been made that might have led to enormous gains by BP (had the oil rig not exploded) that entailed risks to the livelihood of millions of others so dependent upon the Gulf of Mexico? While this chapter does not discuss the answers to these questions specifically, it does provide discussions of sociological concepts necessary for understanding the ways in which groups and organizations are formed and maintained. How do members of groups and organizations develop their ways of thinking, often at times to protect their own interests at the expense of others? What are the intended functions of bureaucratic procedures? How, also, can bureaucracy become a series of rituals that lose site of the initial organizational goals, and thus lead to potential negative consequences? After reading this chapter, you should return to this vignette about the oil spill to see if you can use your knowledge about social structure, groups, and organizations to help explain why preventable catastrophes sometimes occur.

The people who live and interact in a geographical area and share a common culture make up the basic social structure of society. Anything complex has a structure. The building you live in has a physical structure consisting of a certain number of floors, windows and doors, and other physical features. Your body has a biological structure consisting of a brain, digestive system, cardiovascular system, and other anatomical and physiological features. Although we understand the concept of *structure*, what does it mean to say that society is socially structured? Social structure means that society is organized in a way that makes human behavior and relationships predictable. It means that human behavior is socially patterned. These social regularities or patterns are composed of many interrelated parts or components, which sociologists give labels such as social statuses, roles, groups, organizations, and institutions. With the exception of institutions, these major social structures are examined in this chapter.

COMPONENTS OF SOCIAL STRUCTURE

Central to an understanding of social structure are the concepts of statuses and roles. Social structures provide us with familiarity in everyday life, thus allowing us to make sense of our social interactions. We come to expect certain behaviors from people we encounter, and this allows us to predict patterns in group situations. We can assume a great deal about a person simply by knowing their occupation. For example, suppose you are at a social gathering, and you inquire about the occupation of the person with whom you are speaking. If the individual tells you she is a medical doctor, how does that influence what you think about the person? What does her information imply about her character? What if she said she was a restaurant server? Would it change your perception of her? During the process of social interaction, a person's position in society often influences how we act toward them. In addition, we come to expect certain behaviors and actions based on their position.

Status

When we hear the word **status**, we often think of prestige; but status in sociological terms is different. Status is a socially defined position that an individual occupies. While a status does not mean prestige, a position (status) held by an individual can imply esteem standing, such as that of judge, doctor, or bank executive. On the other hand, if a person is a janitor, we may consider his occupation to be less prestigious. Judge, doctor, bank executive and janitor are all statuses within society. They exist independently from the people who occupy them.

An individual will, generally, occupy several statuses at one time. The combination of all the statuses any individual holds at a given time is **status set**. You, for example, are a student if you are enrolled in a school, a son or daughter to a parent, a brother or sister if you have a sibling, a friend or acquaintance to your peers, and a citizen of some country. A status set including student, daughter, sister, friend, and citizen guides what you do and enables others to predict much of your behavior. Students behave differently from teachers (and are expected to), just as children behave differently from adults.

Ascribed and Achieved Status

There are two ways that a person acquires a status; it is either ascribed or achieved. Ascribed statuses are obtained involuntarily or without effort on the part of the individual. Ascribed statuses can be acquired at birth, such as age, race, or sex. For example, being a sister, daughter, woman, white, or poor are statuses that can be given to you at birth without willingness on your part. Achieved statuses are those you choose voluntarily or attain through effort or ability. Examples of achieved statuses include husband, athlete, coach, parent, or deviant. Typically, statuses are obtained through a combination of both ascription and achievement. An individual born into a family where both parents are incarcerated is more likely to be deviant than if he were the son of two prominent lawyers.

Sometimes, a particular status stands out among all the others you occupy and shapes how you and others view you. A **master status** takes priority over all the others in your social identity. As a well-known athlete, chairman of the board, or child of a famous person, you may have doors opened to you that most of us would not have opened to us. On the other hand, suppose that one of your statuses happens to be ex-prisoner, homosexual, citizen of a country the United States dislikes, or a carrier of the AIDS virus. This status may become a master status and cause people to avoid, criticize, or dislike you. All of the other statuses in your status set (husband, father, choir member, employee) may be ignored or subordinated to your master status. Often, societies determine which status becomes your master status. A person's racial status, for example, is a master status in South Africa today. Race is an ascribed status, but other master statuses, such as criminal, are achieved. In the United States it is typically a person's occupation that becomes their master status in adulthood.

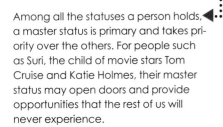

Among all the statuses a person holds, a master status is primary and takes priority over the others. For people such as Suri, the child of movie stars Tom Cruise and Katie Holmes, their master status may open doors and provide opportunities that the rest of us will never experience.

Social Roles

With statuses comes a responsibility to behave a certain way. The second component of social structure is roles. Status and role, like structure and function, parent and child, or student and teacher, are reciprocal concepts. Any given status in your status set has a dynamic aspect, a set of expectations and behaviors associated with it in a given group or society; these are **roles**. Different roles (expectations for behavior) are associated with different statuses (positions). A useful way to think about this is that you *occupy* a status; you *play* a role. A role is a collection of expectations associated with a status. Figure 5.1 oversimplifies the complexity of statuses and roles, but it does illustrate the relationship between the two concepts. Multiple roles attached to individual statuses are **role sets**. These role expectations and behaviors are learned through the socialization process. Learning what to expect from others who occupy given statuses and what behaviors are appropriate for our own statuses are basic aspects of life as a social being. We learn to expect different behaviors from persons who occupy different statuses. For example, what is the role of a mother within our culture? The expected behavior of a mother is that she love, nurture and care for her children. The roles or expectations of the father are different. He is expected to provide for his family financially and to present himself as a strong and secure man.

Sometimes, confusion exists about a given role, in that differences may exist in what is prescribed, what is perceived, and the actual behavior that occurs. To differentiate these, it may help to define prescribed roles, role perceptions, and actual role performance, to clarify any confusion. A **prescribed role** (or roles) describes what society suggests that we should do. The prescribed roles (expectations) for the status of student generally include attending classes, getting to classes on time, listening, taking notes, studying, and getting passing grades. While a student may understand these prescriptions, the student's **role perception** may be that it really is not necessary to attend every class, take complete notes, or get an A or B grade to pass. As a result, some of us have met students whose **role performance** (what they actually do) differs somewhat from the prescribed role. Perhaps you even know students personally who skip class, arrive late when they do attend, and fail to study.

Role perceptions and role performance may differ from the prescription for a variety of reasons. One is that students (or holders of any status or position) may not be deeply committed to the role or may define it as unimportant. A second is that enough flexibility exists in the role that some prescriptions can be fulfilled (such as passing) without the performance (going to class). A third reason may be that the roles associated with other statuses, such as being a boyfriend or girlfriend, athlete, campus leader, and employee, compete for the student's time. These are value role conflicts.

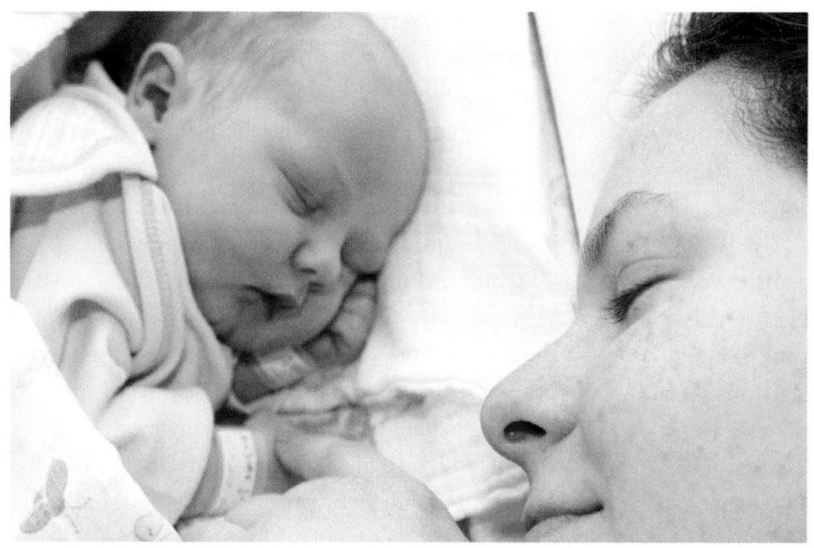

Each status a person holds is associated with an expected role related to that status, and we learn to expect different behaviors from people occupying different statuses. A mother, for example, is expected to provide love and care for her child.

Role Ambiguity, Role Strain and Role Conflict

All of us have experienced role ambiguity, role strain, and role conflict. **Role ambiguity** exists when the expectations associated with particular social statuses are unclear. The behavior or actions that are expected from us is unclear. We may find ourselves asking, "What am I suppose to be doing?" "How am I supposed to act"? We may experience role ambiguity in a variety of situations such as with a new job or with a date.

Role strain results from a single role overload or from contradictory demands placed on a given status. Despite our best efforts, the expectations may exceed the time and energy we have available to fulfill them. There may be no role ambiguity about what is expected, but the demands may exceed our abilities. If your parents expect you to get A or B grades, and you cannot meet their expectations because of other demands on your time such as school work-study, social fraternity or sorority, the college baseball or softball team, or because of the difficulty you have in understanding the material, you are probably experiencing role strain. You are more likely to experience role strain as a college student when you try to be involved in multiple school activities without leaving yourself much time for the academic component. Professors also experience role strain when they are required to be instructor, advisor, researcher, committee member, and sponsor to a student organization all at the same time. Within our individual roles, we must learn to balance the work load if we are to avoid role strain.

Role conflict occurs when the demands or expectations associated with two or more statuses interfere with each other or are incompatible. If you're like most college students, you will be required to work during the semester in order to have money. Most college communities have jobs available for students after school hours, but they may require you to work late into the evening. By the time you get home from work you're exhausted and too worn out to study for the sociology exam you have the next morning. On other days, because you stayed up late studying, you are too tired at work to remain awake and receive a reprimand from the boss. Your job and schooling are getting in the way of each other and are creating role conflict regarding expectations. A student who is an athlete or a performing artist may face a conflict between meeting the expectations of being at practice or rehearsal and also being expected to attend an event for a class that afternoon. These are time and energy role conflicts.

Other role conflicts can result not only from competing demands on the time and energy required to fill different roles but also because of different value expectations that may be built into a single status. Can parents be expected to discipline their children at the same time that they are expected to show them love and affection? Can Christians both love their enemies and shoot them during war? These are value role conflicts.

To sum up, then, role ambiguity results from uncertainty over the expectations of a given role. Role strain results from a role overload or the inability to carry out or live up to the expectations of a given status. Role conflict arises from the need to conform to incompatible expectations (time and energy or values) of the same or differing roles.

Role ambiguity, role strain, and role conflict seem particularly prevalent in industrialized societies where people assume complex status sets with multiple and often unclear and incompatible role expectations. Yet it would be totally misleading to conclude that roles are a negative and troublesome characteristic of human behavior. On the contrary, the role expectations that accompany social statuses are the means by which behavior is made predictable, human relationships become patterned, and society is organized.

APPLYING KNOWLEDGE OF ROLES

Although strict adherence to prescribed role expectations is rare, the power of roles to shape human behavior should not be underestimated. A heatedly debated issue among sociologists, social psychologists, and psychologists is whether the individual shapes the role or the role shapes the individual. Do we often find corruption in high government positions because corrupt people are elected to those positions, or is it because the nature of the role and the power it bestows lead to corruption? Do people have maternal and paternal instincts by nature, or does the role of parent lead one to become nurturing and authoritarian? Are college students "party animals" by nature, or does one become a member of that species because of expectations that students at a particular college should be that way?

The issue will probably never be resolved once and for all. It may be that role and personality are both involved, but some researchers have found strong evidence that we take on or accept the role we are playing. For example, Zimbardo's famous prison experiment demonstrates the power of social structure and roles over personality. He had to cancel his experiment prematurely because of how the students—"the cream of the crop of their generation"—had internalized the roles of guards and prisoners that they were assigned to play.

Zimbardo's research is still relevant today. His conclusions were cited in a *Time Magazine* article as an explanation for the behavior of American soldiers mistreating Iraqi prisoners of war in Abu Ghraib. The Bush Administration had blamed the abusive behavior on a "few bad apples"; however, a look at the backgrounds of the soldiers implicated suggests otherwise. Israeli psychiatrist Dr. Ilan Kutz notes, "During actual wars, if there isn't any particular command figure in charge who puts a stop to it, [torture and sadism by prison guards] can spread like a psychological epidemic." In prisons, Zimbardo concluded, abuse is virtually guaranteed if three key components are not present: clear rules, a staff that is well trained in those rules, and tight management that includes punishment for violations. At Abu Ghraib, the conditions for conforming to the role of abuser were present (McGeary 2004).

How is the knowledge that role expectations play a powerful part in shaping behavior useful to us? Primarily, it alerts us to the possibility that personal and interpersonal behavior is more than a matter of individual personalities or predispositions. This fact, in itself, has important practical implications. Clinical sociologists, for example, are often hired to conduct training programs in stress management in hospital, business, and educational settings. Training programs that teach managers how to restructure work environments and role relationships are usually more successful in reducing stress than programs that focus exclusively on dealing with the psychological problems of individuals (Goldman 1984).

Realizing the importance of role relationships and social structure, applied sociologists have actually helped some industries overcome problematic situations. A classic example is William Foote Whyte's work (1949) in the restaurant industry. Whyte found that role ambiguity among waiters, waitresses, and kitchen workers—not personality conflicts—accounted for the friction, anxiety, and emotional outbursts in many restaurants. His solution relied mainly on creating clear, specific roles for each of the different types of workers in the restaurants. It seems obvious to us now that this is the best way to run a restaurant; however in 1949, Whyte's solution had a major impact on the entire restaurant industry.

All of us—sociologists or not—can use what we know about roles and behavior to our advantage. Administrators and managers might examine how roles are structured—instead of individual personalities—to increase efficiency in their organization. In our personal lives, parents might first try to understand the roles outside the family that their children are expected to play before they try to shape their behavior through a series of rewards and punishments.

Clearly, the way that statuses and roles are structured is as important for the success of an organization as selecting the appropriate personnel.

Thinking Sociologically

1. Make a diagram of your statuses and roles. Which of your statuses are ascribed and which are achieved?

2. Describe a time in your college or work career when you have experienced role ambiguity, role strain, and role conflict.

TYPES OF SOCIAL INTERACTION

When humans interact, they display both intentional and unintentional behaviors. Think back to a time when your mother or father was angry with you for something. Could you recognize their anger even before they said anything? At times our body language provides clues to our thoughts and feelings, even without our intention. What other behaviors indicate the attitude of the person with whom we are interacting? When a person yawns, looks at his watch, looks past us, nods, or shifts posture, what clues does it provide us about the status of our communication? What about eye contact? How long do we feel comfortable maintaining eye contact with someone to whom we are speaking? It generally depends on the status of the person with whom we are talking, but often after ten seconds of constant eye contact, we begin to feel uncomfortable.

Generally, when we interact with others, we are doing so with intention. Following are five types of social interaction in which we intentionally engage with others.

Exchange is the most common type of social interaction that occurs between people. When individuals interact, they do so with the intent of receiving a reward, either extrinsic or intrinsic. For example, two people engaged in an employer/employee relationship expect to receive something in return during the course of their interaction. The employer expects to receive a certain number of days of work from the

FIGURE 5-1 STATUSES AND ROLES

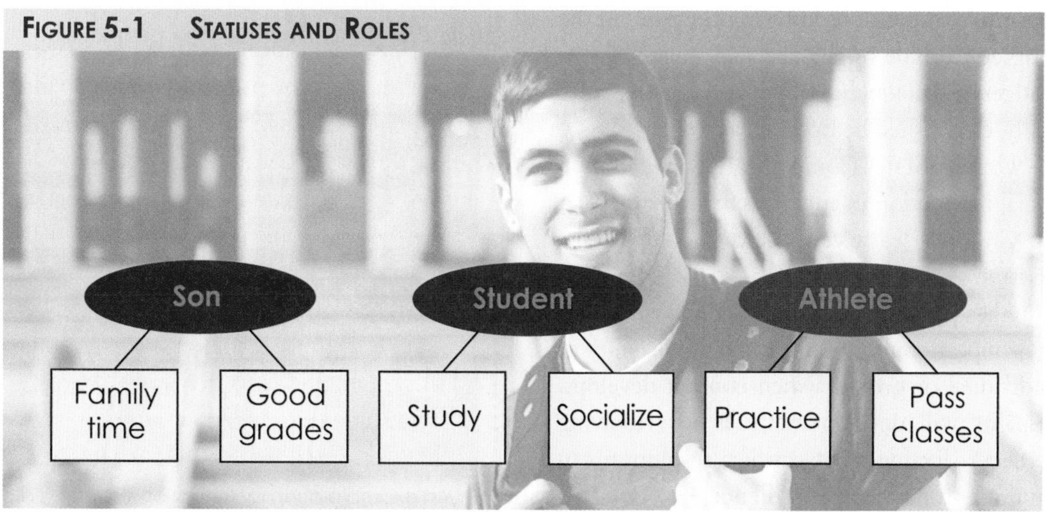

Socializing in groups is beneficial.

employee, while the employee insists on receiving a paycheck for his labor. Rewards don't always have to be material but can, also, be nonmaterial—such as a smile, hug, thank-you, or feeling of satisfaction from helping someone in need.

Cooperation is another type of social interaction that occurs when individuals work to achieve some common goal. Perhaps in one of your college courses you were required to work with others on a group project, with each member expected to contribute to the overall work. As a member of the group, each person must be willing to cooperate with the others to accomplish the goals of the group. Another example would be a football team that works cooperatively together to win a game.

Competition occurs in a great deal of our society. America promotes and respects competitiveness (when two or more individuals compete for a valued prize). Individuals or groups agree to the established rules and consent to play by them during competition. Examples include students competing for grades, employees battling for a leadership promotion, and so on. Sports teams enter into competitions knowing the rules of the game and agree to abide by the decisions made by referees or judges. Consequences for breaking the rules are, generally, established beforehand as well.

In the United States competition is a common form of social interaction in education, work, athletics, and so on. Children learn very early to compete for everything from grades to trophies.

Conflict takes place in social interactions when one person or group attempts to control the behaviors of another individual or group. When conflict develops, the participants will develop methods for resolving their differences. Examples of conflict resolution can include anything from voting to violence.

Coercion is the use of intimidation, or the threat of force or violence, to control the actions of others. Parents may use coercion to influence their teens by threatening to take away car privileges for curfew violations.

TYPES OF SOCIAL GROUPS

While statuses and roles are important in society, another major component of social structure is the social group. Groups can be classified as either non-social or social with the degree of social interaction ranging from none to constant.

Humans are social animals. Even those who think of themselves as loners participate in many groups; and, for most of us, groups are a major source of satisfaction. You may eat with a particular group of friends every day, belong to a drama club, or play tennis every week with your gym class. You probably depend on social groups, social organizations, and social systems for most of your psychological and physical needs. Research indicates that we are influenced not only by the groups to which we currently belong and those we identify with, but also by those we associated with in the past. In fact, life without groups seems impossible. Without group involvements, infants die, adolescents get depressed, middle-aged people suffer psychologically, and the elderly get lonely and lose their will to live. We learn, eat, work, and worship in groups; and deprivation of group involvement is damaging. We need people; and to better understand the concept of groups, we need to learn more about what sociologists mean when they use the word "group."

We have all seen and been a part of a group gathered somewhere. Hence, what exactly is a group? A *group* can be as small as two people who have some-

An example of an organizational group is a band.

thing in common to a very large group with little shared interests. Like most topics in sociology, however, the definition is not that simple. Although the concept of *group* is one of the key elements of sociology, no single definition is universally accepted. The problem is not that sociologists are unable to decide what a group is; rather, there are many types of groups, and sociologists attach different meanings to their forms, their functions, and their consequences.

Throughout this chapter we focus our discussion on *social groups*—those in which people physically or socially interact. However, there are non-social and limited social groups recognized by sociologists as well.

Non-Social Groups

Statistical groups, or—perhaps more accurately—statistical groupings, are formed not by the group members but by sociologists and statisticians. In 2010, for example, some 74.7 million children younger than age eighteen were living in the United States. Of these, 65.7 percent lived with married parents, 3.6 percent lived with two unmarried parents, 26.6 percent lived with one parent and 4 percent lived with no parent present (*Families and Living Arrangements* 2010). The group of women between 5 feet 1 inch and 5 feet 5 inches tall would be another statistical group. Some sociologists do not consider groups of this sort to be groups at all because the members are unaware of their membership and there is no social interaction or social organization (see Table 5-1).

Another type of group is the **categorical group** in which a number of people share a common characteristic. We all belong to categories and share common characteristics with others within society. Blondes, the homeless, single mothers, children, students, and tall people are all categorical groups. Categorical groups are not social groups because the members do not interact with other members who share common characteristic. They are important, however, in the common identity member's share with others like them.

Limited Social Groups

Limited social groups interact minimally, and members are generally not concerned with the feelings and attitudes of the other. An **aggregate** is a group consisting of a collection of people who are together in one place and socialize very little. People standing in line for movie tickets, individuals waiting for the bus, and drivers stuck in a traffic jam—all share a common space but may not see themselves as belonging to a group. Aggregates are basically unstructured, and the participants interact briefly and sporadically. Most members act as if they are alone, except perhaps to comment about the weather, ask the time, or complain about the service. The members of an aggregate need not converse but may do so; they need not know one another but may see familiar faces.

TABLE 5-1 A CLASSIFICATION OF NONSOCIAL AND SOCIAL GROUPS

Type of Group	Awareness of Kind	Social Interaction	Social Organization	Example
Statistical	No	No	No	Average family size
Categorical	Yes	No	No	Redheads
Aggregate	Yes	limited	No	Football crowd
Associational	Yes	limited	Yes	Democratic Party

Another type of group where there may be limited interaction is the **associational** or **organizational** group, which is especially important in complex industrialized societies. Associational groups consist of people who join together in some organized way to pursue a common interest, and they have a formal structure. Most of us belong to a number of them; they can be formed for almost any conceivable purpose. The university, a volleyball team, a Rotary Club, the Democratic Party, General Motors Corporation, and Protestant churches—all are associational groups. They share the major characteristics of other types of groups; but, in addition, they also have a formal structure. Their degree of social interaction may be limited to their participation in the association or organization.

As you can see, a number of different kinds of groups are recognized; and their boundaries are not easy to state clearly. Like other classification schemes, the one we have suggested makes use of some criteria but ignores others that may in some circumstances be equally important. Groups might also be classified on the basis of social boundaries between members and nonmembers, adherence to a special set of norms, awareness not only of kind, as in Table 5-1, but also of membership or a variety of other factors.

Social Groups

Given this range of definitions and possible classification criteria, what types of collectives can we call social groups? Although sociologists do not accept a single definition, there would be widespread agreement that membership in a **social group** involves the following: (a) some type of interaction; (b) a sense of belonging or membership; (c) shared interests or agreement on values, norms, and goals; and (d) a structure—that is, a definable, recognizable arrangement of parts. Thus, the sociological use of *group* involves interaction, a consciousness of membership, shared interests, and a definable structure. From the above discussion, associational or organizational groups are social but less intimate and limited in the amount of interaction.

Social groups are important because they provide us with a social identity, serve as a key to understanding social behavior, link the self with the larger society, and help us understand social structure and societal organization. By studying the individual in a group context, the dynamic interactions within groups, and the organizational network of the larger society, we can improve our understanding of the self, of human interaction, and of the larger social order.

Primary and Secondary Groups

Of all the groups to which we belong the one that provides much of our identity is the family. We feel a sense of individuality or uniqueness when we are with family or friends. The term **primary group**, was coined by Charles H. Cooley (1909) to refer to small, informal groups of people who interact in a personal, direct, and intimate way. Members of our primary group, according to Cooley, were the most important in shaping the human personality. Primary groups involve intimate face-to-face association and interaction; and their members have a sense of "we-ness", involving mutual identification and shared feelings. Their members tend to be emotionally attached to one another and involved with other group members as whole people, not just with those aspects of a person that pertain to work, school, or some other isolated part of one's life. Your family, close friends, girlfriend or boyfriend, and some neighbors are likely to be members of your primary group. A primary group tends to remain intact for a long time, and its members are often considered irreplaceable.

Your family, close friends, girlfriend or boyfriend, and some neighbors are likely to be members of your primary group.

A **secondary group** is a group whose members interact in an impersonal manner, have few emotional ties, and come together for a specific practical purpose. Like primary groups, secondary groups may be small, but also can be large, and may involve face-to-face contacts and cordial or friendly interactions. Secondary group interactions are more formal than primary group interactions; however, they are just as important. Most of our time is spent in secondary groups—committees, professional groups, sales-related groups, classroom groups, or neighborhood groups. As a student, you come together with other students at specified times to learn sociology. While you have the class in common with many others, it is unlikely that you will develop a close relationship with all the individuals enrolled in the course. In fact, it is quite likely you would not recognize many of your classmates if they passed you in the hallways.

The key difference between primary and secondary groups is in the quality of the relationships and the extent of personal intimacy and involvement (Table 5.2). Primary groups are person-oriented, whereas secondary groups tend to be goal-oriented. We allow those with whom we have a close relationship to occupy more of our personal space than members of secondary groups. A primary group conversation usually focuses on personal experiences, feelings, and casual, open sharing, whereas a secondary group conversation is more apt to be impersonal and purposeful.

Primary and secondary groups are important both to individuals and to society. Primary groups are particularly important in shaping the personality, in formulating self-concepts, in developing a sense of personal worth, and in becoming an accepted member of society. They are also an important source of social control and social cohesion. Such famous scholars as Erich Fromm (1965) and Lewis Mumford (1962) contend that the strength and vitality of primary groups are the basis of the health of a society. In an increasingly impersonal world, they are sources of openness, trust, and intimacy. People who are not members of some primary group—a marriage, friendship, or work relationship—experience greater health problems and other difficulties.

Although primary groups are vital to the health of individuals and society, secondary groups are also important because they tend to meet specific goals. They help societies function effectively and permit people who do not know one another intimately to perform their jobs more effectively. Most formal organizations such as schools, corporations, hospitals, and unions comprise many secondary groups and relationships.

It should be recognized that the difference between primary and secondary groups is one of degree. Many formal secondary group situations involve instances of informality and personal openness. In fact, many primary groups develop from secondary groups and organizations. Two students who meet in a formal lecture hall (secondary group) may

TABLE 5-2 CHARACTERISTICS OF PRIMARY AND SECONDARY GROUPS

Primary Groups	Secondary Groups
Informal	Formal
Smaller in number	Larger in number
Intimate	Less intimate
Person-oriented	Goal-oriented
Longer in duration	Shorter in duration

later marry (primary group); coworkers in a large organization may develop an intimate friendship. Conversely, two friends who join a corporation may grow apart and ultimately have only a secondary relationship. The composition of an individual's primary and secondary groups shifts frequently.

In-Groups and Out-Groups

As a college student and probably recent high school graduate, you are familiar with in-groups and out-groups. Your high school most likely had some groups that you felt a sense of belonging to more than others. Like most public schools, there were probably groups labeled as preps, jocks, band geeks, stoners, and nerds—common categories throughout recent years. An **in-group** is a social category to which persons feel they belong and in which the members have a consciousness or awareness of kind. One of the key characteristics of an in-group is the members' sense of belonging. Those who belong think of one another as forming a social unit. This unit has boundaries that separate "us" from "them," that differentiate those who are "in" from those who are "out." Members believe they share a common fate, adhere to a common ideology, come from a common background, or otherwise resemble the other members. In-groups may be primary groups, but are not necessarily so. We can feel "in" with people we have never met or shared personal intimacies with—members of our alumni group, religious group, or veterans group, for example. University of California graduates, Buddhists, or Iraq War veterans may experience feelings of comradeship or a sense of togetherness.

As we feel the we-ness among our group, an **out-group** is one to which we feel we do not belong. Out-groups are made up of those who do not share an awareness of kind. We do not identify or affiliate ourselves with members of out-groups, and we feel little allegiance to them. We treat most members of out-groups with indifference, but at times we may feel hostile toward them because of our tendency toward ethnocentrism—the predisposition to perceive our own in-group as superior to others. The out-group, being inferior, does not deserve the same respect as

We can feel "in" with people we have never met or shared personal intimacies with—such as members of our alumni group.

the in-group. Thus the members of an in-group—friends, classmates, doctors, industrialists—may defend other in-group members even when it does an injustice to those who are "out."

The difference between in- and out-groups is sociologically important for at least two reasons. First, in-group members tend to stereotype out-group members as they notice and compare the differences between their own group and out-groups. Second, when we perceive threats from out-groups, it heightens our in-group solidarity.

Regarding the first reason, although we may notice individual differences among members of the in-group, most of us notice only similarities in the out-group; and we label them accordingly. Americans may recognize a wide range of variations in appearance, beliefs, and behavior among our fellow citizens but fail to recognize that not all Asians look alike, not all Germans love sauerkraut, and not all Iraqis are terrorists. Within the United States, whites (in-group) may label Hispanic immigrants (out-group) as lazy, and blacks (in-group) may label whites (out-group) as racists. Furthermore, the way we interact with others is often based upon prejudices we have towards groups we consider as out-groups. For example, we tend to avoid members of out-groups when the out-group is a group to which we attribute a negative stereotype (Wyer 2010).

Consider what the consequences of such stereotyping might be in our professional and personal relationships. How, for example, might a college professor communicate with students in class and relate to them outside of class if she assumes that all the students are unmotivated and uninterested in serious academic work? Because of her belief that most students are not serious about academics, she might have a tendency to talk down to them, to discuss difficult course material too quickly, or be unavailable for office hours. If she would recognize that her method of communicating and relating to students is based on a stereotype she holds toward an out-group rather than the qualities of the individual students in her class, she might be able to develop more effective ways of teaching and advising. Thus, we might use the knowledge that people tend to stereotype all members of out-groups to help us improve our interpersonal and communication skills.

A second reason the two groups are important to sociologists is because any threat or attack, whether imaginary or real, from the out-group tends to increase the cohesion and solidarity of the in-group. Strange as it may seem, an attack on our in-group can have positive effects. After the September 11, 2001, terrorist attack on the World Trade Center, for example, citizens of diverse backgrounds united as "Americans," and ideological, political, and racial differences within the country were diminished. American flags and other displays of support and patriotism were evident everywhere. Similarly, economic hardships may bring the members of a family closer together; just as flood destruction may bring a community closer together.

After the September 11, 2001, attacks on the World Trade Center, the country united as an in-group of "Americans."

In turn, members of in-groups may overreact toward out-groups in times of crises. When the Alfred P. Murrah Federal Building in Oklahoma City was blown up on April 19, 1995, killing 167 people, we immediately began searching for a member of an out-group. In one of the worst acts of terrorism in America, we quickly discovered that it was a member of our own in-group when Timothy McVeigh, a veteran, was arrested for the bombing. Later we learned that he was a member of a radical anti-government militia group in the U.S, and he was placed into an out-group category.

Knowing that out-group threats often increase the solidarity of members of an in-group is useful for anyone helping a group overcome conflict among its members. A therapist, for example, may work with a group of rehabilitated alcoholics by discussing ways in which they can begin to see drinkers as an out-group rather than an in-group as they had previously done. Similarly, in an effort to overcome the conflict among workers in an industrial plant, a labor union leader may call the workers' attention to the common enemy they face in management. If you were a coach of a high school softball team having difficulty with arguments and competition among the team players, how could you use what you know about out-groups to make the players feel closer to one another?

We all have many in-group identities and loyalties, some of which overlap and some of which cause conflict. We may, for example, strongly identify with both the women's movement and the Catholic Church but find that our belief that a woman should be able to choose whether to have an abortion is in direct conflict with the position of the Catholic Church. In-groups and out-groups can vary in size. They may be large, like the thousands who attend a football game, or as small as a two-person marriage. Our affiliation with a particular in-group may provide us with an identity and a sense of belonging, but it also induces conflict and restricts our relationships and interactions with others.

Peer Groups

One type of group from which in- and out-groups draw their members is the **peer group**, an informal primary group of people who share a similar status and who usually are of a similar age. The unique factor in peer groups is equality. In most groups, even small ones such as marriages or committees, one person or more has a higher status or a position of dominance; however, but in peer groups the members are roughly equal in importance.

Although peer groups are most often discussed in connection with young people, they are found in all age groups. Most friendships, regardless of the friends' ages, share the characteristics of a peer group: They are informal, primary relationships, and the participants are of equal rank and often of the same sex.

Reference Groups

Reference groups are the groups we identify with psychologically. They serve as sources of self-evaluation (comparative reference groups) and influence how we think and act and what we believe (normative reference groups). People need not belong to a group for it to be a reference group for them; groups we aspire to belong to may also be reference groups. Negative reference groups, those with which we do not want to be identified, also serve as sources of self-evaluation. A person might, for example, try to avoid resembling members of a group composed of intellectuals or of football players.

Most attention is focused on positive reference groups. These are the ones we want to be accepted by. Thus, if you want to be an executive, you might carefully observe and imitate the behavior of executives. If you note that they play golf, wear conservative clothes, and read the *Wall Street Journal*, you might do the same.

Comparative reference groups are an important source of information about our performance in a given area. Just as cultures tend to assess themselves on the basis of their own standards, individuals assess themselves in accordance with the standards of their reference group. Receiving a grade of B may be a source of pride to students if their peer reference group did worse; but it may be a source of disappointment to a family reference group if they expected an A from their child. A professor's income may be good relative to an assistant professor's income, but it may be poor relative to the income of someone employed in industry. In brief, we tend to judge our worth, accomplishments, and even our morality in comparison with groups of reference.

Normative reference groups serve not only as sources of current evaluation but also as sources of aspiration and goal attainment. A person who chooses to become a professional baseball player, a lawyer, or a teacher begins to identify with that group and is socialized to have particular goals and expectations associated with that group.

Having knowledge of people's reference groups can sometimes help us understand why they behave as they do. It may explain why a teenager who never smokes or drinks at home will do so with a school group, or why politicians may vary their stances on an issue, depending on the audiences they are addressing. Our aim is to please and to conform to the expectations and behaviors of the groups that are important to us.

APPLYING KNOWLEDGE OF REFERENCE GROUPS

The concept of reference groups also helps us understand why some people are unhappy or dissatisfied with their condition. People often feel deprived, not necessarily because of the objective conditions they face, but because they compare themselves to a reference group. This is known as relative deprivation. Sociological research has turned up many instances of groups that have experienced **relative deprivation.** Thomas Pettigrew (1964), for example, found that the economic and social conditions for black Americans improved greatly after World War II (for example, life expectancy increased, civil-service jobs increased,

SOCIOLOGY AT WORK

Job Rankings

At the beginning of 2009 CareerCast.com, an online job search company, issued its top ten jobs in America today. At the top of the list was mathematician, but in the number eight spot was sociologist. When determining the rankings of over two hundred jobs, Career Cast took into consideration work environment, physical demands, stress, income, and hours worked. *The Wall Street Journal* provides an example with Mark Nord, a sociologist working for the Department of Agriculture. As a researcher, he studies household incomes and writes reports that are used by organizations, the media, and the government to make policy decisions. Mr. Nord's salary is about double that of the $63,195 average income of sociologists reported by Career Cast. The following are the top ten best and worst jobs among the 200 studied (CareerCast.com, 2009).

TABLE 5A TOP JOBS

CareerCast.com rates the top two hundred jobs in the United States based upon income, working environment, stress, physical demands and job outlook, using data from the Labor Dept. and U.S. Census and researchers' own expertise.

Look at the mid-level salaries in this ranking, and note that the higher ranked jobs do not necessarily have the highest incomes. In fact, the two jobs in the ranking that have the highest mid-level salaries are are not in the top twenty: (24) and pharmacist (36). Compare also the salaries of the two jobs that are tied for thirteen. Note that sociologist falls securely in the top 20. It is important to consider a variety of factors, not only salary, in helping you decide what will lead to a satisfying career.

Rank	Title	Mid-level salary
1	software engineer	$87,000
2	mathematician	$94,000
3	actuary	$87,000
4	statistician	$73,000
5	computer systems analyst	$77,000
6	meteorologist	$85,000
7	biologist	$74,000
8	historian	$63,000
9	audiologist	$63,000
10	dental hygienist	$67,000
11	sociologist	$70,000
12	accountant	$60,000
13	paralegal assistant	$47,000
14	physicist	$106,000
15	financial planner	$101,000
16	philosopher	$61,000
17	occupational therapist	$70,000
18	parole officer	$47,000
19	aerospace engineer	$95,000
20	economist	$87,000

Source: From *The Wall Street Journal*, January 5, 2011. For the complete rankings and discussion about how the rankings were formulated, see www.careercast.com

income increased, and college attendance increased), yet blacks became progressively more dissatisfied. Pettigrew pointed out that this was because when compared to whites, a reference group, blacks were and still are considerably lacking equality with whites in many areas. Indeed, the economic and social conditions improved much more for whites, leaving blacks to experience relative deprivation. Relative deprivation has been found to explain many areas of life including health, mortality, suicide bombings, and others. For example, Pham-Kanter (2009) found that people tend to report certain types of illnesses such as ulcers, diabetes and cardiovascular problems at higher rates in very low-income groups and less likely in very high-income groups. Sayre (2010) found evidence that relative deprivation helps to explain the phenomenon of Palestinian suicide-bombings. There is ample research that supports the idea that reference groups indeed have an impact on our social and psychological well-being and on our actions.

Sociologists and economists are finding that employers and administrators would do well to pay attention to relative deprivation when they make decisions about salaries, bonuses, benefits, and other working conditions that affect various groups within an organization (Stark 1990). They could increase their ability to relate to the employees and treat them more fairly if they could understand the reference groups to which their employees compare themselves.

For example, pretend that you are the owner of a construction company, and your staff and your employees are dissatisfied with their wages. Before you consider giving an across-the-board 10-percent raise to all employees, you might first consider the impact of such a raise. The employees making higher salaries to begin with will receive bigger raises in terms of real dollars. So, in effect, you might be giving more money to those who need it the least and less money to those who need it the most. If you do this, do you think that the problem of worker dissatisfaction will be solved? Probably not. Instead, you might consider looking at who the various work groups compare themselves to and try to determine some fair amount that would bring each group more in line with the others or with groups at similar levels in different companies.

On a personal level, the concept of relative deprivation helps us to understand our own feelings of inadequacy and might help us to realize the sources of some of our frustrations. Many of us are happy with our lot in life—or with our car, clothes, stereo equipment, and so on—until we see members of our reference groups with something better. If we could realize that we are experiencing a relative deprivation—not an objective one—we might be able to deal with our feelings of inadequacy.

GROUP SIZE

Small Groups and Large Groups

Group size has an effect on much of our social interaction, such as our family, employment, juries, and protests. Categorizing groups according to size is an imprecise way to differentiate them, but numerous consequences or outcomes result from varying the group size:

1. Size has a dramatic effect on member interactions.
2. As size increases, so does the division of labor.
3. As the size of a group increases, its structure becomes more rigid and formal.
4. As the size of a group increases, so does the need for a more formal type of leadership.
5. As the size of a group increases, communication patterns change.
6. As size increases, cohesion decreases.

Let's look closer at the effects group size has on social interaction. First, it is important to understand how size affects membership interactions. The smallest group, a *dyad*, consists of two people. When just two people are involved, each of them has a special responsibility to interact—if one person withdraws, the group no longer exists. With the addition of a third person, the dyad becomes a *triad*, and the interactions change drastically. If one person drops out, the group can still survive. In a group of three, one person can serve as a mediator in a disagreement or alternatively side with one person and then the other. A third person, however, can also be a source of conflict or tension. The phrase "two's company; three's a crowd" emphasizes the dramatic shift that takes place when dyads become triads. When a triad adds a fourth or fifth member, two subgroups can emerge. As group size increases, the stability of the group decreases. It may be more difficult to choose a leader, arrive at an agreement or consensus, or decide who will perform particular tasks.

At what point does a small group become large? Is it small if it has two, ten, or twenty members? Is it large if it has 25 or 250 or 25,000 members? The type of group, as well as its goals may influence determinations of whether a group is large or small. In a marriage in many cultures, three would be large. In politics, thirty thousand may be small. As you can see, choosing a cutoff point between large and small groups requires that we consider a number of different factors. Even so, such a designation may be largely arbitrary.

Regardless of the distinction between large and small groups, the complexity of group relations increases much more rapidly than the number of members. Two people have only one reciprocal relationship, three people have six reciprocal relationships, four people have twenty-four relationships, five people have 120 relationships, six people have 720 relationships, and seven people have 5,040 relationships. Beyond that, the number of relationships quickly becomes astronomical. Size *does* make a difference.

A second consequence is that as size increases, so does the division of labor. If the group is small, all the members may engage in the same activities. As size increases, however, activities tend to become specialized. The father of one of the authors, for example, once taught eight grades in a one-room school. He covered the three R's and any other subjects, supervised the playground, did some personal counseling, and occasionally had some transportation responsibilities. As schools grew larger, teachers were assigned not only to specific grade levels but also to specific subject areas. They were employed to teach music, art, and other specialized subjects, and a complex system developed to provide transportation, counseling, lunches, sports, and a wide variety of clubs and other school-related activities. Similar changes in the division of labor occur as churches, families, manufacturing concerns, and other groups grow. Generally, as group size increases, so does the division of labor.

The third consequence is that increases in group size result in an increasingly rigid and formal structure. Whereas small groups are likely to operate informally according to unwritten rules, large groups usually conduct meetings in accordance with Robert's Rules of Order or some other standard formula. Also, small groups are more apt to emphasize personal and

The size of group has a dramatic effect on how its members interact. A dyad is the smallest group size and its existence depends on the interaction of both members. In a triad, such as in this photo, the group can survive even if one of its members drops out. Further, one person in a triad may serve as a mediator between the other two and maintain the group's cohesiveness.

primary characteristics. A small grocery store run by a family, for example, may reflect the tastes of the family members. Jobs may be delegated to various people on the basis of their preferences, and work schedules may be drawn up to accommodate one person's going to college or another person's social life. Large groups, on the other hand, emphasize status and secondary characteristics. In a large supermarket chain, committees make decisions. Chairpersons, division heads, or managers are selected, and the problems of bureaucratic red tape begin. In contrast to small groups, employees are expected to conform to the demands of their jobs rather than changing their jobs to meet their personal preferences.

The fourth is that as the size of a group increases, so does the need for a more formal type of leadership. With increasing size come complex problems relating to the coordination of activities and decisions, and this leads to the emergence of group leaders, persons who have the authority, the power, or the potential ability to direct or influence the behavior of others.

In all groups, somebody or some collectivity must make the decisions. In small groups, these decisions may be made informally, in a spirit of mutual sharing and agreement, with no designated leader. In large groups, which, as indicated, have more specialized activities and a more rigid and formal structure, the leadership becomes more formal as well, and the decision-making is more constraining. When the population of these groups bestows the rights to leadership, authority exists. Authority is legitimized power.

In analyzing leadership in small groups, Bales (1953) found that leaders are of two types, instrumental and expressive. **Instrumental leaders** organize the group around its goals by suggesting ways to achieve them and persuading the members to act appropriately. Thus, the instrumental leader directs activities and helps make group decisions. However, this type of leader is more likely to cause or create friction within the group because of the goal-oriented style of leadership. **Expressive leaders**, on the other hand, resolve conflicts and create group harmony and social cohesion. They make sure that the members can get along with one another and are relatively satisfied and happy. For groups to function effectively, Bales concluded, both types of leaders are needed.

Groups reflect the characteristics of the societies of which they are a part. Suppose, for example, that a neighborhood meeting is called to complain about the garbage collection. Six men and six women show up. What would you guess are the odds that a male will be asked to take the notes or a female will be asked to chair the session or take the formal complaint to the official source? It is unlikely that the group will wait to see who can write most effectively (which might be a male) or who can best serve as leader (which might be a female). Similarly, groups may assign the leadership position to the eldest, the most popular, the one with the most formal training, or the one who called the meeting.

Are there particular traits that distinguish leaders from nonleaders? For several decades, psychologists and social psychologists have tried to compile lists of leadership characteristics, but most results have been disappointing. Why? One explanation is that the attempt has been to find characteristics or traits that reside within individuals rather than seeking characteristics or traits relative to a task environment or a specific interpersonal and social context. Leaders and leadership qualities do not exist in a vacuum. Assigned cultural and social statuses, skills for specific tasks, and prior experience and training will influence the choice of leaders, which suggests that there is no such thing as a "born leader." Inborn characteristics, in combination with training, experience, skills, and social circumstances, determine the likelihood that a given person will occupy leadership positions. For example, many in the African American community have called President Barack Obama a "born leader". However, there were many black men and women throughout history possessing the leadership skills needed to run the country but who went unrecognized, simply because of their skin color. Women faced a similar fate not because they lacked the ability but, rather, the social status needed in our culture to be recognized as competent and qualified to lead the government and corporations.

A fifth consequence of increase in group size is a change in communication patterns. In large groups, the leaders tend to dominate the discussions. They talk the most and are addressed the most because the discussion and comments of other members are directed toward them. Although similar patterns of communication may exist in small groups, members who never join the discussion in a large group may do so in a small one. Some teachers prefer either a large or small class for this very reason. In a large class, the communication is both dominated by them and directed toward them. In a small class, the chances increase that most members will participate and that a communication exchange may take place among the group members. Social psychologists have been especially fascinated with "small-group dynamics." What happens when two, five, or eight people get together? Who sits where, who talks to whom, and how are decisions made?

Sixth, as size increases, cohesion decreases. A group is considered cohesive when members interact frequently, when they talk of "we," when they defend the group from external criticism, when they work together to achieve common goals, and when they are willing to yield their own personal preferences for those of the group. Membership stability is important for cohesion because a high turnover rate has a negative effect. Conformity is also important—failure to abide by group norms and decisions lessens cohesiveness. Groups induce conformity by formal means such as fines, not allowing participation, or assigning specific tasks, as well as by informal means such as verbal chides or jokes. Although these informal means become less effective as group size increases, small groups and informal networks exist within the large group or complex organization. The importance of this small group cohesiveness operating in a large group context was evident in World War II; both American and German soldiers admitted to fighting for their buddies, not for the glory and fame of their country.

Social scientists have found that cohesiveness within groups generally improves group performance. Group cohesiveness tends to reduce the anxieties of group members and leads to greater cooperation. A statement such as this suggests that the ability to create cohesion (for example, by reducing group size) can be an important tool for managers and administrators. The adage "many hands make light work" may not apply to all situations.

For example, imagine that you work for an advertising company and are put in charge of forming a committee to develop a new approach to selling a particular product. Considering the findings discussed here, you might be better off putting together a small group of creative people who will become tightly knit and develop a sense of unity, rather than assembling a large team where people do not feel as loyal to one another.

Social Networks

Throughout college you will probably be told that social networking is critical to job attainment after graduation. On a daily basis, each of us is involved in numerous groups of the types just described: primary, secondary, large, small, peer, reference, and so forth. Through these groups, we develop linkages or ties to a total set of relationships: **a social network**. Social networks link people. Think, for example, of your social network. It probably includes your family, your friends, your neighbors, classmates, members of social clubs, people you work with, and others.

Unlike close personal networks, many of our social networks include linkages with people with whom we have little in common and only occasional contact. These may be people whom we only know of or who only know of us. These "weak" ties, however, can be extremely important in getting a job or a "good deal" on a purchase. Perhaps this can be illustrated by the frequently heard phrase, "Whom you know is as important as what you know." This is social networking. The "good old boy" network seems to be effective in perpetuating social privileges to those who already hold positions of higher rank and prestige. Not only is networking important for our professional lives, but evidence of the increasing importance of networking in everyday life can be found in the growing popularity of websites such as Facebook, MySpace, Twitter, and others.

Social networks do not just happen. Over time, we build and establish ties to others, some strong, some weak. Strong ties may be characterized by emotional involvement and are sustained in a variety of ways, including calls, visits, letters, cards, attendance at particular events, and—as suggested by Cheal (1988)—through gifts. Results from intensive interviews led Cheal to suggest that people use gifts to reinforce relationships already in existence. Strong ties were based on numerous small gifts rather than large expensive ones. Marsden (1987) found that the average individual had only three strong ties with individuals with whom they could discuss important matters. This number increases considerably when other criteria, such as with whom you engage in social activities or from whom you would borrow, were used.

The ties to people in social networks do not have to be strong to have an important impact on our lives. Indeed, Malcolm Gladwell in his best-selling book *The Tipping Point: How Little Things Make a Big Difference* (2000) uses the findings of sociologist Mark Granovetter (1974) to explain how it is that the networks that have weak ties that can have some of the most profound effects on our lives. For example, Granovetter found that when finding a job, weak ties are more important than strong ties. We are more likely to have strong ties to close friends, people in our neighborhood, people you work with, members of your church congregation, and so on. They occupy a world that is very similar to yours. However, people who are only acquaintances, rather than close friends, are more likely to inhabit social worlds that are quite different than yours, thus allowing you to cast your net of contacts to places outside of what is immediately accessible to you.

There is little question of the importance of social networks. Women, for example, whose networks include more relatives than those of men, are paying increasing attention to building networks in the world of work. Many professional women are finding support in their ties with other women that they find lacking in settings where men both outnumber and overpower them. Social networks do make a difference in professional advancement, as well as in developing a sense of self-worth and integration into the society and culture of which we are a part.

Thinking Sociologically

1. Provide examples of some of your groups and examine the importance of each in your life.

2. How can you begin early in your college career to establish social networks that would increase your chances of getting jobing offers after graduation?

3. Are you a subscriber to any social networking websites such as Facebook, MySpace, or Twitter? If so, provide some examples of how networking through any of these websites has affected your personal life or professional opportunities.

FORMAL ORGANIZATIONS AND BUREAUCRACY

Many sociologists view the study of social organizations as the key to understanding society, groups, and personal behavior. The organization, they suggest, is different from the sum of the individuals who belong to it. If all the parts of an automobile are put in one pile, we have all the ingredients necessary for a car; but we certainly do not have an operable means of transportation. Only when those parts are properly assembled and interrelated do we get a car that works. Organizations are much the same. The whole is greater than the sum of its parts. In analyzing organizations, we focus not on the individual but on the social structure, the interrelated statuses and accompanying roles, and the norms that specify the rules of conduct and expectations for behavior.

Social organization refers to the stable patterns within our society: its norms, mores, roles, values, communication patterns, social institutions, and the like. One form of social organization is the **formal organization**, a large social group deliberately constructed and organized to achieve some specific and clearly stated goals. The *Encyclopedia of Associations* (2008) provides details of more than 22,200 national professional societies, labor unions, trade associations, fraternal and patriotic organizations, and other types of structured groups in the United States alone, which consist solely of voluntary members. More than 135,000 entries are listed when international as well as regional, state, and local organizations are included.

Organizations tend to be stable, often keeping the same structure and continuing to exist for many years. Those who belong to an organization generally feel a sense of membership. Industrial corporations, professional sports, country clubs, trade unions, schools, churches, prisons, hospitals, and government agencies are formal organizations created to meet

A church is a formal organization created to meet a specific goal.

specific goals. All groups have goals of some sort, but they are often latent, unstated, and general. Group members may even have conflicting goals; but in an organization, the goals are specific, clearly stated, and usually understood precisely by the members.

Consider the case of a family and a school. Both have as goals the education of children. The parents in a family may read to the youngest children and provide the older ones with books, magazines, and newspapers. They may also encourage children to play learning games or take them to museums and concerts. In a formal organization such as a school, however, the education program is much more highly structured. The teachers, administrators, and other staff members have been trained to teach a particular subject to a single group or to meet some other specific goal. The overall educational goals of the school, although perhaps subject to disagreement, are stated and understood more clearly than those of the family. The same holds true with factories (see Figure 5-2) and all other formal organizations, including voluntary associations, which are described at the end of this chapter.

The Importance of Formal Organizations

The importance of formal organizations in modern complex societies can hardly be overestimated. Every day, we deal with some sort of formal organization in connection with work, food, travel, health care, police protection, or some other necessity of life. Organizations enable people who are often total strangers to work together toward common goals. They create levels of authority and channels of command that clarify who gives orders, who obeys them, and who does which tasks. They are also a source of continuity and permanence in a society's efforts to meet specific goals. Individual members may come and go, but the organization continues to function. Thus, formal organizations make it possible for highly complex industrialized societies to meet their most fundamental needs and to pursue their collective aspirations.

Formalization is the process by which the norms, roles, or procedures of a group or organization become established, precise, and valid and by which increasing attention is given to structure, detail, and form. The formalization of organizations is the characteristic that distinguishes complex societies from small tribal societies. Herman Turk (1970) went so far as to state that modern societies are "an aggregate of organizations, which appear, disappear, change, merge, and form networks of relations with one another" (p. 1).

The Goals of Formal Organizations

As you can well imagine, the goals of different organizations vary widely. Businesses are interested chiefly in making a profit. Service organizations assist people with problems such as unemployment or illness. Some organizations, such as unions or stamp collectors, exist to promote the interests of their own group; other organizations, such as governments, the military, and prisons, are established to provide services to the general public.

Given this diversity of goals, it is not surprising that some formal organizations are in conflict with each other. The goals of right-to-life and right-to-choice organizations such as the National Organization for

FIGURE 5-2 HIERARCHY STRUCTURE OF MID-SIZED UNIVERSITY

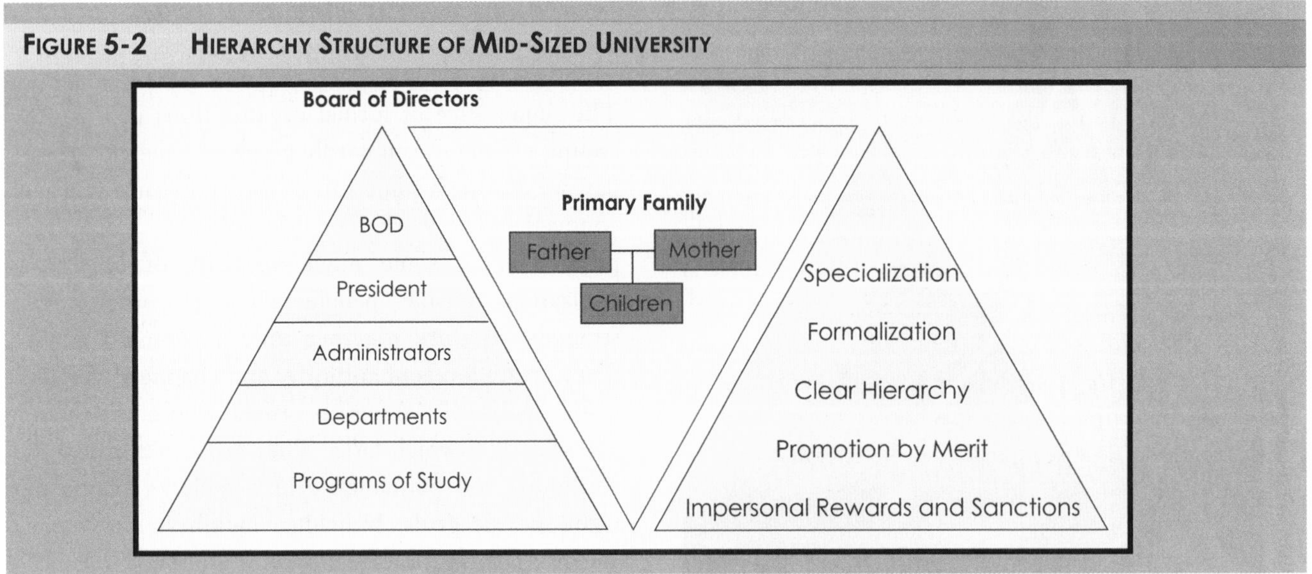

Women (NOW), for example, are very different, and conflict between the two is evident. Also, note the policy debate in this chapter over employee drug testing. The goals of some organizations, such as the Department of Transportation, favor this activity, while the goals of other organizations focus on the right to privacy and the noninterference into our personal matters.

Conflicts appear both between organizations and within them. Universities must determine whether the primary goal of their faculty is teaching or research. Medical organizations must decide whether their chief function is to aid and protect the physician or to improve the health care given to the public. Sometimes, an organization's apparent primary goal (e.g., service) is used to conceal its actual primary goal (e.g., profit). A private mental institution, for example, may emphasize the quality of the care it gives in its literature, but decisions about whether to provide a particular service to its clients may always be made on the basis of its profitability.

There are often conflicts between the goals of an organization's administration and those of its employees or the clients or public it serves. In a university, for example, the main priority for the administration may be to balance the budget. The aim of the faculty may be to do research and publish papers. The students may be most concerned with receiving a good education through exceptional teaching and the use of outstanding library and laboratory facilities, which may conflict with cost-saving measures and cut into professors' research time. Finally, some influential alumni may consider all these goals less important than having an outstanding football team, which brings the school national recognition.

Formal organizations have a particular type of administrative machinery designed to help them meet their goals. This administrative structure is known as bureaucratic organization, or, more simply, bureaucracy.

BUREAUCRACY

A **bureaucracy** is a formal organizational structure that directs and coordinates the efforts of the people involved in various organizational tasks. It is simply a hierarchical arrangement of an organization's parts, based on the division of labor and authority (see Figure 5.2). A hierarchical structure is like a pyramid—the people at each level have authority over the larger number of people at the level below them. The authority resides not in a person but in the office, position, or status within the organization. In other words, the responsibilities and authority associated with a particular job in the hierarchy remain essentially the same, regardless of the person occupying the position. Merton (1968) defines bureaucracy as "a formal, rationally organized social structure involving clearly defined patterns of activity in which, ideally, every series of actions is functionally related to the purposes of the organization" (p. 195).

Bureaucracy as an Ideal Type and Its Functions

One of the pioneers of sociology, Max Weber (1864–1920), authored the classical work on bureaucracy. Weber dealt with bureaucracy as an **ideal type**, which is a model of a hypothetical pure form of an existing entity. In other words, he did not concern himself with describing a specific bureaucracy; rather, he examined a great many bureaucracies in an attempt to discover the general principles that govern how they operate. An ideal type, then, is not to be thought of as a perfect entity in the usual sense of the word ideal. As this chapter later shows, bureaucracies are often far from perfect. As Weber (1914–1947) suggests, bureaucracies typically have the following characteristics:

- *Division of Labor and Specialization* Each member or worker is trained for a specific job. Each member has carefully described responsibilities, and each job is designed to meet a specific need.

- *Hierarchy of Authority* Organizations are run by a chain of command—a hierarchy of bosses and workers who are, in turn, the bosses of other workers. As indicated earlier, the hierarchy is in the form of a pyramid. All officials are accountable to those at a higher level for their own responsibilities and for those of subordinates. The top of the chain of command is often a board of directors or company officers. Below this level are the middle-level managers, administrators, foremen, and department heads. The largest number of workers is at the bottom of the hierarchy (refer back to Figure 5-2).

- *Impersonality* Employees are expected to maintain integrity and to separate their personal lives from their professional lives. The office and the organization's written files are in a separate location from the employees' homes, and families and are not subject to their influence. The organization's money and equipment belong to the organization, not to individuals; and its activity is separate from the activity of private life. Public office implies impersonality, a separation of person and the organization.

- *Qualifications* Organizations select personnel on the basis of merit, using standardized criteria such as civil service examinations or educational training rather than friendship or political or family connections. Those who are hired are expected to have the specialized knowledge or skills necessary to perform their assigned task.

- *Career Pattern* Employees are expected to devote themselves completely to the business of the organization and to recognize that people work their way to the top. As one moves up in the hierarchy, job security and salaries improve. Seniority is recognized, valued, and rewarded. Whether the organization is the U.S. Army, General Motors, or the Catholic Church, increasing time with the organization and adequate job performance are supposed to bring promotions, higher pay and status, and stronger tenure or job security.

- *Written Rules* The operation of the organization is governed by a consistent set of rules that define the responsibilities of various positions, assure the coordination of tasks, and encourage the uniform treatment of clients. Written rules are used rather than informal communication, and the larger the organization the more rules are used to cover rules from regarding almost every possible situation. These rules are quite stable and comprehensive, and they can be readily learned and followed. In a university setting there are student, faculty, and departmental handbooks outlining the rules of the school.

Although in any given formal organization, some members are employed for personal reasons rather than merit, the rules are occasionally ignored, and some customers are not treated impartially, most bureaucracies share the characteristics described here. A hierarchical organization, division of labor, and the other attributes of the bureaucratic ideal type are essential to efficient functioning. As we all know, however, bureaucracies have their shortcomings. Most of us associate them with red tape, mountains of forms to complete, and endless lines. How and why do bureaucracies get so bogged down?

POLICY DEBATE

Employee Drug Testing

Along with their efforts to increase productivity and efficiency, and to try to prevent avoidable accidents, many organizations have deemed it necessary to ensure that their employees are "drug free." There were 17.2 million illicit drug users over age eighteen in the United States in 2005. Of these, 12.9 million (74.8 percent) were employed full or part time. Between 10 percent and 20 percent of U.S. workers who die on the job test positive for alcohol or drugs (www.OSHA.com). Drug testing is typically seen differently by employees than employers. The percentage of full-time workers, age eighteen to forty-nine, who indicated that their employer conducted any type of drug testing programs—whether at hiring, randomly, upon suspicion, or post-accident—increased from 43.6 percent in 1994 to 48.5 percent in 1997. The rationale behind drug testing in the workplace is simple: increasing the consequences to employees who use drugs will deter drug usage. Interestingly, both supporters and opponents of drug testing agree that this is a likely outcome of drug testing (Carpenter 2007).

The American Management Association regularly conducts surveys of workplace surveillance and medical testing. Their survey findings have found that in 1986 only 21 percent of companies subjected their employees or job applicants to drug testing. In 1991, drug testing of some kind was conducted by 63 percent of companies surveyed, growing to 81 percent in 1996, falling to 66 percent in 2000 and then to 62 percent in 2004. The possibility of being drug tested as a new-hire by a company was 48 percent in 1991, growing to 68 percent in 1996, falling to 61 percent in 2000 and then to 54.5 percent in 2004. Chances of being tested randomly by your employer was 52 percent in 1991, rising to 70 percent in 1996, falling to 47 percent in 2000 and then to 44.3 percent in 2004. The research clearly indicates that an employee is more likely to be asked to submit to a drug test before an offer of a job is given. However, the trend also seems to indicate a decrease in the number of companies that are requiring drug testing of any kind and a decrease in the types of companies that are testing (see Table 5.4). What are the possible reasons for the decline and company type?

Varieties of reasons are given to support employee drug testing; most focus on safety and productivity. The pros and cons of drug testing in the workplace are very much the same now as when the debate about drug testing began to become widespread in the mid-1980s. The Department of Transportation, one of the strongest advocates of employee drug testing, rationalizes its decision to routinely test private-industry employees out of concern for the public (Navasky 1990). Airline pilots, railroad engineers, air traffic controllers, and other mass transportation workers under the influence of drugs obviously pose a severe safety hazard. Corporate legal liability and moral responsibility for the actions of its employees has been given as a compelling reason to allow corporations the right to test its employees for drug use (Moore 1989).

Lost productivity is another often-cited reason for drug testing. J. Michael Walsh, head of NIDA's applied research division and a supporter of employee drug testing, claimed that the "cost of drug abuse to U.S. industry" was more than about fifty billion dollars a year and that drug users—from crack addicts to weekend marijuana smokers—are more likely to cause accidents, miss work, and use health benefits (Horgan 1990b).

However, current research indicates that companies are beginning to forego the hiring and random tests and strictly use impairment drug testing if the employee is involved in an accident. Cost is cited as the number one reason why companies are discontinuing mandatory drug testing (Cornell and Smithers 1992). It is estimated that approximately one billion dollars was spent annually in the mid-1990's to drug test twenty million employees (Shepherd and Thomas 1998).

One electronics manufacturer noted that after testing ten thousand employees, only forty-nine of them tested positive for substance abuse. The company argued that given the low number of positive returns, each one cost them approximately $20,000 (Cornell and Smithers 1992).

Dysfunctions of Bureaucracies

Robert Michels (1876–1936), a colleague of Weber, believed inevitably formal organization would be dominated by a small self-serving group of individuals at the top. He coined the term **"the iron law of oligarchy"** in 1911 in reference to his theory. Michels argued that simple power in the hands of those at the top of the pyramid allowed them an opportunity to promote their own self-interests.

Weber focused on many of the positive accomplishments of bureaucracies: precision, coordination, reliability, efficiency, stability, and continuity. Merton (1957) was the most important writer on the dysfunctions of bureaucracy. He observed that people in bureaucracies tend to develop what Veblen called **trained incapacity**, which occurs when the demands of discipline, rigidity, conformity, and adherence to rules render people unable to perceive the end for which the rules were developed. In Merton's words, "Adherence to the rules, originally conceived as a means, becomes transformed into an end-in-itself" (p. 199). This condition is similar to *ritualism*, which is discussed in another chapter.

The debate about drug testing has shifted from testing employees to testing students. According to Columbia University (2003), "Drug testing of students is more prevalent in schools where drugs are used, kept, or sold than in schools that are drug free. While only 23 percent of drug-free schools drug test students, 38 percent of non-drug-free schools conduct some type of drug testing."

Much criticism on drug testing in both the workplace and schools focuses on the right to privacy (Moore 1989). Drug testing has been mostly criticized on the grounds that it violates the Fourth Amendment, which prohibits unreasonable searches and seizures. Victor Navasky (1990, p. 39), editor of the *Nation*, suggests that employee drug testing "is just one small part of a vast campaign of control that seeks to examine every aspect of a person's physical, social, and emotional life—down to the genetic core—and subordinate the right of privacy to the imperatives of state power. . . . The enormously expensive, elaborate, totalitarian testing procedures are meant to control consciousness and regulate behavior." While employers have the right to fire or reprehend employees whose drug use hampers their work performance, they should have no right to sanction employees who perform well who use drugs for recreational use, nor do they have a right to interfere in their personal lives.

In our discussions about the bureaucratization of society, we raised the question, "To what extent does bureaucracy affect our personal lives?" Has the increasing tendency toward bureaucratization and the associated centralization of power cost us some freedom in exchange for increased efficiency and productivity? Which position do you agree with? Consider these questions from the perspectives of both organizations and individuals. Should drug testing be allowed or prohibited in all work situations? If so, where should the line be drawn with regard to control over our private lives? Should any other types of personal behavior be prohibited if they are deemed to be a threat to safety or productivity? Questions such as these are becoming increasingly relevant as advances in technology increasingly enable the examination of our private lives.

TABLE 5B TYPES OF COMPANIES THAT PERFORM EMPLOYEE DRUG TESTS

Type of Business	Test New Hires	Test All Employees
Financial	35.8%	18.8%
Business & Professional	36.0%	18.4%
Other Services	60.3%	34.7%
Wholesale & Retail	63.0%	36.8%
Manufacturing	78.5%	42.2%

Source: American Management Association, A 2000 AMA Survey: Workplace Testing: Medical Testing: New York, NY: American Management Association, 2000, p. 1.

We have all had experiences in which an obsessive adherence to procedures and rules kept us from meeting goals. In corporations, for example, employees are often required to routinely send copies of memos, emails, and letters to people who do not look at them and perhaps would not know what the correspondence meant if they did. It would be much more efficient simply to stop sending them. Often, our training, habits, or traditional ways of behaving blind us to alternatives that might be far more effective than the ones to which we are accustomed.

A second dysfunction comes about when hiring and promotions are based on a rigid set of formal qualifications—five years' experience or a college degree, for example, rather than skill or performance. In one instance, a woman with ten years' experience in her company and an excellent work reputation was passed over for promotion to supervisor because her company's policy dictated that supervisors must have a college degree. There are also instances in which excellent college teachers are denied tenure because they do not have a sufficient number of publishing credits. In bureaucratic organizations, formal qualifications may supersede performance in hiring and promotion.

A third dysfunction of bureaucracy with which we are all familiar is the runaround. Who among us has not called an organization and had our call transferred to two or three other departments, only to be returned to the first person to whom we spoke, with the problem still unresolved? Recall that bureaucracies have rules defining the duties and responsibilities of various offices. The legal department handles legal matters, the personnel office handles recruitment, rank, and salary matters, and the payroll department issues checks, withholds money for benefits, and pays taxes. Other departments handle other matters. Now which one would you get in touch with about a lawsuit concerning the payment of salary? The difficulty is that actual problems do not always fit neatly into the compartments designed to handle them. If a problem does not clearly fall within a department's area of responsibility, or if it involves several departments, the runaround is likely to begin.

Understanding the dysfunctions of bureaucracy may help administrators, managers, and entrepreneurs assess whether the positive aspects of this form of organizational structure outweigh the negative. Bureaucracy as an organizational form is not for every situation. The mom-and-pop grocery store, for example, may attract large numbers of customers precisely because of its friendly, informal, "homey," unbusinesslike atmosphere. Running that business according to bureaucratic principles would probably lead to its demise. Some professional and educational settings where efficiency and production are less important than high-quality interpersonal relationships are also better off without rigid bureaucratic procedures. The large-scale "student-processing" that efficiently pushes students through a university system and hands them a diploma in four years would be dysfunctional in the small liberal arts college. The physician who boasts "family care in a caring way" would probably see a decline in business if she decided that seeing patients without appointments was an inefficient way to run her practice. In situations such as these, the manifest function of the organization might possibly be distorted—and failure might result—if the principles of bureaucracy are applied.

Must Bureaucracies Be Dehumanizing and Impersonal? The Case of Japan

The very impersonality that makes an organization efficient can create problems on the human level. Merton (1957) wrote that bureaucracies stress depersonalization of relationships, categorization, and indifference to individuals. C. Wright Mills (1951) wrote that middle class, white-collar employees of bureaucratic organizations were enmeshed in a vast impersonal structure of rationalized activity in which their own rationality is lost. Interestingly, and perhaps a meaningful indicator of the general public's negative views about bureaucracy, www.dictionary.com defines a *bureaucrat* as "an official of a bureaucracy who is rigidly devoted to the details of administrative procedure." Similarly, another Internet information source, www.infoplease.com, defines a bureaucrat as, "an official who works by fixed routine without exercising intelligent judgment." The prevalence of popular stereotypes about the rigidity and formality suggests that bureaucracies will almost inevitably be dehumanized and impersonal.

Do organizations have to be dehumanizing and impersonal, though? Perhaps a brief look at American and Japanese automotive assembly plants can help us answer this question. Richard Florida and Martin Kenney (1991), in studying whether Japanese industrial organization could be transplanted to the United States, describe the U.S. organizational environment as typically characterized in terms of diversity, individualism, and unrestrained market forces. Japan is characterized in terms of homogeneity, familism, paternalism, and/or welfare corporatism. High levels of functional specialization, large numbers of job classifications, and adversarial labor–management relations among others, distinguish U.S. organization. In contrast, the Japanese manufacturing firm is distinguished by small numbers of job classifications, team-based work organization, and consensual relations between labor and management.

What does this have to do with the issue of dehumanization and impersonality in bureaucracies? It suggests that bureaucracies can be organized in ways that are both more humanizing and personal. Work in

Japanese organizations is generally based on teams that are responsible for planning and carrying out production tasks. The teams have team leaders, but unlike U.S. foremen, those leaders do not supervise workers. While they have managerial responsibility, they are themselves members of the work group.

This is related to another feature of Japanese organization, that of minimal status distinction between management and blue-collar workers. In Japan, workers and managers are likely to eat in the same cafeteria and to wear the same uniforms. Generally, managers do not have enclosed offices but sit at desks on a large open floor adjacent to the production facility. Within the production facility, the workers rotate tasks within their teams. This functions both to train workers in multiple tasks and to reduce the incidence of repetitive-motion injuries.

Unlike U.S. companies, a main objective of the Japanese system of work and production organization is to harness the collective intelligence of workers for continuous product and process improvement (Kenney and Florida 1988). This means that, in Japan, workers actively participate in company suggestion programs and quality-control circles, as well as informal, everyday continuous improvement activities. Workers have significant input into the design of their jobs, the production process, and the operation of the organization.

American individualism stands in contrast to Japanese familism in that Japanese workers become "married" to the organization, with guaranteed lifetime employment. Classes of workers receive uniform wages, with raises at regular intervals based on work effort, absenteeism, willingness to work in teams, and willingness to suggest new ideas. Semiannual bonuses are said to often constitute 30 percent of total remuneration (Aoki 1988). These factors, among others, are related to morale and job security, frequently discussed features of the Japanese system.

Must bureaucracies be dehumanizing and impersonal? Japan provides us with one example of how they can be made less so. Guaranteed lifetime employment, participation in decision making, team-based activities, workers trained and rotated among a variety of specialties, minimal adversarial relationships, and diminished status distinctions between workers and management, all combine to increase the probabilities of greater humanization and personalization within bureaucracies. Other examples of this process may be evident in organizations that people join voluntarily.

Thinking Sociologically

1. Describe how the dehumanization process takes place within an organization with which you are familiar. Consider how statuses and roles within the organization contribute to dehumanization.

2. Discuss how the university you attend is bureaucratic. Using your knowledge of social structure, groups, and organizations, discuss how the college would be different if it became less bureaucratic and more bureaucratic, respectively.

Voluntary Associations

Voluntary associations are organizations that people join because they share their goals and values and voluntarily choose to support them. People join many formal organizations because they are forced to or because they need the income, protection, or training that these organizations offer. Examples include schools, the armed services, insurance companies, and places of work. Voluntary associations, however, are joined out of personal interest, to participate in some social program, or as a channel for political action.

Voluntary associations are instances of associational or organizational groups, which were discussed earlier in this chapter. They typically involve awareness of kind, social interaction, and formal organization. Awareness of kind is central to our voluntary involvement because we share the interests and goals of the membership, whether the group is the League of Women Voters, Boy Scouts of America, National Rifle Association (NRA), National Association for the Advancement of Colored People (NAACP), the Baptist Church, or American Sociological Association. We enjoy socially interacting with other members because of our common focus of attention and shared interests.

Since these associations are formally organized, they have officers and bylaws or a constitution. Some associations are small and highly informal; others are large, formal, bureaucratically organized, and demand dues and conformity to established procedures. Membership is voluntary rather than by ascription; therefore, members can leave if they become dissatisfied.

In studies covering several decades, sociologists have learned a good deal about voluntary associations. We know that they are class-limited—members in any given association usually come from similar socioeconomic levels. Bowling club members are unlikely to join golf clubs; members of a wealthy businessmen's club are unlikely to join the Ku Klux Klan. Churches are voluntary associations that cover the class and wealth spectrum, but those living at a poverty level seldom attend the same church as the affluent. Although people of all ages and socioeconomic levels join voluntary associations, middle-aged people of high social status and education are the most frequent participants. Men are more likely to join than women, but American women are more likely to join associations than women in most other countries.

CHAPTER REVIEW
Wrapping it up

Summary

1. Society is socially structured. It is composed of many parts, including social statuses, roles, groups, organizations, and institutions. Statuses are socially defined positions that individuals occupy. A combination of statuses held by a person is a *status set*. Statuses can be ascribed or achieved but, usually, involve a combination of the two. Sometimes a particular status, a *master status*, takes priority over all the others.

2. All statuses have sets of expectations and behaviors associated with them. These are roles and role sets. What a role prescribes, the perception of it, and the behavior that is actually performed may be very different. Commitment to the role, the flexibility it permits, and competing demands from other roles may clarify these differences.

3. Three difficulties that can result from roles are *role ambiguity*, in which the expectations are not clear, *role strain*, in which contradictory demands or the ability to live up to the expectations of the role produces stress, and *role conflict*, in which inconsistent expectations are associated with the same role. However, roles are basic to social structure and social behavior, making them predictable, patterned, and organized.

4. There are five types of social interactions in which we engage: exchange, cooperation, competition, conflict, and coercion. We are generally engaged in an exchange situation, based on a rewards system; however, we live in a society that increasing encourages competition.

5. Social groups are so fundamental a part of our existence that it is difficult to imagine life without them. Most social groups involve interaction, a sense of belonging or membership, shared interests and values, and some type of structure.

6. Members of statistical and categorical groups, often formed for comparative and research purposes, share common characteristics but are not social groups, in that they do not interact with one another.

7. *Aggregates* are social collections of people who are in physical proximity to one another. They are loosely structured groups that are short-lived and involve little interaction. Members of *associations* and *organizational groups* interact, are aware of their similarity, and, in addition, are organized to pursue a common goal.

8. *Primary groups* are small and informal and emphasize interpersonal cohesion and personal involvement. *Secondary groups* are less personal and intimate, and they are more goal-oriented and purposeful.

9. *In-groups* are those to which people feel they belong. The in-group shares a common allegiance and identity, tends to be ethnocentric, and stereotypes members of the out-group. In-group cohesion is intensified by out-group threats.

10. *Peer groups* are informal primary groups of people who share a similar status and usually are of similar age. *Reference groups* provide self-evaluation and direct aspirations. They are the groups we use to assess our own performance, even if we do not actually belong to them.

11. Groups are also differentiated by size. The addition of even a few people changes group interactions considerably; and, as size increases, there are generally changes in the division of labor, formality, leadership, communication, and cohesion.

12. Formal organizations are deliberately organized to achieve specific goals. They are particularly important in industrialized societies, in which many relationships are impersonal. Formal organizations are sources of authority and of continuity in our efforts to meet basic societal and personal goals, but conflict within and between organizations is common.

13. *Bureaucracy* is a type of administrative structure found in formal organizations. It is a hierarchical arrangement of the parts of an organization, based on a division of labor and authority. Roles in the hierarchy are based on position or office, not on individual characteristics. Bureaucracies operate in a location separate from the homes and families of their employees. They also operate according to objective rules, hire and promote people on the basis of merit, and encourage workers to rise in the hierarchy through hard work. They can have a positive influence on efficiency, precision, coordination, stability, and continuity.

14. Bureaucracies have dysfunctions as well. Trained incapacity, the bureaucratic runaround, dehumanization, and impersonality appear to be negative characteristics of bureaucracies. The iron law of oligarchy refers to a small group of self-serving people, generally at the top of the bureaucratic pyramid, who promote their own interests.

15. The case of Japan illustrates how bureaucracies and formal organizations can be made less dehumanizing and impersonal. Participation in decision-making, team-based activities, work rotation, and diminution of status distinctions between workers and management all may contribute to humanizing the bureaucratic organization.

16. *Voluntary associations* are organizations that people join because they share the goals and values of these organizations and choose to support them. Since membership is voluntary, members can resign if their interest wanes.

Key Terms

aggregate group Any collection of people together in one place that interact briefly and sporadically

associational group A group of people who join together to pursue a common interest in an organized, formally structured way

bureaucracy A hierarchical, formally organized structural arrangement of an organization based on the division of labor and authority

categorical group Group of people who share a common characteristic but do not interact or have any social organization

expressive leader Type of leader that focuses on resolving conflicts and creating group harmony and social cohesion

formal organization Large social group deliberately organized to achieve certain specific, clearly stated goals

ideal type A model of a hypothetical pure form of an existing entity

in-group A social group to which people feel they belong and with which they share a consciousness of kind

instrumental leader A type of leader that focuses on goals, directing activities, and helping make group decisions

iron law of oligarchy An organization dominated by a small self-serving group of people who achieve power and promote their own interests

master status A particular status in one's status set that takes priority over the others

out-group A group to which people feel they do not belong, with which they do not share consciousness of kind, and with which they feel little identity

peer group An informal primary group of people who share a similar or equal status and who are usually of roughly the same age

prescribed role The expectations associated with a given status that are based on what society suggests or dictates

primary group A small, informal group of people who interact in a personal, direct, and intimate way

reference group A group with which people identify psychologically and to which they refer in evaluating themselves and their behavior

relative deprivation A feeling of being deprived, not because of objective conditions, but because of comparison to a reference group

role The social expectations or behaviors associated with a particular status

role ambiguity A situation in which the expectations associated with a particular social status are unclear

role conflict A situation that exists when differing expectations are associated with the same role

role perception The way that expectations for behavior are perceived or defined—which may differ considerably from what is prescribed or actually done

role performance The actual behavior of a person in a particular role, in contrast to the way that person is expected to behave

role set The multiple roles attached to statuses

role strain A situation that occurs when differing and incompatible roles are associated with the same status

secondary group A group in which the members interact impersonally, have few emotional ties, and come together for a specific, practical purpose

social group A group in which people physically or socially interact

social network The linkage or ties to a set of relationships

statistical group A group formed by sociologists or statisticians in which members are unaware of belonging and have no social interaction or social organization

status The socially defined position an individual occupies

status set The combination of all the statuses any individual holds at a given time

trained incapacity The situation that exists when the demands of discipline, conformity, and adherence to rules render people unable to perceive the end for which the rules were developed

voluntary association An organization people join because they share the organization's goals and values and voluntarily choose to support them

Discussion Questions

1. What is meant by the statement, "Society is socially structured"?
2. Answer the question, "Who am I?" in terms of your status set. List several social expectations (roles) that are generally attributed to statuses within the set. From this, discuss the various role conflicts that are part of your life.
3. List some of your primary and secondary groups. Describe the ways you act in each of these. Compare the criterion by which you are judged by others in each of these groups.
4. Discuss some of the most important reference groups in your life. How do they affect how you think about things and about yourself, and how you act? Do you belong to any reference groups of which you are not a member? If so, explain.

5. Illustrate how group processes and outcomes or consequences are influenced by the size of the group.
6. In relation to social networks discuss the statement, "Whom you know is as important as what you know."
7. Must bureaucracies be dehumanizing and impersonal? Contrast Japanese and American corporations in your response
8. Discuss some problems that primary groups in an organization might encounter when faced with increasing bureaucratization.
9. How are statuses and roles in a group, organization, and community affected by bureaucratization?
10. Why do people join voluntary organizations?

Pop Quiz

1. A socially defined position is known as a ______.

a. status
b. role
c. status set
d. role set

2. Ascribed status involves one's ______.

a. age
b. race
c. sex
d. all of the above

3. Which of the following groups is created by sociologists or statisticians?

a. categorical group
b. statistical group
c. societal unit
d. associational group

4. Which of the following is considered to be a social group?

a. an aggregate
b. a statistical group
c. a random group
d. a secondary group

5. A ________ group is an example of an informal primary group.

a. peer
b. statistical
c. reference
d. mutual interest

6. The ________ leader directs group activities and decision-making, while the ________ leader resolves conflict and creates group harmony.

a. expressive; instrumental
b. expressive; informal
c. instrumental; expressive
d. instrumental; formal

7. The process of formalization includes ______.

a. the establishment of norms and roles by an organization
b. less attention to the matter of structure
c. less attention to the details of relationships
d. only a and c above

8. Weber found bureaucracies to have all but which one of the following attributes?

a. a division of labor
b. hierarchy of authority
c. public office
d. selections of personnel by political connections

9. Organizations that people join because of shared interests and values are called ______.

a. peer groups
b. voluntary associations
c. formal organizations
d. aggregates

10. Which one of the following is true regarding voluntary associations?

a. Membership turnover is high
b. They are not class-limited
c. Women are more likely to join than are men
d. One-third of all Americans belong to at least one

11. If a particular status is much more important to you than others, it can be termed your status set. T/F

12. A categorical group is one in which people share a common characteristic. T/F

13. Primary groups are uncommon in industrial societies. T/F

14. Reference groups serve as sources of self-evaluation. T/F

15. Formal organizations are groups deliberately constructed to reach certain specific, clearly stated goals. T/F

1. A	6. C	11. F
2. D	7. D	12. T
3. B	8. D	13. F
4. D	9. B	14. T
5. A	10. A	15. T

CHAPTER 6

Socialization and Social Interaction

TRANSGENDER SOCIALIZATION AND IDENTITY: THE CASE OF JOHN/JOAN

Bruce Reimer (who later changed his name to David) was an identical twin boy born in August 1965. At around eight months of age, both boys were brought in to their doctor to be circumcised. Rather than use a scalpel, which was the more typical method for circumcision, the physician opted to use an electric cauterizing needle to remove Bruce's foreskin because he happened to go to the operating room first. Because of complications to the procedure, Bruce suffered severe burns to his penis that resulted in dismemberment within a few days (Money and Tucker 1975, in Westheimer and Lopater 2005)

Needless to say, the parents were devastated. Several months later, while they were still considering what course of action to take to help their child live a life in which he could normally fulfill his bodily functions and obtain satisfaction as an adult, their doctor referred them to John Hopkins University Medical Center. Concurrently, Dr. John Money, a psychologist who specialized in working with transsexual people (gender reassignments) and had a clinic at Johns Hopkins, was receiving a great deal of publicity. Money presented the Reimers with the option of reconstructing their son's genitals and his undergoing treatments that would ultimately make him biologically a female. Although gender reassignment through genital reconstruction up until that time had been rare (although not unprecedented), gender reconstruction for hermaphrodites (children born with ambiguous genitals) did exist as a viable medical alternative. Today, gender reconstruction of intersexes at birth is highly controversial as it is not clear with which gender the individual will identify as an adult. At the time, however, the Reimer's choice to begin transgender procedures did not seem unreasonable to them. Bruce was twenty-two months of age when he began the process. It is important to mention, however, that until that time he had been socialized as a boy during the period of life in which, arguably, some of the most profound gender imprints on our identity are formed.

On July 3, 1967, Bruce became Brenda, and the Reimers were instructed to never discuss or doubt their decision to have their son undergo gender reconstruction. The transformation to a female was to be absolute and unequivocal. From that moment on, the Reimers raised their child as a girl. Not only did they socialize her as a girl, she also embarked on a series of hormonal treatments through early adolescence that would result in female physical characteristics, such as the development of breasts. In 1997, John Colapinto revealed through an article in *Rolling Stone Magazine* the truth about Brenda, who at age fourteen stopped living as a girl (prior to surgery that would create an organ that simulated a vagina). "Brenda" eventually changed his name to David. The story became known as the "case of John/Joan."

As Colapinto discovered, "Brenda" had never fully embraced "her" identity as a female. She continuously tried to exhibit the same type of masculine behavior as her twin brother. Dr. Money, however, was insistent on maintaining a strict regime of feminine gender role socialization in order to achieve what he felt would lead to a complete gender transformation. Ultimately, when he was fourteen, Bruce's parents told him the truth about his past, and he began to try to live his life as a male.

Bruce eventually had a prosthetic device implanted to simulate a penis, changed his name to David, and married. His marriage lasted for fourteen years. However, the trauma of his childhood continued to plague him as an adult, and he committed suicide in 2004.

The case of John/Joan is important because it demonstrates the interplay and complexity of biology and socialization on the development of gender identity.

WHAT IS SOCIALIZATION?

Socialization is the lifelong process through which people are prepared to participate in society at every level: individual, interpersonal, group, organizational, institutional. It shapes our identities and the skills, norms, values and beliefs that underlie our actions and interactions. This learning occurs in all interactions from the minute a baby is born. Individuals must learn about their culture, including the rules and expectations of the culture. In the United States, most people learn to speak the English language and to eat with a fork. They learn that cereal, bacon, and eggs are breakfast foods and that sandwiches are appropriate for lunch. They find out that some people do work that is defined as important, and that those who do not or will not work are of less value. They discover that particular countries and people are

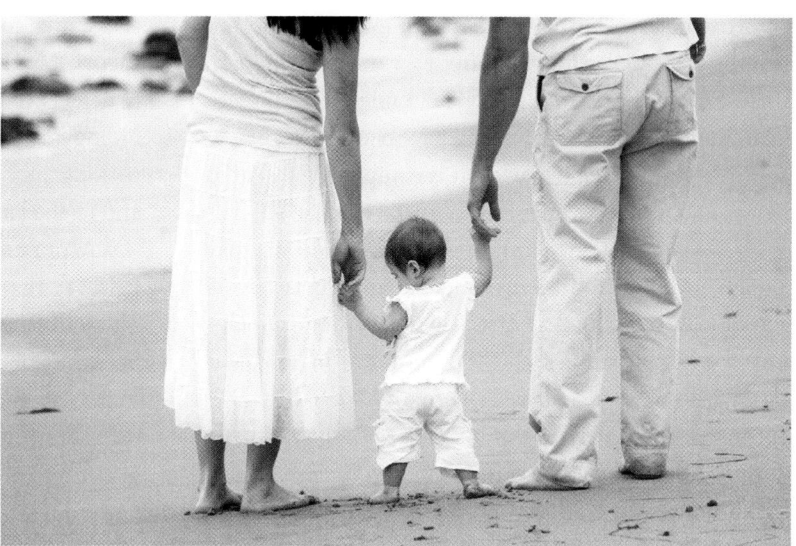

Socialization is a lifelong process that begins the moment a baby is born. It is believed that physically healthy children cannot develop normal social behavior without social interaction.

friendly and others are hostile. Women learn to smile when they are tense and to cry at good news as a release of tension. Men learn that they should not cry, although some do so at times.

Sociologists are interested in socialization because by studying how people learn the rules of society, we hope to understand better why people think and act as they do. If we understand why we think and act as we do, we can change our values, our beliefs, our expectations, and our behavior in ways that might otherwise never occur to us. The study of socialization is a very liberating part of a liberal education. In order to understand socialization, however, we must look to our earliest social interaction.

Why do children develop so little when they are isolated from others? Sociologists believe that even physically healthy children cannot develop normal social behavior without social interaction. The controversy over the extent to which behavior results from predetermined biological characteristics or from socialization is known as the **nature—nurture debate**. This debate has continued for centuries, but it has drawn more interest recently as a result of the new science of sociobiology.

It would be misleading and an oversimplification to suggest that socialization can be directly understood as resulting only from obvious social forces such as family, age, gender, peer groups, race/ethnicity, socio—economic status, and others. Socialization includes the complex interplay of social, cultural, psychological, and biological processes and is a concept that has been undergoing change and refinement within the fields of sociology and psychology since it was first developed (Morawski and St. Martin 2011).

Sociobiology and the Nature-Nurture Debate

Sociobiology is the study of the biological and genetic determinants of social behavior (Wilson 1975). Sociobiologists are biologists by training, although some sociologists and other social scientists support their views. Sociobiologists believe that social behavior is determined by inborn genetic traits, which influence human behavior in much the same way that animals are influenced by their genetic inheritance. An example in sociology would be that sexual preference is determined genetically and that humans have a genetic tendency to have only one or a very few mates (Van den Berghe 1979). Sociobiologists also think that homosexuality is genetically determined, although temporary homosexual behavior (occurring, for example, when opposite—sex partners are not available) may be environmental. They also believe, for example, that altruistic behavior (behavior performed to benefit others without regard for oneself) and warlike behavior are biologically based, although these and other behaviors may be modified by social experience.

Most sociologists criticize the sociobiological viewpoint on the grounds that behavior varies greatly from culture to culture. Sexual behavior, for example, whether with the same sex or the opposite sex, varies enormously. Altruistic behavior also varies widely and is entirely lacking in humans and monkeys who have been raised in isolation. As for warlike behavior, it is completely absent in many societies. According to Hoffman (1985), a specialist in the study of socialization, geneticists do not pay enough attention to environmental and socialization factors in their studies. Thus, when they draw conclusions from their studies, they do not know what effects the environment or socialization might have had.

In addition to the doubts of sociologists, many physiologists believe that there is no genetic basis for human behavior. Biological drives or **instincts**, which are patterns of reflexes that occur in animals, are very powerful. Insects and birds perform many complex behaviors even when they have been reared in isolation. Honeybees perform complicated dances to show other bees where food is located, and birds build intricate nests in the same manner as others of their species, each without having had any environmental opportunities for learning. So far no powerful, fixed drives or instincts have been discovered in human beings. Humans who have been raised in isolation do almost nothing, as we will discuss later in this chapter.

Sexual behavior in human beings, long thought to be a biological drive, varies so much from society to society and from time to time that researchers are now convinced that it is greatly shaped by social learning. Lauer and Handel (1983), for example, report some of the variations. For instance, in the Victorian age, it was assumed that women did not enjoy sexual intercourse, and men were sometimes advised not to have intercourse more than twelve times per year. Today, women who were studied in an Irish community expressed no sexual desire and engaged in intercourse only as a duty. Men in the community avoided intercourse before hard work because they thought it sapped them of their energy. On the other hand, young men in some South Pacific cultures have intercourse several times a night. Appropriate sexual behavior, then, is learned in the context of a particular culture.

There is a resurgence of interest among a growing faction of sociologists in the sociobiological approach. Arcaro (2002), for example, argues that incorporating sociobiology with traditional sociological perspectives is essential for developing a unified body of sociological theory. Sanderson (2001), a contemporary social theorist, feels that if sociologists ignore the importance of biology as an explanation of behavior, "they are going to look increasingly foolish both within the academy and to the larger educated public."

Money (1980), a physiologist and a psychologist, believes that the nature-nurture controversy is based on an illusion. He believes that environmental factors become part of our biology when we perceive them. When a piece of information enters our minds, it is translated into a biochemical form. Although we do not fully understand the workings of the brain, we do know both that the brain stores information permanently and that information in the brain can cause physiological changes in other parts of our bodies. Money contends that the information in our brains shapes our behavior and that distinctions between nature and nurture are irrelevant.

Researchers believe sexual behavior in humans is shaped by social learning.

Although a few sociologists emphasize the sociobiological perspective, most believe that human behavior can be limited by our physiology. For example, we can tolerate just so much heat, cold, or hunger. However, the way in which we respond to our physical limits—or how we behave under any other circumstances—is learned from interacting with other people. This interaction occurs in a manner different from any other animals because humans use language and other symbols. Understanding this, what happens if these things are missing from our environment?

THE EFFECTS OF SOCIAL ISOLATION

Normal human infants are born with all the muscles, bones, and biological organs needed to live. They are utterly helpless, however, and cannot survive without human interaction. Babies not only need food and warmth to survive physically, they also need physical stimulation to grow. When an adult handles them physically, they are stimulated by touch, tones of voice, and facial expressions; these make them aware of their environment and stimulate them to respond to it. Observations of infants and children who were comparatively isolated from human contact have shown that a lack of social interaction can have very serious consequences.

In addition to food and warmth, babies need physical contact and stimulation to grow.

Feral Children

The importance of social interaction is evident in studies of feral children, those who have grown up in the wild. Several feral children were reportedly found in Europe during the past few centuries. Probably the most famous was the wild boy of Aveyron, found in the wilderness in France in 1800 (Shattuck 1980). It is not known when the boy was separated from other humans or how he survived in the wilderness until he reached puberty; however, he did not know any language, so he might have been separated from humans while very young.

The boy's behavior seemed very strange to those who found him. When given a choice of food to eat, he rejected most of it. He liked potatoes, which he threw into a fire and then picked out with his bare hands and ate while they were very hot. He could tolerate cold as well as heat, and he was happy to be outdoors in the winter without clothes. He could swing from tree to tree easily, the wind and the moon excited him.

A young doctor took an interest in the boy and taught him to eat a wider variety of foods, to sleep at regular hours, and to wear clothes. It was determined that he could hear noises and make sounds, so an effort was made to teach him to talk. He learned to say a word for milk, but only after he had been given milk—he never used the word to ask for it. After five years of training, he had not learned to talk. He did, however, learn to cry occasionally and to hug his teacher. He survived for twenty-two years after the training stopped, living a quiet life in a cottage with a housekeeper; however, he never advanced his learning. Those who studied him were interested to note that he never showed any interest in sexual behavior.

A more recent case occurred in 2002 in Romania. Traian Caldarar was raised in an abusive family, and his mother eventually fled the abuse without him (www.telegraph.com.uk). Unable to get him back, the mother lost contact, and she believed another family adopted him. However, little four year-old Traian had not been adopted. Instead, he had fled from his abusive father as well. With nowhere to go, Traian lived with a large number of stray dogs roaming the Transylvanian countryside. When he was discovered at the age of seven, three years after he went missing, Traian was eating a dead dog and displaying animalistic behaviors. He suffered from many diseases, including rickets, which caused him to walk like a chimpanzee. His size was that of a three-year-old; he could not speak, and he possessed no socialization skills necessary to communicate with humans.

While sociologists, researchers, and other specialists believe it is possible for children to live among wild animals, they are less likely to believe that wild animals raise children. Instead, it's more likely that children, such as the wild boy of Aveyron and Traian, somehow learn to adapt once abandoned by their families and denied human interaction.

Children in Institutions

In the early 1900s, children were often placed in orphanages when their parents died or were unable to care for them. While the children's basic needs were met within the institutions, staff usually had very little time for personal interaction beyond routine feedings, baths, and healthcare. When children showed signs of developmental delays, it was believed the cause was due to their family background—not the environment or the care they received at the orphanages. In the 1930s two psychologists, Harold Skeels and Harold Dye, began to suspect that lack of social interaction, rather than family, was the cause of developmental problems in the children. Skeels and Dye learned of two infant girls that had been placed in a women's mental ward due to the lack of space in the orphanage; both girls improved remarkably within the first six months of their replacement. Fascinated by this phenomenon, the two researchers convinced the state to allow them to conduct an experiment using other institutionalized children (Heward 2000).

The researchers placed thirteen children between the ages of one and two, and with an average IQ score of sixty-four (indicating mental retardation), in with young women at the mental institution. The children were considered "unadoptable" by the state, and the women were labeled as "mentally retarded" by the institution. The women were given basic instructions on how to care for the infants and were provided with items such as books and toys. Skeels and Dye also left twelve infants in the orphanage as a control group. These children were under the age of three years and had an average IQ of eighty-six, higher than that of the experimental group. The control group received normal treatment from the caregivers, with no individual attention (Heward 2000). Because of the workload of the caregivers, children typically received minimal adult contact that generally included baths, diaper changes, and medicine. Feedings usually consisted of nourishment from a bottle being propped up in the crib for each baby.

During follow-up exams, Skeels and Dye discovered that while the experimental group steadily gained IQ points, the control group was losing them. By the end of the first year, the children cared for by women in the mental institution had improved considerably. At a two and a half year follow-up, the children in the mental institution had gained on average twenty-eight points while those in the orphanage lost an average of thirty points. Twenty-one years later, the researchers were able to track down all twenty-four participants in the study and found that most of the children in the mental institution had completed school (average of twelve years), while those left in the orphanage had completed an average of four years of schooling. In addition, eleven of the thirteen who had been moved to the mental institution had married, and all were either employed or were housewives. In contrast, the control group had four participants that were still institutionalized; and while some were employed, their jobs were of a lower level status than those in the experimental group. Skeels and Dye contributed the improvement of the children moved to the mental institution to the increased attention and care they received from the women residing there.

Rene Spitz published a similar study in 1946. Spitz observed children who had apparently been healthy when they were born and who had been living in a foundling home for about two years. Nutrition, clothing, bedding, and room temperatures in the home were suitable, and a physician saw every child. A small staff of nurses took care of the physical needs of the children, but other interaction was very limited.

Despite their excellent physical care, 34 percent of the ninety-one children in the home died within two years of the study, and twenty-one other children (23 percent) showed slow physical and social development. They were small, and some could not walk or even sit up. Those who could talk could say only a few words, and some could not talk at all.

Spitz compared these children with infants brought up in another institution, where their mothers were being held for delinquency. Physical care was basically the same as in the foundling home; but their mothers, who had little else to occupy them, enjoyed playing with their children for hours. The infants received a great deal of social stimulation, and their development was normal. Spitz concluded that the difference between the foundling home and the home for delinquent mothers was the amount of attention the children received. This further illustrates the crucial importance of social interactions in child development.

Abused and Neglected Children

Children who have been isolated from others in their own homes also show a lack of development. Kingsley Davis (1940, 1947) described two girls, Isabelle and Anna, found in the 1930s. They had been hidden in the attics of their family homes because they were illegitimate and unwanted.

One child, Isabelle, had been kept in seclusion until she was six and a half years old. Her mother was deaf and mute; and because Isabelle had been confined in a dark room with her mother, she had no chance to develop speech. She communicated with her mother by gestures and could make only a strange croaking sound. Although it was established that Isabelle could hear, specialists working with her believed that she was retarded because she had not developed any social

Children who have been isolated in their own homes show a lack of development.

skills. They believed she could not be educated and that any attempt to teach her to speak would fail after so long a period of silence. Nevertheless, the people in charge of Isabelle launched a systematic and skillful program of training that involved pantomime and dramatization. After one week of intensive effort, Isabelle made her first attempt to speak; and in two months, she was putting sentences together. Eighteen months after her discovery, she spoke well, walked, ran, and sang with gusto. Once she learned speech, she developed rapidly; and at age fourteen years, she had completed the sixth grade in public school.

The second child discovered around the same time was a girl named Anna. She was the second illegitimate child born to an unmarried woman. The mother lived on a farm with her widowed father who did not approve of his daughter's promiscuity and refused to allow her to keep the baby. Anna was moved to several locations but was repeatedly returned to the mother and labeled as unadoptable. Eventually, with nowhere else to go, the grandfather banished Anna to a storage room where she lived until she was discovered. Her mother fed her just enough to stay alive; otherwise Anna had no other human contact. When authorities found her, Anna was unable to speak, smile, or perform basic tasks. After extensive therapy she eventually was able to brush her teeth and comb her hair. She could speak simple sentences and learned to feed herself. Anna's full potential would never be recognized because she died of a brain hemorrhage when she was ten and a half years old.

Perhaps the most well known case of an abused and neglected child is that of Genie, a thirteen -year-old girl discovered in 1970 in Los Angeles, California (Curtiss 1977) Like the previous two cases, Genie was locked in a room for the majority of her life. During the day she was strapped to a potty chair, and at night she was placed in a strait jacket type of contraption made from a sleeping bag and put into a crib that had a wire covering. When discovered, Genie could not talk and; as a result of severe beatings by her elderly father, she made very little noise. She could not eat, constantly spat, sniffed like a dog, and clawed at things. She had a very strange bunny-like walk, and she kept her hands in a bent position at the front of her body—like paws. As a result of being kept in the room, Genie's eyesight was extremely poor; she could only see a distance of twelve feet. After receiving extensive treatment by a team of specialists, Genie's language remained relatively primitive; she could only speak a few words and virtually no sentences. She was able to follow simple commands, but otherwise her development was poor. Eventually, Genie ended up in a series of foster care homes, and then she was sent to an adult group home.

The cases of Isabelle, Anna, and Genie provide a great deal of information about the development of children who experience severe abuse and neglect; however, the cases also leave many questions unanswered. Isabelle was able to overcome her early trauma, while Anna's progress would be left to speculation. Does this provide us with enough information to believe that children who are rescued from abusive situations by the age of six can overcome their developmental delays? Since Genie was unable to overcome her early problems, is there a critical age threshold for language development between the ages of six and thirteen?

Deprived Monkeys

Perhaps one last study will help us understand the effects of social isolation. Psychologist Harry Harlow conducted studies on rhesus monkeys raised in captivity to determine how maternal deprivation affected their development. Just a few hours after their birth, baby monkeys were separated from their mothers and placed in isolation cages. Each cage was equipped with a special feeding device to provide nourishment to the baby monkey. The devices were artificial mothers—made of wire frames, with a head and a device to dispense milk for feeding. The only difference would be that one artificial mother was covered in a soft terry cloth material, and the other remained bare wire mesh.

Harlow discovered that when the wire frame mothers provided nourishment, the monkeys would cling to their terrycloth mothers when they were not feeding. Later, Harlow removed the terrycloth mothers from some of the cages and conducted further experiments. He found that when he scared the monkeys, those in the cages with the terrycloth mothers would cling pathetically to them. Yet, when there were no terrycloth mothers, the monkeys would curl in the corner and rock back and forth to try and soothe themselves, rather than attempt consolation by their artificial mother. Harlow's experiments suggested that more than nourishment is needed for attachment to occur; a physical relationship with the mother was also necessary. The isolated monkeys were deprived of the emotional attachment received during mother-child interaction, which often involves cuddling and soothing during times of stress.

Harlow also discovered that monkeys kept in isolation for eight months or longer were, afterwards, unable to fit in with other monkeys. They did not know how to engage in interaction; and, as a result, the other monkeys often shunned those previously isolated. Behaviors such as pretend fighting and normal sexual behavior did not occur because the isolated monkeys were unaware of how to engage in behaviors found among other monkeys.

After many unsuccessful attempts to place the isolated female monkeys with male monkeys for the purpose of reproduction, Harlow designed a device to allow some of the females to become pregnant. After they gave birth, the mothers were either neglectful or abusive toward their babies. The neglectful mothers did not harm their babies; but they did not feed them, cuddle them or protect them from harm either. The abusive mothers were violent toward their young, often trying to bite, hit, or squash them against the cage floor. In the end, Harlow discovered that when baby monkeys were isolated for no more than ninety days, they could overcome their isolation and live a normal monkey life; however, if isolated any longer, they would be permanently damaged.

What can we learn from studying the cases of feral, institutionalized, and abused and neglected children? Are there critical periods in a child's life that determine how they will ultimately develop? What about Harlow's monkeys? How much of what we learn about animals can we apply to humans? All animals interact, but we humans are unique in our ability to create societies, cultures, and social institutions. We are also unique in our capacity to use language. George Herbert Mead (1863–1931) was the first to describe why language makes humans different from all other animals.

THE DEVELOPMENT OF A SELF

How do we know who we are? If asked to describe yourself ... what would you say? Are you pretty, smart, skinny, witty, funny? Perhaps you see yourself as just the opposite—ugly, dumb, fat, dull, or boring. What factors contribute to the development of our identities? Do we care what others think about us? Scholars such as George Herbert Mead and Charles Horton Cooley contributed to the study of the importance of early socialization on the individual.

George Herbert Mead: Mind, Self, and Society

The students of George Herbert Mead were so impressed with his insights about human interaction that after his death they compiled his lectures and published his book, *Mind, Self and Society from the Standpoint of a Social Behaviorist* (1934). Mead demonstrated that the unique feature of the human mind is its capacity to use symbols, and he discussed how human development proceeds because of this ability. Through language and human interaction an individual develops a **self**. According to Mead (1934:135), "The self is something which has a development; it is not initially there, at birth, but arises in the process of social experience and activity, that is, develops in the given individual as a result of his relations to that process as a whole and to other individuals within that process." Language is the key to the development of self. Words in a language have meaning; and we use language symbols when we think or talk to ourselves, and when we talk to other people. When we see another person in the street, we do not simply react to the person instinctively. We interpret the situation by giving meaning to the other person's behavior. We think, "Is this someone I know, or a stranger? Do I want to know this person, ignore her, say hello to her?" If we say "hello" to the other person, we are using a symbol that means, "I wish to greet you in a friendly manner." The other person knows the meaning of the symbol. This is an example of **symbolic interaction**, the social process that occurs within and among individuals as a result of the internalization of meanings and the use of language.

Mead recognized how important it is for people to interact with others in the development of the self. When infants are born, they cannot differentiate among all the objects they see. The world appears as a kaleidoscope of color and movement. Very soon, however, they learn to distinguish important objects, such as the source of nourishment and the parent who brings it. Infants also eventually learn to differentiate themselves from their surroundings and from other persons. For example, as a father repeatedly brings a bottle to his daughter, she becomes aware that she is the object of her father's attention. She learns to differentiate herself from the crib and other objects. She learns that she is a separate object receiving both the bottle and her father's attention. Infants also develop expectations about their parents' behaviors and about their parents' roles. They expect their parents to bring the bottle.

Role Taking: Significant Others and Generalized Others

Mead used the term **role—taking** to describe the process of figuring out how others will act. The ability to take a role is extremely important to children. In fact, **play** is a way of practicing role-taking. Children often play "house" or "school," taking the role of **significant others**—mother, father, or any other person important to them. By taking the roles of these significant others, children can better understand their own roles as children, students, sons, or daughters.

Mead believed that children develop role-taking skills during play and ultimately learn to take the role of others through the process. He identified three stages in which the self emerges through play, and he labeled them: preparatory, play and game. In the ***preparatory stage***, children are only capable of imitating the people in their lives. They are not yet aware of their sense of self but are learning to become social through meaningful interaction with others. In Mead's second stage, the ***play stage***, children begin to take the role of others significant in their lives. Children enjoy playing dress up and may pretend to be mother, father, fireman, teacher, etc. In the ***game stage***, the child is older and is capable of understanding not merely one individual, but the roles of several others, simultaneously. The child now has the ability to put himself in the place of others and act accordingly. Once the child can do this, Mead contends he or she can "take the role of the generalized other".

By practicing the roles of others in play, children learn to understand what others expect of them and how to behave to meet those expectations. As adults, when we take roles, we figure out what others are thinking and how others will act; and then we can act accordingly. Often, however, we do not have the opportunity to play out the role of others, except in our imagination.

A child who responds differently to each person in his or her life would never develop a sense of self. In order to develop a sense of self, the child learns to see others not as individuals but as **generalized others**, the organized community or social group that provides reference for his own conduct. Mead used the example of a baseball game to illustrate the concept of generalized other. A child playing baseball develops generalized expectations of

In the play stage, children enjoy playing dress up and may pretend to be mother, father, etc.

each position on the team; pitchers throw, fielders catch, batters hit and run, regardless of the individuals playing those positions. These generalized expectations become incorporated into the child's sense of self.

The "I" and the "Me"

Once a child has an idea of the generalized other, he or she can begin to develop a personality, an individual way of behaving. The child learns to meet the expectation of the group in some situations but may argue with the group on other occasions. The child interprets the situation and then decides how to act. That is what makes each person unique.

To analyze each person's unique ability to respond to the generalized other, Mead theoretically divided the person into two parts: The "**I**" and the "**me**". The *I* represents the acting person, as in "I attend class." The *I* is not self-conscious. When taking a test in class, the *I* concentrates on the test, not on the self.

The *me* represents the part of self that sees self as object, the part that is concerned with society's expectations of self, such as, "Society expects me to go to class." It is the *me*, seeing self as an object, which says after class, "You really did great on the exam!" or after the party says, "You really made a fool of yourself!" The socially constructed *me* spends a good deal of time talking to the I.

We use the generalized other to shape our own personality throughout life. We may decide, for example, that attending class is a waste of time or that multiple-choice tests are unfair. We may choose to go along with the norms, or we may choose to argue against them. To do either, however, we must understand the expectations of the generalized other—the school, in this case. We develop our own **mind**, our own ability to think, based on the expectations of the generalized other.

Mead believed that the human mind is entirely social and develops in interaction. Although we are born with a brain, Mead argued, we do not learn to use our mind to think and develop ideas until we have learned the expectations of our society. We learn these expectations mostly through language, and then we use language to talk to ourselves and to develop our own ideas. We get ideas about the usefulness of class attendance and multiple-choice tests. We also get ideas about what we are like, what we want to become in the future, or the relative attractiveness of the persons sitting next to us. It is easy to understand that we would not think about class attendance if there were no classes to attend. It is not as obvious, but just as true, that the relative attractiveness of the persons sitting next to us is based on what we have learned from society about attractiveness. We have learned what color of hair and skin, what size of nose, and what height and weight are valued by society. Based on this, we establish our own definition of attractiveness in others and in ourselves.

APPLYING MEAD'S ROLE-TAKING

Although many of Mead's theories are useful in providing an understanding of how our self develops, his concept of role-taking is particularly helpful. Role-taking is important not only for self-development but also for our personal and professional relationships. For clinical sociologists, therapists, and other counselors who help people deal with problems, role-taking is an important *verstehen* technique. *Verstehen* is Max Weber's concept referring to a deep imagining of how things might be and feel for others. For example, a client undergoing drug counseling may explain his or her fears and feelings of inadequacy to the therapist; however, unless the therapist can see things from a drug user's point of view, the therapy might be cold and meaningless to the client.

Clinicians, counselors, and therapists may also ask their clients to engage in role-taking as part of their treatment. Marriage counselors sometimes help husbands and wives confront their marital problems by having them switch roles temporarily so that they can feel what it is like to be in the other's position. By having the husband take the role of wife and the wife take the role of husband, each spouse may learn to see himself or herself the way the other spouse does. Each spouse's role-taking might help in developing more sensitivity to the partner's needs.

How can you use role-taking in your career or occupation? By engaging in role-taking, you will probably improve how you relate to, organize, and lead other people. As a teacher, you might find examples to which students can relate better if you can imagine how the students see the subject matter. For example, teachers sometimes show movies explaining serious topics; however, if a particular movie is old, the students may find the fashions dated and the movie quaint, thus missing the point of the movie. As a physician, you might develop a better "bedside manner" if you can put yourself in the place of the cancer patient you are treating. Novels, movies, and even jokes make fun of doctors who become patients and are shocked because they had never previously understood how the patient felt. All of us find it difficult to understand the feelings, attitudes, and ideas of every person with whom we interact, so we find more efficient ways to deal with people. We develop a sense of self and a generalized other.

Charles Horton Cooley: The Looking-Glass Self

Charles Horton Cooley (1864–1929), like Mead, theorized that the idea of the self develops in a process that requires reference to other people, a process he called the **looking-glass self**. According to Cooley, the looking-glass self has three components: (1) how we think our behavior appears to others, (2) how we think others judge our behavior, and (3) how we feel about their judgments. We know that we exist, that we are beautiful or ugly, serious or funny, lively or dull, intelligent or stupid, through the way other people treat us. We never know exactly what other people think of us, of course, but we can imagine how we appear to them and how they evaluate our appearance. Ultimately, the looking-glass concept self is based on perception and effect—the perception we believe others have of us, and the effect those perceptions have on our self-image.

Our imagination about our own looking-glass self may or may not be accurate. If it is not accurate, we may think we are clumsy when other people think we move very gracefully. We may think we speak clearly when others think we mumble. We may think we are shy even when others admire our confidence. Whether our ideas about ourselves are accurate or not, we believe them; and we often respond to these imagined evaluations with some feeling, such as pride, mortification, or humiliation.

Cooley noted that when we refer to ourselves, we are usually referring to our looking-glass self, not to our physical being, our heart, lungs, arms, and legs. We usually refer to our opinions, desires, ideas, or feelings (I think, I feel, I want), or we associate the idea of the self with roles (I am a student, an athlete, a friend). This sense of self exists in relation to other people. We compare and contrast ourselves with others; our own sense of uniqueness is based on that comparison. Even the language we use to refer to ourselves must be learned from other people.

In sum, both Mead and Cooley pointed out that the major difference between social theories of the self and psychological theories of the self is that social theories emphasize that society exists first and that the individual is shaped by society. Psychological theories emphasize individual development apart from social processes; that is, the individual develops and then responds to society based on preexisting tendencies to behave in particular ways. (See Jean Piaget, Sigmund Freud, Lawrence Kohlberg.)

APPLYING COOLEY'S "LOOKING-GLASS SELF"

One common manifestation of Cooley's theory is the **self-fulfilling prophecy**, a concept developed by Robert Merton. A self-fulfilling prophecy is a prediction that causes us to act as if a particular definition of others, a situation, or ourselves were true (even if it is not true); and as a result, it becomes true because of our actions.

A classic example of a self-fulfilling prophecy is a bank failure. Banks operate under the reasonable assumption that all the depositors will not want all of their money back at the same time. Banks do not merely keep our money in a vault; rather, they invest it so that they can pay us interest and also make a profit. However, if all the depositors at the

First International Bank believe a rumor (or a prediction) that the bank does not have enough money to give back to them, they might all rush to get their money from the bank at the same time. The resultant bank failure would not be due to any economic or management problems, but solely to a sociological self-fulfilling prophecy.

We now look at the self-fulfilling prophecy and see how it relates to the looking-glass self. If we imagine that others think we are a particular kind of person (even if we are not), we may believe that their perceptions are true. As a result, we may act in a manner that results in our becoming that way. Suppose, for example, that you imagine that others think you are a funny person. (It does not matter whether they really think you are funny; what matters is that you imagine that they think you are funny.) Because you believe that you are a funny person, you may make an extra effort to become funny by learning and telling new jokes, doing amusing things at parties, and generally cultivating your sense of humor. ("Because I am a funny person, I am the kind of person who knows a lot of good jokes, so I had better be prepared.")

The knowledge that the looking-glass self often becomes a self-fulfilling prophecy may be useful in a variety of ways. First, it might be applied in some occupational settings. How, for example, could this knowledge improve your effectiveness as a teacher? If you are aware that people see themselves as they think others (especially significant others) see them, you might try to be especially sensitive to how you react to students when they ask questions in class, when you speak to them in your office, or when you make comments on their papers. If students think that they are being put down or are perceived as unintelligent, they may prematurely give up on learning a subject. Conversely, if students develop positive views of themselves because they think you as the teacher see them as intuitive, creative, and interesting, they may strive to cultivate those qualities even further; and it may play an important part in their interaction with others. As a parent, as well as a teacher, the implications of the looking-glass self on adolescent self-approval are significant (Gamble and Yu 2008).

Erving Goffman: The Presentation of Self

Throughout life, our socialization influences the way we interact with each other. Erving Goffman (1959) was interested in the process of interaction once a self has been developed. Every interaction, Goffman believed, begins with a **presentation of self.** The way we present ourselves gives other people cues about the type of interaction we expect. In formal situations, we usually greet friends with a handshake or a remark, whereas in informal situations, we may greet friends

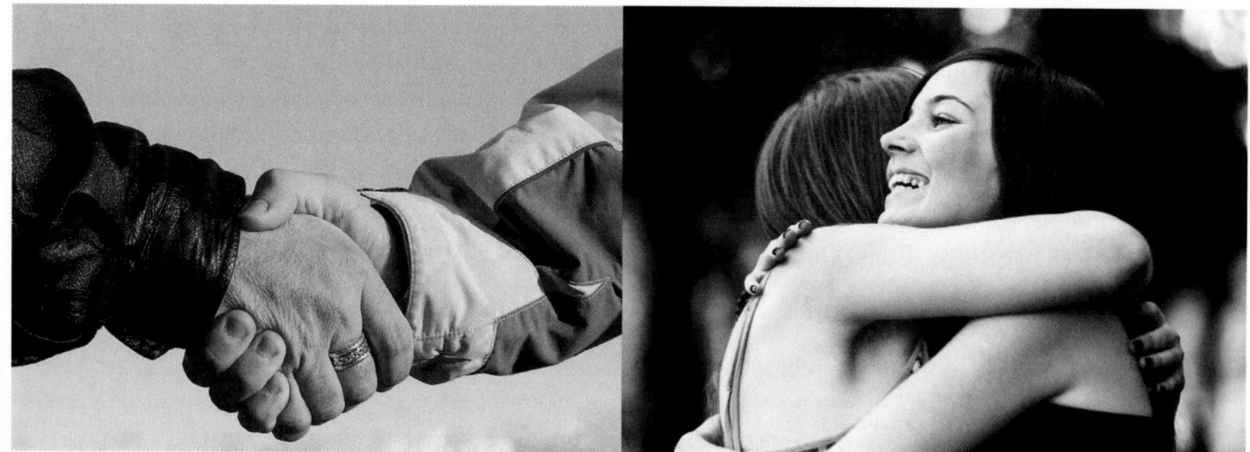

Erving Goffman believed every interaction, such as the greeting of friends, begins with a presentation of self.

with a hug or a kiss. If we are with friends, we talk and laugh; but on a bus or in an elevator, we do not speak to strangers, and we keep a social distance even when space is crowded and we cannot keep physically distant. Psychologists refer to our manner of presentation as "body language." We give cues about ourselves in the way we present and use our bodies in interaction.

In an attempt to analyze how interaction takes place, Goffman (1959) compared social interaction to a drama on stage—a comparison known as the **dramaturgical approach**. Whenever we interact, we prepare ourselves backstage and then present ourselves as if onstage, according to what we have learned in the socialization process. Goffman believed that all behavior, even the most routine, is neither instinctual nor habitual; it is a presentation. Most Americans prepare to present themselves by showering, washing their hair, and using deodorant—in our society, cleanliness and a lack of odor are important. Complexions must be smooth—so men shave, women put on makeup, and adolescents use cosmetics to cover up acne. Suitable clothing is selected so that we can present ourselves formally in formal situations and casually in casual situations. A formal setting such as a church, a more informal setting such as a classroom, and a casual setting such as a basketball arena require very different presentations. In some settings, one can race for a front-row seat, talk loudly, wave to friends, and eat and drink. In other settings, these behaviors would be quite inappropriate.

In illustrating the dramaturgical approach, Goffman described a character, called "Preedy," as he presented himself on a beach on the Riviera. Preedy very consciously tried to make an impression on the people around him. It was his first day on vacation, and he knew no one. He wanted to meet some people, but he did not want to appear too lonely or too eager; so he presented himself as perfectly content in his solitary state.

The following excerpt from Goffman (1959) describes Preedy's behavior:

> If by chance a ball was thrown his way, he looked surprised; then let a smile of amusement lighten his face (Kindly Preedy), looked round dazed to see that there were people on the beach, tossed it back with a smile to himself and not a smile at the people, and then resumed carelessly his nonchalant survey of space.
>
> But it was time to institute a little parade, the parade of the Ideal Preedy. By devious handlings he gave any who wanted to look a chance to see the title of his book—a Spanish translation of Homer, classic thus, but not daring, cosmopolitan, too—and then gathered together his beach-wrap and bag into a neat sand-resistant pile (Methodical and Sensible Preedy), rose slowly to stretch at ease his huge frame (Big-Cat Preedy), and tossed aside his sandals (Carefree Preedy, after all).
>
> The marriage of Preedy and the sea! There were alternative rituals. The first involved the stroll that turns into a run and a dive straight into the water, thereafter smoothing into a strong splashless crawl towards the horizon. But of course not really on the horizon. Quite suddenly he would turn on to his back and thrash great white splashes with his legs, somehow thus showing that he could have swum further had he wanted to, and then would stand up a quarter out of water for all to see who it was.
>
> The alternative course was simpler, it avoided the cold-water shock and it avoided the risk of appearing too high-spirited. The point was to appear to be so used to the sea, the Mediterranean, and this particular beach, that one might as well be in the sea as out of it. It involved a slow stroll down and into the edge of the water—not even noticing his toes were wet, land and water all the same to him—with his eyes up at the sky gravely surveying portents, invisible to others, of the weather (Local Fisherman Preedy). (p. 5)

Notice how much Preedy could tell about himself without saying a word. Whether anyone enters the water in as calculated a manner as Preedy is questionable, but whoever watches someone like Preedy will form an opinion of him from his presentation. The dramaturgical approach helps us understand that how one appears is at least as important as what one actually does or says—and often, it is more important.

Maintaining the Self

Once we have presented ourselves in a particular role and have begun to interact, we must maintain our presentation. In class, students cannot begin to shake hands with fellow students, wander around the room, or write on the blackboard. It would not only disrupt the class, but it would also spoil the presentation of the student, who would be considered disruptive, strange, or worse. If students or others want to maintain the definitions others have of them, they must maintain a performance in accord with the definition.

Sometimes we inadvertently do not maintain our performance, so we try to **account** for or to **excuse** our behavior (Scott and Lyman 1968; Simon and Manstead 1983). If we are late and want to avoid giving the impression that we are always late, we make excuses: "I am usually very prompt, but my car ran out of gas" "I thought the meeting was at eight o'clock, not seven o'clock."

We also try to maintain our presentations by **disclaimers**—that is, disclaiming a role even while we are acting in that role. "I usually don't drink, but this punch is so good" disclaims the role of drinker. "I'm not prejudiced, but..." followed by a racist remark, or "I'm no expert, but..." followed by a remark only an expert could make, are phrases that tell the audience that the self is not what it appears to be.

Often, the audience accepts a person's accounts or disclaimers, and the interaction proceeds smoothly; but sometimes, the drama does not work out so well. We may present ourselves in the role of someone who knows how to act in social situations but not live up to those claims. We may fall down a flight of stairs as we make our grand entrance. We may stand up at a meeting to give a report, claiming to be an expert, but our trembling hands and factual errors will not support these claims. The speaker and those in the audience may attempt to ignore the errors, but at some point, the speaker may get too flustered to continue the pretense of living up to the role or may become embarrassed and laugh, cry, faint, or blush. When a group can no longer support the claims made by an individual, the whole group may become embarrassed or angry (Goffman 1967).

Implicit in interactions is the assumption that presentations will be maintained. Each person agrees to maintain the self and to support the presentations of others. If people's presentations are not supported by the people themselves or by others, they may be followed by an emotional response. For example, in some situations, I may become embarrassed; and if my presentation is ridiculed, I may get angry. In another situation, if someone seems to fill your image of the ideal romantic love, you may fall in love with that individual. If the person then is cruel, unfaithful, or behaves in some other way that tarnishes your image of him or her, you may grow angry and eventually fall out of love.

Not only do we learn behavior in the process of socialization and interaction, but we also learn appropriate feelings about others and ourselves. We learn self-esteem by understanding how others evaluate us; we learn when to be embarrassed, when to be angry, and both when to fall in love and with what type of person. If we are angry with someone who deserves our respect, we feel guilty about our feelings. If we love someone whom others define as entirely inappropriate, we become confused. Again, we have expectations about maintaining these performances of self—both our own and others'—and we respond emotionally when these expectations are not met. This happens in all of our roles and in whatever groups we act.

Thinking Sociologically

1. What is required for babies to develop into full human beings? What are the components that make us human?

2. Think of times you have seen your looking-glass self inaccurately. How has this shaped your actions?

3. Think of a time when your presentation of self was not maintained. How did you respond emotionally?

Kohlberg's Stages of Moral Development

As very young children, we begin the process of moral development—or learning the difference between right and wrong. Psychologist Lawrence Kohlberg spent many years studying children and the process of moral development. He proposed a number of stages which people pass through in their moral development:

- **Pre-conventional Stage (Elementary School Aged)** During this stage of moral development, Kohlberg argued that children act according to what is expected from them by authoritative figures. They view right or wrong as what pleases those in authority, such as their parents and teachers. Morality is external and children are simply trying to avoid punishment.
- **Conventional Stage** At this stage children have internalized what has been taught to them. They began to view right and wrong in terms of what is socially acceptable. Instead of avoiding punishment, they want to be a good person and do what is right, such as obeying the law.
- **Post-conventional Stage (Teen Years)** In this stage, individuals are more concerned with the rights of others rather than the laws of society. A person's basic rights to life, liberty, etc., are more important from a moral standpoint, than laws that would deprive individuals or groups of these things.

Children begin the process of learning the difference between right and wrong at a very young age.

Kohlberg argued that individuals could only pass through one stage at a time and in the order listed. They did not skip stages, nor could they jump back and forth between stages. Kohlberg believed that moral development occurred through the process of social interaction.

Development of a Personality

Sigmund Freud believed that personality consists of three elements: id, ego and superego. When a child is born, we first come into contact with the *id*, or the inborn drives for self-gratification. For example, when the child senses hunger, he will cry if his needs are not immediately met. Freud referred to the id as the pleasure-seeking component, which demands immediate fulfillment of basic instinctual needs that remain unconscious most of the time. The second component is the ego, or balancing principle. The ego's job is to act as a mediator between the id and the superego and to prevent one or the other from becoming too dominant. The third component is the superego, or our conscience. The superego has internalized the norms, values, and beliefs of our culture or society. Unlike the id, the superego is not inherent but, rather, is learned from our social interactions with others.

MAJOR AGENTS OF SOCIALIZATION

Socialization is found in all interaction, but the most influential interaction occurs in particular groups referred to as "agencies of socialization." Among the most important are the family, the schools, peer groups, and the mass media.

The Family

The family is considered the primary agency of socialization. It is within the family that most children encounter the first socializing influence, and this influence affects them for the rest of their lives. For example, families give children their geographical location, as easterners or westerners, and their urban or rural background. The family also determines the child's social class, race, religious background, and

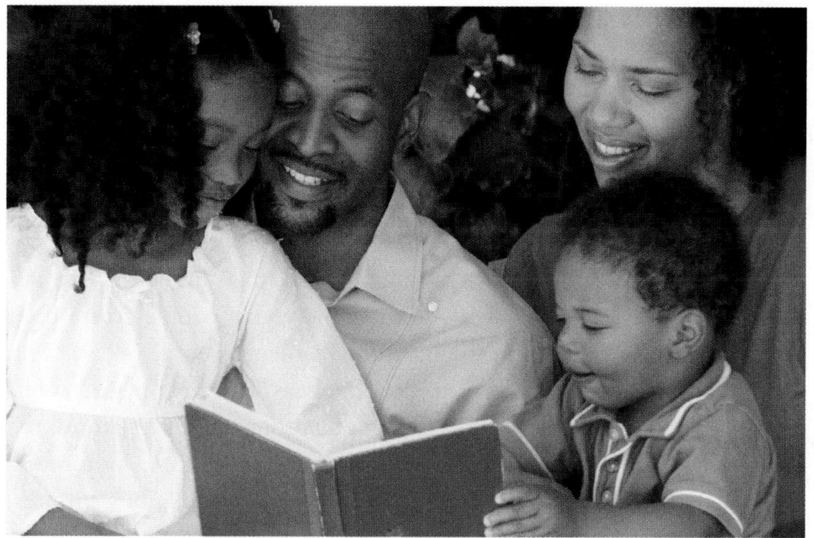

The family is considered the primary agency of socialization. It can determine their social class, religious belief, language, and how they view themselves. This influence will affect them for the rest of their lives.

ethnic group. Each of these factors can have a profound influence on children. They may learn to speak a particular dialect, to prefer particular foods, and to pursue some types of leisure activities.

Families also teach children values that they will hold throughout life. Children frequently adopt their parents' attitudes about the importance of education, work, patriotism, and religion. Even a child's sense of self-worth is determined, at least in part, by the child's parents.

One of the values instilled in the children of most American families concerns the worth of the unique individual. We are taught that we possess a set of talents, personality characteristics, strengths, and weaknesses peculiar to ourselves, and that we are responsible for developing these traits. Our parents tell us that we can be all that we want to be, as long as we work hard and want something badly enough. Ultimately, we are responsible for our successes and failures. This view of the value of the individual is not found in all cultures, however. Many people who emigrated from southern Europe, for example, believe that one's primary responsibility is to the family, not to oneself. The son of a European farm family, for example, is expected to be loyal and obedient to the family, to work for its benefit, and eventually, to take over the management of the farm when the parents are old. In our culture, however, staying with the family is often regarded as a sign of weakness or of lack of ambition on the part of young adults; and when adult children return home to live, both they and their parents often feel uncomfortable (Clemens and Axelsen 1985; Schnaiberg and Goldenberg 1989). Some cultures, such as China, place an emphasis on inculcating both individualist and collectivist values, indicating that modern and traditional values are part of family socialization of children (Lu 2009).

As more and more children spend time in childcare instead of in the family, the question of what type of socialization will take place in these organizations is of major concern. Can nonfamilial childcare really replace family care, and will the quality of socialization be maintained in these organizations? Note the Policy Debate in this chapter and its discussion on child care.

The Schools

In some societies, socialization takes place almost entirely within the family, but in highly technical societies, children are also socialized by the educational system. Schools in the United States teach more than reading, writing, arithmetic, and other basic academic skills. They also teach students to develop themselves, to test their achievements through competition, to self-discipline, to cooperate with others, and to obey rules of which are necessary if a youngster is to achieve success in a society dominated by large organizations.

Schools teach sets of expectations about the work children will do when they mature. The children begin by learning about the work roles of community helpers such as firefighters and doctors, and later, they learn about occupations more formally. They take aptitude tests to discover their unique talents, and with the help of teachers and guidance counselors, they set occupational goals.

Schools also teach citizenship in countless ways. They encourage children to take pride in their communities; to feel patriotic about their nation; to learn about their country's geography, history, and national holidays; to study government, explain the role of good citizens, urge their parents to vote, and pledge allegiance to the U.S. flag; to become informed about community and school leaders; and to respect school property. At times what a child is taught in school may conflict with the values taught within the home. For example, a child who is taught to believe that religion is central to his or her life will find it difficult to understand the separation of church and state in public education. Schools can provide the first time children are challenged to question their family's beliefs.

Most school administrators and teachers reinforce our cultural emphasis on the uniqueness of individuals. Thus, they try to identify the unique talents of students through comparison and competition with other students and then attempt to develop these talents so that they will become useful to the larger society. Japanese schools, operating in a less individualistic society, assume that all students will be able to meet whatever standards the schools set.

Peer Groups

Young people spend considerable time in school, and their **peer group** of people their own age is an important influence on their socialization. Peer-group socialization has been found to have an impact on so many values, attitudes and behaviors concerning things such as dating, homosexuality, ethnic/racial interactions, delinquency, risk taking, overall adjustment, and many other issues of central importance in the lives of young people (cf. eg., Poteat 2007; Rivas-Drake, et al, 2009; Ellis and Zarbatany 2007; Higgins, et al, 2010; Criss, et al, 2009).

Young people today also spend more time with one another outside of school. Unlike young people of earlier decades, few are isolated on farms. Most live in cities or suburbs, and increasingly, they have access to automobiles so that they can spend time together away from their families. Teenagers' most intimate relationships are often those they have with their peers, not with parents or siblings, and they influence one another greatly. In fact, some young people create their own unique subcultures. Coleman et al. (1974), who refer to these groups simply as "cultures," list as examples the culture of athletic groups in high schools, the college campus culture, the drug culture, motorcycle cultures, the culture of surfers, and religious cultures. In part because teenagers are often unsure of themselves, they may prize the sense of belonging that they get from their subculture, although the pressures to conform to group expectations can be quite severe.

Peer groups can be a strong influence on a young person's life. A sense of belonging is important to school-aged children and can influence how they react

Peer groups are an important influence on young people's socialization.

toward themselves. Clothing styles, music, and dating habit preferences are beginning to form during the teen years; and those teens who fail to conform to their group's behavior may be seen as an "outsider", which in turn can lead to feelings of rejection.

Religion

All societies have some form of religion, and how one practices or doesn't practice religion is dependent upon their social interaction with others. Religion can be an extremely powerful influence on a person's social self. Children whose parents encouraged them to attend church early in life are more likely to rely on faith and prayer in much of their adult life, as well. Children learn the language of their religion and the ideas about what is and is not acceptable behavior, particularly regarding morality.

The Mass Media

The American **mass media**—television, popular magazines, and other forms of communication intended for a large audience—play a major role in teaching Americans to consume goods. They devise programs that attract a particular audience and then sell products to that audience. American children spend more than fifty-three hours a week watching TV or using video games, cellphones, and computers (Kaiser Family Foundation 2010). That is more than the equivalent of a full-time-work week. While most advertising takes place on TV, almost all of these other portable devices are vehicles for some form of advertising, especially since TV can be watched on all of them. Thus, younger children, urge their parents to buy the cereals, snack foods, and toys they see advertised. An average of two hundred junk food ads are shown in four hours of children's Saturday morning cartoon programming (*Source Book for Teaching Science* 2001). Teenagers listen to their favorite music on radio or the Internet and buy the products advertised there. At the very least, the mass media teach people what products are available. In addition, by the age of eighteen the average American has seen tow hundred thousand acts of violence on television, forty thousand of these being murders (*Source Book for Teaching Science* 2001).

The mass media also teach values and needs. An advertisement may teach you, for example, that thoughtful, sensitive children send their parents Hallmark cards on special occasions or just to convey "I love you." You may learn that "people on the go," like you, drink Pepsi "uh-huh;" or you may learn that intelligent, frequent travelers should not leave home without their American Express cards.

The mass media also teach viewers something about what life is like, although the view presented may be an idealized version. For example, people learn from television comedy shows that the American family is very happy. Everyday problems of living—such as dented automobiles, lackluster sex lives, occupational failures, trouble juggling two careers and childcare, or a shortage of money—are treated as abnormalities on television. In these media, rich people are often miserable; and poor people, who usually appear in comedies, have a wonderful time and never seem to worry about money. After watching this, viewers may develop unrealistic expectations about the quality of their own lives, becoming unnecessarily frustrated and discontent. If we can understand that our conception of what is normal is one that we have been socialized to accept by the media, perhaps we would not have such unrealistic expectations of our spouses, our children, and ourselves. With more realistic expectations, perhaps we could become more tolerant of ourselves and of others.

Researchers now believe that television shapes not only what we think but also how we think. Healy (1990) believes that television prevents thinking, at least in characteristic ways. Before television, children spent much more time learning about things by talking or reading. This required more use of the imagination. When learning through conversation, a person has to formulate ideas and respond to what is being said in order to maintain the conversation. When learning through reading, a child has to imagine what things look like and how things sound in order to grasp the meaning of the written word. When watching television, children are provided with pictures and sounds and are not required to formulate ideas and respond. As a result, Healy (1990) argues that children who have grown up watching a great deal of television do not think unless the pictures and sounds are provided for them.

Undoubtedly, many more theories about how the mass media shape our thoughts will be forthcoming. Nevertheless, the fact that the mass media play a part in socialization is widely accepted.

Thinking Sociologically

1. How have your parents influenced your development of a self? What are some of the values and beliefs taught to you that remain an important component of your life today?

2. Discuss the importance of education on the development of a self. How did education either enhance or contradict what was taught to you by your parents?

SOCIALIZATION OF GENDER ROLES

Socialization plays an especially important part in determining what children believe to be acceptable behaviors for members of their own sex. Even though the situation has begun to change, our environment bombards both men and women with subtle and not-so-subtle suggestions that some types of behavior are acceptable for women and other types of behavior are acceptable for men. People who diverge significantly from expected gender roles often meet with resistance from individuals and from the social system. The same sources of socialization that influence people in other areas of their lives—home, school, the mass media, and interactions with others—also affect the socialization of gender roles.

Infant and Childhood Experiences

Gender-role socialization in our society begins at birth. When a baby is born, he or she is wrapped in a blue or a pink blanket; and from that moment on, parents respond to the infant on the basis of its gender (Bem and Bem 1976). In decades past, parents could predict the future role expectations of their infants. Boys were expected to grow up to play **instrumental roles**, performing tasks that lead to goals they have set for themselves. Girls were expected to be more verbal, more expressive, more emotional, and when they grew up, more interested in interpersonal relationships, characteristics that have been labeled the **expressive role** by sociologists (Zelditch 1955).

Research has shown that infants are viewed differently, depending on these future role expectations. Infant boys are often described as big, athletic, strong, or alert; however, but girls are usually described as tiny, dainty, sweet, pretty, delicate, inattentive, or weak. Parents tend to notice the dainty fingernails of the baby girl, even though those of the baby boy look identical. Boy and girl infants are also treated differently. Boys are handled roughly and tossed around playfully; girls are held more, cuddled, talked to, and treated as if they were very fragile. Even the tone of voice used is different. Boys are talked to in loud voices, whereas girls are spoken to gently. Parents also give their children different surroundings, toys, and games, based on gender. However, traditional gender roles do not necessarily have to be the outcome of childhood socialization. A study of NCAA Division 1 female athletes revealed that parental influence was a significant influence in both the athletes' desire to participate in and their success in sports. This form of socialization included role modeling on the part of parents, the opportunities and the expectations provided by parents, and the various ways of leading females to interpret sports as a meaningful and realistic pursuit (Dixon, et al, 2008).

Other research shows that infants respond differently to early variations in treatment (Pridham, Becker, and Brown 2000). Children who are touched and talked to cling to their mothers and talk to them more, regardless of their gender; and because girls are held and talked to more than boys, they tend to reciprocate with this kind of behavior (Goldberg and Lewis 1969; Moss 1967).

Parents teach their boys and girls different techniques for solving problems. When doing a puzzle, for example, parents give girls specific advice, but they try to help boys learn problem-solving techniques (Frankel and Rollins, 1983). Toys selected for boys are either constructive (pieces are added to build or change the toy, such as railroads) or aggressive (such as guns), while toys for girls are more nurturant or attractive (such as dolls) (Lorber 2003).

Gender socialization also results in how children's emotions develop. Parents tend to encourage the expression of sadness more for girls than for boys. Gender socialization is not only affected by the gender of the children but also by the parents as well. Fathers tend to inhibit the expression of sadness in their children more than mothers do (Cassano and Perry-Parrish 2007).

Today, parents are beginning to have different role expectations for their daughters. More and more parents realize that their daughters will have to compete in the work force. In Sweden, where the government has long been active in discouraging differential treatment of boys and girls, Lamb et al. (1982) found that parents treated their infant sons and daughters alike. However, the two parents differed from one another. They treated their children the way they were treated as children. Mothers smiled, cooed, and cuddled their infants more than fathers did, and fathers were more playful. These children experienced both types of socialization. As would be expected, the educational and occupational aspirations of boys and girls differ according to whether they are raised by traditional or feminist parents (Blakemore and Hill 2008).

Gender-Role Socialization in Schools

Children continue to learn gender-role behavior in nursery school (Ornstein 1994). Classroom observations of fifteen nursery schools showed that the teachers (all women) treated boys and girls differently. Teachers responded three times more often to disruptive behavior by boys than by girls. The boys usually got a loud public reprimand, whereas the girls were given a quiet rebuke that others could not hear. Disruptive behavior is often an attempt to gain attention, and because the boys received the attention they were seeking, they continued to behave disruptively. When the teacher paid less attention to the boys, this behavior diminished. Teachers were also more willing to help the boys find something to do. The girls who were not doing anything were ignored and received attention only when they were literally clinging to the teacher's skirts.

The teachers spent more time teaching boys. In one instance, the teacher showed boys how to use a stapler; but when a girl did not know how to use it, the teacher took the materials, stapled them herself, and handed them back to the girl. Both problem-solving and analytical abilities are related to active participation, but girls were not given the opportunity to try things as often as boys were. Boys are also praised more for good work and are encouraged to keep trying. Girls are praised for appearance but left in the dark about their academic performance (Sadker and Sadker 1994).

Teachers also evaluate boys differently from girls. If the preschool child is a boy, the teacher evaluates him no differently whether he is compliant or not. However, compliance is a significant factor in evaluating girls. Less compliant girls are viewed as less intellectually competent (Gold, Crombie, and Noble 1987).

Schools teach gender roles in other ways as well. Most teachers are women, but principals and superintendents are men. Women teachers are more likely to teach young children; but as subject matter becomes more sophisticated and specialized, more men are found teaching. Children receive subtle messages about the capability of men and women as they observe the jobs they hold. School counselors also encourage children to follow expected gender roles. Girls who want to enter masculine occupations or boys who want to enter traditionally feminine occupations will be defined by career counselors as in need of more extensive guidance. Efforts are sometimes made to steer them into more "appropriate" occupations.

Gender-Role Socialization in Peer Groups

Children play mainly in same-sex groups, and this contributes to their socialization. Maccoby (1998) notes that children segregate themselves into same-sex playgroups whenever they have a choice of playmates. This tendency begins at the preschool ages and increases until the children reach puberty. Furthermore, this tendency to segregate is stronger when adults do not interfere—in other words, children are more segregated in the cafeteria than they are in the classroom.

Although it is not clear why children segregate themselves in playgroups, at least part of the explanation is that

POLICY DEBATE

Childcare

The use of substitute childcare is becoming increasingly widespread and debated both in the United States and in other developed countries (Saraceno 2011). The long-term effects of substitute childcare on children when they become adults are not fully known. Most of the research to date suggests that extensive non-parental care in the first year of life does have an impact on a child's development. However, some of the earliest studies were contradictory about what the overall effects are, how long they last, and whether they are beneficial or detrimental to the child (cf., e.g., Belsky, 1990; Clarke-Stewart, 1989; Leavitt and Power, 1989; Phillips et al., 1987).

Referring to the widespread use of substitute childcare, in the last decades of the twentieth century, when non-parental day care became widespread social critic Charles Siegel (1990) wrote, "An entire generation of children is the subject of a risky experiment" (p. 37). While the related political debates focus mostly on who should be responsible for ensuring that there is adequate childcare—government, business, or family—the heart of the matter is socialization. How well are children learning to function in society? Is the socialization of children with parental care different than with non-parental care? If so, what are the differences, and are they detrimental or beneficial to the development of the child? Answers to questions such as these will probably have an impact on any national childcare policies that are developed.

Public and political debates about childcare policies have drawn a great deal of attention to the needs of working parents regarding quality placements for their children. Little (2007) argues that there is a growing recognition that quality programs for school-aged children can enhance the learning achievements obtained at school. In addition, federal funding for childcare programs is at an all time high due to the need for stimulating before and after school activities that will expand the knowledge of children both academically and socially.

Research findings for infants and preschoolers are not as positive as they are for school-aged children. Kreader, Ferguson, and Lawrence (2005) argue that efforts need to be made to enhance the quality of childcare for this age group. Infants and preschoolers should have care from individuals properly trained and educated in child development. The ratio of caregivers to children is particularly important at this age. Children at the greatest risk are those from low-income families who may receive less than adequate care from facilities that are often overcrowded and staffed with persons with little knowledge about the socialization process.

The childcare issue is no longer whether democratic societies in developed countries need alternative methods of child- care; it is how we devise child-care policies that can ensure the best possible socialization of children, while addressing the realities of families throughout the world as they exist today (cf. eg., Saraceno 2011; Brennan 2007).

children in mixed groups will be teased for liking or loving a member of the opposite sex (Maccoby 1998). Children who have ongoing friendships with members of the opposite sex often go into hiding about these friendships by age seven years. They will not acknowledge each other in public but only play together in the privacy of their own homes. To the extent that children segregate themselves to avoid teasing, they are responding to the behavior of older members of the society. They are being socialized to play in same-sex groups.

The result of playing in same-sex groups is that girls are socialized to act like girls and boys are socialized to act like boys (Greenwald 1996; Lawson 1992). Maccoby (1998) found that the children did not form groups based on like interests. Whether the girls were passive or aggressive, they played with other girls; and the same was true of boys. Once in the play group, however, girls learn to act in socially binding ways while boys act competitively. In conversation, for example, girls acknowledge each other, agree with each other, and pause frequently to give others a chance to speak. Boys more often use commands, interrupt, boast, heckle each other, tell jokes, and engage in name-calling. When engaged in taking turns, boys use physical means to get a turn, such as pushing and shoving, while girls use conversational means, persuading others to let them have a turn. As they learn how to get along with others of the same sex, girls especially are less interested in playing with those of the opposite sex because their socially binding norms are less influential and powerful than the competitive norms of boys (Maccoby 1988), and when girls do play with boys, girls become passive.

Psychologist Carol Gilligan argues that as young girls progress through early socialization they end up "hitting the wall". In other words, all the negative messages they have received from society about their image, abilities, worth, etc., come flooding back to influence their perceptions of themselves. The gender socialization that begins at birth and continues throughout life has consistently emphasized a male dominated society where power is less likely to be in the hands of females. When girls fail to conform to the standards set for them by society, the blame will fall on their shoulders. They will be viewed as "tomboy", "oddball", "manly" or some other term situated on their unwillingness to act the way they are suppose to. Gilligan suggests that gender related stereotypes are harmful to the socialization of girls. For example, the words of former Harvard President Lawrence Summers in 2005 drew enormous criticism when he suggested at an academic conference on economics that innate differences between men and women might be one reason fewer women succeed in science and math careers. Summers also suggested that discrimination and socialization are not what creates the low number of female professors in science and engineering. He argued that "the real issue is the overall size of the pool", not the size of the pool that was "held down by discrimination".

Mass Media and Socialization of Gender Roles

From childhood on, Americans spend thousands of hours watching television, which has a strong tendency to portray gender-role stereotypes. In children's television programming, male characters are more often portrayed as aggressive, constructive, and helpful, whereas female characters are more often passive and defer to males. Many children and adults watch adult programs, especially the situation comedies. *I Love Lucy,* which was originally produced in the 1950s and is still seen in reruns, featured Lucille Ball as a consistently inept housewife who had to be rescued by her harassed but tolerant husband. Every episode revolved around Lucy's getting into some sort of trouble. Current situation comedies are a little more subtle.

Music videos, however, are usually not at all subtle. They show men acting rough, tough, and even violent. "Their" women follow or even crawl after the men—

Television programs, such as *I Love Lucy*, tend to portray gender-role stereotypes. Lucille Ball's character was portrayed as an inept housewife who had to be rescued by her harassed but tolerant husband.

As was seen in the treatment of Sarah Palin (above) and Hillary Clinton during the 2008 presidential election, news reporting generally follows established gender stereotypes.

waiting, competing, and even suffering for a bit of attention. The focus of the women is usually on their appearance; they wear provocative clothing that suggests they are waiting on men to sexually seduce them.

Advertising on television and in the press also tends to stereotype both men and women or to portray roles that are impossible to live up to. Career women are portrayed as superwomen who combine a successful career, motherhood, and a terrific marriage while cooking a gourmet meal for a small dinner party of ten. At the other extreme, women are portrayed as beautiful, bewildered homemakers, even when they work outside the home. These ads show the woman arriving home from work to cook the family meal or do the family wash but apparently overwhelmed by indecision about what to serve or how to get shirt collars really clean. A male voice heard in the background tells the woman how to solve her problem. Men in ads are stereotyped as forceful, athletic, involved in business of some kind, or at least actively watching a ball game, but always knowing exactly what they want or which beer has more gusto.

News reporting has generally followed the stereotypes established by society when discussing issues related to women. During the 2008 presidential election the focus was on women, particularly with Hillary Clinton as a presidential candidate, Sarah Palin as a vice-presidential candidate, and Nancy Pelosi, as the Speaker of the House. For example, the New York, journalist Amanda Fortini wrote, "In the grand Passion play that was this election, both Clinton and Palin came to represent—and, at times, reinforce—two of the most pernicious stereotypes that are applied to women: the bitch and the ditz." Another example came from a female anchor for *MSNBC Live*, who wondered on air if Pelosi's "personal feelings [were] getting in the way of effective leadership"—a problem she suggested would not surface in "men-run leadership posts"—and whether men were "more capable of taking personality clashes." (Boehlert and Foser 2006).

APPLYING GENDER-ROLE SOCIALIZATION

Understanding that gender-role stereotypes are a product of socialization is important for you in your work life and in your personal life. One important problem in the workplace that results from gender-role stereotypes is discrimination against women. This has taken a variety of forms, including unfair hiring practices, lower wages, sexual harassment, and many others.

Some companies hire consultants to develop training programs to help employees at all levels understand the sources of these gender-related tensions in the workplace. Employees can be made aware of how stereotypes are generated through media and other agents of socialization. Also, exercises may be used to help men and women employees understand each other's work experience a little better. One way is to have the men and women engage in role-reversal role-playing. This can help them to see situations from the other gender's point of view and to become more sensitive to each other's needs and attitudes. The key theme that runs through the training is to get beyond the gender stereotypes that people have learned in their previous socialization.

Stereotypes generated through gender-role socialization may also create problems in your intimate relationships. In her book *Intimate Strangers*, Lillian Rubin (1983) discusses how our **gender identity** as males or females often prevents people of the opposite sex (husbands and wives, boyfriends and girlfriends, or just close friends) from developing true intimacy. That is, as a result of gender-role socialization, males often learn to see themselves in terms of stereotypical instrumental traits (aggressive, unemotional, dominant, career-oriented, and so forth), and females often learn to see themselves in terms of stereotypical expressive traits (passive, emotional, subordinate, relationship-oriented, and so forth). Think of how these perceptions of ourselves might interfere with the ability of men and women to develop close emotional bonds. Since you see yourself as a "real man," for example, you may find it difficult to express your emotions openly, to cry in front of others, or to be sensitive, even if these feelings tend to emerge. Because you see yourself as a "real woman," you may find it difficult or confusing to have an equal say in your relationship, to take charge of a situation, or to be aggressive, even though you may want to. The realization that gender roles and gender identities are learned through socialization and are not an inherent part of our biological makeup can help both sexes to overcome many barriers to intimacy and to relate to each other as whole individuals.

Thinking Sociologically

In the discussion of how the news media portrays female candidates, both journalists were themselves female. Explain why women are likely to criticize other women and to reinforce gender stereotypes?

SOCIALIZATION IN ADULTHOOD

The knowledge we acquire as children shapes the meanings we give to ourselves and to the world, and it can continue to influence us for the rest of our lives. We never stop learning new things, however; every day, we have new experiences, learn new information, and add the meanings of these new facts to what we already know. Adult socialization occurs when we learn new roles that are expected from us, as we get older. Although new knowledge may be different from knowledge acquired as children, the same agencies of socialization are at work.

College and Marriage

Like children, adults are socialized by their families. Adult socialization also occurs in schools. Colleges teach adults of all ages, and the move from home to college can be a period of intense socialization. College freshmen must adapt to their new independence from the family and make their own decisions about health, food, sleep, class attendance, study habits, exercise, and social relationships. They must learn to live in crowded situations and to compete with peers. Some avoid these decisions by going along with the crowd. Others drop the values they learned in the family and adopt a new set of values, whereas some continue to maintain family values in the new setting. Each choice entails some socialization.

Single people must be socialized when they marry in order to live intimately with their spouses and to share living arrangements. Each person is socialized toward marriage based on their own set of experiences and social interactions growing up. Once married, a young couple must decide how to define their marriage based on their own expectations rather than those of others.

Parenthood

When a couple has children, they learn the role of parent and will probably rely on the knowledge of childcare they acquired from their own parents. Because the two parents were themselves brought up by different sets of parents, they will have learned different child-rearing techniques and therefore will have to socialize each other to reach agreement about child-care practices. As the children grow up, the parents must be socialized to allow their children to become independent after years of dependency. All of this learning is a part of adult socialization.

Children themselves are often very active socializers of their parents. As infants, they let their parents know when they need attention. Beginning at about age two years, they become aware of themselves, learn to say "no," and begin to let their parents know when they need some independence. This process of demanding both attention and independence continues as long as the children are at home. It can result in serious conflicts in some youths, particularly those who rebel, fight, take drugs, or run away from home. The socialization of parents can be quite dramatic, but it is often successful. A questionnaire given to mothers and fathers of college students (Peters 1985) found that the parents had learned different attitudes and behaviors about sports, leisure, minority groups, drug use, and sexuality from their children.

Career

Another type of adult socialization is occupational training, which teaches the attitudes and values associated with an occupation, as well as the skills. Acquiring a new job involves taking on new statuses and roles. A new employee in an office has to learn how to conform to the expectations of the other workers and to the business's written and unwritten rules. During this socialization, the employee will discover the answers to questions such as these: Are men and women expected to wear suits, or is less formal clothing acceptable? Do employees address one another by their first names? Is rigid adherence to established procedures expected? Are some department heads more accommodating than others?

Resocialization

Major adaptations to new situations in adulthood may sometimes require **resocialization**. The changes people undergo during this period are much more pervasive than the gradual adaptations characteristic of regular socialization. Resocialization usually follows a major break in a person's customary life; this break requires that the person adopt an entirely new set of meanings to understand his or her new life. Divorce, retirement, or the death of a loved one usually involves the process of resocialization. Retirement from work is sometimes an easy process of socialization to a new situation, but it often requires a great deal of resocialization. Retired people often lose at least part of their income, so they may have to adapt to a new standard of living. With the loss of work, new sources of self-esteem may have to be developed, but society may help in this process by providing education on financial management, health, and housing. Employers may also provide counseling services and support groups for retired persons, especially when they want employees to retire.

Besides loss of income and self-esteem, retirement creates another resocialization problem. Most roles involve social expectations and provide rewards for meeting those expectations. However, there are few social expectations associated with retirement other than the loss of a previous role; as a result, the satisfactory performance of the retirement role goes unrecognized. To compound the problem, the retired person's spouse often dies during this period, so he or she must relinquish the family role, as well as the work role. Nonetheless, if the retired person has enough money to buy nice clothes, enjoy hobbies, and afford travel for social events or volunteer work, then he or she can create a new role that is rewarding.

Mortification of self (Goffman 1961), the most dramatic type of resocialization, occurs in such institutions as the armed forces, prisons, and mental hospitals. People entering these institutions are totally stripped of their old selves. Physically, they are required to strip, shower, and don institutional clothing. All personal possessions are taken away; and they must leave behind family, friends, and work roles. They must live in a new environment under a new set of rules and adopt a new role as a military person, prisoner, or mental patient. Their previous learning must be completely redefined.

Whether dealing with socialization or with resocialization, the human mind is very complex. People learn a varied set of meanings during their lives, and they interpret each situation on the basis of their own biography and their own definition of the situation. How a person presents the self and maintains interactions depends on his or her unique interpretation of self, others, and the situation. It is this ability to interpret that makes socialization and social interaction such a varied, interesting, and challenging area of study.

CHAPTER REVIEW

Wrapping it up

Summary

1. Socialization is the process of learning how to interact in society. Infants must interact in order to survive; and as they interact, they learn about society.
2. Children who have been isolated, abused, or received little attention when very young do not learn to walk, talk, or otherwise respond to people because early social interactions are crucial to development.
3. Sociobiologists believe that inborn genetic traits direct human behavior just as they direct the behavior of animals. They contend that sexual, altruistic, and warlike behaviors occur in humans because we are predisposed to them in our genetic makeup. Most biologists and social scientists, however, sidestep the nature—nurture debate by believing that people's behavior is determined by their biological capacity to learn socially.
4. Human beings are unique because they learn a symbol system—language. Through linguistic interaction, we develop a self—an idea of who we are.
5. Mead used the term *role-taking* to describe the process of figuring out how others think and perceive us. According to Mead, children take the role of only one other person at a time at first. Children *practice* role-taking in play and learn to generalize in team games. The *I* acts, but the *me* sees the self as an object. The interplay between the two allows the self to act freely while aware of social reactions.
6. Charles Horton Cooley used the term *looking-glass self* to describe how people learn about themselves; he argued that our identities are heavily influenced by our perceptions of how others view us. We see ourselves not as we are, and not as others see us, but as we think others see us.
7. Goffman compared interaction to a drama on stage. We present ourselves, as we want other people to define us. Once we have presented ourselves, everyone involved in the interaction is expected to maintain that presentation. We justify our discrepant behavior by making excuses or disclaimers. If we cannot maintain our presentations, we will respond to our failure with emotion, often embarrassment or anger.
8. Kohlberg provided us with the foundation on which to understand moral development in children.
9. Freud believed that personality consisted of three components: the id, superego, and ego.
10. Some of the important agencies of socialization are the family, schools, peer groups, and mass media.

11. From birth, males and females are socialized differently. Men are expected to be instrumental, active, and task-oriented, whereas women are expected to be expressive, nurturing, and people-oriented.

12. Resocialization may be necessary when a person's life changes dramatically and abruptly, such as when he or she goes to prison or retires.

Key Terms

account of behavior An effort at maintaining the self by explaining the reasons for or facts surrounding the behavior

disclaimers An aspect of maintaining our presentation of self in which we deny behavior that contradicts how we wish to be viewed

dramaturgical approach An approach to the study of interaction in which interaction is compared to a drama on stage; the importance of setting and presentation of self are emphasized

excuse of behavior An effort at maintaining the self by justifying or making an apology for the behavior

expressive role A role that emphasizes warmth and understanding rather than action or leadership; traditionally associated more with women than with men

gender identity The social construction of boys and girls, men and women, as opposed to their biological characteristics

generalized other The assumption that other people have similar attitudes, values, beliefs, and expectations, making it, therefore, not necessary to know a specific individual in order to know how to behave toward that individual

I The acting, unselfconscious person

instinct Biological or hereditary impulses, drives, or behaviors that require no learning or reasoning

instrumental role A role that emphasizes accomplishment of tasks, such as earning a living to provide food and shelter; traditionally associated more with men than with women

looking-glass self A process occurring in social interaction and having three components: (1) how we think our behavior appears to others, (2) how we think others judge our behavior, and (3) how we feel about their judgments

mass media Forms of communication, such as television, popular magazines, and radio, intended for a large audience

me The part of self that sees self as object, evaluates self, and is aware of society's expectations of self

mind The process of using a language and thinking

mortification of self Stripping the self of all the characteristics of a past identity, including clothing, personal possessions, friends, roles and routines, and so on

nature—nurture debate A longstanding debate over whether behavior results from predetermined biological characteristics or from socialization

peer group An informal primary group of people who share a similar or equal status and who are usually of roughly the same age

play According to Mead, a way of practicing role taking

presentation of self The way we present ourselves to others and how our presentation influences others

resocialization Socialization to a new role or position in life that requires a dramatic shift in the attitudes, values, behaviors, and expectations learned in the past

role taking Assuming the roles of others and seeing the world from their perspective

self The sense of one's own identity as a person

self-fulfilling prophecy A prediction that comes true because people believe it and act as though it were true

significant others Persons that one identifies with psychologically and whose opinions are considered important

socialization The process of learning how to interact in society by learning the rules and expectations of society

sociobiology The study of the biological and genetic determinants of social behavior

symbolic interaction theory The social theory stressing interactions between people and the social processes that occur within the individual that are made possible by language and internalized meanings

Discussion Questions

1. How could the ideas of Mead and Cooley be used to discuss your own gender-role socialization?
2. Using Cooley's looking-glass self concept, discuss how your perception of how others see you influences the way you think about yourself. What effect does this have on your self?
3. Discuss things you do in college that you believe are important because your peers tell you they are important. Are these messages from your peers making you a better student?
4. Discuss things you do in college that you believe are important because the mass media tell you they are important. Are these messages from the mass media making you a better student?
5. Imagine that you are putting on a skit about getting ready to go to class (or put on such a skit, if possible). What impression are you going to make on professors? On classmates?
6. How does your backstage preparation for class differ from your performance onstage?
7. Think back to your most recent casual conversation, perhaps at lunch. What disclaimers were used in the course of this conversation?
8. Use Goffman's ideas about social interaction to develop an explanation of socialization.

Pop Quiz

1. In Spitz's study, children reared with their mothers in a detention center compared to those in foundling homes were found ______.

   a. to have normal development
   b. to show slow physical and social development
   c. not to be able to talk at all or capable of saying only a few words
   d. to have died within two years of the study

2. The process of learning how to interact in society is called ______.

   a. behaviorism
   b. developmentalism
   c. socialization
   d. interactionism

3. Studies of feral children lend support to what idea?

   a. Children can develop normally even without human interaction
   b. The first two years of life determine the type of later development
   c. Except for learning to speak a language, the physical growth of feral children is only minimally impaired
   d. None of the above

4. The wild boy of Aveyron ______.

   a. learned to talk within four years
   b. learned to use utensils quite readily
   c. died within a few years after being rescued
   d none of the above

5. The study of the biological and genetic determinants of behavior is called ______.

   a. sociobiology
   b. symbolic interaction
   c. socialization
   d. dramaturgy

6. Mead called the process of figuring out how others will act ______.

   a. the presentation of self
   b. behavior modification
   c. developmental growth
   d. role taking

7. Mead's two-part social self consists of ______.

   a. the "I" and the "me"
   b. the "you" and the "me"
   c. the "we" and the "you"
   d. the "me" and the "you"

8. According to Mead, play is a way of practicing ______.

   a. role taking
   b. socialization
   c. gender-role stereotyping
   d. dramaturgy

9. Components of the looking-glass self include ______.

   a. how we think our behavior appears to others
   b. how we think others judge our behavior
   c. how we feel about the judgments of others
   d. all of the above

10. Traditionally, the primary agency of socialization is ______.

    a. the family
    b. educational institutions
    c. peer groups
    d. reference groups

11. Studies show that human interaction is generally necessary for infant survival, but in rare instances infants can become normal, healthy children without it. T/F

12. Although the media are important socializers of children and adolescents, they have little impact on the social learning of adults. T/F

13. Children themselves are active socializers of parents. T/F

14. Peer groups are people roughly about the same age. T/F

15. People learn a varied set of meanings during their lives. T/F

1. A	6. D	11. F
2. C	7. A	12. F
3. D	8. A	13. T
4. D	9. D	14. T
5. A	10. A	15. T

CHAPTER 7

Deviance and Social Control

PRESCRIPTION DRUG ABUSE

Every United States president since Richard Nixon has had the "war on drugs" as a priority. In 1970, Nixon stated, "Public enemy Number one in the United States is drug abuse. In order to fight and defeat this enemy, it is necessary to wage a new, all-out offensive." Nixon's war on drugs budget was $100 million. Today the war on drugs budget is over $15 billion. In the past forty years, the war on drugs has cost the U.S. over $1 trillion and hundreds of thousands of lives (www.cbsnews.com, 2010). Combating drug abuse remains one of the United States' most important domestic and foreign policy issues.

Like many before him, President George W. Bush's anti-drug campaign focused on a law-enforcement model that attacked the "supply-side" of the illegal drug industry—traffickers, smugglers and users (Katel 2006). President Obama's anti-drug strategy shifted from the "supply-side" approach to a policy that treated illegal drug use as a public health issue, putting more resources into prevention and treatment (Hernanel 2010).

Regardless of the various tactics used by presidents from Nixon to Obama, there are still many public misconceptions about the drug abuse problem in the U.S. One common misconception that has existed since the start of the war on drugs is that the word drugs, when considering the drug abuse problem, refers only to illegal drugs such as marijuana, cocaine (and cocaine derivatives such as "crack"), methamphetamine (and "meth" derivatives such as MDMA and ecstasy), phencyclidine (PCP), and LSD and other hallucinogens (Coleman and Cressey 1990). However, alcohol and tobacco are also psychoactive drugs, and they can be more dangerous than illegal drugs and are readily accepted in many social circles. The Institute of Medicine reported in 2007 that tobacco kills more people in the U.S. annually than AIDS, alcohol, cocaine, heroin, homicides, suicides, car accidents and fires combined (Oral Cancer Foundation).

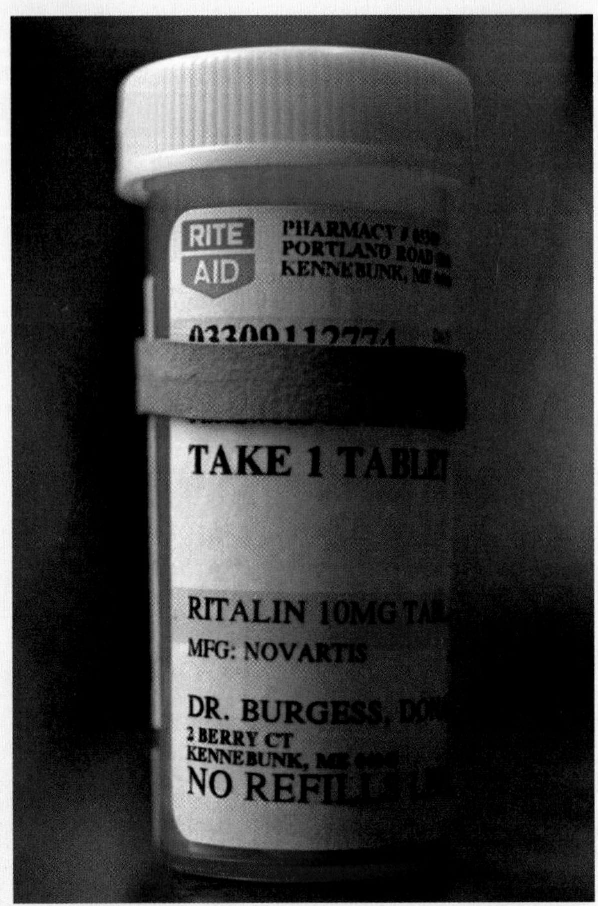

Painkillers and stimulants (such as Ritalin and Adderall) to treat ADHD (attention deficit hyperactivity) has increased significantly in the last few decades

Perhaps one of the most problematic drug problems in the United States today is prescription (legal) drug abuse. While we have seen the news about celebrities who have died or have suffered from prescription drugs (for example, Michael Jackson, Anna Nicole Smith, Heath Ledger, Rush Limbaugh, to name only a few of the most recent ones), celebrities are not the only ones who suffer from medication abuse. In 2005, more people ages forty-five to fifty-four died from prescription drug overdoses than in car crashes (www.CQresearcher.com, 2009). Yet, many people still believe that prescription drugs are safer than illegal drugs. This misconception is an important part of the drug abuse problem today.

Deaths from unintentional overdoses from legal drugs, led by prescription opiods (such as Vicodin, OxyContin, and other tranquilizers), have reached historic highs. Rates of death from overdoses are four to five times more than during the heroin epidemic of the 1970s (Clemmit 2009). The use of legitimate painkillers and stimulants (such as Ritalin and Adderall) to treat ADHD (attention deficit hyperactivity) has increased significantly in the last few decades; and with this increase in prescriptions and availability has been an increase in abuse. Prescription drug overdoses are now more common than deaths from heroin and cocaine combined. Deaths from prescription opiods increased 150 percent in the U.S. between 1999 and 2004.

This overuse and abuse of prescription drugs raises the question as to whom and what should be the focus of the "war on drugs." Should the federal Drug Enforcement Administration enact tighter controls? Does the pharmaceutical industry bear any responsibility, and do they profit excessively? Do physicians prescribe drugs too freely? Should there be more of a focus on combating the availability of drugs on the Internet? Should drug education be re-designed to focus on prescription drugs rather than on "street" drugs? Have the social expectations for achievement and success from parents and schools led to an increase in drug use to combat feelings of inadequacy or to the use of performance-enhancing drugs? These are only questions, not blame.

Sociology does not focus on individual blame to understand social problems but rather explores the structural and cultural factors that create social problems. For example, while it does not deny that some people may be more or less biologically or psychologically prone to drug abuse, it is more concerned with understanding the social nature of the drug world and the wider social environment, and the ways in which they can affect people's tendencies toward drug use. The issue of prescription drug use illustrates how sociological theories of deviance can be used to reconceptualize social problems in ways that might help solve them.

Deviance is universal because people everywhere violate social norms. It exists in all societies, wherever people interact and live in groups. It is found in complex, industrialized, urban areas, as well as in tribal, folk, and agrarian regions. Although it is sometimes claimed that people in some societies cooperate in complete harmony and peace, anthropologists claim that no society or culture, large or small, rural or urban, has complete behavioral conformity and a total absence of deviance.

WHAT IS DEVIANCE?

Deviance means different things to different people. The definition we use influences our explanations of its causes and our attempts to control it. Does deviance reside in the individual? Is it a particular type of act or behavior? Is it defined socially? Are some groups of people immune from being labeled deviants? Our answers to questions such as these will influence how we analyze deviance and whether we ultimately understand it.

We define **deviance** as variation from a set of norms or shared social expectations and deviants as the people who violate these shared expectations. Deviance involves a social audience that defines particular people and behaviors as going beyond the tolerance limits of social norms. The opposite of deviance is conformity, when people follow the norms of their social group or society. Social norms, rules, and expectations about appropriate and inappropriate behavior exist in all societies. People everywhere have social controls to enforce the rules and to punish those who do not conform.

Norms rarely state exactly which behaviors are acceptable and which are unacceptable, and universal adherence to norms is unknown. All societies permit variations in the behavior demanded by the norms. Where variations are possible, people will test their range, and some will inevitably exceed the boundaries of permissible and approved behavior. People's perceptions of deviance rarely correspond to its reality, however, as is shown in the following discussion of some traditional views of deviance and of deviants.

Social Functions of Deviance

While deviance may be viewed as harmful, immoral, antisocial, or a sickness by society, it may have positive effects, as well. Deviance is part of the nature of all social systems and traditionally regarded as evidence of social disorganization. However, many deviant subcultures—such as gangs, organized crime, prostitution, or police corruption, found in highly organized societies —may be highly organized themselves. As early as 1894, Durkheim pointed out that deviations should be regarded as a normal part of a society (Kelly 1979). It appears that deviance performs various social functions, some of which are described next.

Deviance helps to *define the limits of social tolerance.* Indicating the extent to which norms can be violated without provoking a reaction helps to clarify the boundaries of social norms and the limits of behavioral diversity. Methods of social control—such as arrests, psychiatric counseling, criminal trials, and social ostracism—help to define these limits. Arrests and trials indicate to the public the seriousness of some deviations and the extent to which violations of norms are tolerated. For many years, bullying was tolerated as a typical behavior of school children, particularly boys; however, with the current attention given to school violence (both in the US and other countries), most schools

Bullying was tolerated for many years as a typical behavior of school children. Today most schools have implemented a "bullying" policy.

today have implemented "bullying" policies (cf.eg., Farrington and Ttofi 2009; Hilton, et al, 2010). Police may tolerate a person driving a couple of miles over the speed limit; but if the person is in a school zone, he will likely be stopped and ticketed. By observing societal reactions to deviance, members learn the limits of acceptable variation from norms.

Deviance can *increase the solidarity and integration of a group*. Such a label can unite the people who share it. Most people find emotional support and a sense of community among others who share their values and behavior patterns. If the group is considered deviant by society, they tend to defend and protect one another and derive their identities from their group. By the same token, highly integrated groups may form in an attempt to defeat or eliminate deviants because having a common enemy tends to unite group members.

Deviance can serve as a *"safety valve" for social discontent*. When people desire things that the social norms do not permit them to have, they may become frustrated and angry, attacking norms or even attempting to destroy the social system. Some types of deviance permit people to escape from conventional norms and rid themselves of frustration without disrupting the social system as a whole. Cheating on paying income tax may be an outlet for frustration with government spending on wasteful projects or with being underpaid. The use of illegal drugs may be a safety valve against job frustrations or an unhappy marriage. Cheating on income tax or drug use involves risk to individuals, but either may prevent expressions of frustration more injurious to society. Thus, some deviances tend indirectly to support such basic institutions as marriage, the economy, and the government. By funneling off anger and discontent, deviance may remove some of the strain produced by social mores.

Deviance can *indicate defects or inadequacies in the existing social organization*. High rates of some kinds of deviance may expose problems in the social order. Large numbers of parking violations may indicate that there are not enough parking spaces. Outbreaks of violence in prison serve as a warning that the system is inadequate. Activities such as freedom marches by blacks in the South, the burning of draft cards by young men in the 1960s, and the hunger strikes of IRA members in Ireland were organized acts of defiance (and deviance), intended to force leaders and the public to address perceived problems in the social system.

Another functional aspect of deviance, therefore, is that it can *set in motion steps that lead to social change*. Such change can occur in many different forms. It can involve modifications in the existing structure, modifications in behavior, or changes in the definitions of deviance. Until the early 1960s, a black who tried to sit in the front of a bus in Alabama was regarded as deviant. Following bus boycotts, court cases, and rulings against segregation, this behavior is no longer considered deviant. As social norms change, so do their definitions; folkways and mores may be modified as a consequence of deviant acts.

Social Dysfunctions of Deviance

Some consequences of deviance are dysfunctional. Deviances can disrupt, destabilize, or even lead to the complete breakdown of a social system. Given the range of tolerance of norm violations, isolated instances of deviance generally have little effect on the stability of systems. Widespread, long-term, and more extreme norm violations can impair the functioning of groups or of entire systems.

Deviance can *disrupt the social order*. Violations of norms can disturb the status quo, make social life unpredictable, and create tension and conflict. Teachers who refuse to teach, parents who ignore their children, or workers who fail to perform their appointed tasks can keep the system from functioning smoothly. The effect of an alcoholic father on a family system is a good example. The family's income may decrease, the wife may have to assume full responsibility for raising the children, and the children may be ashamed to bring friends home. All routines and social expectations are subject to being disturbed by him. Deviance is, thus, often dysfunctional because it disrupts the order and predictability of life.

Deviance can *disrupt the will of others to conform*. If norm violations are unpunished or if members of society refuse to obey established rules, the desire to conform is decreased. Studying for an exam may seem pointless if you know that other students are going to cheat. Obeying the speed limit can be frustrating if other drivers blow their horns to get you out of the way so that they can speed by. To work hard when others are lazy, to be honest when others are dishonest, or to obey the rules when others ignore them—all can make the efforts seem pointless. When deviance and conformity are not differentiated, deviance disappears. If they receive the same response or reward, what is the motivation to conform? Conformity to a given norm, rule, or law makes sense only if (1) others conform as well, (2) those who conform are differentiated from those who do not in some way, or (3) norm violators receive some type of punishment. Deviance that erodes the desire to follow rules and conform to social norms is dysfunctional.

Deviance can *destroy trust*. Social life is based in part on the assumption that other people are honest and trustworthy. When interpersonal trust decreases, people become more dependent on the legal system to define, interpret, support, and enforce the law. If all car dealers (or car buyers) were honest, written contracts would not be necessary; and a few judges and lawyers would be out of work. In this sense, deviance is functional for the legal system, but it is dysfunctional to the society as a whole. Widespread deviance destroys our confidence and trust in others, just as it disrupts the will to conform.

Deviance can *divert resources* into social rehabilitation and control efforts—resources which otherwise could be used elsewhere. It may be functional in that it provides thousands of jobs for those who rehabilitate and control criminals, drug addicts, the mentally ill, and others; but it is dysfunctional in that the money and other resources used to deal with deviance cannot be used for other constructive and productive purposes. Criminal activities alone cost billions of dollars every year. Most would agree that these funds could be used more profitably elsewhere.

Clearly, deviance is neither all good nor all bad. Some of its consequences lead to the stability and maintenance of the system while others tend to disrupt it. Whatever the case, it is here to stay, an inevitable part of every society.

TRADITIONAL VIEWS OF DEVIANCE AND OF DEVIANTS

Who and what is deviant involves a range of perspectives. Sociologists are likely to focus on social aspects of deviance (and of deviants), including how it is formally and informally controlled. As you might guess, there are also biological, psychological, legal, religious, and other perspectives, including views by those who counsel, treat, punish, or work with those defined as deviant. We begin by noting some traditional views of deviance that are widely held today.

The Absolutist and Moral Views

One common traditional view of deviance, often found in conservative political and religious contexts, is that deviance is both absolute and immoral. That is, particular behaviors—be they extramarital sexual relationships, homosexuality, criminal acts, dishonesty, or the use of psychoactive drugs—are always deviant (absolutism) and bad or wrong (immoral). Black is black, and white is white; there are no shades of grey, and no theory, teaching, or argument will make it otherwise. From this perspective, the social rules are clear, and people should adhere to them. Those who do not are labeled as "bad" people, people who lack proper moral codes, and people who need to be punished.

The Medical and Social-Pathological Views

A second traditional approach is the **medical view** of deviance, in which deviance is assumed to be essentially pathological—evidence that deviants are "sick" people and that society is unhealthy. Just as healthy humans function efficiently without pain or the need for drugs or criminal activities, healthy societies are thought to function smoothly without social problems such as deviance. The prevalence of child abuse, rape, robbery, mental disorders, and alcoholism are thought to indicate that the society in which these occur has a sickness; and the people who do these things or who behave in these ways need to be "cured." Like the absolutist and moral view, the medical view assumes that people are either deviant or not deviant—there is no gray area—but this polarity is expressed in terms of health or illness, not good or evil. The **"Medicalization of Deviance"** is a relatively new term in the world of sociology, but it's becoming increasingly popular in society to explain deviant behavior. Over the last fifty years society has watched certain conditions such as AIDS and alcoholism transform from deviant and moral issues into medical conditions (Kimberlin, et al., 2006).

The Statistical View

A third traditional view of deviance relies on statistics. Any behavior that is atypical—that varies from the average or the mode—is considered deviant. This view is not absolutist. Deviance is assumed to be a variable characteristic that increases the further a behavior is removed from the average. Deviants are viewed not as sick people, as in the medical view, but simply as being different. According to the **statistical view**, any variation from a statistical norm is deviant. Thus, a person who is left-handed, who has red hair, or who belongs to a minority group is defined as a deviant. Everyone fails to conform to the average in some respect, however; so according to this definition, we are all deviants.

DEVIANCE AND SOCIAL CONTROL

The fact that deviance is universal and sometimes has positive social functions does not eliminate the need to control it. If societies are to survive, they must have ways of making people conform to social norms. The mechanisms of social control are ways of manipulating members to conform to the group's norms. The influences can be internal or external, negative or positive, and formal or informal. The norms of society are maintained both by encouraging conformity and by discouraging deviance.

Conformity to social norms is generally explained in terms of two social control processes: (1) **Internal means of control** occurs when members conform to the norms because they believe they should, even when other members of the group are not present. (2) **External means of control** are the responses of others to a member's behavior. Others in the group will utilize pressures or sanctions to attempt to control an individual's behavior. The two types of control tend to operate interactively.

In the statistical view of deviance, any behavior that is atypical and varies from the average is considered deviant. For example, a person who is left handed or has red hair is defined as a deviant. Deviants are viewed as simply being different.

Groups will typically rely on sanctions to control the behaviors of its members. **Sanctions** are rewards and punishments used to encourage proper behavior or to discourage deviant conduct. **Positive sanctions** are actions that encourage individuals to continue a behavior while **negative sanctions**, such as a frown, are utilized to stop a behavior from being repeated. In addition, the type of sanction used can be either formal or informal. Formal sanctions generally occur in a public setting, whereas informal sanctions are spontaneous acts used by other group members to control behaviors. Let's look closer at mechanisms of social control.

Positive Internal Controls of Deviance

Internal controls are those that exist within the particular individual's moral and social codes of behavior. They include a wide range of factors: positive self-image, self-control, ego strength, high frustration tolerance, and a sense of social responsibility, among others. The workings of internal controls can be explained, in part, by socialization theories. These theories explain how we internalize norms, learn what others expect of us, and develop a desire to conform to those expectations. Some types of deviance, such as criminality and mental illness, are widely believed to be caused by inadequate socialization, especially in the years of early childhood.

Most social control is directly related to a person's *social self*—our definitions of who we are in relation to the society in which we live. Internal motivations to conform result not from a fear of being caught or a fear of punishment but because people have been socialized to see themselves in a certain way and to believe that stealing, cheating, murder, and some other behaviors are wrong. Again, the looking glass-self and the self-fulfilling prophecy are relevant here and could be used in personal and professional relationships. The manager of a large department store, for example, might have a problem with employee theft of goods in the store. Instead of dealing with the problem by threats of punishment, the manager might try to get the employees to see themselves as part of a team working together toward a common goal. College teachers who have a problem with students cutting classes or not doing their reading assignments might treat the students as if they were mature, responsible individuals and commend their positive actions. It is true that rewards or punishments might work at times. However, when people act *only* out of fear of punishment or desire for a reward, and the reward or punishment is the only reason for conforming to the desired behavior, people may no longer conform if the reward or punishment is removed.

Parents might use the knowledge that people tend to act in a manner consistent with their view of themselves in a positive way to influence and socialize

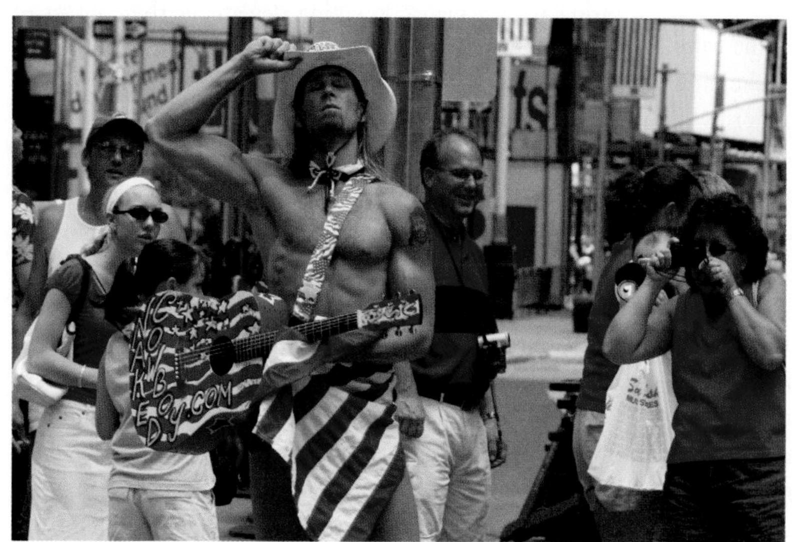

Robert Burck, the "Naked Cowboy" performs in New York. Although his behavior may be called deviant by some, the positive sanctions he receives from passersby encourage him to continue.

children. Instead of trying to control their behavior with rewards or punishments, parents might try to instill a sense of high self-esteem and self-respect in their children by the way they act toward them. If children are constantly ridiculed and put down, they may come to have a low self-esteem and low self-respect; thus, they may act accordingly. On the other hand, if children are often praised or corrected in a more positive way, their positive self-images may motivate them to adopt more positive social values and to act in accordance with these values.

Feelings about right and wrong are sometimes referred to as "conscience." The saying, "Let your conscience be your guide," assumes that you have internalized some notions about deviant and nondeviant behavior. For most people, the conscience develops as a direct result of socialization experiences in early childhood and later in life. Social institutions such as the family and religion significantly aid in the internalization of social norms. Once social norms are internalized, deviations produce feelings of guilt, remorse, or conflict. The relatively high prevalence of conformity in comparison to deviance is largely due to internal controls.

Informal and Formal External Controls of Deviance

External controls are those that come from outside an individual. They can be either informal or formal. **Informal external controls** involve peers, friends, parents, or the other people with whom we associate regularly; these people apply pressure to encourage us to obey the rules and conform to social expectations. The same techniques can be used to encourage conformity to deviant norms.

Informal social controls may be used to control the behaviors of persons within our racial, ethnic, family, or peer group. For example, why are some ethnic groups more prone to problems with alcoholism than others, or more likely to be involved in athletics? Glassner and Berg (1980) found that American Jews avoid alcohol problems through protective social processes such as childhood socialization, adult relationships, and avoidance techniques. These same techniques could be used in African American communities to promote athletics over gangs, drugs, or other deviant behaviors. **Formal external controls,** the systems created by society specifically to control deviance, are probably the least influential. Courts, police officers, and prisons are formal external controls. Unlike internal controls and informal external controls, formal controls are supposed to be impersonal and just. In actuality, however, the legal system tends to favor some groups of people, just as conflict theory suggests. Even in prisons, guards tend to overlook rule violations by some prisoners and to enforce the rules with others. The discretionary power of police officers, prosecutors, judges, and other officials in arresting, prosecuting, and convicting people is often used arbitrarily. It may be highly dependent on factors other than deviance per se. Age, race, sex, social status, known prior deviations, and other factors—all have been shown to affect the nature and outcome of formal control mechanisms.

THE RELATIVE NATURE OF DEVIANCE

More recently, sociologists have begun to advocate a relativistic model. Cultural relativism is the assumption that behaviors, ideas, and products can be understood or evaluated only within the context of the culture and society of which they are a part. In the same way, a **relativistic view** suggests that deviance can be interpreted only in the sociocultural context in which it happens. Is a person who is seven feet tall a deviant in the context of professional basketball? Is a person without a bathing suit a deviant at a nudist beach? Is taking opiate drugs to treat excruciating pain deviant? Is killing deviant in the context of war? Context influences all of these determinations.

If deviance is relative rather than absolute, an act that is deviant in one context may not be deviant in another. A behavior considered "sick" in one society could be thought of as healthy in a different society. An act that might be statistically deviant in one culture might not be in another. Thus, as is generally true of cultural relativism, acts that are defined as deviant in some places are not defined as such everywhere. By the same token, however, the fact that an act is defined as nondeviant in one situation does not mean that it is nondeviant everywhere. Deviance does not consist merely of acts or behaviors, but also of the group responses, definitions, and meanings attached to behaviors; and we, therefore, can expect definitions of deviance to vary with differing circumstances. Some of the most important variations that affect these definitions concern time, place, situation, and social status.

Variation by Time

An act considered deviant in one time period might be considered nondeviant in another. Cigarette smoking, for example, has a long history of changing normative definitions. Nuehring and Markle (1974) note that in the United States, between 1895 and 1921; fourteen states completely banned cigarette smoking, and all other states except Texas passed laws regulating the sale of cigarettes to minors. In the early years of this century, stop-smoking clinics were opened in several cities, and antismoking campaigns were widespread. Following World War I, however, cigarette sales increased, and public attitudes toward smoking changed. Through the mass media, the tobacco industry appealed to women, weight-watchers, and even to health seekers. States began to realize that tobacco could be a rich source of revenue, and by 1927, the fourteen states that had banned cigarettes had repealed their laws. By the end of World War II, smoking had become acceptable, and in many contexts, it was considered to be socially desirable.

An act—such as cigarette smoking , which was acceptable during the middle part of the last century—considered deviant in one time period might be considered nondeviant in another.

In the 1950s, scientists found that smoking could cause a variety of diseases, including lung cancer and heart disease. In 1964, the surgeon general published a landmark report on smoking and health, and soon thereafter, some states began passing anticigarette legislation again. Laws were passed requiring a health warning on cigarette packages, and in 1973, the National Association of Broadcasters agreed to phase out cigarette advertising on television (Markle and Troyer 1979). Another surgeon general's report in 1986 crystallized the push of this public health concern to a new level; smoking not only harms the health of those who choose to smoke, but it is also hazardous to those who must breathe residual smoke while in physical proximity of someone who is smoking.

The result was that by the 1990s, airlines, restaurants, and other public places either prohibited smoking totally or designated segregated sections for smokers and nonsmokers. Many states have completely prohibited smoking in such places as elevators, concert halls, museums, and physicians' offices. In 2006, the State of Ohio enacted the statewide law banning all smoking in any public place including private clubs. It wasn't long before more states followed; and by the beginning of 2009, twenty-three of fifty, plus Washington D.C., had banned smoking in most public places, including restaurants and bars. The latest state to join was Virginia, the home of Marlboro and the world's largest cigarette factory. For over four hundred years Virginia has grown tobacco and for 150 years has been home to Phillip Morris, the largest U.S. tobacco manufacturer. In February 2009, California Senator Alex Padilla, introduced a bill that would ban tobacco sales within one thousand feet of schools and other areas, such as recreational facilities, where children would likely be without adult supervision. All of these actions suggest that smoking is increasingly being considered a deviant behavior. Many other examples could be given to illustrate how behaviors defined as deviant change over time, such as the use of intoxicating products (see the Volstead Act), various other psychoactive drugs, appropriate bathing attire, nonmarital sexual behavior, and so forth.

Variation by Place

Behaviors viewed as deviant in one location, society, or culture may be considered nondeviant in others. In most African cultures, having more than one wife is a sign of wealth, prestige, and high status. In the United States, however, having more than one wife at a time is a punishable offense. Topless bathing is common on certain public beaches in Southern Europe, but is defined as immoral, criminal, or delinquent in American society. Bullfighting in Spain and Mexico and cockfighting in the Philippines are festive, legal gambling activities that produce income, but they are forbidden in the United States. On the other hand, American dating practices, divorce rates, crime rates, and the widespread acceptance of and practice of capital punishment are considered shocking by much of both the Western and non-Western world. For example, the United States remains the leader, in comparison to other countries, in incarceration rates (Wamsley 2009), particularly for female prisoners. Figure 7-1 provides data on the incarceration of women in six countries, including the United States. Note the U.S. is double that of the next largest number, and more women are incarcerated in the U.S. than all the countries listed on the chart, combined.

There are variations in definitions of deviance within cultures as well as among them. Take, for example, the smoking issue, used in illustrating variation of deviance over time. Compared to the United States, countries in Africa are very lenient toward the use of tobacco among their youth. There are only five countries, out of forty-six in the region, which have advertisement bans on tobacco. In addition, no country in Africa requires age verification at the time of tobacco sales.

Variation by Situation

Behavior that is defined as deviant in one situation may not be in another, even in the same time period and geographical area. A man who dresses in women's clothes to act in a play would be considered normal, but a man who dresses in women's clothes in the audience would not. Sex between husband and wife in the home is granted social approval, but sex by the same

FIGURE 7-1 COMPARATIVE RATES OF INCARCERATED WOMEN

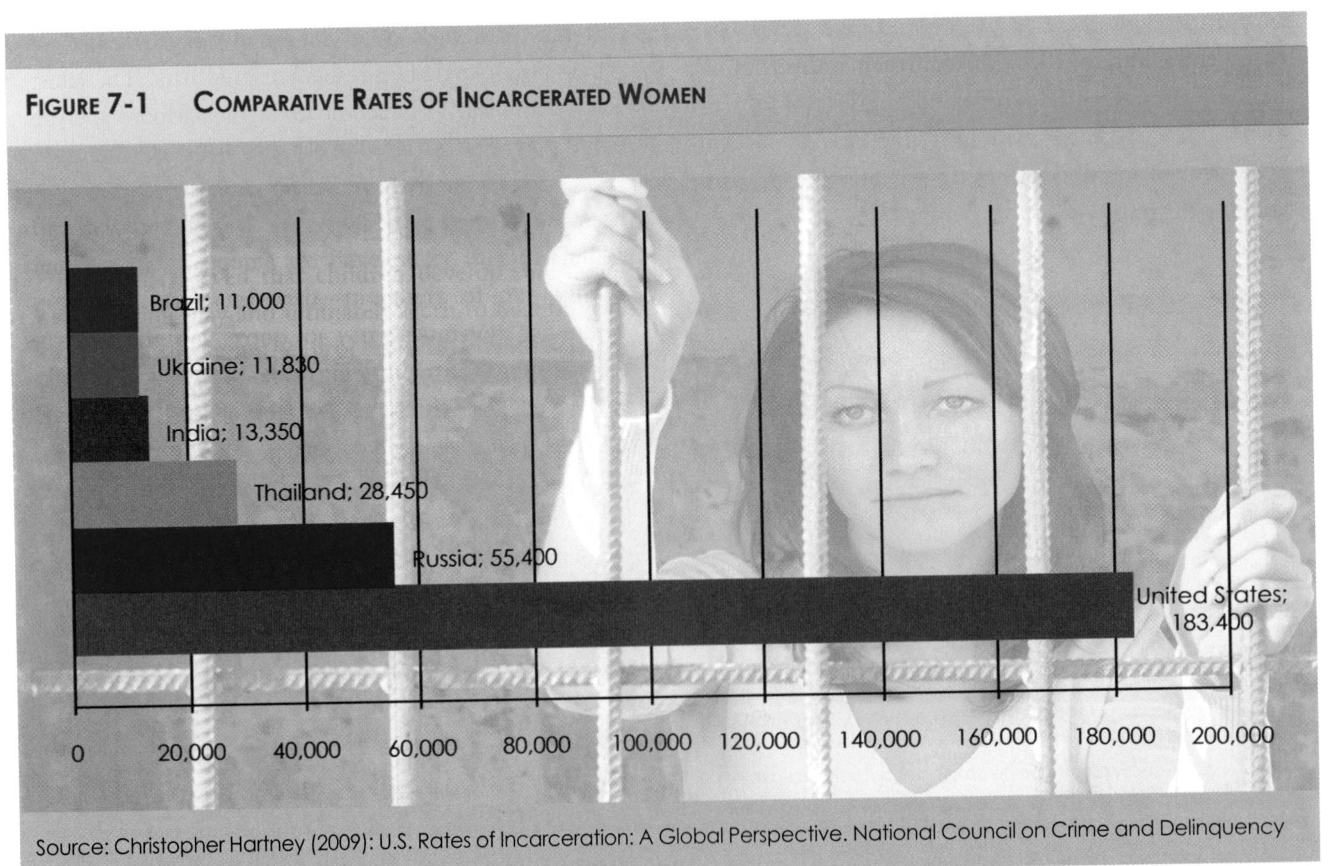

Source: Christopher Hartney (2009): U.S. Rates of Incarceration: A Global Perspective. National Council on Crime and Delinquency

husband and wife at a public beach or on the church altar might land them in jail or in a mental hospital.

When is it okay to lie? Are we conditioned to lie? DePaulo (1997) asked 147 people between the ages of eighteen to seventy-one years to keep journals over the course of one week and to note all the lies they told. People lie at least once or twice a day, and most lies are told during social encounters lasting around ten minutes or longer. The researchers exclude common pleasantries where we commonly admit, "I'm fine" when asked how we are doing. In the study, DePaulo found that college students lie to their mothers in one out of every two conversations.

As children, we are taught not to tell a lie, but our society actually encourages us a lie in certain situations. In fact, there are occupations that are built around the art of deceit—lawyers, car salesmen, etc. Most lies are meant to prevent a negative reaction rather than the other way around. Have you ever told someone they looked good when they did not, or said a particular food item was tasty when it was horrible? There are over five hundred million Facebook users worldwide. Think of how people can manipulate the way they present themselves, or information about their lives, on Facebook and other social network websites. Is it ok to "lie" about where we happen to be in order to protect ourselves or our homes? With Facebook, we have the opportunity to present select parts about ourselves, including aspects of our biography and even the way we look. Is it wrong to control that image so that it is not a complete representation of who we really are?

While many might argue and agree that cheating is always wrong, the social relativity of deviance reminds us that we must carefully select the time, place, and situation in which to behave in particular ways. The identical behavior by the same individual may be appropriate at one time, place, or situation yet not at others.

Variation by Social Status

Deviance also varies with social status both ascribed and achieved. As you recall, ascribed statuses are those acquired at birth such as age, sex, and race. Achieved statuses are those that people gain on their own: marital status, educational status, occupational status, and so on. Until recently, both women and minorities wouldn't have publicly aspired to be President of the United States as such an open aspiration might have been considered deviant. On the other hand, wealthy, educated white males were encouraged to participate in politics. Similarly, members of a country club might try to encourage a rich Mafia member to join, but may treat the drug dealers and prostitutes who provided the Mafia's money with contempt. The status associated with a person's sex, race, age, and income will influence which of his or her behaviors are considered deviant.

Until recently, women and minorities who aspired to be the president of the United States would have been considered socially deviant.

We can examine the influence social status has on deviance by noting differences in appropriate behaviors for males and females. There are variations by time, place, and situation; but some behaviors are generally given greater approval for women than for men, whereas others are given greater approval for men than for women. It is generally considered acceptable for women to wear high heels, panty hose, and lipstick; but in our society, such behaviors in men would be considered deviant. Men can go topless to any beach, but women who do so would be considered deviant.

The relativistic perspective acknowledges the diversity of behaviors, convictions, and sanctions that can be found in society, as well as the variety of meanings and definitions attributed to behaviors and sanctions. This view also recognizes the potential for conflict, both in a large society and in a single person who attempts to conform to the norms of different groups. A teenager may be encouraged to drink alcohol by peers but not by parents. A Catholic couple may wish to use only what are considered "natural" contraceptive methods to coincide with church norms, yet want to use more artificial methods to conform to their own norms and those of their friends and society.

From the relativistic perspective, deviance is not assumed to reside exclusively either in people or in actions. It is, rather, an interactive process involving people's behavior, an audience, societal norms or subgroup norms and definitions, and society as a whole. To understand deviance, we must focus not only on people or acts but also on the time, place, situation, and social status of the deviance and the deviants, on the reactions of others to both, and on the means by which the deviants are controlled or punished.

APPLYING THE RELATIVISTIC VIEW OF DEVIANCE

The view that deviance can be interpreted only in the sociocultural context in which it occurs has important implications for the creation, implementation, and evaluation of many social policies. Social policies and programs often deal with social problems such as poverty, teen pregnancies, the spread of disease, homelessness, drug addiction, and alcoholism, among many others. Although people's lifestyles and choices sometimes do cause their problems, it is incorrect to categorically explain the existence of particular social problems (for example, poverty) as the result of people's failure to conform to societal norms. That type of explanation is based on the absolutist, social—pathological, or statistical views of deviance described earlier in this chapter.

If we do not use the relativistic view of deviance that looks at people's lifestyles in terms of their sociocultural context, it is easy for us to say that people have problems because their behavior is atypical. This type of reasoning, known as **blaming the victim**, implies that the people facing social problems cause them. The way that policy—makers (politicians, legislators, and the people who vote for them) explain social problems directly influences how they propose to deal with them. If you feel that a group is to blame for its situation, you may try to change the group rather than to search for other causes of the problem or to examine the social context or circumstances in which the problems take place.

Governments do not formulate policies exclusively. You probably will formulate policies in your job and even in your personal life, so you, too, may benefit from using the relativistic view of deviance. For example, the value of this view may help you if you are, or decide to become a parent. As a parent, you will find yourself constantly making policies that you want your children to obey. Will you forbid your daughter to ask a boy out on a date because that type of behavior might have been considered immoral in your grandparents' day? Will you prohibit your son from growing his hair long or from wearing an earring because that was considered a sign of rebellion at one time? Both of these behaviors, considered deviant at one time, are acceptable behaviors in contemporary society. You run the risk of alienating your children and breaking down the channels of communication if you judge their behavior by standards of acceptability that no longer apply. Parents may improve their relationship with their children if they keep in mind the relativistic view of deviance. One way of doing this might be for parents to think of some of the things they did as adolescents—things they thought were perfectly justifiable but were abhorrent to their parents.

Thinking Sociologically

1. How have we medicalized deviance within our society?

2. Why are women more likely to be incarcerated within the United States than other countries? Explain how social views concerning women may lead to higher rates of incarceration.

THEORIES EXPLAINING DEVIANCE

As we have illustrated, deviance varies by time, place, situation, and social status. Given the wide variations in deviance, how can it be explained? What causes deviance? Why do people violate social norms? Equally important, why do people conform to and obey social norms? Most people do conform, and conformity is granted greater social approval in most circumstances; thus, theories have tended to focus more on the deviant than the nondeviant. The two are not easily separated, however; and explanations of one are equally applicable to the other.

Scientists have developed a variety of theories to explain deviance, but the fact that many theories exist does not mean that one is correct and the others incorrect. Theories often reflect the discipline from which they were developed. Biological theories tend to focus on genetic, anatomical, or physiological factors. Psychological theories tend to emphasize personality, motives, aggression, frustration, or ego strength. Sociologists usually emphasize sociocultural, organizational, environmental, or group factors. Although some theories have more empirical support than others, these theories help to increase our understanding of the complexities of human behavior—whether deviant or nondeviant—and of the social order.

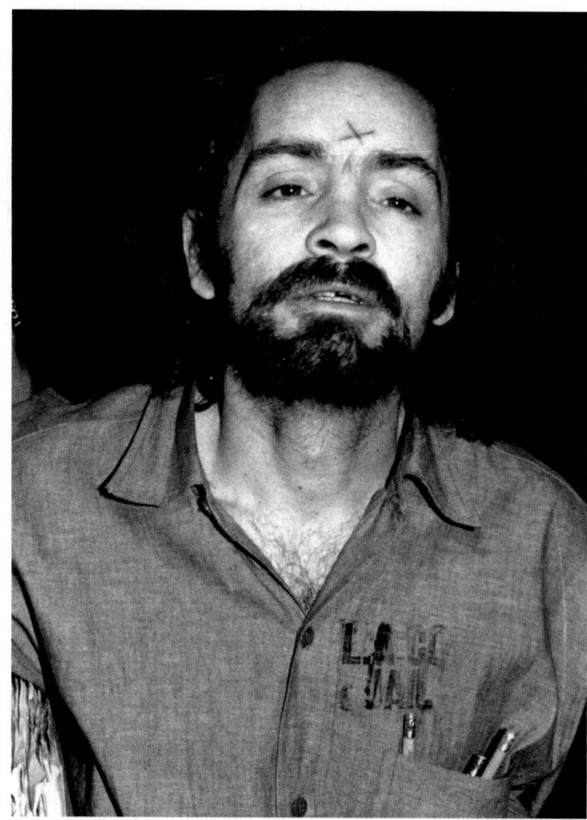

Followers of Charles Manson committed the infamous Tate-LaBianca murders in the late 1960s. The medical model explanation of deviant behavior assumes mental illness is a cause.

Biological Theories of Deviance

Several of the traditional views discussed earlier in this chapter involved biological factors. The view that deviance is a sickness adheres to a medical model, which assumes not just a social pathology or mental illness but an unhealthy biological organism as well. Similarly, the moral model implies that some people possess a biologically based resistance to conformity. These views share the assumption that particular defects or weaknesses in an individual's physical structure produce deviant behaviors.

Biological theories of deviance are often traced back to the Italian physician-psychiatrist Cesare Lombroso (1835–1909). Lombroso, sometimes referred to as the "father of modern criminology," was interested in the scientific study of crime. He believed that attention should be shifted from the criminal act to the criminal—specifically, to the physical characteristics of the criminal. He was convinced that the major determinants of crime (or deviance) were biological—that there was a "born criminal type." Lombroso believed that criminals suffered from atavistic anomalies, genetic traits that would distinguish the criminals from the non-criminals. He identified physical characteristics he believed unique among criminals: long arms, big hands, small ears, prominent cheekbones, and protruding forehead and jaw. Others explored the idea of biological determinism; and Lombroso's ideas were influential for many years, particularly in the United States. Research, however, has basically ruled out the notion of a "born criminal".

Other research on biological explanations of crime and deviance followed. In the 1930s, the American anthropologist Ernest Hooton claimed that criminals were organically inferior to those he called "normal" people (Vold 1958). In the 1940s, William Sheldon attempted to link body type to behavior. He classified people into three categories—*endomorphs*, who are soft, round, and usually fat; *mesomorphs*, who are muscular, stocky, and athletic; and *ectomorphs*, who are skinny and fragile. Endomorphs would more likely be the lazy criminal—selling drugs, fencing stolen property, etc. Mesomorphs were disproportionately identified, as those most likely to be criminal, and ectomorphs were the least likely among the three groups to possess deviant traits and behaviors.

Charles Whitman, who murdered his wife, mother, and fourteen other people, was found to have a malignant brain tumor, which may or may not have caused his violent behavior.

There have been other attempts to identify physical features of people as contributing to their deviant behavior. Phrenology is the scientific study of the bumps and protrusions of the skull. At one time those bumps and protrusions were linked to criminality. These and other studies of genes became very popular in the U.S., ultimately leading to dire consequences for many when eugenics became a popular practice (See Sociological Focus). By the early twentieth century the family pedigree became the focus of attention as it was decided that genes and family background were keys to understanding deviance and conformity; however, later many biological theories were questioned.

The case of Charles Whitman brought a considerable amount of attention back to a possible genetic link to deviance. On August 1, 1966, Charles Whitman killed his wife and mother before climbing the tower stairs on the campus of the University of Texas. As he made his way to the observation deck armed with and arsenal of weapons, Whitman killed a number of people who were in the tower. Before he left, he had killed fourteen and wounded thirty-one in his 96-minute rampage. He was eventually killed by a police officer. After his death an autopsy indicated that Whitman suffered from a malignant brain tumor. Whitman had seen doctors in the past and confided in them his urge to kill people; he had documented his feelings in a journal. After his death, notes left by Whitman gave instructions to donate the money from his estate to an organization studying mental health issues.

Due to the brain tumor, many speculated it might have caused his violence both before and during his killing spree. Researchers believed the tumor was pressing against the part of the brain that handles the fight or flight component. Since the Whitman case, a great deal of attention has focused on neurological conditions and criminal behavior.

In the 1970s and 1980s, considerable excitement was generated by claims that a specific genetic condition, in combination with social influences, may be associated with crimes of physical violence (Jencks 1987; Rowe and Osgood 1984; and Suchar 1978). Some violent criminals were found to have an extra Y chromosome. They had XYY chromosomes rather than the usual XY. Initially, it was believed that Richard Speck, the killer of eight Chicago nurses, suffered from the XYY syndrome. Later, when it was discovered Speck did not have the extra Y chromosome, the popularity of the XYY theory declined, as it was discovered others with the syndrome were not more deviant than those without it.

As you may have guessed, there are many problems with biological theories of crime, delinquency, and deviance; but the recent interest in the new science of sociobiology testifies to the continuing appeal of biological approaches. There are theories suggesting that sexual behaviors, both deviant and nondeviant, are biologically rooted and that alcohol and other drug abuse are caused by some chromosome component or genetic deficiency. Most of these explanations fail to explain, however, why others with a similar biological makeup do not exhibit the same forms of behaviors. In other words, biological explanations do not clearly differentiate the deviant from the nondeviant, and they fail to explain the tremendous variation in deviance, as well as its relative nature. Today, most sociologists reject the notion that biology, heredity, or other creation factors cause deviance; however, a number accept the idea that genetic or biological factors, in combination with social factors, may be predisposing conditions or may increase the likelihood of some types of behaviors that are socially defined as deviant.

Psychological Theories of Deviance

Like biological explanations, psychological theories tend to focus on the person who engages in deviant behavior. Some psychological theories share with biological approaches the notion that the causes of behavior are rooted in a person's physiological or genetic makeup: instincts, needs, drives, and impulses. In psychological theories, however, the emphasis is on the mind rather than the body. Social psychologists often consider the social context of behavior in addition to these factors.

Psychological theories are often tied to the medical model, associating deviance with a sickness, arguing that deviance results from a psychological abnormality, a psychopathic personality, or a mental illness. This explanation assumes that deviant behaviors such as alcoholism, child abuse, and crime are the consequences of mental illness. While mentally ill people may commit deviant acts, this theory does not account for deviance among people who are not otherwise considered mentally ill, nor does it explain why some mentally ill people do not engage in deviant behaviors.

PSYCHOANALYTIC THEORY Sigmund Freud spent his entire life attempting to explain human behavior. Freud believed that all human behavior is motivated by the desire to feel pleasure, based on two instincts—sexuality and aggression. His psychoanalytical approach to working with clients, the patient/doctor conversation, is still very popular today among clinicians, psychologists, psychiatrists, and others.

Sigmund Freud believed the human personality is made up of three components: the id, the ego, and the superego.

FIGURE 7-2 THE ICEBERG METAPHOR OF THE MIND

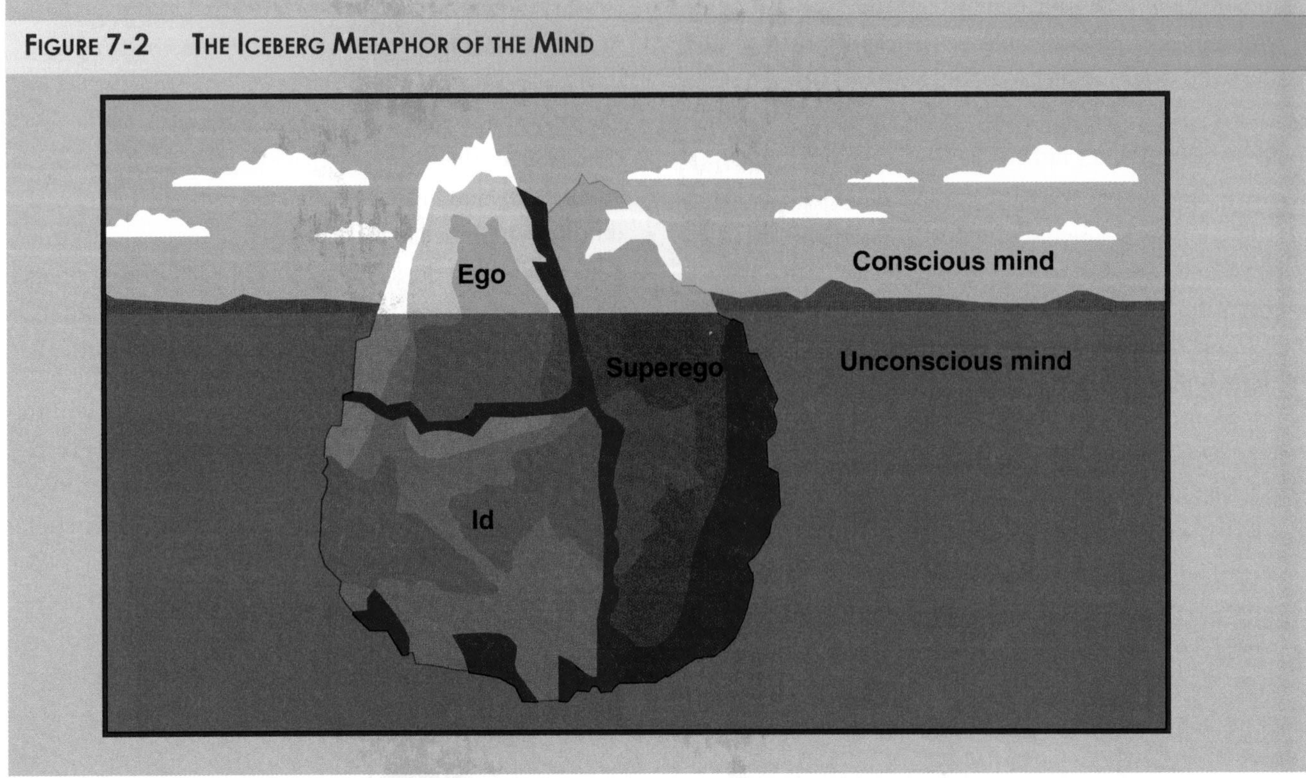

According to Freud, the human personality is made up of three components: the id, the superego, and the ego. The *id, present at birth*, is our pleasure seeking principle, constantly seeking immediate gratification. The superego refers to the internalized norms of society, what we typically think of as our "conscience" or "the morality principle." The ego, sometimes referred to as the "reality principle", mediates between the innate drives of the individual (id) and the demands of society (superego), enabling the individual to postpone immediate gratification at times when it may be socially unacceptable.

Because we are all born with an id, we have the potential to be deviant. If our id dominates the other two components, we are more likely to exhibit deviant behavior. On the other hand, if our superego is the dominating component, we are likely to be rigid in our behavior. The ego acts to balance the two others and maintain social conformity.

Freud also believed we have three layers of psyche: the conscious, preconscious, and subconscious. The *conscious* part of the mind is what we are most aware of and contains our wants, needs, and desires. Our *preconscious* mind is just below the surface of our conscience and can be brought to the surface through a memory or experience. The last component is the one that can cause us the most problems. Our *subconscious* mind is likely to keep painful memories repressed and to hold our biological desires and urges well below the surface. This component of our psyche could contribute to irrational thinking.

Other psychological theories suggest that deviance is a learned behavior much like any other behavior. Through experiences, we will enhance or alter our behavior in order to obtain a desired response from others. Albert Bandura (1959) argued that people are not born with the ability to act violently, but learn to be aggressive through life experiences. A child can learn violent behavior by observing someone acting aggressively and receiving a desired reward for their behavior. For example, a drug dealer in an impoverished neighborhood may be seen as a positive figure if he has money, cars, clothes, and other things generally unattainable when living in poverty. Children may learn to act aggressively by observing domestic disputes within the home. Young boys and girls are more likely to become abusers or marry abusers when they witness violence between their parents.

Some psychological explanations suggest that deviance results from frustration and aggression. When needs are not fulfilled, frustration results, which in turn leads to aggression and often to antisocial, deviant behaviors—the greater the frustration, the more extreme the aggression. Frustration over the lack of money, the loss of a job, or a failure in love can lead to aggressive acts: speeding, child abuse, robbery, or even murder. One difficulty with this explanation is that frustration is defined so broadly that it includes almost any behavior. Another problem is that it does not account for people who are frustrated but do not act deviantly.

In general, psychological explanations based on frustration, aggression, unconscious needs, instincts, guilt, weak egos, personality traits, and so forth have generated much research but have resulted in very inconclusive results. Many theories or ideas, such as those involving instinct and unconscious needs, are extremely difficult—if not impossible—to test empirically. Explanations based on frustration and aggression or on illness, fail to differentiate the deviant from the nondeviant. Another major difficulty with most biological and psychological theories is that they ignore the relative nature of deviance—the influence of social context, variations in rates of deviance, and social responses to deviance. Several sociological theories, some of which incorporate psychological components, consider factors other than acts and actors.

SOCIOLOGICAL THEORIES EXPLAINING DEVIANCE

Sociological theories attempt to explain deviance by looking at sociocultural processes and organizational structures, although acts and actors are considered as well. *Strain and anomie theory*, a structural functional theory, focuses on value conflicts among culturally prescribed goals and socially approved ways of achieving them. *Conflict theory* contends that groups in power define the acts of the weaker groups as deviant in order to exploit them. *Sociocultural learning or Interactionist theories* are concerned with how people interact and learn deviance. *Labeling theory* regards deviance as a process of symbolic interaction and focuses on the meanings, definitions, and interpretations applied to people and acts. *Control theories* concentrate heavily on conformity; they ask why people choose not to be deviant, and they deal with internal and external social controls that inhibit people's involvement in deviance.

The Structural Functionalist Perspective

STRAIN AND ANOMIE THEORY A number of traditional sociological theories are collectively referred to as **strain theories** because they suggest how people adapt to strains experienced by persons within society. The causes of crime are a result of disadvantages within cultures, groups, or among individuals (Agnew 1997; Thornberry 1997). To some theorists, the strain is the inability to realize a success goal. To others, the strain is the failure to achieve high status. For our purposes, we focus on what is perhaps the best-known example of strain theory—namely, anomie theory.

Emile Durkheim concluded that suicide is a social phenomenon related to a person's involvement with group life and membership in a cohesive social unit. Anomic suicide, he said, happens because of social and personal disorganization. People feel lost when the values of a society or group are confused or norms break down. Under most conditions, norms are clear, and most people adhere to them; but during times of social turmoil, people find themselves in unfamiliar situations. Making distinctions between the possible and the impossible, between desires and the fulfillment of those desires, becomes impossible. This condition of social normlessness is termed **anomie**. In an anomic society, the rules for proper behavior are not present, creating confusion or other problems.

Merton (1957) extended Durkheim's explanation of anomie and applied it to the study of crime. His strain theory suggests that deviance arises from the struggle society has between its culturally defined goals and the socially approved means by which they are met. In the United States the goals are to obtain wealth, power, and success while the legitimate means of reaching these goals include education, hard work, and deferred gratification. Such groups as the poor, teenagers, racial minorities, and blue-collar workers are constantly informed through education, the media, and friends that

TABLE 7-1 MERTON'S TYPOLOGY OF MODES OF INDIVIDUAL ADAPTATION

Modes of Adaptation	Culture Goals	Institutionalized Means
I. Conformity	+	+
II. Innovation	+	–
III. Ritualism	–	+
IV. Retreatism	–	–
V. Rebellion	±	±

Note: In this typology, Merton used the symbol + to signify "acceptance," – to signify "rejection," and ± to signify "rejection of prevailing values and substitution of new values."

Source: *Social Theory and Social Structure* by Robert K. Merton. Copyright © 1957, by The Free Press; copyright renewed 1985 by Robert K. Merton. Reprinted with the permission of The Free Press, a division of Macmillan, Inc.

material success is an important goal, but legitimate means for achieving it are often unavailable. Thus, deviance is the result of a strain between a society's culture and its social structure, between culturally prescribed goals and the socially approved ways of achieving them.

Merton listed five ways in which people adapt to the goals of a culture and the institutionalized means of achieving them (see Table 7-1). Only *conformity* to both the goals and the means is nondeviant. The other four methods of adaptations—innovation, ritualism, retreatism, and rebellion—all varieties of deviant behavior. *Innovators* accept social goals but reject the acceptable means of achieving them. Students who want to get good grades are adhering to widely held values; but if they cheat, they are violating a norm for achieving that goal.

A third mode of adaptation is ritualism. *Ritualists* follow rules rigidly without regard for the ends for which they are designed. The office manager that rigidly adheres to all the rules, making sure employees come to work on time and follow all the policies of the company is a ritualist. By focusing on petty rules, he or she loses sight of the real goal of the office. Ritualists

Retreatists, such as alcoholics, adapt by being in society but not of it; they reject both the cultural goals and institutional means.

conform to traditions and never take chances. Merton suggests that lower-middle-class Americans are likely to be ritualists when parents pressure their children to compulsively abide by the moral mandates and mores of society. This form of adaptation is not generally considered a serious form of deviant behavior. People cling to safe routines and institutional norms, thereby avoiding dangers and frustrations that they feel are inherent in the competition for major cultural goals.

Retreatism is a more drastic mode of adaptation. *Retreatists*, such as prostitutes, alcoholics, and drug addicts, reject both the cultural goals and the institutional means. These people are truly aliens; they are in the society but not of it. They are members of their society only in that they live in the same place. Retreatism is probably the least common form of adaptation, and it is heartily condemned by conventional representatives of society. Retreatist deviants are widely regarded as a social liability. According to Merton (1957, 155), this fourth mode of adaptation "is that of the socially disinherited who, if they have none of the rewards held out by society, also have few of the frustrations attendant upon continuing to seek these rewards".

The fifth and final mode of adaptation is rebellion. *Rebels*, such as members of revolutionary movements, withdraw their allegiance to a society they feel is unjust and seek to bring into being a new, greatly modified social structure. Military militia groups such as the one Timothy McVeigh belonged to prior to bombing the Oklahoma City Murrah Building would be considered rebels. This category is seen as the one most likely to be deviant and to reject most societal goals. Merton suggests that it is typically members of a rising class rather than the most depressed strata who organize the resentful and the rebellious into a revolutionary group.

Merton's theory has been criticized on a number of different grounds (Thio 1988). Some critics argue that it erroneously assumes that a single system of cultural goals is shared by the entire society. It has also been faulted for failing to explain why some people choose one response while others choose a different one. Another weakness is that some types of deviance—rape or the behavior of hippies in the 1960s—do not neatly fall into any of his five modes of adaptation. Other critics argue that Merton's theory ignores the influence of societal reactions in the shaping of deviance and the fact that much perceived deviance involves collective rather than individual action. Finally, much criticism has been leveled at Merton's underlying assumption that deviance is disproportionately concentrated in the lower socioeconomic levels.

There are strengths to anomie theory, as well. It provides a framework for examining a wide range of social behavior; it has stimulated many research studies; and it has raised the social consciousness of deviance analysts. This last-mentioned point is particularly true of some members of the new generation of sociologists. These theorists have devised conflict theories of deviance that emphasize the widespread social oppression and basic contradictions found at the heart of our socioeconomic system.

A weakness in Merton's theory is that some types of deviance, such as the behavior of hippies in the 1960s, do not neatly fall into any of his five modes of adaptation.

Conflict Theory

Conflict theorists are the major critics of the assumption of the functionalist and anomie theories that a society shares a single set of values. **Conflict theory** contends that most societies contain many groups that have different, often conflicting, values and that the strongest groups in a society have the power to define the values of weaker groups as deviant. Conflict theorists emphasize the repression of the weak by the powerful, the exploitation of the masses by strong interest groups, and the influential and often wealthy groups who use laws, courts, and other agencies to oppose the interests and activities of lower socioeconomic groups and minorities.

Most businesses exist to make a profit. If in making a profit, they also (intentionally or unintentionally) provide jobs, raise the level of personal gratification, and improve the community, little conflict may result. If, however, high taxes, high wages, fringe benefits, safety requirements, or pollution controls disrupt profits, then lobbying groups, political contributions, and media campaigns are used to influence legislation, taxation, and controls. Part-time workers may be used extensively to eliminate cost of fringe benefits. Members of minority groups, particularly new immigrant groups, may be hired at lower wages than those paid to others. Community tax incentives may be granted to sustain businesses or industries at the expense of the individual. The powerful exploit those with less power, and this exploitation by the elite produces inequality and institutionalized violence. The conflict between the powerful and the weak, therefore, influences both the creation of deviance and our response to it.

People tend to assume that the law is based on the consensus of its citizens, that it represents the public interest, and that it treats citizens as equals and serves the best interests of society. Conflict theorists, however, argue that the law means that legal authorities *ought* to be fair and just but are actually unfair and unjust, favoring the rich and powerful over the poor and weak. This condition exists, they say, not because law enforcement officials are cruel or evil, but because they would antagonize members of the middle and upper classes if they arrested them for their white-collar offenses. These classes might then withdraw their support from law-enforcement agencies, thus leading to loss of law-enforcement jobs. Later in this chapter, we discuss white collar crime. White collar crime, such as fraud in world of investments, is an example of how the rich and powerful can often get away with egregious crimes that have devastating individual and social consequences, yet go unnoticed and often unpunished. While one of the most famous white collar criminals of recent times, Bernie Madoff, was convicted of defrauding investors and received a 150-year-prison sentence, many who contributed to the economic meltdown that occurred in 2008 were completely untouched by the criminal justice system and received exorbitant incomes in the years following the crisis (Pontell and Geis 2010). This is partially because they were protected either by Security Exchange Commission (SEC) policies or a failure of the SEC to adequately police investment brokers.

Quinney (1979) and Spitzer (1975), who agree that deviance and deviants are defined and controlled by the powerful, go a step further and blame the lack of justice directly on the capitalist system. Drawing heavily from Karl Marx, Spitzer contends that populations are considered deviant by capitalists when they disturb, hinder, or question any of the following: (1) capitalist modes of appropriating the products of human labor, (2) the social conditions under which capitalist production takes place, (3) patterns of distribution and consumption in capitalist society, (4) the socialization of productive and nonproductive roles, or (5) the ideology that supports capitalist society.

According to the conflict perspective, the dominant class, for the most part, determines definitions of deviance. Rates of deviance are determined primarily by the extent to which the potentially deviant behaviors threaten dominant class interests, while control of deviance is largely determined by the extent to which the powerful can socialize and reward those who follow their demands. Many conflict theorists perceive their theory as a call for political action to raise a revolutionary consciousness and end the oppression of the powerless by the powerful.

Like other theories, conflict theory has its critics that fault it for not searching for the causes of deviant behavior. They also say it does not explain the crimes and deviances that are basically nonpolitical (vices or trivial deviations such as outlandish forms of dress or

SOCIOLOGY AT WORK

Eugenics as a Consequence of Deviance

In 1883, Sir Francis Galton, a cousin of Charles Darwin, coined the term eugenics with hopes it would eventually replace Christianity. Eugenics, meaning to be well born, became a popular movement in the United States, as scientists believed genetics could be used to determine the importance of a human being. If the person or group was believed to be genetically inferior, a process of "purifying the race" through sterilization was performed. By the 1920s, the U.S. was the center for the world eugenics movement with more than one hundred thousand persons sterilized over the next several decades. Its fall from popularity within the U.S. came after Hitler used harsher methods to rid groups he believed to be genetically inferior in Germany. Human breeding grounds for Aryans, death camps for Jews, and euthanasia or sterilization for the mentally ill and others deemed genetically unworthy—all Hitler's methods of eugenics were seen as radical, cruel, and inhumane; however, even after his defeat in World War II, the U.S. struggled with ways to deal with those seen inferior within society.

Adolf Hitler.

Indiana became the first state to legally enact laws allowing for the sterilization of those deemed genetically inferior, and at one time as many as thirty-three states had statutes allowing the practice of eugenics. By 1924 over three thousand persons had been sterilized in the United States for being "insane", "feebleminded", "epileptic", "idiot" or "defective". When Virginia passed its Eugenical Sterilization Act, it was meant to relieve the tax burden on citizens forced to care for individuals seen as a menace to society.

The first person sterilized in Virginia under such a law was seventeen-year-old Carrie Buck, who had given birth to a baby out of wedlock and whose own mother was institutionalized. Doctors testified that Carrie and her mother shared hereditary traits such as "feeblemindedness" and "sexual promiscuity". Therefore, Carrie was labeled as someone who was the "probable potential parent of a socially inadequate offspring".

Attorneys challenged the sterilization of Carrie on the grounds it was unconstitutional. In court proceedings, sociologist Arthur Eastbrook, of the Eugenics Record Office, testified that Carrie's baby girl, Vivian, was below average and not normal. As a result, the judge ruled that Carrie needed to be sterilized to prevent having any additional children burdening society. Carrie's attorneys appealed the decision all the way to the United States Supreme Court where justices heard the case of *Buck v. Bell*. Ruling in favor of sterilization Justice Oliver Wendell Holmes Jr., wrote in his opinion, "It is better for all the world, if instead of waiting to execute degenerate offspring for crime or to let them starve for their imbecility, society can prevent those who are manifestly unfit from continuing their kind ... Three generations of imbeciles are enough."

What role did the sociologist play in Carrie's sterilization? Years later, records found that Carrie's baby was not the result of promiscuity, but of rape by a relative in the foster home where Carrie had been placed after her mother was institutionalized. In addition, Vivian's school records indicated she was an "A" and "B" student, who suffered no feeblemindedness. Sociologists today recognize the factors that lead to Carrie being socially constructed by society as inferior; however, the practice of eugenics continued through the mid-1970s when a judge ruled in a class action lawsuit in favor of plaintiffs who had been forced to undergo sterilization.

goldfish-swallowing contests). In addition, conflict theorists have been criticized for assuming that in the utopian communist society murder, robbery, rape, and other crimes will disappear after the power to criminalize them is abolished.

The Symbolic Interactionist Perspective

Theories that fall under the interactionist perspective are micro level in analysis and focus on sociocultural learning the processes through which deviant acts are learned and the conditions under which learning takes place. Deviant behaviors are learned through essentially the same processes as other behaviors. Unlike functionalist and conflict theories, interactionist theories emphasize the groups to which people belong and the ways in which they learn the norms prescribed by those groups. In other words, people grow up in groups and situations in which deviance is the norm and, thus, is learned. Three of these theories focus specifically on deviance: cultural transmission theory, differential association theory, and social learning theory.

Cultural transmission theory, sometimes called "subculture theory", stems from the Chicago School of Sociology. This theory suggests that when deviance is part of a subculture's cultural pattern, it is transmitted to newcomers through socialization. Shaw and McKay (1929) noted that high crime rates persisted in some Chicago neighborhoods over several decades even though the areas changed in ethnic composition and in other ways. When there is a tradition of deviance in a subculture, they suggested, the norms of that subculture are passed on by the gang, peer group, or the play group during interaction with newcomers. As a result, they not only become deviant, also, by violating norms but also by conforming to the norms of the subculture.

Other sociologists quickly picked up on the idea that deviance is transmitted culturally through learning and socialization. These scientists extended the theory, suggesting that people learn not only from gangs or peer groups but also from other agents of socialization—parents, teachers, church leaders, business colleagues, and others. A person could learn deviant attitudes by observing that people throw away parking tickets, keep incorrect change from a supermarket, or find ways to avoid paying taxes. One primary source of learning about deviance may be institutions designed to correct deviance, such as juvenile homes, detention centers, reformatories, prisons, and mental hospitals. Even people within these subcultures, however, are exposed to and learn conforming behaviors. So why are some people attracted to deviant behaviors while others are not?

To answer this question and explain how deviance and crime are culturally transmitted, Edwin Sutherland devised the differential association theory (1939; Sutherland and Cressey 1970). Sutherland attempted to determine why crime rates vary among different groups of people. Why is the crime rate higher in the city than in the country and higher in impoverished areas than in other areas? Why do more males than females and more young people than older people commit crimes? Sutherland also wanted to explain why some individuals become criminals and others do not.

Differential association theory suggests that deviance results when individuals have more contact with groups that define deviance favorably than with groups that define it unfavorably. Sutherland contended that criminal behavior is learned rather than inherited or invented and that it takes place through verbal and nonverbal communications, primarily in intimate groups. Learning a criminal behavior involves acquiring a set of motives, drives, rationalizations, and attitudes, as well as specific techniques for committing the act itself. Sutherland did not believe that contact with criminals was necessary for a person to become deviant; exposure to definitions favoring deviance was sufficient, and the influence and frequency of these exposures vary from person to person. According to this theory, deviance is a learned behavior, a set of behaviors transmitted to people through their interactions with others.

Social learning theory is a revision of Sutherland's differential association theory, in accordance with the principles of behavioral theory (Akers 1977; Akers, et al., 1979). Social learning theory suggests that deviant and conforming behaviors are determined by the consequences—rewards or punishment—that follow them. This is known as *operant* or *instrumental conditioning*, whereby behavior is acquired through direct conditioning or through imitating the modeled behavior of others. A behavior is strengthened by rewards (positive reinforcement) or the avoidance of punishment (negative reinforcement) and weakened by aversive stimuli (positive punishment) or loss of rewards (negative punishment). Akers, et al., (1979) state that the acquisition and persistence of either deviant or conforming behavior are functions of what particular behaviors have been rewarded or punished, which is known as **differential reinforcement**. The norms and attitudes people learn from others, especially peers and family, are also influential.

Suppose, for example, that fifteen-year-old John has just moved to a new neighborhood. Initially, he has no friends. One day, unhappy and lonely, he defies a teacher and gets into a violent argument with him. After class, several of his peers comment admiringly on the way he told the teacher off. The attention serves as positive reinforcement because John needs friends. He tells his mother what happened. She says only that she wishes she could tell her boss to go to hell once in a while, which encourages John to think that his behavior is acceptable. He begins to

Akers et al. found that alcohol users were positively correlated with exposure to and association with users.

deliberately provoke arguments with teachers, and gradually he gets a reputation as a rebel. Girls begin to pay attention to him (more positive reinforcement). Eventually, however, he is suspended from school for two weeks, which then deprives him of the attention of his friends (negative punishment). When John returns, he finds that his teachers have collectively decided to ask him to leave the room whenever he acts up; so he learns to be more cautious (negative reinforcement). He is also required to clean the bathrooms after school every time he gets into trouble (positive punishment). The positive reinforcement encouraged him to act in a mildly deviant fashion, but the negative punishment, negative reinforcement, and positive punishment encouraged him to conform to school standards. Eventually, he finds a level of disruption that maintains his reputation without forcing his teachers to try to change his behavior.

Akers et al. (1979) assessed social learning theory of deviant behavior with data on factors that influenced the drinking (alcohol) and other drug use of three thousand adolescents. They found that alcohol and other drug use were both positively correlated with exposure to users and association with users. They also found that the use of drugs such as alcohol increased when it was reinforced more than punished and when use was defined positively or neutrally. Although differential association accounted for most of the adolescents' variations in alcohol and other drug use, differential reinforcement, definitions, and imitation were also influential.

Sociocultural learning theories focus on how deviance is learned. Critics argue that these theories do not explain how deviance originated or how some behaviors came to be defined as deviant. It has also been argued that these theories do not deal adequately with those who commit deviant acts in isolation rather than as part of a group. Furthermore, these theories are often difficult to test empirically without engaging in circular reasoning—deviance is caused by a tradition of deviance, caused by earlier deviance. Another weakness is that it is very difficult to determine precisely what stimuli or learning experience causes a person initially to commit a deviance instead of a conforming act. Nevertheless, sociocultural learning theories have contributed to our understanding of the nature of deviance.

Labeling Theory

The theories of deviance discussed so far have focused on deviant people, deviant acts, the process of learning deviance, and the causes of deviance. **Labeling theory** is concerned primarily with how some behaviors are labeled "deviant" and how being given such a label influences a person's behavior.

Most labeling theorists interpret deviance in terms of symbolic interaction processes. Like other behaviors, deviant behavior is not regarded as a particular type of act undertaken by a person in isolation. It is, rather, a result of human interactions, as well as people's interpretations and definitions of their own actions and those of others. As Kitsuse (1962) stated it, "Forms of behavior *per se* do not differentiate deviants from non-deviants; it is the responses of the conventional and conforming members of the society who identify and interpret behavior as deviant which sociologically transform persons into deviants" (p. 253).

Note that, according to this perspective, deviance is a relative condition. It is not a specific type of act; rather, it is the consequence of applying a particular label. As noted several decades ago by Becker, "Social groups create deviance by making the rules whose infraction constitutes deviance and by applying those rules to particular people and labeling them as outsiders" (Becker 1974). Thus, if two people commit the same act, one might be labeled a deviant and the other might not, depending on the meaning given to the act by their social groups.

Edwin Lemert (1951), one of the first labeling theorists, identified two categories of deviance. *Primary deviance* involves behavior that violates social norms but is temporary and sporadic. Individuals who are involved in primary deviance do not regard themselves as deviant, nor are they regarded as such by those around them. Secondary deviance involves habitual violation of norms by individuals who not only consider themselves deviant but also are labeled as deviant by others. *Secondary deviance* becomes a routine, resulting in a label that leads to further deviance. The behavior, for example, of a student who buys one term paper to turn in to a history professor might be primary deviance. However, if this student consistently cheated on tests and turned in papers that she had not written herself, her behavior would be considered deviant by her peers, her professors, and herself; and it would, therefore, constitute secondary deviance. Sociologist Erving Goffman also believed that when one is labeled, they can assume a "retrospective labeling," which is a re-interpretation of a person's past based on present deviance (Macionis 2006).

What are the consequences of labeling? According to this theory, being labeled as deviant has negative consequences because labeled people tend to see themselves as deviant, which leads them to continue their so-called deviant behavior. Thus, we have the development of a deviant career and a label that becomes a master status—cheat, prostitute, liar, and so on. Getting so labeled leads others to view one in terms of that deviant status, overlooking other qualities or statuses. Beyond that, labeled people may no longer be treated as respectable parents, teachers, or community members; they may lose their jobs, be rejected by friends, or be sent to a prison or a mental hospital. Responses of this sort often push labeled people further into the deviant activity. Ex-convicts who cannot get legitimate jobs may return to robbery or drug dealing. Those labeled as mentally ill lose many of the social supports necessary for mental health. Drug addicts, alcoholics, and prostitutes may turn to others who share the same label for support and companionship, which leads them to organize their lives around their deviance.

Who labels whom? Of labeling, Becker (1974) says, "A major element in every aspect of the drama of deviance is the imposition of definitions—of situations, acts, and people—by those powerful enough or legitimated to be able to do so" (p. 62). The labelers, therefore, would include such social control agents as police, judges, prison guards, and psychiatrists, whereas the labeled would include criminals, delinquents, drug addicts, prostitutes, mental patients, and others. Consistent with the conflict theory described earlier, rich, white, or powerful people are more likely to apply the labels; and poor, black, and otherwise powerless people are more likely to be labeled. A poor or a minority person is more apt to be arrested, prosecuted, and convicted than a rich or a white person for committing the same act.

Data from the Bureau of Justice Statistics, for example, show that in 2007, over 7.3 million people were on probation, in jail or prison, or on parole. Blacks make up approximately 13 percent of the U.S. population but remain overrepresented within the prison population with 3,138 per 100,000 black males incarcerated. In comparison, 1,251 per 100,000 Hispanic males, and 481 per 100,000 white males are serving time in prison. In 2007 blacks constituted 12.8 percent of the U.S. population, but over 39 percent of the prison population (Bureau of Prisons 2009). Similar statistics show a higher arrest, prosecution, and conviction rate among men, the young, the less educated, and the poor. For example, about 93 percent of all state prison inmates are male, 57 percent are under thirty-five years of age, 43 percent have less than twelve years of schooling, and more than one-third (36 percent) were not employed at the time of their arrest (*Bureau of Justice Statistics* 2005).

Although many sociologists accept it, labeling theory has its critics. It does not explain the causes of deviance, nor can it be used to predict who will be labeled and in what contexts. Like other symbolic interaction theories, labeling theory is difficult to test empirically. Another criticism is one that also applies to conflict theory: If the powerful create and impose the deviant label, how is it possible that powerful people are also sometimes labeled as deviant? Critics have also questioned the extent to which the labeling of deviance encourages rather than deters deviant behavior. Finally, are all persons in prisons or mental hospitals there simply because someone chose to label them, or are some behaviors so disruptive that severe sanctions such as institutionalization must be imposed to maintain social order? Other social consequences of deviance are discussed in the next section.

Thinking Sociologically

1. Select one of the theories discussed above, explain why deviant behavior occurs among teenagers within the United States?

2. Discuss what you believe to be the pros and cons of prison. In addition, discuss the functions and dysfunctions of using prison instead of community-based sentencing for non-violent offenses.

SOCIAL CONSEQUENCES OF DEVIANCE

Social systems are composed of many parts, which exist because they perform some function in the maintenance of the system. Any part of a social system may be dysfunctional in some respects, but the part continues to exist because it performs a function that leads to the maintenance and stability of the system. Also, as we stated earlier in this chapter, deviance is universal—it exists in all societies—and, therefore, it seems plausible to argue that deviance continues to exist because it serves some functions in the maintenance of societies.

Deviance and Crime

We have defined deviance as variations from a set of norms or shared social expectations. A **crime** is a violation of criminal statutory law, and a specific punishment applied by some governmental authority generally accompanies the violation. Many types of deviance, such as rape, robbery, and murder, are criminal acts in most states; other types of deviance, such as bizarre behaviors related to mental disorders, wearing unusual clothes, cussing in public, and shouting at strangers passing by are not. Just as definitions of deviance differ from group to group, criminal activities and crime rates vary in different legal jurisdictions, with accompanying differences in rates of enforcement. For example, prostitution, illegal in most states, is legal in Nevada. A decade ago, it was legally impossible for a man to rape his wife. Today, many states have amended their rape laws to make the relationship between the rapist and the victim irrelevant.

Types of Crime

The way crimes are classified in the U.S. implies a great deal about the seriousness of the offense. If someone were to say they were convicted of a felony, we immediately believe they are a violent offender. Consequently, most applications for employment ask the person if they have ever been convicted of a felony; and if the answer is "yes", the applicant is often excluded from consideration. The following section explains some of the common crime categories.

Crimes are most often separated as violent or non-violent offenses. Violent crimes are those we most refer to as street crimes, usually involving a victim. The most common form of violent crime is assault. Violent crime includes four crimes: homicide, forcible rape, aggravated assault, and robbery. These crimes, including robbery, involve a victim because there is a threat of "use of force" against the victim. In 2007, the Federal Bureau of Investigation reports that over 1.4 million violent crimes occurred nationwide.

Property crimes are committed with the intent of gaining property without the threat or use of force. Property crimes include larceny-theft, burglary, motor-vehicle theft, and arson. Arson is included because it involves the destruction of property. Nearly ten million property crimes occurred in the U.S. in 2007, with the most common being larceny-theft. Crimes are also classified in the U.S. as felonies and misdemeanors. *Felonies* are crimes that are punishable by one year or more in a state prison. *Misdemeanors* are less serious crimes, usually punishable by a fine and/or jail time up to one year in a county jail.

Some crimes are seen as victimless crimes, usually associated with a society's moral values and beliefs.

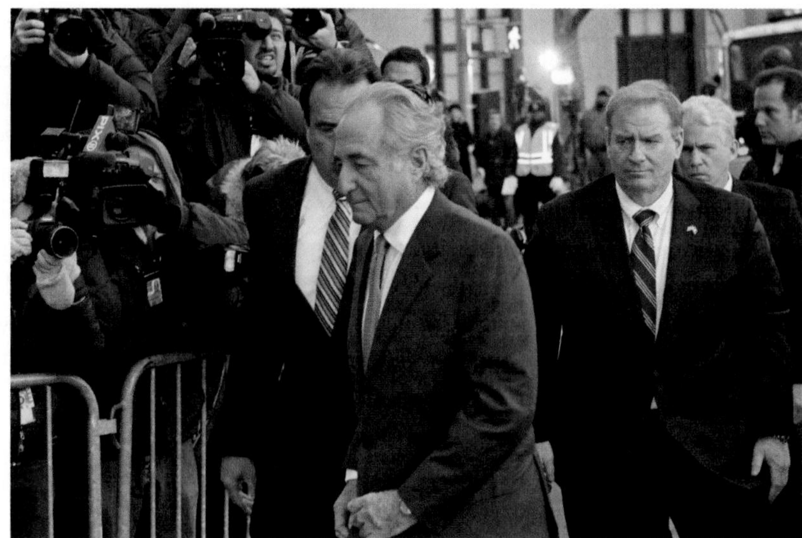

Bernie Madoff pleaded guilty in 2009 to the white-collar crime of bilking investors out of an estimated $65 billion.

Some view victimless crimes as not harming anyone except the persons committing the crimes. Included in victimless crimes are prostitution, vagrancy, gambling, public drunkenness, etc. Who are the victims of these crimes? Do they violate public decency? There is much debate over the impact victimless crimes have on society.

White-collar crime was a term coined by Edwin Sutherland in 1939 to refer to those, generally seen as respectable individuals, who break the law in the course of their employment for the purpose of personal or organizational gain. These individuals are usually corporate or government employees. The FBI reports 189 active cases of white-collar investigations, with at least eighteen of those involving over $1 billion dollars (FBI 2004–2009 Strategic Plan). The case of Bernie Madoff, for example, involved taking an estimated sixty-five billion from investors in a Ponzi scheme (named after con man Charles Ponzi in 1920) over a forty-year period (Pontell and Geis 2010). In the largest scam in U.S. history, Madoff, former chairman of the NASDAQ stock exchange, convinced investors he could make a quick return on their money. His clientele involved nearly five thousand investors, including endowments from non-profit organizations. Confronted by his sons, Madoff finally admitted he was scamming investors out of their money so his sons reported him to the Federal Bureau of Investigation. Madoff was arrested. On March 12, 2009, Madoff plead guilty to eleven counts, including securities fraud, and faced a sentence of up to 150 years in prison. Other examples of white-collar crimes include embezzlement, insider trading, bribery, and kickbacks.

Organized crime consists of groups expressly organized to carry out illegal activities such as the distribution of drugs, the operation of a gambling business, or loan sharking (lending money at excessively high rates). Some consider organized crime to be the tightly knit national organization variously called the "Mafia," the "Cosa Nostra," the "syndicate," or the "mob"; others use the term more loosely to cover any group of organized professional criminals who maintain control of a large-scale illegal business enterprise.

In either case, the organization has a strict hierarchy, ranging from the "lords of the underworld" (who make the important decisions and direct the activities) to those at the lower levels (who follow the orders). Those at the lower levels, who deal directly with the public, are the ones who get caught; however, some may get released through the leader's connections with the police, judges, or relevant professionals. Organized crime groups maintain control within their group or organization through threats, intimidation, bribery, and, when they deem it necessary, violence. Most deviance is not controlled by such severe means, however. It should also be noted that some types of formal and informal means of social control exist in all societies in order to encourage people to conform to social norms.

Another category of crime is juvenile crime, involving those under the age of eighteen years. Juvenile crimes refer to the age of the offender rather than types of crimes committed; therefore, juvenile crimes can involve anything from a felony to a status offense. Status offenses are crimes only because the individual is under age, such as truancy and running away. The most common juvenile crime is theft-larceny, whereas for adults the most common offenses involve drugs. Recidivism, repeating criminal behavior after previous punishment, has been a concern for juvenile offenders. Research suggests the high rate of status offenses contributes largely to the rates of juvenile recidivism.

FIGURE 7-3 CRIME CLOCK, 2009

The crime clock should be viewed with care. Because it is the most aggregate representation of *Uniform Crime Reports (UCR)* data, it is designed to convey the annual reported crime experience by showing the relative frequency of occurrence of the index offenses. This mode of display should not be taken to imply regularity in the commission of offenses; rather, it represents the annual ratio of crime to fixed time intervals.

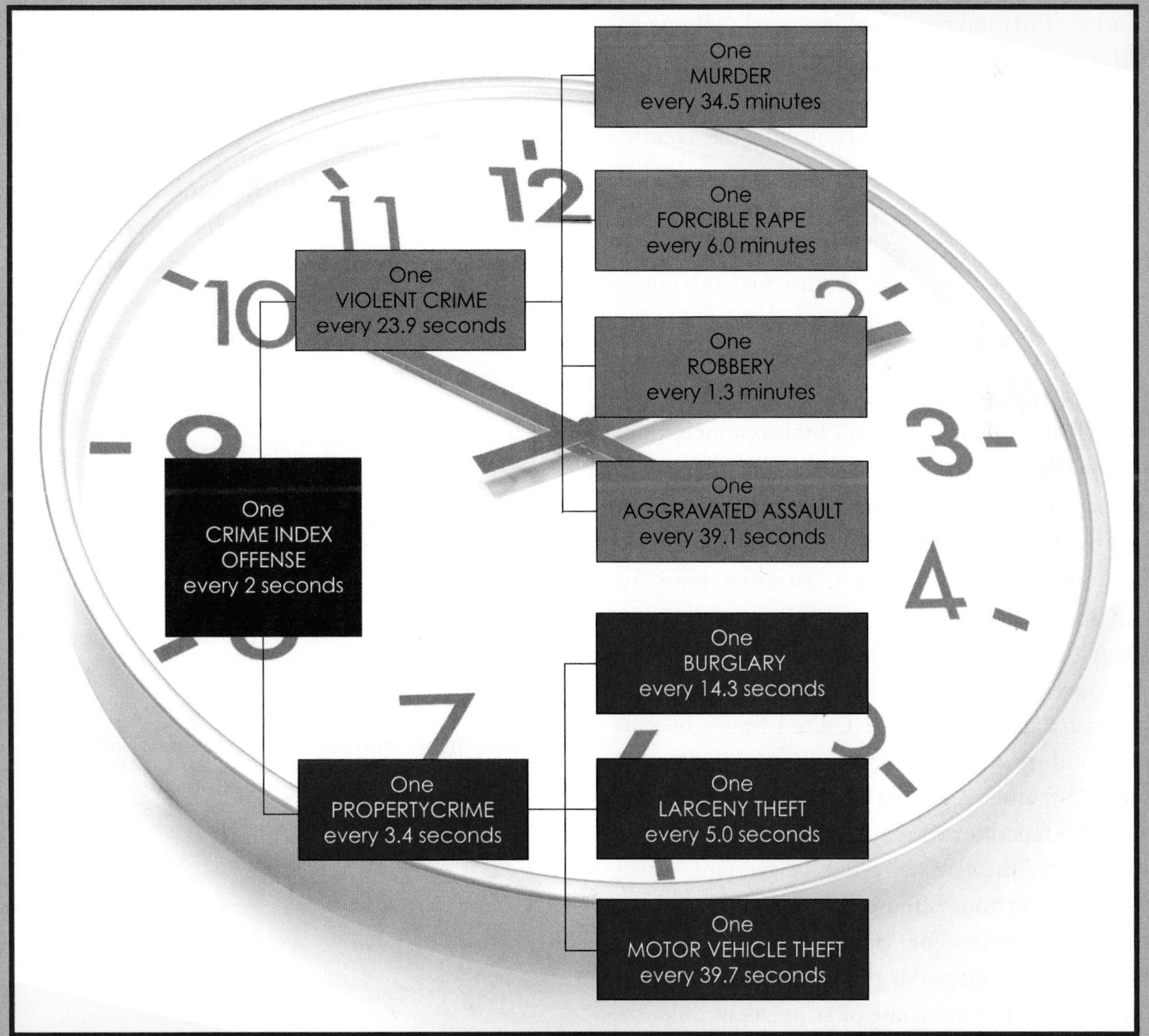
One MURDER every 34.5 minutes
One FORCIBLE RAPE every 6.0 minutes
One VIOLENT CRIME every 23.9 seconds
One ROBBERY every 1.3 minutes
One AGGRAVATED ASSAULT every 39.1 seconds
One CRIME INDEX OFFENSE every 2 seconds
One BURGLARY every 14.3 seconds
One PROPERTYCRIME every 3.4 seconds
One LARCENY THEFT every 5.0 seconds
One MOTOR VEHICLE THEFT every 39.7 seconds

Source: U.S. Department of Justice – Federal Bureau of Investigation, September 2010. http://www2.fbi.gov/ucr/cius2009/about/crime_clock.html

Measuring Crime in the United States

Accurate estimates of crime rates are difficult to make because a high percentage of most crimes go undetected and unreported. Even crimes such as murder, in which the body of a victim can serve as evidence, present classification problems. Official data on crime in the United States typically come from two sources: the Uniform Crime Report and the National Crime Victimization Survey. In addition, self-report surveys provide information on prevalence and types of offenses committed by offenders.

The Uniform Crime Report (UCR) is the official source for statistical data on crimes committed in the United States. Collected by the Federal Bureau of Investigation (FBI) and published in a yearly volume entitled *Uniform Crime Reports*, the statistics are gathered from more than sixteen thousand city, county, and state law-enforcement agencies around the country. While agencies voluntarily report data on criminal offenses, more than 96 percent of the countries law enforcement agencies participate. The crimes recorded in the FBI reports are divided into two categories. One includes *violent crimes*—such as murder, forcible rape, robbery, and aggravated assault—while the other consists of *property crimes*, including burglary, larceny of fifty dollars or more, motor vehicle theft, and arson. Approximately thirteen million property crimes are known to be committed each year. The famous FBI "Crime Clock" for 2008, shown in Figure 7-3, is one dramatic way of illustrating how frequently some offenses are committed.

As with most data collection methods, the UCR has its share of problems. First, it does not provide a clear picture of crime in the United States because only crimes that are recorded by the police are provided. Second, each police department creates its own set of statistics and may report biased information regarding the level of crime in the city. Third, only the most serious offense is recorded when multiple crimes occur. For example, if a person is charged with driving under the influence, aggravated assault, and leaving the scene of an accident, only the aggravated assault will be included in the UCR. Even with its faults, the UCR provides us with important information on crimes in the U.S.

The National Crime Victimization Survey (NCVS) has been conducted by the Bureau of Justice since 1973 and allows for measurements on the likelihood of becoming a victim of crime. The survey is sent to 76,000 U.S. households comprising 136,000 individuals and collects data on rape, sexual assault, robbery, assault, theft, household burglary, and motor vehicle theft—whether reported to the police or not. According to the NCVS, in 2006, only 49 percent of violent crimes and 38 percent of property crimes were reported to the police. Of violent crimes, 57 percent of robberies and 59 percent of aggravated assaults were reported. Given these numbers, it is clear that a many crimes do not show up on the FBI Uniform Crime Report (U.S. Department of Justice 2006).

Like the UCR, the NCVS has problems, including over-reporting or underreporting of information. A person may believe he or she was the victim of theft, when he or she simply misplaced a piece of property. Memory is another concern with getting accurate information on the NCVS. It is not unusual for victims of crime to have problems with dates, times, and locations which can lead to survey mistakes.

Another method of collecting data on crime is self-report surveys. This type of survey is given to offenders, usually juveniles or prison inmates, and asks them to voluntarily report whether they have committed various criminal acts. Self-report surveys also tend to show the incidence of crime to be much higher than the officially reported incidence; again, the data should be used with caution.

Surveys also reveal what conflict and labeling theorists contend is a discriminatory bias in the legal system. Some groups of people are far more likely to be caught and punished for their crimes than others. Young people, blacks, persons from a lower socioeconomic status, and disadvantaged groups, in general, are more likely to be picked up by the police, to have their cases reported, to be arrested, and to be punished.

Criminal Justice System

The criminal justice system consists of our police, courts, and corrections—each equally important in reducing the incidence of crime within the United States.

Policing can be divided into four broad categories: local, county, state and federal agencies. In the United States, policing is mainly the responsibility of local and county agencies, such as city police and county sheriff's departments. State level policing typically involves highway patrols and/or agencies such as the Texas Rangers. At the federal level, law enforcement agencies—such as the Drug Enforcement Agency and the Bureau of Alcohol, Tobacco, and Firearms—assist local, county, and state law enforcement when they are needed.

Another component of the criminal justice system are courts, which have the authority to hear and decide cases within jurisdictional areas. In the United States, there is a dual court system comprised of federal and state level courts. Each state maintains its own state level court system with approximately twelve thousand general jurisdiction courts across the United States. Appellate courts do not hear new cases but, rather, act as a reviewer of those from general jurisdictions. There are twelve state appellate courts and one federal court that hear appeals from the federal circuit. Appellate courts have a great deal of discretion with regard to their rulings which can include ordering a new trial, allowing defendants to go free, or upholding the lower court's verdict. However, all fifty states have a "court of last resort," usually referred to as a state supreme court that can review the appellate court's decision. The United States Supreme Court is the highest law in the country because when it hands down a ruling, all states must abide by it.

When community corrections are not an option, an inmate may be sent to a jail, prison, or private prison.

The third component, corrections, is a growing industry within the United States, with a population of over two million persons either incarcerated in prisons or on some type of community corrections, such as probation or parole. In addition to probation and parole, other community corrections ordered by the courts include home confinement and restitution. Probation is widely used and involves a sentence of imprisonment that is suspended by the court provided the convicted person abides by the rules of the court. Parole occurs when a parole authority releases an inmate before his or her sentence has expired. The released prisoner must report to a parole officer and follow the protocol established upon reentry into society. Home confinement or house arrest is sometimes ordered when a person is not a serious offender and he or she has a job. The individual must be in the home at all times except when working and is monitored using an electronic device usually placed on the ankle. A court may also order a person to pay restitution to his or her victim or volunteer services to the community.

When community corrections are not an option, an inmate may be sent to a jail, prison, or private prison. There are over 3,300 jails in the U.S., housing approximately 750,000 inmates. The majority of jail inmates are pre-trial detainees waiting for their day in court. If an inmate is sent to one of the country's 1,325 state prisons or eighty-four federal prisons, the inmate may encounter some overcrowding with nearly 1.5 million other inmates. In 2001, it cost nearly $60 billion to run the prisons within the United States (Schmalleger, 2008). Private prisons are becoming increasing popular to ease the burden of overcrowding. State governments contract with private firms to provide correctional services for inmates. In 2005, nearly 6 percent of state and 14 percent of federal prisoners were housed in private prisons (Schmalleger 2008).

The Future of the Criminal Justice System

In the future, it is expected that the focus of criminal justice will be on globalization and the effects international and transnational crimes have on our system. Globalization refers to the idea the world is getting smaller and crimes committed in other countries will have an effect on the United States. Louise Shelley, director of the Transnational Crime and Corruption Center, suggests that transnational crime will be as much a defining issue for twenty-first century policymakers as was the Cold War for the twentieth century (Fairchild and Dammer 2005). Crimes such as terrorism, computer crimes, sea piracy, drug and human trafficking, money laundering, and corruption will influence the United States criminal justice system in many ways. Police will need specialized training to deal with specific crimes. For example, the most widely trafficked and most widely abused drug is cannabis, with seizures reported in 98 percent of all countries and territories. Courts will have concerns over jurisdiction and nation sovereignty, as the US Department of Treasury estimates that as much as $100 billion is laundered annually in the US and anywhere from three hundred to five hundred billion worldwide (Fairchild and Dammer 2005). As police and courts work to combat crime, the corrections industry continues to expand with the number of persons incarcerated showing steady growth.

CHAPTER REVIEW

Wrapping it up

Summary

1. Deviance is universal, and every society has people who commit acts defined as exceeding the tolerance limits of social norms.

2. Deviance can influence social systems in several different ways. Some of the consequences are *functional. Specifically*, they can help to define the limits of social tolerance, increase the solidarity and integration of groups, serve as a safety valve for future deviance, indicate inadequacies in the system, and bring about constructive change. Other consequences are *dysfunctional. For example*, deviance can disrupt the social order, decrease the will of others to conform, destroy trust, and divert resources that otherwise could be used elsewhere into social rehabilitation and control efforts.

3. There are several traditional views of deviance. The *absolutist and moral view* assumes that particular acts or people are deviant in all contexts and that these acts and people are bad and immoral. The *medical model* of deviance suggests that deviants are sick people and that deviance is unhealthy. A *statistical model* defines deviance as any behavior that varies from the average or the mode.

4. The mechanisms of social control are used to maintain conformity. Control of deviance is generally explained in terms of two factors: internal controls and external controls. *Internal controls*, which are exerted by individuals on themselves, involve such factors as self-concept, ego strength, high frustration tolerance, and conscience. These controls are believed to be acquired through socialization. *External controls* include both informal interactions with people, such as family and friends, and formal controls, which are carried out by the agencies designated by society to maintain law and order.

5. The *relative nature of deviance* assumes that deviance can be defined only in the context of the society or group in which it takes place. Deviance is not thought to be a particular type of act. It is, rather, a relative condition that varies according to time, place, situation, and social status. This view takes into account the great diversity of meanings that can be associated with people or acts in different situations.

6. Many theories have been developed to explain the causes of deviance and how it can be controlled or modified. Biological theories have attempted to associate it with body type, physical abnormalities, and chromosome aberrations. Psychological theories emphasize such factors as personality, motivation, willpower, frustration, aggression, and ego strength.

7. Sociological theorists do not ignore biological and psychological factors, but they tend to

view theories based on these factors as insufficient. Sociological theories focus on the interaction, organization, and social normative factors through which people learn definitions of deviance. These factors also determine people's behavior, which a social audience labels as either deviant or nondeviant.

8. Functionalist theories, such as *strain* and *anomie theories*, link deviance to conflicts between culturally valued goals and institutionalized means of achieving them. Innovation, ritualism, retreatism, and rebellion are deviant modes of adaptation.

9. *Conflict theories* contend that definitions of deviance are devised by the powerful to repress and exploit the weak. An influential, wealthy elite is assumed to oppose and control the powerless, the poor, and minorities.

10. Interactionist *theories*, which are based on sociocultural learning, examine both social and psychological influences, but emphasize the processes through which deviant acts are learned and the types of conditions under which they are learned. *Cultural transmission theory*, sometimes called "subculture theory," explains the continuity of crime and deviance in some geographical areas as the result of the transmission of deviant norms from one generation to the next.

11. *Differential association theory* contends that deviance is learned through verbal and nonverbal communication, by associating differentially with deviant or nondeviant individuals or groups. The social learning theory of deviance, which draws heavily on differential association theory, suggests that operant (instrumental) conditioning and imitation play important roles in the learning of behaviors. Differential rewards and punishments, as well as exposure to conforming or deviant models, greatly influence whether we develop deviant or conforming attitudes and behaviors.

12. *Labeling theory*, rather than emphasizing acts or individuals in isolation, focuses on why some people and acts are singled out as deviant and also on the effects of being labeled deviant. This approach, which is based on the principles of symbolic interaction, assumes that the definition of deviance and other behaviors is a collective process. People in social contexts define and interpret their own behavior and that of others and apply labels on the basis of their definitions. These labels have a significant effect on the continuation of deviant behavior for both those defined as deviant and the audience who labels them.

13. The social consequences of deviance include crime, in that *crimes* are violations of criminal statutory law. Types of crime include violent and non-violent, property crimes, victimless crimes, white-collar crimes, organized crimes, and juvenile crimes.

14. Rates of criminal activity are measured using two primary sources of data. The UCR measures the amount of crime reported to police, and the NCVS gauges those crimes that go unreported. In addition, self-report surveys are used to appraise crimes committed by the offenders.

15. The criminal justice system includes police, courts, and corrections. Police can be divided into local, county, state, and federal law enforcement. Courts include state and federal level systems with the authority to hear cases based on jurisdiction. Corrections include incarceration and community sentences such as probation, parole, house arrest, and restitution.

16. The future of the criminal justice system will increasingly focus on globalization and the influence of transnational and international crimes on the United States.

Key Terms

absolutist view The view that there is wide agreement about social norms and that certain behaviors are deviant regardless of the social context in which they occur

anomie theory The view that deviance arises from

the incongruenceis between a society's emphasis on attaining certain goals and the availability of legitimate, institutionalized means of reaching those goals

blaming the victim A type of reasoning that implies that social problems are caused by the people facing them

conflict theory A social theory that views conflict as inevitable and natural and as a significant cause of social change

crime A violation of a criminal statutory law accompanied by a specific punishment applied by some governmental authority

cultural transmission theory The theory that a community's deviance may be transmitted to newcomers through learning and socialization

deviance Variation from a set of norms or shared social expectations

differential association theory The theory that deviance results when individuals have more contact with groups that define deviance favorably than with groups that define it unfavorably

differential reinforcement The view that the acquisition and persistence of either deviant or conforming behavior is a function of what behaviors have been rewarded or punished

external controls Pressures or sanctions applied to members of society by others

formal controls Generally occur in a public setting such as a courtroom

immoral view The view that deviance is immoral and antisocial

informal controls Positive and negative controls such as smiling, frowning, and high-fives, used to influence behavior

internal controls Learned patterns of control that exist in the minds of individuals and make them want to conform to social norms

labeling theory A theory that emphasizes how certain behaviors are labeled "deviant" and how being given such a label influences a person's behavior

medical view The view that deviance is essentially pathological evidence that a society is unhealthy

"medicalization of deviance" The transformation of moral and legal deviance into a medical condition

National Crime Victimization Survey Data collected by the Bureau of Justice on crimes that go unreported to the police

negative sanctions Actions that discourage individuals from a particular behavior

organized crime Groups expressly organized to carry out illegal activities

positive sanctions Actions that encourage individuals to continue a behavior

relativistic view The view that deviance can be interpreted only in the sociocultural context in which it occurs

sanctions Rewards and punishments used to encourage proper behavior

social learning theory The view that deviant and conforming behaviors are strongly influenced by the consequences that follow them

sociocultural learning theories Theories that deal with the processes through which deviant acts are learned and the conditions under which learning takes place

statistical view A perspective on deviance that defines deviant as any variation from a statistical norm

strain theories Theories of deviance suggesting that the experience of socially induced strain, such as anomie, forces people to engage in deviant activities

Discussion Questions

1. How do you define deviance? Explain what it means to say that deviance is socially defined.
2. Evaluate why women kill their children. If the mother is found guilty of killing her daughter,

which theory most likely explains why the mother committed the murder?

3. How would you explain the variation in the rates of women incarcerated around the world? Can it be explained using the relativistic view? How do social responses differ in each country?
4. What are the similarities and differences among the anomie, conflict, interactionist, and labeling theories of deviance?
5. How can the definitions of some types of behavior as deviant regardless of their sociocultural context result in misguided social policies? Give some examples other than the ones shown in this chapter.
6. What are some types of behavior that are commonly explained in terms of biological and psychological theories of deviance? Is it possible to explain these in terms of sociological theories? If so, how?
7. Compare the usefulness of the biological and psychological theories of deviance with the sociological theories of deviance.
8. How does being labeled a "deviant" influence interaction patterns? Does "truth" (i.e., accuracy, correctness) matter? Is it ever okay to tell a lie?
9. Discuss some ways in which deviance has positive functions for society. Give examples.
10. Use the sociological theories of deviance to discuss the internal and external controls of deviance.

Pop Quiz

1. Deviance, as defined by the text, refers to behavior that ______.

   a. violates a law
   b. defies moral values
   c. varies from a set of norms
   d. is harmful to the interests of a society

2. The perspective on deviance that suggests that any variation from a norm constitutes deviance is the ______.

   a. absolutist and moral view
   b. medical and social-pathological views
   c. statistical view
   d. biological view

3. What does it mean to say that deviance is relative?

   a. It can be understood only within the context in which it occurs
   b. Relatives know better than others the deviant behaviors of their own family network
   c. All behavior is relative, and nothing is deviant
   d. All violent crimes are considered deviant

4. The view that the creation of deviance is an interactive process, involving people's behavior, an audience, norms, and social definition, is reflected in which of the following perspectives?

   a. biological model
   b. statistical theory
   c. relativistic perspective
   d. absolutist and moral perspective

5. An extra "Y" chromosome is ______.

   a. linked to criminal behavior
   b. associated with physical violence
   c. commonly found in non-deviant males
   d. all of the above

6. Merton's version of anomie theory does not include which of the following modes of adaptation?

   a. conservatism
   b. innovation
   c. ritualism
   d. retreatism

7. The sociological theory of deviance that argues that groups in power define the acts of weaker groups as deviant is known as ______.

a. anomie theory
b. sociological elitism theory
c. sociocultural learning theory
d. conflict theory

8. On what do labeling theorists focus primarily?

a. acts of people who are deviant
b. people who define others as deviant
c. process and effects of defining people as deviant
d. rewards or punishments of deviance

9. Social deviance is dysfunctional when it ______.

a. prevents constructive social change
b. disrupts the will of others to conform
c. destroys the public trust
d. all of the above

10. Which of the following is an example of an informal social control?

a. police officers
b. district judges
c. probation officers
d. peers

11. The medical and social-pathological views classify deviance as an illness. T/F

12. According to the relativistic point of view, deviance resides exclusively in the person and his or her actions. T/F

13. Psychological theories are often tied to the medical model. T/F

14. Sutherland's differential association theory contends that the more deviant contacts people have, the more likely they are to develop into deviants. T/F

15. The Uniform Crime Report depicts an accurate account of serious crimes. T/F

1. C	6. A	11. T
2. A	7. D	12. F
3. A	8. C	13. T
4. C	9. D	14. T
5. D	10. D	15. F

PART THREE

Social Inequality

All animals are equal, but some animals are more equal than others.

GEORGE ORWELL

CHAPTER 8

Social Differentiation and Stratification

HURRICANE KATRINA: NATURAL DISASTERS AND INEQUALITY

In August 2005, one of the worst and costliest hurricanes hit New Orleans causing catastrophic damage and loss of life. Named Katrina by the National Hurricane Center, the storm had reached a Level 3 status with winds as high as 125 miles per hour by the time it made landfall in Louisiana on August 29. Katrina dropped large amounts of rainfall on the state with some areas receiving as much as fifteen inches. The levels of rain created problems for Lake Pontchartrain. As the lake continued to rise, the most disastrous effects of Katrina occurred: the federally built levees in New Orleans began to break.

As the nation watched, people were forced to confront the issues of racism, poverty, and inequality within the United States. The images shown by the media were of poor, mainly black, citizens of New Orleans trapped by the floodwaters. Even though the mayor had called for mandatory evacuations, most of the poor were unable to leave on their own; and no coordinated efforts by the government were put in place to address this problem. However, while the news media plastered the airwaves with pictures of poor black women, children, and the elderly struggling to survive until help could arrive, the attitudes of Americans were not of empathy but of a media bias. Blaming the victim is a common phenomenon in America. Many people believe that everyone has some means, however small, to "make it" when catastrophe occurs—whether it is the help of family and friends, or any other means necessary. We fail to realize that most Americans live from paycheck to paycheck; having the means to leave our house, job, school, etc. is not an immediate option for most of us.

Grusky and Ryo (2006) examined the opinions of Americans after Katrina and suggested that disaster had the potential to re-adjust the mind-set of society toward the poor and poverty in the United States. Their report indicated that while 70 percent of Americans tuned in to hear news about Katrina, not everyone's opinions about poverty were changed by the events. Of those tuned in to the effects of Katrina, 40 percent still felt that there is nothing the government can do to address poverty and inequality or reveal that it is a major problem in the United States. The research conducted by Grusky and Ryo examined what is referred to as "the dirty little secret hypothesis" which says that disasters often reveal injustices in society that exist as a result of inequality. For example, many in the public news media felt that Hurricane Katrina would call attention to how inequality is largely responsible for the devastating effects of natural disasters (due to things such as lack of an adequate infrastructure or slow response rates after the disaster); and as a result of the exposure of that "dirty little secret," U.S. Americans would support a renewed war on poverty to combat the injustices of inequality. This effect was borne out only partially after Hurricane Katrina. Activists who already understood the ramifications of inequality prior to Katrina were hardened in their approach that further steps to eradicate social inequality should take place. Non-activists remained opposed to stepping up government efforts to eradicate inequality and tended to feel that the "dirty little secret" being exposed was being presented as such as a result of a liberal news bias. So, while some individuals saw hopelessness and pain on the faces of those trapped, others saw a group of people who should have gotten out but didn't. How is it that people can see the same images, yet draw vastly different opinions about those affected? If the trapped group had been mainly white and middle class, would the response of those watching been different?

In the U.S., blacks often compete with lower class whites for low-paying unskilled and semi-skilled jobs. After World War II and following the Civil Rights Movement, life chances for blacks began to make positive strides (Wilson 1978). In *The Declining Significance of Race*, Wilson (1978) argues that class became more important than race in determining access to power and privilege. He contends that in American society today many blacks have better opportunities for quality education and positions of prestige than some whites. However, Wilson cautions that not all blacks are experiencing progress. Uneducated, poorly trained blacks are limited in their life chances with many facing unemployment and crime within their inner city environments. Yet, while many blacks are living in poverty, many others are moving up the corporate and government ladders to successful jobs and businesses. Therefore, Wilson argues, "The recent mobility patterns of blacks lend strong support to the view that economic class is clearly more important than race in predetermining job placement and occupational mobility" (1999, p. 165). It is important to note that others feel that disasters such as Katrina undermine Wilson's notion that race is declining in significance. Sherrow Pinder (2009), for example, argues that Katrina drew our attention to the interrelation of race and class inequality that is deeply embedded within America's political, economic, and social structures.

How does class status affect one's life chances? How are other factors, such as race, gender, and age related to social class? As you read this chapter, think about the importance of class on those who experience natural disasters. Does race or economic status influence how we see victims? What other factors influence what we see?

The devastation caused by Hurricane Katrina in 2005 brought to light issues of racism, poverty, and inequality.

UNDERSTANDING SOCIAL STRATIFICATION

Americans emphasize a commitment to equality and a belief in the American middle-class lifestyle. The belief is that people are basically equal and that most are middle class. However, how stratified is the middle class in the United States? Are all people within the middle class equal? We have a tendency to believe that everyone has the ability to pull themselves up by the bootstraps and become whatever they want to be. Those few people who have great wealth excelled at something highly valued and needed within society. The Bill Gate's and Oprah Winfrey's of the world were creative and managed to build their "American Dream" with the opportunities provided them by society. On the other hand, the tendency is to believe that only a few Americans are poor, mostly as a result of not taking advantage of the opportunities the country has to offer.

What Americans seldom realize is how incredibly wealthy a few are and how extremely poor others are. A relatively few people control great wealth and power; yet, most of them have not worked hard for their money—they inherited it. They live in luxury beach houses in the summer and mansions in the winter. Meanwhile, as many as two or three million Americans eat in soup kitchens (when they eat), have no homes at all, and without a home are not qualified to vote. Some of these people work hard for a living, and many are only children. In reality, people are not created equal, nor do they experience equality in their lives.

Inequality—the unequal access to scarce goods or resources—is found in most, if not all, societies. Some goods and resources are hard to come by in some countries. For example, we have a tendency to believe water is plentiful whereas in many African countries it is extremely scarce. Land is a scarce resource in some areas of the world; in others, it is so plentiful that no one bothers to claim ownership. In societies where there are not enough workers, child labor becomes a valuable resource. From their youth, instead of going to school, people work to contribute to the family income.

Of course, people differ in other ways as well. Some people have blue eyes, and some have brown eyes. Some people live and work on the east coast, and some on the west coast. Some people travel in their work, and others prefer to work at a desk. Some people like to work with people, and others prefer solitary work. This is **social differentiation**—how people vary according to social characteristics. Usually, we do not rank people as high or low based on these differences.

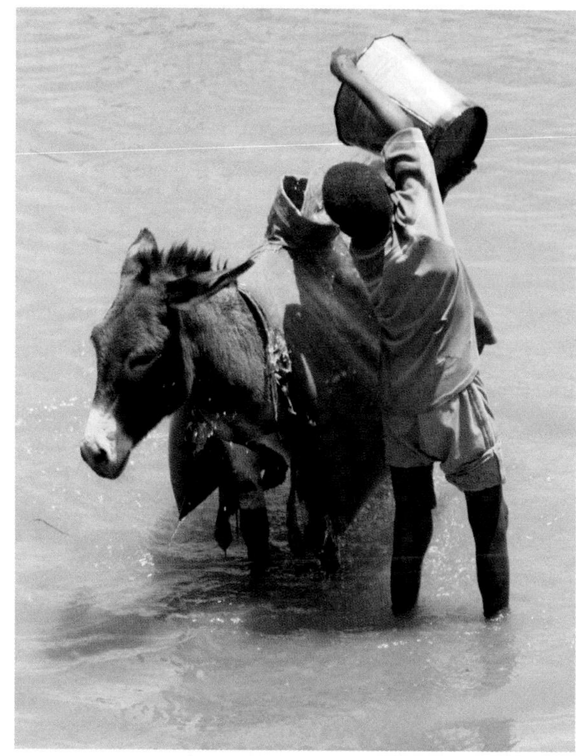

Water is extremely scarce in many African countries.

Rather, people are ranked according to their ability to access scarce resources. Wealth, **power** and prestige are scarce, but valuable, resources within the U.S. Wealth includes money, stock, property, etc, while power and prestige include education, respect, and membership in political and philanthropic organizations. The ranking of people according to their wealth, power, or prestige is known as **social stratification**. Stratification, then, is a hierarchical structure of society.

Our ranking in the stratification system influences every part of our lives: where we live, access to education, what jobs we work, what we eat, how or if we vote, and whom we marry. Our sexual behavior, sports, hobbies, and health are all affected by the rank society gives us. This chapter examines stratification and how it affects people's lives; additionally, we explore how to use this knowledge in our work and in our personal lives. We begin by noting social differentiation in selected types of societies.

TYPES OF SOCIETIES AND SOCIAL DIFFERENTIATION

In simple societies, there is little division of labor—all people perform similar tasks and possess similar wealth. As a result, there is little social differentiation. In complex societies, there are wide divisions of labor, with a wide array of social positions. Stratification develops as we rank these positions in order of importance. Lenski (1966) found that stratification generally increases as societies grow in wealth and become more complex. He differentiated five basic types of societies:

1. Hunting-and-gathering societies
2. Simple horticultural societies
3. Advanced horticultural societies
4. Agrarian societies
5. Industrial societies

Hunting-and-gathering societies consist of about fifty people, or even fewer, who live on what they can find to eat. They are often nomadic, moving from place to place in search of food. They are usually very poor and must share what they find to eat in order to survive. No one can be excused from work. Surpluses of food or supplies are not accumulated, so no one can become wealthy. Some people may gain special respect because of their age, wisdom, skill in hunting, or magical abilities; but they do not derive any power from their status because there is no area to exercise their authority and little to do except work. With so little differentiation in these societies, there is little stratification.

In **simple horticultural societies**, people farm using a digging stick as their basic tool. They have a fairly reliable source of food and may even have a surplus from time to time. Thus, they can remain in one location, build shelters, and make tools. A surplus of food and supplies allows them some leisure time, which they use for sports and ceremonial activities. They, also, occasionally fight wars to protect their land. A **division of labor** develops when some people do certain specialized occupations: warriors, ceremonial and political leaders, for example. Ceremonial leaders are sometimes paid for performing ceremonies, especially those involving healing, and

A digging stick is used as a farming tool.

they may become wealthy. Political leaders, with the assistance of warriors, can capture slaves and enforce their edicts. As labor is divided among different groups and wealth and status accumulate, a stratification system develops.

Advanced horticultural societies farm with irrigation, terracing, and fertilization. These techniques increase the food supply, so the size of the population can grow. Societies at this level have learned how to work metals. This increases the variety of material goods and also the variety of occupations. As the size and wealth of the populations increase and a greater variety of occupations develops, stratification increases. Political leaders in advanced horticultural societies become very wealthy and powerful as they increase the size of their armies and slave labor. Social differentiation and stratification are much greater in these societies than in simple horticultural societies.

Agrarian societies, such as those found in Europe during the Middle Ages, have far more sophisticated

Irrigation is a part of successful farming.

technology than horticultural societies. This advanced technology increases the development of centralized power in two ways. First, as defenses and weapons are improved, arming a warrior with the materials needed to win battles becomes an expensive proposition. By supplying the weapons, the rich are able to develop armies that they use to conquer land and slaves and to control farmers, who then become the serfs of the society. Second, as the variety of goods grows, a merchant class develops to trade those goods. The more powerful rulers tax the wealth accumulated by the merchant class and become extremely rich.

As wealth and power become concentrated in the hands of very few people, society becomes severely stratified. During the Middle Ages, the ruler and governing classes in agrarian societies probably received income of about a quarter to a half of the national income (Lenski 1966).

Industrial societies, such as the United States and western European countries, have the greatest division of labor, the most wealth, and therefore the most stratification, at least at the beginnings of industrial revolutions. Industrialization, which is structured on the factory system of production and the assembly line, requires workers to perform very specialized tasks. Workers specialize in operating a particular piece of equipment, packing a manufactured product, driving a truck to market, advertising the product, selling the product, and so on. Workers do not produce goods for personal consumption. Instead, they do a specific job in exchange for money and then buy personal goods with that money.

Durkheim (1933) argued that in preindustrial times the division of labor created **mechanical solidarity**, a situation in which people do similar work but are not very dependent on each other. Most people farmed and were self-sufficient. He believed that the division of labor could create **organic solidarity** because as each person specializes in one phase of production, he or she becomes dependent on others to produce other products. As a result, Durkheim believed, society would become more integrated and people would become more equal. However, Durkheim's predictions did not come about. Industrial societies have developed a wide gap between those at the top and those at the bottom. The surplus of goods produced, when accumulated in the hands of just a few people, make those people very wealthy compared with others.

SYSTEMS OF STRATIFICATION

The systems of stratification have changed during various time periods and under certain social conditions. Within stratification systems, the status of a person is determined either through ascription or achievement, meaning they are either born into it or they attain it through effort. Most sociologists agree that status is a combination of both. For example, a child born into a wealthy family will have more opportunities to achieve status than a child born into poverty.

There have been four basic types of stratification systems in the world: caste, estate, slavery, and class. In addition, systems are classified as open or closed, allowing for specific degrees of social mobility of its citizens. In **open systems**, individual accomplishments are encouraged and social mobility rewarded with advancements. Equality is not influenced by gender, race, age, etc, as status is based on achievement. In **closed systems**, status is determined at birth and social mobility is based on a person's social position. Individual achievement is not rewarded because status is determined by law or through inheritance.

In a **caste system**, a person's social status is ascribed at birth. Worth is judged on the basis of religious or traditional beliefs about the person or the person's family. The caste system is a very rigid, closed system of stratification.

India, where there are some three thousand castes, provides the best example of a caste system; and status is determined by religion rather than race. The following are the caste of India:

Brahman	Priests or scholars
Kshatriya	Nobles and warriors
Vaishva	Merchants and skilled artisans
Shudra	Common laborers
Harijan	Outcasts

In 1949, India officially outlawed the caste system, but it remains deeply embedded in the culture and is practiced routinely in rural areas. The 2008 Academy Award-winning movie, *Slum Dog Millionaire*, highlighted

The Shudra caste of India is comprised of common laborers.

the influence India's caste system has on the status, identity, education, and employment of individuals within society. The caste into which people are born affects what kind of food they eat, where they live, what kind of medical care they receive, how they are supported in old age, and how they are buried. For example, Harijans were considered to be so low that even their movements were limited during the daytime. The belief was that even the shadow of an "untouchable" would contaminate any person who came into contact with it and that person would then be unclean as a result.

An **estate system** was very similar to a caste, in that status was ascribed and social mobility limited. Law and membership through inheritance determined the identity of a person. An example of an estate system was Europe during the Middle Ages, where three estates existed. The *first estate* was comprised of nobility, wealthy families, and powerful landowners. Their status allowed them great privilege and opportunities, including the right to not work as labor was believed to be beneath them. The *second estate* was made up of clergy from the Roman Catholic Church. Highly powerful, the church owned land and collected taxes. The *third estate* was commoners, or laborers, particularly of the land. Serfs, as they were called, could only move out of their estate if they were knighted or performed a remarkable deed for the king.

The **slave system** of stratification has been less recognized, but is equally important to this discussion. In a slave system, there existed a basic belief in the ownership of humans for labor. A debtor could enslave a person who owed him a debt, and that person's labor could be used as a form of repayment. When a person committed certain types of crimes, that person could be sentenced to slavery and required to work for the family of his victim. The first slaves in the American colonies were purchased from a Dutch ship in 1619 and initially considered as indentured servants who would work for a specific period of time to repay their passage debt. However, when labor demands exceeded the supply of workers, the United States turned to chattel slavery.

In a **class system**, social status is defined in terms of wealth and income. There are no legal definitions of class, so the system is an open system. Classes are fluid—that is, there is unlimited social mobility between one class and another. Anyone can move to a higher or lower ranking by either gaining or losing wealth; as a result, class societies are highly competitive, and power has become increasingly important to maintain a high position in the stratification system.

DIMENSIONS OF A CLASS SYSTEM

Class systems are commonly economic based societies where a person's wealth determines their classification. Marx was the first to use class system as a form of stratification. Weber (1946) pointed out that as the class system developed in industrial civilizations, class, status, and power become scarce resources that people compete for within society.

Social Class

Social class is a ranking generally based on a person's wealth. A number of things contribute to one's wealth—such as income and occupation, power derived from wealth, and the "life chances" to acquire wealth. **Life chances** are opportunities people have

SOCIOLOGY AT WORK

Helping Disabled Drug Addicts

Alexander Boros (1931-1996) received his PhD in sociology from Case Western Reserve University in 1969. He is best known for founding the Association for Applied and Clinical Sociology. Boros' work with Addiction Intervention with the Disabled (AID) in Cleveland, Ohio, is a prime example of Boros' applied and clinical focus. AID focused much of its attention on two groups: deaf people and people who are reading limited.

Boros believed that a sociological perspective is quite different than other approaches that try to help the disabled with alcohol and other drug problems. According to Boros, "Human services people tend to have a very individualistic orientation." "Whether they're doctors or therapists or counselors, they deal with the problem as an individual's problem. Sociologists try to understand the social and cultural conditions in which the problem arises. Most deaf people, for example, live out their lives as members of a closed community. They have their own language and their own culture. They read at, on the average, a third-grade level. The rate of intermarriage within the group is about 90 percent. Deaf people represent a different community with different needs. As a sociologist, I am able to see the social context in which members of this group act out their problems through alcohol and [other] drug abuse."

Boros, who was known for his work in the area of rehabilitation for more than 30 years, began his work on AID when he was approached by a group of deaf people who wanted sign-language interpreters at local meetings of Alcoholics Anonymous. AID organized a national conference on treating deaf alcoholics. It also conducted workshops for people already involved in the treatment of addiction to alcohol and other drugs, regarding the unique needs of the deaf. However, Boros began to perceive a larger need. "About 16 percent of the population is disabled—deaf, blind, retarded, spinal cord-injured, and so on. We have been able to determine that the rate of alcohol and [other] drug addiction among the deaf is about the same as among the general population. However the other disabled lack the kind of cohesive community the deaf have developed. They probably experience a much higher rate—some of us estimate twice as high. Other than in the standard treatment programs, the rate of participation by the disabled is about 1 percent. So it's not just that the need was being met badly. It wasn't being met at all."

The solution was to set up special services for the deaf and those with multiple disabilities, find the alcohol and other drug abusers in that population, and refer them to those services. "The rehabilitation agencies for the disabled tend not to understand alcohol and [other] drug addiction. They see it as a self-inflicted problem. They prefer to work with what they call the 'true disabled.' The people who work in alcohol addiction treatment, on the other hand, are people whose expertise is life experience: They tend to be recovering alcoholics themselves. Many do not have the time or the desire to learn about what the special needs of the deaf or the disabled. Therefore we needed something new."

To meet the need, Boros, his staff, and their volunteer assistants trained alcohol- and other drug-abuse counselors to work in educational programs with the deaf and the disabled. Boros and his staff came up with new ideas. A byproduct of their work is a new "picture-idea methodology" for communicating material about alcohol and other drug abuse to people who are reading-limited. This methodology uses a picture format with a sentence above each picture, simplified to a fourth-grade reading level. "With help," Boros felt, "this methodology enables people that are reading-limited to have access to material about drug ... abuse."

to improve their social class status such as education, health, and autonomy. For example, members of a first generation immigrant farm family will have fewer life chances than subsequent generations.

Social classes typically share similar characteristics such as occupations, education, lifestyles, attitudes and behaviors. In the United States, three classes exist: upper class, middle class, and lower class. However, throughout the years we have increasingly included a working class, as well as stratified the middle class itself. According to the Pew Research Center (2008), America is home to four middle classes: top middle, satisfied middle, anxious middle, and struggling middle—with 53 percent of Americans identifying themselves as belonging to one of these groups.

Social Status

Social status, according to Weber, is the amount of honor and prestige a person receives from others in the community; therefore, it is the social dimension of class. Prestige can be acquired in a number of ways—being born into a highly respected family, living in a high-status neighborhood, attending prestigious schools, or joining high-status groups or clubs. People also gain prestige by being able to buy consumer goods that others admire, such as expensive houses, yachts, or airplanes. Status can also be gained by holding respected positions in the community, such as clergy or professors. In short, doing things and buying things that others admire acquire status. Thus, people's status is very closely related to their wealth. Some people use their wealth to buy status while other wealthy people are content to live quietly, relatively unknown in the community.

Power

Power is another component of social class within the United States. Power is about having authority and respect, usually within an organization in which decisions are made to reach the group's goals—such as to win an election, change a law, revise the banking system, educate children, or any other goal. A person can gain power in the community by being politically active in national, state, or local politics; in special interest groups; in influential clubs; or in any other type of organization in which decisions are made to reach broad-based societal goals. By developing power, people can increase their social status through winning respect and can increase their social class through reaching goals that are profitable to them.

Class, status, and power are often closely interrelated. Status and power can be used to increase wealth. Wealth can be used to buy consumer goods and increase status or to join prestigious clubs and increase political power. These three sources of status do not always go together, however. Wealthy people who are criminals, who live reclusive lives, or who are otherwise atypical have low status if no one respects them. Priests, ministers, college professors, and community leaders may be poor but still have a high status. Powerful leaders who use their position to increase their wealth sometimes do so in such a way that they lose status and the respect of others.

You may better understand characteristics of stratification—class, social status, and power—if you think back to your high school days and the ways in which students could gain recognition. Some students gained recognition in dimensions of class; others gained recognition in

TABLE 8-1 DIMENSIONS OF STRATIFICATION IN A HIGH SCHOOL ELITE

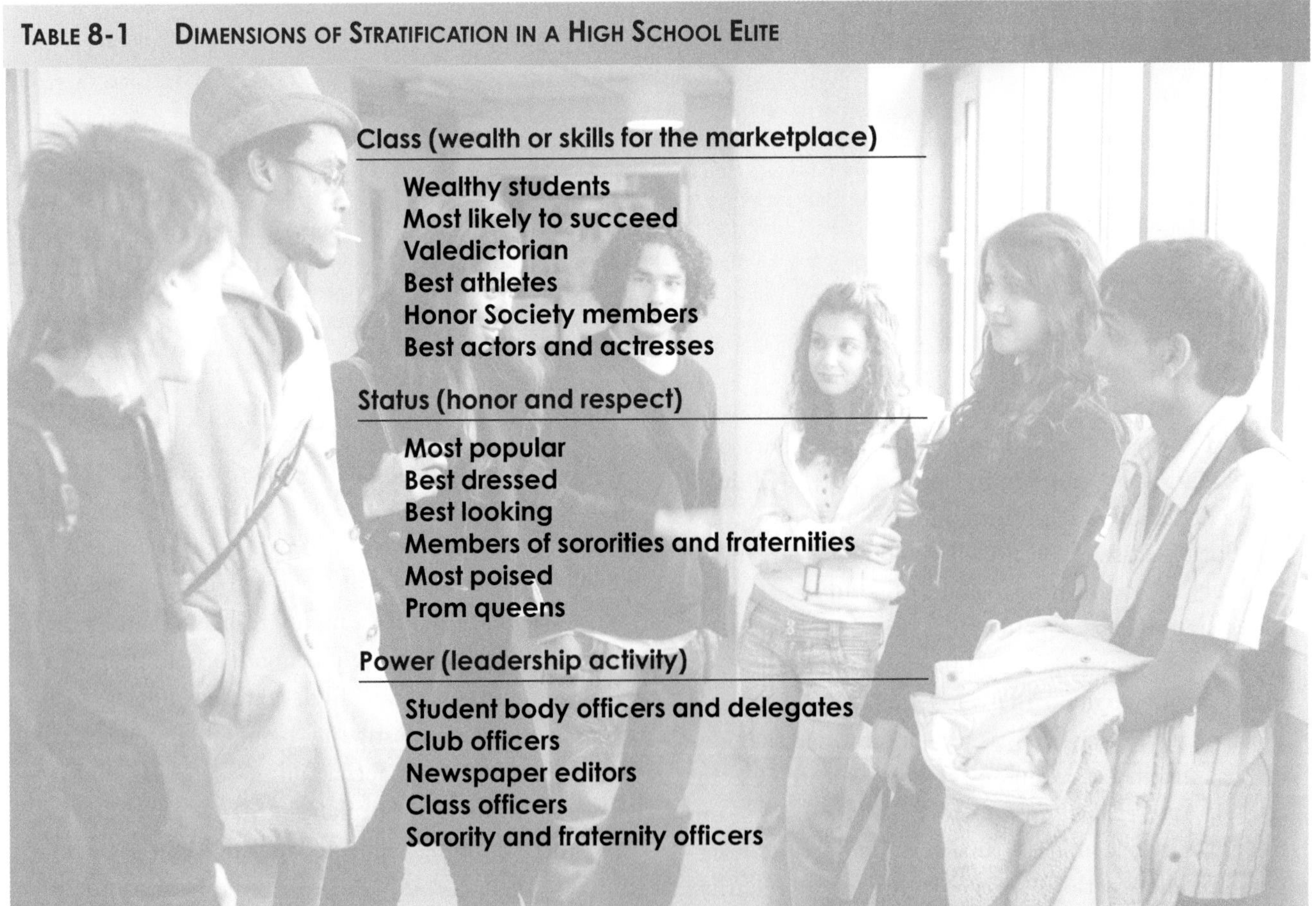

Class (wealth or skills for the marketplace)

Wealthy students
Most likely to succeed
Valedictorian
Best athletes
Honor Society members
Best actors and actresses

Status (honor and respect)

Most popular
Best dressed
Best looking
Members of sororities and fraternities
Most poised
Prom queens

Power (leadership activity)

Student body officers and delegates
Club officers
Newspaper editors
Class officers
Sorority and fraternity officers

dimensions of status, and still others in dimensions of leadership in student organizations. Table 8-1 provides examples of these dimensions of stratification.

Thinking Sociologically

1. Think of ways in which you could gain power if you had great wealth.
2. If you have high social class and status, will you also have increased power? Explain.
3. Discuss the ways in which life chances contribute to having wealth, power, and success.

Socioeconomic Status

It is difficult to place individuals in a particular social stratum because class, status, and power can all influence where they might be placed. Is the widower of a distinguished scholar who lives on a small retirement income in the same class as a mail carrier or a shoplifter who has the same income? Does a rural doctor who serves the poor and receives a small income have the same class position as a suburban doctor who serves the rich and has a large income? As you can see, class boundaries can be difficult to determine. A person who has a high position in one category may have a low position in a different category. Where, then, should that person be placed?

To resolve this problem, sociologists have developed the concept of **socioeconomic status (SES)**. This concept considers income, education, and occupation when assessing a person's status. Someone who earns $50,000 will be ranked higher than a person earning $10,000; a college graduate will be ranked higher than a high school graduate; and anybody in a professional or management occupation will be ranked higher than a laborer. Usually there is a consistent pattern among these three rankings of status. People with many years of education tend to hold occupations that afford high status and high incomes. One of the more interesting problems sociologists study is how to categorize people who have "status inconsistency"—an advanced education but a very low income, for example.

SOCIAL CLASS IN THE UNITED STATES

In the United States we live in an open class system. Access to a specific social class is based on several factors—including family background, wealth, education, occupation, and a variety of other characteristics. A person's placement within a social class will determine his/her access to America's valuable resources. The best way to understand the class system is to look at each one separately.

The Upper Class

The upper class is those individuals who have considerable wealth. Wealth consists of personal property: liquid assets (cash in bank accounts), real estate, stocks, bonds, and other owned assets. This class has net worth in the millions or billions and control as much as they possess. By owning many shares of the major corporations, they influence not just their own fortunes but also those of many others. The Rockefeller family, for example, dominates key banks and corporations and has been known to control assets of more than fifteen times their personal wealth.

There is generally one of two categories into which the upper class fit, old money or new money. In the past, most of those in the upper class inherited their wealth that had been passed down from generation to generation. The Rockefeller and DuPont families would be considered *old money* upper class. *New money* is a fairly new phenomenon as the dot-com industry increased the wealth of many. Individuals such as Bill Gates made their millions either starting Internet companies or investing in them. Others, such as Oprah Winfrey and professional athletes, earned their wealth using creative talents. More recently, some individuals have become very rich by winning a lottery, changing their lives virtually overnight. While lottery winners may be considered wealthy by income standards, access to the realm of upper class involves more than money. It is unlikely they would be invited to rub elbows with the Hiltons, Rockefellers, and others.

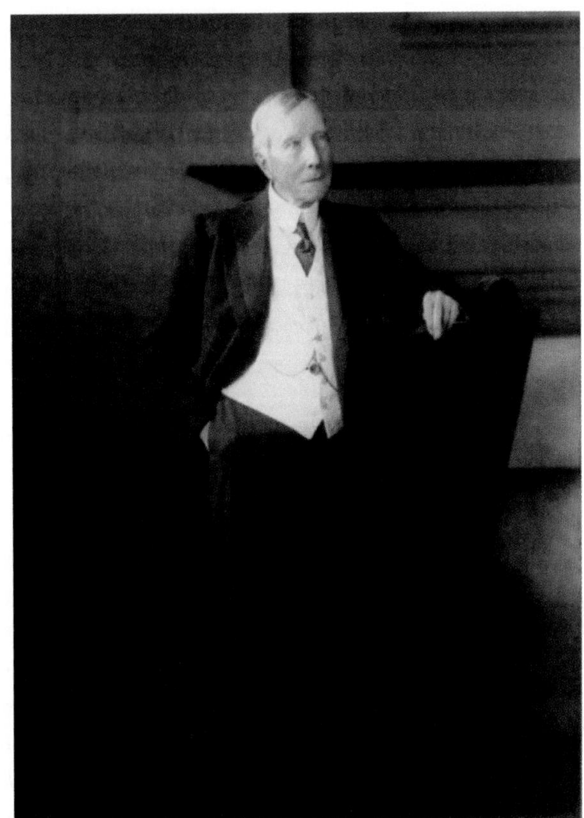

John D. Rockefeller was considered old money upper class.

The Middle Class

As mentioned previously, 53 percent of Americans consider themselves part of the middle class, the largest of all the classes. Most sociologists stratify middle class further into upper middle and lower middle. However, the Pew Research Institute argues the middle class itself is stratified into four distinct groups: top, satisfied, anxious, and struggling (Pew Research, 2008). At the highest point on the stratum are the *top middle* class, and the largest of the four groups, with 39 percent. Income levels for the top middle class range between fifty thousand and one hundred thousand dollars, and they are more likely to have a college degree. White males between the ages of thirty to forty-nine years make up the majority of this level, and 46 percent acknowledge having a high satisfaction with life. Nearly 70 percent of the class is married, and 46 percent believe the lives of their children will be better than their own.

The *satisfied* middle is the next branch and is comprised of 25 percent of those identifying themselves as middle class. The satisfied middle class are more likely to be white women between the ages of eighteen to twenty-nine or sixty-five years and over. This class has an income generally between $30,000–$49,000 and less than a college education. While this group has limited income, their outlook on life is higher than the next two groups. Members are more likely to be unmarried, which is not uncommon for their age group. They see their quality of life as high and believe the lives of their children will be higher.

The *anxious middle* class make up 23 percent of the overall middle class and have higher incomes and education than those in the satisfied group. This group is less optimistic about their futures, even with incomes between $50,000 and $99,000 and some degree of college education. The anxious middle class are more likely to be white, married, and between thirty to forty years of age. They rank their level of satisfaction as either low or medium and see the outlook of their children's lives as less hopeful than the other three groups.

The bottom group is the *struggling middle* class with incomes of $20,000 or less. This group has more minority members than the other three categories, but whites still make up 56 percent of the struggling middle class. Group members are likely to be unmarried and to have a high school degree or less. They have a low satisfaction with life, but an equal number identified themselves as either being medium or highly satisfied with their financial fate. In addition, the majority believes their children will have a better life than theirs in the future.

Is the middle class divided into four distinct groups such as the one suggest by the Pew Research Institute, or is there one large middle class? Has the definition of middle class been too narrow in the past? Those in the upper middle class have distinct lifestyles from those in the lower middle class. Most Americans identify with the middle class than with any other while the media focuses on this class and recognizes it as the norm.

The Lower Class

The lower class consists of individuals who generally have the least amount of education and the most difficulties with employment. The working poor, the displaced, and the unemployed are members of the lower class, with women and children increasingly overrepresented. While income distribution is used to identify members of social classes, self-identification as a member of the lower class is less likely. The term "low class" conjures up images of poverty, uneducated, lazy, and other derogatory visions of people unwilling to pull themselves up and take advantages of life's opportunities.

Poverty

Poverty is defined as having fewer resources than necessary to meet the basic necessities of life—food, shelter, and medical care. The U.S. Department of Health and Human Services has developed a measure of poverty that takes into account the size of the family, the number of children, and whether the family lives on a farm. The Social Security Administration first used the Poverty Index in the 1960s to determine how much a family of four would need to survive on a basic diet. (Note that prior to 1982, the poverty guidelines were issued by the Office of Economic Opportunity/Community Services Administration.) In 2011 the poverty index for a family of four was $22,350, compared to $17,600 in 2001, $13,400 in 1991, and $9,280 in 1981 (www.aspe.hhs.gov/poverty and www.census.gov/hhes/www/poverty). The government reports that in 2009, 14.3 percent of the population was living in poverty, compared to 11.1 percent in 1999, 12.8 percent in 1989 and 10.4 percent in 1979. See Figure 8-1 and Figure 8-2.

Counting the poor has been a difficult task for governmental agencies. First, the government assumes that living on a farm costs less than living in the city; therefore, the poverty index is different for each. Second, no distinction is made between geographical locations of urban cities. For example, a family of four living in New York City is considered no different than a family of four residing in Tulsa, Oklahoma; each would be based on the same poverty index. In reality, there is a difference between absolute and relative poverty. Absolute poverty occurs when people fall below a minimum subsistence level and are unable to function. They don't have the basic necessities such as food, water, and shelter to survive. Relative poverty, on the other hand, occurs when people lack resources relative to others within their economic income level and the overall standards of society. Going back to the previous example, a family of four surviving on $25,000 a year in New York City will suffer relative poverty compared to a family of four living in Tulsa, Oklahoma and having the same income.

Low paying jobs for poor people would not solve the problems of poverty. Of the adult poor, about 40 percent work at jobs that pay so little that they fall below the poverty line even though they work. The adults who are poor and not working or are either retired, ill or disabled, going to school, or keeping house. Approximately one-third of the poor in the United States are children. Most adults who could be working and are not, are unemployed because they cannot find work; they are not unemployed by choice. (Eitzen and Zinn 2007).

Those most likely to live in poverty in the United States are women and children. Referred to as the Feminization of Poverty, increasingly the poor include unwed, separated, and divorced mothers, serving as the heads of households. In 2009, 32.5 percent of female-headed households were living in poverty. Today, women head more than half of all families living in poverty, and many of them receive little support from the fathers of their children.

Inequalities in the United States

CLASS-CONSCIOUSNESS *Class-consciousness* is the awareness that different classes exist in society and that people's fates are tied to the fate of their whole class. Americans, it is argued, are not very class conscious because they believe in social mobility, or the possibility of moving upward to a higher class. However, a study conducted by Jackman and Jackman (1983) found that members of the different classes were aware of others in their class and that they felt a sense of connection and warmth toward people in their own class. Of the social classes in the United States, the upper class is more likely to maintain class-consciousness and to recognize the boundaries between themselves and the middle or lower classes. The upper class will send their children to the same private schools, attend the same social functions, and vacation in the same luxury resorts.

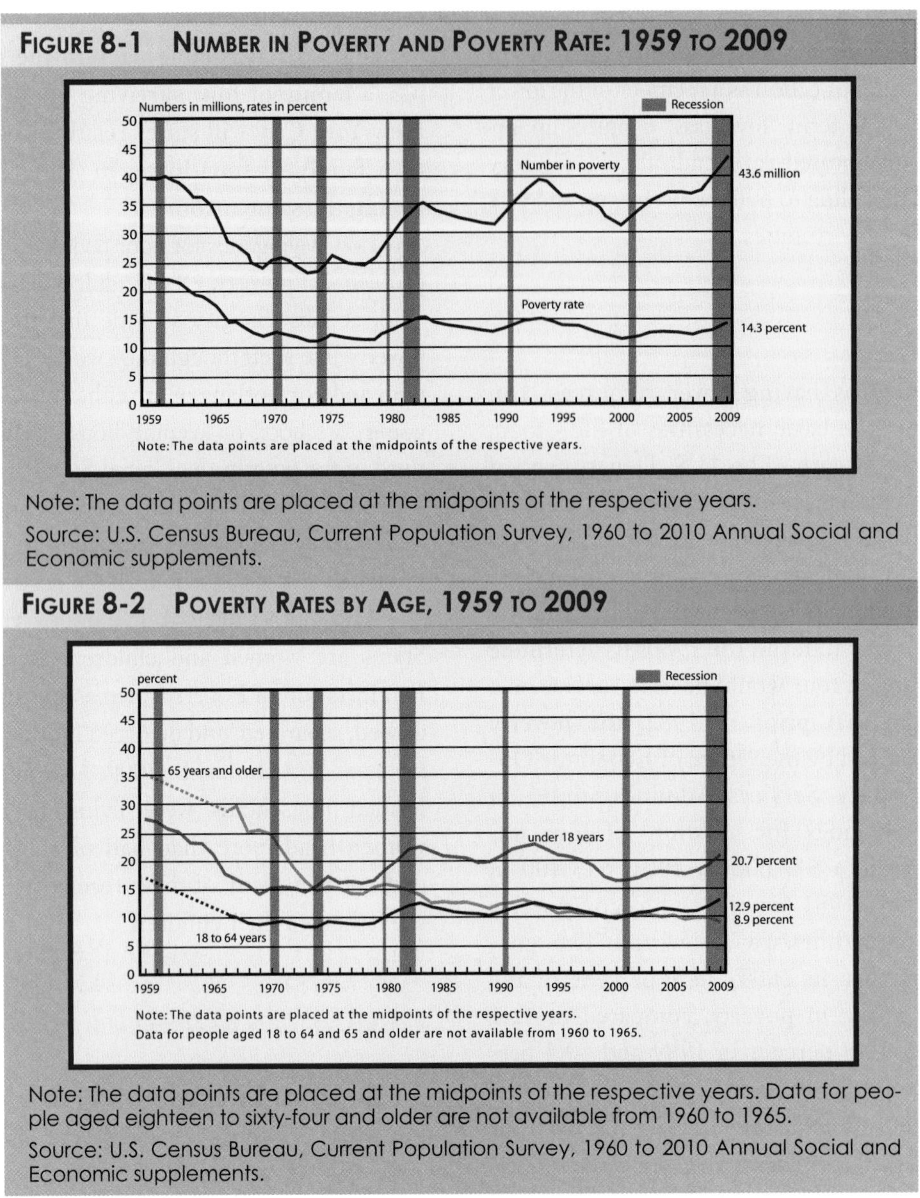

FIGURE 8-1 NUMBER IN POVERTY AND POVERTY RATE: 1959 TO 2009

Note: The data points are placed at the midpoints of the respective years.
Source: U.S. Census Bureau, Current Population Survey, 1960 to 2010 Annual Social and Economic supplements.

FIGURE 8-2 POVERTY RATES BY AGE, 1959 TO 2009

Note: The data points are placed at the midpoints of the respective years. Data for people aged eighteen to sixty-four and older are not available from 1960 to 1965.
Source: U.S. Census Bureau, Current Population Survey, 1960 to 2010 Annual Social and Economic supplements.

INCOME INEQUALITIES Wealth is not evenly distributed within the United States. G. William Domhoff (2011) has spent most of his career studying the relationship between income inequality and power in the United States. Interestingly, a recent study showed that most Americans are unaware of how concentrated the wealth is in the United States (Norton and Ariely 2011). The top one percent of households own nearly 35 percent of the privately held wealth (total net worth), the next 19 percent own 50 percent, leaving 15 percent of the wealth to be shared by the bottom 80 percent of households (Wolff 2010). Put another way, the top 1 percent has more than double the cumulative wealth of the bottom 80 precent. If you look at financial wealth (total net worth minus the value of one's home), the inequality is even greater with the top 1 percent having almost 43 percent of the wealth and the bottom 80 percent sharing seven percent. See Tables 8-2 and 8-3.

In 2007, the median income in the United States for people with full-time jobs was $45,113 for men and $35,102 for women (*Current Population Survey*, 2008). (The *median* is the amount at which half of a given population falls above and half falls below.) The median household income was $49,777 in 2009, down from its peak of $50,303 in 2008 (U.S. Bureau of the Census).

TABLE 8-2 SHARE OF WEALTH HELD BY THE BOTTOM 99% AND TOP 1% IN THE UNITED STATES, 1922-2007.

	Bottom 99 percent	Top 1 percent
1922	63.3%	36.7%
1929	55.8%	44.2%
1933	66.7%	33.3%
1939	63.6%	36.4%
1945	70.2%	29.8%
1949	72.9%	27.1%
1953	68.8%	31.2%
1962	68.2%	31.8%
1965	65.6%	34.4%
1969	68.9%	31.1%
1972	70.9%	29.1%
1976	80.1%	19.9%
1979	79.5%	20.5%
1981	75.2%	24.8%
1983	69.1%	30.9%
1986	68.1%	31.9%
1989	64.3%	35.7%
1992	62.8%	37.2%
1995	61.5%	38.5%
1998	61.9%	38.1%
2001	66.6%	33.4%
2004	65.7%	34.3%
2007	65.4%	34.6%

Source: 1922-1989 data from Wolff (1996). 1992-2007 data from Wolff (2010), in Domhoff (2011)

Problems on Wall Street in 2009 placed a spotlight on the inequalities of income. American International Group (AIG), for example, received billions of dollars from the government to assist the company financially. A short time later it was determined that $165 million of the government's bailout money was given as bonuses to AIG's top executives. A total of 298 top executives received bonuses of $100,000 or more. Add to this type of government assistance the tax breaks for large corporations and salary increases, it is easy to see how income inequalities are likely to occur.

CONCEPT OF STATUS The earliest studies of stratification in America were based on the concept of status—people's opinions of other people. Status can be conferred on others for any reason a person chooses—mystical or religious powers, athletic ability, youth or beauty, good deeds—whatever seems appropriate to the person doing the ranking. It was found that in this country, status was conferred on others on the basis of their wealth. However, wealth used to be more obvious than it is today.

A study completed in Middletown during the Great Depression (Lynd and Lynd 1929, 1937) found status differences between the business class and the working class. When the study was originally done, the business class lived in larger and better quality housing than did the working class. The very wealthy had elaborate mansions with indoor plumbing and central heating, whereas working-class homes were much smaller and often lacked indoor plumbing; water had to be carried in from an outdoor well. A wood or coal stove provided heating.

In another study, Middletown (Caplow, et al., 1982) found that it had become more difficult to identify classes among the population. The working class now lives in houses that are only slightly smaller than those of the business class, and they contain all of the amenities that modern society provides—not only indoor plumbing and central heating but also self-cleaning ovens, dishwashers, and other labor saving devices. The wealthy are likely to live relatively modestly in town while spending more of their money less conspicuously

TABLE 8-3 DISTRIBUTION OF NET WORTH AND FINANCIAL WEALTH IN THE UNITED STATES, 1983-2007

	Total Net Worth		
	Top 1 percent	Next 19 percent	Bottom 80 percent
1983	33.8%	47.5%	18.7%
1989	37.4%	46.2%	16.5%
1992	37.2%	46.6%	16.2%
1995	38.5%	45.4%	16.1%
1998	38.1%	45.3%	16.6%
2001	33.4%	51.0%	15.6%
2004	34.3%	50.3%	15.3%
2007	34.6%	50.5%	15.0%
	Financial Wealth		
	Top 1 percent	Next 19 percent	Bottom 80 percent
1983	42.9%	48.4%	8.7%
1989	46.9%	46.5%	6.6%
1992	45.6%	46.7%	7.7%
1995	47.2%	45.9%	7.0%
1998	47.3%	43.6%	9.1%
2001	39.7%	51.5%	8.7%
2004	42.2%	50.3%	7.5%
2007	42.7%	50.3%	7.0%

Source: From Wolff (2004, 2007, & 2010), in Domhoff, 2011.

out of town. Is it more difficult to assign status today simply on the basis of wealth?

LIFE CHANCES

Occupations

For most people, the most important life chance in a society such as the United States is the opportunity to have a successful and respectable occupation or career that provides an adequate income. The upper middle class holds the majority of professional positions—those of doctors, lawyers, business managers, and other high-ranking workers in large organizations. Many people think of the professional person as the typical American worker—educated, earning a comfortable living, owning a home, and sending children to college. Most people in the ordinary ranks of business management, however, need a second worker in the family to afford this higher standard of living.

The majority of people in the United States are considered working class by sociologists because they work in blue-collar jobs—skilled laborers, labor supervisors, and unskilled laborers in industry, or service workers who provide cleaning, maintenance, and other services to those industries. Some sociologists argue that clerical workers, most of whom are women with routine jobs and low pay, should also be considered part of the working class. Strictly speaking, they are not blue-collar workers because they do not wear work clothes or spend their days in a factory

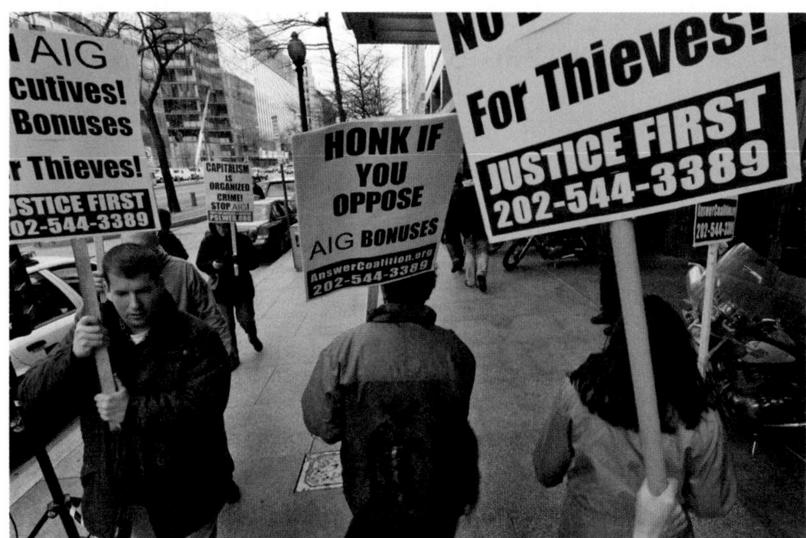

Protesters picket the bonuses and bailout provided to AIG in 2009. With government assistance such as tax breaks to large corporations and salary increases, it's easy to see how income inequalities are likely to occur.

or plant; but they have much in common with working-class people—low wages and strict supervision.

Other working-class occupations pay considerably less than either manufacturing or clerical positions. For one thing, many blue-collar workers, especially construction workers, typically are laid off at some point during the year, which reduces their total annual income. Also, these workers make less than the median income even when there are no layoffs. Many low-paid, working-class people fall below the poverty line and enter the class that has come to be called the "working poor." Most of these people work at jobs that do not pay enough money to bring them out of poverty. The minimum wage in the United States provides income to one person working full-time year-round that is well below the poverty line for a family of four people.

In the widely read work, *Nickel and Dimed: On (Not) Getting By in America* (2001), Barbara Ehrenreich lends a first-hand look at the plight of the working poor in America. Ehrenreich highlights deplorable working conditions, lack of access to affordable housing, and the social isolation endured by those attempting to live on pitifully poor wages.

Housing and Lifestyle

The very rich often own several homes: a family estate, an estate in an exclusive resort area, and a large apartment in an exclusive building in the center of a major city. They spend their leisure time with their wealthy friends and neighbors, and they work together on the boards of banks and corporations. They manage their business affairs with much mutual respect and close cooperation (Domhoff, 2001). Their children usually marry the children of other wealthy families, so that rich families are often related to other rich families; and their wealth remains in the same group. Their housing provides a lifestyle that enables them to know other wealthy people, thereby giving them numerous opportunities to increase their wealth further.

Upper-middle-class managers and professionals, who are near the top 20 percent of earners, are more likely to own homes in the suburbs. Their homes may sometimes be in gated communities or in specific suburban areas. Security alarms, manicured yards, swimming

An estate of the very rich

pools, entertainment rooms, and other luxuries are commonly found in the homes of the upper-middle class. In addition to providing a nice place to live, owning a home has proved to be a good investment because homes increase in value with inflation. The mortgage interest on homes also provides income tax deductions.

The upper-middle class tend to own their homes.

Lower-middle or working-class people are likely to live in the suburbs, but they are less apt to own their own homes. Those who do own homes live in modest neighborhoods and tend to their own yards on the weekends. Those who rent houses or apartments do not have financial buffers from inflation or benefit from homeowner tax deductions. Instead, as prices go up, their rents go up; and they may find it very difficult to maintain their standard of living.

The lower class often finds it very difficult to get adequate, affordable housing. They may live in substandard housing in rural areas or in urban slums, and they often pay high rents for housing. Their neighborhoods may be run down and crime ridden with little pride in the upkeep of properties. Sometimes two or more families share the same overcrowded apartment in order to meet the rent payments.

The lower class may live in substandard housing.

The poorest people in the United States do not have access to housing, living in shelters or on the street. The number of street people is not known, but it is estimated that there are as many as three million homeless in the United States. The homeless have either lost contact with their families or have no families. Some of them may work on a day-to-day basis, but they do not earn enough money to rent a place to live. Others have no income. They sleep in subways, doorways, or on park benches. They are more likely to be the victim of rape or assault, and in winter, they sometimes freeze to death.

In addition, children under the age of eighteen account for 39 percent of the homeless population, one-half million children live in foster homes, and another 130,000 are waiting to be adopted (U.S. Department of Health and Human Services, 2008). Many others are in hospitals, mental health facilities, and detention centers because they have no homes or families who can take care of them.

Homeless children exhibit high degrees of social isolation which is, in turn, related to emotional health concerns such as depression and social anxiety (Anooshian, 2003). Children between kindergarten and 6th grade who live in homeless shelters believe their chances of academic success are virtually unattainable. A recurring theme among shelter parents and children is that their lower social status negatively influences the attitude of school officials toward them (Marcus 2002).

The poor suffer in personal, not so obvious ways, as well. For example, insurance companies have developed the concept of "moral hazards" to justify requiring deductibles from the insured. The idea behind this insurance company practice is that full payment to the insured (without having to pay a deductible) for disasters such as fires or automobile accidents would induce anti-social behavior such as being careless around the home or driving dangerously, thus serving as a "moral hazard." The concept of "moral hazards" has been applied by policy makers to issues such as public assistance, unemployment insurance, and other efforts used to combat unemployment and poverty. Unfortunately, in situations that are completely beyond the control of victims, such as the catastrophic damage caused by Hurricane Katrina, those who can least afford to pay a deductible, the poor, suffer the most consequences. This negative effect of the "moral hazards" approach has led S.M. Miller (2007) to coin the term "immoral hazards"– harming people through governmental or corporate neglect.

Education

The children of the rich are the group most likely to go to private preparatory schools and elite colleges, regardless of their grades. Not only do they earn credentials that are useful in business, but also they make more valuable contacts with influential people who can help them get high-paying positions. Middle-class children ordinarily graduate from public or parochial high schools, and they have an excellent chance of going to college. Working-class children usually complete high school, but only those who achieve very high grades are likely to attend college. Poor children tend to drop out of high school and often live in neighborhoods with poor schools, in which they may not even learn to read and write. Moreover, when they see that high school graduates often have trouble getting jobs, they become discouraged and quit as soon as they are old enough because there is no apparent advantage to staying in school. Education is thus a life chance very closely associated with family wealth.

Medical Care

Medical care is not distributed equally. The rich and the middle classes are usually covered by medical insurance through their employers. Insurance covers most medical expenses, and members of these classes generally receive good medical care. Nearly fifty-one million people in the United States were without health insurance in 2009 (U.S. Census Bureau). The less income you make, the less likely you are to have health insurance. Case in point: 27 percent of people who made less than twenty-five thousand dollars in 2009 did not have health insurance compared to 9 percent of those who made more than seventy-five thousand dollars.

The very poor and homeless see doctors only when the police pick them up and take them to public hospitals. Among the most unfortunate cases seen in emergency rooms are homeless people who are frostbite victims; they may have to have a toe or a foot amputated, only to return to the streets to suffer frostbite again.

In all modern industrialized societies except the United States and South Africa, everyone in the society is covered by a national health system that meets their health needs. As a result, infants are born with full medical care, children are immunized from childhood diseases, and the diseases of adults are treated promptly, usually at no cost to the patient.

On March 23, 2010, President Obama signed into law legislation that would extend health care coverage to thirty-two million people that were not covered. Yet, attorneys general from more than twenty states sought to stop the law from going into effect and every Republican in Congress opposed the law (Clemmit, 2010). The plight of the poor to receive adequate health care will likely continue for some time.

Criminal Justice

Herbert Gans (1971) argues that the poor are punished and identified as deviant more than members of the middle class. The poor are overrepresented within the criminal justice system. Those living in poverty are less likely to be able to afford legal representation and lack the political power to change their fate. The United States incarcerates more people than any other country, with the majority of inmates coming from poverty or low-income homes.

APPLYING KNOWLEDGE OF INEQUALITY AND LIFE CHANCES

Knowledge of the different life chances available to members of different social classes can be used in a number of practical ways. Clinical sociologists and other therapists may use this knowledge to gain a greater understanding of clients from different social classes. As we have seen, people from different social classes have different types of problems and different perspectives on those problems.

Politicians and legislators may rely on this information to help them develop meaningful, relevant, and workable social policies to help the underprivileged. The differential occupational opportunities, living arrangements, education, and medical treatment may strongly influence their psychological makeup. This fact has important implications for what type of policies will or will not succeed. Consider, for example, policies regarding welfare. A welfare program that increases the number of jobs for the poor may look very attractive to someone in the middle or upper class. However, to assume that the mere availability of jobs will enable the downtrodden to compete in the same manner that members of the middle class do is to assume that people from all classes are the same. A welfare program may need to include some type of counseling for recipients to help them gain the confidence and self-esteem necessary for success in a competitive market. Other measures might include education and career training, housing reforms, and improved medical care.

Teachers may also benefit from knowledge of different life chances. The crowded living conditions of some lower-class families may inhibit lower-class students from spending the necessary amount of solitary homework time it takes to understand some subjects. Because their parents may not have experienced the rewards that a good education can bring, lower-class students may not receive the same reinforcement about the importance of studying and achieving good grades that middle-class students do. Lower-class students may not have role models who have achieved upward mobility due to a good education and, as a result, may have a difficult time seeing the value in schoolwork.

Teaching upper-middle-class students and lower-class students, therefore, may require very different teaching strategies. Teachers of lower-class students may need to spend as much time helping their students understand the value and importance of an education as they do with the course material itself; and they may need to explain difficult material more slowly, more intensively, and in more ways during class time rather than expect students to master the material at home.

They might also spend time teaching student about workplace culture and behavioral expectations that might differ from the expectations of their daily lives. Jay McLeod (1995) in his classic ethnography, *Ain't No Makin' It: Aspirations and Attainment in a Low-income Neighborhood,* points out that students adapt to their living conditions by exhibiting behaviors that are not appropriate for the workplace. Therefore, they are unprepared for the social demands and expectations that accompany working in and for the public.

These examples are only a few ways in which knowledge of how life chances relate to position in the stratification system can he used. Consider how you could use this knowledge in a career that you are thinking about entering. Also consider how you can use this knowledge to understand how to get ahead. Are people more or less stuck in their social strata, or can they get ahead?

Thinking Sociologically

1. Social class influences the life chances of individuals in what ways? Choose one of the middle class categories identified by the Pew Research Center and discuss the life chances of a member if he/she lived in your city. Discuss the following: income, neighborhood, work, play, school, church, healthcare, and so on. Use specific examples from your city to illustrate the specific class.
2. Develop an explanation for the inequalities found within school systems that are public education facilities.
3. Discuss the pros and cons of having a national healthcare system where all members of society are covered by insurance, regardless of their social class ranking.

SOCIAL MOBILITY IN THE UNITED STATES

Social mobility—changing social position—can occur in a variety of ways. A change to a job of higher rank or marriage to a person of higher rank is **upward mobility**, and a movement to a job of lower rank is **downward mobility**. Sometimes, marrying someone of a lower rank can produce downward mobility.

Persons who change class or status within their own lifetimes experience **intragenerational mobility**. Mobility between generations, or **intergenerational mobility**, is traditionally measured by comparing the social positions of parents and children. If sons or daughters have higher positions than their parents had, they are upwardly mobile; if the younger generation's position is lower, they are downwardly mobile. Both the social structure and individual characteristics influence upward and downward mobility.

Structural Characteristics of Mobility in the United States

Mobility in this country is influenced by numerous factors: (a) growth of large corporations; (b) increased standard of living; (c) growth of urban areas; (d) maintenance of a split labor market, which splinters the labor pool in ways that minimize mobility; and (e) advanced technology, such as reliance on computers and robots.

The growth of large corporations has influenced the wages people are paid. Those who work in large organizations often earn more than those who work in small firms. People in supervisory positions earn a percentage more than the people they supervise, and their earnings generally increase as the number of people they supervise increases. Thus, as corporations grow larger, supervisors earn more. Many qualified people in large organizations never have the opportunity to be supervisors, however; and despite their high qualifications, they will never be able to earn the income of the supervisor.

The increasing standard of living over the past century has improved the lives of most workers in the United States, even though their relative class or status remains unchanged. This improvement is especially true of factory workers, whose wages and living conditions have improved dramatically since the turn of the century.

The growth of urban areas, where the cost of living is higher, has led to higher wages for city dwellers. Equally qualified people doing the same work are apt to earn more money in the city than in the country. Doctors, for example, earn considerably more in large metropolitan areas than in rural areas.

A split labor market is one in which some jobs afford upward mobility and others do not. The job market is split between manual and nonmanual work and is further segmented within these spheres. White-collar workers cannot move into higher-level manual work or into the professions, which normally require extensive educational certification. Manual workers cannot be promoted into the skilled crafts or into white-collar positions. Farmers are completely outside the main sphere of upward mobility.

The **split labor market** provides even greater obstacles for women, the poor, and minority groups, of whom most work in the lowest ranks of manual and nonmanual occupations. Their jobs often have no career paths at all, and the poor rarely get the opportunity for professional training or apprenticeships in the skilled crafts. In recent years, robots do more and more manual jobs (or corporations have moved such jobs overseas where labor is cheaper). Not only is there no mobility in manual work, but also the number of manual-labor jobs is shrinking. Thus, increased technology has eliminated some jobs involving manual labor and has increased the number of white-collar clerical and service jobs.

Furthermore, even if a move from a low-paying assembly-line job to a low-paying desk job were likely, should it be considered upward mobility; or is it movement that does not bring with it any real advantages? Some sociologists argue that white-collar work has a higher status; but others contend that this shift merely changes the nature of work, not the class or status of the worker.

Individual Characteristics and Upward Mobility

A basic assumption of structural functional theory is that society rewards people who develop leadership skills through education and hard work. Researchers have conducted many studies to learn about the characteristics of individuals who succeed. These studies,

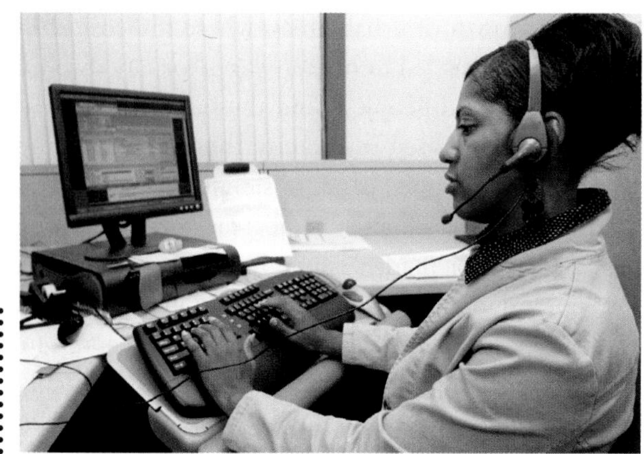

Increased technology has increased the number of white-collar and clerical and service jobs.

most of which were concerned with men, have examined the influence of such factors as family background, grades in school, years of education, and attitudes.

The attitudes of young men from Wisconsin were thoroughly studied by William Sewell (Sewell, et al., 1975), who found no relationship between attitude and success. The research did show that those Wisconsin boys whose attitudes were ambitious (i.e., who desired an occupation of a higher status than that of their fathers) often found it necessary to change their attitudes when they did not have the opportunity to reach their goals. In most cases, people get discouraged when they cannot obtain the training required for a particular occupation and then adjust their attitudes to suit what they can attain.

Family background is the factor that most accurately predicts the future earnings of men, not upward mobility. Anywhere from 15 to 50 percent of the variation in men's earnings appears to be related to family background. Men from families with high incomes generally make more money than those from families with low incomes. The studies do not, however, explain why family income is related to a son's future earnings. Structural functionalists argue that sons from families with high incomes usually have all of the advantages believed to contribute to future moneymaking ability. Their parents can teach their sons important skills, and they live in neighborhoods in which their friends have the same advantages. Because of family advantages, they are likely to do well in high school and to attend college.

Structural functionalists believe that the best way to increase upward mobility in the U.S. is to increase the opportunities available to children from poor families. Such a move would involve providing better preschool education, better public school education (including the opportunity to attend schools with young people from wealthier backgrounds), and the opportunity to go on to college or technical schools.

Conflict theorists criticize the notions that sons from high-income families succeed because they are better educated or that the poor can enter the upper class through increased education. Women and blacks have demonstrated that advanced education does not guarantee upward mobility. This fact may discourage members of minority groups, who may find it difficult to spend the time and money required to receive a higher education if they believe they will not be rewarded for their efforts. Conflict theorists contend that opportunity and equality for the poor will be brought about only through changes in the stratification system and in the distribution of wealth.

THEORIES OF SOCIAL STRATIFICATION

Why are societies stratified? How is it that some people have more of the scarce resources society has to offer? This question was widely debated by early sociologists. As mentioned in Chapter 2, Spencer believed that superior people would educate themselves and become leaders, whereas inferior people would remain in the bottom ranks of society. Society, he said, developed through an evolutionary process, and those who profited from natural selection—"survival of the fittest"—came out on top. This process of natural selection was good for social progress, he argued, and society should not interfere with it.

Marx, who argued that stratification would eventually cause revolution, formulated the opposing view. The upper class in industrial society hired the proletariat to work in their factories, exploited them for profit, and drove them into poverty. As the proletariat became poorer, Marx contended, they would become aware of their plight and would revolt. The theories of these early European writers have had a strong influence on modern theories of stratification and have resulted in the structural functional theory and the conflict theory.

Structural Functional Theory

Structural functionalists have refined Spencer's notion that society, like any other organism, is self-regulating and self-maintaining. It consists of interrelated parts that serve a function in maintaining the system as a whole. When they recognized that stratification was a persistent force in society, they argued that it must serve some function. They hypothesized that because modern society is so complex, people with strong leadership skills are needed to organize and run the complex businesses and industries. People with strong leadership abilities need advanced training and must be willing to work very hard and assume a great deal of responsibility. Society must encourage these efforts by rewarding leaders with wealth and status—scarce resources that in turn can be used to gain power.

In terms of inherent worth as a human being, Davis and Moore (1945) acknowledged that an artist or a teacher might be equal to a corporate executive. The talents of artists and teachers, however, are not as scarce and therefore not as valuable to the society, according to Davis and Moore. Thus, corporate executives who have the talent to lead business and industry are more highly rewarded, not because they are more worthwhile human beings but because they are making greater contributions to the functioning of society. This theoretical perspective permits a belief in human equality at the same time that it explains inequality. If society had an equal need for all types of work, then all its members would be equal in the stratification system.

Conflict Theory

Conflict theorists reject the functional viewpoint (Duberman 1976), arguing that inequality develops as a result of people's desire for power and that close-knit groups compete with one another to gain possession of the scarce resources that are a source of power. According to this view, resources are not rewards for talent or for assuming difficult tasks but are acquired through inheritance, coercion, or exploitation. Inequality results when one group acquires more resources than other groups.

Once a dominant group gets power, according to conflict theorists, the group **legitimates** its power and makes it acceptable by appealing to the values of the masses. Politicians often use democratic values, a mandate from the people, to legitimate their stands on issues. The powerful may point to progress as a value to gain support for everything from expenditures for scientific research to acceptance of a polluted environment. Corporations may appeal directly to patriotic values to justify their opposition to a raise in corporate taxes—what is good for the corporation is good for the nation; or they may appeal to the value of equal opportunity, arguing that such a raise would cost jobs. These beliefs and perceptions, when accepted by the masses, become the prevailing **ideology**. *Ideology* refers to a set of cultural beliefs, values, and attitudes that legitimate the status quo as well as attempts to change it.

If the masses are influenced by elite ideology, they are said to have **false consciousness**, a lack of awareness of their own interests and an acceptance of elite rule. If, on the other hand, the masses are aware that people's fates are tied to the fate of their own class, they are said to have **class-consciousness**. For example, if people realize that which neighborhood school they attend is determined by how much money they have, they have class-consciousness.

Theories of social stratification are important not only because they help us to understand why some basic social inequalities exist, but also because they provide a basis on which politicians and legislators may develop social policies. For example, whether a politician favors increased government spending on social services (such as welfare, Medicaid, food stamps, and shelters for the homeless) may have to do with his or her understanding of why people need such services. A politician who believes that poverty exists because of individuals' unwillingness or lack of motivation to work hard may oppose government spending. Conversely, a politician who believes that poverty exists because of basic inequities in the system may support government spending. Issues such as these often have no clear answers, but theories of social stratification can offer politicians important insights for dealing with them and can prevent them from relying solely on their own values and beliefs.

Attempts at Synthesis

Some sociologists have tried to reconcile the functional and conflict theories of stratification (Dahrendorf 1951;

Lenski 1966; Tumin 1963). Accumulating research suggests that stratification has a wide variety of causes—some based on conflict, some on cooperation. A stratification system based on religion, for example, may emphasize feelings of community and selflessness. Others, based on land ownership or accumulation of money, may emphasize competition and the efforts of individuals. As our understanding of the nature and development of stratification improves, it is becoming increasingly apparent that stratification is influenced by a great many different factors: how food is grown, how supplies are manufactured and distributed, how much wealth accumulates, and how people use their leisure time, only to name a few. Neither functional nor conflict theory offers us a full understanding of how stratification systems develop.

There is, however, widespread agreement that all stratification systems are based on the consensus among members of the society that inequality is good, fair, and just. People may accept stratification because they value the achievements of the wealthy or because the media have misled. Whatever the reason, acceptance of the stratification system confers power on those of high rank.

CHAPTER REVIEW

Wrapping it up

Summary

1. Inequality develops as a result of the unequal distribution of scarce resources. People are differentiated, but not usually ranked, on the basis of many criteria: hair color, height, hobbies, or region of the country in which they live.

2. People are ranked, or stratified, on the basis of their possession of or access to scarce resources.

3. Very simple societies have little division of labor and little stratification. Agrarian and industrial societies have more wealth, greater division of labor, and more stratification.

4. There are four types of stratification systems that have existed in the world: (1) In *caste systems*, positions are assigned at birth, according to the position of the caste, and a person's caste is fixed for life. (2) In *estate systems*, position is determined by law or through inheritance. (3) In *slave systems*, position is assigned at birth, and (4) in *class systems*, found in industrial societies, a person may be able to move into higher or lower strata. Sources of power in a class-based society include class position, status, and party position.

5. Determinants of class position within the United States include social class, social status, and power. Many sociologists are using SES to determine class position.

6. Most people identify themselves as middle class, but lifestyles of Americans vary widely, most importantly in terms of occupation, housing, health care, and educational opportunity, even within the middle class.

7. Life chances for occupations, housing, education, and medical care vary, are in relation to a person's place in the stratification system.

8. Upward mobility is most influenced by structural changes in the workplace. The proliferation and increasing size of large corporations has improved the standard of living for many workers. The segmented or split labor market has limited upward mobility for lower-class people.

9. Structural functionalists believe that systems of stratification develop because societies need scarce leadership skills and reward those who are willing to assume the responsibility of leadership.

10. Conflict theorists contend that stratification develops because some groups gain a monopoly of the scarce resources through either inheritance or conflict, and they use those resources to maintain their high positions.

Key Terms

advanced horticultural societies Societies with irrigation systems and other advanced farming practices

agrarian societies Complex societies with farming, armies, merchants, and a concentration of wealth in the hands of a few people

caste system A system of stratification in which one's social position is ascribed at birth, one's value is assessed in terms of religious or traditional beliefs, and in which upward social mobility is impossible

class consciousness Awareness among members of a society that the society is stratified

class system A system of stratification found in industrial societies in which one's class is determined by one's wealth and in which vertical social mobility is possible

closed system A system of stratification in which there is no movement from one rank to another

division of labor A situation in which some people do certain specialized occupations

downward mobility A move to a position of lower rank in the stratification system

estate system A system of stratification in which one's social position is ascribed by law or through inheritance

false consciousness Lack of awareness of class differences and acceptance of upper-class rule

hunting-and-gathering societies Small, often nomadic societies that have no agriculture and live on food that is found

ideology A set of ideas about what society is like, how it functions, whether it is good or bad, and how it should be changed

industrial societies Societies with great division of labor, highly specialized work, and a great concentration of wealth

inequality Differences between groups in wealth, status, or power

intergenerational mobility A change of social position or rank, up or down, from one generation to the next, such as when children have a higher status than their parents

intragenerational mobility A change of social position or rank, up or down, within one's own lifetime

legitimate To make the power of the dominant group acceptable to the masses so they let the dominant group rule without question

life chances The opportunities a person has to improve his or her income and lifestyle

mechanical solidarity The idea of Durkheim in which people do similar work but are not very dependent on one another (in contrast to organic solidarity, in which people are very dependent on others)

open system A system of stratification in which it is possible to move to a higher or lower position

organic solidarity Durkheim's term for the integration of society that results from the division of labor

poverty Having fewer resources than are required to meet the basic necessities of life. Rates are usually based on a government index of income relative to size of family and farm/nonfarm residence

power The ability to control or influence the behavior of others, even without their consent

simple horticultural societies Societies that grow food using very simple tools, such as digging sticks

slave system A system of stratification in which one's position was ascribed at birth and based on race

social class A category of people who have approximately the same amount of power and wealth and the same life chances to acquire wealth

social differentiation The difference or variation of people based on selected social characteristics such as class, gender, race, or age

social status The amount of honor and prestige a person receives from others in the community; also, the position one occupies in the stratification system

social stratification The ranking of people according to their wealth, prestige, or party position

socioeconomic status (SES) An assessment of status that takes into account a person's income, education, and occupation

split labor market A labor market in which some jobs afford upward mobility and others do not

upward mobility Movement in the stratification system to a position of greater wealth, status, and power

Discussion Questions

1. Discuss the functions of the stratification system in American society. Discuss its dysfunctions.
2. Look through your campus newspaper, and find ways that groups legitimate their political positions.
3. Discuss the extent of class consciousness you would expect to find on your campus and in your community. Do you think people are very aware of class? Would the people you know use the same categories of class used in the Jackman and Jackman study?
4. What people have the most power in your community? Do they have power because of their wealth, their status, or their position in an organization? Explain.
5. Has the quality of your education been influenced by the amount of money your family has?
6. Discuss how poverty affects those involved with the criminal justice system. Are those living in poverty more likely to be victims or offenders? Explain.
7. How does the split labor market lead to further separation between the rich and the poor?

Pop Quiz

1. How people vary according to social characteristics is known as ______.

   a. social differentiation
   b. social stratification
   c. social roles
   d. social status

2. The greatest degree of stratification is found in ________ societies.

   a. simple horticultural
   b. advanced horticultural
   c. agrarian
   d. industrial

3. Durkheim argued that an increased division of labor created ______.

   a. organic solidarity
   b. organic disintegration
   c. mechanical solidarity
   d. mechanical disintegration

4. Which of the following is true in a case system?:

   a. Class does not exist
   b. Class is ascribed at birth
   c. Class is achieved
   d. Classes are fluid

5. Social status refers to ______.

   a. accumulated wealth
   b. accumulated consumer goods
   c. honor and prestige given by the community
   d. life chances to improve income

6. Opportunities that people have to improve their income are termed ______.

   a. social class
   b. life chances
   c. contacts
   d. connections

7. Which of the following is true according to structural-functional theory?

   a. Stratification is an unnecessary aspect of society
   b. Society has an equal need for all types of work
   c. Stratification and inequality are created by the needs of society
   d. Stratification is due to people's desire for power

8. If the masses are influenced by elite ideology, they have what Marx called ______.

   a. class consciousness
   b. caste consciousness
   c. false consciousness
   d. political consciousness

9. In examining the distribution of income and wealth in the United States, which of the following is most true?

   a. A relatively small percentage of the population has a relatively large proportion of the income and wealth
   b. A relatively large percentage of the population controls a relatively large proportion of the income and wealth
   c. A relatively large percentage of the population holds a relatively small proportion of the wealth
   d. Income is spread fairly evenly throughout the population

10. Kristy holds a higher social position than her father, Ken. She has experienced ______.

   a. intergenerational mobility
   b. intragenerational mobility
   c. horizontal mobility
   d. downward mobility

11. The greatest equality is found in hunting-and-gathering societies. T/F

12 Caste systems allow no social mobility. T/F

13. Conflict theorists argue that because stratification is so persistent, it must be functional for societies. T/F

14. Americans are said to be extremely class conscious. T/F

15. The research of Sewell and others found a strong relationship between attitude and success. T/F

1. A	6. A	11. T
2. D	7. C	12. T
3. A	8. C	13. F
4. B	9. A	14. F
5. C	10. A	15. F

CHAPTER 9

Racial and Ethnic Differentiation

HOME WAS A HORSE STALL

Throughout history America has attracted immigrants from places far and wide. It is ironic that while one of America's greatest attractions for immigrants is its ideal of equality, racial and ethnic minorities have been discriminated against since the birth of our nation. The treatment of Native Americans, the first group to encounter immigrants, was harsh and brutal, eventually leading to a near extermination of an entire culture (or cultures) of people. Slavery was the next step in creating differences among the citizens of the United States. Brought to America against their will, Blacks were subjected to the worst kind of torture and humiliation cast upon a group of people. Labeled as two-thirds of a human by the first Census, Blacks were seen as property rather than as people. Given freedom after being enslaved for over two hundred years, Blacks could only dream of equality in a country that refused to recognize their existence. The era of Jim Crow segregation further alienated Blacks from Whites and created harsh divisions that would last for the next one hundred years.

Historically, Americans have professed the belief that people of all races are created equal and that all should have an equal chance to obtain society's benefits. Our actions, which reflect inequality to most racial and ethnic groups migrating from somewhere other than European counties, belie our words. The "melting pot" mentality led us to falsely believe that America was one culture, assimilated from many others, into one. Therefore, as John Macionis (2004) points out, some of our most dominant cultural beliefs actually contradict one another, an observation that echoes the arguments in the early mid-twentieth century advanced in the classic work by Gunnar Myrdal, *An American Dilemma* (1944). More specifically, according to sociologists Elliot Currie and Jerome Skolnick, "American history is also the history of the conquest, enslavement, and exclusion of racial minorities. The vision of racial equality and the harsh reality of unequal treatment have coexisted uneasily from the beginning" (1988, 136).

An example of the level of intolerance inflicted on a group of people can be found in the stories of Japanese-Americans during World War II. Americans, born on American soil, were treated as terrorists by a country that refused to acknowledge their citizenship. An immediate backlash against Japanese-Americans occurred after the bombing of Pearl Harbor. On February 19, 1942, a little more than two months after the bombing, President Franklin D. Roosevelt issued Executive Order 9066, which established military internment camps for all people of Japanese decent. The 112,000 Japanese Americans had one week to prepare for evacuation. Two-thirds of them citizens of the United States, Japanese-Americans had to close their stores, sell their belongings, and discard what couldn't be carried in a suitcase.

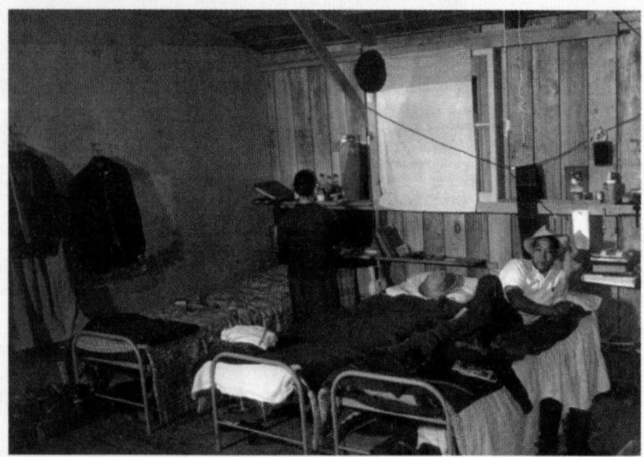

Japanese-Americans were forced to live in military internment camps such as this one during World War II.

For some Japanese-Americans, a horse stall at a racetrack in California became home. Barracks lined the infield for mothers with infants, while the rest were ushered into stalls and given sacks to fill with hay for mattresses. Having five people to a nine-foot by twenty-foot horse stall was not uncommon, and over the next four months life was nearly unbearable. Then, the U.S. government provided them with new quarters that measured twenty feet by twenty-four feet, located in the desert. Barbed wire, police with weapons, and isolation from the outside world, was the everyday norm; and a rule violation could likely end in death.

By 1943 the war was going strong, and President Roosevelt issued a letter to the Secretary of War stating, "Americanism is not, and never was, a matter of race or ancestry. Every loyal American citizen should be given the opportunity to serve this country in the ranks of our armed forces" (Carnes, 2008). Over thirty thousand Japanese-Americans served in the United States Armed Forces during World War II.

In 1944, the Civilian Order was lifted, and within a year the camps were closed. It took another forty years for the United States government to issue the Civil Liberties Act of 1988 granting reparations to the survivors of the internment camps. The treatment of Japanese-Americans serves as a reminder that most minorities wear the invisible tag of minority status. In other words, at any given time, and without much cause, a group of people can be singled out for no other reason than the color of their skin or the country of their origin. When that happens, their tag will be in full view as a reminder to themselves and others that inequality can rear its ugly head in America very quickly.

The Civil Rights Memorial located in Montgomery, Alabama, along with the civil rights museum housed in Memphis,

Tennessee where Dr. King was assassinated, are tributes to the lives lost as a result of racial inequality. Their dedication to the pursuit of racial equality is symbolized in the statement by Martin Luther King, Jr., now found on the wall in the Alabama memorial: "until justice rolls down like waters and righteousness like a mighty stream".

As you read this chapter, keep in mind the contributions that all racial and ethnic groups in America have contributed to making our country so powerful. Understanding the subtleties and intricacies of race and ethnicity and of racism and discrimination is extremely important. With the proportion of minorities expected to increase substantially over the next few decades, the United States will likely experience heightened racial tensions. It is our hope that this chapter will provide you with knowledge to help you reach your own conclusions about the reasons for racial and ethnic inequality and help you to make informed decisions that might have an impact on the future of racial and ethnic equality.

The United States is aptly called "a nation of nations." The diversity of the country's social and cultural life is a result of the many different groups who have migrated here. Can you imagine how monotonous life would be if people were all the same? Almost everyone enjoys the cultural sights, sounds, and smells of Chinatown. Greek, Italian, or Japanese cuisine is a welcome change from the usual American diet of hamburger and French fries. We also benefit from our diverse cultural heritage in many more important ways as well.

Racial and ethnic relations in the United States, however, are far from smooth. Our history has been marked by conflict, competition, prejudice, and discrimination. In this chapter, we identify the major racial and ethnic groups in North America and discuss some of the causes and consequences of stereotyping, prejudice, discrimination, racism, and racial inequality. We also consider two approaches, the pluralistic and integrationist perspectives, which may help to reduce racial and ethnic inequality.

RACIAL, ETHNIC, AND MINORITY GROUPS

The terms *racial*, *ethnic*, and *minority* are often used interchangeably and rather loosely. Although they may be treated as equivalent or overlapping concepts, it is important to differentiate these terms before we discuss the more substantive issues of race and ethnic relations.

Race and Racial Groups

The concept of race has a long history, even though the term "race" has only been around for a short period of time. Race is one of the most arbitrary and misunderstood concepts used by our society. A **racial group** is a socially constructed category of people who are distinguished from each other by select physical characteristics. These traits typically include basic physical attributes such as facial features, body type, skin color, hair texture, and so on. Definitions of race can include biological, physical, and social meanings.

The essential question is whether there are significant variations in the physical traits of different populations of humans. The focus of investigation has ranged from obvious characteristics, such as skin and hair coloring, to less obvious traits, such as blood type and genetically transmitted diseases.

The effects of climate have complicated classification of peoples by skin color. It has been found that varying degrees of exposure to sunlight causes variations in skin shading. Asians and Africans have darker coloring because they live in more tropical climates. Classification by skin color is further complicated by biological mixing—for example, the Creoles of Alabama and Mississippi, the Red Bones of Louisiana, the Croatians of North Carolina, and the Mestizos of South America. Whether members of these groups have Native American or African American ancestors is a matter of dispute.

In reality, truly objective criteria of racial groups based strictly on physical or biological characteristics do not seem to exist. In the past few decades, sociologists and anthropologists have concluded that race is primarily a social construct rather than a biological one. That is, it is a concept that has been defined by humans to help make sense of social worlds, but it is far from clear if we can make distinctions about humans based upon inherited physical characteristics. The trend in current thinking among social scientists and many natural scientists is that we cannot.

What may be of more importance is how and why race has been defined over the years. Some feel that the concept of race developed by the dominant groups in the world as a mechanism to prejudge, divide, rank and control populations that are different than themselves. Regardless of the reasons for the development of the concept of race, it does seem clear that it distorts our ideas about differences among different groups throughout the world and contributes to myths about their behaviors and characteristics, and also contributes to the perpetuation of inequality of dominant groups over minority groups. (American Anthropological Association 1998; Morning 2009).

The concept of race found popularity in the United States during slavery and Jim Crow segregation. In the mid-1600's the fear of a degenerative race led many colonies to create laws forbidding marriage between Blacks, Indians, and Whites. After slavery, a one-drop rule was put in place that required any person with one-drop of African blood to identify themselves as Black. The case of Susie Guillory Phipps, for example, highlights the problems generations of children encountered after the one-drop rule was ended. In 1982, Phipps went to the Department of Vital Records in Louisiana to get a birth certificate. Upon receiving it she noticed the race box on her certificate was marked "Black", rather than "White". Thinking a mistake had clearly been made Phipps brought it to the attention of the employee. The agency informed Phipps that no mistake was made and that she was correctly identified as Black even though her parents, grandparents, and great-grandparents were White. Phipps took her case all the way to the Louisiana Supreme Court which upheld the lower court's ruling that Ms. Phipps was indeed legally "Black". During the trial, the government produced a family tree tracing eleven generations of her family that included a Black slave and White plantation owner. At the time of Phipps birth, the legal one-drop rule was still in place, identifying her as Black, regardless of her social identity.

In the 1600s many U.S. colonies had laws forbidding marriage between people of different races.

Social and cultural conceptions of race, regardless of their lack of having a biological basis, are probably the most important meaning with regard to the individual being labeled. A person will typically associate themselves with those who validate their racial identity. For example, people who are of mixed Black and White heritage and who identify themselves as Black will likely want to authenticate their identity to others including their social circle, peers, class, etc. In 2000, the U.S. Census, which relies on self-definition, for the first time allowed individuals to mark "all that apply" with regard to race. As a result, 6.8 million people, or 2.4 percent of the population, identified themselves as multiracial. In the case of Susie Phipps, legally she is Black; however, her social identity remains White as a result of how she and society sees her race. In 2010, 9 million people identified themselves as multiracial, or 2.9 percent of the population.

In review, social definitions far outweigh biological definitions or race, but these social definitions are based on some combination of some inherited physical traits, regardless of any evidence that there are clear and distinct physical differences or that any such differences can explain human behavior. Some physical traits —such as hair color, height, and size of feet—may be inherited, however, these are rarely used to differentiate people into one racial category or another, where as other physical traits—such as skin color—may be used. Taking these considerations into account, biological differences per se do not constitute racial differences. Rather, a racial group is a socially defined group distinguished by selected physical characteristics, even though such are difficult to ascertain.

ETHNICITY AND ETHNIC GROUPS The word *ethnic* is derived from the Greek word ethnikos, which translates to mean "nations" in English. The word was initially applied to European immigrants such as the Italians, Germans, Poles, and other national groups who came to the United States in large numbers, especially between 1900 and 1925. Today, ethnicity is given a wider definition and may also refer to group membership based on religion, language, or region. Using the word in this sense, Jews, Mormons, Latinos, and White Southerners can be considered **ethnic groups**.

Again, whereas race is based on socially constructed definitions using selected physical characteristics such as skin color, hair texture, or eye color and shape, ethnicity is based on cultural traits that reflect national origin, religion, and language. Characteristics of an ethnic group may include unique cultural traits, ascribed membership, sense of community, ethnocentrism, and territoriality.

Unique cultural traits refer to a group's attributes that set them apart from other groups in society. A group's manner of dress, language, religious practices, or speech patterns can create an ethnic identity. Ethnic groups are often seen as subcultures within a larger society who possess unique cultural traits that set them apart from the dominant group. However, cultural traits alone will not set one group apart from the other. There are many groups within society who display unique behavior who are not seen as an ethnic group. While persons from New York may display differences in language and mannerism from persons in Texas, neither would be seen as an ethnic group.

Ascribed membership means the person's ethnic characteristics were ascribed at birth. When an individual is born into an ethnic group, it is unlikely he/she will leave unless there are unusual circumstances. For example, a person may be born into the Jewish culture, but choose to leave and adopt the culture of another group, such as Christianity or Catholicism.

Sense of community exists when an ethnic group displays a sense of common association among its members. Sociologist Milton Gordon (1964) suggests the ethnic group serves as a social-psychological reference for creating a "sense of peoplehood". This sense of we-ness is derived from a common ancestry or origin when people sense a community, an awareness of belonging to a group. However, the common ancestry does not have to be authentic, as long as the ethnic group (or others) perceive themselves as a community. Therefore, just like race, ethnicity is socially created and maintained.

Among other attributes, an ethnic identity can be created from a group's manner of dress.

Ethnocentrism is another common characteristic among ethnic groups. When a group has a sense of peoplehood, they have a tendency to judge other groups by the standards and values of their own. Group solidarity serves as a source of ethnocentrism, or the belief that one's own group is superior to others. The norms, values, beliefs, attitudes, and behaviors of one's own group are perceived as natural or correct while other groups are seen as unnatural or incorrect.

Territoriality refers to the idea of "nations within nations", where groups occupy distinct territories within the larger society. Enclaves of ethnic groups can be found in larger communities where they have some degree of autonomy away from the dominant culture. Stores, restaurants, community centers and other facilities accommodate or are owned by members of the ethnic group.

In the United States, the largest identified ethnic group is "Hispanic". However, within this category are a number of other ethnic groups including Mexicans, Spaniards, Puerto Ricans, Cubans, and others. Each has distinctive cultures in America, which can create problems when classified as one ethnic group.

Minority Groups

The concept of a **minority group**, according to sociologists, refers to a group's access to power and status within a society. First used in World War I peace treaties, a minority group's size is insignificant to their being labeled as a subordinate category of people. Women, for example, are a numerical majority in American society, yet they have historically held a minority status within society. In the Republic of South Africa, Whites comprise less than one-fifth of the total population, but are considered the dominant majority group. In a similar fashion, Schaeffer (2005) argues that a *minority group*, generally, has significantly less control or power over their own lives than do the members of a dominant or majority group. Schaeffer suggests that minorities, as subordinated members of a society, experience more than a loss of control or power over their own lives: they also experience a narrowing of life's opportunities for success, education, wealth, and the pursuit of happiness. In other words, a minority group does not share, in proportion to its numbers, what a given society defines as valuable (Schaeffer 2005).

In the United States, the most highly valued norms have historically been those created by White, Anglo-Saxon, Protestant (WASP) middle classes. Even today, WASP norms, values, cultural patterns, standards of beauty, and laws are widely observed and enforced. A minority group will be distinguished from other groups (including other minority groups) in terms of where the group is situated in society's social hierarchy. The extent of the group's departure from the norms established by the dominant group will define their social status within society.

According to the above discussion, the elderly, poor people, poor people in Appalachia, southern Whites, disabled persons, gays and lesbians and members of most diversity populations are minority groups in the United States. Prior to discussing any specific racial, ethnic, or minority groups, we examine various types of attitudes, behaviors, and patterns of group interaction.

Thinking Sociologically

1. To what extent is race, based solely on biological, legal, or social criteria in the U.S. today?
2. Using the ideas of interactionist theory, explain the social significance of groups as racial, ethnic, or minority categories.

ATTITUDES, BEHAVIORS, AND THEIR INFLUENCE

One of the most serious problems faced by most racial and ethnic groups in America and around the world concerns how they are perceived and treated by others. For a number of reasons, people tend to treat those they perceive to be different in ways that they would not treat members of their own group. As a result, rising inequalities have increased societal strains and tensions among different groups. To pursue ideals of equality, we must understand how the attitudes underlying unfair practices are formed.

Stereotypes

Stereotypes are exaggerated beliefs usually associated with a group of people and based on race, ethnicity, gender, religion, or sexual orientation. Stereotypes generally begin with a particular belief about an undesirable characteristic of a group. Through interaction with others, the socially constructed belief will persist and be generalized to the entire group, thus creating a stereotype. Stereotypes often, but not always, develop out of fear or when the dominant group feels threatened by a particular group.

Stereotypes can persist over time; however, they usually change regularly. For example, the images of Jews have changed repeatedly throughout history, from shrewd and materialistic to intelligent and savvy. With many racial and ethnic stereotypes there exists a "kernel of truth" with a perceived belief.

In other words, there may be group members who possess the characteristic used as the foundation of the stereotype; however, it does not apply to the entire group, and it may be an exaggeration of that "kernel of truth." Needless to say, stereotypes do not begin to address the great variety of behavior that exists among members of diverse populations.

The media plays a significant role in the establishment and persistence of stereotypes about racial and ethnic groups. Consider the stereotypes that were reinforced by the television series *The Sopranos* that aired for eight years (1999-2007). In 2004, Italian-American groups confronted Dream Works SKG about the ethnic slurs and stereotypes that were perpetuated by the movie *Shark Tale*, especially since the intended audience of the movie was children. In the movie, Don Lino is the godfather of great white sharks. The Italian American groups who protested felt "The movie introduces young minds to the idea that people with Italian names—like millions of Americans across the country—are gangsters" (Reuters 2004).

Stereotypes are rarely used to create positive images of a racial or ethnic group; instead, they are used to tear down the social value of a particular group within society. When stereotyped group members themselves begin to internalize the belief, they will act toward themselves accordingly. Several researchers have focused on how children form racial identities (Clark and Clark 1939; Spencer, Brookin, and Allen 1985), as well as how children form attitudes about others based on race (Ausdale and Feagin 1996). Clark and Clark (1947) examined how Black children see themselves during play. Provided with identical black and white dolls (except for the color), Black children were more likely to see the white doll as more positive, pretty, nice, etc., while identifying the black doll as bad, negative, or ugly. In a similar vein, Radke and Trager's (1950) early studies of Black children support the idea that members of a stereotyped minority tend to internalize the definitions attached to them. In their study, the children were asked to evaluate black and white dolls and to tell stories about Black and White persons in photographs. The children overwhelmingly preferred the white dolls to the black ones; the white dolls were described as good, the black dolls as bad. The black individuals in the photographs were given inferior roles as servants, maids, or gardeners.

Later studies of self-esteem, however, tended to find little or no difference between Blacks and Whites. Zirkel (1971) reviewed over a dozen studies of Black and White students attending grammar and secondary schools and concluded that Black and White children have similar levels of self-esteem. Simmons et al. (1978) found that minority students have even stronger self-concepts than majority students. This change in attitudes can be linked to the civil rights movements of the late 1960s and early 1970s, when emerging ethnic pride began to be expressed in such slogans as "Red Power" and "Black is beautiful." However, in 2006 Kiri Davis, a young filmmaker recreated the Clark and Clark study and found Black children are still influenced greatly by the stereotype that white is socially accepted more than black. In her seven-minute video, Davis asked the children to "pick the doll that is nice", with fifteen out of twenty-one Black children choosing the white doll.

Another effect of stereotypes that has become controversial in recent years is the practice of racial and ethnic profiling. Profiling is the practice of subjecting people to increased surveillance or scrutiny based on racial or ethnic factors, without any other basis (Chan 2011). For example, Black citizens undergo significantly more repeated motor vehicle stops by police than White citizens. Growette-Bostaph found that this was not the result of differences in driving behavior but as the result of being members of different population groups (2008).

Stereotyping is not entirely dysfunctional. Albrecht et al. (1980, 254) argued, that "Stereotypes afford us the comfort of recognition and save us the time and effort of interpreting masses of new stimuli hourly." They help us mentally sort people into predictable categories and make social interaction easier. Most of our encounters are dominated by stereotyped conceptions of how we should act and how others should respond. Most would agree, however, that the dysfunctional aspects of stereotyping far outweigh the functional aspects.

Prejudice

One dysfunction of stereotyping is prejudice. **Prejudice** is an attitude, usually negative, that is used against an entire group, and often based on stereotypes of racial

The battleship *USS Arizona* after it was bombed by the Japanese in a surprise attack at Pearl Harbor on December 7, 1941. Japanese-Americans suffered prejudicial treatment after the event.

or ethnic characteristics (Schaefer 2005). It involves thoughts and beliefs that people harbor, which lead to categorical rejection and the disliking of an entire racial or ethnic group. Prejudice can occur whether the person has contact with the group or not. Prejudices can be formed from social interaction with others within one's own group, through the media, or through direct contact with the outside group.

A variety of theories have been offered to explain prejudice. Early theories were often based on the premise that prejudiced attitudes are innate or biological, but more recent explanations tend to attribute the development of prejudices to the social environment. Locating the source of prejudice in the social environment, rather than in innate or biological traits, means that measures can be taken to curtail prejudice. Some examples of such measures are discussed later in this chapter.

Economic theories of prejudice are based on the supposition that both competition and conflict among groups are inevitable when different groups desire commodities that are in short supply. These theories explain why racial prejudice is most salient during periods of depression and economic turmoil. In California, for example, from the 1840s through the depression of the 1930s, economic relations between European and Chinese Americans were tolerant and amiable as long as the Chinese confined themselves to occupations such as laundry and curio shops. When Chinese Americans began to compete with European Americans in gold mining and other business enterprises, however, violent racial conflicts erupted. Japanese Americans had a similar experience during their internment in camps after the bombing of Pearl Harbor.

The exploitation variant of economic theory argues that prejudice is used to stigmatize a group as inferior, to put its members in a subordinate position, and to justify their exploitation. The exploitation theme explains how systems under capitalism have traditionally justified exploiting recent immigrants who had little money, few skills, and difficulties with English.

Psychological theories of prejudice suggest that prejudice satisfies psychic needs or compensates for some defect in the personality. When people use **scapegoating**, they blame other persons or groups for their own problems. Another psychological strategy involves **projection**, in which people attribute their own unacceptable traits or behaviors to another person. In this way, people transfer responsibility for their own failures to a vulnerable group, often a racial or ethnic group. **Frustration-aggression theory** involves a form of projection (Dollard, et al., 1939). In this view, groups who strive repeatedly to achieve their goals become frustrated after failing a number of times. When the frustration reaches a high intensity, the group seeks an outlet for its frustration by displacing its aggressive behavior to a socially approved target, a racial or ethnic group. Thus, it has been argued that Germans, frustrated by runaway inflation and the failure of their nationalist ambitions, vented their aggressive feelings by persecuting Jews. Poor Whites, frustrated by their unproductive lands and financial problems, drained off their hostilities through anti-Black prejudices. Schaeffer (2005) adds a theory called ***normative theory*** that emphasizes socialization as an explanation for prejudice. The theory maintains that peers and social influences either encourage tolerance or intolerance toward others. In other words, a person from an intolerant household is more likely to be openly prejudiced than someone from a tolerant household.

The **authoritarian personality theory** argues that some people are more inclined to prejudice than others, due to differences in personality. According to this theory (Adorno, et al., 1950), prejudiced individuals are characterized by rigidity of outlook, intolerance, suggestibility, dislike for ambiguity, and irrational attitudes. They tend to be authoritarian, preferring stability and orderliness to the indefiniteness that accompanies social change. Simpson and Yinger (1972) questioned whether these traits cause prejudice and suggested that they may in fact be an effect of prejudice or even completely unrelated to it. In addition, this theory reduces prejudice to a personality trait in individuals.

APPLYING THEORIES OF PREJUDICE

Gordon Allport (1954), in *The Nature of Prejudice*, noted that interracial interaction would reduce prejudice only when the groups are of equal status, they have common goals, and their interaction are sanctioned by authorities. Allport's notion is congruent with the economic theory that says that competition and conflict can heighten prejudice. Using these ideas, a classroom program known as the "jigsaw technique" was developed by Aronson and his associates. Weyant (1995) offers a description of that technique:

> The jigsaw technique involves dividing the class into small groups of usually about five to six students each. Each child in a group is given information about one part of a total lesson. For example, a lesson on Spanish and Portuguese explorers might be divided such that one child in the group is given information about Magellan; another student receives information about Balboa, another about Ponce de Leon, etc. The members of the group then proceed to teach their part to the group. Afterward, the students are tested individually on the entire lesson. Just as all the pieces of a jigsaw puzzle must be put into place to get the whole picture, the only way any one student can master the entire lesson is to learn all the pieces of information from his or her peers. Equal status is attained because every student has an equally important part. The common goal is to put together the entire lesson. (pp. 108–109)

Evaluation studies of the jigsaw technique found very positive results, including increased attraction of classmates for one another and higher self-esteem. These results also helped alleviate some of the causes of prejudice suggested by psychological theories. Furthermore, the results were obtained with only a few hours of "jigsawing" a week, so the goals of desegregation were met without a major restructuring of the schools.

Techniques to reduce prejudice do not have to be confined to the classroom. Community leaders such as local politicians, businesspeople, and ministers might help eliminate racial tensions in a neighborhood by developing programs that require citizen participation. A church, for example, might sponsor a food drive to help the needy. In organizing a committee to run such a drive, the pastor or director could create racially and ethnically integrated committees to handle the various responsibilities necessary to make the drive a success. These might include committees for advertising and publicizing, collection, distribution, setup, and cleanup. Like the classroom, people of different minority groups would come to work with and to depend on each other in a cooperative rather than a competitive situation and thus have an opportunity to overcome some of their prejudices.

Your knowledge of how prejudice occurs could lead to many other programs to help eliminate this serious social problem. For example, as a parent, how do you think you could use what you have learned in this chapter to prevent your children and their friends from developing prejudice against minority groups?

Thinking Sociologically

1. What are some dysfunctional aspects of prejudices and stereotyping? What are some functional aspects?
2. How could the information contained in the section "Applying Theories of Prejudice" be used to make social action programs more effective?

Discrimination

Prejudice is a judgment, an attitude. **Discrimination**, on the other hand, is overt behavior or actions. It is the categorical exclusion of members of a specific group from certain rights, opportunities, and/or privileges (Schaefer 2005). According to the conflict perspective, the dominant group in a society practices discrimination to protect its advantages, privileges, and interests.

Most of us can understand discrimination at the individual level. A person may engage in behavior that excludes another individual from rights, opportunities, or privileges simply on the basis of that person's racial, ethnic, or minority status. For example, if I refuse to hire a particular Japanese American to type this manuscript because he or she does not does not read English; I am not engaging in prejudicially determined discrimination. On the other hand, if I refuse to hire a highly qualified typist of English because he or she is Japanese-American, that is discrimination.

Merton designed a classification system to examine four ways that prejudice and discrimination can be defined.

1. *Unprejudiced non-discriminators (all-weather liberal)* are individuals who are not prejudiced, and they don't discriminate against other racial groups. They believe that everyone is equal. However, they usually won't do anything to stop others from being prejudiced or discriminating.
2. *Unprejudiced discriminators (fair-weathered liberal)* are people who are not prejudice, but will not speak out against those who are. They will laugh nervously when a racist joke is told. Their main concern is to not hurt their own position.
3. *Prejudiced non-discriminators (fair-weathered bigot)* are individuals who don't believe that everyone is equal; but because we live in a "politically correct" society, they will not disclose their prejudice unless they believe they are among like minded people. They don't act on their prejudices.
4. *Prejudiced discriminators (all-weather bigot)* are the hardcore racists. They don't believe races are equal and will share their beliefs with anyone willing to listen. They will openly discriminate against persons due to their race or ethnicity.

Individual discrimination has become more insidious than in the past. Outward acts of discrimination, such as when James Byrd was dragged to his death behind a truck in Texas simply because he was Black, are uncommon today. Instead, individual discrimination is harder to recognize, but still prevalent. Today, a

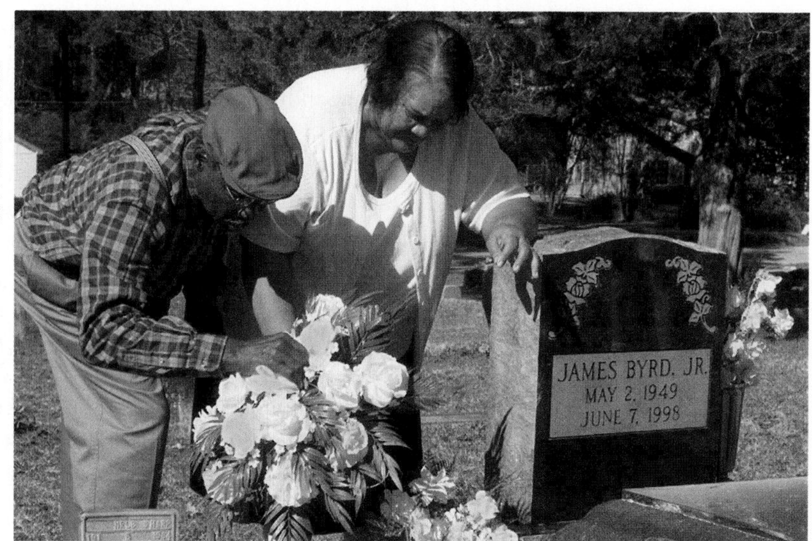

Stella and James Byrd Sr. arrange flowers around the headstone of their son, James Byrd Jr. Byrd was dragged to death in 1998 in Texas simply because he was Black.

Black family may be turned down for a rental house because the owner does not like Blacks or a Mexican worker won't be hired because the manager thinks all Mexicans are lazy. Even though these practices are illegal based on the Civil Rights Act, they are still a common problem for racial and ethnic groups. According to the Southern Poverty Law Center, there were 1002 hate groups in the United States in 2010, up 12.8 percent from 888 in 2007. Hate groups have beliefs and practices that attack or malign a class of people, typically for what are perceived to be inherent, unchanging characteristics. Hate group activities include things such as criminal acts, marches, rallies, meetings, or publications (www.splcenter.org).

Discrimination also operates at the institutional level when prejudices are embedded in the structures of our social institutions. Rothman (2005) defines the institutionalization of inequality at the structural dimension: the collection of laws, customs, and social practices that combine to create and sustain the unequal distribution of rewards based on class, minority status, and gender (Rothman 2005). Therefore, **institutional discrimination** is the continuing exclusion or oppression of a group as a result of criteria established by an institution. In this form of discrimination, individual prejudice is not a factor; instead, groups are excluded based on prejudices that are entrenched in the structure of the institution. Laws or rules are not applied with the intent of excluding any person or group from particular rights, opportunities, or privileges; however, the outcome has discriminatory consequences. Grodsky et al. (2008, 386) conducted research on how "standardized testing in American education has reflected, reproduced, and transformed social inequalities by race/ethnicity, social origins, and gender". Testing does not intentionally contribute to social inequalities, but because some have access to or are denied education that better prepares them for standardized testing, inequality is perpetuated.

Suppose, for example, that a school requires for admission a particular minimum score on a standardized national exam based on middle-class White culture, thus individuals outside of that culture will find the exam to be more difficult. In such a case, no bias against any particular racial or ethnic group may be intended—anyone who meets the criteria can be admitted. However, the result is the same as if the discrimination were by design. Few members of minority or ethnic groups could meet the requirements for admittance to the school or club, and the benefits of belonging would apply mainly to the White students who could pass the test. This would tend to continue existing patterns of educational and occupational deprivation from one generation to the next.

A similar process operates in our criminal justice system. Suppose that individuals from two different ethnic groups are arrested for identical offenses and given the same fine. If one can pay the fine but the other cannot, their fates may be quite different. The one who cannot pay will go to jail while the other one goes home. The result is institutional discrimination against the poor. Once a person has been imprisoned and has probably lost her or his job, that individual may find that other jobs are harder to find.

Racism

Racism is the belief that one racial group or category is inherently superior to others. It includes prejudices and discriminatory behaviors based on this belief. Racism can be regarded as having three major components. First, the racist believes that her or his own race is superior to other racial groups. This component may involve racial prejudice, but it is not synonymous with it. Racial prejudice is an attitude, usually negative, toward the members of other racial groups. The belief in the superiority of one's own group may also involve *ethnocentrism*, which is the belief in the superiority of one's own group on the basis of cultural criteria. A person's own group may be an ethnic group, but it need not be. Thus, racial prejudice and ethnocentrism can be regarded as properties of racism, not synonyms for it.

The second property of racism is that it has an ideology, or set of beliefs, that justifies the subjugation and exploitation of another group. According to Rothman (1978, p. 51), a racist ideology serves five functions:

1. It provides a moral rationale for systematic deprivation.
2. It allows the dominant group to reconcile values and behavior.
3. It discourages the subordinate group from challenging the system.
4. It rallies adherence in support of a "just" cause.
5. It defends the existing division of labor.

Perpetuators of racist ideologies claim their beliefs are based on scientific evidence. Herrnstein and Murray (1994) in the *Bell Curve*, for example argued that Whites are superior to other races based mainly on the scores of standardized tests. Much controversy exists over this type of science because many of the standardized tests used in school settings are geared toward White middle-class students, creating a disadvantage for racial and ethnic groups. Another pseudoscientific theory held that various races evolved at different times. Blacks, who presumably evolved first, were regarded as the most primitive race. As such, they were believed to be incapable of creating a superior culture or carrying on the culture of the higher, White races. The theory further argued that some benefits would come to Blacks by serving members of the White race. This theory is obviously self-serving and completely without scientific foundation; however, it allowed Whites to establish and maintain a paternalistic relationship with Blacks during slavery.

Racism creates dysfunction in a society. Richard Schaeffer identifies six ways that racism is dysfunctional, or disruptive to the stability of a social system, even to

Racism is the belief that one racial group or category is inherently superior to others. The Ku Klux Klan, shown here, holds such a belief concerning Whites.

the dominant members of the society (Schaeffer 2005). These are as follows:

1. A society that practices discrimination fails to use the resources of all individuals. Discrimination limits the search for talent and leadership to the dominant group.
2. Discrimination aggravates social problems such as poverty, delinquency, and crime and places the financial burden of alleviating these problems on the dominant group.
3. Society must invest a good deal of time and money to defend the barriers that prevent the full participation of all members.
4. Racial prejudice and discrimination undercut goodwill and friendly diplomatic relations between nations.
5. Social change is inhibited because change may assist a subordinate group.
6. Discrimination promotes disrespect for law enforcement and for the peaceful settlement of disputes.

Finally, the third property of racism is that racist beliefs are acted upon. Many examples of racist actions in this country could be highlighted. The lynching of Blacks in the U.S. South and the destruction of entire tribes of Native Americans who were regarded as little more than animals are two of the more extreme instances.

Racism, like discrimination, can be of two types. Individual racism originates in the racist beliefs of a single person. Racist storeowners, for example, might refuse to hire Black employees because they regard them as inferior beings. **Institutional racism** occurs when racist ideas and practices are embodied in the folkways, mores, or legal structures of various institutions.

The policy of apartheid in the Republic of South Africa was, and in many ways is, one of the most notorious examples of institutional racism. This policy calls for biological, territorial, social, educational, economic, and political separation of the various racial groups that compose the nation. Only in the past few years have the media brought the South African racial situation to the conscious attention of most Americans. As a result, many schools, foundations, and industries have removed from their investment portfolios companies that have a major investment in that country. Others have taken public stands against the institutionalized racism that supports different rules, opportunities, and activities based on the color of one's skin.

PATTERNS OF RACIAL AND ETHNIC RELATIONS

When different racial and ethnic groups live in the same area, widespread and continuous contact among groups is inevitable; but it rarely results in equality. Generally, one group holds more power and dominates the other groups. In some cases, assimilation, pluralism, segregation, expulsion, or genocide will occur. Whatever the form of group interaction, relations among groups is strongly influenced by their rankings in the stratification system.

Integration and Assimilation

Integration occurs when ethnicity becomes insignificant and everyone can freely and fully participate in the social, economic, and political mainstream. All groups are brought together. **Assimilation** occurs when individuals and groups forsake their own cultural tradition to become part of a different group and tradition. With complete assimilation, the minority group loses its identity as a subordinate group and becomes fully integrated into the institutions, groups, and activities of society. The extent to which integration and assimilation has occurred represents what sociologists call **social distance,** meaning the degree of intimacy and equality between two groups. It is measured by asking questions as to whether one would be willing to have members of a particular ethnic group live in one's neighborhood, have them as friends, or be willing to marry them.

Assimilation in the United States appears to focus on one of two models: the **melting pot** and **Anglo conformity**. The following formulations differentiate these two terms (Newman 1973).

Melting pot:	A + B + C = D
Anglo conformity:	A + B + C = A

In melting-pot assimilation, each group contributes a bit of its own culture and absorbs aspects of other cultures such that the whole is a combination of all the groups. Many sociologists in the United States view the melting-pot model as a popular myth, with reality better illustrated by the Anglo conformity model. *Anglo conformity* is equated with "Americanization," whereby the minority completely loses its identity to the dominant WASP culture.

The degree to which assimilation takes place is different for different ethnic and racial groups. There are two important mechanisms that help to determine the extent to which a group assimilates (and, thus, the extent to which its members retain or lose their cultural identity). The first, and most important, is the group's ownership of society's resources. The more ownership of resources that a group has, the less likely that the group will have to assimilate in order to succeed. The second most important mechanism that affects assimilation is whether or not a group has been cut off from its mother society. In cases where the immigrant population still has strong ties with its mother society, such as with Mexicans and Puerto Ricans, assimilation has been retarded because the groups can maintain their cultural practices. Simply put, groups who have been able to resist domination by the country to which they have migrated are more likely to resist assimilation (Barber 2007).

Integration is a two-way process. The immigrants must want to assimilate, and the host society must be willing to have them assimilate. The immigrant must undergo *cultural assimilation*, learning the day-to-day norms of the WASP culture pertaining to dress, language, food, and sports. This process also involves internalizing the more crucial aspects of the culture, such as values, ideas, beliefs, and attitudes. **Structural assimilation** involves developing patterns of intimate contact between the guest and host groups in the clubs, organizations, and institutions of the host society. Cultural assimilation generally precedes structural assimilation, although the two sometimes happen simultaneously.

Cultural assimilation has occurred on a large scale in American society, although the various minorities differed in the pace at which they were assimilated. With White ethnics of European origin, cultural assimilation went hand in hand with **amalgamation** (biological mixing through large-scale intermarriage). Among Asian ethnics, Japanese-Americans seem to have assimilated most completely and are being rewarded with high socioeconomic status. In contrast, Chinese-Americans, particularly first-generation migrants, have resisted assimilation and have retained strong ties to their cultural traditions. The existence of Chinatowns in many cities reflects this desire for cultural continuity.

Assimilation involves more than just culture borrowing because immigrants want access to the host's institutional privileges. The issue of integration is particularly relevant in three areas: housing, schooling, and employment.

The existence of Chinatowns in many cities, such as this one, reflects the desire by many Chinese immigrants for cultural continuity.

Pluralism

Are the elimination of segregation and the achievement of integration the only choices of societies with racial and ethnic diversity, or can diverse racial and ethnic groups coexist side by side and maintain their distinctive heritages and cultures? This issue is what Lambert and Taylor (1990) address as "the American challenge: assimilation or multiculturalism" and what Lieberson and Waters (1988) state as "melting pot versus cultural pluralism."

Multiculturalism or **cultural pluralism** can be defined as a situation in which the various racial, ethnic, or other minority groups in a society maintain their distinctive cultural patterns, subsystems, and institutions. Perhaps this can be illustrated by the following formula:

Cultural pluralism: A + B + C = A + B + C

Whereas those who support assimilation and integration seek to eliminate ethnic boundaries, a pluralist wants to retain them. Pluralists argue that groups can coexist by accepting their differences. Basic to cultural pluralism are beliefs that individuals never forget or escape their social origin, that all groups bring positive contributions that enrich the larger society, and that groups have the right to be different yet equal.

Several authorities believe that assimilation and pluralism are happening simultaneously in American society. Glazer and Moynihan (1970), in their seminal work on assimilation *Beyond the Melting Pot*, perceive the process of becoming what they call "hyphenated" Americans as involving cultural assimilation. Thus, a Russian-American is different from a Russian in Russia, and an African American is not the same as an African in Africa. On the other hand, they perceive the emergence of minority groups as political interest groups as a pluralistic trend. Gordon (1978) contends that assimilation of minorities is the prevailing trend in economic, political, and educational institutions, whereas cultural pluralism prevails in religion, the family, and recreation.

Cultural pluralism results in separate ethnic communities, many of which are characterized by a high degree of institutional completeness; that is, they include institutions and services that meet the needs of the group, such as ethnic churches, newspapers, mutual aid societies, and recreational groups. These ethnic enclaves are particularly attractive to recent immigrants who have language problems and few skills. Schaefer (2003) compared ethnic communities to decompression chambers. "Just as divers use such chambers to adjust to the rapid change in water pressure, immigrants use the communities to adjust to cultural change they are forced to make upon arriving in a new country" (p. 48).

Today, we are witnessing a resurgence of interest by various ethnic groups in almost forgotten languages, customs, and traditions. This is characterized by people's increased interest in the culture of their ethnic group, visits to ancestral homes, their increased use of ethnic names, and their renewed interest in the native language of their own group.

The general rule has been for American minorities to assimilate, however. Most ethnic groups are oriented toward the future, not toward the past. American ethnics are far more interested in shaping their future within the American structure than in maintaining cultural ties with the past. However, as Rothman (2005) contends, the importance of a multicultural model is accelerated by the recognition that Whites will probably be a numerical minority sometime after the year 2050.

Segregation

Segregation is the physical and social separation of groups or categories or people. It results in ethnic enclaves such as Little Italy, Chinatown, Black ghetto, and Hispanic barrio. The most significant division, however, is between Whites in the suburbs and Blacks and other minorities in the inner cities. At the institutional level, segregation can be attributed to discriminatory practices and policies of the federal housing agencies and of mortgage-lending institutions. Suburban zoning patterns that tend to keep out poorer families are also influential. At the individual level, segregation is the result of some Whites' refusal to sell their houses to non-Whites or the desire of minorities to live in their own ethnic communities.

The city-suburb polarization of Blacks and Whites continues through the early part of this millennium. This pattern of segregation continues in spite of a 1965 federal law that prohibits discrimination in the rental, sale, or financing of suburban housing. Based on this law, all banks

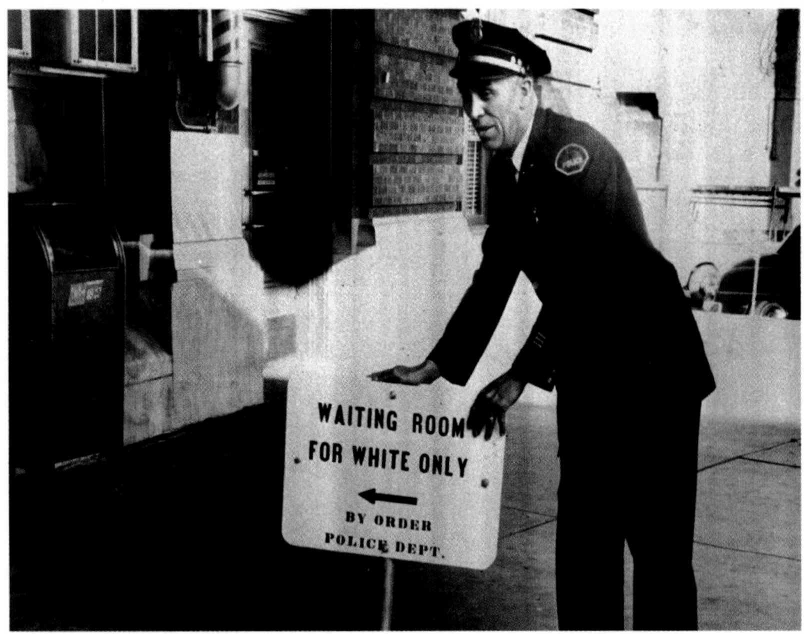

Segregation was common in the U.S. through the 1950s. This photo was taken at the Illinois Central Railroad in 1956.

and savings and loan associations bidding for deposits of federal funds were requested to sign anti-redlining pledges. *Redlining* is the practice among mortgage-lending institutions of imposing artificial restrictions on housing loans for areas where minorities have started to buy. Despite these and other advances, American society has a long way to go in desegregating housing patterns.

School segregation was brought to national attention with the 1954 decision in *Brown verus the Board of Education of Topeka, Kansas*, in which the U.S. Supreme Court ruled that the assignment of children to schools solely because of race—called **de jure segregation** (meaning segregation by law)—violates the U.S. Constitution and that the schools involved must desegregate. For decades prior to the *Brown* decision, particularly in the South, busing was used to keep the races apart even when they lived in the same neighborhoods and communities.

In the past few decades, attention has shifted to the North and West, where school segregation resulted from Blacks and Whites living in separate neighborhoods, with school assignment based on residence boundaries. This pattern, which is called **de facto segregation** (meaning segregation in fact), led to legislation in many cities that bused Blacks and Whites out of their neighborhood schools for purposes of achieving racial balance. Defenders of the legislation argue that minority students who are exposed to high-achieving White middle-class students will do better academically. They also contend that desegregation by busing is a way for Whites and minority groups to learn about each other, which may diminish stereotypes and racist attitudes.

It is not always clear whether segregation is de facto or de jure. School districts may follow neighborhood boundaries and define a neighborhood school so that it minimizes contact between Black and White children. Is that de facto segregation (resulting from Black and White neighborhoods) or de jure segregation (resulting from legally sanctioned assignment of children to schools based on race)? Regardless of what it is, the vast majority of black children in Atlanta, Baltimore, Chicago, Cleveland, Detroit, Los Angeles, Memphis, Philadelphia, and many other cities today attend schools that are predominantly Black.

Mass Expulsion

Mass expulsion is the practice of expelling racial or ethnic groups from their homeland. The United States routinely used expulsion to solve conflicts with Native Americans. In an incident known as "The Trail of Tears," the Cherokees were forced out of their homeland in the region where Georgia meets

Tennessee and North Carolina. The removal was triggered by the discovery of gold in the Georgia mountains and the determination of European-Americans to take possession of it. The exodus went to the Ohio River and then to the Mississippi, ending in what is now Oklahoma. Of the ten thousand Cherokees rounded up, about four thousand perished during the exodus.

Racist thinking and racist doctrine were rampant between 1850 and 1950, which is aptly called "the century of racism." Since 1950, it has declined in many parts of the world, but there is no question that it still exists.

Genocide

Genocide is the practice of deliberately destroying a whole race or ethnic group. Raphael Lemkin coined the term in 1944 to describe the heinous crimes committed by the Nazis during World War II against the Jewish people, which is the supreme example of racism. Of the 9,600,000 Jews who lived in Nazi-dominated Europe between 1933 and 1945, 60 percent died in concentration camps. The British also solved race problems through annihilation during their colonization campaigns overseas. Between 1803 and 1876, for example, they almost wiped out the native population of Tasmania. The aborigines were believed by the British to be a degenerate race, wild beasts to be hunted and killed. One colonist regularly hunted natives to feed his dogs.

Lemkin (1946, 228) defined genocide as the "crime of destroying national, racial or religious groups." As early as 1717, the U.S. government was giving incentives to private citizens for exterminating the so-called troublesome (American) Indians, and Americans were paid generous bounties for natives' scalps. Through the process of displacement, diseases, removal, and assimilation, the Native American population was reduced to meager numbers, less than one percent of the U.S. population today.

In the 1990s the world witnessed the genocide in Rwanda that left over a million men, women, and children dead and many more displaced from their homeland. Today, we are once again witnessing the tragic events of genocide taking place in the Darfur region of Sudan. Since 2003 the conflict in Darfur has left over four hundred thousand dead and 2.5 million people displaced. Tens of thousands of people are being raped and killed based only on their ethnicity. In March 2009, the International Criminal Court charged Sudan's President Omar Hassan al-Bashir with seven counts of war crimes and crimes against humanity.

Because of its moral distinctiveness, genocide has been called the "crime of crimes" (Schabas 2000, in Lee 2010). While international concern about genocide subsided after World War II, events in Rawanda, Darfur and other areas has led to a justification and resurgence of international humanitarian military intervention.

GLOBAL RACIAL RELATIONS

As we discussed in Chapter 8, **stratification** is structured social inequality. It is the ranking of entire groups of people that perpetuates unequal rewards and power in a society (Schaeffer 2005). Stratification in a society takes a variety of forms. Sometimes, it is based on a status ascribed at birth, as in a caste system; and sometimes, it is based on an acquired status, such as income or occupation, as in many industrialized countries. Some societies, including our own, stratify people on the basis of ascribed statuses such as race and ethnic heritage, in addition to the achieved statuses of education and income.

In America, the predominant norms, values, beliefs, ideas, and character traits are those of the WASP majority—described more fully later in this chapter. The more a group diverges from the economic status and norms of the majority, the lower its rank in the social hierarchy. Thus, it may be less advantageous to be Chinese or Mexican than to be Polish or Irish, as well as less desirable to be Polish or Irish than to be a WASP.

The consequences of allocating status on the basis of ethnic or racial membership are most evident in the different lifestyles and opportunities of different groups. When social inequality is based on racial lines, the majority holds the more desirable positions and minorities hold the less desirable ones.

Donald L. Noel (1975) contends that three conditions are necessary for ethnic stratification to occur in a society: ethnocentrism, which is the tendency to assume that one's culture and way of life are superior to all others (Schaeffer 2005), competition for resources, and inequalities in power. The inevitable outcome of ethno-

Since 2003 the Darfur region of Sudan has seen the genocide of thousands of people. Sudan's President, shown here, has been charged with war crimes and crimes against humanity as a result.

centrism is that other groups are disparaged to a greater or lesser degree, depending on the extent of their difference from the majority. Competition among groups occurs when they must vie for the same scarce resources or goals, but it need not lead to ethnic stratification if values concerning freedom and equality are held and enforced. According to Noel, it is the third condition, inequality in power, which enables one group to impose its will upon the others. Power permits the dominant group to render the subordinate groups ineffectual as competitors and to institutionalize the distribution of rewards and the opportunities to consolidate their position.

The rankings of people because of race, nationality, religious, or other ethnic or minority affiliation is clearly not unique to the United States. South Africa serves as an example of ethnic stratification, unmatched by any other society (Marger 2003). White Afrikaners (South Africans of European decent) created a system of apartheid (White supremacy) that had caste-like elements. Blacks were seen as inferior in every way to Whites, and a formal system of racial classification defined the status of all others. Ethnic categories during apartheid included Whites, Coloreds, Asians, and Africans. While Whites made up only 10 percent of the population, they controlled all other aspects of society. Coloreds were those who had a mixture of White and Black parentage; and while treated differently from Whites, they held more privileges than Africans. Asians were mainly indentured servants brought in from India. Their treatment was similar to the Coloreds during apartheid; and once their servitude had ended, they could establish themselves within society. Over 75 percent of the population of South Africa was Black Africans, yet they held the least amount of power within society. Apartheid was legal segregation that allowed for the separation of races based on skin color alone. This system of discrimination stayed in effect from 1948 to 1994, when White Afrikaans (The Nationalist Party) relinquished power and agreed to a democratic state.

History is full of examples where race, ethnicity or religion has been the dominant factor in the treatment of human beings. For example, in Brazil one's outward appearance determines racial classification, much like in the United States. However, social factors can also serve as an indicator. A popular saying in Brazil is "money whitens" (Marger 2003), meaning that as one climbs the social ladder, the more like Whites he or she becomes. The opposite is true as well, the lower one is economically speaking, the darker he or she becomes. Before the Good Friday Agreement in 1998, Northern Ireland had numerous incidents and reports of armed conflict between Protestants and Catholics. While the Agreement was a move in the right direction, it did not create an immediate cease–fire between the two groups. In 2007, and after repeated attempts to unify Northern Ireland, the head of each party was sworn in as leader and deputy leader, in an effort to end the long history of conflict. Other examples of stratification and conflict include the strife between Jews and

TABLE 9-1 POVERTY RATES FOR SELECTED RACE AND ETHNIC GROUPS IN THE UNITED STATES IN 2007 TO 2009

Race	2007 Poverty	2008	2009
Whites	8.2	11.2	12.3
Blacks	24.5	24.7	25.8
Asians	10.2	11.8	12.5
Hispanics	21.5	23.2	25.3
National Average	12.5	13.2	14.3

Source: U.S. Bureau of the Census, Income, Poverty, and Health Insurance Coverage in the United States: 2007 and 2009

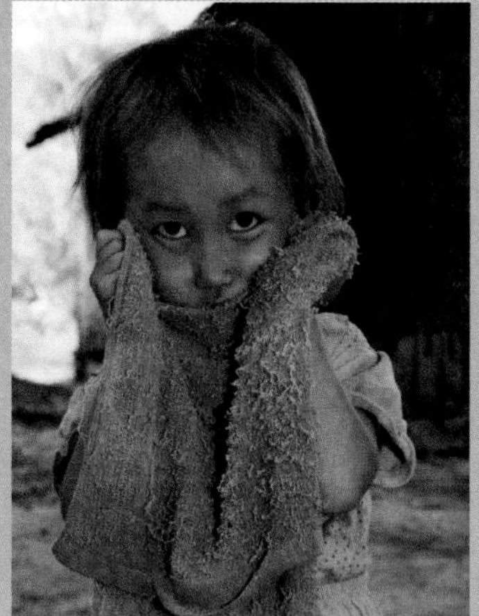

Muslims in Israel and other Middle-Eastern countries and the ethnic war between Croats and Serbs in Yugoslavia.

What positions do ethnic and racial groups occupy in the stratification system of the United States? Table 9-1 lists poverty rates for selected racial and ethnic groups in America, from 2007 to 2009. Figure 9-1 provides a historical perspective on incomes between groups from 1967 to 2009.

In our society, income and education are important indicators of a group's place in the stratification system. As Figure 9-1 and Table 9-2 indicate, Blacks and Hispanics have had the lowest median family incomes since 1967 and continue to do so. As Table 9-3 indicates, Blacks, Native Americans and Hispanics had the lowest levels of education consistently since 1970.

The high income and education levels of Asian Americans reflect the emphasis placed on education by those groups. It probably also reflects the changes in immigration policy in the mid-1960s, which gave priority to highly skilled and professional immigrants. The low incomes of African and Hispanic American families reflect their overrepresentation in less prestigious, less skilled, and lower-paying occupational categories. Native Americans would be in similar lower-level occupational groupings. One common consequence of these income, education, and employment differentials is antagonism among ethnic groups and between the less powerful and the more powerful.

Ethnic Antagonism

Ethnic antagonism is mutual opposition, conflict, or hostility among different ethnic groups. In the broadest sense, the term encompasses all levels of intergroup conflict—ideologies and beliefs such as racism and prejudice, behaviors such as discrimination and riots, and institutions such as the legal and economic systems. Ethnic antagonism is closely linked to the racial and ethnic stratification system. The best-known theory of ethnic antagonism is that of the split labor market, as formulated by Edna Bonacich in a series of articles in the 1970s (1972, 1975, and 1976).

A central tenet of split-labor-market theory is that when the price of labor for the same work differs by ethnic group, a three-way conflict develops among business managers and owners, higher-priced labor, and cheaper labor. Business—that is, the employer—aims at having as cheap and docile a labor force as possible. Higher-priced labor may include current employees or a dominant ethnic group that demands higher wages, a share of the profits, or fringe benefits that increase the employer's costs. Cheaper labor refers to any ethnic group that can do the work done by the higher-priced laborers at a lower cost to the employer.

Antagonism results when the higher-paid labor groups, who want to keep both their jobs and their wages (including benefits), are threatened by the

Figure 9-1 Real Median Household Income by Race and Hispanic Origin: 1967 to 2009

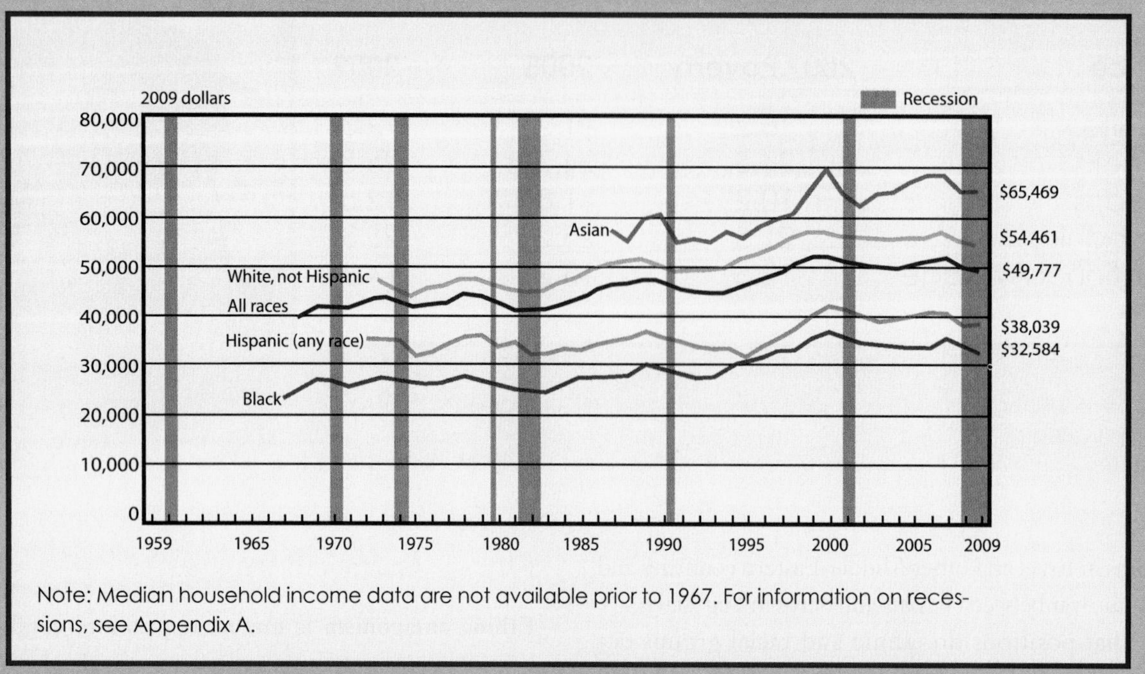

Note: Median household income data are not available prior to 1967. For information on recessions, see Appendix A.

Source: U.S. Census Bureau, Current Population Survey, 1968 to 2010 Annual Social and Economic Supplements.

introduction of cheaper labor into the market. The fear is that the cheaper labor group will either replace them or force them to lower their wage level. This basic class conflict then becomes an ethnic and racial conflict. If the higher-paid labor groups are strong enough, they may try to exclude the lower-paid group. **Exclusion** is the attempt to keep out the cheaper labor (or the product they produce). Thus, laws may be

Table 9-2 Median Family Income and Earnings by Race, 2007 to 2009

Race	2007	2008	2009
White (not Hispanic)	54,920	55,319	54,461
Black	34,091	34,088	32,584
Hispanic	38,679	37,769	38,039
Asian	65,876	65,388	65,469

Source: U.S. Bureau of the Census, Civilian Population: Employment Status by Race, Sex, Ethnicity 1970–2007; U.S. Bureau of the Census, Income and Earnings Summary Measures by Selected Characteristics: 2008 and 2009

TABLE 9-3 EDUCATIONAL ATTAINMENT BY RACE AND HISPANIC ORIGIN:1970-2009

(In percent. for persons 25 years old and over, 1970 and 1980 as of April 1 and based on sample data from the censuses of population. Other years as of March and based on the current Population Survey; see text, Section 1 and appendix III.)

Year	Total[1]	White[2]	Black[2]	Asian and Pacific Islander[2]	Hispanic[3] Total[4]
HIGH SCHOOL GRADUATE OR MORE[5]					
1970	52.3	54.5	31.4	62.2	32.1
1980	66.5	68.8	51.2	74.8	44.0
1990	77.6	79.1	66.2	80.4	50.8
1995	81.7	83.0	73.8	(NA)	53.4
2000	84.1	84.9	78.5	85.7	57.0
2005	85.2	85.8	81.1	[6]87.6	58.5
2006	85.5	86.1	80.7	87.4	59.3
2007	85.7	86.2	82.3	87.8	60.3
2008	86.6	87.1	83.0	88.7	62.3
2009	86.7	87.1	84.1	88.2	61.9
COLLEGE GRADUATE OR MORE[5]					
1970	10.7	11.3	4.4	20.4	4.5
1980	16.2	17.1	8.4	32.9	7.6
1990	21.3	22.0	11.3	39.9	9.2
1995	23.0	24.0	13.2	(NA)	9.3
2000	25.6	26.1	16.5	43.9	10.6
2005	27.7	28.1	17.6	[6]50.2	12.0
2006	28.0	28.4	18.5	49.7	12.4
2007	28.7	29.1	18.5	52.1	12.7
2008	29.4	29.8	19.6	52.6	13.3
2009	29.5	29.9	19.3	52.3	13.2

NA Not available. [1] Includes other races not shown separately. [2] Beginning 2005, for persons who selected this race group only. The 2003 Current Population Survey (CPS) allowed respondents to choose more than one race. Beginning 2003, data represent persons who selected this race group only and exclude persons reporting more than one race. The CPS in prior years only allowed respondents to report one race group. See also comments on race in the text for Section 1. [3] Persons of Hispanic origin may be any race. [4] Includes persons of other Hispanic origin not shown separately. [5] Through 1990, completed 4 years of high school or more and 4 years of college or more. [6] Starting in 2005, data are for Asians only, excludes Pacific Islanders.

Source: U.S. Census Bureau, U.S. Census of Population,1970 and 1980, Vol. 1; current Population reports, p20-550, and earlier reports; and " Educational Attainment," <http://www.census.gov/population/www/socdemo/educ-attn.html>.

passed that make it illegal for Mexicans, Cubans, Haitians, Chinese, Filipinos, or other immigrants to enter the country; taxes may be imposed on Japanese automobiles, foreign steel, or clothes made in Taiwan. Another technique used by higher-paid labor is the imposition of a caste system, in which the cheaper labor can get jobs only in low-paying, low-prestige occupations. As a result, the higher-paid group controls the prestigious jobs that pay well. In one sense, it can be argued that a sort of caste system exists today for women, Blacks, and some Hispanic groups. These groups often hold jobs of lower status and power and receive lower wages.

Bonacich claims that another process, **displacement**, is also likely to arise in split labor markets. Capitalists who want to reduce labor costs may simply displace the higher-paid employees with cheaper labor. They can replace workers at their present location or move their factories and businesses to states or countries where the costs are lower. This is evident in auto parts, clothes, and other products with tags or labels such as "made in Mexico," or "made in Korea," or made in any other country where labor costs are considerably lower than in the United States. Within the United States, the early 1980s witnessed many examples of strike-breaking by powerful business managers and government officials, who replaced union and higher-paid workers with nonunion and lower-paid employees. The steel, airline, and automobile industries are three cases in point.

An alternative to the split labor market is what Bonacich terms **radicalism**, in which labor groups join together in a coalition against the capitalist class and present a united front. When this occurs, Bonacich claims, no one is displaced or excluded, and no caste system is established. Anyone who gets hired comes in under the conditions of the higher-priced labor. Bonacich believes that as long as there is cheap labor anywhere in the world, there may not be a solution to a split labor market within a capitalist system.

Thinking Sociologically

1. Can you identify five ethnic groups in the United States and stratify them? What criteria do you use? What social significance can you attach to the ranking you have given a particular group?

2. Discuss the pros and cons of split labor market theory from the perspective of both the higher-priced worker and the lower-priced worker. How does this influence the opinions one group has toward the other?

RACIAL AND ETHNIC GROUPS IN THE UNITED STATES

As of 2010, minority races made up one-third of the U.S. population; however, it is expected by 2042 they will be the majority. The Hispanic American population is the largest racial, ethnic minority group in the U.S., constituting approximately 16.3 percent of the total population in 2010 up from 12.5 percent in 2000. The Hispanic American classification, however, is very difficult to measure for many reasons, including overlap with other categories and illegal immigration. The African American population is the second largest racial, ethnic, minority group (see Table 9-4), comprising 12.6 percent of the total population up from 12.3 percent in 2000. As of 2010 the total population in the United States was estimated to be nearly 309 million people. Table 9-4 reflects the population estimates regarding racial and ethnic groups in the United States as of 2010 United States Census.

The third largest group, the Asian American community, includes Americans whose historical roots are Chinese, Filipinos, Japanese, Asian Indians (from India), Koreans, Vietnamese, and people in other Asian nations. Between 2000 and 2010 the number of Asians in the United States increased by nearly 4.5 million or 4.8 percent of the total United States population. This is a 43 percent increase in the population of Asian Americans since 2000. Reasons for growths in immigration are (discussed later in this chapter).

Following Asian Americans in size are Native Americans, categorized in the U.S. census as "American Indians" and grouped with the Alaskan Natives, Eskimos and Aleuts (native Eskimoan tribes from the Aleutian Islands, which is a chain of volcanic islands extending some 1,100 miles from the tip of the Alaskan Peninsula). These Native American groups included about 2.5 million people in 2010, slightly less than 1 percent of the U.S. population. Every group except for

Whites experienced an increase in their percentage of the total U.S. population since 2010. The percentage of Whites declined from 75.1 percent of the total U.S. population in 2000 to 72.4 percent in 2010. This is a clear indication of the changing ethnic population composition in the United States.

Hispanic-Americans

As of 2010, there were nearly 50.5 million Hispanics living in the United States, up from 33.3 million in 2000. That is an increase of 43 percent. This category includes those who classify themselves as Mexican American, Puerto Rican, Cuban, Central American, South American, and other Hispanic. These also included those who simply identify themselves as "Spanish-American," "Hispanic," or "Latino." Our discussion focuses on Mexican Americans, who constitute approximately 65.5 percent of the Hispanic-American group.

Mexican Americans are also identified as Chicanos, a contraction of Mexicanos (pronounced "meschicanos" in the ancient Nahuatl language of Mexico). Over one million Mexican Americans are descendants of the native Mexicans who lived in the Southwest before it became part of the United States, following the Mexican American war. They became Americans in 1848, when Texas, California, New Mexico, and most of Arizona became U.S. territory.

TABLE 9-4 POPULATION BY HISPANIC OR LATINO ORIGIN AND BY RACE FOR THE UNITED STATES: 2000 AND 2010

Hispanic or Latino origin and race	2000		2010		Change, 2000 to 2010	
	Number	Percentage of the population	Number	Percentage of the population	Number	Percent
HISPANIC OR LATINO ORIGIN AND RACE						
Total population	281,421,906	100.0	308,745,538	100.0	27,323,632	9.7
Hispanic or Latino	35,305,818	12.5	50,447,594	16.3	15,171,776	43.0
Not Hispanic or Latino	246,116,088	87.5	258,267,944	83.7	12,151,856	4.9
White alone	194,552,774	69.1	196,817,552	63.7	2,264,778	1.2
RACE						
Total population	281,421,906	100.0	308,745,538	100.0	27,323,632	9.7
One Race	274,595,678	97.6	299,736,465	97.1	25,140,787	9.2
White	211,460,626	75.1	223,553,265	72.4	12,092,639	5.7
Black or African American	34,658,190	12.3	38,929,319	12.6	4,271,129	12.3
American Indian and Alaska Native	2,475,956	0.9	2,932,248	0.9	456,292	18.4
Asian	10,242,998	3.6	14,674,252	4.8	4,431,254	43.3
Native Hawaiian and Other Pacific Islander	398,835	0.1	540,013	0.2	141,178	35.4
Some Other Race	15,359,073	5.5	19,107,368	6.2	3,748,295	24.4
Two or More Races	6,826,228	2.4	9,009,073	2.9	2,182,845	32.0

[1] In Census 2000, an error in data processing resulted in an overstatement of the Two or More Races population by about 1 million people (about 15 percent) nationally, which almost entirely affected race combinations involving Some Other Race. Therefore, data users should assess observed changes in the Two or More Races population and race combinations involving Some Other Race between Census 2000 and the 2010 Census with caution Changes in specific race combinations not involving Some Other Race, such as White and Black or African American or White and Asian, generally should be more comparable.

Sources: U S *Census Bureau, Census 2000 Redistricting Data (Public Law 94-171) Summary File*, Tables PL1 and PL2; and 2010 *Census Redistricting Data (Public Law 94-171) Summary File*, Tables P1 and P2.

Minorities such as women, Blacks, and some Hispanic groups often hold jobs of lower status and power and receive lower wages.

These four states plus Colorado contain the largest concentrations of this group today. Most urban Mexican Americans live in California, especially in Los Angeles.

Other Mexican Americans came from Mexico since 1848. They can be classified into three types: (1) legal immigrants; (2) *braceros*, or temporary workers; and (3) illegal aliens. The Mexican Revolution caused large-scale migration in the early 1900s beause of, unsettled economic conditions in Mexico, and by the demand for labor on cotton farms and railroads in California. Before the minimum wage law was passed, agricultural employers preferred braceros to local workers because they could be paid less; and the braceros were not a burden to the federal government inasmuch as they returned to Mexico when their services were no longer needed.

The number of illegal aliens from Mexico is not known; estimates range from one to ten million. Immigration policy concerning legal and illegal Mexican immigrants generally varies with the need for labor, which in turn depends on economic conditions. When the demand for Mexican labor was high, immigration was encouraged. When times were bad, illegal aliens were tracked down, rounded up, and deported. They were scapegoats in the depression of the 1930s and again in the recession of the early 1980s.

Strong family ties and large families characterize traditional Mexican American culture. The extended family is the most important institution in the Chicano community. The theme of family honor and unity occurs throughout Mexican American society, irrespective of social class or geographical location. This theme extends beyond the nuclear family unit of husband, wife, and children to relatives on both sides and persists even when the dominance of the male becomes weakened. It is a primary source of emotional and economic support and the primary focus of obligations.

Most American families have two or three children, but it is not unusual for Mexican American families to have five or more. In 2006, for example, 22.5 percent of Hispanic families had five or more people. About twice as many Hispanic families had five or more members compared to non-Hispanics. Families of this size, when linked with minimal skills and low levels of income, make it difficult for the Mexican American to enjoy life at a level equal to the dominant groups in American society. For example, the median family income for non-Hispanic White families in 2009 was $54,461 compared to $38,039 for Hispanic families. Combining a large family size with a low income makes life very hard for most Hispanic Americans.

To improve the educational and income level of the Mexican American family, several Mexican American social movements have emerged over the past three decades. One movement was directed at having bilingual instruction introduced at the elementary level. Bilingualism emerged into such a politically controversial issue that in 1986 California passed a resolution (joining six other states) making English the state's official language. Today, thirty states have English only laws, and more are considering legislation.

Cesar Chavez, one of the best-known Chicano leaders, led another movement. In 1962, he formed the National Farm Workers Association (later the United Farm Workers Union) and organized Mexican migrant farm workers first to strike against grape growers and later against lettuce growers. The strikes included boycotts against these products, which carried the struggles of low-paid Chicano laborers into the kitchens of homes throughout America. Primary goals of Chicano agricultural and political movements, in addition to increasing wages and benefits for migrant workers, included increasing the rights of all workers and restoring pride in Mexican American heritage.

The Hispanic population is fairly young, with the average age around twenty-seven years for both men and women. Education is perhaps the most influential factor creating income gaps for Hispanic workers. As Table 9-3 indicates, the percentage of Hispanics with less than a high school degree is the largest among all racial groups. This, along with a young workforce and low-skilled or semi-skilled labor, creates economic hardships for Hispanic families.

African Americans

As noted, African Americans comprise the second largest racial minority in the United States. Because of such unique historical experiences as slavery, legal and social segregation, and economic discrimination, many African Americans have lifestyles and value patterns that differ from those of the European-American majority. The relations between Whites and Blacks have been the source of a number of major social issues in the past several decades: busing, segregation, job discrimination, and interracial marriage, to mention a few.

Perhaps these issues can be understood more fully by examining five major social transitions that have affected or will affect African Americans (Eshleman and Bulcroft 2006). The first transition was the movement from Africa to America, which is significant because of three factors: color, cultural discontinuity, and slavery. *Color* is the most obvious characteristic that sets Whites and Blacks apart. *Cultural discontinuity* was the abrupt shift from the culture learned and accepted in Africa to the cultural system of America. Rarely has any ethnic or racial group faced such a severe disruption of cultural patterns. *Slavery* was the unique circumstance that brought many Africans to America. Unlike almost all other groups, Africans did not come to this country by choice. Most were brought as slaves to work on southern U.S. plantations. Unlike many free African Americans in the North, slaves in the South had few legal rights. Southern Blacks were considered the property of their White owners, who had complete control over every aspect of their lives. Furthermore, there were no established groups of Blacks to welcome and aid the newly-arrived Africans, as was the case with other immigrant groups.

A second major transition was from slavery to emancipation. In 1863, a proclamation issued by President Lincoln freed the slaves in the Union and in all territories still at war with the Union. Although the slaves were legally free, emancipation presented a major crisis for many African Americans because most were faced with the difficult choice of either remaining on the plantations as tenants with low wages or none at all for their labor, or searching beyond the plantation for jobs, food, and housing. Many men left to search for jobs, so women became the major source of family stability. The shift to emancipation from slavery contributed to the third and fourth transitions.

The third transition was from rural to urban and from Southern to Northern communities. For many African Americans, this shift had both good and bad effects. Cities were much more impersonal than the rural areas from which most Blacks moved, but they also provided more jobs, better schools, improved health facilities, a greater tolerance of racial minorities, and a greater chance for vertical social mobility. As of 2001, twenty-three million African Americans lived in a metropolitan area and 13.5 million lived within a central city (*Current Population Reports*, Annual Demographic Survey, March 2002). Blacks are no longer confined to the inner-cities, but are active participants in large metropolitan areas.

The job opportunities created by World War I and World War II provided the major impetus for the exodus of African Americans from the South to the North, a trend that continued through the 1960s. In 1900, 90 percent of all African Americans lived in the South. By 1980, this figure had dropped to 53 percent, but increased to 55.3 percent by 2002 (*Current Population Reports*, Series P-20, No. 541, 2003). Today, there are more African Americans in New York City and Chicago than in any other cities in the world, including African cities, and these cities have retained their top rankings for thirty years. Atlanta and Washington, D.C. are the cities with the third and fourth largest African American population. New York and Florida rank first and second, respectively, in states with the highest African American population.

The fourth transition was from negative to positive social status. The African American middle class has been growing in recent years and resembles the European American middle class in terms of education, job level, and other factors. In 2008, 40 percent of Blacks had household incomes of $50,000 or more, up from 29.4 percent in 1980. An even greater advance can be seen in the number of Blacks who have made $100,000 or more: 13.4 percent made more than $100,000 in 2008, up from 4.5 percent in 2008. That is nearly a 300 percent increase. However, it must be pointed out that the percentage of Blacks reaching the middle and upper middle classes is still noticeably lower than for Whites, even when comparing the 2008 figures for Blacks to the 1980 figures for Whites. (See Table 9-5.) A high proportion of African Americans remain in the lower income brackets, however, because of the prejudice, segregation, and discriminatory practices endured by them throughout most of their time in this country; only in the past thirty years have they achieved a measure of equality. Previously, they were routinely denied equal protection under the law, equal access to schools and housing, and equal wages.

The final transition was from negative to positive self-image. A basic tenet of the symbolic interaction approach is that we develop self-image, our identities, and our feelings of self-worth through our interactions with others. Throughout most of our history, African Americans have been the last to be hired and the first to be fired. It would be understandable if Black self-esteem were lower than White; but studies have shown that Blacks' self-evaluations are equal to or higher than those of Whites, and their rate of suicide is about one-half that of Whites. Unfortunately, one major consequence of cuts in social programs that took place under the Reagan and George H. Bush administrations is that the cuts may have conveyed a message to all minority groups in the United States that they are of little importance, compared with the interests of the dominant White middle and upper classes.

Asian Americans

The Asian American community in the United States is a highly diverse group, even more so than the Hispanic community. Asian immigration to the United States has been in two distinct parts: the "Old Asians" and the "New Asians" (Marger 2003). The first group consisted of Chinese immigrants arriving in the middle of the nineteenth century and spanning to the early twentieth century. Japanese, Korean, and Filipino workers—mainly recruited for hard labor, low-income construction jobs—followed the Chinese. The next wave of Asian immigrants to enter the U.S. is the most recent group, comprising a more diverse cultural heritage.

TABLE 9-5 MONEY INCOME OF FAMILIES–PERCENT DISTRIBUTION BY INCOME LEVEL IN CONSTANT (2008) DOLLARS: 1980 TO 2008

Year	Number of Families (1,000)	Percent distribution							Median Income (dollars)
		Under $15,000	$15,000 to $24,999	$25,000 to $34,999	$35,000 to $49,999	$50,000 to $74,999	$75,000 to $99,999	$100,000 and over	
ALL FAMILIES [1]									
1980	60,309	8.8	10.5	11.4	17.1	24.8	14.2	13.2	52,301
1990	66,322	8.6	9.4	10.2	15.6	22.4	14.7	19.1	56,458
2000[2]	73,778	6.7	8.4	9.5	14.1	19.7	15.4	26.2	63,430
2007	77,908	7.6	8.7	9.4	13.4	19.2	14.4	27.4	63,712
2008	78,874	8.1	9.0	9.7	13.6	19.4	14.3	26.0	61,521
WHITE									
1980	52,710	7.0	9.5	11.1	17.3	25.8	15.0	14.1	54,493
1990	56,803	6.7	8.7	9.9	15.8	23.1	15.5	20.4	58,952
2000[2]	61,330	5.5	7.7	9.1	14.0	19.9	16.1	27.7	66,302
2007[3,4]	63,595	6.1	8.1	9.1	13.2	19.5	15.0	29.0	66,903
2008[3,4]	64,183	6.6	8.3	9.3	13.4	19.9	15.1	27.5	65,000
BLACK									
1980	6,317	22.8	18.2	14.1	15.3	16.7	8.2	4.5	31,530
1990	7,471	24.0	14.6	12.6	14.4	17.5	8.8	8.2	34,212
2000[2]	8,731	15.1	13.8	13.0	15.7	18.8	10.5	13.0	42,105
2007[3,5]	9,259	17.9	13.4	12.0	14.6	17.6	10.9	13.7	41,685
2008[3,5]	9,359	17.7	13.8	12.8	15.7	16.9	9.7	13.4	39,879
ASIAN AND PACIFIC ISLANDER									
1990	1,536	8.1	7.8	8.2	11.5	20.8	15.1	28.5	67,466
2000[2]	2,982	5.9	6.1	6.8	11.0	17.3	15.9	37.0	78,290
2007[3,6]	3,302	5.8	6.4	6.8	10.5	18.0	13.7	38.7	80,097
2008[3,6]	3,494	7.3	7.2	7.1	12.4	16.6	12.8	36.6	73,578
HISPANIC ORIGIN [7]									
1980	3,235	15.8	17.1	15.1	19.1	19.0	8.5	5.4	36,611
1990	4,981	17.0	16.3	13.6	17.2	19.0	8.7	8.2	37,419
2000[2]	8,017	11.9	14.3	13.4	18.0	19.4	11.0	12.0	43,063
2007	10,397	12.9	14.8	14.2	16.7	19.0	10.2	12.1	42,125
2008	10,503	14.6	14.3	14.2	16.8	17.8	9.8	12.5	40,466

[1] Includes other races, not shown separately. [2] Data reflect implementation of Census 2000-based population controls and a 28,000 household sample expansion to 78,000 households. [3] Beginning with the 2003 Current Population Survey (CPS), the questionnaire allowed respondents to choose more than one race. For 2002 and later, data represent persons who selected this race group only and excludes persons reporting more than one race. The CPS in prior years allowed respondents to report only one race group. See also comments on race in the text for Section 1. [4] Data represent White alone, which refers to people who reported White and did not report any other race category. [5] Data represent Black alone, which refers to people who reported Black and did not report any other race category. [6] Data represent Asian alone, which refers to people who reported Asian and did not report any other race category. [7] People of Hispanic origin may be any race.

Source: U.S. Census Bureau, *Income, Poverty and Health Insurance Coverage in the United States: 2008*, Current Population Reports, P60-236(RV), and Historical Tables—Table F-23, September 2009. See also <http://www.census.gov/hhes/www/income/income.html> and <http://www.census.gov/hhes/www/income/data/historical/families/index.html>.

This group is distinct from the first group in that educational levels, occupational skills, and social class status has been much higher. While the most numerous groups within the Asian population are those with Chinese, Filipino, and Japanese heritages, Asian Indians, Koreans, Hawaiians, and Guamanians are also included in this category. In the past decade, more immigrants have come from the Philippines, China, Vietnam, Korea, and India than from any country outside of North and South America. Other groups represented in the large amounts of immigrants to America come from Africa, Iran, Cambodia, and the United Kingdom, with recent increases from Poland and Laos.

As mentioned, the Chinese were the first Asians to enter this country in large numbers. Mostly single males, Chinese workers intended to return home after working in the United States. In 1882, due to fear by White workers that Chinese men would take their jobs, an anti-Chinese movement began that culminated in a ban on immigrants from China. The Chinese Exclusion Act was made permanent in 1907 and began a series of restrictions by the United States on other immigrant groups. In 1943 the ban was lifted, but life for Chinese immigrants suffered as a result. The Chinese have historically resisted assimilation and tend to uphold traditional values, such as filial duty, veneration of the aged and of deceased ancestors, and arranged marriages. Chinese American families tend to be male-dominated, and an extended family pattern is the rule. In 1965 large scale immigration from China to the U.S. occurred and increased their population.

Today, most Chinese Americans live in large urban enclaves in Hawaii, San Francisco, Los Angeles, and New York. A tourist visiting a Chinatown is likely to notice only the exotic sights, smells, and sounds; the problems prevalent in Chinatowns are less evident. There is often overcrowding, poverty, poor health, rundown housing, and inadequate care for the elderly. Not all Chinese live in Chinatowns, however. Those who have "made it" live in the suburbs.

Like the Chinese, most early Japanese immigrants were males imported for their labor. For both groups, employment was at physically difficult, low-prestige, and low-paying jobs. Both groups were victims of prejudice, discrimination, and racism. As time went by, a large percentage of Japanese immigrants turned to farming instead of construction and honed their farming skills mainly in California (Marger 2003). Other important differences between the Chinese and Japanese were noted by Kitano (1991), which promoted diverse outcomes. For example, the Japanese came from a nation that was moving toward modernization and an industrial economy, while China (during the time of major emigration) was an agricultural nation that was weak and growing weaker. This meant that the Japanese had the backing of a growing international power, while the Chinese were more dependent on local resources. Another difference focused on marriage and family life. The Japanese men sent for their wives and families almost immediately. In contrast, many Chinese men left their wives in China or remained as bachelors primarily as a result of the Chinese Exclusion Act of 1882, which closed the door to Chinese immigrants. One consequence of this was the birth and presence of children for the Japanese, which meant facing issues of acculturation and a permanent place in the larger community. This process was delayed among the Chinese because they had so few children. Japanese Americans are today more fully integrated into American culture and have higher incomes than the Chinese or other Asian groups.

During World War II, European Americans feared that there might be Japanese Americans working against the American war effort, so the federal government moved most of them to what they called "relocation camps." As noted in the opening story, regardless of their political views or how long they had been in this country, families were forced to pack up whatever possessions they could and to move to camps in Utah, Arizona, California, Idaho, Wyoming, Colorado, and Arkansas, abandoning or selling at nominal prices their land and their homes, severely disrupting their lives. Many were incensed at the suggestion that they were not loyal Americans capable of making valuable contributions to the American war effort. Many also noted that German Americans were not similarly relocated. In addition, some of the relocated families even had sons serving in the U.S. armed forces. Altogether, more than 110,000 people of Japanese ancestry, seventy thousand of them U.S. citizens by birth, were moved. After the war, the Japanese were allowed to return to their homes; but even with the token monetary compensation recently awarded them, they have never been compensated adequately for the time, businesses, or property lost during their internment.

Native Americans

The Native American population is actually a varied group of tribes having different languages and cultures. At the time of the European invasion of America, there were perhaps two hundred distinct groups that traditionally have been grouped into seven major geographical areas (Feagin and Feagin 2002):

1. the Eastern tribes, who hunted, farmed, and fished
2. the Great Plains hunters and agriculturists
3. the Pacific Northwest fishing societies
4. the California and neighboring area seed gatherers
5. the Navajo shepherds and Pueblo farmers of the Arizona and New Mexico area
6. the Southwestern desert societies (e.g., Hopi) of Arizona and New Mexico
7. the Alaskan groups, including the Eskimos

Estimates of the number of Native Americans in the United States at the time of the European settlement range from one to ten million. By 1800, the native population had declined to six hundred thousand, and by 1850, it had dwindled to 250,000, as a result of starvation, deliberate massacre, and diseases such as smallpox, measles, and the common cold. Since the turn of the century, however, their numbers have increased dramatically. In the 1970s, the Native American population exceeded the one million mark for the first time since the period of European expansion, and by 2010, it reached an estimated three million (including Eskimos and Aleuts), according to U.S. Bureau of the Census.

By the 1960s, Native Americans were no longer regarded as nations to be dealt with through treaties. Most tribes were treated as wards of the U.S. government and lived isolated lives on reservations. Today, about half of all Native Americans live on or near reservations administered fully or partly by the

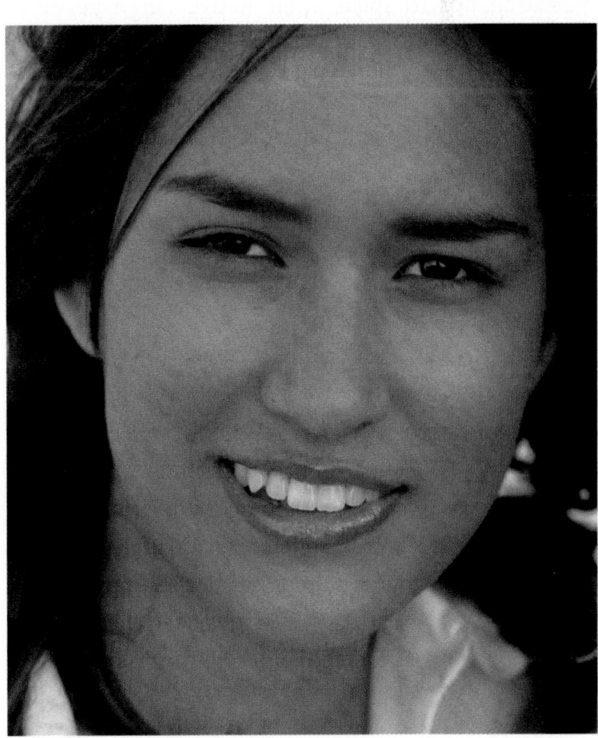

Bureau of Indian Affairs (BIA). Many other Native Americans have moved to urban areas or have been relocated there by the BIA to help in their search for jobs and improved living conditions.

Native Americans are among the most deprived of American minority groups. Their unemployment rate is twice that of European Americans (Feagin and Feagin 2002). Most hold jobs at lower occupational levels and have incomes far below the median for American families. Housing is often severely crowded, and two-thirds of their houses in rural areas have no plumbing facilities. The life expectancy is about two-thirds the national average. It appears that teenage suicide, alcoholism, and adult diabetes are more common among reservation-dwelling Native Americans than among any other group in the country. Studies suggest that Native Americans have the lowest school enrollment rates of any racial or ethnic group in the United States (Feagin and Feagin 2002). The norms, practices, and even materials within public schools often are at variance with those of Native American groups. In the Southwest, at least, many of these public schools are actually boarding schools, removing children entirely from their families and homes. In either type of school, children are often pressured not to speak their native language or to practice their native traditions.

One area in which Native Americans differ from the mainstream culture is in family structure. The Native American equivalent to the family is the band, which includes a number of related families who live in close proximity. The band is composed of kin people who share property, jointly organize rituals and festivals, and provide mutual support and assistance. Bands are egalitarian and arrive at decisions collectively.

Since the 1960s, many Native American tribes united and formed organized collectives to demand a better life for their people. Several tribes have banded together to bargain more effectively with the federal government, and they have sometimes used militant tactics to get results. Nonetheless, Native Americans—the only group that did not immigrate to the United States—remain a subordinate group. Stereotyped as inferior, they have suffered exploitation and discrimination in all of our basic social institutions.

WASPs and White Ethnic Americans

Most of the White population in the United States today emigrated as a result of European expansionist policies of the past 350 years. Earlier immigrants were WASPs, who came mainly from northern and western European countries such as Britain, Ireland, Scotland, Sweden, Norway, Germany, France, and Switzerland. Although within the U.S. population they are a minority group in terms of numbers, they are not a minority in terms of political and economic power. Thus, they have pressured African Americans, Hispanic Americans, Native Americans, and other racial, ethnic, and other minority groups to assimilate or acculturate to the ideal of Anglo conformity, the ideal of Americanization, or the model of A + B + C = A.

Historically, WASP immigrants displayed what became known as the "Protestant ethic." This was an ethic of a strong belief in God, honesty, frugality, piety, abstinence, and hard work. As the majority group in terms of power, they were not subject to the prejudices and discrimination experienced by other, later, immigrants. The pressure on these other groups to be assimilated and integrated into American society meant basically to think and behave like the WASP.

The more recent European immigrants are today's White ethnics. They came largely from southern and eastern European countries, such as Italy, Greece, Yugoslavia, Russia and other formerly Soviet republics, and Poland. Schaefer (2003) states that White ethnics separate themselves from WASPs and make it clear that they were not responsible for the oppression of Native Americans, African Americans, and Mexican Americans that took place before their ancestors had left Europe.

The majority of these immigrants, although they did not totally discard their roots, adopted American norms and values. Many dropped their European names in favor of names that sounded more "American," and most White ethnics have successfully assimilated. Michael Novak (1975), who is of Slovak ancestry, wrote the following about his experiences:

> Under challenge in grammar school concerning my nationality, I had been instructed by my father to announce proudly: "American." When my family moved from the Slovak ghetto of Johnston to the WASP suburb on the hill, my mother impressed upon us how well we must be dressed, and show good manners, and behave—people think of us as "different" and we mustn't give them any cause. (p. 593)

The emerging assertiveness of African Americans and other nonWhites in the 1960s induced many White ethnics to reexamine their positions. Today, many American ethnic communities emphasize more than their folk culture, native food, dance, costume, and religious traditions in establishing their ethnic identities. They have sought a more structured means of expressing, preserving, and expanding their cultures, and many have formed fraternal organizations, museums, and native-language newspapers in an effort to preserve their heritage (Lopata 1976).

Jewish Americans

One of the predominant religious ethnic groups is the Jewish American. America has the largest Jewish population in the world, estimated to be 6.5 million and exceeding the approximately four million Jews in Israel. They are heavily concentrated in the New York City metropolitan area and other urban areas.

Jewish Americans are basically ethnic in nature, in that they share cultural traits to a greater extent than physical features or religious beliefs. As a minority group, they have a strong sense of group solidarity, tend to marry one another, and experience unequal treatment from non-Jews in the form of prejudice, discrimination, and segregation. Although Jews are generally perceived to be affiliated with one of the three Jewish religious groups—Orthodox, Reform, or Conservative—many, if not the majority of Jews, do not participate as adults in religious services or belong to a temple or synagogue; yet, they do not cease to think of themselves as Jews. The trend in the United States seems to be the substitution of cultural traditions for religion as the binding and solidifying force among Jewish Americans.

Injustices to Jewish people have continued for centuries all over the world. The most tragic example of anti-Semitism occurred during World War II, when Adolf Hitler succeeded in having six million Jewish civilians exterminated—the terrifying event that has become known as the "Holocaust." Anti-Semitism in the United States never reached the extreme of Germany, but it did exist. As early as the 1870s, some colleges excluded Jewish Americans. In the 1920s and 1930s, a myth of international Jewry emerged that suggested Jews were going to conquer all governments throughout the world by using the vehicle of communism, which was believed by anti-Semites to be a Jewish movement. At that time, Henry Ford, Catholic priest Charles E. Coughlin, and groups such as the Ku Klux Klan published, preached, and spoke about a Jewish conspiracy as if it were fact. Unlike in Germany or Italy, however, the United States government never publicly promoted anti-Semitism, and Jewish Americans were more likely to face questions concerning how to assimilate than how to survive.

Concern about anti-Semitism seemed to decrease drastically following World War II through the 1960s; but in the 1970s and continuing today, anti-Semitic sentiments and behaviors appear to be on the increase. Whatever the cause, racial or ethnic hostility tends to unify the victims against attackers, and Jewish Americans are no exception.

Thinking Sociologically

1. Using information found in this chapter (and other relevant chapters, if necessary), discuss the racial and ethnic hierarchy found within American society. What has lead to and continues to exacerbate inequality among the various groups?
2. Examine your own family tree and compare your grandparents, great-grandparents, etc., to the early immigrant groups. How would life have been different for them during their generation?

THE FUTURE

What does the future hold for ethnic groups and integration in the United States? Will there be a time when Americans can get past racial and economic injustices and conquer the serious problems that we have yet to overcome. Racism continues to powerfully influence individual lives and the interactions of different ethnic groups, and each step in the integrative process presents new problems. With the election of President Barack Obama, many citizens are eager to suggest that race no longer matters in the United States. While Obama was touted as the "first Black President", it is easy to overlook the obvious one-drop rule that continues to define how we look at race. While Obama is linked to African ancestry through his father from Kenya, he is also equally White through his mother's lineage. The continuation of an "us" and "them" mentality will only serve to divide, rather than unite a nation of people.

Another issue is that of affirmative action which has been drastically weakened over the past five years. In 2003, the Supreme Court handed down two decisions that directly affected affirmative action, especially regarding education. In *Grutter v. Bollinger*, the Court held that schools could use race as a deciding factor in admission decisions. However, the narrowly divided court also seemed to put limits on how much of a factor race can play in giving minority students an advantage in the admissions process. In *Gratz v. Bollinger*, the Supreme Court ruled that giving points to a candidate simply based on race was a violation of the equal protection provision of the Constitution.

Despite the new problems that crop up and the frequent news stories of racial and racist incidents, there is reason for optimism. Just as few would argue that race relations are not everything they should be in this country, few would refute the fact that progress has been made during the past four decades. A number of barriers to equality have been eliminated. Civil rights activism during the 1960s and 1970s brought about reforms in laws and government policies. In 1963, affirmative action policies were established (again, note this chapter's policy debate), and President Kennedy issued an executive order calling for the disregard of race, creed, color, or national origin in hiring procedures, as well as in the treatment of employees. Affirmative action has since become a principal government instrument in eradicating institutional racism (Feagin and Feagin 2002); its laws were later amended to include women, so that today, the laws also prohibit discrimination on the basis of sex.

The reduction of institutional racism has had both indirect and direct effects. According to the "contact hypothesis," interracial contact leads to reductions in prejudice if at least the following conditions exist: (1) The parties involved are of equal status, and (2) the situation in which the contact occurs is pleasant or harmonious. This hypothesis, reflecting an interactionist perspective, claims that these conditions cause people to become less prejudiced and to abandon previously held stereotypes. The importance of both equal status and pleasant contact cannot be overlooked. For example, a Black employee being abused by a White employer (unequal status) or two people of equal status from different ethnic or minority groups competing for the same job opening (unpleasant contact) do little to promote interracial harmony and, in fact, may lead to greater hostility.

Changes in the way that minorities are portrayed in the mass media have also influenced levels of prejudice. During the 1950s and 1960s, when Blacks and other minorities were portrayed, it was usually in stereotyped roles as servants or other low-status workers. Today, although it could be argued that portrayals of minorities in the media still tend to reflect stereotypes, the situation has improved considerably.

Another cause for optimism is the frequent finding of research studies that better-educated people are more likely to express liking for groups other than their own. It may be that the educated have a more cosmopolitan outlook and are more likely to question the accuracy of racial stereotypes. It is to be hoped that the trend in this country toward a more-educated population, along with the other advances that have been made, will contribute to a reduction in prejudice and the more complete realization of the American ideals of freedom and equal opportunity.

Lastly, one needs to look no further than the 2008 presidential election and the forum of candidates who sought the highest office in the land. There has never been a time of such diversity within the political spectrum for President of the United States. This appeared to be the first time predicted front–runners in the election were from such diverse backgrounds. Hillary Clinton was a strong female candidate for the Democratic Party and along side of her was Barack Obama another strong contender who happened to be of mixed ancestry: African American and European American. The field of candidates also included Mitt Romney, a very strong prospect in the Republican Party who happens to be Mormon. As Barack Obama took the oath of office for President of the United States, it was a cold frigid afternoon when thousands and thousands of people lined the streets, courtyards, and Lincoln Mall to witness that historic occasion. We should realize that these are truly positive steps in recognizing the changes that are currently under way towards making the United States of America a land where "All Men Are Created Equal."

CHAPTER REVIEW

Wrapping it up

Summary

Check out our website www.bvtstudents.com for free chapter-by-chapter flashcards, summaries, and self-quizzes.

1. A *race* is a defined group or category of people distinguished by selected inherited physical characteristics. Throughout history race has been defined in biological, legal, and social terms. An *ethnic group* is a collection of individuals who feel they are one people because they have unique cultural traits, ascribed membership, and a sense of community, ethnocentrism, and territoriality.

2. Racial and ethnic groups are considered minorities when they are subordinate to another group in terms of power, social status, and privilege, and when their norms, values, and other characteristics differ from those that prevail in a society.

3. A stereotype is applied to entire groups of people based on a particular belief. *Prejudice* is a negative attitude toward an entire category of people. A variety of theories have been offered to explain prejudice, including economic and psychological ones. Prejudice often involves acceptance of ethnic *stereotypes*, widely held beliefs about the character and behavior of all members of a group.

4. Whereas prejudice is an attitude, *discrimination* is overt behavior on the part of individuals or institutions. It is the categorical exclusion of all members of a group from particular rights, opportunities, or privileges. Merton provides four categories of discriminators.

5. *Racism* includes prejudices and discriminatory behaviors based on three distinguishing characteristics: (1) the belief that one's own race is superior to any other race, (2) an ideology, and (3) actions based on racist beliefs. Genocide and mass expulsion are consequences of extreme forms of racism.

6. *Ethnic stratification* allocates status on the basis of ethnic or racial membership and is most evident in the different lifestyles and opportunities of different groups. Three conditions necessary for ethnic stratification to occur include ethnocentrism, competition, and inequalities in power.

7. Inequality may lead to ethnic antagonism. A leading theory of ethnic antagonism, the split-labor-market theory, suggests that conflict results among business ownership and management, higher-priced labor, and lower-priced labor. The basic fear of those in higher-priced labor is of being displaced by the lower-priced labor, which business owners view as one way of reducing costs.

8. Racial and ethnic inequalities can be resolved through either integration or pluralism. Integration involves assimilation, an event that occurs when individuals and groups forsake their own cultural traditions to become part of a different group or tradition. The extent to which integration and assimilation has or has not occurred represents *social distance*.

9. Two models of assimilation include the *melting pot* and *Anglo conformity*. The former means that different groups contribute something of their

own culture and absorb aspects of other cultures, with an outcome different from any former groups. The latter, equated with Americanization, means that the minority loses its identity to the dominant WASP culture.

10. *Segregation* is the physical and social separation of groups or categories of people. It may be de jure, segregation by law, or *de facto*, segregation in fact.

11. *Cultural pluralism* refers to a situation in which various racial, ethnic, or minority groups exist side by side but maintain their distinctive cultural patterns, subsystems, and institutions. Resurgence in this idea is evident in the ethnic and other minority emphasis on their native language, customs, and traditions.

12. The major racial or ethnic groups in the United States are African Americans, Hispanic Americans, Asian Americans, Native Americans, and European ethnics. The largest of these groups is the African American. African Americans, with the unique historical fact of slavery, have long been in the process of going through a number of social transitions. Today, most live in metropolitan areas with high population concentrations in northern cities.

13. Hispanic Americans include those who classify themselves as Mexican, Puerto Rican, Cuban, Central and South American, and other Hispanics from Spain or other Spanish-speaking countries. Mexican Americans, or Chicanos, are the largest Hispanic American group and are characterized by strong family ties and large families. A number of social movements have emerged over the past few decades to improve the status and living conditions of this group.

14. Numerous other ethnic and other minority groups exist in the United States today. Asian Americans include those with ties to China, Japan, the Philippines, India, Korea, Vietnam, and other Asian countries. Native Americans, the only nonimmigrant group, are often grouped into seven major geographical areas with distinct language patterns and tribal customs.

15. White Anglo-Saxon Protestant (WASP) groups came predominantly from northern and western European countries, while White ethnic groups came predominantly from southern and eastern European countries. Jewish-Americans are basically ethnic in nature, in that they share cultural traits to a greater extent than physical features or religious beliefs.

16. Although relations among ethnic groups are far from perfect in this country, some progress has been made during the past few decades. Government regulations have made discriminatory action illegal, and numerous affirmative action programs have been instituted in political, educational, and economic agencies throughout the country. The election of our first non-White President, changes in the portrayal of minorities in the media and the trend toward a better-educated population may lead to further progress in this area.

Key Terms

amalgamation The process by which different racial or ethnic groups form a new group through interbreeding or intermarriage

Anglo conformity A form of assimilation in which the minority loses its identity completely and adopts the norms and practices of the dominant WASP culture

assimilation The process through which individuals and groups forsake their own cultural tradition to become part of a different group and tradition

authoritarian personality theory The view that people with an authoritarian type of personality are more likely to be prejudiced than those who have other personality types

biological race The view that race is determined based on heredity

cultural pluralism The situation in which the various ethnic groups in a society maintain their distinctive cultural patterns, subsystems, and institutions

de facto segregation School assignment based on residence boundaries in which Blacks and Whites live in separate neighborhoods

de jure segregation The legal assignment of children to schools solely because of race

discrimination Overt unequal and unfair treatment of people on the basis of their membership in a particular group

displacement A process occurring in split labor markets in which higher-paid workers are replaced with cheaper labor

ethnic antagonism Mutual opposition, conflict, or hostility among different ethnic groups

ethnic group A group set apart from others because of its national origin or distinctive cultural patterns, such as religion, language, or region of the country

exclusion Attempts to keep cheaper labor from taking jobs from groups that receive higher pay

frustration-aggression theory The theory that prejudice results when personal frustrations are displaced to a socially approved racial or ethnic target

genocide The deliberate destruction of an entire racial or ethnic group

institutional discrimination The continuing exclusion or oppression of a group as a result of criteria established by an institution

institutional racism Racism that is embodied in the folkways, mores, or legal structures of a social institution

integration The situation that exists when ethnicity becomes insignificant and everyone can freely and fully participate in the social, economic, and political mainstream

legal race The legal definition of race: typically referred to as the rule of hypo-descent or "one-drop" rule

mass expulsion Expelling racial or ethnic groups from their homeland

melting pot A form of assimilation in which each group contributes aspects of its own culture and absorbs aspects of other cultures, such that the whole is a combination of all the groups

minority group A group subordinate to the dominant group in terms of the distribution of social power; such groups are defined by some physical or cultural characteristic and are usually but not always smaller than the dominant group

prejudice A preconceived attitude or judgment, either good or bad, about another group; prejudices usually involve negative stereotypes

projection A psychological explanation of prejudice that suggests that people transfer responsibility for their own failures to a vulnerable group, usually a racial or ethnic group

racial group A socially defined group distinguished by selected inherited physical characteristics

racism Discrimination based on racial characteristics

radicalism Labor groups joining together in a coalition against the capitalist class

scapegoating A psychological explanation of prejudice that involves blaming another person or group for one's own problems

segregation The separation of a group from the main body; it usually involves separating a minority group from the dominant group

social distance The degree of intimacy and equality between groups of people

social race Race is socially constructed and maintained through the process of interaction with others

stereotypes Widely held and oversimplified beliefs about the character and behavior of all members of a group that seldom correspond to the facts

structural assimilation One aspect of assimilation in which patterns of intimate contact between the guest and host groups are developed in the clubs, organizations, and institutions of the host society

stratification The structured ranking of entire groups of people that perpetuates unequal rewards and power in a society

Discussion Questions

1. Discuss the differences between the sociological concepts of racial, ethnic, and minority groups.
2. Do you believe that racial identity is based on biological, legal or social factors? Explain.
3. Select a racial, ethnic, or minority group other than your own, and compare it with your own.
4. Identify a prejudice that you hold, and use the theories of prejudice to discuss why you might have this prejudice.
5. Do you think that anyone has ever held a prejudice or discriminated against you? Why do you think so? Was this prejudice accurate?
6. What is the difference between de jure and de facto segregation? Can you identify either in your local community or state?
7. Differentiate between individual and institutional racism. Give specific examples.
8. Discuss the melting-pot, Anglo conformity, and pluralism models described in the chapter. Show how your community or city would be different, depending on which model was most prevalent.
9. What is the significance of any of the social transitions that have occurred or are occurring for African Americans? For example, is the demographic shift from the rural South to the urban North significant? How?
10. Based on the increases in the African American, Hispanic American, and Asian American population in the United States, social demographers suggest that within the next quarter century, the number of these groups will surpass the number of White-ethnic and WASP Americans. Will White Americans then be the minority? Explain.

Pop Quiz

1. Racial groups are based on ______.

   a. cultural characteristics
   b. biological and inherited physical traits
   c. the definition dictated by the census
   d. socially defined groups distinguished by inherited physical characteristics

2. A group that is subordinate to the majority in power and privilege is a(n) ______.

   a. minority group
   b. majority group
   c. ethnic group
   d. racial group

3. A minority group is a group that ______.

   a. is a minority in number
   b. has less power and fewer privileges than the majority group
   c. does not desire the same things as the majority group
   d. is culturally distinctive from other groups

4. Prejudice ______.

   a. is a negative attitude toward an entire category of people
   b. refers to actions directed against others
   c. is best controlled by public officials
   d. is a practice that attempts to destroy an entire race

5. Widely held beliefs about the character and behavior of all members of a group that operate to sustain prejudice are referred to as ______.

   a. biases
   b. concepts
   c. stereotypes
   d. propositions

6. What did Adorno find in his study of the "authoritarian personality?"

   a. The concept of an authoritarian personality is basically a myth.
   b. Authoritarian individuals tend to be flexible and tolerant.
   c. Authoritarian personalities are more prone than others to welcome and accept social change.
   d. Authoritarian people are more inclined to be prejudiced.

7. The jigsaw technique was developed to ______.

   a. reduce prejudice in the classroom
   b. encourage development of the authoritarian personality
   c. encourage social organizations to fight discrimination
   d. only "b" and "c"

8. Institutional discrimination is ______.

   a. a preconceived attitude about another group
   b. prejudice in prisons and nursing homes
   c. caused by criteria established by institutions
   d. caused by cultural diversity

9. When does institutional racism occur?

   a. Individuals are racist.
   b. The folkways, mores, and laws of a society are racist.
   c. Prejudice occurs in political and educational institutions.
   d. The president of the country is racist.

10. Mass expulsion of a race ______.

    a. has never occurred
    b. was used by the United States on Native Americans
    c. is called genocide
    d. is called exploitation

11. A minority group is any that has fewer members than some other group in a society. T/F

12. Individual prejudice is a factor in institutional discrimination. T/F

13. The Brown v. Board of Education decision was aimed at eliminating de facto segregation. T/F

14. Braceros are illegal immigrants searching for work in the United States. T/F

15. Israel has the largest Jewish population in the world. T/F

1. D	6. D	11. F
2. A	7. A	12. F
3. B	8. C	13. F
4. A	9. B	14. F
5. C	10. B	15. F

CHAPTER 10

Gender Differentiation

We Can Do It!

WOMEN IN AMERICA

In March 2011, the Office of Management and Budget and the Economics and Statistics Administration within the Department of Commerce released a report about the overall condition of women's lives in the United States today. The report, Women in America: Indicators of Social and Economic Well-Being, takes a comprehensive look at how women fare with regard to family life, income, employment, health, crime and violence. This is the first federal government report about the state of women since one produced in 1963 by the Commission on Status of Women, established by President Kennedy. That such a comprehensive document has been created recently, and that so much time has elapsed since the previous report about the state of women in the United States, is an important message in itself.

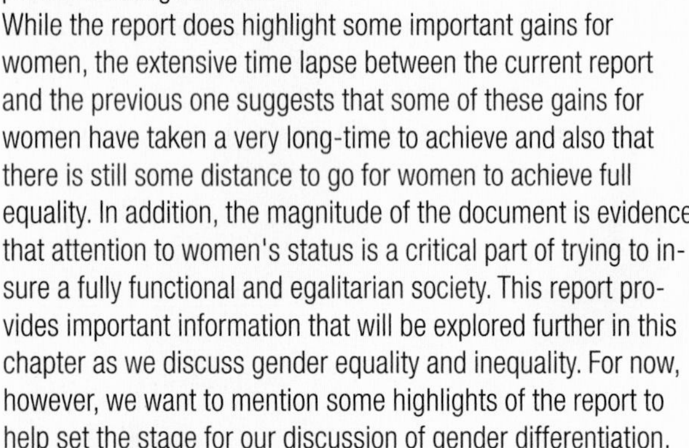

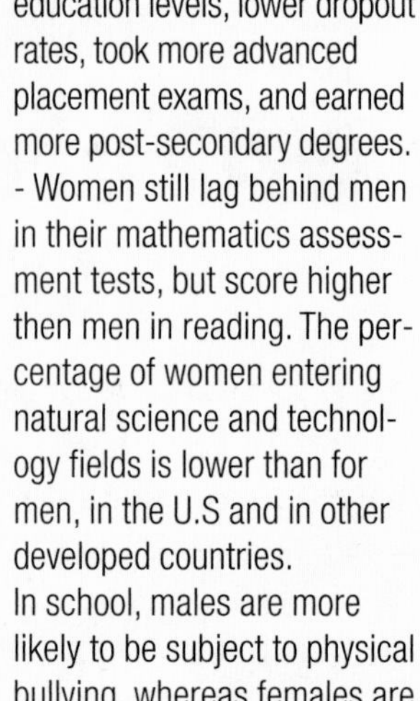

While the report does highlight some important gains for women, the extensive time lapse between the current report and the previous one suggests that some of these gains for women have taken a very long-time to achieve and also that there is still some distance to go for women to achieve full equality. In addition, the magnitude of the document is evidence that attention to women's status is a critical part of trying to insure a fully functional and egalitarian society. This report provides important information that will be explored further in this chapter as we discuss gender equality and inequality. For now, however, we want to mention some highlights of the report to help set the stage for our discussion of gender differentiation.

• People, Families and Income

–Females make up 51 percent of the U.S population.
- Women continue to earn less then men for the same work. Women are two to three times more likely than men to live in poverty.
- Women are more likely than men to live without a spouse. The percentage of women who are married declined from 72 percent in 1970 to 62 percent in 2009, as compared to 84 percent and 66 percent for men, respectively.
- Almost twice as many women in 2008 as in 1970 have never had a child (18 percent compared to 10 percent).

• Education

- Women have made greater educational gains than men in recent decades, across all ethnic groups and in all developed countries.
- In 2008, the college enrollment rate for women was 72 percent, compared to 66 percent of men. As compared to males, White, Black and Hispanic women have higher graduation rates at all education levels, lower dropout rates, took more advanced placement exams, and earned more post-secondary degrees.
- Women still lag behind men in their mathematics assessment tests, but score higher then men in reading. The percentage of women entering natural science and technology fields is lower than for men, in the U.S and in other developed countries. In school, males are more likely to be subject to physical bullying, whereas females are more likely to be victims of electronic bullying.

• Employment

- The labor force participation rate for women in 1950 was 33 percent and was 66 percent in 2009, having held steady since 1999, as compared to 75 percent of men.
- Statistically, 51 percent of all persons employed in management, professional and related occupations in 2009 were women, but they are more represented than men in the lower paying positions within these categories.
- Women still lag behind men in weekly earnings, but have made gains. In 1979, women earned 62 percent of what men earned as compared to 80 percent in 2009.
- Unemployment rates for women have risen less than for men in recent recessions.
- In dual income families in 2009, 87 percent of wives spent time in household activities as compared to 65 percent of husbands.

• Health

- Although the gender gap is closing the area of life span, women still live longer then men. Life expectancy for women in the U.S is lower than in other industrialized countries.
- Mortality from heart disease, the leading cause of death among women, decreased 68 percent since 1950, but the mortality rate for cancer, the second leading cause of death for women,

decreased only 17 percent. The lung cancer rate increased 500 percent. The maternal mortality rate in the U.S. is much lower than it was in the 1950s, but it is significantly higher than in many European countries.

- More women than men have chronic medical conditions such as asthma, emphysema, arthritis, or cancer. Men have a higher rate of heart disease and diabetes.
- The ceasarean rate rose from 21 percent in 1996 to 32 percent in 2008.
- Approximately 15 percent of women and 26 percent of men have no regular source of health care.

• Crime and Violence

- The rate of nonfatal violent crimes against women has declined from 43 per 1000 women in 1993 to 18 per 1000 women in 2008.
- The rate of sexual victimization and intimate partner violence affects women more than five times the instances it affects men. In 2008, intimate partners were responsible for 5 percent of all violence against men as compared to 25 percent of all violence against females. While the rate of rape declined 60 percent between 1993 and 2000 (and has remained consistent since then) between 2004 and 2008, police were not notified in approximately half of all the incidents of rape. Women are much more likely than men to be victims of stalking. In 2006, the number of female victims was 20 per 1000 women as compared to 7 per 1000 men.
- While men commit more crimes, especially violent crimes, than women, the proportion of women arrested for crimes is increasing. Women represented 18 percent of all those arrested for violent felony crimes in 2008, up from 11 percent in 1990. During that same period, the percent of women arrested for larceny increased from 25 percent to 35 percent.
- The number of women under some form of correctional supervision between 1990 and 2008 increased 121 percent.

Women have made important gains in past half century, but also still suffer from inequality in a number of ways. This chapter explores reasons for some of the differences between men and women's behaviors considering gender primarily as a social explanation rather than a biological one.

SEX AND GENDER DIFFERENTIATION

Sex refers to biological characteristics—the genetic, hormonal, and anatomical differences between males and females. **Gender**, on the other hand, is a social status. It refers to social differences between the sexes, specifically to the cultural concepts of masculinity and femininity. Our culture traditionally defines masculinity to mean strong, competent, rational, unemotional, and competitive. It defines femininity to mean nurturant, caring, and able to deal with the emotional side of relationships.

Gender roles refer to the behaviors that are expected of men and women. For example, men are supposed to work hard to get ahead, run the nation's industries, make tough political and economic decisions, and—of course—earn a living for their families. Women are expected to cook, clean, and care for their families, as well as earn additional income if their families require it. Gender roles, in other words, are behaviors assigned on the basis of the assumed characteristics of masculinity and femininity. They are roles required to fill the needs of the society.

Very often, these two concepts—gender and sex—are linked together without good reason. Our biology, or our sex, is often seen as the cause of our gender roles, even when our biology has little or no importance in the performance of these roles. In order to understand the difference between biological sex and socially defined gender roles, we review some of the basic biological differences between men and women.

Biological Bases of Gender Differentiation

Males and females differ from the moment of conception, when sex is determined. The ovum of the mother always carries an X chromosome, one of which is needed to bear the genetic material to develop either a male or a female. The father's sperm may carry either an X or a Y chromosome. If the sperm carries a second X chromosome, the fetus will develop into a female. If the sperm carries a Y chromosome, on the other hand, testes develop that secrete a hormone that causes the embryo to develop as a male. Between birth and puberty, the hormones produced by males and females are the same, so other than the development of either male or female sex organs, these chromosome differences cause very few physical differences between boys and girls.

Physiologists and psychologists have been more interested in behavioral differences between males and females. They ask whether the sex hormones in the fetus affect the central nervous system and, therefore, influence how males and females behave. In order to find answers to this question, they study infants and children.

The research literature is extensive on this point, but it gives no clear indication that boys and girls are born with a predisposition toward different behaviors. In a recent cross-cultural study, researchers observed aggression in 192 children between the ages of three and nine years. They observed children in naturalistic settings in Belize, Kenya, Nepal, and American Samoa. Results showed that boys exhibited aggression in approximately 10 percent of their social behaviors, girls in 6 percent, and in all four cultures the aggression of boys was more frequent than that of girls (Munroe, et al., 2000). These differences could be explained as differences in socialization.

Social Bases of Gender Differentiation

Most people in nurturing roles—such as teachers, counselors, and parents—are unaware that they have a tendency to treat males and females in gender-biased ways in nurturing, counseling, and educational situations (Sadker and Sadker 1985, 1986). It is a profoundly important fact for people in these roles to understand that a person's gender characteristics may be determined as much by social conditions as by heredity. The concept of the self-fulfilling prophecy comes into play here. If children are treated as if they have (or do not have) particular characteristics, they may well develop (or fail to develop) those traits. Teachers play a significant role in shaping the potential of males and females treating students—from kindergarten to graduate school—in terms of stereotypical gender traits. This occurs both in and out of the classroom.

If parents assume, for example, that females are by nature non-aggressive, they might directly discourage—or indirectly discourage by lack of attention or praise—their daughter from engaging in rough-and-tumble activities or contact games. As a result, the girl may not develop aggressive or competitive qualities—not because of her genetic makeup, but because she was never encouraged to develop them.

On the other hand, if parents assume that their son, because he is male, necessarily has good physical dexterity or analytical ability, they might encourage him to play with puzzles and to figure them out on his own. As a result, he may become adept at tasks that require physical coordination and analytical ability. The point is that children often develop the traits that we assume that they have by nature, as a result of the activities we provide for them.

One study, for example, found that in classrooms, boys were more likely than girls to get individual instruction on a task when they asked for it, and they got more tangible and verbal rewards for academic work (Serbin and O'Leary 1975). Girls were responded to less than the boys—usually only when they were physically close to the teacher—and were rarely encouraged to work on their own. Boys received more attention whether they were close to the teacher or not, and they were encouraged to do independent work.

It is important to point out that research about behaviors, such as the differential treatment of boys and girls in educational settings, that contribute to stereotypical traditional gender traits has become a political issue. Sadker (2000), a renowned scholar in the area of gender bias in educational settings, notes that ultraconservative "educational research" organizations have been created to discredit decades of studies documenting gender bias in schools. "In the past," Sadker notes (2000, 83), "the enemies of equity spoke more openly about the beliefs: the 'natural' roles of men and women the 'biological destinies' of each, even biblical references to the second class status of females." Because the Internet and the media do not evaluate research the same way that academic scholars do, politically funded and affiliated commentary is often seen by the public as valid "research," thus perpetuating gender bias and stereotypes that lead to inequity between females and males. By keeping in mind that we often unintentionally send hidden messages to males and females regarding their capabilities, teachers, counselors, and parents might develop more effective ways to give both genders an equal opportunity to excel in all academic areas and might develop ways to advise students (in terms of careers, choice of major, and other areas related to academics) based on their qualities and characteristics as individuals, and not on whether they are male or female.

Adult Sex Differentiation

When children reach adolescence, they begin to produce sex hormones again; the secondary sex characteristics develop—facial hair on men and breasts on women, for example. Most of these secondary sex characteristics are of little importance in behavior. Men do develop more muscular builds than women, especially in the upper part of their body. As a result, men have more muscle strength, greater spurts of energy, and are able to lift heavier objects. Women have a larger proportion of fat on their bodies, particularly through the breast and hip areas. This enables them to have more endurance than men over long periods of time. Women also have greater finger dexterity and should tend to be better able to do fine work with their hands, such as surgery, needlework, or dentistry.

However, socialization to gender roles, rather than physical differences, shape adult behavior. In our society, for example, even though women have greater finger dexterity, most dentists and surgeons are men (but most dental assistants are women). Women's finger dexterity is valued primarily in low-paying factory work, where sewing or electronics work is assigned to women. Cross-cultural studies show that the variety of gender roles men and women play in societies depends on the norms of the society and not on any physical characteristics.

CROSS-CULTURAL GENDER DIFFERENTIATION

In some cultures, men and women occupy roles in ways very unlike those typically found in the United States. In the Chambri (formerly called "Tchambuli") society of New Guinea, for example, the women are the workers. They do the fishing, weaving, planting, harvesting, and cooking, all the while they are carrying and caring for their children. They are generally confident, laughing, brisk, good-natured, and efficient. They have a jolly comradeship that involves much rough joking. The men, on the other hand, are more involved in producing arts and crafts and in planning ceremonies. They tend to be more emotional than the women and also more responsive to the needs of others. The women typically have an attitude of kindly toleration toward the men, enjoying the men's games and parties but remaining rather remote emotionally (Mead 1935).

> **Thinking Sociologically**
>
> Do you think any gender roles might really be sex roles—in other words, based on biological characteristics rather than social experiences? Explain why or why not.

In many African societies, the women have traditionally owned much of the land. Europeans have often tried to impose their own system of ownership on these tribes, sometimes with dire consequences. When Europeans introduced modern farming methods to the Ibo tribe of Nigeria, they took the land from the women and gave it to the men. The men raised cash crops, which they sold, and the women were left without their traditional means of subsistence. In 1923, the Ibo women rioted; ten thousand women looted shops and released prisoners from jail. In two days of intense rioting, fifty people were killed and another fifty were injured. Later, the women became more organized and continued their revolt against land reforms and taxation with more riots, strikes, cursing, and ridicule (Leavitt 1971).

In the Chambri society of New Guinea, the women are the workers and do such tasks as weaving and fishing.

THEORIES OF GENDER DIFFERENTIATION

The gender-role socialization of members of a society seems to differ with the type of society. In hunting-and-gathering societies, in which survival depends on the constant search for food, both males and females must be responsible for finding food; and, therefore, both are socialized to be assertive and independent. As societies grow wealthier and more complex, and as the division of labor increases and hunting is no longer necessary to provide food for people, gender-role differentiation increases. If both men and women are capable of meeting the demands of almost all positions or statuses without being constrained by biological factors, why does role differentiation increase? Why do women have lower status in modern society than men? Sociologists have explored these questions from several theoretical perspectives, including structural functionalism and conflict theory.

Structural Functional Theory

As mentioned previously, structural functionalists believe that society consists of interrelated parts, each of which performs functions in maintaining the whole system. They assume, accordingly, that women have traditionally made important contributions to society. They raised children, maintained the home, and provided food, clean clothing, and other necessities of daily living. They played an expressive role, nurturing and providing emotional support for husbands and children returning home from work or school. The woman in the family created the atmosphere of close interpersonal relationships necessary to a worthwhile human existence, relationships lacking in the competitive workplace (Mann, et al., 1997; Parsons and Bales 1955; Smith 1993). Although these skills are vital to society, they do not command a salary outside of the marketplace. According to this perspective, the traditional function of the male was to play the instrumental role of protecting and providing for his wife and children. He was the head of the household, controlling where the family lived, how money was spent, and making other decisions important to the survival of the family. He also made the political and economic decisions in the community by serving in powerful decision-making positions.

Structural functionalists might argue that many traditional family functions have moved from the family to other social institutions. Most families no longer find support through work at home. Instead, work is more likely to take place in the factory or office. Recreation has also moved away from the family and is sponsored by Little Leagues, tennis clubs, and other organizations at recreation centers. Structural functional theorists believe that because of changing socialization practices and changing beliefs about work, play, and other functions of the family, the complementary roles of husbands and wives are changing to parallel roles, where roles of husbands and wives are similar. The change has been gradual, but both husbands and wives are now likely to work outside the home; and both are increasingly sharing household duties. Most functionalists believe that the family will benefit as equality increases between men and women.

Recreation has moved away from the family and is now sponsored by such organizations as Little Leagues.

Conflict Theory

A conflict theory of gender differentiation focuses on the power and authority discrepancies between men and women. The conflict perspective views women's relative social status, domestic violence, rape, and disparities in wages as resulting from degradation and exploitation by men. Very early in the development of horticultural societies, military force was used to protect land and other valuable private property and also to capture women from other tribes. Women were prized possessions who could work for their captors to increase wealth, provide children who would grow into future workers, and increase the prestige of the men who owned them. It was not just as future workers that children were important. Men needed children to look after the property when they grew old and to inherit it when they died. To know who his children were, a man needed to isolate his women from other men. Thus, women became the protected property of men, so that men could accumulate wealth and have children to inherit it. According to this perspective, from earliest times, men exploited women for the work they did and for the children they bore and reared.

The process of industrialization removed work from the family. Therefore, conflict theorists argue, men were not willing to lose their control over the labor of women. They either tried to keep women out of the work force entirely or used them as a surplus labor force, moving them in and out of the lowest-paying jobs as the economy required. They passed laws regulating the kind of work that women could do and the hours they could work. They also passed laws regulating women's rights to income, property ownership, and birth control; and they made women exclusively responsible for domestic tasks. Men forbade women from joining unions and from entering professions. Legally and by tradition, they prevented women from gaining high positions in the work force. Men increased their position of power and dominance, while sustaining the dependence of women on them. Less powerful men were also hurt by the practice of keeping women in positions with low pay. The existence of a labor force of poorly paid women meant that lower-paid women could easily replace men who asked for higher wages.

As can be seen, these two theories of gender differentiation lead sociologists to diverse approaches in the study and understanding of the behavior and roles of men and women. According to a structural functional perspective, as industrial society develops, women should move into the work force and attain equality with men. According to a conflict perspective, as industrial society creates more wealth and power for men, men will use their wealth and power to improve their own position; and women will lag farther and farther behind. We now turn our attention to gender differentiation in the workplace and, more specifically, to women in the workplace.

GENDER DIFFERENTIATION AND THE WORKPLACE

Women in the Workplace

The status of women in the workplace is often treated as if it were a new issue. However, women have always played an important economic role in society, moving in and out of the work force as the economy required. Throughout much of history, women produced much of what was needed in the home and also made items for sale in the marketplace. With the growth of large cities during the Middle Ages, new options became available to them. They became traders and innkeepers and occasionally ran breweries and blacksmith shops. They often joined guilds (Bernard 1981), which were a type of medieval trade union. Those who did not wish to marry could become **Beguines**, members of urban

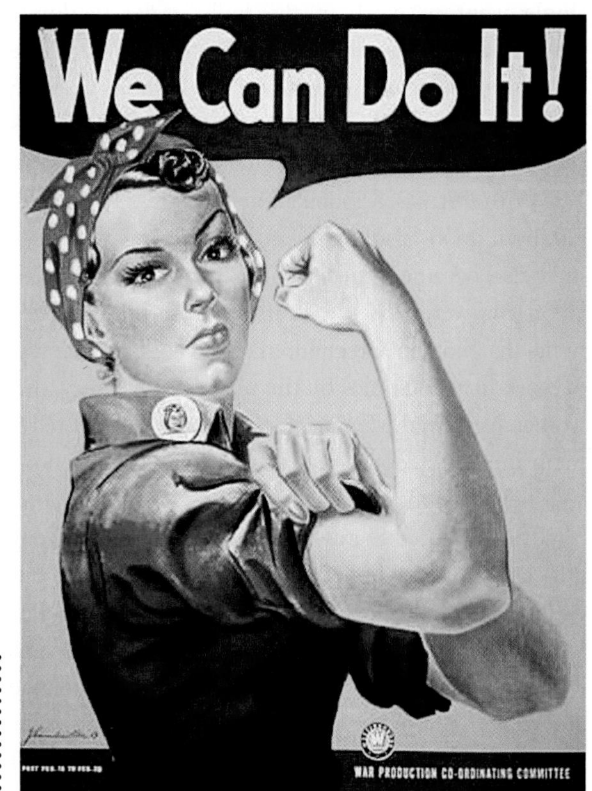

So many women went to work in defense plants during Word War II that they were nicknamed "Rosie the Riveter."

communes of seven or eight women who pursued such occupations as sewing, baking, spinning, and weaving.

Women from the upper class could join convents and become nuns. At that time, some convents had great wealth and beautiful furnishings, and nuns wore beautiful embroidered robes. Some convents also had great scholarly reputations and were political forces to be reckoned with.

When the plagues swept Europe and devastated the population, the powerful Catholic Church and the states of that time wanted women to stay home and have babies to increase the population. The states passed laws banning the Beguine communes, and the Church closed most of the nunneries. In those nunneries that remained open, the nuns were required to wear black habits and to serve the poor. Otherwise, family life was the only secure option for women; and their income was from the goods, particularly textiles, that they could produce in the home.

The textile and other goods traditionally produced by women in the home were the first to be manufactured in factories at the beginning of the Industrial Revolution. Many women who were poor, young, and single went to work in the mills under deplorable working conditions, for very little pay. Married women could seldom leave the home for the 12-hour workdays required in the mills and still maintain their homes, so they lost their ability to earn income.

With increased population growth and industrialization, good farmland became increasingly scarce, so men also became available for factory work. Protective labor laws were passed that limited both the number of hours that women and children could work and the types of work they could do. By the nineteenth century, then, women had lost the few work options that had existed for them in earlier centuries. The only source of economic well-being was marriage.

In the United States at the beginning of the twentieth century, many upper-class women received an education, and some worked in the professions. Poor women who worked were usually employed as servants. The vast majority of women, however, were married and worked in the home to meet the needs of their families. In fact, during the Great Depression in the 1930s, married women who took jobs were considered selfish and unpatriotic. Jobs were scarce. The unemployment rate rose to 25 percent; and if a woman worked, she was seen as taking a job away from a man who needed it to support his family.

In 1941, the country went to war. Men were sent overseas, and women were told that it was now their patriotic duty to help out in the war effort by going to work. Women held every conceivable job, and for many of them, it was their first opportunity to earn a good salary. They not only worked at white-collar jobs but they also did factory work, building the planes and ships needed for war. In fact, so many women went to work in defense plants that they were often nicknamed "Rosie the Riveter."

After the war was over, men returned to their jobs; and many women were seen as dispensable and were fired. Since many of these women had supported themselves and families on their salaries, it was a hardship to give up work. However, as the economy shifted from the needs of wartime to peace, it had become their patriotic duty to go home and have babies. The country had experienced very low birth rates throughout the depression and World War II, and it needed to build its population of future workers. Thus began the "baby boom," which continued until 1960 when the birth rate began to decline.

In the 1960s, there was a labor shortage because of the low birth rates during the depression and World War II. Unemployment was low, and salaries were high. Women were once again welcomed into the labor force, at least to fill low-paying jobs. From that time to the present, wages did not keep up with inflation, and more and more women were required to work to help pay family expenses. As of 2009, 59.2 percent of women were in the work force in the U.S, and they composed 46.8 percent of workers, projected to increase to 46.9 percent by 2018 (U.S. Department of Labor). While the increase in the percentage of women in the workforce by 2018 seems insignificant, this will account for 51.2 percent of the increase in total labor force growth between 2008 and 2018.

Income

The median income for women working full-time year round in 2009 was $35,549—compared to men's median of $45,485 (U.S. Census). In 1960, women earned

61 percent of what men made; but during the 1960s and 1970s, the gap between men and women widened as more women moved into the work force and took low-paying jobs. By the late 1970s, women made only 59 percent of what men made. In 2009, women earned about 78 percent of what men earned. Clearly, this wage differential is now narrowing, largely because the mean income of men is decreasing. There are several reasons for the continuing gap in earnings:

1. More women than men are entering the work force in low-paying occupations, such as clerical, service, or blue-collar work. Often, these jobs have no career lines, so women cannot advance to higher positions.
2. Women are sometimes paid less than men, even though they hold equivalent jobs.
3. People with low salaries receive smaller raises. A 10 percent raise on $20,000 is smaller than a 10 percent raise on $30,000, with the result that income differentials increase even as percentage increases remain equal.

Women have been steadily returning to work for four decades. Surely, many women have gained considerable education and work experience during this time, and the gap in earnings between men and women should be closing more rapidly than it is. (See Tables 10-1 and 10-2.) The question, then, is this: Why do women remain in low-paying occupations?

The Split Labor Market

One reason that women are not advancing is the split labor market. In a split labor market there are two distinct and unequal groups of workers (Bonacich 1972). The **primary labor market** is reserved for elites, people who will advance to high-level positions. Primary-labor-market jobs offer job security, on-the-job training, high wages, and frequent promotions. Corporate managers, professionals, and engineers belong to this labor market.

In the **secondary labor market**, jobs pay poorly, and there is little job security. There are many layoffs but few promotions or salary increases. Most women work in the secondary labor force in secretarial, typing, and clerical jobs, as sales clerks or waitresses, or in manufacturing jobs. This inequality caused by the split labor market accounts for much of the inequality in earnings between women and men (Bose and Rossi 1983; Marshall and Paulin 1985).

The secondary labor market is growing in size, both in the United States and throughout the world. During the decade of the 1980s, unions worldwide lost power. As a result, there has been increasing pressure to weaken job security and to reduce or eliminate minimum-wage regulations. It is now easier for employers to dismiss midlevel managers or highly skilled manufacturing workers. The employer then can automate the job with robotic or other machinery or can divide it into simple, repetitive tasks, which can be done by temporary workers at very low wages. Such workers do not develop complex skills; they have no route into the primary labor force. They are not promoted; they do not receive any company benefits such as child care, health insurance, or pensions, and often are not eligible for social security.

Shifts in union composition in recent years have led to new research about the changing nature of the split-labor market. Global markets have led to shifts in the

In the secondary labor market, most women work in such occupations as secretaries or waitresses.

TABLE 10-1 THE 20 MOST PREVALENT OCCUPATIONS FOR EMPLOYED WOMEN IN 2009

Occupation	Number
Secretaries and administrative assistants	3,074,000
Registered nurses	2,612,000
Elementary and middle school teachers	2,343,000
Cashiers	2,273,000
Nursing, psychiatric, and home health aides	1,770,000
Retail salespersons	1,650,000
First-line supervisors/managers of retail sales workers	1,459,000
Waiters and waitresses	1,434,000
Maids and housekeeping cleaners	1,282,000
Customer service representatives	1,263,000
Child care workers	1,228,000
Bookkeeping, accounting, and auditing clerks	1,205,000
Receptionists and information clerks	1,168,000
First-line supervisors/managers of office and administrative support workers	1,163,000
Managers, all other	1,106,000
Accountants and auditors	1,084,000
Teacher assistants	921,000
Cooks	831,000
Office clerks, general	821,000
Personal and home care aides	789,000

Source: United States Department of Labor

power of balance in labor unions, with membership from workers in the upper tiers declining, and increasing in the lower tiers. In the old split labor market, organized labor drew its strength from the upper tier of the organized workforce to help combat the sometimes unjust practices of employers. Today, we are seeing greater strength within the lower tiers to overcome assaults against labor unions. This movement has the potential to bring more fairness and justice to the most vulnerable members of society (Chun 2008).

Nevertheless, women are still disproportionately poor as compared to men. Many of the jobs in the secondary labor force are being moved from industrialized countries to Third World countries, where labor is even cheaper. There, many rural women are being recruited to leave their homes and take jobs in the new urban industries. Leaving home to go to work is a greater sacrifice in Asian countries than it is in Western countries because in Asia, the women are traditionally very sheltered. Often, once they leave home, they are no longer respectable; they are not welcome to return home, and they also lose their opportunity to marry. In some countries, the women compose almost half the work force. Globally, women earn on average about three-fourths what men earn for the same work (U.N. Fourth World Conference on Women 1995).

Comparable Worth

Some jobs are low paying simply because they are held by women, not because the job does not require considerable skill. For example, some office work requires many skills but is often paid less than maintenance work, a position traditionally held by men. Many women argue that pay scales should be based on **comparable worth**—work of equal value, requiring the same level of skills—should earn equal pay, even when the work is not identical. If clerical

TABLE 10-2 WOMEN IN HIGH PAYING MANAGEMENT AND PROFESSIONAL OCCUPATIONS

Women accounted for 51 percent of all workers in the high-paying management, professional, and related occupations. Here is just a sample of these occupations where women were the larger percentage of those employed:

Occupation	Percent Female
Registered nurses	92.0 percent
Meeting and convention planners	83.3
Elementary and middle school teachers	81.9
Tax examiners, collectors, and revenue agents	73.8
Medical and health services managers	69.5
Social and community service managers	69.4
Psychologists	68.8
Other business operations specialists	68.4
Human resources managers	66.8
Financial specialists, all other	66.6
Tax preparers	65.9
Insurance underwriters	62.8
Education administrators	62.6
Accountants and auditors	61.8
Veterinarians	61.2
Claims adjusters, appraisers, examiners, and investigators	60.6
Budget analysts	59.3
Medical scientists	56.9
Advertising and promotions managers	56.5
Financial managers	54.7

Source: United States Department of Labor

work, for example, is as necessary to an organization and requires the same level of skills as maintenance work, workers in these two occupations should receive equal pay. If the sale of women's clothing is of equal value and requires the same skills as the sale of men's clothing, it is argued that these two occupations should receive equal pay. Currently, they do not.

The idea of comparable worth has met with a great deal of resistance because companies resist increasing salaries, and women have little bargaining power (O'Donnell 1984). Legally, it is discriminatory to pay women less for their low-status jobs if the low status is conferred solely because of the gender of the worker. It is not considered discriminatory to pay a worker less if the job has low prestige.

Upward Mobility

As was noted earlier in the beginning of this chapter, women make up about half of the labor force, yet women who reach management-level positions seem to confront a glass ceiling. Only twelve Fortune 500 companies (2.4 percent) and twenty-five Fortune 1000 companies (2.5 percent) have women CEOs or presidents (www.infoplease.com). In 1995, 8.7 percent of corporate officers in Fortune 500 companies were women,

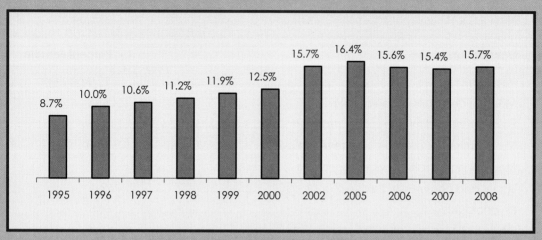

FIGURE 10-1 FORTUNE 500 CORPORATE OFFICER POSITIONS HELD BY WOMEN 2†

1995	1996	1997	1998	1999	2000	2002	2005	2006	2007	2008
8.7%	10.0%	10.6%	11.2%	11.9%	12.5%	15.7%	16.4%	15.6%	15.4%	15.7%

†Note: In 2009, Catalyst instituted a methodology change that makes comparison to previous annual Corporate Officer statistics inappropriate.

Source: [2] Catalyst, 2008 Catalyst Census of Women Corporate Officers and Top Earners of the Fortune 500 (2008); Catalyst, 2007 Census of Women Corporate Officers and Top Earners of the Fortune 500 (2007); Catalyst, 2005 Catalyst Census of Women Corporate Officers and Top Earners of the Fortune 500 (2006).

peaking at 16.4 percent in 2005, and falling back to 15.7 percent as of 2009 (Catalyst 2011). (See Figure 10-1) At the level of vice president or above in major companies, there has been no significant increase in the number of women in these positions during recent years.

Research has shown that in order to increase earnings and to get promoted into executive positions, a person needs experience in two areas: authority and autonomy (Spaeth 1985). **Authority** consists of supervisory experience and experience in a decision-making position. Autonomy on the job means having the ability to decide how work will be done. People who decide for themselves how they will do a job are more committed to their work than people who are told what to do (Spaeth 1985).

Women have less authority and less autonomy in their work than do men (Jaffee 1989). The major reason is that most women work in female-dominated jobs—nurses, teachers, and bank tellers—and these jobs do not generally offer either authority or autonomy. However, discrimination also plays a role in why women do not achieve these more powerful positions. When men enter a female-dominated work field, they often quickly move into one of the few jobs that have authority and autonomy. For example, the majority of elementary school teachers are women, but most school superintendents are male.

When women work in occupations in which the work force is mixed—male and female—women are still less likely than men to get the jobs with authority and autonomy. This lack of opportunity has been shown to occur even when education and work experience are equal and regardless of whether the woman has family responsibilities (Jaffee 1989).

Thinking Sociologically

1. How could the material in this chapter be used to develop a strategy for parents, teachers, employers, and politicians that would help lead to greater equality for women and men in the workplace?
2. Use material (including theories, concepts, and facts) in this chapter to discuss why the glass ceiling exists for women.

Women's Work in the Family

It is generally recognized that women carry the greatest burden in the family, doing the unpaid but necessary labor of housework and childcare (Berk 1985). Understanding spousal perceptions of fairness in housework is necessary because the division of household labor can be a source of dissatisfaction in many marriages, especially for wives. Wives who feel that household work is inequitable tend to be less happy in their marriages and personally, and have higher rates of depression than those who feel that housework is shared equitably (Rogers and Amato 2000; Bird 1999). One thing that contributes to wives' level of satisfaction is how much housework their husbands share equally. Spousal housework hours mean more to wives' perception of fairness then their own housework hours. This is not just an American phenomenon but true in many other countries as well (Ruppanner 2008). It is not just the amount of work that they each do that has to do with wives' happiness. When spouses share housework, wives feel more appreciated and recognized for their household contributions (Lee and Waite 2010). As women enter the work force, they continue to carry this family burden. Working women spend less time on housework than women who do not work; however, working women spend more time on housework than their husbands, even when the wife works forty hours a week and the husband is unemployed (Hochschild 2003). When household chores increase, such as when a child is ill, women are more likely than men to increase their hours of work at home. (In 2007, Salary.com calculated that a stay-at-home mom would have earned $138,095 per year if she were compensated for all of the elements of her job.)

Women who would like more equality in their marriages have been waiting for the time when it would be acceptable for men to share more of the workload. She does most of the unpleasant chores; he makes decisions. When he does household chores, *he is helping her*. The day-to-day activities in the household are rituals that reinforce the ideas that women are different and are subservient to men. Seeing women's and men's work as "different" is one way structural functionalists describe this phenomenon. Viewing disparate roles where women are subservient to men makes is best explained from the conflict perspective.

When women try to manage work, housework, and children, their health suffers under the strain (Arber, Nigel, and Dale 1985). As a group, they are less healthy than working childless women and women over age forty. Also, if their husbands dominate them, doing more than their share of work but having less than a fair share in decision-making processes, they are likely to suffer from depression (Davies and Doyle 2002).

Nonetheless, men are doing more housework today than ever before. Between 1976 and 2005, the amount of housework that husbands do has doubled and has decreased for women. (See Figure 10-2) What's more, husbands today tend to do more housework if they are well-educated and young (Zinn and Eitzen 2005). It also appears that contemporary husbands divide up housework with their wives more equitably if they earn roughly the same amount of money as their wives (Greenstein 2000).

THE WOMEN'S MOVEMENT

Efforts by women to gain political and economic power—known collectively as the **women's movement**—have taken place for more than a century in both Europe and the United States. However, these movements have had different emphasis on either side of the Atlantic.

The Women's Movement in the United States

The women's movement in the United States, instead of seeking special privileges for women, has emphasized equal rights. In an attempt to unite all women behind the cause of equality, the movement has remained separate from any particular political party or union, for fear that such an alignment would divide women.

In fact, however, the cause of equality has divided women. The movement wants equality for women in the workplace and thereby plays down the importance of special treatment for women as homemakers. This

FIGURE 10-2 WEEKLY HOURS OF BASIC HOUSEWORK BY GENDER AND MARITAL STATUS

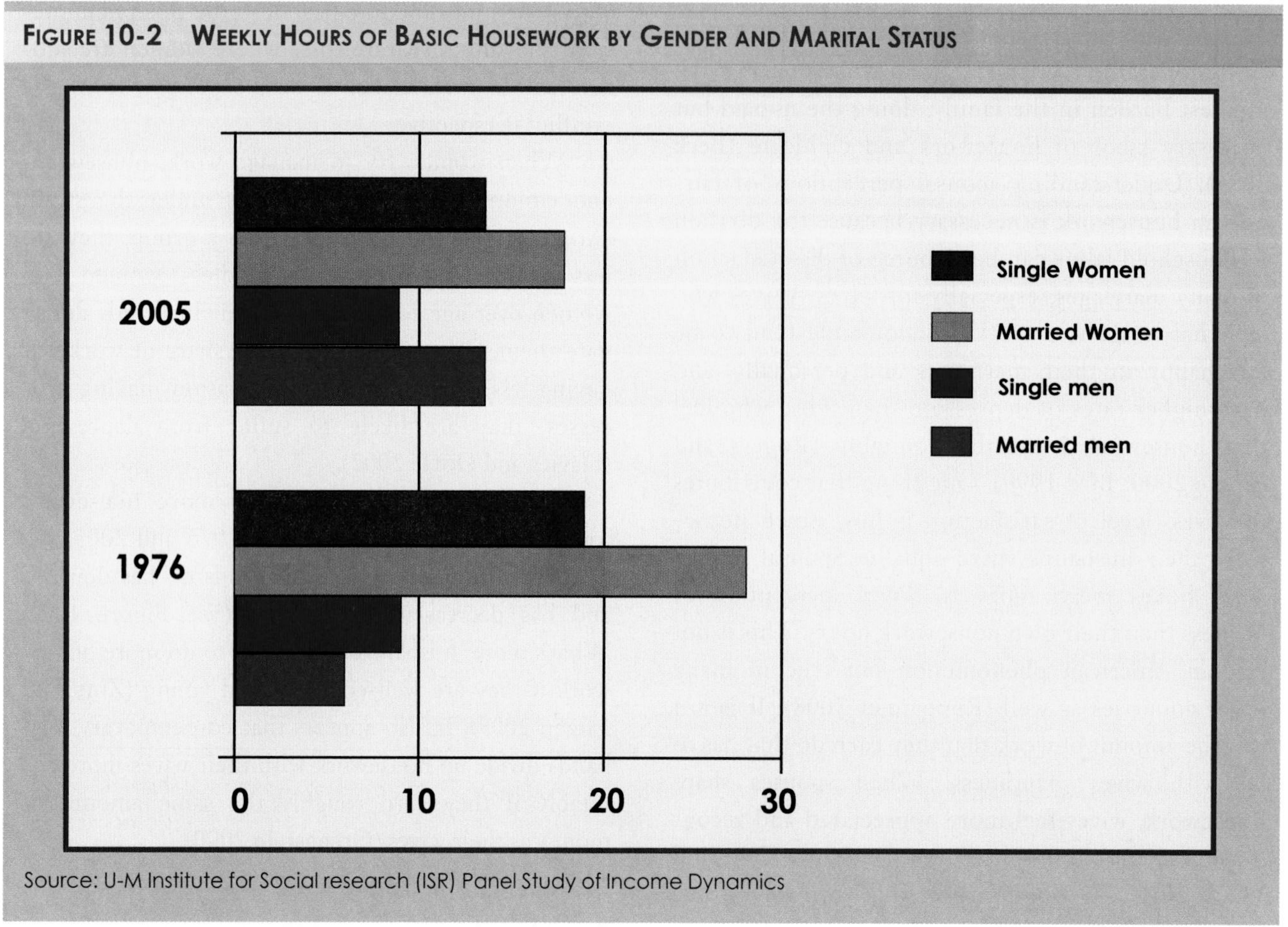

Source: U-M Institute for Social research (ISR) Panel Study of Income Dynamics

has served to alienate women who give primary importance to their roles as homemakers and who want special support and protection in their homemaking roles. In general, the level of benefits that working mothers in this country can expect falls far below the norm for their European counterparts; and they continue to have difficulty being recognized as fully committed workers.

The women's movement has succeeded in gaining many rights for women. Through the women's suffrage movement, women first gained the right to vote in the 1920s; and they can now hold many jobs from which they previously were barred. Today, there are female bartenders, construction workers, and bus drivers, to mention just a few. Laws have been passed guaranteeing them equal pay for equal work, and they have gained the right to practice birth control and to obtain abortions. Except for the right to vote, however, these rights are not guaranteed under the U.S. Constitution; and Congress could change the laws that grant these rights at any time (or their constitutional legitimacy could be changed through new U.S. Supreme Court rulings).

The women's movement supported the **Equal Rights Amendment (ERA)**, a proposed amendment that would have guaranteed women equal rights under the Constitution. The ERA states simply, "Equality of rights under the law shall not be denied or abridged by the United States or any state on account of sex." Congress approved the amendment in 1972; and although most Americans support the ERA (Lansing 1986), the required number of states needed to ratify it as part of the U.S. Constitution did not do so. The women's movement thus failed to gain guaranteed equal rights.

This was a major disappointment to the American women's movement. Their attempts to gain equal rights in the workplace and in the law met with only partial success, but American women gained even less as homemakers and mothers. Without adequate pay, American women who are widowed, divorced, or never married often find themselves and their children living

Women suffragists march in New York City in 1915.

in poverty. The benefits that European women received as a result of their movement assures them that they and their children are not as likely to be poor as they would be if they lived in the United States.

The Women's Movement in Europe

In Europe, the women's movement focused on special privileges for women (Hewlett 1986). Those involved in the movement believe that women have special problems because they assume most of the responsibility for child rearing and therefore need better pay when they work, time off for childbearing, and help from the community in providing child rearing. The movement in European countries has aligned itself with political parties and labor unions that support the programs women need, and this political support has been successful in gaining benefits. Swedish women, for example, have recently been earning more than 80 percent of what men earn. When a child is born in Sweden, either parent may take leave for one year and still receive 90 percent of salary for thirty-eight weeks of that year. In addition, state-supported childcare, noted for its excellence, is usually available for children when the parent returns to work. In Austria, women in manufacturing earn 82 percent of what men earn, and women receive 100 percent of their salaries while on leave for the birth of a child, although the leave granted is shorter than it is in Sweden. Although Sweden has the best benefits for women, almost all European nations pay women a higher proportion of men's earnings than women earn in the United States. In addition, these countries offer both childcare and paid leaves-of-absence for parenting.

THE CONSEQUENCES OF INEQUALITY

The most obvious result of gender inequality in the United States is the high level of poverty among women. However, the stratification system results in other notable gender differences as well. In this section, we discuss the problems of poverty, women's self-esteem, medical care, sexual harassment in the workplace, family violence, and rape.

Gender and Poverty

Given the many problems women face in the workplace, it is not surprising that in 2009 almost 30 percent of women who are heads of families with no husband present have incomes below the poverty line (U.S Census Beureau). Women are said to be *heads of families* if they have children to support. Persons in female-householder families are the most likely demographic group to be chronically poor. U.S. Census and Labor Statistics show a steady trend of poverty, which primarily affects women and children in their care. This increase in the number of women who head families suffering in poverty continues and has been called the **feminization of poverty**. Black and Hispanic women have a much greater likelihood of living in poverty than White or Asian women.

In the older population, the increase in poor women is partly due to their longevity because men die at an earlier age than do women. Also, the death of a man can throw his widow into poverty by reducing the amounts of Social Security and pension she receives and also by reducing any savings she might have had, which were used to pay for medical and nursing care prior to his death.

Those most severely affected by poverty are women who are responsible for both the care and the financial support of children, as well as the children in their care. Children either reduce the hours that a mother can work or increase her child-care costs. Available new jobs tend to be low-paying and frequently do not provide the basics for mother and children. Researchers have identified a new family type in the United States, the "fragile family," that

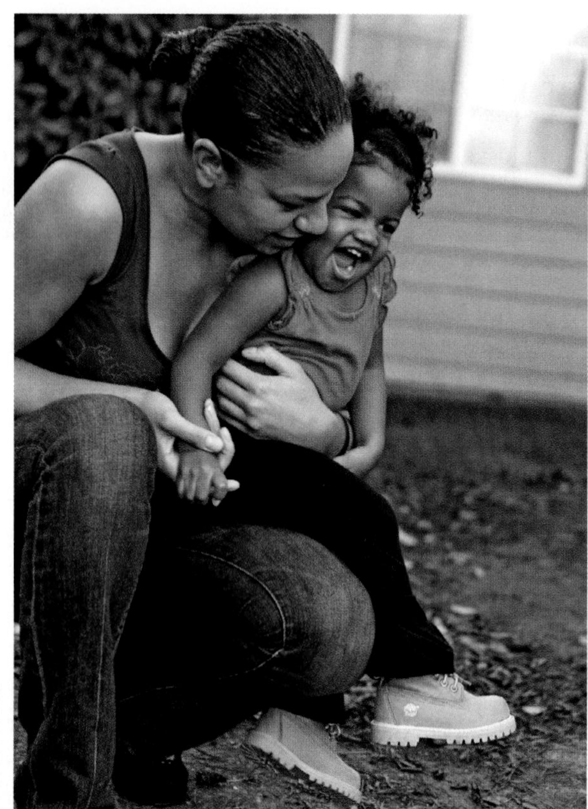

Women responsible for the care and financial support of children and those children in their care are most severely affected by poverty.

also contributes to economic hardships especially for single women with children (Kalil and Ryan 2010). These families are the result of an increase in the rates of non-marital childbirth. These families consist of cohabiting couples as well as single mothers, but single mothers experience the most economic hardships. Public safety nets (such as food stamps, Medicaid, housing, and child care) help. However, single mothers in fragile families increasingly have to turn to private safety nets (such as family and friends) to make ends meet and these are neither consistent nor dependable, nor do they significantly improve mothers' economic circumstances. Because the high rate of non-marital childbirth is likely to continue rise, and at a time when public assistance is coming increasingly under question, single mothers are likely to face economic hardship for some time to come.

An additional cause of the increase of the feminization of poverty relates to single-parent families resulting from no-fault divorce and the rising divorce rate. No-fault divorce laws, first passed in California in 1970 and since adopted in some form by most states, do not require that anyone be blamed for the breakdown of the marriage (Weitzman 1985) and do not allow punitive payments to be paid by one spouse to the other. This is in sharp contrast to traditional divorce laws, in which one spouse, usually the husband, was considered to be at fault. As punishment, he was sometimes required to pay alimony to his wife and sometimes the family home was awarded to her. This could support her for the rest of her life. Under no-fault divorce, both husband and wife are expected to assume equal responsibility for themselves and for their children after the divorce. Alimony, if awarded, is usually awarded as a temporary measure to give the wife time to find a job and adjust to a new life. The family home is usually ordered to be sold so that the proceeds can be divided equally. The child-support payments required of the husband are usually low because the courts assume that the wife will help to support the children. Little consideration is given to the fact that she may not be able to earn much money.

As a result of the no-fault divorce laws, a man who divorces his wife can expect a 42 percent rise in his standard of living (Weitzman 1985). He is allowed to keep half of the family assets and most of his income. He is free from the burden of supporting his wife and needs only to contribute a small portion of his paycheck to his children while they are under the age of eighteen. In contrast, a woman who is divorced will experience a 73 percent decline in her standard of living (as will her children, if she has custody). The woman must provide a home, support herself, and support her children on what is usually a very small paycheck. In the time since no-fault divorce first went into practice in some states, not much has changed in terms of the-long term financial impact on women.

In addition, if a father sues for custody, the low earnings of a woman may be taken into account by the courts. In 70 percent of the cases where the father sues for custody, he will win because he has the financial means to support his children (Weitzman 1985). Often, men threaten to sue for custody even when they do not want it to get women to negotiate smaller child-support payments (Weitzman 1985); some women so fear losing their children that they will sacrifice future income rather than risk a custody battle. Thus, many women are receiving even smaller settlements than they are entitled to under the law, which increases the number of women (and their children) who have incomes below the poverty line.

Women's Self-Esteem

Most women are, sooner or later, housewives and mothers, at least for a time. Because our society gives so little respect and esteem to these roles, it is not surprising that women tend to give themselves little respect for accomplishments in these areas; and they often find the demands of the role stressful. Gove and Geerken (1977), in trying to develop a theory to explain stress, argued that married women experience high rates of stress because the role of a married woman is not respected in American society. To test this theory, a study was conducted comparing American women of European descent with Mexican women (Ross, et al., 1983b). Since previous research had shown that the family is more highly valued in Mexico than it is in the United States, this research hypothesized that Mexican women would feel less stress because they were more valued as family members. It was found that Mexican women did, in fact, suffer less stress and receive more support for their role in the family.

In America, some evidence supports the idea that many women have low self-esteem regarding their personal appearance. They are expected to be thin and beautiful; and as a result, women spend more time, energy, and money than men do on cosmetics, diet, and exercise products. Numerous examples exist of women who are extremely critical of their bodies and diet, to the point of malnutrition. In extreme cases, excessive dieting results in anorexia or bulimia, illnesses most often seen in women, which sometimes result in death from starvation. It is important to point out that gender concern over body image and self-esteem varies across cultures. Whereas most research has found that women are more concerned with their appearance and experience greater body dissatisfaction, and thus lower self-esteem than men, recent research has found that body image disturbances are of concern to Australian men (Mellor, et. al, 2010). This suggests that issues of body image and self-esteem are not inherent to gender in and of itself, but have much to do with the importance that different cultures and societies place on body image for men and for women.

Females at all ages in the U.S also experience depression more often then men. Women in America, the government document discussed at the beginning of this chapter, reports that in any two-week period, 8 percent of women and girls report experiencing clinically significant depression as compared to 5 percent for men and boys. Depression for females is found even more often for those living below the poverty line, Blacks, and those between the ages of forty to fifty-nine.

Medical Care

When men go to their physicians with complaints, they are likely to receive a very thorough physical. When women go to their physician with complaints, they are likely to receive a prescription for tranquilizers or antidepressants instead of a physical (Ehrenreich and English 1979). Even when their symptoms are severe, women receive fewer diagnostic tests for heart disease and receive less treatment; although postmenopausal women have comparable rates of heart disease to men's rates, only half as many women receive heart bypass operations as men. Women also receive only half the number of diagnostic tests for lung cancer (despite women's increasing rates of lung cancer) and are only half as likely to receive a kidney transplant (Trafford 1991). According to Trafford, this indicates negligent health care for women. While women receive less care for the major diseases that kill people in this country, physicians have a tendency to interfere with and over treat the normal reproductive process (Schur 1984); and as a result, the following procedures are done routinely and are unnecessary in 90 percent of cases: fetal monitoring during labor; use of drugs to induce early labor; use of anesthesia, forceps, and related techniques in delivery; performance of *episiotomy* (surgical incision at the opening of the vagina during the birth process); and surgical delivery through cesarean section. Cesarean sections have risen from 5 percent to over 30 percent of births in the past three decades. In 2008, the cesarean rate was the highest ever reported in the U.S (*Women in America*). Recent research has shown that women use more health services and incur greater expenditures for healthcare than men. Women have significantly more annual care visits, diagnostic services, and total medical charges than men, even after controlling for health status and variables related to socioeconomic status and demographic factors such as age and ethnicity (Bertakis and Azari 2010). This is especially problematic since, as noted in *Women in America*, the share of women without health insurance, ages eighteen to sixty-four has increased. In 2009, 18 percent of non-elderly women lacked health insurance compared to 13 percent in 1984. (It should be noted that the percentage of uninsured also rose for men during the same time period, from 16 percent to 24 percent.)

Women also have an excessive number of *hysterectomies*, the removal of the uterus and sometimes of the other female reproductive organs. Physicians have argued that the female reproductive organs are not useful except to have children, and they perform this major abdominal surgery for any number of reasons, sometimes as minor as for the relief of menstruation. However, many women who have had hysterectomies report serious depression and difficulty in adjusting to sexual activity (Stokes 1986).

In recent years, there has been increasing interest in new reproductive technologies. Although research continues to investigate the causes of infertility and birth defects, most research has concentrated on amniocentesis and artificial reproduction. Amniocentesis is early testing of the fetus, and the fetus is usually aborted if defective. The mother often feels little choice in whether to abort (Rothman 1986) because the social pressure to abort a defective baby is so strong. Reproductive technologies also include the work associated with so-called test-tube babies. Some hope that women eventually will be freed of the reproductive role; but others fear that women's status would be lowered further, and their bodies would become no more than a source of spare parts (Corea 1985; Rowland 1985).

Sexual Harassment

Women in all types of jobs suffer from **sexual harassment**, unwelcome sexual advances made by coworkers or superiors at work. Women who reject sexual advances may be denied a job, be intimidated, given poor work evaluations, denied raises or promotions, or fired.

Women in all types of jobs suffer from unwelcome sexual advances by coworkers or superiors.

Sexual harassment is much more widespread than is generally realized. The first questionnaire ever devoted solely to this topic surveyed working women in 1975 (Farley 1978). The results were startling: 92 percent of respondents cited sexual harassment as a serious problem, and 70 percent reported that they had personally experienced some form of harassment. Other more recent studies indicate that sexual harassment is also a major problem in colleges and universities, in offices of the United Nations, in the United States military, in civil service jobs, and in private industry.

In deciding how to respond to sexual harassment, the victim must consider the economic necessity of keeping the job, opportunities for getting another job, the likelihood of obtaining decent work evaluations and future promotions, the possibility of being fired, and the attitudes of family and friends to her situation. The victim usually decides to quit, transfer to another job within the organization, or simply to do nothing and to suffer in silence because probably no one will believe her if she makes a complaint.

Family Violence

Family violence is a widespread problem in the United States. Indeed, "[American] women are more likely to be killed, physically assaulted, sexually victimized, hit, beat up, slapped, or spanked in their own homes by other family members than anywhere else, or by anyone else, in our society" (Gelles 1995:450). The Center for Disease Control (www.cdc.gov, 2011) reports that each year women experience about 4.8 million intimate partner

An estimated 4 million women are battered each year by their husbands or lovers.

related assaults and rapes. Men are the victims of 2.9 milliion intimate partner related assaults. Intimate partner violence resulted in 2,340 deaths in 2007, of which 70 percent were female and 30 percent were male. Battery causes more injury to women than rape (including rape with battery), auto accidents, and muggings combined (Cleage 1993). Nearly one in four women in the U.S reports experiencing violence by a current or former spouse or boyfriend at some point in their life (www.endabuse.org)

When a wife or child is being abused, the wife often does not leave the home or remove the child from the home. Sometimes, the wife believes she deserves to be beaten, but women frequently have no money of their own and no safe place to go (Chasin 1997). It is likewise difficult for a woman to take her children out of her home when she has no means of support, no food, and no shelter. Thus, while the reasons for family violence are complex, one of the major reasons it continues is that women are unable to support themselves and their children and are therefore unwilling to leave home.

Rape

Rape is another form of violence that results in part from gender inequality. The FBI's Uniform Crime Reports show that 78,770 rapes were reported in 1982 and increased significantly to 109,593 one decade later. The number of reported rapes decreased in 2001 to 90,491, but once again increased 3.4 percent to 93,934 in 2006. 10.6 percent of women and 2.1 percent of men have experienced forced sex at some point in their lives; that is more than 11 million women and 2 million men (Basile, et. al., 2007). These numbers are estimates of actual rapes, which are likely two to three times higher than the number reported to authorities. Most sexual assault victimization is not disclosed (Kilpatrick, et. al., 1992 in Basile, et al).

One myth about rape often believed by the public is that rape usually occurs between strangers. However, very often men know the women they rape. In the typical incidence of **acquaintance rape** or *date rape*, the man and woman have been dating for a long time, perhaps a year. In one study of rape on a college campus, 20 to 25 percent of female college students reported having been raped (Fisher, et. al., 2000).

Another myth about rape is that rape is sexually motivated. However, when men rape women, it is often an act of aggressiveness. Men may rape because they hate women, they wish to be cruel or violent, or they seek revenge (Henslin 1990). Nonetheless, because society believes that rape is a sexual act, they believe that women involved in rape have done something sexual to invite rape. Perhaps the women wore enticing clothing, appeared in public at late hours, drank too much, or did not resist the advances of men. Efforts are being made to reduce the tendency to blame the victim of the rape for her victimization. Nevertheless, should the rapist be caught and brought to trial, the reputation of the victim will come under scrutiny. It will be assumed that if she is sexually active, the rapist may have interpreted her behavior as an invitation to him to attack her (Hamlin 2001).

Some feminists have argued that rape and other forms of violence are the end result of the norms of aggressiveness that men learn to display toward women. Pornography, or erotic literature, has been severely criticized, not because it is sexual but because in this society, most pornography depicts women as passive victims of violent men. The message to readers of this type of pornographic literature is that the violent abuse of women is both masculine and normal (Lederer 1980). A society that differentiates the sexes, gives one sex a lower status than the other, and provides little opportunity for mutual respect between the sexes is likely to continue to see violence against one sex by the other.

THE FUTURE OF GENDER INEQUALITY

Will gender differentiation decrease? Will women become economically and occupationally equal to men? If the structural functionalists are correct, women will gradually win promotions and pay increases that will move them into the upper echelons of the bureaucratic work world and that will win them equality with men. According to the U.S. Department of Labor and Statistics in its 2006 report, "At all levels of education women have fared better than men with respect to earnings."

A third alternative is also possible, one that combines aspects of the functionalist and conflict views. Upper-class women may use a college education as a stepping-stone into the primary labor market. Their educational credentials and their family background will help them get good positions, where, like upper-class men, they will be groomed for greater responsibility and will achieve higher and higher positions. Working-class women, without family connections and educational opportunity, are likely to remain in the secondary labor market and to fall farther and farther behind. In such a scenario, gender differentiation could diminish considerably even while class differences remained great. Complete equality between men and women requires an end to class, as well as gender, differentiation.

Thinking Sociologically

1. Do you believe that women will progress through the glass ceiling? What factors explain why they may or may not?
2. If women made it through the glass ceiling, which of the consequences of inequality would disappear?

CHAPTER REVIEW

Wrapping it up

Summary

1. Modern societies differentiate people on the basis of gender, gender roles, and our concepts of masculinity and femininity.
2. Males and females differ in anatomy, chromosomes, and hormones, but research does not show important differences in behavior because of these sex differences. In fact, where one might expect to find differences in behavior based on physical characteristics, such as females having the most important jobs requiring finger dexterity, the opposite is true. Men have the jobs defined as most important, regardless of physical attributes.
3. In other cultures, the definitions of masculinity and femininity differ, so that men and women occupy roles very different from those found in the United States.
4. According to structural functionalists, women play an expressive role in society, nurturing the family, and men play an instrumental role, providing financially for the family. These roles are changing rapidly, and men and women are sharing roles more often now.
5. According to conflict theorists, women have been exploited by men throughout history, kept out of the paid work force, or moved in and out of the lowest-paying jobs, as needed by the economy.
6. Women have been pushed out of the work force when birth rates were low, so their only alternative would be to get married and have babies. Women have also been encouraged to enter the work force when there was a shortage of workers.
7. When women enter the work force, it is often to take positions in the growing secondary labor market, where salaries are low, work is often part-time or temporary, and fringe benefits are practically nonexistent.
8. Even when women have jobs requiring skills equal to men's jobs, they are not paid for comparable worth.
9. Upward mobility for women is limited first by the inability to move from the secondary work force to the primary work force, and then by the inability to move above the glass ceiling to executive positions. Women are not given positions that provide experience in authority and autonomy and therefore are not eligible for promotion.
10. Women who have families do most of the work at home, whether they are married or not. Their physical and mental health often suffers.
11. The women's movement in Europe fought for special privileges for women and made significant gains in women's salaries, child care, and maternity leaves.
12. The women's movement in the United States fought for equality and gained the right to vote

and to work at a wider variety of jobs, but it divided women because there was no support for women's family responsibilities.

13. As a result of all of these discriminating conditions, 34 percent of women in the United States suffer from poverty when they have children to support.

14. *In no-fault divorce*, the father is required to pay only a small portion of the cost of caring for his children because it is assumed that the mother will pay a share, even if she has custody of the children and a low-paying job.

15. Women in the United States suffer low self-esteem because they get little respect for their family responsibilities.

16. Women get less than adequate health care because women's reproductive organs are seen as problematic when they are not, and women's complaints about other organs are not taken seriously enough.

17. Women are subjected to a great deal of violence. They are harassed at work, treated violently at home, and raped by acquaintances and strangers.

18. It is possible that women may gradually win promotions and get ahead, or they may be trapped in the secondary labor market. It is also possible that women of the upper classes will move ahead while women of the lower classes remain in the secondary work force, reinforcing two classes of women.

Key Terms

acquaintance rape Rape by someone who is known to the person being raped (such as in date rape)

authority Power accepted as legitimate by those it affects

Beguines Communes, existing during the Middle Ages, of peasant women who did not choose to marry and who took vows of celibacy

comparable worth Evaluating and rewarding different occupations equally if the work in each occupation requires the same level of skill and is of equal value to the employer

Equal Rights Amendment (ERA) A proposed amendment to the Constitution of the United States giving equal rights to women that was not ratified

feminization of poverty The increase in the number of persons who are below the level of poverty being predominantly women, particularly as found in female headed families

gender A social status that refers to differences between the sexes, specifically to differences in masculinity and femininity

gender roles The cultural concepts of masculinity and femininity that society creates around gender

primary labor market The labor market reserved for people who will advance to high-level positions

secondary labor market The labor market in which jobs pay poorly, there is little job security, and there are few promotions or salary increases

sex The biological and anatomical characteristics that differentiate males and females

sexual harassment Sexual advances made by coworkers or superiors at work

victimization surveys Asking samples of people who have been victims of a particular behavior, such as rape

women's movement The social movements led by women to gain political and economic equality

Discussion Questions

1. Discuss the relationships among sex, gender, and gender roles.

2. Discuss how various explanations of gender differentiation can be used to account for the way that you have developed. In doing so, identify some experiences in your life in which you were treated in a particular way primarily because of your gender.

3. Use the knowledge of cross-cultural gender differentiation to evaluate the merits of social and biological explanations of gender differentiation.

4. How do structural functionalism and conflict theory account for the persistence of traditional gender roles? Use personal examples to illustrate each approach.

5. Why do you think that the status of women in the workplace is often treated as if it were a new issue? What are some factors that have affected women's status and role in the workplace throughout history?

6. Why is there a wage differential between women and men in the workplace?

7. How has the split labor market affected men and women differently?

8. Discuss some structural factors that make upward mobility easier for men than for women.

9. Compare the impact of the women's movement in Europe with the women's movement in the United States. Where do you think that women have the best chance for equality? Why?

10. What are some consequences of gender inequality for men and women in families and at work?

11. How are such issues as sexual harassment, family violence, and rape a result of gender inequality?

Pop Quiz

1. The social basis of gender differentiation means that ______.

   a. socialization is the primary determinant of behavior
   b. society distinguishes between males and females
   c. society determines a person's gender characteristics
   d. all of the above

2. The influence of hormones on the nervous system ______.

   a. varies from culture to culture
   b. is the same for all humans
   c. is the same for men in all cultures, but varies for women
   d. is the same for women in all cultures, but varies for men

3. What do structural functionalists argue?

   a. Men have traditionally played a more important role in society
   b. The roles of husbands and wives are becoming similar
   c. The roles of husbands and wives are becoming more diversified
   d. The family will suffer if equality of roles continues to grow

4. Conflict theorists argue that men have historically ______.

   a. considered women valuable property
   b. advocated equal rights for women
   c. encouraged women to join labor unions
   d. passed legislation to encourage women in the workplace

5. By 1988, what percentage of women held full-time jobs outside the home?

   a. 20 percent
   b. 40 percent
   c. 57 percent
   d. 75 percent

6. In 2000, the median income of women working full-time year-round was ________ compared to men's income of ________.

   a. $30,000; $31,000
   b. $27,355; $37,339
   c. $25,000; $30,000
   d. $35,000; $40,000

7. The ideas of comparable worth calls for ______.

   a. equal recognition for equal work
   b. equal pay for equal work
   c. equal pay for work requiring similar levels of skills, even if not identical
   d. equal pay for different jobs requiring different skills

8. The Women's Movement in Europe ______.

   a. focused on equal rights
   b. focused on both equal rights and special privileges
   c. focused on uniting all women
   d. focused on special privileges for women

9. The amendment that would have guaranteed women equal protection under the Constitution was the _______ amendment.

   a. Equal Rights
   b. Equal Pay
   c. Comparable Worth
   d. Mommy Track

10. Sexual harassment is reported by _______ percent of working women to be ______.

    a. 92; a serious problem
    b. 80; a serious problem
    c. 48; a minor problem
    d. 32; not a problem

11. Studies show that sex hormones affect the nervous system and structure masculine or feminine behavior. T/F

12. Beguines existed for married female workers. T/F

13. The skilled workers with seniority who were laid off in the 1980s were mostly women. T/F

14. The number of women heads of families living in poverty has been decreasing. T/F

15. Women's reproductive organs are viewed as problematic. T/F

1. D	6. C	11. F
2. B	7. C	12. F
3. B	8. D	13. F
4. A	9. A	14. F
5. C	10. A	15. T

CHAPTER 11

Age Differentiation and the Aged

WHEN DOES LIFE END?

When is a person's life over? The answer seems simple enough, and a few decades ago the question probably would have been dismissed as absurd. Traditionally, a person's life was considered over when his or her heart stopped beating or lungs could no longer breathe. However, over the past few decades, medical technology has made the question about when life ends vastly complex. Consider what people might be thinking and feeling regarding someone who is being kept alive by life-support system. Is a person whose vital organs function only with the help of life-sustaining machinery really alive? Is a person in an irreversible coma or in a vegetative state really alive? In addition, is there a specific physical quality of life—other than the ability to sustain life functions on one's own—that now needs to be considered in deciding when life is over? The answers to these questions are not at all simple, as evidenced by highly publicized court battles—such as the cases of Karen Ann Quinlan, Nancy Cruzan and Terri Schiavo—in which patients in irreversible comas are kept alive through life-support systems had relatives fought to allow their loved ones to die. Although the questions about when life ends are not confined to any one age group, they are more relevant to the elderly, as a group, precisely because they are in their later stages of life and are more likely to face such questions than members of other age groups.

While court battles such as those faced by the relatives of Karen Ann Quinlan, Nancy Cruzan, and Terri Schiavo still take place, there is evidence that most adults in the United States would prefer death for themselves or others to living in permanent pain or on life-support systems. Consider the following survey results:

• Gallup Poll (2006): "When a person has a disease that cannot be cured, do you think the doctors should be allowed by law to end the patient's life by some painless means if the patient and his [sic] family request it?" Results: Yes – 69 percent; No – 27 percent; Unsure – 4 percent

• CBS News/*New York Times* (2006): "If a person has a disease that will ultimately destroy their mind or body, and they want to take their own life, should a doctor be allowed to assist the person in taking their own life, or not?" Results: Should be allowed – 56 percent; Should not be allowed – 37 percent; Unsure – 7 percent.

• Fox News (2005): "Do you favor or oppose legalizing physician-assisted suicide for terminally ill patients?" Results: Favor – 48 percent; Oppose – 39 percent; Unsure – 13 percent.

• Pew Research Center (2005): "In some states, it's legal to stop medical treatment that is keeping a terminally ill patient alive, or never start the treatment in the first place if that's what the patient wants. Do you approve or disapprove of laws that let PATIENTS decide about being kept alive through medical treatment?" Results: Approve – 84 percent; Disapprove – 10 percent; Unsure – 6 percent.

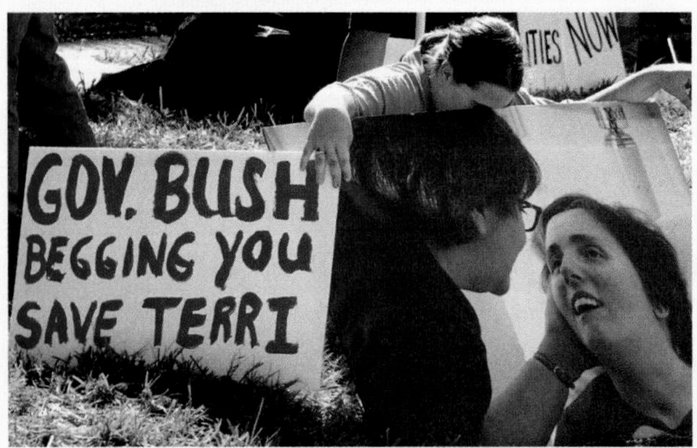

A woman leans against a picture of Terri Schiavo during a vigil outside Schiavo's nursing home in 2003.

• The Harris Poll (2005): "Do you think that the law should allow doctors to comply with the wishes of a dying patient in severe distress who asks to have his or her life ended, or not?" Results: Yes, should allow – 70 percent; No, should not allow – 29 percent; Not sure – 1 percent.

• ABC News (2002): "Do you think it should be legal or illegal for doctors to help terminally ill patients commit suicide by giving them a prescription for fatal drugs?" Results: Legal – 40 percent; Illegal – 48 percent; No opinion – 12 percent. (www.euthanasia. procon.org)

However, the Pew Research Center (2005) also found that only a third of Americans support self assisted suicide if "the person is an extremely heavy burden on the family" (29 percent) or "is ready to die because living has become a burden" (33 percent). "Thus," as an earlier Gallup Poll report (1991) noted, "while Americans certainly are not supportive of a culture in which suicide is condoned under any and all circumstances, they are strongly in favor of societal norms which allow for and support the idea that patients nearing the end of their lives—with incurable diseases and great pain—should be allowed to choose to die, and that doctors should be encouraged to aid and abet in these decisions."

What do the results of these polls suggest that individuals and societies believe about when life ends? Do we feel that life ends only when a person's heart has stopped or a person can no longer breathe independently? Do we feel that life ends when a person can no longer live naturally without support from a life-sustaining system? Do we feel that life ends when a person is in intolerable pain that cannot be alleviated? We cannot infer answers to these questions based on the poll results that have been cited. However, it is reasonable to conclude that many societies are at least beginning to include quality of life among the criteria used to determine when life ends.

While the questions associated with when life ends or should end seem to be more suited to philosophy or biology courses than to sociology, they are significant questions for sociologists as well. We live within a society that has the technological capabilities to sustain physical life well beyond when a person might naturally die, yet we have not yet fully answered the questions about the social implications involved in these life-and-death decisions. Who has the power to decide when a person's life is really over: individuals, families, medical institutions, religious institutions, government? How will the meanings that we attach to illness and death change if euthanasia becomes adopted as one of our cultural norms? How will the social meanings of being elderly or terminally ill change? What types of social expectations will be placed upon the elderly and the terminally ill? Clearly, a cultural lag exists because of a rapidly advancing medical technology and a society that has not yet learned to deal with such questions. The questions are particularly relevant in light of the fact that the number of elderly in our society is becoming larger than ever. In terms of functional theory, this cultural lag represents the manifest functions of medical technology while exposing the latent consequences produced by the aging population in our society.

All societies expect different behaviors from people who are of a different age. In dress, music, leisure, sex, work, and so forth, what may be expected and appropriate for the young might not be expected or appropriate for the elderly. In many countries, including the United States, people are living longer than ever before, and an aging population creates new concerns for both individuals and societies. Many individuals do not look forward to growing old because they associate attractiveness, health, and productivity with the young. For the society as a whole, an increasing aged population arouses concerns about financial support, health care, housing, productivity, and other issues.

An example of how an aging society presents new concerns has been cited in Sweden (Ekman 2001) where bicycling has almost doubled between 1980 and 1992–93 among persons ages twenty-five to sixty-four. For the elderly (age sixty-five or older) the bicycle is a common means of transport, in both Sweden and a number of other countries. The risk of dying due to bicycling was about 3.7 times greater among the elderly than among children ages fourteen or under. The elderly face a greater risk of being injured or killed than their younger counterparts. For all ages, the risk is 7.4 times higher for a bicyclist than for a car driver. The risk for the elderly is about three times greater than for the average bicyclist, and as much as six times higher for the age group seventy-five to eighty-four years. The author states, "With some few exceptions, there is no doubt that society has neglected the problem." He attributes the neglect to the fact that decision-makers have a tendency to focus on the relatively young. However, people are living longer today and the elderly are healthier, which indicates the need for greater interest and more intervention. "We have signs of an epidemic, but one that can be ameliorated or prevented" (Ekman 2001).

AGE, AGING, AND THE AGED

The introductory paragraph uses terms such as *young, old, growing old, age, aging, aged,* and the *elderly.* Although most of us use and understand these terms in everyday language, they refer to different phenomena and have different meanings attached to them at different times and places. Have you noticed, personally, the fact that *who or what* is old changes, as you grow older? Have you ever wished you were of a different age so that you could do things that you could not do at your own age? The former question alerts us to the relative nature of what is young or old. The latter question suggests that the changes are related to chronological time.

Age generally refers to the number of years since birth. It is an ascribed status over which we have no choice or control. As such, each age status includes different social expectations about the appropriate behavior for different age groups. We expect babies to suck their thumbs and crawl on the floor, but we do not expect adults to do these things. We expect children to skip down the sidewalk, teenagers to attend school, and middle-aged executives to wear suits. Expectations about the behavior considered appropriate for people of a given age are called **age norms**. Because these particular expected behaviors are associated with particular ages, we ask people, according to their age, whether they have finished high school, are married, have children or grandchildren, or are retired. These social timetables tell people whether their lives are on schedule. There seems to be wide agreement among adults about age norms within societies, but age norms vary widely among different societies. One society may agree that the aged should be accorded deference, respect, and reverence; another may agree that they should retire and become less productive. One society may expect old people to live with and be cared for by their families; another may expect them to join other elderly persons in retirement communities or be cared for by the government.

A concept related to age, but one that implies something different, is **aging**, which suggest process and change. This broad concept includes biological or physical changes in our bodies; psychological changes in our mental capacities; and social changes in how we are defined, what is expected of us, and what we expect from others; *Biological aging* is the result of many processes; but it includes changes in our physical appearance (such as wrinkled skin, gray hair, and midriff bulge); physiological changes (such as puberty and menopause); and other changes in bodily systems (such as the nervous, endocrine, or immune systems). *Psychological aging,* also the result of many factors, includes changes in our mental functioning (such as learning, thinking, memory, or emotions).

Social aging, while greatly influenced by chronological age, deals with social roles, the life course, and age norms. In family terms, we speak of the family life cycle for heterosexuals in terms of progressive stages, which may include being married, having children, raising preschool and then school-age children, dealing with adolescents, launching the children and entering an empty-nest stage, and progressing through middle age into old age, with its accompanying events of retirement, widowhood, and death. In general sociological terms, frequent reference is made to the **life course**, an age-related progression or sequence of roles and group memberships that people are expected to follow as they mature and move through life. Thus, there is an age or time to go to school, get a job, get married, have children and grandchildren, retire, and so forth. What sociologists make real is an awareness of the wide diversity of paths in the life course, depending on culture, ethnicity, gender, social class, sexuality, and so forth. Life-course events, while related to chronological age, occur over a wide range of years. Both fifteen and fifty-year-old women may be able to get pregnant and have children, and both fifty-five and seventy-five-year-old workers retire. However, to retire at fifteen or get pregnant at age fifty is highly inconsistent with expected behaviors for those ages.

Each age status includes different social expectations about the appropriate behavior for different age groups.

The **aged** refers to one specific age grouping and to a particular stage or point in the life cycle or life course. This is the group we define as old, elderly, or as senior citizens; it occupies the later part of the aging process or the life span. This age segment of our population is the central focus of this chapter.

The systematic study of the aging process is known as **gerontology**, an interdisciplinary field of study that draws heavily on the biological and social sciences. One biological branch of gerontology is **geriatrics**, the medical care of the aged. **Social gerontology** focuses on the social and cultural factors related to age and the aging process.

Many age norms, particularly those concerning the aged in the United States, are inaccurate. Based upon false assumptions, the enforcement of these age norms tends to restrict the lifestyles and limit the personal fulfillment of elderly persons. Many definitions and perceptions of old people or the aging process are *stereotypes*—conventional mental images applied universally to all old people. Although widely held, many of these stereotypes are not supported by empirical evidence. Unfortunately, these misinformed, negative stereotypes can lead to **ageism:** prejudice and discrimination based on age. Like racism and sexism, ageism involves beliefs about the inherent inferiority of a group that are used to justify individual or institutionalized discrimination. We examine a few of these prejudices, stereotypes, and myths in the next section of this chapter.

MYTHS ABOUT OLD AGE

The development of gerontology as a field of study and our increasing body of research on the aging process show that many traditional beliefs about the aged are inaccurate. It is important to understand that many of these beliefs about the aged are, in fact, myths. These beliefs influence (a) the way in which the aged are treated by family and employers, (b) the nature of social policies that are designed with the aged in mind, and (c) the self-esteem of old people. Kart (2000) lists ten misconceptions about old people and the aging process:

1. Old age is inevitably accompanied by senility, a mental infirmity associated with the aging process.
2. In general, old people are miserable.
3. Most old people are lonely.
4. The majority of old people have health problems.
5. Old people are more likely than younger people to be victimized by crime.
6. The majority of old people live in poverty.
7. Most old people are unable to manage a household.
8. Old people who retire usually suffer a decline in health.
9. Most old people have no interest in or capacity for sexual relations.
10. Most old people end up in nursing homes and other long-term care institutions.

Some of these myths are discussed later in this chapter. At this point, we briefly summarize why each of these statements is false.

1. Senility Senility does not inevitably accompany old age. Many people, including a number of the world's leaders and other famous figures, make significant contributions in their seventh and eighth decades of life. In the absence of disease, age-related changes in learning ability appear to be small, even after the keenness of the senses has begun to decline. Dispelling this myth about the elderly could have enormous social consequences. If the elderly are treated as if they are still vibrant and alert human beings, they may be encouraged to see themselves as such. (Remember Cooley's "looking-glass self.") If old people believe that they still have the potential for personal growth, they may make the effort to remain mentally and physically active. However, they will probably not make that effort if they believe they have no potential for growth, and thus mental and physical deterioration may become a self-fulfilling prophecy. It is also essential that policymakers understand that age-related changes in learning ability are relatively small, so that they can strengthen their efforts to combat age discrimination in the workplace.

2. Despondence Most old people are not miserable and lonely. The evidence consistently indicates that old people are satisfied with their lives and do not suffer from depression any more than adults at other ages (Chappell 2008). Life satisfaction is stable across the adult lifespan. That is, adults at all ages have a tendency to retain their relative level of life satisfaction (Schilling 2006). Among Americans ages sixty-five to sixty-nine, 49 percent said, "These are the best years of my life." Many people in their seventies (44 percent) and eighties (33 percent) agreed. (Among Americans of all ages, 66 percent described the present as their best years.) Older Black (60 percent) and older Hispanic (57 percent) responded that these are their best years. In 2002, 58 percent of seventy year–olds and older stated they would be "very happy" to live another ten years ("Myths & Realities of Aging Study," National Council on Aging [NCOA] 2002). Nearly half of older Americans consider themselves to be middle aged or young. Only 15 percent of those seventy-five plus consider themselves "very old" ("American Perceptions on Aging in the 21st Century," NCOA 2002).

3. Loneliness Although many old people are alone, they are not necessarily lonely. The meaning of loneliness appears to change with age. Except for widows who miss their husbands and express higher degrees of loneliness, other groups of older people do not find loneliness to be problematic.

4. Health Problems Although many old people do have some health problems, the majority of those over age sixty-five do not have problems that limit their ability to work, keep house, or engage in routine daily activities. This myth—like the first one mentioned—has enormous implications concerning discrimination in the workplace. If all elderly are stereotyped as having health problems, employers may not hire them or may create policies that force them to take early retirement. The labor force participation rate—the proportion of the population that is either employed or looking for work—rose during the most recent recession in the U.S while unemployment increased for the overall population. Rising labor force participation for older persons is part of a long term pattern that began in the 1990s (U.S. Department of Labor 2010).

5. Victimization Crime against older people is an area of increasing study, and surveys show that the elderly are more fearful of crime than the young. However, the popular belief that elderly persons are victimized more often is false. The victimization rate of old people for assault and robbery, for example, is much lower than it is for others. The one exception may be personal larceny, such as purse- and wallet-snatchings, in which the victimization rates are about equal.

6. Poverty Most old people do not live in poverty. Admittedly, many of the elderly are poor; but taking into account their Social Security benefits, private pension plans, tax relief laws, and income from sources such as rents, annuities, retirement plans, savings, dividends, and so on, plus the high percentage of older people who own their own homes and automobiles, the vast majority are not at the poverty level. In 2009, 8.9 percent (approximately 3.4 million) of all householders age sixty-five and over were below the poverty level (*U.S. Census Bureau*). These figures, by contrast, are considerably lower than the 20.7 percent (almost 15 million) of people under age eighteen and the 12.9 percent (about 24. 5 million) of people eighteen to sixty-four years of age who were below the poverty level the same year.

7. Dependence and Incompetence Most old people can manage a household. In 2000, 89 percent of men and 81 percent of women over age seventy-five lived alone or with their spouse in their own household. Most aged people prefer to live close to their adult children but in separate households from them.

8. Postretirement Decline Not all old people suffer a decline in health when they retire. Although some people do retire because of health problems, the widespread tale of the individual who retired and "went downhill fast" appears to have little empirical support.

9. Sexual Disinterest or Incapacity Although sexual interests, capacities, and functions do change with age, detailed clinical studies of sexuality in late life have demonstrated the lifelong potential for sexual response and reversibility of sexual disorders occurring later in life (Masters and Johnson 1981). Ade-Ridder (1990) joins others (e.g., Janus and Janus 1994; Lindau, et al., 2007) in dispelling the myth that old people have no interest in or capacity for sexual relations. She studied the sexual behavior of 488 married men and women (244 couples) with a mean age of seventy-two years and found that two-thirds of the couples were still sexually active. While the data concur with other reports of a decline in sexual interest with advancing age, it is clear that sexual expression continues late in life and that sexual intimacy, including but not restricted to intercourse, is important to older persons. More recently, the National Council on Aging (1998) found that among sexually active seniors, most (74 percent of the men and 70 percent of the women) said they were as satisfied or more satisfied with their sex lives, compared to when they were in their 40s ("Healthy Sexuality and Vital Aging," NCOA 1998).

10. Institutionalization Most old people are not in nursing homes or other long-term care institutions. U.S. Bureau of the Census data indicate that only about 5 percent of the elderly are in old-age institutions of one kind or another. The vast majority of them live alone or with their spouse in their own household. It is clearly not the case that the elderly are predominantly institutionalized. According to the

U.S. Bureau of the Census (2010), most people aged sixty-five plus live with family members, with over half (55 percent) of noninstitutionalized persons living with their spouses. In 2000, approximately 10.1 million or 73 percent of older men and 7.7 million or 41 percent of older women lived with their spouses. Only 1.56 million (4.5 percent) of the sixty-five plus population lived in nursing homes in 2000.

Thinking Sociologically

1. State two or three ideas or perceptions you hold about old people. Are any of them likely to be myths?
2. Many myths exist about old age and the elderly. (a) Consider the extent to which the myths just presented may not be myths in societies outside of North America; and (b) if such myths differ by culture, how many can be attributed solely or even primarily to the biological effects of aging?
3. Since sociological findings can be used to empower individuals and groups while debunking myths and misinformation, how could educating old people about their actual versus perceived chances of victimization change the quality of their lives?

In general, blind acceptance of these myths can impair the way that family, government, health care personnel, social workers, employers, and even themselves treat the elderly. By understanding that the lifestyles, mental and physical health, sexual attitudes and capabilities, and learning potential of the aged are not markedly different from those of younger people, we might be more sensitive to our treatment of them and learn to overcome our ageist attitudes. It is commonplace to say that people have difficulty overcoming their prejudices against minority groups because they are not members of that minority themselves. However, keep in mind barring any major illness or accident, some day you will be among the elderly. Eliminating discrimination and prejudice against the aged clearly concerns all of us.

DEMOGRAPHIC ASPECTS OF AGING

The study of population is a central concern of sociologists. A number of questions tend to arise in examining any population: How many people are there? Has the number of people changed in the past? How is it likely to change in the future? What are the characteristics of the population? How do these numbers compare with other groups in society and with the numbers of similar groups in other societies? The answers to questions such as these alert us

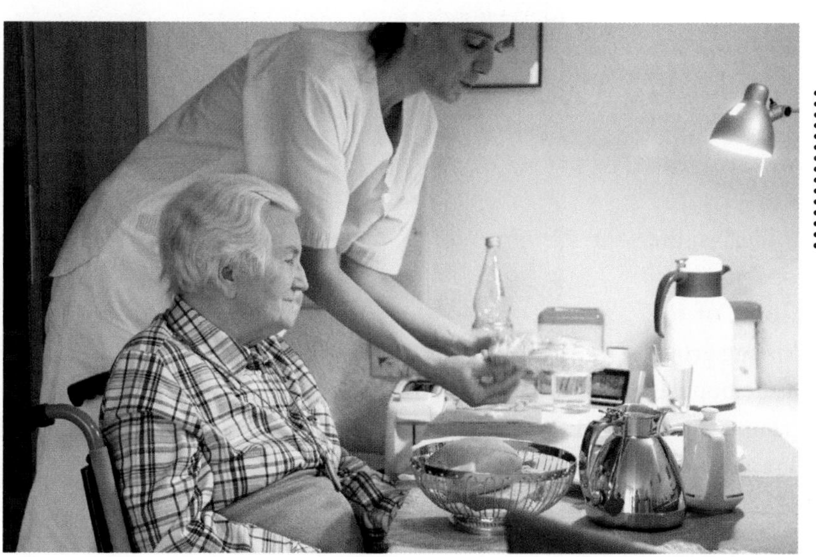

Most people 65 and above live with family members; in 2000, only 4.5 percent of the 65-plus population lived in nursing homes.

to the increasing significance of aging in most industrialized nations because the large number of elderly people is unprecedented in world history. Never have so many people lived so long.

One key question in investigations of an aged population concerns the age at which people are considered elderly. Most of us know of men and women over age seventy years who look, think, and act young and others who seem old at age thirty-five or forty-five. Nevertheless, social policy and much of the available data in the United States define the elderly population as those sixty-five years of age and over. This cutoff point is somewhat arbitrary; however, it is widely used by gerontologists, and we follow it in this chapter. It is not universal, however, and today many gerontologists distinguish between the "young-old" (those ages fifty-five to seventy-four) and the "old-old" (those seventy-five years old and over). You should recognize that numbers such as these are statistical generalizations and that wide variations exist in people's life expectancy, income, activity, and so forth.

Numbers of the Elderly: The Graying of America

The population age sixty-five and older is projected to double over the next three decades from nearly 40 million to nearly 80 million. In 2030, people sixty-five-plus are expected to make up 20 percent of the population. The Census Bureau projects the sixty-five plus populations to be almost 55 million in 2020, 53.7 million in 2020, 72 million in 2030, over 81 million in 2040, and around 88.5 million in 2050. The U.S. will rank third in the world in population of those sixty-five and older.

The population aged eighty and older is the fastest growing segment of the older population. In 2010, the eighty plus made up 3.7 percent of the population; by 2050 the percentage of this age group is projected to grow to be 7.4 percent of the population. The eighty plus population will grow to more than 32.5 million in 2050. The U.S. will rank second in the world in this population sector (U.S. Bureau of the Census, P25-1138, 2010). (See Figure 11-1)

These numbers are not wild speculation. These people have already been born, and—barring any major wars or diseases—nearly three-fourths of those currently living can expect to reach old age. These numbers can, of course, be influenced by migrations of people into or out of the United States, in addition to the unexpected death factor.

This pattern of growth raises many questions relating to work, leisure, health, housing, family life, and other matters. One approach gerontologists have taken in considering how changes in these areas will affect society involves examining the relationship between the elderly and the rest of the population.

One way to examine the relationship between the old and the young is by calculating the **dependency ratio**— the ratio between the number of people in the dependent population and the number of people in the supportive or working population. The dependent population includes both the aged and children. Dependency ratios are an indicator of the potential burden on those in the working-age population. Using data provided by the U.S. Bureau of the Census, we can compute this ratio by dividing the number of people under twenty years old plus the number of people sixty years old and over by the number of people ages

The population of people sixty-five and older is projected to double over the next three decades.

FIGURE 11-1 AGE AND SEX STRUCTURE OF THE POPULATION FOR THE UNITED STATES: 2010, 2030, AND 2050

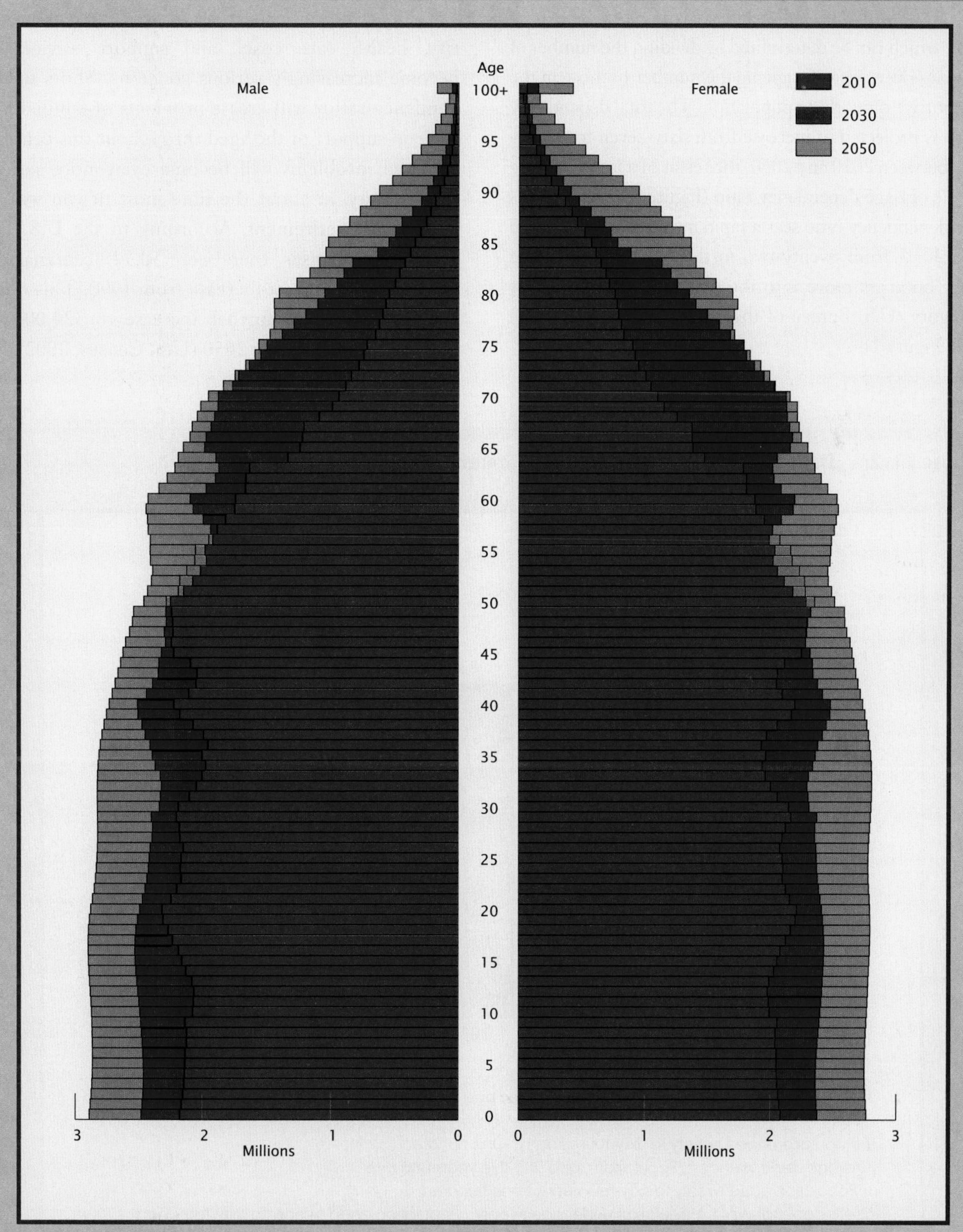

Source: U.S. Census Bureau, 2008.

twenty to sixty-four, and then multiply by one hundred.

A figure that excludes children is an *old-age dependency ratio*, which can be determined by dividing the number of persons over a specific age by the number of those in the supportive or working population. The total dependency ratio is projected to increase from sixty-seven to eighty-five between 2010 and 2050, the result of a large increase in the old-age dependency ratio (Figure 11-2). The old-age dependency ratio sees a rapid increase between 2010 and 2030, from twenty-two to thirty-five, as all of the baby boomers move into the sixty-five years and over category (U.S. Bureau of the Census, P25-1138, 2010) (See Figure 11-2)

Today's lower birth rate will result in fewer workers to support each elderly, non-working person. Thus, we can expect issues such as Social Security, health care costs, and support services to become increasingly serious concerns. Shifts in dependency ratios will create problems of familial and societal support of the aged throughout this century, and such problems will become even more serious mid-century, at about the time most of you will be considering retirement. According to the U.S. Bureau of the Census, there were 50,545 centenarians in 2000, a 35 percent increase from 1990. This number is expected to further increase to 324,000 by 2030 and to 834,000 in 2050 (U.S. Census, 2002).

FIGURE 11-2 DEPENDENCY RATIOS FOR THE UNITED STATES 2010-2050

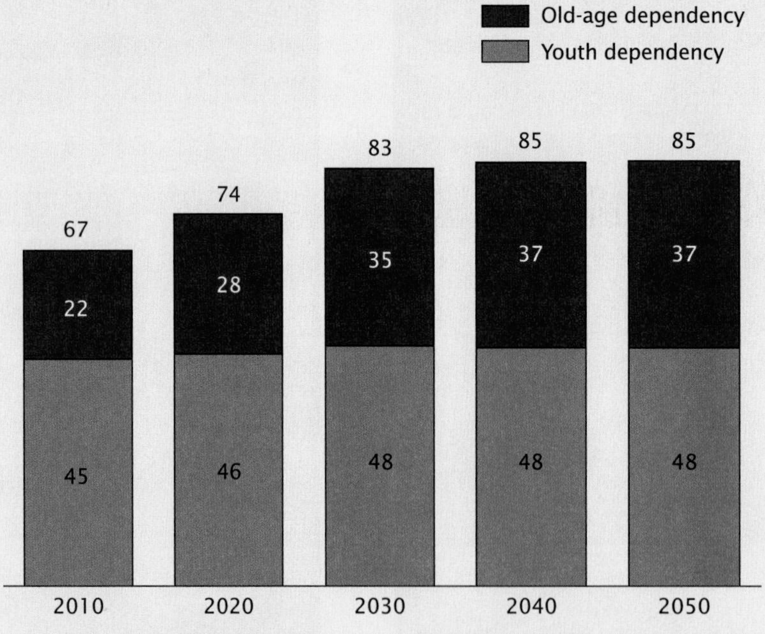

Note: Total dependency = ((Population under age twenty + Population aged sixty-five years and over)
/ (Population aged twenty to sixty-four years)) * One hundred.
Old-age dependency = (Population aged sixty-five years and over
/ Population aged twenty to sixty-four years) * one hundred.
Youth dependency = (Population under age twenty / Population aged twenty to sixty-four years) * 100.

Source: U.S. Census Bureau, 2008.

Life Expectancy

Life expectancy is the average years of life remaining for people who attain a given age. The most commonly cited life expectancy figure is based on birth. In other words, how many years, on average, can infants born in a given year expect to live? A glimpse at Table 11-1 shows these figures for selected countries. In many industrialized countries, the estimated life expectancy at birth as of 2011 was greater than eithty years. However, for many countries in the developing world, life expectancy at birth was less than fifty years, and for some countries less than fifty years. You may want to take a moment to consider some reasons as to why these figures vary so extensively. However, at this point, we focus on the United States and the life expectancy of older persons here.

Within the United States, the projected lifespan for those born in 2009 is 78.2 years (both genders, all races), but this figure varies considerably by sex and race. White females born the same year have a life expectancy of 80.9 years, (white females have the highest level of life expectancy of all races and genders) compared with 76.2 years for white males; black females had a life expectancy of 77.4 years, compared with 70.9 years for black males (*National Vital Statistics*, 2011). Instead of dealing with life expectancy at birth, what about the life expectancy of older persons? Suppose that we consider life expectancy of people who are sixty-five today rather than life expectancy at birth. People who are age sixty-five today (those born around 1950) have a projected life span of an additional 18.8 years. That would give them a total life

Many characteristics of the elderly population are related to the fact that women greatly outnumber men.

TABLE 11-1 LIFE EXPECTANCY AT BIRTH FOR SELECTED COUNTRIES, 2011 (EST.)

Country	Life Expectancy	Country	Life Expectancy
Japan	82.25	Greenland	70.96
Singapore	82.14	Guatemala	70.88
France	81.19	Bangladesh	69.75
Sweden	81.07	Bolivia	67.57
Italy	81.77	India	66.80
United Kingdom	80.05	Kenya	59.48
United States	78.37	Zimbabwe	49.64
Mexico	76.47	Liberia	57.00
China (mainland)	74.68	Uganda	53.24
Brazil	72.53	Namibia	52.19
Peru	72.47	South Africa	49.33
Philippines	71.66	Afghanistan	45.02

Source: CIA World Factbook, 2009.

span of 83.8 years. However, in 1950, their projected lifespan was 68.2 years. The projected life span of someone born in 2000 was 76.8 years. Yet, people who were ten years-old in 2009 are projected to live another 68.8 years, giving them a life span of 78.8 years. This means that the older we get, our projected life span increases and that we cannot look only at the year of birth as the only predictor of lifespan. This suggests that lifespan is not determined by biological factors alone but by a variety of social factors such as gender, race, geographic location, income, and others. (See Table 11-2)

TABLE 11-2 LIFESPAN BY AGE AS OF 2009

Age	Expectation of years to live
0	78.2
1	77.7
5	73.8
10	68.8
15	63.9
20	59
25	54.3
30	49.5
35	44.8
40	40.1
45	35.5
50	31.1
55	26.8
60	22.7
65	18.8
70	15.1
75	11.7
80	8.8
85	6.4
90	4.6
95	3.2
100	2.2

Source: NATIONAL VITAL STATISTICS REPORTS, VOL 59, NO 4, 2011, P. 50

Gerontologists estimate the life span to be slightly over a hundred years, and many believe it has remained basically unchanged throughout recorded history. Therefore, while life expectancy has increased dramatically, and more people are reaching old age than ever before, the life span is virtually unchanged. Despite frequent efforts to find a "fountain of youth," most biologists see no major scientific breakthrough in the near future that will extend the life span. Some time ago, there were reports of many persons in the Ural Mountains who lived to be 130 and individuals who lived to be 150 years old, but according to the Russian gerontologist Medvedev (1974, 1975), these reports were without scientific foundation.

Thinking Sociologically

1. What are some implications of a changing dependency ratio in terms of (a) Social Security, (b) labor force demands, (c) health care, and (d) intergenerational relationships?
2. Recognizing the difference in life expectancy and life span, why has life expectancy increased in the United States and many other countries while the life span has remained virtually unchanged? What possibilities do you see for changes in either life expectancy or the life span over the next several decades?
3. Pretend you are going to take an elderly person on a tour of your university campus. What are things you would consider as you plan your tour? What does this tell you about your own beliefs concerning the elderly?

Social Characteristics of the Elderly

The elderly population, like the rest of the population, varies in terms of sex (male or female), marital status, living arrangements, geographical distribution, labor force participation, and other characteristics. Many characteristics are related in some way to the fact that women greatly outnumber men. Of the 37.8 million people over age sixty-five years of age in the U.S in 2009, 43 percent were men and 57 percent were women. Elderly women far outnumber elderly men.

This factor has a major impact on conditions such as marital status and living arrangements.

Elderly men and women differ sharply in their marital status and living arrangements (see Table 11-3). About three-fourths of all older men are married and living with their spouse, compared with less than half of the women. The most dramatic difference in marital status between the sexes is shown under the category "Widowed." In 2009, of people over sixty-five, nearly 13 percent of the men and 41 percent of the women were widowed. These differences are due to the fact that men tend to marry younger women and die at younger ages. Also, elderly widowed men have remarriage rates about seven times higher than those of women. As noted earlier, the notion that most old people end up in nursing homes and other long-term care institutions is a myth: Only about 5 percent, or one in twenty, is institutionalized.

Geographically, the elderly are heavily concentrated in metropolitan areas and in a few states. Compared with those under age sixty-five, elderly persons are less likely to live in the suburbs. In the early 1990s, as was true a decade earlier, about two-thirds lived in metropolitan areas. Black and Hispanic elderly are especially concentrated in central cities, whereas whites are more likely to live outside the central city. In 2009, there were ten states with more than 1 million people age sixty-five and over: California (4 million), Florida (3 million), New York (2.7 million), Pennsylvania (1.9 million), Texas (2.5 million), Illinois (1.7 million), Ohio (1.6 million), Michigan (1.3 million), North Carolina (1.2 million), and New Jersey (1.2 million). More than half of the total elderly population of the United States is found in these nine states. (U.S. Census Bureau 2010) Alaska has the smallest number of elderly persons—only 53,000 or 7.6 percent of its population. Florida is the state with the highest proportion of persons over age sixty-five—18.9 percent. During the past decade, the largest increases in the elderly population were in the southern and western states.

Applying Demographic Aspects of Aging

The demographic aspects of aging are useful in a number of ways. Politicians and other policymakers are discovering that they need to understand the demographics of this growing constituency, such as knowing how many people will be over age sixty-five years and identifying their social characteristics. This understanding is important in determining the nature and form of policies and laws regarding mandatory retirement, pension plans, Social Security, Medicaid, Medicare, disability provisions, and so forth. Effective politicians realize that millions of older persons are active in special interest groups that can wield strong political pressure and support, such as the Gray Panthers, the National Retired Teachers Association, the National Council of Senior Citizens, and the American Association of Retired Persons (AARP). The AARP alone has a stunning forty million members and more than four thousand local chapters. Organizations such as these often apply their efforts toward improving the lives of older Americans by offering travel possibilities and insurance plans, as well as through selective lobbying efforts at the state and local level. To be politically effective, politicians cannot ignore the needs of this substantial and increasingly powerful group of Americans.

Business leaders and advertisers also need to be aware of the various demographic characteristics of the elderly. How will the needs of consumers change, as the population grows older? What kinds of products should research-and-development (R&D) departments of corporations be concerned with when planning for future corporate growth? Advertisers particularly must be concerned with elderly demographics. No longer can advertising campaigns focus exclusively on the young; as the median age of the population climbs, so does the age of consumers who have a large disposable income. In fact, if you pay close attention to television commercials and magazine ads, you will notice that more and more middle-aged and elderly models, actors, and actresses are being used.

Considering that the percentage of the population over sixty-five years of age is steadily increasing, community planners need to consider this age group in many aspects of their plans for the near future. For example, are there enough municipal parks? Are they conveniently located? Do they contain the facilities that will be needed

TABLE 11-3 PERSONS 65 YEARS OLD AND OVER—CHARACTERISTICS BY SEX: 1990 TO 2009

	Total				Male				Female			
Characteristic	**1990**	**2000**	**2005**	**2009**	**1990**	**2000**	**2005**	**2009**	**1990**	**2000**	**2005**	**2009**
Total (million)......	**29.6**	**32.6**	**35.2**	**37.8**	**12.3**	**13.9**	**15.1**	**16.3**	**17.2**	**18.7**	**20.0**	**21 5**
PERCENT DISTRIBUTION												
Marital status												
Never married..	4.6	3.9	4.1	4.2	4.2	4.2	4.4	4.4	4.9	3.6	3.9	4.0
Married..................	56.1	57.2	57.7	57.2	76.5	75.2	74.9	74.4	41.4	43.8	44.7	44.1
Spouse present	54.1	54.6	54.8	54.8	74.2	72.6	71.7	72.0	39.7	41.3	42.0	41.8
Spouse absent	2.0	2.6	2.9	2.3	2.3	2.6	4.1	4.2	1.7	3.9	4.1	4.2
Widowed...........	34.2	32.1	30.3	29.0	14.2	14.4	13.7	12.9	48.6	45.3	42.9	41.3
Divorced............	5.0	6.7	7.9	9.6	5.0	6.1	7.0	8.3	5.1	7.2	8.5	10.7
Educational attainment:												
Less than ninth grade...........	28.5	16.7	13.4	10.7	30.0	17.8	13.2	10.4	27.5	15.9	13.5	10.9
Completed 9th to 12th grade, but no high school diploma..	[1] 16.1	13.8	12.7	11.0	[1] 15.7	12.7	11.9	10.0	[1] 16.4	14.7	13.3	11.7
High school graduate...............	[2] 32.9	35.9	36.3	36.5	[2] 29.0	30.4	31.6	32.0	[2] 35.6	39.9	39.9	39.9
Some college or associate's degree	[3] 10.9	18.0	18.7	20.2	[3] 10.8	17.8	18.4	19.4	[3] 11.0	18.2	19.0	20.8
Bachelor's or advanced degree	[4] 11.6	15.6	18.9	21.7	[4] 14.5	21.4	24.9	28.2	[4] 9.5	11.4	14.3	16.8
Labor force participation: [5]												
Employed..............	11.5	12.4	14.5	16.1	15.9	16.9	19.1	20.5	8.4	9.1	11.1	12.8
Unemployed........	0.4	0.4	0.5	1.1	0.5	0.6	0.7	1.5	0.3	0.3	0.4	0.8
Not in labor force......	88.1	87.2	84.9	82.8	83.6	82.5	80.2	78.1	91.3	90.6	88.5	86.4
Percent below poverty level [6]..........	11.4	9.7	9.8	(NA)	7.8	6.9	7.0	(NA)	13.9	11.8	11.9	(NA)

[1] Represents those who completed 1 to 3 years of high school. [2] Represents those who completed 4 years of high school. [3] Represents those who completed 1 to 3 years of college. [4] Represents those who completed 4 years of college or more. [5] Annual averages of monthly figures. Source: U.S. Bureau of Labor Statistics, Employment and Earnings, January issues. See footnote 2, Table 584. 6 Poverty status based on income in preceding year.

Source: Except as noted, U.S. Census Bureau, Current Population Reports, The Older Population in the United States: March 2002, P20-546, 2003, and earlier reports; "Educational Attainment," <http://www.census.gov/population/www/socdemo/educ-attn .html>; "Families and Living Arrangements," <http://www.census.gov/population/www/socdemo/hh-fam.html>; and "Detailed Poverty Tabulations from the CPS," <http://www.census.gov/hhes/www/cpstables/032009/pov/toc.htm>.

by the elderly? If the number of elderly people in the population is increasing, it might make more sense to include park facilities that the aged are more likely to use (such as picnic areas, walking paths, botanical areas, and so forth) rather than increasing the number of basketball courts or bicycle paths. Planners also need to ensure that there will be adequate nursing home facilities and retirement villages, increased availability of low-cost housing and apartments, and adequate medical facilities that specialize in the health care of the elderly.

Awareness of the demographics of aging can also be useful for you personally. As you formulate your career plans, you may want to consider what types of services will be needed by the growing population of elderly. Will some careers or occupations be more highly rewarded because of increased demand? How will the increased population of elderly people affect your family planning, finances, and investments? There may be investment opportunities that you can take advantage of by knowing that the population of the United States is getting older. Knowing that there will be increased competition—and thus, rising costs—for retirement homes, cemetery plots, and so forth, may affect the way you plan for your future.

THEORIES OF AGING AND OF AGE DIFFERENTIATION

Tremendous emphasis is given to children and youth in the literature, but the socialization and resocialization needs of the elderly are more likely to be ignored. For the socialization of young people, we have families, schools, peers, jobs, and the community. However, what socialization agents exist to direct the aging process or to train people for retirement, widowhood, illness, or death? How can we explain differences among age groups in income, status, prestige, usefulness, and similar characteristics?

Aging is a biological as well as a social process, and many theories of aging focus on genetic or physiological changes. As we age, our skin wrinkles, our posture becomes stooped, our muscle reflexes become less efficient, and our responses to sexual stimuli are slower. These biological changes are important to note, but they do not explain what happens to humans socially as we grow older. For these explanations, we turn to social-psychological and sociological theories.

Structural Functional Theory

Structural functional theories assess aging in terms of social changes, such as population shifts and industrialization, attempting to determine how they influence social organization. According to the functionalist perspective, societies should be able to provide rewards and meaningful lives for all their citizens, including the elderly. Yet some observers argue that changes in the extended family structure have stripped the elderly of their respected positions as leaders and authorities. With today's rapid changes in industry and high technology, the elderly often lack the skills and training needed to fulfill beneficial economic roles. Today, there are more old people and fewer productive roles for them to fulfill. It could be said that there is an imbalance between the age structures and the role-performance structures of our basic social institutions. This view is reflected in two structural functional perspectives: modernization theory and disengagement theory.

Modernization theory (Cowgill 1974; Cowgill and Holmes 1972) states that with increasing modernization, the status of older people declines, which is reflected in diminished power and influence for the elderly and fewer leadership roles for them in community life. This lower status is a consequence of the processes of modernization: scientific technology, urbanization, literacy and mass education, and health technology. *Scientific technology* creates new jobs primarily for the young, with the elderly more likely to remain in traditional occupations that become obsolete. One illustration of this phenomenon is the gap between generations in the use of computers. *Urbanization* and urban life, unlike farm life, involves a good deal of mobility, especially among the young; and this mobility tends to separate the youthful generation from the older one. *Mass education* is targeted at the young, so younger people rapidly gain a higher level of literacy and greater contemporary skills than their parents. They occupy higher-status positions, and the elderly experience reduced leadership roles and influence.

Health technology has led to declining birth rates and longer lives. Considering all four factors together, early retirement is encouraged; however, the elderly are often denied a chance to participate in the labor market, which reduces their income, prestige, honor, and status.

Modernization theory has received some empirical support in cross-cultural studies, which reveal that as technology, education, and the like increased, and the importance of agriculture declined, the elderly population's control of important information and the esteem and deference accorded to them decreased. However, critics of this theory say that *modernization* is a vague term often used to describe development, progress, and, more specifically, westernization. They note that whatever modernization may be, it is not necessarily a linear process; and the elderly and other age groups may be affected differently by different stages in the process.

For example, as societies move beyond an initial stage of modernization, status differences between generations may decrease and the status of the elderly may rise, particularly when reinforced by social policies such as Social Security and more positive media images of the elderly. Critics also note exceptions, such as the treatment of the elderly in Japan. Keefer (1990), for example, states that in Japan, the prestige and power of the elderly was maintained at fairly high levels throughout the industrialization process. In other words, a decline in status of the elderly did not accompany modernization, and respect for the elderly still remains.

Disengagement theory (Cumming and Henry 1961) states that as people grow older, they go through a period of disengagement or withdrawal. This theory has been widely discussed since the 1960s, but the available evidence lends it little support. Consistent with aspects of structural functionalism, disengagement theory suggests that gradual withdrawal or disengagement of the elderly from jobs and some other roles is functional both for the elderly and for society. It prepares them for the end of life and also opens up opportunities for the younger generations, whereas a sudden withdrawal of the elderly would lead to social disruption.

Implicit in this theory is the idea that society should help older people to disengage themselves from their accustomed roles by separating them residentially

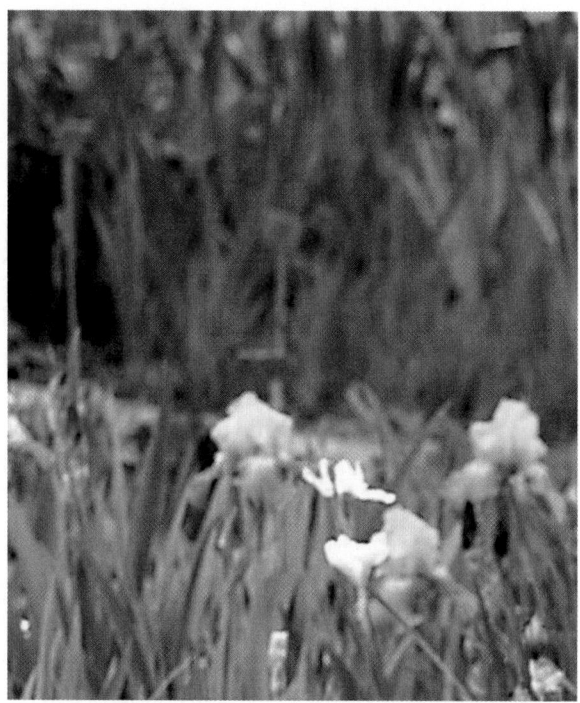

Disengagement theory states that as people grow older, they go through a period of disengagement or withdrawal.

(having them retire to the Sunbelt or to retirement communities), educating them about new activities designed for the elderly, and providing recreational alternatives such as social centers for senior citizens. These steps, which are often initiated by aging individuals themselves, are believed to help the old surrender their roles to a younger segment of the population. This disengagement process also prepares people for their death, with minimal disruption to society.

Disengagement theory did contribute to the view that old age is a normal stage of life. It differentiated this stage of life from middle age and emphasized that a lower level of social involvement and activity can still be highly rewarding. Critics, however, argue that elderly people do not want to be disengaged, do not want to be "put away," and do not want to withdraw from the mainstream of society. Robert Atchley (1991) suggests that disengagement is not a mutually satisfying process but one that is imposed on older people by the withdrawal of opportunities to participate and by circumstances such as ill health. In other words, although disengagement is not what the majority of older people want, it is what many get.

Symbolic Interaction Theory

Symbolic interaction theory focuses on how people define themselves and others, what meanings they give to events, and how they relate to their reference groups. When applied to the elderly, the theory emphasizes how people define the aging process and the status of the aged. Interaction patterns that bring satisfaction to the elderly are also noted. For many older persons, marital and family relationships are primary sources of social involvement, companionship, fulfillment, and happiness. Lee (1978), for example, found that marital satisfaction has a positive effect on morale, which supports the basic tenet of symbolic interaction theory: Interactions with significant others in primary types of group relationships are crucial to personal satisfaction and psychological well-being.

Symbolic interaction theory provides the context for what Lemon and his colleagues (1977) have termed the **activity theory** of aging. In contrast to the disengagement theory, which suggests that aging people go through a process of mutual withdrawal and a severance of relationships, the activity theory argues that the best-adjusted elderly persons are those who remain actively engaged. Many older people may not have the desire or the ability to perform the roles they performed at age thirty or forty, but they have essentially the same need for social interaction that they had years earlier. Activity theory contends that in order to achieve a satisfying adjustment to the aging process, avocations, part-time jobs, and hobbies should replace full-time employment, and friends or loved ones who move away or die should be replaced by new friends and associates.

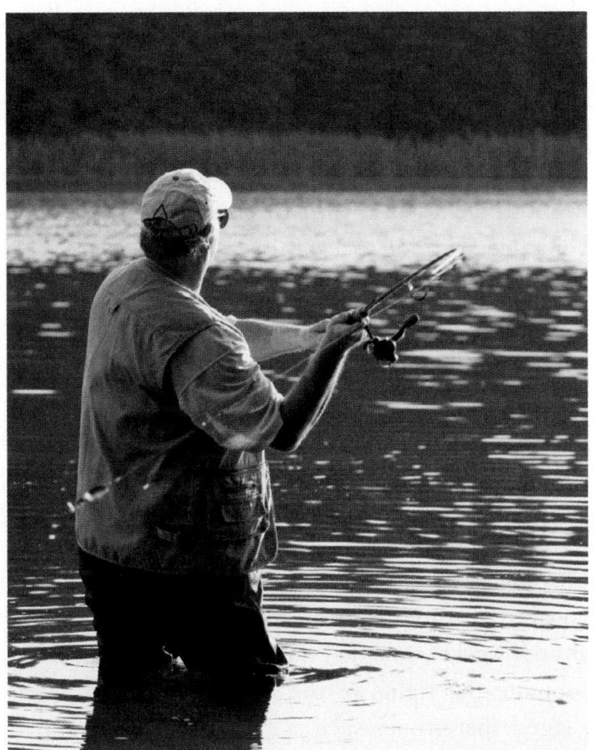

Activity theory argues that hobbies should replace full-time employment in order for a person to achieve a satisfying adjustment to the aging process.

In an attempt to test activity theory, Lemon and his colleagues investigated a sample of more than four hundred potential joiners of a retirement community in southern California. His findings were mixed. He discovered that *informal activity* such as interaction with friends, relatives, and neighbors was significantly related to life satisfaction, whereas solitary activities such as housework and *formal activities* such as involvement in voluntary organizations were not.

This theory, however, presents problems as well. The basic idea of involvement in activities with primary networks of people has merit, but it is not safe to assume that elderly persons have full control over their social lives and ready access to intimate relationships. Widows who see loved ones die or retirees who have too much leisure time and lower incomes may find it extremely difficult to replace loved ones and to fill their time with meaningful activities. Furthermore, the economic resources needed to reconstruct their lives may be lacking. Another questionable assumption is whether activity of any kind can always substitute for the loss of a spouse, job, child, or friend, or particularly of one's health. Psychologists and sociologists would agree that merely knowing a large number of people and being involved in many activities is not enough for a satisfactory life.

In brief, the relationship between aging and life satisfaction, or well-being, is one of the oldest and most persistently investigated issues in studies of aging. The issue took the form of a debate regarding disengagement versus activity. The disengagement theorists held that withdrawal from major social roles would optimize life satisfaction in old age. The activity theorists held that involvement and activity would maximize well-being. While this debate is still given some attention, it is now widely viewed as *specious*—that is, attractively plausible but having a deceptive or false sense of truth. Other theories of aging have emerged, including the application of variants of exchange and conflict theories.

Social Exchange Theory

Social exchange theory, as discussed elsewhere in this book, assumes that people try to maximize rewards and minimize costs. It suggests that voluntary social interactions are contingent on rewarding reactions from others. Each person receives in the exchange something perceived as equivalent to what is given. If the reciprocal exchanges are not fair, one person is at a disadvantage, and the other controls the relationship.

Dowd (1975, 1980) drew on exchange theory to offer an alternative to the disengagement and activity theories of aging. He believes that the problems of the aged in twentieth-century industrial societies are really problems of decreasing power. The low status of the elderly relative to younger people limits their bargaining power. Their economic and social dependence means that they have less power than those in the rest of society, and with the gradual loss of power comes the need to comply. The elderly, who once could exchange their labor and skills for wages, must now exchange compliance for a Social Security pension or for health-care benefits. According to Dowd, the withdrawal from social roles that disengagement theorists view as satisfying to the elderly is the result of a series of exchange relationships in which the aged lose power.

Even those who have financial resources, skills, and good health are often at a disadvantage in an exchange relationship. Their ability to gain new skills, more resources, or better health is limited. Stereotypes about the aged, rules forcing them to retire at a specific age, and declining physical capacities all hinder their ability to compete with their younger counterparts.

Conflict theorists might suggest that the elderly form coalitions to increase their power, but for the majority this has not taken place because the aged lack a shared awareness of common social and economic circumstances. Others might suggest that the AARP, which admits members at age fifty who are not necessarily retired, is one example of a rapidly growing coalition that provides the following: (a) provides a collective consciousness about issues central to the elderly, (b) presses for legislative changes, and (c) uses its large membership size as bargaining power for obtaining favorable rates for insurance, travel, and the like.

Conflict Theory

The conflict theory of the aged emphasizes the inequality and discrimination that occur among all subordinate groups that have little power. According to this view, the aged are a minority group in a youth-oriented society. Because they are less powerful than the younger group, they are treated unfairly, especially in the job market. The corporate elite prefers to hire younger people—who are stronger, healthier, and work for less pay—than older, more experienced employees. Younger workers, concerned about the scarcity of jobs, support laws that force the elderly to vacate jobs that the younger workers need. Faced with the opposition of these two powerful groups, the elderly are forced to retire. Because younger workers do not want to pay high taxes to support large numbers of older people, the elderly are often left with no work and little or no income.

Without income, conflict theorists contend, the elderly have little power. As a result, they are unable to combat the negative stereotypes assigned to them. The aged may often be perceived as unattractive, poor, neglected, sickly, depressed, and senile, and these perceptions are used in turn to justify denying them an equitable share of society's resources. Like other minority groups, they are discriminated against in jobs, wages, housing, and many other areas.

According to conflict theorists, the controversies that result from this inequality are beneficial, insofar as they emphasize aging as a social problem and alert increasing numbers of people to the plight of the elderly. Recognizing the problem is the first step toward organizing for political action. Just as the National Organization for Women (NOW) was established to fight for equal rights for women, Margaret Kuhn, a retired church worker, founded the Gray Panthers in 1971 to promote the rights of the elderly. Conflict theorists suggest that groups such as the Gray Panthers or the AARP are essential to bringing inequalities to public awareness, to campaigning for social reform, and to forcing social-policy changes.

Thinking Sociologically

Review the theories of aging just presented. Using that presentation as a starting point, discuss the following:

1. How is the modernization of societies likely to affect older people?
2. How may the activity theory lead to different results for widows or married people, those having differing degrees of health, or those with different levels of skills or financial resources?
3. Why are older people often at a disadvantage in terms of bargaining and social exchange? In light of the growing numbers of elderly citizens, are there possible advantages to being old?
4. In terms of conflict theory, how are the aged, as a minority group, likely to experience discrimination?

ISSUES OF THE AGED

The issues faced by the elderly in the United States resemble those that some other groups face, but they are compounded by old age. These issues are often magnified among ethnic and minority group members. Here, we discuss just four of these areas of concern: retirement, lifestyles and income, health, and abuse.

Retirement

Retirement is basically a phenomenon of modern industrialized nations. In agrarian societies, there is little paid employment from which to retire. In many areas of the world, the life expectancy is such that too few people live to old age to make retirement an issue of social concern. In Japan, on the other hand, people traditionally retired at age fifty-five years. When life expectancy was relatively short (fifty years in 1945), this allowed Japanese companies to maintain a tradition of "lifetime employment." This tradition of lifetime employment has been threatened, however, by the increased life expectancy to age eighty-two in Japan (see Table 11-1). If retirement was maintained at age fifty-five, the typical Japanese worker could expect to live twenty-five years or more in retirement, which would mean a substantial increase in the ratio of retirees to workers (old-age dependency ratio).

To address this labor and retirement problem, Japan, in contrast to many other industrialized countries that eliminated or lowered a mandatory retirement age for most workers, increased the retirement age to sixty. In a nation with a fairly strict seniority system where age and length of service meant higher pay, discontent resulted when some companies attempted to cut the pay of older workers. Government joined businesses in attempts to encourage part-time employment for older workers (Martin 1989). The Japanese government also created "Silver Talent Centers" (Conner 1992) to provide the retired Japanese workers with an opportunity to make contributions to society, as well as to continue their productivity. Through these government-funded centers, retired Japanese workers were reemployed in public-service jobs, such as tutors, translators, and advisers to selected businesses. Such opportunities for making positive contributions to societies or to communities may be an important ingredient for self-worth, dignity, and satisfaction in old age, for elderly persons in any location.

Retirement is likely to be increasingly problematic when it is nonvoluntary or when it is associated with loss of status, productivity, usefulness, income, or life itself. Voluntary retirement, which appears to be increasing in the United States, is often viewed as an opportunity to travel, enjoy greater freedom and leisure, and work at self-chosen occupations and avocations. When retirement is mandatory, on the other hand, the person involved does not have control over the decision. Retirement of both types involves resocialization to accommodate new roles, new definitions of self, and modified lifestyles.

Mandatory retirement has been the subject of a long and heated debate. According to Harris and Cole (1980), the issue goes back to 1777, when the first American mandatory-retirement laws were enacted in New York. By 1820, six other states had passed laws requiring the mandatory retirement of judges at ages ranging from sixty to seventy years. The decision to begin retirement at age sixty-five dates back to the Social Security Act of 1935. This cutoff point was the standard mandatory retirement age until 1978, when Congress raised it to seventy; and the issue is still not settled today. It is argued that mandatory retirement is discriminatory, fails to consider the abilities of older people, and leads to resentment among those who want to keep working. Others argue that mandatory retirement is not discriminatory because it ensures that everyone is treated equally and serves as a face-saving device when it is necessary to ease out ineffective workers. It also opens up job and promotional opportunities for younger workers.

Having a set retirement age places the emphasis on retirement as an event rather than a process. As an event, we note the age, the year, or the date at which we leave work. There may be an announcement in the company or community newspaper and a ceremony with a token gift and speech making. The process of retirement, however, may cover a span of many years.

Robert Atchley (1976, 1982) conducted some of the earliest research about the retirement process and the stages of adjustment. Atchley believes that the retirement process involves three major periods: preretirement, the retirement transition, and postretirement. Preretirement is the period of looking ahead to retirement: determining when to retire, wondering what to expect, and the like. The *retirement transition* requires leaving a job, ending a career role, and taking up the role of a retired person. The *postretirement* period involves life without the job that was a major focus of time and attention in the preceding years.

Atchley also identified five stages of retirement adjustment: the honeymoon (a euphoric period when retirees relish their newfound freedom); *disenchantment* (when retirees face the reality of their everyday life in retirement); *reorientation* (when retirees develop a realistic view of their social and economic opportunities and limitations); *stability* (when retirees accommodate and adjust themselves to their situation); and *termination* (when retirees eventually lose their independence due to illness and disability).

To investigate the retirement process, Atchley mailed questionnaires to men and women in a small town near a large metropolitan area in 1975, 1977, 1979, and 1981. Of the 1,100 respondents, about 350 were in the preretirement period and employed full-time. About fifty of the respondents did not plan to retire because they were self-employed and in good health or were unmarried women too poor to retire. The average retirement age for those who planned to retire was sixty-four. Women were much more likely than men to plan to retire before age sixty or after age seventy years. The early retirees tended to have high social status and to be married, whereas the late retirees tended to have low social status and to be unmarried. Thus, there appear to be important class differences in retirement, but general statements about women's retirement should be viewed with caution. Less than 1 percent of either sex in this preretirement period had negative attitudes toward retirement.

Between 1975 and 1979, 170 of the persons surveyed went through the retirement transition. Those who had a negative attitude toward retirement (17 percent of the women and 11 percent of the men) were more apt to have poorer health, lower social status, and incomes they regarded as inadequate. Retirement turned out better than they expected, however, and attitude scores went up significantly following retirement. For both men and women in the total sample, retirement tended to improve life satisfaction slightly, regardless of marital status, health, income adequacy, social status, or living arrangements. It also reduced the activity level for both sexes, but the reduction was much greater for women than for men because their level of activity was much higher before retirement. These activities included visiting with friends, being with children or grandchildren, going for walks, attending church, and so on.

About three hundred respondents were in the postretirement period in 1975. This group had very positive attitudes toward their retirement, relatively high activity levels, and positive life satisfaction scores for both sexes. Activity level was a strong predictor of morale among retired men; health was more important among retired women. Interestingly, the older the women, the more positive their attitudes toward retirement were likely to be. It should be noted that the findings in this study were for generally healthy people, in one small community, who had many opportunities for participation. In this context, people look forward to retirement, go through the transition smoothly, and find life in retirement to be satisfying. In more current research, Reitzes and Mutran (2004) found that while there is some variability in how stages of adjustment occur, Atchley's overall conclusions are still accurate.

Lifestyles and Income

The lifestyles of the elderly resemble those of other adult age groups. The very wealthy have access to the best care available, can vacation when and where they choose (influenced by health conditions), and can choose to have a second home in a resort area. The wealthy are better able than others to live with their families and to continue the activities they previously enjoyed.

The middle classes often leave their suburban homes when they retire because their income is reduced to the point where they cannot continue to maintain a house. They may move from urban to rural areas, where the cost of living is lower, or to the warmer climates of the South. Some have enough money to move to retirement villages, where they can enjoy a variety of activities and the companionship of other elderly people. Others do not like the age segregation and retire to small towns or rural areas.

People who have always been poor usually continue to live in the same poor areas when they grow old. They may live in subsidized housing for the elderly, in cheap hotels or rooming houses in the city, or in rural housing. The rural poor occasionally migrate to the city because of the shortage of affordable housing and adequate services in rural areas. The elderly poor, in general, are most likely to suffer from social isolation. They often have no network of friends for socializing and no money to spend on activities. They frequently live in crime-ridden areas and are afraid to venture out into the streets. Their nutrition may be inadequate, so they are more apt to be ill than wealthier people. Thus, the elderly poor suffer from poverty in much the same way that younger groups suffer from poverty.

The aged comprise a large but rapidly decreasing group of the nation's poor. As was mentioned previously, 8.9 percent of family householders age sixty-five and over in 2009 (down from 9.7 percent in 2007) were below the poverty level. Of those below the poverty level, roughly 7.5 percent were white and around 19.5 percent were black. In 2009, the median income of all households with a householder age sixty-five or over was $31,354, compared with a total median income of $49,777 for all families. As might be expected, the figures differed by race and Hispanic origin. For non-Hispanic whites over age sixty-five , the median income was $32,825; for Hispanics, it was $24,051; and for blacks, it was $23,387. Older Asian Americans had the highest median income at $47,319, which may reflect this group's tendency to save and invest money throughout the life cycle (U.S. Census Bureau, Current Population Survey, HINC-02, 2009).

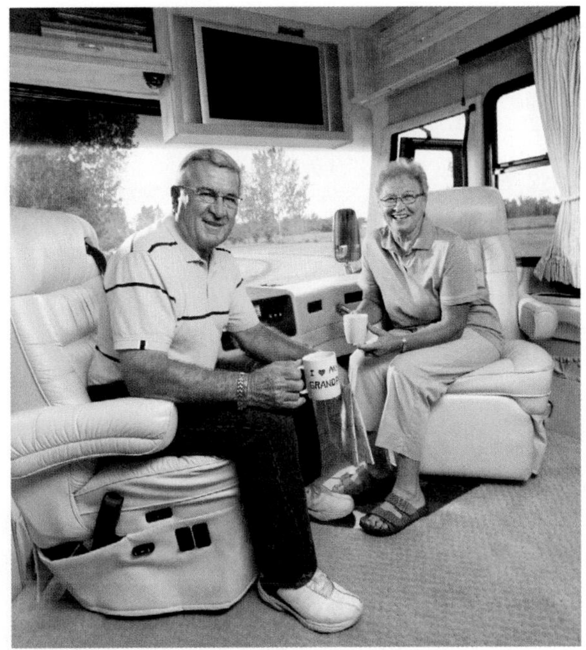

The lifestyles of the elderly resemble those of other adult age groups.

Despite these figures and the sharp decline in income among the elderly, David Cheal (1983), whose research is still relevant despite its age, reminds us that, overall, old people in North America are not as poor as the stereotypes may suggest. Average incomes decline sharply, but so do average expenditures. The ownership of domestic assets such as the family home makes it possible to enjoy a higher standard of living with a lower income than would otherwise be required. In fact, Cheal says that gift giving by old people is more significant than might be expected and that the elderly give more financial aid to relatives than they receive.

The most common source of income for the aged is **Social Security**. If people work to earn additional income, their Social Security may be reduced or

SOCIOLOGY AT WORK

Using Sociology in Nursing Care of the Elderly

Drucilla Tiliakos combines the skills of a registered nurse in psychiatric nursing with the advanced training she received from her graduate studies in sociology at Kent State University. In her doctoral work, she specialized in the study of complex organizations and medical sociology. While she was pursuing her PhD, she worked as an independent consultant in applied sociology, helping organizations to identify, understand, and resolve problems in which patterns of social interaction play an important role.

In several settings, Tiliakos has used her skills to help elderly patients who were victims of Alzheimer's disease and other chronic brain syndromes involving progressive mental and physical deterioration. Tiliakos explains that it is important to understand the sociological aspects of Alzheimer's disease, as well as the psychological and physiological ones. "Alzheimer's disease, apart from being a tragic condition for the victim and his or her family, is sociologically interesting because of the role changes and social stress that occur among the victim and his or her family constellation. It is of further sociological interest because of the demographic trends in our population, in which a growing proportion consists of persons over the age of sixty-five years. The increasing 'graying' of America is expected to place great strains on our health care facilities and social agencies in terms of their capabilities to provide reasonable care and assistance. Most frequently, sufferers eventually require nursing home care because families, when present, are hard pressed to cope with the scope of the patient's mental and physical deterioration. Since full recovery such as we might expect in acute diseases like pneumonia is not yet possible, a setting which emphasizes a rehabilitation philosophy is most appropriate."

The goals of a rehabilitation center differ from those of acute-care facilities such as hospitals, Tiliakos explains. The treatment of acute illness focuses on curing the disease, whereas rehabilitation focuses on "restoration, adjustment, motivation, and training in the skills needed in daily life. As staff in rehabilitation facilities struggle to care for patients, they need support and training in skills to help them manage distressing patient behaviors and provide support systems for victims and their families."

In her work as an independent consultant for rehabilitation centers, then, Tiliakos has relied on a broad range of sociological information. She has applied her knowledge of the changing roles of the aging, of research methods, and of therapeutic techniques. Her eclectic approach reflects her reasons for pursuing the field of medical sociology and the study of complex organizations. "Essentially, I wanted specialties that would complement my considerable experience and training in psychiatric nursing and that would allow me to develop additional skills that would be useful in organizational development, human relations, and health promotion consultation. I am especially interested in the process of change in organizations as they attempt to adapt to increasingly complex technologies. This trend has affected hospitals, home health care, and nursing homes as well, where we are seeing increases in the [intensity] of patient care and, as a result, the level of knowledge, skills, and technology needed to adequately care for patients and their families. The rapidity of change, while bringing progress in treatment methods, often is accompanied by a considerable degree of organizational and personal stress and strain."

eliminated. If retirees are not eligible for Social Security and have no other income, they are eligible for Supplemental Security Income (SSI), which in 2000 paid an aged person an average of $845 a month. In 2008, the amount increased slightly to $1,153 a month (*U.S. Census Bureau, Statistical, Table 544, 2011*).

The United States began the Social Security program during the depression of 1930s, when millions of people were out of work and unable to support themselves. The Social Security Act, signed in 1935, was designed such that working citizens covered by the program paid a part of their wages into the program and at age sixty-five became eligible to receive income based on the amount they had contributed. It was not intended to provide an adequate income, however. It was assumed that savings or pensions that had been accumulated during the working years would also be used during retirement and that Social Security would just provide a secure base on which to build a retirement income.

Social Security benefits have increased steadily since the program began in order to reduce the number of people living in poverty. Whether these benefits will continue to increase is a serious concern to the elderly. As the number of older people increases, the costs of paying benefits may put pressure on the Social Security system, and many expect to see benefits reduced drastically.

Millions of workers in the lowest-paying jobs have never even been covered by Social Security. Either companies that did not have pensions have employed them, or they have lost their pensions when they were laid off or their companies went out of business. The meager wages earned during their working years have not permitted them to save money. Today, many of these people live in poverty even when they are assisted by the small SSI payments.

A married woman receives her husband's Social Security benefits after he dies, but forfeits the additional 50 percent share she received while married. The company pensions of husbands are often stopped when the husband dies. Working women often receive low benefits or none at all because they earned low wages or worked in occupations not covered by Social Security. Thus, on the average, women collect much lower benefits than men.

Health

As mentioned, one of the myths discussed earlier in this chapter is that most old people have health problems. No one denies that organs deteriorate and gradually diminish in function over time, but diminishing function alone is not a real threat to the health of the majority of older people. The older population is living longer and enjoying greater prosperity than any previous generation, but there are still inequalities between the sexes and among income groups and racial and ethnic groups. During the period 2006 to 2008, 75 percent of people over the age of sixty-five rated their health as good, very good, or excellent (Federal Interagency Forum on Aging-Related Statistics, 2010)

Nearly half of older Americans consider themselves to be middle aged or young. Only 15 percent of those seventy-five plus consider themselves "very old" ("American Perceptions on Aging in the 21st Century," NCOA, 2002).

Why, then, is there so much concern about health as a social problem among the elderly? There are several reasons. One is chronic disease. The principal chronic diseases of the elderly in 2007 and 2008 were hypertension (55.7 percent), heart disease (31.9 percent), arthritis (49.5 percent), cancer (22.5 percent), diabetes (18.6 percent), asthma (10.4 percent), bronchitis or emphysema (9 percent), and stroke (8.8 percent). These vary by sex and race. (Federal Interagency Forum on Aging-Related Statistics, 2010) (See Table 11-4)

A second major concern is medical care. Health care costs have risen dramatically for older Americans, from $9,224 in 1992 to $15,081 in 2006. During that same period, the percentage of health care costs going to prescription drugs nearly doubled from approximately 8 percent to approximately 16 percent. The elderly poor were particularly affected with their percentage of household income going towards health care doubling, rising from 12 percent to 28 percent. The elderly are hospitalized approximately twice as often as the non-elderly, stay twice as long, and use twice as many prescription drugs, all of which are very expensive. At the same time, the cost of drugs, hospital care, and physician care has increased at a rate far exceeding that of inflation. Medicaid and Medicare, although widely believed to cover these bills, actually pay for only about half. In addition, both medical programs totally exclude such items as hearing aids, eyeglasses, and some dental services. The problem is compounded by the following facts: (1) The American medical profession has a general lack of interest in the problems of the elderly, who are less likely to be cured. (2) The income of the elderly decreases after retirement and becomes fixed, which means that they cannot keep pace with increasing costs. (3) Qualifying for Medicaid requires *pauperization*—people are eligible only after they have drained their resources and literally have joined the aged poor.

TABLE 11-4 CHRONIC HEALTH CONDITIONS

Percentage of people age 65 and over who reported having selected chronic health conditions, by sex, 2007–2008

	Heart disease	Hypertension	Stroke	Asthma	Chronic bronchitis or Emphysema	Any cancer	Diabetes	Arthritis
Total	31.9	55.7	8.8	10.4	9.0	22.5	18.6	49.5
Men	38.2	53.1	8.7	8.9	8.6	23.9	19.5	42.2
Women	27.1	57.6	8.9	11.5	9.2	21.4	17.9	54.9
Non-Hispanic White	33.7	54.3	8.7	10.2	9.7	24.8	16.4	50.6
Non-Hispanic Black	27.2	71.1	10.8	11.3	5.9	13.3	29.7	52.2
Hispanic	23.8	53.1	7.7	10.9	6.2	12.4	27.3	42.1

Source: Centers for Disease Control and Prevention, National Center for Health Statistics, National Health Interview survey.

A third concern, and one that is often overlooked, is mental health. Depressive symptoms are one indicator of mental health. Among the over-sixty-five population, the percentage of people reporting symptoms of clinical depression remained fairly stable between 1998 and 2006. 10 percent of men and 18 percent of women reported depressive symptoms.

A destructive stereotype suggests that senility is inevitable in old age and that aged individuals who are not in some state of mental deterioration are rare. While the number of elderly mentally ill is projected to swell from about four million in 1970 to fifteen million in 2030 psychiatrists and gerontologists are increasingly reporting that even patients who have senile dementia can be helped if the disability is deemphasized and the general quality of their life is improved (Jeste, et al, 1999).

A closely related mental health problem among the aged is **Alzheimer's disease**. According to the Alzheimer's Association (2010), about 5.3 million persons in the United States have this disease, which causes the brain to gradually atrophy (shrink in both size and weight). 5.1 million are sixty-five years of age or older. 13 percent of people over sixty-five and nearly 50 percent of those over eighty-five have Alzheimer's. The number of people aged sixty-five and older with Alzheimer's is estimated to reach 7.7 million by 2030, and 11 million to 16 million by 2050—more than a 300 percent increase from 2010. A small percentage of people as young as their 30's and 40's get the disease.

Affected individuals gradually lose their memories. Their thought processes slow, their judgment is impaired, communication disturbances develop, and disorientation occurs. Those familiar with this incurable disease recognize the tragedy of watching a healthy, able-bodied person gradually deteriorate, come to no longer recognize his or her own children or best friends, and eventually die. A final mental health concern among the elderly is suicide. The annual suicide rate for all ages in the United States is 14.3 per 100,000 population. White men are at the highest risk with a rate of approximately 31.1 suicides

A male Alzheimer's patient rests on his bed. Due to his loss of short-term memory, he relies on Post-it® reminders on his dresser drawers to remind him how his clothes are organized.

per 100,000 each year and increases to 45.4 per 100,000 for men over eighty-five. The rate of male suicides in late life is 7.3 times greater than for female suicides (www.suicidology.org, 2007).

The following possible reasons for these dramatically higher rates for men have been suggested. Men may be more adversely affected by retirement; may be less willing to endure illness and inactive status; may be more action-oriented, combative, and aggressive; may feel diminished by not being in charge in the home as they were in the workplace; and may be less integrated into an intimate network of friends. In contrast, women are said to be more intimately involved in a circle of supportive friends, better able to handle poverty, and more accustomed to a secondary status in a male dominated society. Clearly, Durkheim's propositions relating the degree of social integration to levels of mental health and suicide seem as applicable to the elderly as to other groups.

Abuse

One problem that has only recently received major research and policy attention is the abuse, exploitation, and neglect of the elderly by the people upon whom they depend. This is one of our newest social problems, and little information about it was available until the late 1970s. Since then, a number of investigations have been conducted, and they show an estimated 293,000 reports of domestic elder abuse nationwide (Tatara and Kuzmeskus 1997).

The severity of mistreatment of older people ranges from reasonably benign neglect to severe emotional and physical abuse. The most common form of neglect is *passive*, such as when an elderly dependent is left alone without essential medical care, food, or clothing. Passive neglect may also happen because a caregiver is inept or unable to provide for the needs of the elderly person. *Active neglect*, which is less common, occurs when needed goods or services are intentionally withheld, and social contacts are forbidden. Caregivers have been known to tie older people to a bed or chair or to lock them in a room while they go out, give them alcohol or excessive medication to make them more manageable, threaten violence to force them to sign over a Social Security check, and deceive them into changing their wills. Many of these examples of passive and active neglect result in severe emotional pain and abuse.

A commonly cited cause of such abuses is that the caregiver is being overtaxed by the requirements of looking after a dependent adult. Pillemer (1985), however, found no support for the hypothesis that the dependency of the elderly leads to abuse. His research suggests that the typical abused elder, rather than being a dependent, may be an older woman supporting a dependent child or, to a lesser extent, a physically or mentally disabled spouse. From an exchange perspective, the victims perceived themselves as being on the losing end, or as giving much and receiving little. Most did not leave the situation but felt trapped by a sense of family obligation.

In addition to benign neglect or emotional abuse is physical abuse. *Physical abuse* may involve beating, hitting, pushing, burning, cutting, mugging, sexually molesting, or otherwise injuring an elderly person. This type of abuse, more than neglect, is likely to come to the attention of police, physicians, community social service workers (caseworkers), or clergy. The professionals involved in such instances are also likely to observe various other forms of emotional abuse, such as threats, fraud or financial exploitation, and intimidation.

With all types of abuse, women are victims more often than men. Victims also tend to be the older elderly (seventy-five or older), people who are frail and mentally or physically disabled. The abuser is usually a son or a daughter of the victim and is often experiencing great stress brought about by alcoholism, drug addiction, marital problems, or chronic financial difficulties, in addition to the burden of caring for an aging parent.

Parallels can be drawn between the abuse and neglect of children. In both cases, the victims are heavily, if not totally, dependent on others for basic survival needs. They both lack resources such as strength, speed, and independent finances to protect themselves. The family or intimate group network is the source of abuse far more often than strangers are. In both cases, the abuse generally occurs in the home. In fact, for all citizens, young or old, rich or poor, the most dangerous place is the home.

It is unlikely that major government-supported programs at a federal, state, or local level will be created to combat neglect and abuse of the elderly, even though governments have taken action to prevent child and spouse abuse. Today's political climate, economic support for social programs, and conservative orientation toward social concerns—all tend to place the emphasis on voluntary responses to human needs. Some local and voluntary agencies have joined together to organize reporting and referral systems and temporary shelters for elderly victims. Other services are needed, however—laws mandating that physicians and others who work with the elderly report their suspicions of abuse, free or low-cost legal service systems, and increased support services, such as transportation, meal preparation, and chore and homemaker services. Many of these services now exist at a minimal level, but the need is too great; voluntary services alone cannot solve the problem.

Thinking Sociologically

What factors do you consider important and in influential in preparation for (a) retirement, (b) a particular lifestyle in old age, (c) a high level of physical and mental health, and (d) the prevention of elder abuse?

DEATH AND DYING

All humans die. Therefore, for most persons, the awareness and the anticipation of death is an important aspect of living. While death may occur at any age, it is most expected, accepted, and understood among the elderly. As a result, groups and societies develop patterns of behavior and institutional arrangements to manage death and its impact (see Marshall and Levy 1990).

The aged must confront two difficult facts—their own death and the death of their friends and loved ones. Surprising though it may seem, socialization plays a role in preparing people for death. As with other types of social behavior, our social institutions, norms, and practices largely determine how we think about dying. Symbolic interaction theory, for example, would suggest that the definitions and meanings we attach to illness and death greatly influence our ability to cope with it. An understanding of reference groups may help us understand the functioning of the church, friends, or a kin network as support systems in facing death. How we mourn, what we do with the physical remains of the dead, how we behave after the death of a family member, how we prepare for our own death—all are influenced by cultural, class, and other social factors.

In the United States and most other cultures, the family and kin network is the major social support in times of illness. Among the elderly, the presence of relatives may make it possible for bedridden persons to live outside of institutions. Elderly people turn first to their families for help, then to neighbors, and finally—only as a last resort—to bureaucratic replacements for families. This sequence is consistent with survey findings that show that most people would like to die at home. Nevertheless, medical attention, nursing care, and social workers for the dying are based in hospitals. Four people wish to die at home for every one who would like to die in a hospital; however, in actual practice, the ratio is reversed (Hine 1979–1980). More recently from the BBC News, a survey found two-thirds of those sampled would want to die at home if they were terminally ill. However, a lack of funding for palliative care means only 25 percent of cancer patients can currently do so (BBC News, U.K. Edition, March 2004).

An alternative to hospital care, the hospice movement is intended to make family interaction with the terminally ill or dying patient easier. A **hospice** is a therapeutic environment designed from the patients' point of view. Unlike a regular hospital with its emphasis on privacy, a hospice provides space for interaction with staff, family, and friends. Instead of subordinating the patient to the needs of the institution, hospice programs are designed to provide as much care in the patient's home as possible. When medical facilities are required, they include a team of medical, nursing, psychiatric, religious, and social workers, as needed, plus family members. The concern is to increase the quality of the last days or months of life and to provide humane care. The family of the institutionalized patient is encouraged to be involved. They can bring in "home cooking," bathe the patient, supply medication, or even bring along the family dog. Hours for visits are unlimited, and patients are allowed to interact with young children or grandchildren. The program is innovative, but it is very expensive as well; and few hospices care for chronically ill people who are expected to live for a year or more.

A controversial issue concerning the terminally ill is **euthanasia**. Euthanasia, sometimes called "mercy killing" or "elective death" is the deliberate ending of a person's life to spare him or her from the suffering that goes with an incurable and agonizing disease. Euthanasia can be passive (not preventing death) or active (causing death).

In *passive euthanasia,* treatment is terminated, and nothing is done to prolong the person's life artificially. In *active euthanasia,* actions are deliberately taken to end a person's life. The person who takes the action may be a physician, a husband or wife who shoots or strangles a terminally ill spouse because the loved one's suffering is unbearable or because the loved one has asked that it be done, or other persons who have been asked by the dying to assist in their deciding their own destiny. A Michigan doctor, Jack Kevorkian, brought the physician-assisted suicide issue to national attention in 1991 when he consented to instruct and assist three women in using his suicide machine to end their lives. As this textbook goes into print, societal and legal responses to his actions are continuing. Thus, in contrast to passive euthanasia, where the decision is made to let a person die without medical intervention, active euthanasia includes the decision to assist in the termination of life.

As noted in this chapter, the growth of the aged population and the increased numbers who will survive to age eighty-five years and beyond will provide major challenges to societies in providing economic assistance and social services to this segment of the population. One of our great challenges will be to devise social structures that will allow the elderly to lead active lives for as long as possible and to live graciously and with dignity even when they can no longer be active.

Thinking Sociologically

While euthanasia is not only relevant to elderly patients, it is clear that it is an issue that is more likely to concern the elderly because they are closer to the point at which life would naturally end, and they are more likely to encounter illness or enter a state of health in which euthanasia might be considered. Using theories of aging and age differentiation—and other material in this chapter—evaluate the pros and cons of both passive and active euthanasia. After you evaluate each side of the debate, take a position as to whether active euthanasia should be allowed.

CHAPTER REVIEW
Wrapping it up

Summary

Check out our website www.bvtstudents.com for free chapter-by-chapter flashcards, summaries, and self-quizzes.

1. All societies differentiate behavior by age. *Age*, an ascribed status, includes social expectations about appropriate behaviors for persons who have lived a certain number of years. *Aging*, the process of growing older, is accompanied by biological, psychological, and social changes as people move through the life course.

2. The systematic study of the aging process is known as *gerontology*. *Social gerontology*, a subfield of gerontology, focuses on the social and cultural aspects of age and of the aging process.

3. Expectations about the behavior considered appropriate for people of a given age are *age norms*. Many such norms reflect inaccurate stereotypes and may lead to ageism, which is prejudice and discrimination based on age.

4. Myths about the aged suggest that they are senile, miserable, lonely, unhealthy, frequent victims of crime, poor, unable to manage households, incapable of and disinterested in sexual relations, and probably live in nursing homes. All of these stereotypes are basically false.

5. The elderly are considered to be those age sixty-five and over. Some gerontologists differentiate between the *young-old* (fifty-five–seventy-four) and the *old-old* (seventy-five and over). Demographically, the percentage of elderly people in the total population is increasing, as is life expectancy, although there are considerable variations due to sex and race. Interestingly, the life expectancy of those who reach old age has increased very little and the life span is basically unchanged. The proportion of older people who do not work is increasing in comparison to the younger working population; this proportion is known as the old-age *dependency ratio*.

6. The social characteristics of the elderly vary widely according to sex, marital status, living arrangements, geographical distribution, labor force participation, and other factors. Women greatly outnumber men, and many women are widows; and most of the elderly live in their own homes or with their families. Geographically, they tend to live in metropolitan areas, and they are heavily concentrated in some states. The proportion of the elderly in the labor force has dropped considerably over the past several decades.

7. There are a number of theories on aging and age differentiation. Theories based on the structural functional perspective include modernization and disengagement theory. *Modernization theory* assumes that the status of old people declines with increasing modernization. *Disengagement theory*, which is less widely accepted, contends that as people grow older, they go through a period of mutual disengagement or withdrawal from the rest of society.

8. A symbolic interaction perspective, *activity theory*, states that those who remain active, particularly with avocations, part-time jobs, and interaction in

primary networks, will be better adjusted than those who do not.

9. *Social exchange theory* suggests that both withdrawal and activity can be best explained in terms of the decreasing power of the elderly. Having less to exchange and a greater dependency on others forces the elderly into social compliance. Finally, *conflict theory*, drawing on exchange theory, assumes that inequalities in areas such as jobs, wages, and housing permit the elderly to be exploited.

10. The aged share many of the problems of the rest of society, but their problems are often compounded because they have fewer resources and less power. Nevertheless, most people look forward to retirement.

11. The lifestyles of the elderly vary greatly, depending on their social class and income. Women and blacks are the groups most likely to live in poverty. The most common source of income for the aged is Social Security. A minimal income is available to those not on Social Security through the Supplemental Security Income (SSI) program.

12. Income and class level greatly influence the health of the elderly. Most say that their health is fair or good, but those whose health is poor often face chronic disease, high medical costs, and prolonged hospitalization. A relatively small proportion of the aged suffer from mental problems such as those related to Alzheimer's disease.

13. The abuse of the elderly has come to be recognized recently as a widespread problem. Like dependent children, the elderly are often neglected or physically abused. They have few resources to protect themselves. In most cases, they are abused in their homes by their caregivers.

14. A *hospice* is a therapeutic environment for terminally ill patients, designed to permit interaction with family and friends and to combine good medical care with humane treatment. Euthanasia, sometimes called "mercy killing," is a controversial issue concerning those who have terminal illnesses.

Key Terms

activity theory The theory of aging that suggests that elderly persons who remain active will be the best adjusted

age The number of years since birth

aged The age group that occupies the later part of the life span, generally meaning the old, elderly, or senior citizens

ageism Prejudice and discrimination based on age

age norms Expectations about the behavior considered appropriate for people of a given age

aging The biological, psychological, or social processes that occur with growing older

Alzheimer's disease A disease affecting primarily older persons in which the brain gradually atrophies, resulting in loss of memory and impairment of thought processes

dependency ratio The ratio between the number of persons in the dependent population and the number of people in the supportive or working population

disengagement theory The theory of aging that suggests that as people get older, they and the younger people around them go through a period of mutual withdrawal

euthanasia Sometimes called mercy killing; deliberately ending a person's life to spare him or her suffering from an incurable and agonizing disease

geriatrics The subfield of gerontological practice that deals with the medical care of the aging

gerontology The systematic study of the aging process

hospice A home for terminally ill patients in which the emphasis is on providing a comfortable, supportive environment for the patient and the patient's family

life course An age-related progression or sequence of roles and group memberships that people go through as they mature and move through life

life expectancy The average years of life remaining for persons who attain a given age

life span The biological age limit beyond which no one can expect to live

modernization theory The view that the status of older people declines with modernization

senility A mental infirmity associated with the aging process

social gerontology A branch of gerontology that focuses on the social and cultural factors related to age and the aging process

Social Security The federal program that provides financial support for the elderly

Discussion Questions

1. List a number of age norms that exist for teenagers or those in their early 20s. How would you explain their existence and differentiation from those existing for younger or older persons?
2. How do myths about old age lead to prejudice against the elderly?
3. Discuss some ways in which shifts in the dependency ratio might affect family life. How have changes in the dependency ratio affected life in your family over the past two or three generations?
4. What types of social changes, social problems, and social benefits might occur from the increase in life expectancy?
5. Discuss changes in marital status and living arrangements by age. What types of factors other than widowhood affect marital status and living arrangements?
6. It was stated that the elderly are heavily concentrated in a few states. Why? What are some social implications (recreation, transportation, consumer spending, health care, etc.) of this geographical distribution?
7. Briefly discuss how structural functional theory, conflict theory, symbolic interaction theory, and social exchange theory could be used to explore the role of elderly people in your family and how they are treated.
8. People are retiring at earlier ages than in the past. Why? What benefits and costs, for society as well as for the individuals themselves, are associated with this change?
9. Examine the lifestyles of the elderly by ethnicity. What differences exist? Why do these differences exist? Is there any need to establish different policies for Hispanic-Americans, Native Americans, African-Americans, or white Appalachian Americans?
10. Describe various health needs that are most prevalent among the elderly, and discuss issues related to them: care, cost, curability, and the like.

Pop Quiz

1. Expectation about the behavior considered appropriate for people of a given age is called ______.

   a. age mores
   b. age norms
   c. age statuses
   d. age differentiations

2. An age-related progression or sequence of roles and group memberships that people are expected to follow is called ______.

   a. social aging
   b. biological aging
   c. social gerontology
   d. life course

3. The branch of gerontology that focuses on the social and cultural factors relating to age and the aging process is known as ______.

   a. social geriatrics
   b. psychological gerontology
   c. social gerontology

d. sociocultural gerontology

4. Prejudice and discrimination based on age are referred to as ______.

   a. age norms
   b. ageism
   c. gerontology
   d. age differentiation

5. Which of the following is true?

   a. In general, old people are miserable
   b. The majority of old people have health problems
   c. Old people generally do not have health problems
   d. Old people usually die in a nursing home

6. The average years of life remaining for people who attain a certain age is ______.

   a. life span
   b. life expectancy
   c. life chances
   d. life course

7. The dependency ratio compares ______.

   a. the number of aged to those under 20
   b. the number of aged and young to the working population
   c. the number of retired aged to the working population
   d. the number of non-retired aged to the working population

8. The group having the shortest life expectancy is ______.

   a. black males
   b. black females
   c. white males
   d. white females

9. The elderly most often live in ______.

   a. metropolitan areas
   b. rural areas
   c. suburbs
   d. small cities

10. The theory that states that as people grow older they go through a period of withdrawal is ______.

   a. disengagement theory
   b. activity theory
   c. modernization theory
   d. conflict theory

11. Today, the elderly comprise about 12 percent of the population. T/F

12. Florida has the highest number of elderly of any state in the United States. T/F

13. Activity theory suggests that the elderly actively withdraw once they retire. T/F

14. Elderly people are hospitalized more often than young people. T/F

15. Men are the most frequent victims of elderly abuse. T/F

1. B	6. B	11. T
2. D	7. B	12. F
3. C	8. A	13. F
4. B	9. A	14. T
5. C	10. A	15. F

PART FOUR

Social: Institutions

The aim of education is the knowledge not of fact but of values.

DEAN WILLIAM R. INGE

CHAPTER 12

Family Groups and Systems

A NEW AMERICAN FAMILY?

The American family is undergoing radical changes. Until recently, families in the United States almost always consisted of a husband and wife, their children, and frequently their extended family. Divorce was rare until the middle of the twentieth century, and sex was a topic not widely discussed in public. However, today, most American families no longer fit the traditional mold. In fact, the modern American family is more diverse than ever. Moreover, tolerance of alternate family forms and family-related behavior is on the rise. To be sure, for the first time in history, homosexual marriage is legal in many parts of the United States. As of 2009, nearly half of all children in the United States are born out-of-wedlock (Ravitz 2009). Cohabitation is, also, on the rise. Even polygamy is slowly gaining legitimacy (Hostin 2008). If these trends continue, the American family will almost certainly appear fundamentally different by the turn of the next century. Consider the cases below.

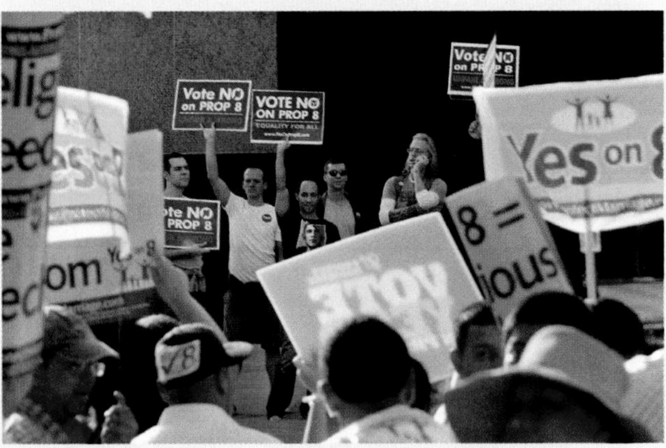

Supporters and opposers of California's Proposition 8 to ban same-sex marriage rally in Los Angeles in November 2008.

Nadya Suleman is an unmarried mother with fourteen children living in California. In January 2009, Nadya gained national attention when she gave birth to octuplets even though she was already a mother of six, unmarried, and living on government money (Richards and Olshan 2009). In 2008, Nadya had six embryos from previous in-vitro fertilizations implanted in her womb. Remarkably, two of the embryos split and all eight were fertilized. Public reaction to the octuplets was mixed. Many asked how an unemployed single-mother could ever raise fourteen children without going bankrupt. Others were dismayed that Nadya wouldn't identify the father. Still more were shocked that Nadya showed no signs of shame in having children out-of-wedlock. Many people only saw Nadya as a quick way to make money, however. To be sure, in February 2009, Vivid Entertainment offered Nadya a million-dollar deal to star in a pornographic film (McKay 2009). Two months later, Nadya sought to trademark her new nickname—the Octomom—for a television show and a line of diapers (Duke 2009).

The second case involves Mary Cheney, the daughter of former Vice President, Dick Cheney. Mary, a lesbian, received considerable media attention concerning her sexuality and delivery of a child out-of-wedlock in 2007. Since 1992, Mary has been cohabiting with her female partner Heather Poe. In December 2006, Mary reported that she was pregnant, but details of who the father was and how the baby was conceived were never released (Argetsinger and Roberts 2006). While Vice President Cheney was reportedly elated about his daughter's pregnancy, many social conservatives were not. The Concerned Women for America, for example, denounced the pregnancy as "unconscionable" (*BBC News*, 7 December 2006).

The third example centers on the pregnancy of Bristol Palin, daughter of the former vice-presidential candidate, Sarah Palin. In 2008, Bristol became pregnant while unmarried (Saul 2009). When news of the pregnancy broke out, Bristol claimed she was engaged to the father (Levi Johnston, a classmate) of the child-to-be and would soon get married. However, Bristol and Levi broke off their engagement several months after their son was born in December 2008 (Saul 2009). That leaves Bristol today as a single-mother with a child born out of wedlock.

While less famous than the above cases, the story of Mia Washington and James Harrison, an unmarried couple from Texas, is no less illustrative of the new American family. In 2008, Mia gave birth to fraternal twins, Justin and Jordan (DeMarco 2009). At first, James thought both twins were his. However, it wasn't long before he could tell Justin and Jordan looked suspiciously unalike. Doubtful that both twins were his, James ordered a paternity test. Sure enough, the boys had different fathers. When James first learned Justin wasn't his biological son, he said of the occasion, "I was hurt, torn apart—didn't know what the next move was gonna be" (*NBC News*, 21 May 2009). In the end, however, James decided to raise Justin as his own. "I raised him from a baby all the way to now. He knows me as his father, and I know him as my son," James said (*NBC News*, 21 May 2009). As of summer 2009, Mia and James were still unmarried.

A final example focuses on the connection between same-sex marriage and polygamy. While polygamy is still not prevalent enough today to threaten monogamy as the dominant form of marriage in the United States, many social conservatives are concerned that the legalization of homosexual marriage may change this (Zeitzen 2008). Proponents of traditional marriage point out that just a generation ago the idea of same-sex marriage was unheard of. Because of pressure from the political left since the 1970s, however, gay marriage has been gaining legitimacy in the United States. Social conservatives argue that, should gay marriage become a federally protected form of marriage, the legalization of polygamy could very well become the next agenda for the political left. As evidence, they point out that in 2005, when the Canadians legalized gay marriage, Ottawa commissioned a series of reports on

Canada's polygamy laws to see if polygamy should be decriminalized in that country (Lak 2008). While no one can say that legalizing gay marriage will definitely lead to the legalization of polygamy, the fact that people are even debating the possibility shows how much the American family is under change.

The above cases underscore a core tenet of this chapter: family systems and the social expectations that go along with them are relative. The United States has traditionally encouraged monogamy and fidelity, while discouraging divorce and adultery. Powerful social and political forces have recently begun to whittle away at these traditions, however. As a result, the appearance of the American family in the years to come may be significantly different than the one Americans think of as usual today.

If we want to understand society and social life, it is impossible to ignore the family. Most of us spend a major portion of our lives in one form of family or another. It is unlikely that any society has ever existed without some social arrangement that could be termed "family," and we cannot overestimate its importance to the individual and to society as a whole.

This chapter considers the family as a group, as a social system, and as a social institution. For most of us, the family serves as a primary social group; it is the first agency of socialization. Sociologists consider the family to be a *social system* because it is composed of interdependent parts, it has a characteristic organization and pattern of functioning, and it has subsystems that are part of the larger system. The family is considered a *social institution* because it is an area of social life that is organized into discernible patterns and because it helps to meet crucial societal goals.

Families do not exist in isolation, of course. They are an interdependent unit of the larger society. If families have many children, for example, schools may become crowded and unemployment may become a problem. If, on the other hand, they have few children, over several generations Social Security, the care of the aged, and an adequate work force may become important issues. It also makes a difference whether one spouse is employed or both are. Do newlyweds live with one set of parents or establish independent residences? Is divorce frequent or infrequent? Do people select their own mates or have them selected for them? Family practices have a profound influence on many aspects of social life.

We begin our discussion by clarifying what we mean by the term *family*. Although the answer may appear quite obvious to most of us, it becomes less obvious to judges who must make decisions on property settlements with cohabiting couples, social service workers who get adoption requests from unmarried persons or same-sex couples, or government agencies who must decide who is eligible for various benefits. Some definitions result in informal stigmatization and discrimination against families who do not meet the qualifications, such as a mother and her child, two men, or an unmarried man and woman.

WHAT IS FAMILY?

The **family** has traditionally been defined as a group of kin united by blood, marriage, or adoption, who share a common residence for some part of their lives, and who assume reciprocal rights and obligations with regard to one another. Today, however, an increasing number of writers are defining *families* differently. They recognize the reality of childless marriages, stepparents, one-parent households, same-sex unions, and cohabiting couples. Currently, we can think about families in terms of intimate relationships, sexual bonds, and family realms.

The traditional definition of *family* suggests ideas of legal unions, permanence, children, intergenerational continuity, and a perceived ideal of what families should be. The nontraditional definition suggests a broader and more comprehensive portrayal of intimate relationships that often fall outside of fixed legal boundaries. Thus, a same-sex (lesbian or gay) couple or a heterosexual cohabiting couple, with or without children, would not be a family in traditional terms of blood, marriage, or adoptive ties. However, in terms of family-like relationships based on what families do (engage in intimate interactions, share household expenses and a division of labor, recognize other members as part of a primary intimate bonded unit), some same-sex or cohabiting partners are being viewed as families for purposes of property settlements, housing regulations for "families only," or employee benefit plans. Up to this point, however, few numbers or figures have existed that include these types of families.

This is not to deny the tremendous variations in traditional family structures and processes that exist in our own culture and in others around the world. There exists recognition of differentiating families as conjugal, nuclear, families of orientation and procreation, as well as extended or modifications of an extended structure. The smallest units are called **conjugal families**, which must include a husband and wife but may or may not include children. **Nuclear families** may or may not include a husband and wife—they consist of any two or more persons related to one another by blood, marriage, or adoption who share a common residence. Thus, a brother and sister or a single parent and child would be nuclear families but not conjugal families. These terms are sometimes used interchangeably, and some families fall under both categories.

The definition used in census reporting in the United States is the nuclear family. Family households are identified when the members of a household are related to the householder. The count of family units, regardless of whether the householder is in that family, is considered a family group. In 2010, there were 78.8 million family households and 83.6 million family groups in the U.S. Of these, 58.4 million were husband-and-wife family households (U.S. Census Bureau, *America's Families and Living Arrangements* 2010, Tables H1 and FG 10). Traditionally, family households made up the majority of all households. In 1970, 81 percent were family households; by 2010, family households made up 67 percent of all households.

Approximately 90 percent of all Americans marry at some time in their lives (Zinn and Eitzen, 2005). In so doing, they become members of two different, but overlapping, nuclear families. The nuclear family into which a person is born and reared (consisting of the person, brothers, sisters, and parents) is termed the **family of orientation**. This is the family in which most basic early childhood socialization occurs. When a person marries, a new nuclear (and conjugal) family is formed, which is called the **family of procreation**. This family consists of the person, a spouse, and children. These relations are diagrammed in Figure 12-1.

In the world as a whole, conjugal and nuclear families as isolated and independent units are rare. In most societies, the norm is the **extended family**, which goes beyond the nuclear family to include other nuclear families and relatives, such as grandparents, aunts, uncles, and cousins.

Is the typical family in the United States nuclear or extended? Actually, it is both. It is not an isolated nuclear unit that is separate from extended kin contacts

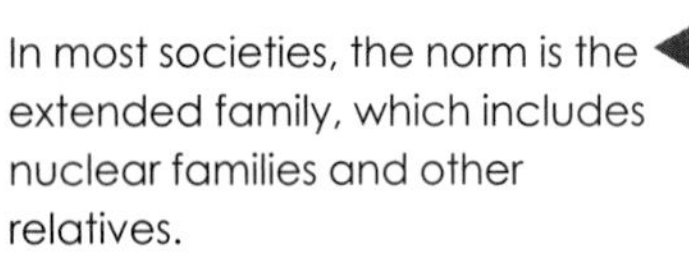

In most societies, the norm is the extended family, which includes nuclear families and other relatives.

FIGURE 12-1 FAMILIES OF ORIENTATION AND OF PROCREATION

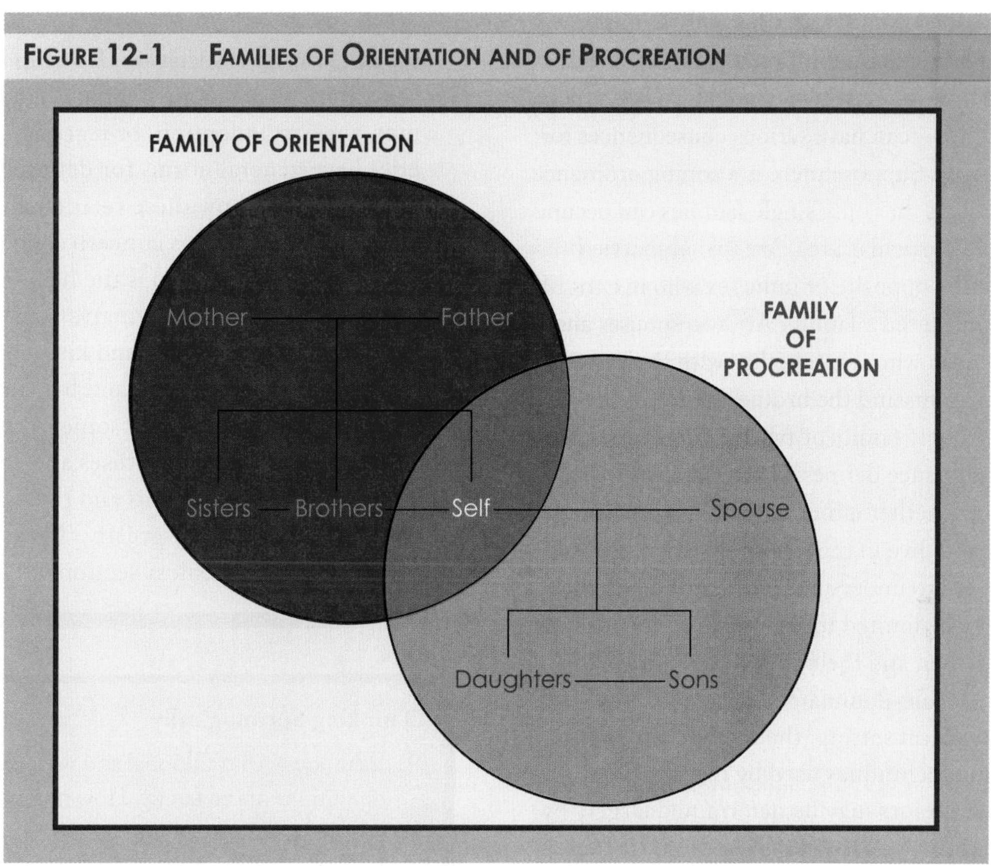

and support, nor is it an extended family in the traditional sense that extended family members share the same household. American families typically have what is called a **modified-extended family structure**, in which individual nuclear families retain considerable autonomy and yet maintain connections with other nuclear families through visits, calls, or the exchange of goods, services, or affective greetings. This type of family differs from the traditional extended family, in that its members may live in different parts of the country and may choose their occupations independently rather than following the parent's occupation.

APPLYING DEFINITIONS OF FAMILY

It is important for many reasons, therefore, to realize that there may be more than one acceptable definition of what a family is. Social scientist Arlene Skolnick (1992) points out that one of the major obstacles to social scientists in studying and understanding the family is the temptation to use our own experience as a basis for generalizations and comparisons. Everyone has a great deal of experience with families—their own—and there is a tendency to use our own family as a basis for insights and theories about families in general. Recognizing that there is a tremendous variety of types of family patterns is an essential part of helping social scientists to overcome their own ethnocentrism, stereotypes, and prejudices, which might get in the way of doing their objective research.

As suggested earlier, it is important for politicians who make policies that affect families to understand that because there are variations in types of families, strict definitions may be problematic. As Skolnick (1997) and many others who have explored the impact of policies upon the family have noted, how a family is defined has important consequences for the nature of policies and how they are carried out. Zoning laws, tax laws, welfare regulations, federally funded student loan guidelines, and many other policies often employ a particular definition of a family. Limiting the definition of what a family is to one type—or even a few—can have serious consequences for people's lives. Suppose there is a zoning ordinance that stipulates that only single families can occupy homes in a particular area. Are two unmarried people of the opposite or same sex who live together considered a family? Are two spouses and their children who live together with both of one spouse's parents and the brother of one of the spouses a single family or two families? How that zoning ordinance defines what a family is would determine whether either of these groups would be allowed to live in the area in question. Policymakers need to understand that families may not necessarily be limited to the middle-class norm of mother, father, and their children residing together in a male-dominated household.

In a clinical setting, the therapeutic and counseling techniques used by marriage and family counselors may be determined largely by how the family is defined. Assuming that there is only one definition of the family could lead some therapists to look at families that fall outside that definition as pathological or troubled. Certainly, some families are in trouble, but not necessarily because they do not fit the norm of the white, middle-class nuclear family. In recognizing that there are many possible ways to live as a family, marriage counselors might be able to be more creative and flexible in what they have to offer their clients.

Finally, and perhaps most important for you, the recognition that there is more than one acceptable definition of a family can lead to more choices and freedom in your own life. This does not mean, however, that you have complete freedom to live the way you want to or that every family pattern will necessarily work. As this chapter shows later, many family and kinship patterns may be workable only in a particular social context that emphasizes the social creation and construction of family and kinship patterns. However, the options that are workable in a particular social context may not be as limited as they were once thought to be.

Family groups and systems are only one type of kinship association. **Kinship** is the web of relationships among people linked by common ancestry, adoption, or marriage. All societies have general norms for defining family and kin groups and how these relationships are organized. These norms concern such matters as who lives together, who is the head of the group, who marries whom, how mates are selected, which relatives in family and kin groups are most important, and how and by whom children are to be raised. Although some general norms tend to determine the statuses and roles of family members, other norms and the kinship systems they govern vary greatly. These variations are discussed in the next section.

Thinking Sociologically

1. Examine both traditional and nontraditional definitions of the family. How might family policies differ, depending on the definition used?
2. In terms of patterns of helping and assistance, visiting, or letter writing, to what extent do families in the United States (or your own family) resemble a modified-extended family?
3. Choose two family forms to compare. Discuss whether or not each can meet the basic tasks required of family units. What can you conclude about "what a family really is"?

VARIATION IN KINSHIP AND FAMILY ORGANIZATION

Each society defines particular patterns of marriage, family, and kinship as correct and proper. Because we tend to be ethnocentric and to favor the family structure found in our own society, we may overlook the wide range of variations that exist. We may also tend to assume that if our current family forms change too drastically, the institution of the family will collapse. It is important to recognize that a tremendous variety of marriage, family, and kinship patterns exist and that any of these patterns may be both appropriate and workable in a particular social context. One fundamental variation concerns marriage and the number of spouses considered acceptable.

Marriage and Number of Spouses

Marital status (single, married, separated, widowed, divorced) and number of spouses (none, one, more than one) are two major variations in family organization. Every society permits some form of marriage although some groups, such as the Catholic Church, take the position that nuns and priests, to devote their lives fully to God, must take vows of chastity and remain unmarried. Totally apart from religious reasons, in the United States today, it seems that remaining single may be emerging as an acceptable lifestyle. It is unclear, however, whether this is a permanent alternative to marriage or just a delay in marriage.

To most Americans, the most "proper" form of marriage is **monogamy**, in which one man is married to one woman at a time. Throughout the world, this form of marriage is the only one universally recognized; it is the predominant form even in societies where other forms exist. However, only about 20 percent of the world's societies are strictly monogamous, considering monogamy the only acceptable form of marriage.

Marital status is just one major variation in the family organization.

While the United States is strictly monogamous, Americans frequently have more than one spouse over a lifetime. This pattern of "marriage, divorce, and remarriage" is called **serial** or **sequential monogamy**. It is both legally and socially accepted to have more than one wife or husband as long as it is done sequentially and not simultaneously. It is completely illegal in every state in the United States to be married to more than one person at any given time.

There are a variety of alternatives to monogamy. Murdock (1957) investigated the frequency of **polygamy**, marriage to more than one spouse, in a sample of 554 societies from around the world. He found that **polygyny**, in which a man has more than one wife, was the norm in 77 percent of these societies, whereas **polyandry**, in which a woman has more than one husband, was culturally favored in less than 1 percent. **Group marriage**, in which several or many men are married to several or many women, has been practiced among selected groups in some societies; but nowhere is it the dominant form.

One example of group marriage in the United States was that of the Oneida Community, the founding group of Oneida Corporation that is listed today on the New York Stock Exchange. For about thirty years in the mid-1800s, John Humphrey Noyes preached that people were capable of living sinless lives based on a spiritual equality of all persons: materially, socially, and sexually. The outcome of this teaching was a group marriage structure where all adults were recognized as married to each other, all adults were parents to all children, and the total emphasis was on "we" rather than "I."

In discussing polygamy or any family structure with a plural number of spouses, several words of caution are in order. First, a distinction must be made between ideology and actual occurrence. The fact that a society permits one to have several spouses does not necessarily mean that a large proportion of all marriages are polygamous. Second, except for group marriage, multiple spouses are possible on a large scale only when the ratio of the sexes is unbalanced. Third, when polygamy is practiced, it is controlled by societal norms like any other form of marriage. Rather than resulting from strictly personal or psychological motives, it is supported by the values and norms of both sexes and is closely linked to the economic conditions and belief systems of the wider society. Fourth, polygamy itself may take a variety of forms. The multiple husbands may all be brothers or the multiple wives may all be sisters, for example.

The most common form of polygamy is polygyny. In many societies, having several wives is a mark of prestige and high status. The wealthy, the leaders, and the best hunters may get a second or third wife. Multiple wives may also be desired as a source of children, especially sons. Polygyny is very common in Africa, among Muslim groups in the Middle East and Asia, and in many tribal groups in South America and throughout the world. In Ibadan, Nigeria, for example, a study of more than 6,600 women (Ware 1979) found that nearly one wife in two was living in a polygamous marriage; the proportion rose to two out of three for wives age forty years and above. The Muslim religion permits men to have up to four wives. In the United States, despite its illegality, some Mormon fundamentalists living in Utah and neighboring states practice polygyny.

While the Mormon Church has officially rejected polygamy for over a century, a (1998) poll by the *Salt Lake Tribune* found that 35 percent of Utah's population opposed the prosecution of polygamists. Not surprisingly, people who know a polygamist, infrequent churchgoers, and older people tend to hold more positive views of polygamy (Nielsen 2009). One of the most recent and shocking cases of polygamy in Utah centered on the now infamous Warren Steed Jeffs, a radical Mormon who ran the Fundamentalist Church of Jesus Christ of Latter Day Saints (FLDS) until 2007. Jeffs gained national notoriety in 2006 when he was placed on the FBI's Ten Most Wanted List for unlawful flight to avoid prosecution in Utah on charges of arranging the rape of a minor. In 2007, Jeffs was found guilty and is now behind bars at Utah State Prison. He was reputed to have seventy wives at the time of his conviction. It is important to note that the Church of Jesus Christ of Latter Day Saints (LDS) does not recognize the FLDS and took steps to further distance itself from FLDS after the Warren Jeffs incident due to the media's lack of attention to distinguishing between the two organizations (Cragun and Nielsen 2009).

Polyandry is quite rare. Where it is practiced, the co-husbands are usually brothers, either blood brothers or clan brothers who belong to the same clan and are of the same generation. Among the Todas, for example, a non-Hindu tribe in India, it is understood that when a woman marries a man, she becomes the wife of his brothers at the same time. This type of polyandry, where brothers are co-husbands, may also be referred to as **fraternal polyandry**.

Members of The Fundamentalist Church of Jesus Christ of Latter-day Saints board a bus for relocation in Texas in 2008.

Norms of Residence

When people marry, they must decide where to live. Decisions about place of residence are typically dictated by societal norms and conform to one of three patterns. In Western societies, the residence norm is **neolocal**—the couple lives alone wherever they wish—but this pattern is rare in the rest of the world. Of the societies Murdock (1949) examined, only about 10 percent considered it appropriate for newlywed couples to move to a place of residence separate from both the husband's and the wife's families. This type of residence pattern seems to be linked with norms of monogamy and individualism. Nearly three-fourths of the societies studied by Murdock were **patrilocal**—the newlywed couple lived not just in the groom's community but also usually in his parents' home or compound. This type of residence is most common in polygamous hunting-and-gathering societies throughout Asia, Africa, and Latin America. In the United States, the Amish communities represent one example of a patrilocal system. A **matrilocal** residence pattern, in which the newly married couple lives with the wife's family, was the norm in about 15 percent of the societies Murdock studied and was generally found where women held title to the land.

Norms of Descent and Inheritance

Children inherit two separate bloodlines at birth, the mother's and the father's. Most societies place more importance on one lineage or the other. In much of the Western world, particularly in the United States, lineage is of small importance. It determines surname but little else. In most societies, however, explicit rules indicate that one bloodline is more important than the other. These rules are known as the "norms of descent and inheritance."

The most common norms of descent are **patrilineal**, in which kinship is traced through the male kin, the father's lineage. In this type of descent system, offspring owe a special allegiance and loyalty to the father and his kin, who in turn protect and socialize the children and eventually pass to the sons their authority, property, and wealth. Under this system, the key ties are those among father, sons, and grandsons. The wife may maintain ties to her kin, and she contributes her genes to her children; however, she and her children are considered members of her husband's family.

In a **matrilineal** system of descent, descent and inheritance are traced through the mother's line. The mother's kin assume the important role among offspring. Matrilineal norms of descent are uncommon, but they do exist. Among the Trobriand Islanders, for example, kinship, wealth, and responsibility for support are traced through the female line.

In the United States, the norm is to assign influence, wealth, and power to both sides of the family. This system is referred to as **bilateral lineage**. Kinship lines are traced equally through the biological relatives of both the mother and the father, and inheritance is passed on in equal proportions to all children regardless of sex. One consequence of this descent system is that, although the kin of both parents are equally recognized and respected, neither kin group exerts much power and influence over the children, which has a significant effect on social change: a newlywed couple coming from families with different values and lifestyles may choose to conform to neither and establish a lifestyle of their own. In addition, the likelihood of marrying someone with different values increases because the parents and kin groups in bilateral systems have relatively little influence over whom their sons or daughters marry.

Norms of Authority

All families and kinship systems have norms concerning who makes important decisions. These norms follow the pattern of other norm variations in that they are aligned with gender. Most societies are **patriarchal**—the men have the power and authority and are dominant. In Iran, Thailand, and Japan, the male position of dominance is even reflected in the law. In matriarchal societies, the authority rests with the females, especially wives and mothers. **Matriarchal** systems are rare, even among matrilineal societies such as that of the Trobriand Islanders, where the wives do not have authority over their husbands.

It is important to recognize that although authority in most families rests with the males, other family members have a strong influence on the decision-making process. Male family members are generally most influential, but wives and mothers often have a strong impact on decisions as well.

The least common pattern of authority is the **egalitarian** model, in which decisions are equally divided between husband and wife. Some have argued that the United States is egalitarian because husbands and wives either make decisions jointly or assume responsibility for different areas of concern. The husband might make decisions related to his job, the automobile, or home repairs, whereas the wife might make decisions related to her job, the home, food, clothing, or the children. Many would argue that the family system in the United States is more patriarchal than egalitarian, however, because males generally control income and other family resources.

Endogamous norms vary from one society to another. For example, marriages between members of different racial groups were considered improper at different times in America.

Norms for Choice of Marriage Partner

Every society, including the United States, has norms concerning the appropriateness or unacceptability of some types of marriage partners. These norms can be divided into two categories: **exogamy**, in which people must marry outside of their own group, and **endogamy**, which requires that people considering marriage share particular group characteristics, such as age, race, religion, or socioeconomic status.

Some exogamous norms are almost universal. **Incest**—sexual relations or marriage with close relatives—is forbidden in almost every society. One cannot marry one's mother, father, brother, sister, son, or daughter. Isolated exceptions to this taboo are said to have existed between Egyptian and Inca royalty. Most societies also forbid marriage between first cousins and between members of the same sex. Argentina, The Netherlands, Belgium, Canada, Iceland, Portugal, Spain, South Africa, and most recently Norway in 2008 and Sweden in 2009 now allow gay marriage. In the UnitedStates as of 2009, the states of Iowa, Connecticut, Massachusetts, New Hampshire, and Vermont, and Washington D.C. recognize and perform same-sex marriages.

Endogamous norms of one sort or another are also very widespread, although they vary greatly from one society to another. In this country, for example, marriages between members of different racial groups were considered improper, or even forbidden by law, at different times.

Why have norms concerning endogamy and exogamy evolved? It seems clear from their universality that they perform an important social function, but the nature of that function is widely debated. A number of authorities have suggested that the incest taboo, for instance, is a result of the dangers of inbreeding. Others contend that the taboo is instinctive, that prolonged associations with people during childhood precludes viewing them as a marriage partner or that marriage within a kinship group would lead to intense conflicts and jealousy. Each of these explanations has its shortcomings, however. Murdock (1949) suggests that a complete explanation of the incest taboo must synthesize theories from the different disciplines that deal with human behavior.

There are also a number of explanations for endogamy. It is widely believed that members of similar groups share similar values, role expectations, and attitudes, which results in fewer marital or kinship conflicts. For example, some suggest that people from similar age groups share similar developmental tasks and interests. Marriage within the race maintains what the race considers to be its pure genetic traits. Marriages between people of the same socioeconomic status keep the wealth and power within the social class. Marriages within the same religious orientation are likely to agree on child-rearing practices, family rituals, and beliefs relating to the sacred. Although the norms of endogamy—and of what determines being in the same social group—vary among and within societies such as the United States, all societies foster suspicion and dislike of groups whose values, behaviors, and customs are unfamiliar or seem strange. This is a manifestation of Merton's in-group virtues to out-group vices. Both exogamy and endogamy, therefore, restrict the eligibility of available marriage partners for both sexes.

Thinking Sociologically

1. Polygyny is known to exist as a legitimate form of marriage in many societies around the world. Why does (or should) the United States not legally permit either polygyny or polyandry?
2. What are some consequences of a particular type of lineage system? Think of examples that illustrate whether families are patrilineal, matrilineal, or bilateral, and what difference it makes.
3. What factors aid in determining "appropriate" societal norms around marriage and family? How does determining these factors help us understand societal unrest around marriage and family in the United States?

A FUNCTIONALIST PERSPECTIVE ON THE FAMILY

The functionalist perspective emphasizes the structures of social systems and the functions of these parts in maintaining the society. Despite the many variations that exist in family structure around the world, families everywhere perform many of the same functions. Among the more important are socialization, affection and emotional support, sexual regulation, reproduction, and social placement.

Socialization

As discussed elsewhere, the family is one of the most important agents of socialization because it teaches its members the rules and expectations for behavior in the society. Reiss (1965) argues that although families perform many functions, only the function of nurturant socialization of children is universal. It is doubtful whether infants could even survive, much less develop into mentally, physically, and socially healthy human beings, outside of the intimate network of the family. The family is not only more permanent than other social institutions but also it provides the care, protection, and love best suited to teaching children the knowledge, skills, values, and norms of the society and subculture. However excellent hospitals, child-care centers, and nursery or elementary schools may be, none seems to perform the socialization and learning functions as well as the family (Elkin and Handel 1989; Spitz 1945). This emphasis on the infant and young child should not cause us to overlook the socialization function of the family on adults, however. Parents learn from each other, from their children, and from other kin as they interact in the intimate network bound by blood and marriage ties. This affective support is a second function provided by the family.

Affection and Emotional Support

More than thirty-five years ago, Parsons and Bales (1955) suggested that the family has two essential functions: (1) the primary socialization of children so that they can become true members of the society in which they were born in, and (2) the stabilization of the adult personalities of the society. This second function, although often ignored, seems to be just as important as the first. Although some individuals enjoy living alone, most people need others who care, show affection, share joys and sorrows, and give support in times of need. Humans are social animals who depend on their families at every stage of the life cycle; and although friends, neighbors, co-workers, and government agencies also provide social support, none is as effective as the family at providing warm, supportive relationships.

The importance of this family function is evidenced in many different ways. Aging persons particularly exemplify this idea. In studies, they often indicated that good relationships with their children are a major source of gratification. In fact, people who have a network of family connections live longer than those who are single, widowed, or divorced.

Sexual Regulation

All societies approve of some sexual behaviors and disapprove of others. As mentioned earlier, there is an almost universal taboo against incest, whereas marriage is the most universally approved outlet for sexual behavior. Both are linked to the family system.

Societies control sexual activity in a number of ways. The chief means is by socializing sexual norms and attempting to enforce them. Secluding single women, for example, might enforce the norm of chastity. Society also differentiates sexual rights in accordance with various roles and statuses (male, female, single, married, priest, teacher) and places taboos on intercourse at some times in the reproductive cycle, such as during menstruation, pregnancy, or immediately following childbirth. The norms of most societies discourage practices such as rape, child molesting, voyeurism, and the like. Sexual norms are concerned with more than just sexual intercourse; they also cover such behaviors as kissing and touching, as well as appropriate attitudes and values.

In the United States, the most pervasive socially approved sexual interest is heterosexual. Sexual relationships are generally defined in terms of the family and marriage, as premarital or extramarital relationships, for example. Other institutions—religion, education, economics, or politics—may also regulate sexual behaviors and attitudes, but it is not one of their primary tasks. Families have the chief responsibility in this area; and because they regulate sexual activity, it seems logical that they also control the function of reproduction.

Reproduction

The family is the most widely approved social context for having children. Children are sometimes born outside the family, of course, but if it is common, it is considered a social problem. According to the functionalist perspective, a society's reproductive practices should conform to institutional patterns and should be integrated with other societal functions, such as sexual regulation, physical and emotional support, and socialization. This view reflects the **principle of legitimacy**, formulated by Bronislaw Malinowski (1930) more than seventy years ago. The principle states that every society has a rule that every child should have a legitimate father to act as the child's protector, guardian, and representative in the society.

Those who are not functionalists may be disturbed at this explanation of the role of the family. It suggests that children born outside of the family are stigmatized in some way, that they are illegitimate. Even functionalists would concede that there are functional alternatives to a biological father; father substitutes can fulfill the essential social tasks and roles of a father. Interactionists would also argue that the biological link between parent and child is less significant than the social links—what is important to the child are role models, social support, and patterns of interaction that will enable the child to develop adequately and to function effectively in society.

Clinicians often deal with problems of adjustment between adopted children and their parents, who may have fears of rejection or inadequacy because they are not biologically related to their child. Counselors can help parents to realize the overriding significance of the social ties between parent and child, and thus help to allay the parents' fears. With today's high divorce

Clinicians often deal with problems of adjustment between adopted children and their parents.

rate (discussed later in this chapter), many of you will remarry and perhaps be involved in **blended families**—families composed of at least one formerly married spouse, the children of the previous marriage or marriages, and new offspring. Sometimes, stepparents feel guilty about not being able to instantly love their stepchildren. Other tensions may develop between biologically unrelated children. Realizing the essential significance of the social links between family members may help family members to overcome some of those tensions. Further, a more active approach by family members and counselors working with such families could involve finding ways to strengthen those links through activities that provide close interaction and communication.

Although it is true that children born outside the family can develop into functioning members of society, it is undeniably the family that universally fulfills the function of giving legal status and social approval to parenthood and reproduction. This function is related to another family function, that of social placement.

Social Placement

The social placement of children is a family function closely associated with socialization and reproduction. Social placement involves determining what roles and statuses the child will occupy in society. As discussed elsewhere, some of the statuses that a person will occupy are ascribed at birth, such as age, sex, and social class position. Children generally assume the legal, religious, and political status of their family as well. Even statuses that are achieved, such as marriage, occupation, and education, are greatly influenced by one's membership in a particular family or kin network.

The family also performs functions other than the five mentioned (i.e., socialization, affection and emotional support, sexual regulation, reproduction, and social placement). It fulfills basic economic, protective, educational, recreational, and religious functions, as well.

A CONFLICT PERSPECTIVE ON THE FAMILY

Conflict theorists, like functionalists, recognize variations in family structure and accept the idea that the family provides basic social needs and goals. The two approaches are fundamentally very different, however. Conflict theorists contend that social systems, including the family, are not static structures that maintain equilibrium and harmony among the parts. They argue, rather, that social systems are constantly in a state of conflict and change. They contend that conflict is natural and inevitable in all human interactions, including those between male and female, husband and wife, and parent and child, and that these conflicts are the result of a continual struggle for power and control. Marriage is one of many contexts in which each person seeks his or her rights. The struggles of parenthood involve not just rivalries among siblings but also between parents and children.

Conflict stems from the unequal distribution of scarce resources. In all systems, some have more resources than others, which gives them dominance and power over others. Feminist theories, like conflict theories, argue that inequalities exist not only in the economic and occupational realm but also in the family. Friedrich Engels (1902) claimed that the family, the basic unit in a capitalist society, serves as the chief means of oppressing women. The husband is the bourgeois and the wife is the proletariat. As general Marxist–feminist theory suggests, when women become aware of their collective interests, they will question the legitimacy of the existing patterns of inequality and will join together against men to bring about changes and the redistribution of resources: power, money, education, job opportunities, and the like. Conflict is as inevitable in the family as it is in society, and it leads to change.

Conflict theory assumes that economic organization, especially the ownership of property, generates revolutionary class conflict. In families, property ownership involves not just one's home and possessions, but people as well. Collins and Coltrane (2000) argue that basic to the institution of sexual stratification is the notion of sexual property, the belief that one has permanent exclusive sexual rights to a particular person. In societies operating under a system of patriarchy that is dominated by males, the principal form of sexual property is male ownership of females, husband ownership of wives.

This pattern of male ownership and male dominance has a long history, stemming from laws in ancient Hebrew society and continuing through the twentieth century. The Hebrew laws stated, among other things, that if a man had sexual intercourse with an *unbetrothed* (not contracted for marriage) virgin, he was required to marry her and to pay her father the bride price. In many societies, women are closely guarded so they will not attract other men and lose their market value. These practices are reflected in such customs as wearing a veil and strict chaperonage. Even in the United States, women could not legally make contracts or obtain credit until recently, and women are still not guaranteed equal rights under the U.S. Constitution. The status of women is also evident in many wedding ceremonies, in which the father "gives away" some of his property—the bride—and the bride vows not just to love but also to honor and obey her new owner (the groom).

How can this inequality and the prevalence of male domination be explained? The most common theory relates power and domination to available resources. Men gain power over women through their physical strength and their freedom from the biological limitations of childbirth. The traditional resource of women, on the other hand, is their sexuality. Before and during marriage, women traditionally control men by giving or withholding sexual "favors."

Conflict theory suggests that the structure of domination shifts as resources shift. In general, those with greater occupational prestige, higher income, or more education have more power. Women who bear children, it could be argued, gain status, prestige, and power because they are fulfilling the important role of mother. However, realistically, exactly the opposite happens. A woman's power declines with the birth of a child and goes down even more with additional children. Why? Women with children are more likely to be confined to the home, with the primary responsibilities of child care, and do not have the time or the liberty to acquire resources such as education, income, or the type of job that would increase their power. Logically, we can argue, and might expect, women today to be in better bargaining positions relative to men because they are having fewer children and are more likely hold jobs. Being free from unwanted pregnancies and from childbirth, combined with an increased education and income, lessens their economic dependence on husbands. The result today is that there seems to be a major trend, at least in the more industrialized nations, toward greater equality between the sexes, both within and outside of marriage and the family.

Conflict in families also occurs over issues other than inequality between men and women. It can arise over a variety of issues: place of residence, inheritance rights, decision-making, selection of mates, violence (especially rape), sexual relationships, and marital adjustment, to mention a few. In every instance, the issue is likely to involve an inequality of power, authority, or resources, which will lead to conflict. This means that these marital conflicts are not necessarily due to personality clashes but rather to inequality, a power imbalance in the relationship.

It is important for married people and marriage counselors to understand this in trying to work out troubled relationships. It may be more important to try to adjust the balance of power between spouses than to try to adjust personalities that are thought to be incompatible. These ideas may be useful for you even if you are not currently married. Consider your relationship with your boyfriend or girlfriend. Can you think of any ways in which an imbalance of power sometimes leads to disagreements? The disagreements do not necessarily mean that there is a loss of affection for one another—although there may be—but may instead reflect inequality in the relationship.

OTHER PERSPECTIVES ON THE FAMILY

An Exchange Perspective

All human interactions, including those between husbands and wives or parents and children, can be viewed in terms of social exchange. Social exchange theory assumes that people weigh rewards and costs in their social interactions. If the exchange is unequal or is perceived as unequal, one person will be at a disadvantage, and the other will control the relationship. In this regard, exchange theory parallels the conflict perspective. If people in a relationship give a great deal and receive little in return, they will perceive the relationship as unsatisfactory. These ideas can be illustrated with mate selection.

Everywhere in the world, selecting a mate involves trying to get the best spouse for what one has to offer. As you know from our earlier discussion of the endogamous and exogamous rules of marriage, selecting a mate is never a matter of completely free and independent choice. One must conform to societal norms.

Marriages may be arranged in several ways. At one extreme, they may be organized by the families of the people to be married; the prospective spouses may have no say in the matter at all. When this practice is followed, the criteria of the exchange involve such factors as money, prestige, family position, or power. When, on the other hand, the people to be married choose their mates themselves, the exchange criteria involve factors such as love, affection, emotional support, beauty, personality, prestige, and fulfillment of needs. The latter procedure is rare in the world as a whole, the United States being one of the few countries that practices it.

One of the most widely researched exchange theories of mate selection is the theory of **complementary needs**. Robert Winch (1954, 1958) believed that although mates tend to resemble each other in such social characteristics as age, race, religion, ethnic origin, socioeconomic status, and education, they are usually complementary rather than similar in respect to needs, psychic fulfillment, and individual motivation. Rather than seeking a mate with a similar personality, one seeks a person who will satisfy one's needs. If both people are dominant, for example, the relationship will not succeed; but if one is dominant and the other submissive, the relationship is complementary, and the needs of both parties are met. A great deal of research was instigated by this theory of complementary needs, but the results did not provide empirical support for the notion that people choose mates whose needs complement their own.

An earlier exchange theory of mate selection was Willard Waller's (1938) analysis of courtship conduct as a process of bargaining, exploitation, or both. In his words, "When one marries he makes a number of different bargains. Everyone knows this and this knowledge affects the sentiment of love and the process of falling in love" (p. 239). Although it is doubtful that only "he makes bargains" or that "everyone knows this," the fact that bargaining and exchanges take place for both males and females in the mate-selection process is today widely recognized and accepted. Good looks, athletic stardom, a sense of humor, clothes, or money are resources commonly perceived as valuable in the exchange process. In mate selection, as in other interaction processes, people rarely get something for nothing, although each person, either consciously or unconsciously, tries to maximize gains and minimize costs. Over the long run, however, actual exchanges tend to be about equal; and if they are not, the relationship is likely to end.

Like conflict theory, exchange theory helps us to recognize the importance of equality in a marriage and may be a useful perspective in dealing with troubled marriages. If a relationship is in trouble, counselors or therapists might try to evaluate the balance of exchange that exists in a marriage. They might find that there is more of a balanced exchange than appears; and if this is the case, they could explain to the couple the resources that each partner provides. If there were, indeed, an imbalance, the clinician would recognize that this is likely to be a major source of trouble and may help the couple to find ways to attain a balanced exchange. Here, again, is a perspective that you can use to examine some of your relationships even if you are not married.

An Interactionist Perspective

An interactionist perspective on the family uses a social-psychological approach to examine interaction patterns, socialization processes, role expectations and behaviors, and the definitions or meanings given to various family issues. This approach considers not just structural variations but also the interactional patterns and covert definitions associated with structural arrangements.

Few relationships are more enduring or more intense than marriage, and few reflect the principles of interactionism so comprehensively. Marriage exemplifies the central ideas of symbolic interaction: shared meanings, significant others, role expectations, role taking, definitions of situations, symbolic communication, and so on.

Marriage is dynamic—the needs of the married individuals and their role relationships change frequently. According to the interactionist perspective, husband and wife have a reciprocal influence on each other. Each partner continually affects the other, so adjustment is a process, not an end result. Good adjustment means "the individual or the pair has a good working arrangement with reality, adulthood, and expectations of others" (Waller and Hill 1951, 362).

Each of us brings to a marriage certain ideas about what is proper behavior for our spouses and ourselves. Inevitably, people find as they interact that some behaviors do not fit their preconceived definitions. Unless the definitions or the behaviors change, one spouse or both may be frustrated in attempting to fulfill their roles. Some argue that these frustrations are increasing because the roles of husband and wife are more flexible and diverse than they were in the past. Others maintain that today's increased flexibility and diversity decrease marital strain by allowing partners a greater range of options. In either case, what the interactionist considers important is that the couple share definitions, perceptions, and meanings. Also, disagreements may not lead to conflict if they involve issues considered unimportant. Suppose, for example, that a wife likes football but her husband does not. The situation will not lead to conflict if the husband defines football as important to his wife and accepts her behavior. In the same way, a husband's desire for only part-time employment or his wish to avoid cooking is a source of conflict only if the wife has different expectations. Adjustment is a result of shared expectations.

To maintain a satisfactory relationship, married couples must continually redefine themselves in relation to each other, which is often an unconscious process. When problems arise, marriage counseling may help by bringing unconscious definitions into consciousness, thus allowing the couple to examine how they influence the relationship.

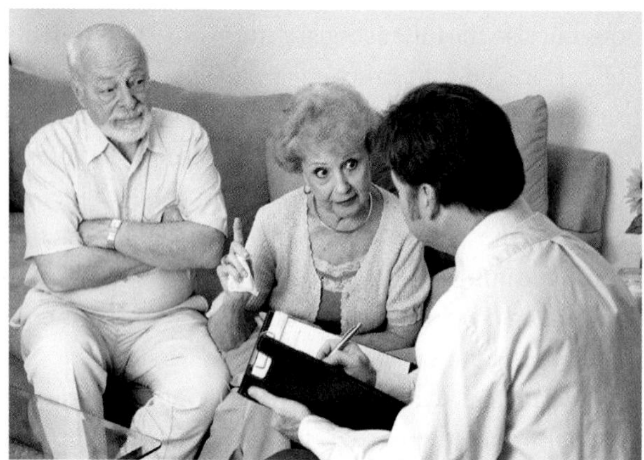

Married couples must continually redefine themselves in relation to each other; marriage counseling may help.

The interactionist perspective stresses the importance of analyzing marriages and other relationships in the context in which they occur. A definition, role expectation, or behavior that is appropriate in one setting may be inappropriate in another. This perspective also emphasizes the notion that a successful marriage involves a process of adjustment, or continual adaptation to shifts in shared meaning.

Interactionism, thus, is a particularly useful perspective for marital therapy. The family is not simply a group of separate people performing separate functions independently. The interactionist perspective helps us to realize that family members act largely on the basis of how they interpret one another's actions. Using the interactionist perspective, clinicians may come to understand that each family has its own context that provides the basis for interaction and for interpretation of each family member's actions. This being the case, a clinician using this perspective might work on making sure that the individual family members understand clearly what the other family members intentions are, and might also help to clarify how each person defines the actions of the others.

A Developmental Perspective

The developmental perspective on the family suggests that families pass through a family life cycle, a series of different responsibilities and tasks. This perspective suggests that successful achievement at one point in the developmental process is essential to effectively accomplishing later tasks, whereas failure in earlier tasks leads to increased difficulty with later tasks. Just as individuals must learn to crawl and walk before they can run, new families must be able to perform various financial, sexual, and interpersonal tasks to maintain the family unit and meet later developmental goals.

During its life cycle, the family passes through a sequence of stages that require different interaction patterns, roles, and responsibilities. The number of stages identified depends on the intent of the researcher. There may be as few as two, but the most typical division is of seven stages. The transition points between stages most often center on the age of the oldest child.

The first stage typically begins with marriage and extends to the birth of the first child. For most couples, this stage involves defining the marital relationship, learning to communicate effectively and resolve conflicts, working out mutually satisfying and realistic systems for getting and spending the family income, and deciding about parenthood. Obviously, not all newlyweds face the same tasks. If the woman is pregnant before the marriage, if it is a teenage, interracial, or second marriage, or if the couple lived together before marriage, their concerns may differ. Nevertheless, the first stage of the family life cycle typically focuses on the married couple and their adjustment to life as a married pair.

Stage two may include families with a preschool child, or be subdivided into families with an infant (birth to age two or three years) and families with an older preschool child (ages two or three to six years). During this stage, the couple changes from a dyad of husband and wife to a triad of parents and offspring. The central tasks are adjusting to parenthood, dealing with the needs and development of the infant and young children, relating to parents and in-laws who are grandparents to the child, assuming and managing the additional housing and space needs, and continuing the communicative, sexual, and financial responsibilities described in stage one.

Stage three may extend from the time the oldest child begins school until he or she reaches the teens. When children enter school, both parents and children face new relationships and responsibilities. In this stage, the family focuses on the education and socialization of children. The increasing significance of peer relationships, children's changing interests and activities, and the management of parent–child conflicts are added to the ongoing marital, work, and other responsibilities. A second or third child, the loss of a job, or the dissolution of the marriage modifies the responsibilities generally associated with this stage.

Stage four is the family with adolescents or teenagers. Data suggest that at the adolescent stage, the family often undergoes economic problems. Medical and dental costs, food, clothing, transportation, entertainment, education, and other expenses often place a strain on the budget. For many families, such issues as drinking, drugs, and sex become additional sources of strain. New types of adolescent dance, music, dress, and jargon must also be accommodated. In addition, families in this stage begin to prepare their teenager to be launched from the home.

Stage five begins when the oldest child leaves home and is frequently called the launching stage. The young person's departure—to marry, to attend college, or to take a full-time job—creates a significant transition for both parent and child. This stage may be very brief, as with a one-child family in which the child marries upon graduation from high school, or it may extend over many years, as happens when there are several children or when an unmarried child remains in the home for many years, dependent on parents for support. When the children have been launched, the family returns to the original two-person conjugal unit; at the same time, however, it may expand to include sons- or daughters-in-law and grandchildren.

Stage six is the period when all the children have left home; this is called the "empty-nest" stage. It starts with the departure of the last child from the home and continues until the retirement or death of one spouse. Again, it may be very brief because of one or more children who remain in the home through their twenties or because of an early death of a parent; or it may cover many years, as when the last child departs when the parents are in their late thirties or early forties and when the parents remain employed until age seventy or later. At this stage, the interpersonal focus is on the married couple, yet intergenerational family responsibilities can arise. The husband and wife in the middle years may have some responsibility for their retired and elderly parents and also for their married children and grandchildren, who may seek emotional and financial support from the middle generation from time to time.

The seventh and final stage generally begins with retirement and extends until the marriage ends with the death of one spouse. Because women live longer than men and are usually younger than their husbands, they are widowed more often than men. With the death of both spouses, the family life span for that family has ended, and the cycle continues with each successive generation.

Family life-cycle stages can be used to analyze a wide range of behaviors and interaction patterns. Frequency of sexual relations, income patterns, recreational activities, and interactions with children have been found to differ by the stage of the family life cycle. Olson and McCubbin (1983), for example, used a seven-stage family life-cycle model to study how 1,140 families managed their lives and why they succeeded in some areas better than in others. One finding consistent with other studies was that adults' satisfaction with marriage and family tends to decline between the birth of the first child and that child's adolescence, and to rise as the children are launched from the nest. One explanation for the dramatic increase in satisfaction following the launching stage concerns the relaxation of sex roles between the parents. Women see themselves as more free to look for work and organizational roles outside the home, and men find themselves with decreased financial responsibilities and allow themselves to be more passive and dependent.

Thinking Sociologically

1. Apply an exchange perspective to several close relationships in your life. What did you have to offer, and in turn, what did you receive? Can you identify instances in which an unequal relationship led to the termination of the relationship?
2. Suppose that you are a sociologist who is called upon to testify as an expert witness in a child custody case. This is a case in which the father wants a joint custody arrangement, but the mother objects and wants sole custody of the child. Assume that there is no violence or any other urgent reason to keep the child away from the father. Develop an argument for or against joint custody, using any or all of the theories just covered.

THE AMERICAN FAMILY SYSTEM

As indicated earlier in this chapter, the American family system emphasizes monogamy, neolocal residence, a modified-extended kinship linkage, bilateral descent and inheritance, egalitarian decision-making, endogamous marriage, and relatively free choice of mate. A number of other structural characteristics have also been described: American families tend to be small and, when compared with families of other countries, rather isolated. Marital and family roles for women and men are becoming increasingly ambiguous. We tend to emphasize love in mate selection, and we are often sexually permissive prior to or outside of marriage; and divorce is granted easily.

Table 12-1 shows the marital status of the population by sex and age. You can see that as of 2010, the population of the United States included 117.7 million males and a little over 124.3 million females age fifteen and over. Approximately 34.2 percent of the men and 27.4 percent of the women were never married. A relatively small number (around 3 million) of the men were widowers, compared with 11.4 million of the women who were widows. Much publicity is given to the breakup of marriages through divorce, but only 8.5 percent of the men and 11.1 percent of the women had a divorced status in 2010. Note how these figures vary by age. Very few older people are single, and very few young and middle-aged people are widowed. The divorced population is concentrated most heavily in the thirty-five to fifty-four age group.

Broad profiles of the sort given in the preceding paragraph, however, do not indicate the frequency or range of specific trends in the evolution of the family. In the following sections, we examine some of these trends in more detail.

Marriage Rates and Age at Marriage

Rates of marriage (the number of people who marry in a given year per 1,000 people [or per 1,000 unmarried women age fifteen and over]) are influenced by a variety of factors. The rate characteristically falls during periods of economic recession and rises during periods of prosperity. The rate also tends to rise at the beginning of a war and after a war has ended. Variations in the age of the population are also influential.

In the United States prior to 1900, the rate was relatively stable, varying between 8.6 and 9.6 marriages per 1,000 population per year. Shortly after the turn of the century, the rate rose until the depression of the early 1930s, when it dropped to a low of 7.9. Marriage rates

TABLE 12-1 MARITAL STATUS OF PEOPLE 15 YEARS AND OVER, 2010 (IN THOUSANDS, EXCEPT PERCENTAGES)

All Races	Total Number	Married Spouse Present Number	Married Spouse Absent Number	Widowed Number	Divorced Number	Separated Number	Never Married Number	Married Spouse Present Percent	Married Spouse Absent Percent
Both sexes									
Total 15 +	242,047	120,258	3,415	14,341	23,346	14,314	71,479	49.9	1.4
15-17 years	12,928	37	65	9	28	86	12,703	0.3	0.5
18-19 years	8151	141	44	13	32	65	7,856	1.7	0.5
20-24 years	21,142	2,655	202	17	195	309	17,765	12.6	1.0
25-29 years	21,445	7,793	406	60	766	594	11,826	36.3	1.9
30-34 years	19,623	10,896	337	72	1,447	632	6,239	55.5	1.7
35-39 years	19,879	12,547	369	123	2,076	672	4,091	63.1	1.9
40-44 years	20,556	13,181	364	222	2,621	659	3,508	64.1	1.8
45-49 years	22,517	14,394	373	445	3,392	717	3,196	63.9	1.7
50-54 years	21,856	14,225	330	635	3,559	578	2,529	65.1	1.5
55-64 years	35,381	23,621	463	1,923	5,750	763	2,861	66.8	1.3
65-74 years	20,938	13,340	216	3,313	2,746	306	1016	63.7	1.0
75-84 years	12,950	6,529	174	4,722	923	139	464	50.4	1.3
85 + years	4,681	1,408	72	2,788	206	19	188	30.1	1.5
65 + years	38,569	21,276	461	10,823	3,875	465	1,668	55.2	1.2
Males									
Total 15 +	117,686	60,384	1,789	2,974	9,981	2,352	40,206	51.3	1.5
15-17 years	6,566	16	33	5	16	39	6,458	0.2	0.5
18-19 years	4,147	45	22	3	14	23	4,040	1.1	0.5
20-24 years	10,677	946	86	3	49	123	9,469	8.9	0.8
25-29 years	10,926	3,343	220	21	318	224	6,800	30.6	2.0
30-34 years	9,759	5,143	188	28	593	246	3,561	52.7	1.9
35-39 years	9,897	6,185	191	29	879	289	2,324	62.5	1.9
40-44 years	10,169	6,429	201	52	1,119	289	2,078	63.2	2.0
45-49 years	11,092	7,145	187	124	1,508	298	1,830	64.4	1.7
50-54 years	10,687	7,135	180	160	1,555	241	1,416	66.8	1.7
55-64 years	16,980	11,958	244	424	2,465	343	1,545	70.4	1.4
65-74 years	9,731	7,316	121	627	1,071	155	441	75.2	1.2
75-84 years	5,426	3,815	84	933	329	72	192	70.3	1.5
85 + years	1,630	908	33	564	64	10	52	55.7	2.0
65 + years	16,786	12,039	237	2,124	1,464	237	685	71.7	1.4
Females									
Total 15 +	124,361	60,384	1,626	11,368	13,760	3,187	34,037	48.6	1.3
15-17 years	6,361	22	32	4	12	47	6,245	0.3	0.5
18-19 years	4,004	96	23	9	18	43	3,816	2.4	0.6
20-24 years	10,465	1,708	116	14	146	185	8,296	16.3	1.1
25-29 years	10,519	4,451	186	39	448	370	5,026	42.3	1.8
30-34 years	9,864	5,753	150	44	854	386	2,678	58.3	1.5
35-39 years	9,982	6,362	178	94	1,197	383	1,768	63.7	1.8
40-44 years	10,387	6,753	163	170	1,501	370	1,430	65.0	1.6
45-49 years	11,425	7,249	186	320	1,885	419	1,366	63.5	1.6
50-54 years	11,169	7,090	151	474	2,004	337	1,113	63.5	1.3
55-64 years	18,401	11,663	220	1,499	3,284	420	1,315	63.4	1.2
65-74 years	11,208	6,024	95	2,686	1,676	151	576	53.8	0.8
75-84 years	7,525	2,713	90	3,789	594	67	272	36.1	1.2
85 + years	3,051	500	39	2,224	142	9	136	16.4	1.3
65 + years	21,783	9,238	224	8,700	2,412	227	983	42.4	1.0

Adapted from Table A1. Marital Status of People 15 years and Over, by Age, Sex, Personal Earnings, Race, and Hispanic Origin/1, 2010

Source: U.S. Census Bureau America's Family Living Arrangements 2010

(continued)

TABLE 12-1 MARITAL STATUS OF PEOPLE 15 YEARS AND OVER, 2010 (IN THOUSANDS, EXCEPT PERCENTAGES)

All Races	Widowed	Divorced	Separated	Never Married
	Percent	Percent	Percent	Percent
Both sexes				
Total 15 +	5.9	9.8	2.3	30.7
15-17 years	0.1	0.2	0.7	98.3
18-19 years	0.2	0.4	0.8	96.4
20-24 years	0.1	0.9	1.5	84.0
25-29 years	0.3	3.6	2.8	55.1
30-34 years	0.4	7.4	3.2	31.8
35-39 years	0.6	10.4	3.4	20.6
40-44 years	1.1	12.7	3.2	17.1
45-49 years	2.0	15.1	3.2	14.2
50-54 years	2.9	16.3	2.6	11.6
55-64 years	5.4	16.3	2.2	8.1
65-74 years	15.8	13.1	1.5	4.9
75-84 years	36.5	7.1	1.1	3.6
85 + years	59.6	4.4	0.4	4.0
65 + years	28.1	10.0	1.2	4.3
Males				
Total 15 +	2.5	8.5	2.0	34.2
15-17 years	0.1	0.2	0.6	98.4
18-19 years	0.1	0.3	0.5	97.4
20-24 years	0.0	0.5	1.2	88.7
25-29 years	0.2	2.9	2.0	62.2
30-34 years	0.3	6.1	2.5	36.5
35-39 years	0.3	8.9	2.9	23.5
40-44 years	0.5	11.0	2.8	20.4
45-49 years	1.1	13.6	2.7	16.5
50-54 years	1.5	14.6	2.3	13.3
55-64 years	2.5	14.5	2.0	9.1
65-74 years	6.4	11.0	1.6	4.5
75-84 years	17.2	6.1	1.3	3.5
85 + years	34.6	3.9	0.6	3.2
65 + years	12.7	8.7	1.4	4.1
Females				
Total 15 +	9.1	11.1	2.6	27.4
15-17 years	0.1	0.2	0.7	98.2
18-19 years	0.2	0.4	1.1	95.3
20-24 years	0.1	1.4	1.8	79.3
25-29 years	0.4	4.3	3.5	47.8
30-34 years	0.4	8.7	3.9	27.2
35-39 years	0.9	12.0	3.8	17.7
40-44 years	1.6	14.5	3.6	13.8
45-49 years	2.8	16.5	3.7	12.0
50-54 years	4.2	17.9	3.0	10.0
55-64 years	8.1	17.8	2.3	7.1
65-74 years	24.0	15.0	1.3	5.1
75-84 years	50.4	7.9	0.9	3.6
85 + years	72.9	4.7	0.3	4.5
65 + years	39.9	11.1	1.0	4.5

Adapted from Table A1. Marital Status of People 15 years and Over, by Age, Sex, Personal Earnings, Race, and Hispanic Origin/1, 2010

Source: U.S. Census Bureau America's Family Living Arrangements 2010

rose dramatically at the outset of World War II, as young men sought to avail themselves of the deferred status granted to married men or simply wanted to marry before going over-seas. The end of the war and the return of men to civilian life precipitated another upsurge in marriages. In 1946, the marriage rate reached 16.4, an unprecedented and to-date unsurpassed peak. Subsequently, it dropped. While there have been fluctuations, it has declined steadily since 1970. In 2009, the marriage rate was 6.8 per 1,000 population (U.S. National Center for Health Statistics, Vital Statistics of the United States, annual; and National Vital Statistics Reports).

In the United States, marriage rates have distinct seasonal and geographic variations. More marriages take place in June than in any other month, followed by August, May, and September. The fewest marriages are in January, February, and March. Interestingly, the favorite month for marriage varies by age group: teenage brides and grooms prefer June; brides ages thirty to thirty-four and grooms ages forty-five to fifty-four most often choose December; and brides thirty-five to fifty-four and grooms fifty-five to sixty-four tend to select July. Most marriages take place on Saturday. Friday is next in popularity, and Tuesdays, Wednesdays, and Thursdays are the least popular.

As an example of a use of sociological statistics, put yourself in the position of a business that has to do with marriage—a florist, bridal boutique, tuxedo rental store, caterer, limousine service, or travel agent. Knowing the times of year that people prefer to get married and what the specific age group preferences are could vastly help these businesses increase their success. This information could help them to plan when and where to advertise, when to have the most personnel available to help potential customers, how to decorate the showrooms and arrange displays to appeal to the age groups most likely to shop at a particular time of year, and so forth.

Suppose that you are a travel agent and you know not only that June is the most popular time to get married, but also that young people prefer it most. You might decorate your showroom with travel posters with young rather than middle-aged people in them, have a large number of low-priced packages available, perhaps have a young travel agent on duty,

SOCIOLOGY AT WORK

Family Counseling

Marie Witkin Kargman,(1914-2009) considered herself a clinical sociologist and obtained both a law degree and a PhD in sociology. She was a family disputes mediator, a marriage counselor, a divorce counselor, and a family counselor. Kargman felt that her law degree and sociology degree offered a variable combination of skills for the type of work that she does.

Kargman told of a realization that she came to early in her career. "Before I trained in sociology at graduate school [Department of Social Relations, Harvard University], I was a practicing lawyer in the juvenile and family courts of Chicago. I discovered that the law is in a very real sense applied sociology: It deals with institutionalized patterns of behavior legitimized by the legal system, and with the sanctions applied when people deviate. I felt I needed to know more about the family, its structure, and its functions to be a better lawyer. Most lawyers rearrange the family, writing divorce and separation agreements that create new family structures, without knowing much about the sociology of the family. I was not comfortable rearranging family relationships when I knew so little theory in the field. However by the time I got my sociology degree I knew that I wanted to be a marriage counselor who worked with lawyers, helping them do a better job."

Using her knowledge gained from her experience as a family counselor, disputes mediator, and sociologist, Kargman wrote a book called *How to Manage a Marriage*. In it, she explained that the family system must be viewed as a combination of subsystems: a political, economic, and kinship system. If a marriage is in trouble, she explains, people have a tendency to blame one another. The advice she offers is, "Attack the problematic subsystem within the family; attack the problem, not the person."

Kargman explained how she applied her sociological knowledge. "In my family disputes mediation, and particularly in child custody disputes, I am apt to say to the divorced parents who have a child custody problem, 'What we are trying to do here is to get two parents and their children to come together to carry out the family functions without the foundation of living in a joint household. Each household is a family group with a political system, an economic system, and a kinship system. The child must now live in two households, juggle two different sets of systems, integrate them, or deal with them as unrelated parts of his or her life.' We then look at the similarities of expectation of the child's two separate households, and try to decide what is in the best interests of the child."

Kargman spoke of one particular case in which she was appointed by the court to represent a child in a custody case. The mother had asked the court for permission to take the child out of Massachusetts; she had remarried, and there were two additional children in the second marriage. This meant that there was an additional family involved besides the child's original one. Because the mother wanted to move across the country with her new family, the question of reasonable visitation for the child's father was in dispute. "Before I got into the dispute, the only persons discussed by the lawyers were the natural father, the natural mother, and the child. That the child was part of many different family relationships was never discussed. From a legal point of view, the family before the court was the original family of procreation. However this child was a member of three families: his original family, the step-family, and the family of his half-sisters. The child wanted to spend holidays with 'his family' and the natural father wanted the holidays on a strict two-parent division. All of the child's social systems were described in my report to the judge, whose decision was made based on the child's multifamily expectations."

and advertise during the preceding months in the magazines that young people are most likely to read.

Statistics about when people get married could also be very useful to you in planning your own marriage. If most marriages occur in June, for example, it will be more difficult to reserve the specific time and place you want for your ceremony; and the rates for caterers, limousines, travel, flowers, and tuxedo rentals are likely to be higher then. Knowing this, you may want to start making your plans as early as possible, or you might decide to change the date of your marriage to a less popular time.

Most marriages in the United States are between people of roughly the same age although people are free to marry someone considerably older or younger, within the legal limits determined by each state. Surprisingly the median ages at first marriage and the age difference between males and females have not varied that much since the turn of the century. In 1900, these figures were 25.9 for males and 21.9 for females, a difference of four years. The median age at first marriage in 2010 was 28.2 for men and 26.1 for women, a difference of 2.1 years (Table 12-2).

Recently, people have been postponing marriage until they are older, which reflects a decision on the part of young people to live independently as they pursue higher education or job opportunities. In the past

TABLE 12-2 MEDIAN AGE AT FIRST MARRIAGE, 1890-2010

The following table shows the median age of men and women when they were first married in the United States from 1890 to 2010. The median age for a man's first marriage was 28.2 years in 2010, up from 26.1 in 1990. The median age for a woman's first marriage was 26.1 years in 2010, up from 23.9 in 1990.

Year	Males	Females
1890	26.1	22.0
1900	25.9	21.9
1910	25.1	21.6
1920	24.6	21.2
1930	24.3	21.3
1940	24.3	21.5
1950	22.8	20.3
1960	22.8	20.3
1970	23.2	20.8
1980	24.7	22.0
1990	26.1	23.9
1993	26.5	24.5
1994	26.7	24.5
1995	26.9	24.5
1996	27.1	24.8
1997	26.8	25.0
1998	26.7	25.0
1999	26.9	25.1
2000	26.8	25.1
2001	26.9	25.1
2002	26.9	25.3
2003	27.1	25.3
2005	27.0	25.5
2006	27.5	25.9
2007	27.7[1]	26.0
2008	27.6	25.9
2009	28.1	25.9
2010	28.2	26.1

1. The margin of error for 2007 is +/- 0.2 years.

Source: U.S. Bureau of the Census; Web: www.census.gov.

two decades, there has been a rapid increase in the percentage of men and women who have never married. In 1970, one in every ten men (10.5 percent) and nearly one in every five women ages twenty-five to twenty-nine years had never married, but by 2008, this proportion had increased to 57.6 percent for men and 43.4 percent for women *(U.S. Bureau of the Census, Statistical Abstract of the United States, 2010)*. (See Table 12-3.)

Teenage marriages are an issue of special concern in the United States. Married teenagers have an increased high school dropout rate and a high unemployment rate. The divorce rate for teenagers is estimated to be from two to four times the rate for marriages that begin after age twenty. Many teenage marriages involve a pregnancy at the time of marriage, and data consistently show a higher divorce rate among marriages begun with a pregnancy (Teachman 1983). In reference to his research on economically disadvantaged couples, Fein (2004) states: "Whereas the vast bulk of first transitions to parenthood among upper middle class couples *follow* first marriages, first births among disadvantaged newlyweds are far more likely to *precede* marriage." Furthermore, among couples who married in 1990, one-third of those in the bottom education category had their first child before marriage, compared with one-tenth of those in the top education category. Among African Americans, the fraction is even higher: over half (51 percent) married after their first transition to parenthood (Fein 2004). Studies indicate that people who marry young, for a variety of reasons, are unprepared for the process of selecting a mate and assuming a marital role and are disproportionately represented in divorce statistics.

Family Size

In this country, as in the rest of the world, most married couples have or want to have children. Voluntarily childless marriages are uncommon although, as the next section describes, a pattern of childless marriages does exist. In the United States in 2000, 34.6 million married couples were without children. Measuring the number of births and the population growth in a country is usually in terms of the "crude birth rate," usually referred to simply as the birth rate. The birth rate is the number of births during a year per 1,000 population. In 2000, the birth rate in the United States was 14.2 per 1,000 population. In 2008 it was 14.18 per 1,000 population, but in 2009 dropped to 13.82 per 1,000 population. While this does not seem like a big change, an examination of birth rates between 2000 and 2009 indicate that drop between 2008 and 2009 was precipitous when looked at comparatively. (See Figure 12-2 and Table 12-4.) Rates, such as birth rates, do not have much meaning unless looked at comparatively. For social scientists, it is usually the variation in rates that is more helpful than the rates in and of themselves. When significant variations occur, such as the change in the birth rate between 2008 and 2009, this

TABLE 12-3 PERCENT NEVER MARRIED, 1970–2008

The following table shows the percent of men and women in the United States ages 20 to 44 who never married from 1970 to 2008.

Age	1970	1999	2000	2002	2004	2008
Male:						
20 to 24 years	35.8%	83.2%	83.7%	85.4%	86.7%	86.9%
25 to 29 years	10.5	52.1	51.7	53.7	56.6	57.6
30 to 34 years	6.2	30.7	30.0	34.0	33.4	32.4
35 to 39 years	5.4	21.1	20.3	21.1	23.4	23.0
40 to 44 years	4.9	15.8	15.7	16.7	18.5	16.9
Female:						
20 to 24 years	54.7%	72.3%	72.8%	74.0%	75.4%	76.4%
25 to 29 years	19.1	38.9	38.9	40.4	40.8	43.4
30 to 34 years	9.4	22.1	21.9	23.0	23.7	24.0
35 to 39 years	7.2	15.2	14.3	14.7	14.6	15.2
40 to 44 years	6.3	10.9	11.8	11.5	12.2	12.9

Source: U.S. Bureau of the Census. From Statistical Abstract of the United States 2010.

indicates to social scientists that there are factors that led to the change that should be explored. Like marriage rates, birth rates fluctuate with wars, socioeconomic conditions, and other variables.

The "baby boom" period of the late 1940s and the 1950s produced an unanticipated but significant rise in the United States birth rate. It may have been caused by increases in the normative pressures on women to have children, the end of the disruption brought about by war, postwar economic prosperity, or the long-term psychological effects of growing up during the Great Depression. Bean (1983) states that while social and cultural conditions during the era supported having families, increased costs tended to discourage couples from having large families. Thus, only a minor part of the baby boom can be attributed to families deciding to have three or more children.

In 2000, 19.5 million married couples had four or more children under age eighteen (*Current Population Reports* 2001). Improved methods of birth control, liberalized abortion laws, and a widespread acceptance of family planning measures have decreased the number of unplanned and unwanted births and have enabled couples to have the number of children they want. It remains to be seen just what impact, if any, the political and legal moves toward restricting abortion that are currently taking place will have on the number of births. Analysis of newly released Census Bureau figures emphasize that over the last decades of the twentieth century, the size of U.S. families has declined very rapidly. Since 1970 the percentage of households containing five or more people has fallen by half. On the other hand, the number of single and two-person households has soared. One group of single households that has increased particularly fast is single women between the ages of thirty and thirty-five (Grier and Miller 2004). The increase in single households has been accompanied by an increase in the number of single households with children. In 1980 in the U.S., 19.5 percent of single parent households had children as compared to 29.5 percent in 2008. This type of increase is seen in many countries throughout the world. (See Tables 12-5 and 12-6.)

Does family size make a difference in interactions among siblings or between children and their parents? Because families are groups and the numbers of people

FIGURE 12-2 UNITED STATES - BIRTH RATE (BIRTHS/1.000 POPULATION)

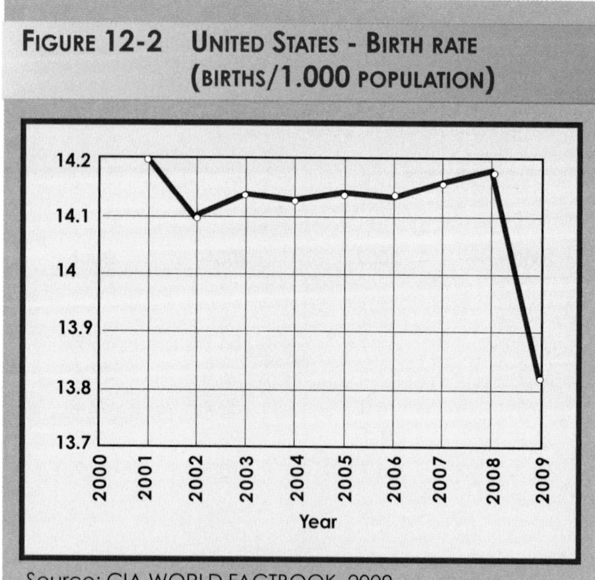

Source: CIA WORLD FACTBOOK, 2009

in a group influences the behavior of its members, the answer is "yes." Specifically, how does family size make a difference? Perhaps the greatest difference in family interaction patterns comes with the birth of the first child because the transition to parenthood involves a major shift in parental role expectations and

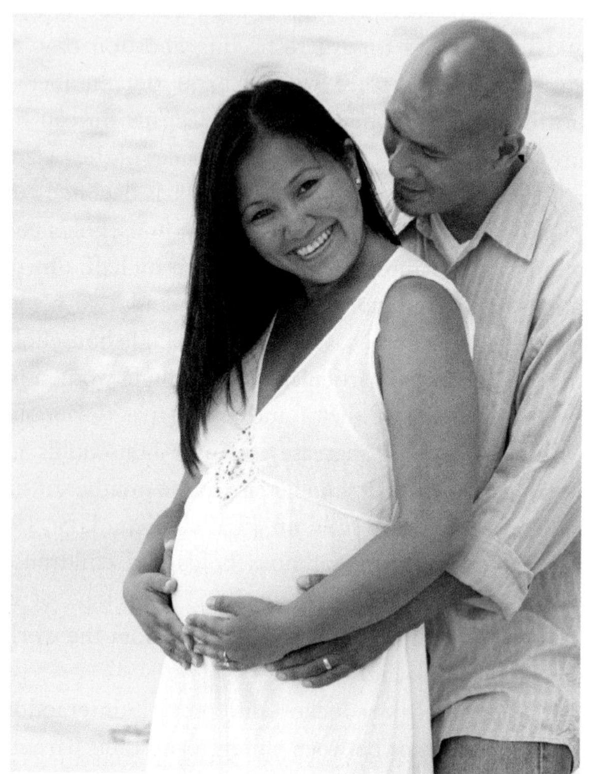

Most married couples have or want to have children.

TABLE 12-4 UNITED STATES - BIRTH RATE (BIRTHS/1.000 POPULATION)

Year	Birth rate (births/1,000 Population
2000	14.2
2001	14.2
2002	14.1
2003	14.14
2004	14.13
2005	14.14
2006	14.14
2007	14.16
2008	14.18
2009	13.82

Source: CIA WORLD FACTBOOK, 2009

behaviors. A number of writers have called the early stages of parenthood a "crisis," a traumatic change that forces couples to drastically reorganize their lives (Hobbs 1965; LeMasters 1957). Later studies concluded, however, that for most couples, beginning parenthood is a period of transition but not a period of change so dramatic that it should be termed a crisis.

With the birth of the first child, the expectation exists that a second and third child should follow. One-child families have generally been viewed as unhealthy for parents and child alike. The "only" child has been described as spoiled, selfish, overly dependent, maladjusted, and lonely. Parents of a single child have been described as selfish, self-centered, immature, cold, and abnormal. Research findings, however, do not support these descriptions.

Findings generally tend to support those of Blake (1981a, 1981b, and 1989), who claims that single children are intellectually superior, have no obvious personality defects, tend to consider themselves happy, and are satisfied with the important aspects of life, notably jobs and health. In fact, Blake's research supports the *dilution hypothesis*, which predicts that, on average, the more children a family has, the less each child will achieve in such areas as educational and occupational attainment. That is, there is a dilution

TABLE 12-5 SINGLE PARENT HOUSEHOLDS 1980-2009

Country and Year	Number (1,000)	Percent of all households with children	Country and Year	Number (1,000)	Percent of all households with children
United States:			Germany		
1980	6,061	19.5	1991	1,429	15.2
1990	7,752	24.0	1995[1]	2,496	18.8
2000	9,357	27.0	2000[1]	2,274	17.6
2008	10,536	29.5	2008	2,616	21.7
Canada:			Ireland:[2]		
1981	437	12.7	1981	30	7.2
1991	572	16.2	1991	44	10.7
2001[1]	1,184	23.5	2002	50	17.4
2006	1,276	24.6	2006	78	22.6
Japan:			Netherlands:		
1980	796	4.9	1988	179	9.6
1990	934	6.5	2000	240	13.0
2000	996	8.3	2009	310	16.0
2005	1,163	10.2	Sweeden:		
Denmark:[2]			1985	117	11.2
1980	99	13.4	1995[1]	189	17.4
1990	117	17.8	2000	240	21.4
2001	120	18.4	2008	200	18.7
2009[1]	165	21.7	United Kingdom:[3]		
France:			1981	1,010	13.9
1982	887	10.2	1991	1,344	19.4
1990	1,175	13.2	2000	1,434	20.7
1999	1,494	17.4	2008	1,750	25.0
2005[1]	1,725	19.8			

11 Break in series. 2 Data are family-based, rather than household-based, statistics. 3 Great Britain only (excludes Northern Ireland).

Source: U.S. Bureau of Labor Statistics, updated and revised from "families and Work in Transition in 12 Cuntries, 1980-2001," *Monthly Labor Review*, September 2003, with national sources, some of which may be unpublished.

of familial resources available for children in large families and a concentration of such resources in small ones. These diluted resources include the parents' time, emotional and physical energy (including that of a mother who is frequently pregnant), attention, personal interaction, and material resources that allow for personal living space and privacy within the home, better neighborhoods surrounding the home, specialized medical and dental care, travel, and specialized instruction, such as music lessons.

These findings are extremely important for you to consider in planning your own families. Would you be more receptive to having just one child, knowing that "only" children do as well as or better than children with siblings? Would you be less willing to have a large number of children, knowing about the dilution hypothesis? Clearly, many factors enter into the decision as to how many children you may personally want or actually have: age at marriage, religious orientation, effective use of contraception, career pattern, and so forth. Nonetheless, what is known about the consequences of having few or many children has important implications for personal decision-making and social policy as well.

Although people may agree that a one-child family is small, there is less agreement about the number of children required to make a family be considered "large." Perceptions of a family as small or large are relative. A family with four children in the United States at the turn of the century would not have been perceived as large. However, today, it generally would be. The more central issue in reference

TABLE 12-6 BIRTHS TO UNMARRIED WOMEN BY COUNTRY 1980 TO 2008

Percent of all live births

Country	1980	1990	2000	2005	2006	2007	2008
United States	18.4	28.0	33.2	36.9	38.5	39.7	40.6
Canada	12.8	24.4	28.3	25.6	27.1	2.3	(NA)
Japan	0.8	1.1	1.6	2.0	2.1	(NA)	(NA)
Denmark	33.2	46.4	44.6	45.7	46.4	46.1	46.2
France	11.4	30.1	43.6	48.4	50.5	51.7	52.6
Germany[1]	(X)	15.1	23.4	29.2	30.0	30.8	32.1
Ireland	5.9	14.6	31.5	31.8	32.7	(NA)	(NA)
Italy	4.3	6.5	9.7	15.2	16.2	17.7	(NA)
Netherlands	4.1	11.4	24.9	34.9	37.1	39.5	41.2
Spain	3.9	9.6	17.7	26.6	28.4	30.2	31.7
Sweden	39.7	47.0	55.3	55.4	55.5	54.8	54.7
United Kingdom	11.5	27.9	39.5	42.9	43.7	(NA)	(NA)

NA Not available. X Not applicable. 1 Data are for 1991 instad of 1990.

Source: U.S. Bureau of Labor Statistics, updated and revised from "Families and Work Transition in 12 Countries 1980-2001", *Monthly Labor Review*, September 2003, with national sources, some of which may be unpublished.

to family size, however, concerns the consequences of having more children in a given family.

It is known that family size increases with factors such as younger ages at marriage, lower educational and socioeconomic levels, and rural residence. Certain religious groups, such as the Amish and the Mormons, place a major value on having children and tend to have large families. It is known that as families increase in size, the chances increase that some children will be unplanned and unwanted. One review of the effects of family size (Wagner, et al., 1985) showed that in larger families, child rearing becomes more rule-ridden and less individualized. There is more corporal punishment and fewer resources to invest per child. Smaller families tend to result in higher IQ, academic achievement, and occupational performance. Large families produce more delinquents and alcoholics. In regard to health, in large families, *perinatal* (surrounding birth), *morbidity* (injury and illness), and *mortality* (death) rates are higher, and mothers are at higher risk from several physical diseases.

Although a number of studies revealed no effect, positive or negative, to be associated with family size, very few exist that associate positive consequences with large families. It is not family size per se, however, that creates health problems or family difficulties. Large families heighten the complexity of intragroup relations, pose problems in fulfilling family needs, and influence how much money and attention can be devoted to each child.

Divorce

Whenever two people interact, conflicts may arise, and one person or both may want to end the relationship. This is true not only of marriage but of other relationships as well. Unlike most relationships, however, marriage involves civil, legal, or religious ties that specify if and how the relationship can end. In countries with strong Roman Catholic traditions such as Ireland, Brazil, and Peru, a divorce is not only extremely difficult to obtain, it is also highly discouraged by society in general. In Switzerland, the Scandinavian countries, Poland, Russia, and several other countries, a divorce is granted if it is shown that the marriage has failed. The laws of Islam and Judaism give a husband the power to terminate his marriage by simply renouncing his wife or wives. In this country, most states, traditionally at least, grant a divorce if it is shown that one party has gravely violated his or her marital obligations. Since 1970, however, many states have moved to a no-fault divorce system, in which marriages can be ended on the basis of what are commonly called "irreconcilable differences." Why are our divorce rates so high in this county? Experts agree that there are six main reasons why this is so today:

1. Individualism: Families are spending less and less time together and are more concerned with personal happiness.
2. Romantic love subsides. The excitement goes away.
3. Women are less dependent on men. They now have careers of their own.
4. Stressful relationships contribute, especially since both work outside of the home.
5. Divorce is now more socially acceptable.
6. Divorce is now easier to legally obtain. (Macionis 2005).

The United States has one of the highest divorce rates in the world. According to the Summary of Vital Statistics, the U.S. rate of divorce per 1,000 persons per year in 2008 was 5.2, compared with 3.5 in Germany, 3.5 in Sweden, 3.1 in Japan, 3.0 in France (2000), and 1.3 in Italy.

Why, then, do we so often hear that one marriage in two ends in divorce? The divorce rate is figured by dividing the number of divorces in a given year by the number of marriages in the same year. For example, in 2008 in the U.S., there were 2,208,000 marriages and 1,212,767 divorces or annulments. Dividing the number of divorces by the number of marriages for that year gives a divorce rate of 55 percent or more than one in two. This is the rate used to illustrate the "breakdown in the American family." It does not, however, provide proof that half of all marriages end in divorce any more than saying that a community that had one hundred marriages and one hundred divorces in a given year would prove that all marriages end in divorce. Few of the divorces that take place in a given year are of the marriages that took place that same year. Rather, they were probably from marriages that occurred two, five, or fifteen years earlier. According to *Current Population Reports*, 2002, approximately 10 percent of marriages end in divorce after five years of marriage while another 10 percent (or 20 percent cumulatively) are divorced by the tenth year. There is, nevertheless, a great deal of concern about the frequency of divorce in the United States. As stated earlier, the divorce rate in the U.S in 2008 was 5.2 per 1,000 population; and even though it is one of the highest rates in the world, it has decreased from 7.9 per 1,000 population in 1980. Divorce rates take on a very different perspective when based on the number per 1,000 population. This tells you that it is critically important to understand how various rates are computed, not only when looking at divorce, but also when looking at all statistics presented in the media.

Like marriage rates, divorce rates tend to decline in times of economic depression and rise during periods of prosperity. They also vary by geographic and social characteristics. Geographically, the general trend in the United States is for divorce rates to increase as one moves from east to west. Demographic figures show that more than one-half of all divorces are among persons in their late 20s and early 30s. While the numbers are fewer, the divorce rate is exceptionally high among teenagers. Divorce is also most frequent in the first three years after marriage, and the incidence is higher among the lower socioeconomic levels. Whether education, occupation, or income is used as an index of socioeconomic level, the divorce rate goes up as the socioeconomic level goes down.

The National Center for Policy Analysis reported in 1999 that states in the Bible Belt lead the United States in divorces. In the southern states included, the divorce rates are roughly 50 percent above the national average (Crary 1999). Rates in the south still tend to be higher than the national average Do southern people just have a harder time getting along? A true sociological explanation will look for trends and patterns. Experts cite low household incomes, the tendency to marry at a younger age, and religious belief systems that allow divorce as major factors in producing such a high divorce rate. After 1999, the Center for Disease Control and the National Center for Health Statistics ceased to publish aggregated divorce counts for all fifty states due to four major states failing to report their statistics. The findings will continue in the U.S. Census Reports.

These variations in rate of divorce give us clues about its causes. The fact that rates are higher in the western United States indicates that divorce may be related to the liberality of the laws and the degree of cultural mixing. Financial problems and emotional immaturity may be factors in the high rates found among teenagers. Difficulties in adjusting to new relationships or discrepancies in role expectations may contribute to the divorce rates in the first three years after marriage. Money problems, lack of education, and working at a low-status job may account for the rates found in the lower socioeconomic levels. Although other factors are involved, and there are some exceptions to these general patterns, divorce is not merely a result of personal characteristics. These variations illustrate how social and cultural factors can influence the chances that a marriage will end in divorce. Since the mid-1990s, a few states have enacted laws providing for "covenant marriages". Couples who marry under the category of a covenant marriage are voluntarily choosing to make divorce more difficult to obtain in the future. Once a couple has chosen the covenant marriage option, they give up the right to divorce under the no-fault system in the state where they were married. In covenant marriages, cause for divorce is usually limited to domestic violence, a felony conviction with jail time, or adultery. The movement to create covenant marriages was heavily driven by evangelical Christians who were alarmed by the rising U.S. divorce rate. As of 2009, three states offer the covenant marriage option: Louisiana, Arkansas, and Arizona.

Thinking Sociologically

1. The research suggests many advantages of small families over large ones. Can you think of ways that large families may be advantageous over small ones?
2. How would you explain the tremendous variation in divorce rates in the following: (a) from one country or society to another; (b) between religious and ethnic groups in a given country such as the United States or Canada; and (c) over time?

NONTRADITIONAL MARITAL AND FAMILY LIFESTYLES

In the United States today, many people are choosing alternatives to the *traditional family*, which consisted of a husband, a wife, and two or more children. The husband was the authority and primary, if not sole, wage earner, whereas the wife was submissive to the husband and served as primary child caregiver and homemaker. Now, however, the diversity of families in this country is greater than ever before, and changes are occurring rapidly. Four nontraditional approaches to family life are discussed in more detail next: (1) nonmarital cohabitation, (2) childless marriage, (3) one-parent families, and (4) dual-career marriages.

Nonmarital Cohabitation

Nonmarital cohabitation, or living together, occurs when two adults who are not related or married to each other occupy the same dwelling as a couple in an intimate relationship or partnership. As mentioned earlier in this chapter, in relation to, "What is a family?" reference was made to defining families in nontraditional ways. Examples used to illustrate families defined in terms of intimate relationships, sexual bonds, and family realms included examples of both heterosexual and homosexual (lesbian and gay) cohabitation.

Both heterosexual and same-sex unions are attracting increasing attention among social researchers, as well as policymakers. A number of churches are recognizing the legitimacy of gay/lesbian unions. A number of businesses are extending spousal benefits to both heterosexual and homosexual cohabitants. A number of communities are accepting the civil registration of such relationships. State and national legislators are being forced to reexamine who is to be included or excluded from social policies covering a range of issues (family/parent benefits, adoption, surrogate parenting, housing, and others).

Most census data on unmarried couples have tended to focus on the heterosexual union. More than 7.5 million unmarried couples lived together in 2010 (U.S. Census Bureau, *Population Survey*), more than ten times the number in 1970. Contrary to a widely held assumption, nonmarital heterosexual cohabitation is not just a college-student phenomenon, nor is it confined to the generation under age twenty-five. Despite these findings, most research on cohabitation has involved college student populations. In a review of this research, (Waite et al., 2000) found that non-married cohabitants are significantly less committed to each other than married couples. With regard to the division of labor, cohabiting couples tended to mirror the society around them and accept gender roles characteristic of other couples their age. The same was true for sexual exclusivity. Most believed in sexual freedom within their nonmarried relationship, but most voluntarily limited their sexual activity with outsiders.

Nonmarital heterosexual cohabitation does not appear to be a substitute for marriage, a cure-all for marital problems, or a solution to the problem of frequent divorce. Most cohabitating relationships are short-term and last only a few months, but the longer that couples cohabit, the more likely they are to eventually marry. However, according to the National Marriage Project completed by Rutgers University in 2005 titled, "The State of Our Unions", while the divorce rates in the U.S. may be declining, more men and women are cohabitating, many with children, rather than marrying. In cohabiting heterosexual couples, as in married couples, women do most of the housework.

Unmarried couples, whether of the same or the opposite sex, experience problems quite similar to those of married couples: concern over financial matters, the division of labor, and relationships with extended family members. Although unmarried cohabitation does not fall within acceptable value limits for everyone, it does appear to have functional value for an increasing number of adults of all ages. For many couples, it provides a financially practical situation (two together can live more cheaply than two separately); a warm, homelike atmosphere; ready access to a sexual partner; an intimate interpersonal relationship; and for some, a highly exclusive, long-term partnership.

Childless Marriage

Most unmarried couples are childless. Among these couples, a desire for children, a pregnancy, or the birth of a child often leads to marriage. On the other hand, what of the legally married couples who have no children and who desire none? In recent years, the subject of the voluntarily childless marriage as an acceptable marital lifestyle has gained increased attention for a number of reasons. First, it is inconsistent with myths about the existence of a maternal instinct, the notion that all women want to have, love, and care for a child or children. Second, it changes the functions of marriage and the family that deal with reproduction, nurturant socialization, and social placement. Third, the availability and reliability of contraceptives and of abortion make it possible for women and couples to have no children if they so choose.

Veevers (1975) conducted in-depth interviews with childless wives living with their husbands and found that they held a number of uncommon beliefs about parenting. Most of these women were married to husbands who agreed that children were not desirable. The wives defined parenthood in negative rather than positive terms and denied the existence of a maternal instinct. They dismissed the accusation that childlessness was abnormal. Pregnancy and childbirth were perceived to be at best unpleasant and at worst difficult and dangerous. They regarded childcare as excessively burdensome and unrewarding and as having a deleterious effect on a woman's life chances. Finally, they defined parenthood as a trap that interfered with personal happiness.

The child-free alternative may be an acceptable family form and lifestyle for a small proportion of families. Under some conditions, as in the dual-career marriages discussed later, childlessness may be conducive to both personal and marital satisfaction and adjustment.

One-Parent Families

One-parent families are those in which the mother or, more commonly, the father does not share the household with the children and the remaining parent. As shown in Table 12-7, 85.5 percent of Asian American, 77.5 percent of white non-Hispanic, 67 percent of Hispanic origin, and 39.2 percent of black children under age eighteen years were living with both parents in 2010. In the traditional view, this is the way families "should be," the most appropriate family structure for the socialization of children. However, 12.4 percent of Asian American, 19.3 per-

TABLE 12-7 LIVING ARRANGEMENTS OF CHILDREN1 BY RACE AND ETHNICITY: 2010 (IN THOUSANDS)

Living Arrangements	All races		White		Black		Asian		Hispanic2	
	#	%	#	%	#	%	#	%	#	%
Children	74,718	100	41,089	100	11,272	100	3,300	100	6,941	100
Living with:										
Two parents[3]	51,823	69.4	31,859	77.5	4,424	39.2	2,658	85.5	11,345	67.0
Married parents	49,106	65.7	30,835	67.5	3,911	34.7	2,777	84.1	10,046	60.9
Unmarried parents	2,717	3.6	1,024	2.5	513	4.6	45	1.4	1,020	6.0
One Parent	19,857	26.6	7,938	19.3	6,007	54.4	408	12.4	4,919	29.0
Mother only	17,285	23.1	6,382	15.5	5,791	53.3	334	10.1	4.456	26.3
Father only	2,572	3.4	1,555	3.8	405	3.6	74	2.2	463	2.6
No parent	3,038	4.1	1,292	3.1	841	7.5	70	2.1	677	4.0
Grandparents only	1,655	2.2	692	1.7	523	4.6	23	.7	330	1.9
Other relatives only	650	.9	196	0.5	206	1.8	22	.7	192	1.1
Nonrelatives only	595	0.8	334	0.8	92	.8	14	0.4	126	0.7
Other arrangement	138	0.2	711	0.2	20	0.2	11	.3	29	0.2
At least 1 biological parent	70,236	94.0	39,033	95.0	10,213	90.6	3,113	94.3	16,008	94.5
At least 1 stepparent	6,156	6.2	2,818	6.9	627	5.6	81	2.5	933	5.5
At least 1 adoptive parent	1,258	1.7	701	1.7	177	1.6	109	3.3	193	1.8

Source: U.S. Bueau, America's Families and Living Arrangements, 2010 Tables FG10. Family Groups; Table C9. Children 1/by Presence and Type of Parent(s), Race and Hispanic Origin/2

cent of white non-Hispanic children, 29 percent of Hispanic-origin children, and 53.3 percent of black children were living with the mother only. Living with the father only were 3.4 percent of all children, 23.3 percent with their mother only and 4.1 percent of all children living with neither parent.

There are approximately seventy-five million families in the U.S. Approximately fifty-six million are married-couple families and nearly fourteen million are female-headed households with no father present. Nearly 10 percent of all families are below the poverty level, 4.8 percent of married-couple families are below the poverty level, and nearly 29 percent of families without a father present are below the poverty level (U.S. Census Bureau, 2005-2009 American Community Survey, S1702). All of these families below the poverty level are likely to receive Medicare, school lunches, and food stamps, and live in subsidized housing. These are the families affected most harshly by middle-class efforts to cut welfare, by religious group efforts to forbid abortion, and by government policies that demand what is called "workfare" (i.e., programs requiring welfare recipients to work full- or part-time in order to receive their below-poverty-level income). Members of such families often have disproportionate school dropout rates, few job-related skills, high unemployment rates, irregular incomes, little dental or other health care, and little control over their own fates.

In a cross-cultural study, Bilge and Kaufman (1983) contend that one-parent families are neither pathological nor inferior. Stigmatizing them in this way, they claim, is a refusal to recognize the economic inequalities of our society. They say that in combination with an extended network of concerned kin (grandparents, siblings, uncles, aunts, etc.) single parent families can offer emotional support and that they are a suitable alternative to the traditional family. Bilge and Kaufman also note that around the world, one-parent female-headed families are able to bring up children and provide emotional support.

What happens to children in American female-headed families? Cashion (1982) reviewed the social-psychological research pertaining to female-headed families published between 1970 and 1980. She concluded that children in these families are likely to have good emotional adjustment, good self-esteem (except when they are stigmatized), comparable intellectual development to others of the same socioeconomic status, and rates of juvenile delinquency comparable to other children of the same socioeconomic standing. The major problems in these families stem from *poverty* and from *stigmatization.* Poverty is associated with problems in school and juvenile delinquency. It also contributes to poor attitudes among mothers about their situations and impairs a mother's sense of being in control. Stigmatization is associated with low self-esteem in children. It results in defining children as problems even when they do not have problems. Cashion's general conclusion is that the majority of female-headed families, when not plagued by poverty, have children who are as successful and well adjusted as those of two-parent families.

As of 2010, 11.9 percent of American households are categorized as female-headed households with children, but there is significant variation in the share of female-headed households by race and ethnicity. About 7.8 percent of white non-Hispanic and 5.9 percent of Asian households were headed by mothers without a father present. In contrast, single mothers with children accounted for 29.3 percent of all Black households and 18.4 percent of Hispanic households. (U.S. Census Bureau, *Current Population Survey*, 2010, Annual Social and Economic Supplement, Table FG10. Over the past twenty-five years, the percentage of female-headed households with children has increased particularly rapidly among Blacks, but this trend appears to have slowed (Ameristat 2003).

Dual-Career Marriages

One of the important social changes since World War II has been the increase of women, generally, and of married women, more specifically, in the labor force. In 1940, despite a sharp increase in the number of working wives during the depression of the 1930s, only 15 percent of all married women living with their husbands held an outside job. By 1960, the proportion had risen to 32 percent, 58.4 percent by 1990, and 61.4 percent by 2009 (U.S Census Bureau, Table 596, 2010).

Women who have children are less likely to hold jobs than those who do not, although with each decade, the presence of children decreases in importance as a factor in whether women are employed. The proportion of married women in the labor force is highest among those who have no children under age six years to take care of at home. However, even among the women who have one or more children under the age of six, more than half are employed. Most of these employed women are in clerical or service work, with earnings well below those of their male counterparts. Arrangements of this type are called "dual-employed marriages." (It is assumed, sometimes incorrectly, that the husband is also employed.)

Although women have been taking jobs in increasing numbers, the "dual-career" marriage is a relatively recent development. The word career is used to designate jobs that are not taken just to produce additional income, but also for the satisfaction involved. Careers typically involve a higher level of commitment than just "paid employment," and they progress through a developmental sequence of increasing responsibility. One study (Burke and Weir 1976) of one- and two-career families found that women in two-career families reported fewer pressures and worries, more communication with husbands, more happiness with their marriages, and better physical and mental health than women who did not work outside the home. In contrast, the men in the two-career families, as opposed to one-career families, were in poorer health and less content with marriage, work, and life in general. It seems that the husband of a career wife loses part of his support system when his wife no longer functions as a servant, homemaker, and mother. Wives who have careers, on the other hand, are able to expand into roles that have a more positive value for them.

Despite these rewards for women, most studies of dual-career marriages suggest that they involve certain strains. One of these strains, particularly for women, develops due to what Fox and Nichols (1983) refer to as "time crunch." Wives are often expected to perform the majority of household tasks whether they have careers outside the home or not. In addition, wives usually accommodate more to the husband's career than vice versa, and husbands and wives have differential gains and losses when both have a career. Although the professional employment of women is gaining increasing acceptance, sexual equality in marriage has not yet been achieved. Wives are generally expected to give up their own jobs for the sake of their husbands and to consider their families their first duty.

Thinking Sociologically

1. Does an increase in nontraditional marital and family lifestyles signify a breakdown of the family?
2. In regard to one-parent families, discuss the following:

(a) the adoption of children by single persons,

(b) the feminization of poverty, and

(c) the need for children to have two parents.

CHAPTER REVIEW
Wrapping it up

Summary

1. The family serves a number of different purposes. It is the primary social group, a system of interdependent statuses and structures, and a social institution organized to meet certain essential societal goals.

2. The smallest family units—nuclear and conjugal families—consist of persons related by blood, marriage, or adoption who share a common residence. Sociologists also distinguish families of orientation, families of procreation, extended families, and modified-extended families.

3. Families throughout the world vary in many different ways, such as in number of spouses. A person may have one spouse (*monogamy*) or two or more (*polygamy*). In group *marriages*, there are several people of each sex. *Sequential monogamy* involves having several wives or husbands in succession but just one at any given time. *Polygyny*, in which one man is married to more than one woman, is the most common form of polygamy; *polyandry*, in which one woman has several husbands, is very rare.

4. Families vary in their norms of residence. Most cultures adhere to one of three patterns: *neolocal*, in which the couple is free to choose its own place of residence; *patrilocal*, in which the couple lives in the groom's community; and *matrilocal*, in which the couple lives in the bride's community. Worldwide, the patrilocal pattern is the most common.

5. Families have different norms of descent and inheritance. The *patrilineal* pattern, in which lineage is traced through the father's kin, is the most common, but there are also matrilineal and bilateral patterns.

6. Families vary in their norms of authority and decision-making. Sociologists recognize systems of three types: patriarchal, matriarchal, and egalitarian. The *patriarchal* pattern of male dominance, power, and authority is the most widespread.

7. Norms vary with regard to the marriage partner considered appropriate. *Endogamous rules* state that a marriage partner should be from a similar group. *Exogamous rules* state that marriage partners should be from a different group. Incest and same-sex marriages are almost universally forbidden; whereas marriage to a person of the same race, religion, and socioeconomic status is widely encouraged.

8. Several theoretical perspectives are widely used to explain family structures, interaction patterns, and behaviors. *Functionalists* examine variations in family structures, such as those just described, in terms of the functions they perform. According to this perspective, the family has many major functions: socialization, affection and emotional support, sexual regulation, reproduction, and social placement.

9. According to the *conflict perspective*, family members continually struggle for power and control. Conflict, which stems from the unequal distribution of scarce resources, is a major force behind social change.

10. The *exchange perspective* assumes that there are rewards and costs in all relationships, including those in marriage and the family. This view suggests that when selecting a spouse, people try to get the best they can with what they have to offer. The *complementary needs theory* proposes that people seek mates who will meet their needs without causing conflicts.

11. The *interactionist perspective* emphasizes the influence of role expectations and how people define situations. In this view, marriage, like other relationships, is a dynamic process of reciprocal interactions.

12. The d*evelopmental perspective* focuses on the time dimension. Change is analyzed in terms of the family life cycle, a series of stages that families go through from their inception at marriage through their dissolution by death or divorce.

13. The American family system emphasizes norms of monogamy, neolocal residence, modified-extended kinship, bilateral descent and inheritance, egalitarian decision-making, endogamous marriage, and relatively free choice of mate. In a number of respects, however, the American family is quite variable.

14. Rates of marriage vary widely in terms of time period, geographical location, economic conditions, and other factors. The number of marriages also varies by season and by day of the week. The age at marriage in the United States, which declined from the turn of the century until the mid-1950s, has since increased; and marriages among teenagers are unlikely to last.

15. Norms concerning family size and parent-child relations are influenced by such variables as socioeconomic status, religion, education, urbanization, and female participation in the labor force. Although most married couples have or want to have children, younger women today generally plan to have small families, compared with earlier generations.

16. The United States has one of the highest divorce rates in the world. Like birth rates, rates of divorce vary with time period, geographical location, and socioeconomic level, and differing techniques of computing the divorce rate yield different figures about the rate of divorce. Variations in these rates illustrate how social and cultural factors influence the chances of marital dissolution.

17. Many marital and family lifestyles exist today that do not conform to the traditional model of two parents, two or more children, with the husband and wife performing fixed roles. The number of unmarried couples of all ages who live together, for example, is increasing dramatically.

18. Childless marriages are increasingly common, in part because of the availability and reliability of contraceptives and abortion.

19. The number of one-parent families is increasing sharply, and many of these families are below the poverty level.

20. Marriages in which both spouses work have been common for a long time, but the dual-career marriage is a relatively recent development. There are many strains in these marriages, but women who have careers report fewer life pressures and worries and more happiness in their marriages. The men involved in two-career marriages tend to be relatively discontent, however.

Key Terms

bilateral lineage A descent system in which influence, wealth, and power are assigned to both sides of the family

blended families Families composed of at least one formerly married spouse, the children of the previous marriage or marriages, and new offspring

complementary needs A theory of mate selection based on the idea that people marry those who provide the maximum need gratification when needs tend to be complementary rather than similar

conjugal families Families consisting of a husband and wife, with or without children

egalitarian The norm of authority in the family in which decisions are equally divided between husband and wife

endogamy A marriage norm requiring a person to marry someone from his or her own group

exogamy A marriage norm requiring a person to marry someone from outside his or her own group

extended family A family that goes beyond the nuclear family to include other nuclear families and relatives such as grandparents, aunts, uncles, and cousins

family A group of kin united by blood, marriage, or adoption who share a common residence for some part of their lives and assume reciprocal rights and obligations with regard to one another

family of orientation The nuclear family into which one was born and in which one was reared

family of procreation The nuclear family formed by marriage

fraternal polyandry A form of polyandry where brothers are co-husbands

group marriage A form of marriage in which several or many men are married to several or many women

incest Socially forbidden sexual relationships or marriage with certain close relatives

kinship The web of relationships among people linked by common ancestry, adoption, or marriage

matriarchal A family structure in which the wife dominates the husband

matrilineal A family structure in which descent and inheritance are traced through the mother's line

matrilocal A family norm that newly married couples should live with the wife's family

modified-extended family structure The family structure in which individual nuclear families retain considerable autonomy yet maintain connections with other nuclear families in the extended family structure

monogamy The marriage of one man to one woman

neolocal A family norm that newly married couples should establish residences separate from those of both sets of parents

nonmarital cohabitation An arrangement in which two unmarried and unrelated adults share a common household or dwelling

nuclear families Families in which two or more persons are related by blood, marriage, or adoption and who share a common residence

patriarchal A family structure in which the husband dominates the wife

patrilineal A family system in which descent and inheritance are traced through the father's line

patrilocal A family norm that newly married couples should live with the husband's family

polyandry The marriage of one woman to more than one husband at the same time

polygamy The marriage of one man or woman to more than one person of the opposite sex at the same time

polygyny The marriage of one man to more than one wife at the same time

principle of legitimacy Malinowski's idea that every society has a rule that every child should have a legitimate father to act as the child's protector, guardian, and representative in society

serial or sequential monogamy Marriage to a number of different spouses in succession, but only one at any given time

Discussion Questions

1. Discuss the importance of definitions of the family with regard to child custody policies.

2. What types of norms for choice of marriage partner—endogamy or exogamy—exist for you? These norms are encouraged and enforced in what ways?
3. Why does the United States insist on monogamy when many countries of the world permit polygamy? Why is polygyny very common and polyandry very rare?
4. How have norms of residence, descent and inheritance, authority, and choice of marriage partner changed in the United States over the past century? What do you think has led to these changes?
5. What types of questions would you ask about parent-child relations, using functionalist, conflict, interactionist, exchange, and developmental perspectives?
6. How do you explain the rapid increase in the median age at first marriage over the past two decades in the United States?
7. What types of social conditions are likely to affect the size of families in the United States and around the world? How does size affect family interaction patterns, educational systems, or the economy?
8. Should divorce be made more difficult to obtain? Why or why not? Discuss the consequences of divorce for men, women, children, and the society at large.
9. Discuss the pros and cons of nonmarital cohabitation. How are these types of relationships similar to or different from marriages?
10. What kinds of problems are encountered in dual-career marriages that do not occur in marriages where only one spouse is employed?

Pop Quiz

1. Sociologists consider the family to be a ________.

   a. social group
   b. social system
   c. social institution
   d. all of the above

2. The family that consists of two or more people related by blood, marriage, or adoption who share a common residence is the ________.

   a. conjugal family
   b. extended family
   c. nuclear family
   d. family of procreation

3. In the United States, the typical family is the ________.

   a. extended family
   b. modified-extended family
   c. one-parent family
   d. nuclear family

4. The most common form of polygamy is ________.

   a. polygyny
   b. polyandry
   c. group marriage
   d. exogamy

5. The pattern of ending a marriage with one spouse and marrying another is called ________.

   a. polygamy
   b. polyandry
   c. polygyny
   d. serial monogamy

6. Buddy and Paulette, who were recently married, live with Paulette's side of the family. This residential pattern is ______.

   a. patrilocal
   b. exogamous
   c. matrilocal
   d. neolocal

7. Keary and Amy, who are married, trace their ancestry through both sides of their families. This illustrates ________ descent.

   a. bilateral
   b. matrilineal
   c. patrilineal
   d. endogamous

8. Which norm requires that people marry outside their group?

   a. patriarchy
   b. matriarchy
   c. endogamy
   d. exogamy

9. The idea that every society has a rule that every child should have a father is called the principle of ________.

   a. cohesiveness
   b. legitimacy
   c. paternity
   d. social placement

10. Marriage rates are influenced by ________.

    a. economic climate
    b. war and peace
    c. seasonal variations
    d. all of the above

11. The typical family in the United States is both a nuclear and an extended form. T/F

12. Polygyny occurs when a woman has more than one husband. T/F

13. The Hebrew laws stated that if a man had sexual intercourse with an unbetrothed virgin, he was required to marry her and to pay the father the bride price. T/F

14. Brides ages 30–34 prefer the month of December for weddings. T/F

15. Women who have children are more likely to hold jobs than those who do not. T/F

1. D	6. C	11. T
2. C	7. A	12. F
3. B	8. D	13. T
4. A	9. B	14. F
5. D	10. D	15. T

CHAPTER 13

Religious Groups and Systems

POLITICAL ISLAM: THE CASE OF SAUDI ARABIA

Saudi Arabia is a theocratic monarchy with Islam as the official religion. The Saudi king holds executive, legislative, judicial, and religious powers. His official title is the Custodian of the Two Holy Mosques, and he is both the prime minister and supreme religious leader of Saudi Arabia. Even so, because the constitution of Saudi Arabia emanates from the Qur'an, the power of the king is not absolute; rather, his power is constrained by the strictures of Islam. The king remains one of the most influential leaders on earth, however, with a fifth of the world's proven oil reserves under his control (*CIA World Factbook* 2009).

The Saudi government strongly encourages and supports Wahhabism, a highly fundamentalist branch of Islam that seeks to purify the Muslim religion of any innovations or practices that stray from the original teachings of the Prophet Mohammed. Because of this, Saudi Arabia has some of the strictest religious laws in the world. What's more, the Saudi government has no legal protection for religious freedom because freedom of religion violates Wahhabism. Infidels are forbidden from practicing religion in public, and non-citizens have to carry identity cards indicating whether they're Muslim or non-Muslim (US Department of State 2007).

The Saudi government censors the press, blocks Internet sites, and prohibits criticism of the royal family and Wahhabism. Not only is this policy enforced inside Saudi Arabia, but it also reaches overseas to such Saudi-owned media outlets as *Al Hayat*, a major pan-Arab newspaper in Lebanon and Morocco (Sharpe 2004). While most local newspapers are privately owned in Saudi Arabia, the Saudi government can vet editors and dismiss journalists at any time without cause. Since 1999, the Saudi government has blocked more than two thousand websites deemed unfit for Muslim viewing (Hermida 2002).

A system of Islamic courts handles all judicial cases in Saudi Arabia. A judge with religious training presides over each court. There are no juries. The king represents the highest court of appeals and has the power to pardon. While the Saudi government officially sanctions five schools of Islamic legal doctrine, Saudi universities focus almost exclusively on the Wahhabi school (U.S. State Department 2008). Accordingly, most judges in Saudi Arabia follow Wahhabism in carrying out justice.

In the Saudi judicial system, institutionalized discrimination against infidels is an acceptable practice. For religious reasons, Jews and Christians face less discrimination than other infidels. However, all infidels are treated with less respect than Muslims. To illustrate, consider how Saudi judges calculate accidental death or injury compensation for male infidels. When a male plaintiff is Jewish or Christian, he can only be awarded half of what a Muslim male would receive under the same circumstances. If a male plaintiff is Buddhist or Hindu, he can only receive a sixteenth of that to which a male Muslim would be entitled (U.S. State Department 2008).

In Saudi Arabia, education revolves around Islam. Accordingly, public schools in Saudi Arabia are also religious institutions. What's more, all Saudi students receive compulsory instruction in Wahhabism. In accordance with Islamic law, girls and boys attend separate schools. In many cases, Saudi students are taught to demean different religions and non-Wahhabi Islam (Blanchard 2008). Infidels may only attend secular private schools because religious schools of any kind are banned for non-Muslims (U.S. State Department 2008).

To enforce Islamic law, the Saudi government utilizes a corps of religious police called the *mutaween*. The *mutaween* has over ten thousand patrolmen working throughout Saudi Arabia (McLeod 2007). The *mutaween* can arrest married women for talking to unmarried men. They can detain anyone displaying homosexual behavior and arrest women for driving. They can punish anyone for eating pork or drinking alcohol. They even have the power to confiscate consumer products deemed un-Islamic. Perhaps the most egregious incident attributed to the *mutaween* in recent years occurred in 2002 when they blocked fifteen schoolgirls from escaping a burning building because the girls weren't wearing proper Islamic dress. All fifteen girls perished as a result of the *mutaween's* actions (*BBC* 2002).

Understanding political Islam in Saudi Arabia is relevant to sociology and this chapter because it underscores how religion can influence society in profound and different ways. The United States, for instance, has no official religion while the Saudis are officially Muslim. The U.S. constitution protects religious freedom. The Saudi constitution forbids it. The point is religion is not only a simple matter of spirituality and personal belief but also a multifaceted social force with major implications for society.

Throughout the world, people meditate, pray, join communes, worry about "being saved," partake in rituals, bow to statues, burn incense, chant, offer sacrifices, torture themselves, and proclaim their allegiance to many gods or to a particular god. Anthropologists suggest that events, acts, and beliefs such as these are part of every society, both today and throughout history. Together, these behaviors constitute a society's religious system.

Religion has always been the anchor of identity for human beings. Religious beliefs give meaning to life; and the experiences associated with them provide personal gratification, as well as a release from the

frustrations and anxieties of daily life. Ceremonies, formal acts, or rituals are essential for both personal identity and social cohesion. We have ceremonies to rejoice about the birth of an infant, to initiate a young person into adult society, to celebrate a new marriage, to bury the dead, and to fortify our belief that life goes on. Most of these ceremonies are linked to religion.

It may make you uneasy to examine these events and rituals objectively, but the goal of sociological investigations of religion is not to criticize anyone's faith or to compare the validity of different religions. Sociologists are interested, rather, in studying how religion is organized and how it affects the members of a given society. They study how people organize in groups in regard to religious beliefs and how these belief systems affect their behavior in other areas, such as family life and economic achievement. Sociologists also examine the kinds of belief systems developed by people in different circumstances and how religious beliefs change over time as external circumstances change.

A SOCIOLOGICAL APPROACH TO RELIGION

What Is Religion?

One of the earliest writers on the sociology of religion was the French sociologist Emile Durkheim. In *The Elementary Forms of the Religious Life* (1915), Durkheim defined *religion* as "a unified system of beliefs and practices relative to sacred things, that is to say, things set apart and forbidden—beliefs and practices which unite into one single moral community called a church, all those who adhere to them" (p. 47).

In this definition, Durkheim identified several elements that he believed to be common to all religions. He viewed the first element, *a system of beliefs and practices*, as the cultural component of religion. The *beliefs* are states of opinion; and the practices, which Durkheim termed "rites," are modes of action. These beliefs and practices exist within a social context, consistent with the values and norms of the culture.

The second element, *a community or church*, he saw as the social organizational component. A *church*, in this sense, is not a building or even a local group that gathers together to worship. Rather it is a collective of persons who share similar beliefs and practices. He claimed that in all history, we do not find a single religion without a community of believers. Sometimes, this community is strictly national. A corps of priests sometimes directs it, and it sometimes lacks any official directing body; however, it always has a definite group at its foundation. Even the so-called cults satisfy this condition, for they are always celebrated by a group or a family. What the community does is to translate the beliefs and practices into something shared, which led Durkheim to think of these first two elements—the cultural and social components of religion—as being linked. Contemporary sociologists of religion do recognize a functional difference between the two, in that a person may accept a set of religious beliefs without being affiliated with a particular church.

The third element, *sacred things*, he saw as existing only in relation to the profane. The **profane** is the realm of the everyday world: food, clothes, work, play, or anything generally considered mundane and unspiritual. In contrast, the **sacred** consists of objects or ideas that are treated with reverence and awe: an altar, bible, prayer, or rosary is sacred. A hamburger, rock song, football, or sociology text is profane. However, Durkheim believed that anything could become sacred. Sacredness is not a property

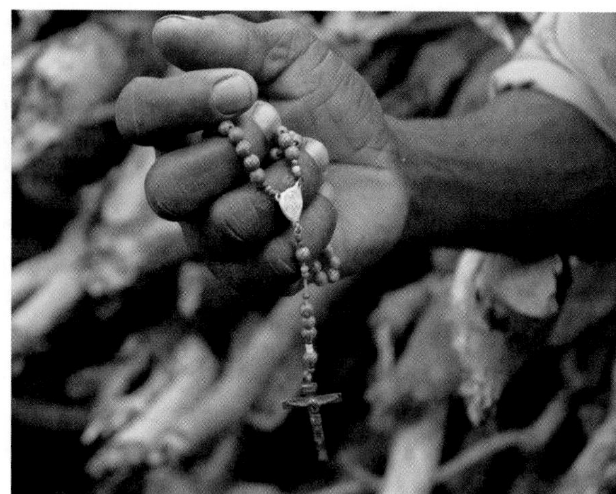

An African child holds a rosary. Emile Durkheim believed that a sacred object could be a rosary, an alter, or a bible. He also believed that sacredness is not a property inherent in an object, but rather it exists in the mind of the beholder.

inherent in an object. It exists in the mind of the beholder. Thus, a tree, a pebble, a ring, a scarf worn by Elvis Presley, or a baseball bat used by Babe Ruth may be considered sacred.

Durkheim hypothesized that religion developed out of group experiences, as primitive tribes came to believe that feelings about sacredness were derived from some supernatural power. As people perform certain rituals, they develop feelings of awe, which reinforce the moral norms of society. When they no longer feel in awe of moral norms, society is in a state of anomie or without norms. Informal social control is possible largely because people have strong feelings that they should or should not do certain things. When they no longer have such feelings, social control breaks down. We see an example of this in some of our cities, where church doors are locked to prevent robberies. In many societies, nobody steals from churches because they believe they will be punished or suffer some form of retribution from their god(s).

Other sociologists present somewhat different views of religion, but most would agree that a **religion** has the following elements:

1. Things considered sacred, such as gods, spirits, special persons, or any object or thought defined as being sacred
2. A group or community of believers who make religion a social, as well as a personal, experience because members of a religion share goals, norms, and beliefs
3. A set of rituals, ceremonies, or behaviors that take on religious meaning when they express a relationship to the sacred—in Christian ceremonies, for example, bread and wine as sacred components of communion that symbolizing the body and the blood of Christ
4. A set of beliefs, such as a creed, doctrine, or holy book, which may define what is to be emphasized and/or how people should relate to society, or what happens to persons after their death
5. A form of organization that reinforces the sacred, unites the community of believers, carries out the rituals, teaches the creeds and doctrines, initiates new members, and so on

THE ORGANIZATION OF RELIGION

People have tried to understand the world around them throughout history, but we do not know exactly how or why they began to believe in supernatural beings or powers. Societies such as the Bushmen of Africa, who rely on hunting and gathering as their primary means of subsistence, often explain things in naturalistic terms. This type of religion is known as **animism**, which is the belief that spirits inhabit virtually everything in nature—rocks, trees, lakes, animals, and humans alike—and that these spirits influence all aspects of life and destiny. Sometimes they help, perhaps causing an arrow to strike and kill a wild pig for food. At other times, they are harmful, as when they make a child get sick and die. Specific rituals or behaviors, however, can sometimes influence these spirits, and pleasing them results in favorable treatment.

Some groups, such as the Tapajos of Brazil, practice a form of religion known as **shamanism**, which revolves around the belief that certain individuals, called "shamans," have special skill or knowledge in influencing the spirits that influence processes and events in their environment. Shamans (spiritual leaders), most of whom are men, are called upon to heal the sick and wounded, to make hunting expeditions successful, to protect the group against evil spirits, and to generally ensure the group's well-being. Shamans receive their power through ecstatic experiences, which might originate from a psychotic episode, the use of a hallucinogen such as peyote, or deprivation such as fasting or lack of sleep. More than 10 million people in the world are identified as shamanists. All but about 250,000 of these are located in Asia.

Within the United States, Native Americans of the Pacific Northwest who live on reservations hold that ancestral spirits work for the good or ill of the tribe through shamans. The shaman is a very powerful spiritual leader among most of the 176 Native American tribes recognized by the federal government. According to Joe Therrien from Michigan—a Chippewa leader, sociologist, and friend of one of the authors of this textbook—this form of religion is more ceremonial than a daily practice. He cautions us that we should not be misled into believing that all Native Americans follow the shaman or tribal spiritual leader. Most (70 percent) are urban, and most are Christian, primarily Roman Catholic. Many have become involved in The Native American Church Movement, started in the late 1960s, which serves as a compromise between traditional ceremonial practices and Christian beliefs.

A third form of religion among selected groups is **totemism**, the worship of plants, animals, or other natural objects, both as gods and ancestors. The totem itself is the plant or animal, which is believed to be ancestrally related to a person, tribe, or clan. Totems usually represent something important to the community, such as a food source or a dangerous predator, and the people often wear costumes and perform dances to mimic the totem object. Most readers are probably familiar with the totem poles used by North American Indians in Ketchikan, Alaska, often depicted in photographs, illustrations, or artifacts purchased by tourists. These tall posts, carved or painted with totemic symbols, were erected as a memorial to the dead. Totemism is still practiced today by some New Guinea tribes and by Australian aborigines. Durkheim believed that totemism was one of the earliest forms of religion and that other forms of religious organization evolved from it.

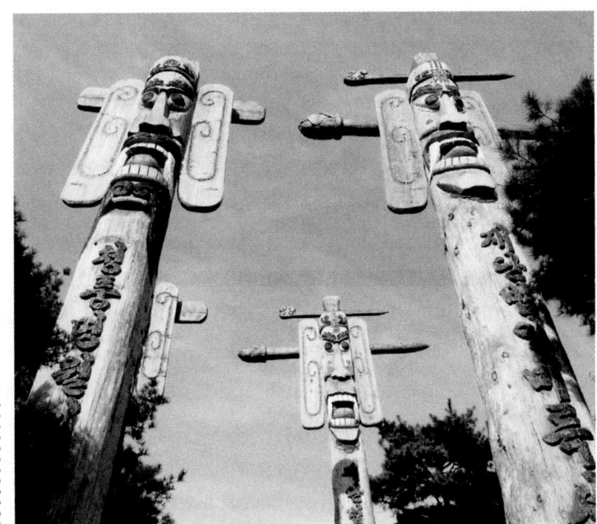

Totems such as these usually represent something important to the community. It is believed that totemism was one of the earliest forms of religion.

Religions may be organized in terms of the number of gods their adherents worship. **Polytheism** is belief in and worship of more than one god. Hinduism, which is practiced mainly in India, has a special god for each village and caste. People believe that these gods have special powers or control a significant life event, such as harvest or childbirth. Monotheism, on the other hand, is belief in only one god. **Monotheism** is familiar to most Americans because the two major religious groups in this country—Christians and Jews—believe in one god.

Most Westerners are less familiar with such major religions as Buddhism, Confucianism, Shintoism, and Taoism. These religions are neither monotheistic nor polytheistic because they do not involve a god figure. They are based, rather, on sets of moral, ethical, or philosophical principles. Most are dedicated to achieving some form of moral or spiritual excellence. Some groups, such as the Confucianists, have no priesthood. Shintoism and Confucianism both place heavy emphasis on honoring one's ancestors, particularly one's parents, who gave the greatest of all gifts, life itself.

Churches, Sects, and Cults

Religious systems differ in many ways, and sociologists have devised numerous ways for classifying them. We have already seen how Durkheim divided the world into the sacred and the profane. We have noted how the religious practices of some hunting-and-gathering societies were described in terms of animism, shamanism, and totemism. Can Christianity be understood in terms of the profane or of shamanism? Most contemporary religious scholars think not. Thus, another scheme of classification is used—that of churches, sects, and cults. This scheme focuses directly on the relationship between the type of religious organization and the world surrounding it.

Max Weber (1905) was one of the first sociologists to clarify the interrelationships between people's beliefs and their surroundings. In his classic essay, *The Protestant Ethic and the Spirit of Capitalism,* he argued that capitalism would not have been possible without Protestantism because Protestantism stressed the importance of work as an end in itself, of personal frugality, and of worldly success as a means of confirming one's salvation and evidence of God's favor. In dealing with this relationship between religion and the economy, he identified two major types of religious leaders. One, the **priest**, owes authority to the power of the office. By contrast, the **prophet** holds authority on the basis of charismatic qualities. Priestly and prophetic leaders are often in conflict, for the priest defends and represents the institution or society in question and supports the status quo. The prophet, not bound to a given institution, is more likely to criticize both the institutions and the general society.

This contrast led Weber to suggest that different sectors of society would develop different types of organizations to accompany their different belief systems. The ruling class or leaders, the better educated, and the more wealthy would need a more formalized type of religion that accepts modern science and the existing social world. The laboring class, the less educated, and the poor would need a type of religion that emphasizes another world or life and an emotional, spontaneous experience to console them for the deprivation in this life.

A German theologian and student of Weber, Ernst Troeltsch (1931), continued this line of thinking. Troeltsch divided religions into three categories: mysticism, churches, and sects. **Mysticism** is the belief that spiritual or divine truths come to us through intuition and meditation, not through the use of reason or the ordinary range of human experience and senses. *Mystics,* persons who believe in mysticism, practice their beliefs outside of organized religion. They often pose problems for other religious groups because they purport to be in direct contact with divine power. Evelyn Underhill, a Christian mystic, defines mysticism in the following way: "Mysticism, according to its historical and psychological definitions, is the direct intuition or experience of God; a mystic is a person who has, to a greater or less degree, such a direct experience—one whose religion and life are centered, not merely on an accepted belief or practice, but on that which the person regards as first-hand personal knowledge."

The church and the sect are differentiated in many ways but in particular by their relationships with the world around them (see Table 13-1). A **church** is an institutionalized organization of people who share common religious beliefs. The membership of churches is fairly stable. Most have formal bureaucratic structures with trained clergy and other officials, and they are closely linked to the larger society and seek to work within it. The majority of the religious organizations in the United States would be considered churches.

Two categories of churches that are sometimes differentiated are the ecclesia and the denomination. An **ecclesia** is an official state religion that includes all or most of the members of society. As a state church, it accepts state support and sanctions the basic cultural values and norms of the society. Sometimes, it administers the educational system as well. The Church of England in Great Britain and the Lutheran churches in the Scandinavian countries are two contemporary examples of national churches. The contemporary power of these churches, however, is not as great as was the power of the Roman Catholic Church in Western Europe during the Middle Ages or even its power today in Spain, Italy, and many Latin American countries.

Churches in the United States are termed **denominations**. They are not officially linked to state or national governments. In fact, various denominations may be at odds with state positions on war, abortion, taxes, pornography, alcohol, equal rights, and other issues, and no nation has more denominations than the United States. The U.S. Bureau of the Census lists approximately eighty denominations with memberships of sixty thousand or more (*Statistical Abstract* 2000), but the list would probably exceed several hundred if all of the small or independent denominations were added.

Whereas churches (ecclesia and denominations) are well established and highly institutionalized, **sects** are small groups that have broken away from a parent church and that call for a return to the old ways. They follow rigid doctrines and emphasize fundamentalist teachings.

TABLE 13-1 CHARACTERISTICS OF CHURCHES, SECTS, AND CULTS

Characteristic	Church	Sect	Cult
Membership based on:	Faith	Conversion	Emotional commitment
Membership is:	Inclusive, regional/ national boundaries	Closely guarded and protected	Closely guarded and protected
Size is:	Large	Small	Small
Class/wealth is:	Middle/higher	Lower, limited	Varies by recruit
Organization is:	Bureaucratic	Informal organization of faithful	Loose, organization around leader
Authority is:	Traditional	Charismatic	Single leader
Emphasis is on:	Brother/sisterhood of all humanity	The select and faithful	New and unusual lifestyle
Clergy are:	Highly trained, professional	Deemphasized, high lay participation	Divinely chosen, individualized
Salvation is through:	Grace of God	Moral purity and being born again	Adherence to leader/cult demands
Relationship to state is:	Compromising, closely aligned	Hostile	Ignored and avoided
Theology is:	Modernistic	Fundamentalistic	Innovative, unique, pathbreaking
Worship is:	Formal, orderly	Informal and spontaneous	Innovative, often radical

As suggested in this chapter's introduction, **fundamentalism** is the belief that the Bible is the divine word of God and that all statements in it are to be taken literally, word for word. Incidentally, this is a position taken by about one-third of the United States population (Wood 1990, 361), most of who are *not* members of sects but are affiliated with institutionalized churches that take very conservative views toward social issues (note the introductory issue in this chapter). The size of this group depends on how fundamentalism is defined. Conservatively estimated, there are at least thirty million Christian fundamentalists in the United States alone. Fundamentalism stands with Pentecostalism as one of the most successful religious movements of the twentieth century (*Religious Movements Homepage* University of Virginia, 2000, http://religious movements.lib.virginia.edu/.)

The creationism controversy, for example, stems from the fundamentalist position that the world was literally created in six days. Sect groups follow this type of literal interpretation of the Bible, although different groups focus their attention on different Bible scriptures. Their religious services often involve extensive member participation, with an emphasis on emotional expression.

The clergy of sects, who frequently preach part-time, often have little professional training and no seminary degrees. Members of sects tend to emphasize otherworldly rewards and are more likely to be of lower occupational and educational status than members of churches. Most of them are dissatisfied with their position in life and believe that the world is evil and sinful. As a result, their degree of commitment to the sect is often far greater than the commitment found among church members. Unwilling to compromise their beliefs, they are often in conflict with the government, the schools, and other social institutions. Although most sects are short-lived, some acquire a stable membership and a formal organizational structure and gradually become denominations.

There are many sects in the United States today including the Jehovah's Witnesses, Jews for Jesus, and a number of fundamentalist, evangelical, and Pentecostal groups. Although evangelical groups, like fundamentalist groups, maintain that the Bible is the only rule of faith, they focus their attention on preaching that salvation comes through faith as described in the four New Testament Gospels: Matthew, Mark, Luke, and John. Pentecostal groups, usually both evangelical and fundamentalist, are Christian sects with a highly emotional form of worship experience. Some contrasting characteristics of churches, sects, and cults are shown in Table 13-1. You may want to place your religious group or affiliation, if any, on this church-sect-cult continuum.

Another form, some would say "extreme form," of religious organization is the **cult**, the most loosely organized and most temporary of all religious groups. Unlike sects, cults—often under the direction of a charismatic leader—call for a unusual lifestyle. Jim Jones and Father Divine, for example, believed that they were divinely chosen to lead humanity, as does the Reverend Sun Myung Moon today. In cults, the emphasis is on the individual rather than on society. Because cults operate outside the mainstream of society and are focused around one leader or prophet, their existence depends on the life and health of their leader. In

Thinking Sociologically

Select your own religion or one with which you are well familiar. Can you identify the following for this religion: (a) things that are considered sacred, (b) selected characteristics of the membership or its adherents, (c) selected rituals or ceremonies in which the adherents participate, (d) key beliefs of the religion, and (e) the form of social organization that exists?

Jim Jones was the founder of the cult the Peoples Temple in Jonestown, Guyana.

some cases, they have given up their more radical teachings and, accepting more mainstream beliefs, have become churches. The Seventh-Day Adventists, for example, began as a cult group that proclaimed the end of the world on a specific date; but when that date passed, it maintained many of its other beliefs. Today, it is a church with a trained clergy, a stable membership, and a formal organizational structure.

THEORIES OF RELIGION

A Functionalist Approach

The universality of religion suggests to the functionalist that religion is a requirement of group life and that it serves both manifest and latent functions. Durkheim's classic study of religion, *The Elementary Forms of the Religious Life* (1915), posed two basic questions: (1) What is religion? (2) What are the functions of religion for human society? In answering the first question, he noted that religion is a unified system of beliefs and practices relative to sacred things. He answered the second question by focusing on religion's social function of promoting solidarity within a society.

Unlike most people today, who view religion as primarily a private and personal experience, Durkheim believed that the primary function of religion was *to preserve and solidify society.* Noting that worship, God, and society are inseparable, he paid little attention to the other functions of religion.

This perspective assumes that religion is the central focus for integrating the social system. By developing the awe that members of society feel for moral norms, religion functions to hold society together. This social solidarity is developed through rituals such as church or synagogue services, baptisms, bar (or bas) mitzvahs, Christmas caroling and gift-giving, and the multitude of observances and ceremonies practiced by specific religious groups.

A second function, related to promoting social solidarity, is to *create a community of believers.* A religion provides a system of beliefs around which people may gather to belong to something greater than themselves and to have their personal beliefs reinforced by the group and its rituals. Those who share a common ideology develop a collective identity and a sense of fellowship.

A third function is to *provide social control.* Religion reinforces social norms, providing sanctions for violations of norms and reinforcing basic values, such as property rights and respect for others. Society's existence depends on its members' willingness to abide by folkways and mores and to interact with one another in a spirit of cooperation and trust.

Religion also serves to *provide answers to ultimate questions.* Why are we here? Is there a supreme being? What happens after death? Religions provide systems of belief based on the faith that life has a purpose and that someone or something is in control of the universe. They make the world seem comprehensible, often by attributing familiar, human motives to supernatural forces.

Religion also provides *rites of passage, ceremonies, and rituals* designed to give sacred meaning and a social significance to birth, the attainment of adulthood, marriage, death, and other momentous events.

Religion helps to *reconcile people to hardship.* All societies have inequality, poverty, and oppression, and everyone experiences pain, crises, prejudice, and sorrow. By belonging to a religion, people may come to feel that they are special in some way—that they will be rewarded in the future for having suffered today. Many religions call for caring, mercy, charity, kindness, and other prosocial behaviors. They may provide moral, ethical, social, and even financial support to those in need.

Religion can also *cultivate social change.* Many religious groups criticize social injustice, existing social morality, and community or government actions. Some take action to change unfavorable conditions. The churches have been a major force in the civil rights movement, for example. Many protests against the Vietnam War were a result of religious teachings about love and peace. Religious groups to oppose social reforms have mounted other major protests, such as opposition to the right to have an abortion, equal rights for homosexuals, and the women's rights movement.

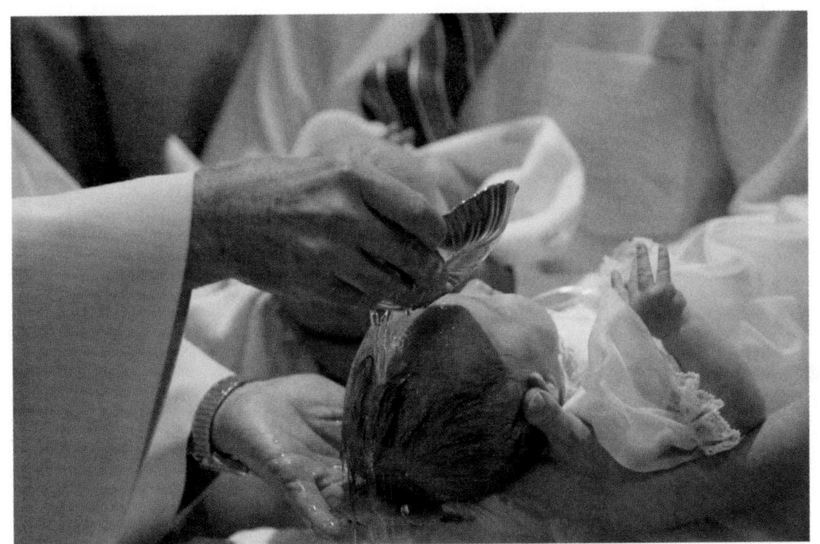

Durkheim believed religion served to preserve and solidify society through rituals such as baptisms, church services, and gift-giving. He also believed that those who share a common ideology develop a collective identity and a sense of fellowship.

This list of *manifest functions* performed by religion could be continued. Some latent functions of religion concern mate selection, experience in public speaking, and psychic rewards for donating funds or labor to worthy causes. Other groups and systems may be able to fulfill some of these manifest or latent functions, but many social scientists argue that particular functions provided by religion cannot be adequately met by other means. Other social scientists might suggest that some of the functions of religion may not be needed by society.

A functionalist approach to religion reminds us that while it performs many basic functions for society and individuals, it is likely to have dysfunctions as well. If it serves to preserve and solidify society, to create a community of believers, to reinforce social norms, and to reconcile people to hardship, it also can serve to divide society, create bias against the nonbeliever, exclude nonmembers of the group, and maintain the status quo. Religion can be dysfunctional in forcing people to accept inequities and in inhibiting its members from acting to change them. It can be dysfunctional in convincing its followers to reject this world for a future life in which rewards are guaranteed, and it can often inhibit the search for and acceptance of new truths, new ideas, and additional knowledge.

Examples of religion as both a source of integration and conflict are evident throughout the world. In Iran, the religious teachings of Islam formed the basis for convincing youth that it was honorable to die for their country in their war with Iraq. In Northern Ireland, protests and violence abound between Catholics and Protestants. In the Middle East, the conflicts between Jews and Moslems are intense. In India and Pakistan, caste and class conflicts linked to religious traditions cause death and destruction. In many countries, Jews are persecuted. Overpopulation and wars can be justified in the name of religion. As mentioned elsewhere, to have in-groups is to have out-groups. To believe that there is only one *Truth* is to reject all ideas that challenge prejudices.

APPLYING THE FUNCTIONALIST APPROACH TO RELIGION

Some useful insights provided by the functionalist approach are that religion serves a variety of essential social functions and that an understanding of religion is closely linked to an understanding of an entire culture. For example, can we understand Israel without knowing about Judaism, Saudi Arabia without knowing about Islam, or the United States without knowing about Christianity? Judeo-Christian religions penetrate most of our lives—even though we may be unaware of it and may not subscribe to any particular religion. This is exemplified even by our legal tender, on every piece of which is the phrase, "In God We Trust." Our entire economic system is imbued with religious overtones.

The knowledge that religion serves basic social functions may be useful in a number of careers. Notably, people whose jobs lead them to deal with foreign cultures might benefit from a thorough understanding of the major religions in those countries. Consider, for example, the difficulties that politicians, diplomats, and military personnel from the United States might have in dealing with the governments in the Middle East if they do not first understand the basic religions in these countries, their influence on Middle Eastern culture, and how they contrast with the Protestant ethic, one of the mainstays of U.S. culture. In the war with Iraq in 2003, many Americans came to realize just how important it is to understand the impact of a country's religious traditions on its culture. Many American soldiers, other military personnel, medical personnel, news reporters, and others who observed the war had to adjust to what they thought were the odd attitudes that the Arab world has toward such things as gender roles, alcohol use, and the female body. Imagine what it must be like for someone from the Middle East who comes to the United States, where many religious viewpoints are tolerated.

Because religion plays such a key part in a society's values, norms, roles, and beliefs, people involved in international business may benefit by fully understanding a country's religious traditions. This could be especially true in the advertising of products. Even though most advertisements in the United States are still geared toward traditional gender roles, for example, much of it is beginning to cater to the changing roles of women and men in American society. Considering again the example of Islam, we see that using this type of advertising would be a serious mistake in Middle Eastern countries, where religion plays a central role in keeping marriage and homemaking the central occupations of women.

A Conflict Approach

As discussed in previous chapters, the conflict approach focuses on the exploitation of the poor by the elite. The classical Marxist perspective suggests that religion, like other social structures, can be understood only in the context of its role in the economic system.

In sharp contrast to the functionalist approach, conflict theorists view religion as a tool that the elite uses to get the poor to obey authority and to follow the rules established by the privileged. Religion counsels the masses to be humble and to accept their condition. In the words of Karl Marx, religion "is the opiate of the masses" because it distracts them from finding practical political solutions to their problems. The powerless find an illusion of happiness through religion and look forward to future life after death, where the streets will be paved with gold and life will be joyful and everlasting. Marx urged revolution so that people could experience during life the joy and freedom that religion postpones until after death. In American society, we supplement that illusion of happiness by focusing upon individualism and meritocracy. Loosely, meritocracy advocates that "you get what you deserve and you deserve what you get." These two belief systems shore up the religious ideas that help to hold the inequality and lack of action in place.

Most theorists today would agree that religion serves interests other than those of the ruling class, but it is unquestionably true that there are strong relationships between religion and social class. Churches are highly segregated along racial and economic lines. In the United States, a number of denominations are largely or wholly black. Although the ideals of religious faith are supposed to unite people across the great chasms carved by race and ethnicity, social scientists have long noted that church attendance is perhaps the most highly segregated activity in the United States. In 2008, in a campaign interview, President Barack Obama reiterated this observation by saying, "The most segregated hour of American life occurs on Sunday morning" (NPR 2008).

Within the white population, different religious groups tend to attract people of similar educational and occupational levels. Few factory workers are Episcopalians, for example; and few professional people and company executives are Baptists or members of Pentecostal groups. Some groups, such as the Roman Catholic Church, have working-class as well as wealthy members; but the data generally show that occupation and income vary with religious affiliation.

Using the same type of advertising in Middle eastern countries as is used in the U.S. would be a mistake as gender roles are viewed differently.

Is religion related to class conflict? In a general way, the answer is yes. Religious affiliation is related to class, and many social controversies result from perceptions that differ according to social class. Opinions on such issues as prayer in the schools, the teaching of creationism, abortion, women as clergy, the Equal Rights Amendment, and homosexuality vary both by class and by religion. The conservative positions are generally supported both by fundamentalist and Pentecostal churches and by people who have lower incomes and less education.

APPLYING THE CONFLICT APPROACH TO RELIGION

In pointing out how religion is related to class conflict, the conflict approach yields some other useful findings. One is that occupation and income vary with religious affiliation. This is an important fact for church leaders to consider. By knowing that the members of a particular religious congregation are likely to be from a particular social class, ministers, priests, deacons, rabbis, and others could address the relevant needs of that congregation and might formulate examples to which the people can relate.

In Latin America, a branch of religious teaching known as "liberation theology" has been gaining wide acceptance. Liberation theology directly applies church policy and intervention to the social and class conflicts that plague Latin American society. Church leaders who support this approach speak out against repressive government policies, promote land reform, and generally act as advocates for the peasant population. Although not condoned by Catholic leadership in Rome, many priests praise liberation theology as an example of the applicability of religion to social welfare.

Understanding the relationship between social class and religious affiliation could be useful for you personally. You can learn a great deal about a community, for instance, by noticing its variety of churches. If you see a fairly broad representation of Baptist, Methodist, Catholic, and Episcopalian churches and Jewish synagogues, you know that the community has a fairly wide range of income and educational levels and probably a diversity of political attitudes. However, a preponderance of one type of church or temple might be a reflection of a community with less cultural diversity and less tolerance for differences.

Thinking Sociologically

1. Evaluate the major social functions of religion provided in this chapter. Can you give examples to illustrate each function? Do these functions exist for all religions?
2. From the conflict perspective, how does religion serve the elite?

RELIGIONS OF THE WORLD

The world population is more than 6 billion. About 16 percent of these people are listed as nonreligious (see Figure 13-1). Thus, whether we refer to Asia, to Russia and other countries in the Commonwealth of Independent States, to North America, or to Africa, the majority of people in the world adheres to or profess adherence to some religion.

It is difficult to obtain accurate counts of the number of adherents to the world's religions. The procedures used by different countries and groups to measure religious membership vary widely. Some assessments include only adults, others include everyone who attends services. Some people may be included in several different religious groups, such as Confucianism, Taoism, and Shintoism. Some religions forbid counts of their members. In countries where a particular religion has prevailed for many centuries (such as Christianity in Europe and Hinduism in India), the entire population may be reported as adherents. While most of us are likely to be familiar with one or two specific religions we may be less familiar with others. We now briefly examine some major ones.

FIGURE 13-1 RELIGIONS OF THE WORLD AND NUMBER OF ADHERENTS

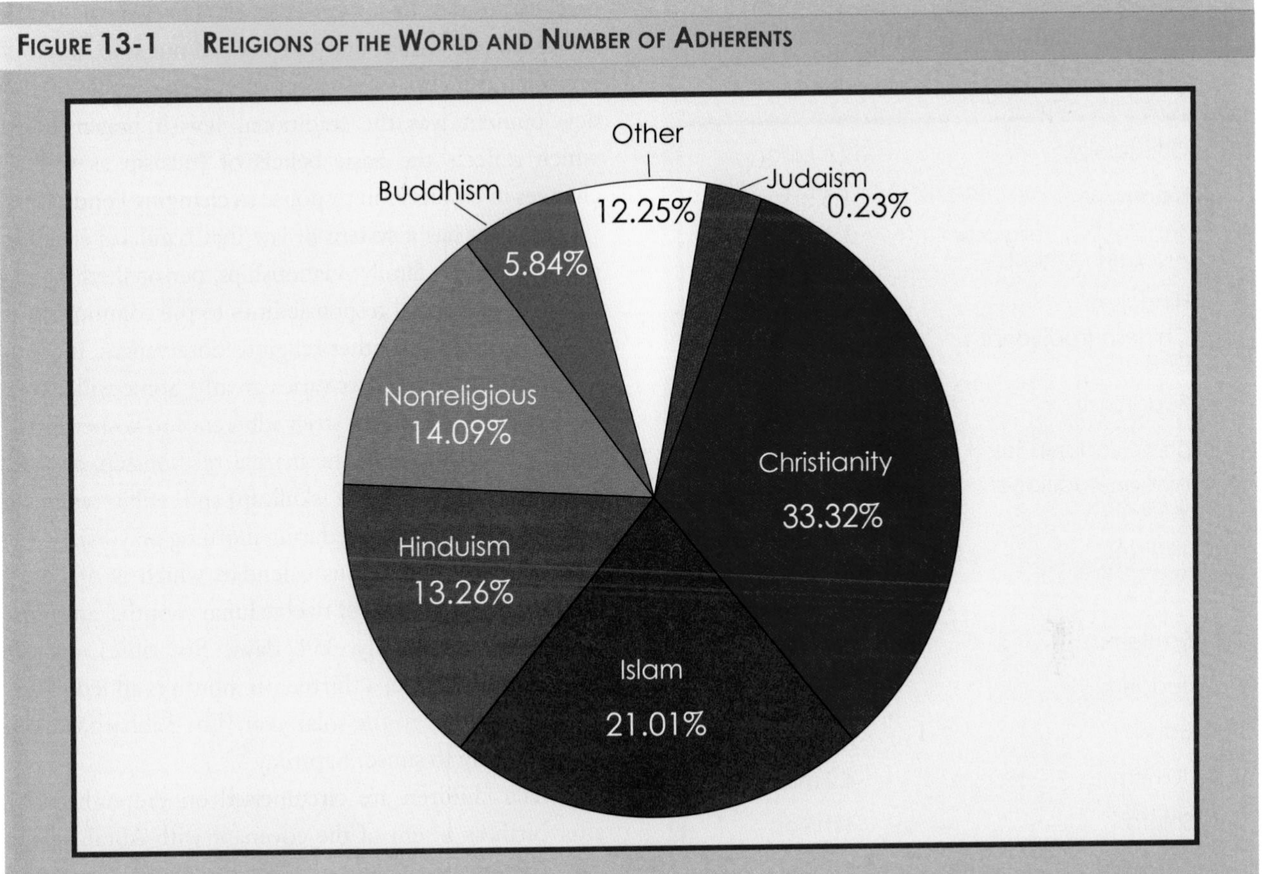

Source: CIA World Factbook 2009. Percentages are based on estimates of the number of adherents of different religions in the world population in 2007.

A Shinto ceremony in Japan

Christianity and Judaism

More than 2 billion people adhere to **Christianity**, and more than 14 million adhere to Judaism in the world today. Christians, who comprise about one-third of the world's population (see Table 13-2) profess faith in the teachings of Jesus Christ, as found in the New Testament of the Bible, whereas adherents to **Judaism** find the source of their beliefs in the Hebrew Bible (called the "Old Testament" by Christians), especially in its first five books, which are called the "Torah." The Torah was traditionally regarded as the primary revelation of God, originally passed on orally and eventually written.

Judaism is the oldest religion in the Western world. It comprises both a religious and an ethnic community. It was the first religion to teach monotheism, which was based on the Old Testament verse "Hear O Israel, the Lord our God, the Lord is one" (Deuteronomy 6:4).

Table 13-2 Estimates of World Adherents to Religions

Christianity:	2.1 billion
Islam:	1.5 billion
Secular/Nonreligious/ Agnostic/Atheist:	1.1billion
Hinduism:	900 million
Chinese traditional religion:	394 million
Buddhism:	376 million
primal-indigenous:	300 million
African Traditional & Diasporic:	100 million
Sikhism:	23 million
Juche:	19 million
Spiritism:	15 million
Judaism:	14 million
Baha'i:	7 million
Jainism:	4.2 million
Shinto:	4 million
Cao Dai:	4 million
Zoroastrianism:	2.6 million
Tenrikyo:	2 million
Neo-Paganism:	1 million
Unitarian-Universalism:	800 thousand
Rastafarianism:	600 thousand
Scientology:	500 thousand

Note: Sizes shown are approximate estimates, and are here mainly for the purpose of ordering the groups, not providing a definitive number. This list is sociological/statistical in perspective.

Source: www.adherents.com

Jews, the people who identify with and practice Judaism, believe that God's providence extends into a special covenant with the ancient Israelites: to bring God's message to humanity by their example. As a result, the emphasis is on conduct rather than on doctrinal correctness. Adherents to Judaism have a considerable measure of latitude in matters of belief because their beliefs have never been formulated in an official creed. This lack of an official creed also meant that Judaism did not stop developing after the Bible was completed. One result of this development was the traditional Jewish prayer book, which reflects the basic beliefs of Judaism as well as changes in emphasis in response to changing conditions.

Judaism has a system of law that regulates civil and criminal justice, family relationships, personal ethics and manners, and social responsibilities to the community, as well as worship and other religious observances. Individual practice of these laws varies greatly. Some widely observed practices concern strict adherence to kosher foods, daily prayer and study, the marital relationship, and the meaning of the yarmulke (skullcap) and tefillin (worn on the forehead and left arm during morning prayers).

The Jewish religious calendar, which is of Babylonian origin, consists of twelve lunar months, amounting to approximately 354 days. Six times over a nineteen-year cycle, a thirteenth month is added to adjust the calendar to the solar year. The Sabbath is from sunset Friday to sunset Saturday.

Male children are circumcised on the eighth day after birth as a sign of the covenant with Abraham. At age thirteen, Jewish boys undergo the rite of becoming a bar mitzvah to signify adult status and a responsibility for performing the commandments. A similar ceremony for girls, the bas mitzvah, is a more recent innovation.

Christianity diverged from Judaism in ancient Israel. Christians considered Jesus to be the Jewish savior, or Messiah, and incorporated the traditional Hebrew writings of Christ's followers into the canon of their faith, the Bible. After Christ's death (and, as Christians believe, his resurrection), his teachings spread to Rome and many other centers of the Roman Empire. When the Roman Empire split in AD 1054, so did the Christian church; it came to be called the Orthodox Church in the East and the Roman Catholic Church in the West. The Roman Catholic Church was united under Popes until the sixteenth century. Today, of the estimated 2 billion plus Christians, nearly 57 percent are Roman Catholic. Slightly more than one-third is Protestant, and the rest are Eastern Orthodox.

Christians, like Jews, believe in one god (monotheism); but for most Christians, their God takes the form of a Holy Trinity: Father, Son, and Holy Spirit. Christians experience God as the Father, Jesus Christ as the Son of God, and the Holy Spirit as the continuing presence of God. Also, most Christians worship on Sunday instead of Saturday, which is the Jewish Sabbath. They also practice baptism by water when they become adherents or give a public testimony of their acceptance of Christ and of Christ's divinity. Christians also take the Eucharist, a sacred meal recalling the last supper that Jesus had with his disciples. The breaking of bread, symbolizing the body of Christ, and the drinking of wine, symbolizing the blood of Christ, are sacred acts (sacraments) to most Christians. Prayer and preaching are also important Christian functions.

Muslim children reading the Koran. Followers of Islam follow the teachings of the Koran and of Muhammad, a prophet.

Islam

There are nearly 1 billion Islamic adherents in the world. Followers of **Islam** follow the teachings of the Koran and of Muhammad, a prophet. Islam means "surrender, resignation," and "submission." A person who submits to the will of Allah, the one and only God, is called a Muslim (sometimes spelled Moslem). This surrender involves a total commitment in faith, obedience, and trust to this one God. The insistence that no one but God be worshiped has led many Muslims to object to the term "Muhammadanism," a designation widely used in the West but thought to suggest that Muhammad, a great prophet of Islam, is worshiped in a manner that parallels the worship of Christ by Christians.

It is sometimes assumed that Islam originated during the lifetime of Muhammad (AD 570–630), specifically during the years in which he received the divine revelations recorded in the Muslim sacred book, the Qur'an (Koran). Many Muslims, however, believe that the prophet Muhammad simply restored the original religion of Abraham.

Islam encompasses a code of ethics, a distinctive culture, a system of laws, and a set of guidelines and rules for other aspects of life. The Muslim place of worship is the mosque, and the chief gathering of the congregation takes place on Fridays. Muslims profess their faith by repeating, "There is no God but God, and Muhammad is the messenger of God." The Muslims also have a deep awareness of the importance of a fellowship of faith and a community of believers.

The Koran includes rules for ordering social relationships. It is especially explicit about matters pertaining to the family, marriage, divorce, and inheritance. The family is basically authoritarian, patriarchal, polygamous, patrilineal, and largely patrilocal. Women are clearly subordinate to men and receive only half the inheritance that male heirs receive. Muslim males may marry non-Muslim women; and in countries where the Muslim holy law is the law of the state, Muslim women may not marry outside their faith. A Muslim male may take up to four wives (polygyny) and traditionally can divorce a wife by simple pronouncement and dowry repayment. Children, especially sons, are perceived as desirable.

Although laws are changing in many Islamic countries and the education of women has increased dramatically, fewer females than males attend school; even fewer women receive a higher education. Marriage and housekeeping are considered the proper occupations of women. It is not surprising, therefore, that Islam is finding it difficult to come to terms with the scientific ideas and the technology of the Western world. Since it is difficult to accurately report the number of Muslims in the U.S. due to the U.S. Census not reporting religious identification, we have to estimate the members to be from seven million to eight million based on recent studies (Ali 2008).

Hinduism

The greatest majority of the 786 million Hindus in the world are residing in India, Pakistan, and Nepal.

SOCIOLOGY AT WORK

Helping Religious Refugees Readjust

Baila Miller received a doctorate in sociology at the University of Illinois at Chicago Circle. She used her sociological training in a variety of ways. She was a member of the faculty doing applied research in gerontology in the Department of Medical Social Work at the University of Illinois at Chicago. Prior to that, she handled publications and training for SPSS, a computer software company, and before that, she was the assistant director of research at the Jewish Federation of Metropolitan Chicago.

It was at the Jewish Federation where Miller first used her sociological training to earn a living. When Miller was asked how she used her sociological training in her work at the Jewish Federation, she responded, "The federation raises charitable funds and allocates them to Jewish causes in Israel and overseas and to local Jewish social welfare, health, and educational institutions. The office of research and planning where I worked was a small department—just three people. We were responsible for analyzing the budgets of some of the agencies we supported, for preparing service statistics for submission to the United Way, for collecting and analyzing data needed by our volunteer committees, and for carrying out special research projects."

It was in these special research projects that Miller found the fullest application of her training. "In one project we completed a survey of the Jewish population of greater Chicago," she says—a survey that presented unique problems among population studies because the U.S. Bureau of the Census does not collect data on religious affiliations in its decennial census. "We wanted to determine many things about the Jewish community: How many people were there? Where did they live? How did they maintain their Jewish identity? Did they participate in religious observances and in Jewish education? What were their service needs and how could a Jewish agency meet [these needs]? Should we have concentrated on services for the elderly or on child care for two-career families? Who were the Jewish poor?"

Clearly, many areas of Miller's sociological training came into play with this one study alone. In addition to needing knowledge of various types of quantitative and qualitative research techniques, she needed to know about substantive areas in sociology, such as minority groups, religious groups, population, community, families, and social psychology, which were invaluable to her research.

Another project with which Miller was involved at the Jewish Federation was a study of the adjustment of Soviet Jewish émigrés to life in various communities in the United States. Miller analyzed data about Soviet Jewish émigrés in a number of ways. First, at the individual level, she studied how these people adjusted to American life in terms of occupational achievement, language acquisition, social and cultural involvement in the Jewish community, and maintenance of Jewish identity. She looked at the effects of *background characteristics*—social and economic status and place of origin in the former Soviet Union; and of *mediating factors*—the type of resettlement services that were offered in various communities in this country. Second, on the community level, she looked at *aggregate measures* of differences in adjustment in various cities in the United States. This included an investigation of comparable studies that were done in thirteen U.S. cities and a cross-cultural analysis of the similarities and differences with other large refugee or émigré groups, particularly Asians and Mexicans. Finally, she did a policy analysis of different programs offered by Jewish agencies and national refugee organizations in order to determine their effectiveness.

The state religion of Nepal is Hinduism. Until 2008, the King of Nepal was considered a dependent of the Hindu god Vishnu. In India, approximately 85 percent of the population is Hindu. **Hinduism** has evolved over about four thousand years and comprises an enormous variety of beliefs and practices. It hardly corresponds to most Western conceptions of religion because organization is minimal, and there is no religious hierarchy.

Hinduism is so closely intertwined with other aspects of the society that it is difficult to describe it clearly, especially in regard to castes. Hindus sometimes refer to the ideal way of life as fulfilling the duties of one's class and station, which means obeying the rules of the four great castes of India: the Brahmans, or priests; the Kshatriyas, warriors and rulers; the Vaisyas, merchants and farmers; and the Sudras, peasants and laborers. A fifth class, the Untouchables, includes those whose occupations require them to handle "unclean" objects.

These classes encompass males only. The position of women is ambiguous. In some respects, they are treated as symbols of the divine, yet in other ways, they are considered inferior beings. Traditionally, women have been expected to serve their husbands and to have no independent interests, but this is rapidly changing.

Although caste is a powerful influence in Hindu religious behavior, a person's village community and

Ganesh is the Hindu god of success. Hindu belief holds that the universe is populated by a multitude of gods (polytheism) who behave much as humans do, and worship of these gods takes many forms.

family are important as well. Every village has gods and goddesses who ward off epidemics and drought. Hindu belief holds that the universe is populated by a multitude of gods (polytheism) who behave much as humans do, and worship of these gods takes many forms. Some are thought to require sacrifices, others are worshiped at shrines or temples, and shrines devoted to several gods associated with a family deity are often erected in private homes.

To Hindus, the word *dharma* means the cosmos, or the social order. Hindus practice rituals that uphold the great cosmic order. They believe that to be righteous, a person must strive to behave in accordance with the way things are. In a sense, the Hindu sees life as a ritual. The world is regarded as a great dance determined by one's karma, or personal destiny; and the final goal of the believer is liberation from this cosmic dance. Hindus also believe in *transmigration of souls:* After an individual dies, that individual's soul is born again in another form, as either a higher or a lower being, depending on whether the person was righteous or evil in the previous life. If an individual becomes righteous enough, the soul will be liberated and will cease to be reborn into an earthly form and will exist only as spirit.

A fundamental principle of Hinduism is that our perceptions of the external world are limitations. When we think about one thing, we are cut off from the infinite number of things we are not thinking about but could be. If we think of nothing, we become in tune with the universe and freed of these limitations. One means of doing this is through meditation.

The actual belief systems of India are extremely confusing to Westerners because so many different tribal religions have been assimilated into Hinduism; but the basic nature of polytheism, in general, and of Hinduism, in particular, permits new gods to be admitted.

Buddhism

Buddhism has about 376 million adherents. It is impossible to precisely determine the number of Buddhists because many people accept Buddhist beliefs and engage in Buddhist rites while practicing other religions, such as Shintoism, Confucianism, Taoism, or Hinduism.

Buddhism is thought to have originated as a reaction against the Brahmanic tradition of Hinduism in the fifth century BC. At this time, a prince named Siddhartha Gautama was born in northern India to a prosperous ruling family. As he grew older, the suffering he witnessed among the people distressed him. At the age of twenty-nine, he left his wife and family to go on a religious quest. One day, sitting under a giant fig tree, he passed through several stages of awareness and became the first Buddha, the enlightened one. He decided to share his experience with others and became a wandering teacher, preaching his doctrine of the "Four Noble

A Buddhist monk prays. Buddhism is thought to have originated as a reaction against the Brahmanic tradition of Hinduism in the fifth century B.C.

Truths": (1) This life is suffering and pain. (2) The source of suffering is desire and craving. (3) Suffering can cease. (4) The practice of an "eightfold path" can end suffering. The eightfold path consisted of right views, right intentions, right speech, right conduct, right livelihood, right effort, right mindfulness, and right concentration. It combined ethical and disciplinary practices, training in concentration and meditation, and the development of enlightened wisdom. This doctrine was Buddha's message until the age of eighty, when he passed into final nirvana, a state of transcendence forever free from the cycle of suffering and rebirth.

After Buddha's death, legends of his great deeds and supernatural powers emerged. Stories were told of his heroism in past lives, and speculations arose about his true nature. Some groups viewed him as a historical figure, whereas others placed him in a succession of several Buddhas of the past and a Buddha yet to come. Differing views eventually led to a diversity of Buddhist sects in different countries. Some remained householders who set up Buddha images and established many holy sites that became centers of pilgrimage. Others became monks, living in monastic communities and depending on the laity for food and material support. Many monks became beggars, and in several Southeast Asian countries they still go on daily alms rounds. They spend their days in rituals, devotions, meditation, study, and preaching. Flowers, incense, and praise are offered to the image of the Buddha. These acts are thought to ensure that the monks will be reborn in one of the heavens or in a better place in life, from which they may be able to attain the goal of enlightenment.

In every society where Buddhism is widespread, people combine Buddhist thought with a native religion, supporting the monks and paying for rituals in the temples. These societies are also organized around other religions, however.

Today, the integration of Buddhism into many cultures has resulted in different interpretations of the way to Buddhahood. Yet we can supposedly reach Nirvana by seeing with complete detachment, by seeing things as they really are without being attached to any theoretical concept or doctrine.

Confucianism

Confucianism, which has about 5.8 million adherents, is associated primarily with China, the home of nearly 180 million adherents to Chinese folk religions. Confucianism has influenced the civilizations of Korea, Japan, and Vietnam, as well as China. Confucianism is the philosophical and religious system based on the teachings of Confucius, who was born to a poor family in 551 BC, in what is today Shantung Province in China, was orphaned at an early age. As a young man, he held several minor government positions, but he became best known as a teacher, philosopher, and scholar.

Distressed by the misery and oppression that surrounded him, he dedicated his life to attempting to relieve the suffering of the people.

By talking with younger men about his ideas to reform government to serve the people rather than the rulers, Confucius attracted many disciples. He emphasized the total person, sincerity, ethics, and the right of individuals to make decisions for themselves. Although Confucius was not a religious leader in the usual sense of the word, he believed that there was a righteous force in the universe; and yet his philosophy was founded not on supernaturalism but on humanity. He said that virtue is to love people, and wisdom is to understand them.

The basic philosophy of Confucius is found in his many sayings: "All people are brothers." "Sincerity and reciprocity should be one's guiding principles." "The truly virtuous person, desiring to be established personally, seeks to establish others; desiring success for oneself can help others to succeed." "The superior person stands in awe of three things: the ordinances of heaven, great persons, and the words of sages." The ideals of Confucius were motivated not by the desire for rewards or an afterlife but simply by the satisfaction of acting in accordance with the divine order.

Confucius had a pervasive influence on all aspects of Chinese life—so much so that every county in China built a temple to him. Everyone tried to live in accordance with the Confucian code of conduct. His values guided human relations at all levels—among individuals, communities, and nations. His thought guided conduct in work and in the family. Even today, the Chinese who profess to be Taoists, Buddhists, or Christians still generally act in accordance with Confucian ideals.

Thinking Sociologically

Given the tremendous variability in religious beliefs and practices around the world, consider statements such as these:

1. Religious truth is only found in a literal interpretation of the Bible.
2. Religion is a social creation.
3. Whether there is no god, one god, or many gods is only relevant in terms of what people believe.

One of the books in the classical literature of Confucius is the *Book of Changes*, or the *I Ching*. This book is familiar to many Americans and is used to guide a person's behavior and attitude toward the future.

RELIGION IN THE UNITED STATES

Of the religions of the world just described, most readers of this text are well aware that Christianity predominates in the United States. The Roman Catholic Church is the largest religious group in the United States with more than 57 million adult members (25 percent of the adult population). When combined, more than half (around 51 percent) of the adult population (around 116 million) in this country are non-Catholic Christians (including around 112 million Protestants, 3 million Mormons, and 800 thousand Greek Orthodox) (U.S. Census Bureau, *Statistical Abstract*, Table 74, 2011). Protestants belong to such churches as the National and Southern Baptist conventions, the Assemblies of God, the United Methodist Church, and the Lutheran Church, to mention just a few. There are about 2.7 million adult members of Jewish congregations. Note that the 2011 Statistical Abstracts contain religious data only on the adult population in the United States. In 2009, a little over 85 percent of the population clearly identified with one or another religious group.

The United States, which has no state church, has more than two hundred denominations and is greatly influenced by a variety of religious groups and belief systems. In addition to churches and denominations, revivalists preach on TV and radio, and religious leaders such as Billy Graham give spiritual advice and seek converts to Christianity. Bumper stickers tell us that "Jesus Saves" or to "Honk if you love Jesus."

Williams (1980) conceptualizes American religion as interplay between two forces: the structured and the unstructured, the major religious communities and the informal groups that he calls "popular religions." These two trends developed, he says, in response to the demands of life in a new country. Faced with a diverse population, a new political system, and rapid technological change, Americans sometimes have found organized religions too limited; and in response to the demands of a new nation, they have developed new religious movements.

A group of Amish children walk along a road. The Amish are considered to be the descendants of the Pietist sect which rejected worldliness in favor of pacifism, communal living, and aspiration toward perfection.

The Development of Religious Movements

Religion in American society has infused with the core American value of individualism. Despite the emergence of religious groups that seemingly are a response to individualism, there is in fact, a strong commonality that runs through the various religious movements in the United States. Although guided by different practices, there is a commonality about the nature of faith and the relationship of faith to social commitments, very much guided by a sacred adherence to individualism (Madsen 2009). Some so-called liberal religious groups have downplayed the supernatural aspects of Christianity and have emphasized the importance of ethical conduct and a remote, depersonalized God. Others worship a personal god and express their beliefs emotionally. Those who worship in this way seek signs of divine intervention in their daily lives.

Another religious movement is the development of sects. (Review Table 13-1.) The proliferation of these groups accompanied the breakdown of the feudal structure and the development of industrialization. One wave of groups, known as the Pietist sects, rejected worldliness in favor of pacifism, communal living, and aspiration toward perfection. The Amish and the Hutterites are American groups descended from these sects.

Another sect is the Religious Society of Friends (Quakers), who came to Pennsylvania from England. Quakers believe in an "inner light," that people mystically partake of the nature of God. Thus, they see no need for a religious structure (e.g., clergy or churches) interceding between God and human beings.

Another theme in American religious life is **millennialism**, the belief that a dramatic transformation of the earth will occur and that Christ will rule the world for a thousand years of prosperity and happiness. One millennial movement took place among the Millerites in the 1830s. William Miller, the founder, was convinced that the Second Coming of Christ would happen in 1843. When it did not, he changed the date to 1844. Again nothing happened. Some of his followers, who believed that the Second Coming had occurred invisibly and spiritually, founded the *Seventh-Day Adventists.* A more recent example of millennialism is Christian Exodus, a group that incorporates Evangelical Christianity and paleoconservative beliefs as a response to social crises that they believe have resulted from liberalized social values and economic uncertainty. Christian Exodus feels that these values have threatened a Christian way of life and that the way to salvation is through the electorate. The group's focus is aimed at dominating South Carolina politics as an attempt to create policies that reinforce traditional Christian values (Sweet and Lee 2010).

Other religious movements have been based on divine revelation. One American prophet who received a divine revelation was Joseph Smith, who founded the *Church of Jesus Christ of Latter-Day Saints* (Mormons) in 1830. His following was recruited from the rural people of upstate New York. About thirty years later, Mary Baker Eddy began a movement in the urban middle class, known as the Christian Science movement. Ms. Eddy's revelation was that illness could be controlled by the mind. This sect developed into a denomination when people of wealth and status became adherents.

Pentecostalism involves a practice similar to divine revelation. Pentecostal Christians hold highly emotional services that resemble revivals. Participants also "speak in tongues" (*glossolalia*), in which they go into ecstatic seizures and utter a rapid flow of apparently meaningless syllables that are claimed to be a direct gift of the Holy Spirit.

An offshoot of Pentecostalism is *faith healing*, which experienced a rapid growth after World War II. In faith healing, the fundamentalist preacher asks members of the congregation who are sick or disabled to come forward. The preacher asks the disabled person and the rest of the congregation to call upon the power of the Lord to heal: "In the name of Jesus, heal." If their faith in Christ is strong enough, the blind will see, the lame can throw away their crutches, and so on. Followers of faith healers come primarily from the poor or working classes, who often do not have health insurance, adequate financial resources, or sometimes an awareness of what is available or where to go for adequate medical treatment.

A recent manifestation of the interplay between churches or denominations and fundamentalist groups of the sect type concerns the teaching of evolution in the public schools. Most educated people in the United States accept Darwin's theory of biological evolution. Many fundamentalist Christians, however, interpret the Bible literally and believe that God created heaven and earth in exactly the six days it specifies. The creationists are urging that creationism be given "equal time" with evolution in school science classes. The basic assumptions of scientists and religious fundamentalists are in direct conflict: Science is based on deductions drawn from empirical reality, whereas creationism is based on divine revelation and denounces empirical evidence that contradicts Biblical accounts. The issue of whether creationism should be taught in the public schools was temporarily muted in 1982 when a federal district judge in Arkansas ruled that the two-model approach of the creationists is simply a contrived dualism that has no scientific factual basis or legitimate educational purpose. The ruling contended that because creationism is not science, the conclusion is inescapable that the only real effect of teaching creation theory is the advancement of religion. What the creation law does, in effect, is to make the teaching of creationism in the public schools unconstitutional.

A ruling in the opposite direction that illustrates the impact of fundamentalism on our judicial system took place in 1987. A federal district judge in Alabama ruled that about forty social studies books be removed from the public schools because they taught what creationists called "secular humanism." The judge ruled that secular humanism was a religion that gave credit to humans rather than to God.

Current Trends in Religion

The use of computers and sophisticated statistical techniques has brought about significant changes in social science research in general and in the scientific study of religion in particular. Researchers can now deal efficiently with large samples of the population and can test some of the theories developed by Durkheim and Weber.

One such study was published in 1961 by Gerhard Lenski, whose book, *The Religious Factor*, is now considered a pioneering quantitative study of religion. Using survey techniques on a probability sample of males in the Detroit area, Lenski tried to test Weber's notions about the Protestant ethic. Lenski reasoned that if Protestants were more oriented toward the Protestant ethic than Catholics, they should show more upward mobility. He found that more white Protestant men than Catholic men rose into the upper middle class or retained that status and that Catholic men were more likely to move into or remain in the lower half of the working class.

Subsequent studies (Greeley 1989) have contradicted Lenski's findings and show no direct relationship between Protestant or Catholic religious beliefs and socioeconomic status. Nevertheless, quantitative research on religion became much more popular

POLICY DEBATE

Should Corporal Punishment of Children Be Allowed?

The concept of corporal punishment is an example of the linkage between religion and other institutions—specifically the family and education—and how religious beliefs have played an important part in shaping cultural practices. Corporal punishment is broadly defined as the infliction of physical pain, loss, or confinement in response to an offense or an occurrence of misbehavior. Typical forms of corporal punishment against children are slapping, spanking, and paddling. Corporal punishment, however, has included other much more abusive practices as well, such as vigorous shaking (often causing concussion), grabbing, dragging, kicking, washing a child's mouth with noxious substances, not allowing a child to use the bathroom, denying a child normal movement, forcing a child to do pushups or run laps, denying adequate free time for recess and lunch, and many others. Corporal punishment usually is discussed primarily in connection with children in schools, but it is also important to consider it in relation to disciplining children at home and in nonparental child-care settings (Clark and Clark 1989; Vockell 1991).

The religious roots of corporal punishment are traceable from ancient Greece, Rome, and Egypt, through medieval Europe, and then early colonial America to the present in America. As was true in the past, religious groups still maintain considerable influence over corporal-punishment legislation. For example, in 1991, legislation in North Carolina banned corporal punishment in public-run child-care centers, but not in church-operated ones. Many religious groups—especially fundamentalist, evangelical, and Pentecostal Protestants—argue that corporal punishment is positively sanctioned in the Bible in the books of Proverbs, Chronicles, Joshua, and Kings in the Old Testament. The key text that is cited in support of corporal punishment is Proverbs 23:14—"Thou shalt beat him with the rod, / And shalt deliver his soul from hell." The more common contemporary expression of this, with which you are probably familiar, is "Spare the rod and spoil the child." The rationale for corporal punishment from the New Testament, although Jesus never urges punishment for children, is derived from the belief that wickedness will be punished in hell, which is taken to imply the need to inflict pain on children in the present to prevent them from evil (Clark and Clark 1989; Silverman 1991). This reasoning prevails in many contemporary fundamentalist child-rearing manuals, some of which offer detailed advice on the discipline ritual, what instruments to use, and where to position children when hitting them (Greven, 1991). The religious basis of corporal punishment has had a strong influence on its acceptance among groups that continue to use it in the United States.

From its inception, American law viewed corporal punishment as an effective and acceptable method of maintaining order both at home and in school. Nevertheless, its morality (or immorality) and long-term effects on children has been a topic long debated by parents, educators, and legislators. In 1867, New Jersey banned corporal punishment in public schools. However, not until more than one hundred years later did another state, Massachusetts, make corporal punishment illegal. In 1977, the United States Supreme Court upheld the constitutionality of corporal punishment in *Ingraham v. Wright*, a case that involved a student whose physical injuries resulted in hospitalization from injuries inflicted by a paddling from school authorities. In *Baker v. Owen*, the Supreme Court ruled that the school has authority over parents in issues involving discipline. These cases upheld corporal punishment as an acceptable means of maintaining discipline in schools, even over a parent's objection to corporal punishment, and the court ruled that the Eighth Amendment—which prohibits cruel and unusual punishment—does not apply to the paddling of children in school (Clark and Clark 1989). Thus, as of 2009, corporal punishment is still legal in twenty-two states. Further, corporal punishment is pervasive around the world. Of the 192 countries that have ratified the United Nations Convention on the Rights of Children, only twenty-four countries have banned corporal punishment (Zolor and Puzia 2010).

While suitable punishment of children is sometimes necessary, justifiable, and effective as a means of maintaining order and for the proper socialization of children, the debate over the use of corporal punishment continues. Besides the religious arguments, there are other important aspects of the debate. In a 1991 article, Edward L. Vockell, professor of education at Purdue University Calumet, discusses some the pros and cons of corporal punishment in education.

One advantage of corporal punishment—because it involves physical pain—is that it is very likely to be perceived by the recipient as unpleasant. Nonphysical forms of punishment, such as being sent to the principal's office or writing an essay on "Why I Should Not Talk in Class," may be thought by the teacher

following Lenski's publication. We now have a profile of American religious beliefs and their relation to social class, race, age, and other factors. One important finding of this research has been that a sizable part of the population has no conventional religious commitment, although they are concerned with ethical and moral beliefs and practices that often have their roots in Judeo-Christian teachings. This movement away from the church is known as "secularization."

to be unpleasant, but may not necessarily be perceived as particularly painful by the child. On the other hand, when a child receives physical punishment (i.e., corporal punishment), the message is unequivocal.

Second, corporal punishment can be administered quickly and can be over with quickly. If a student commits a major offense and receives, for example, three afternoons of detention, the prolonged punishment may affect other interactions between the student and teacher during those three days. As a result, the learning situation may be compromised during that time. Additionally, because the punishment takes up time, the student may not be able to use this time in productive behavior. With corporal punishment, however, the teacher could paddle the student, get it over with, and get back to the business of education more quickly.

Third, corporal punishment has very clear, specific, and obvious consequences. In classrooms where corporal punishment is used, students know exactly what will happen if they misbehave. In settings where corporal punishment is not used as a disciplinary practice, students may not be able to clearly anticipate the consequences for misbehavior; and thus, the teacher may have less control over the class.

The disadvantages of corporal punishment, Vockell suggests, are both theoretical and practical. One theoretical disadvantage is that the punishment is not likely to be logically related to the misbehavior. For example, being paddled is not logically related to smoking in the washroom, talking in class, or failing to turn in homework. As adults, we sometimes engage in similar indiscretions—being late for work, failing to obey the speed limit, inadequately performing our jobs—but we certainly do not expect to be struck or hit violently for doing so. In fact, laws prevent it. In other words, corporal punishment is likely to be an *artificial* form of punishment—a punishment not related directly to the behavior such as paddling someone for not doing a homework assignment—rather than a *natural* form of reinforcement and punishment—punishment directly related to the misbehavior, such as making a student stay after school to complete an assignment. While artificial punishment is sometimes necessary when there are no logical forms of natural punishment available, most theorists feel that natural forms of punishment should be used whenever possible.

A second disadvantage is that it is usually very difficult for the recipient of corporal punishment to behave in a desirable way in order to end the punishment (that is, "time off for good behavior"), whereas for many other forms of punishment, engaging in good behavior is often possible. For example, if a child's television privileges are suspended because he or she fails to complete homework assignments, privileges might be reinstated if the child demonstrates that his or her study habits have changed. If, instead, corporal punishment is used, there is nothing the child can do once the punishment has commenced.

Third, physical punishment affirms the value of physical assault as a means of effecting change and models socially inappropriate behaviors to children. Many studies have clearly shown that children who are spanked more often are more likely to hit other children and to behave aggressively as they grow up. On the other hand, if parents and teachers reason with children and use more natural forms of punishment, children are more likely to learn these behaviors and to use them in their interactions with others.

Fourth, corporal punishment may inflict real injury or may easily escalate into child abuse. This does not mean that corporal punishment is child abuse. Theoretically, corporal punishment is carried out dispassionately, with the goal of correcting a child's behavior. However, corporal punishment can escalate into child abuse when the punishment is not directly related to a specific misbehavior of a child and instead may be employed because the parent or teacher is irritated, frustrated, or angry about past behaviors or about unrelated events.

Fifth, the recipients often perceive corporal punishment as embarrassing and demeaning to their dignity. While this can be an advantage in helping to bring about a change in behavior, it often has the reverse effect. Some children harbor resentment and feel the need to retaliate, thus creating interference with the punisher's future attempts at discipline and instruction.

A final disadvantage of corporal punishment is the practical problem of accidents and lawsuits. A teacher may have the best of intentions and may not be acting abusively. Nevertheless, the child may be hit too hard, may move to block a blow, or something else unexpected may occur that results in serious injury. Aside from the possible physical damage that could occur to the student, lawsuits may also follow. Even in states where corporal punishment is not prohibited, teachers are often prosecuted in such instances.

Secularization

It is widely accepted by social scientists that the dominant trend in modern religion is secularization. **Secularization** means to focus on this world and on worldly things such as science, reason and technology, as distinguished from the church, religious affairs, and faith. It means that problems are solved by humans through their own efforts (the essence of so-called secular humanism), as opposed to unquestioned

A Pentecostal church service in Tucson, Arizona. Pentecostalism involves a practice similar to divine revelation. It is believed that the participants are able to "speak in tongues".

faith in supernatural powers and a focus on the next world or an afterlife. It means a trend toward the declining influence of religion in the lives of people and in the institutions of society. Today, for example, marriages are assumed to be decided between humans, not foreordained by a god. Tragedies such as automobile accidents are explained in terms of human interactions and the laws of science, not as manifestations of divine will.

This secular way of thinking is extremely disturbing to fundamentalists and to right-wing evangelicals. To them, the idea that human beings are in control of their own destiny and that individuals themselves can change the condition of their lives without divine providence or intervention is unimaginable and unbelievable, if not evil and sinful. To emphasize materialism, consumption, and the here and now runs counter to giving up your "sinful ways," trusting in God, and focusing on salvation and the hereafter.

At a Catholic mass in Cameroon, Pope Benedict XVI urged Cameroon's bishops to defend against secularization. Secularization means that problems are solved by humans through their own efforts as opposed to unquestioned faith in supernatural powers.

Stark and Bainbridge (1981) argue that secularization is a major trend but that it is not a new or modern development and does not presage the demise of religion. It is a process that goes on in all societies while countervailing intensification of religion goes on in other parts. The dominant religious organizations are always becoming more *secularized* (worldly) but are supplanted by more vigorous and less worldly religions.

The authors demonstrate that secularization is one of three interrelated processes that constantly occur in all societies. Secularization itself generates two countervailing processes: revival and religious innovation. *Revival* is born out of secularization, as protest groups and sect movement's form to meet the demand for a less worldly religion and to restore vigorous otherworldliness to a conventional faith. *Religious innovation*, also stimulated by secularization, leads to new faiths and new religious traditions. The birth of these new faiths will not be found in the directories of major church listings but will be found in lists of obscure cult movements.

Cults flourish where conventional churches are weakest. Stark and Bainbridge provide evidence that in America, there are very robust *negative* correlations between church membership rates and cult activity rates. The states and cities that have low church membership rates have the highest rates of membership in cults. Centuries ago, Christianity, Judaism, Islam, and Buddhism began as cults that rose to power because of the weaknesses in the dominant religions of their time. Stark and Bainbridge argue that the same process is happening today. Thus, in America, as in most societies, the history of religion is not only a pattern of secularization and decline but also equally one of birth and growth. While the sources of religion are shifting constantly, the amount of religion remains fairly constant.

Researchers from the *Religious Movements Homepage* at the University of Virginia (2000) found that women are more likely than men to describe their outlook as "religious" versus secular. They also found that older Americans are less likely than younger Americans to describe their outlook as religious, and African-Americans are the least likely to describe themselves as secular. Asian Americans are most likely to describe their outlook as secular (*Religious Movements Homepage* at the University of Virginia, http://religiousmovements.lib.virginia.edu/). However, there are reasons that different groups are more likely to become secular than other groups. There is evidence that women are defecting from churches now at a higher rate then men. This is very likely due to changing gender roles in society and the liberation of women from traditional expectations associated with submissive womanhood (Woodhead 2008).

Religiosity and Church Attendance

Religiosity, the level of religious belief and behavior (Grant 2008) is a qualitative factor that is difficult to assess accurately. While very difficult to measure, church attendance is one indication of the importance of religion. According to a 2010 Gallup Poll, 43.1 percent of Americans say they go to religious services weekly or almost weekly, up slightly from 42.1 percent in 2008 (See Table 13-3). Political affiliation, race, age, gender, marital status, education, and geographic location all seem to be related to church attendance. (See Table 13-4) The highest rates of frequent church attendance are found among conservatives (55 percent), Blacks (55 percent), Republicans (55 percent), people over sixty-five years-old (53 percent), Hispanics (52 percent), Southerners (51 percent), married people (48 percent) and women (47 percent). The lowest rates are found among Liberals (27 percent), Asians (31 percent), eighteen to twenty-nine year-olds (35 percent), single people (35 percent), Westerners (37 percent), Easterners (38 percent), Independents (38 percent), and men (39 percent).

Yet church attendance may not be an accurate measure of religiosity because people go to churches, synagogues, temples, or mosques for many reasons: worship God, see friends, enjoy music, meet social expectations, and so on. Public opinion polls consistently indicate that a high percentage of people believe in God (more than 90 percent) and a life after death (about 75 percent) and overwhelmingly want their

TABLE 13-3 CHURCH ATTENDANCE IN THE UNITED STATES

How often do you attend church, synagogue, or mosque?

	% At least once a week	% Almost every week	% About once a month	% Seldom	% Never	Sample size
2010 (Jan - May)	35	8	11	25	20	146,355
2009	35	8	12	25	20	353,849
2008	34	8	12	26	20	311,591

Gallup Daily Tracking

GALLUP

Source: http://www.gallup.com/

Table 13-4 Church Attendance in Selected Groups, 2010

Frequent Church Attendance, January - May 2010
By demograpic group

Conservative	55
Non-Hispanic black	55
Republican	55
65+	53
Black Hispanic	52
South	51
Married	48
Women	47
White Hispanic	46
Midwest	44
College graduate	44
Postgraduate	44
High school or less	44
SAMPLE AVERAGE	43
50 to 64	43
Some college	41
Non-Hispanic white	41
30 to 49	41
Moderate	39
Democrat	39
Men	39
Independent	38
East	38
West	37
Not married	36
18 to29	35
Asian	31
Liberal	27

Percentage saying they attend "at least once a week" or "almost every week"

Gallup Daily Tracking

children to have religious training. The discrepancy between church attendance figures and religious beliefs indicates that factors other than formal religious organizations influence religious thought. Until fairly recently, social scientists have not had a satisfactory way of measuring overall religiosity within societies. Sociologists have used indicators such as attendance at religious services, prayer and meditation, membership in churches and other religious organizations, religious beliefs and attitudes, and the subjective importance of religion. Rather than seeing these as individual indicators, Grant (2008) used them to arrive at an "aggregate religiosity" to measure the overall religiosity of a society. Using this measure, Grant found that there was a sharp rise in religiosity in the United States in the 1950s, a decline beginning in the 1960s, and a slower decline since the 1970s.

The Electronic Church

Through television, many people in the United States "attend church" without ever leaving their homes. Evangelists such as Robert Schuller, Pat Robertson, Jerry Falwell, Oral Roberts, Bob Jones, Jimmy Swaggart, and Jim and Tammy Bakker became national celebrities in the 1980s through this medium. Each of them created a huge financial empire through a variety of marketing techniques.

The notoriety of some of these TV evangelists increased by unusual activities that the press picked up and sensationalized. Oral Roberts announced that God had told him that he would die unless he raised millions of dollars by a certain date. The Bakkers used Praise the Lord (PTL) funds for a Christian theme park, several expensive homes for their personal use, a new Corvette and houseboat, and a luxurious air-conditioned doghouse. Both Jim Bakker and Jimmy Swaggart were caught in indiscrete sexual relationships. Pat Robertson, who "speaks in tongues" and receives prophecies directly from God, ran for President of the United States. Jerry Falwell started the Moral Majority and became actively involved in supporting conservative political candidates and right-wing social causes, before passing away in May 2007. Several, such as Jerry Falwell and Bob Jones, established universities that only accept "born-again" instructors and that serve as bastions of fundamentalist Christian teachings. Some, such as Robert Schuller, who has a congregation of 10,000 at his "Crystal Cathedral" in California as well as international members worldwide, have established worldwide ministries while retaining a direct affiliation with a church or denomination (Reformed Church of America) rather than becoming sect like.

With some exceptions, such as Robert Schuller just mentioned, it might be asked why television religious shows appear to be dominated be right-wing and fundamentalist ministers rather than preachers of mainstream denominations? Although no simple answers are available, some clues may lie in their message and in their organization. The message is simple, clear, precise, and based on a literal interpretation of the Bible. In a pluralistic society with social and moral ambiguities over the role of women, freedom of speech and expression, sexual norms, family planning, abortion and the like, it is comforting to believe that social as well as personal problems can be solved by a doctrinaire return to traditional gender roles and social values and a faith in God. The claim can be made that television is not friendly to intellectual discussions of ambiguous moral issues that are more commonly expressed by seminary graduates and the leadership in more established denominations.

The *organization* is often established around the charismatic quality of a single person (almost always male). These persons select their advisors and boards to back them and to establish an independent media network that is seldom accountable to other organizations or institutions. The leaders understand the value of showmanship and make appeals (often highly emotional) in the name of God to save souls, cleanse an immoral nation, and support their ministry. Unless an organization becomes established and institutionalized to provide continuity of the television program, the ministry is likely to die with the removal or death of the charismatic leader.

In functional terms, the success of the electronic church is explained in terms of what it does for people: that is, its religious functions. Among others, it may provide answers to ultimate questions, reconcile people to hardship, and advocate the return to less complex and more traditional ways. The extent to which it facilitates social integration, creates a community of believers, and provides rituals is questionable, however. It is unlikely that many people kneel for prayer or join hands with others in front of a TV set. On the other hand, the millions of dollars sent to television preachers indicate that they are important to many Americans and fill various needs.

Ecumenism

One response to the current trend toward secularization has been for different denominations to join together in pursuit of common interests. This trend, known as **ecumenism** or the ecumenical movement, calls for worldwide Christian unity. Interdenominational organizations such as the National Council of Churches are attempting to reconcile the beliefs and practices of different religious groups.

Thinking Sociologically

1. Is religion a key factor in maintaining the status quo, a key factor in stimulating social change, both, or neither?
2. What types of variables influence the involvement of religious groups in politics? Do the variables change depending on the sociological theory you are using? Describe and explain.
3. How is secularization related to or caused by changes such as industrialization, urbanization, an increasingly educated population, political conservatism or liberalism, changing roles of women, and so forth?

A New Religious Consciousness

A number of new religious groups have sprung up in the United States over the past few decades. Many of them emphasize the personal religious experience rather than a rational, bureaucratic religious organization. The ideas of many of these new groups, such as the Moral Majority, Children of God, Messianic Jews, and the Christian World Liberation Front, have roots in the Christian tradition. The Reverend Sun Myung Moon's Unification Church (popularly known as "Moonies") is a combination of Protestantism and anticommunism. Others, like Synanon, Erhart Seminars Training (est), Church of

Scientology, and Silva Mind Control, grew out of the "human potential" movement of the 1960s and 1970s. Still others, such as Zen Buddhism, Yoga, and ISKCON (the organization of Hare Krishnas), are rooted in Eastern religions such as Buddhism, Hinduism, and Confucianism. Many of these religious movements demand of their members total conformity to the practices of the group and are generally often rigid in their teachings.

Why have these groups and religious movements arisen? A number of factors may be responsible. Durkheim believed that as societies become more complex and diversified, so do the forms of religious belief and practice. Some see the new religious consciousness as a search for identity and meaning. Some see these movements as a reaction against the militaristic and capitalistic values that are emphasized by contemporary American society. Others contend that the new religions have arisen in response to the climate of moral ambiguity in the United States. The decline of the established churches has undoubtedly been influential as well. In all probability, each of these factors has had an effect.

Religion and Other Institutions

The relationship between the church and other institutions is a complex one. The institutions and the functions they perform are not always easy to differentiate. As was mentioned earlier, Max Weber argued shortly after the turn of the century that capitalism was enhanced by the work ethic of Protestantism. In the 1980s, the entry of television evangelists such as Jerry Falwell and Pat Robertson into the political arena reflected the linkage between religion and politics. Other interinstitutional linkages include the influence of religion on school curricula and prayer, the impact of religious teachings on family size and use of contraceptives or abortion, and the influence of religion on the economy through the ownership or control of many businesses and the endorsement or nonendorsement by religious groups of various products. There is increasing evidence that many evangelical members of the power elite within the United States, especially within politics and business, have strong sense of cohesion because of the salience of their religious beliefs, thus furthering the strength of the evangelical movement (Lindsay 2008).

There is also a strong link between religion and marital status. Those who identify with one of the main religious groups (twenty-two classifications account for 98 percent of the sample) are considerably more likely to be married than those who claim no religion. In particular, individuals in the "no religion" group were far more likely to be either single, never married, or single and living with a partner than any other group. Indeed, the "no religion" group shows the lowest incidence of marriage (just 19 percent) of all twenty-two (identified religious) groups. In sharp contrast, those identifying with the Assemblies of God or Evangelical/Born Again Christians show the highest incidence of marriage, 73 percent and 74 percent, respectively (http://religious movements.lib.virginia.edu/. 2000).

Emile Durkheim noted the key linkage between the sacred and the secular or profane when he stated that anything could be made sacred. Political rituals such as those that accompany the election of a president, family behaviors such as eating dinner together, economic goods such as automobiles, or educational events such as a graduation can all be considered sacred. These interrelationships and religious influences extend beyond the basic institutions. Note, for example, how religious principles have served as the foundation for opposition to war, restrictions on alcohol, or the disciplining of children (note policy debate). In today's society, although the church as a social institution has come under attack, religion and religious values continue to exert a major influence on societies, on all the institutions within them, and on the lives of individuals throughout the world.

Thinking Sociologically

1. How might you define "being religious"? Can you be religious without attending some church or synagogue or participating in some social group of like-minded persons?
2. Using theories and facts about religious groups and systems, discuss how and why religious groups become involved in political activities, both domestically and internationally. Provide specific examples of the types of policies with which religious groups would be concerned.

CHAPTER REVIEW

Wrapping it up

Summary

Check out our website www.bvtstudents.com for free chapter-by-chapter flashcards, summaries, and self-quizzes.

1. A religion is a ritualized system of beliefs and practices related to things defined as sacred by an organized community of believers.

2. People have believed in supernatural powers throughout history. Some societies have believed that supernatural powers inhabit objects such as rocks and trees. This is known as animism. Others have assumed that supernatural powers reside in a shaman, who could be called upon to protect the group or to bring success. A third form of belief is totemism, in which a plant or animal is thought to be ancestrally related to a person or tribe.

3. Religions are sometimes differentiated by the number of gods that adherents worship. Monotheistic religions believe in one god, and polytheistic religions believe in a number of gods.

4. Religion may take a variety of forms. Mysticism is based on the belief in powers that are mysterious, secret, and hidden from human understanding. Churches are institutional organizations with formal bureaucratic structures; they are sometimes differentiated into ecclesia, which are official state religions, and denominations, which are independent of the state.

5. Sects are small separatist groups that follow rigid doctrines and emphasize fundamentalist teachings. Cults are loosely organized religious organizations whose members adopt a new, unique, and unusual lifestyle. Rather than attempting to change society, cults generally focus on the spiritual lives of the individual participants.

6. There are a number of theories about religion. The functionalist perspective examines what religion does for society. Religion is generally perceived as fulfilling social functions, such as preserving and solidifying society, creating a community of believers, cultivating social change, and providing a means of social control. It also fulfills personal functions such as answering ultimate questions, providing rites of passage, and reconciling people to hardship.

7. The conflict perspective views religion as a tool used by the dominant individuals and groups to justify their position and to keep the less privileged in subordinate positions.

8. More than 5 billion people are believed to be identified with or have an affiliation with one of the world's major religions. About 2 billion are Christians, who profess faith in the teachings of Jesus Christ. Another billion believe in Islam and surrender their wills to Allah, following the teachings of the prophet Muhammad.

9. Excluding the nonreligious, the third largest religious group is the followers of Hinduism, which is closely linked to the traditional caste system of India. Hindus have a vast array of religious practices and beliefs.

10. Followers of Buddhism believe that they can avoid human suffering by following an eightfold path of appropriate behavior. Confucianism, based on the life and teachings of Confucius, is both a philosophy and a religion and is closely linked to Taoism and Shintoism, as well as to Buddhism.

11. The United States has no state church, and a wide variety of religious groups exist in this country. There are two contrasting trends in contemporary religious practice. One type of group emphasizes formal religious organization, whereas the other emphasizes an informal, personalized, emotional belief system. Throughout American history, religious life has been influenced by folk religions, sects, Pentecostal groups, and groups that believe in millennialism, divine revelation, and faith healing.

12. Currently, religion is being studied in new ways as a result of developments in qualitative and quantitative research techniques and computer technology. The use of these and other techniques has revealed a trend toward secularization, which is counter intuitively believed to contribute to the emergence of cult activities.

13. U.S. church attendance has leveled off at an estimated 40 percent, but a large majority of the population still professes a belief in God and in life after death.

14. Televised religious programs reach millions of persons in their homes. Along with these developments have come increased ecumenicalism and a new religious consciousness. This new consciousness is professed by many new religious sects and movements, some derived from the Christian tradition, others from the human potential movement and Eastern religions.

15. Several explanations for the creation of these groups have been offered. It has been suggested that they have arisen in response to our diverse culture, search for identity, and need for precise, simplistic answers, or as a protest against secularization and materialism. The institution of religion in America and around the world is closely linked with the family, as well as with economic, political, and educationalinstitutions. These institutions both influence religious beliefs and practices and, in turn, are influenced by religion.

Key Terms

animism The religious belief that spirits inhabit virtually everything in nature and control all aspects of life and destiny

Buddhism One of the world's principal religions; adherents follow the teachings of Buddha, the enlightened one, who preached a doctrine of "Four Noble Truths"

Christianity One of the principal religions of the world, followers of which profess faith in the teachings of Jesus Christ

church An institutionalized organization of people who share common religious beliefs

Confucianism One of the world's principal religions, found mainly in China, adherents of which follow the teachings of Confucius

cults Extreme forms of sects that call for a totally new and unique lifestyle, often under the direction of a charismatic leader

denominations Well-established and highly institutionalized churches

ecclesia An official state religion that includes all or most members of society

ecumenism The trend for different denominations to join together in pursuit of common interests in a spirit of worldwide Christian unity

fundamentalism The belief that the Bible is the divine word of God and that all statements in it are to be taken literally, word for word

Hinduism One of the world's principal polytheistic religions, with no religious hierarchy but a close involvement with society and the cosmic order; it is practiced mainly in India and Pakistan

Islam One of the world's principal religions, followers

of which adhere to the teachings of the Koran and of Muhammad, a prophet

Judaism The oldest religion in the Western world and the first to teach monotheism; today, the Jews are both an ethnic community and a religious group

millennialism The belief prevalent among certain sects that there will be a dramatic transformation of life on earth and that Christ will rule the world for a thousand years of prosperity and happiness

monotheism The belief in one god

mysticism The belief that spiritual or divine truths come to us through intuition and meditation, not through the use of reason or via the ordinary range of human experience and senses

polytheism The belief in and worship of more than one god

priests Religious leaders who owe their authority to the power of their office

profane That which belongs to the realm of the everyday world; anything considered mundane and unspiritual

prophets Religious leaders who have authority on the basis of their charismatic qualities

religion An organized community of believers who hold certain things sacred and follow a set of beliefs, ceremonies, or special behaviors

sacred Involving objects and ideas that are treated with reverence and awe

sects Religious groups that have broken away from a parent church, follow rigid doctrines and fundamentalist teachings, and emphasize "otherworldly" rewards, rejecting or deemphasizing contemporary society

secularization The process through which beliefs concerning the supernatural and religious institutions lose social influence

shamanism The religious belief that certain persons (shamans) have special charm, skill, or knowledge in influencing spirits

totemism The worship of plants, animals, and other natural objects as gods and ancestors

Discussion Questions

1. Discuss some ways in which religion affects our identity and our behavior.
2. How do you think life in America would be different if our culture was based on polytheism rather than monotheism?
3. How would you explain why some people are attracted to churches, others to sects, some to cults, and still others to no religious groups at all?
4. Regardless of an American's specific religious beliefs, we are all affected by the Protestant ethic. Explain how Protestantism has helped to shape our cultural beliefs and values, and how it may have affected you.
5. Compare the functionalist and conflict approaches to religion, and discuss how these views are different from or similar to views that you may have been socialized to believe about religion.
6. Discuss some ways in which religion effects the outcomes of peace, gender roles, politics, and so forth in the Middle East, Ireland, or southern U.S. states, for example.
7. Select one of the religions discussed in the text other than your own (if you do not have a religion, then select any one). Explore how your involvement in family and in political, economic, and educational institutions might be different if you were a member of that religion.
8. Make a list of selected trends in religion. How would you explain them? How can they be changed?
9. Explain the appeal of TV preachers or evangelists. What accounts for their appeal, popularity, fund-raising success, and longevity?
10. Discuss the linkage between religion and life in other institutions, such as the family or school.

Pop Quiz

1. Which of the following is NOT one of the elements Durkheim identified as being common to all religions?

   a. system of beliefs
   b. set of rituals
   c. sacred things
   d. church buildings

2. People in certain societies who are believed to have special knowledge in and influencing spirits are called ________.

   a. priests
   b. shamans
   c. totems
   d. witch doctors

3. The belief and worship of more than one god is known as ________.

   a. monotheism
   b. animism
   c. polygyny
   d. polytheism

4. The largest religious denomination in the United States is ______.

   a. Southern Baptists
   b. Roman Catholics
   c. Lutherans
   d. Mormons

5. Official state religions are referred to as ______.

   a. central churches
   b. ecclesia
   c. denominations
   d. sects

6. Manifest functions of religion include ________.

   a. preserving and solidifying society
   b. reinforcing social norms
   c. answering ultimate questions
   d. all of the above

7. The oldest religion in the Western world is ________.

   a. Judaism
   b. Christianity
   c. Catholicism
   d. Confucianism
   e. Islam

8. The religion that stresses submission to the will of Allah is ________.

   a. Judaism
   b. Hinduis
   c. Confucianism
   d. Islam

9. What religion is usually practiced along with a native religion?

   a. Buddhism
   b. Islam
   c. Judaism
   d. Christianity

10. In the United States, the religious belief that a dramatic transformation of the world will occur and that Christ will rule the world is called ________.

    a. ecumenism
    b. transcendentalism
    c. transformation
    d. millennialism

11. Sacredness is a property inherent in an object. T/F

12. Fundamentalists believes in strict interpretation of the Bible. T/F

13. Sects may in time become denominations. T/F

14. Members of the Reverend Sun Myung Moon's Unification Church are popularly known as "Moonies." T/F

15. Zen Buddhism, Yoga, and Iskcon are rooted in Eastern religions. T/F

1. D	6. D	11. F
2. B	7. A	12. T
3. D	8. D	13. T
4. B	9. A	14. T
5. B	10. D	15. T

CHAPTER 14

Educational Groups and Systems

SCHOOL BULLYING

Bullying, or peer-victimization, has become an increasing problem in schools. Bullying is a specific form of aggression among students that is persistent and results from an imbalance in power between the bully and the victim (Olweus 1993, in Bender and Losel 2011). Bullying in schools is not a new phenomenon and can be found all throughout history (Billiterri 2010). Hyojin Koo (2007 in Billiterri), a Korean scholar who studied the history of bullying, found that the meaning of what bullying includes and attitudes about it have changed over time. In the eighteenth to twentieth centuries, bullying generally included physical or verbal harassment related to a death, isolation, or extortion in school children. Koo found that during the 1950s and 60s, bullying evolved from robbing, stealing, and acting rowdy to persistent inattentiveness and underhandedness. Since the 1980s, the meaning of bullying has come to include direct verbal taunting and social exclusion. This includes cyber-bullying as well as face-to-face.

Dan Olweus, creator of the Olweus Bullying Prevention Program, says, "A person is bullied when he or she is exposed, repeatedly and over time, to negative actions on the part of one or more other persons, and he or she has difficulty defending himself or herself." (www.olweus.org) Olweus includes a variety of concerns:

1. Verbal bullying including derogatory comments and bad names
2. Bullying through social exclusion or isolation
3. Physical bullying such as hitting, kicking, shoving, and spitting
4. Bullying through lies and false rumors
5. Having money or other things taken or damaged by students who bully
6. Being threatened or being forced to do things by students who bully
7. Racial bullying
8. Sexual bullying
9. Cyber bullying (via cell phone or Internet)

Bullying in schools is widespread in the United States. In the past year, 50 percent of high school students admitted that they had bullied someone; and 47 percent said that they had been bullied, teased, or taunted in a way that had upset them. Nearly 40 percent of bullied girls and 46 percent of bullied boys in grades three through twelve have been bullied for a year or longer (Billiterri 2010). Research has found that bullying has no national borders and is found in many countries throughout the world (Borntrager, et al., 2009).

The victims of bullying can suffer serious consequences including depression, low self-esteem, health problems, poor

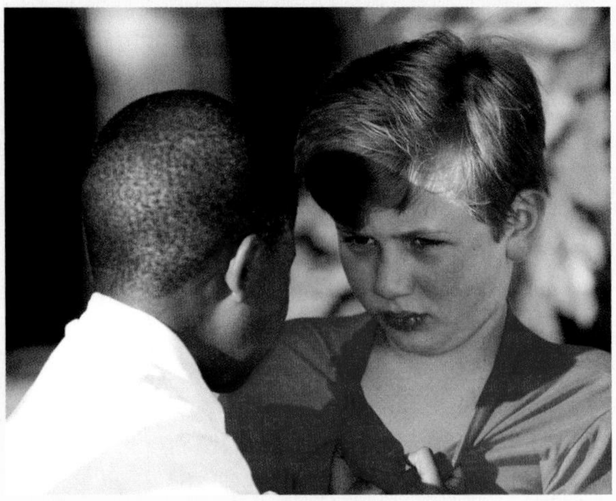

Bullying in schools is widespread in the United States.

grades, and suicidal thoughts. Some of the more catastrophic results have been seen in the news in recent years. Hope Witsell, a thirteen-year-old Florida student, hanged herself in her bedroom after being taunted by classmates after someone had circulated a nude photo she had sent to her boyfriend. Phoebe Prince, a fifteen-year-old, hanged herself after alleged bullying occurred at her Massachusetts high school. Tyler Clementi, eighteen, committed suicide by jumping off the George Washington Bridge after classmates allegedly used a webcam to transmit images of him being involved in a gay relationship. While these are some of the most famous recent cases, the effects of bullying are widespread.

Bullying not only has negative consequences for its victims but for the perpetrators as well. Research has found that bullying at school is often associated with delinquency, violence and other anti-social behavior in adulthood (Bender and Losel 2011).

At least forty-three states and the District of Columbia have laws to address bullying, including six states that address cyber-bullying and thirty that include electronic harassment. However, the creation of the laws is controversial because some feel that they may infringe on students' free speech rights.

The topic of bullying is important to sociology because it is an example of what sociologists would call a dysfunction (a negative latent function) of education. When looking at educational systems, it is important to consider not only its manifest (intended) functions but also the other functions both positive and negative that result from the ways in which the institution of education exists and develops with societies.

Children in the United States are required to go to school. They sometimes begin at age two or three, long before the required age of six or seven, and often stay in school long past age sixteen, when they could legally drop out. Thus, education dominates the lives of children, and it also plays an important role in adult life, as adult students, parents, taxpayers, school employees, government officials, and voters participate in the school system. The high school graduation rate declined in the latter part of the twentieth century but has improved since then. The national graduation rate increased from 72 percent in 2001 to 75 percent in 2008, although there is great deal of variation from state to state and between ethnic and racial groups (Dillon 2010) For example, during that same period, graduation rates declined noticeably in Arizona, Nevada, and Utah, but increased substantially in New York and Tennessee with two states, Vermont and Wisconsin, reaching a graduation rate of almost 90 percent. In 2008, eight states had graduation rates below 70 percent. During that same time, the graduation rate was 81 percent of White students, 64 percent of Hispanic students and 62 percent of Black students (Rotherham 2010).

At the same time, education in the United States produces high school graduates who are not prepared for college. ACT (American College Testing) has been collecting and reporting data on students' academic readiness for college since 1959 (ACT 2010). ACT has benchmarks in English, reading, math and science to assess college readiness. In 2010, 28 percent of graduating high school students met none of the benchmarks, 15 percent met one benchmark, 17 percent met two benchmarks, 15 percent met three benchmarks, and 24 percent met all four benchmarks. (See Figures 14-1, 14-2 and 14-3.) Less than one in four students were academically ready for college coursework in all four subject areas.

Why is education so important? We all know some of the reasons we believe in the value of education. We learn science, the arts, and skills for employment; and we learn to make informed judgments about our leisure activities, our political involvement, and our everyday lives.

Is this all that we get from education? What else does it accomplish for society? What part does our education system play in creating a literate population and in selecting people for occupations that match their talents? What part does it play in maintaining the stratification system and in justifying the unequal distribution of wealth in society? What part does education play in shaping socially acceptable behavior and curtailing inappropriate behavior, such as bullying? How does it affect other parts of our lives such as our identity and self-esteem? Much of the debate about whether schools are doing the job they are supposed to do is really a debate about the proper function of schools. The goal of this chapter is to help you understand how education functions in society today.

STRUCTURAL FUNCTIONAL THEORY OF EDUCATION

Structural functional theory recognizes the family as an important agency of socialization. It is in the family that the child learns the culture's values, norms, and language—how to be a social person. By the age of five or six years, the child has developed a unique social personality; and in a properly functioning family, the child is socialized to adjust to the routines and disciplines of the school system. How does education in the schools differ from education in the home?

The Manifest Functions of Education

The *manifest*, or intended, function of the educational system, according to structural functionalists, is to supplement family socialization. The schools use experts (teachers) to teach children the knowledge, skills, and values necessary to function in the world outside the family (Parsons 1959).

The most obvious teaching in school is the teaching of *skills*. Students today are expected to learn to

FIGURE 14-1 COLLEGE READINESS BENCHMARKS BY SUBJECT

Sixty-six percent of all ACT-tested high school graduates met the English College Readiness Benchmark in 2010. Just under 1 in 4 (24%) met all four College Readiness Benchmarks.

In 2010, 52% of graduates met the Reading Benchmark, while 43% met the Mathematics Benchmark. Over 1 in 4 (29%) met the College Readiness Benchmark in Science.

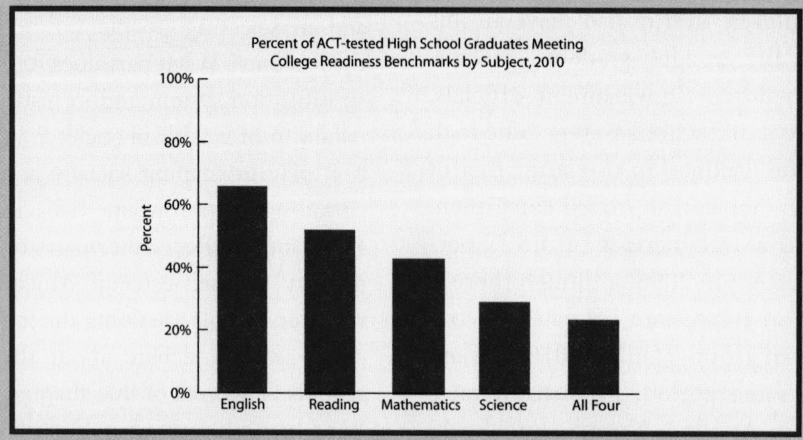

Source: The Condition of College and Career Readiness, 2010 ACT (www.act.org)

FIGURE 14-2 NUMBER OF COLLEGE READINESS BENCHMARKS ATTAINED

About 71% of all ACT-tested 2010 high school graduates met at least one of the four College Readiness Benchmarks in English, Mathematics, Reading, or Science.

Approximately 28% of all graduates met no College Readiness Benchmarks, while 47% met between 1 and 3 Benchmarks. Twenty-four percent of all 2010 ACT-tested high school graduates met all four College Readiness Benchmarks, meaning that less than 1 in 4 were academically ready for college coursework in all four subject areas.

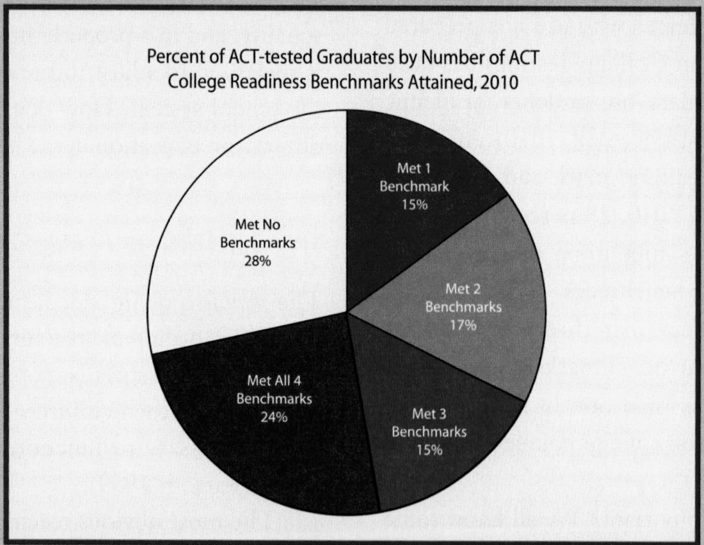

Graph reads: In 2010, 24% of ACT-tested high school graduates met all four College Readiness Benchmarks, 15% met 3 Benchmarks, 17% met 2 Benchmarks, 15% met 1 Benchmark, and 28% met none of the Benchmarks.

Note: Percentages may not sum to 100% due to rounding.

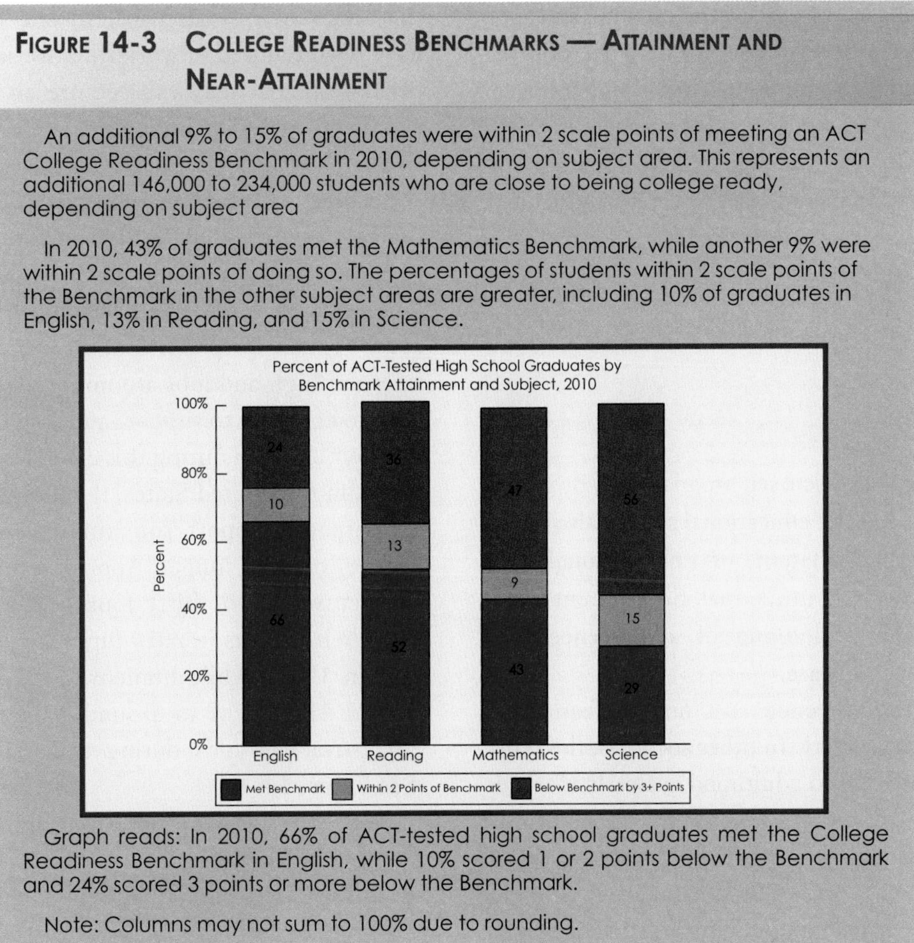
FIGURE 14-3 COLLEGE READINESS BENCHMARKS — ATTAINMENT AND NEAR-ATTAINMENT
An additional 9% to 15% of graduates were within 2 scale points of meeting an ACT College Readiness Benchmark in 2010, depending on subject area. This represents an additional 146,000 to 234,000 students who are close to being college ready, depending on subject area
In 2010, 43% of graduates met the Mathematics Benchmark, while another 9% were within 2 scale points of doing so. The percentages of students within 2 scale points of the Benchmark in the other subject areas are greater, including 10% of graduates in English, 13% in Reading, and 15% in Science.
Percent of ACT-Tested High School Graduates by Benchmark Attainment and Subject, 2010
100%
80%
60%
40%
20%
0%
Percent
24
10
66
36
13
52
47
9
43
56
15
29
English
Reading
Mathematics
Science
Met Benchmark
Within 2 Points of Benchmark
Below Benchmark by 3+ Points
Graph reads: In 2010, 66% of ACT-tested high school graduates met the College Readiness Benchmark in English, while 10% scored 1 or 2 points below the Benchmark and 24% scored 3 points or more below the Benchmark.
Note: Columns may not sum to 100% due to rounding.

read, write, and do arithmetic; specially trained experts teach these skills. Schools also teach students *knowledge* about the larger world through such courses as history, geography, and science. In addition, students learn the *values* of the larger society, including those that pertain to large organizations. They learn to tell time and to be punctual, to cooperate with others to achieve group goals, and to obey the rules necessary for a smooth-running organization.

Another function of education is to select and develop, through evaluation and testing, those young people who have especially useful talents so that each individual will be as productive as his or her abilities permit. Schools give I.Q. tests to determine students' capabilities, and they give grades and achievement tests to find out how much students have learned. They also give psychological tests to help determine which occupations suit the students so that they can then guide them into vocational lines appropriate to their abilities. Some students are guided into vocational courses and the work force; others go to academic high schools and then into two- or four-year colleges. A few of the most talented (or privileged) go to elite colleges and graduate schools and then on to the professions.

A third function of the education system is to transmit new behaviors, skills, ideas, discoveries, and inventions resulting from research. Today, for example, schools teach typing and place less emphasis on penmanship. In some school systems, elementary school students are taught to use a computer terminal before they have mastered their multiplication tables.

The creation of new knowledge is another function of education. Our medical technology is one outstanding example of the knowledge developed in universities. Attempts have also been made to use the educational system to decrease poverty. Education develops the skills necessary to earn income, and special programs have been devised to help the poor to develop these skills. Some high schools and colleges, for example, offer students training in specific vocational skills, such as car repair, computer programming, or restaurant management. Early educational programs such as Head Start are designed to teach disadvantaged children the skills they need to keep up with their peers.

The Latent Functions of Education

The functions so far discussed are manifest, or intentional functions, but the educational system also operates in ways that are latent, or unintentional; and these functions are also influential. Some latent functions include the prolonging of adolescence, age segregation, and child care.

Prolonged adolescence is a unique feature of modern industrial society. In other societies, the transition from childhood to adulthood is clearly marked. The Kpelle of Liberia in West Africa, for example, marks the passage of boy into manhood by a circumcision ritual. After this ceremony, the young man is regarded as having the same responsibilities as the other men of his tribe. In our society, children have been relieved of work roles for increasingly long periods so that they can acquire an education. The age of mandatory school attendance was raised from twelve to fourteen and then to sixteen years, so students today have to remain in school for a longer time than they once did. Another factor that has increased the number of years they spend in school is that many jobs require a high school or college diploma. Students remain in school longer when unemployment rates are high and jobs are not available; and parents have to continue to support and assume responsibility for their children during this extended education. As a result, in the United States, the period of dependency on parental support sometimes continues for two decades or even longer. Approximately 13.5 percent of twenty-five to thirty-four year-olds were living with their parents in 2010 (up from around 10.7 percent in 1983), while homeownership declined from around 41 percent to around 39 percent for under thirty-five year-olds during that same time period (See Figure 14-4).

Age segregation is the separation of some age groups from the larger population. Children in schools spend their time with children of the same age—their peers. The peer group is an important agency of

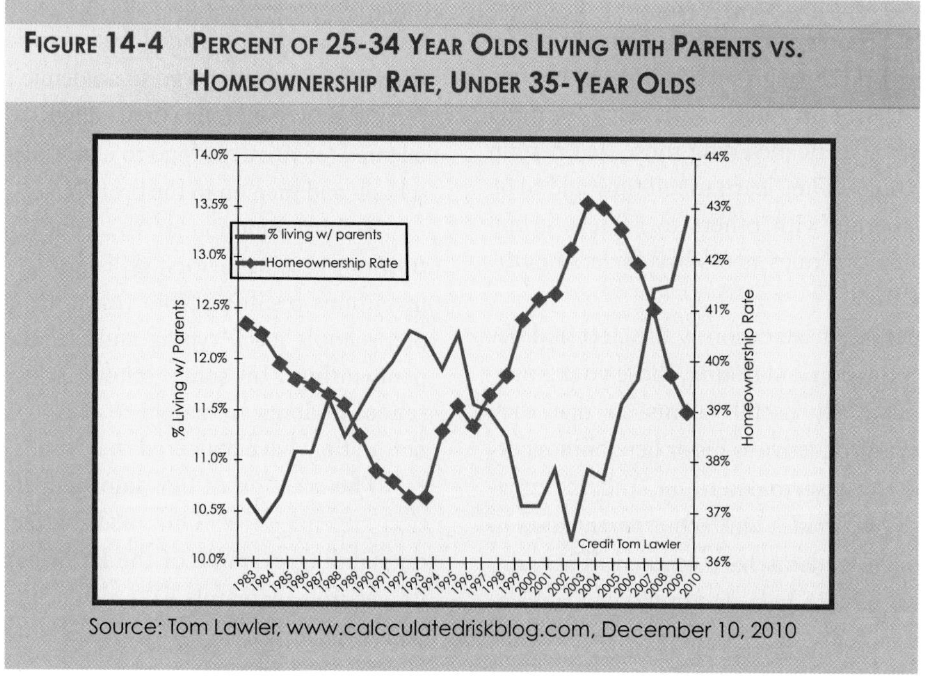

FIGURE 14-4 PERCENT OF 25-34 YEAR OLDS LIVING WITH PARENTS VS. HOMEOWNERSHIP RATE, UNDER 35-YEAR OLDS

Source: Tom Lawler, www.calcculatedriskblog.com, December 10, 2010

Children in schools are segregated according to age so that they may socialize with their peers.

socialization. Peer groups sometimes develop into distinct subcultures, whose members dress alike, listen to the same music, eat the same foods, wear similar hairstyles and makeup, and develop code words and slang—a language of their own. One such age-segregated subculture evolved in the late 1960s. During that decade, adolescents and college students were often in conflict with families, schools, and businesses. Fathers and sons stopped speaking over the length of the sons' hair, and students were expelled from schools and colleges and denied jobs because they wore long hair and blue jeans. The plethora of bare-chested young men and barefooted youths prompted signs to appear on storefronts, announcing "Shirts and shoes required." Students in the late 1960s learned values of equality and individual worth in school but found that the larger society did not reflect these values.

Our education system has also developed other latent functions, such as child care. This function has become increasingly important in American society because in many families, both parents must work simply to make ends meet. Although the hours that children are in school—9 to 3—are often not convenient for working parents, they could not even consider working if their children were not in school. Some school systems are so attuned to their supervisory, child-care function that they offer after-school play groups—at a nominal fee—to take care of children until a parent gets off work and can take the child home.

In sum, structural functionalists believe that the educational system fulfills both manifest and latent functions. It reinforces the socialization process that started with the family, prepares children for work in a complex industrial society, and guides them into the occupations most appropriate to their abilities and to society's needs. Some latent functions of education include the segregation of age groups, the extension of adolescence, and supervisory child care.

APPLYING THE FUNCTIONS OF EDUCATION

Understanding the functions of education is important for teachers, counselors, school administrators, parents, students, and employers. If teachers, for example, concentrate their efforts exclusively on providing specific academic skills to students, the schools may fail to teach values and norms such as honesty, punctuality, respect, trust, civic responsibility, competition, and cooperation. As a result, undue pressure on students by parents and counselors to succeed academically might turn some students into scholars who lack competence in social skills, and academically poor students might become alienated from the entire educational process. By no means are we suggesting that high academic achievement should not be emphasized. However, it may not be the only measure of a successful education for every student.

Understanding the many functions of education is especially important for college students. One of the most difficult decisions you and other students must make early in your college career is your choice of a major. Most often, students lose sight of the many functions of education and focus exclusively—understandably so—on the types of jobs that are available to a graduate with a particular major. It is true that for some career fields, such as accounting, computer programming, architecture, or engineering, students must acquire specific career-related skills and knowledge during their college careers. For the most part, however, the specific occupational skills that people need to do their jobs are learned in some form of on-the-job training or in graduate or other professional

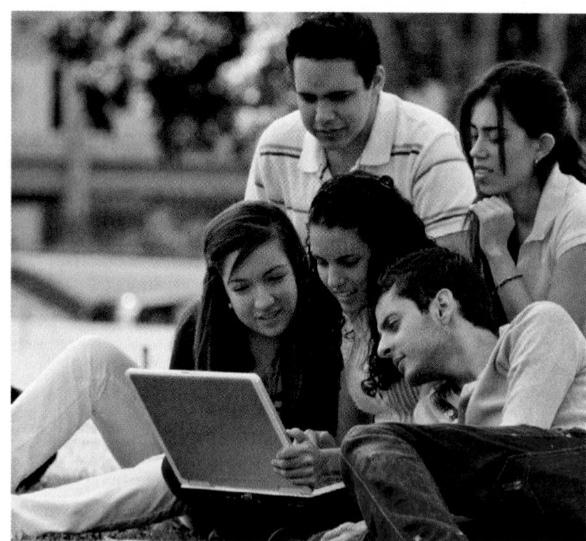
It is important for college students to understand the many functions of education.

schools. Therefore, unless you are pursuing one of the fields that require a specific major—especially in a liberal arts college—you might do just as well to select a major that interests you. Unfortunately, many parents and students do not understand the functions of a college education. The common question asked by parents is, what kind of a job can you get with a major in English (sociology, history, political science, biology, psychology, and so forth)? By mistakenly believing that the sole function of college is to learn specific job skills, students may be pressured to select majors in which they have little interest. However, if you (and just as important, your parents) understand that the functions of a college education include learning social and cultural norms as well as the development of basic communicative, critical thinking, and interpersonal skills, you might select a major that better suits your needs and desires.

College students and their parents are not the only ones who misunderstand the various functions of a college education. Personnel in college placement offices and employers who are hiring college graduates often make similar mistakes in associating careers only with particular major fields. Business majors will not necessarily be better as sales representatives, sociology majors will not necessarily be better as city planners, and English majors will not necessarily be better as journalists. By not understanding the many ways a college education serves a student, college graduates may be channeled into careers for which they are not particularly suited and not considered for jobs in which they might excel.

CONFLICT THEORY OF EDUCATION

Conflict theorists might argue that educational systems help sustain inequalities between the haves and have–nots in a society. Thus, the school system, through a **hidden curriculum**, teaches values and norms that are necessary to maintain the stratification system in society. The educational system is also used to justify giving higher-status jobs to the children of elites and lower-status jobs to children of the poor.

The Hidden Curriculum

Schools require students to learn, albeit subtly, how to behave appropriately for their position in society. This learning is not a part of the stated curriculum—the acknowledged subjects—such as reading, writing, or arithmetic. It is a part of a hidden curriculum, in which students learn such things as obedience, competition, and patriotism. No one ever announces that these qualities are being taught. Nevertheless, if students are to be educated for a job, they must learn to obey rules, to do whatever a superior orders them to do, to work as hard as they can—or at least harder than their coworkers—and to be loyal to the superior, the organization, and the nation in which they work. Both the values and the norms of the elite are a part of the hidden curriculum.

The Teaching of Values

Conflict theorists believe that schools teach children the values of the group in power. Children are taught patriotism by saying the "Pledge of Allegiance" and by studying the history and geography of the United States and of their own states and communities. They learn

Children learn patriotism by reciting the "Pledge of Allegiance".

that the United States is a great country founded by prominent leaders who believed in freedom for all. Students learn about the democratic system of government, the fairness of representation, and the importance of the vote. They are taught to value the capitalist system, in which everyone has the right to accumulate as much private property as possible and to pass it on to their children.

The importance of teaching values can be appreciated by looking at the conflicts that sometimes arise in schools. Teachers may be fired if they teach high school students the advantages of socialism or the disadvantages of capitalism. The topics omitted from school curricula also shed light on the teaching of values. Students are seldom instructed on the family systems or sexual practices of people in other cultures. They are rarely taught about great philosophers who have criticized the United States' political or economic systems, nor are they generally made aware of the people who have suffered under these systems. Students who reach a college sociology course that attempts to analyze both strengths and weaknesses of social systems are often shocked by what they learn.

The Learning of Norms

According to conflict theorists, students learn to conform to the standards of behavior of those in power through the educational process. For example, students are told when to stand in line, when to take turns, when to talk, when to be quiet, when to read, when to listen, when to hang up their coats—the list goes on and on. Students are not taught when to complain, when their rights are being infringed upon, when their time is being wasted, or when to use their freedom of speech. Rules are an important part of the complex organization of a school, and acceptance of certain rules is vital to the maintenance of the social order.

Students are also expected to compete with other students in school. They are taught that they must do better than others to receive attention, good grades, and privileges. Those who do not compete, who pursue the activities they enjoy, may fail, be separated from their peer group, and be labeled as slow, hyperactive, disabled, or otherwise deviant. In short, they are punished.

The competition, however, is unfair because it is based on the norms of the middle class, not those of working-class ethnics or inner-city blacks. Some ethnic groups, for example, find it embarrassing to compete scholastically, to display that they know more than someone else, and do not enter into the competition.

Most teachers come from the middle class and teach students their own values and norms. They tend to teach middle-class literature rather than the literature that might be more germane to their students. When stories about middle-class children in the suburbs with a house, a lawn, a pet dog, and a car are used to teach reading to five-year-old inner-city children who have never had houses to live in, lawns to play on, pet dogs, or cars to ride in, the meaning of the story is as incomprehensible as if the story were written in a foreign language.

Credentialism

Conflict theorists argue that the credentials, diplomas, and degrees given by schools represent learning that is not essential to doing most jobs (Collins 1979). Nevertheless, some jobs afford wealth and prestige to those who hold these credentials. Because such jobs are scarce and so many people want them and compete for them, those who control these jobs can require qualifications of their applicants that have little to do with the skills needed for the job. Instead, the qualifications can serve to place upper-class persons in higher-status or elite jobs, middle-class people in middle-class jobs, working-class people in blue-collar or lower-paying service jobs, and the poor in the lowest-status, lowest-paying jobs society has to offer.

Credentialism is the practice of requiring degrees for jobs whether or not the degrees actually teach skills necessary to accomplish the jobs. Everyone—from assembly-line workers to physicians—learns much more than is necessary to do his or her work. Physicians, for example, must complete four years of college, four years of medical school, and a one-year internship to become general practitioners. Those who want to specialize need an additional three or more years of training. Communist societies such as China and Cuba successfully train people in a much shorter time to take care of most of the health needs of the society. The system in the United States perpetuates the prestige of physicians by demanding credentials that can be obtained only by those who have the time and money to enter this high-prestige profession. In addition, physicians come to form their own subculture of shared values and beliefs during their years of training.

Collins (1979) also argues that the jobs requiring a great deal of education do not necessarily require the skills people learn in school, but the jobs do require the cultural norms learned in school. When college-educated people enter management positions, the elite can rest assured that the managers will make decisions consistent with the cultural norms.

In sum, conflict theorists believe that the group in power, to legitimate their position, runs the educational system. They teach values and norms useful in maintaining their position, use an unfair competitive system to legitimate upper-middle-class success, and insist on certification of skills beyond those necessary to do a job. The upper-middle class has the competitive advantage, but everyone learns the values and norms that maintain the system.

HISTORICAL PERSPECTIVES ON EDUCATION

When sociologists study education, they ask whether it functions to teach a body of knowledge to students, to select the students most capable to perform work in society, or to generate new knowledge. They also ask whether education reflects the conflicts in society by maintaining the stratification system. When we look at historical evidence to analyze how the system functions, we find that from the beginning, education was focused on serving a select group of powerful higher-status persons and was related to occupational training.

Occupational Training

The Puritans, who considered education important, founded Harvard College in Massachusetts in 1636, to educate ministers. Initially, only male students between the ages of twelve and twenty were accepted. The subject matter was morals and ethics, and learning was accomplished through rote memorization. William and Mary (1693), Yale (1701), and Princeton (1746) were founded in quick succession and for the same purpose as Harvard. Founded in 1785 as a "seminary of learning", the University of Georgia is the oldest public university in the United States.

The University of Virginia, founded by Thomas Jefferson in 1819, had a somewhat broader goal than many earlier universities. Aware of the need to train national leaders, Jefferson wanted to form an institution to educate a "natural aristocracy" in a wide range of subjects, including modern languages, science, and mathematics. This curriculum was widely adopted later in the century (Seely 1970).

After about 1850, emphasis on occupational training increased and reached a broader segment of the population. The federal government began to encourage states to begin colleges that would teach agriculture and mechanics (A&M schools). They were provided with *land grants* (i.e., gifts of land) to build the colleges. These land-grant colleges developed into today's public state universities.

During the same period, universities such as Johns Hopkins (1876), which emphasized a scientific curriculum, were founded. Johns Hopkins was also one of the first to systematically support advanced research and the publishing of research findings. Prior to the founding of schools with advanced scientific programs, professions such as medicine, law, and dentistry were learned through the apprenticeship system or were practiced without formal education. Once scientific programs were developed, professionals were required to go to school to be accepted into the profession.

Data show that there are two traits that immigrant children possess: they work hard to achieve and they learn to speak English. Studies also show that they have higher grades and lower dropout rates than native-born American children.

Compulsory public education is public-funded education that is mandatory for all children until a certain age. It developed during the eighteenth and nineteenth centuries, to educate immigrants. The immigrant children who attended public schools learned English and were assimilated into American society. Some then became ashamed of their parents, who often did not learn the new culture (Novak 1972).

More current data show that learning to speak English and working hard to achieve are two traits of immigrant children. Statistics show that children of immigrants are adapting rapidly, surpassing their parents, and utilizing the opportunities that the United States has to offer. Studies also indicate that immigrant children prefer English to the native languages of their parents and that speaking education is linked to their achieving success. Not surprisingly then, studies show that millions of immigrant children have higher grades and sharply lower dropout rates than native-born American children—about one-third the rate. They also do far more homework compared to other children their age—spending an average of two hours per day, in contrast to the national average of about thirty minutes—reflecting their belief that hard work and accomplishment can triumph over any prejudice they've experienced (Immigration Policy Report, 2001). The Public Policy Institute of California found that immigrants continue to make educational gains. In 1970, 17 percent of recently arrived immigrants ages twenty-five to sixty-four had graduated from college, and 33 percent had middle school education or less. In 2009, 35 percent of recently arrived immigrants had college degrees and the percentage of those with middle school education or less dropped to 20 percent (Johnson 2011).

Public schooling met with resistance from a variety of groups. Some religious leaders believed that education should include training in morals and ethics. Catholic religious leaders were afraid that public education would be Protestant education. Landowners did not want to pay taxes for other people's education because they felt that this was socialism. Farmers did not want to lose their sons' labor to the schoolroom, even though concessions were made by giving students summers off to work on the farm. In spite of the objections of these groups, however, local educational systems were developed and run by local leaders. This reflected the strong commitment to local governance in the United States.

Beliefs About Children

The goals and structure of an education system both shape and are shaped by the society's views of the nature and role of children. Are children good or evil, impulsive or rational? Are they fundamentally different from adults in some ways? Are they naturally curious or naturally passive and indolent? The ways in which a society answers questions such as these are manifested in the structure of its education system.

The Puritans believed that children were possessed by the devil. Their education involved memorizing parts of the Bible, catechisms, and other sources of moral wisdom until the evil nature of children was overcome. This process was hurried along by the schoolmaster's liberal use of the switch, stick, whip, or dunce cap to make the children behave (Johnson, et al., 1985). Rather than being isolated from adults, children were encouraged to emulate the adults' good examples because it was assumed that adults had already learned right from wrong.

Early in this century, education became more student centered. Children were not thought to be controlled by the devil, but they were thought to be impulsive; and thus strict discipline was still necessary. Children were required to sit in rows, to memorize their spelling and mathematics, and to raise their hands to recite.

Since 1960, some important changes have taken place. The moral issue of whether children are good or evil has lost importance, but it has come to be believed that children have a natural curiosity—they want to learn. In schools based on this belief, discipline has decreased, rows of chairs have been rearranged to allow freedom of movement, and *learning centers* have been developed and placed around the room so that children can move from center to center as their interests dictate. Under this system, students who fail to learn are likely to be blamed for their failure. It is assumed that they lack curiosity or a desire to learn.

Many parents would like to see a return to an emphasis on basic skills and strict discipline in the schools. They believe that an education is necessary in order to acquire a good job, and they want to be sure their children learn the necessary skills rather than relying on their natural curiosity. Parents may not approve of the way schools are run now, but their power to bring about changes is limited.

WHO RULES THE SCHOOLS?

Most American education is public—the schools are open to everyone. Local and federal governments fund schools, so there are strong ties between the educational system and the political system. Education is paid for through tax dollars; and although it is controlled locally, it complies with all the laws of the land. Those who head federal, state, and local school bureaucracies interpret these laws. Students, parents, and teachers have little opportunity to influence decisions in the bureaucracy.

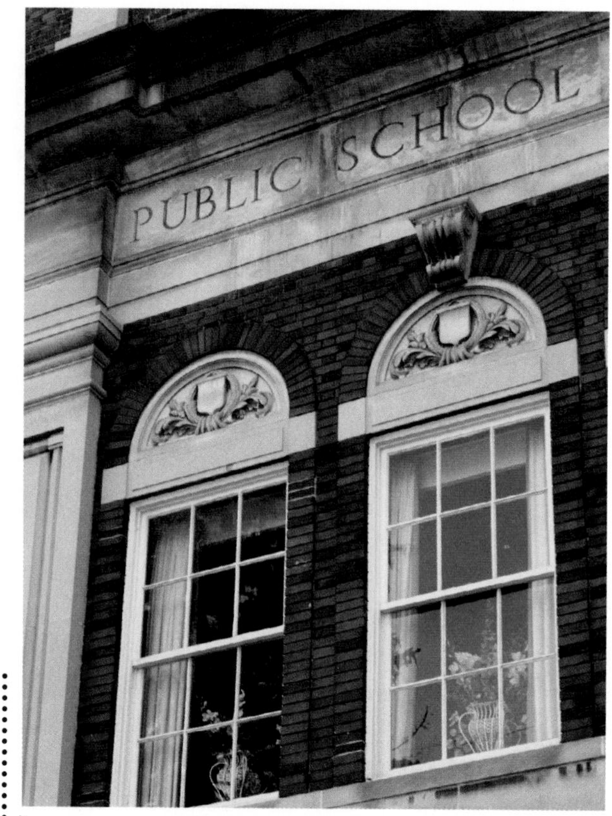

Public schools are open to everyone. Education is paid for through tax dollars.

The bureaucracy of a local school system is headed by a local school board, which adopts a budget, sets policies, and directs the supervisor of schools. The superintendent develops guidelines based on the policies of the school board and directs the principals of the schools in the area. The principals make rules for the local schools, based on the guidelines of the supervisor, and they direct the teachers to carry out the rules. The teacher establishes rules for the classroom in accordance with the principal's direction and teaches the students.

The Center for Public Education lists five reasons that school boards matter (http://www.nsba.org):

1. School boards look out for children, first and foremost. Education is not a line item in a school board's budget—it is the ONLY item.

2. School boards are advocates for their communities when decisions are made about its children's education.
3. School boards set the standards for achievement in their communities, incorporating their community's view of what students should know and be able to do at each grade level.
4. School boards are the public link to public schools. They are accessible to the public and accountable for the performance of their schools.
5. School boards are the education watchdog for their communities, ensuring that taxpayers get the most for their tax dollars.

Although the United States emphasizes local control of schools, it is somewhat misleading to suggest that school boards operate independently because the federal government passes many laws that affect the educational system (e.g., the *No Child Left Behind Act of 2002*). Schools must respect the rights protected by the U.S. Constitution; they must allow religious freedom and offer equal opportunity. The federal government influences such issues as prayer in school, the teaching of evolution, equal opportunity for minorities, and the education of the handicapped, including provisions for children with special educational needs. School boards must comply with federal laws regarding these and other concerns.

With the exception of maintaining the constitutional rights of citizens, the federal government had only a limited role in public education from the founding of the nation until the mid-twentieth century. Early on, some laws—such as the Lands Ordinance Act of 1785, the Northwest Ordinance of 1787, and the Morrill Act during the Civil War—set aside funds from the sale of unsettled land to fund public education. After the Civil War, Congress required new states to establish systems of non-sectarian education. In 1917 Congress approved direct aid to public education. However, it was not until 1950 that the federal government became directly involved in the composition of schools when the U.S Supreme Court ruled that racial segregation in schools was unconstitutional. With the demands of the Cold War and the impending awareness that the United States was starting to fall behind other countries educationally (as evidenced by the Soviet launch of Sputnik, the first space satellite), the federal government began to take direct steps to influence the curriculum in public schools with the passage of the National Defense Act, which provided funds to states for teaching science, math, and foreign languages. Educational concerns have been the part of every presidency since the early 1960s (Jost 2010). (See Table 14-1)

States also have constitutions, which cannot contradict federal law. Within the restrictions of federal law and the state constitution, the states pass laws that set standards for the schools. They certify teachers, set the number of days that students must attend school, determine school holidays, and establish minimum requirements for the curriculum and for graduation.

Within the limits set by the state and federal governments, local school boards set policy to be carried out by school principals and teachers, who must teach course content and follow schedules set by higher authorities (Scimecca 1980). The evaluation of teachers is heavily based on cooperation with the principal and local school board, rather than on creativity or teaching skills. Furthermore, teachers today are overwhelmed with the paperwork of the bureaucracy—seating charts, report cards, attendance records, schedules, and lesson plans—which takes considerable time away from teaching (Ballantine 1983). The National Education Association (NEA) reports that teachers spend an average of fifty hours per week on instructional duties, including an average of twelve hours each week on non-compensated school-related activities such as grading papers, bus duty, and club advising. Furthermore, teachers spend an average of $443 of their own money each year to meet the needs of their students (www.nea.org), and in 2005 the IRS started allowing teachers to deduct $250.00 of those expenses from their yearly tax returns. Also, as with any bureaucracy, the school-system bureaucracy denotes a stratification system.

STRATIFICATION IN THE SCHOOL SYSTEM

Like other social systems, schools reflect stratification and can promote still further stratification. The school

TABLE 14-1 ROLE OF THE FEDERAL GOVERNMENT IN EDUCATION

Through 1950, the Federal government played a limited role with the exception of enacting some laws that lead to setting aside land for public education.

1950s to 1970s	
1954	U.S. Supreme Court ruled racial segregation in public schools unconsitutional.
1958	In response to Cold War threats, National Defense Education Act provided aid to states for teaching math, science and foreign languages.
1965	President Lyndon B. Johnson signed Elementary and Secondary Education Assistance Act, the first broad federal aid for public schools and established Title I which allocates funds to schools with a high proportion of "educationally deprives students."
1979	President Jimmy Carter signs law creating U.S. Department of Education
1980s to 1990s	
1981	President Ronald Regan cut federal spending on education by 20 percent.
1983	Federal government study A Nation at Risk depicted the U.S education system as failing and lagging behind other countries.
1988	President George H. Bush pledged to be the "education president" in his campaign platform.
1989	President Bush hosted "education summit" with few concrete results.
1991	President Bush proposed "America 2000" legislation, but the bill was killed in Congress.
1992	President Bill Clinton stressed education in his campaign platform.
1994	President Clinton enacted "Goals 2000" calling for states to develop education standards and the "Improving America's Schools" act which linked Title I funds to the adoption of standards.
2000 to present	
2001-2002	President George W. Bush enacts "No Child Left Behind" (NCLB) calling for annual testing of students in reading and math and enacting penalties for schools that do not meet standards, tying federal funding to the achievement of standards.
Mid 2000s	Negative reactions to NCLB because of an overemphasis on standardized exams, the perception that schools were unfairly labelled as underpeforming, without providing help to improve them, thus providing incentives for schools to lower standards rather then to raise them.
President Barack Obama stressed education in campaign platform.	
2009	Congress approves $4.3 billion stimulus for "Race to the Top" grants to states with education reform plans. 41 states participate.
2010	State governors and education leaders propose common core standards in English and math and President Obama proposes "Blueprint for Reform" calling for revising NCLB.

Source: Adapted from CQ Researcher, April 16, 2010, Vol. 20., No. 15, p. 347

that children attend can have an enormous influence on their life chances. Those who attend first-rate elementary and high schools can go on to prestigious colleges and can obtain high-paying jobs. At the other end of the spectrum, those who receive a poor education may become so frustrated that they quit without graduating. Some critics contend that schools are biased in favor of middle- and upper class students at all levels, from the federal education bureaucracy to the local school board.

School Boards

The people residing within the school district's boundaries usually elect local school boards although in about 10 percent of the districts the mayor appoints them. They have traditionally consisted primarily of white, male business or professional people, although in the past decades, more women and minorities have won elections to school boards. Sometimes, board members come into conflict with groups in their school districts. Disagreements have ranged from hairstyles to vocational training, from discipline to teaching the basics of reading, writing, and arithmetic.

Some critics argue that school boards would represent their communities better if they consisted of a greater variety of people, including members from ethnic and other minority groups, labor, faculty, and the student body.

Faculty

The faculties in public schools are predominantly middle class. The majority of the faculties in elementary schools are women, most of whom are from the middle class. In high schools, there are more male faculty, many of whom are from the lower socioeconomic class. White males in the public school system often move rather rapidly into administration, normally to vice-principal and then on to more responsible positions in the hierarchy. Women and blacks move into administration much more slowly; and when they do, it is often in special assignments, such as in programs specifically for women and blacks. These moves out of the mainstream then make future promotions for them even more difficult (Ortiz 1982). Although the number of women in the superintendency has increased dramatically since 1970, historical data indicate that women are on the margin of the profession and held fewer chief executive office positions in 1992 than they did in 1910! In sum, in the early 1990s, 96 percent of superintendents in the United States were male, and the census bureau reported this position as being the most male-dominated executive position of any profession in the United States (Glass 1992). This may be changing, however. From 1997 to 2006, the percent of white women as urban superintendents had risen from zero to 12 percent. Moreover, in 2006, almost a

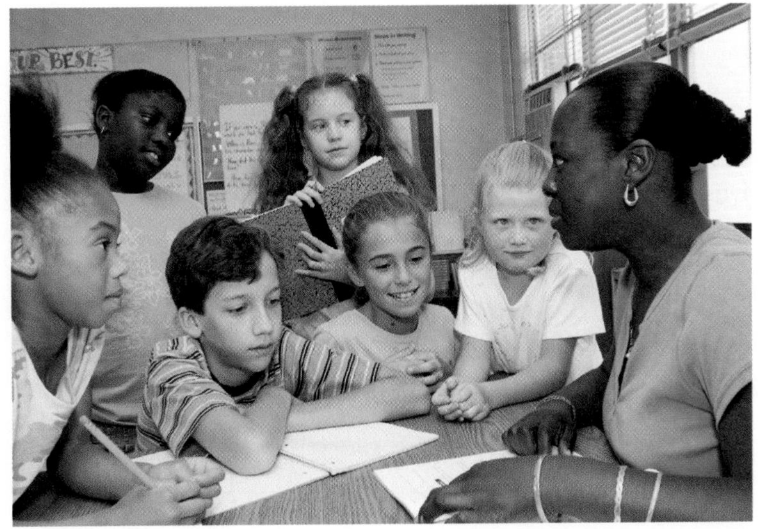

Faculties of public schools are predominantly middle class. The majority of the faculty in elementary schools are women while the majority of administrative positions in general are held by men.

fifth of all urban superintendents were black females. The percent of female urban superintendents who were Hispanic in 2006 was also higher than ever (Council of the Great City Schools 2006).

In colleges and universities, the majority of faculty members are white males, although the number of females has increased. Women are found mostly in the lower ranks; and in spite of laws requiring equal pay for equal work, they are often paid less than their male colleagues of equal rank. Women in some schools have filed complaints to raise their salaries to the level of the men on the faculty; but to date, full equality has not been achieved. Also significant is the fact that blacks are underrepresented in college and university teaching while Asians are over-represented (U.S. Department of Education 2006).

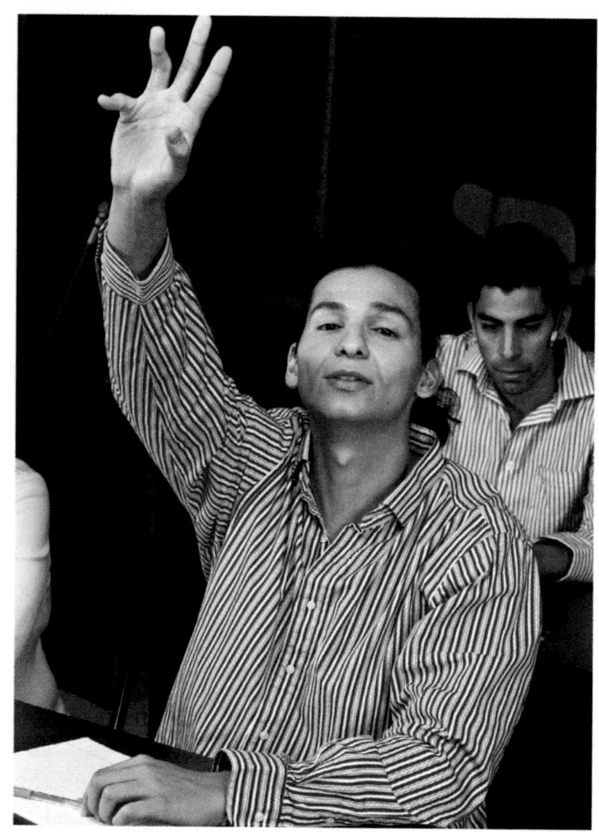

Socioeconomic segregation in neighborhoods seems to define how students see themselves in the social hierarchy.

Students

Traditionally, schools have been segregated by socioeconomic status in the United States because children go to neighborhood schools, and neighborhoods are segregated. Students of different races often attend different schools for the same reason. Many African and Hispanic Americans live in inner-city neighborhoods and go to predominantly African and Hispanic American schools. They also have a higher highschool rate than Whites, although the dropout rate for all groups has declined by almost 50 percent since 1980. (See Table 14-2.)

Lower-class students do not learn to read and write as well as those from higher-class backgrounds. As a result, they may come to believe that they are not capable of accomplishing what their contemporaries at other schools can accomplish. This lowers their

Table 14-2 High School Dropouts 1980-2008 (percentages)

	1980	1990	2000	2005	2008
Total dropouts	12.0	10.1	9.1	7.9	6.8
White	11.3	10.1	9.1	7.9	6.5
Black	16.0	10.9	10.9	9.2	8.6
Hispanic	29.5	26.8	23.5	18.6	15.0

Source: adapted from U.S, Census Bureau, The 2011 Statistical Abstracti, Table 268. High School. Dropouts by Age, Race and Hispanic Origin, 1980 to 2008,

achievement motivation, and they may become apathetic or alienated from the system.

Bowles and Gintis (1976) have theorized that the wealthy, powerful class benefits from neighborhood school systems that segregate students. In segregated school systems, students learn their place in the stratification system. Upper-class students learn about the hierarchy and the need to follow the rules of a hierarchy. They also learn that they, too, can someday take their rightful place among the wealthy and powerful. They are actively socialized into the social system. Lower-class students also come to believe that upper-class people have a legitimate right to rule (Oakes 1982). Intelligence tests have been shown to perpetuate the beliefs of all classes that the wealthy have a right to rule.

Biased Intelligence Tests

In 1916, Lewis M. Terman designed a test to measure what was called an "intelligence quotient," or "I.Q." The test was used for assessing a person's attainment of skills used in upper-middle-class occupations that involved manipulating numbers and words. The purpose of the test was to select students who were good at such manipulations to go on to advanced training. Terman and others believed that it measured an inherited genetic trait called "intelligence." They assumed that those who scored low on the test lacked intelligence and were less capable of learning than those who did well. It was argued that those who did poorly should be assigned to lower-class jobs.

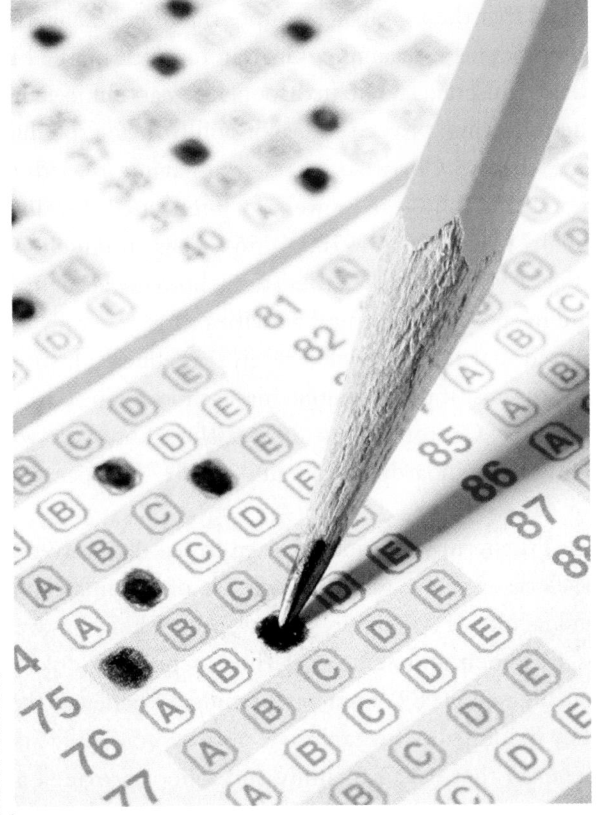

I.Q. tests were used to segregate the upper class from the lower class. Occupations were assigned accordingly.

The initial critics of intelligence tests argued that I.Q. tests measure not an inherited characteristic but, rather, a person's knowledge of upper-middle-class culture, which is why immigrants, the working class, the poor, and blacks score low while upper-middle-class Americans score high. For example, many I.Q. tests are mostly vocabulary tests, and the words that separate the average from the high scorers are words such as "amanuensis," "moiety," and "traduce." While some of the content of intelligence tests has been revised to address these criticisms, research has found that it is not only the content of the intelligence tests that can lead to a bias against lower socioeconomic groups but also the standardized nature of the tests and testing settings. Studies show that standard testing situations have a disruptive effect on how well people from lower socioeconomic groups perform when the students are told that the test is a measure of their intellectual ability. However, the test scores of lower socioeconomic students matched the test scores of students from higher socioeconomic backgrounds when the same test was not presented as a measure of intellectual ability (Croizet and Dutrevis 2004). Studies such as these suggest that standardized intelligence tests do not measure intrinsic ability. Critics say that the test serves the stratification system by creating a myth that convinces the lower classes that their station in life is part of the natural order of things (Karier 1986). They come to believe that they are not capable of advancing in society to the higher positions, partly because they are not capable of attending prestigious private schools.

AMERICAN PRIVATE SCHOOLS

As of 2007, there were 33,740 private schools in the United States. Of these private schools in 2007-2008, 68 percent of private schools in 2007-2008 had a religious orientation (Brougham, et al, 2009). By far the most common private schools in the United States, those serving a broad segment of the population, are the **parochial schools** run by the Catholic Church (22.2 percent of private schools) and founded to serve Catholics who want both an academic and a religious education for their children.

A newer phenomenon in American society is the growth of private religious schools not associated with the Catholic Church. These schools (13.8 percent of private schools) are sometimes referred to as "Christian schools," even though most private schools in the United States already have a Christian tradition. Some of the newer schools are affiliated with Protestant churches, and some have no formal link to traditional religion. Some of these schools developed to provide an alternative to racially integrated schools, and some to provide a place to teach an alternative set of values to students from those taught in the public schools. Currently, the number of students that these schools serve is about one-third the number of parochial-school students.

Other private preparatory schools have a very long history in this country; they are more expensive and they serve a wealthier student body. Finally, private schools of higher education offer an expensive education and serve only a small segment of society. Private systems are generally recognized as providing an education that is superior to those provided by the public schools.

In the following sections, we discuss parochial schools, the traditional private preparatory schools, and private colleges. We are not able to discuss the newer private Christian schools because they are a diverse group with a variety of characteristics, and their impact on society has not yet been adequately studied.

Parochial Schools

Researchers (Lee, Bryk, and Holland 1995; *Financing Schools* 1997) have found that Catholic-school students perform better than public high school students. They also found that school performance was not as closely linked to socioeconomic background in the Catholic high schools as it was in public schools. There are many reasons for the stronger performance of students in Catholic schools, including effective discipline, more monitoring of students' work, and higher expectations of the teachers for all students. For example, students in Catholic schools are more likely to take academic courses than they are in public schools, regardless of their ability or socioeconomic background. Students in Catholic schools are more likely to be groomed for college, whether they are financially able to go or not (Lee, et al., 1995). In public schools, on the other hand, students from lower socioeconomic backgrounds are more likely to be steered into general or vocational curricula, they are less likely to see a future connected with academic performance, and so quite naturally, they will not work hard at academics.

Private Preparatory Schools

The wealthy in America do not usually send their children to public schools, but rather to private **preparatory** ("prep") **schools** and then to private universities. Most of the elite private preparatory schools were founded in the late 1800s, as the American public school system developed. These private schools stated that their goals were more than intellectual development. For example, Groton, founded in 1884 in Massachusetts, stated in its opening announcement the following: "Every endeavor will be made to cultivate manly, Christian character, having regard to moral and physical as well as intellectual development." (McLachlan 1970, p. 256). These prep schools offer a very intensive education, both in academics and in sports and cultural activities. It is generally accepted that these students receive an education superior to most if not all public high schools. The cost of tuition at Groton for the 2010-2011 school year was $48,895 for boarding students and $37,020 per year for day students.

Furthermore, students learn to see themselves as a select, exclusive group. In a study of administrators and faculty of twenty prestigious prep schools, as well as freshmen and seniors at those schools, Cookson and Persell (1989) found that students believed that they belonged to an exclusive, elite group. They also believed that because family and school provided all the friends they needed, they had no interest in meeting other people.

The exclusive nature of preparatory schools bothered both outside critics and the schools themselves, and efforts have been made to admit some students who would normally not be able to finance such an education. One such program was "A Better Chance," also known as the "ABC" program (Zweigenhaft and Domhoff 1993). ABC enabled talented, inner-city minority students to attend some of the most prestigious prep schools with children of some of the wealthiest families in the United States. The minority students flourished both academically and socially, and well over 90 percent continued their education at highly selective colleges and universities. In spite of these accomplishments, these minority students still tended to be limited in their careers to middle-management positions. According to the National Center for Educational Statistics, the average cost for a year at a private school ranged from $9,000 to $36,000 per student in 2006.

Selective Private Colleges

Admittance to selective colleges and universities is no simple task, as many college students know by the time they read this text. The most prestigious colleges do not select students on the basis of intelligence and achievement alone. Studies of how Harvard University (2011-2012 tuition plus fees, $52,650) selects its students (Karen 1990; Klitgaard 1985) demonstrate how selection for college works against the student from a middle-class background who has little to offer except good grades. Harvard does not select only students of high scholastic aptitude. They believe that the quality of their educational program would suffer because those who entered Harvard with very high grades but who found themselves in the bottom 25 percent of the class at Harvard would be unhappy (Klitgaard 1985). Harvard would rather select some students who were not outstanding academically who would be happy to be in the bottom 25 percent of the class. Though Harvard does choose applicants with truly outstanding academic records on the basis of intelligence alone, it also tries to choose students based on other criteria.

Elite institutions, such as Harvard, seek to select young people on the basis of what they will be able to contribute to society.

Harvard's Admissions Committee includes a few faculty members, but it comprises primarily professional admissions officers who specialize in searching for students who would add a "well-rounded" dimension to the student body. They sort applications according to a variety of criteria, such as scholastic aptitude, whether the student is the child of a Harvard graduate, an athlete, a public or private school graduate, from what area of the country the student comes, or whether the student is a foreign candidate.

The outcome of this selection process is, according to Karen (1990), that those from prep schools have an advantage over those from public schools, and those from elite prep schools have the best advantage. Children of alumni and athletes have a great advantage, minority groups have an advantage if they went to elite prep schools, and Asians are at a disadvantage.

Harvard, like many elite institutions, hopes to improve the lives of young people, but it also wants its educational program to have impact on the society as a whole. It attempts to select young people on the basis of what they will be able to contribute to society. A young person who has been educated in one of the best private schools and whose family has important connections in business or government is more likely eventually to hold a key position in society. Education will probably have a greater added value in that person's career than educating a person with no such contacts. Most selective American colleges are believed to have similar procedures.

TABLE 14-3 EXPENDITURE PER PUPIL IN FALL ENROLLMENT IN PUBLIC ELEMENTARY AND SECONDARY SCHOOLS: SELECTED YEARS, 1961-62 THROUGH 2006-07

	Current expenditures in unadjusted dollars	Current expenditures in constant 2007-08 dollars
1961-62	$393	$2,769
1970-71	842	4,489
1980-81	2,307	5,639
1986-87	3,682	7,007
1990-91	4,902	7,749
1995-96	5,689	7,796
1996-97	5,923	7,891
1997-98	6,189	8,101
1998-99	6,508	8,373
1999-2000	6,912	8,644
2000-01	7,380	8,923
2001-02	7,727	9,181
2002-03	8,044	9,351
2003-04	8,310	9,454
2004-05	8,711	9,620
2005-06	9,145	9,729
2006-07	9,683	10,041

Constant dollars based on the Consumer Price Index, prepared by the Bureau of Labor Statistics, U.S. Department of Labor, adjusted to a school-year basis.

NOTE: Beginning in 1980-81, state administration expenditures are excluded from "current" expenditures. Current expenditures include instruction, student support services, food services and enterprise operations. Beginning in 1988-89, extensive changes were made in the data collection procedures.

Adapted from U.S. Department of Education, National Center for Education Statistics. (2010). Digest of Education Statistics, 2009 (NCES 2010-013), Table 182.

Source: http://nces.ed.gov/fastfacts

Although our prestigious colleges are respected worldwide for providing a high-quality education, most of the American educational system has come under attack in the past two decades.

In 2007-2008 the average total price of attendance (tuition plus room and board) for full time students at a public two-year college was approximately $12,000 per year, approximately $19,000 per year at a public four-year college, and approximately $35,000 at a private four-year private institution per year. Studies show no sign of college tuition rates slowing down their rising pace. (National Center for Education Statistics, 2007-2008).

THE FAILURE OF AMERICAN SCHOOLS

Americans and foreign nations alike have been increasingly concerned about the failure of American public schools to educate its young people. Comparisons with other countries reveal that Americans do very poorly on test scores, especially in science and math. As explained in the first part of this chapter, high school graduates are woefully inadequately prepared for college work in English, reading, math and science.

Performance in some other areas is equally poor. The National Association of Education Progress' *The Nations Report Card, Civics 2010* found that fewer than half of American eighth graders knew the purpose of The Bill of Rights and only one in ten demonstrated an acceptable knowledge of the checks and balances of the legislative, executive and judicial branches of the Federal government (Dillon 2011). Unfortunately, 75 percent of high school seniors could not identify the effect of United States foreign policy on other countries, nor could they name a power of Congress granted by the Constitution.

WHY STUDENTS DO NOT LEARN

A variety of reasons are given to explain why American students do not learn in school. They include low socioeconomic statuses of families and pupils, poor resources in school facilities, inadequate curricula, students discouraged from striving toward success, and high dropout rates.

Financial Problems

Whatever the problems are in our educational system, they probably are not due simply to the lack of money. Money spent per pupil on public school education has risen significantly in the past half-century, as shown in Table 14-3. The increase has been more rapid than could be explained by a rising cost of living. Some of this money has been used to increase the number of teachers and staff, with the result being a steady decrease in the number of students per instructional staff member (Table 14-4).

TABLE 14-4 PUBLIC AND PRIVATE ELEMENTARY AND SECONDARY PUPIL/TEACHER RATIOS: SELECTED YEARS, FALL 1955 THROUGH FALL 2015

Year	Pupil/Teacher Ratio Total	Public	Private
1955	27.4	26.9	31.7
1960	26.4	25.8	30.7
1965	25.1	24.7	28.3
1970	22.4	22.3	23.0
1975	20.3	20.4	19.6
1980	18.6	18.7	17.7
1985	17.6	17.9	16.2
1990	17.0	7.2	15.6
1995	17.1	17.3	15.7
2000	15.9	16.0	14.5
2005	15.4	15.6	13.5
2010 (estimate)	15.0	15.3	12.8
2015 (projected)	14.5	14.8	12.5

Source: Adapted from U.S. Department of Education, National Center for Education Statistics, Statistics of Public Elementary and Secondary Day Schools, 1955-56 through 1984-85; Common Core of Data (CCD), "State Nonfiscal Survey of Public Elementary/Secondary Education," 1985-86 through 2007-08; Private School Universe Survey)PPS), 1989-90 through 2007-08; Projections of Education Statistics to 2018; and unpublished data. (This table was prepared September 2009.)

School Facilities

James Coleman and a team of sociologists have done a series of studies (1993, 1997) to compare the facilities of schools in black and white neighborhoods. Coleman found that the schools were the same age, spent the same amount of money per pupil, and had equivalent library and laboratory facilities. Teacher qualifications and class size were also the same. He concluded that the differences in achievement were related to the students' socioeconomic backgrounds, not to differences in the school facilities. Coleman also found that black students performed better in white schools and recommended busing students to promote integration. Busing was carried out in many localities, but both black and white citizens disliked busing children to schools in other neighborhoods. Many argued that it interfered with the concept of neighborhood schools and local control.

Inadequate Curricula

Much of the problem in why students do not learn, according to the National Commission on Excellence in Education, is the deterioration of school curricula in the public schools. Today, about half of all students in high school take a general studies course, compared to only 12 percent in 1964. While most of the courses in a general studies program are traditional academic studies such as English, history, or science, 25 percent of the credits earned in general studies are in physical and health education, work experience, remedial courses, and electives such as bachelor living. Only 31 percent of high school students take intermediate algebra, only 6 percent take calculus, and total homework assignments require an average of less than one hour a night. It has already been noted that parochial schools have an advantage over public schools, in part because they continue to emphasize academic subjects. The National Commission urged a greater emphasis on academic subjects in the public schools, recommending four years of English and three years each of math, science, and social studies. However, most states have failed to meet these standards.

Meanwhile, the United States concerns itself with issues such as a so-called politically correct curriculum, the values that are taught, the future career

SOCIOLOGY AT WORK

Developing Strategies in the Classroom

Victor Gibson has a BA in sociology from Wayne State University (in Michigan), and he currently works as an educational technician for the Detroit Board of Education and as an elementary school teacher. One of his jobs as educational technician is to identify students within third- and fourth-grade classes who need remedial help in language arts—that is, reading, spelling, syntax, grammar, and other areas related to the English language. He works with these students to help them develop the skills they need to proceed at a normal pace with their education. Gibson points out that in addition to providing remedial help in the language arts, he helps these students by facilitating to raise their level of self-esteem. His sociological training has taught him not only how stereotypes lead people to be treated in a way that might hold them back but also how people come to believe certain things about themselves. In situations like this, a self-fulfilling prophecy results when particular types of students believe that they are not capable of doing the work.

The movie *Stand and Deliver* is especially meaningful to Gibson. In that movie, a teacher of predominantly lower-class Hispanic-Americans in a southern California school faced the challenge of getting teachers, parents, and the students to overcome the stereotype that these students were not capable of advanced mathematical learning. The teacher in that movie succeeded in both helping to reinforce the students' self-esteem and teaching them calculus. Gibson's task is similar to this. A sociological concept that Gibson relies upon often in helping him raise his students' self-esteem is Cooley's "looking-glass self." He knows that the way in which he and others react toward students plays a significant part in how they see themselves. Thus, he is very careful to say and do things that will help students to see themselves in a positive light.

Besides using sociology in his specific task of identifying and helping students who need special attention with language arts, Gibson points out that his sociological knowledge has helped him to become a better teacher. "My classroom control is exceptional," he says, "because I understand group dynamics and social theories like social exchange and symbolic interactionism. Cultural sensitivity also plays a major role with transmitting knowledge in terms that the children can readily accept and decode at their level."

Gibson emphasizes that learning the sociological perspective in general has had a significant impact on his teaching style. "In general, sociology has helped me develop a 'holistic' point of view to gaining knowledge. I don't see myself as being a math teacher or a science teacher or social studies teacher. As I'm teaching one subject, I'm also placing the subject in perspective to other subjects. I am constantly thinking about and telling students how each subject relates and interacts with others. No one subject can stand alone in reality. Why teach it in an isolated perspective?"

Additionally, Gibson feels that the continual emphasis on current issues that took place in his sociology classes helps him with his own approach to teaching. "Collectively, understanding today's and tomorrow's demands on future generations was very helpful in preparing me to help children. Understanding how political issues affect program development gives me insight on possible directions of future policy making. This helps me focus students' minds on everyday issues and how these issues might affect their lives. That is something that even young students find very important and can relate to."

potential of students, and other issues not related to academic subjects.

The Self-Fulfilling Prophecy

There are many ways to discourage students from achieving in the classroom. One way is to discourage students from believing that learning and achievement are possible. Rosenthal and Jacobson (1968) found that students do not learn as well when their teachers believe that the students are not very bright. If teachers have learned that lower-class and minority students do not perform well on I.Q. and achievement tests, they will have lower expectations of them in class. Even if they do perform well, teachers may fail to recognize their talents, give them lower grades, and confuse and frustrate them. Thus, a **self-fulfilling prophecy** is at work.

This self-fulfilling prophecy was evident in a study of pupil-teacher interaction, where it was found that teachers asked black students simpler questions than they asked white students. If a black pupil could not answer a question, the teacher asked somebody else. If a white pupil could not answer a question, however, the teacher gave an explanation. Teachers also praised and complimented white students more than black students when they gave correct answers (Weinberg 1977).

High Dropout Rate

Worse than the students who finish without adequate preparation are those who do not finish at all. Dropout rates of young people ages 16–24 has declined from 15 percent to 10 percent between 1972 and 2004. However, these rates are still considered high, and dropout rates are even higher in the Hispanic-American community (24 percent) and the African-American community (12 percent). (NCES, 2006).

Thinking Sociologically

1. Using sociological perspectives about education as the basis for your ideas, what types of changes in your college's curriculum would you recommend to the administration at your school?
2. Discuss the extent to which the curriculum in your college is guided by a traditional Western intellectual perspective or a multicultural perspective. In light of this, what are the functions of your school's curriculum?
3. If you were to become a high school teacher, what personal assumptions would you have to address? Do you hold stereotypes about particular groups? Do you believe that children learn differently because of gender? Social class? How would being an observant sociologist guide your work as a teacher?

IMPROVING THE SCHOOLS

A variety of changes to the public school system are being tested in order to improve the schools in the United States. Some of these changes are discussed in the following sections.

Magnet Schools

In recent years, magnet schools have been developed in segregated school districts. **Magnet schools** are schools with special programs designed to attract exceptional students. These students voluntarily travel outside of their neighborhoods to go to the magnet schools. The

Magnet schools are schools with special programs designed to attract exceptional students. This is one option that is being tested to improve the public school system in the United States.

hope is that white students will be attracted to schools with heavy black enrollment to achieve integration. One fear of magnet school programs is that tax dollars and the best students in a district will be concentrated in magnet schools, and other schools will be left with mediocre programs and students. Most magnet schools are new, so it is too early to judge their success conclusively. Some early research findings suggest that magnet schools are not achieving the goal of integration. One study (Rossell 2003) found that the more magnets that exist in a voluntary desegregation plan, the greater the White flight and the less interracial exposure. This may be because magnet schools are disruptive, and the more magnets, the more disruption. In areas that have mandatory desegregation plans, this is not as much the case since there is already considerable disruption without the magnets. However, in voluntary segregation areas, the effectiveness of magnet schools on achieving integration can be increased if demand, location and structure are considered in their planning.

Decentralized Bureaucracies

Another approach to improving the schools is to **decentralize** the **bureaucracy**, in other words, put more of the decision-making processes in the local schools instead of in the school boards. This approach is being attempted in the Chicago school system (Muwakkil 1990), but with considerable debate and conflict. Chicago is a very large school system, where the relatively elite central Board of

Education has been distant from the less aristocratic local schools over which it rules. Chicago has worked very hard to recruit ethnic and racial minorities onto the school board of this mostly minority-populated school system. Now that they have succeeded in getting minority representation on the school board, critics want to decentralize; and some believe the real intent is to take power away from the now-integrated school board. In other words, the intent is to reinstitute discrimination via a different mechanism.

Instead of the school board running the schools, the schools in Chicago are now to be run by parent-controlled local school councils (LSCs). The LSCs have the right to hire and fire principals, select textbooks, and develop curricula. Many have chosen to fire the principals and are under attack for discrimination and other unfair practices. Some critics argue that parents, especially in the poorest districts, are not equipped to carry out the responsibilities of the LSCs. Whether these changes actually will improve Chicago's schools remains to be seen.

Vouchers

A third approach to improving our educational system is to give parents the choice of a school to which to send their children. If they choose a private school, they will receive a **voucher** for state funds to pay the tuition. The Supreme Court of the State of Wisconsin ruled on June 10, 1998, that the Milwaukee voucher program, which will allow up to fifteen thousand children to attend any religious or private school, does not violate the state or federal constitution. This decision was appealed all the way to the United States Supreme Court. The high court ruled 8–1 not to hear the appeal and thus allowed the verdict in Wisconsin to stand. Government-run voucher programs are very controversial and have been heavily criticized. Those who support the idea of choosing a school believe that parents will choose the best schools for their children. Schools will have to upgrade in order to compete for students, or they will not be able to stay open. Critics of the system argue, however, that parents may not be in the best position to choose a school and may be offered a shoddy product. Furthermore, the number of good schools is limited; and most students will have to remain in the Milwaukee school system, which has admittedly been doing a poor job of educating its students. Lastly, some critics claim vouchers are nothing more than unfair discounts for the rich who can already afford the full cost of expensive private schools like Groton. To be sure, according to the National Conference of State Legislators, over three quarters of the funds for Arizona's voucher program go to students already in private schools, with less than a fifth going to students from public schools (Spartanburg County Legislative Delegation 2005). The end result, say the critics, is that voucher systems not only weaken public

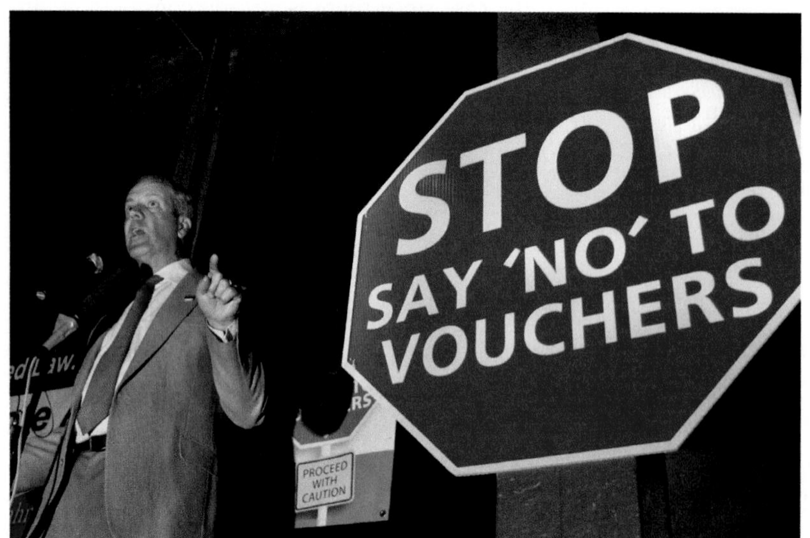

State paid vouchers are given to parents to help pay for private school tuition. However, this method is very controversial and has received much criticism.

education by draining money from public schools, they also fail to provide enough money for middle- and working-class parents to send their children to the same elite private schools that wealthy students attend.

New Management

Chelsea, Massachusetts, has turned over the management of the city schools to Boston University (Ribadeneira 1990), and those educators now run the local schools. This approach has also met with criticism. Critics argue that the university is authoritarian and patronizing. Teachers complain that they are left out of the decision-making process. Hispanic leaders complain that the university has failed to consider bilingual education. This, like other experiments in reform, has met with considerable conflict from the community.

Other approaches being considered or attempted include paying teachers on the basis of merit, involving business and industry more extensively in the educational system, having children begin school at age four years, and increasing the length of the school day and the school year. A wholesale increase in schooling is a risky proposition at best, however, when we do not know why students are not performing well. If schools, however subtly, are encouraging our lower classes and minority students to fail, as would be indicated by the high dropout rate among these students, increasing the school day, the school year, and the number of requirements might also increase the apathy and discouragement felt by these students. Likewise, if school is too strongly oriented toward middle-class occupations and is therefore discouraging to people from the lower classes, and if job opportunities are not increased, might the involvement of the business community in the schools make matters worse? Simple solutions to remedy our very complex problems in education and stratification will probably not work.

Creating Future Goals

Although differences in achievement have been related to family background and to the quality of the schools, one variable—future opportunity—has been given little consideration. However, a program begun almost accidentally may demonstrate that future opportunity is most important when considering achievement. In 1981, multimillionaire Eugene Lang returned to his old school in East Harlem to speak to the sixth-grade graduating class, a group of minority students living in one of the poorest neighborhoods in the country (Bickford 2002). He told them that he would pay for the college education of anyone in the class who would stay in school. He also changed their poor environment by giving them his friendship and moral support through tutoring, career counseling, and other advantages that wealth can bring. In a school where typically only half graduate and where only one or two in a hundred have grades high enough for college admissions, 90 percent of Lang's group of hopeful sixth-graders stayed in school through high school; and more than half had grades that would enable them to attend college. Perhaps a promising future is necessary for success in school, especially if teachers as well as students believe that success is possible. Perhaps a belief that the students can and will attend college is as necessary in public high schools as it is in parochial high schools. Perhaps the United States should look at a different system of rewards for work accomplished in school.

CONTEST AND SPONSORED MOBILITY

In the United States, students can get as much education as they are willing and able to pay for, as long as they maintain the grades necessary for acceptance at the next higher level. This system has been labeled **contest mobility** (Turner 1960) because students can continue as long as they meet the standards of each level. The high school graduate can apply to college, the two-year college graduate can apply to a four-year institution, and the college graduate can apply to a graduate school. Once out of school, the contest continues as students compete with each other for jobs.

However, the contest is not based entirely on performance. As was stressed earlier, the most prestigious schools in America do choose students who have good grades, but they also choose students with lower grades who are likely to make outstanding contributions to society (Klitgaard 1985). These students are often children of people in powerful government or business positions. Education is also limited by the ability to pay. Poor students in the United States have been able to get grants and loans to help pay college costs, but middle-income families in the United States must pay thousands of dollars a year, on average, to attend a public or private college.

By contrast, Japan and most European countries have a system known as **sponsored mobility**. In these countries, students must pass qualifying examinations to gain admittance into different types of high schools and colleges. Once they pass the exams, however, their education is sponsored; and furthermore, if they do their work, they are assured of success both in school and upon completion of their studies. They do not pay any tuition for their higher education (Johnstone 1986). In Britain and in Sweden, students receive grants and loans for living expenses and are discouraged from working while in school. Of course, students in these countries who do not earn good grades cannot further their education.

Within these systems, educational tracks vary. Students may receive a classical education leading to a university degree, a business education, or engineering and technical training. Once they enter a particular track, they rarely change to another type of education. A student in business school, for example, is unlikely to switch to a university.

IS ALL THIS EDUCATION NECESSARY?

In spite of the unequal education received by various groups in the United States, most people have had great faith in education as a means to upward mobility. It is this faith that is largely responsible for the phenomenal growth of our educational institutions, especially public institutions. Community and junior (two-year) colleges have been built and loan programs have been established to assist those who could not otherwise afford a college education. The women's movement has stressed education as a means of upward mobility for women, and poverty programs have focused on training and educating the poor to help them rise out of poverty. Underlying all these steps is the assumption that education leads to upward mobility.

In the past, most sociologists supported this view. Blau and Duncan (1967), for example, argued that if children from large families could get as much education as children from small families, their existing occupational disadvantages would largely disappear. The belief among sociologists that education leads to upward mobility is so widespread that each year presenters at the American Sociological Association conference focus on inequalities in education.

There is, however, reason to doubt that education has much impact on social mobility. Sociologist Ivar Berg (2003) has argued that increasing the educational demands on the disadvantaged creates a hardship for them. They are encouraged to spend more money on education, but when they complete their education, they do not necessarily have additional earning power. Berg refers to this low return on educational investment as "the great training robbery."

The fact that increased education does not necessarily lead to better jobs may come as a surprise. The truth is, however, that factors other than education have a powerful influence on what jobs people take and what salaries they earn. Family background, for example, is more closely related to future occupation than level of education (Jencks 1979). A son from a working-class family is more likely to enter a working-class occupation than a son from a middle-class family, even if he has the same amount of education (Jencks 1979; Lipset and Bendix 1967).

Occupational choice for today's generation is more complicated than in the past. Although the occupation of the parent(s) is still important in predicting occupational choice, other factors appear in the research. For example, Badgett and Folber (2003) propose and support the theory that occupational segregation is perpetuated along gender lines because women (and men) may be penalized in the marriage market for making nontraditional occupational choices. Holding all else equal, their empirical research supports the fact that having a gender-nonconforming occupation reduced the attractiveness of both men and women (Badgett and Folbre 2003). Lupart and Cannon (2002) found significant gender differences in the future career interests of boys and girls. This is true in particular in the career interests of girls, which are falling along traditional paths.

What seems to have remained constant is that "the correlation between parents' education and socioeconomic status and the educational outcomes of their offspring remains a rather universal phenomenon" (Schnabel 2002).

As the level of education for everyone in the society increases, members of the upper class get more education than others, go to the most prestigious schools, and use their influential family and friends to help them find the best jobs. On the other hand, the children of the working class, although they get more education than their parents had, find that working-class jobs now require at least a high school diploma and many jobs in corporations that used to require only a high school diploma now require a college degree or even an MBA. Furthermore, even as educational requirements increase, all credentials are not equal. An MBA from a prestigious university opens doors to jobs that are not available to an MBA from a small public university.

Thinking Sociologically

1. How would you change job qualifications or credentials so that students would be more eager to perform?
2. Do you think that guaranteed jobs for top performers would increase school performance?
3. How would you change the school system so that it would be less costly?

CHAPTER REVIEW
Wrapping it up

Summary

1. Structural functional theory argues that education in a complex industrial society supplements what families can teach their children and that it helps children to acquire both the complex skills and the knowledge necessary to function in the world. The educational system also selects students on the basis of their talents and abilities to meet the needs of society, directing the most talented into advanced education and training for positions of leadership while directing those with less talent to the positions in which they will serve society best. Educational institutions also create new knowledge and new technology, which they teach to the next generation. They create innovation and change so that society can advance.

2. Conflict theory argues that education is a means by which powerful groups prevent change; powerful groups use the educational system to teach children their values and norms so that everyone will believe that the position of the powerful is justified. Powerful groups promote children and give diplomas and degrees on the basis of how well students know their culture. Children of the wealthy usually receive prestigious credentials from prestigious schools and move into high-paying, prestigious jobs, while those from the lower classes tend to remain in lower-class jobs.

3. The American educational system was begun by the Puritans and developed into our modern system of elementary schools, secondary schools, colleges, and universities.

4. Schools are complicated bureaucracies, directed and financed by local, state, and federal boards, which determine curricula, testing procedures, and other requirements for certification. Superintendents, principals, and teachers implement the various rules and standards, and students, upon meeting the standards, receive the appropriate diplomas and degrees.

5. Stratification is pervasive in the educational system. School board members are likely to be business leaders, and teachers are likely to be from the middle or working classes. Students are segregated into rich or poor neighborhood schools. Intelligence tests are biased toward upper-middle-class culture.

6. Private schools in the United States include Catholic and other religious-based parochial schools, private preparatory schools, and private colleges. Select private colleges have a complicated admissions system that does not select exclusively on the basis of grades, thereby allowing class-based differences to play a stronger role in selection.

7. Education in the United States has been criticized because tests show that American students perform well below those in other industrialized countries. Schools have been criticized for lacking funding, strong curricula, and good facilities.

8. School systems are trying solutions such as magnet schools, decentralized bureaucracies, vouchers, and management by universities.
9. European school systems differ from the American system not only by providing a better education but also by sponsoring students who academically qualify for further education. College tuition is provided by the national governments.
10. Some critics argue that too much education is required now and that this requirement is detrimental to the working class, who cannot afford it when, at the end of their courses of study, they do not experience the upward mobility in occupations that they had hoped to gain.

Key Terms

age segregation The separation of groups by age such as occurs in our education system

bureaucracy A hierarchical, formally organized structural arrangement of an organization based on the division of labor and authority

compulsory public education Publicly funded education that is mandatory until a certain age

contest mobility A competitive system of education in which those who do best at each level are able to move on to the next level

credentialism The practice of requiring degrees for most high-paying jobs, whether or not the degrees actually signify skills necessary to accomplish the jobs

decentralized bureaucracies Putting the decision-making processes in the hands of the people or local units rather than in the hands of a centralized few

hidden curriculum The teaching and learning of things such as obedience, competition, and patriotism that are not part of the stated curriculum

magnet schools Schools with special programs designed to attract exceptional students

parochial schools Schools run and maintained by a religious body or organization rather than the public at large

preparatory schools Private schools, usually of a select and elite nature, that are intended to offer an intensive education in both academic as well as social/cultural activities

prolonged adolescence A latent function of education that serves to maintain parental dependency and keep young people out of the job market

self-fulfilling prophecy A prediction that comes true because people believe it and act as though it were true

sponsored mobility A system of education in which certain students are selected at an early age to receive advanced education and training

vouchers Giving parents the choice of a private school for their children to attend and using state funds to pay for the tuition

Discussion Questions

1. What do you see as some specific latent and manifest functions of education in your college?
2. To what extent does your school emphasize credentialism in your selection of courses and major?
3. Discuss ways in which your own educational experience has served to maintain your socioeconomic position in society.
4. If you believed that children were naturally lethargic, how would you structure schools? If you believed that children were naturally geniuses, how would you structure schools? Given the nature of your own school experience, what assumptions about children do you suppose have been made?
5. How might your school experience have been different if you had gone to a more integrated school? A less integrated school? Be specific.
6. How might your school experience have been different if you had gone to a school with more money? A school with less money? Be specific.

7. If there were less opportunity to go to college in the United States, but tuition were free, would this improve your chances of finishing college, or would it diminish your chances? Does your answer have anything to do with your socioeconomic status?

8. If there were fewer educational credentials for jobs and more emphasis on job experiences, would this improve your chances for a good career or make your chances more difficult? Does your answer have anything to do with your socioeconomic status?

9. Discuss the positive and negative functions of contest and of sponsored mobility for individuals and for society.

10. Make up a list of issues for the board of trustees of your college to consider, in order to improve education where you are.

Pop Quiz

1. Which of the following is not a latent function of education?

a. age segregation
b. baby-sitting service for parents
c. prolonging adolescence
d. creating new knowledge

2. Teaching values and norms necessary for maintaining the stratification system is part of the __________.

a. hidden curriculum
b. elite norms
c. upper-class indoctrination
d. functional theory of education

3. According to conflict theorists, how does the American educational system perpetuate inequality?

a. by encouraging conformity to elitist customs and values
b. by selectively teaching certain topics and excluding others
c. by implementing the hidden curriculum
d. all of the above

4. The practice of requiring degrees for most high-paying jobs, even when the degrees do not necessarily signify skills necessary to do the jobs, is called __________.

a. overeducation
b. credentialism
c. undereducation
d. elitism

5. Harvard College was founded in 1636 to educate whom?

a. sociologists, with an emphasis on explaining society
b. architects, with an emphasis on designing buildings
c. physicians, with an emphasis on preventive medicine
d. ministers, with an emphasis on morals and ethics

6. Compulsory U.S. public education __________.

a. helped immigrant children assimilate into the mainstream culture
b. was developed during the eighteenth and nineteenth centuries
c. met with resistance from a variety of groups
d. all of the above

7. Stratification in the United States school system is evident in __________.

a. the composition of school boards
b. the gender of elementary school teachers
c. the gender of school administrators
d. all of the above

8. Magnet schools are those that __________.

   a. attract exceptional students
   b. are run by parent-controlled local school councils
   c. draw financial support from children with vouchers
   d. are run by selected universities

9. Sponsored mobility in education is found in __________.

   a. Japan and most European countries
   b. Thailand
   c. most countries south of the equator
   d. the United States

10. In analyzing education and mobility, which of the following is true?

    a. Family background is more closely related to occupation than is level of education.
    b. There will never be an excess of college graduates in the United States.
    c. Today, few blue-collar jobs require a high school education.
    d. For the disadvantaged, increased education translates into increased earning power.

11. Age segregation is a manifest educational function in the United States. T/F

12. The University of Georgia is the oldest public university in the United States. T/F

13. The majority of faculty in colleges and universities are now white females. T/F

14. "Christian schools" of the past two decades are the first to emphasize Christian tradition. T/F

15. To decentralize the bureaucracy means to put more decision-making processes in the local schools rather than in school boards. T/F

1. D	6. D	11. F
2. A	7. D	12. T
3. D	8. A	13. F
4. B	9. A	14. F
5. D	10. A	15. T

CHAPTER 15

Political Groups and Systems

INFLUENCE PEDDLING

In February 2011, the Pentagon awarded Boeing Company a contract for more than $30 billion for tankers needed by the Air Force for aerial refueling. Boeing won the contract over its biggest competitor EADS North America, a unit of European Aeronautic Defense and Space Company. This is the culmination of a decade-long controversy and scandal about improper communication between the government and Boeing. Up until before the 9/11 terrorist attacks and the financial upheaval they caused to the airline industry, the Air Force had consistently evaluated their refueling tankers to be flight worthy until 2040. Shortly after 9/11, defense contractor Boeing convinced the Pentagon to begin replacing its fueling fleet early. Before near completion of the deal, the process was stalled after evidence of improper communication between Boeing, the Air Force, the Pentagon, OMB (The Office of Management and Budget) and Congress was uncovered. In order to help win a contract with the government, Boeing had enlisted the help of its friends on Capitol Hill, such as Representative Norm Dicks whose state (Washington) houses several Boeing facilities, and other lobbying organizations. One of these organizations was Kerr Consulting, headed by Gordon Kerr who had spent thirty years working for different members of Congress. Boeing also hired PAW and Associates, headed by Paul Weaver, a former high-ranking Air Force officer and Commander of the National Guard for over three decades. Over the course of six years, Boeing paid $3.6 million to Akin, Gump, Strauss, Hauer and Feld L.L.P, one of the most powerful lobbying firms in DC, for a team of former Capitol Hill staffers and political appointees, to capture the "ear" of members of Congress and then Vice-President Dick Cheney (Therkildsen and Bass 2011). This is not the first time, nor the last, that private groups employ those either close to the government or former members of the government to influence policies for private gain. In the mid-1980s former Interior Secretary James G. Watt with the Regan Administration, helped a private housing developer obtain federal funds to rehabilitate low-income housing. Watt did this by making several phone calls to the secretary of housing and urban development and by setting up a meeting between the secretary and the developer. In return, Watt was paid $300,000.

The practice of trying to influence government legislation and decision-making has always been an important part of the American political process. Governmental influence commonly takes one or more of three forms: lobbying, consulting, and public relations.

1. Lobbyists, described in more detail later in this chapter, support and promote an interest group's positions to Congress and federal agencies on specific issues—such as abortion, gun control, environmental regulation, gay rights. Lobbyists muster support for the groups they represent in many ways: making telephone calls, writing letters and emails, setting up Internet blogs, sending petitions to members of Congress, organizing rallies about a specific political issues, and especially through developing alliances with lawmakers.
2. Consultants advise clients seeking government funds. For example, consultants advised Boeing on how to secure a government contract, how best to apply for them in a way that will give them an advantage over other applicants, and how to get through governmental bureaucratic hurdles. They may also try to influence government officials to accept their clients' applications by pointing out their merits.
3. Public relations experts try to influence the government to make the desired decisions by shaping public opinion on an issue. Government officials are more likely to support a policy that will win them votes. Because of the knowledge and contacts they possess, consultants and public relations experts can demand very high fees for their services, giving an advantage to those who can afford them.

The attempts of these three groups—lobbyists, consultants, and public relations experts— to influence governmental legislation by providing knowledge and information to governmental officials constitute a legitimate part of the American democratic political process. However, the legitimacy of "influence peddlers" who try to win governmental support for groups by using their political contacts rather than their knowledge of a subject is questionable. The increasing size and complexity of the government has blurred the distinction between influence that is based on knowledge and influence that is based on political contacts, thus making it increasingly difficult to distinguish legitimate from illegitimate types of influence.

The perception that influence peddling is essential to achieving success when dealing with the government has resulted in a self-fulfilling prophecy. Groups interested in obtaining something from the government—such as funding for a project or passage of legislation that would benefit them—often feel that because competing groups probably have intermediaries working on behalf of the competing groups' interests, it is necessary for them to follow suit. A danger of this, according to James Madison University political scientist Robert N. Roberts, is that the public will become cynical about the integrity of their government and about government's ability to make fair decision without expensive intermediaries (Glazer 1989).

Sociologists, and other social scientists, are interested in the issue of influence peddling because it goes to the heart of a number of other important sociological ideas about political groups and systems. Do political systems reflect the common values and interests of a society or do they reflect the values and interest of those who have the most power and wealth? Do all the people have a say in the policies that govern people, or does a ruling elite determine policy? If it is a ruling elite, who are they, and how do they maintain their power? Stated simply, sociologists are interested in explaining who rules—how, and why.

The United States is a nation of many laws. We register our births, go to school, marry, and divorce according to the law. We paint our houses, mow our grass, shovel our sidewalks, take our driving tests, and park our cars when and where we are supposed to; and we refrain from spitting and other socially unacceptable behaviors in public places. We may get a summons if we do not behave as the law states that we should, but often we are not even aware that there are laws dictating these activities.

Some laws are not obeyed, however. Prohibition of liquor consumption and sales did not stop people from drinking, banning abortions did not stop people from having them, and making marijuana illegal does not stop people from smoking it.

Some laws are not obeyed, such as smoking marijuana.

In large, complex societies, many decisions must be made about the duties and responsibilities of citizens and also about their rights and privileges. If the society is to be orderly, people must obey the rules that are made.

Power is generally viewed as the ability to control the behavior of others, to make the decisions about their rights and privileges, and to see to it that people obey the rules or other expectations of the powerful. **Politics** is the use of power to determine who gets what in society. The political institution establishes and enforces the laws and punishes those who disobey them. It can levy taxes, distribute scarce resources, sponsor education, plan the economy, encourage or ban religion, determine who can marry and who is responsible for children, and otherwise influence behavior. The study of political groups and systems, then, is the study of power.

TYPES OF POWER

Max Weber (1958) pointed out that there are several types of power. **Physical force** is one obvious type. An individual or an army can be captured and put into handcuffs or prison by a stronger individual or army. Often, however, sheer force accomplishes little. Although people can be physically restrained, they cannot be made to perform complicated tasks by force alone.

Latent force, or the threat of force, is more powerful than force alone. Kidnappers can get what they want by demanding ransom in exchange for the victim's life. The kidnappers want the money and hope that the threat of murder will produce it—a dead victim does not do the kidnapper any good. Similarly, a ruler can say, "Either perform your duty or you will go to jail," hoping that the threat of jail will make the citizen perform the desired duty. Putting the citizen in jail, however, does not really help the ruler. In fact, latent force can sometimes produce results in situations in which direct force would not.

Controlling a society through force, whether actual or latent, is expensive and inefficient. It does not bring about the cooperation necessary for society to function productively. A group that relies on force to maintain its power faces a constant threat of being overthrown by its citizens, whereas more reliable types of power do not rely on force for their effectiveness. **Legitimate power**—such as the power to make and enforce rules that benefit all, for example—is power that is accepted by the people in a society as being necessary and beneficial.

Authority is power accepted as legitimate by those it affects. The people give the ruler the authority to rule, and they obey willingly without the need or threat of force. Weber, who was a master at classifying the abstract concepts needed to understand society, identified three types of authority: (1) traditional authority, (2) charismatic authority, and (3) legal authority. In **traditional authority**, the leader of the group leads by tradition or custom. In a patriarchal society, the father is the ruler and is obeyed because this practice is accepted by those ruled. When the father dies, his eldest son becomes ruler and has authority based on the nation's customs. Rulers who have traditional authority are usually born into their positions, and their competence to rule is not usually at issue. Also, the bounds of authority for traditional rulers are fairly broad—their power can range from settling minor disagreements to dictating who can marry whom.

The second type of authority, **charismatic authority**, is based on the personal attributes of the leader. Sometimes, a person can win the confidence, support, and trust of a group of people who then give the leader the authority to make decisions and set down rules. A charismatic leader attracts followers because they judge him or her to be particularly wise or capable.

Martin Luther King, Jr., was this kind of leader. King gained followers because he was a moving speaker who addressed people with sincerity and a sense of mission. He won their respect. With their support, he was able to lead a political fight to improve the position of blacks in the United States.

Another charismatic leader is the Reverend Sun Myung Moon of the Unification Church. Moon has built a following on the basis of his own conviction that he was chosen by God to spread the word of Christianity throughout the world and to rebuild God's kingdom on earth. Moon, who has gained followers in his native Korea and in Japan, Europe, and America, instructs his people to work hard and live a simple life of poverty. When they join the church, they sacrifice their worldly goods and the pleasures they consider evil, such as alcohol, tobacco, and drugs.

The third type of authority, **legal authority**, is based on a system of rules and regulations that determine how the society will be governed. In the United States, the U.S. Constitution sets down the bases for the government's authority, giving Congress the legal authority to enact laws, and the president the legal authority to carry them out. The president also directs the military when it is needed to enforce the law and brings before courts or pardons those who break it. The courts interpret the laws and make judgments about whether the laws have been broken.

Weber was extremely concerned about some of the characteristics of legal authority. The power granted by legal authority is based on the rules and regulations governing the office. The power of the individual officeholder is limited by those rules, and the individual has power only as long as he or she adheres to those rules. Legal authority rests in the organization, and the organization attempts to serve its own interests and to meet its own goals. Thus, power in the United States rests in organizations and not in the will of the individual citizens.

The federal bureaucracy in the United States, for example, has grown so much in recent years that its size has become an issue in presidential elections. Candidates routinely promise to cut back on the number of federal employees. Once in office, however, they find that the bureaucracy has ways of resisting major cutbacks, and it is almost impossible to make substantial reductions—even in the president's own executive branch. Because presidents cannot afford to antagonize the people they rely on to implement their policies, the bureaucracy often continues from administration to administration without significant reduction in size.

APPLYING POWER AND AUTHORITY

Power is not something that is used only by political leaders or army officers. Most of us use it at one time or another in our daily personal and professional lives. If you know the various types of power and authority, you may be able to increase your effectiveness as a parent, employer, business executive, teacher, doctor, politician, police officer, and in many other roles. Although Weber probably did not have these roles in mind when he was developing his ideas regarding power and authority, we can extrapolate how these concepts might be applied to everyday roles. (As you have probably noticed after reading much of this book, the application of sociological concepts and theories often requires thinking about them in ways that extend or go beyond their original meaning.)

As a parent, for example, you have the ability to control your children through traditional authority, for the most part. Typically, you would have little need to justify your demands, and you would not have to rely on latent or physical force when you want them to clean their rooms or to be home by midnight. "Because I said so" is a sufficient explanation for parents to give for demands they make on their children. However, a teacher who uses the same type of explanation to get students to complete a reading assignment will probably suffer a loss of students' respect and diminished overall effectiveness. Often, teachers are more effective when they rely on legal authority, in which the students are

There are different forms of power and authority. For example, parents can rely on a type of traditional authority to control their children rather than use latent or physical force.

firmly reminded that to learn the material and get a passing grade, they must comply with the rules. In some instances, talented teachers can inspire their students to work hard through their charismatic personalities, but charismatic authority would be unlikely to work in most classrooms. However, charismatic authority could be an extremely effective form of control and leadership for political leaders, ministers, or even managers of sports teams. Generally, then, a more effective way of leading people is to be aware of the different forms of power and authority and to be sensitive to what works best in various situations, rather than merely to rely on one method that worked well in one situation.

THE DEVELOPMENT OF POLITICAL SYSTEMS

As societies become wealthier and more complex, political systems grow more powerful. In very primitive and simple societies, there was no ruler and decisions were made as a group. As societies evolved from uncomplicated bands, they grew wealthier, and their rulers were able to control larger areas with their armies. States developed. **States** are institutions organized around a set of social functions, including political regulation (government and laws), military defense, and support for the welfare of the population (Johnson 2000). At first, controlled areas were small, but later, cities and the surrounding areas came under the power of individual rulers. These territories were called **city-states**. Today, most of the world is organized into **nation-states**, large territories ruled by a single institution. Nation-states developed in Europe several centuries ago, but they arose in Africa only during the past century.

When does a nation-state become a cohesive society? How does a country develop laws that will unite the population, create an orderly society, give authority to the governed, and eliminate the need for force? These are two of the oldest questions in political history, but the modern ideas of particular concern to sociologists fall within the basic theoretical approaches discussed throughout this text.

Structural Functional Theory

Structural functionalists believe that a society is built on a common set of values. Our society believes in work, achievement, equal opportunity, and the freedom to run our own lives, to name just a few of our predominant values. These values are learned by young children in the family and passed on to subsequent generations.

In a legal system of authority, a society's values shape its laws and political policies. If people value achievement, the law will protect the right to achieve. If people value freedom, the law will protect freedom, and social policy will encourage freedom. No one will be forced to practice a particular religion, for example, and marriage will be a matter of personal choice. Political institutions pass laws and develop policies that reflect the values of the population. Often, the political institution must extend itself into international affairs to protect the society's values. It may limit the import of foreign goods to protect its own workers and negotiate with other nations in order to allow trade for the benefit of its own citizens. It protects its citizens from aggressive acts and maintains armed forces to carry out its international functions.

Sometimes, however, the values of a society are not mutually consistent. Our views about work and achievement may come into conflict with our view about the freedom to run our own lives: If some people do not want to work, forcing them to do so would impinge on their freedom. Even when values are shared, it is not always easy to determine which values should be translated into laws and which laws will be obeyed. The abortion issue involves two basically conflicting values: one involving the rights of the embryo or fetus and one involving the rights of the mother. Legislatures must decide which rights to protect, and individuals must choose whether to abide by the law or to act according to their own values if they conflict with the law. Predicting which laws will be obeyed becomes even more difficult when different subcultures have conflicting values. Youth groups who do not register for the draft and religious groups who practice polygamy are subcultures with values that conflict with the dominant culture.

Structural functionalists believe that the political institution holds the values of the dominant society and arbitrates conflicts when they arise. One person may act on a value of freedom by marrying more than one spouse, or members of a subculture may feel free to use illegal drugs. It is the political system that decides which values must be upheld and which must be limited to maintain social order. In the United States, where freedom is a value, constant arbitration is necessary to protect the freedoms of the individual without impinging on the other values of society.

Conflict Theory

Conflict theory differs radically from structural functional theory. It assumes not that societies are based on a set of values but, rather, that they are drawn together by people's need for resources: food, shelter, and other necessities. Some groups get a larger share of the resources, and they use these resources to gain power. Just as they hire people to work for their financial interests in the economic sphere, they use their resources to hire people to protect their power interests in the political sphere. They use their wealth to influence political leaders to support their economic interests, and they bring about the downfall of individuals or governments that oppose their interests.

The history of Europe provides many examples of how economic groups have used legal power to protect their own interests (Pirenne 1914). European merchants in the Middle Ages at first sold their goods at strategic points along heavily traveled highways. Eventually, however, they built towns at those points and passed laws restricting others from trading, thus using their political power to create a monopoly of trade. These merchants dominated the cities of Europe for several centuries by passing laws to protect their interests.

In the fifteenth and sixteenth centuries, as worldwide shipping increased, nation-states became powerful and used their political power to protect their shippers. When machinery came into use and manufacturing grew, the manufacturers initially required no political support. They preferred a laissez-faire economy, a free and competitive market. Workers were plentiful, and industry could hire them for very low wages and could fire them at will. The workers, who suffered greatly under this system, eventually caused serious civil disturbances, and the industrialists had to develop a legal system to protect their own interests. Conflict theorists believe that in every age, the wealthy have used both laws and force to protect their wealth.

Why, then, do the great majority of people support the laws of the wealthy? According to conflict theorists, it is because the rich use their wealth and power to control the mass media. They teach their values to the majority of people by controlling the schools, the press, radio, television, and other means of communication. They try to legitimate their power by convincing the population that the rich have a right to their wealth and that they should have the power to restrict trade, hire and fire workers, and otherwise restrict the behavior of the majority to maintain their own position. Unlike the structural functionalists, who believe that the values of the society shape the political system, conflict theorists believe that the political systems shape the values of society.

POLITICAL STRUCTURES IN MODERN SOCIETIES

There are two types of legal political rule in modern societies: democracy, in which the people control the government, and *totalitarianism*, in which the state rules the people. Neither of these types is found in a pure form, and many countries have a mixed power structure. In analyzing modern societies, however, it is useful to describe power structures in terms of their ideal types.

The Democratic State

In its ideal form, a **democracy** is a power structure in which people govern themselves. Philosophers such as Jean Jacques Rousseau, John Locke, John Stuart Mill, and John Dewey believed that people knew what was in their own best interests and could learn how to protect these interests within the political system. They also believed that the experience of being politically involved would develop better citizens (Orum 1978). One major problem with democracies, however, is the likelihood that **oligarchies**, or ruling elites, will develop (Michels 1911). As a result, instead of all people sharing in their own governance, a few people have a monopoly of power and rule for everyone. Michels (1911) believed that in nation-states and other large organizations, the rise of a few to dominate power was inevitable. He called this the **iron law of oligarchy**.

An early attempt to practice democracy was made by the Greek city-state of Athens, but it was actually an oligarchy. Leadership was rotated, and all government responsibility was shared among the citizens. This system is evident in the Greek use of the term **citizen** to refer to those who were considered members of the city-state and who were entitled to the freedoms and privileges granted to members of the state. Only a small percentage of the population of Athens were citizens; and because there were so few, every citizen could participate directly in the political process. However, the great majorities of the city's inhabitants—the slaves, women, and foreigners—were not considered citizens and had no political standing.

Changes in social attitudes have raised women, the lower socioeconomic classes, and other groups from the low status they occupied in ancient Greece to the status of citizens in modern Western civilization. Nonetheless, true democracy continues to be impossible because of the unwieldy size of modern political populations. As a result, modern democracies have chosen a system of representation by which the population elects officials to act as their agents. The elected officials, in turn, appoint the upper-level civil servants and justices of the court. Therefore, when we refer today to "democratic" power structures, we mean those in which people are allowed to vote for elected representatives. It is assumed that the elected representatives will be removed from office if they are not responsive to the desires of the people. Although representative governments of this sort have laws to limit the power of officials and to protect the rights of individuals, especially their rights to equality and to dissent, there is no question that the elected officials and the people they appoint have a great deal of power.

Even in modern democracies, elites may use their power to form an oligarchy. They maintain power by manipulating the electorate. They may, for example, stuff ballot boxes and miscount votes. They may use the mass media to distribute information selectively, advertising favorable information and covering up information that the electorate may not favor. When an oligarchy develops in large bureaucratic governments, the elite sets policy, the bureaucracy carries out that policy, and the citizens believe that the rule is still legitimate, as long as they are allowed to vote (Etzioni-Halevy 1997).

The Totalitarian State

Totalitarianism is a system of rule in which the government has total control. The government dictates the society's values, ideology, and rules. It controls the educational system and plans education based on the skills and technology the rulers believe that the society needs. It also controls economic development, which is planned in advance; and production is based on the needs of the society, as determined by the leaders.

The government has total control in a totalitarian state.

Totalitarian societies do not permit dissent. Their goal is to develop a unified population, one that is not divided by differing religious loyalties or political views. They eliminate dissenters through violence, imprisonment, or expulsion, especially when the societies are just developing.

Democratic and totalitarian societies have several characteristics in common, and they often have similar ideologies. Both types of government may believe in freedom and equality for their citizens; for example, in both types of societies, citizens may be free to vote on some issues. Another ideological similarity is that each considers its own system superior to the other. The most conspicuous similarity, however, is their bureaucratic organization. Both systems are run by bureaucracies of enormous complexity and power, and political parties play an important role in shaping and unifying the organizational structures under each system.

Continuing and escalating turmoil in the Arab world raises questions about whether or not Western-style democracy can take place in Arab countries. Some say no because Islam is not a democratic religion; there is no Arabic word for democracy. Also, due to abundant oil revenues, citizens do not pay taxes in some Arab countries and thus do not hold the government accountable; and Western democracies had reinforced many of the autocratic regimes that protestors are trying to take down. Still others consider support for democracy to be very broad in the Arab world and that it is not affected by degree of religiosity. Evidence of support for democracy, some contend, comes from large voter turnouts in 2005 during times of dire risks to physical safety (Flamini 2011).

Political Parties

Political parties are groups of citizens formed with the express intent of gaining control of the political body of the state. They exist in both democratic and totalitarian states. Parties nominate candidates to run for office, provide personnel for bureaucratic posts, and make public policy. Their goal is not only to influence government but also to manage it.

Political party systems differ in structure, organization, and reasons for existence. Some parties form around a particular person, such as Charles de Gaulle's Gaullist party in France, which was a strong force in French politics even after the death of its founder. Other parties exist to promote a specific issue. The Green Party of West Germany was created to support environmental and antinuclear legislation. The National Woman's Party was founded at the beginning of this century in the United States to represent the interests of a particular minority. Most powerful parties, however, are not organized around a single issue. They concern themselves with managing the entire government and the many issues that government addresses.

A party's role in government is strongly influenced by the number of parties in a particular governmental system. Totalitarian states have only one party, so there is no competition for control of the government. Nevertheless, unless the party is run by the military and order is maintained by force, the political party must react to public opinion while encouraging support for the government. The party also selects candidates for public office and then presents them to the general public. There are no competing candidates in one-party systems, however, so nomination ensures election. In addition, the party defines issues and must convince the electorate to support their stand on these issues. The issues not brought up by the party are not debated, but every effort is made to win support from the public for the activities that the party does undertake.

Two or more political parties are found in democratic countries. This allows competition between candidates and debate over competing issues. In a two-party system, such as in the United States, one party must gain a majority of the votes, so each party tries to attract the voters in the moderate center. Because they have to avoid taking any stand that would alienate this central group of moderate voters, both parties have to be moderate and they dare not offer creative solutions to problems. They can only support the status quo. The voter has little real choice.

In governments with more than two political parties, the parties do not have to seek moderation or win a majority of votes. Instead, they take a definite stand and offer creative solutions to problems in order to satisfy a group of people who are committed to a particular issue—a labor issue, an antiwar issue, or an environmental issue. They then nominate a candidate who will take a strong stand on the chosen one or two issues. Because it is very difficult for such a candidate to get a majority of votes, parties compromise with each other and form coalitions even when they hold opposing positions on a variety of issues. Government policies can change dramatically with each election, depending on which party or coalition of parties gains power. Nevertheless, the voters have a clear choice on a variety of issues when they cast their ballots.

APPLYING KNOWLEDGE OF POLITICAL SYSTEMS

Knowledge of the different types of political structures and systems in modern societies is useful in a number of ways. First, academic sociologists can learn a great deal about a culture by understanding its political systems. By knowing how close a country is to being democratic or totalitarian and knowing the nature of its political parties, sociologists can gain insight into some of the values and behaviors of a people.

Certainly, politicians and diplomats need to know about the nature of the various political systems. A U.S. diplomat could not effectively negotiate with a foreign diplomat without first thoroughly understanding that the rules, policies, and decision-making processes are likely to be very different from those of the United States. Even similar types of political systems do not all operate in the same way. Both France and the United States are democracies, for example; but, as noted in the discussion of France, it is not entirely clear who in the French government is in charge of it.

Corporations involved in international business also need to have a thorough knowledge of foreign political structures. The policies that offer a great deal of freedom to American businesses are not found in all countries. Tax laws, tariffs, import and export laws, and other regulations greatly affect the way a business operates. Before making massive investments in an international business, then, corporate executives need to scrupulously study how the politics of a country will affect their ability to make a profit.

On the clinical side, understanding the nature of various political systems might help therapists and social workers to counsel immigrants who are having problems of adjustment. For someone who is used to being overtly controlled, the freedom offered by some democracies could be difficult to handle. New responsibilities, expectations, and rules about making personal decisions might be disorienting. For immigrants who seek education, teachers and school counselors may also find themselves in a position where they have to help foreign students adjust.

The issue of helping people adjust to new political systems is especially relevant today, considering the sweeping political changes that have been occurring in Eastern Europe. Imagine the psychological and sociological turmoil that could envelop people who have lived within very controlled political environments when their country democratizes almost overnight, or so it seems to have happened in many cases. The classical sociologist Emile Durkheim said that when people are faced with sudden changes in their lives (either positive or negative), they might experience anomie—a condition in which their old goals, values, and norms lose their meaning, leaving them with unclear guidelines for their lives. Perhaps private therapists, teachers, counselors, journalists, politicians, and other public speakers could use a sociological knowledge of political groups and systems to help people adjust to their new situations brought about by rapid political change.

Finally, anyone who travels abroad would benefit by understanding the political systems of foreign countries. Suppose that you decide to visit, work, or attend school in a European or Asian country. Do you know the rights you would have in, say, Greece, Italy, France, or China? If you happened to be accused of a crime, would you have the same rights as a U.S. citizen? Do you know, for example, that possession of marijuana is a more serious crime in many other countries than it is in the United States? To protect yourself and avoid unnecessary expenses or delays in time, you might carefully study the ways in which other political systems operate in such countries before you travel.

THE POLITICAL SYSTEM IN THE UNITED STATES

The United States has a democratic political system. Citizens are expected to rule the country by participating in the political process—debating issues, joining one of the two major political parties or remaining independent, voting for officials, and then expressing their opinions to officeholders.

The elected officials serve in a diverse, decentralized system of federal, state, and local governments. Each level of government has a system of checks and balances. The legislative branch makes the laws, the executive branch carries out the laws, and the judicial branch interprets the laws. Our system of government is representative, but how representative is it in practice? Who holds the power? Which groups influence government the most? There are two opposing perspectives on power in America. The first is that a powerful elite holds all of the power, and the second is that power is divided among many diversified groups.

The Power Elite

C. Wright Mills (1958) argued that a power elite, consisting of leaders in the upper echelons of business, the military, and the government, runs the United States. These leaders, Mills contended, are likely to come from similar backgrounds and have similar beliefs and values. There is no actual conspiracy among these leaders to promote the interests of their own high social stratum; but they, nevertheless, tend to support the same policies, as these policies support their common interests. Recent research, especially by Domhoff (2011) supports the theory that there is a power elite who holds power in United States political affairs.

One example of the operation of a power elite is what has come to be known as the "military–industrial complex." This complex evolved during World War II when some of the checks and balances regulating the defense department were dismantled. The absence of these checks and balances meant that the American defense industry was producing for a consumer, the American taxpayer, for whom price was not negotiable. As a result, unprecedented profits were made. In this way, United States military actions in foreign countries such as Korea and Vietnam kept the defense industry employed, and the industry became a decisive force in governmental policy.

Political Pluralism

Many sociologists believe that numerous groups in the United States play a significant role in political decision-making. David Riesman et al. (1950) described the power system of the United States as one of **political pluralism**—rule by many different groups. A variety of special interest groups try to influence legislation. They form lobbies that represent various industries, labor, religions, educational groups, and other special interests. These groups try to protect their own interests by pressuring politicians for favorable legislation and fighting against legislation they dislike. Thus, Riesman et al. believed, no single group had absolute power because different groups would balance one another's actions when they had competing interests.

There is little question that a variety of interest groups exist in the United States today. The issue for critics of pluralism is whether these various groups have any real power. Political pluralists believe that many groups are equally powerful and balance the power of other groups. Those who believe that a governing class or a military–industrial complex is most powerful fear that other groups are not strong enough to counteract the power of the elite, no matter how active and well organized they are.

Two types of groups are frequently in the news in American politics: *political action committees*, which contribute money to political campaigns, and *lobbies*, which attempt to influence legislation. Both types clearly have more power than individuals who do not belong to such groups. Questions remain about whether either type of group has enough power to counteract the power of elites or whether these groups actually tend to represent and extend the power of elite groups.

Political Action Committees (PACs)

Political action committees (PACs) are organizations formed to raise money for political campaigns. Candidates running for office need a great deal of money for political advertising, office overhead, transportation, and other needs. The expenses can reach tens of millions of dollars per campaign. As a rule, the people who are elected to political office spend more money than their opponents, and PACs help to pay these election expenses.

PACs represent many special interest groups—often groups that are at variance with one another. Business groups, labor groups, and professional groups all sponsor PACs. Some of the largest are the National Conservative PAC, Fund for a Conservative Majority, National Congressional Club, Realtors Political Action Committee, National Rifle Association (NRA), Political Victory Fund, Republican Majority Fund, American Medical Association (AMA), and the Fund for a Democratic Majority. Many of the most powerful favor the Republican Party, but others favor the Democratic Party. Those that have business interests often split their contributions, giving money to members of both parties. Nonetheless, although PACs support both parties and a variety of candidates, they do not represent a cross-section of American voters. Only groups with moneyed connections can possibly raise the sums needed to be influential in funding candidates.

A few PACs, particularly very conservative groups, have used PAC money to try to defeat **incumbents**, the elected officials who already hold office and are trying to be reelected. Most PAC money, however, goes to incumbents and, therefore, tends to maintain the power structure as it is. Currently there exists a very high rate of reelection of incumbents to the U.S. Congress, partly because they have access to PAC money.

Each PAC is allowed to contribute up to $5,000 to each politician per election unless it is a presidential campaign, in which case up to $10,000 is allowed. PACs are not permitted to persuade politicians to take a particular stand, but of course, they support only politicians who will support their cause. Oil and gas PACs, for example, support those members of Congress who vote for bills that will help the oil and gas industry; real estate PACs support only members who vote for bills that will help the real estate industry; and so on.

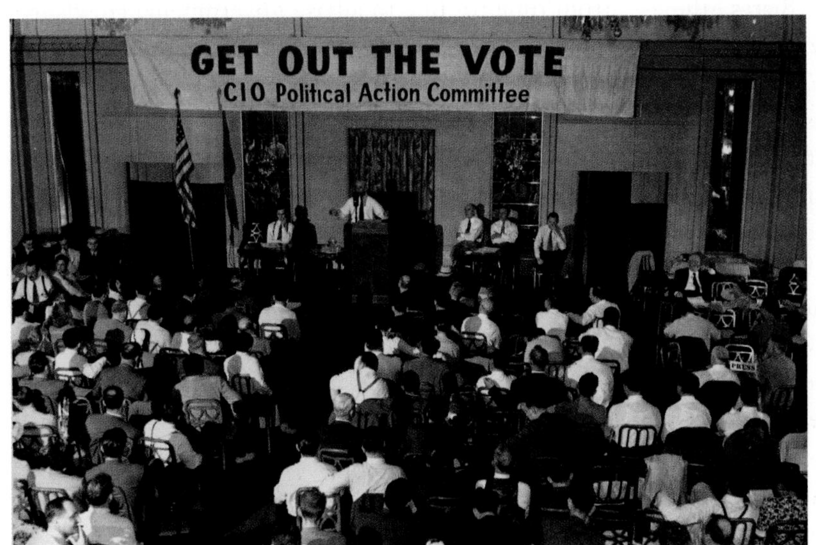

Political action committees (PACs) are organizations formed to raise money for political campaigns. Many special interest groups are represented by PACs. U.S. Congress incumbents who have access to PACs money seem to have a higher reelection rate.

Although PACs are not technically allowed to persuade politicians to take political stands, thousands of associations and groups are permitted to try to influence both politicians and civil servants. These groups are commonly called "lobbies."

Lobbies

Lobbies are organizations of people who wish to influence the political process on specific issues. Unlike political parties, lobbies do not nominate candidates or hope to manage the government. Their goal, rather, is to persuade elected and appointed officials to vote for or against a particular regulation or piece of legislation, as discussed in the introduction to this chapter. Groups of people with a common interest often form an association with the express purpose of influencing the legislative process. Thousands of such associations are based within blocks of the United States Capitol, where they monitor the legislation being considered. They maintain close contact with government officials and scrutinize the work of bureaucrats when budgets are being prepared or hearings are being held, so that they can influence the government to their own best interest. Because most national associations are federations of state and local associations, they have influence at every level of government, from the smallest town to the federal government.

Some of the largest and best-known associations are those involved in manufacturing, such as the National Association of Manufacturers (NAM), the Chamber of Commerce of the United States, the Chemical Specialties Manufacturers Association, the National Asphalt Pavement Association, the Evaporated Milk Association, the National Association of Retail Druggists, and the National Cemetery Association; the list is endless. Whom these organizations hire to lobby for them is a subject of serious debate, as discussed in the policy debate in this chapter.

It is estimated that as many as one in ten Americans depends on defense spending for their livelihood; and these individuals, the corporations for whom they work, and the military are well organized to lobby Congress for money for defense spending. The National Defense Industrial Association, founded in 1997, has eleven hundred corporate members who are defense contractors and twenty-seven thousand additional members from industry, universities, and the Pentagon; the Aerospace Industries Association has 154 associate member companies and 83 member companies. There are also the Navy League, the Air Force Association, the Association of the U.S. Army, the Armed Forces Communications and Electronics Association, the Shipbuilders Council of America, the Electronic Industries Association, and the Society of Naval Architects and Marine Engineers.

There are also some lobby groups who are concerned with issues unrelated to business. They are supported by donations from the public, and they lobby for issues related to the public good. Such groups include Common Cause, the National Wildlife Federation, the ACLU, and the Center for Science in the Public Interest.

The workings of the powerful automobile lobby show how much time, energy, and money are involved in influencing the political process. During the early 1960s, Ralph Nader, a public interest lobbyist, launched an attack on the faulty design of American automobiles in his book *Unsafe at Any Speed.* After the book was published, Nader continued to work for improved auto safety. In response, Congress considered passing legislation to set safety standards for cars, the auto lobby, led by Henry Ford, moved in to stop the legislation (Dowie 1977). Ford went to Washington and spoke to the Business Council, an organization of one hundred executives of large organizations who come to Washington from time to time to advise government. He visited members of Congress, held press conferences, and recruited business support; but he still failed to stop the passage of the Motor Vehicle Safety Act, which was signed into law in 1966. Ralph Nader ran for president of the United States in 2000.

A regulatory agency was then made responsible for setting guidelines for auto safety. The Ford Motor Company responded by sending representatives to the agency to argue that poor drivers, unsafe guardrail designs, poor visibility, and a variety of other highway and driving hazards were responsible for accidents. They contended that not only was the automobile safe but also that the regulations requiring improvements would increase the cost of cars and would save few lives.

A regulatory agency found that 400,000 cars burned up every year and that 3,000 people burned to death. After eight years of delays new safety regulations were finally passed.

Despite these lobbying efforts, in 1968 the regulatory agency issued new safety standards designed to reduce the risk of fire in automobiles after a rear-end crash. As required by law, the agency scheduled hearings on the regulation. Ford responded with a report stating that automobile fires were not a problem. The agency then had to conduct several studies to determine whether fire was a problem. It found that four hundred thousand cars burned up every year and that three thousand people burned to death. It again proposed safety standards; and Ford again responded, arguing that although burning accidents do happen, rear-end collisions were not the cause. The agency researched this question and found that rear-end collisions were, in fact, the cause in most cases. Again, regulations were proposed, again Ford responded, and again research was conducted. The total delay in developing regulations was eight years. The regulations eventually did pass; however, during those eight years, the company managed to defeat regulations requiring other safety measures. For example, it was twenty more years before air bags were finally installed in automobiles.

This account of one corporation's reluctance to comply with a safety regulation shows that big business has enormous, but not absolute, power over government. It also shows how time-consuming and expensive the business of lobbying is. It can be practiced only by organizations with much wealth and power, and bureaucratic organizations have much more power than any individual citizen.

Thinking Sociologically

1. Use the knowledge of political groups and systems provided in this chapter to discuss whether the government should further limit the amount of money that PACs can contribute to political campaigns.
2. Reconstruct the debate about whether there should be restrictions on lobbying by former government officials (see the policy debate) in terms of structural functionalism and conflict theory.
3. Using the information about lobbies and PACs, develop arguments to support and oppose the two views of political power groups offered in this chapter—the power elite and political pluralism.

THE ROLE OF THE INDIVIDUAL

Special interest groups can use their power to try to influence political decisions, but what is the role of the individual? As stated earlier in this chapter, American citizens are expected to participate in the political process by voting, debating issues, either joining one of the two major political parties or remaining

Children learn at an early age that political leaders and other leaders work to make the community a better place to live. They see the President of the United States as a leader, provider and a protector.

independent, and expressing their views to their elected officials. People learn these and other responsibilities through the process of political socialization.

Political Socialization

In most American communities, many children watch the mayor lead the Fourth of July parade and learn that the mayor is a good and benevolent leader. Most youngsters also learn that other leaders, likewise, give time and money to make the community a better place to live. During elections, children often learn about political parties as their families discuss candidates, and frequently they identify with a political party on an emotional level long before they can understand political issues. To a child, the President of the United States is to the country what the father is to the family: a leader, provider, and protector.

Political socialization of this sort continues when children enter school. Through formal courses in history, literature, and government, they learn to respect society's norms and political systems. Leaders are presented in history books as role models for society's norms. In an interesting study of how history books portray George Washington, Schwartz (1991) found that in the early part of the nineteenth century, when the United States believed that our leaders should be genteel, Washington was described in biographies as remote, of flawless virtue, refined, and with a dignified air. After the Civil War, Americans wanted their leaders to be more populist, so historians were criticized for making Washington sound cold, harsh, stern and soulless—a human iceberg. Historians described him at this point as one who loved life, children, flashy clothes, good wine, good houses, cards, and dirty jokes. After 1920, in order to fit into the growth of business, historians began to describe Washington as a good businessman, a captain of industry. Thus, whatever characteristics were considered admirable in a given period, those were the characteristics emphasized when discussing our first president.

Not all children emerge from their family and school socialization with the idea that political leaders are benevolent, caring, achieving people, of course. They may accumulate contradictory evidence along the way, perhaps having experiences with parents, teachers, or others who indicate that leaders are not to be trusted. They may also acquire a distrust of the political system by listening to parental complaints about lack of jobs or other conditions that result from political decisions and that cause family hardship. Schools teaching middle-class values may fail to convince a child living in poverty that the political system is fair and benevolent; realities in the child's environment may provide harsh evidence that not everyone can move from a log cabin to the White House. Children from Appalachia and urban ghettos have been much less apt to support the American political system than middle-class American children (Dowse and Hughes 1972). Political socialization exists as much in the daily interactions between adults and children as it does in the more formalized school settings. This is especially true in both urban and rural lower socioeconomic areas where children become acquainted with the political realities of the gap between the rich and the poor (Lay 2006).

Political Socialization in the Mass Media

By the time that children finish school, they have developed political attitudes that will shape their political behavior in adult life; but political socialization still continues, especially through the mass media, which reinforce childhood socialization. Much mass media socialization presents political issues in emotional terms. Slogans that promise a better America without offering data about how this is to be done are seeking an emotional response from voters, a response resembling the one a child feels for the mayor leading the Fourth of July parade. Although these emotional appeals for voter support are routinely criticized as "flag waving," emotion is believed to play a very large role in voter choice.

What is the price one pays to run for president? The total amount spent by presidential candidates, senate and house candidates, political parties and independent interest groups trying to influence the federal election in 2008 was nearly 5.3 billion dollars, up from 4.1 billion in 2004 and 3.1 billion in 2000. Certainly the majority of this money does not come from PACS, but PACS do play an important contributory role. In the 2004 Presidential election, PACs contributed 384 million dollars to the candidates, (Center for Responsive Politics Oct. 2005, 2011).

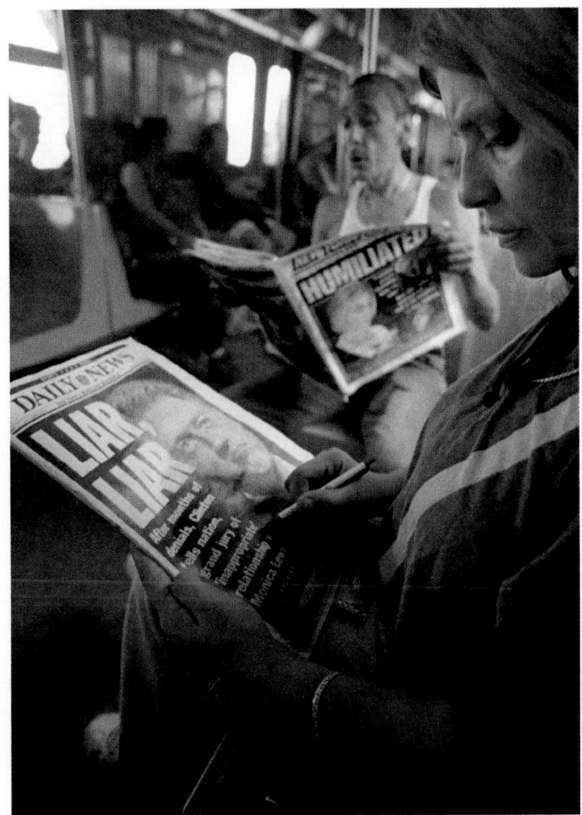

When only one side of an issue is heard, people will tend to believe only that side.

APPLYING POLITICAL SOCIALIZATION

By being aware some politicians often use this emotional ploy, you can increase your ability to critically evaluate their political statements, positions, and campaign platforms. Some politicians—particularly those who have training in acting or public speaking—have mastered this ability to manipulate people's emotions. This skill provides them with a great deal of charismatic authority, which affords them considerable political clout. Often, politicians can muster overwhelming public support for policies that are devoid of any meaningful substance or even—at times—not in the best interests of the population. However, emotion can also be used by politicians to sway the population to accept meaningful and beneficial policies. As voters, you need to be particularly critical of political proposals that are directed more to your hearts to than your minds. The most effective way for the mass media to influence people is to present information in such a way that there is only one obvious conclusion (Goodin 1980). The media often give only one side of an issue; and if the so-called obvious solution is heard frequently enough, it will seem to make sense to most people. Often, for a year or two before an election, we hear a candidate mentioned as the obvious choice for the party. The candidate might even say that if people do not have jobs, they obviously do not want jobs. If people do not vote, they are obviously not interested. These statements are not obvious at all; but unless contradictory information is provided, they may seem obvious enough and will probably be accepted by the majority of the public.

POLICY DEBATE

Should Former Members of Congress or Congressional Staff Be Restricted from Lobbying?

Lobbying has long been a tradition in American politics. In many instances, lobbying has not only been legitimate but also necessary. For example, after the Civil War, many veterans and widows seeking pensions hired lobbyists to help them because the official qualifications for pensions required documents that many eligible citizens did not possess. The lobbyists asked Congress to pass private bills granting pensions to those who could not produce the necessary documents. In The *Spider Web*, a history of lobbying in President Ulysses S. Grant's administration, Syracuse University historian Margaret Thompson writes, "Establishing access, particularly if one's demand was individual and basically indistinguishable from hordes of others, was time-consuming, debilitating, and practically impossible unless someone was continuously on the scene to oversee it. Obviously one's chances were improved if one could afford to hire an advocate—and the better the advocate's record was, the higher his or her fees ... were likely to be" (Thompson 1985, 165). In principle, using experts to influence what goes on in the government is a legitimate part of a representative democracy.

Michael K. Deaver

However, whether it is legitimate and fair for top government officials to trade their government positions for jobs in which they lobby their former congressional colleagues and use their political contacts to help win favors for private organizations is debatable. As mentioned in the introduction to this chapter, this practice of giving up a government position for a position as a lobbyist is known as the "revolving-door" phenomenon. This phenomenon, although not new, received much public attention during the mid-1980s when White House aide Michael K. Deaver left his position in the Reagan administration to set up a high-priced lobbying firm. The political connections, friends, and expertise that Deaver gained as a White House aide provided him with a tremendous potential to influence government legislation. His inside knowledge of the governmental bureaucracy—such as knowing the mechanics about how legislation really gets accepted, the types of policies that Congress might be willing to accept, the specific members of Congress who might be sympathetic to a particular cause, how the president and cabinet secretaries feel about certain matters, and so on—make him highly valuable to private organizations and groups that could benefit from having particular legislation passed. Because of this, private organizations and groups are willing to pay Deaver and his associates enormous salaries—a great deal more money than he was paid in his government job—to counsel them and to help lobby for their cause in

In the United States, there is concern that the mass media express only the views of the large corporations that generally own them. Few newspapers, for example, are still locally owned and compete with other locally owned newspapers. Gannett Company dominates the newspaper business, owning a national newspaper, *USA Today*, plus local newspapers, radio and television stations, and even most of the nation's billboards. There are only a few major television networks, including ABC, CBS, NBC, and FOX. Thus, information about politics may be severely limited, and the information presented may represent only the viewpoint of the mass-media owners.

The federal government also provides information to its citizens regarding health, agriculture,

Congress. This type of activity has led to a debate over whether revolving-door restrictions should be placed on former members of Congress, the congressional staff, and other White House officials.

Opponents to revolving-door restrictions believe that lobbying is an activity that is sanctioned by the Constitution's First Amendment right "to petition the government for redress of grievances" and that it is protected by the Constitutional right to free speech. According to Morton H. Halperin, Director of the American Civil Liberties Union's Washington, D.C., office and Leslie A. Harris, the ACLU's legislative counsel, "Lobbying, at bottom, is political speech entitled to the full protection of the First Amendment. To justify any restriction on that speech, [one] must show that the restrictions serve a compelling state interest and that they are narrowly tailored to serve that interest. We do not believe such a showing can be made with respect to members of Congress." Stated simply, everyone has a constitutional right to lobby.

Those who favor restrictions on revolving-door lobbying feel that revolving-door abuses overstep the boundaries of free political speech guaranteed by the First Amendment, thus disqualifying some people from acting as lobbyists. Archibald Cox, chairperson of a government watchdog group called Common Cause, says, "Nothing in the constitution or judicial precedents supports the view that any individual has an absolute right to speak about government business *in a representative capacity* to a member or agent of the legislative or executive branch. One may well doubt whether the First Amendment gives any right to act in a representative capacity. ... Speaking for another, with or without compensation, involves association—a relationship sometimes protected by the First Amendment but not as absolutely pure speech. ... Ample Supreme Court precedent upholds ... restrictions when designed to preserve the integrity of our political processes and public confidence therein."

A second point of contention is whether the type of lobbying that the revolving door promotes is democratic. Opponents of revolving-door restrictions contend that all citizens have somebody to represent them; and, therefore, lobbying that is connected to the revolving door is democratic. A multitude of associations in Washington represent various age, sex, ethnic, and professional groups. It would, therefore, be undemocratic to disqualify some people from lobbying or to deny some groups access to people who have the influence that they may need to have their interests served.

The problem, according to advocates of restrictions, is that the revolving door grants some lobbyists greater power to influence legislation, thus enabling them to charge a very high fee for their services. What's undemocratic, say advocates of revolving-door restrictions, is that those at the upper end of the income scale can afford the very influential revolving-door lobbyists while those with lower incomes cannot. David Luban, a research scholar at the University of Maryland's Institute for Philosophy and Public Policy, feels that "the idea that everyone's represented [by lobbying groups] is pretty illusory. ... The more diffuse a group is, the harder it is to represent all the interests of that group." Thus, the less-diffuse wealthy groups have a better chance of being served than lower-income, more-diffuse groups.

Luban and other supporters of lobbying restrictions feel that the revolving-door phenomenon also carries the potential for being undemocratic because many revolving-door veterans—with their influence—may, in effect, run the country while no one really knows it and while there is no way to control it. This can have a very corrupting and unhealthy effect on government.

In contrast, opponents of revolving-door restrictions feel that the revolving door is healthy because it helps attract talented people to government service. In order to serve in government, talented lawyers and businesspeople may give up lucrative positions in law firms or businesses. If there was no possibility of economically benefiting from their expertise gained while in government, the most talented might not be interested in serving in government. Thus, they deserve to sell their expertise and their influence to organizations that can afford to pay them once they give up their government service.

Furthermore, the turnover created by revolving-door opportunities is healthy because it enables more talented people to become involved in government at the executive branch. Advocates of revolving-door restrictions counter this by arguing that it is not the government's responsibility to oversee the economic well-being of former officials, nor is it the government's obligation to let former officials profit economically from the expertise they gained at government expense.

This debate is summarized from Sarah Glazer's "Getting a Grip on Influence Peddling," *Congressional Quarterly's Editorial Research Reports*, 2(22) (December 15, 1989: 698–711. Reprinted by permission.)

education, labor, housing, and population statistics. This information is dispensed in a variety of ways: county agricultural agents, public health centers, libraries, newspapers, radio, and television. Many of the statistics used by sociologists are collected and published by government agencies. Sociologists are well aware, however, that the government also attempts to shape public opinion; and it sometimes reports information that presents a misleading description of a problem. Government unemployment figures, for example, count only those unemployed persons who are still known to be actively seeking work; they do not report the number of people who have given up the search for a job. This practice artificially lowers the statistics on unemployment in the country.

Political Participation

The United States has one of the lowest voter turnouts in the democratic world (see Table 15-1). In 2000, only 85.5 percent of registered voters and 51.3 percent of the voting age population chose to vote. (See Table 15-2 and Table 15-3.) Four years later, the statistics looked much the same; of those registered to vote in the 2004 presidential election, only 88.5 percent of registered voters and 55.3 percent of the voting age population cast a ballot. In 2008, 89.6 percent of registered voters and 56.8 percent of the voting-age population voted. Voter turnout hurts the Democratic Party because the blocks of people who do not vote—the young, the poor, and blacks—are statistically more apt to be Democratic. When voter turnout is low, the Republican Party is more likely to win elections, and social programs that help the poor and minority groups are more likely to be ignored.

Table 15-1 Ranking of Voter Turnout Percentages in Selected Democratic Nations in Recent National Election (2008 unless indicated otherwise)

	Country	Vote/VAP % *
1.	Sweden	80.6% (2006)
2.	Italy	79.13%
3.	Spain	77.2%
4.	Austria	75.61%
5.	Germany	71.99% (2005)
6.	Israel	71.16% (2006)
7.	Japan	66.62% (2005)
8.	Mexico	63.62% (2006)
9.	United Kingdom	58.32% (2005)
10.	USA	58.22%
11.	France	54.52% (2007)
12.	Canada	53.59
13.	Republic of Korea	46.49%
14.	Switzerland	39.79% (2007)

* VAP: voting age population (18+)

Source: International Institute for Democracy and Electoral Assistance (International IDEA) http://www.idea.int/vt

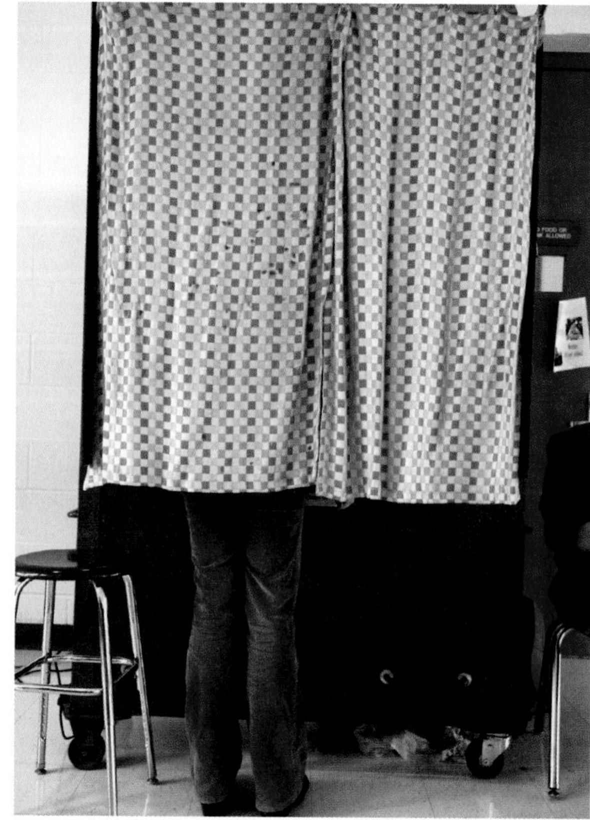

The United States has one of the lowest voter turnouts in the democratic world.

A variety of explanations for the lack of voter participation have been proposed. One set of explanations attributes the lack of voter participation to social-psychological reasons, the attitude of the voter. Potential voters stay away from the polls for a variety of reasons. They may believe that their votes do not make a difference, or they don't feel any civic obligation to participate. Perhaps they do not like either party's candidate, or they may be equally satisfied with all candidates. Voters may lack the education to know either the importance of voting or the issues being considered; they may be too young or too poor to care—in a work, they are *apathetic*. Those who believe that social-psychological reasons are the reasons that people do not vote also tend to believe that if government is less than perfect, the voters have no one to blame but themselves. If they seek change, they should give politics more attention.

However, critics of this theory argue that people are not staying away from the polls because of apathy. In this nation, before the twentieth century, and in

Table 15-2 Voting in Presidential Elections, 1960-2008

Year	Voting-age population	Voter registration	Voter turnout	Turnout of voting-age population (percent)
2008*	231,229,580	NA	132,618,580*	56.8%
2006	220,600,000	135,889,600	80,588,000	37.1%
2004	221,256,931	174,800,000	122,294,978	55.3
2002	215,473,000	150,990,598	79,830,119	37.0
2000	205,815,000	156,421,311	105,586,274	51.3
1998	200,929,000	141,850,558	73,117,022	36.4
1996	196,511,000	146,211,960	96,456,345	49.1
1994	193,650,000	130,292,822	75,105,860	38.8
1992	189,529,000	133,821,178	104,405,155	55.1
1990	185,812,000	121,105,630	67,859,189	36.5
1988	182,778,000	126,379,628	91,594,693	50.1
1986	178,566,000	118,399,984	64,991,128	36.4
1984	174,466,000	124,150,614	92,652,680	53.1
1982	169,938,000	110,671,225	67,615,576	39.8
1980	164,597,000	113,043,734	86,515,221	52.6
1978	158,373,000	103,291,265	58,917,938	37.2
1976	152,309,190	105,037,986	81,555,789	53.6
1974	146,336,000	96,199,020[1]	55,943,834	38.2
1972	140,776,000	97,328,541	77,718,554	55.2
1970	124,498,000	82,496,747[2]	58,014,338	46.6
1968	120,328,186	81,658,180	73,211,875	60.8
1966	116,132,000	76,288,283[3]	56,188,046	48.4
1964	114,090,000	73,715,818	70,644,592	61.9
1962	112,423,000	65,393,751[4]	53,141,227	47.3
1960	109,159,000	64,833,096[5]	68,838,204	63.1

*Source 2008 election results: http://elections.gmu.edu/Turnout_2008G.html.
Read more: National Voter Turnout in Federal Elections: 1960–2008 — Infoplease.com http://www.infoplease.com/ipa/A0781453.html#ixzz1Lsh1hNwl

other nations currently, people have participated at much greater rates than they do in the United States now. The young, the poor, and the less educated—all vote as often as the old, the rich, and the more educated in most European nations. If apathy and social-psychological attitudes are to explain a lack of voter participation, such explanations ought to hold in other twentieth-century democratic, industrialized societies, as they do in the United States.

Critics of social-psychological theories argue that the reasons for a lack of voter participation are found in the social structure of voting procedures. Piven and Cloward (1989), for example, argue that voter participation in this country was high before 1880, and many

SOCIOLOGY AT WORK

Sociology and Municipal Politics

Karen George earned her B.A. and M.A. in sociology at Wayne State University. George has been a councilwoman in the city of Southgate, Michigan, since 1983. Besides serving as councilwoman, she is a licensed cosmetologist and has worked as a secretary, matron, police cadet, and part-time instructor in sociology. She decided to major in sociology after having been involved with the public for many years in a variety of different roles. "I have always been a people watcher and can just sit and watch different groups in a mall," George says. "Having worked with people in such a variety of settings led me to wonder why different groups dressed and acted in the manner in which they did. Sociology gave me some of the answers."

George feels that sociology has been particularly useful to her in her position as city councilwoman. "In my present position as an elected official, I am accountable to all the citizens of the city of Southgate and not to one person or employer. However, I feel that my sociology background has made me much more sensitive to understanding the needs of different groups and individuals. Having been raised in a very traditional religious family and white suburban middle class neighborhood, sociology has made me remove my blinders of prejudice and be more tolerant to those whose lifestyles differ from mine."

"Being in a political position, I could at times take advantage of my position. I must admit that it has opened doors that would not have been opened otherwise. I have experienced first-hand discrimination that went on in me 'before' and 'after' holding public office. My sociological background has helped me to realize that groups will always be in competition with one another. In the political arena, one gets used to a constant power struggle. Conflict theory has helped me understand that politics is much more than a matter of individual personalities. I have come to understand the ways in which groups can use their respective power in order to attempt to obtain what they want."

George notes that sociology has given her more than just an overall perspective that she takes to her political career. Specific sociological knowledge also helps her to serve her constituency better. "My sociology background has made me aware of many aspects of the socialization process. This has made me especially sensitive to the needs of the youth in our cities. I am also keenly sensitive to the needs of single-parent households. The traditional two-parent family is 'history' even in my small homogenous community. The course in the family that I took helped me to view the traditional family and newer family forms in proper perspective. This knowledge has been invaluable to me when dealing with matters that affect children and single-parent households."

Finally, George says that sociology has helped her get beyond simply using common sense. "Sociology as a science has helped me to examine the facts and not to simply see things as they may appear. Many times our common sense leads us to believe one way, while the facts point in another direction." George believes that having this perspective is essential for someone who is in a position to influence the way in which a municipality operates.

of the issues in elections were populist issues that stimulated the participation of farmers and of the working class. However, after the election of 1880, powerful business leaders formed oligarchies in both parties; and as both parties then supported business issues almost exclusively, competition between the parties collapsed. The populists were shut out of party politics.

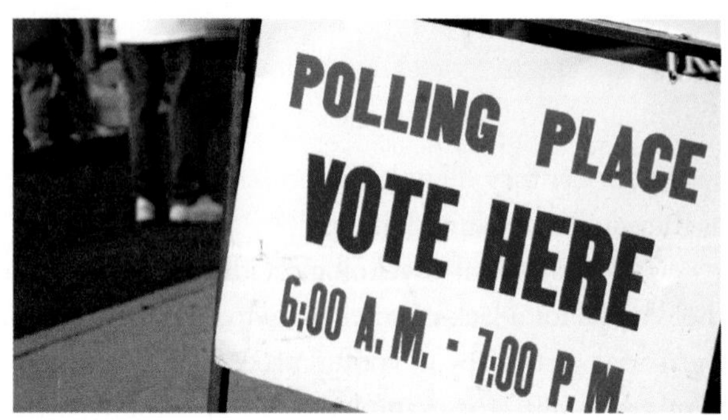

In some countries voting is mandatory.

The business leaders of both parties were concerned about the waves of immigrants flowing into this country and wanted to restrict their power to influence elections; and they were concerned about the power that black people had been developing since the Civil War. In order to restrict these groups, they instituted reforms dealing with registration and voting procedures. They instituted poll taxes, official ballots, registration lists that required a worker to be away from work in order to get on the list, literacy tests, residency requirements, and other complicated voting procedures. While many of these restrictions have been declared illegal, the procedures for registering and voting are still burdensome in this country (Piven and Cloward 1989). Registration sometimes requires traveling to the county seat or even to the state capital. In addition to the difficulties of registering to vote, there are too many elections, too many elected

changing the qualifications of elected officials. In some countries, registration is automatic when the voter reaches an eligible age. In other countries, voting is mandatory, and people who do not vote are fined.

The people in the United States who do vote tend to remain very loyal to either the Republican or the Democratic party, a loyalty based primarily on emotional ties formed during the earlier socialization process. Approximately 85 percent to 95 percent of both parties voted for their own party affiliation in the 2008 election. (See Table 15-4.) Most people do not choose a party on the basis of political opinions, usually because they are not well

TABLE 15-3 WHO VOTED IN THE 2008 PRESIDENTIAL ELECTION?

	Registered	Voted	Registered who Voted
Total, 18 years and older	71%	63.6%	89.6%
Race			
White, non-Hispanic	73.5%	66.1%	90%
African-AmericanBlack	69.7%	64.7%	92.9%
Asian	55.3%	47.6%	86.1%
Hispanic	59.4%	49.9%	84%
Age:			
18-24 year olds	58.4%	48.5%	83%
25-34 year olds	66.4%	57%	85.8%
35-44 year olds	69.9%	62.8%	89.8%
45–54 year olds	73.5%	67.4%	91.6%
55-64 year olds	76.6%	71.5%	93.3%
65-74 year olds	78.1%	72.4%	92.7%
75 and older	76.6%	67.8%	88.6%
Income:			
Under $20,000	63.7%	51.9%	81.5%
$20,000-29,999	67.1%	56.3%	83.9%
$30,000-39,999	71.1%	62.2%	87.5%
$40,000-49,999	72.6%	64.7%	89.1%
$50,000-74,999	78.2%	70.9%	90.7%
$75,000-99,999	81.9%	76.4%	93.3%
$100,000 and above	79.6%	91.8%	91.8%
Income not reported	53.4%	49%	91.7%
Education:			
No high school diploma	50.5%	39.4%	78%
High school graduate or GED	64.1%	54.9%	85.6%
Some college or associate's or degree	75.3%	68%	90.4%
College graduate	81.2%	77%	94.8%
Advanced degree	85.8%	82.7%	96.4%

Source: U.S. Census Bureau, Current Population Survey, November, 2008

TABLE 15-4 HOW PEOPLE VOTED IN 2008 PRESIDENTIAL ELECTION

	How They Voted			
	All Voters		Whites	
	Obama %	McCain %	Obama %	McCain %
Total	53	46	43	55
Age 18-29	66	31	54	44
Republicans	15	84	11	88
Democrats	95	4	92	7
Independents	66	27	62	32
Men	62	34	52	45
Women	69	29	56	42
College experience	65	32	55	42
No college	66	31	50	48
White	54	44		
Black	95	4		
Hispanic	76	19		
Age 30+	50	48	41	57
Republicans	8	90	7	91
Democrats	88	11	83	16
Independents	48	48	44	52
Men	47	51	39	59
Women	52	46	44	54
College experience	49	49	42	56
No college	50	48	38	60
White	41	57		
Black	96	4		
Hispanic	62	36		

Source: National exit poll conducted by NBC News.

informed about political issues, and the parties do not differ significantly on most issues. Instead, they affiliate with a party and then are educated by the party's stand on the issues. Because they are loyal to their party, they accept the stand of the party. In an interesting study, Heritage and Greatbatch (1986) found that people interrupt political speeches with applause after emotion-laden slogans, not after informative analyses of domestic or foreign affairs.

While on most issues, the voters will accept the stand taken by their party, this is not true of the so-called moral issues, such as race, sexual behavior, and religion. People usually have a strong opinion on moral issues; and they will leave their party and either will not vote or else will vote for the other party if they disagree with their own party's stand. As a result, political parties generally try to avoid moral issues altogether and take a middle-of-the-road stand on other issues to attract the largest number of voters.

Some groups outside of the major political parties have attempted to bring moral issues into politics. They recognize that emotional issues often can easily influence a large minority of people, and they have used these issues to attract followers. They cannot, however, attract the majority of voters. If the majority of the voters agreed, for example, that abortions should be outlawed, the major political parties would also express that belief; thus, the issue would cease to be divisive.

Thinking Sociologically

1. What features of the United States political system increase legitimate authority?
2. Given our low voter turnout, is legitimate authority decreasing?
3. Are the social values reflected in the United States political system the values of all the people or the values only of more powerful people?

CHAPTER REVIEW

Wrapping it up

Summary

1. A society's *political institution* is the structure that has the power to rule in a society. Power is the ability to control the behavior of others. Politics is the use of power to determine who gets what in society.

2. Two types of power are physical force and latent force. Physical force is an inefficient way to control a society. *Latent force*, making people comply by threatening them with punishment, is more effective.

3. *Authority* is the most effective means of power and is considered legitimate because the people believe that the ruler has a right to rule; so they comply voluntarily. *Traditional authority* is derived from accepted practices or customs. *Legal authority* is based on a system of legislated rules and regulations. *Charismatic authority* comes from the personal traits of the leader.

4. Structural functionalists believe that political systems reflect societal values. If a society values freedom, monogamy, hard work, and achievement, laws will be passed to enforce these values. Members of the society will comply with the law because it reflects their own beliefs.

5. Structural functionalists also believe that the political system must try to resolve conflicts in values. The value of freedom, for example, may come into conflict with the value of hard work, and the government must arbitrate to ensure that behavior does not infringe on either value. Some subcultures teach values that conflict with those of the larger society, but the government must protect the values of the dominant society.

6. Conflict theorists believe that some groups gain power because they possess a large share of society's resources. They use these resources to acquire power and use the law and the political system to protect their own wealth. The rich teach the population through the schools and the mass media that their wealth, power, and laws are legitimate. In other words, they shape the values of the society to serve their own interests.

7. Modern societies have two types of legal power structures: democratic systems and totalitarian systems. *Democratic systems* allow citizens to participate in their own governance. *Totalitarian systems* have powerful governments that control the society.

8. Political parties are groups of citizens formed with the express intent of gaining control of the political body of the state. They exist in both democratic and totalitarian states. Parties nominate candidates to run for office, provide personnel for bureaucratic posts, and make public policy. Their goal is not only to influence government but also to manage it.

9. Debate about how power is distributed in the United States has continued for many years. Theorists have argued, on the one hand, that a power elite made up of business and government officials controls the power and, on the other hand, that there are a variety of diversified groups that protect their own interests.

10. In the United States, socialization legitimates legal authority, and political socialization begins early. Youngsters learn about political leaders and political parties at home and in the community. Socialization continues in school, and most children learn to respect the political system, although poor children are more likely to question government and its practices.

11. Voter participation is low in this country. Social-psychological explanations do not fully explain why voters do not vote. Instead, the structure of our political parties and our registration and voting procedures explains much of our low voter participation.

12. Most Americans remain loyal to one political party and permit it to guide them on important issues. On moral issues, however, voters tend to act more independently.

Key Terms

authority Power accepted as legitimate by those it affects

charismatic authority Authority granted to someone on the bases of his or her personality characteristics

citizen One who is considered a member of a state and who is entitled to the privileges and freedoms granted to members of the state

city-state A city and the surrounding area ruled independently of other areas

democracy A power structure in which people govern themselves, either directly or through elected representatives

incumbent One holding an elected office

iron law of oligarchy In democratic societies, the inevitable rise of a few elite leaders who dominate power

latent force A type of power in which force is threatened

legal authority Authority based on a system of rules and regulations that determine how a society will be governed

legitimate power Controlling the behavior of others through having people accept the authority as necessary and beneficial to all

lobby An organization of people who want to influence the political process on a specific issue

nation-states Large territories ruled by a single political institution

oligarchy Government by a small elite group

physical force A type of power backed by sheer force such as an army or physical might

political action committees (PACs) Organizations formed to raise money for a political campaign

political parties Groups of citizens formed with the express intent of gaining control of the political body of the state

political pluralism A political system in which many diverse groups have a share of the power

politics The use of power to determine who gets what in society

power The ability to control or influence the behavior of others, even without their consent

power elite A small group of people who hold all of the powerful positions and cooperate to maintain their social positions

referenda Questions on a ballot to be decided by the electorate

states Societies with institutional government and laws as a means of political regulation, a military defense, and a way to finance these activities

totalitarianism A power structure in which the government has total power to dictate the values, rules, ideology, and economic development of a society

traditional authority The right to rule granted to someone on the basis of tradition, as with a patriarch or king

Discussion Questions

1. Discuss how knowledge of different types of power could be useful in your everyday life. Use examples of specific social situations in which you are routinely involved.
2. Discuss the advantages of authority as a source of power.
3. Select a policy or a piece of legislation currently in the news, and examine it from the structural functional and conflict perspectives on political systems.
4. Discuss, which would be a more efficient form of government—democracy or totalitarianism.
5. Discuss the role of political parties in government.
6. Discuss whether you think that power in the United States is monopolized by a few—as in the military–industrial complex—or is broadly distributed, as in a pluralistic model.
7. Discuss the advantages and disadvantages of a one-party political system, a two-party political system, and a political system with multiple parties.
8. What kinds of abuses might result from PACs and lobbies?
9. Examine your own political attitudes and how they have been developed through socialization.
10. Do you believe that a political party educates voters who have chosen the party, or do voters choose a party after educating themselves on issues? Discuss how this difference shapes the nature of authority.

Pop Quiz

1. Power considered legitimate by those it affects is called _________.

   a. authority
   b. latent force
   c. physical force
   d. politics

2. The Queen of England's authority is _________.

   a. legal
   b. traditional
   c. charismatic
   d. latent

3. When is power legitimate?

   a. It is accepted by the people in a society
   b. It is based only on rules and regulations
   c. It is accepted by those in the political system
   d. It is only backed by physical force

4. Which of the following theorists identified three types of authority?

   a. Karl Marx
   b. Max Weber
   c. C. Wright Mills
   d. David Riesman

5. The ________ theory believes that a society is build on a common set of values.

   a. conflict
   b. structural-functional
   c. symbolic interaction
   d. power elite

6. The power structure in which people govern themselves is called _________.

   a. dictatorship
   b. totalitarianism
   c. oligarchy
   d. democracy

7. A system of rule in which the government has total control is __________.

   a. totalitarianism
   b. democratic socialism
   c. fascism
   d. rational

8. Which author is associated with the view that the United States is ruled by a power elite?

   a. G. W. Domhoff
   b. C. Wright Mills
   c. David Riesman
   d. Karl Marx

9. The sociologist who believes that our political system is one of political pluralism is __________.

   a. C. Wright Mills
   b. Max Weber
   c. G. W. Domhoff
   d. David Riesman

10. An organization that attempts to influence the political process on a specific issue is a __________.

    a. special interest group
    b. political party
    c. political action committee
    d. power elite

11. Charismatic authority is based on the personal attributes of a leader. T/F

12. States are societies with institutional means of political regulation. T/F

13. Democratic and totalitarian states have several characteristics in common. T/F

14. The military-industrial complex is an example of a “power elite” in the United States. T/F

15. The people in the United States who do vote tend to remain loyal to either the Republican or Democratic party. T/F

1. A	6. D	11. T
2. B	7. A	12. T
3. A	8. B	13. T
4. B	9. D	14. T
5. B	10. A	15. T

CHAPTER 16

Economic Groups and Systems

GOVERNMENT AND THE AMERICAN ECONOMY

The American Recovery and Reinvestment Act of 2009 underscored the deep ideological divide between Democrats and Republicans about the proper role of government in economic activity. When Congress enacted the economic stimulus package in 2009, nearly every Democrat supported the bill while most Republicans rejected it. The dispute centered on the question of whether the federal government should intervene in the economy by boosting government spending to stimulate economic growth. Republicans claimed the stimulus bill reflected a broader socialist agenda by the Democrats that would undercut economic performance and individual drive in the United States. The Democrats disagreed, saying the stimulus money would not only boost economic growth but also reinforce capitalism by creating thousands of jobs in the private sector.

The political divide over the American Recovery and Reinvestment Act is important because it highlights a major subject of sociological inquiry—the differences between economic systems. The American economy today is essentially capitalist. That is, government regulation and control over the U.S. economy is limited. Moreover, any idea that the U.S. economy is somehow socialist has no merit. Socialist economies are state-run, and everyone has employment for life. Still, it is indisputable that the U.S. government plays a major role in guiding the American economy. Why then do so many Americans oppose socialism? For that matter, why do some Americans criticize capitalism? To answer these questions, it pays to examine the extremes of the two systems. Consider these hypothetical cases. While neither of these descriptions is an accurate depiction of the U.S., they represent stereotypes fostered by critics of each system.

Imagine the United States is completely capitalist with no government regulation or interference in the economy. Everyone is free to accumulate as much wealth as possible. Corporate and personal income taxes are things of the past. Employees are exploited through low wages in order to maximize profits. As competition grows, so does corporate espionage. Without public schools, only the wealthy can afford primary or college educations. Meanwhile, banks raise interest rates as high as 90 percent on business loans, cutting deeply into company profits. Without regulation, banks can do whatever they want. Large corporations have difficulty raising capital as well. With rampant insider trading, confidence in the stock market is perpetually low. Large corporations simply cannot sell enough shares to accumulate adequate amounts of capital. Pollution increases because it is more cost-effective for large corporations not to have pollution-controls. Air and water pollution lead to rapid environmental deterioration as well as an increase in illnesses. Travel becomes prohibitively expensive. First, since everyone pays expensive tolls on all the privately owned roads, it's not cost-effective to send negotiators from place to place. Second, the cost of gasoline is enormous because of price-fixing by multinational petroleum companies.

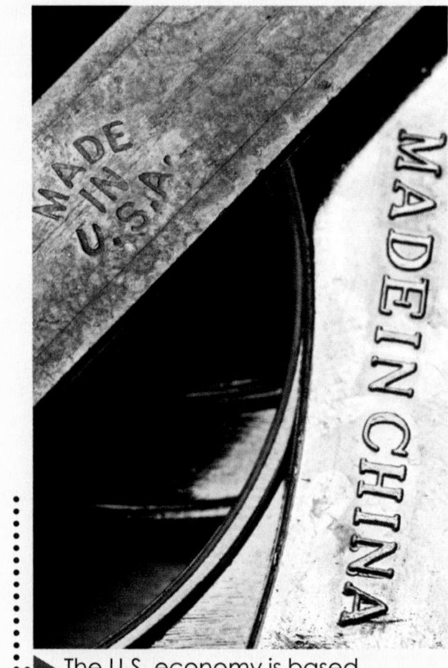

The U.S. economy is based on capitalism.

Now imagine the U.S. economy is entirely socialist. All land, factories, banks, and stores are government owned. The pursuit of profit is a capital crime. Citizens can own personal items, such as clothing and bicycles, but are prohibited from owning any property that generates profit such as apartments for rent. The economy is highly regulated to meet national economic goals. However, to meet these goals, central planners regularly deprive Americans of the latest technology and fashion. Everyone has a free education, but schools are dilapidated because no tax revenue is available to pay for new buildings and equipment. The teachers, moreover, are mostly unqualified because nobody with talent goes to college willingly. Because everyone gets paid equally under socialism, there's no incentive to work hard. Government officials, therefore, resort to tactics of intimidation and tyranny to generate economic productivity. For example, the government may force students to major in certain subjects when professionals in those fields are in short supply. The government may also tell students where to live and work after graduation. It does not matter if anyone agrees with the government; citizens do what they're told. Even with its tyrannical tactics, however, the government never generates the same level of national output as capitalist countries. That's why everyone routinely waits in long lines to get basic amenities such as bread and butter. Meanwhile, citizens who are sick receive free medical care, but the quality of treatment is substandard. Most doctors are mediocre as well. It's easy to understand. When professionals earn the same amount as high-school dropouts, they're not motivated to provide superior service.

Clearly, neither of these scenarios is an accurate depiction of these economic systems. However, it also seems clear that there needs to be a balance between laissez-faire competition and government intervention in order to have a stable economy. The United States is one of the most capitalist countries on earth. However, political wrangling over the government's role in the economy is as old as the republic. In every period, however, one thing remains constant: The government plays a major role in fostering the economic power of the United States. A key goal of this chapter, then, is to provide students with the ability to analyze and evaluate different economic systems and the effects of policies like the American Recovery and Reinvestment Act on society.

To survive, people need food, shelter, and health care. Except for those who live in the tropics, people also need clothing and a source of heat. To be accepted in modern American society, however, we need a great deal more—soap, deodorant, toothpaste, shoes, and various types of clothes for different occasions. We also enjoy the luxuries our society provides—such as plates, knives, forks, furniture, cars, sporting equipment, radios, televisions, the Internet, iPods, Palm Pilots, and so on. All these things, from the most basic necessities to the most expensive luxuries, are produced by our economic system.

The **economic system** is the social system that provides for the production, distribution, and consumption of goods and services. Sociologists study the economic system because it is a major social institution that influences every aspect of society. Sociologists are not economists, however. Economists study the internal workings of the economic system: supply and demand, how much industry is producing, how much consumers are buying, how much government is taxing, borrowing, and spending, and so on. Sociologists, on the other hand, study how the economic system interacts with other social institutions. They study types of economic systems, the size and power of corporations, the occupations of the people in economic systems, how work affects the rest of our lives, and similar issues.

Although sociologists and economists do not study the economy in the same way, they actually cover much of the same material. Economists cannot understand the success or failure of an economic system without considering how it interacts with the rest of society. Sociologists cannot understand how social systems interact unless they understand the internal functioning of each system. Nevertheless, the disciplines have different goals. Economists specialize in studying the economic system as one of society's important interacting parts. Sociologists study the whole of society, including the economic system.

APPLYING SOCIOLOGICAL PERSPECTIVES ON ECONOMIC GROUPS AND SYSTEMS

Developing a sociological perspective about the nature of economic groups and systems is useful in a variety of ways. For example, all of us can learn a great deal about different societies by understanding their economic systems. In addition, sociological perspectives can aid individuals who have specialized interests. For example, politicians can gain important insights because an important aspect of international politics concerns the economic relationships among countries (for example, trade agreements regarding goods, such as oil, wheat, or other natural resources). International business executives need to understand the relationship between social systems and economic systems in order to make prudent business decisions. In addition, on a personal level, individual investors in stocks, bonds, mutual funds, and so on can benefit from insights that may help them understand and predict trends in foreign markets. The world of business and investments is no longer limited to the country of residence or of origin. The practical need to understand the relationship between social systems and economic systems has never been greater and is likely to continue to grow.

TYPES OF ECONOMIC SYSTEMS

To produce goods and services for a society, an economic system requires land on which to produce food and to build factories. It also needs raw materials, tools, and machinery to process them, and it needs labor. Economic systems in modern societies vary according to who owns the land, the factories, the raw materials, and the equipment. These *means of production* may be *privately owned*—that is, owned by individuals, or they may be *publicly owned* by the state. **Capitalism** is a system based on private ownership. **Socialism** is a system based on state ownership of the means of production. Once again, these pure economic systems are only ideal types. In practice, in capitalist societies, some property is owned by the state, and in socialist societies, some property is privately owned, such as small plots of land used to grow food for the local market. No society is purely capitalist or purely socialist. *Mixed economies*, in which private and public ownership are both practiced extensively, are called **welfare capitalism or democratic socialism**.

Although all existing economic systems are based on capitalism, socialism, or some combination of the two, one other system deserves mention, even though it has never been developed in a major nation. **Communism** is an economic system that is the goal of communist political parties throughout the world. It is a system in which the ownership of the means of production is held in common by all citizens. A society's economic system has a powerful influence on how it produces and distributes goods.

Capitalism

The United States has a capitalist economic system; that is, one or more individuals own the means of production, the land and the factories. Most large corporations are owned by the many groups and individuals who own stock, stock being shares of the corporation. Many small businesses are owned by one person, a family, or a few individuals. Individuals who own the means of production are *capitalists*. In this sense, most Americans are not capitalists because they do not derive income from owning a business. They may own cars, clothes, and television sets, but these are consumer goods. They do not provide profit to the owner. Even homes that increase in value over the years and that produce a profit when sold do not produce income when the owners use them as a personal residence. Capitalists earn income from what they own; consumers spend income for what they own.

Capitalism is a **market economy**—that is, the goods sold and the people who buy them and the people who sell them determine the prices at which they are sold. Products no one wants to buy or sell are not traded. If everyone needs a product—fuel, for example—the product will be sold for as much money as people will pay for it. In a **free-market** system, all people are theoretically free to buy, sell, and make a profit, if they can, although there are prohibitions against selling some things, such as illegal drugs, and some services, such as sexual favors. The free-market system is the reason that capitalism is so strongly associated with freedom.

Socialism

Socialism differs from capitalism in that the means of production are owned by the state. Socialist systems are designed to ensure that all members of the society have some share of its wealth. Ownership is social rather than private. So-called communist systems, such as in Cuba, are actually socialist systems because the government owns all of the industries in the country.

Socialism also differs from capitalism in that the marketplace does not control the economy. It has a **planned economy**—the government first decides what goods the society needs, what are luxuries, and what can be done without altogether; then it controls what will be produced and consumed and sets prices for these goods. Thus, there is no free market. The Soviet Union, for example, faced with a severe housing shortage after World War II, gave high priority to building low-cost housing for its population but gave very low priority to building automobiles.

Welfare Capitalism

Welfare capitalism, sometimes called "democratic socialism," is found in most western European countries. In Sweden and Great Britain, some industries are privately owned, and others are state owned. Generally, the state owns the industries most vital to the country's well being, such as the railroads and the communications industry. The most crucial needs—medical care, education, and old-age benefits—all are paid for by the government with tax dollars. As a result, the taxes in welfare capitalist countries are quite high in order to pay for these benefits.

Whether a country is more or less capitalistic can sometimes be determined by comparing the taxes collected to the **gross domestic product (GDP)**, the total value of all final goods and services produced within the borders of a country per year. Often, the greater the proportion of the GDP that goes to taxes, the more social programs the country has. The GDP includes all necessities, luxuries, and military supplies produced for a price within the borders of a country. It does not include anything not produced for profit. The worth of the work of housewives, for example, is the largest item not included in the GDP. As you can see from Table 16-1, GDP in the United States is high compared to other countries.

The GDP does not indicate what the various countries produce; nor does it show for what tax dollars are spent. The United States, which spends much of its tax money on the armed forces, includes military spending in its GDP. Many other countries, on the other hand, spend little of their tax revenue on the military and spend a great deal on health, social planning, and the reduction of poverty. Thus, while the United States has the highest GDP in the world, its GDP per capita (the amount spent per person) falls to tenth place. (See Table 16-2.) As a result, these countries—such as Japan, France, and Sweden—all have populations with longer life expectancies than are found in the United States, with the US being in forty-eighth place (See Table 16-3.) These countries have combined capitalism with social programs paid for through taxation and government spending programs.

TABLE 16-1 TOP 20 COUNTRIES GDP -2009

Rank	Country	GDP (Purchasing Power Parity) (Billion $)
1	United States	13,820
2	China	6,473
3	Japan	4,262
4	Germany	2,816
5	India	2,816
6	United Kingdom	2,154
7	France	2,074
8	Russia	1,985
9	Italy	1,814
10	Brazil	1,794
11	Mexico	1,494
12	Spain	1,337
13	Canada	1,263
14	Korea, South	1,243
15	Turkey	853.6
16	Indonesia	810.9
17	Australia	752.2
18	Iran	733
19	Taiwan	672.9
20	Netherlands	635.9

Source: *CIA World Factbook* 2009 in Index Mundi http://www.indexmundi.com/g/rank.html

Communism—A Utopian Idea

Communism is an economic system that does not exist in any of the world's larger societies. The basic premise of communism is that all property should be held in common and that distribution of goods and services should be based on the principle developed by Marx (1964, 258), "From each according to his ability, to each according to his needs!" Thus, in the ideal communist society, workers would do their best to serve the needs of the society and would be assured of receiving whatever they needed.

Communism has been achieved in some small communities. It was especially popular in the nineteenth century in the United States when there were an estimated one hundred communes with a total of more than one hundred thousand members (Etzioni-Halevy 1997). Religious sects, such as the Shakers, Rappists, Zoarites, Amana Communists, and Perfectionists, formed most. One notable example was the Oneida community in Oneida, New York. All members of this religious society shared the property, buildings, and industries of the community. They also shared the work, rotating in their jobs so that no one would long suffer the burden of the heaviest or the least pleasant work,

TABLE 16-2 TOP 20 COUNTRIES' GDP PER CAPITA - 2009

Rank	Country	GDP - per capita (PPP) (US$)
1	Liechtenstein	118,000
2	Qatar	85,600
3	Luxembourg	79,600
4	Bermuda	69,900
5	Jersey	57,000
6	Norway	54,900
7	Brunei	54,400
8	Kuwait	54,300
9	Singapore	48,500
10	United States	46,300
11	Ireland	45,100
12	Guernsey	44,600
13	Cayman Islands	43,800
14	San Marino	41,900
15	Hong Kong	40,500
16	Iceland	40,100
17	Switzerland	40,000
18	Andorra	38,800
19	Canada	38,700
20	Netherlands	38,600

Source: *CIA World Factbook* 2009 in Index Mundi http://www.indexmundi.com/g/rank.html

and no one would become attached to a particular job. Groups did work, so that fellowship was a part of cooking, cleaning, farming, and whatever else had to be done. There was no monogamous marriage, which they believed would have implied the ownership of another person. The community planned the birth of children; and when children were born, they were members of the community, not possessions of their parents. The Oneida community was very successful in carrying out

TABLE 16-3 LIFE EXPECTANCY AT BIRTH, TOP 50 COUNTRIES

Rank	Country	Life expectancy at birth (years)
1	Macau	84.36
2	Andorra	82.51
3	Japan	82.12
4	Singapore	81.98
5	San Marino	81.97
6	Hong Kong	81.86
7	Australia	81.63
8	Canada	81.23
9	France	80.98
10	Sweden	80.86
11	Switzerland	80.85
12	Guernsey	80.77
13	Israel	80.73
14	Iceland	80.67
15	Anguilla	80.65
16	Cayman Islands	80.44
17	Bermuda	80.43
18	New Zealand	80.36
19	Italy	80.2
20	Gibraltar	80.19
21	Monaco	80.09
22	Liechtenstein	80.06
23	Spain	80.05
24	Norway	79.95
25	Jersey	79.75
26	Greece	79.66
27	Austria	79.5
28	Faroe Islands	79.44
29	Malta	79.44
30	Netherlands	79.4
31	Luxembourg	79.33
32	Germany	79.26
33	Belgium	79.22

(continued)

Table 16-3 Life Expectancy at Birth, Top 50 Countries

Rank	Country	Life expectancy at birth (years)
34	Saint Pierre and Miquelon	79.07
35	Virgin Islands	79.05
36	United Kingdom	79.01
37	Finland	78.97
38	Jordan	78.87
39	Man, Isle of	78.82
40	Korea, South	78.72
41	Puerto Rico	78.53
42	Bosnia and Herzegovina	78.5
43	Saint Helena	78.44
44	Denmark	78.3
45	Ireland	78.24
46	Portugal	78.21
47	Wallis and Futuna	78.2
48	United States	78.11
49	Guam	78.01
50	Albania	77.96

Source: *CIA World Factbook 2009* in Index Mundi http://www.indexmundi.com/g/rank.html

its ideal of communism, and its members were very happy with their fellowship and security. However, neighbors of the commune did not approve of their practices, especially their lack of marriage, and the community was forced to disband.

Communist communities have also been popular in the twentieth century—especially in Europe in the 1930s and in the United States in the 1970s. Most of the recent communes were not religious groups. They did not put a strong emphasis on work, and they failed because they could not sustain themselves.

Communism, like socialism, requires a major redistribution of wealth. Individuals would no longer own the farms, factories, and other means of production. Many capitalists, in fact, confuse socialist systems with communist systems and use these words almost interchangeably. They are, however, very different systems. In socialism, the government controls the economy. In communism, the people themselves control the economy.

THEORIES OF ECONOMIC DEVELOPMENT

Historically, capitalism became the dominant economic system in Europe during the Industrial Revolution. How did this system develop, and why does it persist? Theorists have been considering these questions for several centuries. As in so many areas of sociological inquiry, two basic perspectives have evolved—structural functionalism and conflict theory.

Structural Functional Theory

As discussed previously, structural functional theory suggests that social systems reflect the values of a society and work to meet basic social needs. According to this perspective, the capitalist economic system reflects the social values a society places on the freedom of the individual to accumulate and own private property. Especially in the United States, capitalism is highly valued, and welfare programs are hotly debated. The capitalist system has evolved because immigrants coming to this country brought with them the desire to be free to determine their own economic welfare.

Functionalists argue that capitalism succeeds so well because it meets basic needs. Conservative economists have been describing capitalism as a vast cooperative system for centuries. In *The Wealth of Nations*, written in 1776, Adam Smith pointed out the beautiful balance that is achieved in the ideal functioning of the capitalist economy. This balance, which we know as the "law of supply and demand," ensures that social needs will be met because it is profitable to meet them. When there is a demand, someone will profit from supplying it. People need food, clothing, and medical care, for example; huge industries have developed to meet these needs. By tending to their self-interests, this theory suggests, everyone who produces a necessary product or service will profit and will, thereby, benefit both themselves and society.

In recent years, structural functionalists have been concerned about the large number of people who seem unable to find profitable means of supporting themselves. Most structural functionalists do not fault the capitalistic system, but they do recognize that some dysfunctions make it difficult for some individuals and groups to have an equal opportunity in the marketplace. A child growing up in an urban ghetto or on an impoverished Indian reservation is unlikely to get the education needed to land jobs that pay well. Even when members of minority groups do manage to get a good education, racism and stereotyping may prevent them from finding a profitable occupation. As a result, the benefits of a capitalistic system are not equally available to all. Another dysfunction concerns the development of monopolies, which limit competition and thereby narrow the range of opportunities available in the marketplace. When one corporation dominates the sale of a good or service, it disrupts the market economy and can set its own price.

APPLYING STRUCTURAL FUNCTIONAL PERSPECTIVES OF ECONOMIC SYSTEMS

According to the structural functional perspective, because capitalism reflects our primary American value of individualism, capitalist policies assume that the individual alone is solely responsible for his or her life chances. Understanding the functions and dysfunctions of such capitalist policies—or those of any economic system, for that matter—is essential for policymakers. To create effective economic policies that benefit all people in a society, policymakers would do well to consider both the functions and dysfunctions of particular economic systems, regardless of their reflection of social values. Unfortunately, values—not rationality—form the basis of most public policy (and politicians risk losing public support and reelection when they lose sight of this). Rice (1985) suggests, for example, that it would be rational to have an economic policy in which the government regulates the cost and supply of oil to prevent the oil market from being monopolized by a few giant corporations; but the American value of individualism—as reflected in free enterprise—prohibits this.

Most of you will not be in a position to affect national economic policies, but many of you will be involved in work or business situations that may be arranged to reflect individualism. For example, suppose that you are the manager or owner of a retail–clothing store, and you hope to achieve high sales by basing your employees' salaries on the number of sales each makes. Although individual competition might stimulate them to work harder initially, the store might eventually suffer from this policy. The competition for sales could lead to a lack of trust and lower morale among the sales personnel, and thus to a weakened work team. Some employees might quit because they are dissatisfied with working conditions. Time and money would then be lost to hiring and training new personnel. What seems like a good idea theoretically might turn out, in reality, to contain some serious dysfunctions that could undermine your original goals. By realizing that business and economic policies contain dysfunctions as well as functions and by trying to anticipate what they might be, you might be able to avoid some problems before they arise.

Conflict Theory

In the *Communist Manifesto*, Marx described the development of both capitalism and communism as historical events. When most people produced needed goods directly from farming, there was an agricultural economic system. As industrialization developed and trading of manufactured articles increased, however, the economy came to be based on money, or capital. Marx realized that as some people increased their store of capital, they would be able to buy more and more factories and other means of production. Those who did not own any means of production would be forced to sell their only asset—their labor—to the factory owners. As the owners grew richer and more powerful, they would buy up more and more of the means of production and would force still more people to rely on their labor for subsistence. Eventually, Marx believed, the

number of workers would grow so large that competition would reduce wages to a minimum, and an entire class of impoverished workers would develop. He felt that conditions among the working class would ultimately deteriorate to the point that they would revolt, overthrow the owners, and develop a system in which the means of production would be owned communally and would be operated for the benefit of all.

Max Weber (1946) agreed with Marx's fundamental view of the economic order, but he differed slightly in his assessment of the means and outcome of oppression. Weber was concerned with the growth of bureaucracy. Bureaucracies operate in accordance with rational rules and procedures rather than humanitarian principles. With the compartmentalization of responsibility, it would be possible for a company to become extremely ruthless in the pursuit of profit, even if it meant that thousands of workers and the population at large would suffer. Those who made the decisions would be far removed from those who actually carried them out and who were in a position to observe their consequences. Weber was less optimistic than Marx, believing that eventually bureaucracies would grow so rich and powerful that no human effort could dislodge them. Even today, some conflict theorists contend that giant multinational corporations are too powerful to be controlled by individuals—or even nations—and that the world will come under progressively greater corporate control.

THE AMERICAN ECONOMIC SYSTEM

Most American citizens are convinced that the capitalist system is good and cherish the freedom of the marketplace—the freedom to buy, sell, and earn a living in any way they can. We value these freedoms as much as we value our religious freedom; and, in fact, the two systems arise out of the same tradition.

In *The Protestant Ethic and the Spirit of Capitalism* (1905), Weber discussed the Puritans' influence on the American desire for profit. He noted that capitalism, the exchange of goods for profit, has existed at one time or another in all societies. In the United States, however, profit became a major goal, desired not simply to provide for one's daily needs but also to accumulate wealth.

The Puritans were *Protestant Calvinists*. Their doctrine stated that most people lived in sin but that a few had been predestined for everlasting life by the grace of God. No one on this earth could affect that predestination; God sealed people's fates. The chosen were on earth to build God's kingdom as God intended.

How did people know whether they were among the elect? They could not know; but it was believed that those who were involved in the work of the world, who appeared to be building God's kingdom, must be among the elect. Those who spent their lives in idleness, carousing, drinking, and card playing were obviously not doing God's work and obviously not among the chosen. The Calvinists feared death and sought confirmation that they were among the chosen. They worked to produce goods, taking wealth as a sign that they were among the chosen. They did not spend time or money on comforts, play, or anything else that might indicate that they were not chosen; nor did they associate with people whom they believed to be outside the elect. They worked, and they accumulated wealth, believing it to be an indication of self-worth. We now know this perspective as the **Protestant ethic**.

There is strong evidence that religious values play a role in present day economics as well. "Religion is an important factor in wealth accumulation ... (it) keeps coming up in any model you run to explain wealth" (Keister 2003). Even after considering other ways of accumulating wealth associated with particular denominations, such as inheritance, levels of education, and other factors, the effect of religion is still significant. According to the study, Keister found that families have a powerful influence on how people learn to save, and religion has a powerful impact on shaping family life. The religious beliefs children learn in their families translate into educational attainment, adult occupations, financial literacy, social connections, and other factors that influence adult wealth ownership, according to Keister. For example, conservative Protestants often emphasize prayer and trust in God to meet their needs, which may reduce their desire to invest. These same groups also look forward to the rewards of the afterlife and don't promote acquiring wealth as good for this life. Jews, on the other hand, don't have a strong orientation to the afterlife but do encourage pursuits that will lead to wealth accumulation, such as high-income careers and investing in this life.

Overall, the median net worth of Jewish people in the survey was $150,890, more than three times the median for the entire sample ($48,200). For conservative Protestants (which included Baptists, Jehovah's Witnesses, Seventh-Day Adventists, Christian Scientists, among others), the median net worth was $26,200, or about half the overall average; and median net worth of mainstream Protestants (including Episcopalians, Methodists, Presbyterians, Lutherans, Unitarians, and others) and Catholics were similar to each other, falling at about the average for the whole sample (Keister 2003).

Keister also found that people who regularly attended religious services tended to be wealthier. Going to religious services may provide another opportunity to be indoctrinated with beliefs that help build wealth. Also, attending services provides a social network of like others where one may meet contacts or learn investment tips.

Overall, the results of Keister's study demonstrate the importance of family socialization and processes in shaping wealth accumulation. Furthermore, the results underscore the importance of culture in shaping economic behavior and ultimately in creating social inequality.

The Growth of Large Corporations

The almost religious fervor with which we work for profit has contributed to the growth of large corporations. **Mass production** has also contributed to the growth of corporations. Building one car by hand is very expensive. Obviously, workers on an assembly line, using machinery, can assemble many identical parts and produce many cars in less time, at a lower cost per car. Robots cost even less than workers, and the cars can be sold at a much greater profit. Factories and mass production have replaced the shoemaker, the spinner, the weaver, the dressmaker, the furniture maker, the cigar maker, the glass blower, the potter, the butcher, the baker, and the candlestick maker. Factories, the specialized division of labor, and automation make it possible to mass produce goods that can be sold at low prices and still bring profit to the manufacturer.

Profits have also been increased by **vertical expansion** of businesses, in which a business owns everything from its raw materials to its retail outlets. If a business owns not only the factory that produces the goods but also the source of the raw materials purchased by the factory, the trucks that take the goods to market, and the stores that sell the products, the business can cut its costs at every step of the operation. It does not have to pay part of its profits to the owner of the raw material, the trucker, and the store owner. A business that owns all related businesses, from the raw material to the retailer, can increase its profits at every stage of its operation.

American corporations have expanded their operations to control the entire process from raw material to retail sales (Zwerdling 1976). A large food store chain, for example, may own thousands of food stores and more than a hundred manufacturing and processing plants, including bakeries, milk plants, ice cream plants, soft drink plants, meat processors, and coffee roasting plants. It may manufacture its own soap, peanut butter, and salad oil, and it might own a fleet of thousands of trucks to ship these products to its stores. Members of the board of directors of the chain would also sit on the boards of banks and

Bill Gates

corporations involved in agriculture, food production, food processing, food packaging, gas and electric power, and fuel oil. By owning or influencing every stage of production from the land on which the food is grown to the retail sales outlets, such a chain becomes a very large corporation.

Horizontal expansion, another way to increase profits, refers to the practice of taking over similar businesses in order to gain a monopoly and reduce competition in the field. For example, a company that makes soup may buy all of the competing soup-making companies. Then, when a customer enters the grocery store, most of the soup available for purchase is made by the same company, which can define the quality standards, set the price of soup, and not worry about losing sales to competition. That company controls the market.

Another form of expansion that assures continued profits is **diversification**—entering a variety of businesses in an attempt to ensure a stable rate of profit. Investors might buy a variety of stocks so that if one went down, another might remain stable or go up; and they would be protected from losing their entire investment. In the same way, corporations buy a variety of businesses so that those that are not highly profitable can be supported by those that are. Great Western United owns sugar companies, Shakey's Pizza, and large real estate holdings. The real estate is extremely valuable, but it does not provide income. By diversifying, Great Western United can support its real estate holdings with income from other sources. United States Steel Corporation, when the demand for steel fell, diversified by buying other companies and changing its name to USX.

The legally structured size of corporations tells only half the story of their tremendous power. Corporate links may join corporations that appear to be unrelated. When IBM was developing computers in a highly competitive market, IBM officers and directors were on the boards of Bankers Trust Company of New York, the Rockefeller Foundation, First National City Bank of New York, Chemical Bank, Federal Reserve Bank of New York, Morgan Guaranty Trust Company of New York, the J. P. Morgan Bank, and the United States Trust Company (DeLamarter 1986). According to DeLamarter, these banks made it difficult for competitors of IBM to finance the development of their own computer products, thus aiding IBM in its domination of the field. As corporations grow larger and more powerful, they do not confine their operations to their own country, but instead expand internationally.

Multinational Corporations

Very large corporations own companies in one or more foreign nations, where they employ workers and produce and sell their products. These companies, as mentioned in the introduction, are known as **multinational corporations.** Ford Motor Company is a major example of a multinational corporation. In 1980, one-third of Ford employees were foreigners. In 2002, out of 280,000 workers and 108 plants worldwide, more than half of Ford's employees were foreigners, and 38 percent of Ford sales were in foreign countries (www.ford.com).

Americans owned most multinational corporations. These companies often become involved in political arrangements made between the United States and other countries. They affect the economies of this country and those countries in which they have holdings in several ways. They can buy foreign materials even when the United States would like to reduce overseas spending and would prefer that they "Buy American." They can play one country against another, offering to build a plant in the one that gives them the greatest advantages in taxes, cheap labor, and freedom from regulation. By closing plants, they can create unemployment problems. In a sense, multinational corporations are above the laws of any nation because they can use their vast wealth and power to dominate a nation's economy or evade its laws. The annual sales of either General Motors or Exxon are greater than the GNP of countries such as Austria, Denmark, Norway, Greece, Portugal, and the smaller nations of the world. Corporations can borrow vast amounts of money on the basis of their sales; countries can tax only their GNP. As corporations increase in size, they gain progressively more power to dominate the economies of entire nations.

Multinational businesses have had a great impact on developed nations as well as developing nations. Del Monte and Dole are just two examples of multinational business.

While the major increase in multinational business has been in the developed nations of the world, developing nations have also been powerfully influenced by multinationals. Large agricultural corporations, for example, have converted large tracts of farmland into huge plantations, cultivated by modern machinery to produce cash crops for worldwide shipment. Del Monte and Dole grow pineapples in the Philippines and Thailand, where there is an abundance of cheap labor; and they then ship the pineapples to United States and Japanese markets. The Gulf and Western Corporation controls land in the Dominican Republic, which is used to grow sugar for Gulf and Western's sugar mill. The large corporations often do not own the land but enter into agreements with local landowners to grow what they need for their processing plants; and the local landowners and governments usually cooperate—even when the nutrition of their own local people suffers.

Multinational corporations have such a great impact on the nations in which they do business and are so influential in international relations that some observers believe that nations as we know them today will eventually vanish and that affairs of state will come to be run by the boards of directors of huge corporations. Whether this will happen and whether it would create a more peaceful and orderly world or more poverty for workers is still a matter of speculation, for now. In any case, as corporations change and grow, the nature of work also changes.

Thinking Sociologically

1. Evaluate the structural functional view that capitalism is efficient for a society, especially as corporations grow larger.
2. Evaluate Weber's stance that corporations are becoming so large that they could become ruthless in search of profits and have no regard for people.
3. If you were running a large organization, what would you consider the best way to manage your employees? Incorporating interactionist principles, explain why employers would benefit by creating primary and in-group feelings among their employees. If you were a lower-level employee, would you agree?

THE CHANGING NATURE OF WORK

In simple agricultural societies, most people are **primary workers**. Those who grow food, who fish, who mine, or who otherwise produce raw materials are referred to as "primary workers" because their work is so essential to their country. In an industrial society such as our own, where most farming is done by machine, only a small portion of the population farms for a living. Most of the population works to produce manufactured goods; these workers are called **secondary workers**.

They are the wage earners—the people on the assembly line, the construction workers, and the laborers in industry. The fastest-growing segment of the labor force consists of **tertiary** (or **service**) **workers**, which includes such people as police officers, doctors, lawyers, maids, and plumbers. The following sections describe the nature of secondary and tertiary work in modern society and discuss some important issues for these workers.

Factory Work and Alienation

In an earlier era, the cobbler or the candlestick maker developed a product from start to finish, sold it to the customer, took pride in the finished goods, and stood by his or her reputation as a skilled producer. The factory worker has none of these satisfactions, which has been a continuous problem for worker and manager alike.

Alienation is a term Marx used in describing the working conditions of the factory worker. Factory workers are alienated from their work because they have no control over it and derive no satisfaction from it. Their work involves only a part of the finished product, and they see neither the beginning nor the end of the process. They have no satisfaction in creating a product and no pride in selling it to the customer. They perform one routine task over and over again; and in return they receive money, which may or may not be enough to provide them with a satisfactory lifestyle outside of work.

Factory workers are involved with only a part of the finished product. They seldom see the development of the product from beginning to end.

Factory workers have been studied extensively since the turn of the century. Initially, most studies were designed to improve worker efficiency through scientific management, and this remains an important focus of research in the workplace. More recently, however, the human relations school of management has gained prominence; this perspective suggests that increasing worker satisfaction and decreasing alienation could also increase production.

SCIENTIFIC MANAGEMENT

Scientific management, a term coined by Frederick W. Taylor (1911), is management designed to improve worker efficiency. In an entrepreneurial setting, the workers own the business and are responsible for knowing the best way to do their own job. In companies that practice scientific management, the manager is assumed to know how to accomplish a task most efficiently. By keeping records and using a stopwatch, the manager determines rules for the most efficient work routine and then selects and trains workers to follow directions. The division of labor requires the manager to do the thinking and the worker to do the labor.

Taylor developed his program at Bethlehem Steel Company to improve the efficiency of workers loading pig iron (crude iron) into railroad cars. A crude casting of pig iron, often just called a "pig," weighed about ninety-two pounds. Workers lifted a pig, carried it up a plank, and dropped it into a car. Before Taylor designed his scientific management plan, each worker loaded an average of twelve and one-half tons of pig iron a day. By carefully controlling the pace at which the workers lifted, walked up the plank, rested, and lifted again, Taylor found that he could get the workers to load forty-seven tons of pig iron a day, almost four times as much as they had been loading. The workers were rewarded with a pay increase of 60 percent, and the profit to the company was enormous.

Taylor (1911) described the best type of worker to handle pig iron as follows: "He shall be so stupid and so phlegmatic that he more nearly resembles in his mental make-up the ox than any other type" (p. 51). A man who was alert and intelligent would quickly be dissatisfied and bored with routine labor and the way it was scientifically managed. Nevertheless, scientific management played an important role in increasing the efficient use of workers; the fact that most workers were not as dumb as an ox was overlooked. The intelligence of human workers, however, eventually had to be considered; and it was at that point that the human relations school of management developed.

The Human Relations School

The **human relations school** of management considers the psychological makeup of workers, their attitudes toward management, peer pressures, and similar factors in an attempt to promote worker efficiency. A scientific management study discovered the importance of human relations in the workplace by accident. In the now famous Hawthorne studies, experiments were done to improve the productivity of assembly-line workers making telephone equipment. As indicated by the Hawthorne effect, worker productivity did not increase as scientific management had expected—the workers responded to the attention they received from the researchers. More important, the study found that worker productivity depended on the informal group structure of the workers. When they were allowed to form their own working relationships and develop some of their own rules, they were much more cooperative with management, and their productivity increased. When they felt uneasy about changes handed down by management, they resisted these changes; and productivity did not increase. The findings of the Hawthorne studies made management aware of the importance of informal groups, worker attitudes toward management, and the effects of these factors on productivity.

The human relations school of worker management developed to probe these issues further. Its researchers studied the formal organization of the workplace, company rules and working conditions, and informal organization among the workers themselves, including their customs, traditions, routines, values, and beliefs (Roethlisberger and Dickson 1939). The goal of these studies was to find the best type of person for the job and the best type of environment for maintaining and improving worker attitudes.

Gouldner (1954) conducted a classic study of employee values and their effect on productivity, in a gypsum factory. Initially, the workers had been quite happy with their management, and management had been flexible with the workers. They were occasionally allowed to leave early for personal reasons, and they were sometimes allowed to take supplies for their personal use. They were also encouraged to discuss work problems with management and to make suggestions for improving working conditions. Managers and workers cooperated well together, and neither took advantage of the other.

Then, however, a new management team came to the company. To increase production, they adhered strictly to the rules. Workers were not allowed to leave early or to take supplies, nor were they given a chance to discuss problems with management. The workers, who valued the flexibility of the earlier managers, resented the enforcement of the rules. They believed that they were being treated with less respect, and they no longer cooperated with and supported the company.

APPLYING THE HUMAN RELATIONS MODEL

If you are involved in a management position, you might have the opportunity to apply the human relations model. Schrank (1979), an expert on the human relations style of management, is skeptical about the possibility of making routine work interesting; but he does feel that it is possible to encourage employees to work for you rather than against you and, thus, to increase productivity. Some fairly easy ways to accomplish this could be by having clean restrooms, pleasant dining areas, and an improved social atmosphere in the workplace. Telephones, vending machines, and lounges could be made available.

You may also find ways to apply this management technique in areas other than the office or the factory. You might, for example, become more effective as a teacher if you could encourage your students to work for you instead of against you. This might be achieved by creating an informal atmosphere in the classroom, having students call you by your first name, having an open-door policy with regard to your office hours, having lunch with students, attending campus events with students, or perhaps just by spending a few minutes a day in informal conversations with students. You already may have thought of other ways to encourage employees (or students) to work with you instead of against you.

Although there have been some gains in the area of human relations research during the past few decades, many workers in the United States are still frustrated in their jobs; and management continues to be frustrated with low productivity. In recent years, American managers have turned their attention to Japanese workers to try to understand why they are more productive than American workers.

Modern Trends in Management

The Japanese work force has proven itself to be exceptional in production and efficiency. This efficiency and productivity is attributed to two Japanese employee policies—lifetime jobs and quality control circles.

One example among many found in Japan is Fujio Mitarai, president of Canon Corporation, who has succeeded in making the company one of the most profitable in the word (www.forbesspecialsections.com/SectionPDFs/japan2004/04.html). In Mitarai's seven years as president, Canon's total assets at the current market value increased to 4,400 billion yen, three times as much as when he took over. He maintains the lifetime employment system, but has eliminated the seniority system from it. He sees speed of promotion as being important in American management, whereas in Japanese corporations, many retain the seniority system. Presidents of those companies reward employees who have worked the longest for their companies. Because many have lifetime employment plans, Japanese corporations can pursue their businesses based on long-term plans. Furthermore, they have a system for consensus management, which eliminates the need for employees to take responsibility.

Lifetime jobs are held by only a third of Japanese men and by no women, and they are held only until age fifty or sixty, which creates a hardship for workers when they are older. Nevertheless, a guaranteed job for even this short a "lifetime" creates security for the Japanese man—security most American workers do not have because they can be fired or laid off at any time. The Japanese man is also encouraged to have close personal relationships with other workers and to care about those in his work group just as he cares about his family. The group takes pride in its work, and its members do not need to compete as individuals. They are paid a low base pay and then receive a bonus, often 50 percent of base pay, on the basis of their productivity. The provision of lifetime jobs, commitment to the group, and high productivity works to everyone's advantage.

Knowing that long-term employment leads to efficient, high-quality production may be useful for you someday as an employer. You might not be able to guarantee your employees a lifetime job, but you might be able to provide an atmosphere and benefits that give employees a sense of security and belonging. This could entail having informal employer-employee interactions, discussing long-term company plans with employees, and in general soliciting feedback from your employees.

Quality control circles are meetings held by the group to improve its productivity. Orders do not come down from the manager as they do in American bureaucracies; instead, the groups meet regularly to decide how their work can best be accomplished. They consider such problems as production, flow of work, work roles, worker-management relations, production schedules, improvements in the work environment, innovations in jobs, and ways of enhancing worker profitability, and then they make recommendations to management. If management approves the recommendations, the work group is allowed to change its procedures.

Although these management techniques seem quite revolutionary to American managers–who still value scientific management, efficiency experts, and stopwatches–quality control groups are being tried in a few American companies, with reported success.

Unionization

Workers have for years tried to improve their own working conditions and economic benefits through **unionization**, organizing workers to improve wages and working conditions. Unions can be traced back to the guilds of the Middle Ages, which protected skilled workers in the arts and crafts. As factories developed, workers formed unions to better their work environments. In the United States, skilled artisans were unionized before 1800, and women textile workers united in the early 1800s to protest working conditions in factories.

The later part of the nineteenth century was a period of intense labor-union struggle and conflict, and the result of this struggle continues to shape labor unions today. There was a strong and popular socialist movement in the United States during this period, which was influenced by Marx's theory and his conception of alienation. Workers in various industries saw that they had much in common with one another and wanted to build a strong union covering all workers. They did not expect to cooperate with industry. They wanted, rather, to fight for collective ownership of industry so that they would own the companies they worked in and reap the profits of their own labor. Removing industry from private ownership and placing it in collective ownership would cause a radical redistribution of wealth, of course. The owners of American business, with the aid of federal, state, and local police and military power, forced these more radical labor unions out of existence, deported any of their foreign-born members, tried citizens for treason, and passed laws preventing such unions from forming in the future.

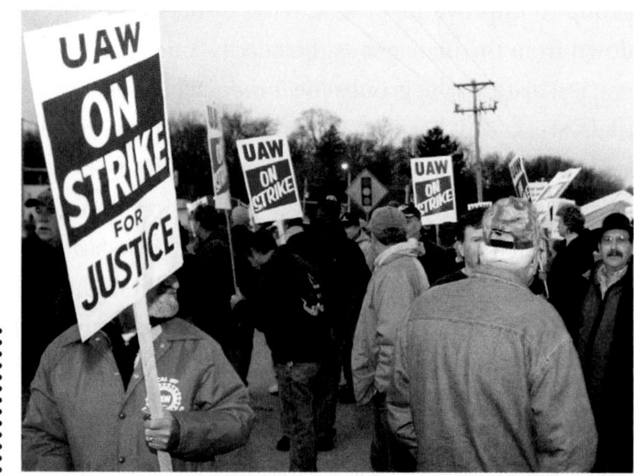

Unions were created to improve wages and working conditions.

The more conservative unions of the period worked to protect their jobs through legislation. Tariff laws were passed to prevent competition from cheap imported goods, and immigration laws prevented cheap foreign labor from entering the country. Protective labor laws kept women and children out of the labor force, thereby eliminating another source of cheap labor. In addition, the unions tried to maintain a cooperative relationship with their employers. They wanted work contracts and preferred to settle disputes by mediation and compromise. Strikes were used only as a last resort.

The owners of American industry put up a fierce struggle against the conservative unions, however (Griffin, Wallace, and Rubin 1986). Manufacturers subdivided tasks into simple units, for example, so that skilled artisans and workers could then be replaced with unskilled workers. They hired workers from different ethnic groups so that the workers could not talk to each other and unionize, and they created antagonism among ethnic groups by discriminating against them. One week an industry would hire only Swedes, the next week only Slavs, and then they would sometimes fire all workers of one ethnic group, building further resentment among groups. Manufacturers also organized themselves into large associations, most notably the National Association of Manufacturers (NAM), to crusade against unionism so that unions would not have the support of the general public. On a more positive note, some industries improved their working conditions and employee benefits so that workers would not want to unionize.

Some small, conservative unions developed, but they were quite powerless to negotiate with large industries. In the 1930s, unions united into large federations, the American Federation of Labor (AFL) and the Congress of Industrial Organizations (CIO), and eventually these two giant federations united to form the AFL-CIO. The federations included all workers, skilled and unskilled, and they practiced conservative policies. The unions were not structured according to class, so that workers would protect the interests of all workers.

Instead, they were organized by industry. Steelworkers, for example, acted in unison when negotiating with the steel industry, and autoworkers acted in unison when negotiating with the auto industry; but other than refusing to cross a picket line, workers could do little to support the efforts of those outside of their own industry.

Unions have been undergoing a decline for almost half-a-century (Godard 2009). This is partially because corporations have provided employee benefits (Cornfield 1986) and partly as a result of corporate expansion (Compa 1986). When a major corporation buys other corporations, it acquires the unions associated with its new acquisition. The owning corporation is then in a position to negotiate with several unions separately. When steelworkers struck against USX, the old U.S. Steel Corporation, the unions representing the newly acquired oil and chemical interests of USX continued to work; and USX could operate very profitable segments of its business even during the steel strike. The other unions were forbidden to strike in support of the steelworkers because of their separate union contracts and because of regulations imposed by the National Labor Relations Board (NLRB), the government agency that regulates the activities of unions.

Through acquisitions, the airline industry has developed a maze of unions serving pilots, mechanics, transport workers, flight attendants, and other specialized workers. For example, a major airline that has acquired several other lines may have several different unions serving just their mechanics. As a result, each of the unions is ineffective in negotiations. Through acquisitions, General Electric was at one point negotiating with a dozen different unions; and until those unions formed their own federation, each was quite powerless. Increasingly, these unions are also covering the lower-paid workers in the service sector.

The airline industry has many different unions that serve workers such as pilots, mechanics, and transport workers.

Some studies show that the decline in the American labor unions is exceptional when compared to labor movements in other countries (Godard 2009). Labor union decline began much earlier than in other countries and was more severe, leading to much lower levels of collective bargaining. Godard argues that the decline of unions is a result of deeply ingrained institutional norms of employer hostility and essentially an atmosphere that labor unions are anti-American, partially stemming from the unique capitalist conditions under which the United States was founded.

Steelworkers acted in unison when negotiating with the steel industry.

Service Work

The increase in the size of corporations has increased the number of tertiary (service) workers, who are not directly involved in producing goods. These are the employees who answer the telephones, keep the records, file the papers, pay the taxes, clean the buildings, and do a host of other jobs necessary to keep large corporations functioning. Another class of service workers meets community rather than corporate needs, and this class has also been growing. As people have moved to urban areas to work, more police officers, firefighters, teachers, doctors, lawyers, and accountants have been needed to serve them.

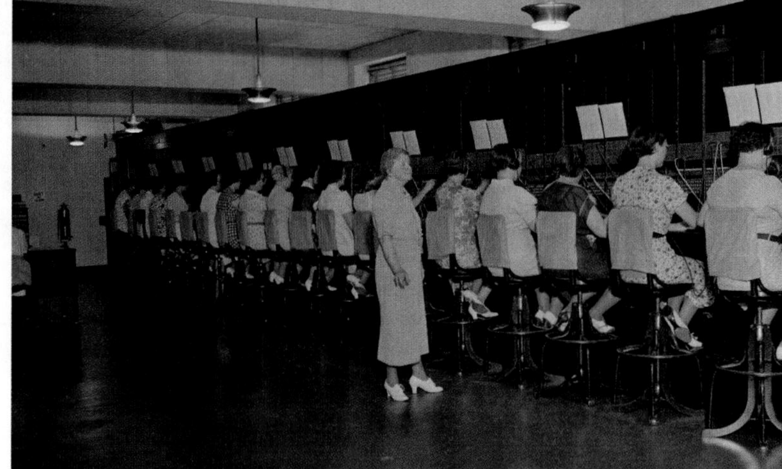

Through new technologies, service workers have become more efficient. For example, it took several thousand switchboard operators to handle one million long-distance telephone calls; today, it takes only a few dozen.

Service workers are an expense to a corporation, part of its fixed overhead costs. They increase the costs of products, but they do not directly increase the production of products. Similarly, in a community, they are a necessary expense to taxpayers, but they do not produce any tangible wealth. Service workers such as filing clerks, typists, police officers, and teachers typically have more education and training than blue-collar workers; however, they do not necessarily receive more pay.

Technology has greatly increased the efficiency of service workers. For example, in 1950, it took several thousand switchboard operators to handle 1 million long-distance telephone calls; today, it takes only a few dozen. This efficiency has not reduced the work of the workers (Howard 2000). Instead, in many ways, it has increased the work they do. Telephone operators' work is less demanding physically now that switchboards are computerized and calls are connected with the touch of a button; and the work is also simpler because computers time the calls and make the necessary computations. However, computers attached to switchboards now keep track of the time that telephone operators spend on each call. These measurements are in seconds.

Each operator can now handle one hundred calls per hour. If one operator is particularly fast, other operators are expected to match that time; thus, there is always pressure for greater speed. Users of long-distance operators may observe this speed when the operator announces that the party does not answer after only four or five rings. A request to please let the phone ring longer may cause the operator to show stress when being timed because waiting for the phone to be answered uses precious seconds.

Like operators, postal workers are timed as to how rapidly they read and sort zip codes—all done on modern computerized sorters. Typists are also timed as they work on word processors. There are no daily quotas that permanently satisfy work requirements. Employers are always looking for faster workers and replacing their slower workers, so quotas tend to creep higher and higher. Many lower-paid service workers are joining unions to improve their working conditions.

Professions

The professions are widely regarded as rewarding service occupations. Professional jobs share five characteristics that set them apart from other types of service work:

1. *A body of knowledge* Professions are based on knowledge not generally available to the public. Because only professionals fully understand this knowledge, they can control how it is applied.
2. *A code of ethics* Professionals gain the confidence of the public by adhering to a code of ethics and promising a specific level of service.

3. *Licensing* Licensing demonstrates to the community that the licensed individuals have in fact mastered the body of knowledge associated with their profession.
4. *Peer control* Because the body of knowledge is specialized, only professionals can judge one another's work. Outsiders do not have the knowledge necessary to make such judgments.
5. *A professional association* The association devises and maintains the profession's educational standards, licensing requirements, peer review procedures, and code of ethics.

Two of the most important professions in the United States are law and medicine. Professionals in these fields are well paid and have some autonomy in their work. The proportion of professionals employed by large bureaucracies, both profit and nonprofit organizations—hospitals, pharmaceutical companies, medical and legal clinics, and large companies in other fields—has been increasing in recent years. Professionals lose some autonomy in these organizations, and their workloads can be increased by the organization. Their workloads are also increased by modern technology—especially car phones and beepers, which keep them constantly in touch with the office. The first major strike by physicians occurred in 1986, when physicians working for a large corporation, Group Health Association, protested increased workloads.

POLITICS AND THE DISTRIBUTION OF WEALTH

The economic system in our society produces wealth, but it has no responsibility to distribute wealth to all of the citizens. It is the political system that determines how the wealth is distributed. The government levies taxes and uses its funds to support programs for its citizens. In recent years, there has been much debate regarding the extent to which government should support the less privileged in society. Critics contend that the country must not drop programs that aid those unable to work because they are too young, too old, or too ill, or simply because no jobs are available. They believe that as long as the needs of society are met only when they provide profits to capitalists, the society will continue to have unemployment and poverty; and human needs will go unmet simply because it is not profitable to meet them. One such debate about government support of the low-income worker centers on the issue of the minimum wage.

Those who encourage government action to help redistribute wealth argue that a more equitable redistribution of money would permit everyone to benefit from the wealth generated by society. Today, most government effort to help those who cannot manage financially takes the form of some type of welfare payment.

Welfare

Welfare consists of government payments to people who have an inadequate income. The United States Federal Government spends more than $400 billion per year to fund welfare programs. Welfare programs include the following:

1. One of the oldest alleviative poverty programs at the national level is Temporary Assistance for Needy Families (TANF), first enacted (under the name Aid to Families with Dependent Children) as part of the landmark Social Security Act of 1935. TANF is jointly funded with state and federal revenues.
2. Medicaid, the medical insurance program for the poor
3. Supplemental Security Income (SSI), part of the Social Security system, which is designed to aid the poorest of the aged, blind, and disabled
4. General Assistance, a program to help poor people not covered by other programs

Piven and Cloward (1993) have shown that historically welfare payments increase when unemployment is high and discontent is widespread, but they decrease when workers are scarce and unemployment is low. They argue that welfare payments are

SOCIOLOGY AT WORK

Counseling Investors; Sociology and the Stock Market

T. Dale Whitsit has worked in two very different fields—the restaurant business and financial services. The two fields, he says, have more in common than one might imagine, however; and restaurant work was good training for brokering. In both areas, his BA in sociology, which he obtained from the State University of New York at Stony Brook, has proven useful. Since 1980, he worked as a financial consultant at Merrill Lynch, Pierce, Fenner & Smith, then for Smith Barney, and now is an independent broker.

"After college, I worked for six years as a bartender at a bar and disco called Tuey's. That experience taught me how to deal with every kind of person imaginable." One of the secrets of being a good bartender, of maintaining control, Whitsit says, is developing the ability to establish a common bond with anybody. "If somebody's getting rowdy, for example, you relate to him; you become his friend. You highlight your similarities, not your differences, and you make him feel important. Once you've established that empathy, that bond, he doesn't want to create problems because he's your friend." Whitsit says that he gained many insights about what creates a sense of cohesion among people from some of the sociology courses he took. "Sometimes I could develop a rapport with a person by letting him or her know that we have similar reference groups, that we might be members of the same in-group, or have some out-groups in common. There are lots of things I learned in sociology about what makes people think in similar ways. Of course, I don't use the sociological jargon when I talk to them."

The ability to interact with people from all different backgrounds is one of the skills that led Whitsit to become a financial consultant. "I wanted a career that would pay me the most money for my ability to communicate one to one with people of any group or background," he says. "I believe my training in sociology has aided me greatly in my field by helping me realize that people, because of their different demographic, ethnic, and financial backgrounds, have uniquely different ideas of how to invest their money and plan for the future."

When he sees new clients, Whitsit's first task is to develop a financial profile. Although he cautions that there are no hard-and-fast rules, he has found that "people who have similar demographics, upbringing, and family situations have similar ideas about how to increase their financial well-being. Young investors, for example, tend to be more aggressive in their investments than older individuals. Younger people feel that they can make up any losses, whereas older people feel that their ability to recover losses is hindered by their age, that their best earnings are behind them. Doctors seem to trust their investment counselors more—they want someone to guide them, perhaps because most successful doctors don't have time to monitor their investments. Teachers, on the other hand, tend to be much more conservative. Furthermore, 'old money' tends to be more confident—and more conservative—than ''new money' because they're used to having money and they know how the system works."

In addition to using his sociology skills to understand people's backgrounds and investment needs, Whitsit makes use of another aspect of sociology—social statistics. "Investment firms, such as Merrill Lynch and Smith Barney, have a large research staff that produces information that can be used to spot trends and guide investment," he says. "One of the factors they take into account is demographic changes." For example, he notes that many members of the baby-boom generation who are having babies themselves are dual-income couples. "Now might be a good time to buy stock in companies that provide day-care centers."

used to keep the unemployed from expressing their discontentment in hard times.

Gans (1996) lists some advantages that the middle and upper classes derive by keeping people poor:

1. They are a source of cheap labor.
2. They can be sold goods of inferior quality that otherwise could not be sold at all.
3. They serve as examples of deviance, thereby motivating others to support the norms of the dominant group.
4. They make mobility easier for others because they are out of the competition.
5. They do the most unpleasant jobs.
6. They absorb the costs of change because they suffer the unemployment when technological advances are made by industry.
7. They create jobs in social work and related fields for the middle class.
8. They create distinctive cultural forms of music and art, which the middle class adopts.

Welfare payments to the poor comprise only a small part of the federal government's efforts to improve living conditions, but most programs are designed to assist classes other than the poor.

Welfare for the Well-Off

There are more government programs to help the middle and upper classes than to help the poor. Following is a partial list:

1. Veterans' benefits, such as life insurance, health care, educational support, housing loans, and burial grounds
2. Housing loans, available to higher-income groups, offering lower interest rates and reduced down payments
3. Business loans on favorable terms, available to owners of both small and large businesses
4. Farming subsidies to landowners who agree not to farm some of their lands or who grow products for which there are powerful lobbies, such as tobacco
5. Social Security, which is not available to the unemployed or to those who work in jobs the program does not cover, and which is not taxed on incomes above a certain level
6. Medical care in hospitals built with government funds, staffed by doctors educated with government support, who use treatments developed with the help of government grants
7. College classrooms and dormitories built with government funds and financial assistance for college students

Even in the face of programs such as these, it is the programs for the poor that generally come under attack when the government tries to cut the domestic budget. Programs that benefit the middle class, especially veterans' and housing benefits, are considered sacred and are never reduced. The next section describes a society that has improved the living conditions of the poor under a very different economic system.

THE CHINESE SYSTEM: AN EXAMPLE OF SOCIALISM

Economic systems, whether capitalist or socialist, are strongly influenced by the societies of which they are a part. We cannot discuss adequately in this chapter all of the variations that exist in the world. However, we do describe one socialist system, that of the Chinese, to provide a comparison with capitalism.

In 1920, China was a nation ruled by local warlords and populated by millions of poor peasants. More than half the peasants owned no land whatsoever, and many who did have land owned so little that they could not support themselves. Chinese workers in the cities were equally poor. Women and children who worked in the silk mills made twelve cents for a fifteen-hour workday. The average wage for male workers was ten dollars a month (Freeman 1979).

Two groups of Chinese organized to fight the warlords and to modernize the Chinese nation. One group, the Kuomintang, was made up of middle-class people, merchants, nationalists, and intellectuals. This group had the support of the United States in their efforts to organize labor and to make China a modern industrial nation. The other group, the Chinese Communist Party, developed around a small number of radical, middle class. This group had the support of the Soviet Union.

For almost thirty years, these two groups fought the warlords, Japanese invaders, and each other. The Japanese invasion of China did much to turn peasant support to the Communist Party. In their response to the Japanese, the Kuomintang leaders treated the peasants cruelly, forcibly drafting them into their army and bringing them to training camps in chains. When the Kuomintang fought the Japanese in open battle, they generally lost; and then they taxed the peasants heavily to rebuild their army. Inflation and corruption were rampant. When World War II ended, the Kuomintang controlled most of Chinese industry and had the support of most of the world's nations. The United States sent them $1.1 billion in aid in 1945 alone. They had no social programs; they specialized in graft and corruption and treated the peasants with contempt.

The peasants, unhappy under Kuomintang rule, turned to the Communist Party, which treated them well. The Communists gave the peasants guns, fought the Japanese in guerrilla warfare, and were better able to protect themselves and the peasants. They preached mutual love and assistance and instructed their army to behave as follows (Freeman 1979, 210):

In 1920s' China, female workers made less money than their male counterparts.

1. Obey orders in all your actions.
2. Do not take a single needle or piece of thread from the masses.
3. Turn in everything captured.
4. Speak politely.
5. Pay fairly for what you buy.
6. Return everything you borrow.
7. Pay for anything you damage.
8. Do not hit or swear at people.
9. Do not damage crops.
10. Do not take liberties with women.
11. Do not ill-treat captives.

Through these policies and practices, the Communists gained the support of the peasants—two million in the army and ten million in village self-defense squads. They eventually won the civil war and created the People's Republic of China on October 1, 1949.

In a matter of months, the Communists made dramatic changes in support of their theme of mutual love and assistance. They outlawed opium-growing, gambling, *female infanticide* (the killing of girl infants), dowries, arranged marriages, the selling of wives and concubines, and many other practices that had existed for centuries. The benefits were great to everyone except the wealthy landowners.

The primary workers were formed into thousands of agricultural communes. The communes of today average fifteen thousand members, each divided into brigades averaging one thousand members each. Brigades are further divided into teams of 150 persons. The peasants were slow to adapt to communes after centuries of working their own plots, but the Communists brought much new land under cultivation by terracing hillsides, digging wells for irrigation, improving the soil, and using new seed strains. They also introduced modern farming equipment, such as machines for planting and transplanting rice. As improvements in farming developed, crop yields increased enormously. The life of the peasants improved, and they have now adapted to communal living.

The Chinese Communists developed successful industries rather quickly. Industries such as iron, steel, machinery, coal, petroleum, electric power, and chemicals were developed in moderate-size factories and plants spread about the country. An effort was also made to keep industry in small-scale plants so that the secondary workers would not feel lost or alienated. In addition, workers were encouraged to feel pride in their individual contribution to the functioning of the plant and to the commune the plant served.

The Communists also made remarkable strides in service (tertiary) areas, such as education and health care. To facilitate education of their people, the Chinese language was simplified, schools and colleges were opened, and teachers were trained. In the ten years after the Communist takeover, enrollment in middle schools, comparable to our junior high and high schools, jumped from one million to twelve million students. The schools emphasize the teaching of Communist doctrine, equality, mutual love and assistance, and pride in the ability to contribute to the good of society.

The Chinese system developed in a very poor nation that now has more than one billion people. China is still poor by U.S. standards, but the planning and setting of priorities required by the socialist system allowed the Chinese to make the most use of their people and their resources. Now that the socialist system has been well established, the system in China is slowly changing to allow more capitalism.

In China, people are expected to put the welfare of the group above their own interests; such cultural norms leave little room for individual self-expression. In fact, reformers who want to increase democracy in China have been treated harshly. The average Chinese worker has sacrificed many of the freedoms that Americans take for granted in the process of developing a socialist economic system.

Thinking Sociologically

1. Carefully go through this chapter, and list all of the topics that could provide insight into the policy debate about raising the minimum wage.
2. How are each of the topics selected in Question 1 useful in evaluating each side of the debate?
3. How are the Japanese models of quality control circles and lifetime jobs at odds with a capitalistic system? In what ways could capitalists benefit from the Japanese models?
4. Although they may be far more subtle, are there employee practices in place today that mirror the tactics of industry owners in their attempts to discourage unionization?

CHAPTER REVIEW

Wrapping it up

Summary

Check out our website
www.bvtstudents.com
for free chapter-by-chapter flashcards, summaries, and self-quizzes.

1. A society's economic system provides for the production and distribution of the goods and services the society uses. Sociologists study economic systems to better understand how the production of goods influences social life.

2. There are currently two basic types of economic systems: capitalism and socialism. In *capitalism*, the property needed to produce resources and goods is privately owned, and goods are sold for a profit. The United States is the most capitalistic of modern nations, but even in this country, some property is not privately owned.

3. In *socialism*, the property needed to produce goods and resources is owned by the state, and production is planned by the state.

4. In a *welfare capitalism* system, some property is private, and some is owned by the state.

5. *Communism* is a system in which the members of the society own the means of production in common. Communism has had some success in small communities, but has not been developed on a national scale.

6. Structural functional theorists point out that capitalism reflects social values favoring private property and the freedom to determine one's own economic course. Functionalists believe that capitalism persists because it functions well, providing profit to whoever supplies any needed goods.

7. Conflict theorists argue that capitalism both creates a monopoly of wealth and alienates workers.

8. The American economic system reflects values held by its people. These values were strongly influenced by the Puritans, who believed that those who accumulated wealth were chosen by God. Americans value *growth*, the individual right to accumulate wealth. In considering the influence of different denominations of religion, there appears to be a correlation between religion, family values, and the accumulation of wealth.

9. Through *vertical expansion*, American corporations have grown from large factories to giant corporations that control every step in the manufacturing process, from raw materials to retail sales. Some corporations have grown through *horizontal expansion* to monopolize most of the sales in a field, and others have grown through *diversification* to own a number of different types of unrelated businesses. Businesses may also be linked by being owned or controlled by the same bank or wealthy individual.

10. Many very large multinational corporations do business in many countries.

11. Work in large factories is said to be alienating when employees cannot control their work or create a product from start to finish.

12. Research has been done to increase productivity, but the scientific management and human relations perspectives offer different views on how to improve efficiency. The Japanese emphasize lifetime jobs and quality control circles to improve efficiency.

13. Employees have formed unions to improve their working conditions. American unions have been conservative, cooperating with management and striking only as a last resort. More radical labor unions, which wanted workers to own the means of production, were outlawed in America.

14. Large corporations and urban areas need many service workers. Most of them are poorly paid, and technology is increasing both their productivity and the stress in their work. Many are forming unions.

15. Professionals are highly trained workers familiar with some specialized bodies of knowledge, who have codes of ethics, licensing procedures, peer controls, and professional organizations. Through legislation, they can limit the practice of their profession and can demand high fees. More and more professionals now work for large corporations.

16. China has a socialist economic system. Through their planned economy, the Chinese have been able to improve the standard of living of a very poor nation. The Chinese Communist party organized workers into communes, built industries, and provided for the country's other basic needs. They are now developing more capitalism.

Key Terms

alienation A feeling of estrangement or dissociation, such as Marx's idea of feeling alienated from work because of no control over it or satisfaction from it

capitalism An economic system in which all of the means of production are privately owned

communism An economic system in which members of the society own the means of production in common

democratic socialism An economic system in which the means of production are owned primarily by individuals or groups of individuals and the goods and services vital to the society, such as transportation systems and medical care, are owned and run by the state

diversification The corporate practice of entering business in a variety of areas of manufacturing in order to protect profits (A decrease in profits in one type of business might be made up by an increase in profits in another type, for example.)

economic system The social institution that provides for the production, distribution, and consumption of goods and services

free market An economic system in which all people are theoretically free to buy, sell, and make a profit

gross domestic product (GDP) The total value of all final goods and services produced within the borders of a country per year

horizontal expansion Corporations taking over similar businesses in order to gain a monopoly and reduce competition

human relations school A form of industrial management in which the workers' psychology, peer pressures, and attitudes toward management are taken into account

lifetime jobs An employment practice in which workers are guaranteed a job for a lengthy period of time

market economy An economy in which the price and production of goods are determined by what people are willing to pay in the marketplace

mass production The production of many items of a product, which lowers the cost per item and reduces the time needed to make it

multinational corporation Corporations that do business in a number of nations

planned economy An economy in which the production and prices of goods are planned by the government

primary workers Workers who produce raw

materials, such as food or minerals

Protestant ethic The view associated with the Puritans that hard work is valuable for its own sake (According to Weber, the Protestant ethic is responsible for the high value placed on capitalism in the United States.)

quality control circles Meetings at which workers discuss ways of improving production and set policy to reach their goals

scientific management A method of managing assembly-line workers such that their every movement is efficient

secondary workers Workers who produce manufactured goods from raw materials

socialism An economic system in which the means of production are owned by all the people through the state

tertiary workers Workers who provide a service, such as doctors, lawyers, politicians, police officers, and secretaries

unionization The process of organizing workers to improve their wages and working conditions

vertical expansion Business expansion in order to own everything related to a business, from raw materials to sales outlets

welfare capitalism A mixed economy in which private and public ownership are both practiced extensively

Discussion Questions

1. Make a list of the socialistic programs that exist in the United States. Which of these programs should be eliminated? What programs do you think should be added to the list?
2. Discuss the traditional values of American society that spur our economy. What values are changing, and what new values are evolving that spur the economy?
3. Consider the advantages and the disadvantages of Sweden's system of having large tax bills and more social programs, compared to the United States having lower taxes and fewer programs.
4. Compare how structural functional theory and conflict theory would explain the growth of multinational corporations.
5. What are some of the positive and negative functions of the scientific management and the human relations school of management?
6. What are the advantages and disadvantages of very meager welfare payments? What would they be for very generous welfare payments?
7. What are some of the reasons for providing government programs to improve the standard of living of the middle class and the wealthy?
8. Discuss how China might have developed under a capitalist system. What would have been the advantages and disadvantages?
9. Discuss the advantages and disadvantages to China's development as a socialist system.

Pop Quiz

1. What does the economic system of a society provide for?

   a. the production, distribution, and consumption of goods and services
   b. the division of labor in industry and society
   c. the basis on which all societies are founded
   d. the distribution of power and authority

2. The economic system based on private ownership is ______.

   a. capitalism
   b. socialism
   c. communism
   d. welfare capitalism

3. A system based on state ownership of the means of production is ______.

   a. capitalism
   b. communism
   c. welfare capitalism
   d. socialism

4. How do socialist systems differ from capitalist ones?

    a. The people themselves control the economy.
    b. Ownership is in the hands of private corporations.
    c. They have free markets.
    d. They have planned economies.

5. Structural functionalists argue that capitalist economies succeed because they ______.

    a. meet basic needs of a society
    b. support the Protestant work ethic
    c. support scientific management
    d. allow for full equality

6. The Communist Manifesto was written by ______.

    a. C. Wright Mills
    b. Karl Marx
    c. Max Weber
    d. William Domhoff

7. Weber's analysis of the political economy of the Western world was called _______.

    a. The Communist Manifesto
    b. The Protestant Ethic and the Spirit of Capitalism
    c. The Wealth of Nations
    d. Capitalism and Economy

8. The business practice of entering a variety of businesses to ensure a stable profit is called ______.

    a. vertical expansion
    b. corporate linkage
    c. multinationalism
    d. diversification

9. Management programs that emphasize the importance of informal groups reflect the beliefs of ______.

    a. the human relations school
    b. the scientific management school
    c. alienation
    d. the Hawthorne effect

10. Which of the following is NOT one of the distinctive characteristics of a profession?

    a. a body of knowledge
    b. a code of ethics
    c. peer control
    d. unions

11. In capitalism, the means of production is publicly owned. T/F

12. The Oneida community was a small-scale communist community. T/F

13. Marx assumed that the workers would eventually revolt and overthrow the capitalist system. T/F

14. Most multinational corporations are owned by the countries of western Europe. T/F

15. Scientific management acknowledges the intelligence of the workers. T/F

1. A	6. B	11. F
2. A	7. B	12. T
3. D	8. D	13. T
4. D	9. A	14. F
5. A	10. D	15. F

CHAPTER 17

Health-Care Groups and Systems

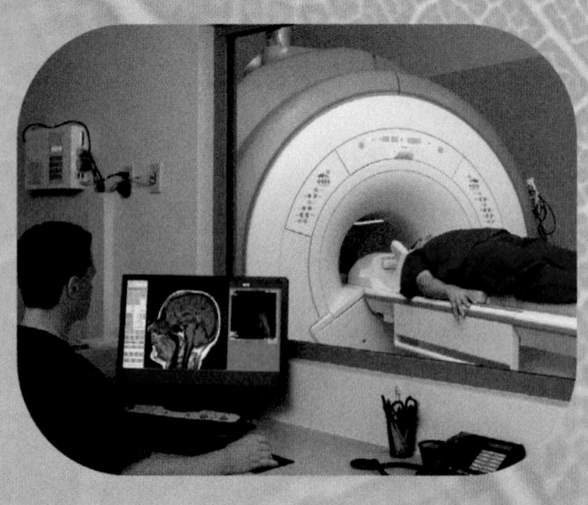

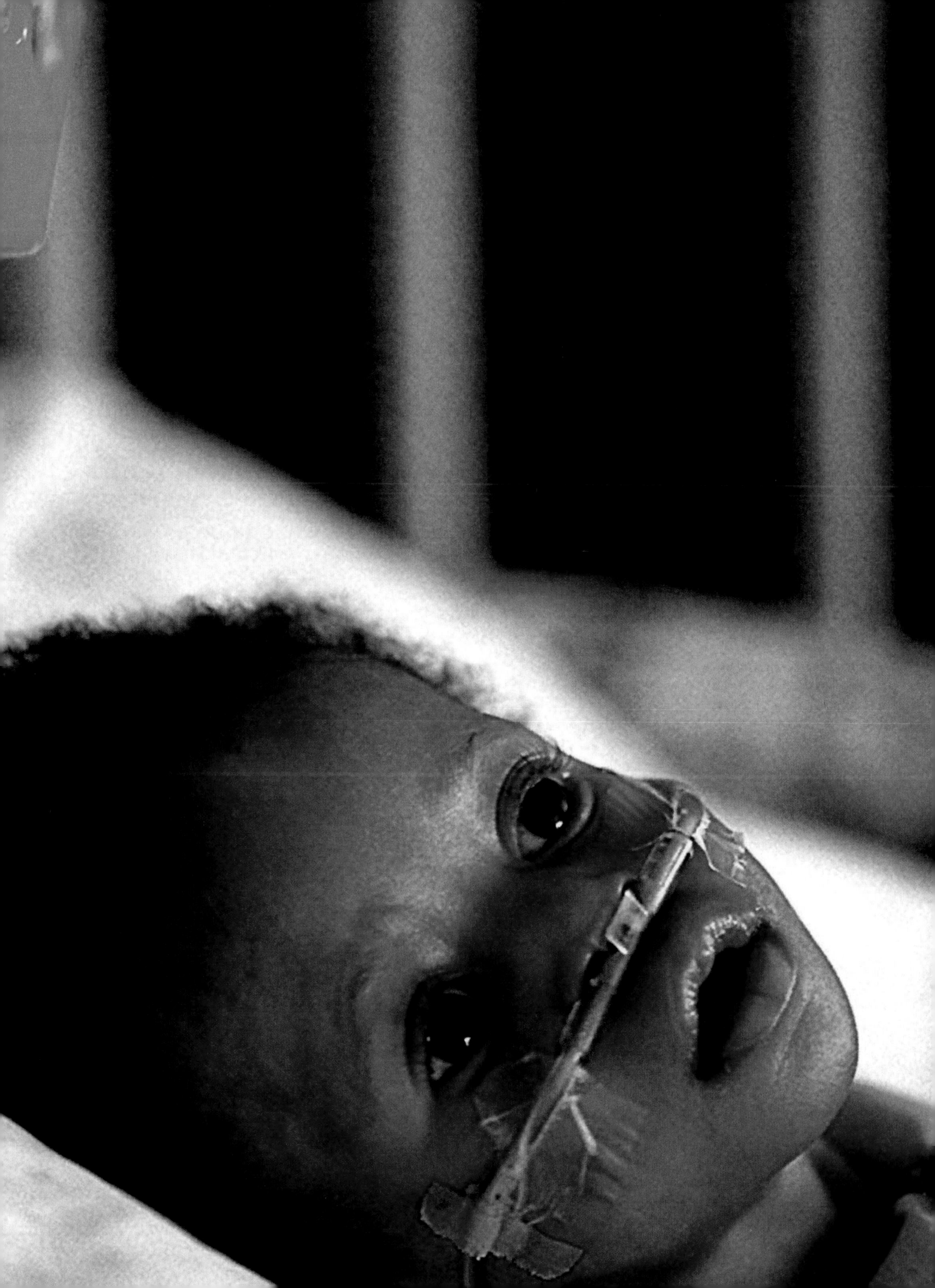

HEALTH AS A SOCIAL FACT

Health, both physical and psychological, is often thought of as an individual condition of people's lives. However, when we look at statistics about health conditions, it becomes clear that health is a social fact. As you read in Chapter 2, Emile Durkheim defined social facts as "every way of acting, fixed or not, capable of exercising on the individual an external constraint." Social facts stem from collective forces rather than individual ones. They are external to individuals and resistant to individual will. While there certainly are aspects of our health that may be affected by our individual decisions (such as the decision to smoke cigarettes), when looked at collectively, the statistics regarding health suggest that health is as much a social fact as it is a biological fact. Consider the following statistics compiled by the *Centers for Disease Control and Prevention (CDC) Health Disparities and Inequalities Report, United States 2011*:

- Lower income residents report fewer average healthy days in all states of the U.S.
- Air-pollution related disparities associated with fine particulates and ozone, which often lead to health problems, are often determined by geographical location. Racial/ethnic minority groups are more likely to live in affected geographic areas and experience a disparately larger impact on their health.
- Infants born to Black women are 1.5 to 3 times more likely to die than infants born to women of other races/ethnicities.
- Men of all races/ethnicities are approximately four times likely to die in motor vehicle crashes than women, and death rates are twice as high among Native Americans.
- Men of all ages and race/ethnicities are approximately four times more likely to die by suicide than females. The suicide rate among Native Americans and non-Hispanic Whites is more than twice that of Blacks, Asian Pacific Islanders and Hispanics.
- Rates of drug-induced deaths increased between 2003 and 2007 among men and women of all race/ethnicities, with the exception of Hispanics, and rates are highest among non-Hispanic Whites. Prescription drug abuse now kills more persons than illicit drugs, a reversal of the situation fifteen to twenty years ago.
- Men are much more likely to die from coronary heart disease, and Black men and women are much more likely to die of heart disease and stroke than their white counterparts.
- Rates of preventable hospitalizations increase as incomes decrease. There also are large racial/ethnic disparities in preventable hospitalizations, with Blacks experiencing a rate more than double that of Whites.
- Racial/ethnic minorities, with the exception of Asians/Pacific Islanders, experience disproportionately higher rates of new human immunodeficiency virus diagnoses than Whites, as do men who have sex with men (MSM).
- Hypertension is by far most prevalent among non-Hispanic Blacks (42 percent vs. 28.8 percent among Whites), while levels of control are lowest for Mexican Americans. Although men and women have roughly equivalent hypertension prevalence, women are significantly more likely to have the condition controlled. Uninsured persons are only about half as likely to have hypertension under control than those with insurance, regardless of type.
- Rates of adolescent pregnancy and childbirth have been falling or holding steady for all racial/ethnic minorities in all age groups. However, disparities persist as birth rates for Hispanics and non-Hispanic Blacks are 3 and 2.5 times those of Whites, respectively.
- More than half of alcohol consumption by adults in the United States is in the form of binge drinking. Younger people and men are more likely to binge drink and consume more alcohol than older people and women. The prevalence of binge drinking is higher in groups with higher incomes and higher educational levels, although people who binge drink and have lower incomes and less educational attainment levels binge drink more frequently. When they do binge drink, they drink more heavily. American Indian/Native Americans report more binge drinking episodes per month and higher alcohol consumption per episode than other groups.
- Tobacco use is the leading cause of preventable illness and death in the United States. Despite overall declines in cigarette smoking, disparities in smoking rates persist among certain racial/ethnic minority groups, particularly among American Indians/Alaska Natives. Smoking rates decline significantly with increasing income and educational attainment.

Consider that each of the above health care disparities pertains to social or demographic characteristics rather than individual traits. While it is true that some of the results (such as alcohol and tobacco consumption) seem to be the result of individual choices, the fact that some behaviors are disproportionate in some social groups suggests that there is something about being in those groups that leads to the disparities.

Health care is one of the most hotly debated and controversial political issues in the United States. Every society must give serious attention to the health of its population if it is to survive. Illness disrupts society inasmuch as members who are ill cannot fulfill their social roles, they use scarce resources such as medicines, and they require the time and attention of healthy persons to take care of them. In extreme instances, illness has even destroyed entire societies, sometimes even killing everyone. Because of these factors, every society has developed ways of coping with illness. We often think of health and illness in strictly biological terms and believe that the diagnosis and treatment of illness are based on a scientific analysis of a biological problem. Social factors, however, play a major role in defining who is well and who is ill; and they also influence how illness is treated. An understanding of these social factors is critical to developing sound health care policies.

THE SOCIAL NATURE OF HEALTH AND ILLNESS

The World Health Organization has defined health to be, in the most idealistic terms, the "complete physical, mental and social well–being and not merely the absence of disease and infirmity." It is difficult to estimate how many people would be considered totally healthy according to this glowing definition. Does anyone ever have complete physical, mental, and social well-being all at the same time? Rather than use such an all-encompassing definition, others in the health field prefer to define *health* as the body in a state of equilibrium. Our biological systems should function in a particular way, and we are healthy when they function, as they should.

Others prefer to define *health* as the absence of illness—but illness is an equally difficult term to define. **Pathological illnesses** are those in which the body is clearly diseased or malfunctioning in some way, as when viruses cause measles and chicken pox, cancer cells develop and grow, or an artery to the heart is blocked. These conditions are either obvious when examining the patient, or they are detected in laboratory tests involving X-rays, microscopes, or the more advanced technology available today. Not all biological abnormalities are considered illnesses, however. Herpes simplex, for example, was not considered an illness until venereal herpes became widespread and life-threatening to newborn infants.

Statistical illnesses are those in which a person's health varies from the norm. For example, high blood pressure is a statistical illness indicating that the person's blood pressure is considerably higher than is deemed normal. The trouble with defining statistical illnesses is knowing whether the norm is actually healthy. In the case of high blood pressure, the norm in the United States (140/95) is probably too high for optimal health. A much lower blood pressure is probably desirable: 100/60. However, that level is so abnormally low in the United States that if it were used as a standard, everyone would be classified as ill.

Iron-deficiency anemia is another example of a statistical disease. How much below the norm does a person have to be before being considered anemic and needing to take iron supplements? The answer is determined by the norm for the majority of the population.

Mental illnesses are even more difficult to define than physical ones. Manic-depressives have more extreme mood swings than normal, but everyone has some mood swings. We are all depressed sometimes. So how depressed must a person be before being labeled as having the illness called "depression"? Comparing an individual's behavior and verbalizations to the norm makes the diagnosis. Medical researchers are searching diligently for biological causes of depression and other behaviors, and they may in time find biological bases for some of these problems. Behavior is social, nevertheless, in that it is learned in social interaction, and whether our behavior is considered healthy or ill, continues to be determined by social criteria.

THEORETICAL PERSPECTIVES ON ILLNESS

How does society handle illness? Who decides when we are ill and when we are well? Why is it that we can sometimes miss school or work while at other times

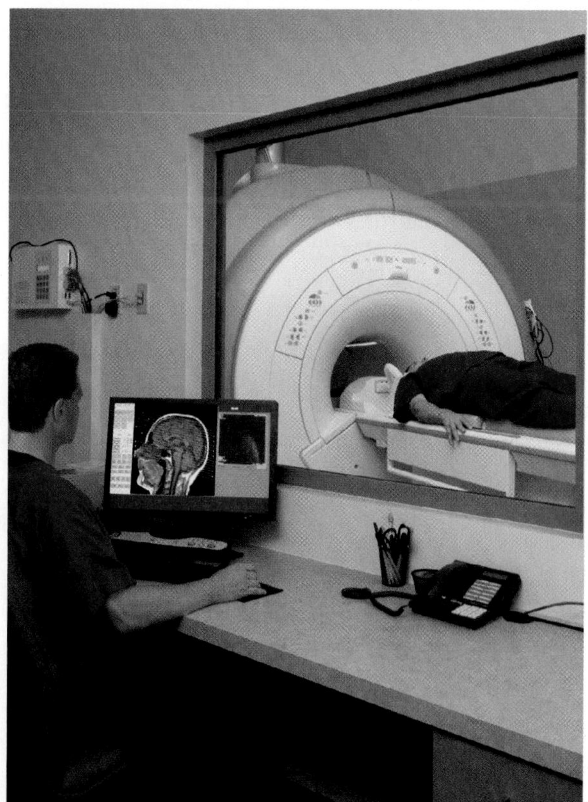

Diagnostic tests using advanced technologies help detect illnesses.

when we feel just as bad we are not excused? Should illness be decided objectively on the basis of biological criteria? Sociologists do not believe that an objective view of illness can ever be achieved because illness is social as well as biological.

A Functional Explanation of Illness

Talcott Parsons (1951) pointed out that people are classified as ill not on the basis of their physical condition, but on the basis of how they are functioning in society. If people do not function well in their social roles, especially in family and work roles, they are considered deviant and disruptive to society. To maintain social order, such people are labeled "ill" and are placed in a **sick role**—a set of expectations, privileges, and obligations related to their illness. The expectations of the sick role vary somewhat, depending on the person and the illness, but they generally involve three assumptions:

1. Sick people are expected to reduce their performance in other roles. Those with a serious case of the flu—who have a high temperature and other symptoms—may be excused from all other roles. Those suffering from a mild case of flu may be expected to perform work or student roles as usual, but they will be expected to reduce social and recreational roles. The sick role reflects a society's need to have members participate in the work of that society. The first roles relinquished are those that are for pleasure. The last ones relinquished are work roles.
2. Sick people are expected to try to get better. They should do whatever they can to improve their health and not linger in their illness.
3. They are expected to take the advice of others. Children must take the advice of parents; and adults must listen to their doctor or to the family members who are caring for them. Sometimes, children take care of their parents; and although they would not usually tell their parents how to behave, in the event of illness, they give extensive advice. Furthermore, if the advice is not accepted, the advice-giver often becomes very hurt or angry.

Society places the power to declare who is sick in the hands of physicians. Only the physician has the legal right to diagnose and treat illness. The physician can excuse you from work or school, admit you to a hospital, or have you declared disabled or too ill to stand trial in a court of law. A person's self-diagnosis is not adequate. He or she must go to a doctor to be seriously considered ill. If the doctor does not agree with the patient's diagnosis, the individual is labeled "well." If the patient disagrees with the diagnosis as well, the individual may be called a **hypochondriac**, a well person who believes that he or she is ill. If people believe they are healthy but a

Depression is considered a form of mental illness. Researchers, however, are looking for biological causes of depression.

physician declares them ill, they can be declared mentally ill, as well as physically ill. A person diagnosed as having cancer who refused to accept such a diagnosis might be sent for psychiatric evaluation, for example.

The sick role varies, depending on a variety of social circumstances such as age, gender, and the influence of caregivers. Elderly people are expected to be ill and are easily placed in the sick role. It is also acceptable for women to be ill unless they have responsibility for young children—women are rarely excused from child care duties. The caregiver also influences the sick role. If he or she accepts the illness, the sick person will play the role more fully; but if the caregiver is someone who works staunchly under all but the most dire circumstances, the sick person may be required to perform work roles. Some mothers are happy to bring soup and tender loving care to their children for long periods of time. Other mothers believe that their children should be up and about as soon as possible. Although the sick role expectations may vary, it does place a person in the social order with a set of both responsibilities and privileges to guide behavior, so that the social order can be kept integrated and functioning.

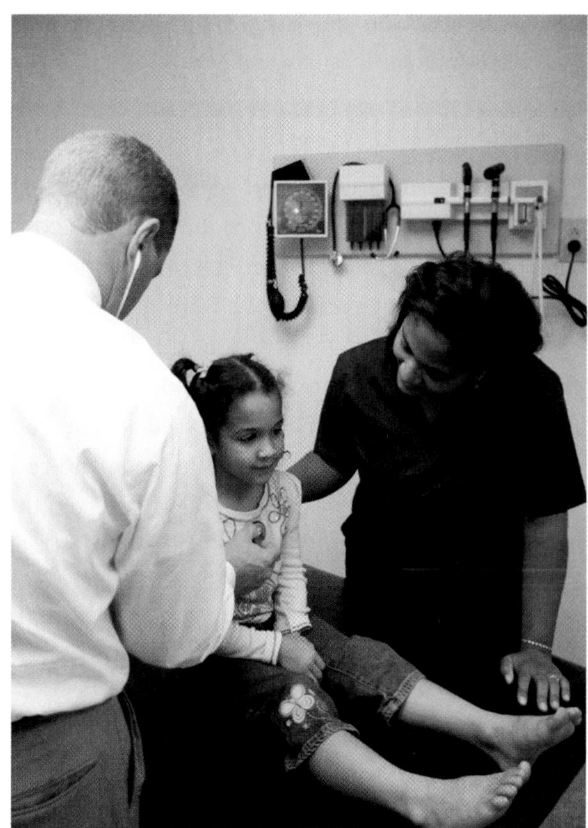

Physicians are deemed as the only individuals legally qualified to diagnose and treat illnesses.

APPLYING THE SICK ROLE

At one time or another, everyone will become sick or be required to care for someone who is sick. It is therefore important to acknowledge the existence and implications of the sick role. If, by being placed in a sick role, a person is expected to reduce his or her performance in other roles, is expected to try to get better, and is expected to take the advice of others, then labeling someone as "sick" becomes a useful device in their treatment and path to recovery. People often have ailments that require them to suspend their routine roles in order to return to proper health. Sometimes, though, people are unable to do this, either because they feel compelled to continue to function in their role as worker, parent, or student, or because they are unable to be excused. Have you ever, for example, felt sick yet continued your routine of play or work, and later, when diagnosed as sick by a parent or a doctor, decided that resting was the proper thing to do? The label "sick" serves the important function of not only allowing but also requiring that the sick role to become the predominant one, at least temporarily.

It is also important to understand the social consequences of such a label and how they might work to a person's disadvantage. Suppose that a person with a physical limitation is labeled as "sick." This can be negative in a few ways. First, although that person might be able to perform adequately in a job, he or she might not be given an opportunity because of the expectation that sick people reduce their performance in other roles. Similarly, some people who are "sick" may be stigmatized or feared. AIDS victims, for example, are often shunned, even though AIDS cannot be transmitted through casual contact. Second, a person with a physical limitation who is labeled "sick" may come to conform to the expectations associated with the sick role. Clearly, the sick role is a powerful social phenomenon that can be applied to the detriment or advantage of people's physical and mental health.

While various factors affect sick role performances, playing the sick role produces various consequences for the sick person. Dr. Christine Laine (1997) found that patients who are active and engaged with regard to their own health care fare better than patients who are less active or adopt the sick role. Although there may be perceived advantages to letting the professionals do the work, the end result is that those who adopt the sick role may lessen their chances of attaining "optimal outcomes" (Laine 1997). As stated earlier, older, sicker, and lesser-educated patients are more likely to adopt the sick role.

The Conflict Perspective of Illness

Conflict theorists believe that the health care system is an elite system intent on maintaining its power. The health care system legitimates its power by claiming a specialized body of knowledge and uses its power to gain wealth and maintain the status quo. Conflict theorists contend, for example, that the system of giving birth in hospitals rather than at home or in birthing centers persists because it is convenient for doctors and profitable for hospitals (Rothman 2000). Deliveries are made by doctors rather than by midwives because it provides employment for doctors, not because it is necessary or better for women and babies. Conflict theorists also note that insurance programs such as *Medicare,* the federal health insurance program for the elderly, are structured such that wealthy people receive more benefits than the poor (Davis 1975).

In the United States, from 2002 to 2011, the cost of health care for a typical family of four has more than doubled from $9,235 to $19,393. (See Figure 17-1). Conflict theorists argue that much of the diagnosis and treatment of diseases benefits the large medical corporations more than the patients. Although drug companies sell drugs of questionable safety and effectiveness for the common cold, they do not like to manufacture **orphan drugs** that are valuable in the treatment of rare diseases but not profitable to the manufacturer. Manufacturers of high-technology medical equipment may sell rarely used, expensive devices to many hospitals within a locality, when one device could be shared by several hospitals (Waitzkin 2000); this raises hospital costs by encouraging physicians to engage in more testing and procedures that must be paid for by the patient, in order to justify the expensive device.

Physicians, who usually represent the upper middle class, may use their power to control patients and to maintain the status quo. Physicians have the power to excuse people from work or to refuse to excuse them. Availability of adequate health insurance often plays a role in patient care. For example, well-paid specialists can put well-insured business executives with back pain into a hospital for days or weeks of treatment. On the other hand, for a similar back condition, public health clinic physicians may give inadequately insured laborers painkillers and send them back to work. Physicians declare who is eligible for insurance payments for illness and disability and who must return to work. Physicians can declare criminals insane and unable to stand trial. Elite criminals are more likely to obtain the services of prestigious psychiatrists, who declare the accused to be insane, whereas lower-class criminals cannot afford such services, and if they receive any psychiatric attention, such services are likely to be publicly funded, which makes it probable that the criminal will stand trial and go to prison. Thus, the sick role and illness are used to perpetuate the existing social system.

Symbolic Interaction and Illness Behavior

Because illness is social, symbolic interaction has played a major role in the study of medical groups and systems. For example, researchers who study symbolic interaction explore the meanings that patients give to symptoms and illness. Patients are the first to recognize their own illness and to decide to visit a doctor, who then takes a medical history. How the patient describes symptoms influences the diagnosis, and patients describe their illness based on what society teaches them. They learn that nausea and dizziness are signs of illness (unless they are smoking their first cigarette, in which case they ignore it).

FIGURE 17-1 MILLIMAN MEDICAL INDEX OF HEALTHCARE COSTS IN THE U.S.

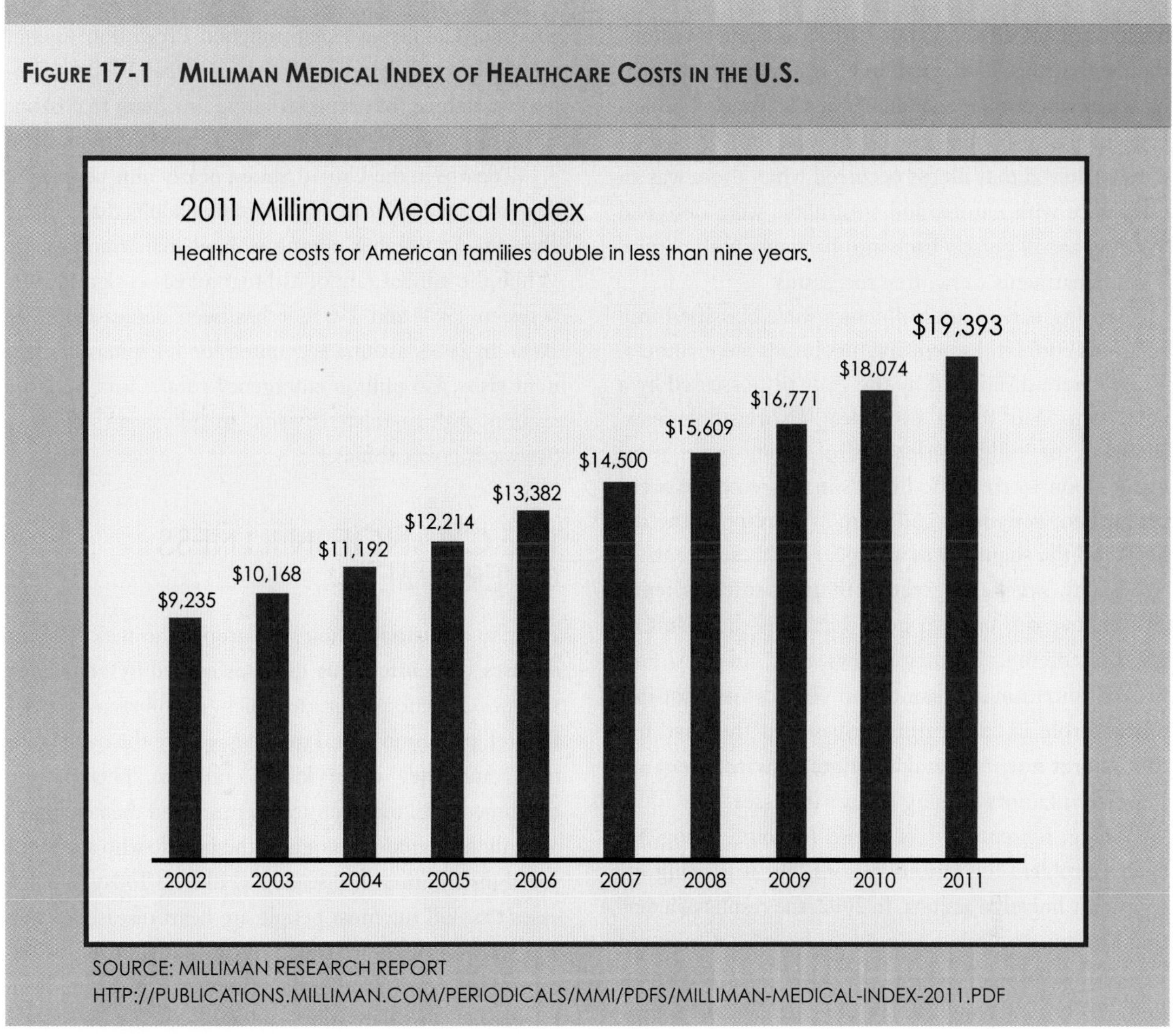

SOURCE: MILLIMAN RESEARCH REPORT
HTTP://PUBLICATIONS.MILLIMAN.COM/PERIODICALS/MMI/PDFS/MILLIMAN-MEDICAL-INDEX-2011.PDF

They learn that headaches or stomach pains require a drugstore remedy, but chest pains require a visit to the doctor. They learn that if they are tired at night, they need to go to bed; but if they are tired in the morning, they must ignore it and go to class or to work, as expected. These experience-based facts and hearsay knowledge are not necessarily good diagnoses, however; pains in the head or stomach, as well as nausea, dizziness, and fatigue, are symptoms that may indicate serious as well as mild diseases.

Children learn about the causes of disease as they grow up. They learn that if they do not wear a sweater, boots, or a coat, they will catch cold. If they do not eat right or get enough sleep, they will get sick. If they go outdoors for fresh air and exercise, they will be healthier. Then, when they get sick, they wonder what they did wrong. As adults, we tend to blame sick people when they develop heart disease or cancer. Did they eat too much or drink too much? Did they live stressful lives? Surely, they must have done something wrong. We accept a great deal of guilt and blame for our health in this society, even though there is no evidence that we can prevent death, little evidence that we can even forestall death significantly, and a great deal of evidence that the environment influences our health more than our own behavior does.

We also learn medical theories of illness as we grow up. We learn that viruses, germs, or other enemies of the body attack us from outside and that we must ward off attack, if not with boots and sweaters, then with drugs, food, vitamin C, rest, exercise, prayer, or whatever else is fashionable at the time. The approach of the Native Americans was more peaceful. They believed that illness occurred when there was an imbalance with nature; and treatments were designed to bring the ill person back into harmony with nature. These treatments were often successful.

During earlier ages, illnesses were classified in a religious context. Lepers and alcoholics were sinners. The ill were disfavored by the gods or possessed by a devil who had to be exorcised. Exorcists, priests, shamans, or religious leaders of other types were called upon to treat the ill person. Ceremonies were performed, gods were called upon to remove the illness, and the shaman was well paid for these talents.

Today, we have great faith in medical science and believe our current good health is the result of good medicine. History shows that, in fact, improved nutrition and sanitation played the most important role in eradicating diseases in the past and that poorer nutrition and a polluted environment are important factors causing today's illnesses.

Smog, for example, is a case in point. Smog has been a problem for various reasons, but it is being increasingly linked to asthma. In 2002, the results of a ten-year study of children funded by the California Environmental Protection Agency's Air Resources Board (ARB) and conducted by the University of Southern California (USC) produced strong evidence that ozone, commonly know as smog, can cause asthma in children (California Environmental Protection Agency (2002). It is widely accepted that smog can trigger or aggravate asthma, but representatives maintain that ozone can also cause asthma. In 2007, asthma accounted for 3,447 deaths in the United States, nearly nine people per day. Asthma deaths are higher among adults than among children, and higher among women than among men. While the annual rate of asthma increased significantly between 1980 and 1995, it has been decreasing since 2000. In 2006, asthma accounted for 1.1 million outpatient visits, 1.6 million emergency room visits, and 106 million asthma-related visits to physician's offices. (www.cdc.gov/asthma).

Asthma appears to be on the rise in the United States.

THE CHANGE IN ILLNESS OVER TIME

Prior to industrialization in Europe, the major killing diseases were **infectious diseases** caused by germs and viruses. Infectious diseases such as tuberculosis, influenza, pneumonia, and the plague were the most common, and they often killed children. This pattern continued until the twentieth century and then changed, according to **epidemiologists**, the people who study the social distribution of disease and illness. Today, the diseases that kill the most people are heart disease, cancer, and stroke, which are called **degenerative diseases** because they slowly disable the body as we get older. Both infectious diseases and degenerative diseases have proven to be related to environmental conditions.

The Age of Infectious Diseases

In the Middle Ages, diseases were widespread. Whenever crops failed, there was a food shortage. Transportation was not good enough to bring in large supplies of food, so the population became undernourished, weak, and increasingly susceptible to infection. Devastating plagues swept Europe from 1370 on. In some areas, one-third to one-half the population died. Often, when the plague hit a city, people fled to the countryside, dying on the way or carrying the plague deep into rural areas.

The causes of the plague and other diseases were not understood. In the cities, human waste was thrown into the streets. People did not concern themselves with cleanliness and did not use soap and water. It was considered immoral to concern oneself with the flesh and immodest to wash below the waist (Thomlinson 1976).

When it was discovered that rats carry the plague and that germs cause infections, urban sanitation systems were developed. Supplies of water were brought to cities, and sewage systems were built. The improvement of sanitation may have added more to the average life expectancy than all modern medical advances.

Improvements in nutrition played an even more dramatic role in reducing the death rate. It is believed that nutrition improved in Europe when the potato came into widespread use, in about the middle of the eighteenth century. The potato is rich in nutrients and easy to store and ship from place to place. Until the development of potato crops, infectious diseases were rampant and the average life expectancy was probably less than forty years.

Modern medicine may have helped to reduce the death rate from infectious diseases in two important ways. *Antibiotics*, such as penicillin, were developed to cure infections; and *vaccines*, such as for measles, were developed to prevent diseases. There is no question that antibiotics save lives; but researchers McKinlay and McKinlay (1981) argue that vaccines actually affected the death rate only slightly, reducing it by 3.5 percent at most. The infectious diseases that were the major causes of death in 1900—influenza, pneumonia, tuberculosis, diphtheria, typhoid, scarlet fever, measles, and whooping cough—were declining steadily as causes of death long before modern vaccines were discovered. They continued to fall after the vaccines were introduced, but not appreciably. Poliomyelitis, commonly called polio, is an exception. It showed a very noticeable decline soon after the vaccine came into widespread use. Otherwise, the reduction in infectious diseases was largely a result of better nutrition, better sanitation, and better housing.

Current Causes of Death

Poor nutrition is still widespread among the poor of most nations, and starvation and infectious diseases are persistent problems. However, the causes of death in industrial societies are dramatically different. Currently, the major causes of death in the United States and most other industrial nations have been heart disease, cancer, and stroke. (See Table 17-1) Although heart disease and strokes have been declining slightly, these and other more rare diseases that damage the heart and blood vessels cause more deaths in the United States than any other disease. The American diet is believed to contribute significantly to these diseases.

The American diet, along with pollution, is also blamed for the increasing cancer rate. Cancer caused 569,490 deaths in 2010 (American Cancer Society 2010). Most experts in the field estimate that 80–90 percent of all cancer cases are the result of environment or diet. In 2010, approximately 171,000 cancer deaths were caused by tobacco use. The American Cancer Society states that all cancers caused by tobacco use and heavy use of alcohol can be prevented completely. About one-third of all cancer deaths are the result of being overweight, obesity, and poor nutrition or physical activity and thus could also be prevented. Cancers related to infectious agents (such as hepatitis B and HIV) are also preventable, as well as cancer caused by overexposure to ultraviolet rays. The risk of *carcinogens* (cancer-causing products) in the environment has

Table 17-1 TEN LEADING CAUSES OF DEATH IN THE UNITED STATES, 2007

Cause	Deaths
Heart disease	616,067
Cancer	562,875
Stroke	135,952
Chronic Lower Respiratory Disease	127,924
Accidents	123,706
Alzheimer's Disease	74,632
Diabetes	71,382
Pneumonia and influenza	52,717
Nephritis, nephritic syndrome, and nephrosis	46,448
Septicemia	34,828

Source: Centers for Disease Control and Prevention, FastStats www.cdc.gov/nchs/faststats/lcod.htm

It is believed that alcoholism is the underlying cause of many deaths. Alcoholism seems to be a physical disease that cannot be cured by willpower.

been known since 1942, when publications urged that measures be taken to minimize cancer hazards on the job (Agran 1975); but little effective action has been taken. Those who work with rubber die of cancer of the stomach and prostate, leukemia, and other cancers of the blood and lymphatic systems. Steelworkers have excessive rates of lung cancer. Workers who produce dyestuffs have high rates of bladder cancer. Miners have a wide range of cancers, and half of them die from some form of cancer. Dry cleaners, painters, printers, petroleum workers, and others who are exposed to benzene have high rates of leukemia. The 1.5 million workers who are exposed to insecticides, copper, lead, and arsenic have high rates of lung and lymphatic cancer. Machinists, chemical workers, woodworkers, roofers, and countless others suffer from cancer risks of one kind or another.

Cancer rates are also higher in neighborhoods where these industries are located, thereby shortening the lives of people who never even enter the plant. If these problems are not successfully checked, increasing cancer rates may shorten life expectancy and cause genetic defects in the next generation.

Accidents, the fifth most common cause of death, are the leading cause of death for persons under age thirty-five years. Motor vehicle accidents, which account for half of these deaths, have declined as speed limits were reduced to fifty–five miles per hour and the use of seat belts increased. White males between the ages of fifteen and twenty–five have the highest death rate from automobile accidents.

Alcoholism: Moral Failure or Major Disease?

Alcoholism is a major killer of Americans and would probably appear on the list of major killers if all deaths due to alcoholism were listed on death certificates. According to the National Institute on Alcohol Abuse and Alcoholism, nearly 17.6 million adults in the U.S have an alcohol problem (*Medline Plus* 2011). Among children ages thirteen to seventeen years, there are three million alcoholics. Untold numbers of heart attack victims are probably victims of alcoholism. Many cancer victims, especially of the mouth, throat, larynx, esophagus, pancreas and liver, are really victims of alcoholism. While the number of alcohol related driving fatalities has decreased from 26,100 (60 percent of fatalities) to 13,486 (37 percent of fatalities), these deaths are still preventable. (See Table 17-2)

In recent decades, experts in the field of alcoholism have found more and more evidence that alcoholism is a physical disease that cannot be cured by willpower any more than could heart disease or cancer. In 1956, the American Medical Association (AMA) declared that **alcoholism** is a disease with identifiable and progressive symptoms; and that if it is untreated, it leads to mental damage, physical incapacity, and early death. The physical nature of the disease was described shortly thereafter by Jellineck (1960). It was demonstrated that alcoholism occurs in people who have inherited a body chemistry that fails to metabolize alcohol the way normal people do. Instead, the body

TABLE 17-2 ALCOHOL-RELATED DEATHS IN THE US SINCE 1982:

	Total fatalities	Alcohol-related fatalities	
Year	Number	Number	Percent
1982	43,945	26,173	60
1983	42,589	24,635	58
1984	44,257	24,762	56
1985	43,825	23,167	53
1986	46,087	25,017	54
1987	46,390	24,094	52
1988	47,087	23,833	51
1989	45,582	22,424	49
1990	44,599	22,587	51
1991	41,508	20,159	49
1992	39,250	18,290	47
1993	40,150	17,908	45
1994	40,716	17,308	43
1995	41,817	17,732	42
1996	42,065	17,749	42
1997	42,013	16,711	40
1998	41,501	16,673	40
1999	41,717	16,572	40
2000	41,945	17,380	41
2001	42,196	17,400	41
2002	43,005	17,524	41
2003	42,643	17,013	40
2004	42,518	16,919	39
2005	43,443	16,885	39
2006	42,532	15,829	37
2007	41,059	15,387	37
2008	37,261	13,846	37

Source: Alcohol Alert http://www.alcoholalert.com/drunk-driving-statistics.html

produces toxic substances that cause widespread damage in the body and changes that cause the body to require more alcohol to function. Thus, the victim is addicted to alcohol because once having introduced alcohol into the body, the victim must continue to drink in order to continue to function. Sooner or later, however, the body will be poisoned to the extent that the victim cannot function with or without alcohol.

Yet alcoholism is not often listed as the cause of death when a patient dies of an alcohol-related disease, and thus it does not appear on the list of common causes of death. Because alcoholism has historically been viewed as a sin, a crime, a moral lapse, or a psychological illness, physicians prefer not to use it as a cause of death in order to protect the reputation of the family.

Thinking Sociologically

1. Because we give personal meanings to health and illness, we do not always recognize the threat of illness objectively. Have you ever thought you were well when you were ill? Have you ever not noticed one of your own symptoms of a disease?
2. At any time, have you learned anything about alcoholism to lead you to believe that alcoholics are weak-willed people rather than people who are ill?
3. What are some possible short-term consequences of assigning someone the "sick role"? Long-term consequences?
   The older, sicker, and less educated are more likely to take on the sick role.
   Sociologically, how do you explain this?

THE AMERICAN HEALTH-CARE SYSTEM

The American health-care system consists of physicians, nurses, and other health-care workers who treat illness primarily as a biological event, to be prevented or cured on an individual basis. Illness, however, can be viewed as a social phenomenon and can often be eliminated in society before many individuals are stricken.

The Social Model of Illness

Historically, the greatest strides in reducing illness have been changes in lifestyle, particularly in nutrition, sanitation, and shelter. The **social model of illness** suggests that much disease is caused by social conditions and that changing those conditions can cure it. Some observers believe that taking a social approach could also reduce death rates from modern causes, such as heart disease, cancer, and automobile accidents Food supplies, for example, could be improved by having a more varied assortment of whole-grain foods on the market, as well as foods that do not contain sugar or excessive amounts of fat or salt. Vegetables and fruits could be improved by practicing farming methods that put nutrients into the soil and keeping pesticides out of the fruit. More efficient water systems could reduce waste and provide purer drinking water. A modern transportation system could reduce air pollution and accidents. Early detection of AIDS and safe sex practices could reduce the spread of this disease. All of these improvements would need to be accomplished through social reorganization and social change, however.

The Medical Model of Illness

Currently, almost all of our research and health care are based on a **medical model of illness**, in which sickness is viewed as an individual problem requiring individual treatment. Cures for heart attacks and cancer are applied after the patient is sick. People are taken to shock trauma centers after the automobile accident occurs. Even when preventive measures are considered, the responsibility rests with the individual. People must seek good food to eat by searching for stores that sell sugar-free and pesticide-free foods, for example; and they must treat their own water if they want pure water to drink. They must find ways to get proper exercise individually.

The American health-care system is designed to maintain the medical model of illness, with a full complement of physicians, nurses, and other staff, plus hospitals, the pharmaceutical industry, and modern medical technology. Ninety-three cents of every health-care dollar is spent trying to cure people after they get sick. Physicians played a major role in building the health-care system we have today.

The Profession of Medicine

The profession of medicine, for which an MD degree is required, is now one of the most prestigious professions in the United States—but this has not always been true. In the early years of United States history, there were very few doctors. Women took care of the ill members of the family and the community, and also delivered babies. Older women often gained considerable experience in these activities and would be consulted whenever someone was particularly ill or a baby was born. Many of the women of the community would gather for births, so younger women observed and understood the birthing process before they had their own children. A doctor was rarely needed.

There were only a few physicians in this country at the time of the American Revolution; and they were trained in Europe, where they studied Latin or Greek. There was little science taught in universities in those days, and no medical science. Most physicians learned to practice medicine by being an apprentice to a physician, taking on more and more responsibility until they were able to venture out on their own, often to the frontier to seek patients who needed their services. The medicine practiced was often **heroic medicine**, a dramatic intervention by the physician. Patients were bled, blistered, and given poisonous laxatives in an attempt to kill the disease. Often, the treatment killed the patient. Most people went to doctors only when they were desperate. Doctors were often poor and had little work to do. They sometimes had to beg in the streets to survive (Rothstein 1992).

By the early 1800s, many physicians were entering the profession, some of whom had been trained in Europe, some trained in apprenticeships, and some not trained at all. There was also a populist health movement at this time. Many groups formed health clubs, started to eat health foods, and learned the best healing remedies from the women in the community. Some populists even set up medical schools to train and graduate physicians in one or another favorite type of remedy. This situation concerned the physicians who had been educated in Europe and knew that in Europe the profession was held in high esteem. They felt that it was necessary to create the same respect for medical authority here in the United States (Starr 1984).

In about 1800, European-educated physicians were able to get state legislatures to pass laws forbidding healers without formal education from practicing medicine, but the laws were unpopular and were soon repealed. In 1847, physicians formed the AMA and adopted the Hippocratic Oath as a vow to practice good and ethical medicine. They lobbied states to ban abortion, which was widely practiced until that time and had been an important source of income to women healers who were not physicians. By this method, the AMA effectively made it impossible for these women to earn a living in the practice of medicine.

In 1910, another major move limited the practice of medicine to wealthy males. Abraham Flexner published the "Flexner Report," which stated that most existing medical schools were inadequate. Congress responded to the "Flexner Report" by giving the AMA the right to determine which schools were qualified to train physicians, an important power in controlling the profession. All seven medical schools for women and most medical schools for blacks were closed, eliminating women and most blacks from the practice of medicine. Part-time schools were also closed, eliminating those who could not afford full-time study. The medical field remained open only to white males of the upper classes, and a shortage of physicians developed, making medicine a very lucrative profession.

Today, medical care has become a huge industry in the United States, with six hundred thousand physicians supported by the pharmaceutical industry, the medical technology industry, the health insurance industry, and more than seven thousand hospitals. The AMA has power and influence over hospitals, medical education, prescription drugs, the use of medical technology, and the qualifications for receiving insurance payments.

The most common type of medical practice is private practice on a **fee-for-service** basis, in which the physician is paid for each visit and each service rendered. In this type of practice, the physician is self-employed and must establish an office with expensive equipment. In the office, the physician provides **primary medical care**, which is the first general, overall care the patient requires. It may include a medical history, checkup, and treatment of minor cuts, colds, sore throats, and other ailments. The primary care physician usually has privileges at a nearby hospital (i.e., the hospital permits the physician's patients to be treated there under the physician's supervision and care). There, patients may go to have surgery, deliver babies, and receive tests or other services.

Hospitals

Hospitals provide **secondary medical care**, which is more specialized than the general practitioner provides; and **secondary caregivers** are those who deliver the specialized care. Hospitals were once poorhouses or places where people went to die. When there was little specialized knowledge of complex treatment procedures, there was no advantage to putting people in the hospital for treatment. Babies were born at home, and tonsils were removed using the kitchen table as an operating table. As medical knowledge increased and hospitals came to be better equipped and more convenient places for doctors to treat patients, hospitals and their specialized staffs of physicians, nurses, and technicians drew large numbers of patients needing short-term specialized care.

There are now many types of hospitals. The most common is the community **voluntary hospital**, a nonprofit facility that treats patients who need short-term care. Most of these hospitals are in the suburbs, and money to build some of them was provided by the Hill-Burton Act of 1954. The only restriction made by Congress was that such hospitals should do some charity work. Otherwise, physicians had complete control over the new buildings and where they were built. As a result of the Hill-Burton Act, a large number of hospitals were built; due to the surplus many have now been closed.

A second type is the **municipal hospital**, which is built by a city or county. These hospitals are often the only ones available to treat the poor and often have names such as "City General" or "County General." They are noted for their busy emergency rooms, which serve as primary care centers for those urban poor who do not have personal physicians. This method of providing primary care is far more expensive than it would be if health clinics were more widely available. Unfortunately, when government budgets are strained, rather than provide more cost-effective clinic care, hospital funding may be cut, emergency rooms may be closed, and sometimes the hospitals themselves are closed, eliminating a vital source of health care for many, especially poor people.This has special impact on people with AIDS.

A third type is the **proprietary hospital**. These are privately owned, usually by physicians or by hospital corporations. Such hospitals have been growing rapidly. They can control costs by refusing patients who cannot pay, by specializing in less expensive short-term procedures, and by not investing in the variety of equipment and services that are costly but not profitable, so they can treat their patients at lower costs than nonprofit hospitals.

A fourth type of hospital, developed with federal funds after World War II, is the **medical center**, which trains new physicians, conducts research, and gives **tertiary medical care**—long-term care requiring complex technology, usually at great expense. It uses specialized modern equipment—such as artificial kidneys, heart-lung machines, computed axial tomography (CAT) scanners, as well as 3-D computed tomography (CT) scanners, magnetic resonance imaging (MRI), positron emission tomography (PET), single photon emission computed tomography (SPECT), coronary care units, electronic fetal-monitoring machines, radioisotopes, ultrasound, and fiber optics. This equipment may or may not be safe or effective, and the federal government does not regulate much of it. It is also extremely expensive. An MRI scanner can cost one million to three million dollars to buy, and each scan costs the patient or the insurance company about $1,000 (Levy 2003).

In a well-planned medical system, the very expensive technology used in tertiary care is centrally located in medical centers, to which patients are referred from their community hospitals. In a free economy such as ours, corporations are eager to sell their very expensive equipment to all hospitals; and hospitals, competing to fill their beds, have sometimes purchased high technology regardless of the community need. Every hospital wants to have its own coronary care unit, CT scanner, fetal monitors, and all of the other technology. Tertiary

Positron emission tomography (PET) technology is used to help diagnose illnesses.

health care, which theoretically should be limited to a few medical centers, is now hardly distinguishable from secondary health care.

This extension of the secondary health-care system to provide tertiary services has the obvious disadvantage of being very costly. Almost forty cents of every medical care dollar is spent in hospitals, much of it to buy and operate equipment. Having spent so much on costly equipment, hospitals and doctors feel pressured to use it. Ordinary head injuries get CT scans, and almost every baby being born is subject to **fetal monitoring**, which measures the heart rate of the infant being born and is not an exact science. Changes in the patterns measured are often treated with alarm, and the mother may be unnecessarily subjected to a cesarean section, which involves surgically opening the womb. Cesarean sections, considered major abdominal surgery, have increased from less than 5 percent to more than 30 percent of all births since the introduction of fetal monitoring. Technology, then, is expensive to buy and use, and it requires teams of medical technicians to operate the equipment. The largest staff group in the hospital, however, consists of the people who actually take care of the patients—the nurses.

Nurses

In the early days of medicine, nurses were considered gentle and caring people who wiped fevered brows and otherwise tenderly cared for patients. Nurses played the roles of wife to the doctor and mother to the patient. In the days before advanced scientific knowledge, nursing duties were not very different from what was done at home. As medicine has changed, the role of the nurse has changed. However, the nursing profession has had difficulty changing its image, partly because of the way in which nurses are educated. Today, there are nearly three million registered nurses in the United States, and they make up the largest healthcare occupation (U.S. Dept. of Health and Human Services, Office of Minority Health, 2009).

To be a nurse, one must get certification as a registered nurse (RN). The educational requirements for RNs vary. Originally, they were trained in hospitals in a three-year program with some classroom work to supplement their on-the-job training. Hospitals gained their labor for three years, while the nurses paid only room, board, and sometimes a modest fee for tuition. Most nurses were from the working class, and the low-cost training gave them entree to a profession that was far superior in salary and working conditions to the typical kind of factory job they might otherwise obtain.

Advances in medical technology brought changes to this educational system. As scientific knowledge accumulated in the 1950s and 1960s, nurses needed more time in the classroom. This was expensive for hospitals, however. During these same two decades, two-year community colleges, four-year colleges, and universities were expanding—and these schools wanted students to prepare for occupations. At that point, the needs of the schools matched the needs of hospitals, so the latter continued to train nurses in the hospital but turned the classroom education over to schools. The two-year colleges awarded the RN certification after two years of school, and the four-year colleges awarded the RN certification after four years. Two-year colleges served the working classes, and four-year colleges served upper-middle-class women. In addition, some nurses were still trained entirely by hospitals.

As a result of this change in education, some nurses have two years of college training, some have four years, and some have no formal college training but more practical hospital training. The goals of the different groups vary. Nurses with four years of college training would like to change the image of nursing to an upper-class profession with more autonomy, more respect, and better salaries. The four-year nurses have not won the support of many less-educated nurses because the new standards would require several more years of education for them. Nurses have not won the support of physicians either. Physicians now have authority over them and do not want to relinquish it.

To date, nurses work at inconvenient hours, such as evenings, nights, and weekends. They work under the strict supervision of the physician; and even though they spend more time with patients, they must follow the physician's directions at all times. They also are not paid as well as many other professionals with four-year degrees. Hospitals, suffering under increasing budgetary pressures, resist the efforts of nurses to improve their professional standing.

Even those who specialize in a field such as nurse midwifery have difficulty in finding autonomous ways to practice their profession. Nurse midwives are trained to deliver babies, and they use methods that are, in the opinion of many, safer than the drugs and surgical procedures used by physicians. At present, nurse midwives also have difficulty obtaining hospital privileges and must practice under the supervision of a physician.

Other Health-Care Workers

Although physicians, hospitals, and nurses make up the core of the American health-care system, many other professionals are involved in health care. Hospital administrators are sometimes physicians, but in recent years, they are more likely to have been trained in business administration or health-care administration (Sager 1986). "A growing recognition among many hospital boards is that the best way to keep physicians happy in times of crisis is to make one of them the boss" (*Modern Healthcare* 2002). They have a staff working with them who have a variety of special skills, such as keeping medical records, purchasing medical supplies, and performing all of the tasks necessary to keep a hospital running.

Medical research is conducted by physicians or by researchers trained in other sciences, such as biology and chemistry. Research takes place at hospitals, in centers devoted to research, or in corporations that produce pharmaceuticals (drugs) or medical equipment.

Registered dietitians (RDs), important members of the hospital staff, plan regular meals and special diets for patients. Registered dietitians are licensed by their own association of dietitians. **Nutritionists** have similar concerns; however, their education, theories, and licenses are quite different from those of dietitians. Dietitians more and more refer to themselves as nutritionists, and in many states, dietitians are lobbying legislatures to ban nutritionists who lack RD certification from advising people on what to eat. Neither group is allowed to diagnose or treat diseases; they can only recommend proper eating programs.

Dentists, who have earned a Doctor of Dental Science (DDS) degree, do not normally work in a hospital setting. They are not allowed to diagnose or treat diseases other than those defined as a part of dentistry, such as gum diseases. Many other diseases, such as oral cancer, are easily detected in the mouth; dentists are expected to be able to detect them and refer patients to a physician.

Chiropractors have been outside of the health-care system for the most part. *Chiropractic* healing is a Greek term for healing by manipulating the body with the hands. Today, chiropractors are primarily concerned with manipulating the spine, but they may also use X-rays and other modern technologies. In addition, they may also educate their patients about nutrition and a healthy lifestyle as preventive measures. Physicians generally do not recognize chiropractic healing as a legitimate form of medicine; and during the nineteenth century, when physicians were building their profession, they lobbied legislatures to have chiropractors outlawed. Chiropractors, who had their own professional association, managed to survive; and today many people recognize that their work is beneficial. A Gallup Poll commissioned by the American Chiropractic Association (ACA) estimates that around twenty-eight million people in the United States see a chiropractor each year.

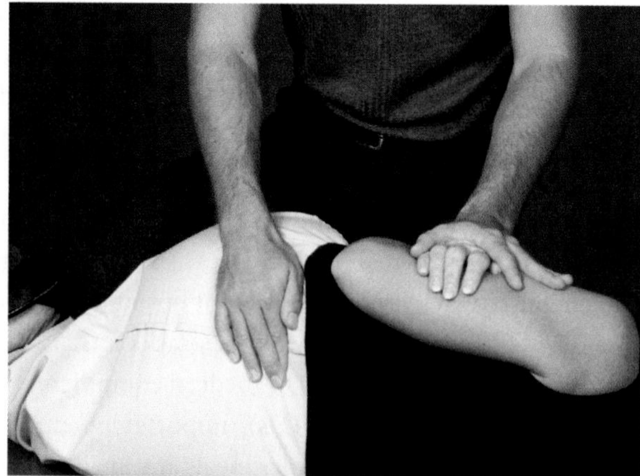

Chiropractic healing is a form of medicine.

Many other health workers are even farther from the mainstream of American medicine. Acupuncture and acupressure are not now generally recognized as legitimate forms of healing in the United States, although recent research is bringing new attention to these methods. Rolfing and other forms of massage are also outside of the mainstream, as are herbal medicines, yoga, relaxation techniques, and a wide variety of other techniques used elsewhere in the world. The American health-care system is dominated by physicians and hospitals, which favor expensive modern technologies and pharmaceuticals.

APPLYING SOCIOLOGY TO HEALTH CARE

Although health care is typically thought to be the sole domain of the medical profession, social science can provide important clues to help diagnose and treat much physical and mental illness. Social scientists can help point out the interplay between social, environmental, and psychological factors in both illness and disease and in their treatment and prevention.

Using a social model of illness in connection with a medical model, health-care workers might be encouraged to explore how the values and norms of a society might help or hinder the development of disease, or how the beliefs and attitudes about a specific illness might affect a return to good health. For example, if alcoholism is still viewed as a moral failure or a lack of willpower, how might this interfere with the prevention of disease in people who are genetically at high risk? How might this hinder a person from admitting to having the disease, being willing to seek help, or gaining the support of friends and family while receiving treatment? If AIDS is seen as a disease caused by males' sexual preferences or by intravenous drug use, how might this interfere with prevention, diagnosis, or treatment of this disease in a heterosexual teenager who does not use intravenous drugs?

PAYING FOR MEDICAL CARE

The United States spends nearly two trillion dollars on healthcare expenses, more than any other industrialized country and more than two-and-a-half times the amount spent by any other member of the Organization for Economic Cooperation and Development (OECD) (Johnson 2010). Yet, it ranks with Turkey and Mexico as the only OECD countries without OECD universal health care. The health-care reform plan signed into law under President Obama in 2010 is designed to make health care more affordable and more accessible. Prior to the reform plan, 45.7 million people in the U.S did not have health insurance (Clemmit 2009). The healthcare reform plan is designed to extend coverage to thirty-two million of uninsured people by expanding Medicaid, providing government subsidies to help low- and middle-income families buy insurance, create regulated insurance markets where people without employer-sponsored insurance can buy subsidized coverage, and use Medicare to cut health costs for individuals (Clemmitt 2010). There are avid supporters and opponents to the plan, and it has become one of the most politically controversial and divisive laws in recent times. Supporters feel that health care is a right for every American and that lack of sufficient health care ultimately hurts U.S. productivity. In addition, supporters feel that the savings to Medicare and Medicaid (as a result of raising Medicare taxes on high income people) will reduce the federal deficit. Opponents believe that the law creates unwarranted entitlements and that the cost of healthcare reform will lead to escalating federal spending on healthcare.

Health Insurance

Private health insurance began during the Great Depression, when physicians had to wait months or even years to get paid for their services (Starr 1982). Physicians developed *Blue Cross*, a nonprofit insurance system, to be sold to groups of workers. Employers offered to pay part of the insurance premium for workers instead of giving them raises; and the program was such a success that in the 1950s, private insurance companies began to offer health insurance. The benefits of health insurance were many. Workers were insured, companies could show their concern for the workers, and there was a large flow of money into the health-care system. The income of physicians increased dramatically; and hospitals were able to afford high-technology medical equipment, which benefited the industries that produced it.

Those who did not benefit from health insurance were the retired, the unemployed, part-time workers, and workers in jobs without fringe benefits. They saw health costs rise and found physicians and hospitals less interested in charity work. To help these people, the United States began the **Medicare** program for retired workers and the **Medicaid** program for the poor. All of these insurance systems paid whatever the physician and hospital charged, and prices soared.

Some people would like to have the federal government provide a national health insurance program that would cover everyone, but others fear that a further infusion of money into the health-care system would cause further cost increases. History has shown us that as more money is available for health care, the costs of health care increase. The medical profession vigorously opposes cost control, considering it an interference with their right to practice medicine as they see fit.

Nevertheless, actions have been taken to resist the rising cost of insurance. In 1983, the federal government began to limit the amount of money it would pay through Medicare and Medicaid. The government devised **diagnostic related groups (DRGs)**, which set a maximum payment for any treatment, and hospitals have had to limit the length of stay and the number of tests given to Medicare and Medicaid patients in order to treat them within the limits of the DRGs. Corporations have responded to rising insurance costs by eliminating insurance as a fringe benefit. Instead, corporations are hiring physicians to run clinics for the specific purpose of providing health care for workers. They find that they are able to contain costs and provide cheaper care directly, rather than through insurance. More and more workers have also responded to the high costs of health insurance by turning to prepaid health care.

Prepaid Health Care

In the United States, the emphasis has been on fee-for-service care, in which the doctor charges a fee for each visit. However, another type of health-care provider, the **health maintenance organization (HMO)**, is growing rapidly. HMOs are prepaid plans in which a fee is paid in advance, and most—if not all—necessary health care is provided at no additional cost.

HMOs have four goals: (1) to provide preventive medicine and early detection of disease; (2) to practice the best scientific medicine possible when a disease is detected; (3) to reduce hospitalization through the use of preventive medicine and early detection of disease; and (4) to reduce medical costs through better use of tests, procedures, and hospitalization.

Because their health care is prepaid, HMO members do not hesitate to have regular checkups and to visit their doctors when illness occurs. Since HMO physicians now practice in large groups, they can communicate with one another easily, they have access to all the necessary equipment and other services, and they have resources and schedules that allow ongoing educational programs. Medical testing can be done knowledgeably, reducing the use of unnecessary tests. Preventive medicine and good medical care reduce hospitalization and medical costs. HMOs also trim costs by using auxiliary medical personnel, such as nurses and physicians' assistants whenever possible. Physicians are motivated to keep costs down because HMOs share cost savings with them in the form of bonuses. Some HMOs even have their own hospitals and are motivated to run these efficiently for further cost savings.

HEALTH MOVEMENTS

In the past, lack of trust in physicians and reliance on home treatment meant that people took responsibility for their own health. Because health was linked to religious values, people considered slovenliness, gluttony, and neglect of one's health to be sinful. It is not surprising, then, that the most notable health movement was inspired by religion.

Health and the Second Great Awakening

The "Second Great Awakening" was a popular religious movement that swept through the northeastern part of the country in the early part of the nineteenth century. This religious movement was accompanied by a health movement, where sweeping changes in attitudes about the care of one's body accompanied concern for one's soul. A leader in this health movement was Sylvester Graham, a Presbyterian minister who believed that foods should be simple, not concocted from complicated recipes. He recommended eating fruits and vegetables, which were unpopular at the time; and although he did not know about vitamins or other scientific nutritional matters, he recommended eating the whole kernel of wheat (Root and de Rochemont 1976). Graham developed a wheat cracker and traveled through the Northeast, preaching his dietary religion and gaining many followers. Boarding houses were set up to serve the Graham crackers and other foods recommended by Graham. Oberlin College reserved part of its cafeteria for those following the Graham diet.

The health movement developed an ecumenical spirit when Seventh-Day Adventists became followers of Dr. Graham. Mother Ellen Harmon White, a Seventh-Day Adventist, founded the Western Health Reform Institute in Battle Creek, Michigan, a sanitarium to restore health to the ailing. She hired Dr. John Harvey Kellogg to manage it. Kellogg thought that chewing on dried, crispy foods would benefit the teeth, and he added them to the menu. One patient, Charles Post, was treated for ulcers at the sanitarium for nine months. Although not cured of ulcers, he believed that the food business might be profitable and developed a drink called Postum and later a cereal, Post Toasties. Kellogg soon followed suit, and the development of packaged foods began. While Americans are still concerned about the food they eat, the more dynamic health movement today is centered on drinking habits.

Alcoholics Anonymous (AA)

Millions of people every day attend AA meetings for the treatment of their alcoholism, a disease that has found no cure within established medical circles. AA is not organized with a bureaucratic structure; it has no membership lists, no dues, no fees, and no hierarchy. Two alcoholics who found that they could stay sober by talking to each other and by following a 12-step program founded AA in the 1930s. Today, AA is the major source of help for one of the most serious diseases in modern society.

Furthermore, this movement is spreading, so that now there are groups reaching people who live or have lived with alcoholics, such as Al-Anon, Al-Ateen, Codependents Anonymous (CoDA), and Adult Children of Alcoholics (ACOA). There are also programs for other addicts, such as overeaters in Overeaters Anonymous (OA), narcotics addicts in Narcotics Anonymous (NA), and smokers in Smokers Anonymous (SA). These groups also have no fees, no dues, and no hierarchy; however, but all practice a series of 12 steps, which each member works individually.

Modern Concerns About Diet and Exercise

Recent concerns about diet and exercise are not religiously motivated and do not have the strength of movements with a religious or spiritual motivation. Modern concerns about diet began with the peace movement of the late 1960s, which also opposed pollution and rejected both chemically filled foods and food packaging that added to litter and pollution. Health food stores sprang up to serve foods without chemicals, such as dyes, hormones, antibiotics, pesticides, and other nonfood ingredients. Foods were sold in bulk and used a minimum of packaging. Food additives account for $1.5 billion in sales for American chemical companies, who assure us that they are safe, and most Americans are satisfied with that assurance.

This is probably the first time in history that exercise could be classified as a social movement. In the past, people got a good deal of exercise quite naturally. Heavy labor had not been replaced by automation; and everyone knows that Abraham Lincoln walked miles to school, as did our grandparents and some of our parents. Today, heavy labor has been replaced by automation, and the automobile has replaced walking. In order to get exercise, a special time of the day must be set aside for such activity, as it no longer occurs naturally in the course of the day.

Americans are showing some concern about diet and exercise in order to reduce their chances of contracting heart disease and cancer. While there may be some improvement in this area, the percentage of overweight people in the United States has not been reduced

Before automation and automobiles people were more physically active out of necessity. This is probably the first time in history that exercise could be classified as a social movement.

SOCIOLOGY AT WORK

Monitoring Medical Billing Practices

Henry Pontell has a BA, an MA and a PhD—all in sociology—from the State University of New York at Stony Brook. He now teaches courses and does research in criminology at the University of California. In addition, he is a general partner in his own consulting firm, Pontell, Jesilow and Associates. One of his most significant projects was to help insurance companies and corporations prevent and detect incorrect billings by health-care providers.

The cost effectiveness of health care is very much an issue today, with health care consuming more than 11 percent of the GNP. It is a major concern of the government, which administers the Medicare and Medicaid Systems; of individual consumers, who must pay ever-increasing insurance premiums or risk having to pay enormous medical bills out of their own pockets; and of businesses, which have traditionally offered health insurance for their employees.

"In many companies," Pontell explains, "health care is the fastest growing operating expense, and they're looking for ways to hold down costs. Some are making greater use of pre-paid plans such as HMOs. Others are going to co-payment, in which the company requires employees to pay part of the cost of insurance themselves. In effect, they're reducing employees' benefits. Another approach is simply to offer plans that provide less extensive coverage."

Pontell's company attacked the problem from a different angle—cutting down the incidence of fraud and abuse on the part of medical practitioners. Improper billing is a sizeable problem. In the Medicare and Medicaid systems, Pontell says, between 10 and 20 percent of all resources are lost to fraud and abuse. *Fraud* occurs when a health-care practitioner knowingly exploits the system, perhaps billing an insurer for services he or she did not actually provide. *Abuse* is unintentionally profiting unfairly, perhaps by mistakenly sending two bills for the same medical procedure.

In essence, the Pontell system is quite simple. Some companies run their own health insurance programs; others contract with insurance companies, in effect paying them to administer the program for their employees. Most companies have some staff dedicated to investigating cases of potential fraud; however, they rarely have the resources to do comprehensive investigations of thousands, or sometimes millions, of claims. Pontell's objective was to help them use their resources more effectively. "Through my research, I've developed a program for reviewing a company's records of claims filed by different physicians." What it yields is a list of names of physicians whose billing of the company is aberrant in some way. It is then up to the company to investigate these practitioners further.

"To conduct this work successfully," Pontell says, "I drew on my training in research methods, human relations, criminological theories relating to white-collar crime, criminal deterrence, medical sociology, law, and the professions. My sociological background is also helpful in two other ways: first, in relating the value of my service to executives in many different industries, and second, in interacting with and coordinating the efforts of corporate executives, insurance investigators, computer analysts, health care personnel, and my research staff."

Besides doing his consulting on medical billing practices, Pontell and his associates have written a book, *Prescriptions for Profit*, which fully describes the ways in which abuses can and have occurred within the health field. Pontell is a prime example of a sociologist who has blended an academic and an applied sociological career. He not only conducts criminological research but also puts to use the knowledge he uncovers.

over the past twenty years. In fact, the incidence of obesity in the United States has risen dramatically over the past twenty years, and research shows the situation may be worsening. A 2007-2008 CDC survey found that 34 percent of adults age twenty and older were obese and an additional 34 percent were overweight but not obese (www.cdc.gov/nchs/fastats/overwt.htm). (See Figures 17-2, 17-3.)

Furthermore, according to the same data, the numbers of children who are overweight continues to increase as well which, in turn, means that these children have an increased chance of being overweight adults. 10 percent of children two to five years of age, 20 percent of six to eleven year olds, and 18 percent of twelve to nineteen year olds were obese. (See Figures 17-4, 17-5.)

Overall, there are a variety of factors that play a role in obesity. In general, behavior, environment, and genetic factors have a part in causing people to be overweight and obese. "Despite obesity having strong genetic determinants, the genetic composition of the population does not change rapidly. Therefore, the large increase in … [obesity] must reflect major changes in nongenetic factors" (Hill and Trowbridge 1998). Behavior and environment are most readily manipulated and are the greatest areas in which prevention could occur.

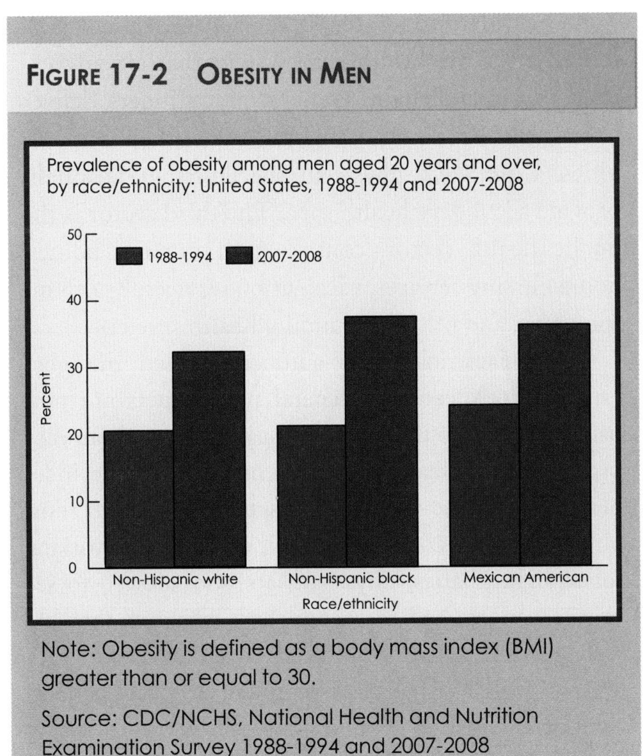

FIGURE 17-2 OBESITY IN MEN

Note: Obesity is defined as a body mass index (BMI) greater than or equal to 30.

Source: CDC/NCHS, National Health and Nutrition Examination Survey 1988-1994 and 2007-2008

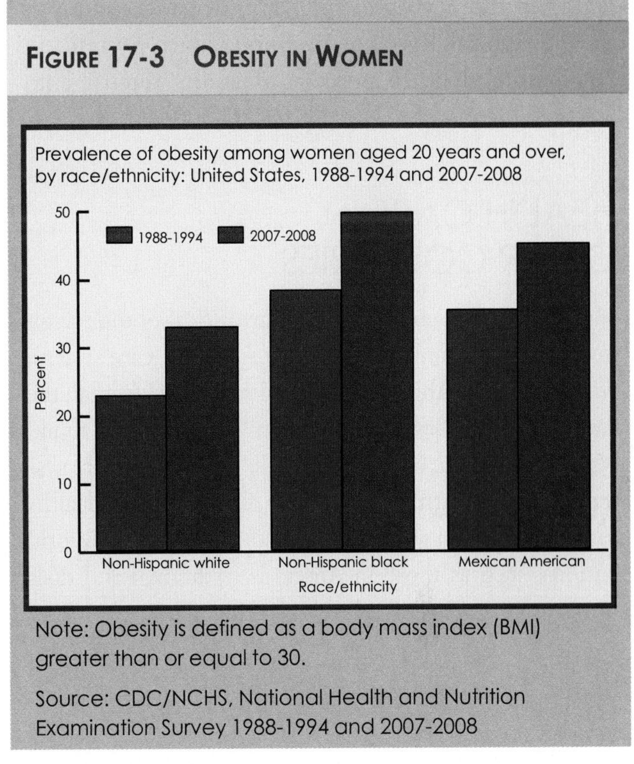

FIGURE 17-3 OBESITY IN WOMEN

Note: Obesity is defined as a body mass index (BMI) greater than or equal to 30.

Source: CDC/NCHS, National Health and Nutrition Examination Survey 1988-1994 and 2007-2008

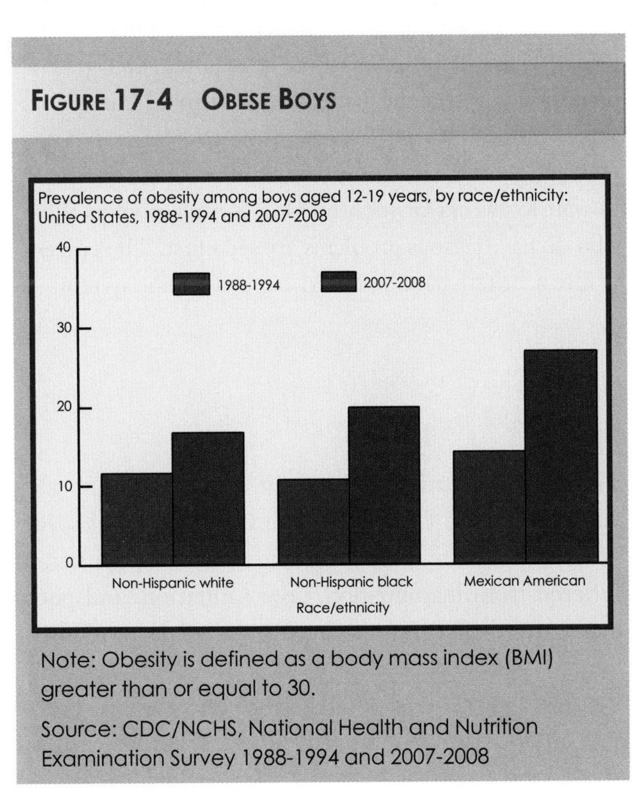

FIGURE 17-4 OBESE BOYS

Note: Obesity is defined as a body mass index (BMI) greater than or equal to 30.

Source: CDC/NCHS, National Health and Nutrition Examination Survey 1988-1994 and 2007-2008

FIGURE 17-5 OBESE GIRLS

Prevalence of obesity among girls aged 12-19 years, by race/ethnicity: United States, 1988-1994 and 2007-2008

1988-1994 2007-2008

Percent

0 10 20 30 40

Non-Hispanic white Non-Hispanic black Mexican American

Race/ethnicity

Note: Obesity is defined as a body mass index (BMI) greater than or equal to 30.

Source: CDC/NCHS, National Health and Nutrition Examination Survey 1988-1994 and 2007-2008

While our culture has succeeded in producing fast and convenient food, more and more options, and super-size portions, we have not succeeded in getting off the sofa. Furthermore, because of technological innovations, our need to exert actual physical energy is diminished so that we increasingly are taking in more calories than we burn. According to the Behavioral Risk Factor Surveillance System, in 2000 more than 26 percent of adults reported no leisure time physical activity (CDC 2004).

HEALTH CARE IN OTHER COUNTRIES

Most modern countries spend a great deal of money on health care; but unlike the American health-care system, where up to one third of the population gets less than the care they need (Basch 1999), other countries have found ways to distribute health care to all. The health-care systems of Great Britain and China illustrate how health-care planning can work. Also, health care in Third World nations, such as those in Africa, is traditional and does not involve expensive technological medicine.

The British Health-Care System

At the beginning of the Industrial Revolution, Great Britain had a **laissez-faire** economy—an economy with little government planning and intervention. Health care depended on **noblesse oblige**, the moral obligation of the rich to give to the poor and the suffering. Unfortunately, the economy produced a great many poor and suffering people whom the rich did not take care of. The British economic system gradually progressed from laissez-faire to welfare capitalism, in which the government takes a major responsibility for the welfare of its people within the capitalist system. The move to welfare capitalism was inspired, in part, by the need for an adequate health care system.

In the nineteenth century, Great Britain was forced to use government money to provide some medical care for its people; and since 1911, Great Britain has had national health insurance, which has covered the medical expenses of workers (Denton 1986, Brown 2000). Their wives and children were not insured, however, and they either did not go to doctors or else postponed treatment until it was too late. After World War II, the poor health of the people and the large number of elderly in the population created a serious problem, and the British developed the National Health Service (NHS), which provides health care for everyone and is funded by tax revenues.

The NHS has three branches, which are patterned after the health care system that already existed in Great Britain. General practitioners deliver primary health care, treating the sick in their communities. *Consultants*, physician specialists in hospitals, provide secondary health care. The third sector is the public health sector, consisting of nursing homes, home nursing services, vaccination services, health inspections, and other community health services.

Physicians lost their autonomy when the government took control. General practitioners are now paid according to the number of patients for whom they provide care. This system does not provide the independence of a fee-for-service practice, but it does allow physicians more control over their income than working for straight salaries. Physicians are also allowed to see private patients and to charge them whatever they are willing to pay. This dual setup has been criticized for creating a two-class medical system, but very few patients want private care.

The working class is especially pleased with the NHS. Any citizen can go to a general practitioner without paying a fee; if hospitalization is required, the general practitioner refers the patient to a hospital consultant, again without charge. To control the costs of such a system, patients who do not have serious problems may have to wait for weeks or months for a consultation, as those who do have serious problems are seen first. The citizens of Great Britain have been very happy with the system.

Health Care in the People's Republic of China

The most dramatic development of a health-care system occurred in China after the Communist takeover in 1949. Before that time, the huge Chinese population suffered from malnutrition, poor sanitation, and poor health. Medical care was almost totally lacking. When the Communists came into power, disease and starvation were rampant (Denton 1978). There was a shortage of doctors, and the few doctors available were divided between Eastern and Western medical practices. Because the Communists had few resources, they had to make efficient use of what little they had.

They did not try to develop scientific medicine after the model set by Western physicians. They

The ancient art of herbal medicine is currently one of the main focuses in the Chinese health care system.

combined Western medicine with traditional Chinese medicine, using acupuncture and herbs along with some Western drugs and technology. The Communists also trained enormous numbers of so-called **barefoot doctors** to serve as unpaid health workers. The peasants in the communes selected commune members for training to become barefoot doctors. Trainees are not chosen on the basis of their academic or intellectual achievements but rather on the basis of their political attitudes and their attitudes toward people. They are required to support the political system, as well as the communes they serve.

To become barefoot doctors, the trainees receive three to eighteen months of training in both Eastern and Western medical techniques. They then serve in their communes, emphasizing preventive medicine by developing sanitary systems and practices in the community, by teaching peasants proper hygiene and health care, and by vaccinating the population. As volunteers, they also work at ordinary jobs, side by side with the peasants for whom they provide care; and they can thereby easily recognize those who have poor health habits or illnesses. They treat simple illnesses and emergencies and direct the more seriously ill to better-trained doctors and nurses.

Urban areas have *Red Guard doctors*, who are not as well trained as the barefoot doctors. In addition, there are *worker doctors*, who work in factories. These doctors receive less training because highly trained full-time physicians and nurses are available in urban areas. The Red Guard and worker doctors serve the same grass roots function as the barefoot doctors—serving without pay, stressing preventive medicine such as sanitation and inoculations, and generally looking after the health of members of their communes.

When hospitalization is necessary for an illness, individuals must pay for it. A variety of insurance plans are available to cover the costs of hospital care, but the costs are not high. Open-heart surgery, the most expensive procedure, costs about two weeks' wages for the average worker—far less than in the United States.

The Chinese Communists emphasize equality. Although most doctors work in urban areas, they are transferred to rural areas if the need develops. They are not free to practice where they wish. They are expected to help nurses to care for patients, and differentiating the various types of doctors and nurses along class lines is forbidden.

When the Communists began their health-care system, the number of educated people available to administer the large bureaucracy was inadequate. Because physicians were the most educated and capable people in the society, they became the leaders of the health-care system regardless of their political leanings. As the Communists increased their power, they became concerned about the independence of the Ministry of Public Health and its practices. They felt that this group did not place enough emphasis on treating rural populations and that this group focused on curative rather than preventive medicine (Maykovich 1980). By 1955, the Communists had developed more political leaders to rule the Ministry of Public Health, along with physicians. Conflicts developed, and some errors were made because the politicians were not trained in medicine; however, the conflicts generally broadened the work of the ministry because the politicians insisted on emphasizing areas that do not ordinarily interest physicians. The conflict between the interests of physicians and political interests has continued. Currently, the emphasis is on what interests the physicians—developing better technology and more sophisticated procedures for treating complicated illnesses.

Along with their interest in technology, the Chinese are doing more than any other country to develop the ancient art of herbal medicine, the use of plants in natural health-care systems (Ayensu 1981). Beijing (formerly known as Peking by Westerners) has an Institute of Medical Materials, and Guangzhou (formerly known as Canton) has the Provincial Institute of Botany for the study of herbal medicines. Thousands of medicinal plants are under cultivation for use in biological evaluations and chemical studies, and every year thousands of barefoot doctors are taught about the use of these herbs in health care. Medicinal plants have been used to treat venereal diseases, leukemia, high blood pressure, ulcers, poor digestion, skin cancer, and countless other diseases. They can be used as heart stimulants, diuretics, sedatives, and to induce abortion. The value of herbs is widely known throughout the world; for example, 25 percent of prescription drugs in the United States are based on flowering plants.

The Herbalist in Underdeveloped Nations

The WHO estimates that between 75 and 90 percent of the world's rural populations have herbalists as their only health-care practitioners. Cultural tradition gives the herbalist an important role, not only as a leading health practitioner but also as an influential spiritual leader who uses magic and religion, as well as herbs, to heal.

There are three types of healers in the African rural tradition, according to Ayensu (1981). The herbalists have the most prestige; but there are also *divine healers*, who cure through religious ceremonies, and *witch doctors*, who intercede against the evil deeds of witches who have possessed a patient. These three types of doctors have kept the native population reasonably healthy throughout history.

Herbalists traditionally have a three-year educational program. The first year often consists of ritual training and ceremony, including abstinence from sex and a ritual bath in a cemetery to make contact with ancestors. Alcohol, quarreling, and either cutting or combing the hair are forbidden. The first year's training serves to set the trainee apart from the rest of the community, in order to develop a distinctive personality.

The second year may begin with practical training in the gathering, identification, and use of herbs. The herbalist is also trained to carefully observe the natural habitats of herbs. Animals have been known to use plants in a medicinal fashion, and they can provide clues to the herbalist in the various uses of plants. Herbalists also learn to be sensitive to any spiritual messages that may increase their knowledge.

After the training program is completed at the end of the third year, herbalists pass through many ceremonies and rituals. They take an oath of allegiance to the trainer and have a graduation ceremony, much as physicians in the United States take an oath and are graduated so that the community will recognize their new status.

Many natives of Third World cultures who are trained in modern medicine in other countries resume using herbs for treatment when they return to their native cultures. The herbs are not only beneficial in themselves, but the tradition and ceremony involved in their use probably provide a **placebo effect** for the patient, a benefit arising from the belief that the medicine will work. It is widely known in our culture that if one believes that a medicine will help, the medicine is very likely to make the patient feel better.

However, some Third World physicians trained in modern medicine and the use of modern chemical pharmaceuticals do not use herbal medicines when they return to their native lands, probably because they are ignorant of the herbs' benefits. This is especially unfortunate because pharmaceutical companies often go to underdeveloped countries and export the very plants that the modern physicians ignore. In fact, the export of medicinal plants to Western pharmaceutical companies is becoming so widespread that some plants—for example, a type of yam used as the foundation material in birth control pills—are becoming rare. After the plants are exported and manufactured into pharmaceuticals, they are then sold back to the country of origin at prices considered by many to be exorbitant.

Thinking Sociologically

1. How could we reduce U.S. health-care costs?
2. How could we provide health care efficiently to all of those who do not have insurance and cannot afford to pay for health care?
3. Why doesn't the United States have a national health service similar to Great Britain?
4. How can the conflict theory of health and illness help to explain the high cost of health care?

CHAPTER REVIEW
Wrapping it up

Summary

1. Health and illness are of interest to sociologists because they are defined socially, as well as biologically, and because society needs a healthy population to survive.

2. *Pathological illnesses* are those in which the body is diseased or malfunctioning.

3. *Statistical illnesses* are those in which a person's health deviates from the norm.

4. Structural functionalists, who emphasize the integrative, functional characteristics of society, note that a sick role exists to integrate ill people into the social structure. This sick role involves certain expectations—for example, sick people are expected to get better and to resume their major roles, thereby ensuring the smooth functioning of society.

5. Conflict theorists contend that physicians share the viewpoint of elite classes in society and use their power over patients to maintain the social system.

6. Symbolic interactionists study the learned meanings associated with illness. In many societies, illness has been associated with sin or demons, and treatment often has had religious overtones.

7. In preindustrial days, when nutrition and sanitation were poor, infectious diseases were the greatest health hazard. The major health hazards now are heart disease, cancer, stroke, and accidents. Many of the occurrences of these diseases are caused by alcoholism.

8. AIDS, an infectious disease, could reach epidemic proportions.

Check out our website **www.bvtstudents.com** for free chapter-by-chapter flashcards, summaries, and self-quizzes.

9. Changing social structures often cause changes in prevailing illnesses—for example, industrialization and its accompanying pollutants are a major cause of cancer.

10. In the American health-care system, the medical model of illness prevails. The individual is considered responsible for prevention, and the health-care system becomes involved only when a person is already sick. The social causes of illness receive little attention.

11. Physicians developed their profession through the nineteenth and twentieth centuries to be powerful and prestigious. Most physicians provide primary health care.

12. Secondary care is provided by hospitals, which have specialized equipment and staff. There are several kinds of hospitals: nonprofit voluntary hospitals, tax-supported municipal hospitals, and privately owned proprietary hospitals.

13. Tertiary health care, the very highly specialized care developed with modern technology, is given in medical centers, which also conduct research and train physicians. Since the other types of hospitals have purchased specialized

technology as well, the cost of medical care has greatly increased.

14. Most nurses work in hospitals. Nursing is still a relatively low-paying profession that reflects its origins as an occupation for working-class women.

15. There is a wide variety of other health-care workers, including technicians, administrators, and dietitians, work in hospitals. Many others work outside of traditional medical settings. Dentists are well-respected health care workers, but nutritionists, chiropractors, and acupuncturists still struggle to have their practices accepted.

16. Health care, with its emphasis on expensive technology, has become very costly. Health insurance—such as Blue Cross/Blue Shield, insurance issued by private companies, and Medicare and Medicaid issued by the federal government—were first designed to help pay costs; but as more money became available, costs rose further.

17. The major departure in health-care delivery from the fee-for-service system and health insurance is the HMO. By using resources more efficiently, HMOs may provide a better, less costly system.

18. Health movements have called for improved diets and have provided treatment for alcoholism and related diseases. These movements typically have a religious or spiritual motivation.

19. Medical care in other countries reflects practices in their social systems. Great Britain's health care system has evolved from the laissez-faire economic system with its belief in noblesse oblige to a welfare system within the capitalist framework.

20. China has developed a health care system using both Eastern and Western medical knowledge. It has been able to integrate the system with its political system, and it has developed a corps of barefoot doctors who provide preventive health care in rural areas. China has also done research on the more sophisticated use of traditional medicines.

21. As they have for centuries, underdeveloped nations continue to depend on herbalists. Herbalists go through an extensive training period, which both sets them apart from other members of their society and teaches them how to use herbs. Herbalists have been successful because their medicines cure illness.

Key Terms

alcoholism A disease related to the drinking of alcohol that has identifiable and progressive symptoms (If untreated, alcoholism can lead to mental damage, physical incapacity, and early death.)

barefoot doctors People chosen by the peasants in the communes in Communist China to provide medicine and treat simple illnesses and emergencies and receive three to eighteen months of training

chiropractors Those who practice healing by manipulating the body, especially the spine

degenerative diseases Those diseases that slowly disable the body as one gets older, such as heart disease and cancer

diagnostic related groups (DRGs) The schedule of payment limits set by the federal government for Medicaid and Medicare recipients

epidemiology The study of the spread of diseases

fee-for-service A medical payment system in which the physician is paid for each visit and each service rendered

fetal monitoring Measuring the vital signs of the infant as it is being born

health maintenance organization (HMO) A prepaid health care plan in which a fee is paid in advance for all necessary health care

heroic medicine Dramatic medical treatments such as bleeding, blistering, or administering poisonous laxatives

hypochondriac A healthy person who believes he or she is ill

infectious diseases Diseases caused by germs and viruses that can be spread from one person to another

laissez faire An economy in which there is no government planning or intervention

Medicaid Federally sponsored health insurance for the poor

medical center A major hospital that trains new physicians, conducts research, and provides tertiary medical care

medical model of illness A model of illness in which sickness is viewed as an individual problem requiring individual treatment

Medicare Federally sponsored health insurance for people age sixty-five or older

municipal hospital A hospital built and operated by a city or county

noblesse oblige The obligation of the rich to give to the poor and suffering

nutritionist A person who specializes in proper eating programs

orphan drugs Drugs that are valuable in the treatment of rare diseases but are not profitable to manufacture

pathological illness An illness in which the body is clearly diseased or malfunctioning in some way

placebo effect A benefit arising from a patient's belief that a medicine will have a beneficial effect

primary medical care The first general, overall care the patient needs

proprietary hospital A hospital that is privately owned, usually by physicians or hospital corporations

registered dietitian (RD) Licensed members of hospital staffs that plan regular meals and special diets for patients

secondary care givers Those who provide more specialized care than that provided by a general practitioner

secondary medical care Care that is more specialized than the care that a general practitioner provides

sick role A set of expectations, privileges, and obligations related to illness

social model of illness The view that much disease is caused by social conditions and that it can be cured by changing social conditions

statistical illness An illness in which one's health varies from the norm

tertiary medical care Long-term care requiring complex technology

voluntary hospital A nonprofit hospital that treats patients who need short-term care

Discussion Questions

1. Discuss why it is important to understand the difference between pathological and statistical illness.
2. What are some positive and negative functions of the sick role for people with pathological illness and for people with statistical illness?
3. If you had the power to set social norms, when would you put people in the sick role, and when would you insist they perform their normal roles?
4. Does your definition of illness match current norms?
5. What are some advantages and disadvantages of the social model of illness and of the medical model of illness? Has the social model of illness become more valued in recent years? Explain and illustrate your answer.
6. Who benefits financially from the current health-care system?
7. Who would lose financially if the United States were to change to a plan similar to the National Health Service in Great Britain?
8. Discuss the relative merits and disadvantages of voluntary hospitals, proprietary hospitals, and medical centers.
9. How does the medical care in various countries reflect their social systems?
10. If you had the power to set social norms, what changes would you make, based on a social model of illness, to end the AIDS epidemic?

11. Discuss your thoughts as to why successful health movements are related to religious or spiritual movements.

12. Compare the training of a physician in this country with that of the herbalist in other societies. Is there a similarity in the way each is learning social roles?

Pop Quiz

1. Most mental illnesses are an example of ______.

   a. pathological illness
   b. statistical illness
   c. adult disorders
   d. physiological disorders

2. When sick people are expected to reduce their performance in other roles, they are fulfilling what Talcott Parsons called the ______.

   a. hypochondriac syndrome
   b. Flexner report
   c. sick syndrome
   d. sick role

3. The perspective that argues that the health-care system uses its power to gain wealth and maintain the status quo is the ______.

   a. functional theory
   b. conflict perspective
   c. symbolic interaction theory
   d. exchange theory

4. Prior to industrialization in Europe, the major killing diseases were ______.

   a. infectious
   b. degenerative
   c. physiological
   d. mental

5. What percentage of all cases of cancer are environmentally induced?

   a. 10–20 percent
   b. 20–30 percent
   c. 60–70 percent
   d. 80–90 percent

6. Which model of illness suggests that sickness is an individual problem requiring individual treatment?

   a. functionalist model
   b. conflict model
   c. social model
   d. medical model

7. The most common type of medical practice is conducted on a ______.

   a. pre-paid care basis
   b. fee-for-service basis
   c. sliding scale basis
   d. state-supported basis

8. Hospitals provide ______.

   a. primary care
   b. secondary care
   c. tertiary care
   d. heroic medicine

9. Which of the following have been considered outside of the health-care system?

   a. nurses
   b. registered dieticians
   c. nutritionists
   d. chiropractors

10. Prepaid medical care is provided by ______.

    a. medical centers
    b. proprietary hospitals
    c. health maintenance organizations
    d. voluntary hospitals

11. Sanitation and nutrition improvements have been as important as medical advances in lowering the death rate. T/F

12. Most health care and research in the United States is based on the social model of illness. T/F

13. Nurses must get certification as registered nurses in the United States. T/F

14. Medicaid is the medical program for retired Americans. T/F

15. Most of the world's rural populations have herbalists as their only health-care practitioners. T/F

1. B	6. D	11. T
2. D	7. B	12. F
3. B	8. B	13. T
4. A	9. D	14. F
5. D	10. C	15. T

PART FIVE

Human Ecology and Change

We have come to a turning point in the human habitation of the earth.

Barry Commoner

CHAPTER 18

Collective Behaviors and Social Movements

CENSORSHIP

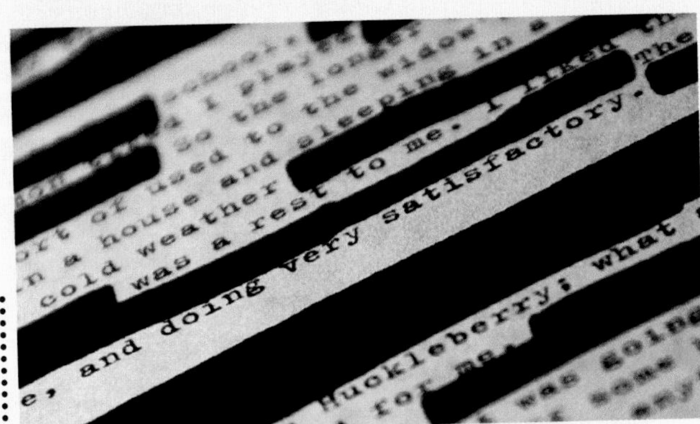

Censorship is a way to prohibit some types of information in order to manipulate public opinion.

After having read much of this book, you probably realize that one of the central themes of sociology—and, some would argue, one of the central themes of a liberal arts education—is the notion that many aspects of social reality are not defined absolutely. For example, political and religious beliefs, standards of morality, and the cultural value of specific works of art and literature are often open to interpretation. Simply stated, people often disagree about what is true, false, good, or bad. When this is the case, competing groups often attempt—through censorship—to manipulate public opinion to accept their respective interpretations. Understanding how public opinion is shaped is an important topic in the study of collective behavior.

One of the most famous cases of censorship in the late twentieth century, and one which brought censorship to international attention, resulted in the death warrant issued by the Iranian leader at the time, Ayatollah Khomeini, against author Salman Rushdie for his book *Satanic Verses.* Khomeini and his followers regarded the book as blasphemy against the Muslim religion, the belief system that lies at the heart of Iranian social and political life (Long 1990). *Censorship*—the prohibition of some types of information—is deeply rooted and openly espoused in many cultures of the Middle East and Asia, and in countries with repressive governments. Within the past few years, censorship in China has become a very contentious issue as the Chinese government has tried, largely unsuccessfully, to limit the freedom of discussion about sensitive issues that could diminish the power of the government. However, censorship also occurs in free countries, including the United States.

Censorship has long been a controversial issue in America, even though the First Amendment to the U.S. Constitution decrees that, "Congress should make no law … abridging the freedom of speech, or of the press." For example, in 1798, John Adams, second President of the United States signed into law the Alien and Sedition Acts, which made it a crime to speak, write, or publish materials "with intent to defame … or bring into contempt or disrepute" members of the government. Under this law, some newspapers were shut down and their editors imprisoned. (It is interesting to note that in 1991, the leaders of the reform movement for democracy in the Soviet Union temporarily shut down *Pravda*, a major newspaper in the Soviet Union because of its overtly communistic orientation.) The Alien and Sedition Acts expired in 1801 under President Thomas Jefferson. Jefferson believed that people should have free access to all information because, he argued, they would be able to recognize falsehood from the truth (Orr 1990). Jefferson felt that Americans should be free to voice any opinion or to express themselves in any way, as long as it does not directly cause harm to any individual or to society. The rationale for this position is that censorship would be a greater harm to America's ideals than the expression itself.

In spite of the dysfunctions of censorship, censorship is still a major issue in the United States. In 1990, many members of the U.S. Congress demanded that the National Endowment of the Arts (NEA) cease its funding of offensive art after Robert Mapplethorpe—a recipient of NEA funding—displayed photographs depicting acts of homosexuality and other sexual behavior.

More recently, the issue of censorship has been in the news surrounding protest songs written in protest to the Iraqi invasion. Many country stations throughout much of the United States pulled recording artists the Dixie Chicks from their play lists after Natalie Maines, the lead singer, expressed embarrassment and shame that the President of the United States is from Texas, the state that is also home to the country trio.

Gumbel (2004) in the *Independent,* a newspaper published in the United Kingdom, noted that the comment might have been a "nonevent" except for the actions of some ardent supporters of the president and some politically sympathetic stations. Brent Staples (2003) in the *New York Times* linked the power of corporate monopolies to the near elimination of protest songs: "… independent radio stations that once would have played edgy, political music have been gobbled up by corporations that control hundreds of stations and have no wish to rock the boat. Corporate ownership has changed what gets played—and who plays it. With a few exceptions, the disc jockeys who once existed to discover provocative new music have long since been put out to pasture".

In April 2007, television stations and radio stations all over the United States once again were faced with the issue of censorship. This time it was radio and television host Don Imus who was pushing it to the limits and was forced off the air by NBC/MSNBC for making comments about a female college basketball team. After the networks (and their advertisers) acknowledged the efforts of many political and community leaders who called for the firing of Mr. Imus, he was terminated from his hosting position.

Perhaps now more than ever, with the widespread use of public forums like Facebook and Twitter, the issue of censorship raises a number of important sociological questions. How are definitions of social reality created and maintained? Who benefits from censorship—society, or the groups that are attempting to prohibit the dissemination of some information? What part does censorship play in accelerating or inhibiting social movements? Should opinions that differ from our own and that could be hurtful to some groups be protected? Is freedom of speech being taken away? Does complete freedom of speech for everyone limit the freedoms of some? How far is too far when speaking over the public airwaves? Who has the power to determine what is censored? This chapter addresses these and other questions about collective behavior and social movements.

Most facets of social life follow patterns of rules and norms. People generally have a daily routine and conform to the roles expected of them. In the same way, such organizations as schools, churches, factories, and governments are highly structured institutions that tend to be stable and relatively static. In these organizations, decisions are made through some semblance of logical, rational discussion.

There is, however, another dimension of social life in which the activities are relatively spontaneous, unstructured, and unstable. This category includes such group activities as panics, demonstrations, riots, fads and fashions, disasters, and social movements. These actions, which may also follow certain patterns and established norms and rules, are instances of what sociologists call "collective behavior."

WHAT IS COLLECTIVE BEHAVIOR?

Sociologists use the term **collective behavior** to refer to spontaneous, unstructured, and transitory behavior of a group of people in response to a specific event. If the term were taken literally, it would incorporate all behaviors involving more than one person—that is, all of sociology—but sociologists use it in a more restrictive sense. The difference between the literal and the sociological definition can be clarified with an example. Take an event such as automobile crashes. To conduct safety tests, car manufacturers have a group of employees perform tests repeatedly and then collect data in an organized fashion about what happens when a car moving thirty-five miles per hour hits something. Compare this with the behavior of a group of people gathered at the site of a highway accident. Although both groups gathered to observe car crashes and are thus behaving collectively in the literal sense, only the second group is engaged in collective behavior in the sociological sense. The car company employees are reacting to a carefully controlled event in which the action is both expected and repeated. The group observing the highway accident reacts to a spontaneous, unstructured, unexpected, nonrecurring event. Panics, riots, crowds, fads, and fashions can all be viewed as spontaneous collective responses to transitory and loosely structured circumstances.

Collective behavior can be contrasted with **institutionalized behavior**, which is recurrent and follows an orderly pattern with a relatively stable set of goals, expectations, and values. In the preceding example, the autoworkers are involved in institutionalized behavior. Other examples of routine, predictable behavior would be going to class, commuting on a train, and going to church. If some unusual event takes place—an earthquake, train wreck, or fire, for example—collective behavior takes over. When people are confronted with an unfamiliar event for which no norms or rules have been established, they may behave in ways that differ radically from their normal conduct. People generally leave a theater in a calm, orderly fashion without pushing or shouting. However, if a fire breaks out, their conventional behavior would change to screams, shoving, and a rush for the exits. The ordinary norms break down and are replaced by new ones. Such actions occur infrequently, however, and only under special conditions.

Sociological theories and perspectives on collective behavior are useful to those whose occupations lead them to deal with large numbers of people. These include police, religious leaders, politicians, organizers of sports events, concert organizers, and others. Others

The term collective behavior refers to spontaneous, unstructured, and transitory behavior of a group of people in response to a specific event. For example, an audience at a concert will sometimes wave their hands to show the band their appreciation.

who do not deal directly with large numbers of people but whose work may affect a large population could also use sociological insights into collective behavior. By understanding, for example, the preconditions of collective behavior or how spatial proximity affects crowds—both of which are discussed in this chapter—architects, designers, and city planners might be able to create more effective ways to channel large numbers of people. Concert halls, sports arenas, convention halls, apartment complexes, subways, airports, and other places that hold large numbers of people could be designed in ways that impede the formation of collective behavior. This chapter explores some theories and perspectives on collective behavior and suggests some ways that they might be used to promote social order in some situations involving large numbers of people.

An example of institutionalized behavior is commuting on a train.

PRECONDITION OF COLLECTIVE BEHAVIOR

Some specific conditions in contemporary societies tend to increase the likelihood of collective behavior. Rapid social change creates tensions and conflicts that sometimes lead to collective actions and violence. Social diversity and the associated inequalities in the distribution of wealth and of opportunities have produced many social movements—the women's movement, the Gray Panthers, the civil rights movement, and the labor movement. The mass media also play an important role in the dissemination of information of all types, from the trends in fashion and trends in music to prison riots. Some critics have suggested that the riots of the 1960s occurred in part because information on riots in other cities was transmitted through the media.

In addition to rapid social change, social diversity, and mass communications, some other preconditions encourage collective behavior. Neil Smelser, in his *Theory of Collective Behavior* (1962), identified six factors that, when they exist simultaneously, will produce collective behavior: (1) structural conduciveness, (2) structural strain, (3) generalized belief, (4) precipitating factors, (5) mobilization for action, and (6) operation of social control.

Structural conduciveness, the most general precondition, is the extent to which a society's organization makes collective behavior possible. A society that has no stock market cannot have a stock market crash. A country that has only one race or religion will not have race or religious riots. Note that structural conduciveness—the existence of banks, stock markets, or different religious or racial groups, for example—does not cause collective behavior. Rather, it is a measure of the existence of conditions in which it can occur. The fact that some aspect of a society is structurally conducive does not mean that collective behavior will happen; it means that, given certain other conditions, it could.

A **structural strain** is any kind of conflict or ambiguity that causes frustration and stress. Structural strains may be caused by conflicts between real and ideal norms, by conflicts between goals and the available means to reach them (anomie), or by the gap between social ideals (full employment, wealth, equality) and social realities (unemployment, poverty, and discrimination by age, race, and gender). Widespread unemployment among teenage blacks is an example of a structural strain.

A third determinant of collective behavior is **generalized belief**. Given structural conduciveness and structural strain, people must identify a problem and share a common interpretation of it for collective action to occur. People develop generalized beliefs about the conditions causing the strain. The women's movement, for example, began to grow only after the belief became widespread that women were discriminated against in employment, education, and other areas. Mobs form and riots take place only when people share a perception of some injustice or unfair treatment. Generalized beliefs may be based on known facts, shared attitudes, or a common ideology. The truth or accuracy of the beliefs is unimportant—the important thing is that they are shared.

Precipitating factors are the fourth determinant. Structural conduciveness, structural strain, and generalized belief alone do not inevitably cause collective behavior. A precipitating event must trigger a collective response. The precipitating event itself is sometimes fairly insignificant. An unwarranted search may start a collective protest in an overcrowded prison. Commodity trading may proceed quietly until a rumor arises that frost has severely damaged the expected orange harvest. The precipitating event can also be a more serious incident, of course. News that a police officer has shot a black youth can inflame a tense racial situation. As was true of generalized beliefs, a precipitating event need not be true or accurately communicated to exert an influence. Even an unfounded rumor can lend focus and support to a belief and can increase the likelihood of a collective response.

Mobilization for action is the fifth determinant of collective behavior. Once a precipitating event has taken place, people have to be persuaded to join the movement. Sometimes, an event mobilizes a group spontaneously, as when the crowd boos the umpire for making a bad call or when a crowd panics if someone yells "Fire!" Sometimes leaders emerge from within the group to encourage participation, which is what occurred during the formation of the Solidarity labor movement in Poland in 1980, when Lech Walesa, an unemployed electrician, quickly became the leader and spokesperson for the group. In other cases, outside leadership steps in to organize the people and push them into action, which is what often happened during the era when labor unions were being formed in this country. Collective behavior begins when mobilization for action takes place.

The **operation of social control** is the sixth and final determinant of collective behavior. Social control consists of the actions of the mass media, government, and other groups when they try to suppress or influence collective behavior. In the case of a potential strike, management might agree to listen to grievances, make a few changes, or raise wages slightly. If the strike takes place, it might fire striking workers and hire new ones. If social control cannot prevent collective action before it starts or halt it once it has begun, the collective behavior continues.

Smelser's approach, then, suggests that a series of six preconditions is necessary to produce collective action. The preconditions are closely interrelated—structural strains will not appear unless the society is structurally conducive to them, for example. This approach has been widely criticized, but it remains the most systematic and important theory of collective behavior.

Smelser's model should be applicable to a wide variety of collective behaviors. As an example, we use the 1991 police assault of a black motorist, Rodney King, in Los Angeles. The incident, shown many times on national television and reported in most newspapers in the country, involved four, white, baton-wielding police officers striking Rodney King more than fifty times after he was pulled over in his car for speeding. What caused this event to make national headlines and led thousands of citizens to demand the resignation of Los Angeles Police Chief Daryl Gates?

First, the circumstances were structurally conducive to a hostile outburst. It involved issues of race differences (black versus white) and power differences (police officers versus a motorist). Second, structural strains in the United States between blacks and whites, as well as between criminals and victims, are common. Note for example, how politicians often exploit fears over racial quotas, affirmative action, the early release of prisoners, and so forth to win elections. Concerns over the rights of the criminal exceeding the rights of the victim are widespread. These and many other structural strains were present in the Los Angeles police incident. Third, a shared generalized belief existed about inequalities, injustices, and unfair treatment of whites toward blacks, as well as of officers toward selected violators of the law. It is likely that most people are aware of instances of racism and brutality in police departments. Nonetheless, the existence of these three conditions, all quite common, seldom leads to collective action. What was different about this event?

A key factor differentiating this event from others was the videotaping of the brutal beating of an unarmed single black man by a group of white police officers. This videotaped film, frequently aired over national television, was a precipitating factor (our fourth precondition) that triggered a collective response. Denial was no longer a possible police or community response. The fifth determinant of collective behavior was the mobilization of people to take action. The action suggested was not merely toward the police officers but also toward the person in charge of them: police chief Daryl Gates. Social control, the sixth determinant, came with a commission report recommending that the chief step down, the involvement of Los Angeles Mayor Bradley in demanding police reform, and other measures to convince the public that corrective actions would follow.

APPLYING KNOWLEDGE OF PRECONDITIONS OF COLLECTIVE BEHAVIOR

One of the preconditions of collective behavior mentioned earlier is the failure of social control to halt collective behavior. Turner and Killian (1987) discuss four ways that the members of the "power structure"—the police, the courts, religious authorities, community leaders, and so forth—attempt to control collective behavior. We now briefly examine these social control measures and discuss their effectiveness in terms of the preconditions of collective behavior.

Repressive measures are used to control collective behavior through such means as banning public assemblies, forbidding the publication of

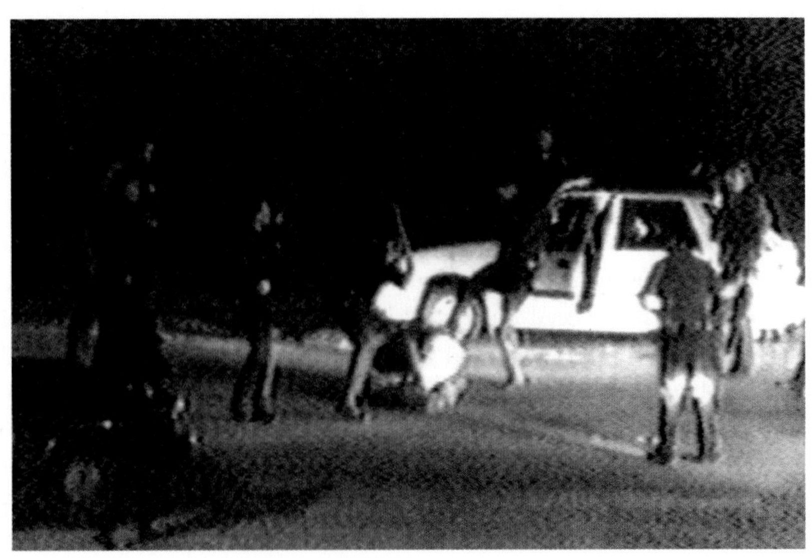

Officers are seen here kicking and beating a man with nightsticks. Rodney King was also treated in the same manner. The witnessing of these events, and existing structural strains within the society, triggered a collective response such as rioting.

subversive views, and punishing individuals who challenge the authorities. This form of social control is likely to be employed in repressive societies. For example, in the 1980s, the South African government outlawed the African National Congress (ANC) when the ANC tried to mobilize black South Africans to overthrow the established order of racial segregation known as "apartheid." In 1989, the Chinese government relied on military force to suppress an impending democratic revolution by its citizens. As is evident from such societies that attempt to use repressive measures, this is neither a practical nor a civil means of social control. Denying the civil liberties of some citizens is likely to be perceived by the populace as reducing freedom for the society in general. This may lead to structural strain and a generalized belief that groups are being treated unfairly.

Ironically, the very measures that some governments use to control collective behavior may function as preconditions for collective behavior. For example, in 1991, there was an attempted coup d'état, in what was then the Soviet Union, in which Mikhail Gorbachev was temporarily ousted from power. At the same time, military tanks filled the streets of Moscow to demonstrate the forceful intentions of those who attempted to take over. Many social scientists and journalists felt that the overt use of the military to suppress the democratic reform movement in the Soviet Union was a very significant factor that generated further public support for reform. Since then, of course, Gorbachev resigned and the Soviet Union disbanded into independent states.

Another means of controlling collective behavior is through the **role of police**, the military, the National Guard, or other formal agents. This type of control is self-explanatory: police force is used to restrain or break up situations in which large numbers of people pose a threat to an existing social order. This differs from the aforementioned repressive measures, however, in that it does not necessarily represent a repressive political or social policy but can be purely situational. Such force may indeed be a part of repressive measures, however. Perhaps the major problem of using police force to control collective behavior is that it may actually heighten the potential for collective behavior rather than eliminate it. In the preceding section, for example, we called your attention to how the police in Los Angeles provided all of the preconditions for collective behavior.

Hidden repression—a means of controlling collective behavior that is not obviously or overtly repressive—is usually a more effective measure of social control. Typically, this occurs when governments manipulate the news through press releases, staged press conferences, and news "leaks." We mentioned earlier that some critics suggested that the ghetto riots of the 1960s were provoked because the media presented news of riots in other cities throughout the country. In the same way, governments can defuse collective social unrest by manipulating the media. The knowledge that the media have the power to help mobilize people to action is important, not only because it can be a means of social control, but because it helps define the limits of responsible journalism. Because journalists and other members of the news media have the power to play a decisive role in creating social conflict or harmony, they need to seriously consider the perspectives they take on news events.

The final technique mentioned by Turner and Killian is **social control through amelioration**. This refers to the elimination of the source of strain that lies behind the collective behavior through the creation of specific policies. If high unemployment among black youths creates the potential for disruptive collective behavior, the government might create a policy that helps to create more jobs for black youths. If CIA recruitment on college campuses appears to cause stress among large numbers of college students, the CIA could change their recruitment policy and look elsewhere for potential employees. This method of social control might function to eliminate the structural strain that serves as a precondition for collective behavior.

Knowledge of collective behavior is useful not only to government policymakers and other members of the power structure but to anyone who deals with large crowds—police, concert promoters, sports event organizers, religious leaders, and others. In the following section, we direct our attention to specific types of collective behavior and demonstrate how that information may be useful in some occupational settings.

Thinking Sociologically

1. Select an example of collective behavior that took place in your state or community. Can you identify preconditions that encouraged it?
2. Assess how social control measures (overt repressive measures, the police, hidden repression, or amelioration) could be or have been effective in controlling the example you used in the first question.
3. Can you cite an example during your lifetime in which collective behavior has produced positive social change?

SPATIALLY PROXIMATE COLLECTIVE BEHAVIORS: CROWDS

Characteristics of Crowds

A **spatially proximate collective** exists when people are geographically close and physically visible to one another. The most common type of spatially proximate collective is the **crowd**, a temporary group of people in face-to-face contact who share a common interest or focus of attention. This common interest may be unexpected and unusual, but it is not necessarily so. Although people in a crowd interact a good deal, the crowd as a whole is organized poorly if at all. According to Spencer and Turner (2000), crowds have four features that make them a unique area for study: anonymity, suggestibility, contagion, and emotional arousability.

Most types of collective behavior involve *anonymity*. People who do not know those around them may behave in ways that they would consider unacceptable if they were alone or with their family or neighbors. During a riot, the anonymity of crowd members makes it easier for people to loot and steal. In a lynch mob, brutal acts can be committed without feelings of shame or responsibility. Whatever the type of crowd, the anonymity of the individuals involved shifts the responsibility to the crowd as a whole.

Because crowds are relatively unstructured and often unpredictable, crowd members are often highly *suggestible*. People who are seeking direction in an uncertain situation are highly responsive to the suggestions of others and become very willing to do what a leader or group of individuals suggests, especially given the crowd's anonymity.

The characteristic of *contagion* is closely linked to anonymity and suggestibility. As people interact, the crowd's response to the common event or situation increases in intensity. If they are clapping or screaming, their behavior is likely to move others to clap or scream; and contagion increases when people are packed close together. An alert evangelist, comedian, or rock singer will try to get the audience to move close to one another to increase the likelihood of contagion and to encourage the listeners to get caught up in the mood, spirit, and activity of the crowd.

A fourth characteristic is *emotional arousal*. Anonymity, suggestibility, and contagion tend to arouse emotions. Inhibitions are forgotten, and people become emotionally charged to act. In some cases, their emotional involvement encourages them to act in uncharacteristic ways. During the Beatles concerts in the early 1960s, for example, teenage girls who were presumably quite conventional most of the time tried to rush on stage and had to be carried away by police. The combination of the four characteristics of crowds makes their behavior extremely volatile and frightening.

Although these four aspects of crowd behavior may be seen in almost any crowd, their intensity varies. Some crowds permit greater anonymity than others, and some have higher levels of suggestibility and contagion; yet one or more of these characteristics may not appear at all. The presence or absence of certain crowd features can be used to organize crowds into different categories.

Types of Crowds

All crowds are spatially proximate and temporary, and every crowd shares a common focus. However, some crowds are very low in emotional arousal and are highly unstructured, whereas others are quite emotional, aggressive, and even dangerous to one's safety.

A concert is an example of a conventional crowd.

The literature on collective behavior, following the lead of Herbert Blumer (1939), tends to label the non-emotional, unstructured crowd as a **casual crowd**. People who stop to look at an animated holiday display or who gather to watch a street musician would be of this type. Another type of crowd, sometimes called a **conventional crowd**, is more highly structured and occurs, for example, when spectators gather at a baseball game, attend a concert, or ride on an airplane. Although the participants are generally unknown to one another (anonymous), they have a specific goal or common purpose and are expected to follow established norms and procedures. At symphony concerts, for example, people applaud at the end of the music (an established procedure). When the music is being played, however, they do not run up and down the aisles or call out to a friend at the opposite side of the concert hall (not an established procedure).

The type of crowds that attract the most public attention are called **acting crowds**, the behavior of which is centered around and typifies aroused impulses. The two most dramatic forms of acting crowds are mobs and riots.

Mobs are groups that are emotionally aroused and ready to engage in violent behavior. They are generally short-lived and highly unstable. Their violent actions often stem from strong dissatisfaction with existing government policies or social circumstances; extreme discontentment with prevailing conditions is used to justify immediate and direct action. Disdainful of regular institutional channels and legal approaches, mobs take matters into their own hands.

Most mobs are predisposed to violence before their actions are triggered by a specific event. When feelings of frustration and hostility are widespread, leaders can easily recruit and command members. With aggressive leadership, an angry, frustrated mob in an atmosphere of hostility can be readily motivated to riot, commit lynchings, throw firebombs, hang people in effigy, or engage in destructive orgies.

Mob violence has erupted in many different circumstances. During the French Revolution of the 1780s and 1790s, angry mobs stormed through Paris, breaking into the Bastille prison for arms and calling for the execution of Louis XVI. In nineteenth-century England, enraged workers burned the factories in which they worked. Lynchings of blacks in the United States for real or imagined offenses continued into the twentieth century, often with little or no opposition from the formal agencies of control—police, courts, and public officials. Although lynch mobs are uncommon today, occasional instances of mob behavior take place over civil rights issues such as busing or housing, during political conventions and rallies, and among student or labor groups angry about perceived injustices. In 1987, for example, mob violence erupted in all-white Forsyth County, Georgia, when a white mob disrupted a march by whites and blacks protesting discriminatory anti-Black housing policy.

A report in the *Seattle Times* titled "Smart Mobs: The Next Social Revolution" examines Howard Rheingold's proposal that cyberspace and the coming generation of fast wireless devices and its experienced users could change the way mobs are created. Rheingold states that "the coming generation of fast wireless devices will make ad hoc 'swarming' a potent force for cultural transformation" (Andrews 2002). Social protesters have managed to use technology effectively, in part because it is still largely unregulated. However, with national security changes taking place, it remains to be seen whether or not technology will change the way action is mobilized.

Riots are collective actions involving mass violence and mob actions. The targets of their hostility and violence are less specific than those of mobs, and the groups involved are more diffuse. Most riots result from an intense hatred of a particular group with no specific person or property in mind. Destruction, burning, or looting may be indiscriminate; and unfocused anger can lead to violent acts against any object or person who happens to be in the wrong area at the wrong time. Like mobs, rioters take actions into their own hands when they feel that institutional reactions to their concerns about war, poverty, racial injustices, or other problems are inadequate.

The race riots of the 1960s in Watts in Los Angeles, Harlem in New York, and many other cities are the most commonly cited examples of rioting. These riots, which generally occurred in black ghettos, involved widespread destruction of property followed by extensive looting. The National Advisory Commission on Civil Disorders (Kerner 1968) found that riots are associated with a number of factors, including discrimination, prejudice, disadvantaged living conditions, and frustration over the inability to bring about change. The incident that triggers a riot can be relatively trivial. In Detroit, for example, riots began after police raided social clubs suspected of permitting illegal gambling and the sale of liquor after hours. The riots of the 1960s, however, took place almost without exception in communities long frustrated by high unemployment, poverty, police harassment, and other factors. In the riots of the summer of 1967, tensions were increased by the sweltering weather. The riots that resulted from the 1991, post–Rodney King verdict are a similar example.

These findings are highly consistent with those of Lieberson and Silverman (1965), who studied conditions underlying seventy-six race riots in the United States between 1913 and 1963. They found that only four of them started without a precipitating event, such as a rape, murder, arrest, or holdup. They also found that race riots are most probable in communities with a history of being unable to resolve racial problems. The characteristics of crowd behavior—anonymity, suggestibility, contagion, and emotional arousal—were present in all the riots studied by Lieberson and Silverman.

THEORIES OF ACTING-CROWD BEHAVIOR

Students of crowd behavior have historically focused on acting crowds. How do acting crowds diminish individualism and encourage people to accept the attitudes and behaviors of the group? We have already examined Smelser's theory about the preconditions of collective behavior. Four additional perspectives are representative of the various other interpretations prevalent today. These include Le Bon's classical perspective, Blumer's interactionist perspective, Turner and Killian's emergent norm perspective, and Berk's game perspective.

The Classical Perspective

The **classical perspective** of acting-crowd behavior suggests that people in a crowd lose their conscious personalities and act impulsively on the basis of their instincts rather than reason. This perspective was articulated in

Riots are collective actions involving mass violence and mob actions. Most riots result from an intense hatred of a particular group with no specific person or property in mind.

When thousands of people are looting, others may join in because they feel that there is less of a chance that they will be arrested.

what is probably the most influential single book ever written on collective behavior, *The Crowd: A Study of the Popular Mind* (1895), by the French sociologist Gustave Le Bon (1841–1931). During Le Bon's life, France was experiencing rapid social change; and earlier, mobs and riots had brought about the French Revolution. Le Bon, who considered crowds pathological, violent, threatening groups, believed that their destructive potential stemmed from "the psychological law of the mental unity of the crowd." According to Le Bon (1895, 2).

> The sentiments and ideas of all the persons in the gathering take one and the same direction, and their conscious personality vanishes. A collective mind is formed, doubtless transitory, but presenting very clearly defined characteristics. The gathering has thus become what, in the absence of a better expression, I will call an organized crowd, or, if the term is considered preferable, a psychological crowd. It forms a single being, and is subjected to the law of the mental unity of crowds.

This quote mentions two key concepts in the classical view of crowds: collective mind and mental unity. Le Bon, the originator of the group-mind concept, believed that crowds cause people to regress. According to this view, crowds are guided by instinct, not by rational decisions. Under the influence of crowds, even conventional, law-abiding citizens may act impulsively and be guided by unconscious influences. Crowds do not reason; they respond instantly to the immediate situation. Why? First, the anonymity of the collective gives each person in a crowd a feeling of power. Then, contagion sweeps through the crowd like a virus passing from one person to another. Finally, the participants become as suggestible as if they had been hypnotized. The result is the unquestioned acceptance of and obedience to the leaders.

The Interactionist Perspective

The **interactionist perspective** assumes that people in crowds reinforce and heighten one another's reactions. Often referred to as the *contagion model*, it was developed by Herbert Blumer (1939), who—like Le Bon—believed that crowd behavior is often irrational and emotional. Blumer, however, rejected the idea that it stems from a group or collective mind. He believed that crowd behavior results from what he called "circular reactions" operating in a situation of social unrest. In Blumer's words, a *circular reaction* is

> a type of interstimulation wherein the response of one individual reproduces the stimulation that has come from another individual and in being reflected back to this individual reinforces the stimulation. Thus, the interstimulation assumes a circular form in which individuals reflect one another's states of feeling and in so doing intensify this feeling. (p. 170)

In other words, in a situation of social unrest, interactions reinforce and heighten the unrest. If one group, for example, shouts, "Let's get him," others model this behavior and usually adopt the same feelings and ways of expressing them. The reactions of these others increase the fervor of the original group, which in turn excites the rest of the crowd even further. In the absence of widespread unrest, such a reaction would never begin. Three types of circular reactions are milling, collective excitement, and social contagion.

In a milling crowd, people move about aimlessly. **Milling** tends to make people preoccupied with one another and less responsive to the usual sources of stimulation. Like hypnotic subjects who become increasingly preoccupied with the hypnotist, milling individuals grow more preoccupied with others in the crowd and become increasingly inclined to respond quickly, directly, and without thinking.

Collective excitement takes place when milling reaches a high level of agitation. People in the grip of collective excitement are emotionally aroused. They respond on the basis of their impulses, they are likely to feel little personal responsibility for their actions, and under the influence of collective excitement they may behave in an uncharacteristic manner (Blumer 1939).

Social contagion comes about wherever milling and collective excitement are intense and widespread. What is fascinating about social contagion is that it can attract people who were initially just indifferent spectators. They get caught up in the excitement and grow more inclined to become involved. Unlike Le Bon's theory, this theory does not suggest the existence of a group mind. Rather, people's interactions tend to heighten in intensity until the group is capable of spontaneous behavior.

The Emergent-Norm Perspective

The **emergent-norm perspective**, first proposed by Turner and Killian (1957), emphasizes how norms influence crowd behavior and how new norms emerge and are maintained. Whereas Le Bon and Blumer stress similarities in the behavior of crowd members, the emergent-norm perspective focuses on differences in crowd members' behavior. As Turner and Killian (1957, 22) state,

> An emergent norm approach reflects the empirical observation that the crowd is characterized not by unanimity but by differential expression, with different individuals in the crowd feeling differently, participating because of diverse motives, and even acting differently.

According to this view, crowds do not behave as a homogeneous unit. Observers may think they act as a unit, but divergent views and behaviors may go unrecognized or be dismissed as unimportant. When attention is focused on the acting crowd, people frequently overlook those who remain silently on the sidelines, those who passively lend their support, and those who express little excitement. People behave differently because they act in accordance with different norms. Norms influence all social conduct, and new norms arise during novel situations such as mob actions or riots. Some may accept norms that make violence and looting acceptable. Others may define the situation differently and choose to leave or remain uninvolved.

As an example and a test of the emergent-norm explanation of collective behavior, Aguirre et al (2011) analyzed the crowd responses to a fire at The Station nightclub in Rhode Island in 2003, which killed one hundred persons and left two hundred injured. The fire was ignited by the pyrotechnics at a Great White rock concert. It was the fourth deadliest fire in U.S. history. Aguirre, et al, discovered that while the fire had all the requisites for panic, panic-like behaviors were not prevalent. While it is true that many of the victims who died competed with each other for escape from the building, Aguirre et al concluded that they were helping each other until the very end. They also found that for the survivors, cooperation and care for each other in their groups was a key factor in their survival. Rather than an expected panic, norms of helping had emerged through interpretation and interaction with one another.

The process by which norms emerge occurs daily in any context of human social interaction and communication. All of us are dependent on those around us to define and determine what a given event means. When others in the group shout, run, or express fear, we are likely to feel tremendous pressure to conform to their behavior. An untrained observer may note the one dominant behavior and describe the group members as unanimous in their definition, mood, and behavior. More careful observation, as emergent norm theory suggests, would reveal that unanimity is an illusion and that differential expression does take place.

The Game Perspective

The **game perspective** on crowd behavior suggests that crowd members think about their actions and consciously try to act in ways that will produce rewards (Berk 1974). Unlike other theories, which assume that crowds behave irrationally, game theory stresses the importance of rational decisions. People weigh the rewards and costs of various actions and choose the course that is most likely to lead to a desired end. Looting, for example, may yield a reward such as a television set. If few people are looting, the chances of arrest may be fairly great, and a potential looter may choose not to take the risk. If, on the other hand, there are thousands of people looting stores, the chances of arrest are quite low, and the person may decide to join in. Milling about before engaging in violent action may be used as a time for assessing various courses of action and for evaluating the strength of support. According to this perspective, violence is not necessarily irrational. It may be the result of a conscious decision that it will be useful in acquiring a desired end: civil rights, jobs, housing, new leaders, or something else. When many people desire the same goal, collective action can increase their chances of achieving it.

APPLYING THEORIES OF ACTING-CROWD BEHAVIOR

Organizers of mass events—sports contests, rock concerts, political conventions—could use knowledge of crowd behavior, especially what causes crowds volatility to help protect against potential disaster. We now look at one example—a stampede in a Chicago nightclub in 2003, in which over seventy people were killed or critically injured—to see how knowledge of crowd behavior could have been used to avert this catastrophe.

MSN news (February 3, 2003) gave the following account of what happened:

> More than twenty people have died and dozens more have been injured following a stampede in a U.S. nightclub. It is believed up to fifteen hundred people fled in panic after security staff at the Chicago club used capsicum spray to stop a fight. The nightclub was still packed at 3 a.m. when a fight broke out. Security guards forced their way through the crowd and in a decision that's already being questioned by police; they used pepper spray and mace to break it up. That had an immediate and deadly effect on the crush of humanity. The gas started to spread, affecting hundreds of club patrons who started to panic. Many were gagging for breath, and others were vomiting. The rush for the one stairway turned into a stampede, and people tripped and were crushed trying to find the exit. So many people tried to get out through the front door that they formed a human wedge. As more clubbers started pushing from behind, few could break out of the crush. "I was pushed down the stairs, then everybody started piling down on my leg and I couldn't move my legs at all," said a victim. Rescuers were confronted with a chaotic scene with emotional survivors looking for partners and screaming at police to arrest the security guards who started the panic. Police in Chicago say at least twenty-one people are confirmed dead and another fifty are injured. Ambulance officers say nineteen people were in cardiac arrest when they arrived but many were eventually revived. Five hospitals were deluged with victims, some critically injured with crushed chests and broken bones, others suffering from asthma-like symptoms. At this early stage, the police say they've already discovered that the club's owners had broken several safety regulations. There were more than fifteen hundred people in the club—way over the permitted number. The emergency exits were also locked.

We now look carefully at the preceding account to see whether there are some precautions that could have been taken, based on knowledge of the theories of acting crowd behavior, that might have prevented the stampede. Three organizational facts leading to the collective behavior that occurred that evening are apparent. First, the club was over capacity. Second, the security officers sprayed mace into the crowd. Third, there were insufficient emergency exits for club participants. Had an interactionist perspective been used beforehand, it could have been deduced that people would begin to become preoccupied with one another (as a result of milling) and would become aroused by any central event such as a fight or start performer (leading to collective excitement), and that this excitement would spread to even the most mild-tempered party-goers (social contagion).

Although it is always easier to understand events in retrospect, knowledge of the theories of crowd behavior could have spurred the club owners to handle the situation differently. First, the club owners could have limited the number of people they admitted. Second, perhaps the club security could have used alternative means to break up the disturbance, a method that would not have caused party goers to panic, gag for breath, or vomit. Third, a greater number of exits could have been available, so that in the event of an emergency, they would have been able to quickly disperse. Using the characteristics of crowd behavior and the theories of crowd behavior discussed so far in this chapter, what would you do to lower the probability of catastrophic collective behavior at a nightclub, concert, or sports event?

Thinking Sociologically

1. How might the emergent-norm and game perspectives be applied to explain the acting-crowd behavior of the Chicago nightclub event?
2. The rock group the Grateful Dead, which came into existence in the late 1960s, is still popular, especially among its faithful fans, known as "Dead Heads." The band has ceased touring since the death of Jerry Garcia. Even though they attracted large crowds, the Grateful Dead concerts were notably peaceful and orderly. This is ironic because the group seemed to represent very free, liberal, nontraditional, anti-establishment values. Use the knowledge of collective behavior found in this chapter to examine why Grateful Dead concerts were usually orderly and devoid of dangerous outbreaks of collective behavior.
3. Use knowledge contained within this chapter, including insights that you have gained from the preceding example of Grateful Dead concerts, to develop a strategy that concert and sporting-event organizers could use to try to protect against the potentially dangerous outbreaks of collective behavior

SPATIALLY DIFFUSE COLLECTIVE BEHAVIORS

Spatially diffuse collectives are collectives that form among people spread over a wide geographical area. The most common types are known as masses and publics.

Masses and Mass Behavior

A **mass** is a collective of geographically dispersed individuals who react to or focus on some common event. We often hear the term *mass* in speech: mass media, mass communication, mass hysteria. The millions of people who watch the Super Bowl or World Series on television or who listen to these on radio constitute a mass. The thousands of people who rush to the store to buy an item rumored to be in short supply constitute a mass. Although dispersed over a large geographical area, they are reacting to a common event.

Members of a mass come from all educational and socioeconomic levels. They are anonymous, and they interact little or not at all. A mass has no established rules or rituals, no shared or common ideology, no hierarchy of statuses or roles, and no established leadership (Blumer 1939).

Fads and fashions are specific types of diffuse collective mass behaviors. Generally, they arrive suddenly and disappear quickly, but they may attract great interest from large numbers of people during their tenure. A **fad** is a superficial or trivial behavior that is very popular for a short time. Some examples of fads are flagpole sitting; crowding into telephone booths; using hula hoops; dancing the jitterbug, twist, or frog; swallowing goldfish; streaking; and buying pet rocks, Trivial Pursuit, "Cabbage Patch" dolls, or more recently Bart Simpson shirts, cups, and other paraphernalia. Most of these fads were or are harmless and have no long-range social consequences.

Aguirre and others (1988) examined the characteristics and effects of fads and tested them with data on over one thousand incidents of streaking—running nude through a public area— at colleges and universities. They reviewed some characteristics of fads listed in the literature, which included their homogeneity, their novelty, their oddness when examined by existing social norms, their non-utilitarian behavior that lacks serious

Fashion influences styles of dress, music, art, literature and sociological theories.

consequences for the participants, their suddenness in appearance, their rapid spread, as well as their quick acceptance and short-lived nature. Contrary to conventional wisdom, their analysis of streaking as a fad revealed that streaking events had clearly identifiable social structures. They suggest that the oddness, impulsivity, inconsequentiability, and novelty of fads have been exaggerated in the literature. To those participating in streaking, the behavior was meaningful and consequential.

Their results conform to the emergent-norm framework of collective behavior that was described earlier. The fad of streaking was made up of compact and diffuse crowds, and was greatly influenced by mass media coverage of previous events; it had a division of labor and clear normative limits and, in the words of Aguirre et al., "was spawned by social organization; it was a product of group life."

In contrast to a fad, **fashions** are more enduring, widespread, and socially significant. A fashion is a temporary trend in some aspect of appearance or behavior. Fashions resemble fads, but they tend to be more cyclical. They are generally thought of as influencing styles of dress, but there are also fashions in music, art, literature, and even sociological theories. To be "in fashion" is to wear the style of hair and the types of clothes that advertisers are pushing and that are currently in vogue. At any given time, hemlines may be long or short, neckties may be wide or narrow, and hairstyles may be straight or curly. Designer clothing, blue jeans, or rap may reveal important information about who is "in" and other important information about social status.

Fads and fashions provide many people with a sense of excitement, feelings of belonging, or a source of identification and self-esteem. Fads and fashions, however, are also big business. Packaging pet rocks, opening a hip-hop club, and selling the latest clothes are ways of making money. Although fads and fashions may seem trivial to the average consumer, they can bring large profits to those who take advantage of them.

Mass hysteria and panic are two other types of diffuse collective mass behaviors. **Mass hysteria** is a widespread, highly emotional fear of a potentially threatening situation. A **panic** occurs when people try to

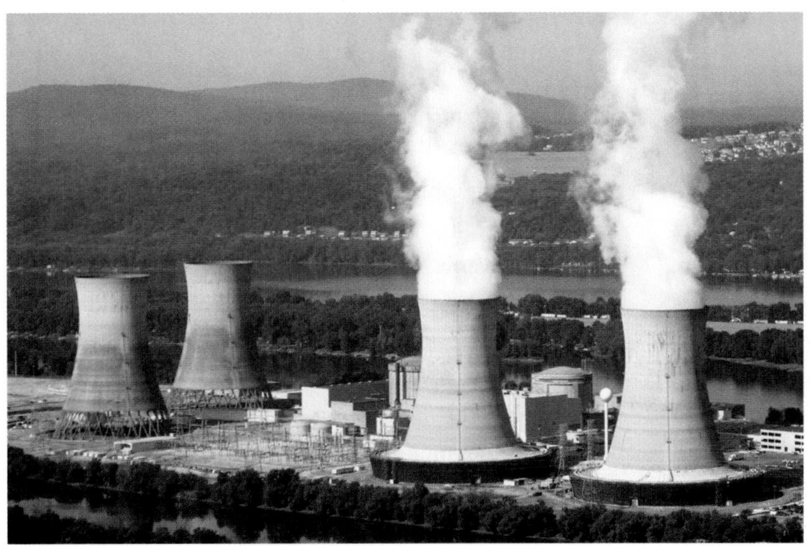

An example of mass hysteria and panic took place at Three Mile Island beginning on Wednesday, March 28, 1979. It was feared that a total meltdown would occur which would have caused serious radiation contamination.

SOCIOLOGY AT WORK

Market Research

A. Emerson Smith is the president of Metromark Market Research, Inc., in Columbia, South Carolina. The firm helps hospitals, utility companies, financial institutions, newspapers, and other businesses identify marketing problems; and it uses opinion and attitude surveys as tools to find solutions to those problems.

Smith began doing market research in 1974 when he was an assistant professor in sociology at the University of South Carolina in Columbia. He and a colleague discovered that marketing researchers were using the methods of sociology and social psychology. "In fact," he says, "we saw other areas in market research where the methods and theory of sociology could be used but weren't. We found that many people in marketing research had business or marketing backgrounds but little training in social theory and research methods."

Smith's job is to help clients identify problems in their business and in marketing, decide on the most appropriate research tools, do the research, interpret the findings, make recommendations to the client on the best ways to solve the problem, and then see that those recommendations are tested and implemented. "The bulk of my time," he says, "is spent talking with clients about problems they have in running their companies and in marketing products and services to their customers."

Smith tells of a particular problem he had to help a client solve. "The marketing director of an investor-owned electric and gas utility came to us with this problem: How can we satisfy the needs of our engineers for investment in equipment, the needs of our customers for a continual improvement in the quality of service, and the needs of our stockholders for a return on investment? The utility's residential customers don't have a choice over their supplier of electricity. To many, a utility is seen as a monopoly, able to take advantage of that situation by raising rates without having to improve services. Yet, the utility is regulated by a state power commission that can either allow or disallow requests for rate increases. Unless the utility gets the support of its customers and improves services, these customers and consumer advocates can argue in front of the power commission to disallow rate increases needed for equipment and stockholder dividends."

How did Smith use his sociological training to help his client? "First, we did library research on studies that had been published on customer satisfaction in power companies and other service industries. Next, we used U.S. census data to describe the customer base, which included rural and urban residents. Our training in demography was helpful here. The problem called for us to do explanatory research. We expected to find that customers with higher incomes would have different evaluations and expectations than would customers with the lowest incomes, whose expenditures on electric bills would constitute a greater proportion of their household income. Here we used our knowledge of social stratification and status, both basic sociological concepts. Our training in research methods helped us design high return mail survey samples that were representative of all customers. We then presented the client with our recommendations on how they could satisfy the needs of customers and, thereby, the needs of their engineers and stockholders."

Smith emphasizes that the skills he learned from sociology courses are very valuable to people in business; and he encourages more sociology students to seek work with companies like his. "All those hours sitting through sociology and social statistics courses really pay off when I have to analyze the impact of social variables on the attitudes and behaviors of utility customers, hospital patients, physicians, or bank customers. Sociology students are not destined to work only in nonprofit or social welfare settings. Sociology students have perspectives and skills that are useful to businesses. Business executives want consultants to help them understand the behavior and lifestyle of consumers. Sociologists can do that."

escape from a perceived danger. An example of mass hysteria and panic took place at Three Mile Island beginning on Wednesday, March 28, 1979, and it continued for several weeks. The incident involved a series of events at the nuclear power plant at Middletown, Pennsylvania. The fear was that a total meltdown of a power unit would cause serious radiation contamination of all people in the area and the destruction of all plant life over a vast land area. When news of the event first broke, commercial telephone lines were jammed with calls to and from people living near the Three Mile Island area. Newspapers around the country carried maps of the area that showed five-, ten-, and twenty-mile concentric circles of danger and reported that evacuation would be the only hope of avoiding contamination. By noon Friday, just two days after the event, the governor of Pennsylvania recommended the immediate evacuation of all pregnant women and preschool children living within five miles of the area. By evening that plan was expanded to include everyone within a twenty-mile radius. By this time, vast numbers (the actual percentages and numbers are unknown) had already departed, many going to stay with relatives and friends in neighboring states or in other areas. To lessen the extent

The world was shocked to learn that Magic Johnson had been diagnosed with AIDS.

of mass hysteria and panic and to convey an impression that all was "safe and under control," President Carter visited the reactor site on Saturday, March 31.

Another example of mass hysteria might be the public reaction to AIDS after basketball star "Magic" Johnson announced in November 1991 that he had HIV. This disease was first reported in 1981, but for ten years was assumed by the major media to be confined to homosexuals and intravenous (IV) drug users. There seemed to be a widespread belief that "I am neither gay nor a user of IV drugs, so it can't happen to me." Public opinion polls (described in the next section) showed that almost everyone knew about AIDS, but about 10 percent thought it could be spread from simply being in the presence of an infected person. These beliefs resulted in instances of children being kept home from school, people refusing to work with AIDS victims, and police being given masks and gloves for protection, responses which, given current medical knowledge about the disease, seem to be overreactions.

With Magic Johnson's announcement that he had contracted the AIDS virus through heterosexual intercourse and his plea to practice "safe sex," the world reacted with surprise and shock. Discussions of condoms became more frequent and more public than ever before in U.S. history. The lack of an existing coherent educational program about AIDS and the lack of a widespread distribution system and an open discussion of condoms helped fuel mass hysteria about the disease. The public is now widely aware of AIDS and HIV, and this awareness has had a significant impact on sexual behavior in non-marital as well as marital relationships.

Thinking Sociologically

1. In what ways and in what contexts over the past decade might an example of AIDS be considered mass hysteria? Can you identify ways in which the emotional fear of this threatening situation could have or can be lessened?
2. Consider the recent anthrax scares in our society. Could public reactions to this perceived threat constitute mass hysteria? Why/why not?

Publics and Public Opinion

A public is another type of spatially diffuse collective. Blumer (1939) defines a **public** as a group of people who are confronted with an issue, who do not agree on how to address the issue, and who discuss the issue. Publics have no culture and no consciousness of themselves as a group. Voters, consumers, magazine subscribers, and stockholders are separate publics. Although these people are geographically dispersed, they share a concern about an issue. As they discuss the issue to resolve their differences about it, a generalized public opinion begins to prevail.

Public opinion is defined variously as any opinion held by a substantial number of people or as the dominant opinion in a given population. Public opinion is especially complex in mass cultures, in which many publics have differing viewpoints. Some publics want their tax money to go to defense; others would prefer to see it spent on social programs. Some publics favor abortion; others oppose it. These conflicts of interest multiply as cultures become more complex. In simpler cultures, most decisions about new issues can be made on the basis of traditional folkways and mores.

A wide range of factors influences the formation of public opinion. Organizations such as the political parties, the National Organization for Women (NOW), and the National Rifle Association (NRA) have a profound effect on public opinion. The mass media are also influential. They do not merely report the news; they can also create it. By choosing to discuss a particular issue, the media focus people's attention on it. The frequency with which an issue is reported often depends entirely on the discretion of the media, particularly with issues that seldom have events, such as homelessness, illiteracy, and common crimes such as rape or murder, or child abuse. If their reporting tends to favor one side of the issue, they may succeed in shifting public opinion in that direction. Opinion is further influenced by a population's cultural values and ethnic and social makeup. Leaders from business, government, or religion also shape public opinion; and it is interesting that elected leaders, who were put in office by the public, often try to use their office to influence those who elected them. Because public opinion is so important in contemporary social life, there is considerable interest in how it is measured.

Knowledge of public opinion is generally obtained through the use of polls, which are a form of survey research. A *public opinion poll* is a sampling of a population representative of a geographical area, of a group of interest to the pollster, or of a society as a whole. The pollster asks the sample population a series of questions about the issue of concern. In most polls, the responses are provided in advance, and the respondents simply state whether they agree or disagree with a statement or answer a yes-no question. These responses are then tabulated and reported to the sponsoring agency.

In recent elections, pollsters have been criticized for announcing results before the voting is completed; but in most cases, increasingly refined polling techniques enable pollsters to make very accurate predictions. There are a number of potential problems in taking accurate polls, however. The sample to be polled and the questions to be asked must be carefully selected because answers to ambiguous or loaded questions may not reflect true opinions. For example, even those who support a woman's right to abortion might find it difficult to answer "yes" to a question such as, "Do you favor a mother's right to murder her helpless unborn children?" A question phrased in this way will not yield representative responses. Polls may also force people to express opinions on subjects they know nothing about. Another problem is that they do not attempt to assess a person's reasons for giving a "yes" or no response.

Those who sponsor polls often use the results to influence public opinion, which may be done through the use of **propaganda**—attempts to manipulate ideas or opinions by presenting limited, selective, or false information. The purpose is to induce the public to accept a particular view. Propagandists rarely present opposing or alternative views; and when they do present those views, the presentations are usually distorted. Propaganda tries to influence people by playing on their emotions rather than by discussing the merits of the various positions. However, if it diverges too far from known facts or personal beliefs, the public may simply dismiss it as nonsense.

The use of propaganda in the early 1980s was evident in the controversy over requiring that both biblical and evolutionary versions of human life on earth be taught in the public schools. Each side issued statements that played on emotions, diverged from known facts, and contained limited and selected information. Each side had the goal of inducing people to accept its own point of view. Those who believe in the literal biblical interpretation that God created all matter and energy in exactly six solar days are not swayed by those who present fossil evidence of evolution covering a time period of millions of years. On the other hand, those who believe in the separation of church and state are not swayed by the argument that evolution and the scientific method is based as much on belief as creation theory is. If propaganda is to be successful, it must not conflict too strongly with a person's existing values and beliefs.

Another way to manipulate public opinion is through **censorship**, prohibiting the dissemination of some types of information. A community may try to prohibit sex education, X-rated movies, or the sale of pornographic magazines. A car manufacturer may refuse to release information about a potential danger in a car's construction. Government officials may withhold controversial information, as the United States government did when it kept secret the bombing of Cambodia during the Vietnam War and kept secret the diversion of funds to the Nicaraguan Contras. Censorship manipulates public opinion not by presenting distorted or incomplete information, as propaganda does, but by withholding information that might influence public opinion.

Thinking Sociologically

1. Select a controversial censorship issue that currently exists in your community. Use the material in this chapter to examine the following: (a) Why is there an attempt to censor the information? (b) Who are the groups that are the force behind the censorship attempts? (c) What are the definitions of social reality that are at stake? (d) Who would benefit from censorship of this information? (e) What would be the individual and social costs, if any, if the information were censored? and (f) Is censorship justified in this particular case?
2. We have been witnessing social movements toward freedom and democracy around the world. Is censorship justifiable if the intention is to bring about social reforms that would provide people with more democratic social systems and government?

SOCIAL MOVEMENTS

A **social movement** is a collective effort to bring about social change and to establish a new order of social thought and action. Movements involve more than a single event or community; they begin during periods of unrest and dissatisfaction with some aspect of society, and they are motivated by the hope that the society can be changed.

Initially, social movements are poorly organized. They have no identity, and their actions are often spontaneous. As they develop, however, they acquire an established leadership, a body of customs and traditions, divisions of labor, social rules and values, and new ways of thinking. This process of institutionalization leads to the development of formal organizations and, ultimately, to new social systems.

Types of Social Movements

In the United States, a number of social movements have had a significant effect on changing public attitudes and the development of policies and laws such as the civil rights movement, the feminist movement, the environmental movement, the peace movement, and the gay rights movement. The recent emergence of the Tea Party in the United States is an example of a contemporary social movement that is having widespread effects. Perhaps some of the most notable social movements today are the pro-democracy movements occurring in the mid-east, such as the youth-led movement in Egypt that led to the resignation of President Hosni Mubarak. Each of these movements has involved a collective effort to bring about social change and to establish a new social order. Various authorities have used different schemes to classify such movements.

Within the past few decades, beginning in the final years of the twentieth century, some social movements have expanded beyond the borders of any one country and have become international in scope. One such movement is the global social justice movement. The global social justice movement emerged both as a critique of the negative social and political environments and the desire to make globalization more socially sustainable and democratic. Some of its manifestations have occurred in the form of protests at top international summits such as the World Trade Organization (WTO), the G8 (representatives of the governments eight major economies), and the International Monetary Fund (IMF). One of the distinguishing features of the global justice movement is that it has been organized across national borders and has challenged traditional nation-state based forms of politics (Wennerhag 2010).

Turner and Killian (1987) organize social movements in terms of their orientation. *Value-oriented movements* advocate social changes concerning various groups, which result in broader adherence to the central values of the larger society. The civil rights, gay liberation, and women's movements, for example, are efforts to fulfill the American values of equality, freedom, and justice. *Power-oriented movements* aim to achieve power, recognition, or status. The Nazi movement in Germany and the Bolshevik Revolution in

Russia are extreme examples of this type of movement. *Participant-oriented movements* focus on personal rewards and fulfillment for their participants. Back-to-nature and evangelical movements are of this type.

Actually, there are as many different kinds of movements as there are goals. *Reactionary movements* advocate the restoration of the values and behaviors of previous times. *Conservative movements* attempt to protect the status quo and resist change. *Resistance movements* are aimed at preventing or reversing changes that have already occurred. *Reformist movements* try to modify some aspect of society without destroying or changing the entire system. *Revolutionary movements* believe in the overthrow of the existing social order as a means of creating a new one. *Nationalistic movements* hope to instill national pride and a sense of identity with one's country. The goal of *utopian movements* is to create the perfect community. *Religious movements* want to convert or modify the existing belief system in accordance with a religious principle. *Expressive movements* would like to change people's emotional reactions to help them cope with prevailing social conditions. Some movements have several purposes or combine the features of several types of movements. Regardless of the way they are categorized, they all involve collective efforts to initiate (or sometimes resist) a new order of social thought and action.

The Development and Life Cycle of Social Movements

Social movements develop most frequently in complex, non-totalitarian societies. They evolve through a series of stages that closely parallel those suggested by Smelser as preconditions of the development of any type of collective behavior. Blumer (1939) divided the development of movements into four steps: social unrest, popular excitement, formalization, and institutionalization. These stages are idealized types, of course, because development varies considerably from one movement to another.

The stage of **social unrest** parallels Smelser's stages of conduciveness and structural strain. This stage is characterized by unfocused restlessness and increasing disorder. Often, people are unaware that others share the same feelings and concerns. Rumors abound, and persons become increasingly susceptible to the appeals of agitators. These agitators do not advocate any particular ideology or course of action; rather, they make people more aware of their discontentment and raise issues and questions to get people thinking.

Social unrest is followed by the stage of **popular excitement**. During this period, unrest is brought into the open. People with similar concerns begin to establish a rapport with one another, and they openly express their anger and restlessness. Then the group begins to acquire a collective identity, and more definite ideas emerge about the causes of the group's condition and how the situation can be changed. Leaders help define and justify feelings, identify the opposition, and point out obstacles that must be overcome. They also offer a vision of what things could be like after the movement succeeds. In the past, social reformers such as Martin Luther King, Jr., charismatic leaders such as Gandhi, and prophets such as Christ have led movements such as these. In other instances, a *group* of individuals clarifies the issues, provides direction, and stirs up excitement. In these cases, the movement becomes increasingly better organized.

During the third stage, **formalization**, a formal structure is developed, and rules, policies, and tactics are laid out. The movement becomes a disciplined organization capable of securing member commitment to stable goals and strategies. At this stage, movements make concerted efforts to influence centers of power (Turner and Killian 1972). The stable organization of the movement and the establishment of various programs and committees serve to keep members involved after the initial urgency has died down. The leadership shifts from agitators, reformers, or prophets to statespersons or intellectual leaders and administrators. The intellectual leaders develop the ideology, symbols, and slogans that keep the movement alive. The administrators work on procedures, tactics, and organization. It is at this stage that movements often split into factions or break down completely due to differences of opinion over such questions as how the movement should proceed, how radical its tactics should be, and what types of concessions should be granted.

In the formalization stage, it becomes clear that the success of social movements requires more than just successful leadership. A group of committed followers is also needed. It has traditionally been assumed that followers are drawn from the ranks of the discontented, the deprived, the frustrated, and the angry. A more recent perspective, **resource mobilization theory**, suggests that the success of a social movement depends not only on those who benefit from it directly but also on their ability to mobilize other individuals and groups to contribute time, money, and influence to the cause—even though they may not directly benefit.

Oberschall (1973) argues that mobilization results not from the recruitment of large numbers of isolated individuals, but from the recruitment of blocs that are already highly organized and politically active. Gamson (1975) agrees, maintaining that collective resources are more important than personal goals in shaping a movement and that one of the most important resources is a group that are already organized. The success of the civil rights movement, for example, depended on the effective mobilization of churches, state and federal agencies, and government leaders, as well as white sympathizers. Martin Luther King, Jr. and his followers could not have been as successful alone. Likewise, the women's movement, to be effective, needed the support of legislation, the mass media, political leaders, men, and existing groups that supported feminist goals.

Thinking Sociologically

Using Blumer's and Smelser's ideas concerning social movements, what role might the Internet play in developing and shaping future social movements? What sort of role, if any, do you currently see the Internet

If adequate resource mobilization takes place, social movements reach the final stage in the life cycle of social movements, **institutionalization**. During this stage, the movement becomes integrated into society. It may have a permanent office and personnel hired to continue its efforts. At this point, it may also have accomplished its primary purpose and may disappear into the network of institutions that already exists. In other instances, the success of a movement leads to the development of new social movements. Some movements never reach this stage—they are suppressed by formal or informal powers and disappear or go underground. At the institutional stage, the unrest, discontent, and popular excitement have largely ceased and are replaced by formal offices, organized groups, and structured activities.

CHAPTER REVIEW

Wrapping it up

Summary

1. Collective behavior is spontaneous, loosely structured, and transitory. Institutionalized behavior, by contrast, is more orderly and has stable goals, expectations, and values.

2. There are two types of collective behavior: *spatially proximate*, in which people are in face-to-face contact or geographical proximity, and *spatially diffuse*, in which people are dispersed over a wide geographical area.

3. Certain conditions increase the likelihood of collective behavior. Smelser described six of them: (1) *structural conduciveness*, the existence of conditions or situations in which collective behavior is possible; (2) *structural strain*, some type of frustration, stress, conflict, or dissatisfaction in society; (3) *generalized belief*, a shared understanding of the reasons for the strain and stress; (4) *precipitating factors*, events that trigger a collective response; (5) *mobilization for action*, in which individuals or groups encourage participation in collective behavior; and (6) *the initiation of social controls*, in order to counter the conditions just listed.

4. The most common type of spatially proximate collective behavior is the *crowd*. The characteristics of crowds are anonymity, suggestibility, contagion, and emotional arousability.

5. Crowds vary in type, ranging from very unemotional and highly unstructured crowds to very emotional, active crowds, such as mobs or rioting crowds.

6. There are four major theories of acting-crowd behavior. The classical theory of Le Bon posited the existence of a collective or group mind that has a regressive influence on behavior, which tends to be irrational, irritable, and impulsive.

7. Blumer's interactionist theory focused on social interactions and a circular reaction process that generates milling, collective excitement, and social contagion.

8. The emergent-norm theory of Turner and Killian emphasized how norms influence crowd behavior and how the emergence of new norms causes a divergence of crowd views and behaviors.

9. Berk's game theory stressed the rational decision-making process involved in crowd behavior and suggested that people consciously weigh the rewards and costs associated with various kinds of collective activity.

10. In spatially diffuse collectives, people who are widely dispersed focus on a common event. The groups who watch a particular television show or buy a given item are considered masses; and although they are geographically separate, they participate in a common behavior.

11. Fads and fashions are mass behaviors in which a large number of people participate for a brief period.

12. Mass hysteria takes place when a potentially destructive or threatening event causes a widespread, highly emotional fear. Sometimes, these fears are accompanied by panic, mass flight, or attempts to escape.

13. A public is a spatially dispersed group confronted with a common issue but divided about how to address it. As the issue is debated or discussed, a variety of public opinions develop, which vary from one public to another.

14. Opinions are influenced by such factors as dominant cultural values, the mass media, group affiliations, and social backgrounds. A type of survey research known as "polling" can measure them. Propaganda and censorship are two ways of manipulating public opinion.

15. Social movements are organized collective efforts to bring about social change and establish a new order of social thought and action. Turner and Killian classify movements in terms of their orientation, whereas other authorities use different classification schemes.

16. As social movements develop, they generally go through four distinct stages: social unrest, popular excitement, formalization, and institutionalization. Although all social movements grow through roughly the same process, the goals of different movements can vary considerably. Their success depends heavily on their ability to effectively mobilize resources.

Key Terms

acting crowd A crowd that acts on the basis of aroused impulse and thus one that may be volatile, aggressive, and dangerous

casual crowd A crowd that is high in anonymity but low in suggestibility, contagion, emotional arousal, and unity

censorship Prohibiting the availability of some type of information

classical perspective A view of acting crowd behavior that suggests that people in a crowd lose their conscious personalities and act impulsively on the basis of their instincts rather than reason

collective behavior The spontaneous, unstructured, and transitory behavior of a group of people in reaction to a specific event

collective excitement In the interactionist perspective on crowd behavior, the stage during which milling reaches a high level of agitation

conventional crowd A crowd, such as the spectators at a baseball game, whose members are anonymous but share a common focus and follow established social norms and rules

crowd A temporary group of people in face-to-face contact who share a common interest or focus of attention

emergent norm perspective A view of collective behavior that emphasizes how new norms emerge and influence the behavior of crowds

fad Superficial or trivial behavior that is very popular for a short time

fashion Temporary trend in some aspect of appearance or behavior that resemble fads but tend to be more cyclical

formalization The stage in the development of social movements in which a formal structure is developed, and rules, policies, and tactics are laid out

game perspective A view of crowd behavior that suggests that members think about their actions and consciously try to act in ways that will produce rewards

generalized belief A stage in the development of collective behavior in which people share a common identification and interpretation of a problem

hidden repression A means of controlling collective behavior that is not obviously or overtly repressive

institutionalization The process by which orderly, stable, structured, and increasingly predictable forms of behavior and interaction are developed

institutionalized behavior Recurrent behavior that follows an orderly pattern with a relatively stable set of goals, expectations, and values

interactionist perspective A view of crowd behavior that emphasizes how people in crowds reinforce and heighten one another's reactions

mass A spatially diffuse collective in which geographically dispersed persons react to or focus upon some common event

mass hysteria A form of diffuse collective behavior involving a widespread, highly emotional fear of a potentially threatening situation

milling The stage in the development of crowd behavior during which people move about aimlessly, grow increasingly preoccupied with others, and become increasingly inclined to respond without thinking

mobilization for action A stage in the development of collective behavior during which people are persuaded to join the movement

mobs Emotionally aroused groups ready to engage in violent behavior

operation of social controls A stage in the development of collective behavior in which the mass media, government, and other groups try to suppress or influence collective behavior

panic An attempt to rapidly escape from a perceived danger

popular excitement The stage in the development of a social movement during which social unrest is brought into the open and people with similar concerns begin to organize

precipitating factors A stage in the development of collective behavior during which an event triggers a collective response

propaganda An attempt to manipulate the ideas or opinions of the public by presenting limited, selective, or false information

public A group of people who are confronted with an issue, who do not agree on how to address the issue, and who discuss the issue

public opinion Any opinion held by a substantial number of people or the dominant opinion in a given population

repressive measures Measures, such as banning public assemblies, used to control collective behavior

resource mobilization theory The theory that the success of a social movement depends not only on those who benefit from it directly but also on its ability to mobilize other individuals and groups to contribute time, money, and influence

riot A form of collective behavior involving mass violence and mob action

role of the police A means of controlling collective behavior through the use of police force

social contagion A stage in the development of crowd behavior during which the crowd's response to a common event increases in intensity and the crowd's behavior moves others to behave in the same way

social control through amelioration The creation of specific policies to eliminate the source of strain that lies behind the collective behavior

social movements Collective non-institutionalized efforts to bring about social change and establish a new order of social thought and action

social unrest The stage in the development of social unrest that is characterized by unfocused restlessness and increasing disorder

spatially diffuse collectives Collectives that form among people spread over a wide geographical area

spatially proximate collectives Collectives in which people are geographically close and physically visible to one another

structural conduciveness The extent to which a society's organization has the conditions that make a particular form of collective behavior possible

structural strain Any conflict or ambiguity in a society's organization that causes frustration and stress; often seen as a precondition for collective behavior

Discussion Questions

1. How does collective behavior differ from institutionalized behavior? Give examples of each type of behavior.
2. Select an incident of collective behavior that has occurred recently, and discuss the preconditions that might have led to it.
3. Explore the different types of crowds and crowd behavior that tend to exist or have existed in your college campus, community, or city where you live.
4. How do mobs and riots differ? Are either or both less likely when and where people know one another?
5. Select examples not provided in the text that illustrate each of the theories of acting-crowd behavior. Discuss how the theories can be used to explain each of the respective examples you have selected.
6. Mass behaviors include fads and fashions. Can you identify any fads that exist at present? What is currently in fashion in terms of hairstyle or clothes among your peer group?
7. Public opinion poll results appear daily in newspapers and magazines. Find one, and discuss: (a) Who was the public that was polled? (b) What issue was raised? and (c) Of what use are the results, and to whom?
8. How does propaganda differ from censorship? Provide examples of each.
9. Propaganda was described as the use of limited or selective information. In what contexts is this useful? Is it ethical or dishonest to not "present the truth, the whole truth, and nothing but the truth"?
10. Examine the development and life cycle of a contemporary social movement or any other social movement in which you might be interested.

Pop Quiz

1. The spontaneous, unstructured, transitory behavior of a group of people in response to a specific event is called ______.

   a. collective behavior
   b. a public
   c. a mass
   d. a social movement

2. The preconditions of collective behavior include ______.

   a. structural conduciveness
   b. structural strain
   c. a generalized belief
   d. all of the above

3. The form of social control that involves creating specific policies to eliminate sources of strain that lie behind potential collective behavior is called ______.

   a. amelioration
   b. hidden repression
   c. repressive measures
   d. police action

4. A temporary group of people in face-to-face contact who share a common interest or focus of attention is a ______.

   a. public
   b. social movement
   c. crowd
   d. mob

5. Which type of crowd acts on the basis of aroused impulse and may be volatile and aggressive?

   a. casual crowd
   b. conventional crowd
   c. expressive crowd
   d. acting crowd

6. A collective action involving mass violence and mob actions is a ______.

    a. mob
    b. riot
    c. casual crowd
    d. conventional crowd

7. Which of the following is NOT a type of mass behavior?

    a. fashion
    b. mass hysteria
    c. panic
    d. fad

8. A superficial or trivial behavior that is very popular for a short time is a ______.

    a. mass
    b. fad
    c. fashion
    d. diffuse collective

9. An attempt to manipulate opinions by presenting limited, selective, or false information is called ______.

    a. public opinion
    b. structural strain
    c. censorship
    d. propaganda

10. An attempt to manipulate opinions by prohibiting the dissemination of some types of information is ______.

    a. censorship
    b. propaganda
    c. public opinion
    d. a social movement

11. In Smelser's theory of collective behavior, the extent to which a society's organization makes collective behavior possible is known as structural strain. T/F

12. The interactionist perspective assumes that people in crowds reinforce and heighten one another's reactions. T/F

13. Cabbage Patch dolls, Trivial Pursuit, and Ninja Turtles are examples of a fashion. T/F

14. Censorship involves prohibiting the dissemination of some type of information. T/F

15. In the institutional stage of the development of a social movement, a formal structure is developed. T/F

1. A	6. B	11. F
2. D	7. C	12. T
3. A	8. B	13. F
4. C	9. D	14. T
5. D	10. A	15. F

CHAPTER 19

Population and Ecology

ENVIRONMENT

Environmental pollution has been a prominent public issue for more than four decades. While the major threats to the environment are now commonplace knowledge—our natural resources are being depleted while our air, land, and water are becoming polluted—people in the United States and many other countries have a history of taking natural resources and the environment for granted. As a result, the environmental damage can be catastrophic.

In the prosperous decades following World War II—the 1950s and 1960s—cultural values in the United States did not include high regard for the environment or concern for energy conservation. For example, Eliott Currie and Jerome Skolnick (1997) cite evidence that U.S. energy consumption doubled between 1950 and 1972, increasing as much during that time as it had in the entire 175 previous years of American history. Table 19-1 shows worldwide oil demand from 1970 to 2009.

The early 1970s, however, marked the end of this "state of environmental unconsciousness." In 1970, President Richard Nixon created the Environmental Protection Agency (EPA), thus demonstrating the federal government's concern about the environment and bringing environmental issues to the fore of national attention, where they have remained since (Melville, 1989). Although there has been some success in environmental protection since the 1970s—for example, the phasing out of leaded gasoline has curtailed *some* forms of air pollution and regulations about the dumping of toxic wastes and raw sewage have improved the water quality in some lakes and streams—the pressures of a growing population and an expanding economy have led to increased environmental pollution and, in the words of William K. Reilly (head of the EPA under former President George H.W. Bush), to "an array of environmental problems even more daunting than the pollution crises of the past generation" (Melville 1988, 4).

In 1988, Keith Melville identified three reasons, still relevant today, why environmental issues are difficult to address. First, many of today's pressing environmental hazards are invisible and thus difficult to call to the public's attention. It is much easier to mobilize public support for problems that are readily apparent, such as polluted water, air, and land. However, it is difficult to reach consensus about problems that cannot be seen easily, such as acid rain, contaminated groundwater, carbon-dioxide emissions and their resultant greenhouse effect, or ozone-layer depletion.

Second, responsibility for environmental pollution is widespread. We are all partially responsible for environmental protection. Melville states, "Virtually everyone who owns a car, operates a power lawn-mower, or uses electricity generated by burning fossil fuels contributes to the build-up of ozone near ground level and carbon dioxide and other greenhouse gases in the atmosphere. While major toxic air emissions from industrial sources are fairly well controlled, many of the current emissions come from relatively small sources, such as dry cleaners and wood stoves."

Third, environmental problems are global in scope. For example, air pollution is not only the result of fossil fuel use in the United States but also because of its use worldwide as well. Because the source of the problem is global rather than local—that is, the result of the habits of seven billion inhabitants of the planet—many people feel that it makes little difference what they do as individuals or perhaps even as a nation. However, this belief took a turn in 2006/2007 when the phrase "**Going Green**" was introduced to the public. The concept of going green—which was started in order to gain the public's interest in cutting back on the usage of oil, electricity, and those machines that require these types of energy to operate—has seen a tremendous boost over the last year. From Hollywood to Washington, DC, the public is becoming more aware of the need for the United States to take the lead in this ecological battle. It provided the platform for many presidential candidates for the 2008 election; and in the early part of 2007, former Vice-President Al Gore won an Academy Award for his documentary film on global warming. This cemented the gap between the film industry and politics, plus it created a platform for the majority of society to be able to not only relate to but also to weigh in on.

Although the environment seems to be a topic more suited to engineers, chemists, biologists, and geologists, it is important to sociologists as well because of the interrelationships that exist between population and the environment. Rapid population growth and the concomitant increased social needs have led to increased industrialization. From the structural functional perspective, the social wellbeing and high standard of living that industry functions to provide are accompanied by the latent dysfunction of environmental pollution. At first glance, this gives the impression that industry itself is to blame for environmental problems. However, as James Coleman and Donald Cressey suggested a few decades ago," The origins of the environmental crisis are not to be found in a few polluting industries but in the basic social organization and cultural outlook of the modern world" (1990, 538). Thus, the key to understanding environmental pollution lies in understanding our cultural ideals and the ways in which our social life is organized. Natural scientists study and explain the physical ways in which the balance of nature is disturbed; sociologists and social scientists study and explain the intricacies of society and culture that often lead to practices that disturb the balance of nature.

If you are like most people, you worry about the population a great deal, even though you may not realize it. By population, we mean the number of people in a society. The population affects your chances of finding a job and a spouse. If you do marry, it is likely to influence the age of your spouse, whether you have children, and how many you will have. It may also affect your chances of being promoted, your taxes, the age at which you will retire, and your income after retirement.

Sometimes, we also worry about population problems in the larger world. Poverty, disease, accident and death rates, world hunger, the problems of crowded cities, vanishing farmlands—all are population problems. To avoid sounding all too gloomy, we should point out that some of the most practical things we can do to resolve these problems involve studying the population in hopes of influencing it. We may be able to better understand our own lives, plan sensible social policies to shape the world's future, and develop sound business, investment, and economic strategies by understanding the size, age, sex ratios, and movements of the population. The study of these various characteristics of society is called "demography."

DEMOGRAPHY AND THE STUDY OF POPULATION

Demography is the study of the size and makeup of the human population and how it changes. Demographers want to know how many babies are being born, what diseases are in the population, how long people live, whether they stay in the same place or move about, and whether they live in remote regions or crowded urban areas.

Collecting the Data

Demographers use many statistics in their work. After all, their main concern is counting people. In fact, the word *demography* is often used to refer to the study of population statistics. Societies have always realized how important it is to know about their members and, since early times, have kept some form of **census**—a count of the population—usually with a record of the age and sex of its members. From such records, estimates of early populations can be made and studied. For hundreds and sometimes thousands of years, family lineages have been recorded and passed on orally to keep track of who was born to whom. Written records of deaths can be found in early Greek and Egyptian accounts. The Bible says that when Jesus was born, Mary and Joseph were on their way to be counted in a Roman census.

Modern nations keep much more reliable records of their populations. The first census in the United States was carried out in 1790, and censuses are still carried out once every ten years, with questionnaires mailed to all known households. In addition, interviewers search door to door for those who are not contacted or do not respond by mail. These large attempts to gather data are very difficult to accomplish.

The census is often criticized for underreporting people, especially the poor and homeless. Some people do not receive the questionnaires or do not bother to return them. Interviewers do not find some people—sometimes because the job is not organized or done properly and sometimes because people avoid being found. State and local governments are quick to complain that their populations have been undercounted because these governments receive federal funds based on their population counts.

A smaller census is made every year and is more accurate than the ten-year census because it is based on a carefully chosen random sample of the population rather than trying to count everyone in the population. A random sample has the advantage of assuring that everyone in the population is represented in the sample without the necessity of finding everyone in the population. The smaller yearly census also has the advantage of being done by more highly experienced interviewers; and there is less need to hire as many temporary, inexperienced people, as is required for the ten-year census.

In addition to population counts, **vital statistics**—records of all births, deaths and their causes, marriages, divorces, some diseases, and similar data—are recorded in each state and reported to the National Center for Health Statistics. Most modern nations keep records as accurate as those of the United States. Underdeveloped

The population—the number of people in a society—affects a number of aspects in life, including your job, your spouse, and your children. Population problems in the larger world can include poverty, disease, and world hunger.

nations also attempt to record their populations; and although data from these countries may be relatively inaccurate, they provide enough information to assess world population trends.

Three variables can cause the size of the population in a given region to change: (1) births, (2) deaths, and (3) migrations. Demographers measure these factors in terms of their rates. **Fertility** is a measure of the rate at which people are born. **Mortality** is a measure of the rate at which people die. **Migration** is the movement of people into or out of a geographical area. To understand how populations change, it is necessary to understand how demographers measure these factors.

Fertility

Fertility data indicate the rate at which babies are born. The crude birth rate is simply the number of births per one thousand people; but if we want to predict how many babies will actually be born, more information is needed. We must know the **age-sex composition** of the society, and the number of males and females in the population, along with their ages. A population with few women will have few children. The ages of the females are especially important because children and older women do not have babies.

In most societies, the number of men and women is about equal. About 105 males are born for each 100 females, but women live longer than men. Thus, there may be more men at younger ages, but there are more women in older groups. During the childbearing years, the number of men and women is usually about equal, except in societies suffering from wars in which large numbers of men are killed, or in societies experiencing a great deal of migration. Areas from which men move away have a surplus of women, whereas the areas they move into have a surplus of men; and a society with unequal numbers of men and women will have a low birth rate. There was an imbalance of this sort in the Soviet Union because so many men were killed during World War I, the Civil War of 1917–1921, World War II, and the repressive era following World War II. As a result, many women were left without husbands and did not have children, and the birth rate dropped dramatically. For years, the Soviets kept secret their great loss of population and low birth rates, but the latest available information indicates that they are now comparable to the United States in birth rates and population size.

Demographers generally assume that women are fertile from age fifteen to age forty-nine. They also know that more children are born to women in the middle of their childbearing years; however, some women in their childbearing years choose not to have children, and few have as many as they potentially could. An individual woman's potential for bearing children is called her **fecundity**. Although women can potentially have twenty to twenty-five children, very few have this many. In recent years, worldwide fertility rates have been declining. (See Figures 19-1A and 19-1B)

Birth rates in societies are affected by the age-sex composition of the society—the number of males and females in the population and their ages. In most societies, the number of men and women is about equal, and more children are born to women in the middle of their childbearing years.

Fertility varies greatly among societies and among subcultures within societies. The number of children born in a society is affected by three major factors: wealth, environment, and societal norms about marriage and children. Generally, richer nations have lower birth rates, and poorer nations have higher birth rates. The same relationship between wealth and birth rates holds within nations: the upper classes usually have lower birth rates than the poor classes.

Fertility rates are also different in rural and urban areas. Women in rural areas usually have more children than those in cities. In rural areas, children are needed to help with farm labor, but in modern urban areas, children are not productive. Rather, they are an expense to house, feed, clothe, and educate. They may also decrease a family's income when a parent must either pay for child care or stay home to care for them. Many demographers believe that the birth rate of the world will decline and perhaps drop sharply as underdeveloped nations become more industrialized and urban.

A society's norms regarding the value of children and the age at which marriage is considered acceptable have a strong effect on fertility rates. In countries in which women marry young, the birth rates are higher than those in which they marry later because of differences in the number of childbearing years. Norms about the number of children a family should have and about the acceptability of birth control and abortion also affect the birth rate. Separation by war, working away from home, and conflicts between spouses also reduce the birth rate, whereas a cultural practice of abstaining from intercourse during menstruation may make intercourse more likely during fertile periods and may result in an increased birth rate.

A low or high fertility rate will, of course, affect the number of people born into the population, but this is only one of several factors that influence population size. Mortality and migration rates are also influential.

Mortality

Mortality, the rate of death in a population, can be measured very simply. The crude death rate is the number of deaths in a given year per one thousand people. Like the crude birth rate, however, the crude death rate does not provide enough information to predict how many people will die or to compare death rates among populations. For a more accurate estimate of the death rate, demographers consider age and gender. A population with many old people will have a higher death rate than a comparatively young population; and because women live longer than men, a population with many women will have a lower death rate. Demographers often use an **age-adjusted death rate**, a measure of the number of deaths at each age for each sex, usually per 100,000 living at that age. Demographers can also compute life expectancy by predicting how many of each age cohort, or age group, will die at each age.

Mortality, like fertility, varies with wealth. When people, especially infants, have adequate food, housing, and

TABLE 19-1 OECD1 COUNTRIES AND WORLD PETROLEUM (OIL) DEMAND, 1970-2009 (THOUSAND BARRELS PER DAY)

	France	Germany	Italy	United Kingdom	OECD Europe	Canada	Japan	South Korea
1970 Average	1,937	2,830	1,710	2,096	13,120	1,516	3,817	199
1971 Average	2,115	2,941	1,838	2,141	13,798	1,564	4,142	232
1972 Average	2,322	3,097	1,947	2,284	14,782	1,664	4,363	235
1973 Average	2,601	3,324	2,068	2,341	15,879	1,729	4,949	281
1974 Average	2,447	3,030	2,004	2,210	14,985	1,779	4,864	287
1975 Average	2,252	2,957	1,855	1,911	14,314	1,779	4,621	311
1976 Average	2,420	3,206	1,971	1,892	15,298	1,818	4,837	357
1977 Average	2,294	3,212	1,897	1,905	15,160	1,850	4,880	422
1978 Average	2,408	3,290	1,952	1,938	15,611	1,902	4,945	482
1979 Average	2,463	3,373	2,039	1,971	16,048	1,971	5,050	525
1980 Average	2,256	3,082	1,934	1,725	14,995	1,873	4,960	537
1981 Average	2,023	2,804	1,874	1,590	13,802	1,768	4,848	536
1982 Average	1,880	2,743	1,781	1,590	13,292	1,578	4,582	534
1983 Average	1,835	2,661	1,750	1,531	12,968	1,448	4,395	561
1984 Average	1,771	2,557	1,720	1,825	12,814	1,520	4,666	554
1985 Average	1,753	2,651	1,705	1,617	12,770	1,526	4,436	552
1986 Average	1,764	2,792	1,734	1,637	13,200	1,531	4,503	592
1987 Average	1,785	2,723	1,815	1,611	13,326	1,607	4,567	627
1988 Average	1,801	2,723	1,829	1,692	13,512	1,681	4,849	746
1989 Average	1,844	2,581	1,897	1,731	13,587	1,754	5,058	860
1990 Average	1,826	2,682	1,868	1,776	13,729	1,737	5,315	1,048
1991 Average	1,942	2,829	1,856	1,803	14,076	1,677	5,389	1,263
1992 Average	1,934	2,841	1,894	1,815	14,287	1,725	5,478	1,527
1993 Average	1,878	2,908	1,891	1,829	14,291	1,751	5,395	1,684
1994 Average	1,865	2,883	1,869	1,833	14,412	1,772	5,655	1,840
1995 Average	1,920	2,882	1,942	1,816	14,714	1,817	5,693	2,008
1996 Average	1,949	2,922	1,920	1,852	14,998	1,871	5,739	2,101
1997 Average	1,969	2,917	1,934	1,810	15,140	1,959	5,702	2,255
1998 Average	2,043	2,923	1,943	1,792	15,447	1,949	5,507	1,917
1999 Average	2,031	2,838	1,891	1,811	15,364	2,036	5,642	2,084
2000 Average	2,000	2,772	1,854	1,765	15,219	2,035	5,515	2,135
2001 Average	2,054	2,815	1,832	1,747	15,393	2,066	5,412	2,132
2002 Average	1,985	2,722	1,870	1,739	15,342	2,087	5,319	2,149
2003 Average	2,001	2,679	1,860	1,759	15,461	2,217	5,429	2,175
2004 Average	2,009	2,665	1,794	1,785	15,531	2,310	5,319	2,155
2005 Average	1,991	2,647	1,755	1,823	15,667	2,341	5,328	2,191
2006 Average	1,991	2,692	1,743	1,804	15,684	2,253	5,198	2,180
2007 Average	1,979	2,468	1,688	1,738	15,453	2,307	5,037	2,241
2008 Average	1,945	2,572	1,633	1,729	15,357	2,242	4,788	2,142
2009 Average	1,828	2,440	1,528	1,667	14,493	2,151	4,367	2,185

(continued)

Table 19-1 OECD1 Countries and World Petroleum (Oil) Demand, 1970-2009 (Thousand Barrels per Day)

	United States	Other OECD	OECD	World
1970 Average	14,697	1,427	34,776	46,808
1971 Average	15,213	1,461	36,412	49,416
1972 Average	16,367	1,646	39,057	53,094
1973 Average	17,308	1,768	41,913	57,237
1974 Average	16,653	1,904	40,473	56,677
1975 Average	16,322	1,885	39,232	56,198
1976 Average	17,461	2,034	41,803	59,673
1977 Average	18,431	2,124	42,868	61,826
1978 Average	18,847	2,289	44,075	64,158
1979 Average	18,513	2,384	44,491	65,220
1980 Average	17,056	2,449	41,870	63,113
1981 Average	16,058	2,583	39,595	60,947
1982 Average	15,296	2,586	37,868	59,545
1983 Average	15,231	2,399	37,002	58,777
1984 Average	15,726	2,504	37,783	59,813
1985 Average	15,726	2,564	37,575	60,083
1986 Average	16,281	2,588	38,694	61,810
1987 Average	16,665	2,652	39,444	63,095
1988 Average	17,283	2,689	40,760	64,965
1989 Average	17,325	2,871	41,455	66,078
1990 Average	16,988	2,784	41,601	66,533
1991 Average	16,714	2,948	42,067	67,197
1992 Average	17,033	2,977	43,026	67,391
1993 Average	17,237	3,046	43,404	67,536
1994 Average	17,718	3,211	44,608	68,858
1995 Average	17,725	3,135	45,092	70,067
1996 Average	18,309	3,206	46,224	71,665
1997 Average	18,620	3,322	46,999	73,436
1998 Average	18,917	3,443	47,180	74,079
1999 Average	19,519	3,512	48,157	75,791
2000 Average	19,701	3,591	48,197	76,772
2001 Average	19,649	3,605	48,257	77,512
2002 Average	19,761	3,558	48,217	78,160
2003 Average	20,034	3,598	48,913	79,722
2004 Average	20,731	3,687	49,733	82,511
2005 Average	20,802	3,800	50,129	84,105
2006 Average	20,687	3,816	49,818	85,255
2007 Average	20,680	3,874	49,593	86,288
2008 Average	19,498	3,846	47,874	85,776
2009 Average	18,771	3,758	45,725	84,337

(continued)

Table 19-1 OECD1 Countries and World Petroleum (Oil) Demand, 1970-2009 (Thousand Barrels per Day)

1 OECD: Organization for Economic Cooperation and Development. See Appendix A for countries in this group at: http://www.eia.doe.

2 Data are for unified Germany, i.e., the former East Germany and West Germany.

3 "OECD Europe" consists of Austria, Belgium, Czech Republic, Denmark, Finland, France, Germany, Greece, Hungary, Iceland, Ireland, Italy,

Luxembourg, the Netherlands, Norway, Poland, Portugal, Slovakia, Spain, Sweden, Switzerland, Turkey, and the United Kingdom.

4 U.S. geographic coverage is the 50 States and the District of Columbia.

5 "Other OECD" consists of Australia, Mexico, New Zealand, the U.S. Territories, and Chile.

Note: The term Demand is used interchangeably with Consumption and Products Supplied.

See Appendix C for definition at: http://www.eia.doe.gov/emeu/ipsr/appc.html

Sources: See sources for Section 4 at: http://www.eia.doe.gov/emeu/ipsr/source4.html

medical care, they are less likely to die of disease. The rate of *infant mortality*, death in the first year of life, was very high in the Middle Ages, but now it is lower; and the average life expectancy has been greatly increased. Infant mortality is low and life expectancy high in more developed nations, such as the United States, Canada, and European countries. When compared to the average infant mortality of all countries worldwide, the United States fares favorably well. (See Figure 19-2A and 19-2B.) However, of the thirty industrialized countries in the world, the United States has the sixth highest infant mortality rates. If we take out the low-income countries from this list, the U.S worsens to the fourth highest rate. (See Table 19-2.)

Researchers have uncovered what they hope to be a one-time blip in infant mortality rates in the United

FIGURE 19-1A A WORLD BIRTH RATES, 2000-2009

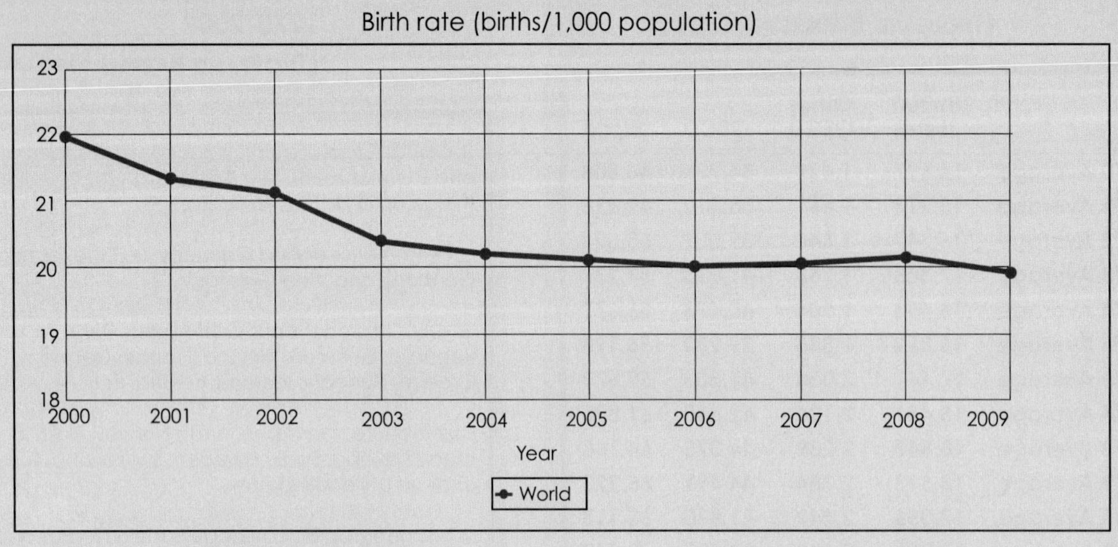

Birth rate (births/1,000 population)

Year

World

Country	2000	2001	2002	2003	2004	2005	2006	2007	2008	2009
World	22	21.37	21.16	20.43	20.24	20.15	20.05	20.09	20.18	19.95

Source: http://www.indexmundi.com/g/

FIGURE 19-1B U.S. BIRTH RATE 2000-2009

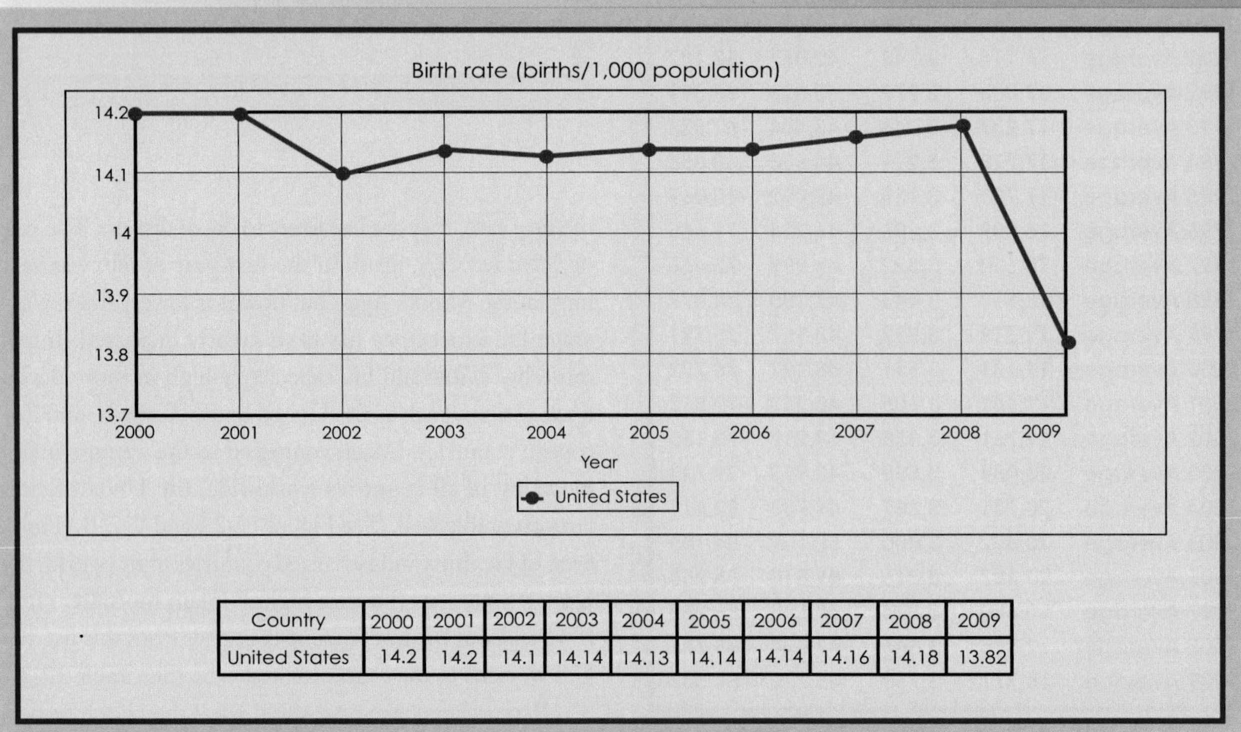

Country	2000	2001	2002	2003	2004	2005	2006	2007	2008	2009
United States	14.2	14.2	14.1	14.14	14.13	14.14	14.14	14.16	14.18	13.82

Source: http://www.indexmundi.com/g/

States. Infant mortality rates rose in 2002 for the first time in decades. Our nation's infant mortality rate edged upward from 6.69 deaths per 1,000 live births in 2001 to 6.75 deaths per 1,000 in 2002 (See Figure 19-2A). In explaining the higher infant mortality rate, researchers point to the surge in older women having babies; the popularity of fertility treatments; and, paradoxically, advancements in identifying and saving fetuses in distress. Because we have the ability to identify fetuses in distress and deliver them early, they are dying at higher rates in early infancy (Stein 2004).

An increase in infant mortality is cause for attention because the infant mortality rate usually reflects the general well-being of the larger society. However, life expectancy in the United States continues to rise because of our ability to prevent, detect, and treat cancer, accidents, stroke, and heart disease.

People in China (Macau), Andorra, and Japan have the longest life expectancies in the world. An infant born in these countries can expect to live, on average, more than eighty years. The death rate is higher and the life expectancy shorter in India, Africa, South America, and Southeast Asia, where poverty is widespread (*CIA World Factbook* 2009).

Death rates also vary by class within nations. In the United States, for example, poor people have a higher rate of infant mortality and a shorter life expectancy than the rich; blacks have a larger proportion of poor people, higher rates of infant mortality, and shorter life expectancies than whites (CDC 2004). The more important factor in infant mortality, however, is poverty, not race. Black infants born to parents living in predominantly white neighborhoods, indicating higher income, have lower infant mortality rates than white infants living in predominantly black neighborhoods, where poverty is greater (Yankauer 1990).

Migration

Migration includes the following: **immigration**, movement into an area, and **emigration**, movement out of an area. Migration is harder to define and measure than birth or death rates. To be considered a migrant, how far must a person move, and how long should the person remain in the new place? In the United States, moving within a county is not considered migration, but moving from one county to another is. *Migrant workers*, who travel about the country doing farm labor, are not technically considered migrants because rather than remaining in a new location after the work season is over, they return to their original starting point and take up jobs in that area.

Why do people move? Demographers speak in terms of push factors and pull factors. **Push factors** are those that push people away from their homes: famines, wars, political oppression, loss of jobs, or bad climate. Some eastern Europeans, for example, have migrated to the west where jobs are more plentiful. **Pull factors** are those that make a new place seem more inviting: the chance to acquire land or jobs, the discovery of riches such as gold or oil, or the chance to live in a more desirable climate. Discoveries of

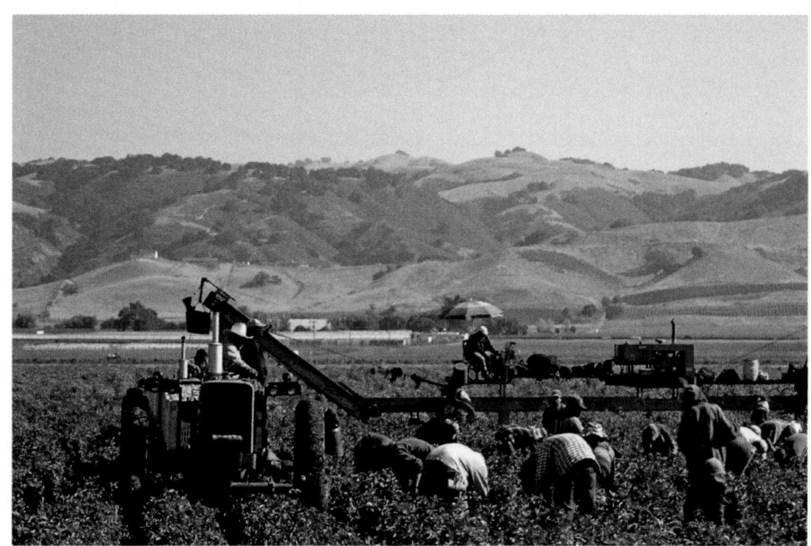

Migration is difficult to define. Migrant workers travel around the country doing farm labor but are not technically considered migrants because they return to their original starting point after the work season is over, rather than remaining in the new locations to which they travel.

FIGURE 19-2 A INFANT MORTALITY RATES IN THE U.S. 2000-2009

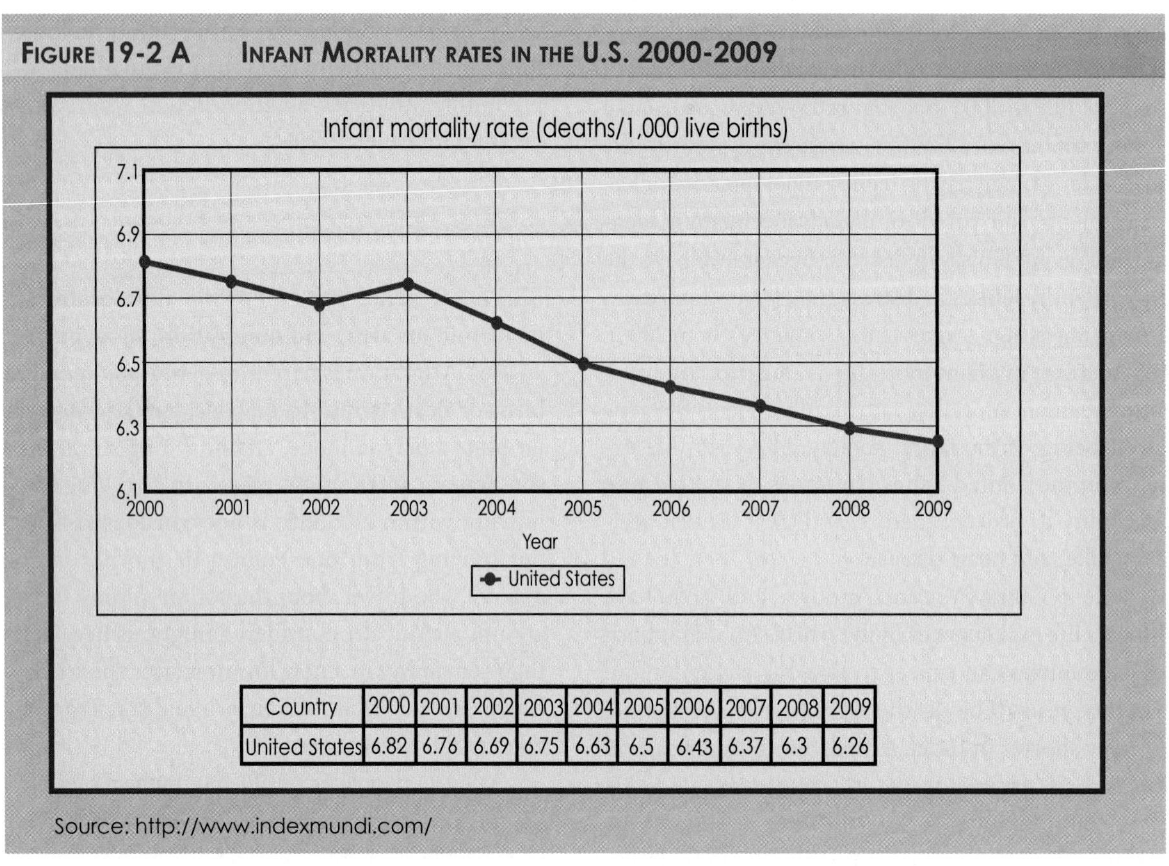

Country	2000	2001	2002	2003	2004	2005	2006	2007	2008	2009
United States	6.82	6.76	6.69	6.75	6.63	6.5	6.43	6.37	6.3	6.26

Source: http://www.indexmundi.com/

FIGURE 19-2 B INFANT MORTALITY RATES IN THE WORLD, 2000-2009

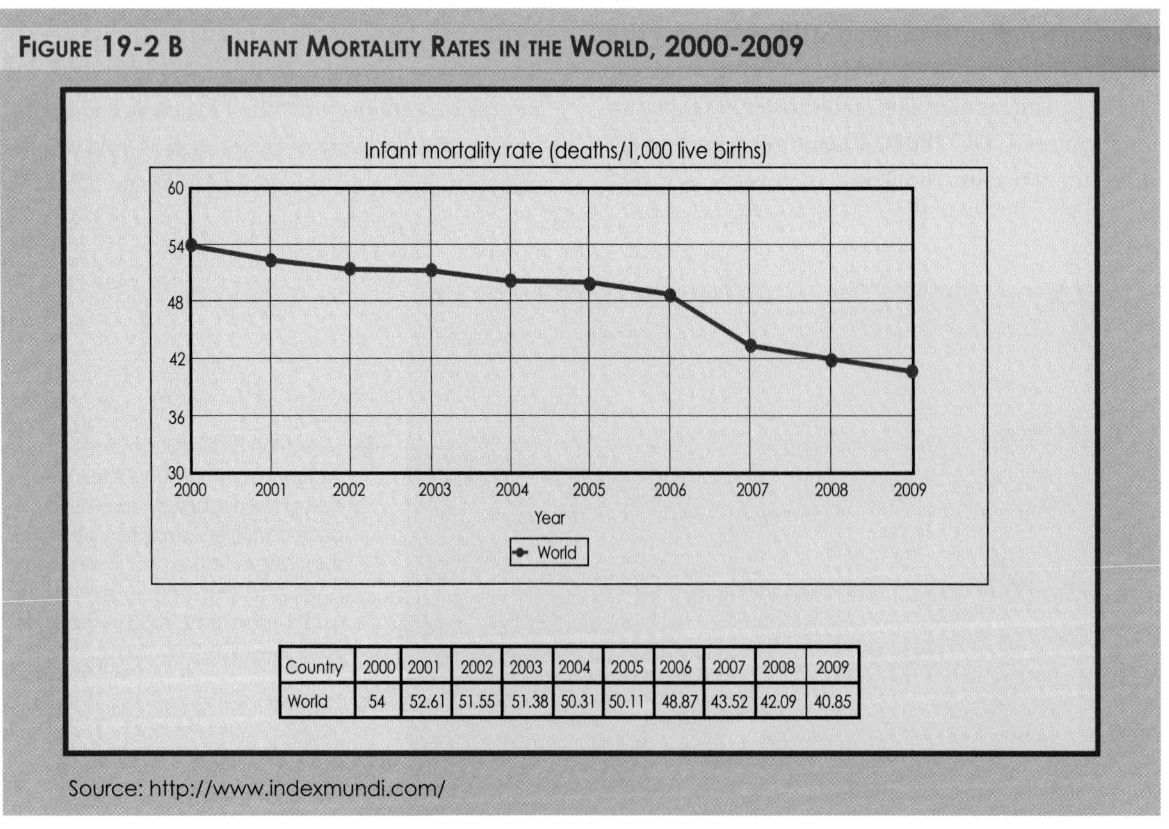

Country	2000	2001	2002	2003	2004	2005	2006	2007	2008	2009
World	54	52.61	51.55	51.38	50.31	50.11	48.87	43.52	42.09	40.85

Source: http://www.indexmundi.com/

TABLE 19-2 INFANT MORTALITY RATE FOR INDUSTRIALIZED (FREE-MARKET) COUNTRIES – 2009 (DEATHS PER 1,000 LIVE BIRTHS)

Country	Rate
Australia	4.75
Austria	4.42
Belgium	4.44
Canada	5.04
Czech Republic	3.79
Denmark	4.34
Finland	3.47
France	3.33
Germany	3.99
Greece	5.16
Hungary	7.86
Iceland	3.23
Ireland	5.05
Italy	5.51
Japan	2.79
Korea (South)	4.26
Luxembourg	4.56
Mexico*	18.42
Netherlands	4.73
New Zealand	4.92
Norway	3.58
Poland*	6.8
Portugal	4.78
Slovak Republic	6.84
Spain	4.21
Sweden	2.75
Switzerland	4.18
Turkey*	25.78
United Kingdom	4.85
United States	6.26

* = low-income country
Source of infant mortality rates: Index Mundi, http://www.indexmundi.com

Source of list of industrialized countries and income status: OECD, Organization for Economic Cooperation and Development

gold in California, for example, drew fortune seekers from all over the world.

In prehistoric times, waves of migrants moved out of Africa and Asia into the Middle East and Eastern Europe. Later, tribes moved further into Europe, spreading their culture as they moved. It is assumed that these waves of migration were caused by push factors, such as changes in climate, changes in food supply, or pressure from increasing populations in Asia, as well as pull factors, such as Europe's more favorable climate.

The population of Europe increased slowly throughout the Middle Ages. When Columbus first came to America, a new wave of migration began. It started slowly, but it is estimated that more than sixty million Europeans eventually left Europe. Many later returned, so the net migration—the actual population change—was much lower (Heer 1975).

Between 1820 and 1970, forty-six million migrants entered the United States (Thomlinson 1976). In a single peak year, 1854, a total of 428,000 immigrants came to this country. This group consisted mainly of Irish leaving their country because of the potato famine and Germans leaving because of political turmoil in their country. A second peak was reached around the turn of the century when immigrants averaged a million per year. Most of the Europeans who entered the United States at that time were from Italy or other southern and eastern European countries.

A more long-term great migration occurred between 1619 and 1808, when four hundred thousand Africans were forced to migrate to the United States as slaves. Considering all the Americas, between ten and twenty million Africans were brought to the Western Hemisphere (Thomlinson 1976).

Immigration restrictions were first imposed in the United States in 1921 and again in 1924 in order to slow the rate of immigration. During this period, most immigrants were from Canada, Mexico, Germany, the United Kingdom, or Italy. After 1965, immigration quotas were relaxed, and a new wave of immigrants entered the country, changing dramatically the origins of American immigrants. About 2.4 million Asians, or about 46 percent of all immigrants, entered the United States during the 1980s. Another two million, or 38 percent of all immigrants, came from Mexico and other parts of Latin America (*Infor-*

mation Please Almanac 1991). What's more, as of 2008, this new pattern of immigration shows no sign of abatement. Certainly, in 2008, a record number of immigrants (1,046,539) naturalized, two-fifths who came from Latin America and Asia. The top countries of birth of new citizens in 2008 were Mexico, India, the Philippines, China, and Cuba.

Besides legal immigration, the United States is also home to one of the largest diasporas of undocumented immigrants in the world. Most illegal immigrants in the United States come from Latin America and enter the country via the U.S.–Mexico border. The lure of the American dream drives these immigrants into the United States by the millions. Indeed, for 2008, the U.S. Department of Homeland Security conservatively estimated that the United States was home to over eleven million undocumented immigrants. Since the terrorist attacks on 9/11/2001, the flow of undocumented immigration into the United States has been curtailed somewhat by stronger border security. However, hundreds of thousands still enter the United States illegally every year. For most Americans, it's a source of pride that so many people from around the world would risk their very lives just to live in the United States. Still, the aftershocks of the 9/11 attacks regularly remind Americans that not every immigrant has the best interests of the United States in mind. As a result, in the decades to come, the issue of undocumented immigration will continue to be a major source of political debate.

Immigrants work at very low-paying jobs, such as in clothing factories or as doormen, when they arrive in the United States. Some are able to begin small businesses of their own. Many immigrants are better off than they were in their country of origin, but others who are more highly educated and trained for professions are unable to find work to match their qualifications; they, too, must work at the very low-paying jobs available to them. There is some research evidence that the influx of low-wage immigrant workers into the Los Angeles area has kept wages there from rising for the population as a whole (Vernez and Ronfeldt 1991). Because of recent restrictions, however, admissions for categories such as temporary agricultural workers and holders of NAFTA visas for professionals declined to 650,000 in 2003, a continued decline from 2002 levels of 688,000 (UNFPA 2004).

Migration within the United States has also been extensive. Throughout this country's history, people

FIGURE 19-3 PERSONS NATURALIZED BY COUNTRY OF ORIGIN TOP FIVE), 2008

Mexico	231,815
India	65,971
Philipines	58,792
China	40,017
Cuba	39871
Total	**436,466**

Source: U.S. Department of Homeland Security.

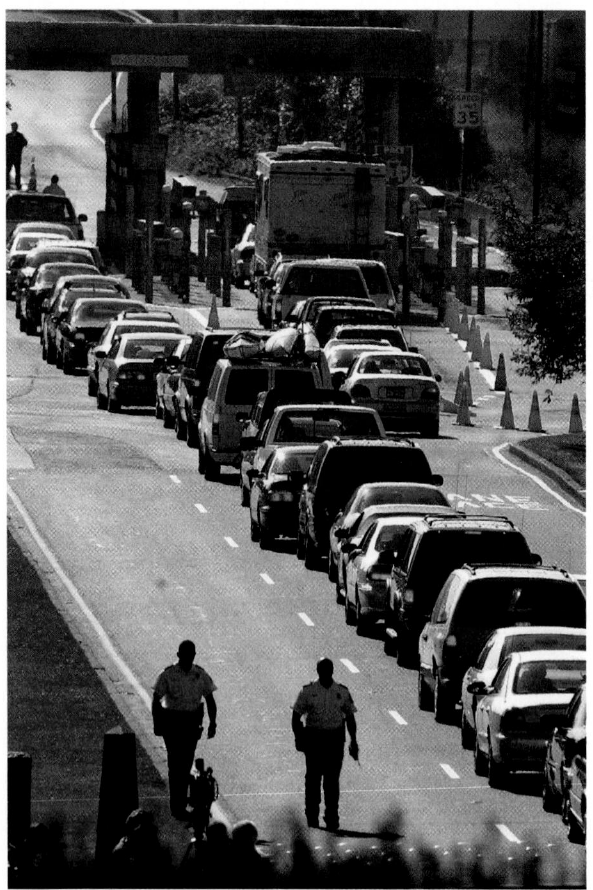

The United States is home to one of the largest populations of illegal immigrants. Although the flow of these immigrants was curtailed somewhat after 9/11, hundreds of thousands of illegal immigrants continue to enter the country for the opportunities it offers.

have moved predominantly from east to west and from rural to urban areas. After World War I, when immigration was restricted and the supply of laborers entering the country was limited, northern cities recruited southern blacks to fill labor jobs. Many blacks moved to northern cities, far exceeding the number of jobs or the housing available. The migrants could not return to the South because they didn't have money to make the return trip nor a home waiting for their return. Even today, we can see the pattern of inadequate jobs and housing for blacks living in northern cities.

The rate of population change is determined by all the foregoing factors. If the birth rate is high and the mortality rate is low, the population increases. If the mortality rate is high compared with the birth rate, the population will decline. Where migration enters the picture, the population can grow or decrease very rapidly. Even relatively small changes in demographic patterns can make long-term, sweeping changes in the lives of people in the population. For example, people born when birth rates are high in the United States have many different experiences from people born when birth rates are low.

POPULATION TRENDS AND LIFE EXPERIENCES

Figure 19-5 is a population pyramid, a graph that shows how many males and females from each age category there are in the United States today. Find in the middle column the category containing your age group, noting that the bars extending to the left and right represent the males and females born in those years. By looking at the bottom of the graph, you can determine the number of people of your age and sex in the population. If your are between fifteen and nineteen years old as of 2010, the left line tells us how many females in your age group live in the United States while the right line tells us how many males of your age group reside in the United States. Notice also how the pyramid bulges out for the ages between forty-five and sixty-four and between fifteen and twenty-nine. The forty-five to sixty-four-year- old bulge represents the people born during what is called the "baby boom" and the fifteen to twenty-nine- year-old bulge represents their children. Compare the 2010 population pyramid of the United States with those of India and Germany that serve as ex-

FIGURE 19-4 UNAUTHORIZED IMMIGRANT POPULATION: 2000-2008* (IN MILLIONS)

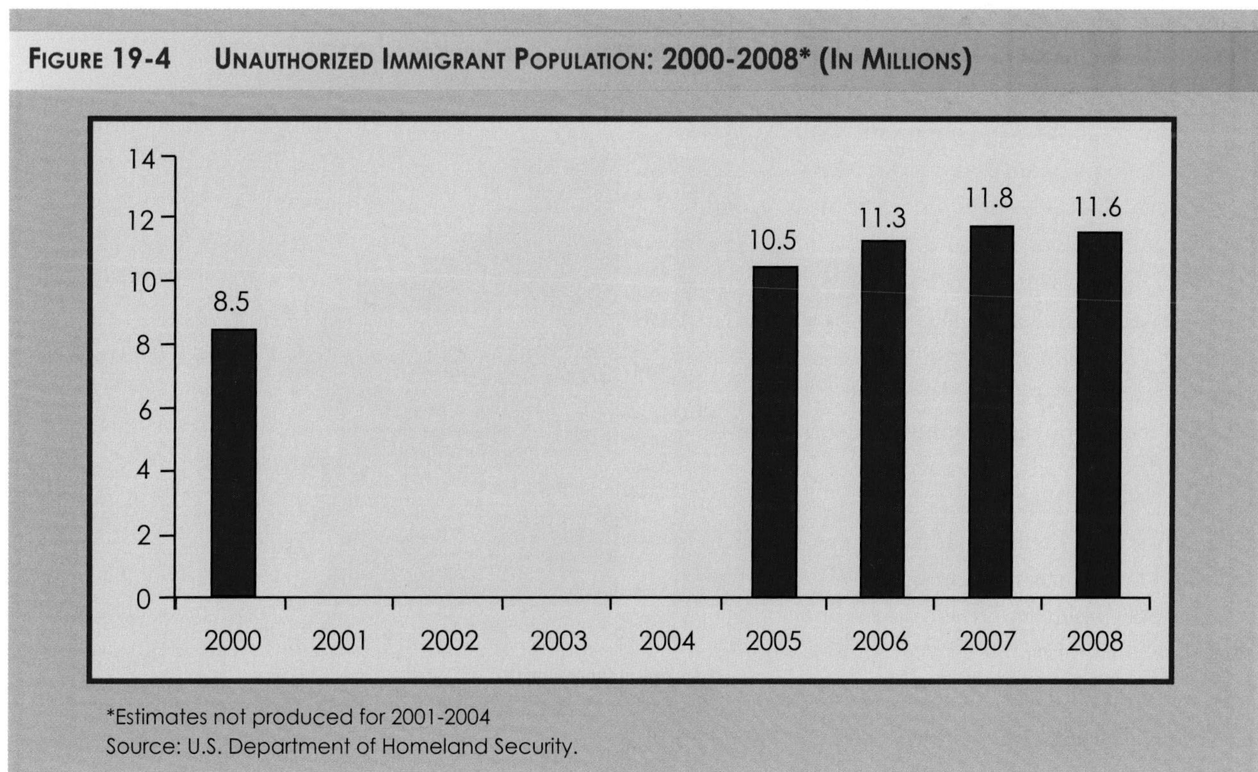

*Estimates not produced for 2001-2004
Source: U.S. Department of Homeland Security.

amples of countries with much older and much younger populations, respectively.

Why were so many people born during those baby boom years? During the depression of the 1930s and World War II in the 1940s, many people postponed having children. After the war, the country was both peaceful and affluent. Those who had postponed having children began families, and those who were just entering their twenties began having children, too. The result was a disproportionate number of babies born in the 1950s and 1960s, compared to other decades.

How has the baby boom affected the lives of people born during those years? First, it may have affected their education. Children might not have gone to nursery school because the schools were full. Schools were crowded because there were not enough schools to take care of so many children, and many children attended schools in temporary classroom buildings. When students reached college age, they faced strong competition to gain entrance to colleges, which were overcrowded trying to deal with the surge in population. At the end of the baby boom, schools closed because there were fewer students to fill all the space that had been created. Some students, especially those in suburban areas, watched their elementary schools close when they left them, went to a junior high school that was closed while they were there, moved to a second junior high, and saw that one close before they had finished senior high school.

Students born between 1975 and 1979 have had a very different educational experience. Their experience is similar to those who were born in the 1930s and followed the baby boom of the 1920s. Harter (1987) describes the generation of the 1930s as the "good-time" cohort. When they went to school, there was plenty of space in school, plus a full complement of athletic teams, glee clubs, debating societies, and other extracurricular activities. The cohort of the 1930s could participate without facing much competition. So it has been with those born between 1975 and 1979. There has been plenty of room in school for them throughout their educational years, and there has not been the extreme competition for a place in college. In fact, colleges have been competing for students to attend their schools and have made every effort to recruit students and provide them with

FIGURE 19-5 AGE-SEX POPULATION PYRAMID, UNITED STATES, FOR THE YEAR 2010

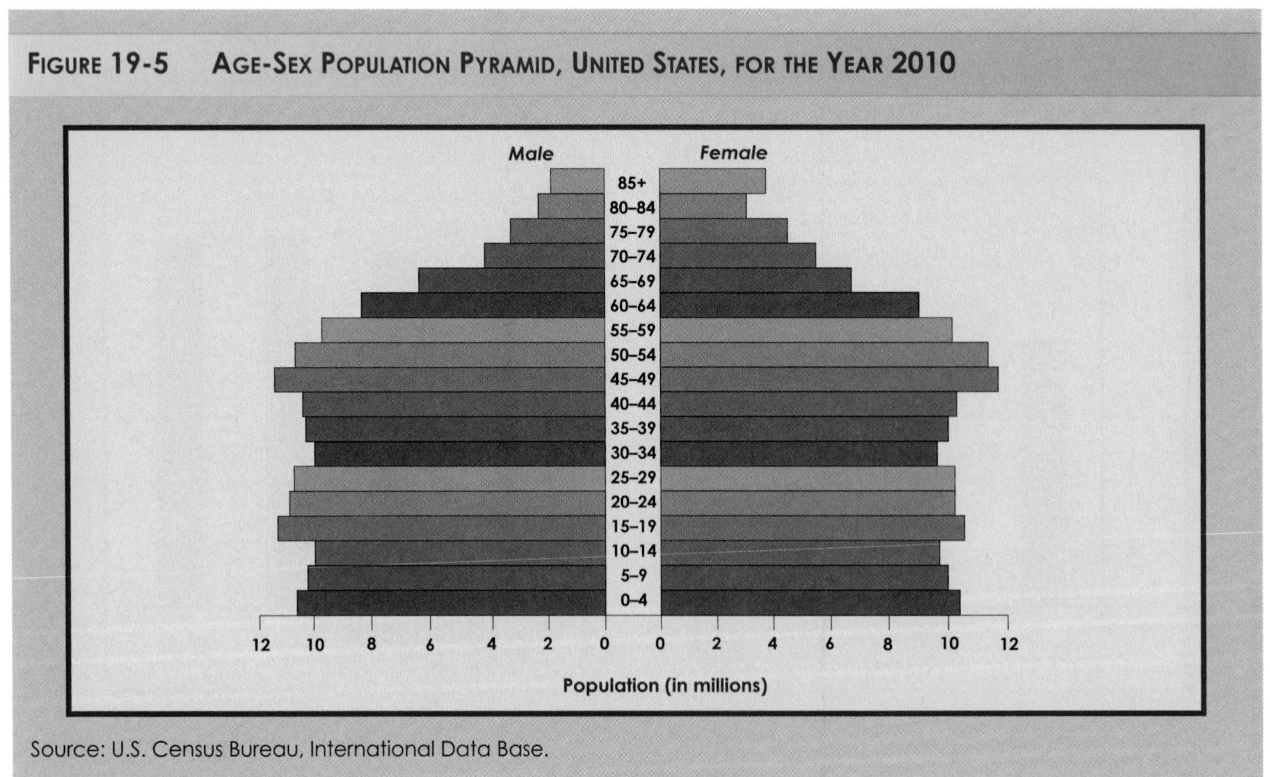

Source: U.S. Census Bureau, International Data Base.

scholarships and loans so that they are able to attend. The lack of competition may also have reduced the amount of studying and learning that has taken place in school.

When baby boom children completed their education, unemployment rates were high. Many people were competing for jobs, and only a small part of the work force was retiring to create more job openings. About a generation later, the drop in the unemployment rate in 1984 was largely a result of a drop in the number of young people entering the job market.

When the people born between 1975 and 1979 entered the job market, there were fewer of them; and they probably had an easier time finding jobs. Furthermore, the bulge of people born between 1920 and 1929 had mostly retired, allowing more room for upward mobility in corporations.

Population trends also affect marriage rates. Women born during the baby boom were more likely to marry at an older age or to stay single than was true in earlier generations. Why? Because of what is referred to as the **marriage squeeze**. Women traditionally marry older men, and a look at the population pyramid shows that there was a shortage of older men for these women to marry (a marriage squeeze). Women born after the baby boom have many older men to marry, so they may marry at a younger age. Men born late in the baby boom who want to follow the normative practice of marrying younger women face a shortage (also a marriage squeeze), and so far they have not shown an inclination to start a new trend and avoid the squeeze by marrying slightly older women.

Population trends also affect clothing styles and fashions. After World War II, the mark of beauty was to have a more well developed figure, like Marilyn Monroe or Betty Grable. Therefore the market for clothes was found among women in their 20s and 30s, who had been unable to buy clothes during the war. Youngsters born during the baby boom, however, represented a big, new market, and manufacturers catered to them beginning in the 1960s. It became stylish to be thin because adolescents tend to be thin during their period of rapid growth, and a whole nation dieted to look like adolescents. When the baby boom generation grew older, clothing manufacturers changed styles to meet the market for clothes for more mature figures; and low-cut jeans were replaced by stretch blue jeans with a fuller-cut thigh and an elastic waist. Also, the health club business began to boom because this age group wanted to stay thin and look young. Ski resorts suffered a slump, however, because as members of the baby boom got older, they began staying home, having children, and watching their budgets. Thus, there were not enough younger people to replace them on the slopes. Golf, a gentler sport, began to increase in popularity.

Thinking Sociologically

1. If the United States were a very young population, such as Mexico, what social problems would probably be more prevalent than they are today? What social problems would probably be less prevalent?

2. If the United States were an older population, such as Sweden, what social problems would probably be more prevalent than they are today? What social problems would be less prevalent?

Housing costs are also affected by population trends. Housing prices increased dramatically when baby boom young adults bought houses, but then dropped as demand eased. Retirement homes also saw a boom when those born in the 1920s retired, but prices fell when those born in the 1930s retired. Through studying population trends, we can see that consumer interests become very predictable.

Population trends may also determine government policies that affect you in your old age. In the year 2020, most of the baby boom will have reached age sixty, and many will be collecting Social Security, while others will still hold powerful positions in business and government. Moreover, because this age group will be a large voting bloc, they may be able to control decisions about continuing the support of Social Security benefits. Because the smaller population just younger than the baby boom may have a large tax burden to help support all the people in retirement, it is to be hoped that the younger population will be fully employed.

Knowledge of this population trend can help us do more than merely hope for the best, however. Because policymakers today know with certainty that there will be massive numbers of people in need of Social Security through 2025, they can take the necessary steps now to avert a future breakdown in the Social Security system. By studying population and predicting how it will affect our lives, we can tailor public policy planning to accommodate these shifts in population trends.

Population trends may affect business and investment decisions, both on the personal and corporate levels. Consider, for example, how corporations that provide services for the elderly will prosper when the baby boom reaches retirement age. Nursing homes, retirement villages, and pharmaceutical products for the aged are likely to experience explosive growth as a result of this population trend. Other services, such as automated car washes, house cleaning and yard services, and restaurants may also develop due to the increased numbers of the elderly. Think of how this knowledge can help businesses plan for those needs. New businesses in new fields may open up and may offer opportunities to those shrewd enough to anticipate the future needs of the population.

Different nations have different population pyramids and, therefore, must plan for very different future needs of the population. As shown in the population pyramid in Figure 19-6, countries in which a large proportion of the population is very young, such as India, can be expected to grow rapidly as children mature and have children of their own. Here the care and education of the young will be of primary importance. In Germany, where the proportion of young people is smaller, the population cannot be expected to grow. However,

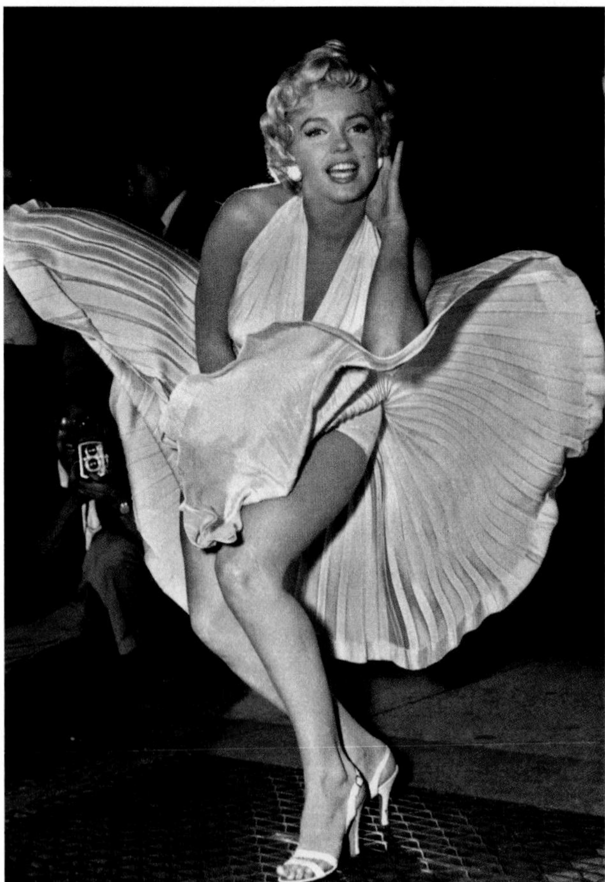

Population trends affect aspects of society including marriage rates and fashion. For example, the mark of beauty after World War II was to have a fuller figure like Marilyn Monroe. In contrast, today's view of beauty is to be thin to mirror the body of an adolescent.

SOCIOLOGY AT WORK

Monitoring Population Trends

Mathew Greenwald received his PhD in sociology from Rutgers University. Prior to opening up his own consulting firm—Mathew Greenwald and Associates, Inc.—he was the director of the social research services department of the American Council of Life Insurance (ACLI). While with the ACLI, he supervised a ten-person staff, designated to monitor past social changes and to predict future social change. Insurance companies use the results of this type of work to construct policies and to prepare for the future.

Greenwald explains that because whole-life insurance policies can run for fifty or sixty years, insurance companies have an interest in the long view. "Of course, some aspects of the social world are so volatile that it's difficult to say what will be happening fifteen years from now," Greenwald says. However, it is still possible to make predictions. "For example, we know that Social Security will be in trouble in 2011. That's when the first year of the baby-boom generation, those born in 1946, will be retiring. We also expect important medical breakthroughs in such areas as cancer research. Certain trends in computerization and global economics will probably also continue. Thus, while there's a lot we can't know, some trends can be accurately predicted; and the more we know, the easier it is to make decisions."

Here is where his sociological training comes in. "The sociological perspective is of crucial importance," Greenwald says. "It's really a certain type of logic, a guide for analysis. It provides a structure for assessing situations. I might approach a family-related problem by looking at it in terms of statuses and roles, for example. More concretely, my training is useful in developing questionnaires and doing survey research. Besides my coursework in methods and statistics being useful, my work in theory, health, population, and the family also has been very valuable."

Greenwald provides an example of how sociological knowledge is useful in making predictions for insurance companies. "The primary purpose of life insurance is to replace income if a family breadwinner dies or is disabled, so the insurance business is bound up with many basic social institutions. We use survey research to keep track of a number of trends on an ongoing basis, including attitudes toward death, retirement, and family responsibility. We also use demographic data about factors such as health, birth rates, death rates, divorce rates, and the number of women working." As you might expect, major social developments influence the sales of life-insurance policies. "Now that families are more dependent on wives' income, women are buying much more insurance than they did previously. We're also finding that sales among Afro-Americans and Hispanics are increasing as these groups become more affluent."

In addition to following demographic trends, Greenwald and his department often undertook special projects. For example, one study concerned the public's sense of control over key aspects of their lives. Their findings: "Sadly, we found that people feel they have less control than they did a few decades ago, especially over the long term." This is probably the result of a number of factors, such as a volatile economic system, political turmoil at home and abroad, terrorism, and wars. "It's unfortunate," he says. "People who don't feel that they have much control are less likely to take a stand and try to change the situation—they don't take advantage of the control they do have. As [that] concerns the insurance business, there's evidence that feelings of lack of control are associated with ill health."

Although Greenwald is no longer with ACLI, he still maintains his ties to the life-insurance industry; his own company mostly does surveys that focus on market research for life-insurance companies. These surveys are used to develop new products, assess the effectiveness of advertising, enhance client relationships, and anticipate how to respond to changes in the social environment.

they have a larger proportion of elderly and will need to plan for their care.

THE WORLD POPULATION EXPLOSION AND THE DEMOGRAPHIC TRANSITION

Until about 200 years ago, both birth and death rates were very high. As a result, the size of the world population remained stable. For every person who was born, someone died. Then a dramatic change took place. First, in industrial nations in the early part of the nineteenth century, the death rate dropped because of improvements in nutrition and sanitation. For several generations, however, the birth rate remained high. (This is the period when what we now refer to as the "population explosion" began.) Then, in about 1850, the birth rate began to decrease, and the rate of population increase slowed. This change from high birth and death rates to low birth and death rates with a period of rapid population growth in between is known as the **demographic transition**. It occurs as a society evolves from a traditional premodern stage to a modern industrial stage; most European nations and other industrial countries have already passed through it. Other countries, particularly those in the developing world, still have very high birth rates in rural areas because children are highly valued for the tasks they do and for the security they provide when their parents reach old age. It is in these countries that population growth continues at very high rates. It took the human race from the beginning of history until 1850 to reach a population of one billion people; it took only an additional 100 years to reach two billion, and only thirty–five more years to reach 4.8 billion. Currently, the world is populated with more than seven billion people, only a dozen years after it reached six billion. In *The World Population Prospects: The 2010 Revision*, the United Nations predicted that the world's population will reach 10.1 billion by the end of the twenty-first century (www.unpopulation.org). While growth in industrialized countries is slowing down, growth in Africa may triple by the end of the century because fertility is not declining as rapidly as expected in some poor countries. Further, the population of the United States is growing faster than in other developed countries because of high immigration and higher fertility

FIGURE 19-6 POPULATION PYRAMIDS OF A YOUNG POPULATION (INDIA) AND AN OLDER POPULATION (GERMANY)

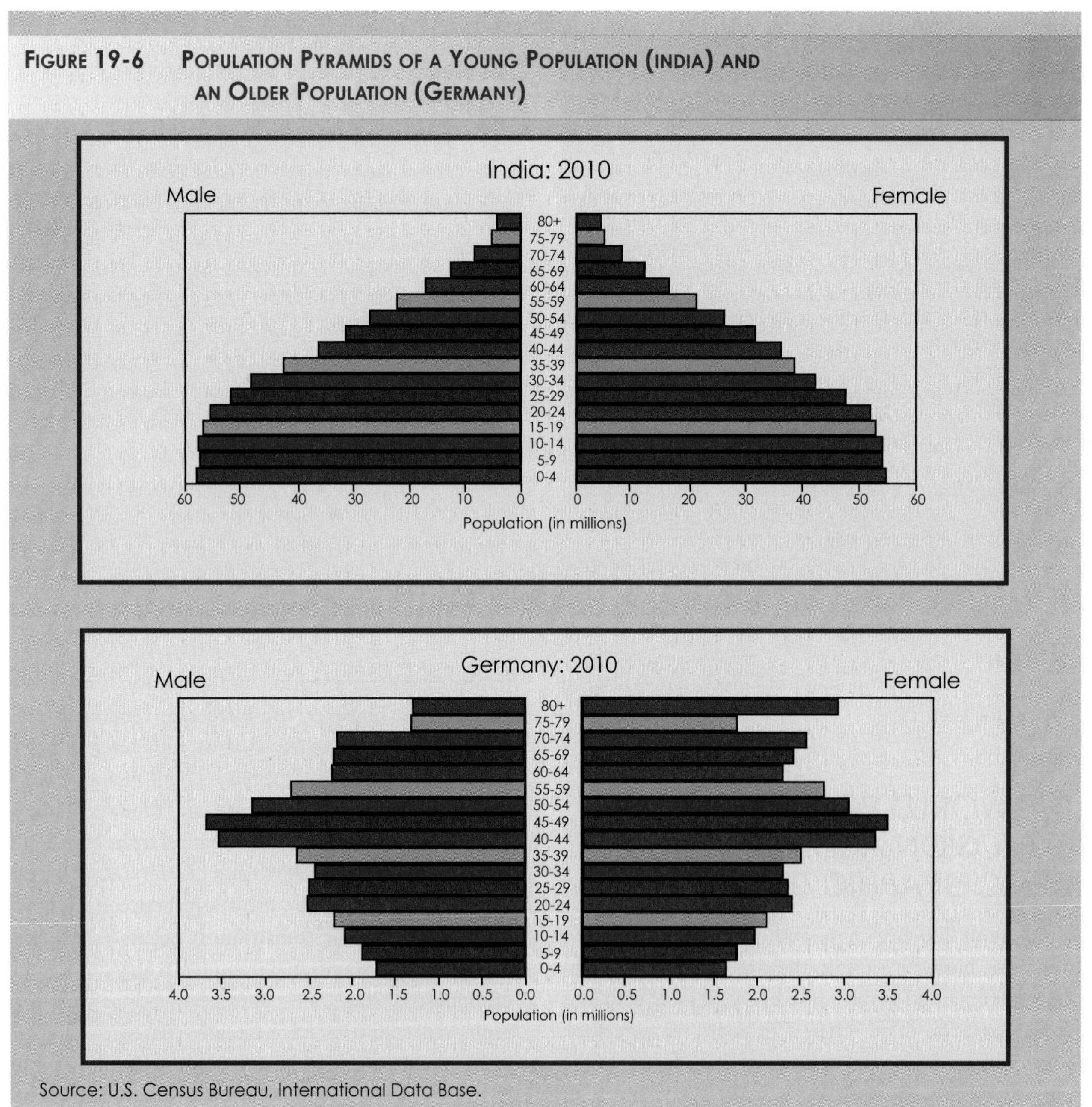

Source: U.S. Census Bureau, International Data Base.

among Hispanic immigrants. The population of the United States, currently around 315 million, is expected to rise to 478 million by 2100. Still, this pales to the projected increase in some countries in Africa, such as Nigeria currently at around 165 million and expected to reach 730 million by century's end (Gillis and Dugger 2011). (See Figures 19-7A and 19-7B.)

Population Density

The population explosion has dramatically increased the number of people in the world, but migrations have not distributed people evenly over the face of the earth. Whereas the population is sparse in many areas of the world, in some regions it is extremely dense. Such areas cannot provide the natural resources needed to maintain their population.

Population density is measured as the number of people per unit area, such as square kilometer or square mile (Rosenberg 2011). The measure can sometimes be confusing, as it is not necessarily related to the size of the population. (See Table 19-3.) The United States, although it has absorbed millions of immigrants, has a relatively low population density. In some remote areas, the density is only five people per square mile. In major cities during the business day, on the other hand, the population density is as high as 100,000 people per square mile. For the entire United States, the density is 83.38 people per square mile (*www.worldatlas.com, 2010*).

The other highly industrialized nations of the world have a higher population density than the United States. In Europe, it is very high. The developing nations are less densely populated than European countries, but they are not highly industrialized and therefore have less wealth to support them. China, the largest nation in the world, now has a population of more than one billion people, but its area is so great that its population density is only 361 people per square mile. There are places in the developing world where the population density is so very high that the land cannot begin to support the human life in the area, and the poverty is devastating.

Population and Ecology

How large a population can survive on the earth's resources? The study of the interrelationships between living organisms and the environment is called **ecology**. In the case of human beings, the concern is that the environment will not be able to support human life with the necessary food, water, and other basic necessities if the population should get too large.

Interestingly, theories about the relationship between population and the environment were initially developed during a period when it was feared that there were too few people to produce what society needed. Between 1450 and 1750, European traders were exporting Europe's products in exchange for gold and silver. In some areas, however, one-third to one-half of the population had been killed by

Although the world's population has dramatically increased over the last 200 years, people are not distributed evenly over the face of the earth. For example, in China, where there are more than 1 billion people, the population density is only 306 people per square mile due to the country's large size; in many smaller countries, on the other hand, the population density is so great, the land cannot support the people.

POLICY DEBATE

Should Stricter Environmental Protection Measures Be Enacted?

As noted in the introduction to this chapter, measures to protect the environment through the regulation of consumer and industrial behavior have accomplished a great deal over the past few decades, but many feel that a great deal more is needed. A variety of environmental protection groups, scientists, and politicians have suggested that further regulatory steps be taken and include the following:

- Ban chlorofluorocarbons (CFCs) and other ozone-depleting chemicals.
- Enforce air-quality standards established by the Clean Air Act.
- Insist upon stringent vehicle emission standards, and require auto manufacturers to produce cars that can yield at least forty miles per gallon of gasoline.
- Reduce the number of miles people drive by requiring car-pooling.
- Ban, highly restrict, or reformulate products that are environmentally unsound, gasoline-powered lawn mowers, charcoal lighter fluid, some kinds of deodorants, polystyrene foam (Styrofoam™), varnishes, adhesives, and hundreds of other products.
- Require rapid reductions in sulfur emissions.

There are many other regulatory measures like these that many consider to be necessary to prevent further environmental destruction (Melville 1988). Yet, despite Americans' heightened environmental consciousness, there still is considerable debate as to whether the government should impose stricter environmental regulations on consumer and industrial behavior. Perhaps this is because many of the proposed environmental regulations would significantly affect both consumer and industrial behavior.

Opponents of strict environmental regulation believe that the aforementioned types of measures would seriously damage the economy and, thus, lead to a decline in our standard of living. It would be very costly in terms of money, time, and reorganization for industries to meet some of the stricter environmental regulations. Opponents, therefore, contend that the cost and complexity of complying with stricter environmental regulations would discourage investment, hinder the construction of new plants, cut into profits, create unemployment, lead to a loss of production, and generally curtail economic growth (Currie and Skolnick 1997).

Advocates of strict environmental regulation argue that putting short-term corporate profits ahead of a cleaner environment is dangerously shortsighted. For example, in 1974, scientists warned of the dangers to the ozone layer that result from the chemicals—such as CFCs—used in aerosol sprays and other products. For many years, manufacturers of CFCs dismissed the warnings as speculative and fought proposed government legislation to restrict their usage on the grounds that eliminating them would lead to serious economic losses. In 1985, however, when a hole in the ozone layer was discovered over Antarctica, the public took notice. CFCs began being phased out of production, nearly two decades after scientists' warnings. The result of acting nearly two decades too late, according to advocates of stricter environmental regulations, is that humans are exposed to higher levels of dangerous ultraviolet rays (Melville 1988).

While most opponents of environmental regulation would probably agree that we would all be better off with a cleaner environment, they contend that a certain amount of pollution and environmental destruction is an unavoidable by-product of

the plague. Many writers argued that if the population were larger, there would be a better ecological balance. More products could be produced and exported, which would bring more gold and silver to the merchants. If the population were large enough, labor would be cheap, wages could be kept low, the people would have little to spend, and increases in imports would not be needed. Thus, all increased production could be traded for gold, silver, or merchandise valuable to the traders.

The political activity of this period was designed to encourage a high birth rate. The birth rate did increase, and by 1750, writers had begun to worry about overpopulation. The most famous of this second group of writers was Thomas Malthus.

Malthus's Theory of Population

Thomas Robert Malthus (1766–1834) argued in his *Essay on the Principle of Population* that because of the strong attraction between the two sexes, the population could increase by multiples, doubling every twenty–five years. According to **Malthusian theory**, the population would increase much more rapidly than the food supply. That is, the population would increase in a geometric progression, as illustrated by the numbers 2, 4, 8, 16, 32, and so on, while the food supply would increase in an arithmetical progression as illustrated by the numbers 1, 2, 3, 4, 5, and so on. The predicted result was a runaway population growth with insufficient food to feed the exploding industrial society. This is part of the price that must be paid for a high standard of living. Opponents feel that the economic dislocation that would be caused by strict environmental regulation would have negative consequences not only for industry but also for all of society. For example, the taxes that large corporations pay help to support public schools, public hospitals, fire departments, police departments, and many other services. In many communities, most of the tax base to support these services is provided by large corporations. Decreased profits for industry would mean that less tax money would be collected and, thus, less money would be available for public services. In order to maintain the same level of service, the tax burden would have to be passed on to the citizens. Opponents of stricter regulation contend that the problem would be even worse for poor people in underdeveloped nations that now can benefit from the economic and technological growth associated with industrialization.

Advocates maintain that while environmental regulation may involve short-range costs to the economy, the long-range economic impact actually is positive. A study conducted by the Council on Environmental Quality found that environmental controls would lower industrial productivity by only a minuscule amount and would entail one-time expenses (Currie and Skolnick 1997). While the cost of stricter environmental regulation could be significant, advocates say that there is no evidence that there would be substantial negative effects on investment. On the contrary, they suggest that environmental regulations carry the potential for increased economic growth. For example, an EPA study projected that unemployment would decrease slightly as a result of newly created jobs in antipollution-equipment industries and services. Another study, conducted by the Conservation Foundation, found no evidence that environmental regulations had caused industries to avoid locating in states with stricter regulations. As Currie and Skolnick note, "California, for example, which has very stringent environmental regulations, also had the largest gain in manufacturing jobs of any state during the 1970s" (1988, 345).

Finally, some opponents of stricter environmental regulation feel that this type of control is an unwarranted intrusion of the government into our lives and contradicts our free-market economy. They feel that government should not control individual behavior or private producers unless it is absolutely necessary (Melville 1988). Advocates of environmental regulation, however, say that it is absolutely necessary for the government to step in because it is unrealistic to trust the free market and consumers to make prudent decisions about environmental effects.

numbers of people. Malthus believed that the more intensively land was farmed, the less the land would produce, and that even by expanding farmlands, food production would not keep up with population growth. Malthus contended that the population would eventually grow so large that food production would be insufficient, and famine and crowding would cause widespread suffering and would increase the death rate—acting as nature's check on overpopulation. Malthus suggested, as an alternative, that the birth rate be decreased, especially through postponing marriage until a later age.

Malthusian theory created much debate. Writers such as John Stuart Mill and the economist John Maynard Keynes supported his theory. Others have argued against it. Karl Marx, for example, contended that starvation was caused by the unequal distribution of the wealth and its accumulation by capitalists.

During the depression of the 1930s, the debate changed because the birth rate fell sharply in industrial nations. Some predicted that the human species would die out—first the Caucasians, then other races. Schemes were proposed to encourage families to have more children by giving them allowances for each child born. Many economists, however, believed that even in societies with smaller populations, people could prosper and industry could grow if the provided wealth were redistributed to poor families to increase consumption. Government spending on programs for the poor and unemployed could be increased;

FIGURE 19-7A WORLD POPULATION GROWTH

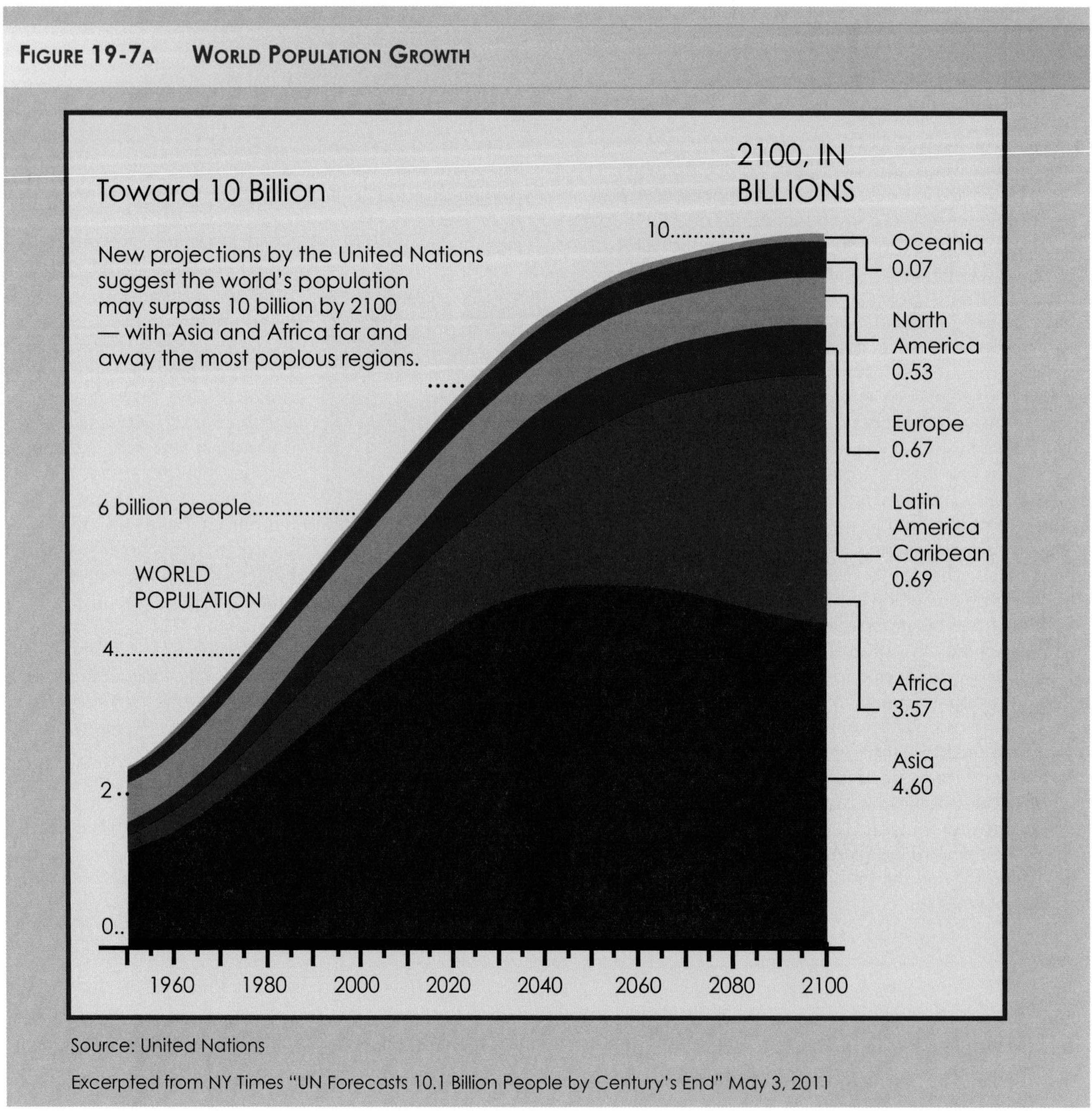

Source: United Nations

Excerpted from NY Times "UN Forecasts 10.1 Billion People by Century's End" May 3, 2011

and low interest rates could be used to encourage spending on houses, cars, and other consumer goods.

The birth rate rose sharply after World War II, especially in the underdeveloped nations; people starved in Bangladesh, Africa, and India. Birth control programs were instituted, and it was argued that the only way to eliminate starvation was to reduce the birth rate. Malthusian theory became popular once again. Malthus's contention that food production could not increase rapidly was much debated when new technology began to give farmers much greater yields. Malthus's contentions were revised. The **neo-Malthusian theory** developed, revising his theory to include more information—such as taking into account the effects of technology—but still predicting the fact that population cannot grow indefinitely without dire consequences.

The debate nevertheless continues, and some social thinkers continue to believe that population explosion is not necessarily a threat. The French sociologist

FIGURE 19-7B WORLD POPULATION GROWTHGROWTH BY SELECTED COUNTRIES

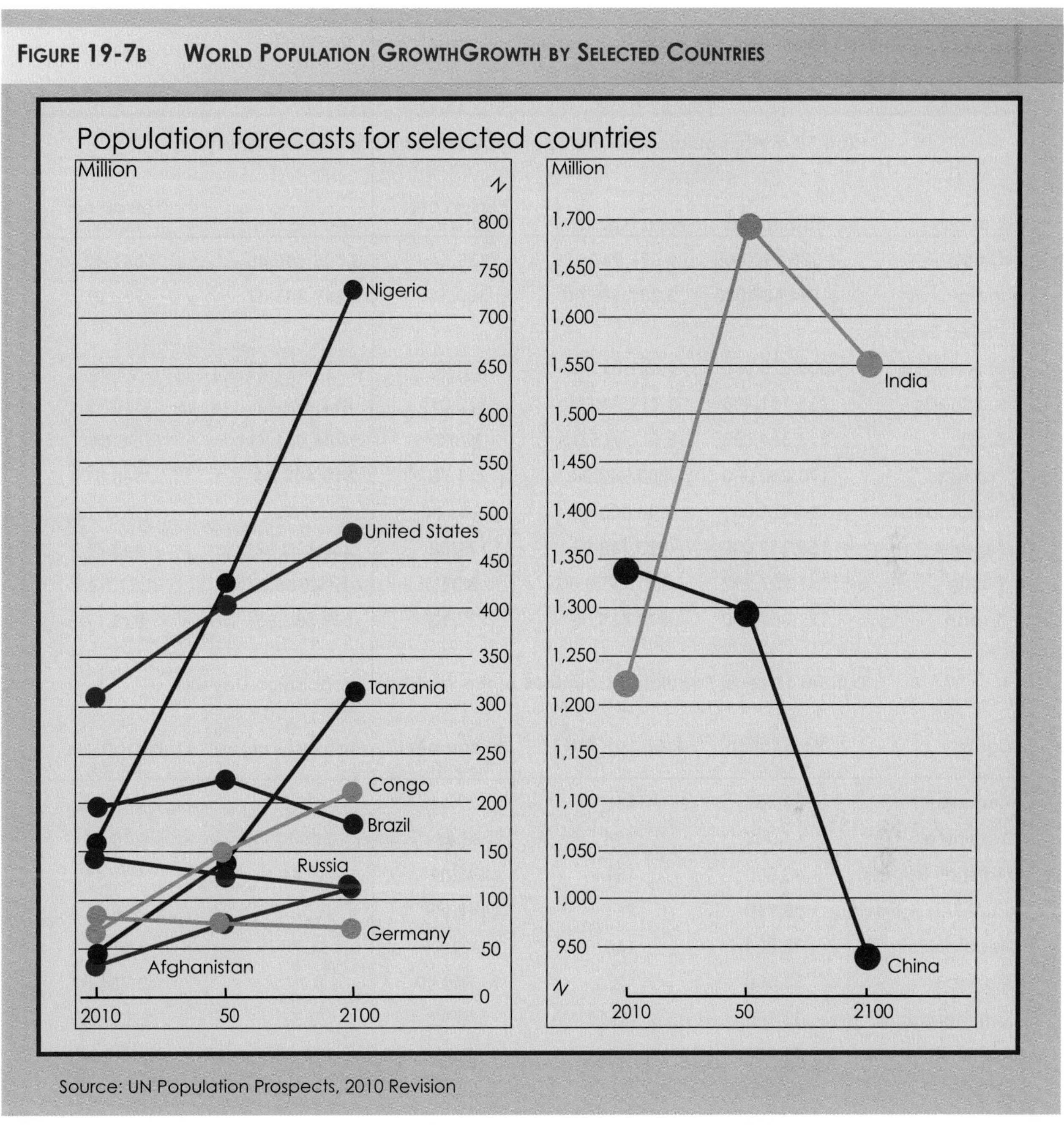

Source: UN Population Prospects, 2010 Revision

Dupreel (1977) argued that an increasing population would spur rapid innovation and development to solve problems, whereas a stable population would be complacent and less likely to progress.

World Food Distribution Today

Before World War II, Africa, India, and Asia exported grain to other nations, primarily to the industrial nations of Europe (George 1977). Why, then, are people in these underdeveloped nations starving today?

Some analysts argue that the land in overpopulated areas has been farmed too intensively to provide food for large populations and thus has been ruined. Even the United States, with its comparatively low population density, has lost 10–15 percent of its farmland through soil erosion since the time of the European immigration (Humphrey and Buttel 1982). In

TABLE 19-3 THE 10 MOST AND 10 LEAST POPULATED COUNTRIES OF THE WORLD AND THEIR POPULATION DENSITY, 2010

Top 10 Most Populated Countries of the World and Population Density

Country	Population	Area (sq. km.)	Person per sq. km.	Area (sq. mi.)	Person per sq mi.
China	1,339,190,000	9,596,960.00	139.54	3,705,405.45	361.42
India	1,184,639,000	3,287,590.00	360.34	1,269,345.07	933.27
United States of America	309,975,000	9,629,091.00	32.19	3,717,811.29	83.38
Indonesia	234,181,400	1,919,440.00	122.01	741,099.62	315.99
Brazil	193,364,000	8,511,965.00	22.72	3,286,486.71	58.84
Pakistan	170,260,000	803,940.00	211.78	310,402.84	548.51
Bangladesh	164,425,000	144,000.00	1,141.84	55,598.69	2,957.35
Nigeria	158,259,000	923,768.00	171.32	356,668.67	443.71
Russia	141,927,297	17,075,200.00	8.31	6,592,768.87	21.53
Japan	127,380,000	377,835.00	337.13	145,882.85	873.17

Bottom 10 Least Populated Countries of the World and Population Density

Country	Population	Area (sq. km.)	Person per sq. km.	Area (sq. mi.)	Person per sq mi.
Andorra	84,082	468	179.66	180.7	465.32
Dominica	67,000	754	88.86	291.12	230.14
Marshall Islands	63,000	181	348.07	69.88	901.49
Saint Kitts & Nevis	38,960	261	149.27	100.77	386.61
Liechtenstein	35,904	160	224.4	61.78	581.19
Monaco	33,000	2	16,500.00	0.77	42,734.82
San Marino	32,386	61	530.92	23.55	1,375.07
Palau	20,000	458	43.67	176.83	113.1
Tuvalu	10,000	26	384.62	10.04	996.15
Nauru	10,000	21	476.19	8.11	1,233.33
Vatican City	800	1	800	0.39	2,071.99

Source: World Atlas, www.worldatlas.com

parts of Asia, Latin America, and Africa, the problem is much worse because overuse of the land is causing it to deteriorate very rapidly. In Africa, the size of the Sahara Desert is estimated to be decreasing by thirty miles a year because the land cannot sustain the population using it.

Other observers of the world food situation have criticized American corporations for creating the world

TABLE 19-4 2000 AND 2009 CRUDE BIRTH RATES AND DEATH RATES FOR SELECTED COUNTRIES (BIRTHS PER 1,000 POPULATION)

Country	Birth Rates 2000	Birth Rates 2009	Death Rates 2000	Death Rates 2009
Afghanistan	41.82	45.46	18.01	19.18
Argentina	18.59	17.94	7.59	7.41
Australia	13.08	12.47	7.12	6.74
China	16.12	14	6.73	7.06
Denmark	12.16	10.54	11	10.22
Egypt	25.38	21.7	7.83	5.08
Finland	10.8	10.38	9.73	10.07
France	12.27	12.57	9.14	8.56
Greece	9.82	9.45	9.64	10.51
Israel	19.32	19.77	6.22	5.43
Italy	9.13	8.18	9.99	10.72
Japan	9.96	7.64	8.15	9.54
Libya	27.68	26.15	3.51	3.45
Mexico	23.15	19.71	5.05	4.8
Netherlands	12.12	10.14	8.72	8.74
Panama	19.53	20.18	4.95	4.66
Romania	10.76	10.53	12.29	11.88
South Africa	24.56	19.93	14.69	16.99
Sweden	10.01	10.13	10.62	10.21
United States	14.2	13.82	8.7	8.38

Source: Index Mundi, http://www.indexmundi.com

food shortage. They contend that because we had a surplus of grain, we encouraged underdeveloped nations to grow nonfood cash crops, such as cotton and rubber, or nonnutritious foods, such as coffee, tea, and sugar. The United States would lend money and supply fertilizer and farm equipment only to nations that agreed to grow products needed in the United States. In Brazil, for example, the United States encouraged soybean production, while American corporations own all the soybean-processing plants and receive most of the profit from soybean production.

Overuse of land in areas, including the U.S., Africa, India, and Asia, has led to deterioration and starving populations. The Sahara Desert in northern Africa is estimated to be decreasing by 30 miles each year because the land cannot sustain the population using it.

In the past few decades, many underdeveloped nations have become increasingly dependent on American grain imports because they use their own land for nonfood products. In the 1970s, the price of grains rose dramatically, and critics argue that the United States, having acquired a monopoly of the food supply, increased prices to make enormous profits. Today, the cash crops grown by other nations cannot be sold at prices high enough to buy all the grain needed from the United States. Thus, poor people everywhere starve because they do not have land on which to grow food or the money to buy food, even when enough food is produced in the world to feed its entire population.

Population and Other Natural Resources

Food production and distribution is only one of the problems that occurs as the world population increases. As was noted in the introduction to this chapter, environmental problems are serious in nature and global in scope. Humans need water just as we need food, and the earth's large human population is rapidly polluting the available water. Waste from modern life, including the many chemicals that are now produced each year, find their way into small streams and large seas, making the water unfit for human consumption. It also makes water unfit for fish, thereby reducing the hope of turning to the sea for a source of additional food.

The increase in the world population is affecting natural resources such as forests, which are rapidly being cut down to provide fuel, houses, furniture, and other products, as well as to make room for people. Such loss of natural resources negatively affects the ecological balance between the earth and the atmosphere, which in turn will cause conflict as people fight to survive the negative effects.

The increased population also affects the air we breathe. As the population increases, more and more rural areas become densely settled; and atmospheric pollution is exacerbated by the toxic elements emanating from cars, planes, industrial smoke, and other sources. Almost every human activity generates dust; when these particles become airborne, they seed the clouds and increase the rainfall. On the east coast, especially in Canada and New England in recent years, pollution from midwestern industries has caused acid rain to fall, killing fish and changing the composition of the land on which it falls. Another pollution-related problem is that as the cloud cover increases with airborne pollutants, it has a *greenhouse effect*, holding warmth from the sun close to the earth rather than letting it escape into the upper atmosphere. As a result, some scientists suggest that the climate of the earth will become warmer and icebergs may even begin to melt, which could raise the sea level and flood coastal areas.

Our forests are also being rapidly depleted. Trees are cut down to make room for people, to provide fuel, and to provide wood for houses, furniture, and other products. The loss of forests not only means the loss of these wood products, it also affects the ecological balance between the earth and the atmosphere. In particular, plants consume an excess of carbon dioxide and give off an excess of oxygen; this crucially affects the ratio of oxygen to carbon dioxide in the air we breathe.

As these natural resources are lost—and the loss will be rapid if we do not use resources wisely—conflict will occur. People who lack the necessary resources to survive will fight those who do have resources. Although conflict in the world is usually expressed in political terms, these conflicts are not based on political ideology. They are conflicts over scarce resources. The United States involvement in the Middle East is motivated largely by our desire to safeguard our supplies of oil. Latin American countries such as El Salvador and Nicaragua cannot provide for the peasants who have been driven off their land by the larger agriculturalists—a dilemma that induces revolution. As suggested by conflict theory, if revolutions and inequalities are to be eliminated, increasing population must be accompanied by an end to the unregulated freedom to pursue wealth and a more equitable rationing of the world's scarce resources.

Note the discussion of environmental protection measures in the policy debate.

Thinking Sociologically

Suppose that you were hired by an environmental protection group to help lobby for stricter environmental regulation. How could you use knowledge of demography and population to help in gathering public support for environmental protection?

Political Policies Regarding Population

Although a more even distribution of resources would solve some of the world's hunger problems, and careful planning would help us to preserve what resources we still have, ultimately, our population must be controlled. The current policies of most governments are now aimed at reducing the birth rate to improve the standard of living. After World War II, Japan initiated a program legalizing abortion and encouraging contraception. Soon afterward, India and most other Asian nations began such programs. In spite of programs to discourage births, however, many nations still experienced a population explosion. China toughened its policies most severely, limiting Chinese families to having only one child.

In the 1960s, the United States began to offer millions of dollars worth of contraceptive aids, especially intrauterine devices and birth control pills, to underdeveloped countries that requested help in controlling their populations. The federal government also provided funds to states to open family-planning clinics and disseminate information about contraceptives in this country. These programs have succeeded in reducing birth rates in many nations, but they have also been severely criticized, for several reasons.

First, some of the contraceptive methods used in underdeveloped nations are those considered unsafe and banned in the United States. Users in other countries, not warned of the dangers, unknowingly risk infection, heart attacks, strokes, and death when they use these contraceptives. Second, lowering the birth rate in underdeveloped nations deprives parents of children, who are an asset in rural areas. They can help carry water and grow food on family plots and care for their parents in illness and old age. Thus, the policies implemented to reduce poverty in industrial nations could well increase poverty for families living in some rural areas. When planning policy, it is crucial to consider all the factors at work in the countries that will be affected.

Zero Population Growth

The goal of current world population policy is **zero population growth**, which is achieved when parents have only two children, just enough to replace themselves. If this practice were followed, the population would remain the same generation after generation. In reality, of course, some people do not have children, and some children die before reaching adulthood; so zero population growth could be attained if couples averaged slightly more than two children each. Given current rates of infant mortality and the number of women who actually have children, the population would remain stable if couples averaged 2.1 children. In the United States, the rate has been steady at 1.9, below the zero growth rate. Many underdeveloped nations have much higher birth rates, however, so the world population explosion is continuing. Increasing population and associated ecological problems will continue to be crucial issues in the future. A more equal and careful distribution of resources is essential to preventing starvation and pollution. This relationship between population and ecology illustrates the need for a scoliotical understanding of the interrelationships between population size and social institutions.

Thinking Sociologically

1. Predict what the future would be like, both the good and the bad, if all birth control and abortion were eliminated from the world.
2. Predict what the future would be like, both the good and the bad, if the entire world achieved zero population growth.

CHAPTER REVIEW

Wrapping it up

Summary

Check out our website www.bvtstudents.com for free chapter-by-chapter flashcards, summaries, and self-quizzes.

1. *Demography* is the study of population statistics. Demographers study census data on the number of people in the population and records of births and deaths to compute the birth and death rates.
2. The crude birth and death rates are computed by determining the number of births and deaths per one thousand people. Neither of these measures takes age or sex into account, but these factors also influence the number of births and deaths.
3. Populations remain stable when people are born at the same rate at which they die. Population increases when the birth rate exceeds the death rate and decreases when the death rate exceeds the birth rate.
4. Populations may also change through migration. Push factors are conditions that encourage people to move out of an area; pull factors encourage people to move into an area.
5. The size of the population affects each of us quite personally. Whether we are born into a growing or a shrinking population has a bearing on our education, the age at which we marry, our ability to get a job, the taxes we pay, and many other aspects of our lives.
6. The population explosion of the past two hundred years occurred because of improvements in nutrition and sanitation, which lowered the death rate. In industrial nations, the birth rate has also dropped, but rapid population growth continues in many Third World countries.
7. Population densities vary greatly in different parts of the world. Generally, the most densely populated countries are industrialized nations of Europe and Japan.
8. *Ecology* is the interrelationship between organisms and their environment.
9. Malthusian theory states that because the population grows faster than the food supply, starvation is inevitable if population growth is not controlled. Although his arguments have received much support through the years, critics contend that the world produces enough food to feed everyone and the problem arises because food is distributed unequally.
10. Some underdeveloped nations raise cash crops that neither feed the people nor bring in enough money to buy food. Some observers believe that the United States, which is the world's largest food exporter, encouraged other countries to grow nonfood cash crops and then, having cornered the grain market, raised prices to increase profits.

11. Other problems affecting food production vis-à-vis population stem from pollution of the air and water and the destruction of forests.
12. Most nations are now attempting to reduce their birth rates, and contraceptives have been distributed throughout the world for this purpose.
13. The goal of world population policy is zero population growth, calculated to be an average of 2.1 children per family.

Key Terms

age-adjusted death rate The number of deaths occurring at each age for each sex, per 100,000 people of that age who are living

age-sex composition The number of men and women in the population, along with their ages

census An official count of the number of people in a given area

demographic transition The change from high birth and death rates to low birth and death rates with a period of rapid population growth in between (This transition occurs as a society evolves from a traditional premodern stage to a modern industrial stage.)

demography The statistical study of population, especially data on birth rates, death rates, marriage rates, health, and migration

ecology The study of the interrelationships between living organisms and the environment

emigration Movement of people out of an area

fecundity A woman's potential for bearing children

fertility A measure of the rate at which people are being born

Going green The phrase that defines people who are mindful of what they consume, mindful of others, and who are working towards protecting the ecology both nationally and internationally

immigration Movement of people into an area

Malthusian theory The theory proposed by Thomas Malthus stating that population expands much faster than the food supply, resulting in starvation for much of the population when it grows too large

marriage squeeze The effects of an imbalance between the number of males and females in the prime marriage ages due to rising or falling birth rates and the median age differences at marriage

migration Movement of people into or out of an area

mortality A measure of the rate at which people die

neo-Malthusian theory Revisions of Malthusian theory about food production and population growth that include more information, such as taking into account the effects of technology

pull factors Natural or social factors that cause people to move into an area

push factors Natural or social factors that cause people to move out of an area

vital statistics Records of all births, deaths and their causes, marriages, divorces, and certain diseases in a society

zero population growth A population policy that encourages parents to have no more than two children to limit the growth of the population

Discussion Questions

1. Discuss how the age and sex of a population can affect its fertility and mortality rates.
2. Based on the conflict perspective, discuss how migration can maintain the position of elites in a society.
3. Based on a functionalist viewpoint, describe when a high fertility rate would be functional and when it would not be.
4. What are some factors that could lead to rapid changes in the rate of population change? Using this information, what kinds of changes do you

predict in the rate of population change in your lifetime?

5. Assume that because of increasing rates of cancer and AIDS, the life expectancy of the United States declines dramatically. How would that change society when you reach age sixty?

6. If the world were purely capitalist, what would happen to the rates of starvation in the world? Why? What if it were purely socialist?

7. Discuss all of the ways in which your life has been shaped by the year of your birth and the number of people your age.

8. Discuss how the relationship between population and ecology is evident today.

Pop Quiz

1. The first census in the United States was carried out in ______.

a. 1776
b. 1790
c. 1800
d. 1850

2. Records of all births, deaths and their causes, marriages, divorces, and similar data are called ______.

a. census data
b. vital statistics
c. demographic statistics
d. the age-sex composition

3. A measure of the rate at which people are born in a society is the society's ______.

a. demography
b. fertility
c. mortality
d. fecundity

4. The number of males and females in a population, along with their age, is called the ______.

a. age-sex composition
b. gender breakdown
c. gender role
d. age-adjusted mortality rate

5. The number of deaths at each age for each sex is the ______.

a. mortality rate
b. crude death rate
c. crude mortality rate
d. age-adjusted death rate

6. The rate of death in the first year of life is the ______.

a. crude death rate
b. infant mortality rate
c. age-adjusted death rate
d. all of the above

7. Movement into an area is called ______.

a. migration
b. emigration
c. immigration
d. demographic transition

8. A graph that shows the distribution of a given population by age and sex is a ______.

a. age-sex ratio
b. demographic transition
c. population pyramid
d. population density

9. The study of the interrelationships between living organisms and their environment is called ______.

a. demography
b. sociology
c. methodology
d. ecology

10. When parents have only two children to replace themselves, they have achieved ______.

    a. demographic transition
    b. cohort transition
    c. population density
    d. zero population growth

11. Fecundity is a measure of the rate at which people are born. T/F

12. The 2000 U.S. Census was criticized for underreporting people. T/F

13. Loss of jobs, famine, and war are examples of a pull factor. T/F

14. The demographic transition suggests that the population explosion occurs in the industrialized countries today. T/F

15. The greenhouse effect measures population density. T/F

1. B	6. B	11. F
2. B	7. C	12. T
3. B	8. C	13. F
4. A	9. D	14. F
5. D	10. D	15. F

CHAPTER 20

The Changing Community

POLICE
GARRETT

HOMELESSNESS

Homelessness can occur anywhere—in any section of the country, in any city, in any neighborhood. Although a great deal of media attention has focused on homelessness in recent years, it is not a new social issue. It has been traced as far back as the Middle Ages in Europe and, at least, to the colonial era in America (Schutt 1990; Wright 1989). What is relatively new, however, is the character of homelessness. Up until fairly recently, the homeless typically consisted mostly of people. Today, the homeless may be a suburban family whose breadwinners have lost their jobs and lost their homes to foreclosure. They might be living with relatives or at a shelter (Katel 2009).

Consider some of the findings from The State of Homelessness, a 2011 report from The National Alliance to End Homelessness examining changes in homelessness between 2008 and 2009 (Sermons and White 2011):

- The homeless population in the U.S. increased by twenty thousand, a 3 percent increase. As of 2009, there were more than 650,000 homeless people in the U.S.
- Thirty-one of fifty states (including the District of Columbia) had increases in homelessness, with Louisiana having the highest increase where homelessness doubled. (See Figure 20-1.)
- The highest increase in homelessness occurred for family households (rather than individuals), an increase of thirty-two hundred households (a 4 percent increase). The number of homeless people within families increased by more than six thousand people (a 3 percent increase). Mississippi experienced a 260 percent increase of the number of people in homeless families. (See Figure 20-2.)
- Nearly four in ten people were living on the street, in a car or in other areas not intended for human habitation, In Wisconsin, the number of homeless living outside of a shelter had doubled.
- There is a vast undercount of the number of people who are homeless.

While not the only reason, the increased cost of housing in conjunction with an economy that has undergone a crisis is major contributing factors to the increase in homelessness. According to The State of Homelessness Report, housing is generally considered affordable when it accounts for 30 percent or less of household income. U.S. renters spend, on average, around 40 percent of their income on rent, with low-income families spending more than 50 percent on rent. When housing accounts for such a significant portion of one's income, any disruption to a family's financial situation could result in a housing crisis for that family. The conditions in four important economic indicators have worsened considerably in recent years, thus exacerbating the homelessness problem. (See Table 20-1.)

Sociologists are particularly interested in explaining the growth of homelessness and in debunking the myths about the homeless. Some of the more common myths are that people are homeless because they are mentally impaired, alcoholics and/or other drug abusers, and lazy, and that they have a choice about their homeless condition. As James Wright states, "Some of the homeless are broken-down alcoholics, but most are not. Some are mentally impaired, but most are not. Some are living off the benefit programs made available through the social welfare system, but most are not" (Wright 1989, 46). There are a number of interrelated and complex reasons for homelessness today that go beyond the popular stereotypes about the homeless and that have been addressed in many books and articles written by sociologists and other social scientists. Most agree that the most basic reasons for homelessness include an insufficient supply of affordable housing, an increase in the poverty rate, a deterioration of the purchasing power of welfare benefits, and a decrease in social supports to help the poor establish themselves (Schutt 1990; Wright 1989). These reasons certainly characterize the increase in homelessness in recent years.

The issue of homelessness is relevant to many areas of sociology—for example, stratification, political systems, economic systems, and minority groups. It is particularly relevant to this chapter because the growth and change of urban communities are partially responsible for homelessness. In order to help overcome the myths about homelessness and to help address the homelessness issue, it is important to understand the structure and process of the community, as well as other areas of sociological concern.

FIGURE 20-1 TOTAL HOMELESS POPULATION BY STATE

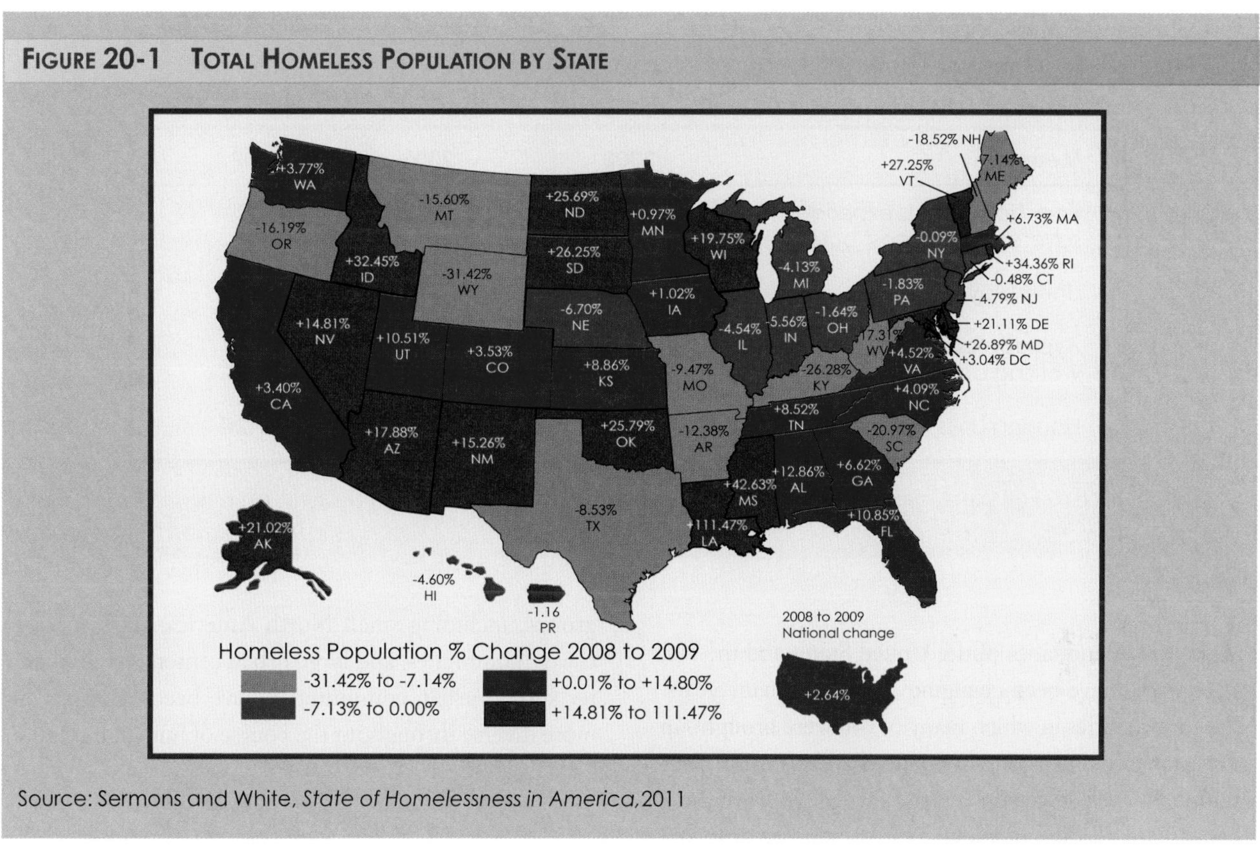

Source: Sermons and White, *State of Homelessness in America*, 2011

FIGURE 20-2 FAMILY HOMELESS POPULATION BY STATE

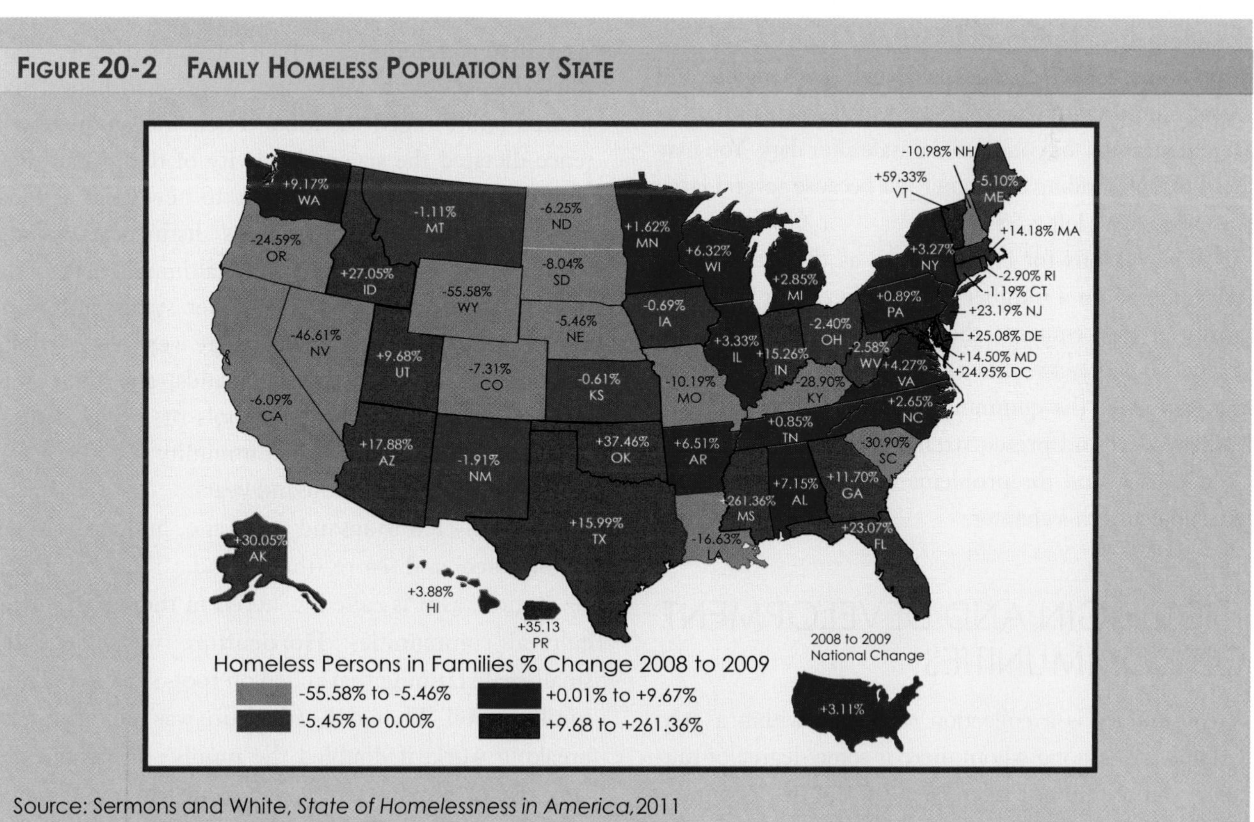

Source: Sermons and White, *State of Homelessness in America*, 2011

TABLE 20-1 NATIONAL CHANGES AMONG ECONOMIC INDICATORS

Measure	2008	2009	2009
Poor households experiencing severe housing cost burden	5,398,379	5,886,293	+9.0%
Unemployed persons	8,924,000	14,265,000	+59.9%
Average annual income of working poor people	$9,353	$9,151	-2.16%
Housing units in foreclosure	2,330,483	2,824,674	+21.2%

SOURCE : SERMONS AND WHITE, STATE OF HOMELESSNESS IN AMERICA, 2011

The towns and cities of the United States and the rest of the world have been changing rapidly for many years. The communities in which many of you were brought up have probably undergone dramatic changes during your lifetime, or even since you entered college. Some of these changes are readily apparent: one of your favorite old buildings may have been razed to make way for a new office complex, or perhaps a new park has been created near your home. Other changes, although less tangible, are equally important. The streets on which you played on as a child may now be considered unsafe after dark. You may have trouble finding a summer job because several large businesses have left your city.

The reasons for changes such as these are many. We touched on a number of them in earlier chapters. Form of government, the family, changing gender roles, bureaucracies, and ethnicity—the list of factors that influence the communities in which we live in is endless. Past and present trends in community living, their causes, and the problems they have brought are the subject of this chapter.

THE ORIGIN AND DEVELOPMENT OF COMMUNITIES

A **community** is a collection of people within a geographic area among whom there is some degree of mutual identification, interdependence, or organized activity. Sociologists apply this term to a variety of social groups, including small North American Indian tribes, towns, communes, and large urban centers. As this chapter shows, urban communities have become larger and more diverse throughout the course of human history.

Early Community and Urban Development

The first communities, which originated more than thirty-five thousand years ago, were small bands that hunted and foraged for food. Their means of subsistence dictated the size and activity of the group; they were *nomadic*, moving frequently to new areas as food ran out. There were few status distinctions among members of these communities, although males and older persons had somewhat higher status and more power than others. Apparently, there were few conflicts among hunting-and-gathering bands, and there was little evidence of war-making tools or group attacks. This rather idyllic form of community predominated for about twenty-five thousand years.

Roughly ten thousand years ago, humans learned to produce and store their food. This Neolithic revolution, as it is called, ushered in the era of horticultural communities. **Horticulture** was essentially small-scale farming that relied on tools such as the hoe to till the soil. Though horticulture was tedious, back-breaking work, it doubled the number of people the land could support—from one to nearly two persons per square mile (Davis 1973). Stable communities developed around fertile agricultural regions; and in the more fertile areas, a surplus of food was produced, which freed some members of the community from agricultural activities. As agricultural techniques improved, horticultural communities became larger and more diverse. Artisans who produced the tools and implements necessary for survival were the first specialists in history (Childe 1951). It was during this era, lasting about seven thousand years, that the first urban communities emerged.

Defining what constitutes an urban community is no simple task. Demographic definitions today are likely to use criteria such as a permanent settlement with a single name that is occupied by a specific minimum of residents. Other definitions, and one that we can use in this context of early urban development, is to define an urban community as one in which people are not primarily engaged in the collection or production of food. In terms of numbers or residents, the earliest cities, which developed along the fertile banks of the Tigris and Euphrates rivers in what is today known as Iraq, were small by modern standards. Cities could grow only as large as the food surplus allowed; that is, the release of a number of people from agriculture required that the remaining members produce more than before. Ancient Babylon, for example, had a population of twenty-five and covered roughly three square miles; Ur, one of the oldest known cities, had about five thousand people and covered less than a square mile (Davis 1970). Urban communities grew slowly for the next several thousand years because of the inefficiency of horticultural techniques—it took about fifty horticulturists to produce enough surplus to support one urban resident—and also because of the primitive political and social organization (Davis 1973).

Nomadic communities are frequently moving to new places as food runs out.

Preindustrial Urban Communities

The introduction of metals, the invention of the plow, the use of animals for transportation and farming, and the refinement of irrigation techniques helped usher in a new era in human history around 3000 BC—the Agrarian Age (Lenski 1966). The development of writing and counting and the evolution of political and social organizations were also essential to the spread of agrarian society. These technological advances increased surpluses so still more people were freed from agriculture. Cities grew larger and their activities became more diverse. Around 1600 BC, Thebes, the capital of Egypt, had a population of over two hundred thousand. Athens had a population of one hundred fifty thousand or so during the same period (Childe 1951). By AD 100, Rome had an estimated population of over five hundred thousand.

This trend of urban growth was not to continue, however. Rome fell in the fifth century AD and subsequent wars and plagues reduced the size of cities. The rate of agricultural innovation was slow because human energies were redirected toward the technology of war. The social system became more rigid; status and occupations were determined on the basis of heredity rather than achievement or ability.

In the eleventh century, cities, especially those along natural routes and junctures, began to flourish after feudal wars subsided. As the food surplus increased, the population in the cities became more specialized. In fourteenth-century Paris, for example, tax rolls listed 157 different trades (Russell 1972). In addition to artisans, cities also had specialists in other areas, such as government, military service, education, and religion. Each major urban activity led to the development of an institution devoted to its performance; and churches, shops, marketplaces, city halls, and palaces became the prominent features of medieval cities.

Community Development in the Industrial Era

It was not until the end of the eighteenth century that cities began to grow rapidly, due largely to the effects of the Industrial Revolution. The social and economic forces that converged at this time eventually changed Western Europe and later the United States from rural to urban societies. The growth of the number of people who live in urban rather than rural areas and the subsequent development of different values and lifestyles are referred to as **urbanization**. Agricultural innovations—crop rotation, soil fertilization, and the selective breeding of animals—brought larger and larger surpluses.

At the same time, the development of manufacturing in the cities attracted many people. As the nineteenth century progressed, cities became much larger and grew into centers of commerce and production; but at the same time, they were the locus of poverty and disease. Also, as migration from rural areas increased, the city population became more heterogeneous. The variety of occupations, ethnic backgrounds, dialects, and lifestyles in these urban areas stood in sharp contrast to the relatively homogeneous populations of small towns and rural communities.

Population diversity, poverty, cramped living quarters, inadequate garbage disposal and sewage facilities, and other social and economic problems placed a tremendous strain on the urban political order. Cities became centers of unrest. Riots and revolutions, strikes by workers, and numerous clashes among members of different social groups were a significant part of nineteenth-century urban history. Many of the problems that arose in European cities during this era persist, to some degree, in all Western nations and, in a different way, in Developing World nations.

Developing World Urbanization

Prior to 1900, urbanization outside of Western Europe and North America was limited in both scale and extent to colonial expansion. Throughout this century, however, the situation has been changing dramatically. During the past fifty years, while the urban population increased in the more developed regions of the world, the increase was most dramatic in Developing World countries, the least industrialized countries. In Latin America and Africa, for example, the urban population increased eightfold.

By the end of World War II, the colonial powers had relinquished control to the local governments of the colonies they had created. In each developing nation, one city became the focus of change and progress. Because these cities had improved health conditions and facilities, more jobs, and better education, they drew masses of people. The newly created governments, usually controlled by military juntas or other totalitarian regimes, were unable to keep pace with this rapid growth, however; and those who had moved from the country found that they had exchanged lives of rural poverty for lives of urban poverty.

Much of this Developing World urban growth became concentrated in what are called "squatter" settlements; people would settle temporarily—*squat*—along railways, highways, the banks of streams, or on vacant government land. Most major cities in developing countries have squatter areas: Manila in the Philippines; Calcutta, India; Lima, Peru; and Saigon, Vietnam. These areas (a) lacked all the basic amenities, (b) were physically decrepit and highly disorganized, and (c) became centers of squalor, illiteracy, sickness, and human depravity. However, they played an important role in solving the housing shortage and the other complex problems associated with migration from rural to urban centers. On closer examination, they were found to provide access to the jobs and services of the central city. Many squatter areas developed highly organized self-help efforts over a period of a few years. The residents gave shelter, security, and assistance to one another, and many of these settlements provided opportunities to continue rural values and ways of living, thereby easing the transition to the density and fast pace of the city.

To Western observers, the solution to these problem areas was to relocate them and provide housing, usually outside the central city limits. However, these solutions rarely solved the problems of most squatters because they involved heavy costs for investment (and interest), maintenance, and transportation and did not originate in the self-help efforts of the squatters themselves. Often funded by developed nations, these efforts tended to follow patterns established in the Western world, ignoring the values and priorities of the Developing World residents themselves. They also tended to overlook the importance of urban community services and failed to follow through on a long-term basis with a commitment to the residents themselves. These problems, which have existed in most Developing World countries throughout modern history, are more severe today than ever before because of rapid urban population growth.

This rapid urban population growth in the Developing World and elsewhere shows no sign of abatement either. Over 250 cities in the world have populations of a million or more. Five of the largest metropolises have over twenty million inhabitants each. In addition, we can see from Table 20-2 that most of the world's mega-cities are located in the Developing World. Given the extreme levels of poverty found in many of these large and densely populated areas, one may question whether solutions are available to deal with the enormous problems and whether living conditions can be made humane and livable. Topics related to this issue are addressed later in this chapter.

Most major cities in developing countries such as Calcutta, India have "squatter" settlements.

Thinking Sociologically

1. The introductory issue described homelessness, and the chapter text described squatter settlements. What similarities or differences exist between the homeless in the United States and squatters in Developing World countries?
2. How can living conditions be made humane in cities with ten, twenty, or thirty million people or in areas with a population density of more than one hundred thousand people in one square mile?

URBANIZATION IN THE UNITED STATES

Population Trends

The Industrial Revolution began approximately half a century later in the United States than it did in Western Europe. The major population shift from rural to urban areas did not begin here until the Civil War. An *urban area*, according to the United States Bureau of the Census, is a city or town that has at least twenty-five hundred inhabitants. In 1800, 6 percent of the population of the United States lived in urban areas. This figure rose to 20 percent by 1860. The period of greatest urban development took place during the sixty-year period between 1860 and 1920; by 1920, slightly more than half the population lived in urban areas. This figure has continued to increase. For example, the urban population of the United States increased from 222.3 million in 2000 to 234.8 million in 2009, an increase of 12.5 million or by 5.6 percent. However, it should be noted that even as the urban population is increasing in size, in recent years the *percent* of people living in urban populations is beginning to stabilize The percent urban population decreased from 79.0 percent in 2000 to 76.5 percent in 2009 (www.proximityone.com/urbanpopulation.htm). Table 20-3 shows the size of the ten largest cities in the United States in 2007 and the total U.S. population they shared.

Why do people live in cities? The answer is that an increasing number of jobs in our society are

TABLE 20-2 WORLD'S LARGEST CITIES (CITY AND SURROUNDING METROPOLITAN AREA POPULATIONS), 2011

World rank	City	Country	City population	Metro population
1	Karachi	Pakistan	15,500,000	18,000,000
2	Shanghai	China	14,900,000	19,200,000
3	Mumbai (Bombay)	India	13,900,000	21,200,000
4	BEIJING	China	12,460,000	17,550,000
5	DELHI	India	12,100,000	16,713,000
6	BUENOS AIRES	Argentina	11,655,000	12,924,000
7	MANILA METRO	Philippines	11,550,000	13,503,000
8	SEOUL	South Korea	11,153,000	24,472,000
9	Sao Paulo	Brazil	11,038,000	19,890,000
10	MOSCOW	Russia	10,524,000	14,800,000
11	JAKARTA	Indonesia	10,100,000	24,100,000
12	Istanbul	Turkey	9,560,000	12,600,000
13	BANGKOK	Thailand	9,100,000	11,970,000
14	MEXICO CITY	Mexico	8,841,000	21,163,000
15	TOKYO	Japan	8,653,000	31,036,000
16	TEHRAN	Iran	8,430,000	13,450,000
17	New York City	USA	8,364,000	20,090,000
18	KINSHASA	Congo D.R.	8,200,000	10,100,000
19	DHAKA	Bangladesh	7,940,000	12,797,000
20	Lagos	Nigeria	7,938,000	9,123,000
21	CAIRO	Egypt	7,764,000	15,546,000
22	LIMA	Peru	7,606,000	8,473,000
23	LONDON	UK	7,557,000	12,200,000
24	Tianjin	China	7,500,000	11,750,000
25	BOGOTA	Colombia	7,320,000	8,361,000

Source: www.citymajors.com

nonagricultural. Thus, the shift of the population from rural to urban areas has paralleled the growth of jobs and opportunities in the industrial and service sectors of the economy. Because of their early industrial and commercial development, northeastern states such as New York and Pennsylvania were among the first to urbanize. A few years later, midwestern cities such as Chicago and Detroit became large urban centers. The western states experienced strong urban growth only after World War II, as a result of the growth of the defense industries.

As of 2009, the West and South were the fastest-growing regions of the United States in terms of population. From 2000 to 2009, the population of the entire United States increased by 8.8 percent. However, the increase in the Northeast and Midwest was only around 3

TABLE 20-3 TEN LARGEST CITIES IN THE UNITED STATES, 2009

City	Population
New York, N.Y.	8,391,881
Los Angeles, Cal.	3,831,868
Chicago, Ill.	2,851,268
Houston, Tex.	2,257,926
Phoenix, Ariz.	1,601,587
Philadelphia, Pa.	1,547,297
San Antonio, Tex.	1,373,668
San Diego, Cal.	1,306,301
Dallas, Tex.	1,299,543
San Jose, Cal.	964, 695

Source: www.infoplease.com

percent whereas in the South and West it was over 12 percent (see Table 20-4). An increasingly aging population in the United States has led many older residents to seek a retirement community in states with warmer climates. In addition, a number of businesses have relocated in the Sunbelt because of the economic advantages this area offers—primarily low wage scales, few problems with unions, cheap land and energy, and low taxes.

One example of this shift was the decision of a number of automobile manufacturers to locate their new plants in the Southeast instead of the North and Midwest where they have been built for many decades. As history demonstrates, people want to move to areas that provide, or at least are perceived as providing, good employment opportunities. A number of Sunbelt businesses have attracted many skilled specialists to Sunbelt areas. This loss of industry and commerce in Snowbelt cities has decreased the tax base of numerous northern cities and states and has magnified their social and economic problems.

The Metropolitan Community

The large, densely populated cities of the early 1900s have given way to the growth of metropolitan areas. The U.S. Bureau of the Census describes a **metropolitan statistical area (MSA)** as a large population nucleus, together with adjacent communities that have a high degree of social and economic integration with that nucleus. The metropolitan community is the organization of people and institutions that performs the routine functions necessary to sustain the existence of both the city and the area around it.

The growth of metropolitan areas has been rapid and dramatic. Because of new developments in technology, in transportation, and in social structures, the concentration of large numbers of people has become possible. These same developments have also enabled a population dispersed over a wide area to become part of a larger, integrated community.

Metropolitan growth was caused initially by a shortage of space for industrial development, new housing, and new highways. Businesses were forced to design their facilities to fit the space that was available. Because streets were narrow and heavily congested, the transportation of goods was tedious and costly. Room for storage and loading was scarce. The land adjacent to the cities was ideal. It was inexpensive, property taxes were low, and businesses could design their facilities to suit their needs. The development of the steam engine and, later, the electric trolley facilitated the transportation of goods and employees over a wider area. After the 1920s, the increase in motor vehicles and the accompanying growth of highway systems stimulated unprecedented metropolitan development. Trucking became

The large, densely populated cities of the early 1900s have given way to the growth of metropolitan areas.

TABLE 20-4 PERCENT CHANGE IN POPULATION FOR REGIONS IN THE US,2000-2009

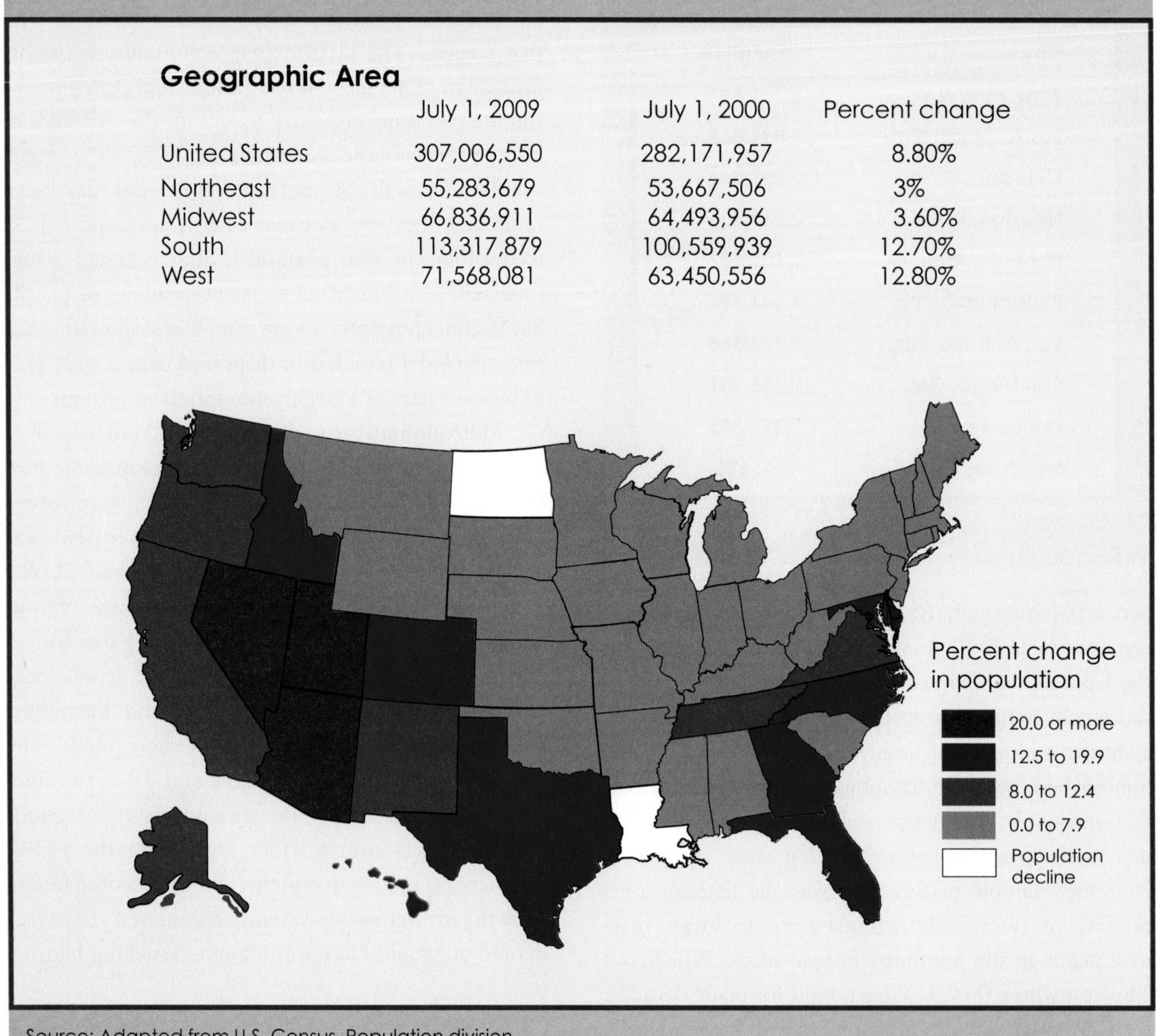

Geographic Area	July 1, 2009	July 1, 2000	Percent change
United States	307,006,550	282,171,957	8.80%
Northeast	55,283,679	53,667,506	3%
Midwest	66,836,911	64,493,956	3.60%
South	113,317,879	100,559,939	12.70%
West	71,568,081	63,450,556	12.80%

Source: Adapted from U.S. Census, Population division

an important method of moving goods and supplies. Manufacturing and industry moved to the suburbs, which drew people and a variety of small businesses and stores to follow. After World War II, hundreds of suburbs developed, each of which had its own government, school system, and public services. The suburban growth paralleled a slower growth and a recent decline in the population of central cities.

A metropolitan area that extends beyond the city and the MSA is the **megalopolis**, which is a continuous strip of urban and suburban development that may stretch for hundreds of miles. One example exists between Boston and Washington, D.C., on the east coast. This megalopolis covers ten states, includes hundreds of local governments, and has a population of nearly fifty million. Other megalopolis areas are forming between San Francisco and San Diego on the west coast and between Chicago and Pittsburgh in the Midwest. Sometime in the next fifty years, half of the United States population may live in one of these three enormous population conglomerations.

FIGURE 20-3 TEN FASTEST GROWING U.S. METRO AREAS, 2000–2006

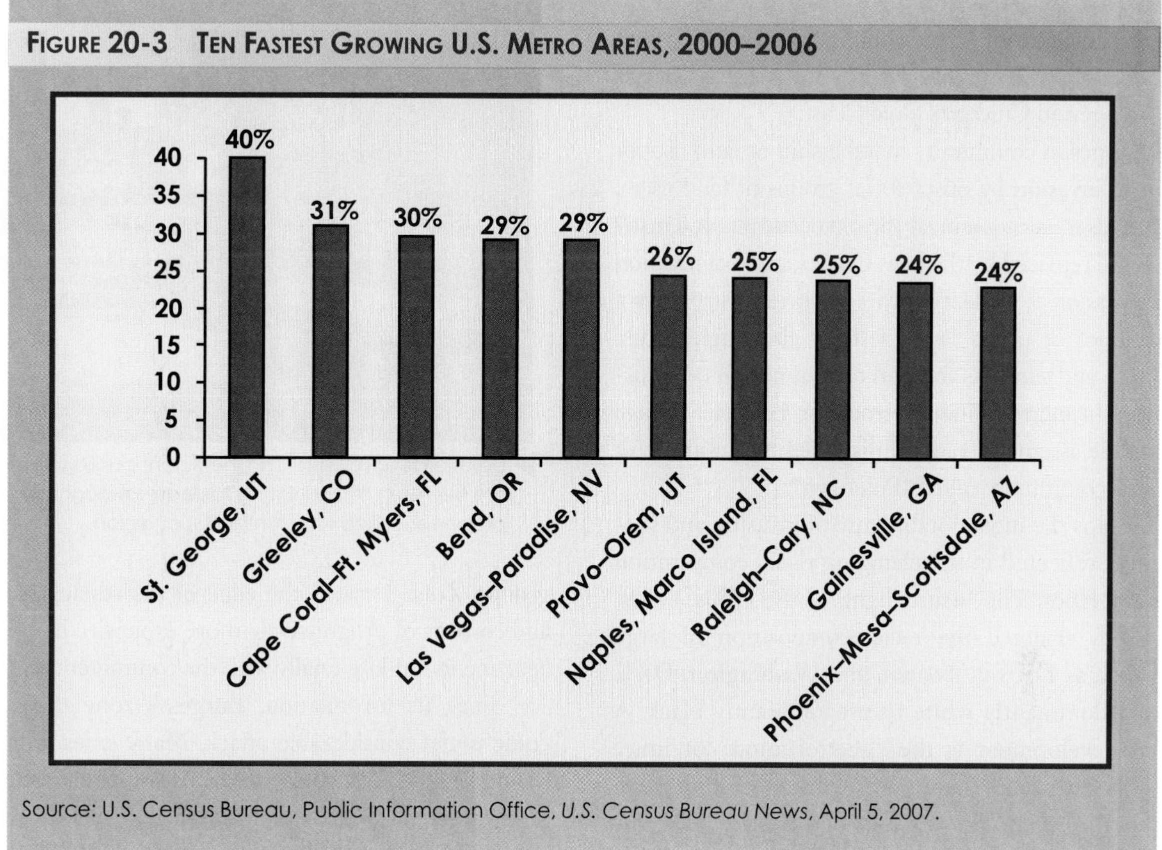

Source: U.S. Census Bureau, Public Information Office, *U.S. Census Bureau News*, April 5, 2007.

URBAN ECOLOGY

In recent years, *ecology* has come to be associated with the biological and natural world of plants and animals and how they are affected by pollution and other environmental influences. However, the term is also concerned with populations and communities. In this context, it is the study of the interrelationships of people and the environment in which they live. **Urban ecology** is concerned not only with urban spatial arrangements but also with the processes that create and reinforce these arrangements.

Urban Processes

Urban areas are not static; they change continually. The urban environment is formed and transformed by three processes: (1) concentration and deconcentration, (2) ecological specialization, and (3) invasion and succession.

The term **concentration** refers to increasing density of population, services, and institutions in a region. As people migrate to the city to find jobs, living quarters become scarce and the institutions that serve the people become strained. This starts an outward trend, called **deconcentration**, as land values and property taxes increase, and the services and public facilities decline. As a result, the core of the city—the central business district—eventually comes to consist of businesses that use space intensively and can afford to pay the economic costs. These consist of prestigious department and retail stores, financial institutions, high-rise luxury apartments, and other highly profitable ventures.

People, institutions, and services are not randomly distributed in the city. Different groups and activities tend to be concentrated in different areas. This phenomenon is called **ecological specialization.** Commercial and retail trade concerns are generally found in a different part of the city than are manufacturing and production. Similarly, public housing and low-rent tenements are seldom located near suburban residences. The basic principle at work is that people and institutions usually sort themselves into spatially homogeneous groups. As we have indicated, this homogeneity may result from economic factors: people gravitate toward places they can afford. Personal preference is also influential, as is evident from the existence of ethnic communities and areas that attract people with a particular lifestyle, such as Greenwich Village and Chicago's Gold Coast.

Changes in community membership or land use result from **invasion** by other social groups or land users, which leads to **succession**, as the old occupants and institutions are replaced by the new. One example of invasion and succession is evident when a major industry buys a sizable tract of urban land, destroys the single-family dwellings, and converts the land to commercial or industrial use. In metropolitan Detroit, for example, a huge automobile assembly complex displaced the residents of an ethnic community called "Poletown".

Perhaps the most notable case of invasion and succession is reflected in the changing racial composition of central cities. The "white flight" of the 1960s, 1970s, and 1980s changed the racial composition of large cities such as Detroit, Atlanta, and Washington, D.C., from predominantly white to predominantly black. A related development is the "ghettoization" of inner cities, which occurs as minorities become trapped in central cities that have diminishing tax bases, deteriorating housing, and inefficient public services.

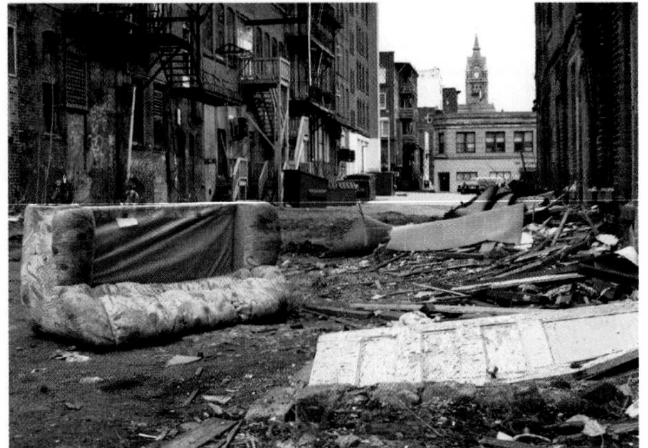

Deteriorating housing and inefficient public services are the result of diminishing tax bases brought on by processes called invasion and succession.

Urban Structure

The three ecological processes just described are the basis for several different models of urban structure. One of the most influential models during the early development of ecological theory was the **concentric zone model**, developed by Ernest W. Burgess (Burgess 1925) in the 1920s. (See Figure 20-4) According to this theory, a city spreads out equally in all directions from its original center to produce uniform circles of growth. Each zone has its own characteristic land use, population, activities, and institutions. At the center of the city is the business district, which consists of retail stores, civil activity centers, banks, hotels, and institutional administrative offices. Zone 2, the transitional zone, contains older factories, wholesale and light manufacturing businesses, and low-rent tenements. It is in this zone that immigrants or migrants are likely to live when they first arrive in the city. At the turn of the century, first-generation European immigrants made their home in this zone; however, today it is populated by minorities—African Americans, Hispanic Americans, and other ethnic groups. Zone 3 marks the edge of the residential areas and consists of progressively more expensive houses and apartments, ending finally with the commuter zone.

Since its formulation, Burgess's zone theory has come under considerable attack. Many cities do not fit the concentric zone pattern, which is more characteristic of commercial–industrial cities than of administrative cities. *Commercial–industrial cities* are those built around industry, such as Detroit, Cleveland, and Pittsburgh. These cities have a high proportion of blue-collar workers. *Administrative cities*, such as Washington, D.C., and New York City, rely heavily on government, education, and nonindustrial businesses. Also, it seems to more accurately describe cities such as Chicago that developed at the turn of the century than cities such as Houston, Phoenix, and San Diego that are developing today.

There are two major alternatives to Burgess's theory. One is the **sector model**, formulated by Hoyt (1939). According to Hoyt, the city is organized into pie-shaped wedges radiating from the central business district. Patterns of land use—industrial, high-income residential, and low-income tenements—tend to extend outward from the city core in internally consistent sectors or wedges. An industrial zone might radiate from the core in one wedge and spread into the suburbs, whereas high-income housing might push outward from the core in another wedge. Hoyt noticed this pattern in several large cities, notably Minneapolis and San Francisco.

The third theory of spatial growth rejects the idea of a single urban core or center, maintaining instead that areas of different land use have different centers. This is

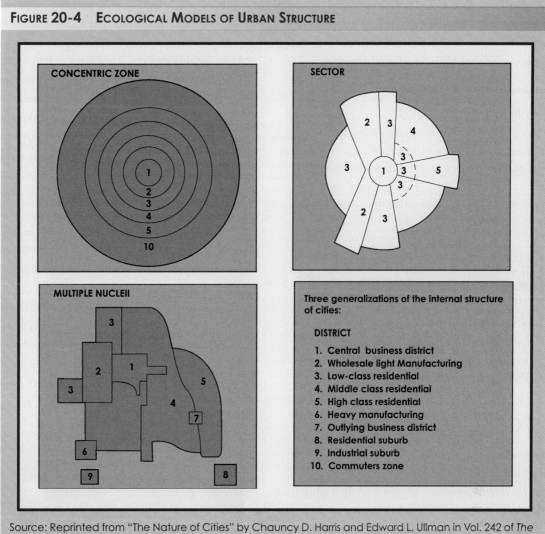

FIGURE 20-4 ECOLOGICAL MODELS OF URBAN STRUCTURE

CONCENTRIC ZONE

1
2
3
4
5
10

SECTOR

2 3 4
3 1 3 3 3 5
2 3

MULTIPLE NUCLEII

3 2 1 3 5 4 7 6 9 8

Three generalizations of the internal structure of cities:

DISTRICT

1. Central business district
2. Wholesale light Manufacturing
3. Low-class residential
4. Middle class residential
5. High class residential
6. Heavy manufacturing
7. Outlying business district
8. Residential suburb
9. Industrial suburb
10. Commuters zone

Source: Reprinted from "The Nature of Cities" by Chauncy D. Harris and Edward L. Ullman in Vol. 242 of *The Annals of the American Academy of Political and Social Science,* November 1945.

the **multiple-nuclei model** formulated by Harris and Ullman (1945). In their view, each area expands from its center, and the form of expansion may fit either the concentric or the sector zone models. In many ways, the multiple-nuclei model describes the growth of metropolitan areas better than the growth of central cities.

These three models do not reflect every possible variety or pattern of growth. Urban expansion is influenced by a variety of factors, including rate of migration into the city, cultural and historical precedents for urban development, and the physical characteristics of the land. As a result of these and other factors, Latin American cities, for example, do not fit American growth patterns, and cities built near major waterways

Hoyt noticed patterns of land use in several large cities such as San Francisco.

grow differently from other cities. Sociologists today are developing more complex models of urban development that take into account a wide variety of factors, including social, economic, and cultural variables.

Thinking Sociologically

1. Locate a map of the city in which you live or a nearby city with which you are familiar. Using the map and what you know about the city, determine which, if any, of the ecological models of urban structure discussed in this chapter it seems to follow. If it does not seem to fit any of these models, try to develop a model that it does fit.
2. Using the same city as in the preceding question, discuss what processes and growth factors might have contributed to the structure of the city. What does the city's structure help you discern and explain about some of the specific problems that the city faces?

LIFE IN CITIES AND SUBURBS

Metropolitan areas, urban areas, cities, and towns are generally defined and described in terms of population. However, the term *community* suggests some degree of interdependence, mutual identification, or organization of activities. The emergence of urban communities has altered human lifestyles and values. The size, complexity, and density of urban communities have given rise to new forms of social organization, new behaviors, and new attitudes. One of the major questions with which sociologists have grappled is why urban communities are different from rural areas in so many ways, rather than just the fact that they are larger and more densely populated. Sociologists have long recognized that there are qualitative differences between urban and rural life; and Ferdinand Tönnies (1887), a German sociologist, made a distinction in this regard over a century ago. He called the small, rural villages of his boyhood gemeinschaft (communities) and the centers of activity *gesellschaft* (associations).

A **gemeinschaft** community is characterized by a sense of solidarity and a common identity. It is a primary community rooted in tradition. Relationships among neighbors are intimate and personal, and there is a strong emphasis on shared values and sentiments, a "we" feeling. People frequently interact with one another and tend to establish deep, long-term relationships. Many small towns and communes have these characteristics.

A **gesellschaft** community, in contrast, is based on diverse economic, political, and social interrelationships. It is characterized by individualism, mobility, impersonality, the pursuit of self-interest, and an emphasis on progress rather than tradition. Shared values and total personal involvement become secondary. People live and work together because it is necessary or convenient, and people are viewed more in terms of their roles than as unique individuals. In a large city, for example, one is likely to interact with a police officer as a public servant or authority figure who has stereotyped characteristics and obligations. In a small town, on the other hand, residents would be likely to know a police officer personally. Rather than viewing the officer as a manifestation of a certain form of authority, one would know the officer as an individual with unique character traits. Historically, there has been a shift from gemeinschaft to gesellschaft

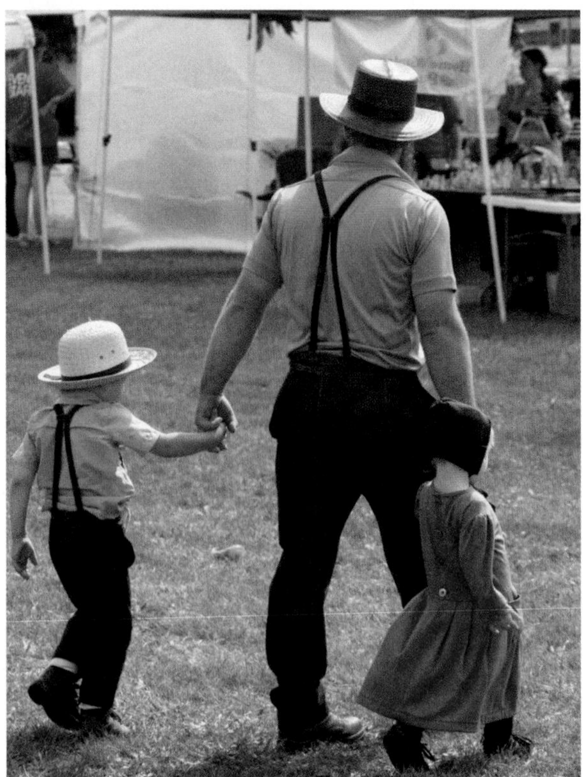
An Amish family is an example of a gemeinschaft community.

relationships as a result of role specialization and, more generally, of bureaucratization. In the nineteenth century, Weber labeled this as a change from a "traditional" to a "rational" society. In the twentieth century, American sociologists have used these ideas as a springboard for their own theories. In the next two sections, we examine some of these theories about the quality of life in cities and suburbs.

City Life

Robert Redfield (1941), an American sociologist, developed a typology similar to those formulated by nineteenth-century scholars. He distinguished a **folk society**, which is small, isolated, homogeneous, and kin oriented, from an urban society, which is large, impersonal, heterogeneous, and fast-paced. Around the same time, Louis Wirth, a colleague of Redfield's at the University of Chicago, described the effects of large numbers, density, and heterogeneity on urban life. In "Urbanism as a Way of Life" (1938), Wirth argued that as the population in an area becomes denser, lifestyles diversify, new opportunities arise, and institutions develop. At the same time, density increases the number of short-term, impersonal, and utilitarian social relationships that a person is likely to have.

According to Wirth, these three factors—large numbers, density, and heterogeneity—create a distinctive way of life, called "urbanism." The distinctive characteristics of urbanism are an extensive and complex division of labor; an emphasis on success, achievement, and social mobility, along with a behavioral orientation that includes rationality and utilitarianism; a decline of the family and kinship bonds and a concurrent rise of specialized agencies that assume roles previously taken by kin; a breakdown of primary relationships and the substitution of secondary group-control mechanisms; the replacement of deep, long-term relationships with superficial, short-term relationships; a decline of shared values and homogeneity and an increase in diversity; and finally, segregation on the basis of achieved and ascribed status characteristics.

Stanley Milgram (1970) has focused on the effects of urbanism. In midtown Manhattan, for example, someone can meet 220,000 people within a ten-minute walking radius of his or her office and not recognize a single person. Such experiences, says Milgram, may cause "psychic overload" and result in the detached, "don't get involved" attitude that is frequently cited as a part of big-city life. There have been a number of recorded incidents, for instance, in which people have been mugged, raped, or beaten in plain view of pedestrians who refused to help the victim.

These views of urban life give the impression that it is cold, violent, and alienating. Scholars have viewed city living conditions as the cause of crime, mental illness, aggression, and other serious problems. However recent

Ethnic communities consisted of working-class individuals who chose a specific area in which to settle. Because of their cultural heritage the area that they settled in developed with their own culture such as Chinatowns.

studies by sociologists have questioned the validity of this assessment. Certainly, these negative aspects of city life do exist; the real question is how typical or widespread they are. Several studies have found that there is considerable cohesion and solidarity in the city, particularly in neighborhoods where the residents are relatively homogeneous in terms of social or demographic characteristics. The findings of early sociologists may have accurately described the central core of American cities such as Chicago during periods of rapid growth. Contemporary research illustrates that a variety of lifestyles and adaptations can be found in cities.

Several decades ago, Herbert Gans (1962) presented research showing the diversity of urban lifestyles that are likely to remain true today. He argues that there are at least five types of residents in the city: cosmopolites, singles, ethnic villagers, the deprived, and the trapped.

Cosmopolites usually choose to remain in the city because of its convenience and cultural benefits. This group includes artists, intellectuals, and professionals who are drawn by the opportunities and activities generally found only in large urban centers. They are typically young, married, and involved in upper-middle-class occupations.

Singles like to live in the city because it is close to their jobs and permits a suitable lifestyle. The central city, with its nightclubs and singles-only apartments, offers a basis for social interaction. It gives singles opportunities to make friends, develop a social identity, and eventually find a mate. Many of these people are not permanent urban residents; they live in the city only until they marry or have children, at which time they move to the suburbs.

The third group identified by Gans, *ethnic villagers*, generally consists of working-class people who have chosen to reside in specific areas of the city. Their neighborhoods often develop a distinctive ethnic color as shops, restaurants, and organizations spring up. The Chinatowns in New York and San Francisco, the Hispanic areas of San Antonio and San Diego, and the Polish communities of Chicago and Detroit are neighborhoods of this type. Because of their strong ethnic ties, they usually do not identify as strongly with the city, nor do they engage in many of the cultural, social, or political activities that take place beyond their ethnic community. Their identity and allegiance are tied to the ethnic group and local community to a far greater extent than to the city. A strong emphasis is placed on kinship and primary group relationships, and members of other groups are often perceived as intruders or outsiders.

The fourth group, the *deprived*, is composed of the poor, the handicapped, and racial minorities who have fallen victim to class inequality, prejudice, or personal misfortune. They live in the city because it offers inexpensive housing and holds the promise of future job opportunities that will enable them to move to a better environment.

Finally, *the trapped* are those who cannot afford to move to a newer community and must remain in their deteriorating neighborhoods. The elderly who live on pensions make up much of this group; and because many have lived in the city all their lives, they tend to identify strongly with their neighborhoods. The deprived and the trapped are the most frequent victims of the problems of the city. They are more likely to be the targets of assault, mugging, extortion, and other crimes than other city residents. In high-crime areas, many of these people live isolated lives and are terrified by the ongoing violence in their neighborhoods.

Suburban Life

The dominance of **suburbs**, communities surrounding and dependent on urban areas, is a recent phenomenon although the population movement to the suburbs began at the end of the nineteenth century. Suburbs grew as a result of both push and pull factors. The problems of the city drove residents to the suburbs, and the positive aspects of suburban life—cleaner air, lower property taxes, larger lots, and a chance to own a home—attracted people. Because the move involved a substantial capital investment, this transition was made primarily by the more affluent.

The growth of the suburbs was also influenced by technological developments, especially those in transportation. Before the 1920s, trains and electric trolleys were the major means of mass transportation to and from the central city. Accordingly, the first pattern of suburban growth was star-shaped, as communities sprang up along the railway and trolley corridors radiating from the center of the city. The automobile gave the suburban movement a significant boost by permitting the development of land not located near a railway or trolley corridor.

After World War II, the suburbs took on a different appearance. The increased affluence of American workers and the mass production of relatively inexpensive housing enabled many lower-middle-class and blue-collar families to become suburbanites (i.e., residents of the suburbs). The type of housing that emerged in the post-World War II suburbs, called "tract housing," was based on mass-production techniques. Neighborhoods and sometimes whole communities of similar houses were constructed. As the population began to shift to the suburbs, so did the retail trade and small businesses. The result was an unprecedented growth of suburban shopping centers.

The rapid growth of suburbs in the 1950s and early 1960s caused a great deal of concern among many social commentators. Suburban life was characterized as a "rat race" dominated by a preoccupation with "keeping up with the Joneses." Suburbanites were seen as anxious, child-oriented, status-seeking people who led empty, frustrating lives (Bell 1958; Gordon, et al., 1961; Mills 1951). The typical suburbanites were viewed as more concerned with household gadgets, status symbols, and getting into what they consider to be the right organizations than with understanding the world around them or achieving individuality. These views generated what sociologists call the "myth of suburbia." Recent research has given us reason to doubt that the patterns of behavior found in the suburbs are due to suburban residence and even that there is a distinctively suburban way of life.

The suburbs and the people who live there are actually quite diverse. Most of you can differentiate suburbs by the types of housing and land areas that accompany it. Most cities have one or two identifiable suburban communities of the affluent, which are occupied by white, upper-middle class executives and professionals. Other identifiable communities consist of white-collar and upper-working-class residents with their three-bedroom, two-and-one-half-bathroom homes with an attached two-car garage. A third type of suburban community is that of the blue-collar, less educated and less affluent resident. These homes, without garages, are small and are the least expensive type of suburban housing. In all categories, a primary reason cited for moving to the suburbs is the desire to own a home. A second important reason is to find a suitable environment in which to raise children. Other factors common to most suburbanites are a desire for open spaces and for a less hectic pace.

Do people change when they move from the city to the suburbs? Is there evidence of a **conversion effect**, a radical shift of interest and lifestyle? Research from the 1960s by Berger (1960) and by Cohen and Hodges (1963) found that blue-collar families had similar values, behavior patterns, and psychological orientations whether they lived in the city or in the suburbs. Similarly, Gans (1967) found that middle-class suburbanites in Levittown were not plagued by the stereotypical problems of boredom, unhappiness, and frustrated status-seeking. He found instead that they were generally happy, well-adjusted, and involved in family and social activities. In short, there was little evidence of a conversion effect.

In recent years, the number of blacks who live in the suburbs has increased sharply. There is little evidence, however, that many suburbs are becoming racially integrated. Because the median income of blacks is still considerably lower than that of whites, many blacks cannot afford to move into the suburbs where most whites reside. Instead, they are moving into the older suburbs with lower property values, which whites are leaving behind in their search for better suburban communities. Though whites often react strongly to blacks who move into their suburban communities because they are perceived as being different, research shows that blacks who move to the suburbs have values and lifestyles similar to those of their white neighbors (Austin 1976).

Hispanics, blacks, and Asians are more likely than non-Hispanic whites to live in central cities (*Changing America* 1998). In 1996 more than half of blacks and Hispanics and nearly half of Asians lived in central cities, compared with less than a quarter of non-Hispanic whites. By contrast, over half of all non-Hispanic whites lived in the suburbs in 1996, as did 48 percent of Asians. Native Americans are by far most likely to live outside cities and suburbs; in 1990 nearly half of the American Indian population lived outside of metropolitan areas (*Changing America* 1998).

Thinking Sociologically

1. Would you say that the town in which you live could be characterized as a gemeinschaft or a gesellschaft? Why? Discuss some features and qualities of the town that lead you to characterize it in this way.

2. Discuss the accuracy of the statement, "People who live in cities are different from people who live in suburban or rural areas."

3. How accurate do you find Gan's classification and description of the five types of urban residents? As you reflect, can you identify these types from your own experiences?

Urban Problems

The most severe problems in urban areas are found in the central cities: poverty, unemployment, crime, noise and air pollution, waste disposal, water purity, transportation, housing, population congestion, and so on. Although the suburbs are by no means immune to these problems, they generally do not experience them to the same degree as central cities. The central cities are beset by a number of crises, some of which are becoming worse. In this section, three problems are discussed: poverty and unemployment, crime, and schooling.

Among the most serious issues facing cities today are the related problems of poverty and unemployment. The economic vitality of central cities has diminished over the years, as industry, affluent taxpayers, and jobs have moved out. The result has been a steady deterioration of housing and public services and the loss of high-paying jobs. The least fortunate of city residents are forced to live in slums and ghettos.

Slums are overcrowded streets or sections of a city marked by poverty and poor living conditions—resulting from the dirt, disease, rodents, and other health hazards that accompany concentrations of housing with poor plumbing, garbage disposal, and sanitation facilities. Slum residents are often victims of social injustice and personal misfortune—such as racial minorities, the elderly, women who head large families, and addicts. Over the years, research has shown that slum living has a number of detrimental effects on health: residents of slums are more likely than others to contract diseases and to become seriously ill; they have poorer overall health and shorter life spans; and they are more apt to have poorer self-images and experience psychological problems such as depression and alienation.

The most serious poverty and its accompanying social problems occur in ghettos. A **ghetto** is an area, usually a deteriorating one, in which members of a racial or ethnic minority are forcibly segregated. Urban areas that are no longer of interest to the more affluent majority tend to become ghettos. A ghetto is a social and economic trap that keeps members of the minority group within a controllable geographic area. Crane (1991) describes ghettos as neighborhoods that have experienced epidemics of social problems: epidemics of crack, gang violence, teenage childbearing, and so forth. His assumption is that social problems are contagious and are spread through peer influence within ghetto neighborhoods. He found that the neighborhood effect on the pattern of dropping out of school and of childbearing—the two variables he studied among teenagers—was precisely the one implied by an epidemic hypothesis. Urban ghettos, the worst areas of large cities, produced sharp, epidemic jumps in both dimensions.

Wilson (1987) argues that the problems of inner-city ghettos indicate the existence of a growing, largely black underclass. In his words,

> Inner-city neighborhoods have undergone a profound social transformation in the last several years as reflected not only in their increasing rates of social dislocation (including crime, joblessness, out-of-wedlock births, female-headed families, and welfare dependency) but also in the changing economic class structure of ghetto neighborhoods...The movement of middle-class professionals from the inner city, followed in increasing numbers by working class blacks, has left behind a much larger concentration of the most disadvantaged segments of the black urban population to which I refer when I speak of the ghetto underclass. (p. 49)

There is evidence that black ghettoization is increasing today. In 2002, 52 percent of all African Americans lived in an urban area, compared to 21 percent whites (*Current Population Reports* 2003).

The jobs for which the less affluent central-city residents are qualified are usually low paying and scarce; and the unemployment rate is twice as high as the rate in the suburbs. The departure of industry and manufacturing jobs has left inner-city residents with jobs characterized by high turnover, low wages, and few opportunities for advancement. It is not unusual to find a person who heads a family and works full-time but barely earns enough to stay above the poverty line. With recent cuts in federal aid to job-training programs, it is unlikely that the situation of these city residents will improve in the near future.

Crime is another serious urban problem. In fact, *The Gallup Poll Monthly* (September 1990, 40) reported that Americans have an overwhelmingly negative perception of the safety of many of America's largest cities. Results from a randomly selected, national sample of adults revealed that New York, leading the list, was seen as an unsafe place to live in or visit by 85 percent of the respondents–followed by Miami (76 percent), Washington, D.C. (71 percent), Detroit (68 percent), and Chicago (65 percent). The picture of cities was not entirely dismal, however. Minneapolis and St. Paul were only viewed as unsafe by 11 and 16 percent, respectively, with less than 30 percent viewing Houston, Dallas, San Diego, and Boston similarly.

Data shows that household perceptions of crime as a problem rose during the late 1980s and early 1990s as the actual crime rate rose. On the other hand, this is not always a predictable correlation. Differences in perception of crime and actual victimization are found because as crime dropped sharply from 1994 to 1995, perceptions that crime was a neighborhood problem remained relatively stable. Black households were much more likely than white households to indicate crime was a neighborhood problem. In 1995, 2.5 times as many black households indicated crime was a problem; but the difference was not nearly as large for actual victimization: 27 percent of black households experienced one or more crimes, compared to 23 percent of white households (Bureau of Justice Statistics 1998).

Furthermore, urban households have historically been, and continue to be, the most vulnerable to property crime, burglary, motor vehicle theft and theft in the United States (Bureau of Justice Statistics 2003).

Crime is at the heart of viewing cities as unsafe places in which to live, visit, and work, and with some justification. Theft, arson, violence, illegal vice activities (such as prostitution, gambling), and the use and sale of narcotics are generally found more in large cities, where there is greater anonymity. In addition, the methods of control are different in large cities and small towns. Whereas towns rely on internalized values and primary-group pressure for enforcement, cities depend on abstract laws and impersonal, bureaucratic agencies such as the police (Dinitz 1973). When high density, heterogeneity, and anonymity are combined with poverty, a physically decayed environment, and other characteristics of inner-city living, there is great potential for social deviance and violence.

Not all areas of a city experience the same crime rate or the same types of crimes. The highest crime rates are found in the inner-city sectors; the rate decreases as one moves toward the fringes of the urban area. Zonal differences in crime tend to persist, however, even when the physical characteristics and the occupants of a zone change.

Using sociological research as a guide, one might argue that there are several ways of reducing urban crime. Increased police surveillance is often an important political issue in cities, but there is some evidence that it has little, if any, effect on the crime rate. Furthermore, research shows that despite the apparent popularity of the community policing approach, community residents may not want closer interaction with the police nor the responsibility for maintaining social control (Grinc 1994). Because high-crime areas are located in similar areas in different cities—generally the most poverty-stricken areas—one might argue that providing the people in these areas with decent living conditions and meaningful jobs would have a greater impact on crime than increasing the size of the police force. One could also argue that voluntary neighborhood organizations in high crime areas might not only provide role models of lawful behavior but also create a sense of community that is frequently lacking in these areas.

A third urban problem area is schooling. Today, city schools are faced with a variety of major problems, two of which are inadequate financing and social disorder, including violence. Many cities have a very difficult time keeping pace with the accelerating costs. This difficulty

Inadequate financing and violence are just two major problems that schools face today.

is accentuated by inequalities in school funding: Urban schools generally have a much lower per-student expenditure allowance than schools in the suburbs. City schools have reacted to this funding problem in several ways. In some areas, school bond increases have been used to retain financial solvency. In recent years, however, irate taxpayers are rejecting an increasing percentage of school bond proposals. As a result of the fiscal crisis, many schools are forced to use outdated or damaged curricular material. Reductions in staff and salary are another means of dealing with the financial woes. These responses to funding cuts have been a factor in recent teacher strikes and walkouts. Staff and salary cutbacks also seem to be related to the morale problems found in many inner-city schools.

School disorder, especially violence, is widespread in many city schools. Incidents that rarely occurred a generation ago happen today on a fairly routine basis: theft, extortion, physical attacks on fellow students and on teachers, and vandalism. In some schools, the halls are routinely patrolled by police officers; in others, the doors of classrooms are locked during class hours to prevent intruders from entering; still other schools have unannounced locker checks to confiscate drugs and weapons, an activity strongly opposed by the American Civil Liberties Union (ACLU). One explanation for the increase in crime in the schools is that schools are no longer immune to the day-to-day problems of the city. Solving some of the problems that cause crime on the streets would, therefore, probably reduce crime in the schools. Another explanation is that the schools themselves are responsible for disorder. Deteriorating buildings, prejudiced or inadequately trained teachers, inequalities in the curriculum (known as "tracking"), and pessimism about the future may all produce an atmosphere of despair and anger. Without adequate funds to buy better equipment and to hire and train more qualified teachers, this problem is likely to persist.

URBAN REJUVENATION: PROBLEMS AND PROSPECTS

What can be done to help our cities survive? Has the central city outlived its usefulness? These are a couple of the serious questions addressed by scholars concerned about the future of our cities. Some feel that the future of cities is dim as the tax base continues to erode, buildings and homes continue to deteriorate, tax rebellions become more frequent, and the people who remain in inner cities constitute the ghetto underclass of racial and class exclusion—single mothers and absent fathers, homeless and unemployed, and so forth (Wilson 1997). Others, such as Feagin and Parke (1990), write about rebuilding American cities with the developers, bankers, and speculators as shapers of cities being joined by protesters of urban redevelopment who want to reinvigorate democracy in urban cities. These protesters are citizens who are demanding more popular control over home and neighborhood spaces and over the quality of life in their communities.

Downtown Revitalization

A person's perspective on and attitude toward the problems and prospects of the city depends greatly on whether the central business district or residential areas are being considered, and on who is doing the considering. The business districts of many cities are being revitalized and are experiencing significant new business construction. Because the downtown areas of our cities are a major center of white-collar employment, financial firms, insurance companies, and private and government services, the future of these areas is relatively secure.

Downtown revitalization programs tend to have a greater impact on white-collar jobs than on blue-collar ones, however. The number of white-collar jobs in cities is increasing, but the number of blue-collar jobs continues to decline. Because the revitalization of the central business district creates a need for well-educated, highly skilled employees, many inner-city residents who have weaker credentials do not directly benefit from these types of economic programs. This has made many city residents angry because they feel that their problems and concerns are secondary to the plans of affluent city and suburban developers and residents. Those who advocate downtown revitalization do not fully acknowledge the dislocating and segregative effects of urban renewal and public housing on central city neighborhoods (Gotham 2001). Feagin and Parke (1990 [Chapter 10]) describe the actions of some citizen protest groups that have voiced their concerns about affordable rental housing, highway projects, shopping malls, high-rise construction, and urban renewal. There is a concern that urban rejuvenation must include residential neighborhoods, as well as the business district, and must create jobs for all city residents, regardless of their levels of skill or education.

Urban Renewal

Urban renewal is, at least in theory, the residential counterpart of downtown revitalization. According to the Urban Renewal Act of 1954, the major goal is to rebuild and renovate the ghettos and slums of American cities, but urban-renewal projects have had several shortcomings. First, local urban renewal agencies were given the power by the federal government to define which areas were considered blighted and, therefore, qualified for renewal. Generally, the better areas of the slums were developed, while the worst were allowed to remain. Sometimes, the reason for this selection was the perception that one area was more likely to produce income than the other. Shopping centers and high-rise apartments for the middle class, for example, often replaced low-income housing. Ironically, many of the residents whose homes were razed did not benefit at all from the structures that were erected, though exactly the opposite effect was intended in the 1954 act. Second, the act specified that the people displaced by urban renewal should be relocated in "decent, safe, and sanitary" housing in other areas of the city. In a number of instances, the new neighborhoods were just as bad as the old ones, and the relocation often destroyed an existing sense of community with friends and neighbors.

The case of the Pruitt-Igoe Housing Project in St. Louis several decades back exemplifies some of the problems associated with urban renewal projects (Newman 1972). The project, which had cleared some of the city's slum dwellings by 1955, consisted of thirty–three buildings, each eleven stories high. It was lauded as a model for all future public housing projects because of its design and use of innovative structures. By 1970, however, the project had become a symbol of all the negative aspects of public housing. The physical deterioration and destruction of elevators, laundry rooms, and stairways were considerable. Residents were afraid to leave their apartments because of the frequency of robbery and rape. The absence of public bathrooms on the ground floors resulted in foul-smelling hallways. Gradually, most of the occupants fled the project, and even the most desperate welfare recipients were unwilling to tolerate the living conditions. The government finally closed down the entire project and later razed it. The basic problem was that human values and lifestyles were not fully considered in the project's design. The high-rise construction isolated residents from one another; the architectural design left too much open space (halls, elevators, laundry rooms) for which no one felt responsible and that made surveillance of children and adolescents very difficult.

Other means of housing the poor were legislated after the problems with urban-renewal projects were publicized in the 1960s. Most of them received mixed reviews. One form of legislation included the Housing and Urban Redevelopment Act, which provided direct subsidies to low-income families so that they could either buy their own homes or rent apartments of their own choosing. The Experimental Housing Allowance Program was implemented in the early 1970s, to help low-income tenants pay their rent. In both cases, part of the rent was paid partly by the government, either to the tenant or directly to the landlord.

Another federal plan that has been implemented is **urban homesteading**. Homesteading programs sell abandoned and foreclosed homes to private families for between one and one hundred dollars if they agree to live in the house for at least three years and to bring the house up to housing code standards within eighteen months. Though the program has limited funds, it has had a significant effect on a number of cities, but there have been pitfalls. Individuals and lending institutions are reluctant to invest in houses surrounded by vandalized, rundown buildings, and despite the low purchase price, repairs may be quite expensive. The Department of Housing and Urban Development (HUD) has acted to alleviate these problems by buying up and making modest repairs on entire neighborhoods. If the federal government were to continue its commitment to urban homesteading, some of our deteriorating neighborhoods could probably be transformed. At the time of this writing, however, this type of commitment by the federal government appears highly unlikely, especially in light of recent concerns over a growing national budget deficit.

A growing number of urban neighborhoods are being rejuvenated by **gentrification**, the movement of middle-class people into old rundown homes that they repair at their own expense. Notable examples of this are found in Chicago's Newtown, the Mission District of San Francisco, and Atlanta's Ansley Park. These people are generally young, white, childless couples who work in the city. They tend to have different values than their suburban counterparts. Many do not want to have families and are turned off by the sameness and the lack of charm of suburban housing. This trend may continue in the future with the increasing costs of transportation and suburban housing.

Urban Planning

Most of our urban development has occurred without a long-term commitment to community living or a strong theoretical understanding of it. Urban planning is a field of study concerned with urban physical structures and spatial configurations and their effects on human attitudes and behavior. Two traditional goals of this field are the reduction of population density and the creation of appealing community structures.

Urban planning became a concern in the nineteenth century when many large cities in Europe and the United States were experiencing severe problems because of rapid industrial and population growth. One early influential figure was Ebenezer Howard. In his *Garden Cities of Tomorrow* (1902), Howard argued that the ideal was to develop cities that combined the benefits of both rural and urban living. All new towns, or "garden cities" as he called them, would be built on undeveloped land in accordance with scientific principles. Population density, a factor he felt was responsible for urban blight, would be carefully controlled. Cities were also to be surrounded by a **greenbelt**, an area preserved for farming and recreation, thus limiting the outward growth of the city. Howard's ideas have had a significant impact on the theoretical orientations of several generations of urban planners, whose major focus has been the construction of new towns, which have a careful mixture of houses, entertainment areas, businesses, and industries.

A number of modern new towns have been carefully designed and monitored. Columbia, Maryland, located between Washington, D.C., and Baltimore, is an example of a city developed with human needs and lifestyles in mind. The city is divided into what are called "villages" and "neighborhoods." Each neighborhood has its own elementary school and recreational facilities, and the villages form a circle around a plaza with a shopping center, office buildings, and medical facilities. The community has also made a conscious attempt to achieve racial balance.

Other, more recent, new towns have not been as successful as Columbia, and federal cutbacks in funding for development have led to the demise of more than half a dozen new towns. The lesson to be learned from these experiences is that the successful development of planned communities requires a long-term investment of money, perhaps as long as fifteen or twenty years, by the federal government. With its present economic woes, our government is unlikely to make such a commitment in the near future.

Diversity of Values

Urban planners must be sensitive to the diverse values and lifestyles of the people who live in urban communities if they are to achieve their goals; however, they have not been completely successful in this area. They have been criticized as having a distinctly middle-class bias. This point can be illustrated with findings about the design and use of space.

Most planners assume that people like a considerable amount of open public space and clearly demarcated areas of private space. Among members of many blue-collar and minority groups, however, the distinction between public and private space is blurred; social interactions tend to flow more freely across private and public regions than they do in middle-class environments.

Thinking Sociologically

1. Make a list of urban problems and a list of rural problems. (a) Is the list different? (b) What are key factors that contribute to both? (c) Who holds primary responsibility (private citizens, private business, local government, federal government, or others) for changing them?
2. Discuss what urban planners or politicians mean when they talk about downtown revitalization and urban renewal. What are some consequences of programs or actions such as the razing of blighted areas, homesteading, and gentrification?

That urban planners and the less affluent have different spatial preferences has been noted with regard to the structure of individual apartments. An experiment in which Hispanic residents of a New York tenement conferred with an architect about the redesign of their apartments revealed that the residents did not like the large areas of open space in an apartment that middle-class couples prefer; they also wanted an apartment entrance that did not open directly into the living room, and they liked an apartment in which the kitchen was isolated from the rest of the house by a wall or a door (Zeisel 1973).

As suggested, the development of attractive, functional physical surroundings cannot be accomplished without a long-term commitment by the government to aid our ailing cities. The rejuvenation of the city also requires the creation of jobs and opportunities for inner-city residents. In the past few decades, major steps have been taken toward the realization of these goals, but many look with despair at the discrepancy between where we are today and where we need to go.

APPLYING SOCIOLOGY TO URBAN PLANNING

Sociological knowledge plays an important part in urban planning. Some professional sociologists have jobs in urban planning as consultants and researchers for state, city, and local governments and for engineers, architects, lawyers, and others involved in planning cities and communities. Before engineers design a new road going through a neighborhood, for example, they might want to know how the increased traffic flow will influence the social organization of the community. Municipal governments might need to know how a neighborhood renewal project might influence the social organization of a particular community before they begin the project. Will the residents' networks of cooperation and exchange be disrupted? How will leisure time and work roles be affected? Will the project impose middle-class values on a lower-class culture? Recall the discussion of how the Pruitt-Igoe Housing Project in St. Louis failed partially because the values and lifestyles of the people who lived there were not considered in the project's design.

Andrew Collver (1983), in an article on housing and environmental planning, suggests six ways in which sociology can contribute to urban planning:

1. Regional data collection and analysis
2. Neighborhood life-cycle analysis
3. Preparation of long-range community plans
4. Critical review and evaluation of alternative courses of action

5. Project evaluation
6. Creation of social inventions or alternate structures

Regional Data Collection and Analysis To plan a workable community or neighborhood, the planners—policymakers, engineers, architects, lawyers, and others—should understand the developmental trends of the larger region in which it is located and how its location both serves and is served by the larger metropolitan system. Is the population of the region growing? How much migration in and out of the area is there? How are the age patterns of the population changing? What are the various types of income, religious, and ethnic groups within the community, and how well integrated are they? Answers to questions such as these require some knowledge of social stratification, minority groups, and demography, as well as knowledge of sociological research methods.

Neighborhood Life-Cycle Analysis This entails examining the history of the neighborhood and its trend of growth or decline, rather than just examining the neighborhood at a single point in time. Is the average income level of the residents rising or declining? Are new businesses opening, or are old businesses closing, or both? Is the middle class moving in or out? As Collver (1983, 281) points out, "to try to attract middle-class homeowners back to an inner-city neighborhood that lacks such essential elements as architectural charm, good schools, and convenient access to work and recreation would be an exercise in frustration." A sociological analysis of a community can help to create plans that are more in line with the natural tendencies of the community.

Preparation of Long-Range Community Plans Long-range plans are not always effectively carried out, but they are a useful way for urban planners to reach common understandings and assumptions about what should be done. This increases the level of communication among the planners and helps to make them of one mind. Sociological knowledge can be a helpful way to create workable plans from the stated goals of community leaders. Suppose, for example, that one of the stated goals of the community government is to create an ethnically and racially diverse neighborhood of middle-income people. Knowledge of prejudice, minority groups, values, norms, roles, culture, and so forth would be useful in devising a means to achieve the community's goals.

Critical Review and Evaluation of Alternative Courses of Action What kind of impact will the proposed urban plan have? What are some possible alternatives to the plan? If they are inferior to the plan chosen, why are they inferior? How can architectural and environmental impact be assessed and managed? Knowledge of people's lifestyles and the effects of spatial arrangement, density, crowding, heterogeneity, and other factors offer insight into the impact of a plan. Field experiments are a means of testing policies before they are actually implemented. Similarly, field experiments can be conducted to assess the impact of various alternative-planning measures before selecting one. Collver notes also that impact analysis is required by federal and state regulations.

Project Evaluation Once a project has been completed, planners must determine whether it met its goals. Outcome evaluation would be one way of assessing the results of an urban planning project. Knowledge of the methodology of outcome evaluation research could be used to help fine-tune the plan being evaluated. There are four steps in evaluation research: specification (defining or identifying the goals of the project), measurement (the information needed to evaluate the goal), analysis (the use of the information to draw conclusions), and recommendation (the advice given regarding what should be done, based on the analysis).

Creation of Social Inventions or Alternative Structures How can the necessary functions of a community be met in new and better ways? Developing such inventions might require changes in basic ideologies and institutions. Could a neighborhood or community, for example, share the use and maintenance of common property rather than having individual property owners? This would require a restructuring of our basic ideology of private ownership, but this seemingly revolutionary idea is what lies behind the movement toward condominiums and cooperative apartments. A sociological analysis of our basic ideologies and institutions may help free us from some confinements that are not practical or beneficial in every situation.

CHAPTER REVIEW

Wrapping it up

Summary

1. Urban communities can exist only when there is a group of people to grow and process food for the urbanites. A degree of social organization is also necessary to transform a crowded group of people into a social group that behaves in an orderly and predictable manner.

2. The first urban communities developed approximately ten thousand years ago during the horticultural era. This development was possible because of increased food production and the creation of regular surpluses. Several thousand years later, technological advances—the plow, metallurgy, use of animals, counting, and writing—and the increasing complexity of social and political organization—enabled cities to grow to unprecedented sizes.

3. The fall of Rome in the fifth century AD marked the beginning of a precipitous decline in city size and complexity that lasted for nearly six hundred years. Urban communities did not begin to grow substantially again until the late eighteenth century with the dawn of the industrial age. Urban populations then increased dramatically, and within a few decades, more people lived in cities than in rural areas.

4. The most dramatic increase in urban population is in Developing World countries, the least developed countries. Some of this urban growth became concentrated in squatter settlements. Today, there are about 250 cities in the world with increasing populations of more than one million people, and there is little hope of this trend abating.

5. In the United States today, three-fourths of our population live in urban areas, which have increased in size as well as in number. The rapid industrial and population growth in large cities during the early part of this century caused people and industries to move from central cities to the sparsely populated areas outside of them. This process resulted in the modern metropolis.

6. *A metropolitan statistical area (MSA)* is a large population nucleus combined with adjacent communities that have a high degree of social and economic integration with that nucleus. A *megalopolis* results from the overlap of two or more metropolitan areas.

7. Urban ecology is the study of the interrelationships of people and the environment in which they live. It includes urban processes of (a) concentration and deconcentration as people move into and out of geographical areas, (b) ecological specialization, and (c) invasion of and succession by new and different social groups and land areas.

8. Various models of urban structure and spatial growth include the *concentric zone model of cities*, spreading out equally in all directions producing uniform circles of growth; the *sector model of cities*, as organized into pie-shaped wedges radiating

from the central business district; and the *multiple nuclei zone models of cities*, as having various centers as well as duplicate areas of business, industrial, shopping, and residential locations.

9. Cities and suburbs, while often described in terms of population, also involve a sense of community. *Gemeinschaft* communities are characterized by a sense of intimacy, common identity, and tradition, in contrast to *gesellschaft* communities, which are characterized by impersonality, self-interest, and an emphasis on progress.

10. In contrast to popular stereotypes, cities and suburbs have quite diverse populations. Early sociologists believed that city living was unhealthy and encouraged family breakdown, violence, and depersonalization. Recent research, however, shows that a variety of people and lifestyles are found in the city. A number of people prefer the city because of its social and economic advantages.

11. Suburban life is also quite diverse, and suburbanites do not differ in lifestyle or values from city residents with similar demographic and social characteristics.

12. Our cities face a number of problems today, notably poverty and unemployment, crime, and inadequate schools. Slum areas and ghetto areas experience the most serious social problems. Attempts to remedy these problems are not likely to succeed without a considerable influx of money and the creation of social and economic opportunities.

13. The downtown areas of many cities are being revitalized, and a number of residential neighborhoods are being given a new appearance as a result of urban renewal and urban homesteading projects. Some urban neighborhoods are being rejuvenated by gentrification efforts.

14. The field of urban planning may play an important role in the future of our cities and can have a significant impact on the quality of urban social and cultural life—if it is sensitive to the needs and values of different groups of city residents.

Key Terms

community A collection of people within a geographic area among whom there is some degree of mutual identification, interdependence, or organization of activities

concentration An urban ecological process in which population, services, and institutions come to be gathered most densely in the areas in which conditions are advantageous

concentric zone model A model of urban structure showing that cities grow out equally in all directions from their original centers, producing uniform circles of growth that have their own distinctive land use, population, activities, and institutions

conversion effect A radical shift of interests and lifestyle that occurs when people move from one type of area to another, as from an urban area to a suburb

deconcentration Movement outward from the city because of increases in land values and taxes and declines in services and public facilities

ecological specialization The concentration of homogeneous groups and activities into different sections or urban areas

folk society A community described by Redfield as small, isolated, homogeneous, and kin-oriented

gemeinschaft A traditional community characterized by a sense of solidarity and common identity and emphasizing intimate and personal relationships

gentrification The rejuvenation of urban neighborhoods by middle-class people who move into and repair run-down houses

gesellschaft A modern community characterized by individualism, mobility, and impersonality, with an emphasis on progress rather than tradition

ghetto An area in a city in which members of a racial or ethnic minority are forcibly segregated

greenbelt An area surrounding cities that is preserved for farming and recreation and that limits the growth of cities

horticulture Small-scale farming that relies on tools such as the hoe to till the soil

invasion An ecological process in which new types of people, organizations, or activities move into an area occupied by a different type

megalopolis A continuous strip of urban and suburban development that may stretch for hundreds of miles

metropolitan statistical area (MSA) A county or group of counties with a central city with a population of at least 50,000, a density of at least 1,000 persons per square mile, and outlying areas that are socially and economically integrated with the central city

multiple-nuclei model The model of urban development showing that cities have areas of different types of land use, each of which has its own center or nucleus

sector model An explanation of the ecology of cities as a series of pie-shaped wedges radiating from the central business district, each with its own characteristics and uses

slums Sections of a city marked by poverty, overcrowding, substandard housing, and poor living conditions

suburbs The communities that surround a central city and are dependent on it

succession An urban process of replacing old occupants and institutions with new ones

urban ecology The study of the interrelationships between people in urban settings and the social and physical environment in which they live

urban homesteading A federal plan in which abandoned and foreclosed homes are sold to private families at extremely low prices if they agree to live in the house and bring it up to code standards

urbanization The growth of the number of people who live in urban rather than rural areas and the process of taking on organizational patterns and lifestyles characteristic of urban areas

Discussion Questions

1. Discuss the types of factors that historically led to the location and growth of urban areas.
2. What are some of the problems associated with Developing World urbanization?
3. What are some factors that have led to urbanization in different areas of the United States?
4. Why are southern and southwestern states and cities the fastest-growing areas of the United States? Why have numerous midwestern and eastern cities lost population during the past decade?
5. Compare the reasons for the growth of metropolitan statistical areas and of nonmetropolitan areas.
6. Discuss how the urban processes of concentration and deconcentration, ecological specialization, and invasion and succession form the basis of different models of urban structure.
7. Does your city, or one with which you are familiar, fit any one of the three models of urban structure described in this chapter? Why or why not?
8. Why is it argued that relationships and communities shift from gemeinschaft to gesellschaft characteristics with increasing urbanization?
9. Describe conditions that characterize a slum and a ghetto. Why does either exist?
10. Identify two urban problems in the city in which you live or a nearby city, and discuss them, using a sociological perspective.
11. What is meant by urban renewal? Discuss the impact on families of tearing down houses in blighted areas to build new apartments or housing units.
12. Examine the pros and cons of such activities as downtown revitalization, homesteading, and gentrification.

Pop Quiz

1. Which of the following is NOT one of the characteristics of a community?

   a. It is a collection of people in a geographic area
   b. It involves some degree of mutual identification
   c. It has some type of organized activity
   d. It has a strong central government

2. As migration from rural areas increases, the city population becomes ______.

   a. more heterogeneous
   b. more homogeneous
   c. more agricultural oriented
   d. more technological

3. In the United States today, which areas are experiencing the fastest growth?
   a. the Northeast and Northwest
   b. the Northeast and Southeast
   c. the South and Southwest
   d. the Northwest and Midwest

4. A continuous strip of urban and suburban development that may extend for hundreds of miles is a ______.

   a. megalopolis
   b. planned community
   c. Metropolitan Statistical Area
   d. metropolis

5. Which of the following is NOT one of the processes that forms and influences the urban environment?

   a. concentration
   b. ecological specialization
   c. invasion
   d. diversification

6. Which theory of urban structure suggests that cities spread out equally in all directions to produce uniform circles of growth?

   a. standard growth model
   b. sector model
   c. concentric zone model
   d. multiple nuclei model

7. Which theory of urban structure suggests that each area of land use has its own center from which growth proceeds?

   a. multiple nuclei model
   b. standard growth model
   c. concentric zone model
   d. sector model

8. In a gesellschaft community, neighbors ______.

   a. have close, personal relationships
   b. are impersonal and individualistic
   c. live very close together
   d. have shared values

9. According to Gans, which of the following choose to remain in the city because of its convenience and culture benefits?

   a. ethnic villagers
   b. singles
   c. cosmopolites
   d. the deprived

10. A deteriorating area in which members of a racial or ethnic minority are forcibly segregated is a/an ______.

    a. slum
    b. sector
    c. ethnic village
    d. ghetto

11. The term community can be applied both to a commune and Indian tribe. T/F

12. The most populated city in the world as of 2000 was Mexico City, Mexico. T/F

13. A megalopolis is one large metropolitan area, according to the census. T/F

14. New York City would be considered a gesellschaft community. T/F

15. Most observers agree that urban renewal has been a resounding success. T/F

1. D	6. C	11. T
2. A	7. A	12. F
3. D	8. B	13. F
4. A	9. C	14. T
5. D	10. D	15. F

CHAPTER 21

The Nature of Social Change

CHINA'S EMERGENCE AS A SUPERPOWER

China is not only a rising political power; it also constitutes the chief foreign rival of the United States in the twenty-first century. China's growing strength is most clearly seen in three areas: militarily, economically and technologically.

China has one of the most ambitious, military modernization programs in the world. For example, since 2006, the Chinese have been actively purchasing Kilo class submarines from Russia, including the stealthy Type-636. China has also accelerated production of its Song-class submarines and has carried out sea trials of its new Jin-class nuclear powered, ballistic missile submarines. Between 1995 and 2005, China launched thirty-one new submarines, an average of three per year. By creating a powerful submarine fleet, China seeks to break American control over maritime security in Asia. John Tkacik (2006), an expert in Chinese military power, explains,

"Sea-power trends in the Pacific Ocean are ominous. By 2025, China's navy could rule the waves of the Pacific. By some estimates, Chinese attack submarines will outnumber U.S. submarines in the Pacific by five to one; and Chinese nuclear ballistic missile submarines will prowl America's Western littoral, each closely tailed by two U.S. attack submarines that have better things to do. The United States, meanwhile, will likely struggle to build enough submarines to meet this challenge."

China is emerging as an economic force in its sophisticated economic statecraft to boost its power relative to the United States. For instance, Beijing is accumulating billons of dollars of U.S government securities and thus has the ability to manipulate the value of the yaun against the dollar, which in turn can lead to massive U.S monetary debt (Morrison and Labonte 2009). With so many U.S. government securities under its control, China could potentially use the threat of currency manipulation to control the United States in the years ahead. If China ever sold its U.S. government securities on the international market, it could sharply devalue the dollar and severely damage the American economy. Morrison and Labonte (2009), two experts in Chinese monetary policy, explain,

"As of October 2008, China's Treasury securities holdings were $653 billion ... making [China] the largest foreign holder of U.S. Treasuries. [As a result], some U.S. policymakers [are] concerned that China might use its large holdings of U.S. securities, including U.S. public debt, as leverage against U.S. policies it opposes. For example, various Chinese government officials are reported to have suggested that China could dump (or threaten to dump) a large share of its holdings to prevent the United States from implementing trade sanctions against China's currency policy.

China's strategic use of soft power— the ability of one country to influence other countries through nonmilitary tactics such as cultural exchange, diplomacy, and foreign aid— in Southeast Asia has challenged U.S. power as well. By expanding economic ties, joining regional organizations, and touting shared Asian values, the Chinese have begun to dispel lingering fears that Beijing could pose a threat to Southeast Asia and thus have gained a considerable amount of respect in the region relative to the United States. According to a 2007 Pew Research poll, 29 percent of Indonesians and 27 percent of Malaysians polled had a favorable view of the United States as opposed to 83 percent of Malaysians and 65 percent of Indonesians who had favorable views of China" (Lum, Morrison, and Vaughn 2008).

The Chinese are also competing against the United States in outer space. Over the past forty years, China has made visible progress in developing a robust, modern space program. China has launched more than a hundred orbital missions since 1970. The Chinese completed human spaceflight missions in 2003 and 2005. In 2007, China successfully launched its first lunar probe mission, making it the fourth country to send a probe around the moon and back. That same year, the Chinese also conducted their first successful anti-satellite weapons test. While Beijing never explained why it carried out the test, some experts saw it as "a demonstration of strategic Chinese deterrence" against the United States (Logan 2008). China is also a global leader in annual space launches, and it spends roughly the same amount as France and Japan on its space program (around $1.8 billion annually in 2006).

The rise of China is relevant to sociology and this chapter because it illustrates social change on a global scale, not only within the U.S. For example, in 2009 China replaced the U.S as Brazil's biggest trading partner. Bilateral trade between China and Brazil rose from $2.3 billion a decade ago to $56 billion in 2009. Chinese companies' investments in Brazil, totaled $17 billion, sixty times more than in 2008 (Chang 2011). As a result, there has been frequent contact between the two cultures which have radically different views about the role of workers, government regulations, and unions. As China exercises such a strong economic foothold in Brazil, what type of cultural ramifications will occur in Brazil? What other global ramifications, culture clashes and shifts in cultural practices of countries will occur as China begins to usurp a global military, economic, and technological environment that has been dominated by the U.S and western democratic countries for so long?

In our rapidly changing society, sociology is largely the study of **social change**, change in the structure of society and in its institutions. This chapter discusses some approaches used to understand social change, with an emphasis on changes in social structures and social institutions.

Sociologists have tried to answer three basic questions about social change. First, earlier sociologists wanted to know whether social change was good or bad. As societies change, do they get better, or do they deteriorate? Because they were writing at the beginning of the Industrial Revolution, they saw their traditional family-oriented society vanish and watched it being replaced by urbanization and factory work.

Today, we are more likely to accept social change, but we are still interested in the reasons for it. Thus, the second basic question: What causes the change? Also, like the early sociologists, we are still concerned with the third question: What happens to the people in a society when their society changes?

THEORIES OF SOCIAL CHANGE

Evolutionary Theory of Change

During more optimistic periods of our history, social change was regarded as progress. When society changed, it was assumed to be getting better. Evolutionary theory suggests that societies evolved from the simple and primitive to the more complex and advanced, just as animal life progressed from the simplest one-celled organisms to the most complex animal, the human being. Herbert Spencer, a classic evolutionary theorist, believed that as a society grows, the functions of its members become more specialized and better coordinated into the larger system; and thus, there is progress. Spencer was very influential for many years, especially in the United States, where growth was equated with progress.

Evolutionary theory is less popular today. Change may create social problems rather than social progress, and Spencer's optimistic theory is regarded with some skepticism. Conflict theorists are among those who do not believe in the continuous evolution of progress.

Conflict Theory of Social Change

Conflict theorists are in many ways as optimistic as evolutionary theorists, but they do not assume that societies smoothly evolve to higher levels. Instead, change comes about as oppressed groups struggle to improve their lot. Thus, change is a result of conflict and struggle; however, the result still is, generally, an improvement in society. Each stage of conflict leads to a higher order. As oppressed groups are able to work their way out of oppression, society is able to provide more justice and equality for all. This is a positive view and very optimistic, especially compared with the views of some cyclical theorists.

Cyclical Theories of Change

The most pessimistic cyclical theorists think that decay is inevitable. One such theorist was the historian Oswald Spengler (1918), whose **cyclical change theory** suggests that every society is born, matures, decays, and eventually dies. The Roman Empire rose to power and then gradually collapsed, just as the British Empire grew strong and then deteriorated. Spengler contended that social change might take the form of progress or of decay but that no society lives forever.

Most sociologists believe this view is too rigid and that although societies may have cycles of change, the cycles are not preordained. Pitirim Sorokin (1889–1968), a Russian social theorist who lived through the Russian Revolution of 1917, did not equate change with progress; but neither did he believe that all societies are

The cyclical change theory is the belief that a society is born, matures, decays, and dies. The Roman Empire is one such example.

inevitably destined to decay. He noted, rather, that societies go through various stages. At different stages, he suggested, they emphasize religious beliefs, scientific beliefs, or the pleasures of art, music, and the beauty of nature. They shift from one cycle to another, moving first in one direction, then in another, as the needs of the society demand. Sorokin is still respected for these ideas and has greatly influenced the attempts of structural functionalists to explain social change.

Structural Functionalism and Social Change

Structural functionalists, who believe that society is a balanced system of institutions, each of which serves a function in maintaining society, suggest that when events outside or inside the society disrupt the equilibrium, social institutions make adjustments to restore stability. An influx of immigrants can bring new ideas into a community that then spread throughout the society. A natural disaster, a famine, or a war may disrupt the social order and force the social institutions to make adjustments. Like Sorokin, the structural functionalists do not necessarily consider social change per se to be good or bad—rather, it is the process through which societies lose and regain their equilibrium.

The term *cultural lag* is often used to describe the state of disequilibrium. When an event such as an increase in population or a depletion of natural resources causes a strain in a society, it takes some time for the society to understand the strain and to alter its values and institutions to adapt to the change. Just as the human body must adjust its functioning to adapt to changes, societies adjust to maintain and restore themselves.

Social Change Theory: A Synthesis

Few theorists today are so optimistic that they believe societies inevitably improve; and few are so pessimistic that they believe that societies inevitably decay. Most integrate the ideas of Sorokin, the structural functionalists, and the conflict theorists. Societies do change, but the changes are not necessarily good or bad. Societies attempt to remain stable; and although a stable one is usually better than a chaotic one, stability sometimes causes harsh conditions, injustice, and oppression. When this happens, conflicts arise, and society is forced to change, perhaps for the better, but not necessarily so.

Change and stability, then, are processes that can take place simultaneously in any society. At any given time, one or the other will dominate, depending on the society's needs. Change is inevitable, and it is often beneficial.

Thinking Sociologically

1. Which theory or combination of theories do you think best describes how society changes?
2. Is your own understanding of social change described adequately by theories in this chapter?

WHAT CAUSES SOCIAL CHANGE?

Sociologists believe that social systems change when powerful internal or external forces influence them such that the previous social order can no longer be maintained. However, societies are complex, inter-dependent systems of values, norms, and institutions; they are often amazingly resistant to change and rarely transformed by the ideas or behavior of a single person. When a major change does occur, however, it influences the entire society; each social institution must adapt to the new order.

Sociologists have determined that **ecological changes**—variations in the relationship between population and geography—are a powerful source of social change. They can shape the ideology and political arrangements of a society and can also bring about other innovations.

Population, Geography, and Political Power

Chirot (1994) described the nature of the social changes that brought about the industrialization of Western Europe. He began by comparing the influence of geography on early civilizations in tropical regions with its influence on civilizations in the temperate zones of Northwestern Europe. The first civilizations developed in tropical areas

Ecological change, such as drought, can shape the ideology and political arrangements of a society as opposed to the behavior of a single person.

of the Middle East, India, and northern Africa, where parasitic diseases were rampant (Boserup 1981). The favorite places to settle in these tropical areas were fertile valleys surrounded by arid lands. As the populations grew, irrigation was developed to make use of the arid lands; but these populations could grow only while the water supply lasted. When the population grew too large to be supported by the natural resources, the people became weak and sickly, and disease reduced their numbers. As a result, the size of these populations remained stable.

Later civilizations developed in Northwestern Europe, where the cold winters controlled parasitic diseases and abundant rainfall produced plenty of food without the need for irrigation. Agriculture in northern Europe could potentially support a large population. Furthermore, the geography of northern Europe protected the inhabitants from invasion. Recall that great waves of Asians migrated to the Middle East and to eastern and southern Europe long before written history began. It is assumed that this migration was largely the result of changes in the Asian climate, perhaps increasing cold weather or severe droughts. The waves of migration continued until the Middle Ages. The migrants were warring nomads who raided the civilizations in the warmer climates, destroying their irrigation systems and plundering the wealth of the people. They did not enter Northwestern Europe, however; the geography was not suitable for their nomadic lifestyle because it lacked grazing lands and room to maneuver.

The Europeans, free from disease, drought, and war, were left to accumulate wealth in the form of animals and improved farmlands. The animals provided food, fertilizer, and labor, pulling the plows that improved the farmland.

Chirot (1994) describes how European geography also played an important role in the type of political system that developed. Europe has many river valleys, and settlements were scattered everywhere along these rivers, making the region difficult to conquer. In contrast, it is easier to conquer a civilization if its people are dependent on one river; China, which has only two major rivers, had fewer centers of power that needed to be conquered to gain control of the entire population. Once in control, the conquerors generally imposed excessive taxes and repressive policies. With the tax money, the government in power could build a powerful kingdom.

In Europe, however, because the people were spread about, it was more difficult for conquerors to gain control and to collect taxes. Without the ability to tax, it became impossible to build a strong state. The kingdoms that developed were not very powerful. Instead, feudal estates developed to provide some security for farmers against invaders. Eventually, cities, to which merchants and artisans could escape the feudal lords, grew. Later, the Catholic Church gained power and challenged the kingdoms, further dividing power. The kings, the Church, the feudal lords, and the merchants finally agreed to share power; and their parliaments gave each group a voice in the rule of the various countries. In England, the Magna Carta of 1215 marked this turn of events.

The effect of this division of power was a change from authoritarian to rational rule. Whereas elsewhere in the world, powerful rulers could dictate at whim, in Western Europe, rights and obligations were debated and negotiated and finally set down as law. The powerful elites, especially the merchants in the cities, eventually developed a rational way to deal with disagreements.

Changing Ideology

Chirot (1994) argues that the rational political system of northwestern Europe led eventually to a rational ideology, an ideology based on reason rather than on magic or mystical beliefs. Most of the great early civilizations had *rational legal systems,* laws that stated what could or could not be done; but those systems were religious in nature and not very flexible in their outlook. Islamic or Christian laws, for example, did not rationally negotiate the day-to-day needs of peasants. The peasants, who worked the land, depended on magic, mysticism, and the whims of nature for sun, rain, successful crops, and good health.

In northwestern Europe, the political practice of negotiating law made rational rule the predominant ideology. It was especially important to the city dwellers, who were traders and whose livelihood depended on the buying and selling of goods. Ledgers and accounts regulated their lives, and they could predict rational outcomes. They carried this rational ideology into their religion. No longer settling for mystical explanations, they developed a practical explanation for personal salvation, which eventually led to the Protestant Reformation.

Max Weber, in *The Protestant Ethic and the Spirit of Capitalism,* describes how this rational ideology, which is reflected in religion and business practices, motivated business persons to develop the Industrial Revolution. The Protestant ethic promised its believers that they would be rewarded in heaven for an honest, hard-working, disciplined lifestyle, and these rewards would be apparent in this life. The Protestant businessmen who led the Industrial Revolution did work hard; they did not indulge in sins such as gambling or extravagant living, saved their money, and accumulated wealth, which they believed to be visible proof of their Christian lifestyle. Furthermore, because of the power they had in European parliaments, they were able to keep that wealth and continue to operate with considerable freedom.

The rational ideology also made scientific inquiry acceptable; before the Reformation, science had been frowned upon, especially when it led to discoveries that went against the teachings of the church. The new acceptance of scientific inquiry then led to discoveries and inventions, new sources of social change.

Discoveries and Inventions

Discoveries and inventions have caused far-reaching changes in modern societies, which are becoming increasingly technological. Discoveries and inventions are called innovations, changes that offer something new to society and that alter its norms or institutions. A **discovery** is the act of finding something that has always existed but that no one previously knew about. Discovering the world was round opened new possibilities in exploration and navigation. The discovery of America led to the great migrations from Europe and the creation of new countries. The discovery of gold and other scarce resources in the American West led Americans to continue their migration. The discovery of oil today leads to great social changes in the areas where it is found.

An **invention** is a device constructed by putting two or more things together in a new way. Navigational equipment, factories, and the assembly line were all invented by putting together in new ways materials already discovered and available.

Inventions can be social as well as technological. An example of a social invention is bureaucratic organization. Max Weber noted that bureaucracies were rational organizations based on rules, not on the word of rulers, such as emperors, queens, or other regents. By the time Weber wrote in the nineteenth century, rational systems of organization were rapidly replacing the traditional patriarchal systems throughout Europe, in business as well as in government. Modern societies would not be able to function without them because bureaucracies can organize highly complex groups of people and highly complex tasks into a working whole. No one can deny that modern societies have developed complex bureaucratic organization.

Discoveries and inventions must be acceptable to a society, however, if they are to create social change; and they are not always accepted, no matter how worthwhile they may be.

Diffusion

Diffusion is the process by which an innovation is spread throughout a social system. The rate at which diffusion occurs depends on the values and beliefs of a society. Rogers (2003) points out that after the British navy discovered that citrus fruits (e.g., lemons, limes, and oranges) could cure scurvy, the biggest killer of the world's sailors, it was two hundred years before they began to supply sailors with oranges and lemons. Other remedies were more popular, even though they did not work.

We can be just as slow today in accepting new innovations. The current typewriter keyboard was carefully designed to slow down the typist's speed so that touch typists would not jam up the keys on the first mechanical typewriters. Now, typewriters are more efficient, and computer keyboards could accommodate very rapid speeds. A more efficient arrangement of the keyboard that allows for more speed was designed in 1932, but it has yet to be adopted (Rogers 1983).

Innovations are sometimes most rapidly adopted when an authority enforces their use. For example, laws requiring installation and use of seatbelts made them acceptable to many people. The automobile itself, however, did not need the force of law to become widely adopted.

Improvements on older technologies can increase efficiency.

The Automobile: Impact of an Innovation

Perhaps no single development has changed the United States more than the invention and diffusion of the automobile. The automobile is considered by many historians to have played a major role in the social changes of the Progressive era in American history.

The Automobile and Economic Growth

Progressive reformers used the automobile to help create a more stable system in which capitalism might grow and flourish, according to Ling (1992). One action necessary to create this better environment for capitalism was to open rural areas by improved methods of transportation. At first, railroads and trolleys—and later, the widespread adoption of the automobile—brought rural

The availability of railroads to rural areas helped bring the people into the mainstream of American life and into the influence of centralized social institutions.

areas into the mainstream of American life and brought rural people into the influence of centralized social institutions—educational, religious, and economic.

A second action taken to create an environment better for capitalism was to encourage consumerism. As assembly lines developed and became an alienating work experience, reformers wished to create a compensating culture of consumerism. Even while the work itself was not rewarding, the fruits of the work, the goods that money could buy, could become the reward for work. The most promising consumer item was the automobile (Ling 1992).

While railroad and trolley systems opened rural areas to urban markets, the automobile was immediately successful as a consumer product. By the end of the 1920s, mass production of the automobile brought the price down to the point where the majority of middle-class families in the United States who wanted an automobile had bought one. Demand decreased; but General Motors needed new markets (Snell 1976), so they began to produce buses. They bought interurban electric railways and urban trolley systems, dismantled them, and replaced them with buses. By 1949, General Motors, working with companies such as Greyhound, Standard Oil of California, and Firestone Tire, had replaced more than one hundred relatively clean electric transit systems with buses.

Buses were slow, inefficient, dirty, and expensive to operate. People did not enjoy riding in them. However, when people were bombarded with advertisements encouraging them to buy cars not only as a means of transportation but also as status symbols, they turned from using public transportation and bought more automobiles. In the meantime, the automotive industry lobbied to have the federal interstate highway system constructed. Between 1945 and 1970, state and local governments spent $156 billion to build hundreds of thousands of miles of roads. Only sixteen miles of subway were built during the same period. Thus, the automobile became a necessity as a means of transportation, and Americans bought them in ever-increasing numbers.

Ironically, the road system that was built to accommodate the widespread use of the automobile is itself on the verge of disintegration from neglect; and while the present road system verges on collapse, few new roads are being built. As the population continues to increase, the use of the automobile grows; all these cars must compete for space on the deteriorating road system. Major traffic jams are more and more common as roadways approach their capacity for handling traffic.

The Automobile and the Environment

The heavy use of automobiles and diesel buses causes pollution, and smog from automobile emissions has become a serious problem in American cities. The bad urban air burns the eyes, damages lung tissues, and increases the levels of poisons in the human body and in food products. The automobile has also vastly increased our need for oil. The United States, even though it has huge supplies of oil, uses so much oil that it imports more than half of what is used in this country.

Oil is the major pollutant of the ocean. Huge tankers routinely leak, spill, or purposely dump oil into the sea. In addition, hundreds of accidents involving tankers take place at sea each year. This issue was brought to international attention in 1989 when an Exxon oil tanker dumped eleven million gallons of oil into Prince William Sound, oil that spread over three thousand square miles of Alaskan waters, and then again, recently, with the BP oil rig explosion that spewed 185 million gallons into the Gulf of Mexico over the course of eighty-six days—discussed in Chapter 5 of this book. Spilled oil poisons, smothers, burns, or coats sea plants and animals, thus killing them. The oceans of the world from the Arctic to the Antarctic are slowly being covered with oil slicks, and to date there is no effective way to clean them up.

The demand for oil as a fuel is so substantial that the United States is willing to go to war to protect its supply from foreign oil fields. Since World War II, this country has built up a vast military force, and the government has vowed to use it to protect oil-producing nations that sell to the United States, such as Kuwait.

Thus, we see that the United States has become so economically dependent on the automobile and on oil that it is willing to pollute land and sea, and go to war to prevent risk to our oil supply. Steps to diminish this dependence have not been taken, and still are not being implemented, however. It is obvious that these factors have serious worldwide consequences.

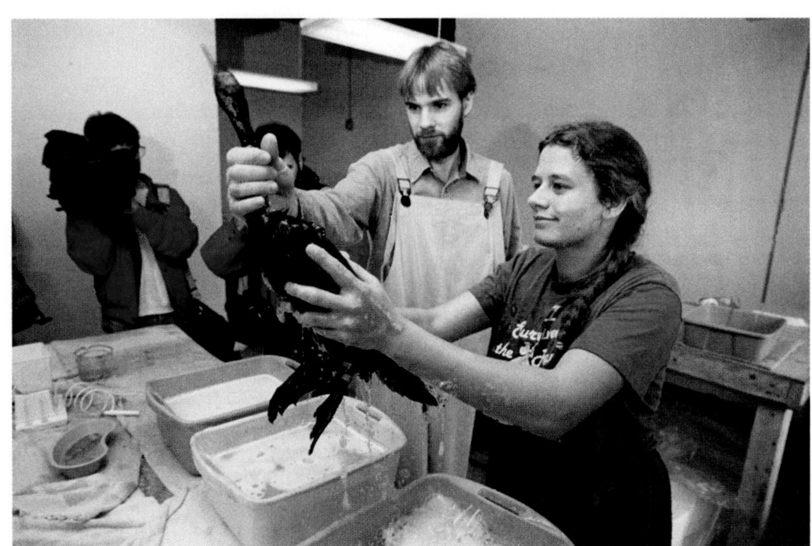

Oil is considered a major pollutant of the ocean. It kills sea plants and animals. Birds were rescued from a massive oil spill when the tanker Exxon Valdez ran aground in the Prince William Sound on March 24, 1989.

THE INTERNET AND SOCIAL CHANGE

There can be no question that one of the biggest impacts on human life in history has been the development of the Internet. The Internet has radically transformed almost every area of social and personal life. A partial list includes dating, shopping, marketing, investing, banking, academic research, medical care, entertainment, education and communication. In 2008, 2.5 billion text messages were sent everyday, an increase of more than 100 percent from the previous year. Ninety trillion emails were sent on the Internet in 2009, approximately 247 billion a day, with 1.4 billion users worldwide, an increase of more than 100 million users in one year (www.royalpingdom.com). There are more than 500 million subscribed Facebook users with 50 percent of subscribers logging on everyday. Interpersonal feedback has become almost instantaneous. This has affected everything from decision making to identity formation. Internet usage is pervasive, world-wide and rapidly expanding. (See Table 21-1). While the Internet has led to vast improvements in many areas of our lives, it has also posed risks, challenges and threats. Identity-theft, terrorism, stalking, and unwanted interruptions are a few areas in which cultural changes are also occurring as a result of the extensive use of the Internet.

Thinking Sociologically

Evaluate the advantages and disadvantages of the development of the automobile in this country.

SOCIAL CHANGE IN UNDERDEVELOPED NATIONS

Although Europe (and later the United States) industrialized, other nations did not. Attempts to explain this lack of development have evolved around two different theoretical points of view—modernization, which has its roots in evolutionary theory, and dependency theory, which is also known as world systems theory.

Modernization in Underdeveloped Nations

Evolutionary theorists tend to assume that today's underdeveloped nations in Africa, South America, and other areas that do not have modern industry, such as is found in Europe and North America, will pass through the same stages that industrialized nations passed through in their quest for modernization. **Modernization** is the process whereby preindustrial countries emerge as urban societies with lower birth rates, more goods and services, better nutrition and health care, improved housing, and some luxuries.

TABLE 21-1 WORLD INTERNET USAGE AND POPULATION STATISTICS

World	Population (2011 Est.)	Internet Users Dec. 31, 2000	Internet Users Mar. 31, 2011	Penetration (% population)	Growth 2000-2011	Users % of Table
Africa	1,037,524,058	4,514,400	118,609,620	11.4%	2,527.4%	5.7%
Asia	3,879,740,877	114,304,000	922,329,554	23.8%	706.9%	44.0%
Europe	816,426,346	105,096,093	476,213,935	58.3%	353.1%	22.7%
Middle East	216,258,843	3,284,800	68,553,666	31.7%	1,987.0%	3.3%
North America	347,394,870	108,096,800	272,066,000	78.3%	151.7%	13.0%
Latin America/Carib.	597,283,165	18,068,919	215,939,400	36.2%	1,037.4%	10.3%
Oceania/ Australia	35,426,995	7,620,480	21,293,830	60.1%	179.4%	1.0%
WORLD TOTAL	**6,930,055,154**	**360,985,492**	**2,095,006,005**	**30.2%**	**480.4%**	**100.0%**

A closer comparison, however, suggests that contemporary nations may not be able to take the same course as those that are already industrialized. The United States developed into an industrial society due to its work ethic, its lack of competition from other countries, and its vast supply of natural resources, including its excellent land for agriculture and its minerals, such as iron and coal. The United States can also bring in the labor it requires through immigration and can stop immigration when no more workers are needed.

Many underdeveloped nations simply lack the same abundance of natural resources. Tropical forests and arid deserts cannot easily be developed to produce grain. Oil, coal, iron, and lumber are unavailable in many countries. Many of these items must be purchased from other countries to meet the needs of the ever-growing native population. To purchase these necessities, Developing World countries have borrowed enormous sums and now have huge debts to Western banks, especially to the large banks in the United States.

To pay these debts, Developing World countries have tried to develop cash crops that can be exported to pay for the goods the country must buy. These agricultural products are usually not foods, but such products as coffee, cotton, and flowers. Unfortunately, because the land has been taken over for cash crops, the native population no longer has land on which to grow food. They do not have jobs in agriculture either because most of the work is done with farm machinery. Part of the rural population has moved into the already crowded cities hoping to find work; but work is scarce, and pay is poor. Often the poor live in the streets or in makeshift homes that provide little shelter. Dysentery and pneumonia are common, especially among children. The need for medical care puts further strain on the resources of the population.

Inasmuch as undeveloped nations cannot compete with the large multinational industries, they sometimes invite those industries to come into their countries to do business, hoping that these industries will provide employment for the natives and income for the country. This is rarely successful. Employment opportunities are usually too few and are limited to the lowest-paying jobs. When the

Products such as coffee are used as cash crops to pay for goods that the country needs to buy.

goods are exported, the profits go to the multinational corporation and not to the host country.

Thus, while the United States developed its industry with control over its population, abundant natural resources, and no competition from other world industries, developing nations have tried to modernize with too large a population, too few natural resources, and too much competition from worldwide industries. Not surprisingly, they have been unable to support their people. In trying to do so, they have gone into debt to such an extent that the world banking system is threatened by bankruptcy from the unpaid debts of these nations.

Dependency theorists agree that underdeveloped nations are suffering. However, their understanding of the cause of the problems is very different.

Dependency or World Systems Theory

Dependency theory was inspired by Marx and has been developed by conflict theorists, who believe that underdeveloped nations cannot industrialize as the Western world did because they have been made dependent on the Western world. One must look at the entire world system, and not just at individual regions, if one is to understand social change. **World systems theory** states that **core nations** (those that are already industrialized) dominate the economies of **peripheral nations** (underdeveloped nations), taking wealth from the peripheral nations to further their own development.

Wallerstein (2000) argues that the northwestern European core nations first exploited the eastern and southern European nations; and when exploration opened trade in the sixteenth century, they went on to exploit North and South America, Africa, and India. The Europeans took raw materials from the rest of the world, used them to produce manufactured goods, and then sold manufactured goods to the peripheral nations at high cost, driving these nations into poverty.

This exploitation is still common. Del Monte and Dole, multinational corporations, grow pineapples in the Philippines and Thailand and ship them to the United States, now a core nation. The Gulf and Western Corporation grows sugar in Central America for sale in the United States. Coffee and bananas are other major products taken exploitatively from Latin American nations. The pharmaceutical industry also takes raw materials from peripheral countries, manufactures medicines, and sells them back to these countries at high prices (Gereffi 1983). The profits from these diverse ventures go to the core nations' stockholders, not to the peripheral nations that provided the raw materials.

Gereffi (1983) suggests that these exploited countries could begin to remedy this situation by putting a ban on the purchase of all but the most essential manufactured products until they develop their own industries; and they could nationalize the industries of foreign corporations in their own countries. However, this would require a revolutionary change in ideology in many cases. As long as the elites in peripheral nations cooperate with business from the core nations, such changes are not possible.

Coffee and bananas are other major products taken exploitatively from Latin American nations.

SOCIOLOGY AT WORK

Societal Analysis in the Auto Industry

Carroll DeWeese has worked as a staff research scientist in the Societal Analysis Department of General Motors (GM) Research Laboratories. The objectives of GM Research Laboratories are to generate new technical knowledge of commercial interest to GM, to evaluate outside technical advances for possible application to GM products and processes, to anticipate future technological needs and develop the expertise to meet those needs, and to assist in the analysis of corporate priorities, policies, and programs. The Societal Analysis Department is an interdisciplinary department, the mission of which is to study the impact of GM on society and vice versa. DeWeese led a group with degrees in applied mathematics, economics, operations research, psychology, and sociology.

Research in the department is generally interdisciplinary, problem oriented, and quantitative. Researchers have worked on a variety of topics, including air pollution, auto safety, auto service, customer satisfaction, energy usage and efficiency, product quality, diesel odor, and other areas of public concern.

DeWeese studied sociology at the University of Houston and at Purdue. He joined GM Research Laboratories immediately on completing his PhD at Purdue. DeWeese talks about what makes researchers successful in an environment such as this. He has been able to identify several characteristics. "They must be pragmatic, not ideological—interested in doing whatever is necessary to solve a problem. They are persons looking for tools to solve problems, not persons with some particular tool trying to find problems to solve. They must be able to communicate, to excite and convince others about their ideas. Brevity is a virtue here. After a year's work, they should be able to convince a decision maker of the importance of the problem studied and the results found on a single sheet of paper or in five minutes of conversation. They must know how to identify critical problems—the more critical the problem, the more attention any actionable results will receive. They must know how to work as part of a team, to secure the cooperation and support of their colleagues. Finally, they must have quantitative ability combined with qualitative flexibility. That's where the interdisciplinary arrangement, the variety of perspectives, pays off." In sum, to be successful in this type of setting, people should have research skills, critical-thinking and problem-solving skills, communication skills, and interpersonal skills.

Interestingly, DeWeese's list of characteristics of the successful researcher in his department does not include specific substantive knowledge. This does not mean that substantive knowledge is not important in this type of work. Instead, he says, "People are expected to acquire whatever substantive knowledge is needed to solve the problems on which they are working. On the other hand, use of the sociological imagination is critical for identifying, studying, and solving problems. The strength of sociology is the perspective it gives a person. I am not saying substantive knowledge is unimportant. When we hire people, we have problem areas in mind and we look for people with substantive backgrounds in those problem areas. However, that substantive knowledge is a given. It is not a characteristic of success." The important thing that a person needs to come to this type of job, DeWeese suggests, is to be able to look at situations and problems from a variety of different perspectives and to be able to recognize the relative merit of each perspective. The sociological imagination enables a person to do this.

Wallerstein (2000) believes that there are worldwide forces uniting to change this ideology and to oppose such extreme inequality. He believes that these movements are growing in strength and, over the next two centuries, will bring an end to capitalistic exploitation and the powerful national systems we know today.

As mentioned in the introduction to this chapter, the totalitarian nations of Eastern Europe saw dramatic social changes in the past decade. These are clearly conflicts over extreme inequality. Many of the people involved in these changes see capitalism as a means to greater equality, but others may not be willing to give up the personal security of socialism in exchange for the economic insecurity of capitalism. It will be interesting to watch what solutions the countries of Eastern Europe find to solve their problems and how the rest of the world responds to the needs of these countries. World systems theory has done a great deal to alter our perception of the world, and it has generated a great deal of scholarly research by viewing the world as one large, complex system. It will be interesting to see whether world systems theory will influence ongoing political actions of nations.

SOCIAL CHANGE AND THE INDIVIDUAL

How does social change affect the individual? In developing nations, increasing population and the removal of people from their land have had a devastating effect on the individual. Whenever social change is so disruptive to the social order that individuals cannot obtain the basic necessities of life, change can be terrifying. However, when the social change is generally perceived as progress, what are its effects? This question has always been of interest to sociologists.

Most early sociologists believed that industrialization alienates people from their work and from one another. Durkheim was one of the few who believed that complex industrial societies would have a positive effect on human relationships. Noting that peasants were moving to European cities in large numbers, he recognized that this changed the nature of their labor. Peasants had been self-sufficient and performed all of the work necessary to meet their personal needs; but in the city, work was specialized, and workers were not self-sufficient. Each person specialized in a particular product and then traded that product for money to meet personal needs. Thus, the cobbler sold shoes and bought food and clothing. In *The Division of Labor* (1893), Durkheim endorsed the move toward specialization, arguing that this interdependence would create a more integrated society.

Marx, on the other hand, was concerned that the move from agrarian to industrial societies would alienate people from their work. The factory owner, not the worker, would own the goods produced. Marx believed that this arrangement was so unfair that it would not survive. Workers would rebel and a more equitable system of work would be developed.

Tönnies (1887) was also concerned that interpersonal relationships would suffer in industrial society. Peasant society, he contended, was characterized by *gemeinschaft relationships*, in which people knew one another totally, whereas in urban society they would be strangers. Those who worked together would know nothing about their coworkers' families or religious or political views, for example. Tönnies referred to these impersonal relationships as *gesellschaft.*

Weber was concerned about the increasing rationalization of society. The traditional beliefs of the family were rapidly disappearing, and in Weber's day, society was becoming more bureaucratic. Decisions were no longer being based on traditional family concerns. The system in which people performed tasks according to their capabilities and were taken care of when they were unable to be productive gave way to one in which decisions about employment were made on the basis of the employer's needs. Employees were hired or fired regardless of their own needs for work, income, or self-respect.

Sociologists realize that modern socialization encourages individuals to behave in a fashion compatible with industrial society. In the nineteenth century, when frontiers were being conquered and industries were being built, people were encouraged to be highly innovative; even the most ruthless could find a place in society taming the frontier or building new industries. Also, people on the frontier far from neighbors did not have to worry about being popular, getting along with others, cooperating, or making a good impression. They did, however, need the skill and wit to stay alive. Riesman (1950) described these people as **inner-directed**.

The same skills were needed in the business world. Businesses were small; and whether one owned a store or began a small factory, survival depended on one's own skill and hard work. The most successful industrial leaders of the nineteenth century, the so-called robber barons, were noted for their extreme ruthlessness.

Today, the nature of work has changed dramatically. Most people work in corporations with many other individuals. In a large corporation, a competitive person who lives by skill and wit, and is concerned exclusively with his or her own survival, makes many enemies and can create chaos rather than cooperation. Many jobs in corporations today require cooperation, teamwork, and a concern for others. Riesman described the cooperative person, the person who is concerned with the reaction of others, as **other-directed**. Maccoby (1977) has called this other-directed person the **gamesman**, the person who is highly competitive and innovative but who prefers to function as the leader of a team. The gamesman thus occupies a position similar to that of a quarterback on a football team. Interestingly, football surpassed baseball as the most popular American sport in the mid-1960s. The more individualistic sport of baseball has given way to a type of sport requiring a team effort and cooperation. It seems that changes in the way we spend our leisure correspond to changes in the types of managers sought in the job market.

The economic prosperity of a country can affect the generation of young people growing up at the time, as has been shown by Elder (1974), who studied children of the Great Depression, and by Jones (1980), who studied children of the prosperous baby-boom generation. Generally speaking, children raised during periods of prosperity and whose families are economically secure develop fairly positive views of the world and are interested in self-development. Children raised during hard times, especially if their families suffered, are more pessimistic and assume that life will be a struggle. They come to value independence, hard work, and security (Stewart and Healy 1989).

Television and the other mass media have also affected individual lifestyles. The media encourage us to buy consumer products such as cosmetics and designer clothes, and we watch programs depicting middle-class lifestyles. We listen to news broadcasts that tell us what is important in the world. If we have learned to be good team players, we buy our products and let the politicians worry about the state of the world.

Thinking Sociologically

How have social changes in the past decade shaped your personal development?

APPLYING SOCIOLOGY TO THE FUTURE

Futurists, people who attempt to describe what the future will be like, range from the most pessimistic doomsayers to the greatest optimists. The doomsayers predict an economic depression far worse than the depression of the 1930s. The wisest investment, they say, is to buy a piece of land in a very remote part of the country, build a substantial shelter that will be well hidden from the hordes of the poor and starving who will be roaming the countryside when the economy collapses, and bury near the shelter a supply of dehydrated food, guns, and other basic equipment needed to survive alone in the wilderness.

The optimists predict an end to poverty and drudgery and believe that human innovation will solve our problems. For example, computers may make a more individualistic society possible. People may be able to remain at home and earn their livings by telecommunications, engendering for themselves and their children a more unique and creative individual lifestyle.

Sociologists are more hesitant to make predictions. One realistic method of determining what the future will be like is to analyze the possibilities and problems that it might hold and to use social planning to strive for future goals and to avoid future disasters.

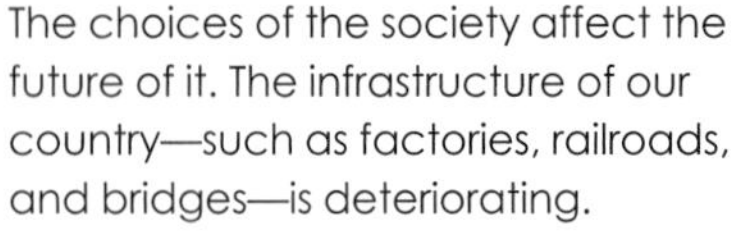

The choices of the society affect the future of it. The infrastructure of our country—such as factories, railroads, and bridges—is deteriorating.

Etzioni (1980) followed this course in making his predictions. He argues that society should make choices and should plan for a future that will provide a satisfactory lifestyle to its members. Our economy is currently based on the consumption of vast amounts of goods, and we are using up our natural and economic resources. Meanwhile, our factories, transportation systems, roads, railroads, and bridges are deteriorating rapidly. We must choose either to continue to spend money on goods—or to spend hundreds of billions of dollars to modernize our factories and to build an efficient transportation system. This rebuilding would reduce the hazards of pollution and would improve the quality of life for all, but it might mean we would have to cut back on our consumption of goods.

Etzioni used the typical approach of sociologists in his study of social change, which is to try to understand the social system. Our social system is based on a profit-oriented economy, and we manufacture products that can be sold for a profit. Our system functions to support a cycle of production and consumption, but it does not support modernization of factories or an efficient use of resources unless such actions provide a profit. By understanding that our system now functions only when profits are made, it is possible to predict what will happen if we continue to function as we have in the past. We will use up all our resources.

Nonetheless, innovations can be made, institutions can be changed, and values and goals can be altered. A society can change its course and move in a new direction. We cannot, today, optimistically assume that progress will be inevitable and that we do not have to plan to reach our goals. Neither is there reason to be so pessimistic that we resign ourselves to becoming victims of a social system in decline. Furthermore, we cannot blithely assume that society will run its course from good times to bad and then bounce back to good times again; we could in the meantime destroy all life on earth. By understanding how societies function, we can make choices, alter our social institutions, and develop lifestyles that will reduce conflict, avoid ecological devastation, and support human life in the ever-increasing numbers that seem inevitable. We can plan to use our resources wisely.

Sociologists who study society from a historical perspective, observing the relationship between social changes and social problems—for example, increased automobile use and today's energy problems—are likely to be frustrated by the practice of solving problems as they arise rather than trying to find long-range solutions. These solutions might require better technology to control auto emissions or clean up oil spills, for example. In any case, more effective solutions can be developed if we understand the social basis of the problems.

Our problems are caused, in part, by a cultural lag in our awareness of future needs. Social planning could help us to change our social systems and to improve the situation. Those who have a vested interest in our current system might resist change, which would create a certain amount of conflict; but such conflict might be beneficial to society. Sociology, by helping us to understand social change, can help us to direct it. Academic sociologists will continue to study how changes affect our social institutions and will help us to predict future trends; professional sociologists in the workplace may use knowledge of sociology to help policymakers and social planners design long-range solutions to social and technological problems; nonprofessional sociologists in the workplace may use knowledge of social change to help them foresee and plan for business trends and consumer needs; and you may use knowledge of social change and other sociological theories to plan for your family's future.

Sociology originally grew out of an attempt to understand and do something about the social problems related to changes brought about by modernization. Thus, as Shostak (1985, 172) notes, "it was conceived as a way of managing social change and helping humankind stay in charge of events." Although it may be impossible to predict with certainty the impact of technological or institutional changes on the whole social system, sociology does alert us to the important fact that a change in one part of the system will continue to reverberate throughout the system long into the future. Armed with this knowledge and with the knowledge of the other theories, perspectives, and concepts sociology offers, humankind may be better equipped to shape its social institutions, and you may be better equipped to shape your own life. The authors hope that this introduction to the study of sociology has sparked your own sociological imagination so that you can think about the good life for you in terms of social as well as individual accomplishments.

CHAPTER REVIEW

Wrapping it up

Summary

1. Society is changing so rapidly that sociology has become, in many respects, the study of social change.

2. Evolutionary theory proposes the optimistic view that change is progress, which growth is always good, and that stagnation leads to decay.

3. Conflict theorists are also optimistic about social change, but they believe that conflict will occasionally arise to correct adverse social developments. The outcome of such conflict, they say, will be better social systems.

4. Cyclical theorists can be very pessimistic. They assume that societies grow, reach a peak, and then inevitably decay. Some cyclical theorists, however, do not assume that change is always for the better or the worse. Societies move back and forth, they contend, emphasizing first one value, then another, as the needs of the society change.

5. Structural functionalists have been concerned primarily with stability, but they recognize that society changes occasionally. Often, a change that affects one social institution will be followed by cultural lag, a disruption in the functioning of society until other institutions adjust to the change.

6. Most sociologists agree that society is orderly and that social institutions function to maintain order. They also agree that conflicts may arise when the existing social order causes hardship for the members of a society but that such conflicts can be beneficial.

7. Some major causes of social change and conflict are population changes, geographic changes, political arrangements, and ideology. In northwestern Europe, the geography allowed many small communities to grow, develop political systems through negotiation, and develop a rational ideology that led to the age of exploration. The migration that followed brought different cultures into contact with one another, spreading the ideas of one culture to another.

8. Discoveries, inventions, and the diffusion of these innovations also cause social change. The automobile has had enormous impact on life in industrial nations.

9. Modernization theorists believe that underdeveloped nations have different natural resources, different values, and a different work ethic—all of which have caused their patterns of growth to differ from those of the developed, or core nations.

10. Dependency or world systems theorists believe that less developed nations are exploited by the nations that developed first.

11. Changes in modern industrial societies have changed the nature of human relationships. From the peasant's concern for family and community, we moved to a period of competitive individualism, and we are now moving into an era of competitive team play.
12. In the future, it is hoped that we will be able to plan innovations that will improve our ecology and our ways of relating to one another.

Key Terms

core nations Industrial nations that exploit underdeveloped, peripheral nations

cyclical change theory The view that societies go through a cycle of birth, maturation, decline, and death

dependency theory Conflict theory stating that underdeveloped nations cannot industrialize because they are dependent on the nations already industrialized

discovery The act of finding something that has always existed but that no one previously knew about

ecological change Change brought about by the way a population uses the natural resources available to it

eamesman The type of manager sought by corporations today: a person who is highly competitive and innovative but who prefers to function as the leader of a team

inner-directed A description by David Riesman of people who are independent, innovative, and focused on their own survival with little concern with what others think

invention A device constructed by putting two or more things together in a new way

modernization The process whereby preindustrial countries emerge as urban societies with lower birth rates, more goods and services, and better nutrition and health care

other-directed A description by David Riesman of people who focus on making a good impression, being popular, getting along with others, and being cooperative

peripheral nations Underdeveloped nations who are exploited by core nations

social change Changes in the structure of a society or in its social institutions

world systems theory Conflict theory stating core nations dominate the economics of peripheral nations

Discussion Questions

1. Discuss how the geography of the United States led to its development as a modern industrial nation.
2. Discuss how closely linked American ideology is to what Weber called "rationalism," as opposed to an ideology linked to traditionalism.
3. Discuss how the American political system developed as a result of geography and of rationalism.
4. Why does the United States have a less developed railroad system than Europe and Japan?
5. Discuss ways in which the United States could change its transportation system and the advantages and disadvantages to such changes.
6. Discuss the reasons why Developing World nations cannot develop industries the way the United States did.
7. Predict the future. Are you an optimist or a pessimist?

Pop Quiz

1. Which theory equates social change with progress?

   a. evolutionary theory
   b. cyclical theory
   c. structural-functional theory
   d. progressional theory

2. Which theory suggests that societies progress to a higher order as oppressed groups improve their lot?

a. evolutionary theory
b. cyclical theory
c. conflict theory
d. structural-functional theory

3. Which theory suggests that social institutions act to restore equilibrium when society is disrupted by social changes?

a. conflict theory
b. cyclical theory
c. structural-functional theory
d. evolutionary theory

4. Variations in the relationship between population and geography are called ______.

a. ecological changes
b. structural changes
c. societal changes
d. cyclical changes

5. The document that provided for shared political power in Europe was the ______.

a. Natural Vindication of the Rights of Man
b. Magna Carta
c. Natural Vindication of the Rights of Woman
d. Declaration of Interdependence

6. What did Max Weber argue about Protestantism?

a. It provided a rational ideology that motivates businesses.
b. It stressed the work ethic.
c. It provided for accumulated wealth and political influence.
d. All of the above

7. Finding something that has always existed but that no one previously knew about is called a/an ______.

a. innovation
b. discovery
c. invention
d. creation

8. A device constructed by putting two or more things together in a new way is a/an ______.

a. discovery
b. invention
c. innovation
d. creation

9. The process whereby preindustrial countries emerge as urban societies with lower birth rates, more goods and services, and some luxuries is known as ______.

a. modernization
b. development
c. dependency
d. industrialization

10. Which of the following types of nations are dominated and exploited?

a. core nations
b. industrialized nations
c. peripheral nations
d. developed nations

11. According to conflict theory, societies progress to a higher order only if oppressed groups improve their lot. T/F

12. Most theorists today agree that social change is inevitably for the better. T/F

13. Ecological changes are a powerful source of social change. T/F

14. Most of the great early civilizations had rational legal systems. T/F

15. Inventions can be social as well as technological. T/F

1. A	6. D	11. T
2. B	7. B	12. F
3. C	8. B	13. T
4. A	9. A	14. T
5. B	10. C	15. T

Glossary

absolutist view The view that there is wide agreement about social norms and that certain behaviors are deviant regardless of the social context in which they occur

account of behavior An effort at maintaining the self by explaining the reasons for or facts surrounding the behavior

achieved status A social position, such as teacher, graduate, or wife, obtained through one's own efforts

acquaintance rape Rape by someone who is known to the person being raped (such as in date rape)

acting crowd A crowd that acts on the basis of aroused impulse and thus one that may be volatile, aggressive, and dangerous

activity theory The theory of aging that suggests that elderly persons who remain active will be the best adjusted

advanced horticultural societies Societies with irrigation systems and other advanced farming practices

age The number of years since birth

age-adjusted death rate The number of deaths occurring at each age for each sex, per 100,000 people of that age who are living

aged The age group that occupies the later part of the life span, generally meaning the old, elderly, or senior citizens

ageism Prejudice and discrimination based on age

age norms Expectations about the behavior considered appropriate for people of a given age

age segregation The separation of groups by age such as occurs in our education system

age-sex composition The number of men and women in the population, along with their ages

aggregate group Any collection of people together in one place; participants interact briefly and sporadically

aging The biological, psychological, or social processes that occur with growing older

agrarian societies Complex societies with farming, armies, merchants, and a concentration of wealth in the hands of a few people

alcoholism A disease related to the drinking of alcohol that has identifiable and progressive symptoms (If untreated, alcoholism can lead to mental damage, physical incapacity, and early death.)

alienation A feeling of estrangement or dissociation, such as Marx's idea of feeling alienated from work because of no control over it or satisfaction from it

Alzheimer's disease A disease affecting primarily older persons in which the brain gradually atrophies, resulting in loss of memory and impairment of thought processes

amalgamation The process by which different racial or ethnic groups form a new group through interbreeding or intermarriage

analytical or explanatory studies The studies used to help explain what causes certain events or problems

Anglo conformity A form of assimilation in which the minority loses its identity completely and adopts the norms and practices of the dominant WASP culture

animism The religious belief that spirits inhabit virtually everything in nature and control all aspects of life and destiny

anomie theory The view that deviance arises from the incongruences between a society's emphasis on attaining certain goals and the availability of legitimate, institutionalized means of reaching those goals

anthropology The study of the physical, biological, social, and cultural development of humans, often on a comparative basis

applied science The area of science in which the knowledge gained from the "pure" sciences is put into practice

applied social research The use of sociological knowledge and research skills to obtain information for groups and organizations

artifacts Physical products or objects created through human actions

ascribed status A social position assigned to a person on the basis of a characteristic over which he or she has no control, such as age, sex, or race

assimilation The process through which individuals and groups forsake their own cultural tradition to become part of a different group and tradition

associational group A group of people who join together to pursue a common interest in an organized, formally structured way

authoritarian personality theory The view that people with an authoritarian type of personality are more likely to be prejudiced than those who have other personality types

authority Power accepted as legitimate by those it affects

barefoot doctors People that are chosen by the peasants in the communes in Communist China to provide medicine and treat simple illnesses and emergencies and receive three to eighteen months of training

blaming the victim A type of reasoning that implies that social problems are caused by the people facing them

Beguines Communes of peasant women who did not choose to marry and who took vows of celibacy (These communes existed during the Middle Ages.)

bilateral lineage A descent system in which influence, wealth, and power are assigned to both sides of the family

biological race The view that race is determined based on heredity

blended families Families composed of at least one formerly married spouse, the children of the previous marriage or marriages, and new offspring

bourgeoisie The class of people who own the means of production

Buddhism One of the world's principal religions in which adherents follow the teachings of Buddha, the enlightened one, who preached a doctrine of "Four Noble Truths"

bureaucracy A hierarchical, formally organized structural arrangement of an organization based on the division of labor and authority

capitalism An economic system in which all of the means of production are privately owned

caste system A system of stratification in which one's social position is ascribed at birth, one's value is assessed in terms of religious or traditional beliefs, and in which upward social mobility is impossible

casual crowd A crowd that is high in anonymity but low in suggestibility, contagion, emotional arousal, and unity

categorical group A group of people who share a common characteristic but do not interact or have any social organization

censorship Prohibiting the availability of some type of information

census An official count of the number of people in a given area

charismatic authority Authority granted to someone on the bases of his or her personality characteristics

Chicago School An approach developed by Cooley, Mead, Thomas, and others in the 1920s that emphasized the importance of social interactions in the development of human thought and action

chiropractors Those who practice healing by manipulating the body, especially the spine

Christianity One of the principal religions of the world, followers of which profess faith in the teachings of Jesus Christ

church An institutionalized organization of people who share common religious beliefs

citizen One who is considered a member of a state and who is entitled to the privileges and freedoms granted to members of the state

city-state A city and the surrounding area ruled independently of other areas

class consciousness Awareness among members of a society that the society is stratified

classical perspective A view of acting crowd behavior that suggests that people in a crowd lose their conscious personalities and act impulsively on the basis of their instincts rather than reason

class system A system of stratification found in industrial societies in which one's class is determined by one's wealth and in which vertical social mobility is possible

clinical sociology The use of sociological perspectives, theories, concepts, research, and methods for consulting and providing technical assistance to individuals or organizations

closed system A system of stratification in which there is no movement from one rank to another

collective behavior The spontaneous, unstructured, and transitory behavior of a group of people in reaction to a specific event

collective conscience A collective psyche that results from the blending of many individual mentalities, but exists above any one individual

collective excitement In the interactionist perspective on crowd behavior, the stage during which milling reaches a high level of agitation

community A collection of people within a geographic area among whom there is some degree of mutual identification, interdependence, or organization of activities

comparable worth Evaluating and rewarding different occupations equally if the work in each occupation requires the same level of skill and is of equal value to the employer

complementary needs A theory of mate selection based on the idea that people marry those who provide the maximum need gratification (Needs tend to be complementary rather than similar.)

compulsory public education Publicly funded education that is mandatory until a certain age

communism An economic system in which members of the society own the means of production in common

concentration An urban ecological process in which population, services, and institutions come to be gathered most densely in the areas in which conditions are advantageous

concentric zone model A model of urban structure showing that cities grow out equally in all directions from their original centers, producing uniform circles of growth that have their own distinctive land use, population, activities, and institutions

concept An abstract system of meaning that enables us to perceive a phenomenon in a certain way

conflict theory A social theory that views conflict as inevitable and natural and as a significant cause of social change

Confucianism One of the world's principal religions, found mainly in China, adherents of which follow the teachings of Confucius

conjugal families Families consisting of a husband and wife, with or without children

content analysis The procedure of systematically extracting thematic data from a wide range of communications

contest mobility A competitive system of education in which those who do best at each level are able to move on to the next level

control group In an experiment, the group not exposed to the independent variable that is introduced to the experimental group

conventional crowd A crowd, such as the spectators at a baseball game, whose members are anonymous but share a common focus and follow established social norms and rules

conversion effect A radical shift of interests and lifestyle that occurs when people move from one type of area to another, as from an urban area to a suburb

core nations Industrial nations that exploit underdeveloped, peripheral nations

counterculture A subculture that adheres to a set of norms and values that sharply contradict the dominant norms and values of the society of which that group is a part

credentialism The practice of requiring degrees for most high-paying jobs, whether or not the degrees actually signify skills necessary to accomplish the jobs

crime A violation of a criminal statutory law accompanied by a specific punishment applied by some governmental authority

crowd A temporary group of people in face-to-face contact who share a common interest or focus of attention

cults Extreme forms of sects that call for a totally new and unique lifestyle, often under the direction of a charismatic leader

cultural lag The tendency for changes in nonmaterial culture to occur more slowly than changes in technology and material culture

cultural pluralism The situation in which the various ethnic groups in a society maintain their distinctive cultural patterns, subsystems, and institutions

cultural relativism The belief that cultures must be judged on their own terms rather than by the standards of another culture

cultural transmission theory The theory that a community's deviance may be transmitted to newcomers through learning and socialization

cultural universals Aspects of culture that are shared by all people, such as symbols, shelter, food, and a belief system

culture The systems of ideas, values, beliefs, knowledge, norms, customs, and technology shared by almost everyone in a particular society

cyclical change theory The view that societies go through a cycle of birth, maturation, decline, and death

decentralized bureaucracies Putting the decision-making processes in the hands of the people or local units rather than in the hands of a centralized few

deconcentration Movement outward from the city because of increases in land values and taxes and declines in services and public facilities

de facto segregation School assignment based on residence boundaries in which blacks and whites live in separate neighborhoods

degenerative diseases Those diseases that slowly disable the body as one gets older, such as heart disease and cancer

de jure segregation The legal assignment of children to schools solely because of race

democracy A power structure in which people govern themselves, either directly or through elected representatives

democratic socialism An economic system in which the means of production are owned primarily by individuals or groups of individuals and in which goods and services vital to the society, such as transportation systems and medical care, are owned and run by the state

demographic transition The change from high birth and death rates to low birth and death rates with a period of rapid population growth in between (This transition occurs as a society evolves from a traditional premodern stage to a modern industrial stage.)

demography The statistical study of population, especially data on birth rates, death rates, marriage rates, health, and migration

denominations Well-established and highly institutionalized churches

dependency ratio The ratio between the number of persons in the dependent population and the number of people in the supportive or working population

dependency theory Conflict theory stating that underdeveloped nations cannot industrialize because they are dependent on the nations already industrialized

dependent variable A variable that is changed or influenced by another variable

descriptive research Research that describes social reality or provides facts about the social world

descriptive studies Studies used primarily to obtain information about a particular social problem, event, or population

deviance Variation from a set of norms or shared social expectations

diagnostic related groups (DRGs) The schedule of payment limits that is set by the federal government for Medicaid and Medicare recipients

differential association theory The theory that deviance results when individuals have more contact with groups that define deviance favorably than with groups that define it unfavorably

differential reinforcement The view that the acquisition and persistence of either deviant or conforming behavior is a function of what behaviors have been rewarded or punished

direct relationship A relationship between two variables in which an increase in one variable is accompanied by an increase in the other; compare with *inverse relationship*

disclaimers An aspect of maintaining our presentation of self in which we deny behavior that contradicts how we wish to be viewed

discovery The act of finding something that has always existed but that no one previously knew about

discrimination Overt unequal and unfair treatment of people on the basis of their membership in a particular group

disengagement theory The theory of aging that suggests that as people get older, they and the younger people around them go through a period of mutual withdrawal

displacement A process occurring in split labor markets in which higher-paid workers are replaced with cheaper labor

diversification The corporate practice of entering business in a variety of areas of manufacturing in order to protect profits (A decrease in profits in one type of business might be made up by an increase in profits in another type, for example.)

division of labor A situation in which some people do certain specialized occupations

downward mobility A move to a position of lower rank in the stratification system

dramaturgical approach An approach to the study of interaction in which interaction is compared to a drama on stage; the importance of setting and presentation of self are emphasized

dysfunction In structural functional theory, factors that lead to the disruption or breakdown of the social system

ecclesia An official state religion that includes all or most members of society

ecological change Change that is brought about by the way a population uses the natural resources available to it

ecological specialization The concentration of homogeneous groups and activities into different sections or urban areas

ecology The study of the interrelationships between living organisms and the environment

economic determinism The idea that economic factors are responsible for most social change and for the nature of social conditions, activities, and institutions

economics The study of how goods, services, and wealth are produced, consumed, and distributed

economic system The social institution that provides for the production, distribution, and consumption of goods and services

ecumenism The trend for different denominations to join together in pursuit of common interests in a spirit of worldwide Christian unity

egalitarian The norm of authority in the family in which decisions are equally divided between husband and wife

emergent norm perspective A view of collective behavior that emphasizes how new norms emerge and influence the behavior of crowds

emigration Movement of people out of an area

endogamy A marriage norm requiring a person to marry someone from his or her own group

epidemiology The study of the spread of diseases

Equal Rights Amendment (ERA) A proposed amendment to the Constitution of the United States giving equal rights to women (It was not ratified.)

ethnic antagonism Mutual opposition, conflict, or hostility among different ethnic groups

ethnic group A group set apart from others because of its national origin or distinctive cultural patterns, such as religion, language, or region of the country

ethnocentrism The view that one's own culture is superior to others and should be used as the standard against which other cultures are judged

ethnographic research A form of descriptive research focusing on the sociology of meaning through close observation of sociocultural phenomena

euthanasia Deliberately ending a person's life to spare him or her suffering from an incurable and agonizing disease and sometimes called mercy killing

evaluation research Research that measures how well a program or project works in relation to its goals

evaluative studies Studies used to estimate the effects of specific social programs or policies

evolutionary theory A theory of social development that suggests that societies, like biological organisms, progress through stages of increasing complexity

exchange theory A theory of interaction that attempts to explain social behavior in terms of reciprocity of costs and rewards

exclusion Attempts to keep cheaper labor from taking jobs from groups that receive higher pay

excuse of behavior An effort at maintaining the self by justifying or making an apology for the behavior

exogamy A marriage norm requiring a person to marry someone from outside his or her own group

experimental design A scientific procedure in which at least two matched groups, differing only in the variable being studied, are used to collect and compare data

experimental group In an experiment, the group to which an independent variable is introduced; this variable is not introduced in the control group

explanatory research Research that attempts to explain why things do or do not happen by examining the relationship between social variables

expressive leader A type of leader that focuses on resolving conflicts and creating group harmony and social cohesion

expressive role A role that emphasizes warmth and understanding rather than action or leadership; traditionally associated more with women than with men

extended family A family that goes beyond the nuclear family to include other nuclear families and relatives such as grandparents, aunts, uncles, and cousins

external controls Pressures or sanctions applied to members of society by others

fad Superficial or trivial behavior that is very popular for a short time

false consciousness Lack of awareness of class differences and acceptance of upper-class rule

family A group of kin united by blood, marriage, or adoption who share a common residence for some part of their lives and assume reciprocal rights and obligations with regard to one another

family of orientation The nuclear family into which one was born and in which one was reared

family of procreation The nuclear family formed by marriage

fashion Temporary trend in some aspect of appearance or behavior (Fashions resemble fads but tend to be more cyclical.)

fecundity A woman's potential for bearing children

fee-for-service A medical payment system in which the physician is paid for each visit and each service rendered

feminization of poverty The increase in the number of persons who are below the level of poverty being predominantly women, particularly as found in female headed families

fertility A measure of the rate at which people are being born

fetal monitoring Measuring the vital signs of the infant as it is being born

folk society A community described by Redfield as small, isolated, homogeneous, and kin-oriented

folkways Norms of conduct of everyday life that bring only mild censure or punishment if they are violated

formal external controls Formal systems of social control applied to the individual by others; examples include courts, police, and prisons

formalization The stage in the development of social movements in which a formal structure is developed, and rules, policies, and tactics are laid out

formal organization A large social group deliberately organized to achieve certain specific, clearly stated goals

fraternal polyandry A form of polyandry where brothers are co-husbands

free market An economic system in which all people are theoretically free to buy, sell, and make a profit

functional alternatives Alternate ways to achieve an intended goal in order to avoid dysfunctions

frustration-aggression theory The theory that prejudice results when personal frustrations are displaced to a socially approved racial or ethnic target

fundamentalism The belief that the Bible is the divine word of God and that all statements in it are to be taken literally, word for word

game perspective A view of crowd behavior that suggests that members think about their actions and consciously try to act in ways that will produce rewards

gamesman The type of manager sought by corporations today: a person who is highly competitive and innovative but who prefers to function as the leader of a team

gemeinschaft A traditional community characterized by a sense of solidarity and common identity and emphasizing intimate and personal relationships

gender A social status that refers to differences between the sexes, specifically to differences in masculinity and femininity

gender identity The social construction of boys and girls, men and women, as opposed to their biological characteristics

gender roles The cultural concepts of masculinity and femininity that society creates around gender

generalized belief A stage in the development of collective behavior in which people share a common identification and interpretation of a problem

generalized other The assumption that other people have similar attitudes, values, beliefs, and expectations (It is therefore not necessary to know a specific individual in order to know how to behave toward that individual.)

genocide The deliberate destruction of an entire racial or ethnic group

gentrification The rejuvenation of urban neighborhoods by middle-class people who move into and repair run-down houses

geography The study of the physical environment and the distribution of plants and animals, including humans

geriatrics The subfield of gerontological practice that deals with the medical care of the aging

gerontology The systematic study of the aging process

gesellschaft A modern community characterized by individualism, mobility, and impersonality, with an emphasis on progress rather than tradition

ghetto An area in a city in which members of a racial or ethnic minority are forcibly segregated

going green The phrase that defines people who are mindful of what they consume, mindful of others, and who are working toward protecting the ecology both nationally and internationally

greenbelt An area surrounding cities that is preserved for farming and recreation and that limits the growth of cities

gross domestic product (GDP) The total value of all finished goods and services produced within the borders of a country per year

group marriage A form of marriage in which several or many men are married to several or many women

health maintenance organization (HMO) A prepaid health care plan in which a fee is paid in advance for all necessary health care

heroic medicine Dramatic medical treatments such as bleeding, blistering, or administering poisonous laxatives

hidden curriculum The teaching and learning of things such as obedience, competition, and patriotism that are not part of the stated curriculum

hidden repression A means of controlling collective behavior that is not obviously or overtly repressive

high culture The materials and ideas of wealthy, affluent, or upper classes (in contrast to popular culture)

Hinduism One of the world's principal polytheistic religions, with no religious hierarchy but a close involvement with society and the cosmic order (It is practiced mainly in India and Pakistan.)

history The study of the past; social history is concerned with past human social events

horizontal expansion Corporations taking over similar businesses in order to gain a monopoly and reduce competition

horticulture Small-scale farming that relies on tools such as the hoe to till the soil

hospice A home for terminally ill patients in which the emphasis is on providing a comfortable, supportive environment for the patient and the patient's family

human relations school A form of industrial management in which the workers' psychology, peer pressures, and attitudes toward management are taken into account

hunting-and-gathering societies Small, often nomadic societies that have no agriculture and live on food that is found

hypochondriac A healthy person who believes he or she is ill

hypothesis A statement about the relationship between variables that can be put to an empirical test

I The acting, unselfconscious person

ideal culture The norms and values that people profess to follow

ideal type A model of a hypothetical pure form of an existing entity

ideology A set of ideas about what society is like, how it functions, whether it is good or bad, and how it should be changed

idioculture The system of knowledge, beliefs, behaviors, and customs that is unique to a given group

immigration Movement of people into an area

immoral view The view that deviance is immoral and antisocial

incest Socially forbidden sexual relationships or marriage with certain close relatives

incumbent One holding an elected office

independent variable A variable that causes a change or variation in a dependent variable

industrial societies Societies with great division of labor, highly specialized work, and a great concentration of wealth

inequality Differences between groups in wealth, status, or power

infectious diseases Diseases caused by germs and viruses that can be spread from one person to another

informal (external) controls Pressure applied by peers, friends, parents, and other people with whom one associates regularly that are intended to encourage one to obey rules and conform to social expectations

in-group A social group to which people feel they belong and with which they share a consciousness of kind

inner-directed A description by David Riesman of people who are independent, innovative, and focused on their own survival with little concern with what others think

instinct Biological or hereditary impulses, drives, or behaviors that require no learning or reasoning

institution A stable cluster of values, norms, statuses, and roles that develops around a basic social goal

institutional discrimination The continuing exclusion or oppression of a group as a result of criteria established by an institution

Institutional Review Boards (IRBs) Committees on college/university campuses and in research organizations that provide oversight of research that is conducted on human subjects

institutionalization The process by which orderly, stable, structured, and increasingly predictable forms of behavior and interaction are developed

institutionalized behavior Recurrent behavior that follows an orderly pattern with a relatively stable set of goals, expectations, and values

institutionalism of inequality The collection of laws, customs, and social practices that combine to create and sustain the unequal distribution of rewards based on class, minority status, and gender

institutional racism Racism that is embodied in the folkways, mores, or legal structures of a social institution

instrumental leader A type of leader that focuses on goals, directing activities, and helping make group decisions

instrumental role A role that emphasizes accomplishment of tasks, such as earning a living to provide food and shelter; traditionally associated more with men than with women

interactionist perspective A view of crowd behavior that emphasizes how people in crowds reinforce and heighten one another's reactions

integration The situation that exists when ethnicity becomes insignificant and everyone can freely and fully participate in the social, economic, and political mainstream

intergenerational mobility A change of social position or rank, up or down, from one generation to the next, such as when children have a higher status than their parents

internal controls Learned patterns of control that exist in the minds of individuals and make them want to conform to social norms

intragenerational mobility A change of social position or rank, up or down, within one's own lifetime

invasion An ecological process in which new types of people, organizations, or activities move into an area occupied by a different type

invention A device constructed by putting two or more things together in a new way

inverse relationship A relationship between two variables such that an increase in one variable is accompanied by a decrease in the other; compare with *direct relationship*

iron law of oligarchy In democratic societies, the inevitable rise of a few elite leaders who dominate power

Islam One of the world's principal religions, followers of which adhere to the teachings of the Koran and of Muhammad, a prophet

Judaism The oldest religion in the Western world and the first to teach monotheism (Today the Jews are both an ethnic community and a religious group.)

kinship The web of relationships among people linked by common ancestry, adoption, or marriage

labeling theory A theory that emphasizes how certain behaviors are labeled "deviant" and how being given such a label influences a person's behavior

language The systematized use of speech and hearing to communicate feelings and ideas

laissez faire An economy in which there is no government planning or intervention

latent force A type of power in which force is threatened

latent functions The unintended consequences of a social system

law of human progress Comte's notion that all knowledge passes through three successive theoretical conditions: the theological, the metaphysical, and the scientific

laws Formal, standardized expressions of norms enacted by legislative bodies to regulate certain types of behaviors

legal authority Authority based on a system of rules and regulations that determine how a society will be governed

legal race The legal definition of race; typically referred to as the rule of hypo-descent or "one drop" rule

legitimate To make the power of the dominant group acceptable to the masses so they let the dominant group rule without question

legitimate power Controlling the behavior of others through having people accept the authority as necessary and beneficial to all

life chances The opportunities a person has to improve his or her income and lifestyle

life course An age-related progression or sequence of roles and group memberships that people go through as they mature and move through life

life expectancy The average years of life remaining for persons who attain a given age

life span The biological age limit beyond which no one can expect to live

lifetime jobs An employment practice in which workers are guaranteed a job for a lengthy period of time

lobby An organization of people who want to influence the political process on a specific issue

looking-glass self A process occurring in social interaction which has three components: (1) how we think our behavior appears to others, (2) how we think others judge our behavior, and (3) how we feel about their judgments

macrosociology A level of sociological analysis concerned with large-scale units such as institutions, social categories, and social systems

magnet schools Schools with special programs designed to attract exceptional students

Malthusian theory The theory proposed by Thomas Malthus stating that population expands much faster than the food supply, resulting in starvation for much of the population when it grows too large

manifest functions The intended consequences of a social system

market economy An economy in which the price and production of goods are determined by what people are willing to pay in the marketplace

marriage squeeze The effects of an imbalance between the number of males and females in the prime marriage ages due to rising or falling birth rates and the median age differences at marriage

mass A spatially diffuse collective in which geographically dispersed persons react to or focus upon some common event

mass expulsion Expelling racial or ethnic groups from their homeland

mass hysteria A form of diffuse collective behavior involving a widespread, highly emotional fear of a potentially threatening situation

mass media Forms of communication, such as television, popular magazines, and radio, intended for a large audience

mass production The production of many items of a product, which lowers the cost per item and reduces the time needed to make it

master status A particular status in one's status set that takes priority over the others

matriarchal A family structure in which the wife dominates the husband

matrilineal A family structure in which descent and inheritance are traced through the mother's line

matrilocal A family norm that newly married couples should live with the wife's family

me The part of self that sees self as object, evaluates self, and is aware of society's expectations of self

mean A measure of central tendency computed by adding the figures and dividing by the number of figures; also known as the average

mechanical solidarity The idea of Durkheim in which people do similar work but are not very dependent on one another (in contrast to organic solidarity, in which people are very dependent on others)

median A measure of central tendency in which half the figures fall above and half the figures fall below; also known as the midpoint

Medicaid Federally sponsored health insurance for the poor

medical center A major hospital that trains new physicians, conducts research, and provides tertiary medical care

medical model of illness A model of illness in which sickness is viewed as an individual problem requiring individual treatment

medical view The view that deviance is essentially pathological evidence that a society is unhealthy

Medicare Federally sponsored health insurance for people age 65 or older

megalopolis A continuous strip of urban and suburban development that may stretch for hundreds of miles

melting pot A form of assimilation in which each group contributes aspects of its own culture and absorbs aspects of other cultures, such that the whole is a combination of all the groups

metropolitan statistical area (MSA) A county or group of counties with a central city with a population of at least 50,000, a density of at least 1,000 persons per square mile, and outlying areas that are socially and economically integrated with the central city

microsociology The level of sociological analysis concerned with small-scale units such as individuals in small group interactions

middle-range theory A set of propositions designed to link abstract propositions with empirical testing

migration Movement of people into or out of an area

millennialism The belief prevalent among certain sects that there will be a dramatic transformation of life on earth and that Christ will rule the world for a thousand years of prosperity and happiness

milling The stage in the development of crowd behavior during which people move about aimlessly, grow increasingly preoccupied with others, and become increasingly inclined to respond without thinking

mind The process of using a language and thinking

minority group A group subordinate to the dominant group in terms of the distribution of social power (Such groups are defined by some physical or cultural characteristic and are usually but not always smaller than the dominant group.)

mobilization for action A stage in the development of collective behavior during which people are persuaded to join the movement

mobs Emotionally aroused groups ready to engage in violent behavior

mode The most frequent response in a body of data

modernization The process whereby preindustrial countries emerge as urban societies with lower birth rates, more goods and services, and better nutrition and health care

modernization theory The view that the status of older people declines with modernization

modified-extended family structure The family structure in which individual nuclear families retain considerable autonomy yet maintain connections with other nuclear families in the extended family structure

monogamy The marriage of one man to one woman

monotheism The belief in one god

mores Norms of conduct associated with strong feelings of right or wrong, violations of which bring intense reaction and some type of punishment

mortality A measure of the rate at which people die

mortification of self Stripping the self of all the characteristics of a past identity, including clothing, personal possessions, friends, roles and routines, and so on

multinational corporation Corporations that do business in a number of nations

multiple-nuclei model The model of urban development showing that cities have areas of different types of land use, each of which has its own center or nucleus

municipal hospital A hospital built and operated by a city or county

mysticism The belief that spiritual or divine truths come to us through intuition and meditation, not through the use of reason or via the ordinary range of human experience and senses

nation-states Large territories ruled by a single political institution

national crime victimization survey Data collected by the Bureau of Justice on crimes that go unreported to the police

nature–nurture debate A longstanding debate over whether behavior results from predetermined biological characteristics or from socialization

negative sanctions Actions that discourage individuals from a particular behavior

neolocal A family norm that newly married couples should establish residences separate from those of both sets of parents

neo-Malthusian theory Revisions of Malthusian theory about food production and population growth that include more information, such as taking into account the effects of technology

noblesse oblige The obligation of the rich to give to the poor and suffering

nonmarital cohabitation An arrangement in which two unmarried and unrelated adults share a common household or dwelling

norms Formal and informal rules of conduct and social expectations for behavior

nuclear families Families in which two or more persons are related by blood, marriage, or adoption and who share a common residence

nutritionist A person who specializes in proper eating programs

observational research Research in which the researcher watches what is happening and makes no attempt to control or modify the activity being observed

oligarchy Government by a small elite group

open system A system of stratification in which it is possible to move to a higher or lower position

operational definition A definition of a concept or variable such that it can be measured

operation of social controls A stage in the development of collective behavior in which the mass media, government, and other groups try to suppress or influence collective behavior

organic solidarity Durkheim's term for the integration of society that results from the division of labor

organized crime Groups expressly organized to carry out illegal activities

organizational deviance Occurs when events that are created by or exist within organizations that do not conform to an organization's goals or expectations and produce unanticipated and harmful outcomes

orphan drugs Drugs that are valuable in the treatment of rare diseases but are not profitable to manufacture

other-directed A description by David Riesman of people who focus on making a good impression, being popular, getting along with others, and being cooperative

out-group A group to which people feel they do not belong; they do not share consciousness of kind, and they feel little identity to the group

panic An attempt to rapidly escape from a perceived danger

parochial schools Schools run and maintained by a religious body or organization rather than the public at large

party An organization in which decisions are made to reach certain goals, the achievement of which affects society

pathological illness An illness in which the body is clearly diseased or malfunctioning in some way

pathology of normalcy The concept that cultural norms are not always beneficial for a society, group, or individual

patriarchal A family structure in which the husband dominates the wife

patrilineal A family system in which descent and inheritance are traced through the father's line

patrilocal A family norm that newly married couples should live with the husband's family

peer group An informal primary group of people who share a similar or equal status and who are usually of roughly the same age

peripheral nations Underdeveloped nations who are exploited by core nations

physical force A type of power backed by sheer force such as an army or physical might

placebo effect A benefit arising from a patient's belief that a medicine will have a beneficial effect

planned economy An economy in which the production and prices of goods are planned by the government

play According to Mead, a way of practicing role taking

political action committees (PACs) Organizations formed to raise money for a political campaign

political parties Groups of citizens formed with the express intent of gaining control of the political body of the state

political pluralism A political system in which many diverse groups have a share of the power

politics The use of power to determine who gets what in society

political science The study of power, government, and the political process

polyandry The marriage of one woman to more than one husband at the same time

polygamy The marriage of one man or woman to more than one person of the opposite sex at the same time

polygyny The marriage of one man to more than one wife at the same time

polytheism The belief in and worship of more than one god

popular culture Trends, social activities, and shared experiences of everyday people (in contrast to elite culture)

popular excitement The stage in the development of a social movement during which social unrest is brought into the open and people with similar concerns begin to organize

positive sanctions Actions that encourage individuals to continue a behavior

poverty Having fewer resources than are required to meet the basic necessities of life (Rates are usually based on a government index of income relative to size of family and farm/nonfarm residence.)

power The ability to control or influence the behavior of others, even without their consent

power elite A small group of people who hold all of the powerful positions and cooperate to maintain their social positions

precipitating factors A stage in the development of collective behavior during which an event triggers a collective response

prejudice A preconceived attitude or judgment, either good or bad, about another group; prejudices usually involve negative stereotypes

preparatory schools Private schools, usually of a select and elite nature, that are intended to offer an intensive education in both academic as well as social/cultural activities

prescribed role The expectations associated with a given status that are based on what society suggests or dictates

presentation of self The way we present ourselves to others and how our presentation influences others

priests Religious leaders who owe their authority to the power of their office

primary group A small, informal group of people who interact in a personal, direct, and intimate way

primary labor market The labor market re-served for people who will advance to high-level positions

primary medical care The first general, overall care the patient needs

primary workers Workers who produce raw materials, such as food or minerals

principle of legitimacy Malinowski's idea that every society has a rule that every child should have a legitimate father to act as the child's protector, guardian, and representative in society

profane That which belongs to the realm of the everyday world; anything considered mundane and unspiritual

projection A psychological explanation of prejudice that suggests that people transfer responsibility for their own failures to a vulnerable group, usually a racial or ethnic group

proletariat The group in capitalist societies that does not own the means of production and has only labor to sell

prolonged adolescence A latent function of education that serves to maintain parental dependency and keep young people out of the job market

propaganda An attempt to manipulate the ideas or opinions of the public by presenting limited, selective, or false information

prophets Religious leaders who have authority on the basis of their charismatic qualities

proposition A statement of the relationship between two or more concepts or variables

proprietary hospital A hospital that is privately owned, usually by physicians or hospital corporations

Protestant ethic The view associated with the Puritans that hard work is valuable for its own sake (According to Weber, the Protestant ethic is responsible for the high value placed on capitalism in the United States.)

psychology The study of human mental processes and individual human behavior

public A group of people who are confronted with an issue, who do not agree on how to address the issue, and who discuss the issue

public opinion Any opinion held by a substantial number of people; or, the dominant opinion in a given population

pull factors Natural or social factors that cause people to move into an area

pure science The area of science in which knowledge is sought for its own sake with little emphasis on how the knowledge might be applied

push factors Natural or social factors that cause people to move out of an area

qualitative methods The gathering and reporting of non-numerical data used to determine the essential characteristics, properties, or processes of something or someone

quality control circles Meetings at which workers discuss ways of improving production and set policy to reach their goals

quantitative methods The gathering and reporting of data based on numbers or amounts of something

racial group A socially defined group distinguished by selected inherited physical characteristics

racism Discrimination based on racial characteristics

radicalism Labor groups joining together in a coalition against the capitalist class

random sample A sample selected in such a way that every member of a population has an equal chance of being chosen

range The span between the largest and smallest amount of a variable.

real culture The norms and values that people actually follow and practice (The real culture may or may not be the same as the ideal culture, which represents the norms and values people profess to follow.)

reference group A group with which people identify psychologically and to which they refer in evaluating themselves and their behavior

referenda Questions on a ballot to be decided by the electorate

registered dietitian (RD) Licensed members of hospital staffs that plan regular meals and special diets for patients

relative deprivation A feeling of being deprived, not because of objective conditions, but because of comparison to a reference group

relativistic view The view that deviance can be interpreted only in the sociocultural context in which it occurs

reliability The extent to which repeated observations of the same phenomena yield similar results

religion An organized community of believers who hold certain things sacred and follow a set of beliefs, ceremonies, or special behaviors

repressive measures Measures, such as banning public assemblies, used to control collective behavior

resocialization Socialization to a new role or position in life that requires a dramatic shift in the attitudes, values, behaviors, and expectations learned in the past

resource mobilization theory The theory that the success of a social movement depends not only on those who benefit from it directly but also on its ability to mobilize other individuals and groups to contribute time, money, and influence

retrospective labeling The term coined by Erving Goffman to describe a person's past based on some type of present deviance

riot A form of collective behavior involving mass violence and mob action

role The social expectations or behaviors associated with a particular status

role ambiguity A situation in which the expectations associated with a particular social status are unclear

role conflict A situation that exists when differing expectations are associated with the same role

role of the police A means of controlling collective behavior through the use of police force

role perception The way that expectations for behavior are perceived or defined—which may differ considerably from what is prescribed or actually done

role performance The actual behavior of a person in a particular role, in contrast to the way that person is expected to behave

role set The multiple roles attached to statuses

role strain A situation that occurs when differing and incompatible roles are associated with the same status

role taking Assuming the roles of others and seeing the world from their perspective

sacred Involving objects and ideas that are treated with reverence and awe

sample A number of individuals or cases drawn from a larger population

sanctions Rewards and punishments used to encourage proper behavior

Sapir-Whorf Hypothesis The hypothesis that societies with different languages perceive the world differently because their members interpret the world through the grammatical forms, labels, and categories their language provides

scapegoating A psychological explanation of prejudice that involves blaming another person or group for one's own problems

scientific management A method of managing assembly-line workers such that their every movement is efficient

scientific method A procedure that involves systematically formulating problems, collecting data through observation and experiment, and devising and testing hypotheses

secondary analysis The use of existing information that was gathered or exists independently of one's own research

secondary care givers Those who provide more specialized care than that provided by a general practitioner

secondary group A group in which the members interact impersonally, have few emotional ties, and come together for a specific, practical purpose

secondary labor market The labor market in which jobs pay poorly, there is little job security, and there are few promotions or salary increases

secondary medical care Care that is more specialized than the care that a general practitioner provides

secondary workers Workers who produce manufactured goods from raw materials

sector model An explanation of the ecology of cities as a series of pie-shaped wedges radiating from the central business district, each with its own characteristics and uses

sects Religious groups that have broken away from a parent church, follow rigid doctrines and fundamentalist teachings, and emphasize "otherworldly" rewards, rejecting or deemphasizing contemporary society

secularization The process through which beliefs concerning the supernatural and religious institutions lose social influence

segregation The separation of a group from the main body; it usually involves separating a minority group from the dominant group

self The sense of one's own identity as a person

self-fulfilling prophecy A prediction that comes true because people believe it and act as though it were true

senility A mental infirmity associated with the aging process

serial or sequential monogamy Marriage to a number of different spouses in succession, but only one at any given time

sex The biological and anatomical characteristics that differentiate males and females

sexual harassment Sexual advances made by coworkers or superiors at work

shamanism The religious belief that certain persons (shamans) have special charm, skill, or knowledge in influencing spirits

sick role A set of expectations, privileges, and obligations related to illness

significant others Persons that one identifies with psychologically and whose opinions are considered important

simple horticultural societies Societies that grow food using very simple tools, such as digging sticks

slave system A system of stratification in which one's position was ascribed at birth and based on race

slums Sections of a city marked by poverty, overcrowding, substandard housing, and poor living conditions

social change Changes in the structure of a society or in its social institutions

social class A category of people who have approximately the same amount of power and wealth and the same life chances to acquire wealth

social conflict A view of Karl Marx that social conflict—class struggle due to economic inequality—is at the core of society and the key source of social change

social contagion A stage in the development of crowd behavior during which the crowd's response to a common event increases in intensity and the crowd's behavior moves others to behave in the same way

social control through amelioration The creation of specific policies to eliminate the source of strain that lies behind the collective behavior

social differentiation The difference or variation of people based on selected social characteristics such as class, gender, race, or age

social distance The degree of intimacy and equality between groups of people

social dynamics Comte's term for social processes and forms of change

social engineering Attempting to change the way a society, community, organization, institution, or group is arranged so that a particular goal may be achieved

social facts Reliable and valid items of information about society

social gerontology A branch of gerontology that focuses on the social and cultural factors related to age and the aging process

social group A group in which people physically or socially interact

socialism An economic system in which the means of production are owned by all the people through the state

socialization The process of learning how to interact in society by learning the rules and expectations of society

social learning theory The view that deviant and conforming behaviors are strongly influenced by the consequences that follow them

social model of illness The view that much disease is caused by social conditions and that it can be cured by changing social conditions

social movements Collective noninstitutionalized efforts to bring about social change and establish a new order of social thought and action

social network The linkage or ties to a set of relationships

social organization Refers to the stable patterns within our society

social psychology The study of how individuals interact with other individuals or groups and how groups influence the individual

social race Race is socially constructed and maintained through the process of interaction with others

social science A science that has as its subject matter human behavior, social organizations, or society

Social Security The federal program that provides financial support for the elderly

social statics Comte's term for the stable structure of a society

social status The amount of honor and prestige a person receives from others in the community; also, the position one occupies in the stratification system

social stratification The ranking of people according to their wealth, prestige, or party position

social structure Refers to the idea that society is organized in a way that makes human behavior and relationships predictable

social system A set of interrelated social statuses and the expectations that accompany them

social unrest The stage in the development of social unrest that is characterized by unfocused restlessness and increasing disorder

social work The field in which the principles of the social sciences are applied to actual social problems

society A group of interacting people who live in a specific geographical area, who are organized in a cooperative manner, and who share a common culture

sociobiology The study of the biological and genetic determinants of social behavior

sociocultural learning theories Theories that deal with the processes through which deviant acts are learned and the conditions under which learning takes place

socioeconomic status (SES) An assessment of status that takes into account a person's income, education, and occupation

sociological imagination The ability to see how history and biography together influence our lives

sociological perspective A way of looking at society and social behavior that involves questioning the obvious, seeking patterns, and looking beyond the individual in an attempt to discern social processes

sociology The study of human society and social life and the social causes and consequences of human behavior

spatially diffuse collectives Collectives that form among people spread over a wide geographical area

spatially proximate collectives Collectives in which people are geographically close and physically visible to one another

split labor market A labor market in which some jobs afford upward mobility and others do not

sponsored mobility A system of education in which certain students are selected at an early age to receive advanced education and training

statistical group A group formed by sociologists or statisticians; members are unaware of belonging and there is no social interaction or social organization

states Societies with institutional government and laws as a means of political regulation, a military defense, and a way to finance these activities

statistical illness An illness in which one's health varies from the norm

statistical view A perspective on deviance that defines deviant as any variation from a statistical norm

stereotypes Widely held and oversimplified beliefs about the character and behavior of all members of a group that seldom correspond to the facts

stratification The structured ranking of entire groups of people that perpetuates unequal rewards and power in a society

stratified sampling Sampling in which a population is divided into groups and then subjects are chosen at random from within those groups

status The socially defined position an individual occupies

status set The combination of all the statuses any individual holds at a given time

strain theories Theories of deviance suggesting that the experience of socially induced strain, such as anomie, forces people to engage in deviant activities

structural assimilation One aspect of assimilation in which patterns of intimate contact between the guest and host groups are developed in the clubs, organizations, and institutions of the host society

structural conduciveness The extent to which a society's organization has the conditions that make a particular form of collective behavior possible

structural functionalism The theory that societies contain certain interdependent structures, each of which performs certain functions for the maintenance of society

structural strain Any conflict or ambiguity in a society's organization that causes frustration and stress; often seen as a precondition for collective behavior

subcultures Groups of persons who share in the main culture of a society but also have their own distinctive values, norms, and lifestyles

suburbs The communities that surround a central city and are dependent on it

succession An urban process of replacing old occupants and institutions with new ones

survey research A quantitative research technique that involves asking people questions about the subject being surveyed

symbolic interaction theory The social theory stressing interactions between people and the social processes that occur within the individual that are made possible by language and internalized meanings

symbol Something that is used to represent something else, such as a word, gesture, or object used to represent some aspect of the world

systematic sampling Obtaining a sample from a population by following a specific pattern of selection, such as choosing every tenth person

taboos Mores that prohibit something

technology The application of nonmaterial and material knowledge by a society to maintain its standard of living and lifestyle

temporocentrism The belief that one's own time is more important than the past or future

tertiary medical care Long-term care requiring complex technology

tertiary workers Workers who provide a service, such as doctors, lawyers, politicians, police officers, and secretaries

theory A set of logically and systematically interrelated propositions that explain a particular process or phenomenon

totalitarianism A power structure in which the government has total power to dictate the values, rules, ideology, and economic development of a society

traditional authority The right to rule granted to someone on the basis of tradition, as with a patriarch or king

traditional indigenous Refers to ethnic groups who are native to a land or region, usually before the arrival of a foreign and possibly dominating culture

totemism The worship of plants, animals, and other natural objects as gods and ancestors

trained incapacity The situation that exists when the demands of discipline, conformity, and adherence to rules render people unable to perceive the end for which the rules were developed

unionization The process of organizing workers to improve their wages and working conditions

upward mobility Movement in the stratification system to a position of greater wealth, status, and power

urban ecology The study of the interrelationships between people in urban settings and the social and physical environment in which they live

urban homesteading A federal plan in which abandoned and foreclosed homes are sold to private families at extremely low prices if they agree to live in the house and bring it up to code standards

urbanization The growth of the number of people who live in urban rather than rural areas and the process of taking on organizational patterns and lifestyles characteristic of urban areas

validity The extent to which observations actually measure what they are supposed to measure

values Ideas and beliefs shared by the people in a society about what is important and worthwhile

variable A characteristic such as age, class, or income that can vary from one person to another; a concept that can have two or more values

variance A descriptive statistic that tells how the data are spread over the range

verstehen Understanding human action by examining the subjective meanings that people attach to their own behavior and the behavior of others

vertical expansion Business expansion in order to own everything related to a business, from raw materials to sales outlets

victimization surveys Asking samples of people if they have been victims of a particular behavior, such as rape

vital statistics Records of all births, deaths and their causes, marriages, divorces, and certain diseases in a society

voluntary association An organization people join because they share the organization's goals and values and voluntarily choose to support them

voluntary hospital A nonprofit hospital that treats patients who need short-term care

vouchers Giving parents the choice of a private school for their children to attend and using state funds to pay for the tuition

welfare capitalism A mixed economy in which private and public ownership are both practiced extensively

women's movement The social movements led by women to gain political and economic equality

world systems theory Conflict theory stating core nations dominate the economics of peripheral nations

xenocentrism The belief that what is foreign is best and that one's own lifestyle, products, or ideas are inferior to those of others

zero population growth A population policy that encourages parents to have no more than two children to limit the growth of the population

References

Absolam Collection. *Polygamy-Frequently Asked Questions.* (1999). www.absalom.com/mormon/, (accessed on 13 April 2009).

Abrahamson, Mark. *Sociological Theory: An Introduction to Concepts, Issues, and Research*, 2nd ed. Englewood Cliffs, NJ: Prentice Hall, 1990.

Abu-Lughod, Janet. *Changing Cities.* New York: Harper Collins, 1991.

ACT. "The Condition of College and Career Readiness 2010," www.act.org.

Ade-Ridder, Linda. "Sexuality and Marital Quality Among Older Married Couples," in Timothy H. Brubaker, ed., *Family Relationships in Later Life*, 2nd ed. Newbury Park, CA: Sage Publications, 1990.

Adler, Jerry., Mark Starr, Farai Chideya, Lynda Wright, Pat Wingert, and Linda Haac. "Taking Offense: Is This the New Enlightenment on Campus or the New McCarthyism?" *Newsweek*, December 24, 1990, 48–54.

Adorno, T. W., Else Frenkel-Brunswik, Daniel J. Levinson, and R. Nevitt Sanford. *The Authoritarian Personality.* New York: Wiley, 1950.

Agnew, Robert. "A Revised Strain Theory of Delinquency," *Social Forces 64* (September 1985): 151–167.

Agran, Larry. "Getting Cancer on the Job," *The Nation*, April 12, 1975, 433–437.

Aguirre, B. E., E. L. Quarantelli, and Jorge L. Mendoza. "The Collective Behavior of Fads: The Characteristics, Effects, and Career of Streaking," *American Sociological Review 53* (August 1988): 569–584.

Aguirre, B. F., and Manuel R. Torres, Kimberly B. Gill and Lawrence H. Hotchkiss. "Normative Collective Behavior in the Station Building Fire," *Social Science Quarterly* (March 2011): 92 (1): 100-118.

Akers, Ronald L. *Deviant Behavior: A Social Learning Approach*, 2nd ed. Belmont, CA: Wadsworth, 1977.

Akers, R. L., M. D. Krohn, L. Lonza Kaduce, and M. Radosevich. "Social Learning and Deviant Behavior: A Specific Test of a General Theory," *American Sociological Review 44* (August 1979): 636–655.

Albrecht, Stanley L., Darwin L. Thomas, and Bruce A. Chadwick. *Social Psychology.* Englewood Cliffs, NJ: Prentice-Hall, 1980.

Ali, Lorraine. "Islam & Obama," *Newsweek*, November 2008. http://www.newsweek.com/id/168062, (accessed April 14, 2009).

Allen, Irving Lewis. *Unkind Words: Ethnic Labeling from Redskin to WASP.* New York: Bergin and Garvey, 1990.

Allport, Gordon. *The Nature of Prejudice.* Boston: Beacon Press, 1954.

Arcaro, Thomas., and Rosemary Haskell, (eds.) *Understanding the Global Experience: Becoming a Responsible World Citizen*. Allyn and Bacon. 2010.

Alzheimer's Association. "Alzheimer's Disease Facts and Figures 2010," *Alzheimer's and Dementia* (2010) 6.

American Anthropological Association. "Statement on Race," (1998).

American Cancer Society. "Cancer Facts and Figures, 2010," Atlanta: American Cancer Society. www.cancer.org

American Sociological Association. *21st Century Careers with an Undergraduate Degree in Sociology*. Washington, D.C.: American Sociological Association, 2009.

AmeriStat. "Diversity, Poverty Characterize Female-Headed Households. Tabulations from the Census Bureau's Current Population Survey," (March 2003).

Andrews, Edmund L. "It's Not Just the Jobs Lost, but the Pay in the New Ones," *New York Times*, August 9, 2004.

Anooshian, Linda J. "Social Isolation and Rejection of Homeless Children," *Journal of Children and Poverty* 9, no. 2 (September 2003): 115–134.

Aoki, Masahiko. *Information, Incentives and Bargaining in the Japanese Economy.* Cambridge, England: Cambridge University Press, 1988.

Arber, Sara., Gilbert G. Nigel, and Angela Dale. "Paid Employment and Women's Health: A Benefit or a Source of Role Strain?" *Sociology of Health and Illness* 7 (November 1985): 375–400.

Argetsinger, Amy., and Roxanne Roberts. "Mary Cheney and Partner Are About to Be Moms," *The Washington Post*, December 6, 2006.

Aronson, E., C. Stephan, J. Sikes, N. Blaney, and M. Snapp. *The Jigsaw Classroom.* Beverly Hills, CA: Sage Publications, 1978.

Atchley, Robert. *The Sociology of Retirement*, NY: John Wiley, 1976.

Atchley, Robert C. "The Process of Retirement: Comparing Men and Women," in Maximiliane Szinovacz, ed., *Women's Retirement: Policy Implications of Recent Research.* Beverly Hills, CA: Sage Publications, 1982, 153–168.

Atchley, Robert. *Social Forces and Aging: An Introduction to Social Gerontology*, 6th ed. Belmont, CA: Wadsworth, 1991.

Atkinson, A. B. *The Economics of Inequality*, 2nd ed. Oxford, England: Clarendon Press, 1983.

Austin, Sarah. "Crisis in New York City," *New York Times*, January 4, 1976. 40.

Ayensu, Edward S. "A Worldwide Role for the Healing Powers of Plants," *Smithsonian 12* (November 1981): 86–97.

Babbie, Earl. *Society by Agreement*. Belmont, CA: Wadworth Publishing Co. 1977, 1980.

Badgett, M. V. Lee, and Nancy Folbre. "Job Gendering: Occupational Choice and the Marriage Market," *Industrial Relations* 42, no. 2 (2003).

Bakanic, Von, Clark McPhail, and Rita J. Simon. "The Manuscript Review and Decision-Making Process," *American Sociological Review 52* (October 1987): 631–642.

Bales, Robert F. "The Equilibrium Problem in Small Groups," in Talcott Parsons, Robert F. Bales, and Edward A. Shils, *Working Papers in the Theory of Action*. Glencoe, IL: Free Press, 1953.

Ballantine, Jeanne H. *The Sociology of Education*. Englewood Cliffs, NJ: Prentice-Hall, 1983.

Bart, Pauline B. "Rape as a Paradigm of Sexism in Society—Victimization and Its Discontents," *Women's Studies International Quarterly 2* (1979): 347–357.

Barber, Melvin. "An Assimilation Theory of Ethnicity and Race," *American Sociological Association Conference* (2007).

Basile, Kathleen C., Jieru Chens, Michele C. Black, and Linda Saltzman. "Prevalence and Characteristics of Sexual Violence Victimization Among U.S. Adults, 2001-2003," *Violence and Victimization* (2007), 22 (4): 437-448.

Basirico, Laurence A. "The Art and Craft Fair: A New Institution in an Old Art World," *Qualitative Sociology 9*(4) (Winter 1986): 339–353.

Basirico, Laurence A. *Glass Consciousness: Social Organization and Social Interaction in the Stained Glass World*. Ph.D. dissertation, Department of Sociology, State University of New York at Stony Brook. Ann Arbor, MI: University Microfilms International, 1983.

Basirico, Laurence A., and Anne Bolin. "The Joy of Culture," in Arcaro, Thomas and Rosemary Haskell (eds.) *Understanding the Global Experience: Becoming a Responsible World Citizen*. Allyn and Bacon. 2010: 26-48.

Bayles, Fred. "First a Puzzle, Then a Plague: A Decade of AIDS," *Greensboro News and Record* [AP], June 2, 1991, 1, 8.

BBC News. *Cheney Lesbian Daughter Pregnant*. (7 December 2006). http://news.bbc.co.uk/1/hi/world/americas/6217056.stm, (accessed on 22 May 2009).

BBC News. *Saudi Police 'Stopped' Fire Rescue*. (15 March 2002). http://news.bbc.co.uk/2/hi/middle_east/1874471.stm, (accessed on 4 June 2009).

Bean, Frank D. "The Baby Boom and Its Explanations," *Sociological Quarterly 24* (Summer 1983): 353–365.

Bearer, Doris., and Friedrich Losel. "Bullying at School as a Predictor of Delinquency, Violence, and Other Anti-Social Behavior in Adulthood," *Criminal Behavior and Mental Health* 21 (2011):99-106.

Becker, Howard S. "The Labeling Theory Reconsidered," in Paul Rock and Mary McIntosh, eds., *Deviance and Social Control*. London: Tavistock, 1974.

Becker, Howard S. *Outsiders: Studies in the Sociology of Deviance*. New York: Free Press, 1963.

Becker, Howard. "Whose Side Are We On?" *Social Problems 14* (Winter 1967): 239–249.

Bell, Terrell. "Key to Education Problem: More Government ...," *New Perspectives Quarterly* (Winter 1991): 70–71.

Bell, Wendell. "Social Choice, Life Styles, and Suburban Residences," in W. Dobriner, ed., *The Suburban Community*. New York: Putnam, 1958.

Belsky, Jay. "Infant Day Care, Child Development, and Family Policy," *Society 27* (July/August 1990): 10–12.

Bem, S., and D. Bem. "Training the Woman to Know Her Place: The Power of a Nonconscious Ideology," in S. Cox, ed., *Female Psychology: The Emerging Self.* Chicago: SRA, 1976, 180–191.

Berg, Ivar. *Education and Jobs: The Great Training Robbery.* New York: Praeger, 1970.

Berger, Bennett. *Working Class Suburbs*. Berkeley, CA: University of California Press, 1960.

Berk, Richard A. *Collective Behavior*. Dubuque, IA: Brown, 1974.

Berk, Sarah Fenstermaker. *The Gender Factory: The Apportionment of Work in American Households*. New York: Plenum Press, 1985.

Bernard, Jessie. *The Female World*. New York: Free Press, 1981.

Bernard, Thomas J. "Control Criticisms of Strain Theories: An Assessment of Theoretical and Empirical Adequacy," *Journal of Research in Crime and Delinquency 21* (November 1984): 353–372.

Bernstein, Richard. "In U.S. Schools: A War of Words," *New York Times Magazine* (October 14, 1990): 34.

Bertakis, Klea D., and Rahman Azari. "Patient Gender Differences in the Predictors of Medical Expenditure," *Journal of Women's Health*, (2010) 19 (10): 1925-1932.

Beutler, Ivan F., Wesley R. Burr, Kathleen S. Bahr, and Donald A. Herrin, "The Family Realm: Theoretical Contributions for Understanding its Uniqueness," *Journal of Marriage and the Family 51* (August 1989): 805–816.

Bilge, Barbara., and Gladis Kaufman. "Children of Divorce and One-Parent Families: Cross-Cultural Perspectives," *Family Relations 32* (January 1983): 59–71.

Billiterri, Thomas J. "Preventing Bullying." *CQ Researcher* (December 10, 2010), 20 (43): 1013-1036

Bird, C. "Gender, Household Labor, and Psychological Distress: the Impact of the Amount and Division of Housework," *Journal of Health and Social Behavior* 40 (1999): 32-35.

Blake, Judith. *Family Size and Achievement*. Berkeley: University of California Press, 1989.

Blake, Judith. "Family Size and the Quality of Children," *Demography 18* (1981a): 421–442.

Blake, Judith. "The Only Child in America: Prejudice Versus Performance," *Population and Development Review* 7 (March 1981b): 43–54.

Blakemore, Judith E. Owen., and Craig A. Hill. "The Child Gender Socialization Scale: A Measure to Compare Traditional and Feminist Parents," *Sex Roles*, (2008), 58: 192-207.

Blanchard, Christopher M. "The Islamic Traditions of Wahhabism and Salafiyya," CRS Report, Order Number RS21695, (24 January 2008).

Blau, Peter. *Exchange and Power in Social Life.* New York: Wiley, 1964.

Blau, Peter M., and Otis Dudley Duncan. *The American Occupational Structure.* New York: Wiley, 1967.

Blits, Jan H., and Linda S. Gottfredson. "Equality of Lasting Inequality?" *Society* 27 (March/April 1990): 4–12.

Blumer, Herbert. "Collective Behavior," in Alfred McClung Lee, ed., *Principles of Sociology.* New York: Barnes and Noble, 1939.

Blumstein, Philip., and Pepper Schwartz. *American Couples: Money, Work and Sex.* New York: William Morrow, 1983.

Bonacich, Edna. "Abolition, the Extension of Slavery, and the Position of Free Blacks: A Study of Split Labor Markets in the United States, 1830–1863," *American Journal of Sociology 81* (November 1975): 601–628.

Bonacich, Edna. "Advanced Capitalism and Black/White Race Relations in the United States: A Split Labor Market Interpretation," *American Sociological Review 41* (February 1976): 34–51.

Bonacich, Edna. "A Theory of Ethnic Antagonism: The Split Labor Market," *American Sociological Review* 37 (October 1972): 547–559.

Borntrager, Cameo., Janet I. Davis, Adam Bernstein, and Heather Gorman "A Cross-National Perspective on Bullying," *Child Youth Care Forum* 38 (2009): 121-134.

Bose, Christine E., and Peter H. Rossi. "Prestige Standings of Occupations as Affected by Gender," *American Sociological Review 48* (June 1983): 316–330.

Boserup, Ester. *Population and Technological Change.* Chicago: University of Chicago Press, 1981.

Bostpath, Lisa M. Growette. "Repeat Citizens in Motor Vehicle Stops," *Journal of Ethnicity in Criminal Justice*, (2008), 6 (1): 41-63.

The Boston Globe, *What's Up with This Health Law?*, (29 December 2006), www.boston.com/news/globe/editorial_opinion/editorials/articles/2006/12/29/whats_with_this_health_law/, (accessed on 10 June 2009).

Bourdieu, Pierre. *The Forms of Capital.* In John Richardson, ed., *Handbook of Theory and Research for the Sociology of Education.* New York: Greenwood Press, 1986, 241–258.

Bowles, Samuel., and Herbert Gintis. *Schooling in Capitalist America.* New York: Basic Books, 1976.

Bowman, Madonna E., and Constance R. Ahrons. "Impact of Legal Custody Status on Fathers' Parenting Post-divorce," *Journal of Marriage and the Family* 47 (May 1985): 481–488.

Boyer, Ernest. "College: The Undergraduate Experience in America," *Chronicle of Higher Education, 33*(10) (November 5, 1986): 16.

Bradbard, Marilyn R. "Sex Differences in Adults' Gifts and Children's Toy Requests at Christmas," *Psychological Reports 56* (1985): 969–970.

Brennan, Deborah. "The ABC of Child Care Politics," *Australian Journal of Social Sciences*, (Winter, 2007), 42 (2): 213-225.

Brougham, Stephen P., Nancy L. Swain, and Patrick W. Keaton. "Characteristics of Private Schools in the U.S.: Results From the 2007-2008 Private School Universe Survey, 2009-2013" (2009), National Center for Education Statistics, Institute of Education Sciences, U.S. Department of Education, Washington, DC.

Brockway, George P. "Minimum Wage vs. Maximum Confusion," *The New Leader* 7 (April 3, 1989): 14–15.

Broder, John. "Firms Knew of Cement Flaws Before Spill, Panel Says," *New York Times* (October 28, 2010), www.nytimes.com.

Brown, Cynthia Stokes. "No Amen for School Prayer," *Learning* (August, 1983) 42–43.

Brown, Henry Phelps. *Egalitarianism and the Generation of Inequality.* New York: Oxford University Press, 1988.

Browne-Miller, Angela. *The Day Care Dilemma: Critical Concerns for American Families.* New York: Plenum Press, 1990.

Bureau of Justice Statistics, U.S. Department of Justice (May 11, 1998). www.ojp.usdoj.gov/bjs

Burgess, Ernest W. "The Growth of the City," in Robert E. Park and Ernest W. Burgess, eds., *The City.* Chicago: University of Chicago Press, 1925, 47–62.

Burke, Ronald J., and Tamara Weir. "Relationship of Wives' Employment Status to Husband, Wife and Pair Satisfaction and Performance," *Journal of Marriage and the Family 38* (May 1976): 279–287.

Calavita, Kitty., and Henry N. Pontell. "Other's People's Money Revisited: Collective Embezzlement in the Savings and Loan Industries," *Social Problems 38* (February 1991): 94–112.

Caldecott, Helen. *Missile Envy: The Arms Race and Nuclear War.* New York: Bantam Books, 1986.

California Environmental Protection Agency Air Resources Board. "Study Links Air Pollution and Asthma," January 31, 2002.

Callahan, Daniel. In Robert Landers, "Right to Die: Medical, Legal & Moral Issues," *Congressional Quarterly's Editorial Research Reports* (September 28, 1990): 554–567.

Caplow, Theodore., Howard M. Bahr, Bruce A. Chadwick, Reuben Hill, and Margaret Holmes Williamson. *Middletown Families: Fifty Years of Change and Continuity.* Minneapolis: University of Minnesota Press, 1982.

Carison, Margaret. "Only English Spoken Here," *Time*, December 5, 1988, 29.

Carpenter, Christopher. "Workspace Drug Testing and Drug Use," *Health Services Research*, (April, 2007), 42 (2):795-810.

Cashion, Barbara G. "Female-Headed Families: Effects on Children and Clinical Implications," *Journal of Marital and Family Therapy* (April 1982): 77–85.

Cassano, Michael., and Carisa Perry-Parrish. "Influence of Gender on Parental Socialization of Children's Sadness Regulation," *Social Development*, (2007), 16 (2): 210-231.

Catalyst. www.catalyst.org.

CBS News. "War on Drugs Unsuccessful, Drug Car Says," (May 13, 2010), www.cbsnews.com.

"Catholic Schools Serving Disadvantaged Students," *Financing Schools* 7, no. 3 (Winter 1997).

Centers, Richard. *The Psychology of Social Classes.* Princeton, NJ: Princeton University Press, 1949.

Centers for Disease Control and Prevention (CDC). "Births: Preliminary Data for 2003," *NVSR* 53, no. 9 (2004): 18.

Centers for Disease Control and Prevention (CDC). "Morbidity and Mortality Weekly Report," 60 (Jan 14, 2011).

Chan, Janet. "Racial Profiling and Police Subcultures," *Canadian Journal of Criminology and Criminal Justice*, (January, 2011), 53 (1): 75-78.

"Changing America: Indicators of Social and Economic Well-Being by Race and Hispanic Origin," Council of Economic Advisers for the Presidents Initiative on Race, September 1998.

Chang, Jack. "Culture Clash Complicates China's Brazil Push." (May 25, 2011). Associated Press.

Chappell, Neena L. "Aging and Mental Health," *Social Work in Mental Health* (2008) 7 (1-3): 122-138.

Chasin, Barbara H. (1997) *Inequality and Violence in the United States.* Atlantic Highlands, NJ: Humanities Press.

Cheal, David. *The Gift Economy.* Boston: Routledge & Kegan Paul, 1988.

Cheal, David J. "Intergenerational Family Transfers," *Journal of Marriage and the Family 45* (November 1983): 805–813.

Chesler, Mark A., and William M. Cave. *A Sociology of Education: Access to Power and Privilege.* New York: Macmillan, 1981.

Childe, V. Gordon. "The Urban Revolution," *Town Planning Review 21* (April 1951): 3–17.

Chirot, Daniel. "The Rise of the West," *American Sociological Review 50* (April 1985): 181–195.

Church, George. "Thinking the Unthinkable," *Time*, May 30, 1988, 12–19.

Chun, Jennifer Jihye. "The Limits of Labor Exclusion: Redefining the Politics of Split Labor Markets Under Globalization," *Critical Sociology* , (2008) 34 (3):433-452.

CIA World Factbook, Field Listing-Life Expectancy at Birth (2009), https://www.cia.gov/library/publictions/the-world-factbook/fields/2102.html, (accessed April 11, 2009).

CIA World Factbook, Saudi Arabia, (2009), [www.cia.gov/library/publications/the-world-factbook/geos/sa.html], accessed on June 4, 2009.

CIA World Factbook, United States, (2007), https://www.cia.gov/library/publications/the-world-factbook/geos/us.html#People, (accessed on April 14, 2009).

Clark, Robin E., and Judith Freeman Clark. *The Encyclopedia of Child Abuse.* New York: Facts on File, 1989.

Clarke-Stewart, K. Alison. "Infant Day Care: Maligned or Malignant?" *American Psychologist 44* (February 1989): 266–273.

Clemens, Audra W., and Leland J. Axelsen. "The Not-So-Empty Nest: The Return of the Fledgling Adult," *Family Relations 34* (April 1985): 259–264.

Clemmit, Marcia. "Health Care Reform: Is Universal Coverage Too Expensive?" *CQ Researcher*, (August 8, 2009), 19 (9): 693-715.

Clemmit, Marcia. "Health Care Reform: Is the Landmark New Plan a Good Idea?" *CQ Researcher*, (June 11, 2010), 20 (22): 505-528.

Clemmit, Marcia. "Medication Abuse," *CQ Researcher* (October 19, 2009), 19 (35): 837-860.

Cohen, Albert K., and Harold M. Hodges, Jr. "Characteristics of Lower Blue-Collar Class," *Social Problems 10* (Winter 1963): 307–321.

Cohen, Harry S. "Sociology and You: Good Living," in Roger A. Strauss, ed., *Using Sociology: An Introduction from the Clinical Perspective.* New York: General Hall, 1985.

Colapinto, John. "The True Story of John/Joan," *Rolling Stone Magazine*, (December 11, 1997): 54-97.

Coleman, James W., and Donald R. Cressey. *Social Problems*, 4th ed. New York: HarperCollins Publishers, 1990.

Coleman, James., Thomas Hoffer, and Sally Kilgore. *Public and Private High Schools: An Analysis of High Schools and Beyond.* Washington, D.C.: National Center for Education Statistics, 1982.

Coleman, James S., et al. *Equality of Educational Opportunity.* Washington, D.C.: U.S. Government Printing Office, 1966.

Coleman, James S., et al. *Youth: Transition to Adulthood. Report of the Panel on Youth of the President's Science Advisory Committee.* Chicago: University of Chicago Press, 1974.

Collver, Andrew. "Housing and Environmental Planning," in Howard Freeman, Russel R. Dynes, Peter H. Rossi, and William Foote Whyte, eds., *Applied Sociology.* San Francisco: Jossey-Bass, 1983, 275–286.

Collins, Randall. *The Credential Society: A Historical Sociology of Education and Stratification.* New York: Academic Press, 1979.

Collins, Randall., and Scott Coltrane. *Sociology of Marriage and the Family: Gender, Love, and Property*, 3rd ed. Chicago: Nelson-Hall, 1991.

Colson, Charles. "Half-Stoned Logic," *Christianity Today* (March 5, 1990): 64.

Compa, Lance. "To Cure Labor's Ills: Bigger Unions, Fewer of Them," *Washington Post* (November 16, 1986): H1.

Connelly, Julie. "How Dual-Income Couples Cope," *Fortune*, (September 24, 1990) 129–130, 133–134, 136.

Conner, Karen A. *Aging America: Issues Facing an Aging Society.* Englewood Cliffs, NJ: Prentice Hall, 1992.

Cookson, Peter W. Jr., and Caroline Hodges Persell. *Preparing for Power: America's Elite Boarding Schools.* New York: Basic Books, 1985.

Cooley, Charles H. *Social Organization.* New York: Scribner's, 1909.

Corea, Genoveffa. "How the New Reproductive Technologies Could Be Used to Apply the Brothel Model of Social Control over Women," *Women's Studies International Forum 8* (1985): 299–305.

Cornfield, Daniel B. "Declining Union Membership in the Post–World War II Era: The United Furniture Workers of America, 1939–1982," *American Journal of Sociology 91* (March 1986): 1112–1153.

Cose, Ellis. "Are Quotas Really the Problem?" *Time* (June 24, 1991): 70.

Coser, Lewis. *Masters of Sociological Thought.* New York: Harcourt Brace Jovanovich, 1977.

Council of the Great City Schools. "Urban School Superintendents," *Urban Indicator* 8(1) (June 2006), http://www.cgcs.org/images/Publications/Indicator_06.pdf, (accessed on April 14, 2009).

Cowgill, Donald. "Aging and Modernization: A Revision of the Theory," in J. Gubrium, ed., *Late Life Communities and Environmental Policy.* Springfield, IL: Charles C. Thomas, 1974.

Cowgill, Donald., and Lowell Holmes. *Aging and Modernization.* New York: Appleton-Century-Crofts, 1972.

Coyne, William J. "Pro: Should the House-Passed Wage Proposal Be Enacted?" *Congressional Digest 68(5)* (May 1989): 154, 156.

Cragun, Ryan T., and Michael E. Nielsen. "Fighting Over 'Mormon': Media Coverage of the FLDS and LDS Churches," *Dialogue: A Journal of Mormon Thought*, (2009), 42 (1):65-1004.

Crane, Jonathan. "The Epidemic Theory of Ghettos and Neighborhood Effects on Dropping Out and Teenage Childbearing," *American Journal of Sociology 96* (March 1991): 1226–1259.

Crary, David. "Bible Belt Leads U.S. in Divorces," Associated Press, November 12, 1999.

Crawford, James. "Is Bilingual Education Best for English-Language Learners?" *CQ Research* (December 11, 2009), (19 (43): 1045.

Criss, Michael M., and Daniel S. Shaw, Kristin L. Moilanen, Julia E. Hitchings and Erin N. Ingoldsby. "Family, Neighborhood and Peer Characteristics as Predictors of Child Adjustment: A Longitudinal Analysis of Additive and Mediation Models," *Social Development*, (August, 2009), 18 (3): 511-535,

Croziet, Jean-Claude., and Marion Outrevis. "Socioeconomic Status and Intelligence: Why Test Scores Do Not Equal Merit," *Journal of Poverty*, (2004), 8 (13):91-107.

Cumming, E., and W. Henry. *Growing Old: The Process of Disengagement.* New York: Basic Books, 1961.

Current Population Reports (see U.S. Bureau of the Census, *Current Population Reports).*

Currie, Elliott. *Confronting Crime: An American Challenge.* New York: Pantheon Books, 1985.

Currie, Elliott., and Jerome H. Skolnick. *America's Problems: Social Issues and Public Policy.* Glenview, IL: Scott, Foresman/Little, Brown, 1988.

Curtis, Susan. Genie: *A Psycholinguistic Study of a Modern Day Wild Child.* NY: Academic Press. 1977.

Cuzzort, R. P., and E. W. King. *20th Century Social Thought*, 3rd ed. New York: Holt, Rinehart and Winston. 1980.

Dahrendorf, Raif. *Class and Class Conflict in Industrial Society.* Palo Alto, CA: Stanford University Press, 1951.

Davis, Karen. "Equal Treatment and Unequal Benefits: The Medicare Program," *Milbank Memorial Fund Quarterly 53*(4) (1975): 449–458.

Davis, Kingsley. "Extreme Social Isolation of a Child," *American Journal of Sociology 45* (1940): 554–565.

Davis, Kingsley. "Final Note on a Case of Extreme Isolation," *American Journal of Sociology 50* (1947): 432–437.

Davis, Kingsley. "The First Cities: How and Why Did They Arise?" in K. Davis, ed., *Cities: Their Origin, Growth, and Human Impact.* San Francisco: W. H. Freeman, 1973.

Davis, Kingsley., and Wilbert E. Moore. "Some Principles of Stratification," *American Sociological Review 10* (April 1945): 242–249.

Davis, Wayne H. "Overpopulated America," *New Republic*, (January 10, 1970): 13–15.

Dedman, Bill. "Facts on the Mass. Health Reform," *MSNBC.com*, (16 August 2007), www.msnbc.msn.com/id/20266957/ns/us_news-gut_check/, (accessed on 10 June 2009).

Dedman, Bill. "Massachusetts is Health Care Lab," *MSNBC.com*, (17 August 2007), www.msnbc.msn.com/id/20255585/ (accessed on 10 June 2009).

DeJong, G. F., and A. B. Madamba. "A Double Disadvantage? Minority Group, Immigrant Status, and Underemployment in the United States," *Social Science Quarterly*, 82, no. 1 (2001):117–130.

DeLamarter, Richard Thomas. *Big Blue: IBM's Use and Abuse of Power.* New York: Dodd, Mead, 1986.

Demarco, Geerald. *Mother Gives Birth to Twins with Different Dads.* (2009). http://today.msnbc.msn.com/id/30864533/?GT1=43001 (accessed on 22 May 2009).

Demo, David H., and Alan C. Acock. "The Impact of Divorce on Children," *Journal of Marriage and the Family 50* (August 1988): 619–648.

Dennis, Richard J. "Bill Bennett Won't You Please Come Home," *New Perspectives Quarterly* (Winter 1991): 69.

Denton, John A. *Medical Sociology.* Boston: Houghton Mifflin, 1978.

Dentzer, Susan., and Tom Hughes. "Going After the Rich," *U.S. News and World Report,* (August 19, 1990): 49–50.

Department of Health and Human Services, Office of Minority Health, 2009, www.omhrc.gov.

Deutscher, Guy. "Does Your Language Shape How You Think?" *New York Times Magazine,* (August 26, 2010).

Devas-Walt, C., Proctor, B.D., & Smith, J. 2007 "Income, Poverty, and Health Insurance Coverage in the United States: 2006." U.S. Census Bureau, *Current Population Reports:* 60–233. www.census.gov/prod/2007pubs/p60-233.pdf. (accessed August 27, 2007).

Diamond, Milton. "Sexual Identity, Monozygotic Twins Reared in Discordant Sex Roles and a BBC Follow-up," *Archives of Sexual Behavior 11*(2) (April 1982): 181–186.

Dillon, Sam. "U.S. Graduation Rate Is Rising," *New York Times* (November 30, 2010), www.nytimes.com.

Dinitz, Simon. "Progress, Crime, and the Folk Ethic," *Criminology 11* (May 1973): 3–21.

Dionne, E. J. Jr.. "Loss of Faith in Egalitarianism Alters U.S. Social Vision," *Washington Post,* April 30, 1990: 1.

Dilip, Jeste V., George S. Alexopoulos, Stephen J. Bartels, Jeffrey L. Cummings, Joseph Gallo, Gary L. Gottleib, MaureenC. Halpain, Barton W. Palmer, Thomas L. Patterson, Charles F. Reynolds III and Barry Lebowitz. "Consensus Statement on the Upcoming Crisis in Geriatric Mental Health: Research Agenda for the Next 2 Decades," *Archives of General Psychiatry* (1999), 56: 848-853.

Dixon, Marlene., Stacey M. Warner and Jennifer Bruening. "More Than Just Letting Them Play: Parental Influence On Women's Lifetime Sport Involvement," *Sociology of Sport Journal,* (2008), 25:538-559.

Dobson, James C. *Attorney General's Commission on Pornography, Final Report.* Washington, D.C.: U.S. Government Printing Office, June 1986, 71–87.

Dollard, John., Neal E. Miller, Leonard W. Doob, O. H. Mowrer, and Robert R. Sears. *Frustration and Aggression.* New Haven, CT: Yale University Press, 1939.

Domhoff, G. William. *The Higher Circles: The Governing Class in America.* New York: Vintage (Random House), 1971.

Domhoff, G. William. *The Power Elite and the State: How Policy Is Made in America.* Hawthorne, NY: Aldine de-Gruyter, 1990.

Domhoff, G. William. *The Powers That Be: Process of Ruling Class Domination in America.* New York: Vintage (Random House), 1979.

Domhoff, G. William. *Who Rules America Now? A View for the Eighties.* Englewood Cliffs, NJ: Prentice-Hall, 1983.

Domhoff, G. William. "*Who Rules America,*" (2011), www.sociology.usc.edu/whorulesamerica/power/wealth.html.

Dority, Barbara. "Feminist Moralism, 'Pornography,' and Censorship," *The Humanist* (November/December 1989): 8–9, 46.

Douglas, Richard L. "Domestic Neglect and Abuse of the Elderly: Implications for Research and Service," *Family Relations 32* (July 1983): 395–402.

Dowd, James. "Aging as Exchange: A Preface to Theory," *Journal of Gerontology 30* (September 1975): 584–594.

Dowd, James. *Stratification Among the Aged.* Monterey, CA: Brooks/Cole, 1980.

Dowie, Mark. "Pinto Madness," *Mother Jones, 2*(8) (September–October 1977): 43–47.

Dowse, Robert E., and John A. Hughes. *Political Sociology.* New York: Wiley, 1972.

D'Souza, Dinesh. "Illiberal Education," *Atlantic Monthly,* March 1991: 51–79.

D'Souza, Dinesh. "In the Name of Academic Freedom, Colleges Should Back Professors Against Students' Demands for 'Correct' Views," *The Chronicles of Higher Education 37* (April 24, 1991b): B1, B3.

Duberman, Lucile. *Social Inequality: Class and Caste in America.* Philadelphia: Lippincott, 1976.

Duke, Alan. *'Octomom' Seeks to Trademark for TV, Diaper Line.* (2009). www.cnn.com/2009/US/04/15/octuplet.mom/index.html?iref=newssearch, (accessed on 22 May 2009).

Dupreel, Eugene G. "Demographic Change and Progress," in Johannes Overbeek, ed., *The Evolution of Population Theory.* Westport, CT: Greenwood Press, 1977, 80–85. (Originally published in 1922)

Durkheim, Emile. *The Division of Labor in Society.* New York: Free Press, 1933. (Originally published in 1893)

Durkheim, Emile. *The Elementary Forms of the Religious Life.* New York: Free Press, 1926. (Originally published in 1915)

Eccles, Jacquelynne. "Sex Differences in Math Achievement and Course Enrollment." Paper presented at the annual meeting of the American Educational Research Association, New York, March 1982.

Ehrenreich, Barbara. "A Conservative Tax Proposal," *Time,* August 27, 1990, p. 70.

Ehrenreich, Barbara. *Nickel and Dimed: On (Not) Getting By in America.* New York: Metropolitan Books, 2001.

Ehrenreich, B., and D. English. *For Her Own Good: 150 Years of the Experts' Advice to Women.* Garden City, NY: Anchor Books, 1979.

Ehrlich, Elizabeth. "The Mommy Track," in Kurt Finsterbusch, ed., *Annual Editions.* Guilford, CT: Dushkin, 1991, 83–85.

Eitzen, Stanley., and Maxine Baca Zinn. *In Conflict and Order: Understanding Society*, 11th ed. Boston: Allyn and Bacon, 2007.

Eitzen, D. Stanley., and Maxine Baca Zinn. *Social Problems*, 4th ed. Needham Heights, MA: Allyn and Bacon, 1989.

Ekman, R., et al. "Bicycle-Related Injuries Among the Elderly—A New Epidemic?" *Public Health* 115, no. 1 (January 2001): 38–43. Karolinska Institutet, Department of Public Health Sciences, Division of Social Medicine, Stockholm, Sweden.

Elder, Glenn. *Children of the Great Depression.* Chicago: University of Chicago Press, 1974.

Elkin, Frederick., and Gerald Handel. *The Child and Society: The Process of Socialization*, 5th ed. New York: Random House, 1989.

Ellis, Wendy., and Lynne Zarbatany. "Peer Group Status as a Moderator of Group Influence on Children's Deviant, Aggressive, and Prosocial Behavior," *Child Development*, (July/August, 2007), 78 (4): 1240-1254.

Encyclopedia of Associations, Vol. 1, 25th ed., "National Organizations of the U.S." Detroit: Gale Research, 1991.

Engels, Friedrich. *The Origin of the Family, Private Property and the State.* Chicago: Charles H. Ken, 1902.

Erikson, Kai J. *Everything in Its Path: Destruction of Community in the Buffalo Creek Flood.* New York: Simon and Schuster, 1976.

Eshleman, J. Ross., and Richard A. Bulcroft. *The Family: An Introduction*, 11th ed. Boston: Allyn and Bacon, 2006.

Etzioni, Amitai. *A Sociological Reader on Complex Organizations*, 3rd ed. New York: Holt, Rinehart and Winston, 1980.

Etzioni-Halevy, Eva. *Social Change.* Boston: Routledge and Kegan Paul, 1981.

Facts on File. World News Digest with Index 46 (August 1, 1986): 622C2.

Fahrenthold, David A. "Mass. Bill Requires Health Coverage," *The Washington Post*, (5 April 2006), www.washingtonpost.com/wp-dyn/content/article/2006/04/04/AR2006040401937.html, (accessed on 10 June 2009).

Falco, Mathea. *Winning the Drug War: A National Strategy.* New York: Priority Press, 1989.

Farley, Lin. *Sexual Shakedown.* New York: Warner Books, 1978.

Farmer, Rod. "The School Prayer Issue," *Education*, Spring, 1984, 248–249.

Farrington, David P., and Maria M. Ttofi. "How to Reduce School Bullying," *Victims and Offenders*, (2009), 4: 321-326.

Feagin, Joe R. *Racial and Ethnic Relations.* Englewood Cliffs, NJ: Prentice-Hall, 2nd ed., 1984; 3rd ed., 1989.

Feagin, Joe R., and Robert Parke. *Building American Cities: The Urban Real Estate Game*, 2nd ed. Englewood Cliffs, NJ: Prentice Hall, 1990.

Fein, David J. "Married and Poor: Basic Characteristics of Economically Disadvantaged Couples in the U.S." ABT Associates (2004). www.mdrc.org/publications/393/workpaper.html.

Feldman-Summers, Shirley., and Gayle C. Palmer. "Rape as Viewed by Judges, Prosecutors and Police Officers," *Criminal Justice and Behavior* 7 (March 1980): 19–40.

Federal Interagency Forum on Aging-Related Statistics. "Older Americans 2010: Key Indicators of Well-Being," (July, 2010), U.S. Government Printing Office, Washington, D.C.

Ferraro, Kenneth F., "Health Beliefs and Proscriptions on Public Smoking," *Sociological Inquiry 60* (August 1990): 244–255.

Fierman, Jaclyn. "Why Women Still Don't Hit the Top," *Fortune 122* (July 30, 1990): 40.

Finkelstein, E. A., I. C. Fiebelkorn, and G. Wang. "National Medical Spending Attributable to Overweight and Obesity: How Much, and Who Is Paying?" *Health Affairs* W3 (2003): 219–226.

Fine, Gary Alan. "Small Groups and Culture Creation: The Idioculture of Little League Baseball Teams," *American Sociological Review 44* (October 1979): 733–745.

Finsterbusch, Kurt., and Annabelle Bender Mars. *Social Research for Policy Decisions.* Belmont, CA: Wadsworth, 1980.

Finsterbusch, Kurt., and George McKenna, eds. *Taking Sides: Clashing Views on Controversial Social Issues*, 4th ed. Guilford, CT: Dushkin Publishing, 1986; 6th ed., 1990.

Fisher, Bonnie S., Frances T. Cullen, and Michael G. Turner. *The Sexual Victimization of College Women.* (December, 2000). Washington: Department of Justice (U.S.), National Institute of Justice, Publication NCJ182369.

FitzGerald, Kathleen Whalen. *Alcoholism: The Genetic Inheritance.* New York: Doubleday, 1988.

Flamini, Roland. "Turmoil in the Arab World." *CQ Global Researcher* (May 3, 2011), 5 (9): 209-236

Florida, Richard., and Martin Kenney. "Transplanted Organizations: The Transfer of Japanese Industrial Organization to the U.S." *American Sociological Review 56* (June 1991): 381–398.

Foster, George M. "Relationships Between Theoretical and Applied Anthropology," in Alvin W. Gouldner and S. M. Miller, eds., *Applied Sociology: Opportunities and Problems.* New York: Free Press, 1965.

Fox, Cybelle., and David J. Harding. "School Shootings as Organizational Deviance," *Sociology of Education*, (January, 2005), 78: 69-97.

Fox, Karen D., and Sharon Y. Nichols. "The Time Crunch: Wife's Employment and Family Work," *Journal of Family Issues 4* (March 1983): 61–82.

Frankel, Marc T., and Rollins, Howard A. Jr.. "Does Mother Know Best? Mothers and Fathers Interacting with Preschool Sons and Daughters," *Developmental Psychology 19* (1983): 694–702.

Freeman, Harold. *Toward Socialism in America.* Cambridge, MA: Schenkman, 1979.

Freeman, Howard E., and Peter H. Rossi. "Furthering the Applied Side of Sociology," *American Sociological Review 49* (1984): 571–580.

Frenzel, Bill. “Con: Should the House-Passed Wage Proposal Be Enacted?” *Congressional Digest 68*(5) (May 1989): 151,153.

Fromm, Erich. *The Sane Society.* New York: Holt, Rinehart and Winston, 1965.

Fuchs, Stephen. "What Makes Sciences 'Scientific'?' in Turner, Jonathan H. *Handbook of Sociological Theory*. New York: Springer Sciences and Business Media. 2006.

Fullerton, Howard N. Jr.. “Labor Force Participation: 75 Years of Change, 1950–98 and 1998–2025,” *Monthly Labor Review* (December 1999).

Galbraith, John Kenneth. “Why Arms Makers Must Be Checked,” *Scholastic Update*, April 29, 1983: 19–20.

Gallup, George Jr., and Frank Newport. “Major U.S. Cities Seen as Unsafe Places to Live and Work,” *The Gallup Poll Monthly 300* (September 1990): 40–41.

The Gallop Poll Monthly June 1990, 36; January 1991, 52.

Gamble, Wendy C., and Jedding Jin Yu. "Adolescent Siblings' Looking Glass Self-Orientations: Patterns of Liabilities and Associations of Parenting," *Journal of Youth Adolescence*, (2008), 37:860-874.

Gamson, William A. *The Strategy of Social Protest.* Homewood, IL: Dorsey Press, 1975.

Gans, Herbert J. *The Levittowners: Ways of Life and Politics in a New Suburb.* New York: Random House, 1967.

Gans, Herbert J. *More Equality.* New York: Pantheon Books, 1972.

Gans, Herbert J. *The Urban Villagers.* New York: Free Press, 1962.

Garcia, Robert. “Pro: Should the House-Passed Wage Proposal Be Enacted?” *Congressional Digest 68*(5) (May 1989): 152, 154.

Gardner, David Pierpont. “If We Stand, They Will Deliver,” *New Perspectives Quarterly* 7 (Fall 1990): 4–6.

Gelfand, Donald E. *Aging: The Ethnic Factor.* Boston: Little, Brown, 1982.

Gelles, Richard J. (1995) *Contemporary Families: A Sociological View.* Thousand Oaks, CA: Sage.

George, Susan. *How the Other Half Dies: The Real Reasons for World Hunger.* Montclair, NJ: Allanheld, Osmun, 1977.

Gereffi, Gary. *The Pharmaceutical Industry and Dependency in the Third World.* Princeton, NJ: Princeton University Press, 1983.

Gillis, Justin., and Celia Dugger. "UN Forecasts 10.1 Billion People by Century's End." (2011). NY Times, May 3.

Gladwell, Malcom. *The Tipping Point: How Little Things Can Make a Big Difference*. 2000. Little Brown and Co.

Glass, T. *The 1992 Study of the American School Superintendency: America's Education Leaders in a Time of Reform.* Arlington, VA: American Association of School Administrators, 1992.

Glassner, Barry., and Bruce Berg. “How Jews Avoid Alcohol Problems,” *American Sociological Review 45* (August 1980): 647–664.

Glazer, Nathan., and Daniel P. Moynihan. *Beyond the Melting Pot*, 2nd ed. Cambridge, MA: Massachusetts Institute of Technology Press, 1970.

Glazer, Sarah. “Getting a Grip on Influence Peddling,” *Congressional Quarterly's Editorial Research Reports 22* (December 15,1989): 697–711.

Glazer, Sarah. “Joint Custody: Is it Good for the Children?” *Congressional Quarterly's Editorial Research Reports 1* (February 3, 1989): 58–71.

Godard, John. "The Exceptional Decline of the American Labor Movement," *Industrial and Labor Relations Review*, (October 2009), 63 (1): 82-108.

Goering, John M. “The Emergence of Ethnic Interests: A Case of Serendipity,” *Social Forces 48* (March 1971): 379–384.

Goetz, Harriet. “Euthanasia Should Be Considered for Terminally Ill Patients,” in *Opposing Viewpoints Sources: Death/Dying, 1990 Annual.* San Diego: Greenhaven Press, 1990, 1–3. (Originally published by Harriet Goetz as “Euthanasia: A Bedside View,” *The Christian Century* [June 21, 1989])

Goffman, Erving. *Asylums: Essays on the Situation of Mental Patients and Other Inmates.* Garden City, NY: Anchor/Doubleday, 1961.

Goffman, Erving. *Encounters.* Indianapolis, IN: Bobbs-Merrill, 1961.

Goffman, Erving. *Interaction Ritual: Essays on Face-to-Face Behavior.* Garden City, NY: Doubleday/Anchor, 1967.

Goffman, Erving. *The Presentation of Self in Everyday Life.* Garden City, NY: Doubleday/Anchor, 1959.

Goffman, Ethan. “The Income Gap and Its Causes,” *Dissent*, Winter, 1990, p. 8.

Gold, Dolores., Gail Crombie, and Sally Noble. “Relations Between Teachers' Judgments of Girls' and Boys' Compliance and Intellectual Competence,” *Sex Roles 16* (1987): 351–358.

Gold, Mark S. “Legalize Drugs: Just Say Never,” *National Review*, April 1, 1990, 42–43.

Goldberg, S., and M. Lewis. “Play Behavior in the Year-Old Infant: Early Sex Differences,” *Child Development 40* (1969): 21–30.

Grant, J. Tobin. "Measuring Aggregate Religiosity in the United States, 1952-2005," *Sociological Spectrum*. (2008) 28: 460-476.

Goldman, Kathryn L. “Stress Management: The Importance of Organizational Context,” *Clinical Sociology Review 2* (1984): 133–136.

Goodin, Robert E. *Manipulatory Politics.* New Haven, CT: Yale University Press, 1980.

Gordon, Milton. *Assimilation in American Life.* New York: Oxford University Press, 1964.

Gordon, Milton M. *Human Nature, Class and Ethnicity.* New York: Oxford University Press, 1978.

Gordon, Richard., Katherine Gordon, and Max Gunther. *The Split Level Trap.* New York: Bernard Geis Associates, 1961.

Gouldner, Alvin W. *Patterns of Industrial Bureaucracy.* New York: Free Press, 1954.

Gove, Walter R., and Michael R. Geerken. "The Effect of Children and Employment on the Mental Health of Married Men and Women," *Social Forces 56* (February 1977): 66–76.

Grant, Linda., Kathryn B. Ward, and Xue Lan Rong. "Is There an Association Between Gender and Methods in Sociological Research?" *American Sociological Research 52* (December 1987): 856–862.

Granovetter, Mark. *Getting a Job: A Study of Contacts and Careers.* 1974. Cambridge, Mass: Harvard University Press.

Greeley, Andrew. *Religious Change in America.* Cambridge, MA: Harvard University Press, 1989.

Greenstein, Theodore N. (2000). "Economic Dependence, Gender, and the Division of Labor in the Home: A Replication and Extension." *Journal of Marriage and the Family* 62 (May): 322–335.

Greven, Phillip. *Spare the Child: The Religious Roots of Punishment and the Psychological Impact of Child Abuse.* New York: Knopf, 1991.

Griffin, Larry J., Michael E. Wallace, and Beth A. Rubin. "Capitalist Resistance to the Organization of Labor Before the New Deal: Why? How? Success?" *American Sociological Review 51* (April 1986): 147–167.

Grodsky, Eric., John Robert Warren, and Erika Felts. "Testing and Social Stratification in American Education," *Annual Review of Sociology*, (2008), 34: 385-404.

Grossman, Richard. *The Other Medicines: An Invitation to Understanding and Using Them for Health and Healing.* Garden City, NY: Doubleday, 1985.

Grusky, David., and Emily Ryo. "Did Katrina Recalibrate Attitudes Toward Poverty of Inequality? A Test of the 'Dirty Little Secret' Hypothesis," *DuBois Review*, (2006), 3 (1): 59-82.

Grzelkowski, Kathryn., and Jim Mitchell. "Applied Curriculum Can Enhance Liberal Arts Learning," *ASA Footnotes, 13*(9) (December 1985): 5–6.

Guillemin, Jeanne Harley., and Lynda Lythe Holmstrom. "The Business of Childbirth," *Society 23* (July/August 1986): 48–53.

Guterman, Stanley S., ed. *Black Psyche: Modal Personality Patterns of Black Americans.* Berkeley, CA: Glendessary Press, 1972, 87.

Hakuta, Kenji. *Mirror of Language: The Debate on Bilingualism.* New York: Basic Books, 1986.

Hall, Douglas T. "Promoting Work/Family Balance: An Organization Change Approach," *Organizational Dynamics*, Winter, 1990, 5–18.

Hall, Edward T. *The Silent Language.* New York: Anchor Books. 1959, 1973, 1981, 1990.

Hall, Richard H. *Organizations: Structures, Processes, and Outcomes*, 4th ed. Englewood Cliffs, NJ: Prentice Hall, 1987.

Hall, Thomas D. "Incorporation in the World System: Toward a Critique," *American Sociological Review 51* (June 1986): 390–402.

Hampton, David R., Charles E. Summer, and Ross A. Webber. *Organizational Behavior and the Practice of Management*, 4th ed. Glenview, IL: Scott, Foresman, 1982.

Harris, Chauncy., and Edward L. Ullman. "The Nature of Cities," *Annals of the American Academy of Political and Social Science 242* (November 1945): 7–17.

Harris, Diana K., and William E. Cole. *Sociology of Aging.* Boston: Houghton Mifflin, 1980.

Harter, Carl L. "The 'Good Times' Cohort of the 1930s: Sometimes Less Means More (and More Means Less)," in Scott W. Menard and Elizabeth W. Moen, *Perspectives on Population: An Introduction to Concepts and Issues.* New York: Oxford University Press, 1987, 372–376.

Hartmann, Heidi. "Capitalism, Patriarchy, and Job Segregation by Sex," in Nona Glazer and Helen Youngelson Waehaer, eds., *Woman in a Man-Made World*, 2nd ed. Chicago: Rand McNally, 1977, 71–84.

Haseltine, Robert W. "The Minimum Wage: Help or Hindrance?" *USA Today Magazine*, July, 1989, p. 31.

Haugen, Emar. *Blessings of Babel: Bilingualism and Language Planning.* Berlin: Mouton de Gruyter, 1987.

Hayes, C. *The Ape in Our House.* New York: Harper and Row, 1951.

Healy, Jane M. *Endangered Minds: Why Our Children Don't Think.* New York: Simon and Schuster, 1990.

Heer, David M. *Society and Population.* Englewood Cliffs, NJ: Prentice-Hall, 1975.

Hefley, Joel. "Con: Should the House-Passed Wage Proposal Be Enacted?" *Congressional Digest 68*(5) (May 1989): 159.

Heilbroner, Robert L. *The Making of Economic Society.* Englewood Cliffs, NJ: Prentice-Hall, 1980.

Henry, William A. "Upside Down in the Groves of Academe," *Time*, April 1, 1991, 66–69.

Henry, William A. "Beyond the Melting Pot," *Time*, April 9, 1990, 28.

Henslin, James M. *Social Problems*, 2nd ed. Englewood Cliffs, NJ: Prentice Hall, 1990.

Hermida, Alfred. "Saudis Block 2,000 Websites," BBC News, (31 July 2002), http://news.bbc.co.uk/2/hi/technology/2153312.stm, (accessed on June 4, 2009).

Hernanel, Sam. "Obama Shifts Strategy Away From War on Drugs, Will Now Focus on Prevention and Treatment," www.Boston.com (May 12, 2010).

Heritage, John., and David Greatbatch. "Generating Applause: A Study of Rhetoric and Response at Party Political Conferences," *American Journal of Sociology 92* (July 1986): 110–157.

Hewlett, Sylvia Ann. *A Lesser Life: The Myth of Women's Liberation in America.* New York: William Morrow, 1986.

Heyzer, Noeleen. "Asian Women Wage-Earners: Their Situation and Possibilities for Donor Intervention," *World Development 17*(7) (1989): 1109–1123.

Higins, George E., Melissa L. Ricketetts, Catherine D. Marcum, and Margaret Mahoney. "Primary Socialization Theory: An Exploratory Study of Delinquent Trajectories," *Criminal Justice Studies*, (2010), 23 (2): 133-146.

Hill, James O., and Frederick L. Trowbridge. "Childhood Obesity: Future Directions and Research Priorities," *Pediatrics* (1998 supplement): 571.

Hilton, Jeanne M., Linda Anngela-Cole, Juri Wakita. "A Cross Cultural Comparison of Factors Associated With School Bullying in Japan and the U.S.," *The Family Journal: Counseling and Therapy for Couples and Families*, (2010), 18 (4): 413-422.

Hine, Virginia H. "Dying at Home: Can Families Cope?" *Omega 10* (1979–1980).

Hobbs, Daniel F., Jr. "Parenthood as Crisis: A Third Study," *Journal of Marriage and the Family* 27 (August 1965): 367–372.

Hodge, Nathan. "Boeing Bid Beats Europe For Tanker." *Wall Street Journal* (February 25, 2011). www.wjs.com

Hoffman, Lois Wladis. "The Changing Genetics/Socialization Balance," *Journal of Social Issues 41* (Spring 1985): 127–148.

Homans, George C. *Social Behavior: Its Elementary Forms.* New York: Harcourt, Brace and World, 1961; 2nd ed., Harcourt Brace Jovanovich, 1974.

Horgan, John. "Test Negative: A Look at the 'Evidence' Justifying Illicit-Drug Tests," *Scientific American 262* (March 1990a): 18–19.

Horgan, John. "Your Analysis Is Faulty," *The New Republic*, April 2, 1990b, 22–24.

Hostin, Sunny. *Commentary: Appellate Court Wrong on FLDS.* (2008). www.cnn.com/2008/CRIME/05/23/flds.appeals/index.html?iref=newssearch, (accessed on 22 May 2009).

Howard, Ebenezer. *Garden Cities of Tomorrow.* London: Faber and Faber, 1902.

Howard, Robert. "Brave New Workplace," in Jerome H. Skolnick and Elliott Currie, eds., *Crisis in American Institutions*, 7th ed. Glenview, IL: Scott, Foresman, 1988.

Hoyer, Steny H. "Con: Should President Bush's Minimum Wage Proposals Be Adopted?" *Congressional Digest 68*(5) (May 1989): 145, 147.

Hoyt, Homer. *The Structure of Residential Neighborhoods in American Cities.* Washington, D.C.: Federal Housing Administration, 1939.

Humphrey, Craig. R., and Frederick R. Buttel. *Environment, Energy and Society.* Belmont, CA: Wadsworth, 1982.

Humphreys, Laud. Tearoom Trade: *Impersonal Sex in Public Places.* New York: Aldine. 1975.

Hunt, J. G., and L. L. Hunt: "Race, Daughters and Father-Loss: Does Absence Make the Girl Grow Stronger?" *Social Problems 25* (February 1977a): 90–102.

Hunt, Janet G., and Larry C. Hunt. "Racial Inequality and Self-image: Identity Maintenance as Identity Confusion," *Sociology and Social Research 61* (July 1977b): 539–559.

"Immigrant Children Exceed Expectations. Studies Show That Immigrant Children Are Assimilating," *Immigration Policy Report (2001).* www.ailf.org/ipc/policy_reports_2001_childre.asp.

Information Please Almanac Atlas & Yearbook, 1991, 44th ed. Boston: Houghton Mifflin, 1991.

Jackman, Mary R., and Robert W. Jackman. *Class Awareness in the United States.* Berkeley: University of California Press, 1983.

Jacob, John E. "Racism Denies Minorities Equal Opportunities," in Carol Wekesser, ed., *Social Justice: Opposing Viewpoints.* San Diego: Greenhaven Press, 1990, 107–114.

Jaffee, David. "Gender Inequality in Workplace Autonomy and Authority," *Social Science Quarterly 70*(2) (June 1989): 375–388.

Jardim, Anne., and Margaret Hennig. "The Last Barrier: Breaking into the Boys' Club at the Top," *Working Woman 15* (November 1990): 130.

Jellinek, E. M. *The Disease Concept of Alcoholism.* New Haven, CT: Yale University Press, 1960.

Jencks, Christopher. "Genes and Crime," *The New York Review*, February 12, 1987, 33–41.

Jencks, Christopher. *Who Gets Ahead? The Determinant of Economic Success in America.* New York: Basic Books, 1979.

Johnson, Doyle Paul. "Using Sociology to Analyze Human and Organizational Problems: A Humanistic Perspective to Link Theory and Practice," *Clinical Sociology Review 4* (1986): 57–71.

Johnson, Hans. "Immigrants and Education," (April, 2011), Public Policy Institute of California, Just the Facts, www.ppic.org.

Johnson, James A., Harold W. Collins, Victor L. Dupuis, and John H. Johansen. *Introduction to the Foundations of American Education*, 6th ed. Boston: Allyn and Bacon, 1985.

Johnson, Tony. "Health Care Costs and U.S. Competitiveness," Council on Foreign Relations, (March 23, 2010), www.cfr.org.

Johnstone, D. Bruce. *Sharing the Costs of Higher Education.* New York: College Board Publications, 1986.

Jones, Charles O. *An Introduction to the Study of Public Policy*, 3rd ed. Monterey, CA: Brooks/Cole, 1984.

Jones, L. Y. *Great Expectations: America and the Baby Boom Generation.* New York: Coward, McCann & Geohegan, 1980.

Jost, Kenneth. "Revising No Child Left Behind," *CQ Researcher* (April 16, 2010), 20 (15): 336-360.

Jost, Kenneth. "Bilingual Education vs. English Immersion," *CQ Research* (December 11, 2009), (19 (43):1029-1052.

Kagan, Sharon Lynn., and James W. Newton. "For-Profit and Nonprofit Child Care: Similarities and Differences," *Young Children*, November 1989, 4–10.

Kalil, Ariel., and Rebecca Ryan. "Mother's Economic Conditions and Sources of Support in Fragile Families," *Future of Children* (Fall, 2010), 20 (2): 39-61.

Kaiser Commission. "Massachusetts Health Care Reform: Two Years Later," *The Henry J. Kaiser Family Foundation*, (May 2008), www.kff.org/uninsured/upload/7777.pdf, (accessed on 10 June 2009).

Kaiser Family Foundation. "Daily Media Use Among Children and Teens Up Dramatically from Five Years Ago," (January 10, 2010), www.kff.org.

Kanter, Rosabeth Moss. *The Change Masters*. New York: Simon and Schuster, 1983.

Karen, David. "Toward a Political-Organizational Model of Gatekeeping: The Case of Elite Colleges," *Sociology of Education 63* (October 1990): 227–239.

Karier, Clarence J. "Testing for Order and Control in the Corporate Liberal State," in NJ Block and Gerald Dworkin, eds., *The I.Q. Controversy: Critical Readings*. New York: Pantheon, 1976, 339–373.

Kart, Cary S. *The Realities of Aging: An Introduction to Gerontology*. Boston: Allyn and Bacon, 1981.

Kasarda, John. "The Changing Occupational Structure of the American Metropolis," in Barry Schwartz, ed., *The Changing Face of the Suburbs*. Chicago: University of Chicago Press, 1976, 113–136.

Kasarda, John D. "The Jobs-Skills Mismatch," *New Perspectives Quarterly* 7 (Fall 1990): 34–37.

Kass, Leon R. "Active Euthanasia Is Inhumane," in *Opposing Viewpoints Sources: Death/Dying, 1990 Annual*. San Diego: Greenhaven Press, 1990, 1–3. (Originally published as "Neither for Love nor Money: Why Doctors Must Not Kill." *The Public Interest 94* (Winter 1989): 25–46.

Katel, Peter. "Housing the Homeless." *CQ Researcher* (December 18, 2009) 19 (44): 1053-1076,

Katel, Peter. "War on Drugs: Should Nonviolent Drug Users Be Subject to Arrest?" *CQ Researcher*, (June 2, 2006), 16 (21): 481-504.

Kathan, Boardman W. "Prayer and the Public Schools: The Issue in Historical Perspective and Implications for Religious Education Today," *Religious Education 84*(2) (Spring 1989): 232–248.

Katzman, Kenneth. "Iraq: Post Saddam Governance and Security," Congressional Research Service, RS21968, (2 March 2009).

Keister, Lisa A. "Religion and Wealth: The Role of Religious Affiliation and Participation in Early Adult Asset Accumulation," *Social Forces* 82, no. 1 (September 2003): 175–207.

Kellogg, W. N., and L. A. Kellogg. *The Ape and the Child*. New York: McGraw-Hill, 1933.

Kelly, Delos H. *Deviant Behavior: Readings in the Sociology of Deviance*. New York: St. Martin's Press, 1979.

Kennedy, Robert E., Jr. *Life Choices: Applying Sociology*. New York: Holt, Rinehart and Winston, 1986.

Kenney, Martin., and Richard Florida. "Beyond Mass Production: Production and the Labor Process in Japan," *Politics and Society 16* (1988): 121–158.

King, John. *Interview with General Ray Odierno*, CNN (11 April 2009) www.cnn.com/video/#/video/bestoftv/2009/04/13/sotu.gen.odierno.cnn?iref=videosearch, (accessed on 28 May 2009).

King, Rufus. "A Worthless Crusade," *Newsweek*, January 1, 1990, pp. 4–5.

Kinsley, Michael. "Stat Wars," *The New Republic*, March 26, 1990, p. 4.

Kitano, Harry H. L. *Race Relations*, 4th ed. Englewood Cliffs, NJ: Prentice-Hall, 1991.

Kitsuse, John I. "Societal Reaction to Deviant Behavior: Problems of Theory and Method," *Social Problems 9* (Winter 1962): 247–256.

Klitgaard, Robert. *Choosing Elites: Selecting the "Best and Brightest" at Top Universities and Elsewhere*. New York: Basic Books, 1985.

Kilpatrick, D.G., C.N. Edwards, A. K. Seymour, *Rape in America: A Report to the Nation*. 1992 Arlington, VA.: National Victim Center and Medical University of South Carolina.

Konos, Susan. "For-Profit Programs in the Child Care Delivery System: Bane or Benefit?" *Child and Youth Care Quarterly 19* (Winter 1990): 211–213.

Kozol, Jonathan. "Distancing the Homeless," *The Yale Review*, Winter, 1988, p. 158.

Kraut, Robert E. "Deterrent and Definitional Influences on Shoplifting," *Social Problems 23* (February 1976): 358–368.

Ksir, C., Hart, C., Ray, O., *Drugs, Society, and Human Behavior*. 12th. Edition. McGraw Hill, Boston. 2007

Kupfer, Andrew. "Is Drug Testing Good or Bad?" *Fortune 118* (December 19, 1988): 133–140.

LaBeff, Emily E., Robert E. Clark, Valerie J. Haines, and George M. Dickhoff. "Situational Ethics and College Student Cheating," *Sociological Inquiry 60* (May 1990): 190–198.

Laine, Christine. "Should Physicians Discourage Patients from Playing the Sick Role?" CMAJ 157 (1997): 393ñ394

Lak, Daniel. *Polygamy in Canada: Can It Be Banned?* (25 April 2008), www.cbc.ca/news/background/polygamy/, (accessed on 22 May 2009).

Lamanna, Mary Ann., and Agnes Riedmann. *Marriages and Families: Making Choices and Facing Change*, 10th ed. Belmont, CA: Thompson Wadsworth, 2009.

Lamb, Michael E., Ann M. Frodi, Carl Philip Hwang, Majt Frodi, and Jamie Steinberg. "Mother- and Father-Infant

Interaction Involving Play and Holding in Traditional and Nontraditional Swedish Families," *Developmental Psychology 18* (1982): 215–221.

Lambert, Wallace E., and Donald M. Taylor. *Coping with Cultural and Racial Diversity in Urban America.* New York: Praeger, 1990.

Landers, Robert K. "Benefits and Dangers of Opinion Polls," *Congressional Quarterly's Editorial Research Reports*, October, 1988, 454–463.

Landers, Robert K. "Is Affirmative Action Still the Answer?" *Congressional Quarterly's Editorial Research Reports*, April, 1989, 198–211.

Landers, Robert K. "Right to Die: Medical, Legal & Moral Issues," *Congressional Quarterly's Editorial Research Reports*, September 28, 1990, 551–567.

Landers, Robert K. "Why Homeless Need More Than Shelter," *Congressional Quarterly's Editorial Research Reports*, March 30, 1990, 173–187.

Lane, Charles. "To Help or Not to Help," *Newsweek*, September 2, 1991, 54–56.

Lansing, Marjorie. "The Gender Gap in American Politics," in Lynne B. Igletzin and Ruth Ross, eds., *Women in the World, 1975–1985.* Santa Barbara, CA: ABC-CLIO, 1986.

Lapinski, Susan. "Now, They Have a Dream," *Parade Magazine*, September 7, 1986, 8–11.

Larson, Calvin J. "Applied/Practical Sociological Theory: Problems and Issues," *Sociological Practice Review 1*(1) (June 1990): 8–18.

Lauer, Robert H., and Warren H. Handel. *Social Psychology: The Theory and Application of Symbolic Interactionism*, 2nd ed. Englewood Cliffs, NJ: Prentice-Hall, 1983.

Lay, J. Celeste. "Learning About Politics in Low-Income Communities." *American Politics Research* (May, 2006) 34 (3):319-340.

LeBlanc, Steve. "Costs Soar for Mass. Health Care Law," *FOXNews.com*, (12 April 2008), www.foxnews.com/wires/2008Apr12/0,4670,MassHealthCareLaw,00.html, (accessed on 10 June 2009).

Le Bon, Gustave. *The Crowd: A Study of the Popular Mind.* London: Ernest Benn, 1895; 2nd ed., Dunwoody, GA: Norman S. Berg, 1968.

Leavitt, Fred. Research Methods for Behavioral Scientists. Dubuque, IA: Brown, 1991.

Leavitt, Robin Lynn., and Martha Bauman Power. "Emotional Socialization in the Postmodern Era: Children in Day Care," *Social Psychology Quarterly 52* (1989): 35–43.

Leavitt, Ruby R. "Women of Other Cultures," in Vivian Gornick and Barbara K. Moran, eds., *Women in Sexist Society: Studies in Power and Powerlessness.* New York: New American Library, 1971.

Lederer, Laura. ed. *Take Back the Night: Women on Pornography.* New York: Morrow, 1980.

Lee, Alfred McClung. *Sociology for People: Toward a Caring Profession.* Syracuse, NY: Syracuse University Press, 1988.

Lee, Gary R. "Marriage and Morale in Later Life," *Journal of Marriage and the Family 40* (February 1978): 131–139.

Lee, Steven P. "The Moral Distinctiveness of Genocide," *The Journal of Political Philosophy*, (2010), 18 (3): 335-356.

Lee, Valerie E., and Anthony S. Bryk. "A Multilevel Model of the Social Distribution of High School Achievement," *Sociology of Education 62* (July 1989): 172–192.

Lee, Yun Suk., and Linda Waite. "How Appreciated Do Wives Feel For the Housework They Do?" *Social Science Quarterly* (June, 2010) 91 (2):466-492.

LeMasters, E. E. "Parenthood as Crisis," *Marriage and Family Living 19* (November 1957): 352–355.

Lemert, Edwin. *Social Pathology.* New York: McGraw-Hill, 1951.

Lemon, B. L., V. L. Bengtson, and J. A. Peterson. "An Exploration of Activity Theory of Aging: Activity Types and Life Satisfaction Among In-Movers to a Retirement Community," *Journal of Gerontology 27* (1977): 511–523.

Lengermann, Patricia M. "The Founding of the American Sociological Review: The Anatomy of a Rebellion," *American Sociological Review 44* (April 1979): 185–198.

Lengermann, Patricia Madoo., and Jill Niebrugge-Brantley. "Contemporary Feminist Theory," in George Ritzer, ed., *Contemporary Sociological Theory.* New York: Knopf, 1988, 282–325.

Lenski, Gerhard. "Hungary in April," *Society 26* (January/February 1989): 11–12.

Lenski, Gerhard. *Power and Privilege.* New York: McGraw-Hill, 1966.

Lenski, Gerhard. *The Religious Factor.* New York: Doubleday, 1961.

Levison, Andrew. *The Working-Class Majority.* New York: Coward, McCann and Geohegan, 1974.

Lieberson, Stanley., and Arnold R. Silverman. "The Precipitants and Underlying Conditions of Race Riots," *American Sociological Review 30* (December 1965): 887–898.

Lieberson, Stanley., and Mary C. Waters. *From Many Strands: Ethnic and Racial Groups in Contemporary America.* New York: Russell Sage Foundation, 1988.

Lin, Nan., Walter M. Ensel, and John C. Vaughn. "Social Resources and Strength of Ties: Structural Factors in Occupational Status Attainment," *American Sociological Review 46* (August 1981): 393–405.

Lindau, S.T., Schumm, L.P., Laumann, E.O., Levinson, W., O'Muircheartaigh, C.A., & Waite, L.J. 2007. "A study of sexuality and health among older adults in the United States." *New England Journal of Medicine*, 357, 762–774.

Lindsay, D. Michael. "Evangelicals in the Power Elite: Elite Cohesion Advancing a Movement," *American Sociological Review*, (February 2008), 73: 60-82.

Ling, Peter J. *America and the Automobile: Technology, Reform and Social Change, 1893–1923.* Manchester, England: Manchester University Press, 1990.

Lipset, S. M., and Reinhard Bendix. *Social Mobility in Industrial Society.* Berkeley: University of California Press, 1967.

Lipton, Eric., Charlie Savage, and Scott Shane. "Arizona Suspect's Recent Acts Offer Hints of Alienation," *New York Times*, (January 8, 2011).

Lischko, Amy M., Sara S. Bachman, and Alyssa Vangeli. "The Massachusetts Commonwealth Health Insurance Connector: Structure and Functions," *The Commonwealth Fund*, (May 2009), www.commonwealthfund.org/Content/Publications/Issue-Briefs/2009/May/The-Massachusetts-Commonwealth-Health-Insurance-Connector.asp, (accessed on 10 June 2009).

Logan, Jeffrey. "China's Space Program: Options for U.S.-China Cooperation," *CRS Report for Congress*, (Order Code: RS22777), (29 September 2008).

Long, Theodore E., and Jeffrey K. Hadden. "A Reconception of Socialization," *Sociological Theory 3* (Spring 1985): 39–49.

Lopata, Helena Z. *Polish Americans: Status Competition in an Ethnic Community.* Englewood Cliffs, NJ: Prentice-Hall, 1976.

Lu, Luo. "'I" or 'We': Family Socialization Values in a National Probability Sample in Taiwan," *Asian Journal of Social Psychology*. (2009). 12: 145-150.

Lueptow, Lloyd B. "Social Structure, Social Change and Parental Influence in Adolescent Sex-Role Socialization: 1964–1975," *Journal of Marriage and the Family 42* (June 1980): 93–104.

Lum, Thomas., Wayne M. Morrison, and Bruce Vaughn. "China's 'Soft Power' in Southeast Asia," *CRS Report for Congress*, (Order Code: RL34310), (4 January 2008).

Lundberg, George. *Can Science Save Us?* 2nd ed. New York: David McKay, 1961.

Lupart, Judy., and Elizabeth Cannon. "Computers and Career Choices: Gender Differences in Grades 7 and 10 Students," *Gender, Technology and Development* (May–August 2002): 233–248.

Lyke, Bob. Z. "Health Care Reform: An Introduction," CRS Report, Order Code R40517, (14 April 2009).

Lynd, Robert S., and Helen Merrell Lynd. *Middletown.* New York: Harcourt, Brace and World, 1929.

Lynd, Robert S., and Helen Merrell Lynd. *Middletown in Transition.* New York: Harcourt, Brace and World, 1937.

Maccoby, Eleanor E. "Gender As a Social Category," *Developmental Psychology 24* (1988): 755–765.

Maccoby, Eleanor., and Carol N. Jacklin. *The Psychology of Sex Differences.* Stanford, CA: Stanford University Press, 1974.

Maccoby, Michael. "The Changing Corporate Character," in Gordon J. DiRenzo, ed., *We, The People: American Character and Social Change.* Westport, CT: Greenwood Press, 1977.

Macionis, John. Social Problems. 2004. Prentice Hall.

Macklin, Eleanor D. "Nonmarital Heterosexual Cohabitation: An Overview," in Eleanor D. Macklin and Roger H. Rubin, eds., *Contemporary Families and Alternative Lifestyles.* Beverly Hills, CA: Sage Publications, 1983, 49–74.

MacLeod, Jay. *Ain't No Makin' It: Aspirations and Attainment in a Low-income Neighborhood.* Boulder, CO: Westview Press, 1995.

MacLeod, Scott. "Vice Squad," *Time Magazine*, (July 26, 2007), www.time.com/time/magazine/article/0,9171,1647239,00.html (accessed on 4 June 2009).

Madsen, Richard. "the Archipelago of Faith: Religious Individualism and Faith Community in America Today," *American Journal of Sociology* , (March, 2009), 114 (5): 1263-1301.

Magner, Denise. "Piercing the 'Posturing and Taboo' of Debate on Campus Reforms. *The Chronicles of Higher Education 37* (April 10, 1991): A3.

Malinowski, Bronislaw. "Parenthood: The Basis of Social Structure," in V. F. Calverton and Samuel D. Schmalhausen, eds., *The New Generation.* New York: Macaulay, 1930.

Mann, Susan A., Michael D. Grimes, Alice Abel Kemp, and Pamela J. Jenkins (1997) "Paradigm Shifts in Family Sociology? Evidence from Three Decades of Family Textbooks." *Journal of Family Issues* 18 (May): 315–349.

Marcus, Warren Stewart. "Tracing the Bitter Roots of Personal Violation and Social Displacement: A Comparative Phenomenological Study of the Life Histories of Homeless Mothers and Their Dependent Children," *Dissertation Abstracts International, A: The Humanities and Social Sciences*, 2002, 63, 1, July, 137–A–138–A.

Markle, Gerald E., and Ronald J. Troyer. "Smoke Gets in Your Eyes: Cigarette Smoking as Deviant Behavior," *Social Problems 26* (June 1979): 611–625.

Marklein, Mary Beth. "Learning Despite Language Differences," *USA Today*, February 20, 1991, p. 9D.

Marsden, Peter V. "Core Discussion Networks of Americans," *American Sociological Review 52* (February 1987): 122–131.

Marshall, Ray., and Beth Paulin. "The Wages of Women's Work," *Society 22* (July–August 1985): 28–38.

Marshall, Victor W., and Judith Levy. "Aging and Dying," in Robert H. Binstock and Linda K. George, eds., *Handbook of Aging and the Social Sciences*, 3rd ed. New York: Academic Press, 1990 245–260.

Martin, Linda G. "The Graying of Japan," *Population Bulletin 44* (July 1989): (Washington, D.C.: Population Reference Bureau).

Marx, Karl. *Selected Writings in Sociology and Social Philosophy;* T. B. Bottomore, trans. New York: McGraw-Hill, 1964.

Marx, Karl., and Friedrich Engels. *Communist Manifesto.* Baltimore: Penguin Books, 1969. (Originally published in 1847)

Masters, William H., and Virginia E. Johnson. *Human Sexual Inadequacy.* Boston: Little, Brown, 1970.

Masters, William H., and Virginia E. Johnson. *Human Sexual Response.* Boston: Little, Brown, 1966.

Maxwell, Nan L. *Income Inequality in the United States: 1947–1985.* New York: Greenwood Press, 1990.

Maykovich, Minako K. *Medical Sociology.* Palo Alto, CA: Mayfield Publishing, 1980.

McIntyre, Robert S., Douglas P. Kelly, Michael P. Ettlinger, and Elizabeth A. Fray. *A Far Cry from Fair: CTJ's Guide to State Tax Reform,* Washington, D.C.: Citizens for Tax Justice, April, 1991.

McKay, Hollie. *Porn Plot: Vivid's Sordid Plans for Nadya 'Octomom' Suleman.* (2009). www.foxnews.com/story/0,2933, 500688,00.html (accessed on 22 May 2009).

McKinlay, John B., and Sonja M. McKinlay. "Medical Measures and the Decline of Mortality," in Peter Conrad and Rochelle Kern, eds., *The Sociology of Health and Illness: Critical Perspectives.* New York: St. Martin's Press, 1981, 12–30.

McLachlan, James. *American Boarding Schools: A Historical Study.* New York: Charles Scribner's Sons, 1970.

McLanahan, Sara S., Annemette Sorensen, and Dorothy Watson. "Sex Differences in Poverty, 1950–1980," *Signs: Journal of Women in Culture and Society 15*(1) (1989): 102–122.

McNeely, D. L., and John L. Calen, eds. *Aging in Minority Groups.* Beverly Hills, CA: Sage Publications, 1983.

Mead, George Herbert. *Mind, Self and Society from the Standpoint of a Social Behaviorist.* Charles Morris, ed. Chicago: University of Chicago Press, 1934.

Mead, Margaret. *Sex and Temperament in Three Primitive Societies.* New York: Morrow, 1935.

Mechanic, David. *Medical Sociology,* 2nd ed. New York: Free Press, 1978.

Medline Plus. www.nih.nih.gov/medlineplus/alcoholism.html.

Medvedev, Zhores A. "Aging and Longevity: New Approaches and New Perspectives," *Gerontologist 15* (1975): 196–201.

Medvedev, Zhores A. "Caucasus and Altay Longevity: A Biological or Social Problem?" *Gerontologist 14* (1974): 381–387.

Mellor, David., Mathew Fuller-Tyskiewicz, Marita P. McCabe and Lina Ricciardelli. "Body Image and Self Esteem Across Age and Gender: A Short-Term Longitudinal Study," *Sex Roles* (2010) 63: 672-681.

Melville, Keith. *The Drug Crisis: Public Strategies for Breaking the Habit* (National Issues Forum Series). Dayton, OH: The Kettering Foundation and the Kendall/Hunt Publishing Company, 1989.

Melville, Keith. *The Environment at Risk: Responding to Growing Dangers* (National Issues Forum Series). Dayton, OH: The Kettering Foundation and the Kendall/Hunt Publishing Company, 1989.

Merton, Robert K. *Social Theory and Social Structure.* New York: Free Press, 1949; rev. eds., 1957 and 1968.

Meyers, Deborah., and Jennifer Yau. "U.S. Immigration Statistics in 2003," *Migration Policy Institute* (2004).

Michels, Robert. *Political Parties.* New York: Free Press, 1911.

Milgram, Stanley. "The Experience of Living in Cities," *Science 167* (March 13, 1970): 1461–1468.

Miller, Cindy Faith., Leah E. Lurye, Kristina M. Zosuls and Diane Ruble. "Accessibility of Gender Stereotype Domains: Developmental and Gender Differences in Children," *Sex Roles,* (2009), 60: 870-881.

Miller, Cynthia L. "Qualitative Differences Among Gender-Stereotyped Toys: Implications for Cognitive and Social Development in Girls and Boys," *Sex Roles 16* (1987): 473–487.

Mills, C. Wright. *The Power Elite.* New York: Oxford University Press, 1958.

Mills, C. Wright. *The Sociological Imagination.* New York: Oxford University Press, 1959.

Mills, Charles W. *White Collar: American Middle Classes.* New York: Oxford University Press, 1951.

Mirowsky, John. "Depression and Marital Power: An Equity Model," *American Journal of Sociology 91* (November 1985): 557–592.

Money, John. *Love and Love Sickness: The Science of Sex, Gender Difference, and Pair-Bonding.* Baltimore: Johns Hopkins University Press, 1980.

Money, John., and P. Tucker. *Sexual Signatures: On Being a Man or a Woman.* Little, Brown and Co. 1975

Monroe, Sylvester. "Does Affirmative Action Help or Hurt?" *Time,* May 27, 1991, 22–23.

Moore, Jennifer. "Drug Testing and Corporate Responsibility: The 'Ought Implies Can' Argument," *Journal of Business Ethics 8* (1989): 270–287.

Morawski, Jill G. and Jenna St. Martin. "The Evolving Vocabulary of the Social Sciences: The Case of Socialization," (2011), 14 (1): 1-25.

Morning, Ann. "Toward a Racial Conceptualization for the 21st Century," *Social Forces,* (2009), 87 (3): 1167-1192.

Morrison, Wayne M., and Marc Labonte. "China's Holdings of U.S. Securities: Implications for the U.S. Economy," *CRS Report for Congress,* (Order Code: RL34314), (13 January 2009).

Morrison, Wayne M., and Marc Labonte. "China's Currency: A Summary of the Economic Issues," *CRS Report for Congress,* (Order Code: RS21625), (13 April 2009).

Morriss, Frank. "Euthanasia Is Never Justified," in *Death and Dying: Opposing Viewpoints.* San Diego: Greenhaven Press, 1987, 146–149.

Moss, H. "Sex, Age and State as Determinants of Mother–Infant Interaction," *Merrill-Palmer Quarterly 13* (1967): 19–36.

Mostert, Noel. "Supership," in Jerome H. Skolnick and Elliott Currie, eds., *Crisis in American Institutions*, 3rd ed. Boston: Little, Brown, 1976, 286–304.

Muehlenhard, Charlene L., and Melaney A. Linton. "Date Rape: Familiar Strangers," *Journal of Counseling Psychology 34* (1987): 186–196.

Mumford, Lewis. *The Transformation of Man.* New York: Collier, 1962.

Murdock, George P. *Social Structure.* New York: Macmillan, 1949.

Murdock, George P. "World Ethnographic Sample," *American Anthropologist 59* (August 1957): 664–687.

Muwakkil, Salim. "Schools in Transition," *The Washington Post Education Review*, August 5, 1990, 1.

Myrdal, Gunna. *An American Dilemma: the Negro Problem and Modern Democracy*. 1944. Harper and Row Publishers.

Nanto, Dick K., and Emma Chanlett-Avery. "The Rise of China and Its Effect on Taiwan, Japan, and South Korea: U.S. Policy Choices," *CRS Report for Congress*, (Order Code: RL32882), (12 April 2005).

National Advisory Commission on Civil Disorders. *Kerner Report.* New York: Bantam Books, 1968.

National Center for Health Statistics. "Annual Summary of Births, Marriages, Divorces, and Deaths: United States, 1990," *Monthly Vital Statistics Report 39*(13) (August 28, 1991): 4 (Public Health Service, Hyattsville, MD).

National Commission on Excellence in Education. *A Nation at Risk: The Imperative for Educational Reform.* Washington, D.C.: U.S. Government Printing Office, 1983.

National Education Association (2011). www.nea.org/home/126611.htm

National Opinion Research Center. *General Social Surveys, 1972–1982: Cumulative Codebook.* Chicago: National Opinion Research Center, 1982.

NBC News. *Mother Has Twins with Two Fathers.* (21 May 2009). www.msnbc.msn.com/id/21134540/vp/30863181#30863181, (accessed on 22 May 2009).

Neilsen, Michael E., and Ryan T. Cragun. "Religious Orientation, Religious Affiliation and Boundary Maintenance: The Case of Polygamy," *Mental Health, Religion and Culture*, (November/ December 2010), 13 (7/8): 761-770.

Nielsen, Michael E. "Opinions Regarding Polygamy Among LDS Church Members: Demographic Predictors," *Archive for the Psychology of Religion*, (2009), 31: 261-270.

New York Times. "Gulf of Mexico Oil Spill," (2010), www.nytimes.com.

NPR (National Public Radio), *Interview with then-Illinois Senator Barack Obama*, (March 2008), http://www.npr.org/templates/story/story.php?storyId=88478467, (accessed on April 14, 2009).

Navasky, Victor. "Body Invaders," *The Nation 250* (January 8, 1990): 39–40.

Nelson, Margaret K. *Negotiated Care: The Experience of Family Day Care Providers.* Philadelphia: Temple University Press, 1990.

Neubeck, Kenneth J. *Social Problems: A Critical Approach*, 3rd ed New York: McGraw-Hill, 1991.

Newman, Oscar. *Defensible Space.* New York: Macmillan, 1972.

Newman, William M. *American Pluralism: A Study of Social Groups and Social Theory.* New York: Harper and Row, 1973.

Newsweek, "Islam & Obama" (November 2008) by Lorraine Ali. http://www.newsweek.com/id/168062, (accessed on April 14, 2009).

Nicholson, David. "Schools in Transition," *The Washington Post Education Review*, August 5, 1990, 1.

Noel, Donald L. "A Theory of the Origin of Ethnic Stratification," in Norman R. Yetman and C. Hoy Steele, eds., *Majority and Minority: The Dynamics of Racial and Ethnic Relations.* Boston: Allyn and Bacon, 1975.

Norton, M.I. and D. Ariely. "Building a Better America One Wealth Quintile at a Time," *Perspectives on Psychological Science*, (January 2011), 6 (1): 9-12.

Novak, M. *The Rise of the Unmeltable Ethnics.* New York: Macmillan, 1972.

Novak, Michael. "White Ethnic," in Norman R. Yetman and C. Hoy Steele, eds., *Majority and Minority: The Dynamics of Racial and Ethnic Relations.* Boston: Allyn and Bacon, 1975.

Nuehring, Elane., and Gerald E. Markle. "Nicotine and Norms: The Reemergence of a Deviant Behavior," *Social Problems 21* (April 1974): 513–526.

Nye, Joseph. "The Rise of China's Soft Power," *Wall Street Journal*, (29 December 2005).

Oakes, Jeannie. "Classroom Social Relationships: Exploring the Bowles and Gintis Hypothesis," *Sociology of Education 55* (October 1982): 197–212.

Oberschall, Anthony. *Social Conflict and Social Movements.* Englewood Cliffs, NJ: Prentice-Hall, 1973.

O'Donnell, Carol. "Major Theories of the Labour Market and Women's Place Within It," *Journal of Industrial Relations 26* (June 1984): 147–165.

Ogburn, William F. *Social Change.* New York: Viking, 1950.

Okin, Susan Joller. *Justice, Gender and the Family.* New York: Basic Books, 1989.

Olson, David H., and Hamilton I. McCubbin. *Families: What Makes Them Work.* Beverly Hills, CA: Sage Publications, 1983.

Olweus, D. *Bullying at School: What We Know and What We Can Do*,. Blackwell, 1993.

Oral Cancer Foundation. www.oralcancerfoundation.org/tobacco/problem_tobacco.htm.

Orr, Lisa. (ed.). *Censorship: Opposing Viewpoints.* San Diego, CA: Greenhaven Press, 1990.

Ortiz, Flora Ida. *Career Patterns in Education: Women, Men and Minorities in Public School Administration*. New York: Praeger, 1982.

Orum, Anthony M. *Introduction to Political Sociology: The Social Anatomy of the Body Politic*. Englewood Cliffs, NJ: Prentice-Hall, 1978.

Ouchi, William G. *Theory Z: How American Business Can Meet the Japanese Challenge*. Reading, MA: Addison-Wesley, 1981.

Ovadia, Seth Alan. "Urban Structure and Individual Outcomes: The Effects of Economic and Racial Segregation on the Black-White Gap in Employment Rates," *Dissertation Abstracts International, A: The Humanities and Social Sciences*.64, no. 6 (December 2003), 2270–A.

Parillo, Vincent N., John Stimson, and Ardyth Stimson. *Contemporary Social Problems*, 2nd ed. New York: Macmillan, 1989.

Park, Robert E., and Ernest W. Burgess. *Introduction to the Science of Sociology*. Chicago: University of Chicago Press, 1921.

Park, Robert E., Ernest W. Burgess, and Roderick D. McKenzie. *The City*. Chicago: University of Chicago Press, 1925.

Parsons, Talcott. "The School Class as Social System: Some of Its Functions in American Society," *Harvard Educational Review 29*(4) (1959): 297–318.

Parsons, Talcott. *The Social System*. Glencoe, IL: Free Press, 1951.

Parsons, Talcott., and Robert F. Bales. *Family, Socialization and Interaction Process*. New York: Free Press, 1955.

Parsons, Talcott., and Edward A. Shils, eds. *Toward a General Theory of Action*. New York: Harper and Row, 1951.

Pearce, Diana M. "The Feminization of Ghetto Poverty," *Society 21* (November–December 1983): 70–74.

Perrow, Charles. *Complex Organizations: A Critical Essay*, 3rd ed. New York: Random House, 1986.

Peters, John F. "Adolescents as Socialization Agents to Parents," *Adolescence 20* (Winter 1985): 921–933.

Peters, Thomas J., and Robert H. Waterman. *In Search of Excellence*. New York: Harper and Row, 1982.

Pettigrew, Thomas F. *A Profile of the Negro American*. Princeton, NJ: Van Nostrand, 1964.

Pham-Kanter, Genevieve. "Social Comparisons and Health: Can Having Richer Friends and Neighbors Make You Sick," *Social Science and Medicine*, (2009), 69: 335-344.

Phillips, Deborah., Kathleen McCartney, and Sandra Scarr. "Child-Care Quality and Children's Social Development," *Developmental Psychology 23* (1987): 537–543.

Pifer, Alan., and Lydia Bronte. *Our Aging Society: Paradox and Promise*. New York: Norton, 1986.

Pillemer, Karl. "The Dangers of Dependency: New Findings on Domestic Violence Against the Elderly," *Social Problems 33* (December 1985): 146–158.

Pillemer, Karl., and David Finkelhor. "The Prevalence of Elder Abuse: A Random Sample Survey," *The Gerontologist 28* (1988): 51–57.

Pinder, Sherrow. "Notes in Hurricane Katrina: Rethinking Race, Class and Power in the United States," *21st Century Society*, (November 2009), 4 (3): 241-256.

Pirenne, Henri. "Stages in the Social History of Capitalism," *American Historical Review 19* (July 1914): 494–515.

Piven, Frances Fox., and Richard A. Cloward. *Regulating the Poor: The Functions of Public Welfare*. New York: Vintage Books, 1971.

Piven, Frances Fox., and Richard A. Cloward. *Why Americans Don't Vote*. New York: Pantheon Books, 1989.

Pogrebin, Letty Cottin. *Family Politics: Love and Power on an Intimate Frontier*. New York: McGraw-Hill, 1983.

"Polygamy: Frequently Asked Questions." Statistical data provided by numerous organizations from 1998–2002. www.absalom.com/mormon/polygamy/faq.htm. Provenzo, Eugene F. *Religious Fundamentalism and American Education: The Battle for the Public Schools*. New York: State University of New York Press, 1990.

Pontell, Henry., and Gilbert Geiss. "How to Effectively Get Crooks Like Bernie Madoff in Dutch," *Criminology and Public Policy*. (2010), 9 (3): 475-481.

Porter, Rosalie Pedalino., Crawford, James. "Is Bilingual Education Best for English-Language Learners?" *CQ Research* (December 11, 2009), (19 (43): 1045.

Poteat, Paul. "Peer Group socialization of Homophobic Attitudes and Behavior During Adolescence," *Child Development*, (November, 2007), 78 (6): 1830-1842.

Powe, L. A. Scot. Jr. "Alter Calls: Constitutional Amendments: The Winners And Losers," *Village Voice* (March 3–9, 2004). www.villagevoice.com/issues/0409/powe.php.

Prowse, Michael. "U.S. Schools: Nearly Bottom of the Class," *Financial Times*, May 4, 1990, 18.

Quinney, Richard. *Criminology*. Boston: Little, Brown, 1979.

Radke, Marian J., and Helen G. Trager. "Children's Perceptions of the Social Roles of Negroes and Whites," *Journal of Psychology 29* (1950): 3–33.

Ruppanner, Leah. "Fairness and Housework: A Cross National Comparison," *Journal of Comparative Studies*, (Autumn, 2008) 39 (4): 509-526.

Ravitz, Jessica. *Out-of-Wedlock Births Hit Record High*. (2009). www.cnn.com/2009/LIVING/wayoflife/04/08/out.of.wedlock.births/index.html?iref=newssearch, (accessed on 22 May 2009).

Redfield, Robert. *The Folk Culture of Yucatan*. Chicago: University of Chicago Press, 1941.

Reich, Robert B. "As the World Turns," *The New Republic*, May 21, 1989, 23–28.

Reich, Robert B. "Secession of the Successful," *New York Times Magazine*, March 17, 1991, 16–45.

Reiss, Ira L. "The Universality of the Family: A Conceptual Analysis," *Journal of Marriage and the Family* 27 (November 1965): 443–453.

Reitzes, Donald C., and Elizabeth J. Mutran. "The Transition to Retirement: Stages and Facts That Influence Retirement Adjustment," *Aging and Human Development*, (2004) 59 (1): 63-84.

Religious Movements Homepage at the University of Virginia (2000). http://religiousmovements.lib.virginia.edu.

Ribadeneira, Diego. "Schools in Transition," *Washington Post Education Review*, August 5, 1990, 1.

Riccio, James. "Religious Affiliation and Socioeconomic Achievement," in Robert Wuthnow, ed., *The Religious Dimension: New Directions in Quantitative Research*. New York: Academic Press, 1979, 199–231.

Rice, Thomas. "American Public Policy Formation and Implementation," in Roger A. Strauss, ed. *Using Sociology: An Introduction from the Clinical Perspective*. Bayside, New York: General Hall, 1985.

Rich, Spencer. "Hunger Said to Afflict 1 in 8 American Children," *Washington Post*, March 27, 1991b, p. A4.

Rich, Spencer. "Nearly 500,000 Children Rely on Government Care," *Washington Post*, December 12, 1989, 1.

Rich, Spencer. "U.S. Poverty Rate up: Median Income Falls," *Washington Post*, September 27, 1991a, 1.

Richards, Tori., and Jeremy Olshan. *Egg on His Face: Fertility Doc Ripped by Octomom's Dad.* (2009). www.nypost.com/seven/02112009/news/nationalnews/egg_on_his_face_154516.htm, (accessed on 22 May 2009).

Ridley, F. F., ed. *Government and Administration in Western Europe*. New York: St. Martin's Press, 1979.

Riesman, David., with Nathan Glazer and Reuel Denney. *The Lonely Crowd: A Study of the Changing American Character.* New Haven, CT: Yale University Press, 1950.

Risley, Robert L. "Legalizing Euthanasia Would Be Beneficial," in *Opposing Viewpoints Sources: Death/Dying, 1989 Annual.* San Diego: Greenhaven Press, 1989, 49–54. (Originally published by Robert L. Risley as "In Defense of the Humane and Dignified Death Act," *Free Inquiry*, Winter, 1988–1989)

Ritzer, George. *Contemporary Sociological Theory*, 3rd ed. New York: McGraw-Hill, 1991.

Rivas-Drake, Deborah., and Diane Hughes. "A Preliminary Analysis of Associations Among Ethnic-Racial Socialization, Ethnic Discrimination and Ethnic Identity Among Urban Sixth Graders," *Journal of Research on Adolescence*, (2009), 19 (3): 558-584.

Roethlisberger, Fritz J., and William J. Dickson. *Management and the Worker.* Cambridge, MA: Harvard University Press, 1939.

Rogers, Everett M. *Diffusion of Innovations.* New York: Free Press, 1983.

Rogers, S., and P. Amato. "Have Changes in Gender Relations Affected Marital Quality?" *Social Forces* (2000) 79: 731-753.

Romaine, Suzanne. *Bilingualism.* Oxford, England: Basil Blackwell, 1989.

Root, Waverley., and Richard de Rochemont. *Eating in America: A History*. New York: Ecco Press, 1976.

Rose, Vicki McNickle., and Susan Carol Randall. "The Impact of Investigator Perceptions of Victim Legitimacy on the Processing of Rape Sexual Assault Cases," *Symbolic Interaction* 5 (Spring 1982): 23–36.

Rosenberg, Matt. "Population Density," (2011), www.geography.about.com/od/populationgeography/a/popdensity.htm, March 2.

Rosenthal, Robert., and Lenore Jacobson. *Pygmalion in the Classroom: Teacher Expectation and Pupil's Intellectual Development.* New York: Holt, Rinehart and Winston, 1968.

Ross, Catherine E., John Mirowsky, and Patricia Ulbrich. "Comparison of Mexicans and Anglos," *American Journal of Sociology 89* (November 1983b): 670–682.

Rossell, Christine. "The Desegregation Efficiency of Magnet Schools," *Urban Affairs Review* (2003), 38 (5): 697-725.

Rossi, Peter. *Down and Out in America: The Origins of Homelessness.* Chicago: University of Chicago Press, 1989.

Rossi, Peter. *Without Shelter: Homelessness in the 1980s.* New York: Priority Press, 1989.

Rossi, Peter H., and William Foote Whyte. "The Applied Side of Sociology," in Howard E. Freeman, Russel R. Dynes, Peter H. Rossi, and William Foote Whyte, eds., *Applied Sociology*. San Francisco: Jossey-Bass, 1983.

Rotherham, Andrew. "Dropout Rates Dropping, But Don't Celebrate Yet," (November 30, 2010). Time. www.time.com

Rothenberg, Paula. "Critics of Attempts to Democratize the Curriculum Are Waging a Campaign to Misrepresent the Work of Responsible Professors," *The Chronicles of Higher Education* 37 (April 10, 1991): B1, B3.

Rothman, Barbara Katz. "Midwives in Transition: The Structure of a Clinical Revolution," in Peter Conrad and Rochelle Kern, eds., *The Sociology of Health and Illness: Critical Perspectives,* 2nd ed. New York: St. Martin's Press, 1986a.

Rothman, Barbara Katz. *The Tentative Pregnancy: Prenatal Diagnoses and the Future of Motherhood.* New York: Viking, 1986b.

Rothman, Robert A. *Inequality and Stratification in the United States.* Englewood Cliffs, NJ: Prentice-Hall, 1978.

Rothman, Robert A. *Inequality and Stratification: Race, Class, and Gender*, fifth edition. Englewood Cliffs, NJ: Pearson Prentice Hall, 2005.

Rothstein, William G. *American Physicians in the Nineteenth Century: From Sects to Science.* Baltimore: Johns Hopkins Press, 1970.

Rovner, Sandy. "Battered Wives: Centuries of Silence," *Washington Post Health* [Washington, D.C.], August 20, 1991, 7.

Rowe, David C., and D. Wayne Osgood. "Heredity and Sociological Theories of Delinquency: A Reconsideration," *American Sociological Review 49* (August 1984): 526–540.

Rowland, Robyn. "A Child at Any Price? An Overview of Issues in the Use of the New Reproductive Technologies, and the Threat to Women," *Women's Studies International Forum 8* (1985): 539–546.

Rubin, J., F. Provenzano, and Z. Luria. "The Eye of the Beholder: Parents' Views on Sex of Newborns," *American Journal of Orthopsychiatry 44* (1974): 512–519.

Rubin, Lillian. *Intimate Strangers.* New York: Harper and Row, 1983.

Rubin, Zick. *Liking and Loving.* New York: Holt, Rinehart and Winston, 1973.

Ruopp, R., J. Travers, F. Glantz, and C. Coelen. *Children at the Center: Summary Findings and Their Implications.* Cambridge, MA: Abt Books, 1979.

Russell, John. *British Medieval Population.* Albuquerque: University of New Mexico Press, 1972.

Ryan, William. *Equality.* New York: Pantheon Books, 1981.

Sadker, David. "Gender Equity: Still Knocking at the Classroom Door," (April 2000) 53 (1).

Sadker, Myra., and David Sadker. "Sexism in the Classroom: From Grade School to Graduate School," *Phi Delta Kappan*, March, 1986, 512–515.

Sadker, Myra., and David Sadker. "Sexism in the Schoolroom of the '80s," *Psychology Today*, March, 1985, 54–57.

Sager, Alan. "Opiate of the Managers," *Society 23* (July/ August 1986): 65–71.

Sakamoto, Arthur., and Changhwan Kim. "The Declining Significance of Race, The Increasing Significance of Class, and Wilson's Hypothesis," *Working Papers Series.* Austin: Population Research Center, University of Texas, 2001.

Salholz, Eloise. "Say It in English," *Newsweek*, February 20, 1989, 22–23.

Salinger, Lawrence M., Paul Jesilow, Henry N. Pontell, and Gilbert Geiss. "Assaults Against Airline Flight Attendants: A Victimization Study," *Transportation Journal 25* (Fall 1985): 66–71.

Sanderson, Stephen. *The Evolution of Human Sociality: A Darwinian Conflict Perspective.* Rowan and Littlefield. 2001.

Saraceno, Chiara. "Childcare Needs and Childcare Policies: A Multi-dimensional Issue," *Current Sociology*, (2011): 59 (1) 78-96.

Saul, Michael. *Sarah Palin's Feud with Bristol Palin's Ex-Boyfriend Levi Johnston Hits New Level.* (2009). www.nydailynews.com/news/politics/2009/04/05/2009-04 05_sarah_palins_feud_with_bristol_palins_ex.html, (accessed on 22 May 2009).

Saulny, Susan. "Race Remixed: Black? White? Asian?: More Young Americans Choose All of the Above," *New York Times*, U.S. Section (June 29, 2011).

Sayre, Edward. "Relative Deprivation and Palestinian Suicide Bombings," *Asian Journal of Social Science*, (2010), 38 (3): 442-461.

Scanzoni, John., Karen Polonko, Jay Teachman, and Linda Thompson. *The Sexual Bond: Rethinking Families and Close Relationships.* Newbury Park, CA: Sage Publications, 1989.

Schabas, William. *Genocide in International Law: The Crime of Crimes*, 2000. Cambridge: Cambridge University Press.

Schaefer, Richard T. *Race and Ethnicity in the United States*, third edition. Englewood Cliffs, NJ: Pearson Prentice Hall, 2005.

Schaefer, Richard T. *Racial and Ethnic Groups*, 4th ed. New York: Harper Collins, 1990.

Schillling, Oliver. "Development of Life Satisfaction in Old Age: Another View on the "Paradox," *Social Indicators Research* (2006) 75: 241-271.

Schnabel, Kai U., et al. (2002). "Parental Influence on Students' Educational Choices in the United States and Germany: Different Ramifications—Same Effect?" *Journal of Vocational Behavior* 60, no. 2 (April 2002): 178–198.

Schnaiberg, Allan, and Sheldon Goldenberg. "From Empty Nest to Crowded Nest: The Dynamics of Incompletely-Launched Young Adults," *Social Problems 36* (June 1989): 251–267.

"School Prayer Controversy: Pro and Con," *Congressional Digest 63* (May 1984). Washington, D.C.

Schrank, Thomas. "Schmoozing with Robert Schrank: An Interview with a Common Sense Sociologist," *Successful Business* (Spring 1979).

Schur, Edwin M. *Labeling Women Deviant: Gender, Stigma, and Social Control.* New York: Random House, 1984.

Schutt, Russell K. "The Quantity and Quality of Homelessness: Research Results and Policy Implications," *Sociological Practice Review 1*(2) (August 1990): 77–87.

Schwartz, Barry. "Social Change and Collective Memory: The Democratization of George Washington," *American Sociological Review 56* (April 1991): 221–236.

Schwartz, Felice. "Management Women and the New Facts of Life," *Harvard Business Review*, January–February, 1989, 66–76.

Schwartz, Herman. "In Defense of Affirmative Action," in Leslie Dunbar, ed., *Minority Report.* New York: Pantheon Books, 1984.

Scimecca, Joseph A. *Education and Society.* New York: Holt, Rinehart and Winston, 1980.

Scott, Marvin., and Stanford Lyman. "Accounts," *American Sociological Review 33* (December 1968): 46–62.

Sears, Alan E. "The Legal Case for Restricting Pornography." In Dale Zillman and Jennings Bryant, eds., *Pornography:*

Research Advances and Policy Decisions. Hillsdale, NJ: Erlbaum, 1989.

See, Patricia., and Roger Strauss. "The Sociology of the Individual," in Roger A. Strauss, ed., *Using Sociology: An Introduction from the Clinical Perspective.* Bayside, NY: General Hall, 1985.

Seely, Gordon M. *Education and Opportunity: For What and for Whom?* Englewood Cliffs, NJ: Prentice-Hall, 1970.

Serbin, L., and K. O'Leary. "How Nursery Schools Teach Girls to Shut Up," *Psychology Today,* December 1975, 56–58.

Sermons, M. William and Peter White. "State of Homelessness in America. January 2011: A Research Report," (2011) *National Alliance to End Homelessness.* Washington D.C.

Sewell, William H. "Inequality of Opportunity for Higher Education," *American Sociological Review 36* (October 1971): 793–809.

Sewell, William H., and Robert M. Hauser. *Education, Occupation, and Earnings: Achievement in the Early Career.* New York: Academic Press, 1975.

Shannon, Elaine. "A Losing Battle," *Time,* December 3, 1990, 44–48.

Sharp, Jeremy M. "Saudi Arabia: Reform and U.S. Policy," CRS Report, Order Code RS21913, (13 October 2004).

Shattuck, Roger. *The Forbidden Experiment: The Story of the Wild Boy of Aveyron.* New York: Farrar, Straus and Giroux, 1980.

Shaw, Clifford R., and Henry D. McKay. *Delinquency Areas.* Chicago: University of Chicago Press, 1929.

Sheremet, Konstantin. "Law and Social Change in the USSR of the 1990s," *Society 27* (May/June 1990): 90–97.

Shostak, Arthur. "How Can We All Survive? Managing Social Change," in Roger A. Strauss, ed. *Using Sociology: An Introduction from the Clinical Perspective.* Bayside, New York: General Hall, 1985, 172–182.

Siegel, Charles N. "The Brave New World of Children," *New Perspectives Quarterly* 7 (Winter 1990): 34–45.

Silverman, Kenneth. "Cruel and Usual Punishment" [Review of *Spare the Child: The Religious Roots of Punishment and the Psychological Impact of Physical Abuse* by Phillip Greven], *The New York Times Book Review,* February 17, 1991, 5–6.

Simmons, Roberta G., Leslie Brown, Diane M. Bush, and Dale A. Blyth. "Self-esteem and Achievement of Black and White Adolescents," *Social Problems 26* (October 1978): 86–96.

Simon, G. R., and A. S. R. Manstead. *The Accountability of Conduct: A Social Psychological Analysis.* New York: Academic Press, 1983.

Simpson, George Eaton., and J. Milton Yinger. *Racial and Cultural Minorities: An Analysis of Prejudice and Discrimination.* New York: Harper and Row, 1972.

Skolnick, Arlene. *The Intimate Environment: Exploring Marriage and the Family,* 5th ed. New York: HarperCollins, 1992; 4th ed., Boston: Little, Brown, 1987.

Smart, Carol. "Power and the Politics of Child Custody," in Carol Smart and Selma Sevenhuijsen, eds., *Child Custody and the Politics of Gender.* London: Routledge and Kegan Paul, 1989.

Smart, Carol., and Selma Sevenhuijsen, eds. *Child Custody and the Politics of Gender.* London: Routledge and Kegan Paul, 1989.

Smelser, Neil J. *Theory of Collective Behavior.* New York: Free Press, 1962.

Smith, Dorothy. (1993). "The Standard North American Family." *Journal of Family Issues* 14 (March): 50–65.

Snell, Bradford. "American Ground Transport," in Jerome H. Skolnick and Elliott Currie, eds., *Crisis in American Institutions,* 3rd ed. Boston: Little, Brown, 1976, 304–326.

Snipp, C. Matthew. "Occupational Mobility and Social Class: Insights from Men's Career Mobility," *American Sociological Review 50* (August 1985): 475–493.

Spaeth, Joe. "Job Power and Earnings," *American Sociological Review 50* (1985): 603–617.

Spain, Daphne., and Suzanne M. Iancdhi. (1996). *Balancing Act.* New York: Russell Sage Foundation.

Spartenburg County Legislative Delegation. *Minutes.* (February 2005) http://www.co.spartanburg.sc.us/govt/depts/legdel/docs/Delegation/Minutes/February72005minutes.pdf (accessed April 14, 2009).

Spengler, Oswald. *The Decline of the West.* New York: Knopf, 1962. (Originally published in 1918)

Spitz, Rene A. "Hospitalism," *The Psychoanalytic Study of the Child 1* (1945): 53–72.

Spitz, Rene A. "Hospitalism: A Follow-Up Report," *The Psychoanalytic Study of the Child 2* (1946): 113–117.

Spitzer, Steven. "Toward a Marxist Theory of Deviance," *Social Problems 22* (June 1975): 638–651.

Squires, Sally. "Million-Dollar Images," *Washington Post Health,* November 6, 1990, 12–13.

Sroka, Stephen R. "Common Sense on Condom Education," *Education Week 10*(5) (March 13, 1991): 39–40.

Standing, Guy. "Global Feminization Through Flexible Labor," *World Development 17* (July 1989): 1077–1095.

Stark, Oded. "A Relative Deprivation Approach to Performance Incentives in Career Games and Other Contests," *Kyklos 43* (1990): 211–227.

Stark, Rodney., and William Sims Bainbridge. "Secularization and Cult Formation in the Jazz Age," *Journal for the Scientific Study of Religion 20* (December 1981): 360–373.

Starr, Paul. *The Social Transformation of American Medicine.* New York: Basic Books, 1982.

Statistical Abstract (see U.S. Bureau of the Census, *Statistical Abstract of the United States*).

Stearns, Elizabeth., Claudia Buchmann, and Kara Bonneal. "Interracial Friendship Networks in the Transition

From High School to College," *Sociology of Education*, (2009), 82: 173-195.

Stearns, Peter R. "Texas and Virginia: A Bloodied Window Into Changes in American Public Life," *Journal of Social History*, (2008): 299-318.

Stein, Rob. "U.S. Infant Mortality Rate Rises 3%: First Increase Since '58 Surprises Officials as Other Health Indicators Keep Improving," *Washington Post*, February 12, 2004.

Stewart, Abigail J., and Joseph M. Healy, Jr. " Linking Individual Development and Social Changes," *American Psychologist 44* (January, 1989): 30–42.

Stokes, Naomi Miller. *The Castrated Woman: What Your Doctor Won't Tell You About Hysterectomy*. New York: Franklin Watts, 1986.

Stoller, P. "The Language Planning Activities of the U.S. Office of Bilingual Education," *International Journal of the Sociology of Language 11* (1976): 45–60.

Stone, Geoffrey R. "Repeating Past Mistakes," *Society 24* (1987): 5.

Strauss, Roger A., ed. *Using Sociology: An Introduction from the Clinical Perspective*. Bayside, NY: General Hall, 1985.

"Study: More Grain Needed to Feed World in 2020," *Telegraph Herald* (Dubuque, IA), November 7, 1999.

Suchar, Charles S. *Social Deviance: Perspectives and Prospects*. New York: Holt, Rinehart and Winston, 1978.

Sumner, William G. *Folkways*. New York: New American Library, 1980. (Originally published in 1906)

Sutherland, Edwin H. *Principles of Criminology*. Philadelphia: Lippincott, 1939.

Sutherland, Edwin H. *White Collar Crime: The Uncut Version*. New Haven, CT: Yale University Press, 1983.

Sutherland, Edwin H. "White-Collar Criminality," *American Sociological Review 5* (February 1940): 1–11.

Sutherland, Edwin H., and Donald R. Cressey. *Criminology*. Philadelphia: Lippincott, 1970.

Swan, L. Alex. *The Practice of Clinical Sociology and Sociotherapy*. Cambridge, MA: Schenkman, 1984.

Swanstrom, Todd., Peter Dreier, and John Mollenkopf. "Economic Inequality and Public Policy: The Power of Place," *City & Community* 1, no. 4 (December 2002): 349–372.

Sweet, Joanna., and Martha F. Lee. "Christian Exodus: A Modern American Millenarian Movement," *Journal for the Study of Radicalism*, (2010), 4 (1): 1-24.

Szymanski, Albert. *The Capitalist State and the Politics of Class*. Cambridge, MA: Winthrop, 1978.

Tavris, Carol., and Carole Wade. *The Longest War: Sex Differences in Perspective*, 2nd ed. New York: Harcourt Brace Jovanovich, 1984.

Taylor, Frederick Winslow. *Scientific Management*. New York: Harper and Row, 1911.

Taylor, Humphrey. "2–1 Majorities Continue to Support Rights to Both Euthanasia and Doctor-Assisted Suicide" The Harris Poll, Harris Interactive (January 9, 2002).

Taylor, Steven J. "Observing Abuse: Professional Ethics and Personal Morality," *Qualitative Sociology 10* (1987): 288–302.

Teachman, Jay D. "Early Marriage, Premarital Fertility, and Marital Dissolution," *Journal of Family Issues 4* (March 1983): 105–126.

Telegraph. "Wolfboy is Welcomed Home by Mother After Years in the Wild," (2002), www.telegraph.co.uk.

Therkildsen, Gary., and Gary D. Bass. "Reducing Influence Peddling in Government Contracting." (May 8, 2011). www..truthout.org

Thio, Alex. *Deviant Behavior*. Boston: Houghton Mifflin, 1978; 3rd ed., Harper and Row, 1988.

"The 13th British Social Attitudes Report," ed. Roger Jowell, et al. (Dartmouth, 1996).

Thomlinson, Ralph. *Population Dynamics: Causes and Consequences of World Demographic Change*. New York: Random House, 1976.

Thomlinson, Ralph. *Urban Structure*. New York: Random House, 1969.

Thompson, Margaret Susan. *The "Spider Web": Congress and Lobbying in the Age of Grant*. New York: Cornell University Press, 1985.

Thornton, Billy., Michael A. Robbins, and Joel A. Johnson. "Social Perception of a Rape Victim's Culpability: The Influence of Respondents' Personal-Environmental Causal Attribution Tendencies," *Human Relations 34* (March 1981): 225–237.

Tifft, Susan. "Better Safe Than Sorry?" *Time*, January 21, 1991, 66–67.

Tkacik, John. J. Jr. "China's Submarine Challenge," *The Heritage Foundation*, (March 2006), [www.heritage.org/research/asiaandthepacific/wm1001.cfm], accessed on 15 June 2009.

Tönnies, Ferdinand. *Community and Society;* C. P. Loomis, trans. New York: Harper and Row, 1963. (Originally published in 1887)

Towell, Pat. "Plowshare Plan Beaten," *Congressional Quarterly*, November 16, 1991a, 3393–3395.

Towell, Pat. "Soviet Aid Package May Be Doomed by Calls to Keep Money at Home," *Congressional Quarterly*, November 9, 1991b, 3293–3297.

Trafford, Abigail. "Gender Bias in Health Care Is No Myth," *Washington Post Health*, July 30, 1991, 4.

Troeltsch, Ernst. *The Social Teachings of the Christian Churches*. New York: Macmillan, 1931.

Tumin, Melvin. "On Social Inequality," *American Sociological Review 28* (February 1963): 19–26.

Turk, Herman. "Interorganizational Networks in Urban Society: Initial Perspectives and Comparative Research," *American Sociological Review 35* (February 1970): 1–19.

Turner, Castellano B., and Barbara F. Turner. “Gender, Race, Social Class, and Self-evaluations Among College Students,” *The Sociological Artery 23* (Autumn 1982): 491–507.

Turner, Jonathan H. *Sociology: The Science of Human Organization*. Chicago: Nelson-Hall, 1985.

Turner, Jonathan H. *Handbook of Sociological Theory*. New York: Springer Sciences and Business Media. 2006.

Turner, R. H. “Sponsored and Contest Mobility and the School System,” *American Sociological Review 25* (December 1960): 855–867.

Turner, Ralph H., and Lewis M. Killian, eds. *Collective Behavior.* Englewood Cliffs, NJ: Prentice-Hall, 1957; 2nd ed., 1972; 3rd ed., 1987.

Turner, Stephen P., and Jonathan H. Turner. *The Impossible Science: An Institutional Analysis of American Sociology*. Newbury Park, CA: Sage Publications, 1990.

Tyson, Will. "Residence Hall Segregation and Roommate Assignment as Determinants of Interracial Friendship Among First Year College Students," *American Sociological Association Annual Meeting*, (2004), San Fransciso.

Underhill, Evelyn. “Christian Mystics: The Site for Christian Mystics, Traditional and Contemporary,” (2004). www.christianmystics.com.

UNFPA, “State of World Population 2004,” (2004). www.unfpa.org.

United Nations. *Demographic Yearbook, 1989*. New York: 1991.

“Unstoppable Canon,” *Shukan Post*, December 24, 2004. www.japantoday.com/e/?content=executive&id=176

U.S. Bureau of the Census, *Current Population Survey* (HINC-02) "Age of Householder- Households by Total Money Income in 2009, type of Household, Race and Hispanic Origin of Householder.

U.S. Bureau of the Census, "Annual Estimates of the Resident Population by Age for States and for Puerto Rico: April 1, 2000-July1,2009.

U.S. Bureau of the Census, *Statistical Abstract of the United States: 2011*, Table 75, "Self-Described Religious Identification of Adult Population: 1990-2008.

U.S. Bureau of the Census, *American Families and Living Arrangements 2010*, Table FG10 "Family Groups" (2010).

U.S. Bureau of the Census, *American Families and Living Arrangements 2010*, Table C9, "Children by Presence and Type of Parents, Race and Hispanic Origin," (2010).

U.S. Bureau of the Census, *American Families and Living Arrangements 2010*, Table H1, "Households by Type and Tenure of Householder for Selected Characteristics," (2010).

U.S. Bureau of the Census, *American Families and Living Arrangements* 2010, Table H1, "Households by Type and Tenure of Householder for Selected Characteristics," (2010).

U.S. Bureau of the Census, *American Families and Living Arrangements 2010*, C3. "Living Arrangements of Children Under 18 Years/1 and Marital Status of Parents by Age, Sex, Race, and Hispanic Origin/ 2 and Selected Characteristics of the Child for All Children" (2010).

U.S. Bureau of the Census. *Statistical Abstract of the United States*. Table 544, "Social Security¬Beneficiaries', Annual Payments, and Average Monthly Benefit, 1990-2009, and by State and Other Areas, 2009."

U.S. Bureau of the Census. www.census.gov/hhes/www/poverty/data/threshld/thresh81.html.

U.S. Department of Labor. "Record Unemployment Among Older Workers Does Not Keep Them Out of the Job Market," *Issues in labor Statistics* (March 2020). Summary 10-04.

U.S. Misery Index. 2010. www.miseryindex.us/urbymonth.asp.

U.S. Department of Justice. “Crime in the United States.” *Uniform Crime Reports*. Washington, D.C.: U.S. Government Printing Office, 1990.

U.S. State Department. “Saudi Arabia” *International Religious Freedom Report*. Bureau of Democracy, Human Rights and Labor, 2008.

U.S. State Department. “Saudi Arabia” *International Religious Freedom Report*. Bureau of Democracy, Human Rights and Labor, 2007.

Van den Berghe, Pierre L. *Human Family Systems: An Evolutionary View*. New York: Elsevier, 1979.

van der Sluis, I. “People Should Not Have the Right to Die,” in *Opposing Viewpoints Sources: Death/Dying, 1990 Annual*. San Diego: Greenhaven Press, 1990, pp. 13–16. (Originally published by I. van der Sluis as “The Practice of Euthanasia in the Netherlands,” *Issues in Law and Medicine 4* [Spring 1989])

.Vaughan, Dianne. "The Dark Side of Organizations: Mistake, Misconduct and Disaster," *Annual Review of Sociology*. (1999), 25: 271-305.

Veevers, J. E. “The Moral Careers of Voluntary Childless Wives: Notes on the Defense of a Variant World View,” *The Family Coordinator 24* (October 1975): 473–487.

Vernez, Georges., and David Ronfeldt. “The Current Situation in Mexican Immigration,” *Science 51* (March 8, 1991): 1189–1193.

Vockell, Edward L. “Corporal Punishment: The Pros and Cons,” *Clearing House*, March/April, 1991, pp. 278–283.

Vold, George B. *Theoretical Criminology*. New York: Oxford University Press, 1958.

Wagner, Mazie Earle, Herman J. P. Schubert, and Daniel S. P. Schubert, “Family Size Effects: A Review,” *Journal of Genetic Psychology 146* (March 1985): 65–78.

Waitzkin, Howard. “A Marxian Interpretation of the Growth and Development of Coronary Care Technology,” in Peter Conrad and Rochelle Kern, eds., *The Sociology of*

Health and Illness: Critical Perspectives, 2nd ed. New York: St. Martin's Press, 1986.

Waller, Willard. *The Family: A Dynamic Interpretation.* New York: Cordon, 1938.

Waller, Willard., and Reuben Hill. *The Family.* New York: Dryden Press, 1951.

Wallerstein, Immanuel. *The Capitalist World-Economy.* Cambridge, England: Cambridge University Press, 1979.

Wallerstein, Immanuel. *The Politics of the World Economy: The States, the Movements, and the Civilizations.* New York: Cambridge University Press, 1984.

Wallerstein, Judith S., and Sandra Blakeslee. *Second Chances: Men, Women, and Children a Decade After Divorce.* New York: Ticknor and Fields, 1990.

Walters, Pamela Barnhouse. "Educational Expansion in the United States," *American Sociological Review 49* (October 1984): 659–671.

Wanzer, Sidney H., Daniel D. Federman, S. James Adelstein, Christine K. Cassel, Edwin H. Cassem, Ronald E. Cranford, Edward W. Hook, Bernard Lo, Charles G. Moertel, Peter Safar, Alan Stone, and Jan van Eys. "Doctors Should Sometimes Help Dying Patients Commit Suicide," in *Opposing Viewpoints Sources: Death and Dying 1990 Annual.* San Diego: Greenhaven Press, 1990, 17–19. (Originally published by Wanzer et al. as "The Physician's Responsibility Toward Hopelessly Ill Patients: A Second Look," *The New England Journal of Medicine 13* [March 30, 1989])

Ware, Helen. "Polygyny: Women's Views in a Traditional Society, Nigeria, 1975," *Journal of Marriage and the Family 41* (February 1979): 185–195.

Watson, Russell. "A Death Trap in Sheffield," *Newsweek*, April *24*, 1989, 54.

Weber, Max. *The City.* New York: Free Press, 1958.

Weber, Max. *From Max Weber: Essays in Sociology;* trans. and eds., H. Gerth and C. Wright Mills. New York: Oxford University Press, 1946.

Weber, Max. *The Protestant Ethic and the Spirit of Capitalism;* trans. Talcott Parsons. New York: Scribner's, 1930. (Originally published in 1905)

Weinberg, M. *Minority Students: A Research Appraisal.* Washington, D.C.: U.S. Government Printing Office, 1977.

Weinberger, Caspar W. "The State of the Union's Schools," *Forbes*, July 23, 1990, 27.

Weiss, Carol H., and Michael J. Bucavalas. *Social Science Research and Decision-Making.* New York: Columbia University Press, 1980.

Weiss, Ted. "Pro: Should the House-Passed Wage Proposal Be Enacted?" *Congressional Digest 68*(5) (May 1989): 150, 152.

Weitzman, Lenore J. *The Divorce Revolution: The Unexpected Social and Economic Consequences for Women and Children in America.* New York: Free Press, 1985.

Wennerhag, Magnus. "Another Modernity is Possible? The Global Justice Movement and the Transformation of Politics," *Distinktion: Scandanavian Journal of Social Theory*, 2010, 21:25-49.

Westheimer, Ruth K. and Sanford Lopater. *Human Sexuality: A Psychosocial Perspective.* 2nd edition. 2005. Philadelphia, PA: Lippincott, Williams and Wilkins.

Weyant, James M. *Applied Social Psychology.* New York: Oxford University Press, 1986.

Whitebook, M., C. Howes, and D. Phillips. *Who Cares? Child Care Teachers and the Quality of Care in America.* Oakland, CA: Child Care Employee Project, 1989.

Whorf, Benjamin L. "The Relation of Habitual Thought and Behavior to Language," in Leslie Spier, A. Irving Hallowell, and Stanley S. Newman (eds.), *Language, Culture and Personality: Essays in Memory of Edward Sapir.* Menasha, WI: Sapir Memorial Publication, 1941.

Whyte, William Foote. *Human Relations in the Restaurant Industry.* New York: McGraw-Hill, 1949.

Wiley, Kim Wright. "Up Against the Ceiling," *Savvy*, June 1987, 51–52.

Williams, Peter. *Popular Religion in America: Symbolic Change and the Modernization Process in Historical Perspective.* Englewood Cliffs, NJ: Prentice-Hall, 1980.

Williams, Robin M., Jr. *American Society: A Sociological Interpretation*, 3rd ed. New York: Knopf, 1970.

Willie, Charles. V. "The Inclining Significance of Race," *Society 15* (1978).

Wilson, E. O. *Sociobiology.* Cambridge, MA: Harvard University Press, 1975.

Wilson, William Julius. *The Declining Significance of Race.* Chicago: University of Chicago Press, 1978.

Wilson, William Julius. *The Truly Disadvantaged: The Inner City, the Underclass, and Public Policy.* Chicago: University of Chicago Press, 1987.

Wilson, William Julius (ed.). "The Ghetto Underclass: Social Science Perspectives," *Annals of the American Academy of Political and Social Science 50* (January 1989).

Winch, Robert F. *Mate Selection.* New York: Harper, 1958.

Winch, Robert F., Thomas Ktsanes, and Virginia Ktsanes. "The Theory of Complementary Needs in Mate Selection: An Analytic and Descriptive Study," *American Sociological Review 19* (June 1954): 241–249.

Wirth, Louis. "Urbanism as a Way of Life," *American Journal of Sociology 44* (July 1938): 3–24.

Wolf, A. "What Is the Economic Case for Treating Obesity?" *Obesity Research* 6 (1998 supplement): 2S–7S.

Wolf, A. M., and G. A. Colditz. "Current Estimates of the Economic Cost of Obesity in the United States," *Obesity Research* 6, no. 2 (1998): 97–106.

Wolff, E. N. "Recent Trends in Household Wealth in the U.S.: Rising Debt and the Middle Class Squeeze," Working Paper, No. 589 (2010), Annandale-on-the-Hudson, N. Y.: The Levy Economics Institute of Bard College.

Wood, Floris W., ed. *An American Profile—Opinions and Behavior, 1972–1989.* Detroit: Gale Research, 1990.

Woodhead, Linda. "Gendering Secularization Theory," *Social Compass*, (2008), 55 (2): 187-193.

World Almanac and Book of Facts, 1992. New York: Pharos Books, 1991.

World Factbook. (2009) Central Intelligence Agency, Washington, D.C.

Wright, James D. "Address Unknown: Homelessness in Contemporary America," *Society 26*(6) (September/ October 1989): 45–53.

Wyer, Natalie A. "Salient Egalitarian Norms Moderate Activation of Out-Group Approach and Avoidance," *Group Processes and Intergroup Relations*, (March, 2010), 13 (2): 151-165.

Yankauer, Alfred. "What Infant Mortality Tells Us," *American Journal of Public Health 80* (June 1990): 653–654.

Yinger, J. Milton. "Countercultures and Social Change," *American Sociological Review 42* (December 1977): 833–853.

Zeisel, John. *Sociology and Architectural Design.* New York: Russell Sage Foundation, 1973.

Zeitzen, Miriam. *Polygamy: A Cross-Cultural Analysis*. Berg Publishers, 2008.

Zelditch, M., Jr. "Role Differentiation in the Nuclear Family," in Talcott Parsons, Robert F. Bales, James Olds, Morris Zelditch, and Philip E. Slater (eds.), *Family, Socialization and Interaction Process.* Glencoe, IL: Free Press, 1955.

Zimbardo, Philip G. "The Pathology of Imprisonment," in James H. Henslin, ed. *Down to Earth Sociology: Introductory Readings*, 6th ed. New York: Free Press, 1991, 287–293.

Zinn, Maxine Baca., and D. Stanley Eitzen (2005). *Diversity in Families.* 7th Ed. New York: Allyn and Bacon.

Zoloton, Adam J., and Megan E. Puzia. "Bans Against Corporal Punishment: A Systematic Review of the Laws, Changes in Attitudes and Behaviors," *Child Abuse Review*, (2010): 19:229-247.

Zirkel, P. A. "Self-concept and the Disadvantage of Ethnic Group Membership and Mixture," *Review of Educational Research 41* (1971): 211–225.

Zweigenhaft, Richard L., and G. William Domhoff. *Blacks in the White Establishment: A Study of Race and Class in America.* New Haven, CT: Yale University Press, 1991.

Zwerdling, Daniel. "The Food Monopolies," in Jerome H. Skolnick and Elliott Currie, eds., *Crisis in American Institutions*, 3rd ed. Boston: Little, Brown, 1976, pp. 43–51.

Zhu Xiao Di, Yi Yang and Xiaodong Liu. "Young American Adults Living in Parental Homes," *Joint Center for Housing Studies* (Winter 2002– 2003).

Photo Credits

Chapter 1: iStockphoto, 2 (top); iStockphoto, 2 (middle); iStockphoto, 2 (bottom); iStockphoto, 3; AP Wide World Photos, 4; Shutterstock images, 6; iStockphoto, 8; iStockphoto, 10 (left); iStockphoto, 10 (right); iStockphoto, 14 (top); iStockphoto, 14 (bottom).

Chapter 2: Wikimedia Commons, 20 (top); Wikimedia Commons, 20 (middle); Wikimedia Commons, 20 (bottom); iStockphoto, 21; Library of Congress, 23; Wikimedia Commons, 24; Wikimedia Commons, 26; AP Wide World Photos, 27; Wikimedia, 28; Dreamstime, 30; Wikimedia Commons, 31; iStockphoto, 32; Wikimedia Commons, 33; Wikimedia Commons, 35; AP Wide World Photos, 37; iStockphoto, 42; iStockphoto, 44; AP Wide World Photos, 48.

Chapter 3: AP Wide World Photos, 58 (top); iStockphoto, 58 (middle); Dreamstime, 58 (bottom); iStockphoto, 59; iStockphoto, 60; AP Wide World Photos, 62 (left); AP Wide World Photos, 62 (right); AP Wide World Photos, 63; iStockphoto, 64 (table); AP Wide World Photos, 65; iStockphoto, 68; AP Wide World Photos, 70; AP Wide World Photos, 71; iStockphoto, 73; iStockphoto, 75; Dreamstime, 76; iStockphoto, 77; Dreamstime, 80; iStockphoto, 83; iStockphoto, 84; iStockphoto, 85.

Chapter 4: iStockphoto, 96 (top); iStockphoto, 96 (middle); iStockphoto, 96 (bottom); iStockphoto, 97; iStockphoto, 99 (left); iStockphoto, 99 (middle left); iStockphoto, 99 (middle right); iStockphoto, 99 (right); iStockphoto, 100; iStockphoto, 104; iStockphoto, 105; AP Wide World Photos, 107; Library of Congress, 109; iStockphoto, 111; AP Wide World Photos, 112; iStockphoto, 112 (top); iStockphoto, 116; AP Wide World Photos, 117; iStockphoto, 118.

Chapter 5: iStockphoto, 124 (left); iStockphoto, 124 (middle); iStockphoto, 124 (right); AP Wide World Photos, 125; AP Wide World Photos, 126; AP Wide World Photos, 128; iStockphoto, 129; iStockphoto, 131; iStockphoto, 132 (bottom); iStockphoto, 132 (top); iStockphoto, 134; iStockphoto, 136; AP Wide World Photos, 137; iStockphoto, 139; iStockphoto, 141; iStockphoto, 145; iStockphoto, 148; iStockphoto, 149 (table).

Chapter 6: iStockphoto, 158 (top); iStockphoto, 158 (middle); iStockphoto, 158 (bottom); iStockphoto, 159; iStockphoto, 161; iStockphoto, 162; iStockphoto, 163; iStockphoto, 168; iStockphoto, 168; iStockphoto, 171 (left); iStockphoto, 171 (right); iStockphoto, 174; iStockphoto, 175; iStockphoto, 176; iStockphoto, 180 (top); iStockphoto, 180 (bottom); AP Wide World Photos, 181; AP Wide World Photos, 182.

Chapter 7: AP Wide World Photos, 190 (top); iStockphoto, 190 (middle); iStockphoto, 190 (bottom); iStockphoto, 191; AP Wide World Photos, 192; iStockphoto, 194; iStockphoto, 196; AP Wide World Photos, 197; iStockphoto, 199; iStockphoto, 200 (table); AP Wide World Photos, 201; AP Wide World Photos, 203; AP Wide World Photos, 204; AP Wide World Photos, 205; iStockphoto, 208; AP Wide World Photos, 209; Library of Congress, 211; iStockphoto, 211 (top) iStockphoto, 211 (bottom); AP Wide World Photos, 216; iStockphoto, 217 (table); iStockphoto, 219.

Chapter 8: iStockphoto, 228 (top); iStockphoto, 228 (middle); iStockphoto, 228 (bottom); AP Wide World Photos, 229; iStockphoto, 230; iStockphoto, 231; iStockphoto, 232 (top); iStockphoto, 232 (bottom); iStockphoto, 234; iStockphoto, 235; iStockphoto, 236 (table); Library of Congress, 238; AP Wide World Photos, 243 (top); iStockphoto, 243 (bottom); iStockphoto, 244 (top); iStockphoto, 244 (bottom); iStockphoto, 248.

Chapter 9: iStockphoto, 256 (top); iStockphoto, 256 (middle); iStockphoto, 256 (bottom); iStockphoto, 257; Library of Congress, 258; iStockphoto, 259 (left); iStockphoto, 259 (middle); iStockphoto, 259 (right); iStockphoto, 260; iStockphoto, 261; AP Wide World Photos, 264; AP Wide World Photos, 267; AP Wide World Photos, 268; iStockphoto, 270; AP Wide World Photos, 272; AP Wide World Photos, 274; iStockphoto, 275 (table); iStockphoto, 276 (table); iStockphoto, 280; iStockphoto, 281; iStockphoto, 284; iStockphoto, 285; iStockphoto, 286.

Chapter 10: iStockphoto, 296 (top); AP Wide World Photos, 296 (middle); AP Wide World Photos, 296 (bottom); AP Wide World Photos, 297; iStockphoto, 298; iStockphoto, 301; iStockphoto, 302; AP Wide World Photos, 303; iStockphoto, 305; Library of Congress, 311; iStockphoto, 312; iStockphoto, 314; iStockphoto, 315.

Chapter 11: iStockphoto, 322 (top); iStockphoto, 322 (middle); iStockphoto, 322 (bottom); iStockphoto, 323; AP Wide World Photos, 324; iStockphoto, 326; iStockphoto, 329; iStockphoto, 330; iStockphoto, 333; iStockphoto, 338; iStockphoto, 339; iStockphoto, 343; iStockphoto, 344 (middle); iStockphoto, 344 (top); Getty Images, 347.

Chapter 12: iStockphoto, 356 (top); iStockphoto, 356 (middle); iStockphoto, 356 (bottom); AP Wide World Photos, 357; AP Wide World Photos, 358; iStockphoto, 360; iStockphoto, 363; AP Wide World Photos, 364; iStockphoto, 366; iStockphoto, 368; iStockphoto, 372; iStockphoto, 377; iStockphoto, 380.

Chapter 13: AP Wide World Photos, 394 (top); iStockphoto, 394 (middle); iStockphoto, 394 (bottom); iStockphoto, 395; iStockphoto, 397 (left); iStockphoto, 397 (middle); iStockphoto, 397 (right): iStockphoto, 398; iStockphoto, 399; AP Wide World Photos, 402; iStockphoto, 403; iStockphoto, 405; iStockphoto, 407; iStockphoto, 409; iStockphoto, 410; iStockphoto, 411; iStockphoto, 412; AP Wide World Photos, 414; iStockphoto, 416; AP Wide World Photos, 418 (top); AP Wide World Photos, 418 (bottom).

Chapter 14: iStockphoto, 428 (top); iStockphoto, 428 (middle); iStockphoto, 428 (bottom); iStockphoto, 429; iStockphoto, 430; iStockphoto, 435; iStockphoto, 436; iStockphoto, 437; iStockphoto, 439; iStockphoto, 440; iStockphoto, 443; iStockphoto, 444; iStockphoto, 445; iStockphoto, 447; iStockphoto, 450; AP Wide World Photos, 451; AP Wide World Photos, 452.

Chapter 15: iStockphoto, 460 (top); AP Wide World Photos, 460 (middle); iStockphoto, 460 (bottom); AP Wide World Photos, 461; iStockphoto, 463; iStockphoto, 465; AP Wide World Photos, 468; AP Wide World Photos, 471; iStockphoto, 473; AP Wide World Photos, 474; AP Wide World Photos, 475; AP Wide World Photos, 476 (middle); AP Wide World Photos, 476 (top); iStockphoto, 478; iStockphoto, 480 (top); iStockphoto, 480 (bottom).

Chapter 16: AP Wide World Photos, 488 (top); AP Wide World Photos, 488 (middle); AP Wide World Photos, 488 (bottom); iStockphoto, 489; iStockphoto, 490; AP Wide World Photos, 498; AP Wide World Photos, 500; iStockphoto, 501; AP Wide World Photos, 504; iStockphoto, 505 (top); iStockphoto, 505 (bottom); Library of Congress, 506; iStockphoto, 508; AP Wide World Photos, 510.

Chapter 17: Shutterstock images, 516 (top); iStockphoto, 516 (middle); iStockphoto, 516 (bottom); AP Wide World Photos, 517; iStockphoto, 519; iStockphoto, 520; Shutterstock images, 521; iStockphoto, 524; iStockphoto, 526; AP Wide World Photos, 530; iStockphotos, 532; iStockphoto, 535; iStockphoto, 536; iStockphoto, 539.

Chapter 18: AP Wide World Photos, 548 (top) iStockphotos, 5484 (middle); iStockphotos, 5448 (bottom); AP Wide World Photos, 549; iStockphotos, 550; iStockphoto, 552 (top); iStockphoto, 552 (bottom); AP Wide World Photos, 554; iStockphoto, 557; AP Wide World Photos, 558; AP Wide World Photos, 559; iStockphoto, 563 (top); iStockphoto, 563 (bottom); iStockphoto, 564; AP Wide World Photos, 565.

Chapter 19: iStockphoto, 576 (top), iStockphoto, 576 (middle); AP Wide World Photos, 576 (bottom); AP Wide World Photos, 577; iStockphoto, 580; iStockphoto, 581; iStockphoto, 585; AP Wide World Photos, 588; AP Wide World Photos, 592 (left); AP Wide World Photos, 592 (right); iStockphoto, 593; iStockphoto, 595; iStockphoto, 596; AP Wide World Photos, 597; iStockphoto, 601; iStockphoto, 602.

Chapter 20: AP Wide World Photos, 608 (top); AP Wide World Photos, 608 (middle); iStockphoto, 608 (bottom); AP Wide World Photos, 609; AP Wide World Photos, 613; AP Wide World Photos, 615; iStockphoto, 617; iStockphoto, 620: Shutterstock images, 621; Shutterstock images, 622; Shutterstock images, 623; AP Wide World Photos, 628.

Chapter 21: Shutterstock images, 640 (top); iStockphoto, 640 (middle); iStockphoto, 640 (bottom); AP Wide World Photos, 641; iStockphoto, 643; courtesy of R. Rappeport, 645; iStockphoto, 647 (top left); iStockphoto, 647 (top right); iStockphoto, 647 (bottom); AP Wide World Photos, 649; iStockphoto, 651 (top); iStockphoto, 651 (bottom); iStockphoto, 652; iStockphoto, 654.

Index

sources, including oil, gold, gas, and timber; and a coastline of pristine beaches that could turn out to be the hot new tourist spot. Vietnam is the world's twelfth most populous nation and southeast Asia's second largest market.

Amid all the excitement, however, are some notes of caution. The per-capita income of most Vietnamese is $280 a year, and Vietnam's transportation and communication systems rank among the world's worst. While the country and its markets develop, marketers are spending their money cautiously. Because most consumers are seeing products for the first time, companies are investing most of their marketing dollars in very simple advertising campaigns. For this reason, radio and billboards are fruitful venues for advertising. One billboard in Ho Chi Minh City boasts a single word: Sony.

Cuba: Watching and Waiting

Cuba is an important emerging market with considerable potential for Canadian exporters and investors. It comprises half the land mass of the Caribbean, and with a population of about 11 million, it is the largest market in the region. Canada and Cuba have a long history of trade. Today, Cuba is Canada's first trading partner in the Caribbean, while Canada is Cuba's second largest trading partner globally; Russia is still number one. Tourism, mining, and agriculture are the main areas of trade focus. Twenty-six Canadian import and export companies have registered as operating offices in Cuba, and over 200 000 Canadians visited the island in 1999. Two-way trade in 1999 totalled $701.8 million. Canadian exports to Cuba were $396.0 million in 1999. As with the emerging markets of China and Vietnam, Cuba's infrastructure needs years of rebuilding. Some places have no running water, gasoline, sewer systems, and energy sources. "They'll have to take care of the basic concept of survival before they can think about pizza and Pepsi," says Joe Zubizarreta, a Cuban-born advertising executive. Thus, it isn't surprising that Canada's main exports to Cuba are metal structures and hardware, industrial machinery and parts, motor vehicles and parts, electrical equipment, and fertilizers.

Not only has the US-led embargo against Cuba dampened the country's economic prospects, but American political pressure has also caused problems for Canadian firms that do business in Cuba. However, while these American laws increase the risk for Canadian companies, they also prevent American competitors from entering the ma
stead of having to challenge ent
American competitors as Canadia
do in other Latin American market
principal competitors in Cuba are m
from Latin America (especially Mex
and Europe (especially Spain, Italy, a
France), as well as from Asia.

Sources: Melana Zyla, "Polish your connections to prosper in business," *Globe and Mail,* 1 July 1997:C13; "Central and Eastern Europe: A market ready to harvest," *Advertising Supplement, Canadian Business,* July 1997; Nattalia Lea, "Passage to the China market," *Marketing,* 12 September 1994:8; Marlene Piturro, "Capitalist China?" *Brandweek,* 16 May 1994:24–7; Mark L. Clifford, "How you can win in China," *Business Week,* 26 May 1997:66–9; "Hong Kong means business," *Financial Post,* 30 June 1997:HK4; Department of Foreign Affairs and International Trade, "Team Canada 2001 concludes with $5.7 billion in new deals," news release, 17 February 2001; Cyndee Miller, "U.S. firms rush to claim share of newly opened Vietnam market," *Marketing News,* 14 March 1994:11; Thomas A. Kissane, "What are we doing in Vietnam?" *Sales & Marketing Management,* May 1996:96–7; Christy Fisher, "U.S. marketers wait for opening in Cuba," *Advertising Age,* 29 August 1994:1,6; Sean Mehegan, "Is Castro convertible?" *Restaurant Business,* 1 May 1996:36–8; Department of Foreign Affairs and International Trade, *Cuba: A Guide for Canadian Businesses,* 2nd ed., June 1999, www.infoexport.gc.ca/docs/view-e.asp?did=214&gid=193.

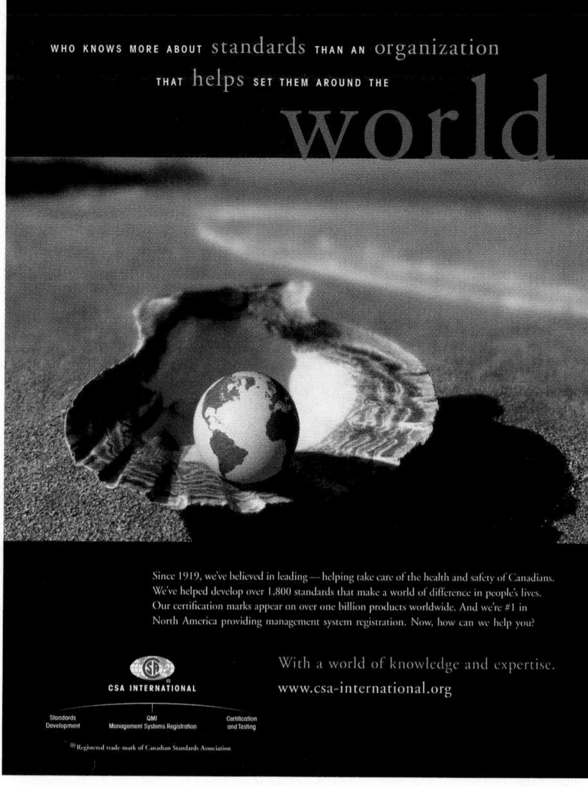

The Canadian Standards Association International can help firms with their market-entry decisions.

very different product and distribution strategies to meet the needs of customers in different countries. For example, in Canada, 90 percent of pools are sold through specialized pool retailers, which offer their customers installation service. In Europe, however, just the opposite is true. Ninety percent of people buying pools do their own installation. Therefore, Vogue realized, these consumers would need help. Since Vogue representatives couldn't join buyers in their backyards to offer a helping hand, they did the next best thing. Pools were redesigned to simplify the installation process. In fact, Vogue took the "Ikea approach." Customers must still dig a hole, but they can use a single tool to assemble their Vogue pool and no longer need to use a confusing array of nuts and bolts. Differences in behaviour didn't stop with customers. Distributors had unique perspectives as well. Gilles Lebuis, VP of marketing, notes, "A distributor in France will know his market much better . . . than someone from Switzerland. . . ." Thus, even though it might have been cheaper to use a single European distributor, Vogue chose different distributors for each country. It sells through major do-it-yourself chains in France and pool distributors in Belgium, Switzerland, Germany, and Austria. Sales have topped $11 million using these strategies, keeping Vogue stroking along.[16]

Deciding Whether to Go International

While many firms view themselves as local businesses serving their immediate communities, they must become aware of the globalization of competition even if they never plan to go overseas themselves. Too many companies have recognized the dangers too late and have gone out of business when faced with new competitors such as the category killers from the United States or abroad. Companies that operate in global industries, where their strategic positions in specific markets are affected strongly by their overall global positions, have no choice but to think and act globally. Thus, Nortel must organize globally if it is to gain purchasing, manufacturing, financial, and marketing advantages. Firms in a global industry must be able to compete on a worldwide basis if they are to succeed.

Several factors may draw a company into the international arena. Global competitors may attack the company's domestic market by offering better products or lower prices. The company may want to counterattack these competitors in their home markets to tie up their resources. Or it may discover foreign markets that present higher profit opportunities than the domestic market does. The company's domestic market may be shrinking, or the company may need a larger customer base to achieve economies of scale. Or it may want to reduce its dependence on any one market to reduce its risk. Finally, the company's customers may be expanding abroad and require international servicing.

Before going abroad, the company must weigh the risks and assess its ability to operate globally. Can the company learn to understand the preferences and buyer behaviour of consumers in other countries? Can it offer competitively attractive products? Will it be able to adapt to other countries' business cultures and deal effectively with foreign nationals? Do the company's managers have the necessary international experience? Has management considered the impact of regulations and the political environments of other countries?

Because of the risks and difficulties of entering international markets, most companies do not act until some situation or event thrusts them into the global arena. Someone—a domestic exporter, a foreign importer, a foreign government—may ask the company to sell abroad. Or the company may be saddled with overcapacity and must find additional markets for its goods.

Deciding Which Markets to Enter

Before going abroad, the company must set its international *marketing objectives and policies.* First, it must decide what *volume* of foreign sales it wants. Most companies start small when they go abroad. Some plan to stay small, seeing international sales as a small part of their business. Other companies have bigger plans, seeing international business as equal to or even more important than their domestic business.

The company must choose *how many* countries it wants to market in. Generally, it makes sense to operate in fewer countries with deeper commitment and penetration in each. The Bulova Watch Company decided to operate in many international markets and expanded into over 100 countries; unfortunately it had spread itself too thin, made profits in only two countries, and lost around $55 million.

In contrast, although consumer-product company Amway is now breaking into markets at a furious pace, it is doing so only after decades of gradually building up its overseas presence. Known for its neighbour-to-neighbour direct-selling networks, Amway expanded into Australia in 1971, a country far away but similar to its North American market. Then, in the 1980s, Amway expanded into 10 more countries, and the pace increased rapidly from then on. By 1994, Amway was firmly established in 60 countries, including Hungary, Poland, and the Czech Republic. Following its substantial success in Japan, China, and other Asian countries, the company entered India in 1998. Entering the new century, international proceeds account for over 70 percent of the company's overall sales.[17]

Next, the company must decide on the *types* of countries to enter. A country's attractiveness depends on the product, geographical factors, income and population, political climate, and other factors. The seller may prefer certain country groups or parts of the world. In recent years, many major markets have emerged, offering both substantial opportunities and daunting challenges (see Marketing Highlight 17-3).

After listing possible international markets, the company must screen and rank each one. Consider this example:[18]

> Many mass marketers dream of selling to China's more than 1.2 billion people. For example, Colgate is waging a pitched battle in China, seeking control of the world's largest toothpaste market. Yet, this country of infrequent brushers offers great potential. Only 20 percent of China's rural dwellers brush daily, so Colgate and its competitors are aggressively pursuing promotional and educational programs, from massive ad campaigns to visits to local schools to sponsoring oral care research. Through such efforts, in this $350 million market dominated by local brands, Colgate has expanded its market share from seven percent in 1995 to 24 percent today.

Colgate's decision to enter the Chinese market seems fairly straightforward: China is a huge market without established competition. Given the low rate of brushing, this already huge market can grow even larger. Yet we still can question whether market size *alone* is reason enough for selecting China. Colgate must also consider other factors. Will the Chinese government remain stable and supportive? Does China provide for the production and distribution technologies needed to produce and market Colgate's products profitably? Will Colgate be able to overcome cultural barriers and convince Chinese consumers to brush their teeth regularly? Can Colgate compete effectively with dozens of local competitors? Colgate's current success in China suggests that it could answer yes to all of these questions. Still, the company's future in China is filled with uncertainties.

A company should rank possible global markets on several factors, including market size, market growth, cost of doing business, competitive advantage, and risk level. It can use indicators like those shown in Table 17-1 to determine the potential of each market, and then decide which ones offer the greatest long-run return on investment.

General Electric's appliance division uses what it calls a "smart bomb" strategy for selecting global markets to enter. GE executives microscopically examine each potential country, measuring such factors as strength of local competitors, market growth potential, and availability of skilled labour. The company then targets only markets where it can earn more than 20 percent on its investment. The

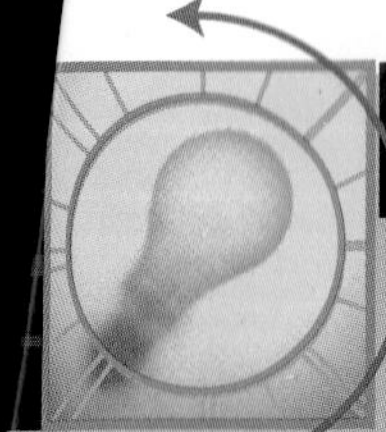

marketing highlight 17-3

The Last Marketing Frontiers: Eastern Europe, China and Vietnam, and Cuba

As communist and formerly communist countries reform their markets, and trade barriers are dismantled, North American companies are eagerly anticipating the profits that await them. Here are "snapshots" of the opportunities and challenges that marketers face in three of the world's global marketing frontiers.

Eastern Europe: A Market Ready to Harvest

As Central and Eastern Europe continue the transition to free-market economies, the market for Canadian goods and services is expanding. Rapid economic growth and the privatization of state-owned companies point the way to increasing opportunities. The Canadian Development Corporation (CDC), a Crown corporation, has helped Canadian firms expand into the region by providing them with financial and risk management services. The Canadian International Development Agency (CIDA) runs other federal government programs designed to help firms ease their way into these markets.

Russia, a challenging market, boasts 250 Canadian companies that have thrived in the oil and gas, agricultural, housing and construction, and telecommunications markets. However, as Russia's economy struggles, Canadian exports have been falling: In 1997, Canada exported $379 million to Russia, but in 1999 (the most recent data available) exports fell to $174 million. Poland is Canada's second largest trade partner in the area. Canada has long enjoyed an excellent reputation in Poland. While charting a course through Poland's business channels is no easy task, perseverance pays, and Canadian firms exported $205 million to the country in 1999. Since the Czech Republic is one of the most stable and fastest-growing former communist countries in Europe, Canadians firms have been working diligently to build relationships there. Hungary is another target of Canadian firms. The new airport in Budapest, built by a Canadian-led consortium, bears witness to the country's open and friendly business environment. Canadian exports to Hungary increased by 500 percent over a 10-year period.

China: 1.2 Billion Consumers

In Guangdong province, Chinese "yuppies" walk department-store aisles to buy $140 Nike or Reebok running shoes or think nothing of spending $6 on a jar of Skippy peanut butter in the supermarket section. Although Chinese consumers make as little as $190 a month, they still have plenty of savings and spending money because of subsidized housing and health care. In Shenzen, Guangdong's second largest city, consumers have the highest disposable income in all of China—$5600 annually. With purchasing power like this, a population of 1.2 billion, and the fastest-growing economy in the world, China is encouraging companies from around the world to set up shop there. Instead of the communist propaganda of yore, modern Chinese billboards exclaim, "Give China a chance."

Since the prime minister's first highly publicized "Team Canada" trade delegation to China in 1994, Canadian exports to China have grown tremendously. The most recent mission, Team Canada 2001, to Beijing, Shanghai, and Hong Kong, wrapped up 27 new business for Canadian enterprises totalling $5.7 billion. Hong Kong is a major financial and high-technology hub and a key gateway for Canadian companies doing business in Asia. It is already home to the largest Canadian business community in Asia.

Yet for all its market potential, there are many hurdles to jump in entering mainland China and marketing to the Chinese. Even firms that have been highly successful in the Chinese market, such as Nortel or Bombardier, still face prolonged and difficult negotiations. Firms are often unsure about who has the authority to close a deal or make a final decision. Moreover, China is not one market, but many, and regional governments may discriminate against certain goods. Distribution channels are undeveloped, consisting of thousands of tiny mom-and-pop stores that can afford to stock only a few bottles or packages at a time. And China's dismal infrastructure can turn a rail shipment travelling from Guanzhou to Beijing into a month-long odyssey. As Canadian firms expand from Hong Kong into mainland China, *guanxi*, or connections, have become one of the keys to doing business. Many believe that businesses will need a Chinese partner with local political connections to be successful. Others acquire Chinese business partners who can help them penetrate distribution channels and hire experienced personnel. Another major concern is China's distressing human rights record. Levi Strauss has turned its back on China's vast market for blue jeans because of such concerns. But other firms counter that industry can be part of the solution. "Supporting the business sector will result in economic and political freedoms for the Chinese people," says a 3M spokesperson.

Vietnam: An Untapped Market Vietnam seems like a marketer's dream: 72 million consumers, 80 percent of whom are under 40 years old; loads of natural re-

Pepsi in China—a huge marketing opportunity?

TABLE 17-1 Indicators of Market Potential

1. Demographic characteristics	4. Technological factors
Size of population Rate of population growth Degree of urbanization Population density Age structure and composition of the population	Level of technological skill Existing production technology Existing consumption technology Education levels
2. Geographic characteristics	**5. Sociocultural factors**
Physical size of a country Topographical characteristics Climate conditions	Dominant values Lifestyle patterns Ethnic groups Linguistic fragmentation
3. Economic factors	**6. National goals and plans**
GNP per capita Income distribution Rate of growth of GNP Ratio of investment to GNP	Industry priorities Infrastructure investment plans

Source: Susan P. Douglas, C. Samuel Craig, and Warren Keegan, "Approaches to assessing international marketing opportunities for small and medium-sized businesses," *Columbia Journal of World Business,* Fall 1982:26–32, © 1982, 1999, Columbia Journal of World Business, reprinted with permission. Also see Tamer S. Cavusil, "Measuring the potential of emerging markets: An indexing approach," *Business Horizons,* January–February 1997:87–91.

goal: "To generate the best returns possible on the smallest investment possible." Once targets are selected, GE zeroes in with marketing "smart bombs"—products and programs tailored to yield the best performance in each market. Using this strategy, GE is trouncing competitors such as Whirlpool and Maytag in Asian markets.[19]

Deciding How to Enter the Market

Once a company has decided to sell in a foreign country, it must determine the best mode of entry. Figure 17-2 shows three market-entry strategies—*exporting, joint venturing,* and *direct investment*—along with the options each one offers. As the figure shows, each succeeding strategy involves more commitment and risk, but also more control and potential profits.

FIGURE 17-2 Market entry strategies

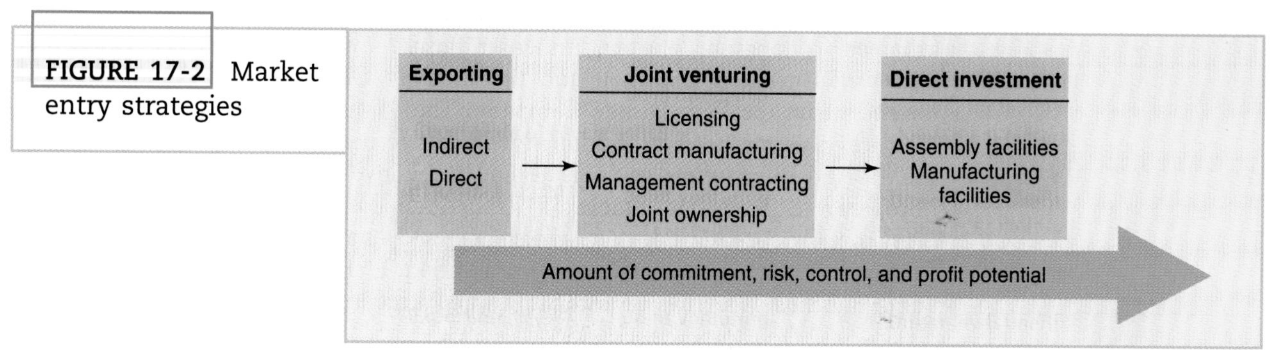

Exporting

Exporting
Entering a foreign market by sending products and selling them through international marketing intermediaries (indirect exporting) or through the company's own department, branch, or sales representatives or agents (direct exporting).

The simplest way to enter a foreign market is through **exporting.** The company can passively export its surpluses from time to time, or it can make an active commitment to expand exports to a particular market. In either case, the company produces all of its goods in its home country, possibly modifying them for the export market. Exporting involves the least change in the company's product lines, organization, investments, or mission.

Companies typically start with *indirect exporting,* working through independent international marketing intermediaries. Indirect exporting involves less investment because the firm does not require an overseas sales force or set of contacts. It also involves less risk. International marketing intermediaries—domestic-based export merchants or agents, cooperative organizations, and export-management companies—bring know-how and services to the relationship, so the seller normally makes fewer mistakes.

Sellers may eventually move into *direct exporting* and handle their own exports. The investment and risk are somewhat greater in this strategy, but so is the potential return. A company can conduct direct exporting in several ways. It can set up a domestic export department that carries out export activities. It can set up an overseas sales branch that handles sales, distribution, and perhaps promotion: The sales branch gives the seller more presence and program control in the foreign market and often serves as a display centre and customer service centre. The company also can send home-based salespeople abroad at certain times to find business. Finally, the company can do its exporting either through foreign-based distributors who buy and own the goods or through foreign-based agents who sell the goods on behalf of the company.

Joint Venturing

Joint venturing
Entering foreign markets by joining with foreign companies to produce or market a product or service.

A second method of entering a foreign market is **joint venturing**—joining with domestic or foreign companies to produce or market products or services. Joint venturing differs from exporting in that the company joins with a partner to sell or market abroad. It differs from direct investment in that an association is formed with someone in the foreign country. The four types of joint ventures are licensing, contract manufacturing, management contracting, and joint ownership.

Licensing

Licensing
A method of entering a foreign market in which the company enters into an agreement with a licensee in the foreign market, offering the right to use a manufacturing process, trademark, patent, trade secret, or other item of value for a fee or royalty.

Licensing is a simple way for a manufacturer to enter international marketing. The company forms an agreement with a licensee in the foreign market. For a fee or royalty, the licensee buys the right to use the company's manufacturing process, trademark, patent, trade secret, or other item of value. The company gains entry into the market at little risk; the licensee gains production expertise or a well-known product or name without having to start from scratch.

Coca-Cola markets internationally by licensing bottlers around the world and supplying them with the syrup needed to produce the product. Molson Breweries ditched its longtime partner, Anheuser Busch, and licensed its beers to Coors. Tokyo Disneyland is owned and operated by Oriental Land Company under licence from the Walt Disney Company: The 45-year licence gives Disney licensing fees plus ten percent of admissions and five percent of food and merchandise sales. And in an effort to bring online retail investing to people abroad, online brokerage E*Trade has launched E*Trade-branded Web sites outside North America, initially forming licensing agreements and launching sites in Australia, New Zealand, France, and Scandinavia. In addition, E*Trade established joint ventures and launched Web sites in both the United Kingdom and Japan.[20]

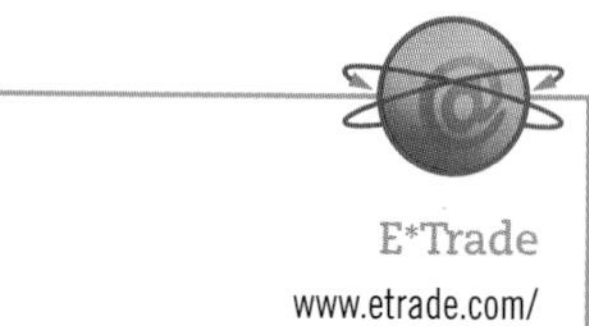

E*Trade
www.etrade.com/

Licensing has potential disadvantages, however. The firm has less control over the licensee than it would over its own production facilities. If the licensee is very successful, the firm has given up these profits, and if and when the contract ends, it may find it has created a competitor.

Contract Manufacturing

Contract manufacturing
A joint venture in which a company contracts with manufacturers in a foreign market to produce the product.

With **contract manufacturing,** the company contracts with manufacturers in the foreign market to produce its product or provide its service. Sears used this method in opening up department stores in Mexico and Spain, where it found qualified local manufacturers to produce many of the products it sells. The drawbacks of contract manufacturing are the decreased control over the manufacturing process and the loss of potential profits on manufacturing. The benefits are the chance to start faster, with less risk, and the later opportunity either to form a partnership with or to buy out the local manufacturer.

Management Contracting

Management contracting
A joint venture in which the domestic firm supplies the management know-how to a foreign company that supplies the capital; the domestic firm exports management services rather than products.

Under **management contracting,** the domestic firm supplies management know-how to a foreign company that supplies the capital. The domestic firm exports management services rather than products. Canada's 2000 trade mission to Russia resulted in a number of management contracts including the $220-million deal signed between Moscow-based Aeroflot and Montreal-based engineering giant SNC-Lavalin to build a rapid transit system linking Sheremetyevo Airport with downtown Moscow.[21]

Management contracting is a low-risk method of getting into a foreign market, and it yields income from the beginning. The arrangement is even more attractive if the contracting firm has an option to buy some share in the managed company later on. The arrangement is not sensible, however, if the company can put its scarce management talent to better uses or if it can make greater profits by undertaking the whole venture. Management contracting also prevents the company from setting up its own operations for a period of time.

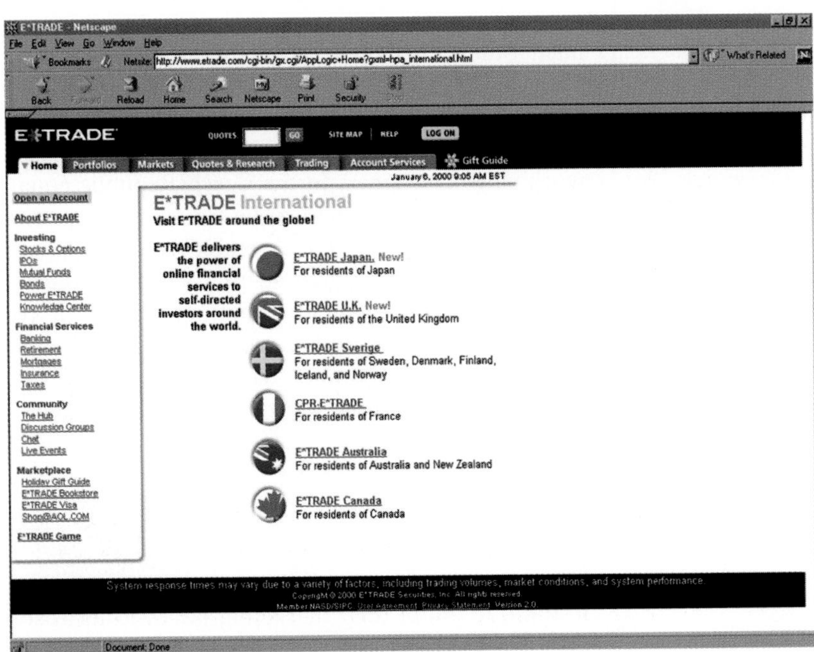

Online brokerage E*TRADE used licensing agreements to launch sites in Australia, New Zealand, France, and Scandinavia.

Joint Ownership

Joint ownership
A joint venture in which a company joins investors in a foreign market to create a local business in which the company shares joint ownership and control.

Joint ownership ventures consist of one company joining forces with foreign investors to create a local business in which they share ownership and control. A company can buy an interest in a local firm, or the two parties can form a new business venture. Magna International, the Canadian auto parts manufacturer, acquired much of UK firm Marley PLC to expand its business into the European Union.[22] Joint ownership may be needed for economic or political reasons. The firm may lack the financial, physical, or managerial resources to undertake the venture alone, or a foreign government may require joint ownership as a condition for entry.

Joint ownership has drawbacks. The partners may disagree over investment, marketing, or other policies. Whereas many Canadian firms like to reinvest earnings for growth, local firms often like to take out these earnings; whereas Canadian firms emphasize the role of marketing, local investors may rely on selling.

Direct Investment

Direct investment
Entering a foreign market by developing foreign-based assembly or manufacturing facilities.

The greatest involvement in a foreign market comes through **direct investment**—the development of foreign-based assembly or manufacturing facilities. If a company has gained experience in exporting and if the foreign market is large enough, foreign production facilities offer many advantages. The firm may have lower costs in the form of cheaper labour or raw materials, foreign government investment incentives, and freight savings. The firm may improve its image in the host country because it creates jobs. Generally, a firm develops a deeper relationship with government, customers, local suppliers, and distributors, allowing it to better adapt its products to the local market. Finally, the firm keeps full control over the investment and can, therefore, develop manufacturing and marketing policies that serve its long-term international objectives.

Bata Shoes
www.bata.com/

The main disadvantage of direct investment is the many risks—restricted or devalued currencies, falling markets, or government takeovers. In some cases, a firm has no choice but to accept these risks if it wants to operate in the host country. These lessons were only too clear when Toronto-based Bata Shoes decided to return to its Czech homeland and begin operations through the route of direct investment. The route, however, wasn't an easy one. Negotiations with government officials to re-establish the family shoe business took years of wrangling. Legal and political hurdles represented only half the battle, as marketing manager Jeanne Milne quickly learned. She faced problems ranging from lack of customer research to redesigning window displays. She discovered that offering sales didn't work since consumers in the Czech Republic equate discounts with inferior quality. Service providers had to be trained since providing service had become a foreign concept. As one Czech employee complained, "Why should I smile at customers? They don't smile at me." Even customers had to be re-educated. When employees went to the stockroom to search for correct sizes, customers followed them, believing that shoe clerks were going elsewhere to avoid serving them. The struggle has been worth it. Bata is held up as an exemplar of one of the few truly successful privatization efforts in Eastern Europe.

Deciding on the Global Marketing Program

Companies that operate in one or more foreign markets must decide how much, if at all, to adapt their marketing mixes to local conditions. At one extreme, some global companies use a **standardized marketing mix,** primarily selling the same

Standardized marketing mix
An international marketing strategy for using basically the same product, advertising, distribution channels, and other elements of the marketing mix in all of the company's international markets.

Adapted marketing mix
An international marketing strategy for adjusting the marketing mix elements to each international target market, bearing more costs but hoping for a larger market share and return.

products and using the same marketing approaches worldwide. At the other extreme, some companies use an **adapted marketing mix,** adjusting the marketing mix elements to each target market, bearing more costs but hoping for a larger market share and return.

How does a firm choose whether to adapt or standardize the marketing mix? The marketing concept holds that marketing programs will be more effective if tailored to the unique needs of each targeted customer group. If this concept applies within a country, it should apply even more in international markets. Consumers in different countries have widely varied cultural backgrounds, needs and wants, spending power, product preferences, and shopping patterns. Because these differences are hard to change, most marketers adapt their products, prices, channels, and promotions to fit consumer desires in each country.

However, some global marketers are bothered by what they see as too much adaptation, which raises costs and dilutes global brand power. As a result, many companies have created so-called world brands—more or less the same product sold the same way to all consumers worldwide. Marketers at these companies believe that advances in communication, transportation, and travel are turning the world into a common marketplace. These marketers claim that people around the world want basically the same products and lifestyles. Despite what consumers say they want, all consumers want good products at lower prices.

Such arguments ring true. The development of the Internet, the rapid spread of cable and satellite television around the world, and the creation of telecommunications networks linking previously remote places have all made the world a smaller place. American TV programming beamed into homes in the developing world has sparked a convergence of consumer appetites, particularly among youth. One economist calls these emerging consumers the "global MTV generation": "They prefer Coke to tea, Nikes to sandals, Chicken McNuggets to rice, and credit cards to cash," he says.[23] Fashion trends spread almost instantly, propelled by TV and Internet chat groups. Around the world, news and comment on almost any topic or product is available at the click of a mouse or twist of a dial. The resulting convergence of needs and wants has created global markets for standardized products, particularly among the young middle class.

Proponents of global standardization claim that international marketers should adapt products and marketing programs only when local wants cannot be changed or avoided. Standardization results in lower production, distribution, marketing, and management costs, and thus lets the company offer consumers higher quality and more reliable products at lower prices. In fact, some companies have successfully marketed global products formats—for example, Coca-Cola soft drinks, McDonald's hamburgers, Black & Decker tools, and Sony Walkmans.

However, even for these "global" brands, companies make some adaptations. Moreover, the assertion that global standardization leads to lower costs and prices, causing more goods to be snapped up by price-sensitive consumers, is questionable. Consider these cases in which the incremental revenues from adapting products far exceeded the incremental costs:[24]

- Mattel Toys had sold its Barbie doll successfully in dozens of countries without modification. But in Japan, it did not sell well. Takara, Mattel's Japanese licensee, surveyed eighth-grade Japanese girls and their parents and found that they thought the doll's breasts were too big and that its legs were too long. Mattel, however, was reluctant to modify the doll because this would require additional production, packaging, and advertising costs. Finally, Takara won out, and Mattel made a special Japanese Barbie. Within two years, Takara had sold over two million of the modified dolls.

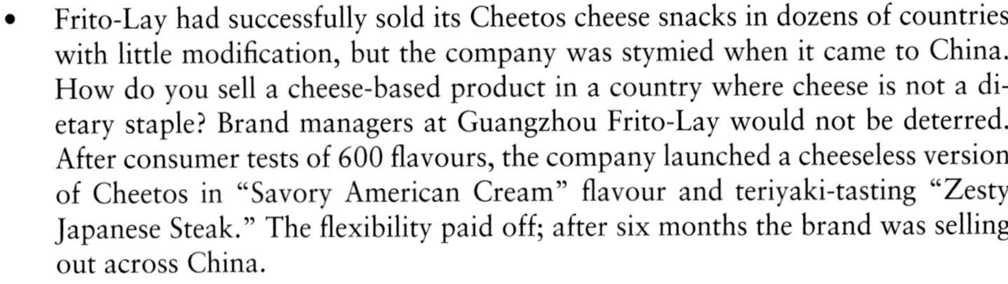

- Frito-Lay had successfully sold its Cheetos cheese snacks in dozens of countries with little modification, but the company was stymied when it came to China. How do you sell a cheese-based product in a country where cheese is not a dietary staple? Brand managers at Guangzhou Frito-Lay would not be deterred. After consumer tests of 600 flavours, the company launched a cheeseless version of Cheetos in "Savory American Cream" flavour and teriyaki-tasting "Zesty Japanese Steak." The flexibility paid off; after six months the brand was selling out across China.

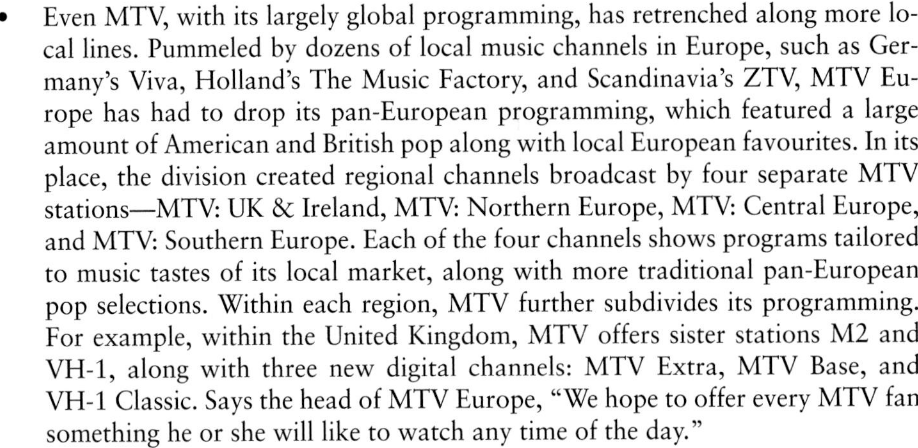

- Even MTV, with its largely global programming, has retrenched along more local lines. Pummeled by dozens of local music channels in Europe, such as Germany's Viva, Holland's The Music Factory, and Scandinavia's ZTV, MTV Europe has had to drop its pan-European programming, which featured a large amount of American and British pop along with local European favourites. In its place, the division created regional channels broadcast by four separate MTV stations—MTV: UK & Ireland, MTV: Northern Europe, MTV: Central Europe, and MTV: Southern Europe. Each of the four channels shows programs tailored to music tastes of its local market, along with more traditional pan-European pop selections. Within each region, MTV further subdivides its programming. For example, within the United Kingdom, MTV offers sister stations M2 and VH-1, along with three new digital channels: MTV Extra, MTV Base, and VH-1 Classic. Says the head of MTV Europe, "We hope to offer every MTV fan something he or she will like to watch any time of the day."

MTV Europe
www.mtveurope.com/

So which approach is best—global standardization or adaptation? Clearly, global standardization is not an all-or-nothing proposition but rather a matter of degree. Companies should look for more standardization to help keep down costs and prices and to build greater global brand power. But they must not replace long-run marketing thinking with short-run financial thinking. Although standardization saves money, marketers must make certain that they offer what consumers in each country want.[25]

Many possibilities exist between the extremes of standardization and complete adaptation. For example, although Whirlpool ovens, refrigerators, clothes washers, and other major appliances share the same interiors worldwide, their outer styling and features are designed to meet the preferences of consumers in different countries. Coca-Cola sells virtually the same Coke beverage worldwide and pulls advertisements for specific markets from a common pool of ads designed to have cross-cultural appeal. However, Coca-Cola is less sweet or less carbonated in some countries. The company also sells a variety of other beverages created specifically for the taste buds of local markets and modifies its distribution channels according to local conditions.

Similarly, McDonald's uses the same basic operating formula in its restaurants around the world but adapts its menu to local tastes. For example, it uses chili sauce instead of ketchup on its hamburgers in Mexico. In India, where cows are considered sacred, McDonald's serves chicken, fish, vegetable burgers, and the Maharaja Mac—two all-mutton patties, special sauce, lettuce, cheese, pickles, onions on a sesame-seed bun. In Vienna, its restaurants include "McCafes," which offer coffee blended to local tastes, and in Korea, it sells roast pork on a bun with a garlicky soy sauce.[26]

Some international marketers suggest that companies should "think globally but act locally." They advocate a "glocal" strategy in which the firm standardizes certain core marketing elements and localizes others.[27] The corporate level gives strategic direction; local units focus on the individual consumer differences. They conclude: global marketing, yes; global standardization, not necessarily.

Product

Figure 17-3 shows the five strategies for adapting products and promotions to a foreign market.[28] We first discuss the three product strategies and then turn to the two promotion strategies.

Straight product extension
Marketing a product in a foreign market without any change.

Straight product extension is marketing a product in a foreign market without any change. Top management tells its marketing people: "Take the product as is and find customers for it." The first step, however, should be to find out whether foreign consumers use that product and what form they prefer.

Straight extension has been successful in some cases and disastrous in others. Coca-Cola, Kellogg cereals, Heineken beer, and Black & Decker tools are all sold successfully in about the same form around the world. But General Foods introduced its standard powdered Jell-O in the British market only to find that British consumers prefer a solid-wafer or cake form. Straight extension is tempting because it involves no additional product development costs, manufacturing changes, or new promotion. But it can be costly in the long run if products fail to satisfy foreign consumers.

Product adaptation
Adapting a product to meet local conditions or wants in foreign markets.

Product adaptation involves changing the product to meet local conditions or wants. For example, Procter & Gamble's Vidal Sassoon shampoos contain a single fragrance worldwide, but the amount of scent varies by country—less in Japan, where subtle scents are preferred, and more in Europe. General Foods blends different coffees for the British (who drink their coffee with milk), the French (who drink their coffee black), and Latin Americans (who prefer a chicory taste). In Japan, Mister Donut serves coffee in smaller and lighter cups that better fit the hands of the average Japanese consumer; even the doughnuts are a little smaller. Gerber serves the Japanese baby food fare that might turn the stomachs of many Western consumers: Local favourites include flounder and spinach stew, cod roe spaghetti, mugwort casserole, and sardines ground up in white radish sauce. In Brazil, Levi Strauss developed its Femina jeans featuring curvaceous cuts that provide the ultratight fit traditionally preferred by Brazilian women. Finnish cellular phone superstar Nokia customized its 6100 series phone for every major market. Developers built in rudimentary voice recognition for Asia where keyboards are a problem and raised the ring volume so the phone could be heard on crowded Asian streets.[29]

In some instances, products must also be adapted to local superstitions or spiritual beliefs. In Asia, the supernatural world often relates directly to sales. Hyatt Hotels' experience with feng shui is a good example:[30]

> A practice widely followed in China, Hong Kong, and Singapore (and which has spread to Japan, Vietnam, and Korea), feng shui means "wind and water." Practitioners of feng shui, or geomancers, will recommend the most favourable conditions for any venture, particularly the placement of office buildings and the arrangement of desks, doors, and other items within. To have good feng shui, a building should face the water and be flanked by mountains. However, it should not block the view of the mountain spirits. The Hyatt Hotel in Singapore was designed

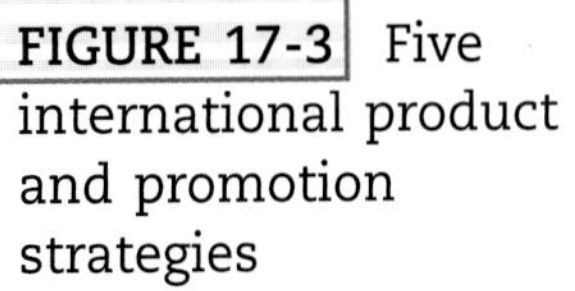

FIGURE 17-3 Five international product and promotion strategies

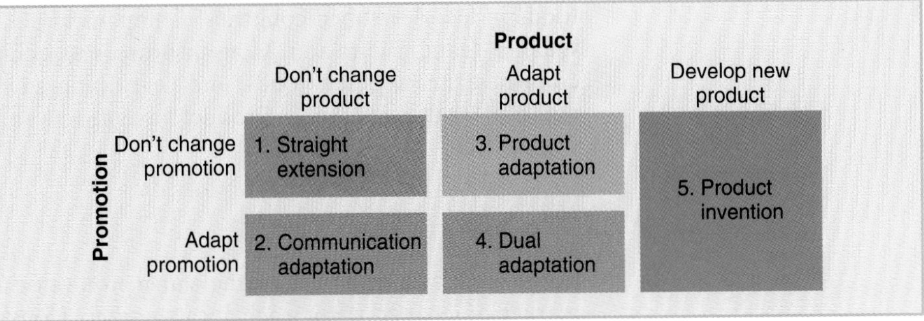

"I'LL BE BACK AT 2:00, I'M JUST TAKING THE CLIENT OUT TO LUNCH."
NOKIA 8890 | ONE PHONE FOR ONE WORLD
The world just got smaller thanks to the new Nokia 8890 – the only world phone you'll ever need in North America, or anywhere else for that matter. Cast in metal, the 8890 features: GSM worldwide coverage, infrared connection between phones/printers/data devices, voice dialing, picture messaging, and the ability to send your business card. Altogether, the Nokia 8890 keeps you in control no matter where you are. 1-800-OK NOKIA www.nokia.ca
NOKIA
CONNECTING PEOPLE

Nokia positions its 8890 as the only phone international businesspeople need: "One phone for one world."

without feng shui in mind and, as a result, had to be redesigned to boost business. Originally the front desk was parallel to the doors and road, and this was thought to lead to wealth flowing out. Furthermore, the doors were facing northwest, which easily let undesirable spirits in. The geomancer recommended design alterations so that wealth could be retained and undesirable spirits kept out.

Product invention Creating new products or services for foreign markets.

The **product invention** strategy, creating something new for the foreign market, can take two forms. It may mean reintroducing earlier product forms that happen to be well adapted to the needs of a given country. For example, the National Cash Register Company reintroduced its crank-operated cash register at half the price of a modern cash register and sold large numbers in Asia, Latin America, and Spain. Or a company can create a new product to meet a need in another country. For example, an enormous need exists for low-cost, high-protein foods in less developed countries. Companies such as Maple Leaf Foods, McCain, Quaker Oats, Swift, and Monsanto are researching the nutrition needs of these countries, creating new foods, and developing advertising campaigns to gain product trial and acceptance. Product invention can be costly, but the payoffs are worthwhile.

Promotion

Companies can either adopt the same promotion strategy they use in their home market or change it for each local market. Consider advertising messages: Some global companies use a standardized advertising theme around the world. For example, to help communicate its global reach, IBM Global Services runs virtually identical "People Who Think. People Who Do. People Who Get It." ads in dozens of countries around the world. However, even in highly standardized promotion campaigns, some small changes may be required to adjust for language and minor cultural differences. For instance, when Heinz Pet Food introduced its 9 Lives cat food in Russia, it used its standardized advertising featuring Morris the Cat. It turns out, however, that Morris needed a makeover. Russian consumers prefer a fatter-looking spokeskitty—it's considered healthier—so Heinz put a beefier Morris on the package.[31]

Companies must also change colours sometimes to avoid taboos in some countries: Purple is associated with death in most of Latin America; white is a mourning colour in Japan; and green is associated with jungle sickness in Malaysia. Even names must be changed: In Sweden, Helene Curtis changed the name of its Every Night Shampoo to Every Day because Swedes usually wash their hair in the morning; Kellogg had to rename Bran Buds cereal in Sweden, where the name roughly translates as "burned farmer." See Marketing Highlight 17-4 for more on language blunders in international marketing.

Communication adaptation
A global communication strategy of fully adapting advertising messages to local markets.

Other companies follow a strategy of **communication adaptation,** fully adapting their advertising messages to local markets. Kellogg ads in North America promote the taste and nutrition of Kellogg's cereals over competitors' brands. In France, where consumers drink little milk and eat little for breakfast, Kellogg's ads must convince consumers that cereals are a tasty and healthful breakfast.

To help communicate its global reach, IBM Global Services runs virtually identical ads in dozens of countries around the world on the theme: "People Who Think. People Who Do. People Who Get It." These ads ran in Canada and the UK.

Media also need to be adapted internationally because their availability varies from country to country. Television advertising time is very limited in Europe, for instance, ranging from four hours a day in France to none in Scandinavian countries. Advertisers must buy time months in advance, and they have little control over airtimes. Magazines also vary in effectiveness. For example, magazines are a major medium in Italy and a minor one in Austria. Newspapers are national in the United Kingdom but are only local in Spain.

The Institute of Canadian Advertising, which represents most of Canada's major agencies, launched a 1997 marketing initiative aimed at achieving better recognition of the strong track record and worldwide capabilities of Canadian agencies. In an effort that integrated public relations, ads in trade publications, direct marketing, a Web site (www.goodmedia.com/ica), and the 126-page book *Canadian Advertising, Push the Boundaries,* the institute worked to convey the message that Canadian-produced advertising travels well beyond Canada's borders. The campaign featured work done by Canadian agencies such as a promotion for Visa ads that helped to reinforce the leadership position of the card in Canada and South America.[32]

Price

Companies face many problems in setting their international prices. For example, how might Black & Decker price its power tools globally? It could set a uniform price all around the world, but this amount would be too high a price in poor countries and not high enough in rich ones. It could charge what consumers in each country would bear, but this strategy ignores differences in the actual costs from country to country. Finally, the company could use a standard markup of its costs everywhere, but this approach might price Black & Decker out of the market in some countries where costs are high.

Feathercraft
www.feathercraft.com/

Regardless of how companies go about pricing their products, their foreign prices probably will be higher than their domestic prices. Makers of Feathercraft kayaks discovered the problem of price escalation as they market in Japan. Even though the kayaks cost the Japanese consumer twice as much as they do Canadian purchasers, the firm makes its lowest margins on Japanese sales. The problem results from Japan's multi-level distribution system. A kayak may have to pass through five intermediaries before reaching the consumer, and each intermediary gets a cut of the price pie.

Another problem involves setting a price for goods that a company ships to its foreign subsidiaries. If the company charges a foreign subsidiary too much, it may end up paying higher tariff duties even while paying lower income taxes in that country. If the company charges its subsidiary too little, it can be charged with *dumping*—charging less than the good costs or less than it charges in its home market. Harley-Davidson accused Honda and Kawasaki of dumping motorcycles on the US market.[33] Canadian farmers have been charged with dumping wheat on the US market. The U.S. International Trade Commission also ruled recently that Japan was dumping computer memory chips in the United States and laid stiff duties on future imports. Various governments are always watching for dumping abuses, and often force companies to set the price charged by other competitors for the same or similar products.

Canadian advertisers have produced award-winning ads that have successfully promoted products and services around the world.

Recent economic and technological forces have had an impact on global pricing. In the European Union, the transition by 11 countries to a single currency, the euro, will certainly reduce the amount of price differentiation. In 1998, for instance, a bottle of Gatorade cost 3.5 European currency units (ECU) in Germany but only about 0.9 in Spain. Once consumers recognize price differentiation by country, com-

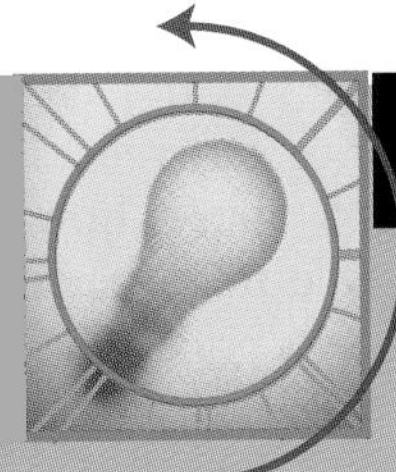

marketing highlight 17-4

Watch Your Language!

Many global companies have had difficulty crossing the language barrier, with results ranging from mild embarrassment to outright failure. Seemingly innocuous brand names and advertising phrases can take on unintended meanings when translated into other languages. Careless translations can make a marketer look foolish to foreign consumers.

We've all run across examples when buying products from other countries. Here's one from a firm in Taiwan attempting to instruct children on how to install a ramp on a garage for toy cars: "Before you play with, fix waiting plate by yourself as per below diagram. But after you once fixed it, you can play with as is and no necessary to fix off again." Many North American firms are guilty of similar atrocities when marketing abroad.

The classic language blunders involve standardized brand names that do not translate well. When Coca-Cola first marketed Coke in China in the 1920s, it developed a group of Chinese characters that, when pronounced, sounded like the product name. Unfortunately, the characters actually translated to mean "bite the wax tadpole." Now, the characters on Chinese Coke bottles translate as "happiness in the mouth." When the Allies dropped food packages into war-torn Germany after the Second World War, no one opened them since they were labelled "gift," a word that means poison in German.

Several carmakers have had similar problems when their brand names crashed into the language barrier. Chevy's Nova translated into Spanish as no va—"it doesn't go." GM changed the name to Caribe, and sales increased. Ford introduced its Fiera truck only to discover that the name means "ugly old woman" in Spanish. Rolls-Royce avoided the name Silver Mist in German markets, where mist means "manure." Sunbeam, however, entered the German market with its Mist Stick hair curling iron: As should have been anticipated, the Germans avoided the "manure wand." A similar fate awaited Colgate when it introduced a toothpaste in France called Cue, the name of a notorious porno magazine.

One well-intentioned firm sold its shampoo in Brazil under the name Evitol. It soon realized it was claiming to sell a "dandruff contraceptive." An American company reportedly had trouble marketing Pet milk in French-speaking areas. It seems that the word pet in French means, among other things, "to break wind." Hunt-Wesson introduced its Big John products in Quebec as Gros Jos before learning that it means "big breasts" in French. This gaffe had no apparent effect on sales. Interbrand of London, the firm that created such household names as Prozac and Acura, recently developed a brand name "hall of shame" list, which contained these and other foreign brand names you're never likely to see inside the local supermarket: Krapp toilet paper (Denmark), Crapsy Fruit cereal (France), Happy End toilet paper (Germany), Mukk yogurt (Italy), Zit lemonade (Germany), Poo curry powder (Argentina), and Pschitt lemonade (France).

Travellers often encounter well-intentioned advice from service firms that takes on meanings very different from those intended. The menu in one Swiss restaurant proudly stated: "Our wines leave you nothing to hope for." Signs in a Japanese hotel pronounced: "You are invited to take advantage of the chambermaid." At a laundry in Rome, it was: "Ladies, leave your clothes here and spend the afternoon having a good time." The brochure at a Tokyo car rental offered this sage advice: "When passenger of foot heave in sight, tootle the horn. Trumpet him melodiously at first, but if he still obstacles your passage, tootle him with vigor."

Advertising themes often lose—or gain—something in the translation. The Coors beer slogan "Get loose with Coors" in Spanish came out as "Get the runs with Coors." Coca-Cola's "Coke adds life" theme in Japanese translated into "Coke brings your ancestors back from the dead." In Chinese, the KFC slogan "finger-lickin' good" came out as "eat your fingers off." Frank Perdue's classic line, "It takes a tough man to make a tender chicken," took on added meaning in Spanish: "It takes a sexually stimulated man to make a chicken affectionate." Even when the language is the same, word usage may differ from country to country. Thus, the British ad line for Electrolux vacuum cleaners—"Nothing sucks like an Electrolux"—would capture few customers in Canada or the United States.

Sources: See David A. Ricks, "Products that crashed into the language barrier," *Business and Society Review,* Spring 1983:46–50; David A. Ricks, "Perspectives: Translation blunders in international business," *Journal of Language for International Business* 7(2), 1996:50–5; David W. Helin, "When slogans go wrong," *American Demographics,* February 1992:14; "But will it sell in Tulsa," *Newsweek,* 17 March 1997:8; "What you didn't learn in Marketing 101," *Sales & Marketing Management,* May 1997:20; Ken Friedenreich, "The lingua too franca," *World Trade,* April 1998:98; and Richard P. Carpenter, "What they meant to say was . . ." *Boston Globe,* 2 August 1998:M6.

panies will be forced to harmonize prices throughout the countries that have adopted the single currency. The Internet will also make global price differences more obvious. When firms sell their wares over the Internet, customers can see how much products sell for in different countries. They may even be able to order a product directly from the company location or dealer offering the lowest price. This will force companies toward more standardized international pricing.[34]

Distribution Channels

Whole-channel view Designing international channels that take into account all the necessary links in distributing the seller's products to final buyers, including the seller's headquarters organization, channels between nations, and channels within nations.

The international company must take a **whole-channel view** of distributing products to final consumers. Figure 17-4 shows the three major links between the seller and the final buyer. The first link, the *seller's headquarters organization,* supervises the channels and is part of the channel itself. The second link, *channels between nations,* moves the products to the borders of the foreign nations. The third link, *channels within nations,* moves the products from their foreign entry point to the final consumers. Some North American manufacturers may think their job is done once the product leaves their hands, but they would do well to pay attention to its handling within foreign countries.

Channels of distribution within countries vary greatly from nation to nation. First, there are the large differences in the *numbers and types of intermediaries* serving each foreign market. For example, a Canadian company marketing in China must operate through a frustrating maze of state-controlled wholesalers and retailers. Chinese distributors often carry competitors' products and frequently refuse to share even basic sales and marketing information with their suppliers. Hustling for sales is an alien concept to Chinese distributors, who are used to selling all they can obtain. Working with or getting around this system sometimes requires substantial time and investment.

Another difference lies in the *size and character of retail units* abroad. Whereas large-scale retail chains dominate in North America, much retailing in other countries is done by many small independent retailers. In India, millions of retailers operate tiny shops or sell in open markets. Their markups are high, but the actual price is lowered through price haggling. Supermarkets could offer lower prices, but supermarkets are difficult to build and open because of many economic and cultural barriers. Incomes are low, and people who lack refrigeration prefer to shop daily for small amounts rather than weekly for large amounts. Packaging is not well developed because it would add too much to the cost. These factors have kept large-scale retailing from spreading rapidly in developing countries.

Deciding on the Global Marketing Organization

Companies can manage their international marketing activities in at least three different ways. Most companies first organize an export department, then create an international division, and finally become a global organization.

A firm normally gets into international marketing by simply shipping out its goods. If its international sales expand, the company organizes an *export depart-*

FIGURE 17-4 Whole-channel concept for international marketing

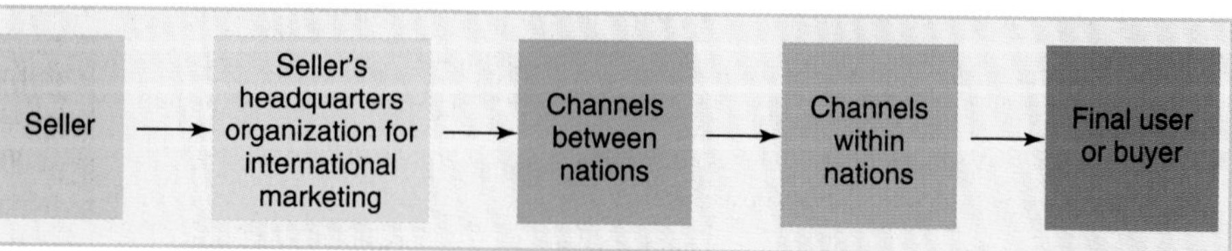

ment with a sales manager and a few assistants. As sales increase, the export department then can expand to include various marketing services so that it can actively pursue business. If the firm moves into joint ventures or direct investment, the export department will no longer be adequate.

Many companies become involved in several international markets and ventures. A company can export to one country, license to another, have a joint ownership venture in a third, and own a subsidiary in a fourth. Sooner or later, it will create an *international division* or subsidiary to handle all of its international activity.

International divisions can be organized in several ways. The international division's corporate staff consists of marketing, manufacturing, research, finance, planning, and personnel specialists. They plan for and provide services to various operating units, which can be organized in one of three ways. They can be *geographical organizations,* with country managers who are responsible for salespeople, sales branches, distributors, and licensees in their respective countries. Or the operating units can be *world product groups,* each responsible for worldwide sales of different product groups. Finally, operating units can be *international subsidiaries*, each responsible for its own sales and profits.

Several firms have passed beyond the international division stage and become truly *global organizations*. They stop thinking of themselves as national marketers who sell abroad and start thinking of themselves as global marketers. The top corporate management and staff plan worldwide manufacturing facilities, marketing policies, financial flows, and logistical systems. The global operating units report directly to the chief executive or executive committee of the organization, not to the head of an international division. Executives are trained in worldwide operations, not just domestic *or* international. The company recruits management from many countries, buys components and supplies where they cost the least, and invests where the expected returns are greatest.

Consider the history of Nortel Networks, Canada's premium high-tech manufacturer. In the early 1970s, it sold most of its production to another member of the BCE family, Bell Canada. By the 1980s, with its state-of-the-art digital switching technology, it was making over 50 percent of its sales to the United States, and five percent to other world markets. By 1994, however, 32 percent of Nortel's $8.9 billion in revenue came from global markets. Today, it operates in over 100 countries and has offices and facilities in Canada, Europe, Asia-Pacific, the Caribbean and Latin America, the Middle East, Africa, and the United States. It employs over 70 000 people worldwide.

In the twenty-first century, major companies must become more global if they hope to compete. As foreign companies successfully invade their domestic markets, companies must move more aggressively into foreign markets. They will have to change from companies that treat their international operations as secondary concerns to companies that view the entire world as a single borderless market.[35]

Review of Concept Connections

North American companies used to pay little attention to international trade. If they could pick up some extra sales through exporting, that was fine. But the big market was at home, and it teemed with opportunities. Companies today can no longer afford to focus only on their domestic market, regardless of its size. Many industries are global, and firms that operate globally achieve lower costs and higher brand awareness. At the same time, global marketing is risky because of variable exchange rates, unstable governments, protectionist tariffs and trade barriers, and several other factors. Given the potential gains and risks of international marketing, companies need a systematic way to make their international marketing decisions.

1. Discuss how the international trade system, economic, politico-legal, and cultural environments affect a company's international marketing decisions.

A company must understand the global marketing environment, especially the international trade system. It must assess each foreign market's economic, politico-legal, and cultural characteristics. The company must then decide on the volume of international sales it wants, how many countries it wants to market in, and which specific markets it wants to enter. This last decision calls for weighing the probable rate of return on investment against the level of risk.

2. Describe three key approaches to entering international markets.

The company must decide how to enter each chosen market—whether through exporting, joint venturing, or direct investment. Many companies start as exporters, move to joint ventures, and finally make a direct investment in foreign markets. In exporting, the company enters a foreign market by sending and selling products through international marketing intermediaries (indirect exporting) or the company's own department, branch, or sales representative or agent (direct exporting). When establishing a joint venture, a company enters foreign markets by joining with foreign companies to produce or market a product or service. In licensing, the company enters a foreign market by contracting with a licensee in the foreign market, offering the right to use a manufacturing process, trademark, patent, trade secret, or other item of value for a fee or royalty.

3. Explain how companies adapt their marketing mixes for international markets.

Companies must decide how much their products, promotion, price, and channels should be adapted for each foreign market. At one extreme, some global companies use a standardized marketing mix worldwide. At the other, some use an adapted marketing mix, in which they adjust the marketing mix to each target market, bearing more costs but hoping for a larger market share and return.

4. Identify the three major forms of international marketing organization.

The company must develop an effective organization for international marketing. Most firms start with an export department and graduate to an international division. A few become global organizations, with worldwide marketing planned and managed by the top officers of the company. Global organizations view the entire world as a single, borderless market.

Key Terms

Adapted marketing mix *(p. 725)*
Communication adaptation *(p. 729)*
Contract manufacturing *(p. 723)*
Countertrade *(p. 715)*
Direct investment *(p. 724)*
Economic community *(p. 709)*
Embargo *(p. 708)*
Exchange controls *(p. 708)*
Exporting *(p. 722)*
Global firm *(p. 706)*
Global industry *(p. 706)*
Joint ownership *(p. 724)*
Joint venturing *(p. 722)*
Licensing *(p. 722)*
Management contracting *(p. 723)*
Non-tariff trade barriers *(p. 708)*
Product adaptation *(p. 727)*
Product invention *(p. 728)*
Quota *(p. 708)*
Standardized marketing mix *(p. 724)*
Straight product extension *(p. 727)*
Tariff *(p. 708)*
Whole-channel view *(p. 732)*

Discussing the Issues

1. With faster communication, transportation, and financial flows, the world is shrinking rapidly. The terms *global industry* and *global firm* are becoming more common. Define these terms and provide an example of each. Explain your examples.
2. When exporting goods to another country, a marketer may face various trade restrictions. Discuss the effects that each of these restrictions can have on an exporter's marketing mix: (a) tariffs, (b) quotas, and (c) embargoes.

3. What is a free trade zone? What have been the positive and negative benefits of NAFTA to each of its member nations? Why have trade unions been against NAFTA? How could General Motors use NAFTA to build and market better vehicles?
4. A country's industrial structure shapes its product and service needs, income levels, and employment levels. Discuss examples of countries exhibiting each of the four major types of industrial structures.
5. With all of the problems facing companies that "go global," explain why so many companies are choosing to expand internationally. What are the advantages of expanding beyond the domestic market?
6. Before going abroad, a company should define its international marketing objectives, policies, and modes of entry. Assume that you are a product manager for Nike. Outline a plan for expanding your operations and marketing efforts into Africa.
7. Once a company has decided to sell in a foreign country, it must determine the best mode of entry. Assume that you are the marketing manager for Mountain Dew and devise a plan for marketing your product in China. Pick a mode of entry, explain your marketing strategy, and comment on possible difficulties you might encounter.
8. Which type of international marketing organization would you suggest for the following companies: (a) Chapters.ca, (b) a European perfume manufacturer that plans to expand into the United States, and (c) DaimlerChrysler planning to sell its full line of products in the Middle East.

Marketing Applications

1. "Defend Our Forests—Clear-cut the WTO!" "WTO Breeds Greed." "WTO: Fix It or Nix It!" These statements were issued by protesters at the 1999 World Trade Organization talks in Seattle, Washington. The protests even led to riots, and the US National Guard was called to restore order. Why all the mobilization against globalization? It used to be that free trade and globalization talks involved mostly discussions about tariffs and quotas. Now the two equate with culture, sovereignty, and power. Trade talks were once held in smoke-filled rooms by diplomats. Today, they are conducted via television and the World Wide Web. The Seattle protesters feel damaged by globalization. They argue that globalization is about exploitation and environmental destruction. They feel that it will result in the assimilation of people, markets, and cultures into a more generic whole. For more information, visit the Centre for International Business Education and Research—Michigan State University (ciber.bus.msu.edu/busres.htm), the International Trade Association (www.ita.doc.gov), the CIA 1998 World Fact Book (www.odic.gov/cia/publications/factbook/index.html), the World Bank (www.worldbank.org), and the World Trade Organization (www.wto.org).
   a. What does the World Trade Organization attempt to do? Who are the member nations?
   b. Why were so many protesters against globalization at the WTO's Seattle conference? How should the WTO proceed in the face of such protests?
   c. Write a short position paper either defending or rejecting globalization.
   d. What are the ramifications of China joining the World Trade Organization?
2. Nowhere is international competition more apparent than in the digital camera market. Overnight, the advent of digital cameras has changed the way many photographers view their equipment. Digital cameras offer opportunities for reproduction and Internet viewing unmatched by more traditional products. However, the market is also uncharted, chaotic, and increasingly crowded, with more than 20 manufacturers worldwide. A recent entrant is film giant Fuji (www.fujifilm.com). As the world's number two producer, Fuji now plans to meet or beat Kodak (www.kodak.com), Sony (www.sony.com), Olympus (www.olympus.com), and Konica (www.konica.com) in digital camera products. Fuji introduced its first digital cameras in its own backyard—Japan, which is also a Sony stronghold. One factor motivating the move into digital cameras was its inability to erode Kodak's worldwide share of the film market. If the wave of the future turns out to be digital, Fuji plans to ride the wave's crest for as long as it can.

a. Analyze Fuji's strategy of entering the digital camera market. What challenges will Fuji most likely face? How can Fuji's traditional strengths in film aid its efforts in the new digital camera market?

b. What world markets should Fuji consider after Japan? Explain.

c. If you were the marketing manager of Fuji, what advertising strategy would you suggest for Fuji's new product venture? What distribution strategy?

d. What actions will Kodak, Olympus, Konica, and Sony probably take to counter Fuji's entry?

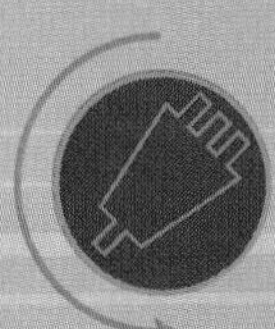

Internet Connections

"World Wide Web" Is Not a Misnomer

Canadian-based Web sites often offer different services and products in different markets. One fertile market for Canadian firms is Europe. Visit www.yahoo.co.uk and compare the services offered there with their Canadian-branch counterparts. Complete the following table.

Service	Offered by Yahoo! UK but not by Yahoo! Canada	Offered by Yahoo! Canada but not by Yahoo! UK

Now visit www.amazon.co.uk and complete a similar table.

Service	Offered by Amazon UK but not by Amazon US	Offered by Amazon US but not by Amazon UK

For Discussion

1. What is the size of the Canadian Internet market versus that of the UK? Visit Cyberatlas (cyberatlas.internet.com) or Nua (www.nua.ie) for help in answering this question.
2. What proportion of the Canadian population is online? The UK population?
3. How are the ads different on Yahoo!'s UK site?
4. What different search option is available on Yahoo!'s UK site?
5. Why do you think Amazon offers fewer services in the UK market?
6. Yahoo! provides free Internet access in the UK market. Why don't they do the same in the North American market? Hint: Research a company called FreeNet (www.freenet.com).

Savvy Sites

- The Department of Foreign Affairs and International Trade (www.dfait-maeci.gc.ca/menu-e.asp) is dedicated to assisting Canadian companies that compete globally.
- The CIA World Factbook (www.odci.gov/cia/publications/factbook), maintained by the Central Intelligence Agency, has economic and other information about most countries in the world.

Notes

1. Extracts and quotes from Ken Derrett, "NBA Canada grabs a rebound," *Marketing On-Line,* 22 February 1999; Stuart Foxman, "Sponsored supplement: The NBA in Canada: Celebrating Season II," *Strategy,* 6 January 1997:31; Marc Gunther, "They all want to be like Mike," *Fortune,* 21 July 1997:51–3: ©1997 Time, Inc.; and Warren Cohen, "Slam-dunk diplomacy," *U.S. News & World Report,* 8 June 1998:7. Also see Tracy Atkinson, "The teen fun zone," *Marketing On-Line,* 2 August 1999; Astrid Van Den Broek, "NBA deal shoots for higher ratings," *Marketing On-Line,* 10 April 2000; Stefan Fatsis, "NBA bravely plans for post-Jordan era," *Wall Street Journal,* 6 February 1998:B1; "NBA will face difficult recovery from lockout," *Greensboro News Record,* 24 December 1998:C2; Mark Hyman, "Another ruined season that wasn't," *Business Week,* 7 June 1999:40; David Bauder, "Mike takes the air out of NBA ratings," *Raleigh News & Observer,* 24 June 1999:E7; "Worldwide TV coverage of the 1999 NBA finals," accessed online at www.nba.com, September 1999; and Daniel Roth, "The NBA's next shot," *Fortune,* 21 February 2000:207–15.
2. "Trade and the Canadian Economy: Why Trade Matters," Department of Foreign Affairs and International Trade (www.dfait-maeci.gc.ca/tna-nac/text-e.asp).
3. Bruce Little, "Who exports Canada's goods to the world?" *Globe and Mail,* 29 January 2001:B10; Department of Foreign Affairs and International Trade, "Pettigrew announces finalists for 2000 Canada export awards," press release No. 172, 4 July 2000; "International Trade Minister Pettigrew—Talking trade," www.infoexport.gc.ca/canadexport/docs/active/view-e.asp?fn'vol.%2018,%20no%209"33-e.htm; John Alden, "What in the world drives UPS?" *International Business,* April 1998:6–7; Karen Pennar, "Two steps forward, one step back," *Business Week,* 31 August 1998:116; Michelle Wirth Fellman, "A new world for marketers," *Marketing News,* 10 May 1999:13.
4. Department of Foreign Affairs and International Trade, "1997 Canada exports awards," *Report on Business Magazine,* July 1997.
5. "The unique Japanese," *Fortune,* 24 November 1986:8. For more on non-tariff and other barriers, see Warren J. Keegan and Mark C. Green, *Principles of Global Marketing,* Upper Saddle River, NJ: Prentice Hall, 1997:200–3.
6. Douglas Harbrecht and Owen Ullmann, "Finally GATT may fly," *Business Week,* 29 December 1993:36–7; Ping Deng, "Impact of GATT Uruguay Round on various industries," *American Business Review,* June 1998:22–9. Also see Charles W. L. Hill, *International Business,* Chicago: Richard A. Irwin, 1997:165–8; "Special article: World trade: fifty years on," *The Economist,* 16 May 1998:21–3; and Helene Cooper, "The millennium—trade & commerce: trading blocks," *Wall Street Journal,* 11 January 1999:R50; www.wto.org/index.htm.
7. Stanley Reed, "We have liftoff! The strong launch of the euro is hailed around the world," *Business Week,* 18 January 1999: 34–7.
8. James Welsh, "Enter the euro," *World Trade,* January 1999: 34–8.
9. For more on the European Union, see "Around Europe in 40 years," *The Economist,* 31 May 1997:S4; "European Union to begin expansion," *New York Times,* 30 March 1998:A5; Joan Warner, "Mix us culturally? It's impossible," *Business Week,* 27 April 1998:108; Paul J. Deveney, "World watch," *Wall Street Journal,* 20 May 1999:A12; and www.dfait-maeci.gc.ca/english/geo/europe/EU/fact-eur.htm.
10. Alan Freeman, "Leaders aim for free trade at APEC forum," *Globe and Mail,* 12 November 1994:B3; "The Vancouver Summit," *Globe and Mail,* 19 November 1997:D1–4.
11. Larry Rohter, "Latin America and Europe to talk trade," *New York Times,* 26 June 1999:2.
12. Bruce Little, "Who exports Canada's goods to the world?" *Globe and Mail,* 29 January 2001:B10; Peter Vamos, "Fairmont Hotels puts on ad blitz," *Strategy,* 29 January 2001:6.
13. David Woodruff, "Ready to shop until they drop," *Business Week;* 22 June 1998:104–8.
14. For this and other examples, see Louis Kraar, "How to sell to cashless buyers," *Fortune,* 7 November 1988:147–54; Nathaniel Gilbert, "The case for countertrade," *Across the Board,* May 1992:43–5; Kwanena Anyane-Ntow and Santhi C. Harvey, "A countertrade primer," *Management Accounting (USA),* April 1995:47; Darren McDermott and S. Karen Witcher, "Bartering gains currency," *Wall Street Journal,* 6 April 1998:A10; and Anne Millen Porter, "Global economic meltdown boosts barter business," *Purchasing,* 11 February 1999:21–5.
15. Rebecca Piirto Heath, "Think globally," *Marketing Tools,* October 1996:49–54.
16. Adam Pletsch, "Vogue Pool products dives into Europe," *Maclean Hunter Publishing Limited,* 1999, www.plant.ca/Content/1999/990118/pla01189904.html.
17. Charles A. Coulombe, "Global expansion: The unstoppable crusade," *Success,* September 1994:18–20; "Amway hopes to set up sales network in India," *Wall Street Journal,* 17 February 1998:B8; Gerald S. Couzens, "Dick Devos," *Success,* November 1998:52–7.

18. See "Crest, Colgate bare teeth in competition for China," *Advertising Age International,* November 1996:I3; Mark L. Clifford, "How you can win in China," *Business Week,* 26 May 1997:66–8; and Ben Davies, "The biggest market retains its luster," *Asia Money,* January 1998:47–9.

19. Linda Grant, "GE's 'smart bomb' strategy," *Fortune,* 21 July 1997:109–10; Richard J. Babyak, "GE appliances: The polar approach," *Appliance Manufacturer,* February 1997:G22; Joe Jancsurak, "Asia to drive world appliance growth," *Appliance Manufacturer,* February 1999:G3–6.

20. Robert Neff, "In Japan, they're goofy about Disney," *Business Week,* 12 March 1990:64; "In brief: E*Trade licensing deal gives it an Israeli link," *American Banker,* 11 May 1998.

21. Department of Foreign Affairs And International Trade, "Pettigrew's trade mission to Russia continues to bear fruit: SNC-Lavalin signs deal with new Russian partner," news release, 18 December 2000.

22. Greg Keenan, "Magna buys U.K. business," *Globe and Mail,* 21 March 1996:B1.

23. Lawrence Donegan, "Heavy job rotation: MTV Europe sacks 80 employees in the name of 'regionalisation,'" *Guardian,* 21 November 1997:19.

24. Karen Benezra, "Fritos 'round the world," *Brandweek,* 27 March 1995:32,35; Cyndee Miller, "Chasing global dream," *Marketing News,* 2 December 1996:1,2; Christian Lorenz, "MTV Europe launches channels," *Billboard,* 27 February 1999:48.

25. See Theodore Levitt, "The globalization of markets," *Harvard Business Review,* May–June 1983:92–102; David M. Szymanski, Sundar G. Bharadwaj, and Rajan Varadarajan, "Standardization versus adaptation of international marketing strategy: An empirical investigation," *Journal of Marketing,* October 1993:1–17; Ashish Banerjee, "Global campaigns don't work; multinationals do," *Advertising Age,* 18 April 1994:23; Miller, "Chasing global dream"; Jeryl Whitelock and Carole Pimblett, "The standardization debate in international marketing," *Journal of Global Marketing,* 1997:22; and David A. Aaker and Ericj Joachimsthaler, "The lure of global branding," *Harvard Business Review,* November–December 1999:137–44.

26. See "In India, beef-free Mickie D," *Business Week,* 7 April 1995:52; Jeff Walters, "Have brand will travel," *Brandweek,* 6 October 1997:22–6; and David Barboza, "From abroad, McDonald's finds value in local control," *New York Times,* 12 February 1999:1.

27. See Martha M. Hamilton, "Going global: A world of difference," *Washington Post,* 10 May 1998:H1.

28. See Warren J. Keegan, *Global Marketing Management,* 4th ed., Upper Saddle River, NJ: Prentice Hall, 1989:378–81; and Keegan and Green, *Principles of Global Marketing*:294–8.

29. For these and other examples, see Andrew Kupfer, "How to be a global manager," *Fortune,* 14 March 1988:52–8; Maria Shao, "For Levi's: A flattering fit overseas," *Business Week,* 5 November 1990:76–7; Joseph Weber, "Campbell: Now it's m-m-global," *Business Week,* 15 March 1993:52–3; Zachary Schiller, "Make it simple," Business Week, 9 September 1996:102; Chester Dawson, "Gerber feeding booming Japanese baby food market," *Durham Herald-Sun,* 21 February 1998:C10; and Jack Neff, "Test it in Paris, France, launch it in Paris, Texas," *Advertising Age,* 31 May 1999:28.

30. J. S. Perry Hobson, "Feng shui: Its impacts on the Asian hospitality industry," *International Journal of Contemporary Hospitality Management* 6(6), 1994:21–6; Bernd H. Schmitt and Yigang Pan, "In Asia, the supernatural means sales," *New York Times,* 19 February 1995:3,11; Sally Taylor, "Tackling the curse of bad feng shui," *Publishers Weekly,* 27 April 1998:24.

31. Erika Rasmusson, "Global warning," *Sales & Marketing Management,* November 1998:17; Bradley Johnson, "IBM talks global clout, in foreign languages," *Advertising Age,* 7 June 1999:10.

32. "The showcase," *Marketing Magazine,* 20 October 1997:14–9.

33. See Michael Oneal, "Harley-Davidson: Ready to hit the road again," *Business Week,* 21 July 1986:70; and "EU proposes dumping change," *East European Markets,* 14 February 1997: 2–3.

34. Ram Charan, "The rules have changed," *Fortune,* 16 March 1998:159–62.

35. See Kenichi Ohmae, "Managing in a borderless world," *Harvard Business Review,* May–June 1989:152–61; William J. Holstein, "The stateless corporation," *Business Week,* 14 May 1990: 98–105; and John A. Byrne and Kathleen Kerwin, "Borderless management," *Business Week,* 23 May 1994:24–6.

Company Case 17

WAL-MART: PILING 'EM HIGH AND SELLING 'EM CHEAP ALL AROUND THE GLOBE!

The internal point of view: "Wal-Mart employees who do not think globally are working for the wrong company."—David Glass, chief executive, Wal-Mart

The external point of view: "Wal-Mart must think and act as if it's a global company. Otherwise, it can't grow enough in North America to maintain its stock price. It needs to be in South America. It needs to be in Asia. It needs to be in Europe."—George Rosenbaum, Leo J. Shapiro Associates

When a major retailer like Wal-Mart sets its mind and cash to global expansion, it's amazing what it can do. At the end of the 1980s, Wal-Mart was a mostly

US phenomenon; by the end of the 1990s, it was a global presence, poised to become the world's dominant retailer. From a base of about 2200 US stores and sales of less than $125 billion in the early 1990s, Wal-Mart expanded to more than 3600 stores worldwide, with sales of $205 billion and a net income of $6.64 billion. Not bad for a company that began its international expansion in 1993 with the purchase of 122 Woolco stores in Canada.

Spurred on by NAFTA, Wal-Mart quickly moved into Mexico using joint ventures to end the decade with more than 400 Mexican stores. In Hong Kong, through a joint venture with Ek Chor Distribution System Co. Ltd., Wal-Mart established several Value Clubs, which became stepping stones to mainland China, the most populous country in the world and a market with an emerging middle class. Because Ek Chor is actually owned by CP Pokphand of Bangkok, Wal-Mart also entered Thailand, and then Indonesia. In 1995, the retailing giant once again looked south, moving into South America with stores in Brazil, Argentina, and Chile.

Most of these countries appear to be good markets for Wal-Mart, as each constitutes a heavily populated emerging market. Although not high in discretionary income, each of these markets exhibits growing income, giving people more money to shop while still retaining their price sensitivity. Wal-Mart's inventory of discounted brand-name merchandise offers consumers in these markets the quality they desire at prices they can afford.

Initially, Wal-Mart's moves into emerging markets matched the expectations of industry analysts. Most experts predicted that Wal-Mart's next move would be into Eastern Europe, where the populace still sought discount prices rather than high-end goods. But in 1998, Wal-Mart confounded the experts by buying the 21-unit Wertkauf chain in Germany. In 1999, it purchased a second German retailer, the 74-unit Interspar hypermarkets chain. Within only one and a half years, Wal-Mart moved from having no presence in Germany to being the country's number four retailer.

Why was this move into Germany so surprising? The Germany countryside is littered with the carcasses of other retailers, such as Toys 'R' Us, which tried and failed to penetrate the market. Although Germany is the third largest market in the world (behind the United States and Japan), it is an especially tough market. First, zoning laws, scarcity of land, and high real estate prices make it almost impossible to find affordable space for new supercentres or hypermarkets. Second, German retailing is dominated by a few large chains, such as Metro, Rewe, and Edeka. As a result, the market is characterized by excessive price competition and extremely narrow margins—two percent or less.

Third, Germany has very strong unions, and German workers are among the most highly paid in the world. Wal-Mart will find it very difficult to make these workers gather early in the morning as they do in the United States to do the Wal-Mart cheer ("Give me a W! W! Give me an A! A!") Fourth, German laws governing retailing severely limit store hours. No retailers (except for bakeries and gas stations) are open on Sunday. And until recently, all stores closed at noon on Saturday (now, it's 4 p.m.) and stayed open late (until 8 p.m.) only one night a week—not an appealing policy for a company that keeps many of its North American stores open 24 hours a day.

Fifth, in attempting to apply the same low-price strategy in Europe as in North America, Wal-Mart would run afoul of some manufacturers' marketing strategies. For example, many clothing brands that are positioned more as commodities and sold in many stores at discount prices (such as Levis) are positioned as more high-end products in Europe. Thus, selling in Wal-Mart as a discount item would undercut such brands' positioning and damage international profits. Sixth, sales in Germany had been flat for the past four years, and no increases were expected given the country's high level of unemployment. Finally, consumers in Western Europe are considered to be more sophisticated and more demanding than North American consumers—not the kinds of buyers likely to be swayed by a greeter at the door who asks, "How are you today?" (or, rather, "Wie geht's?").

So, who was wrong here—Wal-Mart or the analysts? With so much seemingly going against it, how could Wal-Mart expect to be successful in Germany? What did it have to offer that established retailers didn't? The answer—service. In a country full of surly store clerks, sometimes described as having perfected "service with a snarl," customers might respond well to service with a smile. They might like to shop where their patronage is valued—where store clerks are trained when asked, "Who's number one?" to respond, "The customer!" and where customers' purchases are bagged for them instead of by them.

In a country where it's difficult to get to the store because of its limited hours, Wal-Mart has pushed its store hours to the legal limit. It opens at 7 a.m. (the earliest allowed) despite the customary 8 a.m. or 9 a.m. opening times. Customers who work might appreciate the extra hour of time to shop. Also, Wal-Mart helps shoppers reduce shopping time by using common North American practices, such as locating steak sauce or seasoning packets near the meats and salad dressings near the produce so that shoppers don't have to walk back and forth in the store to find complementary goods.

To make shopping more pleasant, Wal-Mart has begun to renovate its German stores, many of which were badly run down. It has created wider aisles, refurbished fixtures, piled the goods higher, and renamed its stores Wal-Mart. Most important, in a land of *pfennig* pinchers, Wal-Mart has introduced everyday low pricing, or EDLP. "Jeden Tag Tiefpriese" signs throughout its stores proclaim drastically slashed prices on over 4000 items. Wal-Mart's EDLP/JTT strategy has worked so well that other German retailers, who previously relied on specials and sales to reduce prices, have been forced to reduce their daily prices.

In a sense, low prices have pulled customers into Wal-Mart's German stores while other attributes, such as friendly clerks and wider aisles, have made shopping more pleasant. What allows Wal-Mart to out-discount the European discounters? The answer lies in its 101-terabyte computer system. Wal-Mart is the country's most sophisticated retailer in terms of using information systems. Every second, data from around the globe are transmitted via satellite to the Wal-Mart computer. Store managers can point handheld scanners at a product on their shelves and find out how much of the product the store has sold today at what price and profit contribution, what its inventory levels are (by colour, size, and other characteristics), and whether more is on order. Analysts pore over thousands of pages of output to track sales everywhere. If a product is moving slowly in one store, it's shipped to another rather than being cleared through reduced prices. Very few goods sit in inventory for very long, which reduces costs. Orders and reorders are placed strictly on the basis of sales. Wal-Mart knows faster than any other retailer what's selling and what's not.

In addition, Wal-Mart's sophisticated distribution system backs up this information system. Wal-Mart has applied for and obtained several free-trade-zone distribution centres in Arizona and Georgia. Goods pour into these centres, where they are repackaged, marked, labelled, and reshipped. While goods remain in the zone, Wal-Mart pays no duty on them: Duties are paid only when goods are shipped. Each zone saves Wal-Mart more than $750 000 annually. Such close attention to distribution costs saves Wal-Mart money and supports rapid shipment of goods.

The analysts expected that, following its move into Germany, Wal-Mart would expand next into France. However, the company confounded the experts once again by buying ASDA, the third largest chain in the United Kingdom. Why? UK retailing has the highest margins in Europe—ranging from five to seven percent. If Wal-Mart can survive on less than two percent in Germany, it can do very well with the higher margins in the UK.

Wal-Mart now poses a serious threat to European retailers. With the purchase of one more major European chain next year, Wal-Mart will become the largest retailer in Euroland, irrevocably changing the face of European retailing. And it will have accomplished this feat in only four years.

How are European retailers retaliating? Wal-Mart's entry spawned a series of mergers, which can result only in a concentration of retailers worldwide. Carrefour and Promodes in France have merged to become the largest retailer in five European countries—France, Spain, Belgium, Portugal, and Greece. Through its holdings in other firms, it will have significant shares of the Argentine, Brazilian, Taiwanese, and Indonesian markets. Metro, the largest retailer in Germany, bought the Allkauf chain and Kriegbaum-Unternemensgruppe in southwest Germany to consolidate its lead in Germany. Ahold, the major Dutch retailer, bought up several chains in Spain.

QUESTIONS

1. Describe Wal-Mart's global strategy? What tactics has it used to become a major global retailer?
2. Can Wal-Mart sustain its competitive advantage in global retailing?
3. Explain the importance to the Wal-Mart strategy of selling only brand-name merchandise.
4. Choosing markets to enter is of major importance in global expansion. If you were in charge of Wal-Mart, what European country would you enter next? Why? Would entering this country require adaptation of Wal-Mart's marketing strategy and tactics? If so, how?
5. If you were running Wal-Mart, what non-European country in the world would you enter next? Why? Would entering this country require adaptation of Wal-Mart's marketing? If so, how?

Sources: "A foothold in Europe's heartland," *Discount Store*, October 1999:77; "Europe seen as tough, while Asia's a natural on Wal-Mart's globe," *WWD*, 23 August 1994:1; "How is Wal-Mart doing in Germany?" *Eurofood*, 1 July 1999:11; "Wal-Mart doubles its size in Europe," *Eurofood*, 17 December 1998:11; Stephen Armstrong, "Wal-Mart goes shopping in Europe," *European*, 2 March 1998:23; Carol Emert, "Wal-Mart sets up to enter Europe, Central America," *WWD*, 22 August 1994:8; Richard Halverson, "Wal-Mart 'walks the walk' of a global retailer; eyes all corners of the globe," *Discount Store News*, 5 December 1994:95; Samer Iskander, "Retailers plan biggest store chain in Europe," *Financial Times*, 30 August 1999:1; Tony Lisanti, "Europe's abuzz over Wal-Mart," *Discount Store News*, 3 May 1999:11; David Moin, "Wal-Mart to enter Europe with buy of German chain," *WWD*, 19 December 1997:2; Elliot Zwiebach, "Europe: In Wal-Mart's wake," *Supermarket News*, 20 September 1999:40.

video case 17

Air Transat's Global Tour

Air Transat, headquartered in Montreal, is the only surviving Canadian-owned tour operator in the $5-billion Canadian tour industry. While just a few years ago, there were several other Canadian operators, they have either been bought out by European firms or gone bankrupt. Jean Marc Eustache, the owner of Transat, is now trying to become an international player himself by expanding into Europe. He has already purchased a French tour operator and is considering the purchase of a British firm, which will give him even more access to the European tourist market.

Eustache started in the travel industry over 20 years ago when he was a university student. At the time, he was a Marxist and a student leader in Quebec. Believing that travel should be accessible to all, he started a travel company specializing in affordable student travel, even though he was afraid of flying. Although still in the travel business, his philosophical orientation has changed significantly. Eustache is now a capitalist who is not afraid of making profits. His company boasts three-percent margins, which are among the highest in the industry. He is, however, still afraid of flying.

In the tour industry, size is important. The larger the firm, the more cost advantages it can enjoy. For example, as the firm becomes larger it has more power with hotels and other suppliers to negotiate better deals. These cost advantages are important in an industry that has regular price wars between operators. Consumers often hold out for last-minute specials, which forces the tour operators to sell below cost. To compete effectively in this industry, Transat has grown through the purchase of other firms and has become vertically integrated. In addition to purchasing two Canadian tour operators, it owns its own travel agency, baggage-handling organization, and airplanes. Eustache hopes to eventually purchase hotels and ships to achieve even greater size and further vertical integration. He thinks of his company as a "leisure group," a perspective that presents several opportunities for growth.

Air Transat's moves to expand to Europe not only will provide cost advantages but also will allow the company to better manage consumer demand cycles in North America. The consumer purchase cycles of vacations are different in Europe and North America. While Canadians want to travel in the winter and not in the summer, consumers in such European countries as the United Kingdom and France want to travel in the summer, not the winter. By servicing both markets, Transat Air will be able to avoid overcapacity during the traditional, North American non-peak times.

As Eustache looks at companies to purchase, he must be careful that Transat does not itself become the target of a takeover. A few years ago, a larger company tried, unsuccessfully, to take over Air Transat. Eustache's goal is to have Air Transat become one of the largest tour companies in the world. But as he strives to achieve that goal, Eustache will need to be one step ahead of competitive moves in the global tourism marketplace.

Questions

1. What mode of entry is Air Transat using to enter international markets?
2. How is the choice of mode of entry into international markets different for a service firm such as Air Transat compared to a manufacturing firm?
3. As Air Transat expands globally, what factors should it consider in deciding whether to standardize or adapt aspects of its marketing mix?

Source: This case was prepared by Auleen Carson and is based on "Transat Air," *Venture,* 16 March 1997.

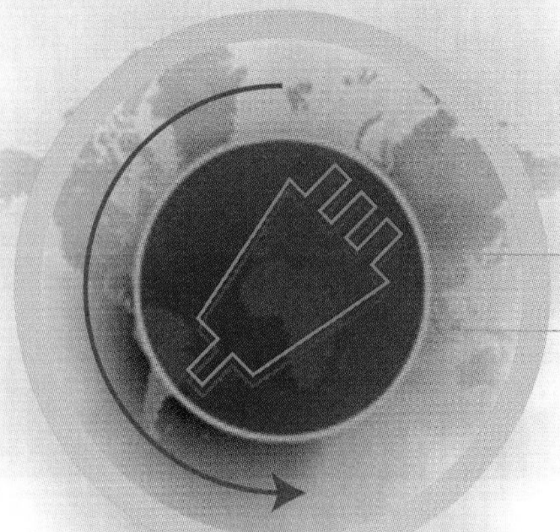

Concept Connections

When you finish this chapter, you should be able to

1. Identify the major social criticisms of marketing.
2. Define consumerism and environmentalism and explain how they affect marketing strategies.
3. Describe the principles of socially responsible marketing.
4. Explain the role of ethics in marketing.

chapter 18

Marketing and Society: Social Responsibility and Marketing Ethics

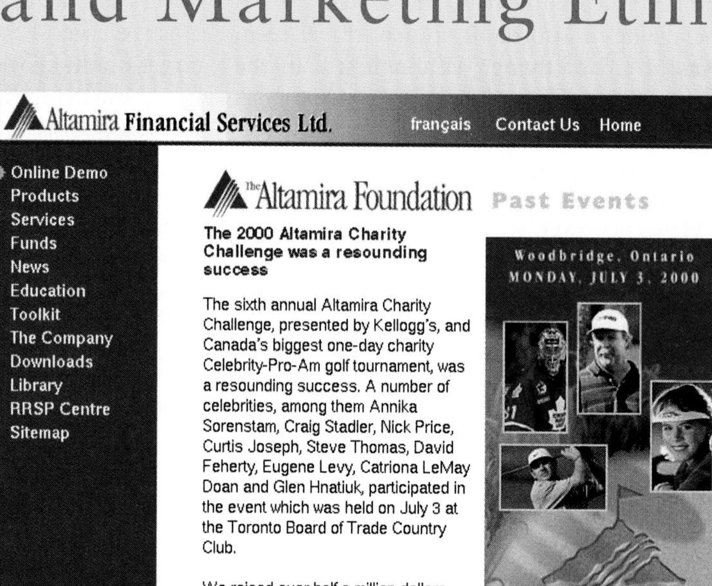

Altamira Financial Services Ltd.
français Contact Us Home
Online Demo
Products
Services
Funds
News
Education
Toolkit
The Company
Downloads
Library
RRSP Centre
Sitemap
Sitemap
The Altamira Foundation
Past Events
The 2000 Altamira Charity Challenge was a resounding success
The sixth annual Altamira Charity Challenge, presented by Kellogg's, and Canada's biggest one-day charity Celebrity-Pro-Am golf tournament, was a resounding success. A number of celebrities, among them Annika Sorenstam, Craig Stadler, Nick Price, Curtis Joseph, Steve Thomas, David Feherty, Eugene Levy, Catriona LeMay Doan and Glen Hnatiuk, participated in the event which was held on July 3 at the Toronto Board of Trade Country Club.
We raised over half a million dollars from the Charity Challenge, which was donated to several children's charities, including: The Kids' Help Phone, The Toronto Star Fresh Air Fund, Ronald McDonald Children's Charities of Canada, Reach for the Rainbow, The Mix/CFRB Children's Fund in support of the Hospital For Sick Children, Nike's P.L.A.Y. Fund (Participate in the Lives of All Youth), The Learning Partnership, Big Brothers/Big Sisters of Toronto, and the Geneva Centre for Autism.
The Altamira Charity Challenge, sponsored by The Altamira Foundation, has raised over $3 million for children's charities since 1995. We believe that children are our most precious resource and that our contribution to their well being will make a positive difference in their lives.
Woodbridge, Ontario
MONDAY, JULY 3, 2000
The Altamira Charity Challenge
presented by Kellogg's
Foundation

"New models of philanthropy are emerging [that emphasize] a far closer relationship among business, individuals, and communities. Corporations are not just giving donations to charity but are entering partnerships that exemplify the best creative approaches to meeting community needs." These words, uttered by Courtney Pratt, former CEO of Noranda, are the hallmark of an era in which corporations are redefining what it means to act in a socially responsible manner. It wasn't long ago that moral philosophers like Milton Friedman stated that the only social responsibility of a firm was to create wealth for its stockholders while acting within the bounds of the law and the moral dictate of society. But Environics International's Millennium Poll on Corporate Social Responsibility revealed that just being profitable isn't enough in today's world. Consumers from North America to Australia want businesses that not only make profits and create jobs, but also help build a better society. In fact, the poll revealed that 88 percent of Canadians want companies to contribute to broader societal goals.

Firms that are sensitive to the demands of the public and consumers are starting to define social responsibility as the "triple bottom line." Not only are they working to be economically responsible, but they are also being environmentally and socially responsible. In other words, rather than just focusing on business problems and their shareholders, many firms are taking a stakeholder perspective, realizing that they need to further and respect the rights of their customers, their employees, their suppliers, their communities, and even their competitors.

Rather than just spouting words about this mandate, they are "walking the walk." Many are actively working not just to be profitable, but also to improve the quality of life in their communities. They contribute the time and energy of their employees; they share their expertise and knowledge; they donate their products, services, and money to resolve a number of social dilemmas. These efforts range from cause-related marketing programs, in which firms donate a portion of the sales revenue from a product to a specific cause, to social alliances in which firms join with non-profit organizations in an effort to resolve complex, long-term social issues.

The list of firms undertaking these types of efforts is growing daily. Firms come from every sector of the Canadian economy, and their efforts are as varied as the social needs themselves. On the

list of socially active firms are Bell Canada, long-time sponsor of the Kids Help Phone, which receives over 4000 calls a day from young people who need to talk over problems or are crying out for help. Compaq Canada's Go for Green environmental program includes an extraordinary Web site (www.TrailPaq.ca) that lets the world know about the thousands of hiking trails Canada has to offer. Compaq believes that anyone who hikes a trail will have a heightened sense of the need to protect the fragile environment.

Molson Breweries also takes a leading place with its long history of social marketing. Molson and its co-sponsors have raised millions of dollars for AIDS research. McDonald's Restaurants of Canada is well known for its long-standing Ronald McDonald House program. Procter & Gamble supports the Canadian Breast Cancer Foundation, while Nissan Canada partners with Meals on Wheels to deliver hot lunches to the elderly and shut-ins. Nortel Networks works diligently to support the Childhood Cancer Foundation, while Sears Canada joined forces with Industry Canada to provide over 100 000 refurbished computers to classrooms and libraries across Canada in its Computers for Schools program. And it's not just large companies that are responding to calls for help. SaskEnergy's employees collaborated with the United Way and collected more than 200 000 sweaters to be distributed to the needy throughout Saskatchewan, while Winnipeg's Assiniboine Credit Union collected used cars to raise funds for the kidney disease research.

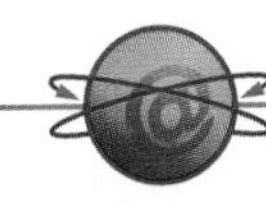

Altamira Financial Services
www.altamira.com/

Let's look at one case in detail. Altamira Financial Services Ltd. was given the 1999 Imagine "New Spirit of Community" award in recognition of its ongoing efforts. As its award submission noted: "Sharing and caring is part of the Altamira way of life. That is why the Altamira Foundation reaches out to charitable organizations and communities that are most in need. Our corporate giving program is focused on areas in which we believe we can make a difference." The Altamira Foundation, established in 1995, "invests in Canada's most precious and critical future resource—its children." Altamira believes that children have the right to grow up in a safe environment, the right to an education, and the right to become productive citizens. To foster these rights, Altamira donates at least one percent of its pre-tax profits and also sponsors on a continuing basis a range of events that support specific programs.

Altamira undertakes a number of initiatives to accomplish its goals. Since 1997, Altamira and its corporate partners, such as Kellogg Canada, have convinced some of the world's best golfers to donate their time and skills to raising money for children's charities. These efforts resulted in the Altamira Charity Golf Challenge, the largest one-day event of its kind in Canada. The event has raised over $3 million, which has supported a number of children's charities including the Raptors Foundation, the Toronto Star Fresh Air Fund, the Hospital for Sick Children, the Kids Help Foundation, Reach for the Rainbow, and the Learning Partnership. Working with the Canadian Opera Company, Altamira sponsored the No Load Opera Concerts and Opera Summer Camps for Children. The $135 000 raised has been donated to various community-based groups, such as the Canadian Feed the Children Fund, which funds breakfast and lunch programs for hungry children throughout the country and across the globe, giving them a better opportunity to learn.

While undoubtedly important, raising money isn't enough. Through the Altamira Homework Club, over 40 Altamira staff have volunteered their time to tutor and mentor students and promote literacy in communities across Canada. Each week during the school year, grade eight students from a local school visit Altamira for help in reading, writing, and doing their homework.

Why are companies taking on these expanded roles and responsibilities? Many businesses see social marketing as a means of reaching their target customers and enhancing the value of their brands. They align themselves with non-profit organizations to break through the clutter of traditional advertising and add distinctiveness and value to their offerings. Molson believes its program helps build stronger relationships with customers, enhances its corporate image, and creates a sense of pride among its employees. Sears believes it is reinforcing its position as Canada's family store and its reputation as a company that supports communities. Other firms want to create lifestyle associations between themselves and the causes they support. They develop social marketing programs to address corporate or brand image problems, to build brand loyalty, and to address issues of low employee morale and productivity.

While a business-related mandate may form part of the motivation behind these efforts, it must be stressed that the marketers involved in these programs are sincerely involved in the causes they choose to support. These firms are leaders—not just market leaders, but leaders in their communities. They take on the full breadth of challenges community membership presents. These firms work diligently with their non-profit partners to resolve social issues. Social marketing appears to be here to stay, according to 82 percent of Canadian executives recently surveyed: Almost two-thirds of companies polled use some form of social marketing, and many plan to expand these efforts.[1]

Responsible marketers discover what consumers want and respond with the right products, priced to give good value to buyers and profit to the producer. The *marketing concept* is a philosophy of customer service and mutual gain.

Not all marketers follow the marketing concept, however. In fact, some companies use questionable marketing practices, and some marketing actions that seem innocent in themselves strongly affect society. Consider the sale of cigarettes. Theoretically, companies should be free to sell cigarettes, and smokers should be free to buy them. But this transaction affects the public interest. First, smokers may be shortening their own lives. Second, smoking places a health-care burden on smokers' families and on society at large. Third, people around smokers may suffer discomfort and harm from second-hand smoke. Thus, private transactions may involve larger questions of public policy.

This chapter examines the social effects of marketing practices. We examine several questions: What are the most frequent social criticisms of marketing? What steps have private citizens taken to curb marketing ills? What steps have legislators and government agencies taken to curb marketing ills? What steps have enlightened companies taken to carry out socially responsible and ethical marketing? We examine how marketing affects and is affected by each of these issues.

Social Criticisms of Marketing

Marketing is often criticized. Some of the criticism is justified; much is not. Social critics claim that certain marketing practices hurt individual consumers, society as a whole, and other business firms.

Marketing's Impact on Individual Consumers

Consumers have many concerns about how well the marketing system serves their interests. Surveys usually show that consumers hold mixed or even slightly unfavourable attitudes toward marketing practices. Consumer advocates, government agencies, and other critics have accused marketing of harming consumers through high prices, deceptive practices, high-pressure selling, shoddy or unsafe products, planned obsolescence, and poor service to disadvantaged consumers.

High Prices

Many critics charge that the marketing system causes prices to be higher than they would be under more "sensible" systems. They point to three factors—*high costs of distribution, high advertising and promotion costs,* and *excessive markups.*

High Costs of Distribution. A long-standing charge is that greedy intermediaries mark up prices beyond the value of their services. Critics charge either that there are too many intermediaries or that intermediaries are inefficient and poorly run, that they provide unnecessary or duplicate services, and that they practise poor management and planning. As a result, distribution costs too much, and consumers pay for these excessive costs in the form of higher prices.

How do retailers answer these charges? First, intermediaries do work that would otherwise have to be done by manufacturers or consumers. Second, markups reflect services that consumers themselves want—more convenience, larger stores and assortment, longer store hours, return privileges, and others. Third, the costs of operating stores keep rising, forcing retailers to raise their prices. Fourth, retail competition is so intense that margins are actually quite low. For example, after taxes, supermarket chains are typically left with one to three percent profit on their sales. If some resellers try to charge too much relative to the value they add, other resellers will step in with lower prices. Low-price stores such as the Dollar Store, Zellers, and Wal-Mart pressure their competitors to operate efficiently and keep their prices down.

High Advertising and Promotion Costs. Modern marketing is accused of pushing up prices because of heavy advertising and sales promotion. For example, a dozen tablets of a heavily promoted brand of pain reliever sell for the same price as 100 tablets of less promoted brands. Differentiated products—cosmetics, deter-

A heavily promoted brand of antacid sells for much more than a virtually identical generic or store-branded product. Critics charge that promotion adds only psychological value to the product rather than functional value.

gents, toiletries—include promotion and packaging costs that can amount to 40 percent or more of the manufacturer's price to the retailer. Critics charge that much of the packaging and promotion adds only psychological value to the product rather than functional value. Retailers use additional promotions—advertising, displays, and sweepstakes—that add several cents to retail prices.

Marketers answer these charges in several ways. First, consumers want more than the merely functional qualities of products. They also want psychological benefits—they want to feel wealthy, beautiful, or special. Consumers usually can buy functional versions or products at lower prices but are often willing to pay more for products that also provide desired psychological benefits. Second, branding gives buyers confidence. A brand name implies a certain quality, and consumers are willing to pay for well-known brands even if they cost a little more. Third, heavy advertising is needed to inform millions of potential buyers of the merits of a brand. If consumers want to know what is available on the market, they must expect manufacturers to spend large sums of money on advertising. Fourth, heavy advertising and promotion may be necessary for a firm to match competitors' efforts. The business would lose "share of mind" if it did not match competitive spending. At the same time, companies are cost-conscious about promotion and try to spend their money wisely. Finally, heavy sales promotion is needed at times because goods are produced ahead of demand in a mass-production economy, and special incentives must be offered to sell inventories.

Excessive Markups. Critics charge that some companies mark up goods excessively. They point to the drug industry, where a pill costing five cents to make may cost the consumer 40 cents to buy. They point to the pricing tactics of funeral homes that prey on the emotions of bereaved relatives and to the high charges for television and auto repair.

Marketers respond that most businesses try to deal fairly with consumers because they want repeat business. Most consumer abuses are unintentional. When shady marketers take advantage of consumers, they should be reported to the police, better business bureau, and the provincial ministry of consumer and commercial relations. Marketers also respond that consumers often don't understand the reason for high markups. For example, pharmaceutical markups must cover the costs of purchasing, promoting, and distributing existing medicines plus the high research and development costs of finding new medicines.

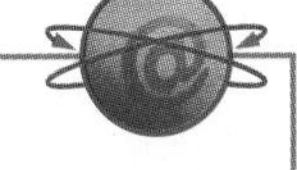

Better Business Bureau
www.bbb.org/

Deceptive Practices

Marketers are sometimes accused of deceptive practices that lead consumers to believe that they will get more value than they actually do. Deceptive practices fall into three groups: deceptive pricing, promotion, and packaging. *Deceptive pricing* includes such practices as falsely advertising "factory" or "wholesale" prices or a large price reduction from a phony high retail list price. The Competition Bureau has taken action against merchants who advertise false values, sell old merchandise as new, or charge too much for credit. For example, in 1995 the Competition Bureau fined Montreal-based Suzy Shier Ltd., which operates 375 outlets across Canada, $300 000 after it was found to be double-tagging merchandise. While this practice of placing a sales ticket showing an original price and another ticket showing a sales price on a piece of clothing is not illegal, Suzy Shier violated the law because it had not sold a substantial volume of goods at the original price. In fact, much of the double-tagging was done at the factory.[2]

Deceptive promotion includes such practices as overstating the product's features or performance, luring the customer to the store for a bargain that is out of stock, or running rigged contests. *Deceptive packaging* includes exaggerating package contents through subtle design, not filling the package to the top, using misleading labelling, or describing size in misleading terms.

Phone fraud has become a significant deceptive practice. According to PhoneBusters, the national reporting centre for telemarketing fraud, Canadians have lost about $40 million as a result of this activity since 1995. Criminals use telecommunications to prey on innocent victims, especially those most vulnerable, such as senior citizens. The Canadian Marketing Association (CMA) has partnered with government to develop initiatives aimed at preventing and combating this crime. Bill C-20 has equipped enforcement agencies with stronger investigative tools and imposed more restrictions on telemarketers. Information on Bill C-20 is available on the CMA Web site.

CMA: Bill C-20
www.the-cma.org/members.html/

Since deceptive practices hurt the reputation of all marketers, the CMA works to develop codes of ethics and standards of good practice so that industry can regulate itself better. It works with policy makers to strengthen the *Competition Act.* In the case of telemarketing fraud, it joined the Deceptive Telemarketing Prevention Forum to launch a public education campaign designed to help consumers avoid becoming victims of telephone fraud. The campaign, "Stop Phone Fraud, It's a Trap!" consists of posters, pamphlets, public service announcements, an upgraded Web site for PhoneBusters, and educational materials to help consumers learn how to tell the difference between an honest telemarketer and a scam artist. Training videos are also made available to volunteer groups that work with seniors.[3]

Deceptive practices have led to industry self-regulation standards as well as legislation and other consumer protection actions. The *Competition Act* forbids many of the practices. Advertising Standards Canada has published several guidelines listing deceptive practices. The toughest problem is defining what is "deceptive."

Telemarketing fraud hurts consumers and the marketing profession. Members of the Deceptive Telemarketing Prevention Forum developed a campaign to educate consumers about phone scams.

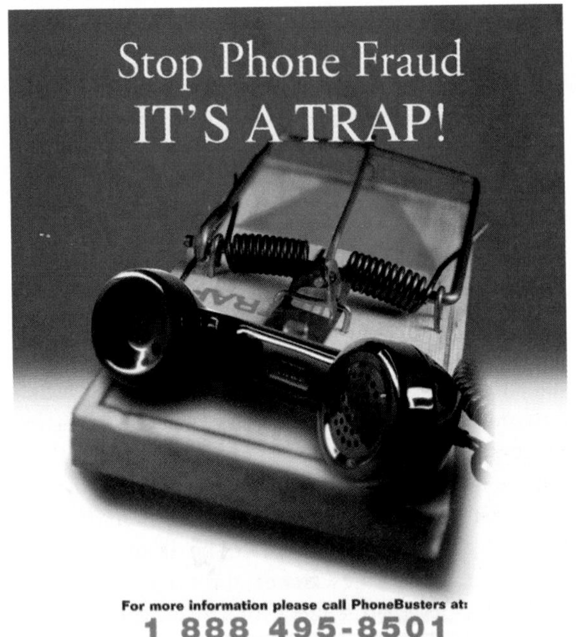

High-Pressure Selling

Salespeople are sometimes accused of high-pressure selling to persuade people to buy goods they had no intention of buying. It is often said that encyclopedias, insurance, real estate, cars, and jewellery are *sold,* not *bought.* Salespeople are trained to deliver smooth, canned talks to entice purchase. They sell hard because sales contests promise big prizes to those who sell the most.

Marketers know that buyers often can be talked into buying unwanted or unneeded things. Laws re-quire door-to-door salespeople to announce that they are selling a product. Buyers in most provinces also have a "three-day cooling-off period" in which they can cancel a contract after rethinking it. In addition, when they feel that undue selling pressure has been applied, consumers can complain to the better business bureau or to their provincial ministry regulating commerce.

Shoddy or Unsafe Products

Another criticism is that products lack the quality they should have. Consumers often complain that many products are not made well or that services did not perform well. Such complaints have been lodged against such products as home appliances, automobiles, and clothing, and such services as home and auto repair.

A second complaint is that many products deliver little benefit. For example, some consumers are surprised to learn that many of the "healthy" foods being marketed today—from cholesterol-free salad dressings and low-fat frozen dinners to high-fibre bran cereals—may have little nutritional value. In fact, they may even be harmful:[4]

> [Despite] sincere efforts on the part of most marketers to provide healthier products, . . . many promises emblazoned on packages and used as ad slogans continue to confuse nutritionally uninformed consumers and . . . may actually be harmful to that group. . . . [Many consumers] incorrectly assume the product is "safe" and eat greater amounts than are good for them. . . . For example, General Foods' . . . new . . . "low-cholesterol, low-calorie" cherry coffee cake . . . may confuse some consumers who shouldn't eat much of it. While each serving is only 90 calories, not everyone realizes that the suggested serving is tiny [one-thirteenth of the small cake]. Although eating half a . . . cake may be better than eating half a dozen Dunkin Donuts . . . neither should be eaten in great amounts by people on restrictive diets.

A third complaint concerns product safety. Product safety has been a problem for several reasons, including manufacturer indifference, increased production complexity, poorly trained labour, and poor quality control. For years, Consumers Union—the organization that publishes *Consumer Reports*—has reported hazards in tested products: electrical dangers in appliances, carbon-monoxide poisoning from room heaters, injury risks from lawn mowers, and faulty automobile design, among many others. The organization's testing and other activities have helped consumers make better buying decision and encouraged businesses to eliminate product flaws (see Marketing Highlight 18-1).

Most manufacturers *want* to produce quality goods. The way a company deals with product quality and safety problems can damage or help its reputation. Companies selling poor-quality or unsafe products risk damaging conflicts with consumer groups and regulators. Moreover, unsafe products can result in product liability suits and large awards for damages. Moreover, consumers who are unhappy with a firm's products may avoid future purchases and talk other consumers into doing the same. Today's marketers know that customer-driven quality results in customer satisfaction, which in turn creates profitable customer relationships.

Consumer Reports
www.consumer.org/

Planned Obsolescence

Critics have charged that some producers follow a program of planned obsolescence, causing their products to become obsolete before they actually should need replacement. Critics charge that some producers continually change consumer concepts of acceptable styles to encourage more and earlier buying: An example is constantly changing clothing fashions. Other producers are accused of holding back attractive functional features, then introducing them later to make older models obsolete: Critics claim that this occurs in the consumer electronics and computer industries. Still other producers are accused of using materials and components that will break, wear, rust, or rot sooner than they should.

Marketers respond that consumers *like* style changes: They get tired of the old goods and want a new look in fashion or a new design in cars. No one has to buy the new look and, if too few people like it, it will simply fail. Companies frequently withhold new features when they are not fully tested, when they add more cost to the product than consumers are willing to pay, and for other good reasons. But they do so at the risk that a competitor will introduce the new feature and steal the market. Moreover, companies often put in new materials to lower

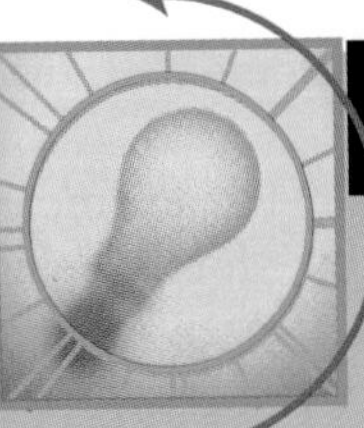

marketing highlight 18-1

When *Consumer Reports* Talks, Buyers Listen

For over 60 years, *Consumer Reports* has given buyers the lowdown on everything from sports cars to luggage to lawn sprinklers. Published by Consumers Union, a nonprofit product-testing organization, the magazine's mission can be summed up by CU's motto: "Test, Inform, Protect." With more than five million subscribers and several times that many borrowers, as dog-eared library copies will attest, *Consumer Reports* is one of North America's most read magazines. It's also one of the most influential. In 1988, when its car-testers rated Suzuki's topple-prone Samurai as "not acceptable"—meaning don't even take one as a gift—sales plunged by 70 percent the following month. In 1992, when it raved about Saucony's Jazz 3000 sneakers, sales doubled, leading to nationwide shortages.

Although non-readers may view *Consumer Reports* as a deadly dull shoppers' guide to major household appliances, the magazine does a lot more than rate cars and refrigerators. It also looks at such items as mutual funds, prostate surgery, home mortgages, retirement communities, and public health policies. In the 1930s, Consumers Union was one of the first organizations to urge a boycott of products imported from Nazi Germany. In the 1950s, it warned that fallout from US nuclear tests was contaminating milk supplies. In the 1960s and 1970s, it prodded carmakers to install seat belts, then air bags.

Yet the magazine is rarely harsh or loud. Instead, it's usually understated, and it can even be funny. Lifebuoy soap was itself so smelly that it simply overwhelmed your BO with LO. And what reader didn't delight to find in a 1990 survey of soaps that the most expensive bar, Eau de Gucci, at 31 cents per handwashing, wound up dead last in a blind test?

Consumer Reports readers clearly appreciate CU and its magazine. It is unlikely that any other magazine in the world could have raised $24 million toward a new building simply by asking readers for donations. To avoid even the appearance of bias, CU has a strict no-ads, no-freebies policy. It buys all of its product samples on the open market, and anonymously. A visit to CU's maze of labs confirms the thoroughness with which CU's testers carry out their mission. A chemist performs a cholesterol extraction test on a small white blob in a beaker; a ground-up piece of turkey enchilada, you are told. Elsewhere you find the remains of a piston-driven machine called Fingers that added 1 + 1 on pocket calculators hundreds of thousands of times or until the calculators failed, whichever came first. You watch suitcases bang into one another inside a huge contraption—affectionately dubbed the "Mechanical Gorilla"—which looks like a three-metre-wide clothes dryer.

Down the hall in the appliance department, a pair of "food soilers" will soon load 20 dishwashers with identical sets of dirty dishes. A sample dinner plate is marked with scientific precision in eight wedge-shaped sections, each with something different caked on it—dried spaghetti, spinach, chipped beef, or something else equally difficult to clean. Next door, self-cleaning ovens are being tested, their interiors coated with a crusty substance—called "Monster Mash" by staffers—which suggests month-old chili sauce. The recipe in-

their costs and prices. They do not design their products to break down earlier, because they do not want to lose customers to other brands. Instead, they implement total quality programs to ensure that products will consistently meet to exceed customer expectations. Thus, much of so-called planned obsolescence is the working of the competitive and technological forces in a free society—forces that lead to ever-improving goods and services.

Poor Service to Disadvantaged Consumers

Finally, the marketing system has been accused of poorly serving disadvantaged consumers. Critics claim that the urban poor often have to shop in smaller stores that carry inferior goods and charge higher prices. A recent Consumers Union study compared the food shopping habits of low-income consumers and the prices they pay relative to middle-income consumers in the same city. The study found that the poor pay more for inferior goods. The results suggested that the presence of large national chain stores in low-income neighbourhoods made a big difference in keeping prices down. However, the study also found evidence of "redlining," a type of economic discrimination in which major chain retailers avoid placing stores in disadvantaged neighbourhoods. Similar redlining charges have been levelled at the home insurance, consumer lending, and banking industries. When disadvantaged consumers are identified and discriminated against in the online environment, the practice is called weblining.[5]

cludes tapioca, cheese, lard, grape jelly, tomato sauce, and cherry pie filling—mixed well and baked one hour at 425 degrees. If an oven's self-cleaning cycle doesn't render the resulting residue into harmless-looking ash, five million readers will be so informed.

Some of the tests that CU runs are standard, but many are not. Several years ago, in a triumph of low-tech creativity, CU's engineers stretched paper towels across embroidery hoops, moistened the centre of each with exactly ten drops of water, then poured lead shot into the middle. The winner held seven pounds of shot; the loser, less than one. Who could argue with that? There is an obvious logic to such tests, and the results are plainly quantifiable.

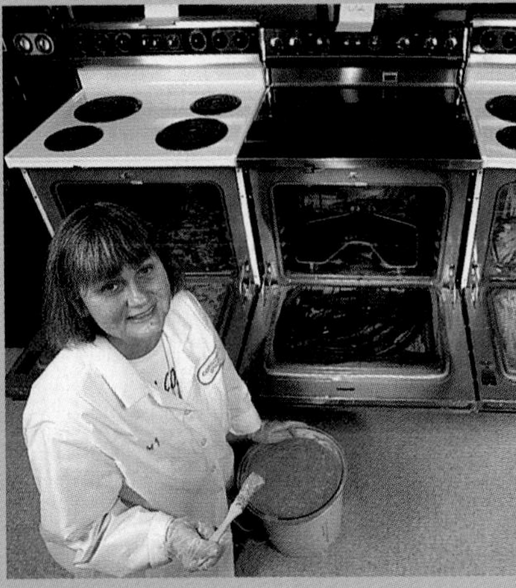

Consumers Union carries out its testing mission: Suitcases bang into one another inside the huge "Mechanical Gorilla," and a staffer coats the interior of self-cleaning ovens with a crusty concoction called "Monster Mash."

From the start, Consumers Union has generated controversy. The second issue dismissed the Good Housekeeping Seal of Approval as nothing more than a fraudulent ploy by publisher William Randolph Hearst to reward loyal advertisers. *Good Housekeeping* responded by accusing CU of prolonging the Great Depression. To the business community, *Consumer Reports* was at first viewed as a clear threat to business. During its early years, more than 60 advertising-dependent publications, including the *New York Times, Newsweek,* and the *New Yorker,* refused to accept CU's subscription ads.

Through the years, many manufacturers have filed suit against CU, challenging findings unfavourable to their products. However, the controversy has more often helped than hurt subscriptions, and to this day Consumers Union has never lost or settled a libel suit.

Source: Adapted from Doug Stewart, "To buy or not to buy, that is the question at *Consumer Reports,*" *Smithsonian,* September 1993:34-43.

Clearly, better marketing systems must be built in low-income areas—one hope is to get large retailers to open outlets in low-income areas. Moreover, low-income people and other vulnerable groups clearly need consumer protection.

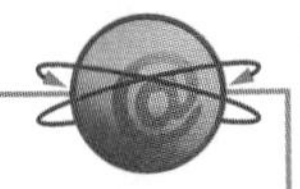

American Association of Advertising Agencies
www.aaaa.org/

Marketing's Impact on Society as a Whole

The marketing system has been accused of adding to several "evils" in society at large. Advertising has been a special target—so much so that the American Association of Advertising Agencies launched a campaign to defend advertising against what it felt to be common but untrue criticisms.

False Wants and Too Much Materialism

Critics, led by Professor Rick Pollay of the University of British Columbia, have charged that the marketing system urges too much interest in material possessions. Pollay wrote an article in the *Journal of Marketing* that outlined the unintended consequences of advertising. The article documented the work of a range of social critics who claim that advertising promoted materialism, undermined family values, reinforced negative stereotypes, and created a class of perpetually dissatisfied consumers.[6] People are judged by what they *own* rather than by who they *are*.

Such critics as Adbusters do not view this interest in material things as a natural state of mind but rather as a matter of false wants created by marketing.

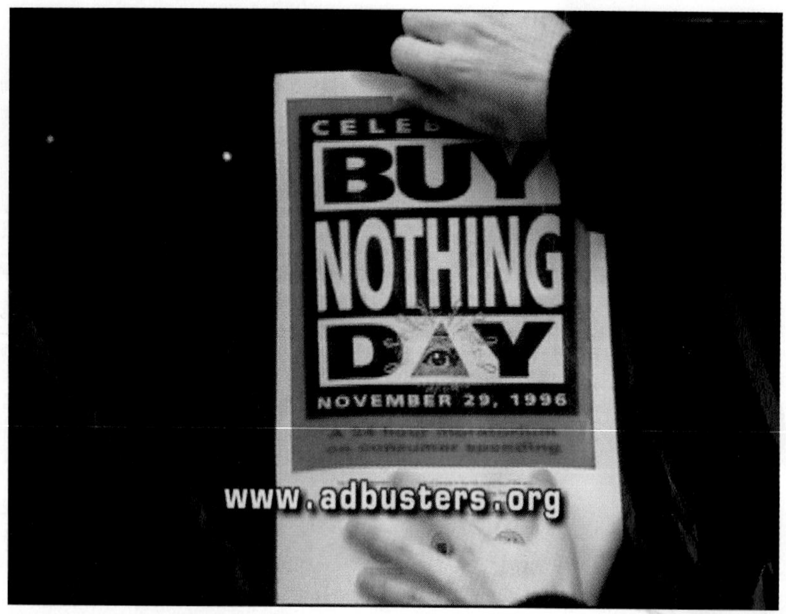

Social critics, like Adbusters, decry the materialism they claim advertising creates.

Businesses hire advertisers to stimulate people's desires for goods, and advertisers use the mass media to create materialistic models of the good life. People work harder to earn the necessary money. Their purchases increase the output of North American industry, and industry in turn uses advertisers to stimulate more desire for the industrial output. Thus, marketing is seen as creating false wants that benefit industry more than they benefit consumers.

Others believe that these criticisms overstate the power of business to create needs, however. People have strong defences against advertising and other marketing tools. Marketers are most effective when they appeal to existing wants rather than when they attempt to create new ones. Furthermore, people seek information when making important purchases and often do not rely on single sources. Even minor purchases that can be affected by advertising messages lead to repeat purchases only if the product performs as promised. Finally, the high failure rate of new products shows that companies are not able to control demand.

On a deeper level, our wants and values are influenced not only by marketers, but also by family, peer groups, religion, ethnic background, and education. If North Americans are highly materialistic, these values arose out of basic socialization processes that go much deeper than business and mass media alone could produce.

Too Few Social Goods

Business has been accused of overselling private goods at the expense of public goods. As private goods increase, they require more public services that are usually not forthcoming. For example, an increase in automobile ownership (private good) requires more highways, traffic controls, parking spaces, and police services (public goods). The overselling of private goods results in "social costs." For cars, the social costs include traffic congestion, air pollution, and deaths and injuries from car accidents.

A way must be found to restore a balance between private and public goods. One option is to make producers bear the full social costs of their operations. For example, the government could require automobile manufacturers to build cars with more safety features and better pollution-control systems. Automakers would then raise their prices to cover extra costs. If buyers found the price of some cars too high, however, the producers of these cars would disappear, and demand would move to those producers that could support the sum of the private and social costs.

Cultural Pollution

Critics charge the marketing system with creating *cultural pollution*. Our senses are being assaulted constantly by advertising. Commercials interrupt serious programs; pages of ads obscure printed matter; billboards mar beautiful scenery. These interruptions continuously pollute people's minds with messages of materialism, sex, power, or status. Although most people do not find advertising overly annoying (some even think it is the best part of television programming), critics call for sweeping changes.

Marketers answer the charges of "commercial noise" with these arguments. First, they hope that their ads reach primarily the target audience; but, because of mass-communication channels, some ads are bound to reach people who have no interest in the product and, therefore, become annoyed. People who buy magazines addressed to their interests—such as *Harrowsmith* or *Canadian Business*—rarely complain about the ads because the magazines advertise products of interest. Second, ads make it possible for consumers to receive commercial television and radio free of charge and keep down the costs of magazines and newspapers. Many people think commercials are a small price to pay for these benefits.

Too Much Political Power

Another criticism is that business wields too much political power. Oil, tobacco, auto, and pharmaceutical firms lobby governments to promote their interests against the public interest. Advertisers are accused of holding too much power over the mass media, limiting their freedom to report independently and objectively. One critic has asked: "How can *Life* . . . and *Reader's Digest* afford to tell the truth about the scandalously low nutritional value of most packaged foods . . . when these magazines are being subsidized by such advertisers as General Foods, Kellogg's, Nabisco, and General Mills? . . . The answer is *they cannot and do not*."[7]

North American industries promote and protect their interests. They have a right to representation in Parliament and the mass media, although their influence can become too great. Fortunately, many powerful business interests once thought to be untouchable have been tamed in the public interest. For example, Petro-Canada was formed to give Canadians greater control over the oil industry. Ralph Nader caused legislation that forced the automobile industry to build more safety into its cars. Amendments to the *Tobacco Products Control Act* made it necessary for cigarette manufacturers to place stronger warnings on their packages about the dangers of smoking. Warnings, which must appear in black type on a white background on the top of the package, include such messages as "Cigarettes cause strokes and heart disease" and "Smoking reduces life expectancy."[8] Because the media receive advertising revenues from many advertisers, it is easier to resist the influence of one or a few of them. Too much business power tends to result in counterforces that check and offset these powerful interests.

Marketing's Impact on Other Businesses

Critics charge that a company's marketing practices can harm other companies and reduce competition. Three problems are involved: acquisitions of competitors, marketing practices that create barriers to entry, and unfair competitive marketing practices.

Critics claim that firms are harmed and competition reduced when companies expand by acquiring competitors rather than by developing their own new products. During the past decade, Corel bought out WordPerfect; Interbrew SA, a Belgian company, acquired Labatt in a $2.7 billion takeover in the summer of 1995; Procter & Gamble gobbled up Richardson-Vicks, Noxell, and parts of Revlon. Acquisition is a complex subject. Acquisitions can sometimes be good for society. The acquiring company may gain economies of scale that lead to lower costs and lower prices. A well-managed company may take over a poorly managed company and improve its efficiency. An industry that was not very competitive may become more competitive after the acquisition. But acquisitions also can be harmful and, therefore, are regulated by the government.

Critics have charged that marketing practices bar new companies from entering an industry. Large marketing companies can use patents and heavy promotional spending, and can tie up suppliers or dealers to keep out or drive out competitors. Nowhere are these issues more apparent than in Canada's pharmaceutical industry. In 1993, Canada revised the regulations dealing with patent protection for drugs. Patent protection was extended from 17 to 20 years. Manufacturers of branded drugs claimed that this increased protection has made the Canadian pharmaceutical industry more competitive internationally. The report is hotly disputed, however. The generic manufacturers want patent protection reduced to 10 years. They claim that the branch of the pharmaceutical industry composed of branded drug firms has actually cut jobs since being granted extended protection.

Finally, some firms have used unfair competitive marketing practices with the intention of hurting or destroying other firms. They may set their prices below costs, threaten to cut off business with suppliers, or discourage the buying of a competitor's products. Various laws work to prevent such predatory competition. It is difficult, however, to prove that the intent or action was really predatory. In recent years, Wal-Mart, Air Canada, Intel, and Microsoft have all been accused of predatory practices:[9]

> For the fiscal year ending June 2000, Microsoft's $9.42 billion in net income significantly overshadowed the profits of the 10 largest publicly traded software companies. Its reach extends beyond the PC into everything from computerized toys and TV set-top boxes to selling cars and airline tickets over the Internet. In its zeal to become a leader not just in operating systems but on the Internet, the company bundled its Internet Explorer browser into its Windows software. This move sparked an antitrust suit by the American government, much to the delight of Microsoft's rivals. After all, Web-browsing innovator Netscape has seen its market share plummet as it tries to sell what Microsoft gives away for free.

Citizen and Public Actions to Regulate Marketing

Because some people view business as the cause of many economic and social ills, grassroots movements have arisen from time to time to keep business in line. The two major movements are *consumerism* and *environmentalism*.

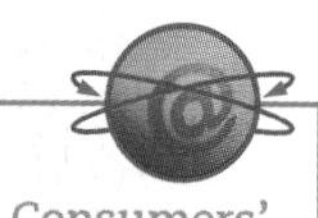

Consumers' Association of Canada
www.consumer.ca/

Consumerism
An organized movement of citizens and government agencies to improve the rights and power of buyers in relation to sellers

Consumerism

The first consumer movements took place in the early 1900s and in the mid-1930s. Both were sparked by an upturn in consumer prices. Another movement began in the 1960s. Consumers had become better educated; products had become more complex and hazardous; and people were questioning the status quo. Many accused big business of wasteful and unethical practices. Since then, many consumer groups have been organized, and several consumer laws have been passed. The consumer movement has spread beyond North America and is especially strong in Europe.

But what is the consumer movement? **Consumerism** is an organized movement of citizens and government agencies to improve the rights and power of buyers in relation to sellers. The Consumers' Association of Canada (CAC) has acted as a consumer advocate and has provided information to Canadian cosumers for over 50 years. It is a volunteer-based, non-governmental organization dedicated to representing the interests of Canadian consumers. Founded in 1947, it is the only nationally organized group of consumers in Canada, with offices in every province. The association lobbies government to secure consumer rights in areas of food, health care, environment, consumer products and services, regulated industries (phone, electricity, telecommunications, cable), financial institutions, taxation, trade, and any other issue of concern to Canadians facing complex buying decisions. The association establishes annual priorities. Recent issues include health-care reform; the information highway; interprovincial trade barriers; consumer education and purchasing literacy; GST reform; price visibility; package downsizing; and environmental rights and responsibilities. The association has also outlined the following as fundamental consumer rights:[10]

- *The right to safety.* Consumers have the right to be protected against the marketing of goods that are hazardous to health or life.
- *The right to be informed.* Consumers must be protected against fraudulent, deceitful, or grossly misleading information, advertising, labelling, or other practices. They are to be given the facts needed to make an informed choice.
- *The right to choose.* Consumers have the right to choose, wherever possible, among a variety of products and services at competitive prices. In industries where competition is not workable and government regulation is substituted, consumers must be assured of satisfactory quality and service at fair prices.
- *The right to be heard.* It is important that consumers' voices be heard. Thus, they must receive full and sympathetic consideration in the formulation of government policy, and fair and expeditious treatment in its administrative tribunals.
- *The right to redress against damage.* Consumers have the right to seek redress from a supplier of goods and services for any loss or damage suffered because of bad information, or faulty products or performance, and shall have easy and inexpensive access to settlement of small claims.
- *The right to consumer education.* Canadian consumers have the right to be educated as school children so that they will be able to act as informed consumers through their lives. Adults also have the right to consumer education.

Consumer desire for more information led to putting ingredients, nutrition, and dating information on product labels.

Each proposed right has led to more specific proposals by consumerists. The right to be informed includes the right to know the true interest on a loan (truth in lending), the true cost per unit of a brand (unit pricing), the ingredients in a product (ingredient labelling), the nutrition in foods (nutritional labelling), product freshness (open dating), and the true benefits of a product (truth in advertising). Proposals related to consumer protection include strengthening consumer rights in cases of business fraud, requiring greater product safety, and giving more power to government agencies. Proposals relating to the quality of life include controlling the ingredients that go into certain products (detergents) and packaging (soft-drink containers), reducing the level of advertising "noise," and appointing consumer representatives to company boards to protect consumer interests.

In addition to the CAC, some better business bureaus offer tips to consumers to protect themselves from fraud or shady business practices. The one for mainland British Columbia, for example, provides information on the dangers of advertisements that promise consumers easy ways of earning money at home, explains the rules about the cooling-off periods, tells how to differentiate between legitimate and fraudulent requests for charitable contributions, and discusses the legality of pyramid schemes.

Consumers have not only the *right* but also the *responsibility* to protect themselves instead of leaving this function to someone else. Consumers who believe they got a bad deal have several remedies available, including writing to the company president or to the media; contacting federal, provincial, or local agencies; and going to small claims court.

Environmentalism

Environmentalism
An organized movement of concerned citizens and government agencies to protect and improve people's living environment.

Environmentalism is an organized movement of concerned citizens, businesses, and government agencies to protect and improve people's living environment. Environmentalists are not against marketing and consumption; they simply want people and organizations to operate with more care for the environment. The marketing system's goal should not be to maximize consumption, consumer choice, or consumer satisfaction, but rather to maximize life quality. And "life quality" means not only the quantity and quality of consumer goods and services, but also the quality of the environment. Environmentalists want environmental costs included in both producer and consumer decision making.

In response to these concerns, the Canadian government has undertaken a number of initiatives to improve the environment. It froze production levels of chlorofluorocarbons (CFCs), the major cause of ozone layer depletion, at 1986 levels, and committed itself to reducing production by a further 50 percent by the year 2000. In December 1999, environmental ministers from around the world met in Beijing and agreed to even stronger controls. Canada was one of the first countries to agree to a freeze of ozone-depleting chemicals. Subsequently, Canada's *Ozone-Depleting Substances (ODS) Regulations, 1998* were revised to enable Canada to accept what became known as the Beijing Amendment, which came into force on 1 January 2001.[11]

Canada's environment ministers established a voluntary program intended to reduce excessive packaging by 50 percent by the year 2000. Patterning itself after the successful Blue Angel program in West Germany, the Canadian government developed an environmentally friendly labelling program and endorsed the goal of sustainable development put forward by the World Commission on Environment and Development. The *Canadian Environmental Assessment Act* is one piece of legislation developed to promote its goal of improving the environment.

Marketers cannot ignore the urgency of environmental issues or be blind to the fact that governments are increasingly willing to take action and pass regula-

Many companies, such as DaimlerChrysler Canada and Honda, are responding positively to Canadians' concerns about environmental issues.

tions restricting marketing practices. All parts of the marketing mix are affected. Advertisers are accused of adding to the solid waste problem when they use direct mail or newspaper inserts. Manufacturers are criticized for making products that incorporate materials that increase pollution or cannot be recycled.[12] Distribution systems have been cited for adding to air pollution as trucks move products from the factory to the store. Critics claim that even when environmentally friendly products are available, they are priced too high for many consumers to afford.

Buying behaviour has changed as sensitivity to this issue has grown. The late 1980s saw the birth of a new product attribute—environmentally friendly. A recent survey conducted by the Grocery Product Manufacturers of Canada found that 80 percent of respondents said they would be willing to pay more for "green" products. Companies began to respond to these changes in demand. Retailers in both Canada and the United States are demanding more environmentally sensitive products. Wal-Mart has asked its suppliers to provide more of these products. Loblaw has developed an entire line of products under its "green" President's Choice label. Governments are demanding that newsprint be made with a high proportion of recycled paper. The City of Toronto has stated it will favour products that are "green."

Some people claim that "green marketing" is dead. If you think that is true, just consider some of the initiatives by the Canadian packaging industry:[13]

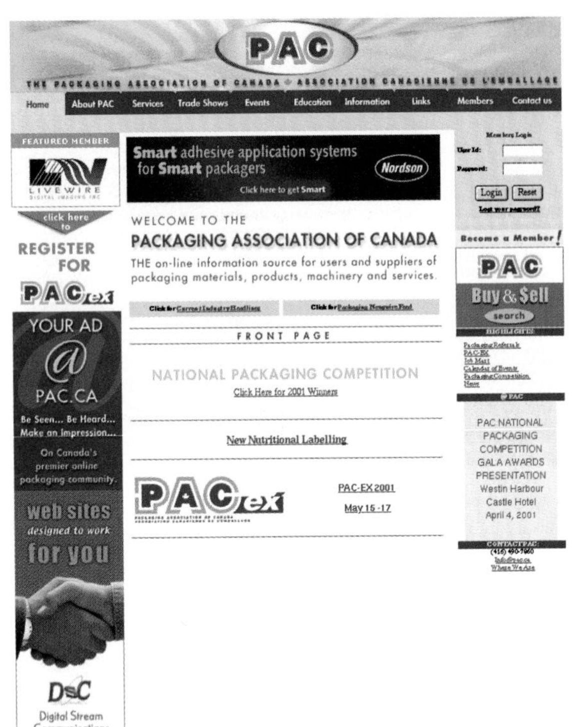

Members of the National Packaging Association of Canada have worked to reduce the amount of packaging going into landfills and have gained international marketing opportunities in return.

> Canada's packaging industry has been working diligently to meet the goals established by the National Packaging Protocol, a voluntary agreement formulated to reduce the amount of packaging sent to landfills by 50 percent relative to what was sent to the trash in 1988. Thus, in the early 1990s, when Canada's major laundry detergent manufacturers introduced concentrated powders to the market, they not only reduced the amount of detergent that people used, they also resulted in a 40 percent reduction in packaging materials. This is only part of the commitment of the packaging industry, which has invested more than $2 billion in infrastructure to reduce, reuse, and recycle its packaging. Compared to a decade ago, there is almost no packaging produced in Canada that hasn't been improved from an environmental perspective. For example, the average glass container has a 34 percent recycled content. Weights of containers have been reduced by at least 10 percent, saving fuel and shipping costs. Because the Canadian packaging industry had a jump on almost every other country in the world in designing better environmental packaging, there is strong export demand for Canadian packaging, especially in the US. It's a good initiative when you can sell more by using less.

The first wave of modern environmentalism was driven by environmental groups and concerned consumers; the second wave was driven by government, which passed laws and regulations governing industrial practices affecting the environment. As we move into the twenty-first century, the first two environmentalism waves are merging into a third and stronger wave in which more companies are accepting responsibility for doing no harm to the environment. They are shifting from protest to prevention, and from regulation to responsibility. Companies are adopting policies of environmental sustainability—developing strategies that both sustain the environment and produce profits for the company. According to one strategist, "The challenge is to develop a sustainable global economy: an economy that the planet is capable of supporting indefinitely. . . . [It's] an enormous challenge—and an enormous opportunity."[14]

Figure 18-1 shows a grid that companies can use to gauge their progress toward environmental sustainability. At the most basic level, a company can practise pollution prevention. This involves more than pollution control—cleaning up waste after it has been created. Pollution prevention means eliminating or minimizing waste before it is created. Companies have developed ecologically safer products, recyclable and biodegradable packaging, better pollution controls, and more energy-efficient operations (see Marketing Highlight 18-2). They are finding that they can be both green and competitive. Consider how the Dutch flower industry has responded to its environmental problems:[15]

> Intense cultivation of flowers in small areas was contaminating the soil and groundwater with pesticides, herbicides, and fertilizers. Facing increasingly strict regulation, . . . the Dutch understood that the only effective way to address the problem would be to develop a closed-loop system. In advanced Dutch greenhouses, flowers now grow in recirculated water and rock wool, not in soil. This lowers the risk of infestation, and reduces the need for fertilizers and pesticides. The . . . closed-loop system also reduces variation in growing conditions, thus improving product quality. Handling costs have also gone down. . . . The net result is not only dramatically lower environmental impact but also lower costs, better product quality, and enhanced global competitiveness.

Ethical Funds
www.ethicalfunds.com/

At the next level, companies can practise *product stewardship*—minimizing not only pollution from production, but all environmental impacts throughout the full product life cycle. Many companies, such as Nortel, are adopting *design for environment* (DFE) practices, which involve thinking ahead in the design stage to create products that are easier to recover, reuse, or recycle. DFE practices not only help to sustain the environment, but also can be highly profitable:[16]

FIGURE 18-1 The environmental sustainability grid

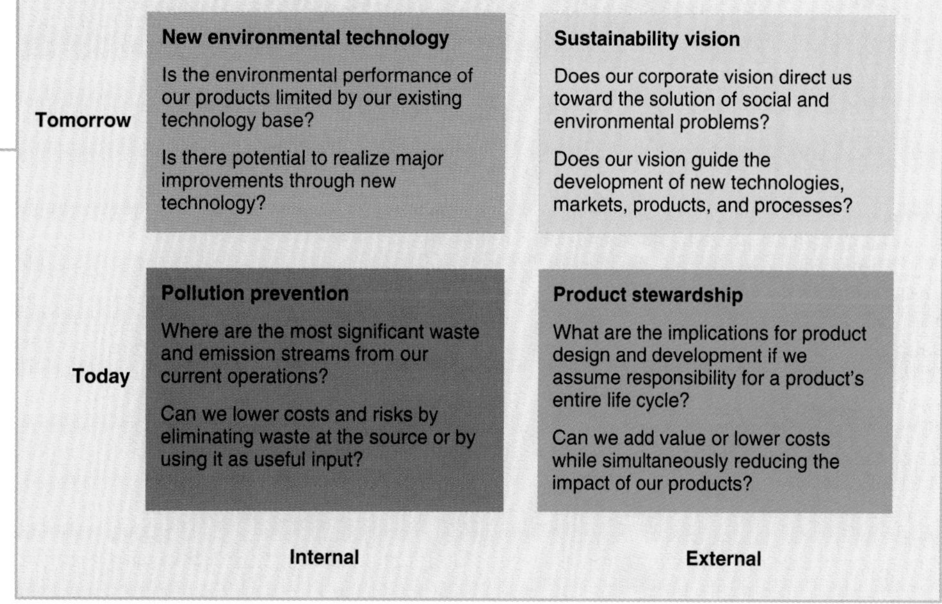

New environmental technology
Is the environmental performance of our products limited by our existing technology base?
Is there potential to realize major improvements through new technology?
Sustainability vision
Does our corporate vision direct us toward the solution of social and environmental problems?
Does our vision guide the development of new technologies, markets, products, and processes?
Tomorrow
Pollution prevention
Where are the most significant waste and emission streams from our current operations?
Can we lower costs and risks by eliminating waste at the source or by using it as useful input?
Product stewardship
What are the implications for product design and development if we assume responsibility for a product's entire life cycle?
Can we add value or lower costs while simultaneously reducing the impact of our products?
Today
Internal
External

Source: From Stuart L. Hart, "Beyond greening: Strategies for a sustainable world," *Harvard Business Review,* January–February 1997:74. © 1997 by the president and fellows of Harvard College; all rights reserved; reprinted by permission.

> Consider Xerox Corporation's Asset Recycle Management (ARM) program. A well-developed [process] for taking back leased copiers combined with a sophisticated remanufacturing process allows . . . components to be reconditioned, tested, and then reassembled into "new" machines. Xerox estimates that ARM savings in raw materials, labour, and waste disposal in 1995 alone were in the $400 million to $500 million range. . .. Xerox has discovered a way to add value and lower costs. It can continually provide lease customers with the latest product upgrades, giving them state-of-the-art functionality with minimum environmental impact.

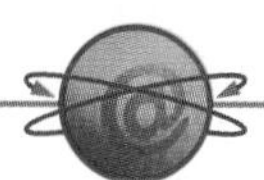

Monsanto Company
www.monsanto.com/

At the third level of environmental sustainability, companies look to the future and plan for *new environmental technologies.* Although many organizations have made significant headway in pollution prevention and product stewardship, they are limited by existing technologies and need to develop new technologies. Monsanto, for example, is tackling this problem with biotechnology. By controlling plant growth and pest resistance through bioengineering rather than through the application of pesticides or fertilizers, it hopes to find an environmentally sustainable path to increased agricultural yields.[17]

Finally, companies can develop a *sustainability vision,* which serves as a guide to the future. It shows how the company's products and services, processes, and policies must evolve and what new technologies must be developed to get there. This vision of sustainability provides a framework for pollution control, product stewardship, and environmental technology.

Most companies today invest in pollution prevention. Some forward-looking companies practise product stewardship and are developing new environmental technologies. Few companies have well-defined sustainability visions. However, emphasizing only one or a few cells in the environmental sustainability grid in Figure 18-1 can be short-sighted. While investing only in the bottom half of the grid puts a company in a good position today, it will be vulnerable in the future. In contrast, undue emphasis on the top half suggests good environmental vision, but not the skills needed to implement it. Therefore, companies should work at developing all four dimensions of environmental sustainability.

Environmentalism creates some special challenges for global marketers. As international trade barriers come down and global markets expand, environmental issues are having a growing impact on international trade. Countries in North

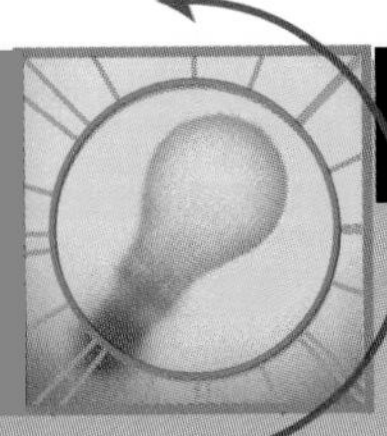

marketing highlight 18-2

The New Environmentalism and Green Marketing

On Earth Day 1970, a newly emerging environmentalism movement made its first large-scale effort to educate people about the dangers of pollution. This was a tough task: At the time, most folks weren't all that interested in environmental problems. By 1990, however, Earth Day had become an important day across North America, marked by articles in major magazines and newspapers, prime-time television extravaganzas, and countless events. It turned out to be just the start of an entire "Earth Decade" in which environmentalism became a massive worldwide force.

These days, environmentalism has broad public support. People hear and read daily about a growing list of environmental problems—global warming, acid rain, depletion of the ozone layer, air and water pollution, hazardous waste disposal, the buildup of solid wastes—and they are calling for solutions. The new environmentalism is causing many consumers to rethink what products they buy and from whom. These changing consumer attitudes have sparked a major new marketing thrust—*green marketing,* the movement by companies to develop and market environmentally responsible products. Committed "green" companies pursue not only environmental cleanup but also pollution prevention. True "green" work requires companies to practise the three Rs of waste management: reducing, reusing, and recycling waste.

Nortel has developed a program in which the company examines all of the components it designs into products to help ensure that they are made from more environmentally responsible materials, and that finished products can be recycled once their life cycle is complete. Spencer Francey Group, a Toronto-based communications firm, is developing more environmentally friendly media kits, trade-show displays, and information packages. In developing more environmentally friendly advertising and promotion materials for its clients, the firm reduced the amount of materials used, incorporated recycled materials whenever possible, and reduced inclusion of superfluous information. Not only did it improve the environmental sensitivity of its products, but it also found that it produced clearer, more concise, and more memorable messages in the process. One of the firm's programs was so successful that *Time* named it one of the best designs of the year.

Specialized products and services have been developed to meet the demands of green consumers. Such products are even being offered on the financial market. Ethical Funds, the largest family of "green funds" in Canada, invests only in firms that pass an ethical screening process that includes such criteria as records of good labour relations and charitable giving, as well as sound environmental policies.

McDonald's provides another example of green marketing. It used to purchase Coca-Cola syrup in plastic bags encased in cardboard, but now the syrup is delivered as gasoline is, pumped directly from tank trucks into storage vats at restaurants. The change saved 34 million kilograms of packaging a year. All napkins, bags, and tray liners in McDonald's restaurants are made from recycled paper, as are its carry-out drink trays and even the stationery used at headquarters. For a company the size of McDonald's, even small changes can make a big difference. For example, just making its drinking straws 20 percent lighter saved the company 500 000 kilograms of waste per year. Beyond turning its own products green, McDonald's purchases recycled materials for building and remodelling its restaurants, and it challenges its suppliers to furnish and use recycled products.

Producers in a range of industries are responding to environmental concerns. For example, 3M runs a Pollution Prevention Pays program, which has led to substantial pollution and cost reduction. Dow built a new ethylene plant in Alberta that uses 40 percent less energy and releases 97 percent less waste water than its previous plant.

During the early phase of the new environmentalism, promoting environmentally improved products and actions bal-

America, Western Europe, and other developed regions are developing stringent environmental standards. A side accord to the North American Free Trade Agreement (NAFTA) set up a commission for resolving environmental matters. And the European Union's Eco-Management and Audit Regulation provides guidelines for environmental self-regulation.[18]

However, environmental policies vary widely from country to country, and uniform worldwide standards are not expected for many years. Although countries such as Canada, Denmark, Germany, Japan, and the US have fully developed environmental policies and high public expectations, major countries such as China, India, Brazil, and Russia are only in the early stages of developing such policies. Moreover, environmental factors that motivate consumers in one country may have no impact on consumers in another. For example, PVC soft-drink bottles cannot be used in Switzerland or Germany. However, they are preferred in France, which has an extensive recycling process for them. Thus,

Corporate environmentalism: Enlightened companies are taking action not because someone is forcing them to, but because it is the right thing to do.

looned into a big business. In fact, environmentalists and regulators became concerned that companies were going overboard with their use of terms like *recyclable, biodegradable,* and *environmentally responsible.* Perhaps of equal concern was that, as more marketers used green marketing claims, more consumers would view them as mere gimmicks.

Responsible green marketing is not an easy task and is full of many contradictions. Even companies like The Body Shop, while admired for increasing awareness of such issues as degradation of the rain forests and the use of animal testing, are criticized for exaggerating their progressive practices. However, as we enter the twenty-first century, environmentalism appears to be moving into a more mature phase. Gone are the hastily prepared environmental pitches and products designed to capitalize on, or even exploit, growing public concern. The new environmentalism is now going mainstream—broader, deeper, and more sophisticated. In the words of one analyst:

> Dressing up ads with pictures of eagles and trees will no longer woo an environmentally sophisticated audience. People want to know that companies are incorporating environmental values into their manufacturing processes, products, packaging, and the very fabric of their corporate cultures. They . . . want to know that companies will not compromise the ability of future generations to enjoy the quality of life that we enjoy today. . . . As a result, we're seeing the marriage of performance benefits and environmental benefits . . . one reinforces the other.

Some companies have responded to consumer environmental concerns by doing only what is required to avert new regulations or to keep environmentalists quiet. Others have rushed to make money by catering to the public's mounting concern for the environment. But enlightened companies are taking action not because someone is forcing them to or to reap short-run profits, but because it is the right thing to do. They believe that environmental far-sightedness today will pay off tomorrow—for both the customer and the company.

Sources: Quote from Robert Rehak, "Green marketing awash in third wave," *Advertising Age,* 22 November 1993:22. Also see Joe Schwartz, "Earth Day today," *American Demographics,* April 1990:40–1; Eric Wieffering, "Wal-Mart turns green in Kansas," *American Demographics,* December 1993:23; David Woodruff, "Herman Miller: How green is my factory," *Business Week,* 16 September 1991:54–6; Jacquelyn Ottman, "Environmentalism will be the trend of the '90s," *Marketing News,* 7 December 1992:13; Peter Stisser, "A deeper shade of green," *American Demographics,* March 1994:24–30; Jon Entine, "In search of saintly stock picks," *Report on Business,* October 1995:45; and Carolyn Leitch, "PR firm delivers fewer pounds in the ruff, in the aid of less waste," *Report on Environmental Protection, Globe and Mail,* 27 February 1990:C1.

international companies are finding it difficult to develop standard environmental practices that work around the world. Instead, they are creating general policies and then translating these into tailored programs to meet local regulations and expectations.

Public Actions to Regulate Marketing

Citizen concerns about marketing practices usually will lead to public attention and legislative proposals. New bills will be debated—many will be defeated, others will be modified, and a few will become workable laws. Many of the laws that affect marketing are listed in Chapter 3. The task is to translate these laws into the language that marketing executives understand as they make decisions about competitive relations, products, price, promotion, and channels of distribution. Figure 18-2 illustrates the major legal and ethical issues facing marketing management.

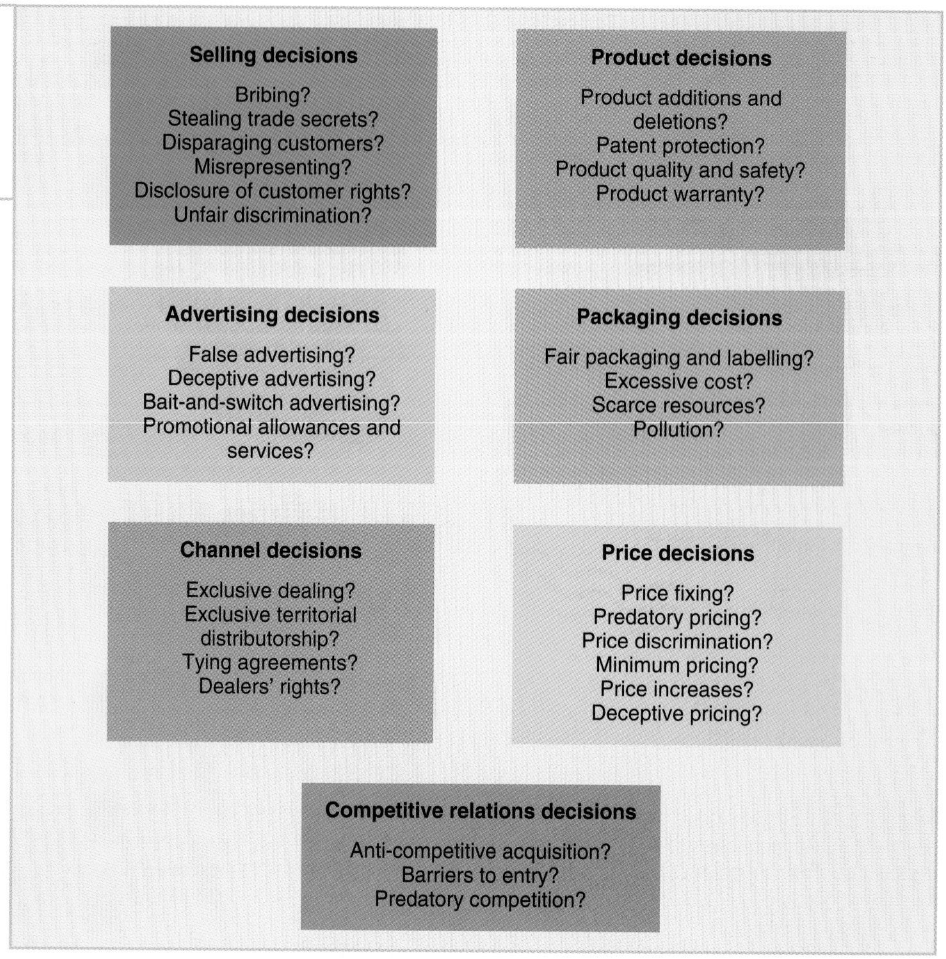

FIGURE 18-2 Legal issues facing marketing management

Selling decisions
Bribing?
Stealing trade secrets?
Disparaging customers?
Misrepresenting?
Disclosure of customer rights?
Unfair discrimination?

Product decisions
Product additions and deletions?
Patent protection?
Product quality and safety?
Product warranty?

Advertising decisions
False advertising?
Deceptive advertising?
Bait-and-switch advertising?
Promotional allowances and services?

Packaging decisions
Fair packaging and labelling?
Excessive cost?
Scarce resources?
Pollution?

Channel decisions
Exclusive dealing?
Exclusive territorial distributorship?
Tying agreements?
Dealers' rights?

Price decisions
Price fixing?
Predatory pricing?
Price discrimination?
Minimum pricing?
Price increases?
Deceptive pricing?

Competitive relations decisions
Anti-competitive acquisition?
Barriers to entry?
Predatory competition?

Business Actions toward Socially Responsible Marketing

At first, many companies opposed consumerism and environmentalism: They thought the criticisms were either unfair or unimportant. However, most companies have grown to accept the new consumer rights, at least in principle. They may oppose certain pieces of legislation as inappropriate for solving certain consumer problems, but they recognize the consumer's right to information and protection. Many companies have responded positively to consumerism and environmentalism to serve consumer needs better.

Enlightened marketing
A marketing philosophy holding that a company's marketing should support the best long-run performance of the marketing system; its five principles are consumer-oriented marketing, innovative marketing, value marketing, sense-of-mission marketing, and societal marketing.

Enlightened Marketing

The philosophy of **enlightened marketing** holds that a company's marketing should support the best long-run performance of the marketing system. Enlightened marketing consists of five principles: *consumer-oriented marketing, innovative marketing, value marketing, sense-of-mission marketing,* and *societal marketing.*

Consumer-oriented marketing
A principle of enlightened marketing that holds that a company should view and organize its marketing activities from the consumer's point of view.

Consumer-Oriented Marketing

Consumer-oriented marketing means that the company should view and organize its marketing activities from the consumer's point of view. It should work hard to sense, serve, and satisfy the needs of a defined group of customer. Consider this example:[19]

Montreal-based Walsh Integrated Environmental Systems Inc. focused on solving the waste management problems of hospitals. The owner, David Walsh, fresh out of business school, wanted to found his own business. After conducting a 12-week waste audit at Montreal's Royal Victoria Hospital, he realized what a huge waste management problem hospitals faced. Disposing of biohazardous waste costs 20 times as much as getting rid of regular waste and can result in bills of over $450 000 per year. Yet Walsh also saw that other materials, from pop cans to newspapers, were thrown in the biohazardous containers the hospital was using. In fact, about 65 percent of the material in the garbage could go into the regular waste stream. Walsh's new business developed a system called the Waste Tracker that allows hospital staff to track the waste from each department, identify how much is biohazardous, and uncover who is misusing the system. His system now saves hospitals over $200 000 per year. Walsh is confident that his focus on solving hospitals' problems will be as valuable to US hospitals as it is to Canadian institutions so he plans to expand his business. He hopes his Web site (www.walshenvironmental.com/) that allows users to download a sample system as well as video material will help crack this market.

Innovative marketing
A principle of enlightened marketing that requires that a company seek real product and marketing improvements.

Value marketing
A principle of enlightened marketing that holds that a company should put most of its resources into value-building marketing investments.

Innovative Marketing

The principle of **innovative marketing** requires that the company continuously seek real product and marketing improvements. The company that overlooks new and better ways to do things will eventually lose customers to another company that has found a better way. Cosmair Canada Inc.'s ability to be an innovative marketer has enabled it to retain its lead in the $2.5 billion Canadian cosmetic and fragrance market over its two major rivals, Procter & Gamble and Lever-Ponds. The Canadian subsidiary of Paris-based Cosmair markets well-known consumer brands L'Oréal, Lancôme, Biotherm, Maybelline, Ralph Lauren, and Drakkar Noir, and professional products in its Redken and L'Oréal lines. It carefully monitors consumer trends and competitors' offerings so that it can launch a constant stream of successful new products designed to fill every niche of the cosmetic and fragrance marketplace. It dominates the channels of distribution, and spends more than $20 million annually on advertising.[20]

Canada's Forrec Limited, an attraction design firm, has become a world leader by creating value for clients like Universal City.

Value Marketing

According to the principle of **value marketing,** the company should put most of its resources into marketing investments that build long-run consumer loyalty by continually improving the value that consumers receive from the firm's marketing offer. Lowering costs and prices, making services more convenient, and improving product quality are some value-adding strategies. The value-adding strategy of Canada's Forrec Limited has made it a leader in international theme park design. While the company name isn't exactly a household word, Forrec has been responsible for creating Canada's Wonderland north of Toronto and the casino in Niagara Falls. It also brought a South Pacific beach to the middle of Edmonton, created the streets of San Francisco in the heart of Florida, added a rooftop waterpark to the Bangkok horizon, built a theme park at the edge of the Pyramids of Giza, and is developing an aquarium in Shanghai. Steve Moorehead reveals the secret of his company's success as follows: "We make the site a place where people want to be, and provide a sense of enjoyment, where they know that they're not being ripped off, and we entice them to come back again and again."[21]

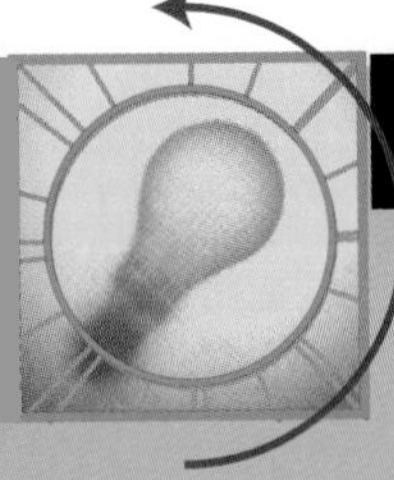

marketing highlight 18-3

Mission: Social Responsibility

In a recent poll, 92 percent of consumers said they believe it's important for marketers to be good corporate citizens. More than three-quarters said that they would switch brands and retailers when price and quality are equal for a product associated with a good cause. Companies have responded to this call for social responsibility with actions ranging from supporting worthwhile causes to writing social responsibility into their underlying mission statements.

Today, acts of good corporate citizenship abound. For example, American Express's Charge against Hunger program—through which the company donates three cents from every transaction made during the traditional holiday season—has raised more than $30 million for hunger relief. Maxwell House, a division of Kraft Foods, recently created a partnership with Habitat for Humanity to build 100 homes in as many days, while working to raise awareness for the organization. Post Cereal celebrated its one hundredth anniversary by donating to Second Harvest—one of the largest networks of hunger-relief charities—enough cereal to feed more than one million people. In addition, Post partnered with grocery retailers to sponsor a 100-day food drive supported by national and local ads to increase hunger awareness and to encourage consumer participation in the drive.

It seems that almost every company has a pet cause. Alarm company ADT gives away personal security systems to battered women. Avon Products helps fund the fight against breast cancer. Dow donates employees' time and home construction materials to Habitat for Humanity. Coca-Cola sponsors local Boys and Girls Clubs, Petro-Canada funds the Canadian Cancer Society's Information Service, while RBC Dominion Securities works with Raising the Roof.

In the chapter opener example, we examined the socially responsible mission of some of Canada's firms that have won awards for their efforts. Here are two more examples of companies working to better their communities:

Saturn. From its inception, Saturn Corporation has worked to distinguish itself as a "different" car company. As its slogan states, Saturn is "A different kind of company. A different kind of car." The company claims to focus more on its employees, customers, and communities than on revenues and bottom lines. Saturn president and chairman Don Hudler notes that "a part of Saturn's business philosophy is to meet the needs of our neighbours." An example of this philosophy in action is Saturn Playgrounds, a company program for employee involvement and community betterment. The goal of the program is to provide young children in poor communities with a safe, fun environment during non-school hours as an alternative to gangs, drugs, and crime. Backed by Saturn retail facility dollars, local Saturn employees and customers join with community members to build a community playground in a single day. So far, Saturn and its customers have built over 50 playgrounds in towns across Canada. When Saturn dedicated the new playground built on the grounds of the Toronto Zoo, 6700 owners and their families participated. But playgrounds aren't the only things needed by communities. Saturn retailers are the eyes and ears of the company, and when a community need arises, Saturn tries to respond. Saturn planted trees in areas hard hit by the 1997 ice storm. In North Bay, it provided funds for a new heart-monitoring unit. As a member of one local United Auto Workers union commented: "The Saturn Playgrounds project is a perfect example of the partnership we've built at Saturn. Working together can bring powerful results, not just in our jobs, but in our communities."

Sense-of-mission marketing
A principle of enlightened marketing that holds that a company should define its mission in broad social terms rather than narrow product terms.

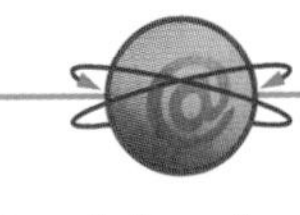

Ben & Jerry's
www.benjerry.com/

Sense-of-Mission Marketing

Sense-of-mission marketing means that the company should define its mission in broad *social* terms rather than narrow *product* terms. When a company defines a social mission, employees feel better about their work and have a clearer sense of direction. For example, defined in narrow product terms, ice-cream marketer Ben & Jerry's mission might be "to sell ice cream and frozen yogurt." However, on its Web page, the company states its mission more broadly as one of "linked prosperity":

> Our mission consists of three interrelated parts: *Product:* To make, distribute, and sell the finest quality all natural ice cream and related products in a wide variety of innovative flavors made from Vermont dairy products. *Economic:* To operate the company on a sound financial basis of profitable growth, increasing value for our shareholders, and creating career opportunities and financial rewards for our employees. *Social:* To operate the company in a way that actively recognizes the central role that business plays in the structure of society by initiating innovative ways to improve the quality of life of a broad community—local, national, and international. The underlying mission of Ben & Jerry's

The Body Shop: In 1976, Anita Roddick opened The Body Shop in Brighton, England, a tiny storefront selling beauty products out of specimen bottles. Now the company and its franchisees operate nearly 1600 stores in 47 countries. Fundamental to this rapid growth, Roddick advocates including social responsibility alongside financial performance as a measure of company success. The Body Shop's mission is "to dedicate our business to the pursuit of social and environmental change." In keeping with that mission, the company manufactures and sells natural-ingredient-based cosmetics in simple and appealing recyclable packaging. All the products are formulated without any animal testing, and supplies are often sourced from developing countries. Each franchise is required to participate in annual projects designed to better its community. In addition to these projects, The Body Shop is committed to continuous activism. For example, to promote AIDS awareness, the company has handed out condoms and pamphlets about safe sex. The Body Shop also donates a percentage of profits each year to animal-rights groups, homeless shelters, Amnesty International, Save the Rain Forest, and other social causes. As The Body Shop grows, however, it appears to be moving from rebel to mainstream. As its markets are invaded by other retailers not shackled by The Body Shop's "principles before profits" mission, the retailer's sales growth and profits are flattening. Still, says Roddick, "Business innovation is no longer just about product [and profits]. It's about the very role of business itself."

Backed by local Saturn retailers, Saturn retail team members and Saturn owners join with community members to build a community playground in a single day.

Sources: Quotes from Anat Arkin, "Open business is good for business," *People Management*, January 1996:24–7; David Lennon, "Roddick isn't finished yet," *Europe*, March 1997:39–40; "Saturn dealers build six new playgrounds in one weekend," *PR Newswire*, 4 June 1997; and The Body Shop Web site, accessed online at www.bodyshop.com, January 2000. Information also provided by Chuck Novak, Brand Manager Saturn Canada in an interview with Peggy Cunningham on 21 July 1999. Also see David Bosworth, "GM attracts site seers," *Strategy*, 22 June 1998:D1; Sinclair Steward, "Putting the customer first," *Strategy*, 9 November 1998:21; Daniel Kadlec, "The new world of giving," *Time*, 5 May 1997:62–4; Heather Salerno, "From selling cars to building playgrounds," *Washington Post*, 9 June 1997:F11; "Can doing good be good for business?" *Fortune*, 2 February 1998:148G–J; Ernest Beck, "Body Shop founder Roddick steps aside as CEO," *Wall Street Journal*, 13 May 1998:B14; and Cathy Hartman and Caryn Beck-Dudley, "Marketing strategies and the search for virtue: A case analysis of The Body Shop, International," *Journal of Business Ethics*, July 1999:249–63.

is the determination to seek new and creative ways of addressing all three parts, while holding a deep respect for the individuals, inside and outside the company, and for the communities of which they are a part.

Reshaping the basic task of selling consumer products into the larger mission of serving the interests of consumers, employees, and others in the company's various "communities" has allowed the firm to grow and prosper while simultaneously accomplishing a social agenda. Many companies today are undertaking socially responsible actions or even building social responsibility into their underlying missions (see Marketing Highlight 18-3).

Many non-profit and special interest organizations also use mission marketing. Vancouver ad agency Lanyon Phillips Partners helped Friends of Animals, a New York-based group opposed to the wearing of fur for fashion, when it developed an award-winning 1995 campaign. Vickers and Benson's "Little Girl" ad showing a little girl talking to the audience was another recent award winner. The dialogue, "I went out last night and got totally hammered. Beer. Shooters, I puked

HOW FUR LOOKS BEFORE THE GASSING, CLUBBING AND ELECTROCUTION.
Friends of Animals

Vancouver ad agency Lanyon Phillips Partners created this award-winning ad for Friends of Animals, to help them to fulfill their mission of preventing the use of fur for fashion.

my guts out. I don't even know how I got home. . . ." dramatically brought attention to the problems of youth alcohol abuse.

Societal Marketing

Societal marketing A principle of enlightened marketing that holds that a company should make marketing decisions by considering consumers' and society's long-run interests.

Following the principle of **societal marketing,** an enlightened company makes marketing decisions by considering consumers' wants and interests, the company's requirements, and society's long-run interests. The company is aware that neglecting consumer and societal long-run interests is a disservice to consumers and society. Alert companies view societal problems as opportunities.

Hewlett-Packard Canada is proud of its commitment to the local communities in which it operates. In fact, it points out that citizenship is one of its seven corporate objectives. The company articulates this belief as follows: "HP Canada sees its contribution to societal needs as creating better places for Canadians to live, including HP employees and our customers." This sense of citizenship is more than corporate public relations. The company works to translate its words into practice. It actively works to protect the environment by carefully following the three Rs (reduce, recycle, reuse), and it supports important causes such as education and health care since it believes "that the betterment of our society is not a job to be left to a few; it is a responsibility to be shared by all."[22]

Deficient products Products that have neither immediate appeal nor long-run benefits.

A societally oriented marketer wants to design products that are not only pleasing but also beneficial. The difference is shown in Figure 18-3. Products can be classified according to their degree of immediate consumer satisfaction and long-run consumer benefit. **Deficient products,** such as bad-tasting and ineffective

Alcohol and Drug Concerns Inc. used mission marketing to dramatically bring attention to the problem of youth alcohol abuse.

FIGURE 18-3 Societal classification of products

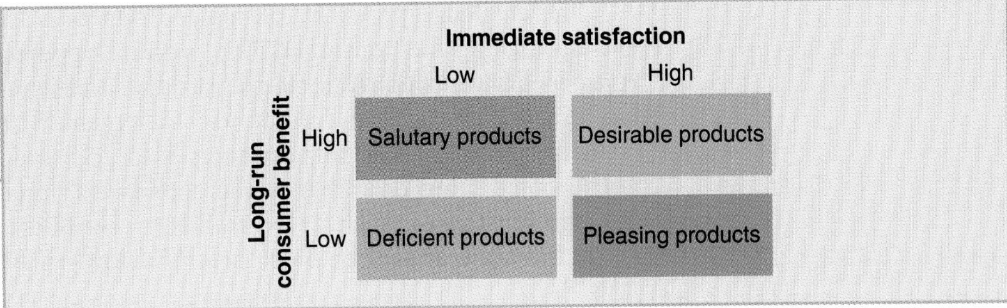

Pleasing products
Products that give high immediate satisfaction but may hurt consumers in the long run.

Salutary products
Products that have low appeal but may benefit consumers in the long run.

Desirable products
Products that give both high immediate satisfaction and high long-run benefits.

medicine, have neither immediate appeal nor long-run benefits. **Pleasing products** give high immediate satisfaction but may hurt consumers in the long run: An example is cigarettes. **Salutary products** have low appeal but benefit consumers in the long run: Insurance is a salutary product. **Desirable products** give both high immediate satisfaction and high long-run benefits. President's Choice "Too Good to Be True" soup mixes have been cited as healthful products. Developed for people with special dietary needs, they have been welcomed by a range of consumers who want good-tasting, high-fibre, low-fat, easy-to-prepare, healthful food. Another example of a desirable product is Herman Miller's Avian office chair, which is not just attractive and functional but also environmentally responsible:[23]

> Herman Miller, one of the world's largest office furniture makers, has received numerous awards for environmentally responsible products and business practices. In 1994, the company formed an earth friendly design task force responsible for infusing the company's design process with its environmental values. The task force carries out life cycle analyses on the company's products, including everything from how much of a product can be made from recycled materials to how much of the product itself can be recycled at the end of its useful life. For example, the company's Avian chair is designed for the lowest possible ecological impact and 100 percent recyclability. Herman Miller reduced material used in the chair by using gas-assist injection molding for the frame, which resulted in hollow frame members (like the bones of birds, hence the chair's name). The frame needs no paint or other finish. All materials are recyclable. No ozone-depleting materials are used. The chair is shipped partially assembled, thus reducing the packaging and energy needed to ship it. Finally, a materials schematic is embedded in the bottom of the seat to help recycle the chair at the end of its life. This is truly a desirable product—it's won awards for design and function and for environmental responsibility.

Herman Miller's earth-friendly design task force infuses the company's design process with environmental values. It designed the Avian chair for the lowest possible ecological impact and 100-percent recyclability.

The challenge posed by pleasing products is that they sell very well but may end up hurting the consumer. The product opportunity, therefore, is to add long-run benefits without reducing the product's pleasing qualities. For example, Sears developed a phosphate-free laundry detergent that was also very effective. The challenge posed by salutary products is to add some pleasing qualities so that they will become more desirable in the consumers' minds. For example, synthetic fats and fat substitutes, such as NutraSweet's Simplesse and P&G's Olestra, promise to improve the appeal of more healthful low-calorie and low-fat foods.

Marketing Ethics

Conscientious marketers face many moral dilemmas. The best thing to do is often unclear. Because not all managers have fine moral sensitivity, companies need to develop *corporate marketing ethics policies*—broad guidelines that everyone in the organization must follow. These policies should cover distributor relations, advertising standards, customer service, pricing, product development, and general ethical standards.

The finest guidelines cannot resolve all the difficult ethical situations the marketer faces. Table 18-1 lists some difficult ethical situations that marketers could

TABLE 18-1 Some Morally Difficult Situations in Marketing

1. You work for a cigarette company and up until now have not been convinced that cigarettes cause cancer. A report comes across your desk that clearly shows the link between smoking and cancer. What do you do?
2. Your R&D department has changed one of your products slightly. It is not really "new and improved," but you know that putting this statement on the package and in advertising will increase sales. What do you do?
3. You have been asked to add a stripped-down model to your line that could be advertised to attract customers to the store. The product won't be very good, but salespeople will be able to switch buyers up to higher-priced units. You are asked to give the green light for this stripped-down version. What do you do?
4. You are considering hiring a product manager who just left a competitor's company. She would be more than happy to tell you all the competitor's plans for the coming year. What do you do?
5. One of your top dealers in an important territory has recently had family troubles, and his sales have slipped. It looks like it will take him some time to straighten out his family trouble. Meanwhile, you are losing many sales. Legally, you can terminate the dealer's franchise and replace him. What do you do?
6. You have a chance to win a big account that will mean a lot to you and your company. The purchasing agent hints that a "gift" would influence the decision. Your assistant recommends sending a fine colour television set to the buyer's home. What do you do?
7. You have heard that a competitor has a new product feature that will make a big difference in sales. The competitor will demonstrate the feature in a private dealer meeting at the annual trade show. You can easily send a snooper to this meeting to learn about the new feature. What do you do?
8. You have to choose between three ad campaigns outlined by your agency. "A" is a soft-sell, honest information campaign. "B" uses sex-loaded emotional appeals and exaggerates the product's benefits. "C" involves a noisy, irritating commercial that is sure to gain audience attention. Pretests show that the campaigns are effective in the following order: C, B, and A. What do you do?
9. You are interviewing a capable woman applicant for a job as a salesperson. She is better qualified than the men just interviewed. Nevertheless, you know that some of your important customers prefer dealing with men, and you will lose some sales if you hire her. What do you do?
10. You are a sales manager in an encyclopedia company. Your competitor's salespeople are getting into homes by pretending to take a research survey. After they finish the survey, they switch to their sales pitch. This technique seems to be very effective. What do you do?

face during their careers. If marketers choose immediate sales-producing actions in all these cases, their marketing behaviour may well be described as immoral or even amoral. If they refuse to go along with *any* of the actions, they may be ineffective as marketing managers and unhappy because of the constant moral tension. Managers need a set of principles that will help them to determine the moral importance of each situation and decide how far they can go in good conscience.

But *what* principle should guide companies and marketing managers on issues of ethics and social responsibility? One philosophy is that such issues are decided by the free market and legal system. Under this principle, companies and their managers are not responsible for making moral judgments. Companies can in good conscience do whatever the system legally allows.

A second philosophy puts responsibility not in the system but in the hands of individual companies and managers. This more enlightened philosophy suggests that a company should have a "social conscience." Companies and managers should apply high standards of ethics and morality when making corporate decisions, regardless of "what the system allows." History provides an endless list of examples of company actions that were legal and allowed but were highly irresponsible. Consider this example:[24]

> Prior to the [US] *Pure Food and Drug Act,* the advertising for a diet pill promised that a person taking this pill could eat virtually anything at any time and still lose weight. Too good to be true? Actually the claim was quite true; the product lived up to its billing with frightening efficiency. It seems that the primary active ingredient in this "diet pill" was tapeworm larvae. These larvae would develop in the intestinal tract and, of course, be well fed; the pill taker would in time, quite literally, starve to death.

Each company and marketing manager must work out a philosophy of socially responsible and ethical behaviour. Under the social marketing concept, companies and managers must look beyond what is legal and allowed and develop standards based on personal integrity, corporate conscience, and long-run consumer welfare. According to a survey of the CEOs of Canada's top 500 companies, 84 percent agreed that there was a good understanding of ethics in their companies, and 90 percent said that ethics was a priority for senior managers. Many Canadian companies (80%) have developed codes of ethics to help their managers make better decisions. Even more important, 70 percent of the codes were written to develop standards that go beyond mere legal compliance. However, only 27 percent of the firms surveyed offered ethics training programs, and only 25 percent have ethics compliance officers. Nonetheless, 75 percent of the companies studied reported that employees of their firms had been disciplined because of lack of ethical behaviour.[25]

The issue of ethics provides special challenges for international marketers. Business standards and laws vary widely from one country to the next. For example, while Levi Strauss, Nike, and Gap have forward-thinking human relations policies in North America, these firms have been accused of exploiting workers working for their subcontractors in Latin America and Southeast Asia. Like many other international firms, Nike has responded by developing a code of ethics that applies to their international businesses as well as to their domestic operations.

Gift giving, always a thorny issue in international business negotiations, is often covered under these codes. Some firms, such as General Motors and Bata Industries Ltd., have very strict codes that forbid the acceptance of gifts, entertainment, or other gratuity. The codes rule out acceptance of any token including tickets to a football game, birthday presents from suppliers, or even a watch sent through the mail. GM realizes that in some countries, like China, where gift giving is part of the business culture, refusal to accept a gift would have significant negative implications. Therefore, GM's representatives working there can accept a gift as long as they do it in the name of the company and turn it over for display on the company premises. Bata believes that such a strict policy is necessary because it is impossible to differentiate between a gift and a bribe. Either can lead a decision maker into a conflict of interest and an inability to make a purchase decision that represents the best value for the company.[26]

When firms go beyond gift giving to influence decisions into the realm of bribery—giving a covert payment to a government official to obtain a concession—they are no longer just committing an unethical act, they are committing an illegal one violating the *Corruption of Foreign Public Officials Act* tabled by the Canadian government in 1998.

Many professional associations and firms have developed codes of ethics to better manage ethical issues related to marketing. For example, the Canadian Direct Marketing Association has a code to regulate practices of its members. The American Marketing Association, an international association of marketing managers and scholars with many Canadian members, developed the code of ethics shown in Table 18-2. Companies are also developing programs to teach managers about important ethics issues and help them find the proper responses. They hold ethics workshops and seminars and set up ethics committees.

Some organizations, like Ontario Power Generation Inc. and Imperial Oil, have appointed high-level ethics officers to champion ethics issues and to help resolve ethics problems and concerns facing employees. Nynex created a new position of vice-president of ethics, supported by a dozen full-time staff and a million-dollar budget. Since 1991, the ethics department has trained some 95 000 employees. This training includes sending 22 000 managers to full-day workshops that include case studies on ethical actions in marketing, finance, and other business functions.[27]

Many companies have developed innovative ways to educate employees about ethics:[28]

> Citicorp has developed an ethics board game, which teams of employees use to solve hypothetical quandaries. General Electric employees can tap into specially designed software on their personal computers to get answers to ethical questions. At Texas Instruments, employees are treated to a weekly column on ethics over an electronic news service. One popular feature: a kind of "Dear Abby" mailbag, answers provided by the company's ethics officer, . . . that deals with the troublesome issues employees face most often.

Whirlpool Corporation
www.whirlpool.com/

Still, written codes and ethics programs do not ensure ethical behaviour. Ethics and social responsibility require a total corporate commitment. They must be a component of the overall corporate culture. According to David R. Whitman, chairman of the board of Whirlpool Corporation: "In the final analysis, 'ethical behaviour' must be an integral part of the organization, a way of life that is deeply ingrained in the collective corporate body. . . . In any business enterprise, ethical behaviour must be a tradition, a way of conducting one's affairs that is passed from generation to generation of employees at all levels of the organization. It is the responsibility of management, starting at the very top, to both set the example by personal conduct and create an environment that not only encourages and rewards ethical behaviour, but which also makes anything less totally unacceptable."[29]

Canada's 74 000 charities and non-profit organizations are not immune to questions of ethics. While few question the importance of these worthy causes, there has been growing criticism about some of the fundraising methods they use. Two major concerns have surfaced. More charities are using lotteries to raise funds. These not only add to the pressures on people to gamble, they may often jeopardize the welfare of the non-profit. Use of professional telemarketers is another source of ethical concern. They raise funds on the part of non-profit organizations, but the charity may only see a small portion of the money raised. In the face of growing public scrutiny, non-profits have to be as ethically aware and socially responsible as their for-profit counterparts.

The future holds many challenges and opportunities for marketing managers as they move into the twenty-first century. Technological advances in solar energy,

TABLE 18-2 American Marketing Association Code of Ethics

Members of the American Marketing Association are committed to ethical, professional conduct. They have joined together in subscribing to this Code of Ethics embracing the following topics:

Responsibilities of the Marketer

Marketers must accept responsibility for the consequences of their activities and make every effort to ensure that their decisions, recommendations, and actions function to identify, serve, and satisfy all relevant publics: customers, organizations, and society.

Marketers' professional conduct must be guided by:

1. The basic rule of professional ethics: not knowingly to do harm;
2. The adherence to all applicable laws and regulations;
3. The accurate representation of their education, training, and experience; and
4. The active support, practice, and promotion of this Code of Ethics.

Honesty and Fairness

Marketers shall uphold and advance the integrity, honour, and dignity of the marketing profession by:

1. Being honest in serving consumers, clients, employees, suppliers, distributors, and the public;
2. Not knowingly participating in conflict of interest without prior notice to all parties involved; and
3. Establishing equitable fee schedules including the payment or receipt of usual, customary, and/or legal compensation for marketing exchanges.

Rights and Duties of Parties in the Marketing Exchange Process

Participants in the marketing exchange process should be able to expect that:

1. Products and services offered are safe and fit for their intended uses;
2. Communications about offered products and services are not deceptive;
3. All parties intend to discharge their obligations, financial and otherwise, in good faith; and
4. Appropriate internal methods exist for equitable adjustment and/or redress of grievances concerning purchases.

It is understood that the above would include, but is not limited to, the following responsibilities of the marketer:

In the area of product development and management,

- disclosure of all substantial risks associated with product or service usage;
- identification of any product component substitution that might materially change the product or impact on the buyer's purchase decision;
- identification of extra cost-added features.

In the area of promotions,

- avoidance of false and misleading advertising;
- rejection of high-pressure manipulations, or misleading sales tactics;
- avoidance of sales promotions that use deceptions or manipulation.

In the area of distribution,

- not manipulating the availability of a product for purpose of exploitation;
- not using coercion in the marketing channel;
- not exerting undue influence over the reseller's choice to handle a product.

In the area of pricing,

- not engaging in price fixing;
- not practising predatory pricing;
- disclosing the full price associated with any purchase.

In the area of marketing research,

- prohibiting selling or fundraising under the guise of conducting research;
- maintaining research integrity by avoiding misrepresentation and omission of pertinent research data;
- treating outside clients and suppliers fairly.

Organizational Relationships

Marketers should be aware of how their behaviour may influence or impact on the behaviour of others in organizational relationships. They should not demand, encourage, or apply coercion to obtain unethical behaviour in their relationships with others, such as employees, suppliers, or customers.

1. Apply confidentiality and anonymity in professional relationships with regard to privileged information;
2. Meet their obligations and responsibilities in contracts and mutual agreements in a timely manner;
3. Avoid taking the work of others, in whole, or in part, and represent this work as their own or directly benefit from it without compensation or consent of the originator or owner;
4. Avoid manipulation to take advantage of situations to maximize personal welfare in a way that unfairly deprives or damages the organization of others.

Any AMA member found to be in violation of any provision of this Code of Ethics may have his or her Association membership suspended or revoked.

personal computers, interactive television, modern medicine, and new forms of transportation, recreation, and communication provide abundant marketing opportunities. However, forces in the socioeconomic, cultural, and natural environments increase the limits under which marketing can be carried out. Companies that are able to create new values in a socially responsible way will have a world to conquer.

Review of Concept Connections

Responsible marketers discover what consumers want and respond with the right products, priced to give good value to buyers and profit to the producer. A marketing system should sense, serve, and satisfy consumer needs and improve the quality of consumers' lives. In working to meet consumer needs, marketers may take some actions that are not to everyone's liking or benefit. Marketing managers should be aware of the main criticisms of marketing.

1. **Identify the major social criticisms of marketing.**

   Marketing's impact on individual consumer welfare has been criticized for its high prices, deceptive practices, high-pressure selling, shoddy or unsafe products, planned obsolescence, and poor service to disadvantaged consumers. Marketing's impact on society has been criticized for creating false wants and too much materialism, too few social goods, cultural pollution, and too much political power. Critics have also criticized marketing's impact on other businesses for harming competitors and reducing competition through acquisitions, practices that create barriers to entry, and unfair competitive marketing practices.

2. **Define consumerism and environmentalism and explain how they affect marketing strategies.**

   Concerns about the marketing system have led to citizen action movements. Consumerism is an organized social movement intended to strengthen the rights and power of consumers relative to sellers. Alert marketers view it as an opportunity to serve consumers better by providing more consumer information, education, and protection. Environmentalism is an organized social movement seeking to minimize the harm done to the environment and quality of life by marketing practices. The first wave of modern environmentalism was driven by environmental groups and concerned consumers; the second wave was driven by government, which passed laws and regulations governing industrial practices affecting the environment. Moving into the twenty-first century, the first two environmentalism waves are merging into a third and stronger wave in which companies are accepting responsibility for doing no environmental harm. Companies now are adopting policies of environmental sustainability—developing strategies that both sustain the environment and produce profits for the company.

3. **Describe the principles of socially responsible marketing.**

   Many companies originally opposed these social movements and laws, but most of them now recognize a need for positive consumer information, education, and protection. Some companies have followed a policy of enlightened marketing, which holds that a company's marketing should support the best long-run performance of the marketing system. The five principles of enlightened marketing are consumer-oriented marketing, innovative marketing, value marketing, sense-of-mission marketing, and societal marketing.

4. **Explain the role of ethics in marketing.**

   Increasingly, companies are responding to the need to provide company policies and guidelines to help their managers deal with questions of marketing ethics. Even the best guidelines cannot resolve all of the difficult ethical decisions that firms must make, but there are some principles that marketers can choose among. One principle states that such issues should be decided by the free market and legal system. A more enlightened principle puts responsibility not in the system but in the hands of individual companies and managers. Each firm and marketing manager must develop a philosophy of socially responsible and ethical behaviour. Under the societal marketing concept, managers must look beyond what is legal and allowable and develop standards based on personal integrity, corporate conscience, and long-term consumer welfare.

   Because business standards and practices vary among countries, the issue of ethics poses special challenges for international marketers. The growing consensus among today's marketers is that it is important to make a commitment to a common set of shared standards worldwide.

Key Terms

Consumerism *(p. 754)*
Consumer-oriented marketing *(p. 762)*
Deficient products *(p. 766)*
Desirable products *(p. 767)*
Enlightened marketing *(p. 762)*
Environmentalism *(p. 756)*
Innovative marketing *(p. 763)*
Pleasing products *(p. 767)*
Salutary products *(p. 767)*
Sense-of-mission marketing *(p. 764)*
Societal marketing *(p. 766)*
Value marketing *(p. 763)*

Discussing the Issues

1. Many firms, like Molson, Canada Trust, Procter & Gamble, Bell Canada, and Imperial Oil, have been practising cause-related marketing as a means of fulfilling their social responsibilities. Cause-related marketing is the practice of associating a for-profit firm's products or services with a non-profit cause. While the primary purpose of the program is the accomplishment of marketing objectives, the non-profit also achieves significant benefits from these campaigns. Describe some of the cause-related campaigns you have seen. Do you think they are a legitimate means for firms to fulfill part of their social responsibility?
2. You have been invited to appear along with an economist on a panel assessing marketing practices in the soft-drink industry. You are surprised when the economist opens the discussion with a long list of criticisms, focusing on the unnecessarily high marketing costs and deceptive promotional practices. Abandoning your prepared comments, you set out to defend marketing, in general, and the beverage industry, in particular. How would you respond to the economist's attack?
3. Comment on the state of consumers' rights on the Internet and in e-commerce. Design a "Bill of Rights" that would protect consumers while they shop for products and services on the Internet. Consider such issues as government regulation, ease and convenience of use, warranties, guarantees and return policies, privacy, security, and cost-efficient commerce.
4. Figure 18-1 shows a grid that companies can use to gauge their progress toward environmental sustainability. Where do most firms begin on this grid? Which cells are most difficult to achieve?
5. Which of the following firms, if any, practise enlightened marketing: (a) McDonald's, (b) your local credit union, (c) General Motors, and (d) Mountain Equipment Co-op?
6. Compare the principle of sense-of-mission marketing with the principle of societal marketing. How do these two concepts relate to the marketing concept and societal marketing concept presented in Chapter 1?
7. Products can be classified according to their degree of immediate consumer satisfaction and long-run consumer benefit. Give examples of products in each of the four cells of Figure 18-3 and prepare a brief strategy statement for marketing each one.
8. You are the marketing manager for a small firm that makes kitchen appliances. While conducting field tests, you discover a design flaw in one of your most popular models that could potentially cause harm to a small number of consumers. However, a product recall would likely bankrupt your company, leaving all of the employees (including you) jobless. What would you do?

Marketing Applications

1. The "greening of North America" has much more to do with lifestyles than forestry management. Adopting a green lifestyle means that consumers demand products and services that are environmentally responsible. As consumers turn greener, companies respond with environmentally responsible products and programs. McDonald's, Wal-Mart, Loblaw, and Procter & Gamble are a few of

the companies that have now adopted a more green way of thinking and acting. See the "Community" section of the McDonald's Web site (www.mcdonalds.com) and the Internet Green Marketplace Web site (www.envirolink.org) for more information.

a. Assume that you are a marketing manager for Crayola Crayons (www.crayola.com) and formulate a "green policy" that will make your product both competitive and environmentally responsible. As you formulate this policy, consider the product itself, packaging, distribution, promotion, and merchandising with distributors.
b. Visit the McDonald's Web site. What is the company's green policy? Comment on the appropriateness of this policy.
c. One organization that has been at the centre of promoting an environmentally responsible green policy to corporations is Greenpeace (www.greenpeace.org). Do you find Greenpeace's proposals to be radical? Explain. How might Greenpeace react to the policies you devised for Crayola?
d. Develop a set of rules that would guide organizations toward being environmentally responsible.

2. As a small child, you were probably taught that it is better to give than to receive. This advice is one of the cornerstones of philanthropy, including corporate philanthropy. Although it is sometimes hard to go from being a receiver to being a giver, Ted Turner and Bill Gates seem to have mastered the transition. In the mid-1990s, Ted Turner pledged $1 billion (spread over 10 years) to the United Nations to help fight world hunger and other problems. Bill Gates's wife, Melinda, heads one of the world's largest philanthropies, with $17 billion at her disposal. This organization targets education and health programs for the poor. Other wealthy entrepreneurs and executives have chosen different paths to charitable giving. Financial wizard Warren Buffett, worth an estimated $30 billion and the world's second richest person behind Bill Gates, has chosen to keep his money working for him until his death. To date, the Buffett Foundation has received only a sliver of his wealth. For more information on charitable giving by business organizations, see the Canadian Centre for Philanthropy (www.ccp.ca), the National Charities Information Bureau (www.give.org), and the American Institute of Philanthropy (www. charitywatch. org).

a. Given the new social responsibility in North America today, what should be an organization's view toward charitable giving? Explain.
b. What are the marketing ramifications of an organization's philanthropic activities?
c. Many corporations support worthy causes and contribute generously to their communities. Check out the Web sites of one of the following or some other company and report on its philanthropic and socially responsible activities: Johnson & Johnson (www.jnj.com), Nike (www.nikebiz.com), Coca-Cola (www.coca cola.com), Avon (www.avon.com), and Prudential Life Insurance (www.prudential.com).
d. How does philanthropy by corporations relate to the social criticisms of marketing?

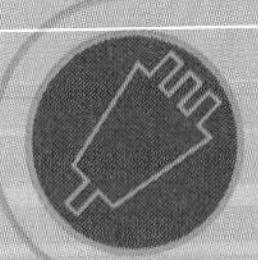

Internet Connections

Spamming

Spamming is the bulk distribution of unsolicited, and often unwanted, e-mail messages. Because e-mail carries no postage cost, this form of direct marketing has grown rapidly in the past few years. Used properly, online direct marketing can inform consumers of products or updates of interest to them. When abused, spamming becomes at best an annoyance to Internet users and at worst offensive—for example, adult sites that spam to underage users. There are two ways for consumers to stop spam. Technological solutions filter the spam either at the Internet service provider

(ISP) level or right on the user's PC. Spam can also be controlled by industry self-regulation and government legislation. Marketers who want to build customer relationships and positive brand equity will add customers to e-mail lists only with their prior consent. Customers thus opt in rather than having to opt out of the list. Complete the following table—leave blank any items for which the organization does not offer a position.

For Discussion

1. Do these organizations promise to stop direct marketing entirely or just filter it for the items that you want?
2. If marketers were doing their job correctly, would consumer filtering be necessary? Explain why or why not.
3. A particularly venal form of spamming disguises the sender's e-mail address to make it impossible to request removal from the list. Do you believe that this practice should be allowed?
4. Many e-mail programs now allow you to block mail coming from specific addresses. Is this an effective way to stop spamming?
5. Based on your understanding of spamming, write another item for the consumers' rights listed in this chapter. Then write an item for the marketers' rights list.
6. A service called BrightMail (www.brightmail.com) helps to remove spam at the ISP level. How does this service work?

Item	Canadian Marketing Association www.the-cma.org	Direct Marketing Association www.the-dma.org	American Marketing Association www.ama.org
Support opt-in lists only			
Support requiring spammers to reveal their return address			
Support consumer's right to be removed from lists			
Provide tips on how to be removed from lists			

Savvy Sites

- CAUCE, the Coalition Against Unsolicited Commercial E-mail (www.cauce.com), is a grassroots organization that advocates legislation against spam.
- Consumer Reports Online (www.consumer reports.org) offers tips about products as well as information about product recalls, product safety alerts, and other consumer issues.
- The Canadian Marketing Association's Web page provides tips to help consumers protect themselves and their families from deceptive marketing practices (www.the-cma.org/main.html).

Notes

1. Quotes from Canadian Centre for Philanthropy, "1999 Imagine New Spirit of Community, Mutual Fund Industry Corporate Industry Award presented to Altamira Investments Services Inc." press release, www.ccp.ca/Imagine; Canadian Centre for Philanthropy, "Tis the season for some good news," press release, Toronto, 15 December 2000; and Bruce Pope, CEO Molson Breweries, Queen's University, School of Business, 27 March 1996. Also see Environics, "Consumers worldwide expect businesses to achieve social as well as economic goals," *The Millennium Poll on Corporate Social Responsibility*, press release, 20 September 1999 www.environics.net/eil/millennium/press; Janet MacPhail, "Event marketing: Social marketing a process, not a program," *Strategy*, 29 September 1997:20; David Menzies, "All for a good cause," *Marketing*, 26 September 1994:13–5; Erica Zlomislic, "Sears backs PC donation effort," *Strategy*, 24 November 1997:1; "And the winners are," *Inter Sector: A Newsletter for Imagine's Community Partners*, 3(6):1; Bell Canada Web site www.bell.ca.
2. Barrie McKenna, "Suzy Shier fined $300,000," *Globe and Mail*, 18 July 1994:B7.
3. John Gustavson, "The new fraud busters," *Marketing On-Line*, 16 August 1999.
4. Sandra Pesmen, "How low is low? How free is free?" *Advertising Age*, 7 May 1990:S10; Karolyn Schuster, "The dark side of nutrition," *Food Management*, June 1999:34–9.
5. See Judith Bell and Bonnie Maria Burlin, "In urban areas, many more still pay more for food," *Journal of Public Policy and Marketing*, Fall 1993:268–70; Alan R. Andreasen, "Revisiting the disadvantaged: Old lesson and new problems," *Journal of Public Policy and Marketing*, Fall 1993:270–5; Tony Attrino, "Nationwide settles redlining suit in Ohio," *National Underwriter*, 27 April 1998:4; Angelo B. Henderson, "First Chicago unit agrees to lend $3 billion in Detroit," *Wall Street Journal*, 26 June 1998; and Kathryn Graddy and Diana C. Robertson, "Fairness of pricing decisions," *Business Ethics Quarterly*, April 1999:225–43.
6. Richard W. Pollay, "The distorted mirror: Reflections on the unintended consequences of advertising," *Journal of Marketing*, April 1986:18–36.
7. From an advertisement for *Fact* magazine, which does not carry advertisements.
8. Ann Gibbon, "Smoking's labelling perils," *Globe and Mail*, 5 May 1994:B1–2.
9. Steve Hamm, "Microsoft's future," *Business Week*, 19 January 1998:58–68; Ronald. A. Cass, "Microsoft, running scared," *New York Times*, 28 June 1999:17; www.microsoft.com/presspass/fastfacts.asp.
10. Consumers' Association of Canada, 404–267 O'Connor Street, Ottawa, ON K2P 1V3; www.consumer.ca.
11. Government of Canada, "Canada shows continued leadership on protecting the ozone layer," news release, Ottawa, 18 December 2000, www.ec.gc.ca/press/001219_n_e.htm.
12. Ken MacQueen, "Ministers declare war on excess packaging," *Whig-Standard*, 22 March 1990:11.
13. Alan M. Robinson, "It's easy being green: Environmentalism isn't dead," *Marketing On-Line*, 11 October 1999.
14. Stuart L. Hart, "Beyond greening: Strategies for a sustainable world," *Harvard Business Review*, January–February 1997: 66–76. Also see Jacquelyn Ottman, "What sustainability means to marketers," *Marketing News*, 21 July 1997:4; and James L. Kolar, "Environmental sustainability: Balancing pollution control with economic growth," *Environmental Quality Management*, Spring 1999:1–10.
15. Michael E. Porter and Claas van derLinde, "Green and competitive: Ending the stalemate," *Harvard Business Review*, September–October 1995:120–34.
16. Hart, "Beyond greening":72. For other examples, see Jacquelyn Ottman, "Environmental winners show sustainable strategies," *Marketing News*, 27 April 1998:6.
17. Hart, "Beyond greening":73; Linda Grant, "Monsanto's bet: There's gold in going green," *Fortune*, 14 April 1997:116–8; Carl Pope, "Billboards of the garden wall," *Sierra*, January–February 1999:12–3.
18. See John Audley, *Green Politics and Global Trade: NAFTA and the Future of Environmental Politics*, Georgetown: Georgetown University Press, 1997; Lars K. Hallstrom, "Industry versus ecology: Environment in the new Europe," *Futures*, February 1999:25–38; Joe McKinney, "NAFTA: Four years down the road," *Baylor Business Review*, Spring 1999:22–3; Andreas Diekmann and Axel Franzen, "The wealth of nations and environmental concern," *Environment and Behavior*, July 1999:540–9.
19. Linda Sutherland, "Brothers find focus in waste," *Globe and Mail*, 6 January 1997:B8.
20. Louise Gagnon, "Cosmetic changes," *Marketing Magazine*, 21/28 July 1997:18.
21. Ian Cruikshand, "Fun factory," *Report on Business Magazine*, August 1997:30–4.
22. "Getting involved in the community: The HP way," supplement sponsored by Hewlett-Packard (Canada) Ltd.., *Report on Business*, April 1996:30.
23. Information accessed online at www.HermanMiller.com/company/environment/conservation.html, January 2000.
24. Dan R. Dalton and Richard A. Cosier, "The four faces of social responsibility," *Business Horizons*, May–June 1982:19–27.
25. Survey data collected by Peggy Cunningham and Derek Gent, Queen's University, 1995.
26. Janet McFarland, "When is a gift a bribe?" *Globe and Mail*, 15 January 1996; "GM's gift policy covers the bases," *Globe and Mail*, 11 September 1997:B17.
27. Mark Hendricks, "Ethics in action," *Management Review*, January 1995:53–5.
28. Kenneth Labich, "The new crisis in business management," *Fortune*, 20 April 1992:167–76.
29. From "Ethics as a practical matter," a message from David R. Whitman, chairman of the board of Whirlpool Corporation, reprinted in Ricky E. Griffin and Ronald J. Ebert, *Business*, Upper Saddle River, NJ: Prentice Hall, 1989:578–9. For more on marketing ethics, see Lynn Sharp Paine, "Managing for organizational integrity," *Harvard Business Review*, March–April 1994:106–17; Tom McInerney, "Double trouble: Combining business and ethics," *Business Ethics Quarterly*, January 1998:187–9; John F. Gaski, "Does marketing ethics really have anything to say?" *Journal of Business Ethics*, February 1999:315–34; and Thomas W. Dunfee, N. Craig Smith, and William T. Ross, "Social contracts and marketing ethics," *Journal of Marketing*, July 1999:14–32.

Company Case 18

Dying to Be Thin?

In 1995, Ann Gilmore just wanted to lose a little weight. Her doctor prescribed a diet pill in the hope that losing weight would help relieve her chronic back pain. Gilmore lost some weight, but not much, so she quit taking the medication after only three months. About a month later, she underwent a series of tests and was diagnosed with primary pulmonary hypertension, or PPH, a rare and deadly lung condition that kills most of its victims within two years. Too late for Gilmore, research revealed that diet drugs containing fenfluramine and dexfenfluramine increased the chance of developing PPH by 23 times. In Canada, the drugs went under the names of Ponderal and Redux.

While some Canadians like Gilmore seek to lose weight for medical reasons, others diet to improve their appearance. North Americans spend almost $60 billion a year trying to stay thin. A recent survey found that 90 percent of respondents believe that they weigh too much, even though only 25 percent were deemed to be medically overweight. Even more troubling is the fact that this number includes underweight women who still view themselves as fat.

No one denies that being medically overweight is a serious problem. The medical community considers obesity to be the second greatest health hazard, right behind smoking. But there is a difference between people who are actually overweight and those who perceive themselves to be in this category even though they are well within their recommended weight limits.

Perceptions of obesity may make people susceptible to unscrupulous marketing tactics. They may purchase premium-priced products with dubious benefits. For example, products sold by Weight Watchers or Jenny Craig are priced significantly higher than other food items in the same product category, yet people purchasing these diet foods keep cash registers humming. Millions join expensive health clubs and get no more benefit than they would by going for a daily walk. While these products and services may eat up consumers' dollars, they probably don't result in significant long-term harm.

This just wasn't the case for the more than 150 000 Canadians who took diet drugs. Twelve have developed PPH and recent Health Canada documents show that two people have died. Dozens more have developed heart and lung problems. These people, including Gilmore, have launched a class action suit against the French drug manufacturer and the Canadian distributor, Servier Canada. Seeking $750 million in damages, they're hopeful of a quick victory since a US firm has already agreed to pay up to $4.5 billion in damages to people who took the drugs. Many people wonder why Health Canada didn't ban these drugs sooner given the growing number of research studies that pointed to the drugs' dangers.

Redux was first launched in North America after receiving approval by the US Federal Drug Administration (FDA). In just five years, after a major promotional program, annual sales of Redux soared to an estimated $1.4 billion. It wasn't long, however, before serious questions were raised about Redux. The prestigious *New England Journal of Medicine* published a study linking the main ingredient in Redux to a rare but fatal lung disorder. Even though sales declined and Redux was withdrawn from the market, it was already too late for consumers who had suffered and died from taking a seemingly harmless item—diet pills.

Why do such tragedies occur? Are consumers to blame for their obsession with being thin? Certainly this obsession has driven sales of diet soft drinks to a level of $25 billion a year. Health clubs rake in an additional $14 billion; exercise-equipment manufacturers have sales of $6 billion a year; and commercial weight-loss programs, such as Weight Watchers, earn more than $3 billion a year. Not only is this a large market, but it has also been experiencing considerable growth potential. If nothing else, it is almost guaranteed repeat business. Almost all of the North Americans who shed pounds each year put them back on eventually, and the dieting-exercising cycle starts again.

Dieting and exercising require effort and time. People must forgo what they want most—lots of tasty food—and suffer the pain and discomfort of exercise to lose only a pound or two a week. Doctors and public health officials frequently caution against losing too much weight too quickly. Consequently, the deprivation and suffering can go on for a long time. No wonder diet pills look so good. Taking pills is easy, requires no immediate or obvious pain, and doesn't force you to give up what you want.

Redux was a prescription drug, but certainly word of mouth had its effect, and taking a pill is easier than exercising. Moreover, Redux succeeded in curbing people's appetites. Users found that they would sit down to a normal meal but never finish it. They felt satisfied before eating everything on their plate. As a result, they ate less. Some users lost up to 40 pounds in just two months—instant success with little effort or pain. Given news of the product's success, it's not surprising that overweight North Americans flooded doctors' offices seeking prescriptions for the product.

But why would medical practitioners concerned with people's health recommend or prescribe such a product? Some of the blame can be placed at the door of manufacturers, who were overly zealous in their attempts to sell the product. Pharmaceutical salespeople pitched the drug to family physicians, psychiatrists, cardiologists, interns, and even gynecologists—people who are less likely to be familiar with the drug or treatment of obesity. According to one analysis, Redux salespeople logged 140 000 doctor visits in the first three months alone—making it one of the largest drug launches in 1996. Doctors received patient starter kits that contained coupons for joining Weight Watchers and Jenny Craig diet centres. Consultants believed that receipt of the kits encouraged doctors to prescribe the drug without monitoring a patient's weight loss.

While some health risks were known at the time of the launch, some salespeople either were unaware of them or neglected to mention them during their sales calls. Physician Dr. Gary Huber says that the salesperson who called on him touted Redux as safe for lifetime use—even though the company's own brochures admit that the drug had been tested for only one year—and hardly addressed the lung disease risk. "I was amazed at how little the salesman knew," Dr. Huber said. Thus, poorly prepared or overly aggressive salespeople were calling on doctors who might be unfamiliar with either weight-loss methods or drugs, and who in turn might prescribe the product to people whose weight loss they did not monitor.

Although many doctors believe that an approved drug is a safe drug, Redux was initially approved with a caveat. Doctors were to prescribe it only for use by obese patients—individuals who were at least 15 to 20 pounds overweight. The FDA knew that pulmonary hypertension, a constriction of blood vessels near the heart that can lead to heart failure, was associated with Redux. An international study indicated that use of Redux could lead to the death of as many as 46 people per million when taken for just three months. However, ordinary Aspirin can kill more individuals per million than Redux. For obese persons, the risk of death or debilitation from Redux was acceptable precisely because the risk of death or debilitation from obesity is higher. Consequently, some of the risk associated with Redux was known to the FDA and was considered acceptable under certain conditions.

The major problem, however, was not with medically obese people who were closely supervised by their doctors. Rather, it was with the millions of individuals who wanted Redux to shed a few pounds so that they would look better. For these people, Redux raised the risks of death to unacceptable levels. Some knew the risks and wanted the drug anyway, but others did not. Again, the obsession with being thin, coupled with the willingness of doctors to prescribe a heavily marketed drug, led to use of Redux by the wrong market segment.

When one reads of cases such as Redux, one wonders who is to blame for such tragic occurrences. Was it government regulators who approved a drug with known side effects? Was it salespeople who were motivated to earn their commissions regardless of the consequences for final consumers? Was it harried doctors who were too busy to follow up with their patients? Or was it consumers themselves who pursue an elusive body image that few can actually attain?

Questions

1. Consider the buyers' and sellers' rights listed in this chapter. Which rights were violated in the Redux case?
2. The Redux case is an example of a product that caused extreme harm. While the outcomes may be less severe, do other products with diet positionings—labelled as "lite," cholesterol free, or calorie reduced—exploit consumers in the same way?
3. Many critics blame advertising for people's obsession with thinness. Are these criticisms valid? Can you find specific ads that help support your claim? What is the effect of campaigns like the one by The Body Shop showing a model with a rounded figure, or Special K's efforts to make women more aware of the need for a healthy diet? While women are most often viewed as the victims of poor body images, do men feel pressured by images of slim, muscular male models in ads?
4. If you were the marketing manager for a firm marketing a diet pill, what methods could you develop that would prevent a case like Redux from repeating itself? What would a code of ethics for such a firm look like?

Sources: L. Davis, A. Gardiner, D. Greene, K. Harness, and S. Mickle, "The ethics of the diet industry," case written for Comm 338, Queen's University; Robert Langreth, "Is marketing of diet pill too aggressive?" *Wall Street Journal,* 21 November 1996:B1; Robert Langreth, "Diet-drug mix may damage heart valves," *Wall Street Journal,* 9 July 1997:B1; Robert Langreth, "Eminent journal urges moratorium on diet-drug use," *Wall Street Journal,* 28 August 1997:B1; Jay Palmer, "Hey, Fatso!" *Barron's,* 1 July 1996:25–9; Michael D. Lemonick, "The miracle drug?" *Time,* 23 September 1996, www.pathfinder.com/time/magazine/domestic/1996/960923/test.html. Timothy Sawa, "Dying to be thin," *CBC Radio News In-Depth,* May 9, 2001 (http://cbc.ca/consumers/indepth/dietdrug).

video case 18

CLASSROOMS FOR SALE

Public schools, like many public-sector organizations, are facing cutbacks in government funding. As a result, some have been considering partnerships with businesses to generate cash to maintain expensive programs like sports and buy costly equipment such as computers. Art Kelly, principal of Assumption Catholic Secondary School in Brampton, Ontario, has encouraged business partnerships in his school. A basketball scoreboard sponsored by Coca-Cola for about $500 a month is just one of his partnership programs that critics claim is exposing his students to subtle and unethical methods of persuasion.

Business involvement in schools was evident in Canada as far back as the 1920s, when Ivory soap sponsored soap-carving contests and provided songbooks to schools containing "company" songs. While there was little questioning of such activities at that time, the anti-establishment sentiments that characterized the 1960s put an end to corporate involvement in schools until recently. With fiscal pressures on schools mounting, many administrators are faced with the choice of seeking out business financing or not being able to offer what many would consider important school programs.

Some of the most vocal critics of school and business partnerships are teachers. Some teacher associations have opposed the influence of corporations in schools, arguing that schools are a place of learning and should be a shelter for children against commercialization. To answer this criticism, Kelly wonders why we would want to protect students from the very world they have to live in.

The business–school partnership often goes beyond providing capital or equipment. At Kelly's school, for example, several local entrepreneurs and businesspeople are brought into the classroom to assist in curriculum delivery. In one class, a local car dealer discusses the differences between buying and leasing a car. While some students and teachers claim that these guest lectures enhance the learning that students will experience, others recognize that from the businessperson's perspective, students and their parents are a lucrative target market. By giving a lecture to students, the businessperson has the opportunity to influence perceptions about the company and its products or services. While that opportunity may cost thousands of dollars to purchase in mass media such as television or magazines, the guest lecture offers that opportunity free of charge.

Art Kelly has no problem providing his students as marketing opportunities for businesspeople. "I'm a businessperson," he says, "involved in running, if you like, a school, but also a franchise. You are going to have to be able to draw in corporate dollars to keep your schools going." As he looks at his school's Coca-Cola scoreboard, he is open about the fact that he is not loyal to Coca-Cola. If Pepsi or another competitor in the industry came in with more money, he would displace the Coca-Cola logo. "They are going to drink something," says Kelly.

Questions

1. Is there a difference between the ethics of guest lectureships compared to corporate sponsorships in public schools?
2. Do partnerships between businesses and schools violate the "principle of consumer education and information" and the "principle of consumer protection," which are two of the principles for public policy toward marketing outlined in the text? Do they violate the "right to consumer education" outlined by the Consumers' Association of Canada?
3. Why don't more corporations donate money to schools without having their name associated with that donation?
4. What is the nature of corporate sponsorships in universities? Are these sponsorships ethical?

Source: This case was prepared by Auleen Carson and is based on "Marketing in the classroom," *Undercurrents,* 14 March 1997.

Foxy Originals

In February 2000, Foxy Originals (Foxy), based in Toronto, Ontario, faced an important decision regarding its distribution and pricing strategies for the upcoming season. Foxy Originals manufactured and sold its own exclusive line of hand-made necklaces at weekend festivals and to retailers in southern Ontario. The company's partners, Suzie Orol and Jen Kluger, were in the process of planning their second year of operations and sales. A number of retailers were upset that Foxy's retail prices at festivals were below the retail prices charged in stores. The partners had to decide whether to continue selling at festivals and to retailers at different prices, or to focus on a single distribution method and pricing strategy.

The Company

Suzie Orol and Jen Kluger founded Foxy Originals in January 1999. Orol and Kluger were first-year students at the University of Western Ontario who had become friends and were interested in starting their own jewelry business. Orol's mother and stepfather owned a metal jewelry manufacturing company that serviced Anne Klein, Jackie Spector, and other designers in the jewelry industry. Orol was involved in the business and had experience in the design and production of jewelry. Kluger had been designing and selling her own line of necklaces since grade eleven and had experience selling to retailers in Toronto.

Orol and Kluger spent their free time on nights and weekends designing and manufacturing the Foxy line of necklaces in their dormitory room. By April 1999, Foxy had sold necklaces to six independent retailers in the London area: Frilly Lizard, From Mars, Backstage Pass, Saffron Road, Artifex, and George and Trixy. Both partners worked full-time during the summer of 1999 to grow their business.

Tim Silk prepared this case under the supervision of Elizabeth Grasby solely to provide material for class discussion. The authors do not intend to illustrate either effective or ineffective handling of a managerial situation. The authors may have disguised certain names and other identifying information to protect confidentiality.

Richard Ivey School of Business
The University of Western Ontario

Success at Festivals

During the summer of 1999, Foxy had been very successful in launching its two product lines at seven festivals (see Exhibit 3). Selling at festivals required detailed planning to secure vendor permits and project adequate production (see Exhibit 4 for the steps involved in selling at festivals).

Demand for Foxy's necklaces was split equally between the two product lines. The Floating Necklace sold for $12.00 and the Berlin Bead Necklace sold for $22.00. Exhibit 5 shows Foxy's sales volumes and the attendance records for the festivals. Although the festivals required long hours, they were also a lot of fun for the partners. Kluger commented:

> The good thing about festivals is that they are always fun to participate in and there is a reliable market. The contact with people is valuable because we can see what people like and what designs will sell. This helps us immensely in designing our product line. We start with an inven-

EXHIBIT 3
Newspaper article:
The Mirror

Foxy jewellery up for grabs at Beach arts & crafts show

15th annual event set for this weekend

By HILARY FORREST
Special to The Mirror

"We're both business students at Western. We were getting a ride together and complimented each other on our jewellery."

So begins this "handmade's" tale of how Jen Kluger and her partner Suzanne Orol started Foxy, a growing jewellery enterprise whose wares will be showcased at the 15th annual Beaches Arts and Crafts Show this weekend.

The two young women fashion "floating" necklaces from tiger wire and Czechoslovakian glass beads, which they sell to small stores in Toronto and London.

The Beach is the first outdoor show of seven they plan to attend this summer.

"It's a cool summer job, we get to meet so many people," said Orol, who with Kluger will return to Western in the fall.

The pair are among 198 exhibitors, including sculptors, folk artists, potters and clothing designers, who will set up shop for two days in Ashbridge's Bay Park, at Coxwell and the Lakeshore.

"This year's going to make it or break it with the move," said show organizer Gaye Hachie, who waxes nostalgic about the first show, held at its traditional locale, Kew Gardens.

"We had 25 exhibitors—and a tornado!" she said.

Rain or shine, this year's show, the first of several Beach summer events to be moving west from the central Beach park, will run from 10 a.m. to 6 p.m. Saturday and Sunday.

As usual, 20 per cent of booth fees will be donated to Senior Link, a local agency that provides services for seniors.

Last year's donation topped $15,000.

Source: The *Beaches/Riverside Mirror*, June 1999

EXHIBIT 4 Steps Involved in Selling at Festivals

Step 1	Find a festival that is a good fit with our product line and our target market.
Step 2	Call to get the name of the festival organizer in charge of vendors.
Step 3	Complete a vendor application form. Requires professional photos of the product line and company information. Meeting with festival organizers is sometimes necessary when there is strong competition for vendor permits.
Step 4	Produce inventory for the festival. Total time for production averaged 30 hours per festival.
Step 5	Attend festival. Average day is 12 hours. Travel time averages 1.5 hours per festival. Set-up time averages 1.5 hours per day.

> tory of 500 necklaces at the beginning of the season and replenish our inventory between festivals. One drawback of festivals is that customers are price-sensitive, so although our designs are unique, we must price competitively. We are also dependent on the weather; if the weather is bad, our sales are directly affected. We were fortunate to lose only one day to bad weather in the summer of 1999.

In the winter of 1999, the partners constructed a booth, at a cost of $500, to use at festivals (see Exhibit 6). They estimated that the booth could be used for three summers before a replacement would be necessary. The only additional cost was the vendor space, which averaged $180 per festival, and transportation, which averaged $40.00 per festival.

Success with Retailers

Foxy had been successful in growing from six retail accounts—all in London—in April 1999, to 21 accounts—14 in Toronto, six in London, and one in Winnipeg, Manitoba—in the fall of the same year. Selling to retailers required an immense time commitment (see Exhibit 7 for the steps involved in selling to retailers). The partners had to be very persistent and some stores did not make large enough orders to justify the partners' hard work. Kluger commented on their success:

> Suzie and I always go to sales appointments together. We work as a team. Buyers choose our products over our competitors' because our necklaces are hand-made, unique in design, and Canadian. Also, and maybe most importantly, they like our product because of our image. When Suzie and I go to stores, we tell the buyer all about ourselves. They ask us a lot of questions and are fascinated by the idea that we are young and we have an established business. Buyers have a much harder time saying no to us compared to regular sales reps. This is because we don't just represent the company, we *are* the company! We had considered hiring sales reps if we were to expand, but we realized that it is the two of us who make our product marketable.

EXHIBIT 5 Sales Volumes and Attendance Records for 1999 Summer Festivals

Festival	Sales Volume (Before tax $)	Festival Attendance	Sales per Person Attended
Churchill Fun Fair	325.00	2,000	0.16
Beaches Art and Craft Show	2,616.00	40,000	0.07
Oakville Festival	2,057.24	60,000	0.03
Friendship Festival	2,487.00	60,000	0.04
Collingwood Arts and Crafts Show	1,500.00	6,000	0.25
Dockside Festival of Arts	1,797.80	25,000	0.07
Lilith Fair	1,982.96	60,000	0.03
Total	$12,766.00	253,000	Average = $0.09

EXHIBIT 6 Festival booth

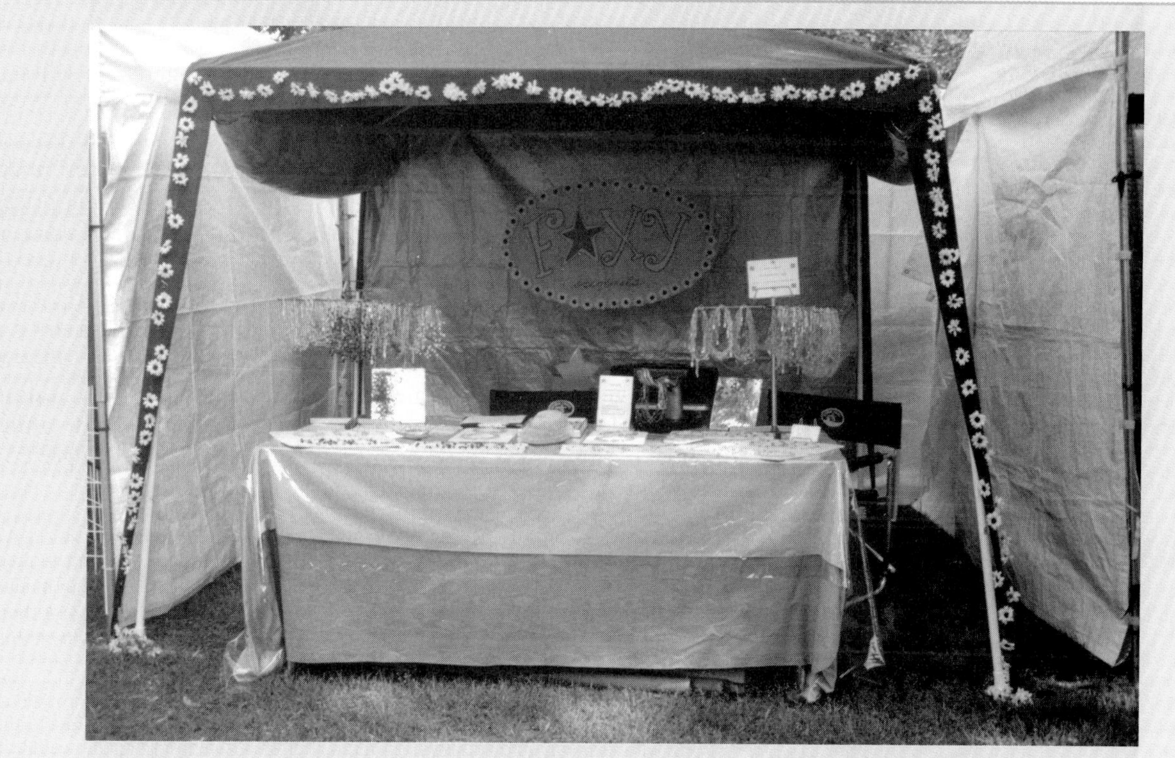

After analysing their 1999 sales efforts, the partners concluded that 83 per cent of the stores they visited bought necklaces as the result of a sales appointment, and the average order size of their 21 established accounts was approximately $300 per account. On average, retailers placed orders every four months. Additional Christmas orders, roughly $300 per retailer, were placed for the month of December. The partners estimated it cost them $60 per account per year for transportation. Usually, it took two weeks for Foxy to manufacture and deliver each order. Foxy's wholesale price to retailers was the same as its retail price at festivals. The average $300 order was usually split equally between the two product lines.

Foxy's product line was very attractive to retailers because of the large markups fashion retailers made on jewelry products. It was standard practice for retailers to mark up the wholesale price by 150 per cent to arrive at the retail price. Although selling to retailers was a lot of work for the partners, retail accounts provided sales volumes throughout the year, unlike sales from summer festivals. Re-

EXHIBIT 7 Steps Involved in Selling to Retailers

Step 1	Find a store that is a good fit with our product line (fashion or accessory retailer).
Step 2	Call to get the name of the store's product buyer.
Step 3	Make an appointment to meet with the buyer. This often takes three or more calls.
Step 4	Meet with the buyer. Total time including the drive and meeting averages 2.5 hours.
Step 5	Buyer either does or does not order.

tail accounts also provided good exposure for the Foxy brand name and gave Orol and Kluger a sense of accomplishment.

The Decision

By the end of 1999, retailers were clearly upset that Orol and Kluger were selling at festivals. The retailers were unhappy for two reasons. First, the retailers were angry that the same product lines available in stores were being sold at low-end festivals in small towns in Ontario. Retailers claimed it was damaging to their stores' image. Second, the partners were selling the necklaces at festivals at the wholesale price—less than half of the retailers' selling price for the same product. Retailers were unwilling to lower their standard 150 per cent mark-up on the Foxy product lines and believed that festival sales were cannibalizing their retail sales. Consequently, retailers wanted Orol and Kluger to stop selling at summer festivals. The partners now had to decide whether to continue selling at festivals and to retailers at different prices, or to focus on a single distribution method and pricing strategy. In addition to wages received for making the necklaces, the partners wished to draw annual salaries of $7,500 each to help cover the costs of attending university. Kluger commented:

> We need to decide which direction to take our company. We got into this business because we wanted to prove that we could succeed and we wanted to have fun doing it. Making money is important to us, but so is having fun. Suzie and I are both committed to growing this business if it is profitable, and we will continue to be full-time students for the next two years. Although we want to keep our retailers happy, I am not convinced that the cannibalization argument is valid. I'm wondering if there is a way to sell at festivals and to retailers without upsetting our retailers. If we can't find a solution, then we'll need to analyse our sales efforts and develop a pricing and distribution strategy that focuses on either festivals or retailers. The growth potential is equally strong with festivals and retailers, so it's a matter of which option represents the most profit and fun.

If the decision was made to focus on festival sales alone, the partners believed that the annual sales volume associated with this distribution channel would grow by 10 per cent to 20 per cent for 2000. Alternatively, if the partners chose to concentrate solely on their retail accounts, they thought they could increase the number of accounts they serviced to 25 or 30 in 2000. Finally, if the decision was made to continue to sell to both festival goers and retail stores, Kluger and Orol had decided that the best way to alleviate the retailers' concerns was to sell separate product lines to each distribution channel. This would require new product designs which would be time consuming. Under this scenario, the partners believed that they would be lucky to grow festival sales by five per cent to 10 per cent and that they would not have the time to pursue additional retail accounts.

Notes

[1]Tiger wire is an attractive, thin-diameter metal wire used to manufacture necklaces.

[2]Crimps are small pieces of metal that are squeezed with pliers to hold the necklace beads in place.

An NHL IMAX/Ridefilm Attraction

It was March 17, 1997, when Frank Supovitz, vice-president of Special Events, handed a memo to Bryant McBride, director of New Business Development with National Hockey League Enterprises (NHLE).[1] The memo contained preliminary financial data on establishing IMAX/Ridefilm attractions within existing NHL SKATE[2] rinks. Similar IMAX/Ridefilm attractions were located at theme parks throughout the United States and Canada; however, this one would be the first to feature a professional sport. McBride was keen on the idea since NHLE was battling in a competitive market to increase exposure to hockey throughout the United States. Although funded by team owners, NHLE had a limited financial budget and would not acquire additional funds easily. Therefore, should he decide to allocate funds toward the IMAX/Ridefilm project, McBride knew he would need to present a convincing case to the NHL board of directors.

The Game of Hockey

The sport was played with teams of five skaters (three offensive and two defensive), a goaltender, and a number of reserve players who rotated into the game from the team bench. Every 45 seconds to 1 1/2 minutes, a reserve player would replace a player on the ice either at a stoppage in play or by a process called "changing on the fly" whereby players substituted while play was still in progress.

The object of the game was to score more goals than the opposing team over the course of three 20-minute periods. A goal was recorded when a player used his stick to shoot a small, solid rubber disk (puck) past the opposing team's goaltender. Participants were required to wear ice skates and protective equipment such

Shawn Flick prepared this case under the supervision of Elizabeth M.A. Grasby solely to provide material for class discussion. The authors do not intend to illustrate either effective or ineffective handling of a managerial situation. The authors may have disguised certain names and other identifying information to protect confidentiality.

Richard Ivey School of Business
The University of Western Ontario

as helmets, gloves, shoulder pads, etc. due to the physical nature of the game and the high speed that players could reach during games.

Three officials (two linesmen and a referee) monitored the progress of the game to enforce the rules and to stop play if players violated the rules. The linesmen were responsible for logistical matters such as illegal passing, while the referee was concerned with infractions that usually took the form of illegal actions against an opposing player (tripping, high sticking, hooking, roughing, etc.). While penalties were enforced, body contact was encouraged as players scrambled to obtain the puck from the opposition. The playing surface was a pad of ice measuring 200 feet in length by 85 feet in width.

The National Hockey League (NHL)

The NHL was the professional league for the sport of ice hockey. Founded on November 22, 1917, the NHL was composed of four teams including the famed Montreal Canadiens, the Montreal Wanderers, the Ottawa Senators, and the Quebec Bulldogs. It was the second oldest league of the four major team sports in North America and possessed the oldest trophy in North American professional sport—the Stanley Cup.

By 1926, the league had grown to 10 teams in two divisions: one Canadian and one American. Most of hockey's tradition, however, was established by the six franchises existing in 1942—Boston Bruins, Chicago Blackhawks, Detroit Redwings, Montreal Canadiens, New York Rangers, and Toronto Maple Leafs—which together came to be known as the "Original Six". Many of the rivalries formed during this time were still active since all six teams still remained in the league.

The league remained intact for the next 25 years until 1967 when the NHL doubled its number of franchises to include six more American-based teams. An additional six teams were granted entrance in 1970. In 1980, the NHL merged four more teams from the competing World Hockey Association (WHA) after it dissolved. More recently, the 1990s have seen the NHL expand to include 26 franchises while establishing a presence in "non-traditional" hockey centres including San Jose, Tampa Bay, Anaheim, and Florida.[3]

The Challenge Ahead

Most of hockey's roots could be traced to Canada since the vast majority of NHL players were originally of Canadian decent. By the late 1960s, however, American-born players started to enter the ranks of the NHL. More recently, highly skilled European players from Sweden, Finland, Russia, and the Czech Republic have had a presence in the NHL. While hockey was becoming more of an international game, it did not enjoy the mainstream following of other team sports throughout the United States.

The rise in the popularity of hockey throughout North America resulted from a vision brought about by a new management team at the NHL. In the early 1990s, Gary Bettman, a long-time aide to the National Basketball Association's commissioner David Stern, was the NHL's first league Commissioner. It was hoped Bettman could transfer his marketing experience that dramatically impacted support for the game of basketball to hockey. Bettman surrounded himself with a management group including Stephen Solomon from ABC Sports, Rick Dudley from Major League Baseball, Glenn Adamo from NBC, and Bernadette Mansur from Reebok to accomplish this task. Bettman himself had characterized hockey as a "misunderstood" game: "These are likable, good-looking athletes in a fast, hard-hitting sport. It's just suffering from underexposure."[4]

Two Options to Consider

There appeared to be two distinct options to increase the exposure of the NHL throughout the United States: a top-down (entertainment) approach or a bottom-up (grass roots) approach. The former strategy leveraged off the pure entertainment value offered by the game. The concept was to first attract people to the arenas with high energy mascots, flashy colors and logos, cheerleaders, and intermission entertainment. It was hoped that eventually people new to the sport would become more knowledgeable and, at some point, would be converted into true fans of the game. The latter strategy involved developing programs that would "get sticks in hands." Advocates of this approach argued that a person needed to play the sport before that person could become a fan. Nevertheless, there was still much debate over which strategy would produce the desired results.

In support of the top-down (entertainment) approach, new franchises were established in "non-traditional" centres including Tampa Bay (1991), Anaheim (1993), and Florida (1993). Concurrently, the management team introduced NHL SKATE rinks as well as mass media educational initiatives including access to videos explaining hockey's rules and strategies at Blockbuster Video outlets. The league also negotiated a network television contract with Fox and developed corporate partnerships with several large companies: Nike, Coca-Cola, and Anheuser-Busch. Following an exciting 1994 Stanley Cup playoff, exposure was on the rise.

The momentum created throughout the first half of the 1990s was hindered, however, in 1995. During that year, a labor dispute ensued as the owners locked out[5] the players over the refusal to accept a salary cap.[6] The lockout lasted 103 days and soured the image of NHL hockey in the minds of many fans. Furthermore, the playoffs were considered by fans to be boring because the New Jersey Devils swept the Detroit Red Wings in four games using a defensive strategy to win. NHL broadcast ratings were sluggish because the 1995 Stanley Cup Playoffs were the most poorly viewed in many years. Determined to get the momentum back, the league was eagerly anticipating the arrival of its new teams in Nashville, Atlanta, Minnesota, and Columbus. In addition, NHLE managers and directors were also becoming more receptive to innovative ideas designed to increase the game's exposure.

IMAX/Ridefilm Project Description[7]

The IMAX/Ridefilm project would involve the installation of motion simulator rides in NHL SKATE rinks. These simulators were intended to provide riders with high-sensory impact experiences through motion, however, not to the degree perceived by the human mind and body. The projection of the high resolution film that covered a wide range of view enhanced the perception of falling great distances, bone-jarring collisions, sudden rotation, and acceleration.

A hydraulically controlled motion base simulator which moved up to 30 inches along three axes (front/back, left/right and up/down) had the capacity to handle a maximum of 18 riders per ride. Film illusions, while again primarily sensory rather than physical, also added to the impression of motion in a multitude of axes. As a result, those with heart and back conditions, as well as pregnant women, were discouraged from using the ride.

The 35-millimetre film was projected at 48 frames per second which was twice the speed of conventional theatrical projections. Thus, the resulting image was remarkably clear and lifelike. Typically, the experience lasted for four minutes—considered adequate for a high-impact ride. Examples of ride simulators included the "Days of Thunder" ride at Canada's Wonderland, the "Back to the Future" ride at Universal Studios in Florida and California, and the "Luxor" ride in Las

Vegas. The latter two were designed and installed by IMAX/Ridefilm. The IMAX/Ridefilm technology was clearly superior to similar ride simulators developed by competing companies in terms of sensory impact.

An NHL-branded simulator would be the first sports-oriented experience of its kind. While most rides of this kind featured the illusion of being enclosed in some type of vehicle, a test film of 15 to 20 seconds in length had been successfully completed by IMAX/Ridefilm which effectively demonstrated the potential for simulating physical personal contact between the film and the viewer. Based on the successful pilot, the NHL developed a preliminary creative script in which the viewer experienced hockey from the perspectives of a runaway jet-powered Zamboni and a hockey player in the midst of intense action on the ice (see Appendix 1). While the riders awaited seating, a brief pre-show video outside of the ride itself would promote the show and build excitement by describing the NHL, its players, and its personalities.

Financial Forecasts

Through discussions with IMAX, it was determined that one-time production costs for the film itself would be $2.5 million maximum. This figure included the cost of the production and the programming of the motion base simulator. In addition, IMAX had quoted a price of $850,000 for a motion-based simulator (the physical ride structure). Construction costs to build the interior and exterior theater enclosure (in which the simulator, and the screen and projector would be housed) were estimated to be $470,000.

Other expenditures included a ticketing cost of $0.25 per rider as well as $680,000 in yearly operating expenses for personnel, marketing, operations, administration, utilities, leasehold improvements, and system service and maintenance.

Ticket prices for the ride would be set at $6 per person. McBride envisioned the ride running 10 hours per day, 350 days a year. Each ride would take approximately four minutes and another four minutes would be needed for one group of riders to exit and the next group of riders to enter. Although confident that an NHL IMAX/Ridefilm would attract enough interest to operate at close to 50 per cent capacity, McBride wanted to know the results of operating at only 30 per cent capacity before making a decision.

Finally, given the fact that the setting of the film was inside a hockey rink, there would be numerous opportunities for corporate sponsorship within the film itself. Examples included advertisements on the rink boards, Zamboni decals, and product placements on the beer truck, broadcast truck, and concession stands shown in the film. It was estimated that $100,000 in corporate advertising could be raised in the form of contracts that would extend through the useful life of the film.

Next Steps

A lot of questions were racing through McBride's mind. It was estimated that the useful life of the film would be five years. McBride initially believed that the project had to be able to pay for itself within this time frame. He was also concerned with obtaining approval for such a large initial investment. However, regardless of the quantitative results, he was also aware that this initiative could prove valuable as the NHL struggled to build long-term popularity in the United States market. On the other hand, was money better spent on developing a "grass roots" strategy? Were there any other alternatives available that might make this project more attractive financially or otherwise? Whichever option he chose, McBride knew he would have to present a solid case to both Supovitz and the NHL board of directors.

APPENDIX 1 Preliminary Treatment for a Hockey-Themed IMAX/Ridefilm

OBJECTIVES

To create . . .

- an exciting, cutting-edge entertainment attraction which, in part, confronts customers with a player's three-dimensional perspective of the high speed, jarring contact, and sudden redirection of NHL hockey.
- a must-see, must-do fantasy experience which incorporates enough whimsy and pure entertainment value to ensure maximum appeal to amusement seekers, as well as hockey fans.
- an anchor attraction for NHL-branded hockey rink/entertainment centres and major retail/restaurant locations, and potentially NHL member club rinks.
- an experience with a long enough shelf life to enable recovery of investment, as well as potential profit after market distribution

Preliminary Creative

The Ridefilm experience begins with a pre-show on video monitors, setting the scene for the ride itself . . . .

Pre-Show

You are a Zamboni driver in training. Your supervisor coaches you on the importance of careful driving across the ice as you resurface just before the player's practise skate. He knows that it has always been your fantasy to be an NHL player, but that's the stuff of dreams. You're a driver now. Keep your fantasies to yourself, and your mind on your work, and you'll have a long career in hockey—if only as the person who cleans the ice.

The new ice-making machine you will be learning on is the latest model—and it has been equipped with a turbo-drive to give the most experienced drivers the ability to complete their circuit of the ice in much shorter time. But, you're not ready for that at this stage of your career. Not by a long shot. The players are almost here. Better get on the machine, and get ready to go . . . .

The Zamboni jerks into forward in the garage. "Easy on the gas", your supervisor says. You emerge onto the ice. "There's only a short time left until the players come onto the ice, but careful driving is most important—you can't leave any part of the ice not cleaned. Check your gauges. Check your lights." He said . . . "check the lights." That's the red button. Suddenly, the Zamboni begins shaking up and down as a jet engine screams. "The black button! The black! Not the red!" A screeching skid of tires and the Zamboni fishtails toward the other end of the ice, as the supervisor runs out of the way. As the machine reaches the corner, it picks up speed. The next corner is even faster. The Zamboni circles around the ice faster and faster—this new machine is really great, and not so hard to maneuver that it requires an expert!

Or maybe it does . . . . Now, you're moving so fast, you can't take the corner. You miss and crash through the dasherboards. Now you're speeding through the winding locker room corridor, and as your machine ricochets off the hallways on either side, trainers, players, cameramen, and journalists are scattering everywhere.

From the confines of the locker room area, you enter the larger service area under the stands. There are television trucks, beer trucks, food service wagons everywhere. You succeed in hitting just about every one of them. You even use grandstands as ramps that enable the Zamboni to become airborne.

A quick turn puts you on a ramp that snakes upward, bursting through a door into the public concourse. Ushers, popcorn-toting fans and program vendors take cover, until you emerge through an aisle vomitory[8] at the top of the arena. The machine seems to have run out of fuel as the jet engine sputters, but it balances precariously at the top of the aisle.

A little too far, though. The Zamboni bounces down the aisle, narrowly missing fans, and crashing through the rail at the bottom, it takes flight until it crashes through the Jumbotron screen showing the player practice which has already begun.

Now, by some fantastical quirk, you're in the game. You're a player, just as you've always wanted to be. You float to the ice, and you're about to take a face-off at centre ice. A teammate tells you, "make sure you run the play just like the coach said in the locker room." The face-off is won, and the puck passes to your teammate. You both skate toward the goal, passing back and forth. You are nudged, bounced, and finally checked into the boards. You recover and turn toward the play. You skate toward the other end as the opposing team misses a shot from the point. Your goaltender flips the puck back toward you, but another player skates in to intercept. You skate toward him, and knock him to the ice before he has a chance to let his shot fly. You've got the puck now, and there is nothing but open ice between you and the goal. You shoot, the puck flies toward the goal. It flips end-over-end until it hits the crossbar. You're charging too fast, the puck ricochets back toward your face and you see stars.

continued

APPENDIX 1 Continued

You drop to the ice, but regain your footing. You think you're going after the puck again, but you are obviously disoriented. Everybody seems to be skating in the opposite direction, bumping and spinning you as you go. You're heading toward the net—the opposing goaltender is waving you off, then he gets out of the way. You skid to a stop in front of the crease, and turn toward the neutral zone. The play is coming back toward you. As your teammate crosses the blue line, he fires you the puck. You take it, turn, and shoot. You score!

As the red light glares, the end-of-game horn blares. Your team hoists you above their shoulders, bouncing you around in celebration. The crowd goes wild. They carry you to the Zamboni garage, where your Zamboni supervisor awaits. "You're fired!" he screams, as your team jubilantly carries you off to the locker room.[9]

APPENDIX 2 National Hockey League Enterprises Canada Organizational Chart

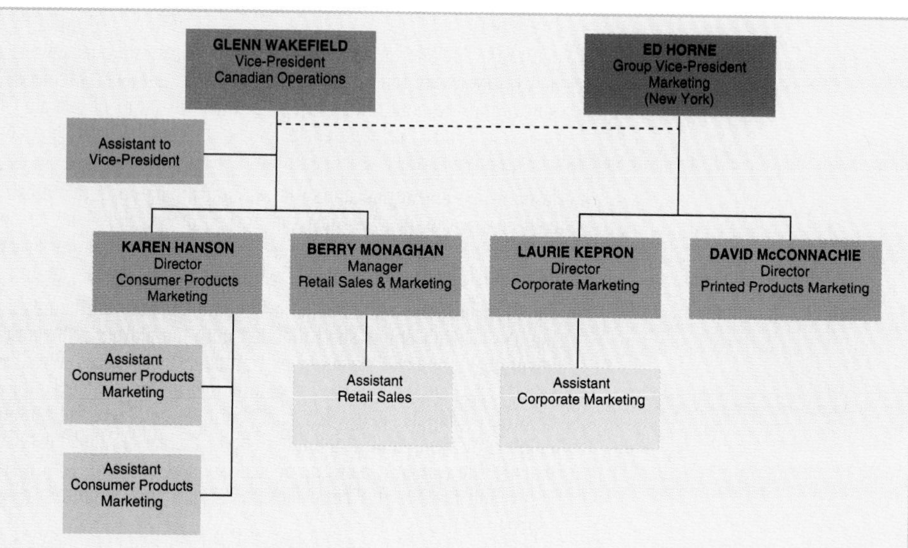

Notes

[1]NHLE was the marketing arm of the National Hockey League (NHL). Established by the team owners, its mandate was to operate profitably by generating corporate partnerships (e.g., NIKE, McDonalds), licensing royalties (10 per cent of manufacturers' gross revenues on items with NHL or member team marks and logos), publishing, and national broadcast revenues. NHLE was also responsible for technological and fan development.

[2]NHL SKATE rinks were NHL theme arenas targeting fan development. Each possessed interactive displays about hockey and its history supported by an extensive retail presence featuring NHL-licensed product. Various hockey skill and instructional initiatives were also operated out of these arenas.

[3]*Total Hockey,* 1998, Dan Diamond & Associates.

[4]*Marketing The National Hockey League,* 1995, Harvard Business School.

[5]The term "lockout" refers to an owner-initiated work stoppage whereby the owners prevent the players from playing.

[6]"Salary cap" refers to a term in the labor agreement whereby teams are prohibited from having a total salary in excess of a stated maximum level.

[7]NHL Enterprises internal memorandum, March 1997, Frank Supovitz.

[8]Each of a series of passages for entrance and exit

[9]NHL Enterprises internal memorandum, May 1997, Frank Supovitz.in (amphi) theatre.

Branding Metro Credit Union

On 5 May 2000, Larry Gordon, vice-president of development of Metro Credit Union (MCU), sat in his office overlooking Brown's Line in Etobicoke and wondered how he could develop a break-through branding strategy for the company. Larry knew that MCU offered its members many benefits as a banking alternative; however, MCU had not clearly established what it stood for in the minds of its current or potential members. In the past, it had focused on marketing its specific products and services, and although it had its own brand symbol—a capital M inside a box (see Exhibit 1), Larry realized that MCU hadn't developed a brand that communicated everything it stood for.

In late 1999, the senior management team formally adopted a retail value proposition (RVP) on which to base its future development (see Exhibit 2). However, even with this RVP, they didn't know exactly how MCU should differentiate itself. While MCU was moving to restructure its operation to become more customer centred to improve service quality, Larry knew that its competitors were doing likewise. However, MCU's additional focus on accountability to consumers and communities, which was anchored by its member-ownership and democratic control structure, was quite distinctive, as was MCU's corporate commitment to social responsibility. He wondered if this aspect of the firm could be used as the foundation of the core brand message.

Market research from 1999 appeared to reinforce this position. Members who had joined in the previous three years had been asked why they had considered MCU. Traditional consumer choice factors were evident: convenience (10%), recommendations (14%), products or prices (18%). But, most interesting, 38 percent reported that "credit union philosophy" or "bank alternative" were their primary reasons for joining MCU.

EXHIBIT 1 Metro Credit Union logo

This case was prepared by Phil Connell under the supervision of Dr. Peggy Cunningham for use in the Inter-Collegiate Business Competition and is not intended to illustrate either effective or ineffective handling of a management situation. Some information may have been disguised in the interest of confidentiality. We thank Larry Gordon of Metro Credit Union for his help and support in developing this case.

EXHIBIT 2 MCU's Retail Value Proposition

Retail Value Proposition (RVP)

- The primary element in our RVP is the *distinctive Metro customer experience,* which is *based on accountability* (i.e., *co-op membership*) and *high quality service.*
- While remaining anchored in financial services, we will move *beyond banking* to meet the needs of our members and their communities.

Related Strategic Issues

- We will ensure the delivery of quality service by developing a *member-centric* corporate structure and operation.
- We will be a *niche player* focused on *specific market segments (to be identified)* where we are most likely to present a competitive advantage.
- We will offer *in-house and brokered products and services,* as appropriate, to meet the needs of our target markets.
- Our *diversification program* will take place through a combination of developing new inhouse offerings, incorporating subsidiaries, and/or forming strategic alliances that:
  1) complement our core financial services, and/or
  2) support our branding strategy, and/or
  3) build on our internal expertise, and/or
  4) generate revenue to support the overall corporate operation.

Larry also thought that MCU's commitment to providing helpful and objective advice to members, through both direct consulting services and educational programs, could be part of the branding strategy. MCU advised both individuals and small businesses on a number of issues, from investment and insurance products to automobile purchases. In addition, MCU had plans to launch a series of educational seminars for members on a variety of financial planning and other topics, particularly on issues or for groups that were not well served (e.g., socially responsible investment seminars, financial planning for single parents).

While any of these facets of Metro's services could be used as a foundation on which to build brand image, Larry wondered which would be the most powerful for a successful brand. He knew that MCU would have to assure consumers that a credit union was just as professional, secure, and able to offer state-of-the-art financial services, as a major bank. At the same time, he knew that MCU would have to offer benefits that were not available from large traditional banks.

Before he could decide on a brand positioning strategy, Larry first had to decide whom to target. The MCU proposition, he realized, was not for everyone. MCU knew it would have to be a niche player. Larry was concerned that having multiple messages aimed at multiple targets would result in brand confusion. Traditionally, MCU's customers were older, educated individuals and small businesses. But Larry was aware that the non-profit sector was under-targeted by financial service providers. He believed that many non-profit organizations in Toronto, along with their employees and supporters, would welcome a committed financial institution to support them. And this would be consistent with the credit union philosophy of serving the community.

Finally, there was the question of how to communicate the new brand to current and potential members. Unfortunately, with a total marketing budget—for agencies, market research, advertising, and promotion—of only $450 000, Larry knew he couldn't afford advertising on TV, radio, and daily newspaper ads in Toronto (see Exhibit 3). He knew MCU would have to rely on highly targeted promotional outreach, special offers and events, direct marketing, and word of mouth, supplemented by targeted advertising in weeklies or special interest publications.

EXHIBIT 3 Media and Advertising Costs

Prime Time Television Commercial Rates (30 seconds)[1]

Network	Number of Stations	Basic Average Cost
Regional television		
ASN	1	$ 90
ATV	4	$ 650
CBC Regional		
Atlantic	5	$1000
Central	15	$6000
Western	12	$2500
Pacific	6	$1000
Global	1	$7000
MITV	2	$ 500
BBS Ontario	8	$5000

Newspaper Advertising[2]

Newspaper	Cost of Advertisement	Cost per 1000 People Reached (CPM)
Toronto Star	$11 340	$2438
Globe and Mail	$16 938	$5314
Toronto Sun	$ 5 463	$2366

Larry shook his head. How was he going to synthesize all of this information into a single brand positioning strategy and program that would clearly communicate what MCU was all about?

The Financial Services Industry

Overview

Canada was renowned for having an efficient, low-cost financial services industry. For many years, it was a relatively stable industry due to strict government regulation. Today, many believe it is entering an era of hypercompetition—an industry stage defined by economies of scale and the war for customers.

The dominant force in the Canadian financial services industry is the Big Five banks—Royal Bank, CIBC, Bank of Montreal, TD Bank, and Bank of Nova Scotia, accounting for about 85 percent of the banking market in Canada. The Big Five along with a number of smaller banks employ 221 000 people, whereas credit unions employ about 20 000. In addition, banks operate 8211 branches and 15 481 automated teller machines (ATMs).

Currently, there are about 750 credit unions in Canada. Many of these have multiple branches. Credit unions and caisses populaires, the Quebec version of credit unions, have a total membership of over 10 million people. However, while membership is increasing, the number of credit unions is decreasing: For example, in Ontario there are now only 350 credit unions; just a few years ago, there were 500. This is a result of an increased number of mergers and acquisitions among credit unions so that they can better compete with the large banks.

Other competitors are mutual fund companies, which have been expanding aggressively: In 1999, close to 40 percent of Canadians made mutual fund investments compared with the 14.9 percent who did in 1991. Over 20 percent of Canadians also own stocks and bonds; 33 percent own GICs or term deposits, and 22 percent own Canada savings bonds or term deposits. With the new online stock trading, the percentage of people owning stocks is expected to increase. This is occurring at a time when the percentage of people having savings accounts is dropping. In 1999, 73.3 percent of people had a savings account compared with 76.6 percent only a year earlier.

Finally, a number of non-traditional players are entering the financial services market to compete with both banks and credit unions. The *Bank Act* does not regulate these organizations. For example, such large manufacturers as General Motors and General Electric and such retailers as Loblaws, Sears, and Canadian Tire are all offering a range of financial products. They compete for customers and members with loan and mortgage companies, life and health insurance firms, pension funds, and mutual fund providers. Furthermore, a number of "category killers" are coming into the marketplace, including American credit card companies MBNA and First USA.

Industry Segmentation

Canada's financial service providers market to four broad categories of customers: retail, commercial and corporate, investment, and international.

The Retail Market: The financial needs of consumers have been changing rapidly. Today, Canadians expect information, choice, and convenience from retail financial institutions. They are aware of the trends in the marketplace and are quick to adapt to them. For example, 87 percent of Canadian consumers believe that it is important to have a good understanding of how the economy functions for the purposes of financial planning. Furthermore, 67 percent believe that having a better understanding of how the economy functions could actually improve economic conditions.[3] There are many financial services and products from which they can choose, and multiple channels in which they can perform their transactions. Financial service providers are becoming more aware of the need to segment the marketplace to address the needs of specific groups. For example, education loans are targeted to university and college students and their families, loans for mortgages are targeted to young families; RRSPs are aimed at people in their peak earning years (45 to 55 years of age); and wealth management products are designed to meet the needs of people aged 55 to 65.

The Commercial and Corporate Market: As with the retail market, commercial and corporate clients of the financial institutions are being offered more choice in financial products and services. These include credit products and services such as risk management, cash management, and payroll services. Financial institutions provide businesses with working capital as well as funds to support capital projects and export operations. Small and medium-sized enterprises (SMEs) make up the majority of firms in this marketplace. Industry Canada works with members of the financial sector to inform small business owners of the various sources and types of funding available.

The Investment Market: There are financial products and services for end-consumers, corporations, and public-sector organizations within this segment of the market. Individual Canadians are offered investment products by a variety of financial institutions, from banks and credit unions to mutual fund firms and stockbrokers. They can choose among stocks, bonds, fixed-return products (such as GICs), and derivatives. Many Canadians put their savings into mutual funds instead of relying on savings accounts and government savings bonds. Mutual fund companies manage about 66 percent of these assets, while banks manage about 26 percent.

The International Market: Many financial institutions also export their financial services. Increasingly, the ability to be a player on the world stage is the rationale used to lobby for recent mergers among the big banks. Products and services offered internationally include collection services, foreign exchange, travellers' cheques, commercial letters of credit, and risk management.

The Technological Environment

Technological changes affect every aspect of the financial services industry. Technology has empowered buyers who can now access a world of information with the click of a mouse. This has lowered members' switching costs if they are interested in the services of a competitor. Credit is now portable, and buyers no longer have to belong to a financial institution to be credit worthy. Technology has also affected the economics of financial institutions, allowing many to lower their costs and increase their revenues.

Technology has created new channels for service delivery. While the branch is still an important distribution channel in the retail sector, more people are using such self-service channels as ATMs and telephone and computer transactions. In fact, Canada has the highest use of ATMs and smart cards of any country in the world. Furthermore, the Bank of Montreal forecasts that by the end of the year 2000, almost 30 percent of bank profits will be derived from Internet banking households. Technology has enabled the use of credit and debit cards, two very popular options with Canadians.

Accelerating technological change has affected credit union operations in several ways. It has increased efficiency and created alternative distribution systems. For example, ATMs and debit cards have increased member access to services at multiple distribution points. Technology has also changed buyer behaviour: To receive certain products, such as credit cards, many consumers are happy to use such direct means as the mail. However, for mortgages and loans, they want to personally interact with a service provider. Desire for personal service varies by customer segment, however. Younger (under 35), more affluent people with higher education are more likely to deal with a financial institution using the direct means of online banking and ATMs.

In this era of rapid technological change, Larry thinks that building a strong brand is of growing importance. In an era of less personal interaction between people and their financial institution, having a brand that speaks to members and potential members is critical.

Metro Credit Union

Metro Credit Union was founded in 1949 as the University of Toronto employees' credit union. Over the years, it has merged with and acquired other credit unions that have served teachers, health care workers, and workers in various other industries. Since the 1980s, MCU has been open to the general public.

Today, MCU is a mid-sized credit union, serving over 44 000 member-owners in the Greater Toronto Area (GTA) through 10 different branches. While most of MCU's members are individual consumers or households, about 3000 are small businesses and community organizations. MCU has over $400 million in assets, and $100 million assets under administration, that is mutual funds. Under its current by-laws, MCU may serve only customers within the GTA, though up to three percent of the membership may come from outside that area. Provincial regulators would have to approve any expanded service area. MCU is the largest credit union focused exclusively on the GTA.

Certain trends have emerged in MCU's growth. Loans to small businesses have grown rapidly, so rapidly that the MCU never needed to advertise. MCU, however, will soon reach the limit on how much of its portfolio it can have in commercial loan assets. For the first time in years, the personal loan portfolio is also growing, largely because of market-leading rates for car loans. The residential mortgage portfolio, on the other hand, is stagnating due to intense rate competition in the market. Total personal deposits are not growing, as individuals shift some of their deposits to mutual funds. MCU is experiencing significant deposit growth, however, from its 1000 non-profit organizational members. Mutual fund sales are also growing significantly.

Most credit unions are similar to banks in that they offer a full range of financial products and services, including chequing and savings accounts, personal loans, mortgages, RRSPs, RRIFs, Internet banking, automated telephone banking, and financial planning, and have investment and insurance services available through affiliated suppliers. In addition to its standard financial services, MCU also offers automobile advisory services, car purchase services, and distinctive consumer education seminars (see Exhibit 4 for a list of all MCU's service and product offerings).

Credit unions differ from banks in that they are financial cooperative whose customers are both members and owners: In fact, credit unions refer to customers as members. The member-owners democratically control the credit union by electing the board of directors at the annual general meeting. MCU prides itself on having the largest annual meeting of any financial institution in Canada, generally with 900 to 1000 attendees. Although MCU's membership is diverse, it is largely composed of highly educated and older individuals (see Exhibit 5 for MCU's organizational structure).

EXHIBIT 4 MCU's Service and Product Offerings

- Telephone banking
- PC banking
- Tele-service centre
- Payroll deposit
- Premium savings
- Regular chequing
- Daily interest chequing
- US $ savings/chequing
- Flat-fee chequing packages
- 14 cash machines
- ATM/debit card
- Interac direct payment
- Interac and PLUS networks
- Personal loans
- Personal lines of credit
- Car leasing
- Car loans
- Business accounts
- Business loans
- Business lines of credit
- First and second residential mortgages
- Reverse mortgages
- Home equity lines of credit
- Multi-option mortgage
- RRSPs
- Financial education seminars
- Term deposits
- Index-linked term deposits
- Canada Savings Bonds
- Seniors' package
- Children's account
- Electronic bill payment
- Travellers' cheques/insurance
- Foreign exchange
- Money orders and drafts
- Safety deposit boxes
- Club accounts
- Organization accounts
- MasterCard
- Gold MasterCard
- Car Facts Centre
- AutoBuy car purchasing services
- Loss of job mortgage insurance
- Credit insurance
- Home insurance
- Term life insurance
- Auto insurance
- RRIFs
- Over 600 mutual funds
- Socially responsible mutual funds
- Financial planning

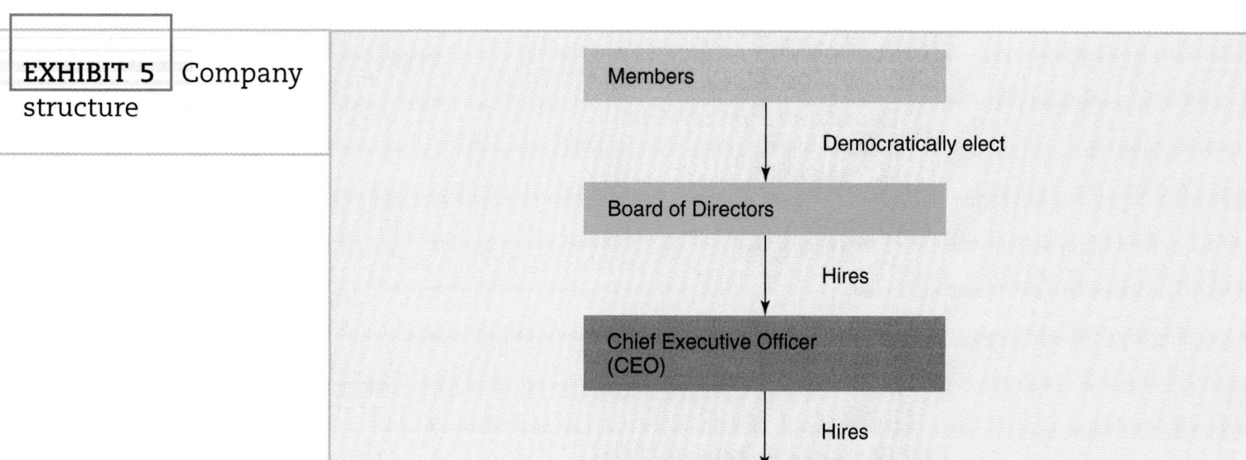

EXHIBIT 5 Company structure

Membership, Fees, and Financial Performance

Member Shares

Although a credit union's customers are also its owners, investment in the credit union is unlike an investment in a publicly traded corporation, as the values of owners' shares do not fluctuate over time.

To join MCU, members are required to make an initial investment of $5. Through a specified formula, their investment must gradually increase to $125 over a period of five to nine years. Membership shares cannot be redeemed until the owners close their accounts with MCU. Members may receive an annual dividend on their investment.

Fees

In general, the fee structure of financial institutions varies according to the type of account, the number of different transactions that a customer typically makes, and the way in which they conduct transactions—branch banking, telephone banking, Internet banking, ATM. The fee structure of MCU is no exception.

In general, MCU maintains relatively low to average fees for most standard transactions. However, it is about to introduce a new fee schedule with several distinctive features. MCU will be eliminating fees for use of its 10 ATMs for all members, regardless of their account balances, transaction volumes, and number of accounts. In addition, it will be introducing a relationship pricing benefit: Any member household with a total banking relationship—all deposits and loans—exceeding $75 000 will also have unlimited free Interac ATM service, as well as free chequing and Interac direct payment services for all members of that household. MCU expects both of these offers to be popular with current members and attractive to those who may consider joining MCU. The credit union hopes that latter relationship pricing benefit will help counter the accessibility problem in having only 10 branches in the GTA.

Financial Performance

The 1999 fiscal year was very successful for MCU: Total assets grew by 4.8 percent, deposits by 7.3 percent, and loans by 2.2 percent. Earnings before interest and taxes were $1 594 249 (see Exhibits 6 and 7 for balance sheet and income statement). Given 1999's healthy financial performance, the board of directors

EXHIBIT 6 MCU Balance Sheet

Metro Credit Union Limited
Balance Sheet
(March 31, 1999)

	March 31, 1999	April 1, 1998
Assets		
Cash resources	**$ 7 670 767**	$ 4 645 813
Loans to members	**311 322 592**	304 603 478
Investments	**38 906 855**	33 220 946
Capital assets	**5 366 920**	4 287 428
Other assets	**4 755 588**	4 489 112
	368 022 722	351 246 777
Liabilities		
Members' deposits	**339 767 349**	316 783 382
Operating loan	—	7 000 000
Other liabilities	**4 878 114**	5 317 970
	344 645 463	329 101 352
Liabilities qualifying as regulatory capital		
Class A investment shares	**7 672 970**	7 222 214
Class B bonus shares	**741 498**	609 893
Membership shares	**4 000 063**	4 544 451
	12 414 531	12 376 558
Total liabilities	**357 059 994**	341 477 910
Members' equity		
Retained earnings	**10 962 728**	9 768 867
	368 022 722	**351 246 777**

announced a five percent dividend on shares. Over recent years, the most significant area of growth occurred in the investment services area: Assets under administration—mostly member mutual fund investments—grew by 63 percent. In total, MCU's income increased by 119 percent.

MCU is very clear about how its profits are earned and distributed. Like all credit unions, it operates under the philosophy that its profits are member profits. Since credit unions are member owned, all of the profits are returned to members in the form of improved services, financial reserves, dividends, or community donations. This is in sharp contrast to what the Big Five banks do with their profits, which were over $9 billion in 1999.

MCU's Distinctive Offerings

As a socially responsible, community-owned, democratically controlled financial institution, MCU presents a distinctive, accountable, and high-quality alternative to consumers, small businesses, and organizations. It also offers its members some products and services that differentiate it from its rivals.

Beyond Banking: Car Facts Center and AutoBuy

Car purchasing is a major financial decision for consumers, most of whom are not prepared to make well-informed decisions in their own interest. Car Facts, which is used by about 1000 members each year, is a free advisory service for all MCU

EXHIBIT 7 MCU Income Statement

Metro Credit Union Limited
Statement of Earnings and Retained Earnings
(Year ended March 31, 1999)

	1999
Revenue	
Interest on loans:	
Residential mortgage loans and home equity lines of credit	14 112 802
Personal loans and lines of credit	6 549 219
Commercial loans and mortgages	1 778 080
Investment income	1 635 557
Other income	3 966 920
Other assets	
	28 042 578
Financial expenses	
Interest on members' deposits:	
Demand deposits	837 963
Term deposits	3 890 735
Registered savings plans	4 901 940
Registered income funds	1 255 136
Dividend on Class A Investment shares	505 555
Dividend on Class B bonus shares	27 685
Dividend on membership shares	127 870
Interest on external borrowings	162 813
	11 709 697
Operating margin	16 332 881
Expenses	
Amortization of capital assets	991 497
Amortization of goodwil	27 560
Data processing costs	1 194 242
Deposit insurance premium	688 848
General and administration	2 979 225
Occupancy	1 635 957
Provision for impaired loans	111 063
Salaries and benefits	7 046 083
Loss on disposal of capital asset	64 157
	14 738 632
Earnings before income taxes	1 594 249
Income taxes	
Current	413 724
Deferred	−13 336
	400 388
Net earnings	1 193 861
Retained earnings, beginning of year	9 768 867
Retained earnings, end of year	10 962 728

members considering the purchase or lease of a new car. A Car Facts advisor provides all the information and advice a member purchasing a car could need, including financial and non-financial information. The former may include which dealers are providing the best deals or how to finance a purchase at the lowest rates. The latter may include actual information about different vehicles that a dealer may be reluctant to reveal. The AutoBuy program goes one step further. On a fee-for-service basis, the AutoBuy advisor shops for the car for the member, doing all the legwork and getting the best deal on the desired car.

Socially Responsible Investment Centre

Like other financial institutions, MCU offers a full range of investment and mutual fund services. Its point of differentiation is in its being one of the largest Ontario retail centres for the sale of socially responsible mutual funds. The national credit union system owns the family of Ethical Funds, the largest and most successful socially responsible funds in Canada. This family is considered the MCU "house brand" mutual fund.

MCU's financial advisory service department provides members with free personalized financial planning, financial education seminars, and direct assistance with investments. As well, branch staff also serve as investment advisors to assist members with basic investment planning and mutual fund purchases. However, despite MCU's sales of socially responsible mutual funds, it does not have a single specialist in this field, which may be a shortcoming in the future.

Fair Pricing Policy

MCU is one of only two financial institutions in Canada that have formalized a *fair* pricing, or rate guarantee, policy which guarantees that the best rates are automatically applied to qualified members. This policy stipulates that any two members meeting the same criteria will pay the same price for services. For example, all members who maintain a certain balance in their accounts or purchase a certain number of products or services will be offered the same rate on a new loan. Effectively, this means that members should not have to question staff and service personnel about the "best offer." There are no hidden deals in their product mix that are offered to one type of member that are not offered to all people in this class.

While MCU is very proud of this policy, it has both advantages and disadvantages in its business. The upside is that it clearly illustrates a business relationship based on trust and integrity. As a part-owner of the business, the member should expect nothing less. This characteristic will appeal to some consumers. The downside is that MCU is vulnerable with other consumers. In a market in which rates are often negotiated, the more aggressive, better-educated consumers can sometimes walk across the street and get a slightly better rate from a competitor. MCU will disclose and apply its best rate upfront, where other institutions will more selectively disclose and apply their best rates and selectively one-up the competition. As a result, the policy most likely helps to retain some business, while other business is lost. After extensively reviewing the pros and cons of this policy, MCU remains committed to it, as both the right thing to do and a marketing strategy that helps ensure that pricing benefits are going to the best—loyal, long-term—customers. Larry believed the policy was part of a package of values benefits provided by MCU to its members, but was less certain that it could be a major component of MCU's marketing strategy.

"Trusted" versus "Accountable" Advisor

Larry believed that its services helped present Metro as a consumer-oriented, consumer-driven and consumer-owned, beyond-banking company. In fact, he thought that promoting MCU as the "trusted advisor" or the "cooperative advisor" could be an excellent strategy. However, this idea was not without controversy. Senior management had discussed the internal conflict inherent in being both an advice-giving intermediary and a product-selling organization. For example, if a member paid the AutoBuy advisor to find the "lowest cost deal" and the advisor found low-cost dealer financing, MCU could lose a loan. Likewise, an investment advisor might tell a member to take deposits out of the MCU and put them in external investments, which would provide much lower return for MCU. In both cases, MCU hoped to strengthen a profitable long-term relationship, but sometimes at a short-term cost. At this time, however, MCU management had held back from using "trusted advisor" as the central point in the retail value proposition, instead focusing on the concept of credit union "accountability" to members.

New MCU Branch at Bay and College

In September 2000, MCU would be launching a major initiative that it expected would dramatically increase its exposure to the Toronto community. It was opening a new branch on the corner of Bay and College Streets in Toronto to be a "new showcase service centre." It was to become a high-profile symbol of the "new" Metro Credit Union, and it would make MCU the first credit union on Bay Street, right around the corporate offices of the Big Five banks.

The new branch design incorporated leading-edge retailing concepts. Designers were given the mandate to create a branch that looked nothing like a bank. The result: an exterior dominated by two large video screens, one facing Bay Street, the other facing College. The video boards would broadcast an eclectic range of visuals, statements and photos about the Credit Union, membership benefits, and special offers. MCU hoped the video boards would become the focal point of this very busy intersection, which 10 500 pedestrians and 21 100 vehicles cross daily.

Inside, the branch would display such things as the history of MCU with creative storyboards and imagery. A member information board would display postings by and for members. An expanded Car Facts Center would be stocked with helpful books, brochures, and a service specialist. There would be a "Welcome New Members" area so that existing members could avoid what MCU hopes to be a very busy part of the branch. There would be a Member Education Centre with easy chairs and many books and pamphlets, newspapers, magazines, and videos with helpful consumer financial planning information. The waiting line would feature reading material to reduce the monotony of being in a line-up. A full-size café would feature live music and lunch seminars on financial planning and other interesting topics.

Larry Gordon and the rest of the management team were very excited about the grand opening in the fall. They intended that the new facility be part of a "progressive, happening urban scene." Larry had no doubt that developing a branding strategy that could be rolled out at the same time as the opening of the new branch would increase Metro's presence in the Toronto marketplace.

Social Responsibility at MCU

Since its inception, MCU has been committed to social responsibility, manifested through a number of initiatives.

Social Audits

MCU is a pioneer in the social audit process, which assesses how well an organization is meeting its objectives in regard to social responsibility and member, community, and employee relations. To its knowledge, MCU was the first Canadian financial institution to publish a social audit report, which was in 1993. In 1996, MCU had its social audit externally verified—another first. MCU's 1998 social audit examined the organization's commitment to its internal and external community, including: an assessment of MCU's membership, specifically MCU as a democracy; its consumer policies; its responsiveness to its members; and its employee relations, including compensation, work environment, and employee support.

Socially Responsible Investment

MCU also manifests its social responsibility and community-service philosophy through counselling its members on socially responsible investment. MCU sells no-load Ethical Funds, which meet high standards in both financial performance and social responsibility; the First Ontario Fund, which invests in job-creating businesses and cooperatives in Ontario; the Clean Environment Fund; and several other socially responsible funds.

Donations

The Canadian Centre for Philanthropy's Imagine campaign suggests that corporations donate one percent of pre-tax profits to charitable causes: MCU makes contributions at a rate double this standard. While the banks are major charitable donors in the community, MCU donates a higher percentage of profits than any of the major banks.

Another MCU innovation, believed to be the first in Canada, is its Spare Change Program. Most members have spare change in their accounts—not round dollar figures—and generally regard these sums as insignificant. MCU encourages members to sign on to the Spare Change Program, which takes their spare change once a month and applies it to one of three special donation funds, which the member designates. The money in these funds are donated to community groups working on environmental issues, homelessness, or children's issues. More than 2000 members joined the program in the first year.

Community Development

Serving the community within the GTA is central to MCU's operating model. It tries to provide support in many ways in addition to making donations. About 85 percent of every dollar deposited in MCU is reinvested locally in the form of loans and mortgages to individuals, organizations, and small businesses.

MCU recently concluded an agreement with the Calmeadow Foundation to take over ownership and operation of Metrofund, Canada's largest micro-enterprise loan fund. Metrofund specializes in providing very small loans to disadvantaged people who are starting self-employment businesses and would not qualify for traditional commercial financing.

In another initiative, MCU will be partnering with a downtown Toronto community service agency for a Community Banking Program. This program will provide a half-time on-site MCU community banker who will help provide basic banking services and information to the clients of the community service agency.

Defining the Target—Financial Services Consumers

Larry had no doubt that the target market decision and branding decision were connected. Since MCU served two major constituencies—end consumers and the small business and organizational marketplace, Larry started to compile information on these markets to help him in his decision-making process.

Canadian Attitudes toward Financial Institutions

Credit Union Central of Canada commissions an annual survey of Canadian attitudes toward financial institutions. Goldfarb Research conducts these studies using a panel of 1600 Canadians. One of the first trends noted in these annual surveys is Canadians' negative attitudes toward banks.

- Eighty-two percent think banks make too much money, compared with only 31 percent who think credit unions make too much money.
- While only 25 percent of the sample think banks are working well, 41 percent think that credit unions are. Despite these attitudes, most Canadians still deal with banks, often because they don't perceive any features differentiating financial institutions.

Canadians select financial institutions that they believe will keep their deposits safe. Once they have this assurance, they look for financial institutions to provide other things including:

- knowledgeable, friendly service
- ease in completing transactions
- the presence of deposit insurance
- convenient locations
- a range of diverse products and services

If these criteria are not met, Canadians may switch institutions. Fees and rates of return may influence switching. It must be stressed, however, that these price-based reasons are well down the list of reasons for switching. Items that link to the quality of service ranked higher in importance (see Exhibit 8 for individual reasons for switching financial institutions as outlined in Goldfarb's report). Finally, the studies note that Canadian's respect for banks has fallen to an 18-year low. Respon-

EXHIBIT 8 Goldfarb's Report: Reasons for Switching Financial Institutions

% of Those Who Switched . . .	1992	1993	1994	1995	1996	1997	1998
Poor service	34	34	33	36	40	34	37
More convenient location	33	31	29	33	27	30	27
Moved to another city	18	13	17	14	13	15	14
Preferred staff at new location	8	8	11	12	12	16	13
Better rates on loans	10	13	14	12	12	15	12
More convenient hours	14	12	11	17	17	14	11
Offered additional products and/or services	6	7	9	8	9	8	8
Better rates on savings	6	8	5	8	7	10	6
Better rates on term deposits	8	5	6	6	7	8	6
ATM available	7	8	7	8	7	8	5
Offered promotion	1	2	1	2	3	3	2
Other	8	8	11	13	13	10	11

dents were asked to rate the institutions, where 100 points was the maximum rating they could give the institution. Credit unions consistently received the highest rating (see Exhibit 9 for the complete results).

Overall, Canadians negative attitudes toward banks may present an opportunity for credit unions to grow their market share if they can communicate why or how they differ from banks.

The 10th Annual Financial Attitude Survey conducted by Investors Group of Winnipeg provided Larry with more helpful information. This survey revealed that Canadians are an increasingly well-informed and confident group of investors. Over one in three Canadians now have a written financial plan to guide their investment: Men are somewhat more likely to have a financial plan than are women. Fewer Canadians are relying on the media, co-workers, or friends for financial information, and more are seeking guidance from financial advisors. Over 20 percent go to their financial institution for investment information, while 18.7 percent seek out financial advisors. Sixteen percent of Canadians see themselves as aggressive investors, while 42.1 percent take a more conservative stance. In general, Canadian investors are well educated, sophisticated, and confident.

Finally, the National Credit Union System's market growth opportunities working committee has identified a number of demographic trends that are having an impact on credit unions' strategies:

Baby boomers with increasing wealth are targets for retention: Over the next 20 to 30 years, parents of baby boomers will pass away leaving their estates to their children. This will be the single biggest transfer of wealth in history. Baby boomers are, therefore, key members that credit unions must retain.

Youth is an important target for growth: People in the 19-to-24 age bracket are consolidating their relationships with financial institutions. This is the stage in their lives when lifetime relationships with institutions form. The youth market, therefore, is a major opportunity for credit unions to secure customers. Many of these people are students struggling to pay higher tuition costs and, while they may be costly to serve now, they will soon be productive wage earners struggling to deal with the debt they acquired as students. Surveys have shown that this group prefers technology-based, convenient financial solutions to their problems. They demand speed and services that immediately meet their expectations.

Teens are a new target with increased spending power: Teens are increasingly independent consumers. They look for products and services directed specifically at them. They will be experimenting with financial institutions for the first time.

Demographic trends also exist within local marketplaces. Toronto, Montreal, and Vancouver are some of the world's most ethnically diverse communities, for example. Some credit unions, like VanCity, have branches in predominantly Chinese sections of Vancouver where service providers are trained to meet the specific needs of this community. Manitoba has some of the largest concentrations of Aboriginal people; therefore, Assiniboine Credit Union tailors some of its offering to

EXHIBIT 9 Goldfarb's Report: Comparative Ranking of Financial Institutions

	1992	1993	1994	1995	1996	1997	1998
Credit unions	59	60	58	57	56	56	56
Caisses populaires	N/A	69	62	56	53	53	54
Trust companies	51	52	51	52	50	49	50
Banks	57	57	56	53	47	47	44

the Aboriginal community. Credit unions know they must respond to the local trends in their own marketplaces to be successful.

Changing Attitudes toward Social Responsibility

In addition to consumer attitudes about banks, Larry was aware of other key public attitudes. According to the Canadian Centre for Philanthropy, a recent national opinion poll found that 72 percent of Canadians are more likely to buy goods or services from a company that commits resources to social and community concerns; 68 percent are more likely to invest their money in companies that demonstrably support the community; and 41 percent believe successful businesses should focus on social and community issues rather than profits.

While these attitudes work in MCU's favour, Larry also knows that expressed attitudes do not necessarily produce follow-through behaviour by consumers. Consumers are increasingly interested in corporate social responsibility, but few are willing to sacrifice anything related to price, convenience, or service quality.

Small Business and Non-Profit Market

Many credit unions, like MCU, hope to take a bigger bite of the small and medium-sized business market. Credit unions currently have about 13 percent of this marketplace; but regional differences determine whether commercial lending is a prime area of their business. Caisse Centrale Desjardins du Quebec is a leader in business financing. Commercial lending is substantial in Alberta, BC, Saskatchewan, and Manitoba, but it is low in Ontario and much of Atlantic Canada.

Although similar in some ways to those affecting end-consumers, variables affecting buying decisions made by business buyers are different: In general, business buyers are more technical, price oriented, highly trained, and risk averse than the end-consumer.

MCU segments the commercial and corporate market, or non-personal market, into four groups:

- businesses (any size)
- non-profit organizations
- housing co-ops
- clubs, or informal, non-incorporated groups

MCU provides each of these four groups with tailored services and pricing designed to address its distinct banking needs. For example, businesses are more likely to be seeking credit than non-profits. The non-profits, on the other hand, are very deposit and transaction service oriented. The housing co-ops, being large housing projects, have service needs that relate to having a monthly cash deposit (monthly rent cheques and coin deposits). They also need consolidated information on rent cheques written on accounts with insufficient funds. Thus, for the housing co-op sector, MCU set up a successful partnership program to provide special banking benefits to housing co-ops with special rates and a growth-related marketing fee paid to the local federation.

Up to this point, MCU has never actively advertised to small businesses. It had relied on word-of-mouth communications that generated enough business to fill its loan capacity. It has a full-time dedicated salesperson, George, who does outreach for this marketplace. He has been very successful at bringing in accounts. George has found that MCU's community orientation and its approach to social responsibility are very important in reaching parts of Metro's market, especially housing co-ops and non-profit organizations. Being a community-owned and controlled bank is something that community groups can relate to.

The Non-Profit Market in Ontario

Given that the non-profit sector had been a small but important part of MCU's customer base, Larry thought that this market might be a very lucrative area for MCU to pursue more aggressively. In addition, the community-focused and socially responsible operating philosophy of non-profit organizations in general was similar to that of MCU. Thus, by targeting non-profit organizations, it would be pursuing not only a potentially promising business market but also a market that was congruent with MCU's objectives as a community-serving organization.

Larry knew that there were little market data available on non-profit organizations, particularly in the GTA: To pursue this market, he would have to make some good market-sizing estimates. He did know that the Ontario non-profit sector as a whole received $39 billion in revenues in 1994. Of these, 31 percent went to hospitals and 22 percent to teaching institutions, which together composed only five percent of the number of charities in Canada. Larry also knew that Ontario's charitable sector had the largest revenues per capita. He was able to gain some additional data from the Canadian Centre for Philanthropy (see Exhibits 10 through 11).[4] These data, however, do not isolate the GTA market. MCU would not be able to service very large institutions such as major hospitals and universities. Its market would be the smaller and mid-sized community institutions and organizations in the GTA, which Larry estimated to have many hundreds of millions of dollars in banking business.

Public

Larry knew that the choice of a primary target was an important aspect of brand strategy development. However, he also hoped to find a brand positioning that would speak to the selected primary target on one hand without alienating or con-

EXHIBIT 10 Distribution of Charity Types within Ontario

Type of Charity	Percentage	Number
Arts and culture	5	1138
Community benefit	7	1653
Education	6	1604
Health	5	1190
Hospitals	1	271
Libraries and museums	2	475
Places of worship	37	9253
Private foundation	6	1479
Public foundation	5	1134
Recreation	2	612
Religion	7	1644
Social services	13	3147
Teaching institutions	4	885
Other	2	405
Total	100	24 890

EXHIBIT 11 Total Revenues and Percentage of Total Revenues Received by Type of Charity

Type of Charity	Percentage	Dollars
Arts and culture	3.2	1 234 937
Community benefit	2.5	951 738
Education	5.5	2 131 859
Health	8.8	3 415 459
Hospitals	30.7	11 917 017
Libraries and museums	1.7	661 562
Places of worship	6.0	2 317 142
Private foundation	1.9	720 978
Public foundation	3.2	1 236 028
Recreation	0.5	197 136
Religion	4.0	1 546 401
Social services	9.8	3 818 284
Teaching institutions	22.2	8 592 525
Other	0.1	45 465
Total	100	$38 786 531

fusing Metro's other important markets on the other. The thought entered his mind that perhaps he should be looking for something with more universal appeal, but just what that "something" was eluded him.

Decisions

The slogan that MCU used on all of its promotional materials referred to MCU as "Much more than a bank." Promotional materials also used such titles as "Frustrated with your bank?" MCU's main objective with these slogans was to present itself as a banking alternative. Larry was increasingly unsure whether simply presenting MCU as a general alternative to banks was really powerful. He also questioned what this did to differentiate Metro from other credit unions. Larry had no doubt that MCU had some attributes that differentiated it from its competitors: Its operating philosophy, its policies and procedures, its products and services were drastically different.

Larry was still uncertain of which direction to move. What market niche could MCU best serve? How could MCU build and present a powerful and distinctive brand in a very competitive market? While MCU had been very successful in past years, Larry was concerned that MCU needed a break-through branding strategy focused on some clearly identified market segments. The task was like beginning a giant jigsaw puzzle: Larry felt he had most of the pieces, but he just wasn't confident he knew how to fit them all together. Fortunately, a member of his marketing department had sent him a memo regarding branding and positioning that he hoped might give him some academic insight into his problem (see Exhibit 12). Reading through this reinforced the importance of the task to MCU's future success. Maybe he needed a consultant to guide him through this complex process.

EXHIBIT 12 Metro Credit Union

Memo

To: Larry Gordon

From: Marketing Department

Date: May 2, 2000

Re: Some information on branding and positioning

Hi Larry,

I gather Jack Trout and Steve Rivkin are real authorities on branding and positioning. I found some material in a couple of articles they have written.

The first one gave some insight into differentiation, here's what it said:[5]

The principles of simple, common-sense thinking can be applied to any discipline in marketing. Companies have to differentiate; they must supply customers with reasons to buy from them instead of their competition. That reason then gets packaged into a simple work or phrase and positioned in the minds of customers and prospects. Differentiation comes in three parts:

- *Having a simple idea that separates a company from its competitors*
- *Having the credentials or product that makes this concept real and believable*
- *Building a program to make customers and prospects aware of the difference*

The second one suggested some similar *"guidelines"* on a branding strategy:[6]

- *A marketer's message has to make sense in the context of the category*
- *The secret to brand differentiation is understanding that your differentness does not have to be product related*
- *To build a logical argument for your difference, you must have the credentials to support your differentiating idea—to make it real and believable*
- *Every aspect of a marketer's communications should reflect its difference: advertising, brochures, Web site, sales presentations*

Hopefully that'll give you some academic insight into your strategy Larry. Good luck!

Notes

[1]"Estimated cost of network commercials," *Media Digest,* 1999–2000:22.

[2]Keith J. Tuckwell, *Canadian Advertising in Action* 5th ed., Toronto, ON: Pearson Education, 2000:332.

[3]Canadian Bankers Association, "Survey of Canadian attitudes," 6 June 2000, www.cba.ca.

[4]Canadian Centre for Philanthropy, "A provincial portrait of Canada's charities," research bulletin, 17 May 2000, www.ccp.ca.

[5]Jack Trout and Steve Rivkin, *Marketing News,* 7 December 1998.

[6]Jack Trout, *Advertising Age,* 22 November 1999.

Landmark Sports Group: Athlete Relationships and Olympic Promotions

In July 1998, Sharon Podatt, vice-president of Landmark Sports Group, was approached by a small Canadian investment firm Patrick Ross Financial Limited to develop a sponsorship program to increase awareness of the firm among Canadian investors. Patrick Ross believed that it could benefit from the excitement surrounding the upcoming Sydney Olympics. While the firm knew that the Olympics was a powerful attraction through which many firms had enhanced their image, it didn't have the resources to be an official Olympic sponsor. The request caused Sharon to review some of her past projects at Landmark Sports Group. She couldn't believe how many hours had gone into each one. Especially challenging had been her efforts combining Olympic athletes with programs that would benefit their corporate sponsors. Landmark represented many Canadian athletes and worked to develop sponsorship opportunities that matched athletes' images and skills with the communication needs of Canadian companies. Sharon enjoyed her role as vice-president of Landmark and knew that the upcoming Sydney Olympics was a great sports marketing opportunity. One of her most memorable promotions with an Olympic theme had focused on Kerrin Lee-Gartner and her sponsor Midland Walwyn (acquired by Merrill Lynch in 1998) for the 1994 Olympics.

Much had changed since 1994. Sharon was particularly concerned about the new, strict regulations on athlete sponsorship and "ambush marketing." The Sydney Olympic Committee defined "ambush marketing" as the unauthorized association of businesses and their goods and services with the marketing of an event, such as the Games, without paying for those marketing and association rights: "Ambush marketing is detrimental and damaging to the success of the Games and to the rights of official Games sponsors and licenses and has the potential to mislead the public." Given the regulations, Sharon knew it would be difficult to develop a powerful campaign for her new client. It would take considerable brainstorming to develop another comprehensive and exciting sports marketing promotion.

History of Landmark Sports Group

Elliot Kerr, president of Landmark Sports Group, was the driving force in the company. He built the company from almost nothing to its current status as a major competitor to International Marketing Group (IMG). In the early 1990s, IMG was the largest sports marketing firm in Canada. Having worked at IMG himself, Elliott took a hands-on approach and developed most of Landmark's earliest clients by cold-calling companies in various industries.

This case was prepared by Lauren Dmytrenko and Phil Connell under the supervision of Dr. Peggy Cunningham for use in the 2001 Inter-Collegiate Business Competition and is not intended to illustrate either effective or ineffective handling of a management situation. Some information may have been disguised in the interest of confidentiality.

Sharon Podatt, fresh out of university and completing a one-year post-graduate degree in marketing and public programs at Humber College, approached Elliot to work as a six-month, pay-free intern at Landmark. Initially, Landmark operated with just the two of them at the helm. Sharon's experience with event management through her volunteer work at the Special Olympics and related sports activities proved to be invaluable.

Landmark's activities include acting as an agent for many sporting and related industry personalities. Its extensive and impressive client list includes such famous names as Silken Laumann and Elvis Stojko. (See Exhibit 1 for the full client list.)

EXHIBIT 1 LSG Athlete Client List

Golf	
• Rob McMillan	–Member of the 2000 Canadian Tour –Winner of the 1996 Manitoba Open –1996 Canadian Amateur Champion
• Dawn Coe-Jones	–Winner of Three LPGA Tour Events –1995 Winner of the LPGA Tournament of Champions
• Liz Earley	–Member of the LPGA Tour –1999 Second Place at Canadian Women's Professional Golf Championship
Diving	
• Eryn Bulmer	–2000 World Cup Bronze Medallist, 3m –1999 Canadian National Women's Diving Champion 1m, 3m. –1998 National Women's Record Holder, 1m & 3m Springboard –1998 Canadian National Women's Diving Champion, 1m, 3m –1997 World Cup Champion
Mountain biking	
• Alison Sydor	–1999 World Cup Champion –1999 Silver World Championships –1999 & 1998 First Overall World Cup Title –1999 Gold Medallist, Sydney, Australia, Pre-Olympic World Cup –1996 Olympic Silver Medallist –Three Time World Champion (1994, 1995 & 1996)
Equestrian	
• Ian Millar	–Two-time World Cup Champion –Canada's Premier Equestrian –7 time Olympian
• Jonathon Millar	–Grand Prix Rider
• Amy Millar	–Grand Prix Rider
Speed skating	
• Catriona LeMay Doan	–2000 Canadian Sprint Champion –1999 First Overall World Cup Standings, 500m –1998 Canadian Female Athlete of the Year –1998 First Overall World Cup Standings, 500m & 1000m –1998 Olympic Gold Medallist, 500m (set Olympic record) –1998 Olympic Bronze Medallist, 1000m
Hockey	
• Jayna Hefford	–Two Time Gold Medallist Women's World Hockey Championships (1997 & 1999) –1999 World Championships Tournament Leading Scorer, All-Star Selection –1998 World Championships MVP –1998 Olympic Silver Medallist
• Vicky Sunohara	–Three Time Gold Medallist Women's World Hockey Championships (1990, 1997, 1999) –1998 Olympic Silver Medallist, Two Time Gold Medallist Women's World Hockey Championships
• Lori Dupuis	–Two Time Gold Medallist Women's World Hockey Championships (1997 & 1999) –1998 Olympic Silver Medallist

EXHIBIT 1 Continued

Curling	
• Russ Howard	–Two Time World Champion (1987 & 1995)
Figure skating	
• Marie-Claude Savard-Gagnon and Luc Bradet	–1997 Canadian National Pairs Champions
• Elizabeth Manley	–1988 Olympic Silver Medallist
Kayaking	
• Caroline Brunet	–Three-Time World Champion (1997, 1998, 1999)
• Karen Furneaux	–World Champion (1998)
Alpine skiing	
• Allison Forsyth	–Two-time World Cup Silver Medallist
Wrestling	
• Daniel Igali	–1999 World Champion
Broadcasters	
• Michael Lansbury	–Director of the Toronto Blue Jays on CTV Sportsnet –Director of the NHL—Canada Cup, 1987 (CTV) and the 1994, 1996–1999 Canadian Figure Skating Championships (CTV) –Director Live/Host Studio of the 1994 Winter Olympics, Lillehammer –Director of Stanley Cup Playoffs 1995–1999 (CBC)
• John Shannon	–Executive Producer CBC "Hockey Night in Canada" –Producer of the 1994 Winter Olympics—Lillehammer and the 1992 Summer Olympics—Barcelona –Producer of the 1993 NHL All-Star Game—NBC
• Rod Black	–CTV Sports
• Don Cherry	–CBC Hockey Night in Canada
• Bob Cole	–CBC Hockey Night in Canada
• Chris Cuthbert	–CBC Sports
• Kerrin Lee-Gartner	–CBC Sports –1993 Sports Federation Female Athlete of the Year –1992 Olympic Gold Medallist—Downhill, Albertville
• Paul Martini	–CBC Sports
• Daren Millard	–CTV Sportsnet
• Greg Millen	–CBC Hockey Night in Canada –Colour analyst, 1994 Winter Olympics for CTV
• Jim Nelford	–Golf Commentator
• Scott Oake	–CBC Sports
• Leo Rautins	–CTV Sports, Raptors Basketball Analyst –ESPN Basketball Analyst
• Elfi Schlegel	–NBC Sports
• Michael Smith	–CBC Sports –1996 Gold Medallist Gotzis Decathlon –1995 World Championships Bronze Medallist Decathlon
• Barbara Underhill	–CTV Sports
• Debbi Wilkes	–CTV Sports
• Al Strachan	–CBC Hockey Night in Canada –Toronto Sun
Motivational speakers	
• Silken Laumann	–Former Olympic Rower
• Rubin "Hurricane" Carter	–Former Boxer
• Stephen Brunt	–*The Globe and Mail*
• Cary Mullen	–1994 World Cup Champion Downhill
• Richard Peddie	–President, Maple Leaf Sports and Entertainment
Other	
• Michael Burgess	–Singer

Kerr's focus on developing long-term relationships with the athletes proved to be very rewarding, and most of the firm's first clients still remained with it even after they retired from professional sport.

Landmark's reputation as a respected athlete agency grew to include strong capabilities in event management. Golf tournaments, skating tours, and other promotions were developed in-house. Much of Landmark's early business arose after Elliot developed programs and initiated contact with prospective companies whose public relations could benefit from including a sports marketing component. A unique characteristic of Landmark's sponsorship drive was its interest in pursuing non-traditional sponsors rather than the Coca-Colas and Nikes of the world: Landmark had been particularly successful in showing smaller firms the power of sports sponsorship. (See Exhibit 2 for a profile of Landmark.)

EXHIBIT 2 Landmark Sports Group Agency Profile

Our Philosophy

The Landmark Group, a sport and special event marketing company, was founded in February 1987, based on the principles of integrity, honesty, old-fashioned hard work, and the mandate to always approach a client's business in an innovative manner. These principles have been strictly adhered to, and as a result, the Landmark Group has grown into a truly national sport and special event marketing company operating from our base in Toronto.

The business philosophy at Landmark is simple. We work harder than the competition with desire, determination and dedication.

- Desire to deliver value for the dollars our clients spend.
- Determination to ensure our service always exceeds our clients' expectations.
- Dedication to excellence, because excellence is not just an ideal to strive for, but an expectation to be met.

The first order of business in everything we do, is to understand our clients needs, assist in creating realistic expectations, and then develop partnerships with them to achieve their stated goals. This is truly evident in the four main divisions of our organization: event management, corporate consulting, athlete representation and sponsorship, and media sales.

Event Management

The organization, planning and implementation of any type of special event is a major undertaking. After studying a client's needs and objectives, involving them in targeted events, acquiring secondary sponsors, negotiating facility contracts, and overseeing the thousands of details around such an exercise, the Landmark Group implements all aspects of sport and non-sport involvement. This includes development of all collateral materials associated with events, as well as all required public relations. In effect, we offer a complete service on a fully turnkey basis.

Securing Sponsorships

Mounting and staging an event can be costly depending on the size and scope. Many events are conducted annually, while others are held on a one-time basis. With each type of event, sponsorship and/or donation dollars are required to competently and effectively conduct the activity. The Landmark Group has developed a reputation for efficient and expedient sponsor acquisition at all levels.

Public Relations

Our staff are skilled and experienced in their public relations activities which include: preparation of news releases, orchestrating press conferences, liaising with the media, organizing special media functions, and developing full public relations plans.

Collateral Material

The Landmark Group has the resources to design and produce a wide range of collateral materials for any event. These may include items such as logos, posters, brochures, print advertisements, pins and assorted clothing (T-shirts, sweatshirts, hats etc. . .).

Corporate Consulting

The Consulting Division of the Landmark Group is enjoying tremendous growth with a diversified group of clients. Our philosophy is not to simply be a supplier to our clients, but to interact with each of them to develop innovative, 'trailblazing' programs. The Landmark Group believes our clients should lead with a proactive mentality as opposed to a reactive response in the special event industry.

EXHIBIT 2 Continued

Whether it is guiding our present client base in the corporate sector on the use of sport or non-sport (environment, arts, music, cause related) activities to meet marketing and communication needs, or analyzing current activities for new and/or prospective clients, the Landmark Group has developed a reputation for providing insightful, critical analysis and artful marketing strategies.

With rising costs, increased clutter, and perceived ineffectiveness of mass media on one side, and the phenomenal growth and use of events for a targeted marketing approach on the other, there is a fiduciary responsibility to choose events wisely and thereafter measure their effectiveness objectively.

The Landmark Group is capable of providing a careful analysis of your organization's marketing and communication objectives, undertaking a creative review of programs that would most effectively meet those objectives, developing an integrated strategy of involvement in an event program (e.g., sponsorship, trade and consumer promotions, cause related activities, additional extensions) and then detailing a qualitative and quantitative evaluation (pre and post) of all event marketing and program activity.

Athlete & Personality Representation

Over the last ten years, the Landmark Group has established many solid relationships with Canada's elite amateur, Olympic, and professional athletes, and television personalities. Each athlete in their own way possesses attributes we all strive to acquire and use in our personal, social, and business lives.

Many of today's blue chip corporations have discovered, through the use of sponsorship, how athletes can enhance a company's business image for the consumer.

The Landmark Group secures and negotiates on behalf of the athletes and personalities with respect to their availability and remuneration for a given event or sponsorship opportunity.

The Landmark Group also:

- Negotiates merchandise/endorsement relationships
- Negotiates equipment contracts
- Develops and coordinates personal appearances
- Develops and manages media relations strategies
- Provides financial management

Sponsorship

Sponsorship Packaging

In addition to professionally preparing and printing a final document, the Landmark Group can accurately develop targeted and fully descriptive sponsorship packages that will:

- Review and analyze the specific property/properties
- Determine and define objectives
- Develop strategies and tactics
- Create uses for the property to meet specific industry/corporate needs

Sponsorship Solicitation

Through our database system, the Landmark Group has an enhanced ability to service current clients in addition to developing a working file on prospective partners.

- More than 2000 companies on our database
- Companies available by industry category
- Cross-referenced to individual contacts
- Key variable fields include:
  –Most recent meeting/contact
  –Response/Feedback
  –Status
  –Budgeting process/timing

The Landmark Group is able to easily retrieve, manipulate, and report this data to deliver an accurate and quick response.

Sponsorship Servicing

- Once a corporate partner is secured, servicing the relationship becomes key.
- Regular communication is mandatory to maintain corporate relationships.
- Landmark can develop a communication link and provide feedback, support, and other service elements to maintain and help the partnership grow.

continued

EXHIBIT 2 Continued

- Regular contact/meetings can be arranged by Landmark.
- We would work together to develop cross-promotional opportunities with other sponsors.

Speakers Network

This area provides sports related speakers from diverse backgrounds, which include present and former top Canadian athletes and prominent media personalities.

The focus and topics they discuss can be tailored to suit any audience, for example, team work, leadership, striving for personal growth and excellence, staying competitive, and the pursuit of a dream.

Our speakers network gives you access to a wide variety of speakers to accommodate any event from annual meetings, open houses, workshops, clinics, to employee functions.

Landmark's Relationship with Kerrin Lee-Gartner

Kerrin Lee-Gartner (see Exhibit 3), one of Canada's premier downhill skiers, grew up in the small British Columbia mining town of Rossland, the home of another famous Canadian skier, Nancy Greene. Kerrin began skiing at three and proved a natural downhiller. She participated in racing programs at the local Red Mountain Ski Club, eventually competing in provincial races. A one-year break from the sport at age 13 and not meeting provincial team standards at age 15 only strengthened her determination and desire to win.

Named to the National C team in 1984, Kerrin joined the World Cup circuit a year later. Despite significant potential, she initially had her share of bad luck. She suffered a number of serious injuries, which demanded months of rehabilitation and a significant amount of time off the snow. In an elite athlete's world, time away means time lost keeping pace with the sport as well as an inability to compete. However, determination to win allowed Kerrin to finally reach her first World Cup top-three podium result in 1991.

In the period before the Olympics in Albertville, France, the Canadian Alpine Ski Team had been demoralized by injuries and mediocre performances. But as happens so often at big ski-racing events, one individual can turn a team around. Kerrin stepped forward and lifted team spirit and Canadian hopes onto her shoul-

EXHIBIT 3 Kerrin Lee-Gartner

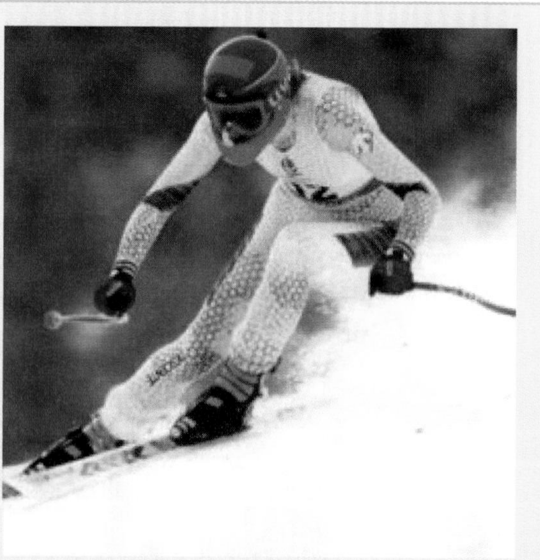

Source: Kerrin Lee-Gartner, 22 June 2000, www.kerrinlee-gartner.com.

ders. She won a first-ever Olympic gold medal in the downhill event, realizing a lifelong dream.

The early 1990s was a period of rapid evolution for sports marketing firms. Suddenly, agencies that could represent the interests of amateur and professional athletes were in demand. Kerrin, following the success in Albertville, selected Landmark to act as her agent to help her coordinate her obligations as an athlete. Furthermore, as training costs increased, athletes also found that sponsorship was necessary to help them cover living, training, medical, and travelling costs. Landmark's straightforward and honest approach to the agency–athlete relationship helped set the stage for some exciting sponsorship opportunities for Kerrin, as the 1994 Winter Olympics in Lillehammer, Norway approached.

Working with Midland Walwyn

In mid-1992, Landmark approached Midland Walwyn (MW) with a sponsorship program designed with Kerrin in mind. Given that the next Winter Olympics was only two years away in Lillehammer (due to the change to split the Winter and Summer Olympics to alternating every two years), this was an ideal opportunity to capitalize on Kerrin's latest success and market MW.

Instead of waiting for a firm to approach Landmark, Elliot Kerr approached MW with a sponsorship plan. Created at a time of deregulation in the Canadian financial services industry, MW had unique regional and market strengths, which meant, to Elliot, that a "nationally" focused program would be ideal for it. MW was one of the country's top five underwriting firms, with about 600 000 client accounts. Its strength in IPOs, knowledge of a number of industry sectors, expertise in developing innovative products, and relationship-focused client service accounted largely for the firm's success. Its asset management business, Atlas Asset Management, offered 24 externally managed mutual funds. MW also ranked high among institutional investors for its equity research group. (See Exhibit 4 for financial data on MW.) Landmark recognized that RRSPs and investment-based companies were starting to gain a high profile among the Canadian public. Furthermore, competition between investment firms was growing, as the baby boomers neared the height of their working careers and began to think of retirement. Elliot believed that the ability to create goodwill for the company through sponsorship was an ideal way to attract new clients as well as retaining current ones.

Landmark knew that the key to successful sponsorship programs was having a multi-faceted, integrated, high-impact program. While much of the sponsorship fee paid by MW was to obtain rights to have its logo placed on Kerrin's clothing,

EXHIBIT 4 Midland Walwyn Five-year Summary Data

Year	Sales*	Net income*
1993	496.00	63.04
1994	471.50	29.08
1995	517.97	18.66
1996	719.20	49.45
1997	846.71	58.53
Growth Rates	14.30	−1.84

*Millions of dollars

Source: Industry Canada, 15 May 2000, strategis.ic.gc.ca.

this was only the start of the program. For alpine skiers, their headgear—helmet, toque, or headband—was the only piece of equipment where they could exhibit names of sponsors. The remaining space on their uniforms often had advertising, but it belonged to the Canadian Ski Team sponsors and to the organizers of each race or tour. Knowing that Kerrin would have a lot of exposure in the upcoming World Cup season, MW prominently displayed its logo on both her helmet and her toque and cap that she would wear immediately after the races. It considered the exposure of the MW logo as equivalent to free television and print advertising, especially if Kerrin reached the podium.

Kerrin and Landmark worked with MW to develop a series of videos that centred on her relationship with her MW broker. These videos had credibility because Kerrin already had a very successful working relationship with a MW broker from Calgary before her sponsorship deal attained through Landmark. This also kept the videos from violating the dictates of the Canadian Advertising Standards. (See Exhibit 5 for excerpts from the code.) As well as showing Kerrin meet-

EXHIBIT 5 Excerpts from the Canadian Advertising Code

Canadian Code of Advertising Standards
May 1999 Revision

Self-Regulation of Advertising in Canada

The Canadian Code of Advertising Standards (Code), which has been developed to promote the professional practice of advertising, was first published in 1963. Since that time it has been reviewed and revised periodically to keep it contemporary. The Code is administered by Advertising Standards Canada/Les normes canadiennes de la publicité (ASC) (formerly the Canadian Advertising Foundation/la Fondation canadienne de la publicité). ASC is the industry body committed to creating and maintaining community confidence in advertising.

The Code sets the criteria for acceptable advertising and forms the basis upon which advertising is evaluated in response to consumer or trade complaints. It is widely endorsed by advertisers, advertising agencies, media that exhibit advertising, and suppliers to the advertising process.

Consumer complaints to ASC about advertising that allegedly does not comply with the Code are reviewed and adjudicated by the English national and regional Consumer Response Councils and by their counterpart in Montreal, le Conseil des normes (collectively referred to as Councils and individually as a Council). These autonomous bodies of senior industry and public representatives are supported and co-ordinated by, but altogether independent from, ASC.

Trade complaints about advertising, based on the Code, are separately administered under ASC's Trade Dispute Procedure.

Definitions

For the purposes of the Code and this document:

- "Advertising" is defined as any message (the content of which is controlled directly or indirectly by the advertiser) expressed in any language and communicated in any medium (except those listed in Appendix "A" to the Code) to Canadians with the intent to influence their choice, opinion or behaviour.
- "Advertising" also includes "advocacy advertising", "political advertising", and "election advertising", as defined below.
- "Advocacy advertising" is defined as "advertising" which presents information or a point-of-view bearing on a publicly recognized controversial issue.
- "Political advertising" is defined as "advertising" by any part of local, provincial or federal governments, or concerning policies, practices or programs of such governments, as distinct from election advertising.
- "Election advertising" is defined as "advertising" regarding a political party, a political or government policy or issue, an electoral candidate, or any other matter before the electorate for a referendum, that is communicated to the public within a time-frame that starts the day after a vote is called and ends the day after the vote is held. In this definition, a "vote" is deemed to have been called when the applicable writ is dropped.

EXHIBIT 5 Continued

Application

The Code applies to "advertising" by (or for):

- advertisers promoting the use of goods and services;
- corporations, organizations or institutions seeking to improve their public image or advance a point of view; and
- governments, government departments and crown corporations.

Exclusions

Canadians are entitled to expect that election advertising will respect the standards articulated in the Code. However, it is not intended that the Code govern or restrict the free expression of public opinion or ideas through election advertising, which is excluded from the application of this Code.

Scope of the Code

The authority of the Code applies only to the content of advertisements and does not prohibit the promotion of legal products or services or their portrayal in circumstances of normal use. The context and content of the advertisement and the audience actually, or likely to be, or intended to be, reached by the advertisement, and the medium/media used to deliver the advertisement, are relevant factors in assessing its conformity with the Code. In the matter of consumer complaints, Councils will be encouraged, when in their judgment it would be helpful and appropriate to do so, to refer to the principles and standards expressed in the Gender Portrayal Guidelines (as amended from time to time) in order to identify acceptable standards respecting the representations of women and men in advertisements.

The Code

The Canadian Code of Advertising Standards is widely supported by all participating organizations, and is designed to help set and maintain standards of honesty, truth, accuracy, fairness and propriety in advertising.

No advertising shall be prepared or knowingly exhibited by the participating organizations which contravenes this Code of Standards.

The provisions of the Code should be adhered to both in letter and in spirit. Advertisers and their representatives must substantiate their advertised claims promptly when requested to do so by one or more of the Councils.

1. Accuracy and Clarity

(a) Advertisements must not contain inaccurate or deceptive claims, statements, illustrations or representations, either direct or implied, with regard to price, availability or performance of a product or service. In assessing the truthfulness and accuracy of a message, the concern is not with the intent of the sender or precise legality of the presentation. Rather, the focus is on the message as received or perceived, that is, the general impression conveyed by the advertisement.

(b) Advertisements must not omit relevant information in a manner which, in the result, is deceptive.

(c) All pertinent details of an advertised offer must be clearly and understandably stated.

(d) Disclaimers and asterisked or footnoted information must not contradict more prominent aspects of the message and should be located and presented in such a manner as to be clearly visible and/or audible.

(e) Both in principle and practice, all advertising claims and representations must be supportable. If the support on which an advertised claim or representation depends is test or survey data, such data must be reasonably competent and reliable, reflecting accepted principles of research design and execution that characterize the current state of the art. At the same time, however, such research should be economically and technically feasible, with due recognition of the various costs of doing business.

(f) The entity that is the advertiser in an advocacy advertisement must be clearly identified as the advertiser in either or both the audio or video portion of the advocacy advertisement.

2. Disguised Advertising Techniques

No advertisement shall be presented in a format or style, which conceals its commercial intent.

ing with her broker to help answer typical client concerns, the video productions used footage of her races and training. The finished videos were used at sales meetings to encourage new clients to work with MW.

The success of Kerrin and MW's relationship depended on Landmark's ability to coordinate and organize programs between the two. In addition to the clothing and video production, it produced a number of promotional commercials showing Kerrin racing and winning, posters, and photo cards. Kerrin also took an active role in contributing columns to MW sales brochures and client newsletters.

Her personal interest in assuring that her own future was secure was evident in the commitment she made to her sponsorship deal with MW. Representatives at MW often proclaimed to Sharon at Landmark how happy they were with this great friendship with Kerrin. Having worked on many other sponsorship deals, Sharon found that these relationships were much more successful when the athletes took it upon themselves to contribute as much as they could to the sponsoring company.

Developing an Olympic Promotion

Knowing that Kerrin would not be allowed to display its logo during the Olympics, MW sat down with Landmark to brainstorm about how it could capitalize on the growing popularity and spirit of the Olympic Games. MW was not large enough internationally to justify the expense of becoming an official Olympic sponsor, and regulations outlining what symbols and phrases non-official Olympics sponsor could use were becoming more stringent. The discussions between Landmark and MW representatives always came back to the idea of providing their current clients with the opportunity to travel to the Olympic Games in Lillehammer to personally cheer Kerrin on.

Sharon knew from the outset that organizing the trip would be an enormous challenge, given that the final decision to use the trip as a contest prize was not made until late summer of 1993. MW agreed to pay all the expenses for the trip as well as pay Landmark a management fee to compensate for the time and effort it put into the design and execution of the trip. (See Exhibit 6 for a full budget for this campaign.) The trip promotion began with the distribution of 300 000 magnets that featured the draw date for the contest and the prizes available to

EXHIBIT 6 Budget for the Execution of the Kerrin Promotion

Banners	500
Business-class air travel	10 000
Entertainment (sleigh ride, tours, etc.)	1 500
Expenses	1 000
Gas	500
Gift baskets	300
Ground transportation	400
Hired guide	1 000
Hotel	12 000
Landmark management fee	10 000
Meals/snacks/drinks	6 000
Olympic event tickets	10 000
Parking	150
Photography	500
Promotional materials	500
Tolls	100
Van rental	1 000
Pre-tax total	55 450
Taxes	8 318
Total	**$ 63 768**

MW's current client base. Each magnet had printed on it the client's identification number for the draw. The primary objective for the Olympic promotion was not to attract new clients, but rather to reward current customers for their commitment to the company—a goodwill building tactic.

That was the easy part. Sharon then had to coordinate the full logistics of the trip that would be rewarded to three individuals and their guests for a total of six adults. The original plan was to have personnel from MW accompany the winners on their trip abroad. However, MW executives found that they couldn't spare this much time away from the office, so Sharon was put in charge of acting as the winner's host. The trip was to include airfare, hotel, meals, tickets to Olympic events, and all travel during the stay in Lillehammer. A full itinerary had to be planned. It was fortunate that Sharon had contacts in the media who helped her find accommodations and tickets, given their scarcity and her tight timeline.

The objectives of the trip were to provide the winners with an experience that few individuals have the opportunity to enjoy, given the high costs of attending the Olympic Games, and to focus on providing Kerrin with Canadian support while in Norway. Therefore, Landmark and MW would provide all winners with clothing emblazoned with the MW logo as well as signs to display while cheering Kerrin on during her races. To kick off the promotion, Kerrin flew to Toronto to participate in drawing the winners' names and to telephone them to say that they had won the draw. (See Exhibit 7 for Landmark's Olympic Plan.)

While the promotion complied with the laws and regulations governing advertising and promotions, Sharon was concerned that some might regard this contest as a form of ambush marketing, since the official Olympic sponsors and the Canadian Olympic Association (COA) might see it as implying that the sponsoring company was an Olympic sponsor, when MW had not actually paid for that entitlement. In fact, ambush marketing is often considered the practice of deceiving the public through taking advantage of subtle (and not so subtle) messages that cre-

EXHIBIT 7 Olympic Plan for Kerrin Lee-Gartner

Plan A: Kerrin medals

- Determine Midland Walwyn identified apparel requirements.
- Obtain media list from Canadian Olympic team media attaché who is responsible for media/athlete relations.
- Tour downhill and GS sites to determine athlete accessibility after race.
- Determine athlete protocol post-event including possibility of drug test, required media interviews, etc.
- Ensure Midland Walwyn apparel is on site at all times.
- Identify appropriate Midland Walwyn representative and coordinate interviews and photos.
- Make any arrangements to send information and photos to Canadian media in Canada.
- Medal presentations
  - –No sponsor identification possible.
  - –Midland Walwyn group to be present with banners.
  - –Arrange possible photos with group.
- Determine plan for Kerrin's return to Canada (airport greeting, luncheon, press conference)

Plan B: Kerrin does not medal

- Determine (if possible) the "story" behind not medalling (for example, a fall).
- Plan to coordinate interviews with Kerrin and Midland Walwyn representative.
- Show Midland Walwyn support.

ate an association between a company running a promotion and the Olympics. Therefore, Sharon maintained close contact with the COA to ensure that Landmark did not violate any regulations with regard to ambush marketing.

Events at Lillehammer

MW received exposure at the Olympic Games a number of ways. First, Sharon and all the winners and their guests received clothing emblazoned with the MW logo to wear to all the events they attended. At the downhill events, they carried huge banners featuring the MW logo to cheer Kerrin on. Although it was exciting for Kerrin to see these banners—she later exclaimed that no one had ever made banners for her races before, they weren't as successful promotional tool as hoped. All MW logos had to be taped over after an encounter with the Olympic "logo police." Nonetheless, MW's contest winners looked impressive in their sponsored clothing, and they caught the eye of the local media who profiled the group in a large newspaper spread. (See Exhibit 8 for translated copy.)

EXHIBIT 8 Oslo Newspaper Photo and Article Translation

Caption under photo: "Lucky Ones: 'They like ski jumping,' says the six lucky winners of an Olympic trip from Canada. From left to right: Rosalyn and Jack Shuster, Bonny Thomson, Glen and Jane Hodge and George Thomson."

Canadians with Winner Luck

Not all Canadians win an Olympic Gold Medal but the six above won 10 days of luxury at the Lillehammer Olympics.

Glen Hodge from Trail in BC has always had winner's luck. Bonny Thomson from Nanaimo in the same province has never had winner's luck. Neither has Jack Shuster from Montreal been surrounded by luck in all his life. But in November last year the lucky star shined over their Canadian sky. Among 300 000 people, they were drawn to take their guest to 10 days of luxury in Lillehammer, Norway.

Why? The Canadians put their savings in a national investment company by the name of Midland Walwyn.

"Unbelievable! I didn't believe when the company called and told me about the trip to Lillehammer. In Canada it is forbidden by law to receive a prize without a competition. To bypass this law, they had to answer a skill testing question like how much is $25 \times 4/5 - 3$? You were allowed to use a calculator so I answered 17 immediately," says Glenn Hodge with a smile.

When he, his friend Jane, and the two other couples boarded the plane in Canada, their life of luxury started. It was first-class flying, big comfortable chairs, multi-course meals, and an endless supply of drinks. And since the flight, the luxury has continued.

"'Please sign here" says a waitress when she arrives with the bill, and I sign, and sign," says Glenn Hodge. "I grab my golden pen and sign thousands of Kroners. Everything is being paid for us, food, hotel, drinks, tickets to all of the events, closing ceremony."

"Yesterday we had dinner with the Gold medallist from Albertville, Kerrin Lee-Gartner, and tomorrow we are going shopping to Oslo," his friend Jane says. "And Friday is a sleigh ride. We are so busy," she continues.

On their hasty trips between the arenas in the Olympic cities, Hamar, Gjovik, and Lillehammer, they are taken by private driver, a 24-year-old Norwegian music student whom the Canadians think is the most polite, nice, and friendly person they've ever met. If all Norwegians are like him, they have reason to be proud people, says six happy Canadians.

Post-Event Recommendations

Feedback from the trip was generally positive. (See Exhibit 9 for the winners' comments.) The detailed schedule was both a benefit and a liability: At times, the group felt they had to follow the schedule, even though more exciting events were taking place, such as a medal presentation. Nevertheless, the winners did see more of the Olympic Games than most people could manage independently. For MW, the initial objectives of the promotion were met, though it later wondered how it could have targeted some of its higher-end investors, who had a much higher stake in the company.

Overall, Sharon was very pleased with the outcome of the Kerrin promotion and, more importantly, she believed that MW achieved its objectives. She believed the program was successful in a number of ways and hoped that her experience with this Olympic promotion would benefit future endeavours surrounding the Olympic Games. However, as with any promotion, there were areas that could be improved. Sharon noted the following recommendations in her post-event report to MW:

- Consider the contest qualifiers by their level of investment with Midland Walwyn.
- Project coordinator should be in Lillehammer at least a day before the arrival of the group. That way this person can already be oriented to the surroundings, determine and deal with any concerns with the schedule, have knowledge of any local items, and generally be prepared for their arrival.

EXHIBIT 9 Quotes from Trip Winners Sent to Midland Walwyn

Jack

- Experience of a lifetime!
- Warm friendly people, interesting activities, and truly exciting events.
- Became a Viking for an evening!

Rosalyn

- Beautiful country with picturesque sunny days. Excellent hospitality, interesting meals, a new experience every day.
- Overwhelmed by the work involved and the thousands of volunteers that it takes to organize the Olympic Games and to organize our trip. Everyone should be proud.

Bonnie

- Lots of exciting things to see and do. Beautiful setting, charming people, fun activities.
- A great chance to enjoy a different culture and experience new foods.

George

- Had a great time! We laughed, took a sleigh ride in the snow, met new friends, and took home many fond memories.
- First class trip all the way!

Glen

- Fun group to travel with and great hospitality.
- Really enjoyed meeting so many people and trying out a new language.
- All the events were thrilling to be at live and experience the Olympics first hand.

Jane

- Truly enjoyed the experience. The events were exciting, the Norwegian people were enthusiastic and hospitable, and we had an opportunity to see many new and interesting things.
- Will talk about the trip for many years.

- The attendees should wear Midland Walwyn-identified ski suits. Every sponsor or group of clients at the Games were easily identified by their matching ski suits. It looks great as well as official when a group is all together in corporate-identified ski suits.
- It was not necessary to provide every meal for the group. Breakfast was included with the room, every lunch was arranged usually at the hotel because it was convenient and accessible, and dinners were all pre-reserved. It would have been enough for breakfast and some dinners to be arranged and paid for and have the group pay for their own meals outside of the planned ones.
- It would be better not to print a schedule with all activities planned. Just letting the group know what events you have purchased tickets for and the travel itinerary worked fine. Other events, such as the broadcast centre tour or the dinner with Kerrin, are difficult to schedule precisely, and a printed itinerary makes incorporating changes difficult. The printed schedule didn't leave room for such spontaneous Olympic activities as Canadian athlete presentations and receptions.

A New Decade in Olympic Sponsorship

Sharon learned a great deal from her first Olympic promotion. Kerrin Lee-Gartner was also happy with the event. In fact, although Kerrin's sponsorship deal ended after she retired from the World Cup Tour, she remained with Landmark as she jumped into an active post-skiing career. As a commentator on CBC, Kerrin has seen many other television commentators join Landmark's prestigious list of athletes and celebrities.

Now Sharon had a new challenge. She had moved up to VP of Landmark through her years of dedication to the company and its innovative practices. The financial management industry had also taken a huge jump, and with the introduction of e-commerce, the marketing opportunities were endless, and the competition was fierce. It was summer of 1998. The Sydney Olympics were coming up in September of 2000, and excitement was building.

Patrick Ross Financial had approached Landmark with the question of how it could jump on the "Olympic bandwagon." Although, it was much smaller than MW, with only 100 000 clients and operating only in Ontario and Quebec, it was a similar organization in terms of its business and customers. One executive who had worked at MW with Landmark on the Kerrin promotion had left MW after Merrill Lynch acquired the company and taken a senior position at Patrick Ross. He was so pleased with the Kerrin promotion that he wanted Landmark to develop a whole promotion strategy for the Summer Olympics in Sydney.

Patrick Ross didn't have any ideas about whom it wanted to sponsor or how it wanted to run the promotion. It contacted Sharon to ask her to develop a promotional strategy. Its only guideline was that the budget for the promotion could not exceed $150 000. It wasn't sure how it wanted to target the promotion to its 100 000 clients, but knew that the promotion would have to have wide appeal to reach as many of its clients as possible. Patrick Ross gave the demographic and financial profiles of its customers to Sharon to assist her in developing the promotion. (See Exhibit 10 for the profiles.) It knew that Landmark had a great list of individual athletes and that it was very experienced in developing sports marketing opportunities. Therefore, it simply left it up to Sharon to come up with a great idea. There was a fundamental difference between this program and the Kerrin promotion. During the Kerrin promotion,

EXHIBIT 10 Client Profiles

Patrick Ross Financial Demographic Profiles

Age	Percentage	Clients
Under 30	15	15 000
30–45	30	30 000
45–65	40	40 000
Retired	15	15 000
Total	**100**	**100 000**

Sex	Percentage	Clients
Males	73	73 000
Females	27	27 000
Total	**100**	**100 000**

Occupation	Percentage	Clients
Blue collar	14	14 000
Professional	20	20 000
Retired	15	15 000
White collar	51	51 000
Total	**100**	**100 000**

Financial Profiles

Income Bracket	Percentage	Clients
Under 30 000	7	7 000
30 000–50 000	13	13 000
50 000–70 000	18	18 000
70 000–90 000	24	24 000
90 000–100 000	19	19 000
100 000+	19	19 000
Totals	**100**	**100 000**

Amount Invested	Percentage	Clients
Under 50 000	27	27 000
50 000–100 000	25	25 000
100 000–250 000	17	17 000
250 000–500 000	18	18 000
500 000+	13	13 000
Totals	**100**	**100 000**

Total assets under administration: $15.4 billion

Landmark was responsible only for the execution of the promotion rather than its development. For Patrick Ross, however, Landmark would have to select an athlete, put together an innovative promotional strategy, and implement and execute the plan in September 2000.

Before Sharon could begin developing a promotional strategy for Patrick Ross, she would have to carefully review the issue of ambush marketing. She knew that many of the regulations had become more strict since Lillehammer and that she would have to familiarize herself with them.

Ambush Marketing at the Sydney Olympics

For years, companies have used ambush marketing at the Olympic Games. Many smaller companies simply cannot afford to become official Olympic sponsors. And since the Olympics allows only one official sponsor per product category, some large firms who are shut out of official sponsorship use ambush marketing, finding unauthorized ways to exploit the Olympics as a promotional opportunity. They accomplished this through indirectly connecting the Olympics with another promotion. (See Exhibit 11 for examples of ambush marketing.)

EXHIBIT 11 Examples of Ambush Marketing Techniques

- "At the Atlanta Games, non-sponsors Nike and Samsung employed classic ambush tactics, using special sports centers as well as billboards near the main stadiums to promote their brands. Post-Games research showed they made their mark with consumers many of whom thought the two companies were official sponsors."
- "Molson's 'I Am Canadian' ads crossed the ambush line, so the COA took action. The ads, parodying famous horror movie scenes, ended with the line: 'The three scariest words in Japan this winter: 'I am Canadian'."
- ". . . a MasterCard ad featuring Elvis Stojko didn't refer to the Olympic Games. However, Patricia Staker, senior manager of sponsorship marketing at the Royal Bank of Canada (an issuer of VISA cards), points out that the fans in the background were waving Japanese flags. She says that's an example of how sophisticated ambushers have become."[4]
- "Nagano Olympic Organizing Committee (NAOC) official covered up the brand name of giant TV screens installed in two ice hockey venues. . . . It cost the NAOC more than 1 million yen to have the inconspicuous name removed. . . . The Hotel's shuttle bus had an advertisement for Pepsi on its side, but it was changed to Coca-Cola, a long-time Olympic sponsor, while maps of the city produced by American Express were collected and distributed elsewhere since VISA paid a minimum of US$40 million to be the official credit card."[5]
- "While Chrysler Canada was the Canadian Olympic Association's (COA) automotive sponsor, it did not pick up the TV sponsor rights from the CBC, partly because of the cost. . . . Instead GM bought those rights which is perfectly legitimate. . . . The problem was newspaper banner ads by GM that used the words 'Nagano' and 'Olympics.'. . . These were stopped by the COA."[6]
- "Take Timex, for instance, whose competitor, Swatch, was the official Olympic timekeeper. The company, which sponsors athletes including Anne Montminy, rolled out a brilliant multi-media campaign through Ogilvy & Mather of Toronto that ran in Canada during the Olympics. One of the print ads had a turquoise Indiglo dot marking Atlanta on a map of North America. There was no use of trademarks or anything else 'official,' but Timex found a way in nonetheless."[7]

"Industry analysts say ambush marketing has become a big problem for Olympic organizers in recent times as the cost of sponsorship packages has soared while exclusivity for sponsors has become virtually impossible to guarantee."[1] The Atlanta games were often criticized for the sheer amount of commercial material that was present during them.[2] Therefore, the IOC, COA, and Sydney Olympic organizations are under pressure from potential "official" sponsoring companies to regulate ambush marketing to maintain sponsorship exclusivity. It is in the best interests of these Olympic regulatory bodies to respond to these companies because the marketability of the sponsorship opportunities depends on the level of exposure that the companies receive.

Therefore, increasingly strict regulations have been placed on advertising and promotions using Olympic themes for the Sydney Olympics. In fact, the Sydney Organizing Committee for the Olympic Games (SOGOG) is so concerned about non-sponsors that it intends to run its own promotional campaign to explain the difference between official and non-official sponsors to the public.[3] SOGOG has outlined specific regulations for non-sponsoring companies and has branded many of the "Olympic" trademarks as belonging to SOGOG before, during, and after the Olympics. In fact, it is virtually impossible to associate a company with the Olympics in a legal and ethical manner. The regulations include about 30 words and phrases that cannot be used for any commercial use without licence from SOGOG. (See Exhibit 12 for the full publication.)

EXHIBIT 12 The Sydney Organizing Committee for the Olympic Games (SOGOG) Brand Protection[8]

Introduction

The Sydney 2000 Games (Indicia and Images) Protection Act 1996 (the "Act") is a Commonwealth Act, which came into effect on 28 June 1996. The Act provides that the Sydney Organizing Committee for the Olympic Games (SOGOG) and the Sydney Paralympic Organizing Committee (SPOC) have the power to use and license others to use various "indicia and/or images" for commercial purposes. Any unlicensed commercial use of the protected indicia and images is prohibited.

The "indicia", or words and phrases, which are protected are listed in the Act and are set out in the brochure. The images which are protected are "any visual or aural representations that to a reasonable person, in the circumstances of the presentation, would suggest a connection with the Sydney Olympic Games or Paralympic Games."

Who Does the Legislation Apply To?

The legislation applies to:

- any person who applies the indicia or images to any goods or services (i.e., a manufacturer)
- any person who contracts a manufacturer to do so
- any participants in the supply chain (e.g., retailers, distributors)
- any person aiding, abetting, counseling or procuring a breach of the Act

Protected Words and Phrases

- Olympic, Paralympic, Olympiad, Paralympiad, Games City, Millennium Games, Sydney Games, Sydney 2000, Share the Spirit, Summer Games, Team Millennium
- Any combination of the word "Games" and the number "2000" or the words "Two Thousand"
- Any combination of "24th", "Twenty Fourth" or "XXIVth" and the word "Olympic" or "Games"
- Any combination of "11th", "Eleventh" or "XIth" and the word "Paralympic" or "Games"

The following combinations of words are also prohibited, namely any combination of a word in List A with a word, words, phrase or number in List B.

List A	List B
Olympian	Bronze
Olympics	Games
Paralympian	Gold
Paralympics	Green & Gold
	Medals
	Millennium
	Silver
	Spirit
	Sponsor
	Summer
	Sydney
	Two thousand
	2000

Aim of Legislation

The purpose of the legislation is to assist SOGOG in raising revenue and therefore preserving the financial integrity of the Games by regulating the use of indicia and images associated with the Games. Without this protection, the value of an official license to use the indicia and images could be diminished by ambush marketing, with a loss of revenue to the licensed person and to SOGOG.

"Ambush marketing" refers to the unauthorized association of businesses and their goods and services with the marketing of an event, such as the Games, without paying for those marketing and association rights. Ambush marketing is detrimental and damaging to the success of the Games, to the rights of official Games sponsors and licenses and has the potential to mislead or deceive the public.

Commercial Use

The protected indicia or images must not be used "commercially." That is, that may not be applied:

- To a person's goods or services for advertising or promotional purposes in a manner likely to enhance the sales of those goods or services, and;
- Where it would suggest that the person is or has been a sponsor of the Olympic or Paralympic Games or both, or is or has been a provider of other support for the Games or any event organized by SOGOG, SPOC or other Games-related bodies such as the Australian Olympic Committee

Use of the indicia in a language other than English is prohibited, as is using other words and phrases, which are so similar to the protected indicia that a reasonable person would be likely to mistake them for protected indicia.

There are several jurisdictions sponsorship regulation. The COA has jurisdiction over all Olympic sponsorship issues within Canada; the IOC has international jurisdiction; and together with SOGOG, the IOC has jurisdiction during the Sydney Olympic games. The COA prohibits any use of the word "Olympics" or the Olympic rings symbol for commercial purposes at any time without proper registration with the COA. It may waive that prohibition, but will rarely do so for a non-official sponsor. Therefore, using the Olympics for any commercial (other than editorial) purposes is strictly prohibited, regardless of whether a company is an Olympic athlete sponsor.

The Olympic charter, developed by the IOC, specifies regulations during the Olympic Games themselves. "Except as permitted by the IOC Executive Board, no competitor who participates in the Olympic Games may allow his/her person, name, picture or sports performances to be used for advertising purposes *during the Olympic Games*."[9] Therefore, any athlete or other individual whom Patrick Ross chose to endorse or sponsor would be unable to promote Patrick Ross in any way in Sydney, including wearing any form of apparel bearing a logo other than that of an official Olympic sponsor.

Sharon learned that the promotion that Landmark ran in 1994 would no longer be considered appropriate. She was beginning to realize that running any kind of promotion during the games or one using Olympic symbols was in direct violation of these regulations. Sharon decided that she was not interested in challenging the legal and ethical issues inherent in ambush marketing. She intended to make the promotion that she developed for Patrick Ross legal and ethical in the eyes of the COA, IOC, and SOGOG, and did not want to take any chances by breaching those regulations. She knew that promotions that were a little closer to those ethical boundaries might be more powerful, but it was not worth Landmark or Patrick Ross's reputation to take any chances.

While Sharon was confident in her decision to remain within these boundaries, she was also aware that this major constraint would challenge her creative abilities. She would have to ensure that any promotion would focus entirely on the athlete or individual. She had been in contact with the COA directly and was told that the regulations became a little less restraining *after* the Olympics and that a promotion that focused on a "personality" without direct association with the Olympics was entirely acceptable because it promoted the individual, not the Olympics. However, the more she explored the issue, the more complex it seemed to become. Sharon was glad she had done this research. The COA had instructed her that their tolerance for violations of the various regulations was very low and they were willing to shut down any promotion that crossed its boundaries.

A Challenging New Promotional Opportunity

Sharon didn't have much time to put the promotion together. She thought about her athlete list and about the advantages of the promotion with Kerrin. Given the strict regulations on ambush marketing, she'd have to use her creative prowess. She reviewed the boundaries of this promotion: It would have to be legal and ethical and follow all the rules and regulations established by the COA, IOC, and SOGOG. She had a small budget of $150 000 for the entire promotion, and she had just over two years to put it together. (See Exhibit 13 for media costs.) She also considered what she had learned running the MW promotion. How, for example, could Patrick Ross specifically target higher-end investors but

EXHIBIT 13 Sample Media Costs

Prime Time Television Commercial Rates (30 Seconds)[10]

Network	Number of Stations	Basic Average Cost
Regional Television		
ASN	1	$90
ATV	4	$650
CBC Regional		
Atlantic	5	$1 000
Central	15	$6 000
Western	12	$2 500
Pacific	6	$1 000
Global	1	$7 000
MITV	2	$500
BBS Ontario	8	$5 000

Newspaper Advertising[11]

Newspaper	Cost of Advertisement	Cost per 1000 People Reached (CPM)
Toronto Star	$11 340	$2 438
Globe and Mail	$16 938	$5 314
Toronto Sun	$ 5 463	$2 366

also use the promotion as a tool to create general goodwill? What individual or individuals on their client list would be most effective in reaching the customers of a small but mature financial institution? How could they use a "personality" effectively in this strategy, and how would they translate that idea into an executable plan with a tangible, measurable result to which customers would respond? Sharon knew it would be challenging, but sports marketing was her passion, and she knew that she could come up with something that would be both successful and memorable.

Notes

[1]Chris Prichard, "Aussie Olympic committee takes on ambush marketing," *Marketing Magazine,* 1 September 1997, Web site.

[2]Jeremy Barker, "Nagano makes Olympian efforts to protect its sponsors," *Marketing Magazine,* 16 February 1998, Web site.

[3]Official Web site of the Olympic Games www.olympic.org, Section 45 of the Olympic Charter, By-Law Number 3.

[4]Prichard, "Aussie Olympic committee takes on ambush marketing."

[5]Barker, "Nagano makes Olympian efforts to protect its sponsors."

[6]Lesley Daw, "Guardians of the rings," *Marketing Magazine,* 13 April 1998, Web site.

[7]Lara Mills, "Ambush marketing as an Olympic event," *Marketing Magazine,* 19/26 August 1996, Web site.

[8]SOGOG brochure on brand protection.

[9]Barker, "Nagano makes Olympian efforts to protect its sponsors." collections.ic.gc.ca/heirloom_series/volume4/380-381.htm

[10]"Estimated cost of network commercials," *Media Digest,* 1999–2000:22.

[11]Keith J. Tuckwell, *Canadian Advertising in Action* 5th ed. Scarborough: Prentice-Hall, 2000:332.

Becel Margarine: Reinvigorating Growth

On December 15, 1999, Ross Hugessen, brand manager at Unilever Canada, reflected on the last several months of managing Becel margarine, one of the company's most important brands. Becel had just been awarded a *Cassie* for advertising effectiveness and it appeared as though Becel would end the year with a record market share in the $450M margarine/butter category. It seemed as though things had never been better for the business. Ross knew however that as soon as he returned from Christmas break, he would be faced with some important issues regarding the brands' future in the New Year.

For some time, Becel had been a very strong player in the market, having grown substantially in its relatively short history. But while Becel was still growing, the growth trend was below that of prior years and well below what senior management had come to expect. Positioned as the "best margarine for your heart's health," Becel had a compelling point of differentiation that seemed to be one of the key reasons the brand had done so well. However, this positioning had been attracting several new competitors at a price point considerably below the premium price around which Becel had built its business. In addition, marketers in the margarine category had to deal with some very tight regulations. For example margarine in Quebec had to be white, not butter coloured. These regulations limited the potential for margarine brands like Becel to come forward with much innovation.

Ross had to evaluate the brand from all angles in order to determine the best strategic plan to deliver the significant short and long-term growth that was expected by Unilever. Even though the brand had met with record share, the rate of growth had fallen below what was expected for 1999. Becel had been built by targeting older, educated and affluent adults, but Ross began to question the ability of Becel to gain a higher share among members of this target market. Furthermore, although the Becel communication strategy had been very successful, it didn't seem to be driving the rates of growth it had initially, although clearly advertising had been proven to drive sales. The advertising campaign had been running for many years and had been developed by his boss. Ross knew it would be difficult to justify the same amount of spending on advertising for his brand if the returns were less than before, especially as other brands in the company were vying for the same budget dollars.

Ross wondered if the brand team could determine a convincing strategy that would shape the future success of Becel margarine and maintain its share leadership and growth momentum.

Unilever Canada

Unilever Canada is a division of the international Unilever group, which is headed by two parent companies, Unilever NV and Unilever PLC headquartered in Rotterdam

This case was prepared by Phil Connell under the supervision of Dr. Peggy Cunningham. We gratefully acknowledge the support provided by Mr. Ross Hugessen and Ms. Jan Mollenhauer of Unilever Canada. They took time out of very busy schedules to work on this case. The case is not intended to illustrate either effective or ineffective handling of a management situation. Some information may have been disguised in the interest of confidentiality.

and London respectively. Unilever was formed in 1930 when the British soap-maker Lever Brothers merged with the Dutch company Margarine Unie. This allowed both companies to benefit from many raw materials and resources that they had in common. Today, Unilever is one of the world's largest consumer products companies.

In 1999, Becel Margarine fell under the foods division, Lipton. In addition to having a category leading position in the margarine market with over 8 brands, including Becel's competitor Fleischmann's, Lipton also sold products in the tea, soup, packaged side dish and pasta sauce markets. Unilever's other major division was Personal Products, marketing such products as Dove, Sunlight Detergent, Salon Selectives and Degree. The Personal Products brands often took priority for marketing budgets due to the competitive nature of their markets.

Becel Margarine

A History of the Becel Brand

Becel Margarine was launched in 1978 as a premium priced product, positioned as the heart healthy margarine choice. Lipton's intention at the time was to create a brand that helped consumers meet their needs for heart health, as had been the position in Europe for 20 years prior to the Canadian introduction. Becel entered the market using very direct communication about the health advantages of the product.

Over the years, as Becel began to gain some success with its positioning, it increasingly attracted competitive attention. Nabisco with their Fleischmann's brand was most threatened, since it was the leader in the health segment of the market. Kraft also responded as it realized that the health segment growth was taking share away from mainstream brands like Parkay. Also, the Dairy Bureau (butter) increased its marketing efforts since it perceived that the target market for butter and Becel seemed to be the same. Furthermore, private label brands launched their own products using "me-too" positioning strategies, at significantly reduced prices.

Despite the uniqueness of Becel's positioning, the brand struggled for many years. By 1991 the brand had only managed to establish an 8.1% share of the market, and had very limited growth at only 1–2% per year. Furthermore, as a result of new legislative guidelines, many of the direct, rational messages about Becel's heart health benefits could no longer be used. By 1991, Lipton knew they had to take the brand in a new direction or risk discontinuing the brand.

The company considered several options for growing the Becel brand. Lipton considered a price decrease, to increase volume; however, health brands in other categories typically had large price premiums that successfully delivered strong profits. Moreover, many consumers perceived a relationship between price and quality. The company also thought about re-positioning the product—maybe not enough Canadians were concerned with heart health? Finally, Lipton considered dramatic increases in advertising support for Becel, but getting approval for heavy investment in a brand with poor volume was not really an option. Management decided that the only viable alternative was to try to grow the brand through a new break-through communication strategy without any change in expenditure. The advertising budget would have to support Becel margarine, as well as the newly launched line of cooking oil and spoonable dressings.

In 1991, Lipton was finally able to devise a strategy that would eventually make Becel the leading brand of margarine in Canada. It developed a communication strategy that would revolve around the notion of "living a life that is young at heart." This strategy allowed Lipton to communicate a simple message that became the emotional benefit associated with consuming Becel.

Becel's "Young at Heart" advertising campaign depicted the benefits of being young at heart through consumer's hope and optimism as expressed in the tagline

"Becel takes your health to heart". The actual ads featured active, fit outgoing seniors enjoying life to the fullest while enjoying a heart healthy diet—which included the consumption of Becel. Seniors were used to create an association between Becel and living life to the fullest at a time in life that is often associated with health deterioration. The TV campaign, featuring the famous Jimmy Durante song, focused on the emotional benefits of Becel, while a comprehensive print campaign delivered the rational heart health messages of Becel (See Exhibit 1 for sample Becel print ads). Together, this communication strategy provided consumers with a powerful reason to believe in the product. Becel was ready to embrace mass consumption.

In addition, Becel started to educate consumers and health professionals about the dietary benefits of margarine through the Becel Heart Health Information Bureau. The Becel Heart Health Information Bureau sought to disseminate key brand messages based on sound scientific principles, while maintaining its objectivity and credibility. With increased marketing spend directed to Health professionals, Becel built a solid reputation as a leader in Heart health and nutrition education.

In 1998, Becel continued to develop the communication strategy even further and launched an interactive web site (www.becelcanada.com). The website was an extension of the Becel Heart Health Information Bureau and provided information on meal planning, cooking recipes, the basics of heart-health and of course, product information on the Becel line-up. In addition, there was a portion of the site dedicated exclusively to health care professionals.

Becel Today

Brand Performance

As a result of the comprehensive Becel communication strategy, the brand went from being a small player to being the market leader within a relative short time frame. In 1992 when the "Young at Heart campaign" was launched, Becel had a 17.7% dollar share of the market. By early 1997, the dollar share had increased to 28.4%. Sustained growth and impressive market share results had been achieved. This was not small feat since at the same time Becel had commanded the highest price premium of any brand in its category. This price premium helped the brand management team justify the high levels of spending on advertising. (See Exhibits 2A and 2B for a full analysis of the market share data and Exhibit 3 for a profit/loss statement. See also Exhibit 8 for media costs.)

Brand Awareness, Trial and Loyalty

The success of this communication and positioning strategy was even further realized in consumers' awareness of Becel in the market. Brand awareness of Becel increased substantially from 1992 onwards. In addition to consumer brand awareness, the actual the number of consumers in the market who had tried Becel had also increased substantially. Even more impressive was that Becel had the highest consumer loyalty of any brand in the category at 50%—in a category where brand switching was very high (see Exhibit 4 for full analysis).

Given that brand awareness was so high, it is not surprising that consumers also had a very good understanding of Becel's position in the marketplace. It was very clear that Becel's heart health message was getting through, substantial portions of the market believed that Becel was the heart health expert. Overall, there was no question that Lipton had developed a successful strategy for a strong product.

The Spreads Category

Competitive Environment

By 1999 the health segment of the margarine market had become very competitive, with many brands attracted by the success of Becel and consumer interest in healthy

EXHIBIT 1 Sample Becel print ad

MARION IRVINE IS ON THE RIGHT PATH.

Making the choice to pursue a heart healthy lifestyle is important. Staying on that path is equally important.

Perhaps that's why so many choose Becel. It's low in saturated fat and non-hydrogenated (and therefore contains virtually no trans fat). No wonder more doctors and dietitians recommend Becel than any other margarine.

And to help you on the path to heart health, Becel is proud to support and make available the Heart and Stroke Foundation's booklet: "Heart Healthy Eating On the Go."

takes your health to heart.®

Please write to us for your free copy:

Becel Heart Health Information Bureau
PO Box 12073, Saint John, NB, E2L 5E7

www.becelcanada.com

EXHIBIT 1
Continued

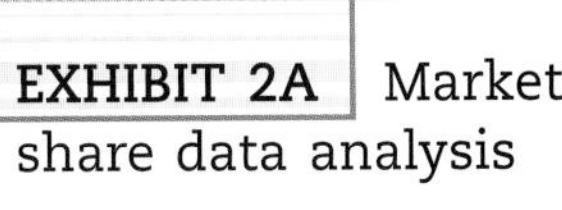

EXHIBIT 2A Market share data analysis

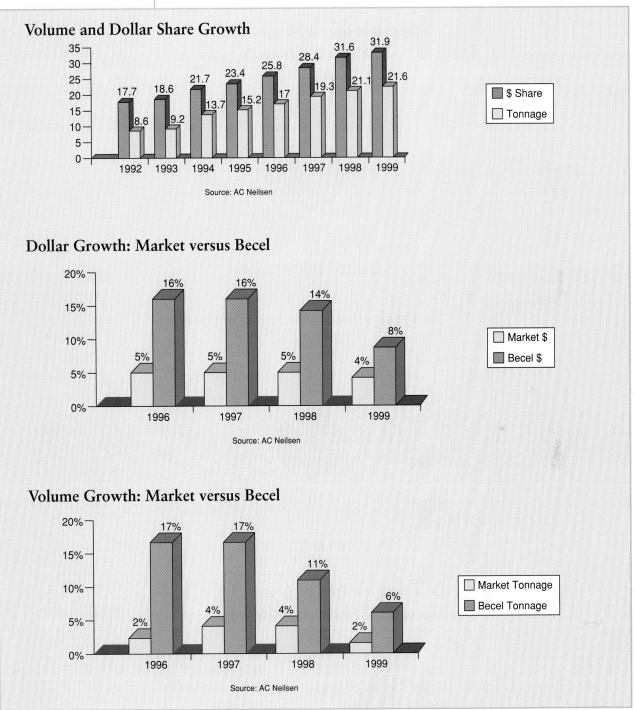

Volume and Dollar Share Growth

Year	$ Share	Tonnage
1992	17.7	8.6
1993	18.6	9.2
1994	21.7	13.7
1995	23.4	15.2
1996	25.8	17
1997	28.4	19.3
1998	31.6	21.1
1999	31.9	21.6

Source: AC Neilsen

Dollar Growth: Market versus Becel

Year	Market $	Becel $
1996	5%	16%
1997	5%	16%
1998	5%	14%
1999	4%	8%

Source: AC Neilsen

Volume Growth: Market versus Becel

Year	Market Tonnage	Becel Tonnage
1996	2%	17%
1997	4%	17%
1998	4%	11%
1999	2%	6%

Source: AC Neilsen

products. Even with the health segment growing, Becel's most formidable competitor was butter. Butter had just over 50% of the market in Canada and Ross knew that in order for Becel to grow, it had to make further inroads with butter users. The Dairy Bureau (who markets butter on behalf of Canadian dairy farmers) was very aggressive with positioning butter on its primary benefit of taste and naturalness. Its campaign highlighted the "naturalness" of dairy over the perceived "processed food" reputation

EXHIBIT 2B Market share data analysis (Continued)

Total Margarine/Butter Market
SPREADS MARKET
$ 450m +2%

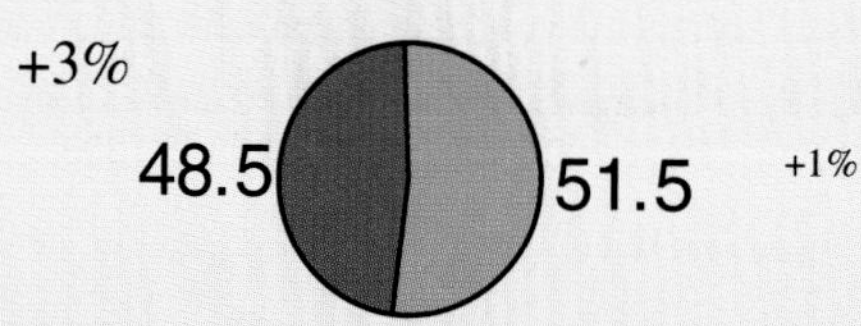

Butter Margarine

Total Margarine/Butter Spreads Market
Tonnage +2

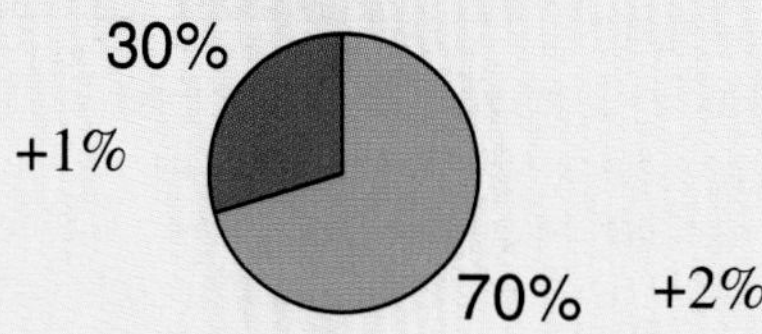

Butter Margarine

Competitive Brand Shares - Margarine 1999 - $ 222M +3

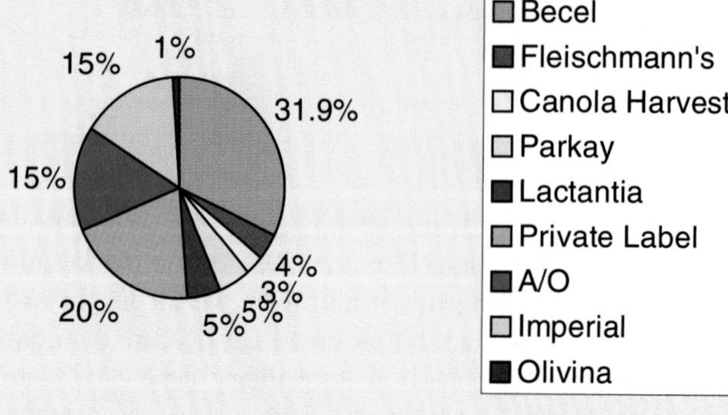

EXHIBIT 3 Becel Profit/Loss Statement

	Actual 98	Actual 99
	(000s)	(000s)
Standard Cases	1 537	1 562
Gross Sales	55 629	58 746
Total Costs	36 567	39 947
Gross Profit	19 062	18 799
Market Expenditure	5 200	3 800
–Advertising	3 200	1 800
–Promotion	2 000	2 000
Profit before indirects	13 862	14 999

of margarine. The butter industry led the category in advertising spending with over a 50% share of voice, with about $7M in spending every year with television and print.

Another competitive threat was posed by Parmalat, a large producer of butter. Parmalat had recently begun to promote its Lactantia margarine using a positioning strategy that leveraged the firm's association with butter: "the makers of great tasting butter now bring you great tasting margarine." Parmalat only had a small portion of the margarine market share, but it was increasing. Ross could not ignore the potential threat that this product posed.

Finally, there were two other brands that Ross knew he had to keep an eye on. Canola Harvest was a product that had a small share of the national market with its strongest market being in Western Canada. This product was positioned as the margarine with the best taste and best health because it contains canola oil. Retailers liked the product because it seemed to offer many of the same benefits of Becel, but at a much cheaper price. The other product Ross viewed as a competitive threat was Olivina, which was positioned using a "Mediterranean diet" association. This product had only secured about 0.6% of the national market, but was showing strong growth. Ross knew that health professionals were starting to recommend the use of olive oil instead of margarine. Ross also knew about the growing interest in olive oil since Unilever had recently bought the Bertolli brand. This caused Ross to wonder if he had the right range of products. (See Exhibit 5.)

Examining the Marketing Mix

Targeting the Market

The demographics of people who use margarine and butter are quite diverse. An analysis of the demographic characteristics do show some interesting trends in the consumers that Becel and its competitors attract. Specifically, there is an interesting dichotomy between the types of consumers that purchase margarine versus those that purchase butter. A substantial portion of the volume of margarine purchased is by people with large families, particularly ones with four or five members and who tend to have lower than average incomes. (See Exhibit 9.)

Conversely, the total volume of butter consumed was disproportionately weighted towards families without children and families with older children. Furthermore, a large portion of butter consumers tended to be over 55 years of age and the most affluent buyers. The target market for Becel tended to be very close to that of butter. However, most households bought both margarine and butter. Ross knew that the reasons people bought butter were quite different from the reason they bought a health margarine.

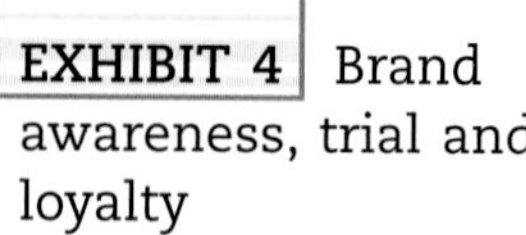

EXHIBIT 4 Brand awareness, trial and loyalty

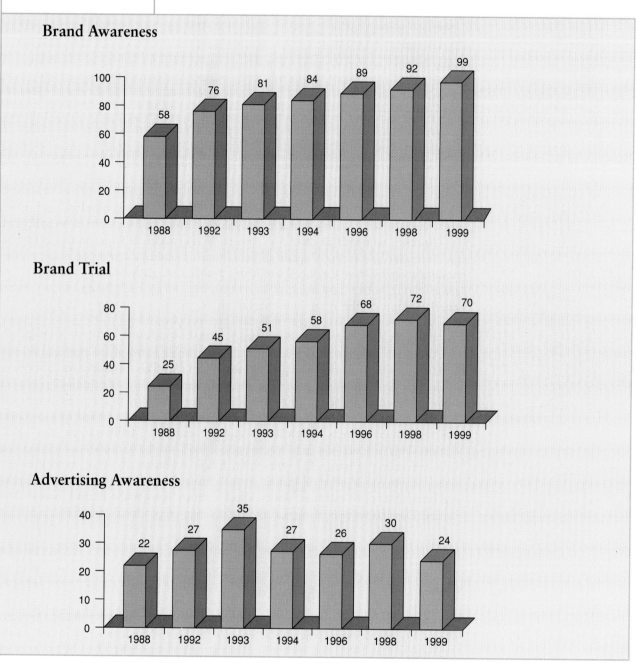

Brand Awareness

1988	1992	1993	1994	1996	1998	1999
58	76	81	84	89	92	99

Brand Trial

1988	1992	1993	1994	1996	1998	1999
25	45	51	58	68	72	70

Advertising Awareness

1988	1992	1993	1994	1996	1998	1999
22	27	35	27	26	30	24

Looking at this data made Ross's job more difficult. The demographics showed that Becel had been doing exactly what it was intended to do, serving the needs of those pursuing heart-healthy lifestyles. In addition, they had secured very high customer loyalty. Those who purchased Becel satisfied almost half of their margarine volume requirements with Becel. Other brands weren't remotely close to this degree of brand loyalty. Yet Becel's growth rates were beginning to slow down. Ross wondered why?

Ross had a look at some market data that showed what consumers tend to look for when purchasing margarine (see Exhibit 6). The data showed that individuals who purchase margarine exclusively on the basis of taste seemed to account

EXHIBIT 5 Becel's line-up of products

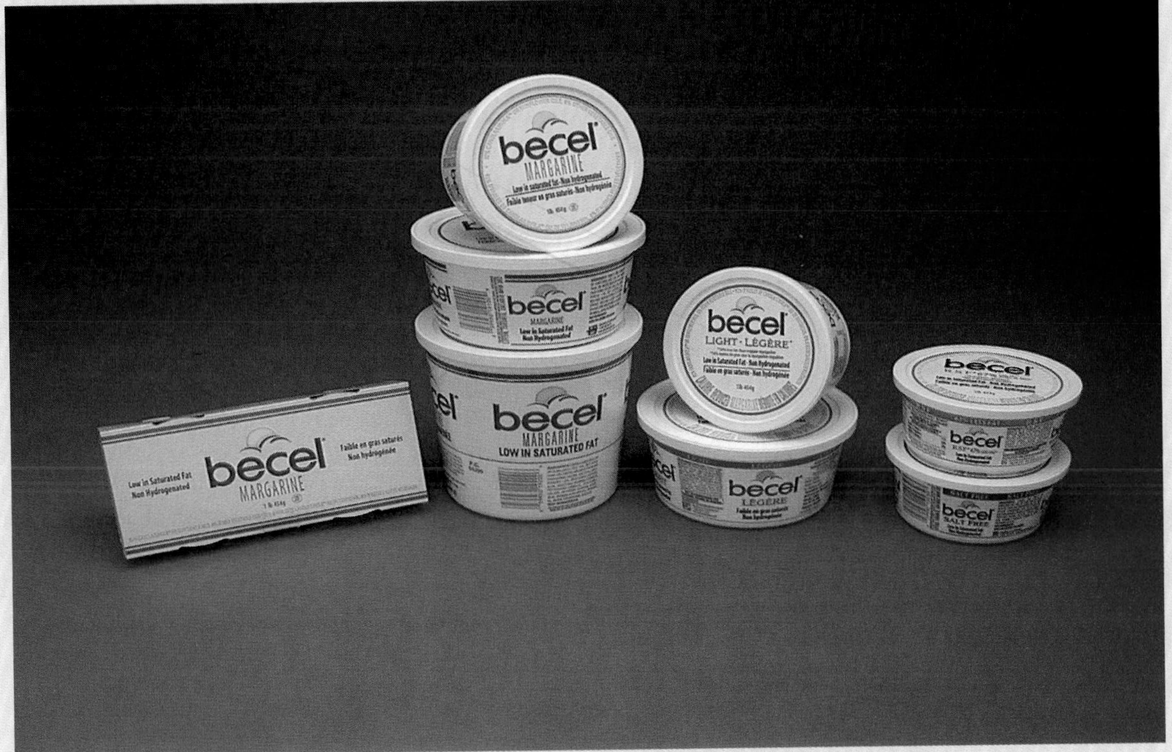

Description of products:

Becel Regular – Becel margarine is Canada's most popular choice for heart healthy eating. It is:

- low in saturated fat and non-hydrogenated
- an excellent source of Vitamin D and a good source of Vitamin E.

Becel Light – Becel Light is an ideal choice for people who want the benefits of Becel and who need to reduce their caloric intake. Becel Light has:

- 50% less fat and calories than regular margarine or butter;

- **Becel RSF** (Reduced Saturated Fat) – For people that need to significantly reduce the saturated fat

- 67% less fat than regular margarine or butter;
- 65% fewer calories than regular margarine or butter.

- **Becel Salt Free** - Becel Salt Free is a good choice for Canadians who would like all the benefits of Becel, but must adhere to a sodium-restricted diet.

Becel Oil – Canola Based Liquid Oil

for the lowest volume of margarine purchased. Those who purchase exclusively on the basis of health or price reasons accounted for almost the same percentage of volume of margarine sold. However, this was really just scratching the surface.

For the most part, consumers purchase products for a variety of reasons and margarine is no exception. Thus, the data further showed what percentage of margarine consumption was based on the interaction between taste, health and price. Apparently individuals considering all three attributes purchased the largest percentage volume of margarine. Looking at this data, Ross realized that he would have to consider the complex interaction of taste, health and price in deciding what his new marketing strategy would be.

Pricing Considerations

Becel's price has remained relatively consistent over time, but since its inception Becel has been priced at a premium to other margarines to reflect the premium quality formulation. See Exhibit 7 for further pricing information.

Interestingly though, all margarines are priced lower than butter. Butter was the highest priced spread in the category and had the ability to demand a premium price because of its strong heritage and loyal user base. Butter had always been the gold standard for taste and best for baking. Margarine had always been considered a cheaper alternative to butter and so the largest share of the margarine market was held by more price-driven brands. In fact in consumer surveys, price/value was the biggest reason for buying margarine over butter. Thus, pricing strategy was an important area Ross had to give more consideration to, if he wanted to grow volume.

Channel Considerations

The channels of distribution for packaged goods are quite broad: grocery stores (Loblaws, Sobeys), convenience stores (Beckers), discount super stores (Wal-Mart, Zellers) and club stores (Costco) are just a few examples of the retail outlets through which packaged goods are sold. However, the dominant force in these channels is the grocery channel. Throughout Canada in the last decade, the grocery industry has seen intense consolidation and increased growth of private label products. In 1999, the consolidation became even greater as Canada's biggest grocery chain, Loblaws, acquired Quebec's Provigo chain. Historically, Quebec had been the biggest market for butter and Becel's weakest market.

The Future of Becel

Ross glanced out his office window as he considered the various strategies that Becel could follow. Becel was an important business and any strategy taken also got lots of attention from the European head office. In fact, the Europeans were strongly considering using the Canadian advertising idea. Ross needed to carefully review what he saw to be some of his major alternatives before proceeding with a decision that would reinvigorate the expected growth for Becel.

Ross began to prepare his recommendation and outline the long-term vision for Becel. He had to get going since it was due within a month. Just as he sat down to consider his options, the phone rang. It was his new advertising agency telling him about some new butter advertising that challenged the health benefit claims made by margarine. The ad actually made a specific reference to the ingredients for Becel, paralleling butter as "Nothing but Good Stuff." This was going to be a difficult day.

EXHIBIT 6 Margarine Buyer Considerations

Taste vs Health vs Price Homescan—National	**Buyers (Projected)**	**% Buyers**	**Eq. Vol**	**% Volume**
Taste or Health or Price	9 776	100.0	239 253	100.0
Excl. Health	1 644	16.8	27 646	11.6
Excl. Taste	1 333	13.6	21 118	8.8
Excl. Price	1 359	13.9	28 765	12.0
Health and Taste	1 176	12.0	27 842	11.6
Health & Price	711	7.3	17 925	7.5
Price & Taste	1 766	18.1	52 685	22.0
Taste and Health and Price	1 786	18.3	63 271	26.4

Taste vs Health vs Price
1999 - Buyer Interaction – 100%
Total Margarine

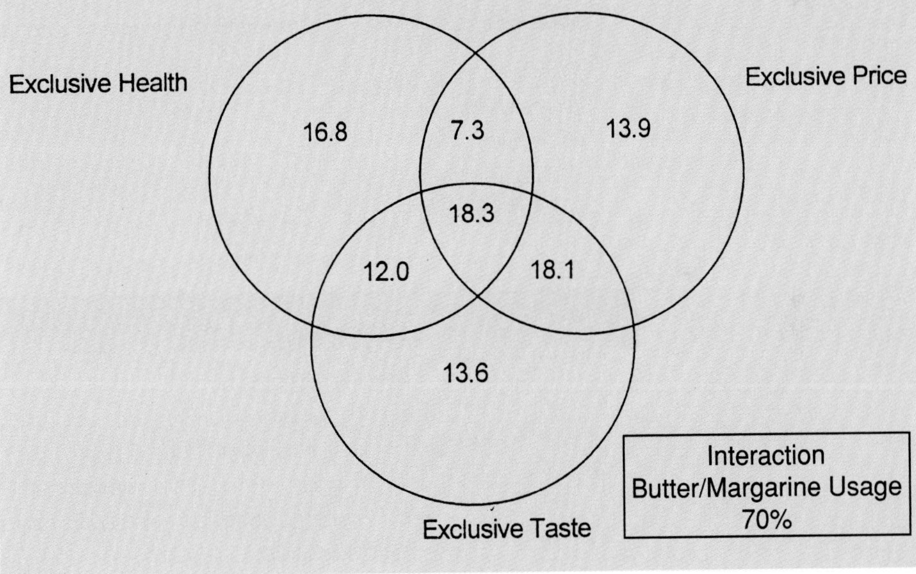

EXHIBIT 7 Spreads Category Pricing Information

Product	**Average Retail Price**
General Butter	\$3.08
General Margarine	\$1.45
Health Margarines	\$2.09
Taste Margarines	\$1.51
Price Margarines	\$0.98
Becel	\$2.10

EXHIBIT 8 Media and Advertising Cost Estimates

1
Primetime Television Commercial Rates (30 Seconds)

Network	Number of Stations	Basic Average Cost
Regional Television		
Atlantic TV Network	1	$90
ATV	4	$650
CBC		
Atlantic	5	$1 000
Central/Quebec	15	$6 000
Western	12	$2 500
Pacific	6	$1 000
Global	1	$7 000
MITV	2	$500
BBS Ontario	8	$5 000
Cost of Production: one commercial $300.00		

2
Newspaper Advertising

Newspaper	Cost of Advertisement	Cost per 1000 People Reached (CPM)
Toronto Star	$11 340	$2 438
Globe and Mail	$16 938	$5 314
Toronto Sun	$5 463	$2 366
Cost of Production: one ad $25.00		

EXHIBIT 9 Consumer Household Profiles

Margarine Households
- 4+ members
- head of household 45+
- strongest in lower income households
- families/empty nesters and childless couples (< $70 000)

Butter Households
- 3+ members
- head of household 45+
- strongest in high income households (+$70 000)
- strongest with empty nesters

Becel Households
- Strongest with empty nesters
- 65+
- Affluent with high incomes

Source: Nielsen Homescan

Notes

[1]"Estimated Cost of Network Commercials" *Media Digest* 1999–2000 ed., p.22.
[2]Tuckwell, Keith J., *Canadian Advertising in Action* 5th ed., p. 332. Pearson Education Canada: Toronto, 2001
Becel, Lipton, Sunlight, Salon Selectives, Dove, Degree, Fleischmann's are all trademarks of Unilever Canada.

Company>Brand Name Index

Subject Index

Photo/Ad Credits

Chapter 1 PAGE 2, Courtesy of Mountain Equipment Co-op; PAGE 5, Courtesy of the Sisters of Charity of Quebec (Marketing Conception: Martial Menard, Klaxon et Mechant Boris); PAGE 9, EyeWire, Inc.; PAGE 10, Courtesy of State Health Products; PAGE 11, © 1999 Microsoft Corporation; PAGE 12, General Motors Media Archives; PAGE 16, Gage Rob/FPG International LLC; PAGE 19, L.L. Bean; PAGE 24, George B. Diebold/The Stock Market; PAGE 25, Courtesy of Just White Shirts; PAGE 27, Courtesy of Chapters; PAGE 31, © Bettmann/CORBIS/Magma Photos; PAGE 33, The Arthritis Society; PAGE 35, Robert Johnston

Chapter 2 PAGE 46, Courtesy of Nortel Networks; PAGE 51, *Dralion*™ ad for the New York market © Cirque du Soleil, Inc.; PAGE 53, 3M; PAGE 55, IBM Corporation; PAGE 59, Alene M. McNeill; PAGE 61, Courtesy of Monsanto; PAGE 63, Courtesy of *Marketing Magazine;* PAGE 64, Bob Sachs/Stew Leonard; PAGE 69 (top) Layne Kennedy/Corbis, (bottom) Courtesy of www.tide.com; PAGE 75, Bentley Motor Cars; PAGE 79, Bruce Ayres/Tony Stone Images; PAGE 81, Robert Johnston

Chapter 3 PAGE 96, Arnold Communications; pages 99 and 102, The Terry Wild Studio; PAGE 106, Courtesy of Wal-Mart Canada and Communicorp Studios; PAGE 111, Reprinted with permission of Houston Effler Herstek Favat; PAGE 112, Courtesy of Ch!ckaboom; PAGE 115, Reprinted with permission of Kraft Canada, Inc.; PAGE 119, Courtesy of Air Canada; PAGE 120, Courtesy of www.enablelink.org; PAGE 128, Courtesy of © 1997 Microcell Solutions, Inc. and Graphiques M & H ; PAGE 132, Reprinted with permission of Farmers Dairy/PAGE & Wood Design; PAGE 133, "Whale," a commercial produced by the Canadian Heritage Commission for its "The World Needs More Canada" campaign, reprinted with permission of Canadian Tourism Commission; PAGE 134, Reproduced with permission of Imperial Oil Limited; PAGE 136, David McLain/Aurora & Quanta Productions

Chapter 4 PAGE 148, Courtesy of Labatt; PAGE 156, SPSS, Inc.; PAGE 159, Courtesy of Direct Protect; PAGE 164 (top) Courtesy of NPD Group, (bottom) Courtesy of www.lexis-nexis.com; PAGE 165, Stern Associates; PAGE 167, Reprinted with permission of Information Resources Inc.; PAGE 170 (top) Focus Vision Network, Inc., (bottom) Courtesy of YOUtv; PAGE 175, Courtesy of YOUtv; PAGE 176, Reproduced with the permission of the Minister of Public Works and Government Services Canada, 2001; PAGE 179, Courtesy of Vanessa Vachon; PAGE 180, Roper Starch Worldwide, Inc.

Chapter 5 PAGE 192, Courtesy of Harley-Davidson; PAGE 199, CIBC Aboriginal Banking; PAGE 200, LCBO and Klaxonnez, Inc.; PAGE 201, Courtesy of Air Canada and Hamazaki Wong; PAGE 202, Courtesy of Harley Davidson; PAGE 205, General Motors Media Archives; PAGE 208, Courtesy of General Motors of Canada; PAGE 209, Courtesy of www.forester.com; PAGE 216, Photographer: Dominique Malaterre (Ad agency: PNMD); PAGE 194, Bell Sports; PAGE 221, Reprinted with permission of Kraft Canada Inc.; PAGE 224, Photo Courtesy of Gerber Products Company

Chapter 6 PAGE 238, Courtesy of Bombardier; PAGE 245, Copyright 1999 Acer America Corp. and Acer Inc. Intel; PAGE 246, Asian Advertisers; PAGE 247, Reprinted with permission of Dow Chemical Company; PAGE 251, Reprinted with permission of Nokia Products Ltd.; PAGE 252, Volvo Trucks North America; PAGE 253, © Jim Feingersh/Stock Market; PAGE 255, Reprinted with permission of PMAC; PAGE 256, Courtesy of UUNet Canada, Inc.; PAGE 263 (top) Reprinted with permission of Computing Devices Canada, (bottom) © Dell Computer Corporation

Chapter 7 PAGE 272, Courtesy of Roche Macaulay & Partners Advertising Inc.; PAGE 277, Courtesy of Marriott Hotels; PAGE 279, Courtesy of Reflect.com; PAGE 281, Courtesy of Seagram Canada; PAGE 283, Reprinted with permission of Johnson and Johnson; PAGE 283, Reprinted with permission of Fruit of the Loom Canada, Inc.; PAGE 286, Courtesy of Beatrice Cheese Inc.; PAGE 287, © ***Lea & Perrins***® is a registered trademark of Lea & Perrins Ltd. Courtesy of Lea & Perrins Ltd. and Young & Rubicam Ltd.; PAGE 290, Reprinted with per-

Photo/Ad Credits

Chapter 1 PAGE 2, Courtesy of Mountain Equipment Co-op; PAGE 5, Courtesy of the Sisters of Charity of Quebec (Marketing Conception: Martial Menard, Klaxon et Mechant Boris); PAGE 9, EyeWire, Inc.; PAGE 10, Courtesy of State Health Products; PAGE 11, © 1999 Microsoft Corporation; PAGE 12, General Motors Media Archives; PAGE 16, Gage Rob/FPG International LLC; PAGE 19, L.L. Bean; PAGE 24, George B. Diebold/The Stock Market; PAGE 25, Courtesy of Just White Shirts; PAGE 27, Courtesy of Chapters; PAGE 31, © Bettmann/CORBIS/Magma Photos; PAGE 33, The Arthritis Society; PAGE 35, Robert Johnston

Chapter 2 PAGE 46, Courtesy of Nortel Networks; PAGE 51, *Dralion*™ ad for the New York market © Cirque du Soleil, Inc.; PAGE 53, 3M; PAGE 55, IBM Corporation; PAGE 59, Alene M. McNeill; PAGE 61, Courtesy of Monsanto; PAGE 63, Courtesy of *Marketing Magazine;* PAGE 64, Bob Sachs/Stew Leonard; PAGE 69 (top) Layne Kennedy/Corbis, (bottom) Courtesy of www.tide.com; PAGE 75, Bentley Motor Cars; PAGE 79, Bruce Ayres/Tony Stone Images; PAGE 81, Robert Johnston

Chapter 3 PAGE 96, Arnold Communications; pages 99 and 102, The Terry Wild Studio; PAGE 106, Courtesy of Wal-Mart Canada and Communicorp Studios; PAGE 111, Reprinted with permission of Houston Effler Herstek Favat; PAGE 112, Courtesy of Ch!ckaboom; PAGE 115, Reprinted with permission of Kraft Canada, Inc.; PAGE 119, Courtesy of Air Canada; PAGE 120, Courtesy of www.enablelink.org; PAGE 128, Courtesy of © 1997 Microcell Solutions, Inc. and Graphiques M & H ; PAGE 132, Reprinted with permission of Farmers Dairy/PAGE & Wood Design; PAGE 133, "Whale," a commercial produced by the Canadian Heritage Commission for its "The World Needs More Canada" campaign, reprinted with permission of Canadian Tourism Commission; PAGE 134, Reproduced with permission of Imperial Oil Limited; PAGE 136, David McLain/Aurora & Quanta Productions

Chapter 4 PAGE 148, Courtesy of Labatt; PAGE 156, SPSS, Inc.; PAGE 159, Courtesy of Direct Protect; PAGE 164 (top) Courtesy of NPD Group, (bottom) Courtesy of www.lexis-nexis.com; PAGE 165, Stern Associates; PAGE 167, Reprinted with permission of Information Resources Inc.; PAGE 170 (top) Focus Vision Network, Inc., (bottom) Courtesy of YOUtv; PAGE 175, Courtesy of YOUtv; PAGE 176, Reproduced with the permission of the Minister of Public Works and Government Services Canada, 2001; PAGE 179, Courtesy of Vanessa Vachon; PAGE 180, Roper Starch Worldwide, Inc.

Chapter 5 PAGE 192, Courtesy of Harley-Davidson; PAGE 199, CIBC Aboriginal Banking; PAGE 200, LCBO and Klaxonnez, Inc.; PAGE 201, Courtesy of Air Canada and Hamazaki Wong; PAGE 202, Courtesy of Harley Davidson; PAGE 205, General Motors Media Archives; PAGE 208, Courtesy of General Motors of Canada; PAGE 209, Courtesy of www.forester.com; PAGE 216, Photographer: Dominique Malaterre (Ad agency: PNMD); PAGE 194, Bell Sports; PAGE 221, Reprinted with permission of Kraft Canada Inc.; PAGE 224, Photo Courtesy of Gerber Products Company

Chapter 6 PAGE 238, Courtesy of Bombardier; PAGE 245, Copyright 1999 Acer America Corp. and Acer Inc. Intel; PAGE 246, Asian Advertisers; PAGE 247, Reprinted with permission of Dow Chemical Company; PAGE 251, Reprinted with permission of Nokia Products Ltd.; PAGE 252, Volvo Trucks North America; PAGE 253, © Jim Feingersh/Stock Market; PAGE 255, Reprinted with permission of PMAC; PAGE 256, Courtesy of UUNet Canada, Inc.; PAGE 263 (top) Reprinted with permission of Computing Devices Canada, (bottom) © Dell Computer Corporation

Chapter 7 PAGE 272, Courtesy of Roche Macaulay & Partners Advertising Inc.; PAGE 277, Courtesy of Marriott Hotels; PAGE 279, Courtesy of Reflect.com; PAGE 281, Courtesy of Seagram Canada; PAGE 283, Reprinted with permission of Johnson and Johnson; PAGE 283, Reprinted with permission of Fruit of the Loom Canada, Inc.; PAGE 286, Courtesy of Beatrice Cheese Inc.; PAGE 287, © ***Lea & Perrins***® is a registered trademark of Lea & Perrins Ltd. Courtesy of Lea & Perrins Ltd. and Young & Rubicam Ltd.; PAGE 290, Reprinted with permission of Steelcase Canada Inc.; PAGE 291, © Jeff Greenberg/Photo Researchers, Inc.; PAGE 292, Reprinted with permission of Altimira Investment Services Inc.; PAGE 296, Courtesy of Cadbury Chocolate Canada Inc.; PAGE 298, Messner Vetere Berger McNamee/Euro RSCG; PAGE 303, Reproduced with permission of CMA Canada; PAGE 305, Courtesy of Unilever PLC

Chapter 8 PAGE 318, Courtesy of Intrawest Corporation; PAGE 320, Courtesy of Graphics; PAGE 324, Sony Corporation of America; PAGE 325, Courtesy of TELUS Mobility; PAGE 329, Courtesy of Parallel Strategies; PAGE 331, Courtesy of Apple iMac; PAGE 333, Courtesy of Canadian Pacific Railway; PAGE 334, Harlequin Enterprises web page; PAGE 336, Courtesy of Outward Bound; PAGE 338, Loblaw Brands Limited; PAGE 339, The Coca-Cola Company; PAGE 340, Martha Stanitz/Martha Stanitz Photography; PAGE 346, Tetra Pak, Inc.; PAGE 350, © Mercedes-Benz of North America, Inc.; PAGE 352, John C. Hillary; PAGE 356, The Ritz-Carleton Hotel Company, LLC; PAGE 357, Allstate Insurance Company; PAGE 359, Courtesy of Whistler; PAGE 361, Munshi Ahmed Photography

Chapter 9 PAGE 376, Brooks Kraft/Corbis Sygma Photo News; PAGE 379, © 2001 Used by permission of About.com, Inc. which can be found on the Web at www.about.com. All rights reserved; PAGE 381, Robert Haller/New Products Showcase and Learning Center; PAGE 383, © 2000 Kellogg Canada Inc. Used with permission of Kellogg Canada Inc. JACKS' PACK is a registered trademark of Kellogg Canada Inc. in Canada; PAGE 386, Liaison Agency, Inc.; PAGE 388, Heinz Canada/Smith Locke Associates Inc.; PAGE 389, ©2000 Procter & Gamble; PAGE 392-3, Courtesy of Discreet Logic; PAGE 394, Black & Decker; PAGE 396, Hershey Foods Corporation; PAGE 398, Courtesy of Discreet Logic; PAGE 399, Reprinted with permission of Kraft Canada Inc.; PAGE 401, Courtesy of Birks Jewelers

Chapter 10 PAGE 412, The Terry Wild Studio; PAGE 417, Courtesy of www.mysimon.com; PAGE 420, Maytag Corporation; PAGE 424, Reprinted with permission of Bick's Pickles; PAGE 425, Courtesy Ault Foods; PAGE 427, Churchill & Klehr Photography; PAGE 428, Courtesy of Toyota Canada, Inc.; PAGE 434, Courtesy of Bell Canada and Cossette Communications; PAGE 436, Reprinted with permission of Zellers; PAGE 437, Eastman Kodak Company; PAGE 439, Reprinted with permission of Ramada Franchise Systems, Inc.; PAGE 440, Courtesy of Zero-Knowlege Systems and Red Whistle Communications; PAGE 442, Charles Gupton/Stock Boston; PAGE 444, Reprinted with permission of Leo Burnett Company, Inc. and Procter & Gamble Company

Chapter 11 PAGE 456, Courtesy of Caterpillar; PAGE 463, Courtesy of Tilley Endurables; PAGE 466, Courtesy of HEPCOE; PAGE 468, Courtesy of Air Canada; PAGE 469, Courtesy of www.ibm.com; PAGE 472, Courtesy of ING Direct; PAGE 474, Michael Rizza/Stock Boston; Dan Rubin/Medichrome/The Stock Shop, Inc.; PAGE 475, Courtesy of Ship to Canada; PAGE 476, © Dan Rubin/The Stock Shop; PAGE 477, Charles Gupton/Stock Boston; PAGE 479, Courtesy of www.ge.com; PAGE 481, Courtesy of Diamond Information Center/New York; PAGE 482, Reprinted with permission of INTERLINK Freight Systems, creative design by The Greaves & Allen Advertising Studios, Willowdale, Ontario; PAGE 485, Courtesy of Roadway Express, Inc.; PAGE 488, Reprinted with permission of Toys 'R' Us

Chapter 12 PAGE 498, Courtesy of Roots; PAGE 505, Courtesy of Eddie Bauer, Inc.; PAGE 506, Courtesy of A.Van Houtte; PAGE 508, Courtesy of Costco; PAGE 510, Courtesy of Cinnzeo/A division of Cinnaroll Bakeries Limited; PAGE 514, A. Ramey/Photo Edit; © Katherine Lambert; PAGE 515, Courtesy of Virgin Megastore, Vancouver; PAGE 516, Courtesy of Canada Post; PAGE 518, Courtesy of West Edmonton Mall; PAGE 522, Alene M. McNeill; PAGE 526, Courtesy McKesson-HBOC

Chapter 13 PAGE 536, William Cornett/Image Excellence Photography; PAGE 541, Hachette Filipacchi Magazines; PAGE 545, Jeff Jacobson, NJ; PAGE 546, © Copyright Hewlett-Packard (Canada) Ltd., 2001; PAGE 549, Courtesy of Mr. Alan Quarry/Quarry Integrated Communications; PAGE 550, Copyright Nissan 1989; PAGE 551, Courtesy of TELUS/Palmer Jarvis DDB; PAGE 552, With permission of W. K. Buckley Ltd.; PAGE 554, Courtesy of Labatt Breweries and Axmith, McIntyre, Wicht; PAGE 559, Courtesy of Volkswagen; PAGE 560, Jon Feingersh/Stock Boston; PAGE 563, Reprinted with permission of Toys 'R' Us

Chapter 14 PAGE 574, Alene M. McNeill; PAGE 579, Courtesy of Mr. Elwood; PAGE 580, Courtesy of Rogers @Home; PAGE 582, Courtesy of Kellogg Canada Inc.; PAGE 584, The Absolute Company; PAGE 586, Reprinted with permission of Outpost.com Marketing; PAGE 587, Courtesy of Rogers Media; PAGE 589, Courtesy of Peter Knight-Art Director and Dan Zimmerman-Writer; PAGE 590, By permission of Lanyon Phillips Partners; PAGE 591, Michael J. Treola/AP/Wide World Photos; PAGE 595, © 1997 The Gillete Company; PAGE 598, Courtesy of www.pertplus.com; PAGE 600, By permission of Pepsi-Cola Canada Ltd.; PAGE 601, © Jeff Scheid/Gamma-Liaison, Inc.; PAGE 603, Courtesy of www.ibm.com; PAGE 604, Cindy Lewis Photography/© 1991 Cindy Lewis; PAGE 606, The Image Works; PAGE 607, Courtesy of www.butterball.com

Chapter 15 PAGE 618, Courtesy of Lear Corporation; PAGE 622, © First Light; PAGE 626, DuPont Canada; PAGE 629, Dan Bosler/Tony Stone Images; PAGE 631, Courtesy of Canadian Professional Sales Association; PAGE 634, Ron Watts/First Light; PAGE 636, Rob Nelson/Black Star; PAGE 637, American Express Incentive Services; PAGE 641, © Lawrence Migdale/Photo Researchers, Inc.; PAGE 641, Courtesy of Advanced Sterilization Products, Irvine, CA

Chapter 16 PAGE 654, Darren Carroll/Liaison Agency, Inc. ; PAGE 659, Courtesy of www.lexus.com and www.ebay.com; PAGE 661, Courtesy of ClubLink; PAGE 665, Courtesy Fingerhut; PAGE 666, Courtesy of Canadian Wildlife Federation; PAGE 668, Ronald McDonald House Charities; PAGE 670 (top) Courtesy of Tilley Endurables, (bottom) Courtesy of Sears; PAGE 672, Karen Leitza; PAGE 673, Courtesy of Sympatico; PAGE 674, Robert Johnston; PAGE 675, Reproduced with the permission of the Minister of Public Works and Government Services Canada 2001; PAGE 677, Richmond Savings Credit Union; PAGE 678, Reproduced with permission of Yahoo! Inc. © 2001 by Yahoo! Inc. Yahoo! and the Yahoo! Logo are trademarks of Yahoo! Inc.; PAGE 679, Courtesy of www.candystand.com; PAGE 681, Courtesy of www.travelocity.com; PAGE 682, © Kevin Fleming/CORBIS/Magma Photos ; PAGE 683, Courtesy of BMW Canada Inc.; PAGE 687, Courtesy of American Standard Canada

Chapter 17 PAGE 700, Kevin Frayer/Canadian Press; PAGE 704 (bottom) Courtesy IBM, (top left) Caroline Parson, (top right) © Catherine Karnow/CORBIS/Magma Photos; PAGE 705 (left) Courtesy Feathercraft Products Ltd., (right) Courtesy of Blitz Design & Graphic Garage; PAGE 707, © 2001 SMART Technologies Inc.; PAGE 709, Used by permission of Canada Department Foreign Affairs and International Trade; PAGE 711, © Allison Wardman Photography; PAGE 713, Young & Rubicam, New York; PAGE 716, Cary S. Wolinsky/Trillium Studios; PAGE 719, Courtesy of Pepsi-Cola Canada Ltd.; PAGE 720, Courtesy of CSA International; PAGE 723, Courtesy of www.etrade.com; PAGE 728, Nokia Products Limited; PAGE 729, Courtesy of International Business Machines Corporation. Unauthorized use not permitted; PAGE 730, Courtesy of Visa Canada

Chapter 18 PAGE 742, Courtesy of Altamira Financial Services Ltd.; PAGE 746, Churchill & Klehr Photography; PAGE 748, Courtesy of PhoneBusters; PAGE 751, Enrico Ferorelli/Stock Boston; PAGE 752, Image used by permission of www.adbusters.org; PAGE 755, Courtesy of Campbell Soup Company Ltd.; PAGE 757 (left) Courtesy of Daimler Chrysler Canada Inc., (right) Honda of Canada Mfg.; PAGE 758, Courtesy of Packaging Association of Canada; PAGE 761, Church & Dwight Co. Inc.; PAGE 763, Courtesy of Forrec; PAGE 765, Copyright 1998 GM Corp. Used with permission of GM Media Archives; PAGE 766 (top) Courtesy of Friends of Animals, Inc., (bottom) Courtesy of Concerns Canada; PAGE 767, Herman Miller, Inc.